T0181024

Lecture Notes in Artificial Intelligence 11873

Subseries of Lecture Notes in Computer Science

More information about this series at http://www.springer.com/series/1244

Editors
Matteo Baldoni 🆔
Università degli Studi di Torino
Turin, Italy

Mehdi Dastani 🆔
Utrecht University
Utrecht, The Netherlands

Beishui Liao 🆔
Zhejiang University
Hangzhou, China

Yuko Sakurai 🆔
National Institute of Advanced Industrial
Science and Technology
Tokyo, Japan

Rym Zalila Wenkstern 🆔
University of Texas at Dallas
Richardson, TX, USA

ISSN 0302-9743   ISSN 1611-3349   (electronic)
Lecture Notes in Artificial Intelligence
ISBN 978-3-030-33791-9   ISBN 978-3-030-33792-6   (eBook)
https://doi.org/10.1007/978-3-030-33792-6

LNCS Sublibrary: SL7 – Artificial Intelligence

This Springer imprint is published by the registered company Springer Nature Switzerland AG
The registered company address is: Gewerbestrasse 11, 6330 Cham, Switzerland

Matteo Baldoni · Mehdi Dastani · Beishui Liao ·
Yuko Sakurai · Rym Zalila Wenkstern (Eds.)

PRIMA 2019: Principles and Practice of Multi-Agent Systems

22nd International Conference
Turin, Italy, October 28–31, 2019
Proceedings

 Springer

Preface

Welcome to the proceedings of the 22nd International Conference on Principles and Practice of Multi-Agent Systems (PRIMA 2019) held in Torino, Italy, during October 28–31, 2019. Originally started as a regional (Asia-Pacific) workshop in 1998, PRIMA has become one of the leading and most influential scientific conferences for research on multi-agent systems. Each year since 2009, PRIMA has brought together active researchers, developers, and practitioners from both academia and industry to show-case, share, and promote research in several domains, ranging from foundations of agent theory and engineering aspects of agent systems, to emerging interdisciplinary areas of agent-based research. PRIMA's previous editions were held in Nagoya, Japan (2009), Kolkata, India (2010), Wollongong, Australia (2011), Kuching, Malaysia (2012), Dunedin, New Zealand (2013), Gold Coast, Australia (2014), Bertinoro, Italy (2015), Phuket, Thailand (2016), Nice, France (2017), and Tokyo, Japan (2018).

This year, we received 112 full paper submissions from 28 countries, including 10 papers submitted to the social science track, chaired by Michael Mäs. Each submission was carefully reviewed by at least three members of the Program Committee (PC) composed of 84 prominent world-class researchers. In addition, 28 sub-reviewers were called upon to review submissions. The PC and senior PC (SPC) included researchers from 23 countries. The review period was followed by PC discussions moderated by SPC members. The PRIMA SPC has been part of the PRIMA reviewing scheme since 2010, and this year it included 15 members. At the end of the reviewing process, in addition to the technical reviews, authors received a summary meta-review by a SPC member. PRIMA 2019 accepted 29 full papers (an acceptance rate of 26%) and 30 submissions were selected to appear as short papers. Four papers were accepted to be presented in the social science track. In total, 25 full papers and 25 short papers are included in the present proceedings. Papers accepted into the social science track were fast-tracked into the *Journal of Artificial Societies and Social Simulation*, and are not included in the present proceedings. In addition to the paper presentations and poster sessions, the conference also included two keynote talks: Prof. Frank Dignum and Prof. Ugo Pagallo.

We would like to thank all individuals, institutions, and sponsors that supported PRIMA 2019. Mainly we thank the authors for submitting high-quality research papers, confirming PRIMA's reputation as a leading international conference in multi-agent systems. We are indebted to our PC and SPC members and additional reviewers for spending their valuable time by providing careful reviews and recommendations on the submissions, and for taking part in follow-up discussions. We also thank EasyChair for the use of their conference management system.

September 2019

Matteo Baldoni
Mehdi Dastani
Beishui Liao
Yuko Sakurai
Rym Zalila Wenkstern

Organization

General Chairs

Matteo Baldoni   Università degli Studi di Torino, Italy
Yuko Sakurai   National Institute of Advanced Industrial Science
         and Technology, Japan

Program Chairs

Mehdi Dastani   Universiteit Utrecht, The Netherlands
Beishui Liao   Zhejiang University, China
Rym Zalila Wenkstern   University of Texas at Dallas, USA

Social Science Track Chair

Michael Mäs   University of Groningen, The Netherlands

Financial, Sponsorship, and Local Arrangement Chair

Roberto Micalizio   Università degli Studi di Torino, Italy

Web Chair

Stefano Tedeschi   Università degli Studi di Torino, Italy

Workshop and Tutorial Chairs

Cristina Baroglio   Università degli Studi di Torino, Italy
Francesco Olivieri   DATA61, CSIRO, Australia

PRIMA Steering Committee

Guido Governatori (Chair)   NICTA, Australia
Takayuki Ito (Deputy Chair)   Nagoya Institute of Technology, Japan
Aditya Ghose   University of Wollongong, Australia
     (Immediate Past Chair)
Abdul Sattar (Treasurer)   Griffith University, Australia
Makoto Yokoo   Kyushu University, Japan
     (Chair Emeritus)
Hoa Dam   University of Wollongong, Australia
Jeremy Pitt   Imperial College, UK

Yang Xu	University of Electronic Science and Technology, China
Jane Hsu	National Taiwan University, Taiwan
Andrea Omicini	Università di Bologna, Italy
Qingliang Chen	Jinan University, China
Paolo Torroni	Università di Bologna, Italy
Serena Villata	Inria Sophia Antipolis, France
Katsutoshi Hirayama	Kobe University, Japan
Matteo Baldoni	University of Torino, Italy
Amit K. Chopra	Lancaster University, UK
Tran Cao Son	New Mexico State University, USA
Michael Mäs	University of Groningen, The Netherlands
Leon van der Torre	University of Luxembourg, Luxembourg
Ana Bazzan	Universidade Federal do Rio Grande do Sul, Brazil
Joao Leite	Universidade Nova de Lisboa, Portugal
Bo An	Nanyang Technological University, Singapore
Itsuki Noda	AIST, Japan
Tony Savarimuthu	University of Otago, New Zealand
Nir Oren	University of Aberdeen, UK
Tim Miller	University of Melbourne, Australia
Yuko Sakurai	AIST, Japan

Senior Program Committee

Bo An	Nanyang Technological University, Singapore
Cristina Baroglio	Università degli Studi di Torino, Italy
Cristiano Castelfranchi	Institute of Cognitive Sciences and Technologies, Italy
Amit Chopra	Lancaster University, UK
Paul Davidsson	Malmö University, Sweden
Yves Demazeau	CNRS - Laboratoire d'Informatique de Grenoble, France
Sylvie Doutre	University of Toulouse 1 - IRIT, France
Rino Falcone	Institute of Cognitive Sciences and Technologies-CNR, Italy
Mingyu Guo	The University of Adelaide, Australia
Katsutoshi Hirayama	Kobe University, Japan
Brian Logan	University of Nottingham, UK
Tim Miller	The University of Melbourne, Australia
Nir Oren	University of Aberdeen, UK
Toshiharu Sugawara	Waseda University, Japan
Makoto Yokoo	Kyushu University, Japan

Program Committee

| Moustafa Ahmed | Nagoya Institute of Technology, Japan |
| Mohammad Al-Zinati | Jordan University of Science and Technology, Jordan |

Ryuta Arisaka   Nagoya Institute of Technology, Japan
Thomas Ågotnes   University of Bergen, Norway
Pietro Baroni   University of Brescia, Italy
Francesco Belardinelli   Imperial College London, UK
Federico Bergenti   Università degli Studi di Parma, Italy
Floris Bex   Utrecht University, The Netherlands
Stefano Bistarelli   Università di Perugia, Italy
Olivier Boissier   Mines Saint-Etienne, Institut Henri Fayol, Laboratoire
                                 Hubert Curien UMR CNRS 5516, France
Jean-Pierre Briot   Laboratoire d'Informatique de Paris 6 (Paris6-CNRS),
                                 France, and PUC-Rio, Brazil
Martin Caminada   Cardiff University, UK
Luciano Cavalcante Siebert   Delft University of Technology, The Netherlands
Rem Collier   University College Dublin, Ireland
Silvano Colombo Tosatto   CSIRO, Australia
Stefania Costantini   Università degli Studi dell'Aquila, Italy
Matteo Cristani   University of Verona, Italy
Aleksander Czechowski   Delft University of Technology, The Netherlands
Célia Da Costa Pereira   Université Nice Sophia Anipolis, France
Hoa Khanh Dam   University of Wollongong, Australia
Dave De Jonge   Western Sydney University, Australia
Dario Della Monica   Università degli Studi di Udine, Italy
Louise Dennis   University of Liverpool, UK
Dragan Doder   IRIT, Université Paul Sabatier, France
Barbara Dunin-Kęplicz   Institute of Informatics, University of Warsaw, Poland
Animesh Dutta   National Institute of Technology, Durgapur, India
Soheil Eshghi   Yale University, USA
Angelo Ferrando   University of Liverpool, UK
Nicoletta Fornara   Università della Svizzera Italiana, Switzerland
Katsuhide Fujita   Tokyo University of Agriculture and Technology,
                                 Japan
Naoki Fukuta   Shizuoka University, Japan
Rustam Galimullin   University of Nottingham, UK
Scott Gerard   IBM, USA
The Anh Han   Teesside Univeresity, UK
Hiromitsu Hattori   College of Computer Science and Engineering,
                                 Ritsumeikan University, Japan
Koen Hindriks   Vrije Universiteit Amsterdam, The Netherlands
Nghia Hoang   MIT-IBM Watson AI Lab, IBM Research, USA
Takayuki Ito   Nagoya Institute of Technology, Japan
Yichuan Jiang   Southeast University, China
Hiroyuki Kido   Sun Yat-Sen University, China
Malte Kliess   Delft University of Technology, The Netherlands
Antonio Lieto   University of Torino, Italy
Emiliano Lorini   IRIT, Université Paul Sabatier, France
Xudong Luo   Guangxi Normal University, China

Additional Reviewers

Arai, Sachiyo
Areyan Viqueira, Enrique
Borg, Annemarie
Campeanu, Theodor
Changder, Narayan
Charrier, Tristan
De Vos, Marina
Dimitri, Nicola
Dong, Huimin
Ghose, Aditya
Gonzalez Leon, Borja
Hoang, Quang Minh
Jana, Nanda Dulal
Johora, Fatema
Kamienski, Piotr
Malvone, Vadim

Mazumdar, Kingshuk
Mercanti, Ivan
Nomura, Shoshin
Padmanabha, Anantha
Parent, Xavier
Qiao, Jianglin
Queffelec, Arthur
Reymond, Mathieu
Rüb, Inga
Sankur, Ocan
Sulis, Emilio
Szałas, Andrzej
Taticchi, Carlo
Testerink, Bas
Yun, Bruno

Contents

Short Papers

Full Papers

Deliberation Towards Transitivity with Unshared Features

Arthur Boixel[1], Pierre Bisquert[2], and Madalina Croitoru[3]($\boxtimes$)

[1] ILLC, University of Amsterdam, Amsterdam, The Netherlands
[2] IATE, INRA, Montpellier, France
[3] University of Montpellier, Montpellier, France
croitoru@lirmm.fr

Abstract. We place ourselves in a decision making setting where a set of agents needs to collectively decide upon a set of alternatives characterised by their features. We introduce the notion of unshared features and show that if such features do not exist then we can reach a Condorcet consensus. We provide a deliberation protocol that ensures that, after its completion, the number of unshared features of the decision problem can only be reduced.

1 Introduction and Motivation

Social choice theory allows to study the way in which the aggregation of individual preferences can lead to the expression of a collective preference. Unfortunately, well-known impossibility results prevent the construction of simple and satisfactory preference aggregation methods [4]. In this paper we focus on a well-known topic in social choice: single-peakedness preferences and their link to the Condorcet paradox. The Condorcet paradox is a situation noted by the Marquis de Condorcet in the late 18th century [5], in which the aggregation of individual preferences *via* pairwise majority can result in cyclic collective preferences, even if the individual preferences are not cyclic. For example, if we consider three agents 1, 2 and 3 and three alternatives *bike*, *car* and *train*, one can encounter the situation where agent 1 prefers *bike* to *car* to *train*, agents 2 prefers *car* to *train* to *bike* and agent 3 prefers *train* to *bike* to *car*. In this case no alternative beats the other in pairwise majority. The *car* is strictly preferred to the *train* by a majority (agents 1 and 2) but the *train* is strictly preferred to the *bike* by an other majority (agents 2 and 3) and the *bike* is strictly preferred to the *car* by a majority (agents 1 and 3). Thus we have no Condorcet winner here (i.e. an alternative that is preferred, pairwise, to all other alternatives by a majority) and we obtain a non transitive result. Although satisfying properties which are desirable in democracy[1] [1], in such cases, pairwise majority cannot be used to aggregate individual preferences.

---

[1] The pairwise majority aggregation method is known to be unanimous, independent to irrelevant alternatives and non-dictatorial.

© Springer Nature Switzerland AG 2019
M. Baldoni et al. (Eds.): PRIMA 2019, LNAI 11873, pp. 3–18, 2019.
https://doi.org/10.1007/978-3-030-33792-6_1

One way of going around this situation is to look for necessary or sufficient conditions on the individual preferences that will ensure a well-defined result [15]. But restricting the expression of individual preferences is a non democratic way for their aggregation. Indeed, it forces our preference aggregation method to violate the universality property [1]. To take advantage of the latter conditions without violating this property, we have to better understand them. In the forties, Duncan Black studied cyclic preferences and introduced the notion of *single-peakedness* [3]. A group of agents is said to have single-peaked preferences if each agent has an ideal choice in the set of alternatives, and for each agent, alternatives that are—according to a fix order on the alternatives—further from her ideal choice are less preferred. Single-peaked preferences have the desired property of allowing for a Condorcet winner [3]. For example if we alter the preferences from the previous example and we consider that agent 3 prefers *train* to *car* and *car* to *bike* then the set of individual preferences is single-peaked according to the order $>$: $bike > car > train$. Therefore we can conclude that there exists a Condorcet winner, in that case, the *car* alternative. In this paper we place ourselves in a decision making setting where a set of agents needs to collectively decide upon a set of alternatives characterised by their features [6]. The agents have desired features and the satisfaction of these features by the alternatives induces agents' individual preferences. The more an alternative satisfies the desired features of an agent, the higher its rank will be in the agent's individual preferences. In this setting, as explained above, using voting rules satisfying desirable properties as a collective decision making procedure can lead to situations (such as the Condorcet Paradox) where no decision can be made. In this paper we address this problem by studying conditions on the alternatives' features that ensure the avoidance of the Condorcet Paradox. We introduce the notion of *unshared features* and show that if such features do not exist then we can reach a Condorcet consensus. Moreover, we conjecture and empirically prove that the less unshared features there are, the closer we get (with respect to well-known distance measures in the literature) to reaching a Condorcet consensus. Last, we provide a deliberation protocol that ensures that, after its completion, the number of unshared features can only be reduced.

2   Individual Desires and Preference Formation

In this section, we will explore how agents can form their individual preferences based on the amount of satisfaction alternatives can provide them and how the consequences of dissatisfaction affect preferences.

Let us consider a set N of n agents that will express preferences over a set X of possible alternatives. Each alternative x is objectively described by a set P_x of *features* that represents the satisfaction, or dissatisfaction, of several criteria. More precisely, given a set of criteria $\mathcal{C}$, for each criterion $c \in \mathcal{C}$, P_x will either contain p_c (criterion c is satisfied) or $\mathbf{n}p_c$ (criterion c is not satisfied). We say that x *satisfies* p_c if $p_c \in P_x$, otherwise $\mathbf{n}p_c \in P_x$.

Inspired by the work of Dietrich et al. [6] we suppose in this work that agents' preferences are based on *desired features*. In particular, we assume that each agent $i \in N$ has a set W_i of desired features which will induce a preference relation over X, i.e. i will prefer an alternative $x \in X$ over an alternative $y \in X$ if the number of features in W_i satisfied by x is greater than or equal to the number of features in W_i satisfied by y.

Definition 1 (Features-induced preference formation). *Given a set W of desired features, two alternatives $x, y \in X$ and their respective set of satisfied properties P_x and P_y, x is preferred to y according to W ($x \succeq_W y$) if and only if*

$$|\{p \in P_x \ s.t. \ p \in W\}| \geq |\{p \in P_y \ s.t. \ p \in W\}|$$

If x is preferred to y and y is not preferred to x according to W, then x is strictly preferred to y according to W ($x \succ_W y$). Otherwise, we suppose that x and y are equivalent according to W ($x \sim_W y$).[2] Given an agent $i \in N$ and her desired features W_i, we will denote by $\succeq_{W_i}$ or $\succeq_i$ her preferences.

Among these desired features, some are desired by all agents in the group, while others are more personal. Some of these personal features can lead to modifications in the agents preferences which bring the collection of individual preferences (so-called *preference profile*) farther from consensus. Intuitively, the more the agents want personal features, the more heterogeneous their preferences will be and the lower the probability of obtaining a transitive result *via* pairwise majority. Following this idea we will qualify as *unshared* every feature which is not desired by the entire set of agents, the others are considered as *consensual*.

Definition 2 (Consensual and unshared features). *Given a set N of agents and, for each agent $i \in N$ its set of desired features W_i, we denote by*

- $W_\forall = \bigcap_{i \in N} W_i$ *the set of* consensual *features*,
- $W_\exists = \{p \in \bigcup_{i \in N} W_i \ s.t. \ p \notin W_\forall\}$ *the set of* unshared *features*.

Hence, it is possible to consider the preferences induced by the consensual features, $\succeq_{W_\forall}$, which correspond to a ranking that can be seen as an approximation of the group's collective preferences. The aim of our work is to provide agents with a means to reach a situation where the Condorcet paradox can be circumvented thanks to a deliberative dialogue. But accounting for every particular case of induced preferences following a deliberation is nearly impossible as it depends on what the agents want and their justifications, which can be considered as infinitely diverse.

Hence, we need to introduce a notion that will help to represent disagreement within the group. Disagreement between agents is caused by diverging goals and

---

[2] Please note that Dietrich et al. [6] suppose that agents can have a preference relation over features and thus they can discriminate between two alternatives satisfying the same number of desired features. Intuitively, the importance given to a feature depends on the context.

Table 1. The six possible rankings for three alternatives.

#	Ranking	#	Ranking
1	$A \succ B \succ C$	4	$C \succ A \succ B$
2	$B \succ A \succ C$	5	$B \succ C \succ A$
3	$A \succ C \succ B$	6	$C \succ B \succ A$

contradicting means to satisfy them. In particular, due to unshared features, agents might distance themselves from the preference relation induced by the consensual features ($\succeq_{W_\lor}$) by swapping alternatives in this approximate ranking. We will see in Sect. 4.2 how to formally link these swaps—called *alternative escalations*—to the number of unshared features.

In other words, this notion aims to represent the quality of the deliberation: the smaller the number of alternative escalations, the higher the level of consensus, and the more "decisive" the deliberation has been.

3 Empirical Results

In this section, we will first define the metrics allowing to assess the distance between a given profile of preferences and some kind of idealised preference structure. We next present the experimental setup as well as the results we obtained.

3.1 Profile Distance

Single-Peakedness and Single-Cavedness. In 2004, Gehrlein [8] considers a variation of the measure proposed by Niemi et al. [13]. Consider the case of an election with three alternatives $X = \{A, B, C\}$. The individual preferences of the agents on these alternatives are limited to the six rankings in Table 1.

Let n_l be the number of agents whose individual preferences correspond to ranking #l. We therefore have $n_1 + n_2$ equal to the number of agents who ranked the alternative C in last position. Similarly, $n_3 + n_4$ agents ranked B last and $n_5 + n_6$ agents ranked A last. In our case, if one of the three alternatives is never ranked last, then the preference profile will be—according to an order in which this alternative is ranked second—*single-peaked* [15]. We thus define our *measure* of proximity: if there exists a candidate rarely ranked last by the agents, then it is probably a unifying candidate in the sense that very few agents would regard her election as the worst possible result. If there are such candidates, it will be easier to find a Condorcet winner [9].

Definition 3 (Proximity to single-peakedness). *Given n agents, 3 alternatives, a preference profile $\mathcal{P}$ and the rankings in Table 1, let n_l be the number* *of agents whose individual preferences $\succeq_i \in \mathcal{P}$ correspond to ranking #l. The* single-peakedness *proximity measure m_{sp} is defined as*

$$\frac{min(n_1 + n_2, n_3 + n_4, n_5 + n_6)}{|\mathcal{P}|}$$

When the value of the metric is 0, a candidate is never ranked last, so the preference profile is *single-peaked* and there is a Condorcet winner[3]. A trivial upper bound for this measure is $\frac{n}{3}$.

A similar metric m_{sc} can be set up in order to compute the proximity to *single-cavedness*, a mirror property of *single-peakedness* which is also a sufficient condition ensuring the existence of a Condorcet winner [11]. A triplet of alternatives is *single-caved* when there is an alternative that is never ranked first by the agents.

Separability into Two Groups. In 2005, based on the work of Inada [11], Gehrlein [9] proposes another measure, variant of the previous ones. Still in the case of three alternatives, if there is a candidate rarely ranked second by the agents, then it is a polarizing candidate. Indeed, it is either very appreciated by some agents (ranked first), or very little appreciated by others (ranked last). In such a situation, it will be easier to extract a structuring dimension from the individual preferences [9]. We can then, in the same way as before, define m_{sg} as a measure of the proximity to *separability into two groups* of a preference profile. In the case $m_{sg} = 0$, there is a candidate who is never ranked second, the preference profile satisfies the condition of *separability into two groups* and a Condorcet winner exists. The same upper bound of $\frac{n}{3}$ applies to this measure.

Triple Wise Value Restriction. The previous measures can be combined to compute a proximity to *triple wise value restriction* which is a generalisation of the three previous conditions introduced by Sen [15].

Definition 4 (Distance to triple wise value restriction). *Given n agents, 3 alternatives, a preference profile $\mathcal{P}$ and the rankings in Table 1, let n_l be the number of agents whose individual preferences $\succeq_i \in \mathcal{P}$ correspond to ranking #l. The* triple wise value restriction *proximity measure m_{tw} is defined as*

$$min(m_{sp}, m_{sc}, m_{sg})$$

In Sect. 3.2, we will use variants of these measures—normalised over all triplets of alternatives—in order to study the consequences that the number of unshared features may have on the proximity of preference profiles to these structural properties.

---

[3] In this case, the Condorcet winner is the most preferred alternative of the median voter [3].

3.2   Simulation Results

The notion of alternative escalations introduced in the previous section lets us control the *quality* of the deliberation that takes place between the agents. A small amount of alternative escalations after deliberation indicates that the agents managed to reduce the quantity of unshared features. On the contrary, a high amount of alternative escalations indicates that they did not manage to agree on a large amount of desirable features and each agent potentially has a significant amount of residual unshared features. More precisely, we will answer in this section the following question: *does proximity to interesting structural properties increase when the number of unshared features decreases?*

Experimental Settings. The experiment, which aims at simulating a deliberation outcome, is fixed by the following parameters: the number n of agents, the number k of alternatives and the maximum number e of alternatives escalations an agent can do. The experimental protocol is the following. One takes a linear order $\succeq_{W_\forall}$ of k alternatives in order to simulate the preference relation induced by the set $W_\forall$ of features considered as desirable by all the agents after deliberation. Then, each agent can do at most e random alternatives escalations in $\succeq_{W_\forall}$ (by using her residual unshared features). Once the new preferences generated, one computes the proximity of the preference profile to a given preference structure (*single-peakedness, separability into two groups, triple wise value restriction*): the proximity measure is the ratio between the number of triplets of alternatives satisfying the preference structure and the total number of triplets. A measure of $m_s = 1$ indicates that all the triplets are satisfying the structure $s \in \{sp, sg, tw\}$. On the contrary, a measure $m_s = 0$ indicates that all the triplets are problematic and thus the preference profile is not satisfying the preference structure, which will give rise to a non-transitive result in most cases. In order to treat and harmonise the different cases that we can encounter, each point on the graphs corresponds to an average performed on $10,000$ repetitions.

Single-Peakedness. The first proximity measure we want to observe is the one to *single-peakedness*. Figure 1 shows the results of the experiment for $n = 200$ agents. For $k = 3$ to $k = 10$ alternatives, the proximity to *single-peakedness* has been computed according to e.

Proximity to *single-peakedness* increases when e (and thus the number of unshared features) decreases. This result supports the hypothesis that agreeing on features allows agents to restructure their individual preferences in an interesting way. However, this increase in proximity is at different speeds depending on the number of alternatives. Indeed, with three alternatives, it is easy to obtain a non *single-peaked* preference profile by modifying very little the same ranking[4]. On the other hand, with more alternatives, and thus more triplets to consider, more personal modifications from the agents in their new preferences are necessary to move away from *single-peakedness*. Thus, for a fixed number

---

[4] Case of the Condorcet paradox for example.

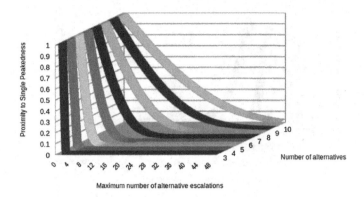

Fig. 1. Proximity to *single-peakedness*: 200 agents.

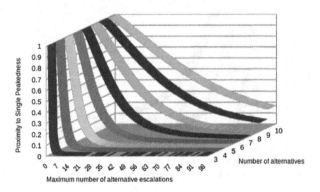

Fig. 2. Proximity to *single-peakedness*: 20 agents.

of modifications, the probability of obtaining a good proportion of *single-peaked* triplets increases with the number of alternatives.

Please note that good proximity to *single-peakedness* does not guarantee a transitive result *via* pairwise majority. We can still hope, in these cases, to obtain a Condorcet winner even if the overall ranking of alternatives is not totally transitive. Indeed, even if there is a cycle in the ranking, a Condorcet winning alternative may exist and may dominate this cycle. This is why the search for a unifying candidate is interesting.

Figure 2 shows the results of the same experiment with a set of 20 agents. The proximity to *single-peakedness* decreases less rapidly here. This can be explained by the fact that, for a triplet of alternatives, the probability that it is not *single-peaked* increases with the number of times it has to be considered. The more agents there are, the more unlikely their individual preferences will be *single-peaked*. Deliberation seems therefore to be more efficient with a reduced number of agents. Although intuitive, this result is interesting because the implementation of a deliberation protocol in real life situations seems difficult if it is necessary to consider a large number of agents.

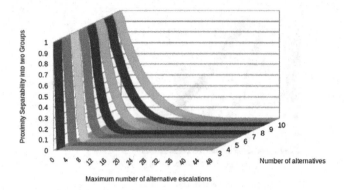

Fig. 3. Proximity to *sep. into two groups*: 200 agents.

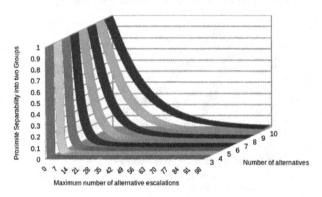

Fig. 4. Proximity to *sep. into two groups*: 20 agents.

Separability into Two Groups. The second experiment aims to study the proximity to *separability into two groups* as introduced in Sect. 3.1. The results obtained are given in Fig. 3 (200 agents) and Fig. 4 (20 agents). The general shape of the curves is the same as before, so we can conclude that the proximity to *separability into two groups* increases when e (and therefore the number of unshared features) decreases. However, the proximity value to this property decreases faster than the proximity to *single-peakedness*, this can be explained by the way in which the new individual preferences are generated. The alternatives ranked first and last in $\succ_{W_{\forall}}$ are half as likely as the others to change their position when performing alternatives escalations (the first one cannot go up and the last one cannot go down). In case the alternative ranked first moves, then it has to go down to the second place, increasing the probability that a triplet of alternatives containing this alternative will not satisfy the *separability into two groups* condition. The same holds for the alternative ranked last in $\succ_{W_{\forall}}$. The final preference profile will therefore be more likely to be *single-peaked* or *single-caved* than to satisfy the *separability into two groups* condition.

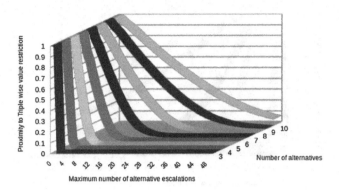

Fig. 5. Proximity to *Triple wise value rest.*: 200 agents.

Triple Wise Value Restriction. In the same way as before, we look at the proportion of triplets of alternatives satisfying this condition: checked if the triple is *single-peaked, single-caved* or satisfies the *separability into two groups* condition. As expected and shown in Fig. 5, the shape of the curves remains the same. Proximity to *triple wise value restriction* increases as the number of residual unshared features decreases. There is also again a rapid drop in the value of proximity when few alternatives are considered. The same experiment was performed for $n = 20$ agents, the results are given in Fig. 6. As for the proximity measure to *single-peakedness* (but to a lesser extent since the measure of proximity to *separability into two groups* comes into play), with less agents the proximity decreases less drastically and this regardless of the number of alternatives considered. Another positive observation is the fact that for a large number of alternatives, a significant proportion (around 25%) of triplets of alternatives always satisfy one of the three conditions that make up the *triple wise value restriction* even with a very large and seemingly unrealistic number of residual unshared features.

Now that we observed the critical impact that alternative escalations can have on the deliberation outcome, it is necessary to study means to reduce their amount. In the next section, we will assess how a simple deliberation protocol can be used to achieve this goal.

4   Deliberation Around Unshared Features

In this section, we will first define a simple yet effective deliberation protocol, we will then assess its ability to impact the number of possible alternative escalations an agent will be able to do once the deliberation is over.

4.1   Protocol Definition

The deliberation protocol will take place in two phases. Before the first phase, each agent $i \in N$ has a preference relation $\succeq_i$ over the alternatives based on

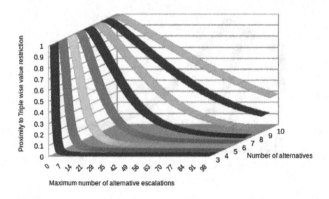

Fig. 6. Proximity to *Triple wise value rest.*: 20 agents.

(*i*) her desirable features in W_i and (*ii*) the *a priori* knowledge she has on the alternatives.

The goal of the protocol is to provide the agents with a way to revise these preferences by refining their set of desired features and the knowledge they have about the alternatives. Intuitively, agents will share knowledge and opinions through arguments. During this process, agents might discover new features that they were not aware of before as well as new arguments leading them to change their opinion on a particular question. Hopefully, this discussion will give agents more insights on the situation and will allow them to refine their preferences, namely their set of desired features and their knowledge about the alternatives. At the end of the second phase, each agent will have modified preferences $\succeq_i'$ over the alternatives which she will use to vote.

During the **first phase**, agents will deliberate to collectively agree upon a—final—set $W_\forall'$ of features, considered as relevant by the group, that they will use in order to choose among the alternatives. Throughout the deliberation, the goal for an agent i is to make her desired features from W_i accepted as relevant by the group. To achieve this goal, agents will assert arguments to justify their preferences. During this first phase, by referring to accepted arguments stored in her *commitment store*, each agent will change her desired features as she gets eventually convinced by other agents' arguments. In this phase, agents will talk in a round robin manner (one after another) but each agent can, if desired, skip her turn. The first phase ends after n successive turn skips. At the end of the first phase, the set $W_\forall'$ of consensual features after deliberation is obtained.

The goal of the **second phase** is to determine, for each alternative $x \in X$, and at least for each criterion $c \in \mathcal{C}$ such that $p_c \in W_\forall'$ or $\mathbf{n}p_c \in W_\forall'$, whether or not x satisfies the criterion c. Agents will use arguments to justify their position. This process results in an attribution for each alternative $x \in X$ of a set P_x of satisfied features. Based on this outcome, the agents will then revise their preferences over the alternatives by considering their own desired features and the features considered as relevant by the group. Once again, agents will deliberate in a round robin manner and can skip their turn. The second phase ends after n successive turn skip.[5]

The way an agent can revise her preferences is to agree that the features chosen by the group are desirable for her too as she is part of the group. Then, each agent i can merge the features contained in $W'_\forall$ with her own set of desired features W_i constructing thus a new set W'_i of desired features, being careful not to leave opposite features in W'_i. In case of a conflict, the feature extracted from $W'_\forall$ is more relevant than its opposite one initially in W_i. The new preference relation of agent i ($\succeq'_i$) is then induced by W'_i and the collective knowledge gained on the alternatives.

Definition 5 (Desired properties after deliberation). *Let N be a set of agents, each agent i in N has a set of wanted properties W_i. Let $W'_\forall$ be the set of consensual features obtained after deliberation. For all i in N, the new wanted features of i are defined as follows:*

$$W'_i = (W_i \cup W'_\forall) \backslash (\{p \in W_i \mid np \in W'_\forall\} \cup \{np \in W_i \mid p \in W'_\forall\})$$

Let us formally define how the agents can interact with each other. In order to get a desired feature or a piece of knowledge accepted as relevant by the group, agents must justify their claims. To achieve this goal, arguments will be used. Classically, in this paper, we assume that agents possess a logical language allowing the construction of arguments. Here, an argument is a triple containing a set of premises, a set of rules and a conclusion which is derived from the premises using the rules [2,7]. Agents can use arguments for different purposes according to possible actions. We define these actions as a set of possible speech acts [14]. This set contains the following locutions:

- ASSERT(.):
    - **Meaning:** an agent uses this locution to formally prove a claim.
    - **Usage:** ASSERT(i, arg) where i is in N and arg is an argument whose conclusion is the statement agent i wants to prove.
- REJECT(.):
    - **Meaning:** an agent uses this locution to formally reject a statement another agent made before. To achieve this goal, the agent uses an argument which proves that the statement she wants to reject is false.
    - **Usage:** REJECT(i, j, F, arg) where i and j are in N and F is a set of premises previously used by j to prove a statement. Note that the conclusion of the argument arg and the rejected premises F are logically incompatible.
- CHALLENGE(.):
    - **Meaning:** an agent uses this locution to ask another agent to justify some premises she used in order to prove a statement.

---

[5] Please note that for simplicity purposes, we assume here that both phases always succeed, *i.e.* all the agents manage to agree on a set of desired features and on the features satisfied by the alternatives.

Table 2. Locutions and their respective attacks and surrenders.

Locutions	Attacks	Surrenders
ASSERT(.)	REJECT(.) CHALLENGE(.)	CONCEDE(.) RETRACT(.)
REJECT(.)	CHALLENGE(.) REJECT(.)	RETRACT(.)
CHALLENGE(.)	ASSERT(.)	RETRACT(.)
RETRACT(.)	$\emptyset$	$\emptyset$
CONCEDE(.)	$\emptyset$	$\emptyset$

- **Usage:** CHALLENGE(i, j, F) where i and j are in N and F are premises used by j in order to prove a statement.
- RETRACT(.):
  - **Meaning:** an agent uses this locution when she is unable to justify some premises she used to prove a statement.
  - **Usage:** RETRACT(i, arg) where i is in N and arg is an argument using premises i is unable to prove.
- CONCEDE(.):
  - **Meaning:** an agent uses this locution to explicitly accept a statement made by another agent.
  - **Usage:** CONCEDE(i, j, arg) where i and j are in N and arg is an argument previously asserted by j whose conclusion is accepted by i.

These locutions allow agents to justify their positions. We will now see how they can use it to deliberate constructively.

Reply Structure. In order to maintain a coherent dialogue, agents have to use locutions in a constructive way. Speech acts are subject to a particular reply structure ensuring that each locution is used for a correct purpose. This reply structure is described in Table 2. We can see, for example, that the RETRACT(.) locution might be used by an agent to respond to a CHALLENGE(.) locution. This CHALLENGE(.) locution, in turn, might be used by someone else to ask for a justification about a claim made earlier using the ASSERT(.) or the REJECT(.) locution.

Correctness Conditions. In order to avoid misuses of the locutions, they are subject to a set of conditions which comply with the reply structure. The conditions that must be satisfied in order to use a specific locution are listed in Table 3. These conditions ensure that agents deliberate in a focused manner.

Commitment Store Effects. Due to the previous conditions, each action performed by an agent is done for a particular purpose. In order to track the effects of these actions on the dialogue, the use of some speech acts is subject to post conditions which imply commitment store modifications. For each agent $i \in N$,

Table 3. Locutions and their using conditions.

Locutions	Using conditions
ASSERT(i, arg)	The arg argument was never asserted before
REJECT(i, j, F, arg)	The rejected premises in F were used by j to prove some statement that i is rejecting. The conclusion of argument arg and the premises in F are logically incompatible with respect to the logical language considered
CHALLENGE(i, j, F)	The challenged premises in F were used by j to prove some statement that i has not yet accepted
RETRACT(i, arg)	The argument arg was asserted by i
CONCEDE(i, j, arg)	The argument arg was asserted by j

$CS(i)$ is the set of arguments that i has explicitly accepted, her *commitment store*. The effects of each locution on agents' commitment stores are shown in Table 4. By applying these modifications, each agent can know, at any time, the status of her preferences. This is necessary as agents have to revise their preferences after the deliberation ends.

Now that the deliberation protocol has been formally defined, we can assess its quality for reaching consensus by characterising its impact on the number of possible alternative escalations agents will be able to do.

4.2 Impact of the Protocol on the Number of Possible Alternative Escalations

At the end of the deliberation process, each agent has a new set of desired features built according to Definition 5. As a consequence, we can make a first trivial observation: if there is a consensus on which features are desirable and as they all share the same knowledge over the alternatives, then all the agents will have the same preferences and the application of pairwise majority will always give a transitive result.

Lemma 1 (Absence of unshared features). *When deliberation ends, if no agent desires an unshared feature then the result of pairwise majority on the induced agents' preferences is transitive.*

We have seen that absence of unshared features benefits transitivity, it is thus interesting to track their evolution during the deliberation phase. The Lemma 1 guarantees a transitive result in case of consensus. The following result ensures that the deliberation process allows agents to move closer to such consensus. The proof consists in verifying that (i) an *unshared* feature can only become a *consensual* one and (ii) a *consensual* feature cannot become an *unshared* one.

Table 4. Locutions and their effects on commitment stores.

Locutions	Commitment store effects
ASSERT(i, arg)	Add arg to $CS(i)$
REJECT(i, j, F, arg)	Add arg to $CS(i)$
CHALLENGE(i, j, F)	–
RETRACT(i, arg)	Remove arg from $CS(i)$
CONCEDE(i, j, arg)	Add arg to $CS(i)$

Lemma 2 (Diminution of unshared features). *The number of unshared features can only decrease during the deliberation.*

At the end of the deliberation, the agents agree on a set $W'_\forall$ of desirable features for the group that induces a preference relation $\succeq_{W'_\forall}$. Then, the unshared features of each agent $i \in N$ will let her modify $\succeq_{W'_\forall}$ in order to obtain her new individual preferences $\succeq'_i$. Let us try to identify the *alternative escalations* that an agent can perform on $\succ_{W'_\forall}$ according to her residual unshared features. Let $x, y \in X$ be two alternatives such that $x \succ_{W'_\forall} y$ and $i \in N$ an agent. In order to obtain $y \succ'_i x$ by changing $\succeq_{W'_\forall}$, i needs a certain number of unshared features. Let us suppose that x satisfies exactly one more feature of $W'_\forall$ than y. Then, i will strictly prefer y over x only if there exist two unshared features (not in $W'_\forall$) p_1 and p_2 in W'_i desired by i such that y satisfies both and x satisfies none. One can generalise this result for scenarios in which the difference $di(x, y)$ of number of features in $W'_\forall$ satisfied by x and y is greater than 1. In such cases, at least $di(x, y) + 1$ unshared features satisfied by y but not by x must be desired by i to obtain $y \succ'_i x$.

Based on this observation, we can now use Lemma 2 to obtain the following theorem which links the *alternative escalation* parameter used in the experiments of Sect. 3.2 to the number of *unshared features*.

Theorem 1 (Maximum number of possible modifications). *Given Max the maximum value of $di(x, y)$ among all pairs of alternatives $(x, y) \in X^2$, an agent $i \in N$ with u_i unshared features will be able to do at most $\lfloor \frac{u_i}{Max+1} \rfloor$ alternative escalations in $\succeq_{W'_\forall}$.*

Hence, during the deliberation, the more the agents are able to bring effective arguments, the less they will get away from the preference relation $\succeq_{W'_\forall}$ induced by $W'_\forall$, which will bring them closer to consensus.

5 Discussion

In this paper, we tried to answer the following question: *is it possible to assess formally the possibility of defining a deliberation protocol moving agents' preferences closer to particular structures (single-peakedness, triple wise value restriction, etc.) ensuring a transitive result under pairwise majority?* We started by defining agents' preference formation based on the notion of *desired features* and used the notion of *alternative escalations* to represent how agents might diverge from the preference relation induced by the group's desired features. Using these notions, we proposed an experimentation showing that less alternative escalations leads to agents' preferences being closer to useful preference structures. Finally, we defined a simple deliberation protocol and characterised it in terms of its impact on the number of possible alternative escalations. While the presented work answer our initial problem, it raises many other questions. We present them in the following paragraphs.

Preferences Formation. Although the results of the experiment seem to confirm the hypothesis that the deliberation protocol improves the agents' preferences structure[6], we observed that our simulation choices have some consequences. In particular, the way in which individual preferences are generated through alternative escalations impacts the *separability into two groups* measure. In our experiment, agents are assumed to be completely independent of each other and to perform alternative escalations in a random way. This way to deal with agents is reminiscent of how one can generate individual preferences under the impartial culture assumption [10]. Unfortunately, impartial culture is known to be unrealistic and seems likely to maximise the probability of obtaining majority cycles [16]. For these reasons, it would be interesting to study other ways of generating preferences and disagreements between agents.

Deliberation Protocol. We deliberately chose to leave aside the argumentation part of the deliberation protocol. However, considering the argument exchange part it is necessary to decide on several points. For instance, what would happen if two agents have rational justifications for opposite features? Or if they desire the same feature but with contradictory justification? Considering argumentation systems [7] during the deliberation could allow the resolution of such conflicts and help agents deciding which justifications should be taken into account.

Measures Generalisation. In the experiment carried out, we have chosen to generalise the various measures of proximity to the whole set of triplets of alternatives by observing the proportion of triplets satisfying the desired condition. Several reasons motivated this choice, such as the fact that for extreme values the measure remains consistent (a measure of 1 means that the condition is true for the preference profile as a whole, a measure of 0 means that the condition is absolutely unverified).

That being said, it would be interesting to consider other approaches to measure the efficiency of the deliberation, for instance by studying the link between the distribution of unshared features and the probability of obtaining a nontransitive result using pairwise majority.

---

[6] This observation is in line with the experimental results obtained by List et al. [12] in 2012.

Real-Life Situation. Finally, setting up a real-life experimentation would allow to focus on other aspects of deliberation. Indeed, in addition to confirming or refuting the experimental results of this work, it would let us assess to which extent people are able to identify desirable features and to defend them using rational arguments.

References

1. Arrow, K.J.: Social Choice and Individual Values. Wiley, New York (1951)
2. Besnard, P., Hunter, A.: A logic-based theory of deductive arguments. Artif. Intell. **128**(1–2), 203–235 (2001)
3. Black, D.: The median voter theorem. J. Polit. Econ. **56**(1), 23–34 (1948)
4. Brandt, F., Conitzer, V., Endriss, U., Lang, J., Procaccia, A.D.: Handbook of Computational Social Choice, 1st edn. Cambridge University Press, New York (2016)
5. de Condorcet, M.J.A.N.C.M.: Essai sur l'application de l'analyse à la probabilité des décisions rendues à la pluralité des voix. L'imprimerie royale (1785)
6. Dietrich, F., List, C.: Where do preferences come from ? Int. J. Game Theory **42**(3), 613–637 (2013)
7. Dung, P.M.: On the acceptability of arguments and its fundamental role in non-monotonic reasoning, logic programming and n-person games. Artif. Intell. **77**(2), 321–357 (1995)
8. Gehrlein, W.V.: Consistency in measures of social homogeneity: a connection with proximity to single peaked preferences. Qual. Quant. **38**(2), 147–171 (2004)
9. Gehrlein, W.V.: Probabilities of election outcomes with two parameters: the relative impact of unifying and polarizing candidates. Rev. Econ. Des. **9**(4), 317–336 (2005)
10. Guilbaud, G.T.: Les théories de l'intérêt général et le problème logique de l'agrégation. Économie appliquée **5**, 501–584 (1952)
11. Inada, K.I.: A note on the simple majority decision rule. Econometrica: J. Econometric Soc. **32**, 525–531 (1964)
12. List, C., Luskin, R.C., Fishkin, J.S., McLean, I.: Deliberation, single-peakedness, and the possibility of meaningful democracy: evidence from deliberative polls. J. Politics **75**(1), 80–95 (2012)
13. Niemi, R.G.: Majority decision-making with partial unidimensionality. Am. Polit. Sci. Rev. **63**(2), 488–497 (1969)
14. Searle, J.R.: Speech Acts: An Essay in the Philosophy of Language, vol. 626. Cambridge University Press, Cambridge (1969)
15. Sen, A.K.: A possibility theorem on majority decisions. Econometrica: J. Econometric Soc. **34**, 491–499 (1966)
16. Tsetlin, I., Regenwetter, M., Grofman, B.: The impartial culture maximizes the probability of majority cycles. Soc. Choice Welf. **21**(3), 387–398 (2003)

K-ACE: A Flexible Environment for Knowledge-Aware Multi-Agent Systems

Stefania Costantini[✉] and Valentina Pitoni

Dipartimento di Ingegneria e Scienze dell'Informazione e Matematica,
Università degli Studi dell'Aquila, L'Aquila, Italy
stefania.costantini@univaq.it,
valentina.pitoni@graduate.univaq.it

Abstract. In this paper we consider complex application scenarios, typically concerning smart Cyber-Physical Systems, where several components and subsystems interact among themselves, with human users and with the physical environment, and employ forms of intelligent reasoning for meeting the system's requirements and reaching its overall objectives. We propose a new multi-component multi-level architecture called K-ACE, which provides a high degree of flexibility in the system's definition, though within a formal semantics.

1 Introduction

There are nowadays many application fields where agents and multi-agent systems are situated in complex, open, dynamic computational environments which include heterogeneous software components, physical devices and sensors including wearable devices, third part services, data centers, expert systems and other knowledge sources available on the Internet. The availability of components evolves in time, as new knowledge can be discovered, and components may join or leave the environment, or become momentarily unreachable. Such environments can actually constitute Cyber-Physical Systems (CPSs), and they may include physical components that interact with or are integrated into the computational "ecosystem". A suitable denomination of a wide class of such systems can be "Dynamic Proactive Expert Systems" (DyPES). In fact, these systems can be aimed at supporting human experts and personnel or human users in a knowledgeable fashion, in applications such as eHealth and many others: so, they are reminiscent of the role of traditional expert systems. However, they are proactive in the sense that such systems may have objectives (e.g., monitoring and assisting patients, rationalizing access to medical doctors, ambulances helicopters, beds in hospital) that they pursue autonomously, requiring human intervention only when needed. They are also dynamic, because they are able to exploit not only a predefined set of knowledge bases and/or resources: rather, they must be able to locate upon need new knowledge sources and reasoning services. DyPESs can be Cyber-Physical Systems: so, they can be able to perform complex event processing, i.e., to actively monitor events in order to make automated decisions and take time-critical actions.

In this paper we propose a software architecture for DyPESs, called K-ACE (standing for 'K-level ACE'). K-ACE aims to gather and organize agents, components and

© Springer Nature Switzerland AG 2019
M. Baldoni et al. (Eds.): PRIMA 2019, LNAI 11873, pp. 19–35, 2019.
https://doi.org/10.1007/978-3-030-33792-6_2

sub-systems, seen as "lower-level" K-ACEs, so that the resulting system is able to implement a specific application or to perform tasks or to reach overall objectives. Each subsystem may have however its own local objectives, not made known to the others. No assumption is therefore done about subsystems, save that in order to be allowed to join a K-ACE they should implement some basic simple mechanisms illustrated below. The wide review [1] strongly advocates the adoption of agents and MAS for Cyber-Physical Systems (CPS) in an industrial perspective. It reviews ongoing projects and existing implementations and discusses relevant aspects and principles. Importantly, it notices that "The technical challenges [about CPS] are complemented by a lack of widely acceptable models on how to design and manage cyber–physical industrial systems". In this sense, the K-ACE proposal makes one first step ahead.

The proposed architecture takes as basic blocks DACMACS (Data-Aware Commitment-based managed Multi-Agent-Context Systems, [2,3]) and ACEs (Agent Computational Environments, [4]). With K-ACE we intend to generalize, unify and empower the DACMACS-ACE features within a smoothly integrated framework. To manage knowledge flow from-to agents and reasoning modules and external contexts and lower level K-ACEs we adopt a very general and versatile mechanism. Precisely, we embrace the use of *bridge-rules*, inspired to those of MCSs (Multi-Context Systems) [5,6]. Bridge rules are thus a basic element of K-ACEs, as they allow knowledge to flow among components in a clearly-specified principled way. Agents composing a K-ACE are not required to be aware of the system's structure in order to be able to retrieve the components that may be useful to their aim. Rather, at each level the system includes a special entity, called "Institutional Agent", which is in charge of the management of system dynamics. The Institutional Agent is in fact able to locate components based upon their *role*, where the *role* indicates the kind of information or operation that a component is able to provide/perform, along with operational information to retrieve and access the component itself. Whenever the required component cannot be found at the present level but might be found at lower levels, the Institutional Agent locates within the system a suitable lower-level K-ACE and defers the search to its Institutional Agent, and so on recursively until a component with the desired role (or a more general one, if none is found) is retrieved.

In this paper we introduce K-ACEs, provide their definition and explain their functioning, and specify their semantics. The paper is organized as follows. In Sect. 2 we introduce and discuss a motivating example. In Sects. 3 and 4 we provide the necessary background knowledge about MCS, ACE and DACMACS. In Sect. 5 we present the new architecture, and provide its formal definition. In Sect. 6 we illustrate the semantics of the proposed framework. In Sect. 7 we discuss related work and conclude.

2   Motivating Example

In this section we introduce a motivating example inspired to our previous work discussed in [7], that concerns the exploitation of smart Cyber Physical Systems, i.e., in the terminology introduced in this paper, DyPESs, for applications in the e-Health field. We assume to have modeled an eHealth system as a K-ACE. We assume also that, in this system, each human patient is monitored by a PMA ("Personal Monitoring

Agent") which is defined as an 1-ACE (seen below in Sect. 5) which is, essentially, an agent equipped with local knowledge bases, complex event processing capabilities, and reasoning modules. These additional components may provide the agent with, e.g., the patient's clinical history, patient's preferences and needs, information about the patient's standard treatment and about possible actions to undertake in case of changes in some of the patient's parameters (e.g., by rearranging the quantity of a medicine according to certain values in blood test). The complex event processing modules can for instance detect symptoms, and decide whether they correspond to a potentially serious or unexpected situation. The reasoning modules can for instance devise a plan for coping with such situation. A K-ACE can encompass several PMAs each one in charge of a patient. The system may include other K-ACEs, for instance a "Diagnostic Center" providing intelligent modules for plausible interpretation of symptoms, a "Medical Center" providing consultation with human specialists, an "Emergency Center" managing hospital beds and transportation facilities, etc. Each PMA can proactively resort to such systems, by means of rules such as:

$$G\langle 8h \rangle \; high\_blood\_pressure \; \textbf{enables}$$
$$communication(pma, helpdesk@Inst@medcenter,$$
$$cardiological\_consultation\_required(patient_{pma},$$
$$high\_blood\_pressure)$$

Here, G stands for "always" where $\langle 8h \rangle$ indicates an interval including the last 8 h. So, if the patient in charge of a certain PMA has had high blood pressure for the last eight hours, this enables the PMA to undertake suitable countermeasures. Here, the PMA communicates with the agent in charge of dispatching requests in an available Medical Center, identified by the expression $helpdesk@Inst@medcenter$. This in order to require a cardiological consultancy. Precisely, the reference to a suitable helpdesk agent $helpdesk$ at an available Medical Center $medcenter$ (which is itself modeled as a K-ACE) is provided by the K-ACE's Institutional Agent $Inst$, inquired by role. So, the PMA can locate the required service without the necessity of being aware of the entire system's topology. This is quite convenient, also considering that such a system can be of big dimensions and that its topology may vary in time, with components joining/leaving the system. In the rule below, a PMA in charge of an emergency is enabled to require an urgent transportation of the patient in its charge to the hospital because of emergency condition E. The request is issued to the manager agent of the Emergency Center K-ACE, identified by role (as explained above) via the expression $emergency\_manager@Inst@emergencies$. Thus:

$$emergency(E) \; \textbf{enables}$$
$$communication(pma, emergency\_manager@Inst@emergencies,$$
$$hospital\_transportation\_required(patient_{pma}, condition(E)))$$

We may notice that the inter-agent communication modalities (that may for instance be based upon *commitments*, which is a relatively recent though very well-established general paradigm for agent interaction, cf. [9] and the references therein), play indeed a fundamental role. In fact, the agents receiving a request will commit to satisfy such request in a certain way and within a certain time: e.g., the Medical Center will provide a video-conference with Dr. House, and the Emergency Center will commit to send, e.g., an ambulance by the hour of, if deemed necessary, an helicopter by twenty minutes.

Notice that, in this example, the involved sub-systems may have different objectives: a PMA has the objective to keep the health of its assigned patient under control. The emergency center will have the objective of an optimal or quasi-optimal usage of the available resources, such as doctors, ambulances, helicopters, and so on. The overall system will have the objective to care in the best possible way about patients' health while staying within budget limits and resource availability. Notice also that ontology and ontological reasoning are very useful in such a context in order to describe, e.g., resources, patients, diseases. etc. In the rest of this paper we will specify and discuss the K-ACE architecture as a tool for the formalization of this example and of many others.

3   Background: MCS

The (Managed) multi-context systems approach (cf. [5,6] and the references therein) aims to make it possible to specify applications involving multiple possibly heteroge-neous data/knowledge/reasoning sources, that in the approach are called "contexts". Information flow among contexts is modeled via "bridge rules", whose form is simi-lar to datalog rules with negation (cf. any standard textbook). Bridge rules allow for inter-context interaction: in fact, each element in their "body" explicitly includes the indication of the context from which information is to be obtained.

In order to account for heterogeneity of sources each context is supposed to be based on its own *logic*. We do not see this as an essential limitation: in fact, many sources are logical by nature (including, e.g., relational databases and ontologies), others can be built in any of the many available logic-based approaches, and others can be wrapped within a logical shell. Reporting from [5], a logic L is a triple $(KB_L; Cn_L; ACC_L)$, where KB_L is the set of admissible knowledge bases of L, which are sets of KB-elements ("formulas"); Cn_L is the set of acceptable sets of consequences, whose ele-ments are data items or "facts" (these sets can be called "belief sets" or "data sets"); $ACC_L : KB_L \rightarrow 2^{Cn_L}$ is a function which defines the semantics of L by assigning each knowledge-base a set of "acceptable" sets of consequences. A managed Multi-Context System (mMCS) $M = (C_1, \ldots, C_n)$ is a heterogeneous collection of contexts with $C_i = (L_i; kb_i; br_i)$ where L_i is a logic, $kb_i \in KB_{L_i}$ is a knowledge base and br_i is a set of bridge rules. Each such rule is of the following form, where the left-hand side $o(s)$ is called the *head*, denoted as $head(\rho)$, the right-hand side is called the *body*, also denoted as $body(\rho)$, and the comma stand for conjunction.

$$o(s) \leftarrow (c_1 : p_1), \ldots, (c_j : p_j), not\, (c_{j+1} : p_{j+1}), \ldots, not\, (c_m : p_m).$$

For each bridge rule included in a context C_i, it is required that $kb_i \cup o(s)$ belongs to KB_{Li} and, for every $k \leq m$, c_k is a context included in M, and each p_k belongs to some set in KB_{L_k}. The meaning is that $o(s)$ is added to the consequences of kb_i when-ever each atom p_r, $r \leq j$, belongs to the consequences of context c_r, while instead each atom p_w, $j < w \leq m$, does not belong to the consequences of context c_s. While in stan-dard MCSs the head s of a bridge rule is simply added to the "destination" context's knowledge base kb, in managed MCS kb is subjected to an elaboration w.r.t. s according to the specific operator o and to its intended semantics. Formula s can in fact be elaborated by o, for instance with the aim, e.g., of making it compatible with kb's format, or via more involved elaboration, or exploited for belief revision. A *management function*, specific for each context, provides a semantics to the operator o which is applied to the conclusion of a bridge rule. Thus, such function is crucial for the incorporation of new knowledge.

If $M = (C_1, \ldots, C_n)$ is an MCS, a data state or, equivalently, belief/knowledge state, is a tuple $S = (S_1, \ldots, S_n)$ such that each S_i is an element of Cn_i. Desirable data states are those where each S_i is acceptable according to ACC_i. A bridge rule ρ is applicable in a knowledge state iff for all $1 \le i \le j : p_i \in S_i$ and for all $j + 1 \le k \le m : p_k \notin S_k$. Let $app(S)$ be the set of the heads of the bridge rules which are applicable in a data state S.

Semantics of mMCS is in terms of *equilibria*. A data state $S = (S_1, \ldots, S_n)$ is an equilibrium for an MCS $M = (C_1, \ldots, C_n)$ iff, for $1 \le i \le n$, $S_i \in ACC_i(kb'_i)$, with $kb'_i = mng_i(app(S), kb_i)$. Thus, an equilibrium is a global data state composed of acceptable data states, one for each context, encompassing inter-context communication determined by bridge rules and the elaboration resulting from the operational statements and the management functions. Equilibria may not exist.

Notice that bridge rules are intended to be applied whenever they are applicable, so they are basically a *reactive* device. In dynamic environments, a bridge rule in general will not be applied only once, and it does not hold that an equilibrium, once reached, lasts forever, because contexts should be able to incorporate new data items.

4 Background: ACE and DACMACS

DACMACS (Data-Aware Commitment-based managed Multi-Agent-Context Systems) [2,3] extend DACMAS (Data-Aware Commitment-based Multi-Agent Systems) [8], a quite general model of multi-agent systems which remains very general about an agent program's definition. So, this model allows for the adoption of virtually any agent-oriented language/formalism. In DACMAS/DACMACS knowledge and data are supposed to be represented via logic ontologies described, e.g., in DLR-Lite description logics. Communication among agents in DACMACS occurs according to the specific agent-oriented language adopted, where however it is assumed that the semantics of communicative acts and the definition of communication protocols are specified via the approach of *commitments*, a very general and flexible paradigm for the definition of agents' interaction (cf. [9] and the references therein). Precisely, a DACMACS (Data-Aware Commitment-based managed Multi-Agent-Context System) is a tuple

$$\langle \mathcal{X}, \mathcal{N}, \mathcal{Y}, \mathcal{E}, \mathcal{T}, \mathcal{A}, \mathcal{I}, \mathcal{C}, \mathcal{B} \rangle$$

where:

(i) $\mathcal{T}$ and $\mathcal{A}$ are the global TBox and ABox respectively, and are common to all agents participating in the system; they represent respectively definition of a knowledge base and its current instance, which is shared by all agents in the system; access to ABox and TBox is not a substitute of inter-agent communication via message-passing, rather it is an additional empowering feature.

(ii) $\mathcal{X}$ is a finite set of agent specifications, defined in any agent-oriented programming language; each agent is assumed to be equipped with a local ABox; the local ABox which is required to be consistent with the global ABox and TBox, where however the ABoxes of the various agents are not required to be mutually consistent; in fact, each agent's knowledge base can be seen as composed of the union the global ABox and TBox and the local ABox.

(iii) $\mathcal{N}$ is a set of agents' names, listing the agents (beyond the Institutional agent) composing the MAS, together with their *roles* in the system.

(iv) $\mathcal{Y}$ is a set of contexts' names, listing the contexts that are globally known to the MAS, together with their *roles* in the system.

(v) $\mathcal{I}$ is a specification for the "Institutional" agent *Inst*; this special agent is responsible of managing message-passing among agents, and is also in charge of locating agents and contexts based on their roles: a query *role@Inst* issued by an agent a will return the name of an agent/context with role *role*; in general, if more that one agent/context fulfills the required role, a query *role@Inst* can return *a set* of names, among which agent a will choose according to some policy.

(vi) $\mathcal{C}$ is a contractual specification, $\mathcal{B}$ is a Commitment Box (CBox), $\mathcal{E}$ is a set of predicates denoting events (where the predicate name is the event type, and the arity determines the content of the event); all these elements are involved in the management of commitment-based communication, performed by the Institutional agent.

Components $\mathcal{T}, \mathcal{E}, \mathcal{X}, \mathcal{I}, \mathcal{C}$ and $\mathcal{B}$ are analogous to those of DACMASs. However, agents' specifications can now include: a set of contexts, and a set of bridge rules for gathering new knowledge from these contexts; *trigger rules* for proactive activation of bridge rules; *bridge-update rules* for incorporating the acquired knowledge into the agent's knowledge base upon specific conditions, thus implementing a proactive counterpart of the MCSs' management function. Contexts in bridge-rule bodies can be now identified by their names, whenever they are locally known to the agent, or by a query *role@Inst* returning the name of an agent/context with the required role. The Institutional agent *Inst* is a special agent that: manages the messages which are exchanged in the system, and is also responsible of the management of commitments, whose concrete instances are maintained in the Commitment Box $\mathcal{B}$; it does so based on the *Commitment Rules* in $\mathcal{C}$, defining the commitment machine. The Institutional agent is also responsible of returning agents' and context's names via their role, by answering queries of the form *role@Inst*. A semantics for DACMACS in terms of equilibria, inspired by the MCSs' semantics but extended with timed data states, timed equilibria and execution trajectories is provided in [2].

An Agent Computational Environment (ACE) [4] is defined as a tuple $\langle A, M_1, \ldots, M_r, C_1, \ldots, C_s, R_1, \ldots, R_q \rangle$ where module A is the "basic agent", i.e., an agent program written in any agent-oriented language. The "overall" agent is obtained by equipping the basic agent with the following facilities. The M_is are "Event-Action modules", that are special modules aimed at Complex Event Processing. The R_js are "Reasoning modules", that are specialized in specific reasoning tasks. The C_ks are contexts in the sense of MCSs, i.e., external data/knowledge sources that the agent is able to locate and to query about some subject, but upon which it has no further knowledge and no control: this means that the agent is aware of the "role" of contexts in the sense of the kind of knowledge they are able to provide, but is unable in general to provide a description of their behavior/contents or to affect them in any way. Interaction among ACE's components occurs via *bridge rules*, inspired by those of MCSs.

The "local" agent's modules, i.e., main agent program, event-action modules, and reasoning modules can be defined in any agent-oriented and/or computational-logic-based programming language or also in other logic formalisms. Notice that in case $r, q, s = 0$, i.e, no auxiliary components are provided, an ACE reduces to a "traditional" agent. Bridge rules have been extended in [10] to become *bridge rule patterns* where each c_i in the body can be either a constant indicating a context name, or a term of the form $m_i(k_i)$, called *context designator*, indicating the *kind* of context (rather than the specific one) to be queried, to be specified before bridge-rule execution. Such a rule, once context designators have been instantiated to actual context names, can become *applicable* as seen before for MCS.

In ACE, bridge rules are proactively enabled (and thus applies whenever applicable) upon conditions internal to the agent. In particular, such conditions are specified via *trigger rules* of the form $Q(\hat{y})$ **enables** $A(\hat{x})$ where: $\hat{x}$, $\hat{y}$ are tuples composed of constants and variables, $Q(\hat{y})$ is a query to the agent's internal knowledge-base and $A(\hat{x})$ is the conclusion of one of agent's bridge rules, that is "fired" whenever $Q(\hat{y})$ evaluates to *true*. The result of $Q(\hat{y})$ can partially instantiate $A(\hat{x})$.

The results returned by a bridge rule with head $A(\hat{x})$ can be exploited via a *bridge-update rule* of the form **upon** $A(\hat{x})$ **then**$\beta(\hat{x})$ where $\beta(\hat{x})$ specifies both the conditions for acquiring $A(\hat{x})$ into the agent's knowledge base, and the elaboration to be performed. So, also the incorporation of bridge-rule results occurs in a proactive way as dictated by $\beta(\hat{x})$, which constitutes the agent-oriented counterpart of MCS's management function.

The merit of the ACE approach is to make an agent fully modular. This is permitted by a semantics which generalizes that of mMCS, and is thus fully parametric w.r.t. formalization of components. The generalization of bridge rules to bridge rule patterns overcomes the limitation to have to specify statically which are the knowledge sources to consult. In ACE, such sources can be determined dynamically, where suitable bridge-rule patterns can be instantiated accordingly.

5 K-ACE

In this section we present K-layers-ACE, or simply K-ACE. It is a generalization of ACE and DACMACS, where: each agent in a DACMACS can be an ACE (more precisely a 1-ACE, which is a slight extension seen below); a DACMACS (now renamed K-ACE) may be composed now not only of agents and contexts, but also of other (lower-level) K-ACEs. This "nesting" is allowed over an arbitrary number "K" of layers. This proposal is introduced in the perspective of DyPESs where an application/organization, represented as a K-ACE, might dynamically resort to other external applications/organizations/systems to obtain data or to perform elaborations. So, such external entities that are accessible by a DypES/K-ACE are seen as (lower-level) K-ACEs that can be reached though a uniform interface, represented by these systems'

Institutional agents. Recursively, lower-level K-ACEs can have other K-ACEs as components, along an arbitrary number of levels. 1-ACEs are, together with contexts, the basic building blocks of the system. Notice that which are the higher-lower levels is not fixed: each K-ACE implementing some application and/or pursuing its own objective considers the other K-ACEs it needs to access, from its own perspective, as lower level. As a metaphor, we might see the whole system with all the composing K-ACEs as a galaxy, and each composing K-ACE as a stellar system composed of solar systems (1-ACEs); each solar and stellar system is able to observe (to some extent) the rest of the galaxy.

Any component or subsystem in a K-ACE is not necessarily always available. Also, not every component is allowed to reach every other one: rather, accessibility can be subject to permissions. Bridge-rules activation may itself be subject to norms, i.e., not only an agent proactively seeks to obtain or distribute new knowledge, but may do so according to either organizational rules or deontic obligations. Each component may in turn choose to access the *best preferred* components among those which may provide certain knowledge or services.

K-ACE systems may evolve in time, so we now define a K-ACE relative to a time T. Except for the Institutional agent and (possibly) for the global TBox and ABox and commitments' contractual specification, whose definition may remain stable, all the other components can evolve over time. A reachability relation, that itself evolves in time, dynamically establishes which component can reach which other. As done in Linear Temporal Logic (LTL) we assume a discrete, linear model of time and represent each state/time instant as an integer number. The actual evolution from time T to $T' = T + 1$ and the interval $\delta = T' - T$ is considered to be peculiar of each specific instance of the architecture given its application domain.

The basic building blocks of K-ACEs are thus ACEs, augmented with some features that make them more suitable to be included in a wider system. Empowered ACEs are defined below, and are called 1-ACEs to mean that they are intended to be the unitary components of K-ACEs.

Definition 1. *Let a 1-ACE be an extension of ACE, where:*

– *a 1-ACE is characterized by a unique name and a list of roles; the name must include sufficient information for locating the 1-ACE and communicating with it;*
– *a 1-ACE's main agent is supposed to be equipped with a local ABox;*
– *in 1-ACE's bridge rules, that are still of the general form:*

$$s \leftarrow (\mathcal{C}_1 : p_1), \dots, (\mathcal{C}_j : p_j), not\,(\mathcal{C}_{j+1} : p_{j+1}), \dots, not\,(\mathcal{C}_m : p_m).$$

each $\mathcal{C}_i$ can now be one of the following:
   • *a constant denoting a context name;*
   • *a term of the form $m_i(k_i)$ that we call* context designator, *indicating the kind of context (rather than the specific one) to be queried; such term must be substituted by a constant denoting a context name before bridge-rule execution; an expression of the form role@Inst to be substituted by a constant denoting a context name before bridge-rule execution.*

As previously seen, an expression of the form $role@Inst$ denotes a query to a special "Institutional" agent, returning the name of a context with the required role. When no ambiguity can arise 1-ACEs can be called simply "agents". By some abuse of notation, for a 1-ACE with name a we will often say "1-ACE a" or "agent a".

Definition 2. *Let a K-ACE ($K \geq 1$) at time T be a tuple*

$$\langle \mathcal{N}^T, \mathcal{X}^T, \mathcal{Y}^T, \mathcal{T}^T, \mathcal{A}^T, \mathcal{R}^T, \mathcal{C}^T, \mathcal{B}^T, \mathcal{E}^T, \mathcal{I} \rangle$$

identified by a unique name n_K, a role r_{n_K}, and an expression denoting its "Institutional" agent $Inst@n_K$, where:

(i) *$\mathcal{N}^T$ is the list of 1-ACEs' that are part of the K-ACE at time T; each one is identified by a unique name and by its role(s); we say that such agents participate to the (K-ACE) system at level K; the specification of 1-ACEs is considered to be external to the system, though when joining the system the agents can be reached via their names and roles;*

(ii) *if $K > 1$, $\mathcal{X}^T$ is a finite list of K'-ACEs, $K' = K - 1$, i.e., the lower-level subsystems taking part in the K-ACE at time T; each one is identified by a unique name $n_{K'}$ and by its role(s) $r_{n_{K'}}$, and by an expression denoting their Institutional agent $Inst@n_{K'}$;*

(iii) *$\mathcal{Y}^T$ is a set of contexts' names, listing the contexts that are globally known to the K-ACE at level K and time T; contexts' definitions is considered to be external to the system.*

(iv) *$\mathcal{T}^T$ and $\mathcal{A}^T$ are the global TBox and ABox respectively, and are common to all agents participating in the system at level K;*

(v) *$\mathcal{R}^T$ is a reachability relation, establishing*

    (a) *which elements of $\mathcal{N}^T$ can reach each other, thus specifying constraints on inter agent communication;*

    (b) *which elements of $\mathcal{Y}^T$ are reachable by each element of $\mathcal{N}^T$, i.e, which contexts are reachable by each agent (at level K);*

    (c) *which lower level K'-ACEs (i.e., which elements of $\mathcal{X}^T$) are reachable by each agent in $\mathcal{N}^T$;*

    (d) *which elements of $\mathcal{Y}^T$, i.e., which contexts, are reachable from the outside, precisely from higher-level K-ACEs (if any); such external agents are designated herein via the standard name outag.*

    We introduce a special distinguished predicate $kreach(C_1, C_2, T)$, that is true whenever component C_2 is accessible from component C_2 at time T according to $\mathcal{R}^T$. The binary version $kreach(C_1, C_2)$ takes T to be the current time.

(vi) *like in DACMACS, $\mathcal{C}^T$ is a contractual specification, $\mathcal{B}^T$ is a Commitment Box (CBox), $\mathcal{E}^T$ is a set of predicates denoting events, and all these elements are exploited by the Institutional agent for the management of (commitment-based) inter-agent communication. Note that communication among 1-ACEs A and B is possible at any time t only if $kreach(A, B, t)$ holds.*

(vii) *$\mathcal{I}$ is a specification for the Institutional agent $Inst@n_k$; specifically, the Institutional agent is in charge of inter-agent communication, of contexts' identification via their roles, and of acting as an interface with the lower-level K-ACEs (see (ii));*

a query to the Institutional agent for obtaining a (set of) agent(s) or a (set of) context(s) with role role issued by the 1-ACEs is now of the form $role@Inst@n_K$, and returns the set of agent/contexts with the specified role; we assume that the Institutional agent is a special 1-ACE that does not encompass Event-Action modules or contexts; however, it may encompass reasoning modules that can be exploited for performing its functions; we assume $Inst@n_k$ to have direct access to all other K-ACE's elements, and to be able to communicate with Institutional agents of lower-level K'-ACEs by means of queries $role@Inst@n_{K'}$. We assume that, given a 1-ACE participating in K-ACE n_K, a query $role@Inst@n_K$ to the "local" Institutional agent takes the simplified form $role@Inst$. Notice that the Institutional agent is the unique "entry point" of a K-ACE; in fact, higher-level components or other components of the same K-ACE can locate and therefore access components only through results of queries of the kind $role@Inst$. In case possible alternative results are available, Inst can apply its own internal policies for selecting one.

We assume the structures $\mathcal{N}^T$, $\mathcal{X}^T$, $\mathcal{R}^T$ to be dynamic, in the sense that, as previously remarked, components may join or leave the system, or become momentarily unreachable.

Therefore, we have constructed a modular architecture where the basic elements are agents, i.e., 1-ACEs, and contexts; they can be part of a K-ACE, that provides, via the Institutional agent with the support of a number of specialized knowledge bases, a suitable infrastructure for communication and for the location (by role) of other agents and of required knowledge bases; K-ACEs can be in turn part of other (higher-level) K-ACEs, where the interface among levels is provided by the Institutional agents.

A more precise specification of the Institutional agent's operation needs to be provided. We suppose that Institutional agent is able to reason about roles, so that in case a module with the specified role could not be found directly it might be possible to find instead another one whose role is either equivalent or more general.

Notice that, given query $role@Inst@n_K$, this query must be issued by an agent and, given the syntactic place where the query occurs, it can be determined whether the agent seeks to find either other agents or contexts with the specified role. The Institutional agent returns a set of agents/contexts including exactly those which are accessible from A and are pertinent to role *role*.

Definition 3. *Let role1 and role2 be expressions denoting roles of agents/contexts in a given K-ACE. Let subs(role1, role2) be a predicate that is true whenever role2 is either equivalent or more general than role1 w.r.t. a background ontological role definition R.*

We assume that the Institutional agent owns a private background knowledge base including the ontological role definition R. It is thus able to compute, given *role1*, roles *role2* such that $subs(role1, role2)$ holds. This may be possibly achieved via a suitable reasoning module.

Definition 4. *Given a K-ACE identified by its name n_K, role r_{n_K}, and Institutional agent $Inst@n_K$ with background ontological role definition R, a query $role@Inst@n_K$ issued by a 1-ACE (agent) A returns a set S that can be: (i) a set of contexts if the query* *occurs in the body a bridge rule; (ii) a set of agents if the query occurs elsewhere in the agent's program. The set S in fact includes:*

1. *all those components that are reachable from A according to $\mathcal{R}^T$ at level K, i.e., within the K-ACE without resorting to lower-level K'-ACEs with role role, or, if none can be found,*
2. *all those components that are reachable from A according to $\mathcal{R}^T$ at level K though with role role1 where $subs(role, role1)$ holds (i.e., a more general role is seeked whenever the specific one could not be identified), or, if none can be found,*
3. *the result of a query $role@Inst@n'_K$ where K'-ACE with name n'_K is reachable from A according to $\mathcal{R}^T$, and has role $r_{n_{K'}}$, where $subs(role, r_{n_{K'}})$ holds; I.e., if a component with the required role (or with a more general role) cannot be found within the K-ACE, then it is looked for in lower level K-ACEs.*

In a K-ACE, the reachability relation $\mathcal{R}^T$ defines a graph structure where: (i) nodes are all the components, namely agents, contexts and K'-ACEs included in the system; i.e., the set $V_{n_K}^T$ of vertices is composed of the elements of $\mathcal{N}^T$, $\mathcal{Y}^T$ and $\mathcal{X}^T$; (ii) the set $E_{n_K}^T$ of edges corresponds to couple of nodes (components) that are connected according to $\mathcal{R}^T$, i.e., at the present time.

The problem of determining all components of a certain kind reachable from a given "starting" one, this can be understood as the problem of finding a spanning tree with that component as root. Therefore,

Proposition 1. *Given a K-ACE, the complexity of determining (at any time T) which set of components is reachable from a given one is $\mathcal{O}(|V_{n_K}^T| + |E_{n_K}^T|)$.*

In case more than one suitable component is retrieved, one will be chosen by the Institutional Agent according to some policy, e.g., by taking into account agents' *preferences*.

We can now establish when a bridge rule occurring in an agent can actually be triggered.

Definition 5. *Given bridge rule ρ occurring in the main agent program of a 1-ACE a that is a component of a K-ACE at time T is executable at time T iff each C_i in its body has been substituted by a constant c_i denoting a context (this either by performing a specific action or by executing a query $role@Inst@n_K$ to the K-ACE's Institutional agent) and $kreach(a, c_i, T)$ holds.*

Note that the notion of bridge-rule being executable is preliminary to bridge rule applicability. Reporting to K-ACEs the notion introduced in [2], each bridge rule ρ is *potentially applicable* in a system's state if such a state entails its body. For contexts, each bridge rule is applicable whenever it is potentially applicable. For agents instead, a bridge rule with head $A(\hat{y})$ is applicable whenever it is potentially applicable and there exists in the main agent program a trigger rule of the form $Q(\hat{y})$ **enables** $A(\hat{x})$ where the agent's present state satisfies $Q(\hat{y})$, where such trigger rule "triggers" or "activates" the bridge rule.

So, for making such applicability formally precise we have to define a K-ACE state at time T, and how such state evolves in time. However, for K-ACE we also propose a generalization of trigger rules. We may notice that trigger rules, that determine proactive activation of bridge-rules, can be modeled in terms of Linear Time Logic expressions. In fact, let us consider the *Separated Normal Form* (SNF) for LTL formulas specified in [11]. In such normal form, all formulas have syntax: $\phi \Rightarrow \bigcirc \psi$ where ϕ is a conjunction of propositional formulas. A trigger rule $Q(\hat{y})$ **enables** $A(\hat{x})$ can thus be understood as $Q(\hat{y}) \Rightarrow \bigcirc A(\hat{x})$ that is in turn implicitly understood as $\Box(Q(\hat{y}) \Rightarrow \bigcirc A(\hat{x}))$.

I.e., whenever $Q(\hat{y})$ is entailed by the present state, bridge rule with head $A(\hat{x})$ will be activated in next state. The advantage of such a reformulation is that it requires no modification to the semantics of the adopted agent-oriented language, as it suffices (as formally seen below) that the system's evolution respects such rules. A similar use of this notation is made in [12] to make agents adapt their behavior to comply with norms without modifying the agent's semantics. We refer to the left-hand-side of a trigger rule as its "premise" and to the right-hand-side as its "consequence", and we say that the rule is fired in a system's current state whenever at previous state the premise holds, and so in current state the consequence is executed.

We can further generalize trigger rules by introducing a temporal element also in the premise, to state that a bridge rule should be activated if something happens (i.e, if $Q(\hat{y})$ becomes true, or is always true, or is never true) at a certain time or within a certain time interval. So, we might have, in 1-ACE A, rules such as for instance $N\langle m, n \rangle\, Q(\hat{y})$ **enables** $A(\hat{x})$ meaning that if $Q(\hat{y})$ has never become true in given time interval $\langle m, n \rangle$ then the bridge rule in the consequence is indeed enabled. Note that time instants, line m and n above, refer to the agent's local time. The temporal operators that we consider (with or without an associated interval, which is in fact optional), with the usual intuitive meaning, are the following. $\Diamond_{m,n}\, \varphi$, also indicated with $F\langle m, n \rangle\, \varphi$, means (*eventually*, or "finally", (in the given time interval, if any); $\Box_{m,n}\, \varphi$, also indicated with $G\langle m, n \rangle\, \varphi$, means *always* (in given time interval, if any); $N\langle m, n \rangle\, \varphi$, means *never* (in given time interval, if any). Consider however that, in expressions occurring in the premise of a trigger rule, using G or N without an interval does not make much sense, as in this case the consequence of the rule cannot be enabled within a finite time.

6 Semantics

A K-ACE includes diverse components. K'-ACEs, 1-ACEs and contexts can be seen as "active", in the sense that 1-ACEs can perform actions (among which communicative acts), and there is a knowledge flow via bridge rules among 1-ACEs and contexts, and 1-ACEs and K'-ACEs. There are, in addition, some "passive" components, namely the reasoning modules, and the components $\mathcal{T}^T, \mathcal{A}^T, \mathcal{R}^T, \mathcal{C}^T, \mathcal{B}^T, \mathcal{E}^T$, that are elaborated (and thus possibly modified) only by the Institutional agent. In the semantics, we manage to ignore the latter by considering them as a part of the Institutional agent's knowledge base. Agents, contexts and reasoning modules are called *basic components*. Contexts, reasoning modules and also the main agent program in 1-ACEs are called *unitary components* as they do not have an internal structure, i.e., they do not in turn consist of components. A 1-ACE is seen itself as a unitary component whenever it consists of the main agent program only.

Agents work in time, and in fact can employ, for instance, timed trigger rules. Agents are in principle asynchronous. However, for a K-ACE we assume a *global* system time where states/time instants can be represented as $t_0, t_1, \ldots$. We take $t_{i+1} - t_i = \delta$, where δ is the actual interval of time after which we assume the overall system to have evolved. In this way, we can approximate each agent's local time instant t with $\min t_i$ such that $t_{i-1} < t < t_i$. This means that each agent's time can be a little asynchronous w.r.t. system's global time, though agents cannot evolve faster than the system.

Every component of a K-ACE, including the K-ACE itself, can be seen (analogously to MCSs) as a tuple $C^l = (C_1^{l'}, \ldots, C_n^{l'})$ where now the $C_i^{l'}$s are themselves *components* with the same structure. More formally:

Definition 6. *A multi-level multi-component MAS (mmMAS) of depth k is formed out of components of the form C_i^l, where l is the* level *of the component, with $0 \leq l \leq k$. A component C_i^l is either a unitary component or it is a* compound component *of the form $C_i^l = (C_{i_1}^{l'}, \ldots, C_{i_n}^{l'})$ where for each i_j $i \geq 1$, $j > 1$, each $C_{i_j}^{l'}$ is a component of level $l' \leq k$, and we have that:*

- *there exists a unique a topmost component C_1^0 of level 0.*
- *for $C_i^l = (C_{i_1}^{l'}, \ldots, C_{i_n}^{l'})$, $l' = l + 1$.*

So, a K-ACE can be seen in abstract terms from the point of view of a topmost component of a multi-level multi-component MAS, though the choice of the topmost components is in general not unique (i.e., there can be different "perspectives" over the same K-ACE). In the following, by abuse of notation we often write $M^l = (C_1, \ldots, C_n)$ to denote a component at level $l \geq 0$ of an mmMAS, thus omitting the level of inner components that is intended to be $l + 1$.

Every unitary component C_i in an mmMAS can be seen as an extension of the notion of a context in MCSs. An acceptable data state for a compound component is however composed of the acceptable data states of its elements (for elements which are in turn compound components of level l in an mmMAS, this will be recursively iterated over the remaining levels). For better defining 1-ACEs we introduce a new function, that we call Act, which, for the basic agent program, returns the actions that the agent is enabled to execute in each state. Bridge rules are the same as for MCSs for unitary contexts except for agents, where each bridge rule, in order to be applicable, must also have been triggered. So, we associate to a main agent program the set tr_i of its trigger rules that can determine bridge-rule executability and the function Act.

Definition 7. *A unitary component $\bar{C}$ of an mmMAS is a tuple $(\bar{L}; \bar{kb}; \bar{br}; \bar{tr})$ with associated functions $ACC_{\bar{C}}$, $mng_{\bar{C}}$, $Cn_{\bar{C}}$ and $Act_{\bar{C}}$ where the differences from a DAC-MACS's context are the following, all concerning the case where the component is a main agent program of an 1-ACE, say A:*

- *$ACC_{\bar{C}}$ returns a single set of consequences $\bar{S}$, that constitutes the unique acceptable data state of the agent;*
- *$\bar{tr}$ is the set of trigger rules associated to the agent, of the form $Op_I Q(\hat{y})$ **enables** α where Op is a temporal operator, I an interval (optional, and possibly reduced to a single time instant), $Q(\hat{y})$ is as in DACMACS trigger rules, and α is a bridge-rule head $A(\hat{x})$.*

– $Act_{\bar{C}} : Cn_{\bar{C}} \rightarrow 2^{Act_A}$, where Act_A is the set of actions feasible by agent A, is a
  function that returns, given $\bar{S}$, the set of actions that the agent is allowed to perform
  in such state.

In dynamic environments, components are in general able to incorporate new
knowledge and data items, e.g, as discussed in [6], the input provided by sensors. We
intend to explicitly take into account not only sensor input, but more generally the
interaction of agents and contexts with an external environment. We assume then that
each component is subjected at each time point to a (possibly empty) finite update.
Updates can be of many kinds: recordings of sensor input, communications from other
agents, insertion/deletion of tuples or entire tables in a relational database, etc. Thus,
for mmMAS $M = (C_1, \ldots, C_n)$ let $\Pi_T = \langle \Pi_T^1, \ldots \Pi_T^n \rangle$ be a tuple composed of the
finite updates performed to each component at time T, where for $1 \leq i \leq n$ Π_T^i is
the update to C_i. Let $\Pi = \Pi_1, \Pi_2, \ldots$ be a sequence of such updates performed at
time instants $t_1, t_2, \ldots$. Let us assume that each context copes with updates in its own
particular way, so let $\mathcal{U}_i$, $1 \leq i \leq n$ be the *update operator* that module C_i employs for
incorporating the new information, and let $\mathcal{U} = \{\mathcal{U}_1, \ldots, \mathcal{U}_n\}$ be the tuple composed of
all these operators. Therefore, each context's knowledge base will evolve in time, and
for component C_i we can talk about "C_i at time T" and "data state S_i^T of C_i at time T"
where C_i's knowledge base has been updated step by step until time T.

Consequently, we allow data states to evolve in time by introducing the concept
of *timed* data state of an mmMAS at time T, defined as follows (building upon our
previous work [13]). This allows us to properly define bridge-rule applicability in a
main agent program, that may depend upon a temporal formula to be true. Formally:

Definition 8. *A timed data state S^T at time T of a mmMAS $M = (C_1, \ldots, C_n)$ of
depth k is a tuple $(S_1^T, \ldots, S_n^T)$ and each S_i^T is:*

– *an acceptable data state S_i^T of C_i at time T if C_i is a unitary component, or*
– *a timed data state S_i^T of C_i otherwise (i.e., for compound components).*

A timed data state of a given K-ACE can thus be seen as a tuple recursively composed of both simple elements and tuples, the latter corresponding to the timed data
state of a subsystem. Given timed data state S^T, we can define entailment of temporal
formulas.

Definition 9. *Given a timed data state S^T at time T of a mmMAS $M = (C_1, \ldots, C_n)$
and unitary component $\bar{C}$ with relative data state element $\bar{S}^T$, S^T entails formulas and
temporal formulas occurring in $\bar{C}$ according to what follows, where, given previously-
established approximation, we assume agent's and mmMAS time to coincide. The considered time interval, if omitted in given formula, is understood as $\langle 0, \infty \rangle$.*

– $S^T \models \varphi$ *iff given its element $\bar{S}^T$ relative to $\bar{C}$, we have that $\bar{S}_i^T \models \varphi$.*
– $S^T \models F\langle T_1, T_2 \rangle \varphi$, *where $T2 = \infty$ or $T_1, T_2 \leq T$, iff there exists $\hat{T}$ where $T_1 \leq
  \hat{T} \leq T_2$ such that given $S^{\hat{T}}$ and its element $\bar{S}^{\hat{T}}$ relative to $\bar{C}$, we have that $\bar{S}^{\hat{T}} \models \varphi$.
  In case of $F\langle T_1 \rangle \varphi$ this reduces to $\bar{S}^{T_1} \models \varphi$.*
– $S^T \models G\langle T_1, T_2 \rangle \varphi$, *where $T2 = \infty$ or $T_1, T_2 \leq T$, iff for every $\hat{T}$ where $T_1 \leq \hat{T} \leq
  T_2$, given $S^{\hat{T}}$ and its element $\bar{S}_i^{\hat{T}}$ relative to $\bar{C}$, we have that $\bar{S}^{\hat{T}} \models \varphi$.*

– $S^T \models N\langle T_1, T_2 \rangle \varphi$, where $T2 = \infty$ or $T_1, T_2 \leq T$, iff there not exists $\hat{T}$ where $T_1 \leq \hat{T} \leq T_2$ such that given $S^{\hat{T}}$ and its element $\bar{S}^{\hat{T}}$ relative to $\bar{C}$, we have that $\bar{S}^{\hat{T}} \models \varphi$. In case of $F\langle T_1 \rangle \varphi$ this reduces to $\bar{S}^{T_1} \not\models \varphi$.

We can now redefine bridge-rule applicability, by exploiting the reading of trigger rules as LTL rules.

Definition 10. *Given mmMAS $M = (C_1, \ldots, C_n)$, and given unitary component $\bar{C} = (\bar{L}; \bar{kb}; \bar{br}; \bar{tr})$, rule $\rho \in \bar{br}$ is applicable in S^T, and therefore (the head of) $\rho \in app(S^T)$ iff $\bar{S}^T \models body(\rho)$ and, if $\bar{C}$ is a basic agent program, there exists a trigger rule in $\bar{tr}$ of the form ε enables $head(\rho)$ and $S^{T-1} \models \varepsilon$.*

The timed data state S^0 is assumed to be an equilibrium according to the DAC-MACS's definition, since no trigger rule has fired yet. Later on however, transition from a timed data state to the next one, and thus the definition of an equilibrium, is determined both by the update operators and by the application of bridge rules. Therefore:

Definition 11. *A timed data state S^{T+1} of mmMAS M at time $T + 1$ is a timed equilibrium iff, for each unitary component $\bar{C}$ of M,*
$\bar{S}^{T+1} \in ACC_{\bar{C}}(mng_{\bar{C}}(app(S^T), \bar{kb}'))$ *where* $\bar{kb}' = \mathcal{U}_{\bar{C}}(\bar{kb}, \Pi_T^{\bar{C}})$.

Complexity of the approach is not discussed for lack of space, but it is easy to believe that the discussion is analogous to that of MCSs.

7   Concluding Remarks

In this paper we have introduced the concept of "Dynamic Proactive Expert Systems" (DyPES), and we have defined K-ACE, that is a very general agent-based multi-level architecture for defining suck kinds of systems. K-ACE does not commit to specific languages/formalism or agent models, in this sense making a considerable difference with respect to other existing approaches. We have spent in fact some effort in order to be independent of the agent-oriented programming language adopted, and of predefined organizational aspects. Concerning related work, JaCaMo (http://jacamo.sourceforge.net) is a methodology for the design and implementation of agents and MAS with AgentSpeak under the Jason interpreter as a programming language [14][1], and CArtAgO, as a platform for programming distributed artifact-based environments [16] in accord to the Moise organizational model.

Our work is indebted to [17], where agents and multi-agent systems are specified as multi-context systems; each single agent is seen as divided into components, and bridge rules are adopted for both communication within an agent's components and communication among different agents. On this line, the recent approach of [18] proposes Sigon, a framework for the definition of agents and multi-agent systems as multi-context systems. The framework has been implemented, and the implementation is freely available.

---

[1] Where AgentSpeak is a very popular language based on the BDI agent model [15], and Jason is a performant interpreter for an extended AgentSpeak language.

The difference with our approach is that we do not intend to model multi-agent systems as multi-context systems, rather we aim to integrate the two approaches, so as to leave the designer of a practical architecture free to adopt any inter-agent communication device, rather than being forced to bridge rules only. Sigon can however be a good candidate as an implementation language for K-ACE.

Many future directions are ahead of us. As a first step we intend to elaborate an execution semantics for K-ACE, that can be for instance obtained by extending the one provided for DACMASs in [8]. This will allow us to devise a principled implementation of the K-ACE framework. So far in fact we have performed no real practical evaluation, that would require to experiment the K-ACE architectural approach within a significantly big project. We are trying to obtain funds for a project in the field of eHealth, as suggested by our small case study.

References

1. Leitão, P., Colombo, A.W., Karnouskos, S.: Industrial automation based on cyber-physical systems technologies: prototype implementations and challenges. Comput. Ind. **81**, 11–25 (2016)
2. Costantini, S.: Knowledge acquisition via non-monotonic reasoning in distributed heterogeneous environments. In: Calimeri, F., Ianni, G., Truszczynski, M. (eds.) LPNMR 2015. LNCS (LNAI), vol. 9345, pp. 228–241. Springer, Cham (2015). https://doi.org/10.1007/978-3-319-23264-5_20
3. Costantini, S., DeGasperis, G.: Exchanging data and ontological definitions in multi-agent-contexts systems. In: RuleML Challenge track, Proceedings. CEUR Workshop Proceedings, vol. 1417 (2015)
4. Costantini, S.: ACE: a flexible environment for complex event processing in logical agents. In: Baldoni, M., Baresi, L., Dastani, M. (eds.) EMAS 2015. LNCS (LNAI), vol. 9318, pp. 70–91. Springer, Cham (2015). https://doi.org/10.1007/978-3-319-26184-3_5
5. Brewka, G., Eiter, T., Fink, M., Weinzierl, A.: Managed multi-context systems. In: Walsh, T. (ed.) Proceedings of the 22nd International Joint Conference on Artificial Intelligence IJCAI 2011, IJCAI/AAAI, pp. 786–791 (2011)
6. Brewka, G., Ellmauthaler, S., Pührer, J.: Multi-context systems for reactive reasoning in dynamic environments. In: Schaub, T. (ed.) Proceedings of the 21st European Conference on Artificial Intelligence ECAI 2014, IJCAI/AAAI (2014)
7. Aielli, F., et al.: FRIENDLY & KIND with your health: human-friendly knowledge-intensive dynamic systems for the e-health domain. In: Bajo, J., et al. (eds.) Highlights of Practical Applications of Scalable Multi-Agent Systems. The PAAMS Collection. PAAMS 2016. Communications in Computer and Information Science, vol. 616. Springer, Cham. https://doi.org/10.1007/978-3-319-39387-2_2
8. Montali, M., Calvanese, D., De Giacomo, G.: Specification and verification of commitment-regulated data-aware multiagent systems. In: Proceedings of AAMAS 2014 (2014)
9. Singh, M.P.: Commitments in multiagent systems: Some history, some confusions, some controversies, some prospects
10. Costantini, S., Formisano, A.: Augmenting agent computational environments with quantitative reasoning modules and customizable bridge rules. In: Osman, N., Sierra, C. (eds.) AAMAS 2016. LNCS (LNAI), vol. 10003, pp. 104–121. Springer, Cham (2016). https://doi.org/10.1007/978-3-319-46840-2_7

11. Fisher, M.: A normal form for temporal logics and its applications in theorem-proving and execution. J. Logic Comput. **7**(4), 429–456 (1997)
12. van Riemsdijk, M.B., Dennis, L.A., Fisher, M., Hindriks, K.V.: A semantic framework for socially adaptive agents: towards strong norm compliance, pp. 423–432. ACM (2015)
13. Cabalar, P., Costantini, S., De Gasperis, G., Formisano, A.: Multi-context systems in dynamic environments. Ann. Math. Artif. Intell. **86**(1–3), 87–120 (2019)
14. Bordini, R.H., Hübner, J.F., Wooldridge, M.: Programming Multi-Agent Systems in AgentSpeak Using Jason. Wiley Series in Agent Technology. Wiley, Chichester
15. Rao, A.S., Georgeff, M.P.: Modeling agents within a BDI-architecture. In: Proceedings of International Conference on Principles of Knowledge Representation and Reasoning (KR) (1991)
16. Ricci, A., Viroli, M., Omicini, A.: CArtA gO: a framework for prototyping artifact-based environments in MAS. In: Weyns, D., Parunak, H.V.D., Michel, F. (eds.) E4MAS 2006. LNCS (LNAI), vol. 4389, pp. 67–86. Springer, Heidelberg (2007). https://doi.org/10.1007/978-3-540-71103-2_4
17. Sabater, J., Sierra, C., Parsons, S., Jennings, N.R.: Engineering executable agents using multi-context systems. J. Logic Comput. **12**(3), 413–442 (2002)
18. Gelaim, T.Â., Hofer, V.L., Marchi, J., Silveira, R.A.: Sigon: a multi-context system framework for intelligent agents. Expert Syst. Appl. **119**, 51–60 (2019). https://github.com/sigon-lang/sigon-lang

Formal Analysis of Responsibility Attribution in a Multimodal Framework

Daniela Glavaničová[1] and Matteo Pascucci[2,3(✉)]

[1] Department of Logic and Methodology of Sciences,
Comenius University in Bratislava, Bratislava, Slovakia
daniela.glavanicova@gmail.com
[2] Institute of Logic and Computation, TU Wien, Vienna, Austria
matteo.pascucci@tuwien.ac.at
[3] Institute of Philosophy, Slovak Academy of Sciences, Bratislava, Slovakia

Abstract. The present article is devoted to a logical treatment of some fundamental concepts involved in responsibility attribution. We specify a theoretical framework based on a language of temporal deontic logic with agent-relative operators for deliberate causal contribution. The framework is endowed with a procedure to solve normative conflicts which arise from the assessment of different normative sources. We provide a characterization result for a basic system within this framework and illustrate how the concepts formalized can be put at work in the analysis of examples of legal reasoning.

Keywords: Multi-agent deontic logic · Legal reasoning · Norm interpretation · Responsibility

1 Introduction

The philosophical literature on responsibility is so rich that is almost intractable, while considerably less attention has been devoted to this notion in the logical literature until recent decades; nowadays formal accounts of responsibility are being developed in various frameworks, such as action logic [8,12], STIT logic [15,16], game theory [4], lambda calculus [17] or precedence logic [2]. Each account focuses on certain aspects of responsibility that are relevant in the underlying framework, without aiming at an exhaustive picture, since responsibility attribution involves an impressive variety of levels of analysis.

To give an idea of this variety we start by pointing out, as in [12], that an individual (or a group) may be held responsible either for an action or for some consequences of an action. Responsibility for an action does not entail responsibility for its consequences, given that an individual cannot foresee all consequences of what he/she does. However, an individual may deliberately act in order to obtain a given outcome. In the latter case responsibility can be attributed with respect to both the action performed and the state-of-affairs achieved. If we restrict our attention to responsibility for consequences of actions,

© Springer Nature Switzerland AG 2019
M. Baldoni et al. (Eds.): PRIMA 2019, LNAI 11873, pp. 36–51, 2019.
https://doi.org/10.1007/978-3-030-33792-6_3

then, as observed in [8], an individual may be taken to be responsible either for some state-of-affairs that should obtain in the future or for some state-of-affairs that occurred in the past. *Future-oriented* responsibility can be sometimes thought of as allocation of duties, which is especially important in scenarios involving many agents that need to coordinate their behaviour in order to achieve a common goal. *Past-oriented* responsibility can be sometimes thought of as culpability for something that has happened.

Focusing on past-oriented responsibility, one can further distinguish, along the lines of [15], between *causal* and *agentive* responsibility—where the former encompasses also cases of accidental contribution to the attainment of a relevant state-of-affairs, while the latter makes explicit reference to voluntary contribution—or between *active* and *passive* responsibility. Active responsibility means that an agent did something to produce a certain outcome, while passive responsibility means that an agent could have prevented something from being the case but did not.

In the present article, we take a novel perspective on the analysis of responsibility and add another piece to the puzzle by looking at the role played by *normative sources and their interpretation*. We introduce a very simple logical framework where it is possible to make explicit reference to normative sources from which obligations, permissions and prohibitions arise and whose content may vary with time and be interpreted in different ways. We will see that this framework allows one to capture many aspects of the debate around responsibility that are directly relevant in the legal domain and that have not been formally addressed so far. For instance, it allows for a treatment of cases of *responsibility alleviation* related to normative conflicts (e.g., when a more important normative source permits or prescribes something forbidden by a subordinated normative source), as well as of cases of *retrospective attribution of responsibility* (i.e., when some law now in effect is used to evaluate something that occurred in the past, where the relevant laws were possibly different).

The structure of the paper is as follows: Sect. 2 provides some theoretical background for the notions of responsibility we will be dealing with; Sect. 3 outlines the formal framework, which is based on a multimodal language; Sect. 4 is devoted to the formal rendering of various concepts involved in responsibility attribution in the legal domain; the applicability of the proposed framework will be illustrated with examples; Sect. 5 concludes the paper, pointing to some interesting applications and directions for future research.

2   The Theoretical Framework

In this section we will illustrate some core aspects of the theoretical framework for responsibility attribution we want to formalize: causal contribution, context of evaluation and interpretation of norms. To this aim, we will employ useful distinctions taken from the philosophical analysis of responsibility.

Causal Contribution. The first distinction is that between responsibility for actions and responsibility for outcomes. An outcome of an action can be identified with a state-of-affairs. Our attention will be restricted to cases of responsibility for outcomes. An agent may *causally determine* an outcome or just *causally contribute* to an outcome. As [3,4] acknowledge, a general definition of responsibility cannot rely on an agent's causal determination of the outcome, since this would not apply to cases in which the realization of the outcome depends on the behaviour of several agents. For instance, Alfred attempted to poison Carl, but his attempt failed due to Barbara's intervention: in this case we still want Alfred to be responsible for "creating the possibility" of Carl's being poisoned. Therefore, the causal contribution of an agent is intended to represent a *triggering condition* for a certain outcome, even if the outcome is in the end avoided due to the behaviour of other agents. An analogous argument can be used in cases of *causal overdetermination* (see [5] for a detailed discussion): both Alfred and Barbara attempted to poison Carl and in the end it was Barbara who managed to achieve the goal. Responsibility is not restricted to Barbara: Alfred is indeed responsible for an attempted crime.

Furthermore, sometimes responsibility for an outcome is attributed to a group of agents even if only some of the members of the group causally contributed to the outcome (see the notion of *collective responsibility* in [7]); therefore, the role played by causal contribution is different in the case of individual and group responsibility. For instance, before the introduction of video surveillance systems in stadiums it was sometimes the case that a football team was punished with some sanction due to the behaviour of a restricted number of ultras. In similar scenarios it was common to say that the supporters of the team (as a group) were responsible for the sanction, since it was not always possible to identify the specific individuals who misbehaved.

In judicial reasoning it is important to assess whether the causal contribution of an agent to an outcome was *deliberate* or not. Our analysis will be focused on deliberate causal contribution which will be represented in terms of *hyperintensional operators* for causal contribution: an agent can deliberately contribute to realizing the proposition expressed by a formula ϕ without being aware that he/she is contributing to realizing the proposition expressed by a formula ψ logically equivalent to ϕ.

Context of Evaluation. Responsibility attribution will be here treated as a relative issue, depending on a certain context of evaluation. First, a person might be held responsible with reference to a certain normative source (set of norms) and not responsible with reference to another. The ultimate decision on whether a person or a group of people is to be blamed for something often depends on a *hierarchy* of normative sources [1]. Different norms can disagree, giving rise to normative conflicts; in this case, a norm can be derogated due to its incompatibility with a more important one. To capture this aspect, which is fundamental both for responsibility attribution and for responsibility alleviation, we will employ a mechanism for conflict resolution which produces *all-things-considered* norms relative to a specified ordering of normative sources.

Second, normative sources can change with time and thus norms valid at the time of an agent's conduct need not be valid at the time of a responsibility ascription (and the other way around). For instance, a law currently in effect may be used to evaluate the conduct of an individual if it is more favourable to him/her than the law in effect when the relevant conduct occurred. Changes in normative systems often occur due to the growth of our knowledge. For instance, if it is not known that a certain compound is toxic, that compound will not appear on the list of chemicals to be avoided, and the relevant regulation on compounds will not prohibit its usage in commercial products. As soon as a certain part of our society acknowledges that the compound is toxic, it is added to the list of toxic chemicals and its usage becomes prohibited. Thus, the relevant regulation changes.

In our framework the interaction between normative sources and time will be central to define three types of responsibility: *prospective*, *historic* and *retrospective*. Prospective responsibility is responsibility for something that should obtain either now or in the future, according to some norm currently in effect. Historic responsibility is responsibility for something that obtained in the past but was at that time prohibited by some norm. Retrospective responsibility is responsibility for something that obtained in the past but is prohibited by some norm currently in effect. We will illustrate how prospective responsibility can be used to define both historic and retrospective responsibility.

Interpretation of Norms. Another important aspect of norms is their interpretation. Since norms are written in a natural language, they often have an ambiguous meaning and different readings can give rise to controversies in courts. The interpretation of norms is especially challenging when a new regulation is released or when a regulation written in one language has to be translated into another language. In legal reasoning it is therefore convenient to keep track of the *different interpretations of a norm* in order to see which are their consequences. In our account we will focus on the role played by *propositional synonymy* in norm interpretation. For instance, consider the following sentences, which are parts of the police caution used, respectively, in the UK and in the US [6]:

A. "You do not have to say anything unless you wish to do so, but what you say may be given in evidence."
B. "You have the right to remain silent. If you give up the right to remain silent, anything you say can and will be used against you in a court of law."

One may interpret B as a way of paraphrasing A (hence, as expressing a logically equivalent proposition) or as a sentence with a more specific meaning (hence, as expressing a proposition strictly entailing the one expressed by A), arguing that the fact that what one says can and will be used against this person in a court entails that it may be given in evidence, but not vice versa.

The problem of establishing when two sentences express logically equivalent propositions recently raised a certain interest also in the area of deontic logic. Borrowing an example from [10], the proposition expressed by the sentence "You ought to drive" is logically equivalent to the proposition expressed by the sentence "You ought to drive or to drive and drink" in many traditional systems of deontic logic, such as **SDL** (Standard Deontic Logic). In our framework, we will employ hyperintensional deontic operators to avoid problems of this kind.

3   The Formal Framework

Consider a countable set of propositional variables $Var = \{p_1, p_2, p_3, ...\}$ and let $Agt = \{a_1, ..., a_n\}$ and $Src = \{s_1, ..., s_m\}$ be a finite set of agents and a finite set of normative sources, respectively. A normative source represents a set of norms. Here we restrict ourselves to the case in which sets of norms are *pairwise disjoint*; that is, each pair of normative sources $s, s' \in Src$ does not include any shared norm.

Definition 1. *The language $\mathcal{L}$ is defined by the following grammar:*

$$\phi ::= p \mid \neg\phi \mid \phi \to \phi \mid \phi \sim \phi \mid H\phi \mid G\phi \mid C_{a_i}\phi \mid O_{a_i}^{s_j}\phi$$

The modal operators used in $\mathcal{L}$ can be interpreted as follows: H means "in all possible past states", G "in all possible future states", C_{a_i} "agent a_i deliberately contributed to" and $O_{a_i}^{s_j}$ "according to normative source s_j, it is obligatory for agent a_i that". The operator $\sim$ is used for the relation of *propositional synonymy*: an expression like $\phi \sim \psi$ means that the formulas ϕ and ψ have the same semantic content (i.e., they denote synonymous propositions).[1] The boolean operators for conjunction ($\wedge$), disjunction ($\vee$) and material equivalence ($\equiv$), as well as the temporal operators for "in some possible past state" (P) and "in some possible future state" (F) can be defined in the usual way, in particular: $P\phi =_{def} \neg H\neg\phi$ and $F\phi =_{def} \neg G\neg\phi$. Furthermore, we provide also a straightforward definition for two source-relative operators of obligation concerning a *group of agents* $X \subseteq Agt$:

$$O_{\forall X}^{s_j}\phi =_{def} \bigwedge_{a_i \in X} O_{a_i}^{s_j}\phi \qquad O_{\exists X}^{s_j}\phi =_{def} \bigvee_{a_i \in X} O_{a_i}^{s_j}\phi$$

In other words, an expression like $O_{\forall X}^{s_j}\phi$ means that all agents belonging to X have a duty with respect to the realization of ϕ, while an expression like $O_{\exists X}^{s_j}\phi$ means that some agent belonging to X has a duty with respect to the realization of ϕ. Notice that in both cases we can speak of a duty of the group X with respect to the realization of ϕ. A duty of all agents can therefore be expressed via $O_{\forall Agt}^{s_j}\phi$.

Definition 2. *The system RNS ('Responsibility and Normative Sources') is specified by the following axiomatic basis (for every $a_i \in Agt$):*

A0 All substitution instances of tautologies of the Propositional Calculus;
A1 $\phi \sim \phi$;
A2 $(\phi \sim \psi) \to (\psi \sim \phi)$;
A3 $(\phi \sim \psi) \to ((\psi \sim \chi) \to (\phi \sim \chi))$;

---

[1] We here adopt a Fregean notion of proposition [11]: a proposition is the thought (or semantic content) expressed by a sentence, rather than a function from possible states to truth-values. Therefore, we can say that two logically equivalent formulas denote different propositions. In the models used for our logical system a particular interpretation of the norms establishes whether two propositions are synonymous.

A4 $(\phi \wedge \psi) \sim (\psi \wedge \phi)$;
A5 $H(\phi \rightarrow \psi) \rightarrow (H\phi \rightarrow H\psi)$;
A6 $G(\phi \rightarrow \psi) \rightarrow (G\phi \rightarrow G\psi)$;
A7 $\phi \rightarrow HF\phi$;
A8 $\phi \rightarrow GP\phi$;
A9 $(H\phi \rightarrow HH\phi)$;
A10 $(G\phi \rightarrow GG\phi)$;
A11 $(H\phi \wedge G\phi \wedge \phi) \rightarrow GH\phi$;
A12 $C_{a_i}\phi \rightarrow (\phi \vee F\phi)$;
A13 $(\phi \sim \psi) \rightarrow (H(\phi \sim \psi) \wedge G(\phi \sim \psi) \wedge HG(\phi \sim \psi))$;
A14 $(\phi \sim \psi) \rightarrow (\phi \equiv \psi)$;
A15 $(\phi \sim \psi) \rightarrow (\chi \sim \chi')$, *where* χ' *results from* χ *by replacing some occurrence*
of ϕ *with* ψ;
R1 if $\vdash_{RNS} \phi$ *and* $\vdash_{RNS} \phi \rightarrow \psi$, *then* $\vdash_{RNS} \psi$;
R2 if $\vdash_{RNS} \phi$, *then* $\vdash_{RNS} H\phi \wedge G\phi$.

Axioms A1–A4 and A14–A15 concern properties of the relation of propositional synonymy, axioms A5–A11 and rule R2 concern properties of temporal operators; axioms A12 and A13 concern interactions among different operators. Even if the axiomatic basis of *RNS* does not include any specific principle for operators of obligation and only the principle A12 for operators of causal contribution, a consequence of A14 and A15 is the following *First Fundamental Theorem*, that will be discussed later:

$$FT1(\phi \sim \psi) \rightarrow ((O^{s_j}_{a_i}\phi \equiv O^{s_j}_{a_i}\psi) \wedge (C_{a_i}\phi \equiv C_{a_i}\psi)).$$

Note that if $\vdash \phi \equiv \psi$ but ϕ and ψ are not in a relation of propositional synonymy, then it may be the case that an agent deliberately contributed to ϕ but not to ψ. Also, if $\vdash \phi \equiv \psi$ but ϕ and ψ are not synonymous, it may be the case that s_j prescribes ϕ but not ψ. In this way our framework captures the hyperintensional flavour of deliberate causal contribution and of deontic modals.

Definition 3. *The language* $\mathcal{L}$ *is interpreted on relational models of kind* $\mathfrak{M} = \langle W, Cnt, \prec, f, c, o, V \rangle$ *where:*

- *W is a set of states denoted by w, w', w'', etc.;*
- *Cnt is a set of semantic contents (propositions) denoted by k, k', k'', etc.;*
- *$\prec \subseteq W \times W$ is a relation that can be called* temporal precedence;
- *$f : \mathcal{L} \times W \longrightarrow Cnt$ is a function that can be called* content assignment;
- *$c : Agt \times W \longrightarrow \wp(Cnt)$ is a function that can be called* causal contribution assignment;
- *$o : Agt \times Src \times W \longrightarrow \wp(Cnt)$ is a function that can be called* obligation assignment;
- *$V : Var \longrightarrow \wp(W)$ is a valuation function.*

For every $w \in W$, $p \in Var$, $\phi \in \mathcal{L}$, $a_i \in Agt$ and $s_j \in Src$, $f(\phi, w)$ is the semantic content of (i.e., the proposition expressed by) formula ϕ at state w, $c(a_i, w)$ is the set of propositions towards whose realization agent a_i provides a deliberate causal contribution at state w, $o(a_i, s_j, w)$ is the set of propositions that are obligatory for agent a_i (i.e., the duties of a_i) with reference to normative source s_j at state w and $V(p)$ the set of states at which the propositional variable p holds. Since in our framework a normative source can vary with time, there are cases in which $o(a_i, s_j, w) \neq o(a_i, s_j, v)$ for $w \neq v$; hence, an agent may have different duties with respect to the same normative source at different states. Furthermore, notice that the semantic content of a formula may vary with states as well; however, we will see that it does not vary in an arbitrary way. Finally, given two states $w, v \in W$ s.t. $w \prec v$, we will say that v is a *successor* of w.

Definition 4. *Truth-conditions for formulas of $\mathcal{L}$ with reference to a state w in a model $\mathfrak{M}$ are specified below:*

- $\mathfrak{M}, w \vDash p$ *iff* $w \in V(p)$, *for any* $p \in Var$;
- $\mathfrak{M}, w \vDash \neg\phi$ *iff* $\mathfrak{M}, w \nvDash \phi$;
- $\mathfrak{M}, w \vDash \phi \rightarrow \psi$ *iff either* $\mathfrak{M}, w \nvDash \phi$ *or* $\mathfrak{M}, w \vDash \psi$;
- $\mathfrak{M}, w \vDash \phi \sim \psi$ *iff* $f(\phi, w) = f(\psi, w)$;
- $\mathfrak{M}, w \vDash H\phi$ *iff* $\mathfrak{M}, v \vDash \phi$ *for all* $v \in W$ *s.t.* $v \prec w$;
- $\mathfrak{M}, w \vDash G\phi$ *iff* $\mathfrak{M}, v \vDash \phi$ *for all* $v \in W$ *s.t.* $w \prec v$;
- $\mathfrak{M}, w \vDash C_{a_i}\phi$ *iff* $f(\phi, w) \in c(a_i, w)$;
- $\mathfrak{M}, w \vDash O_{a_i}^{s_j}\phi$ *iff* $f(\phi, w) \in o(a_i, s_j, w)$.

The notions of validity of a formula in a model (denoted by $\mathfrak{M} \vDash \phi$) and in a class of models are defined in the usual way.

Definition 5. *We say that two states w and v in a model $\mathfrak{M}$ are related by a temporal path (in symbols, $w \bowtie v$) iff there is a sequence of states $(w_0, ..., w_n)$ s.t. $w_0 = w$, $w_n = v$ and, for every i s.t. $0 \leq i \leq n-1$, either (I) $w_i \prec w_{i+1}$ or $w_{i+1} \prec w_i$.*

Definition 6. *We denote by C_m the class of all models $\mathfrak{M}$ satisfying the following properties (for every $w, w', w'', v \in W$ and $a_i \in Agt$):*

P1 $(w \prec w'$ *and* $w' \prec w'')$ *implies* $w \prec w''$;
P2 $(w' \prec w$ *and* $w'' \prec w)$ *implies* $(w' \prec w''$ *or* $w'' \prec w'$ *or* $w'' = w')$;
P3 $f(\phi \wedge \psi, w) = f(\psi \wedge \phi, w)$;
P4 $f(\phi, w) \in c(a_i, w)$ *implies* $(\mathfrak{M}, w \vDash \phi$ *or* $\exists u(w \prec u$ *and* $\mathfrak{M}, u \vDash \phi))$;
P5 $w \bowtie v$ *implies* $(f(\phi, w) = f(\psi, w)$ *implies* $f(\phi, v) = f(\psi, v))$;
P6 $f(\phi, w) = f(\psi, w)$ *implies* $\mathfrak{M}, w \vDash \phi \equiv \psi$;
P7 $f(\phi, w) = f(\psi, w)$ *implies* $f(\chi, w) = f(\chi', w)$, *whenever* χ' *is obtained from χ by replacing some occurrence of ϕ with ψ.*

P1 and P2 describe two fundamental features of (possibly) indeterministic representations of time: transitivity and no branching towards the past. P3 says that the semantic content of a conjunction does not depend on the order of the conjuncts. P4 says that if an agent a_i deliberately contributed to ϕ, then a_i *created the possibility* for ϕ: either ϕ holds now or it holds in some possible future state (consider the examples involving Alfred, Barbara and Carl discussed in

Sect. 2). P5 says that the relation of propositional synonymy is invariant across states related by a temporal path. P6 means that two formulas have the same semantic content at a state only if they have the same truth-value. P7 represents the idea that the semantic content is at least *weakly compositional* (see, e.g., [19]), in the sense that the semantic content of a formula is determined by the semantic content of its subformulas. For instance, if the sentences "Alan is drunk" and "Alan is inebriated" are taken to have the same semantic content (i.e., to express synonymous propositions), then "It ought to be that Alan is not drunk while driving" and "It ought to be that Alan is not inebriated while driving" have the same semantic content as well.

Let us have a closer look at the shape of models for S and at some intuitions they can represent. Due to the properties P1 and P2, a model $\mathfrak{M}$ is the union of a family of *disjoint trees* $\mathfrak{T}, \mathfrak{T}', \mathfrak{T}'',...$ which possibly branch towards the future.[2] Given a state w in a tree $\mathfrak{T}$, a *branch* b stemming from w is a maximal chain of successors of w. Every tree $\mathfrak{T}$ is a maximal set of states that are pairwise related by a temporal path; hence, due to P5, the relation of propositional synonymy is invariant across all states of $\mathfrak{T}$. A tree can be used to represent the temporal evolution of an indeterministic scenario according to a certain interpretation of the norms; such an interpretation is given by the relations of propositional synonymy holding in the tree. Therefore, a model can be used to compare the temporal evolution of a scenario according to different interpretations of the norms (one for each tree).

We will now prove that the system RNS is characterized by the semantics provided. Let $[\phi]_{RNS} = \{\psi \colon \vdash_{RNS} \phi \equiv \psi\}$ and $Eq_{RNS} = \{[\phi]_{RNS} : \phi \in \mathcal{L}\}$.

Proposition 1. *The class of models C_m is non-empty.*

Proof. Immediate, by taking a model $\mathfrak{M} = \langle W, Cnt, \prec, f, c, o, V \rangle$ s.t. $W = \{w_1\}$, $\prec = \emptyset$, $Cnt = Eq_{RNS}$ and for all $\phi \in \mathcal{L}$, $a_i \in Agt$ and $s_j \in Src$, $f(\phi, w_1) = [\phi]_{RNS}$, $c(a_i, w_1) = o(a_i, s_j, w_1) = \emptyset$. It can be easily verified that $\mathfrak{M}$ satisfies properties P1–P7.

Proposition 2. *RNS is sound with respect to the class of models C_m.*

Proof. The validity of A0, A5–A11 and R1–R2 is straightforward, in the light of well-known results in correspondence theory for tense logic [20]. The validity of A1–A3 easily follows from the truth-conditions of $\phi \sim \psi$ and the validity of A4 from P3. Concerning A12, suppose that $\mathfrak{M}, w \vDash C_{a_i}\phi$; then $f(\phi, w) \in c(a_i, w)$ and, by P4, one can infer that either (I) $\mathfrak{M}, w \vDash \phi$ or (II) there is some $u \in W$ s.t. $w \prec u$ and $\mathfrak{M}, u \vDash \phi$, so $\mathfrak{M}, w \vDash C_{a_i}\phi \rightarrow (\phi \vee F\phi)$. Concerning A13, assume that $\mathfrak{M}, w \vDash (\phi \sim \psi) \wedge \neg(H(\phi \sim \psi) \wedge G(\phi \sim \psi) \wedge HG(\phi \sim \psi))$; then $\mathfrak{M}, w \vDash \neg H(\phi \sim \psi) \vee \neg G(\phi \sim \psi) \vee PF\neg(\phi \sim \psi)$. This means that there is some $v \in W$ s.t. $\mathfrak{M}, v \vDash \neg(\phi \sim \psi)$ and either (I) $v \prec w$ or (II) $w \prec v$ or (III) there is some u s.t. $u \prec w$ and $u \prec v$. In all cases (by Definition 5) $w \bowtie v$, so, by P5, we

---

[2] In these models the past of a state is deterministic, given that there is no branching towards the past; hence, we can simplify the reading of H and P as "in all past states" and "in some past state", respectively.

must have that $\mathfrak{M}, v \vDash (\phi \sim \psi)$: contradiction. Finally, the validity of A14 and A15 follows immediately from P6 and P7.

Proposition 3. *RNS is complete with respect to the class of models C_m.*

Proof. For any formula ϕ which is not provable in RNS, there is a maximally RNS-consistent set of formulas Γ including $\neg\phi$. The canonical model for RNS will be denoted by $\mathfrak{M}^+ = \langle W^+, Cnt^+, \prec^+, f^+, c^+, o^+, V^+ \rangle$. W^+ is the set of all maximally RNS-consistent sets of formulas. Cnt^+ is a set of semantic contents having the cardinality of $\mathcal{L}$. The relation $\prec^+$ is such that for every $w, v \in W^+$, $w \prec^+ v$ iff $\{\phi : G\phi \in w\} \subseteq v$ iff $\{\phi : H\phi \in v\} \subseteq w$.[3] The function f^+ is s.t. for every $w \in W^+$ and $\phi, \psi \in \mathcal{L}$, we have $f^+(\phi, w) = f^+(\psi, w)$ iff $\phi \sim \psi \in w$. The relations c^+ and o^+ are s.t. for every $w \in W^+$, $a_i \in Agt$, $s_j \in Src$, and $\phi \in \mathcal{L}$, we have $f^+(\phi, w) \in c^+(a_i, w)$ iff $C_{a_i}\phi \in w$ and $f^+(\phi, w) \in o^+(a_i, s_j, w)$ iff $O_{a_i}^{s_j}\phi \in w$. The valuation function V^+ is defined in the standard way: $V^+(p) = |p|^+ = \{w \in W^+ : p \in w\}$. Relying on the definition of $\mathfrak{M}^+$, it can be easily proven, using an induction on the complexity of formulas, that for every $w \in W^+$ and $\phi \in \mathcal{L}$, we have $\mathfrak{M}^+, w \vDash \phi$ iff $w \in |\phi|^+$.

We now show that $\mathfrak{M}^+ \in C_m$; from this it follows that if ϕ is not provable in RNS, then it is not valid in C_m. The part of the proof concerning P1 and P2 follows from well-known results concerning completeness theory of tense logic [20]. In the case of P3, since, by A4, $(\phi \wedge \psi) \sim (\psi \wedge \phi) \in w$ for every $\phi, \psi \in \mathcal{L}$ and every $w \in W^+$, then $\mathfrak{M}^+, w \vDash (\phi \wedge \psi) \sim (\psi \wedge \phi)$, which entails $f^+(\phi \wedge \psi, w) = f^+(\psi \wedge \phi, w)$. In the case of P4, suppose that there is $w \in W^+$, $a_i \in Agt$ and $\psi \in \mathcal{L}$ s.t. $f^+(\psi, w) \in c^+(a_i, w)$. Then, $C_{a_i}\psi \in w$ and, by A12, $\phi \vee F\phi \in w$; if neither $\mathfrak{M}^+, w \vDash \phi$ nor $\mathfrak{M}^+, u \vDash \phi$ for some u s.t. $w \prec^+ u$, then $\mathfrak{M}^+, w \nvDash \phi \vee F\phi$, whence $\phi \vee F\phi \notin w$: contradiction. In the case of P5, suppose that $w \bowtie v$ and that, for some formulas $\phi, \psi \in \mathcal{L}$, we have $f^+(\phi, w) = f^+(\psi, w)$ while $f^+(\phi, v) \neq f^+(\psi, v)$. Then, $\mathfrak{M}^+, w \vDash (\phi \sim \psi)$ while $\mathfrak{M}^+, v \vDash \neg(\phi \sim \psi)$; however, by A13, $\mathfrak{M}^+, w \vDash H(\phi \sim \psi) \wedge G(\phi \sim \psi) \wedge HG(\phi \sim \psi)$, so, as a consequence of the definition of the relations $\bowtie$ and $\prec^+$, we also have $(\phi \sim \psi) \in v$ and $\mathfrak{M}^+, v \vDash (\phi \sim \psi)$: contradiction. In the case of P6, we have that $f^+(\phi, w) = f^+(\psi, w)$ entails $\phi \sim \psi \in w$, so, by A14, $\phi \equiv \psi \in w$ and $\mathfrak{M}^+, w \vDash \phi \equiv \psi$. In the case of P7, suppose that for some state w we have $f^+(\phi, w) = f^+(\psi, w)$ but $f^+(\chi, w) \neq f^+(\chi', w)$ for some χ' obtained from χ by replacing some occurrence of ϕ with ψ. Then, $\mathfrak{M}^+, w \vDash \phi \sim \psi$ and, by A15, $\mathfrak{M}^+, w \vDash \chi \sim \chi'$, which means $f^+(\chi, w) = f^+(\chi', w)$: contradiction.

Notice that, as a consequence of the characterization result obtained and of the principle FT1, in every model in the class C_m the set of propositions which are obligatory for an agent a_i at a state w with respect to a normative source s_j (i.e. $o(a_i, s_j, w)$) and the set of propositions towards whose realization

---

[3] Here we take for granted the fact that in canonical models for systems of tense logic the derivability of A7 and A8 makes it possible to have only one accessibility relation for temporal reference, rather than two (one for H and one for G). See [20] for details.

a_i deliberately contributed at w (i.e. $c(a_i, w)$) are *closed under propositional synonymy*.

We will now show that obligations and deliberate causal contributions also preserve the commutative property of binary boolean operators.

Proposition 4. *Let* $\clubsuit \in \{\wedge, \vee, \equiv\}$; *then* $\vdash_{RNS} O_{a_i}^{s_j}(\phi \clubsuit \psi) \rightarrow O_{a_i}^{s_j}(\psi \clubsuit \phi)$ *and* $\vdash_{RNS} C_{a_i}(\phi \clubsuit \psi) \rightarrow C_{a_i}(\psi \clubsuit \phi)$ *for any* $a_i \in Agt$ *and any* $s_j \in Src$.

Proof. Axioms A4 and A15 tell us that the result holds for $\clubsuit = \wedge$; hence, we need to show that $\vdash_{RNS} (\phi \vee \psi) \sim (\psi \vee \phi)$ and $\vdash_{RNS} (\phi \equiv \psi) \sim (\psi \equiv \phi)$ in order to apply A15 also in the cases $\clubsuit = \vee$ and $\clubsuit = \equiv$. We can rely on the semantic characterization of RNS with respect to C_m. Assume that $f(\phi \vee \psi, w) = k$ for some w in a model $\mathfrak{M}$ belonging to C_m. Since $(\phi \vee \psi) =_{def} \neg(\neg\phi \wedge \neg\psi)$, then $f(\neg(\neg\phi \wedge \neg\psi), w) = k$. By A4, we know that $f(\neg\phi \wedge \neg\psi, w) = f(\neg\psi \wedge \neg\phi, w)$; hence, by A15, $f(\neg(\neg\psi \wedge \neg\phi), w) = f(\psi \vee \phi, w) = k$. Assume that $f(\phi \equiv \psi, w) = k'$. Since $\phi \equiv \psi =_{def} \neg(\phi \wedge \neg\psi) \wedge \neg(\psi \wedge \neg\phi)$, then $f(\neg(\phi \wedge \neg\psi) \wedge \neg(\psi \wedge \neg\phi), w) = k'$. By A4, we know that $f(\neg(\phi \wedge \neg\psi) \wedge \neg(\psi \wedge \neg\phi), w) = f(\neg(\psi \wedge \neg\phi) \wedge \neg(\phi \wedge \neg\psi), w)$; hence, $f(\neg(\psi \wedge \neg\phi) \wedge \neg(\phi \wedge \neg\psi), w) = f(\psi \equiv \phi, w) = k'$.

The system RNS is supported by a mechanism for conflict resolution. First, we introduce a relation $\ll$ over the set Src so that $s \ll s'$ means that normative source s is *overridden* by normative source s'; we take $\ll$ to be a strict partial order, namely (for all $s, s', s'' \in Src$):[4]

- $\neg(s \ll s)$;
- $(s \ll s' \wedge s' \ll s'') \rightarrow s \ll s''$.

A normative source that is not overridden by any other can be called *maximal*. Due to the properties of $\ll$, Src always includes at least one maximal normative source. Second, we define an operator $O_{a_i}^*$ for agent-relative *all-things-considered obligation*, as follows:

$$O_{a_i}^* \phi =_{def} O_{a_i}^{s_j} \phi \text{ for some maximal } s_j \in Src.$$

Notice that the set of all-things-considered obligations for an agent is not required here to be consistent, differently from what usually is the case in the literature (see, e.g., [13]). Indeed, in real-life scenarios there are sometimes conflicts among two or more normative sources that neither override each other nor are overridden by other normative sources. Such conflicts *cannot* be solved, unless one revises some of the normative sources involved or rearranges their hierarchy. We omit the analogous truth-conditions for the two operators of all-things-considered obligation making reference to groups of agents, that is $O_{\forall X}^*$ and $O_{\exists X}^*$.

We would like to point out that a normative source need not correspond to the set of norms found in a specific legal text, it may also be a proper subset of all norms in a text or a collection of norms taken from different texts, provided

---

[4] For a more elaborated formulation of a hierarchy among normative sources, see [1].

that they have a common status. For instance, a maximal normative source may be also thought of as a collection of *peremptory norms*. A peremptory norm (*jus cogens*), such as the prohibition of torture in international law, is a principle which, by definition, does not admit any derogation (namely, it cannot be overridden by any other). Something prescribed by a peremptory norm can be represented in this framework via an expression of kind $O^*_{\forall Agt}\phi$.

4   Formal Analysis of Responsibility Attribution

The most basic notion used in the present section is that of *prospective responsibility*. We will adopt the following very general definitions for this notion:

Prospective Responsibility (single agent)
$\mathbb{PR}_{a_i}\phi =_{def} O^*_{a_i}\phi$, provided that ϕ does not include any operator for past reference (H or P).

Source-specific Prospective Responsibility (single agent)
$\mathbb{PR}^{s_j}_{a_i}\phi =_{def} O^{s_j}_{a_i}\phi$, provided that ϕ does not include any operator for past reference (H or P).

Prospective responsibility in this sense means that an agent has a certain obligation (or prohibition, when ϕ is a negative formula) *towards the present or the future*—either an all-things-considered obligation, or an obligation with reference to a specific normative source. An attribution of prospective responsibility may also concern a sequence of states to be achieved and duties of other agents. For instance, the expression $O^{s_j}_{a_i}(p \wedge F(q \wedge FO^{s_j}_{a_k}r))$ means that, according to normative source s_j, agent a_i is responsible for the sequential achievement of p and q and for successively ensuring the duty of agent a_k towards the achievement of r. Variations of the definitions of prospective responsibility involving groups of agents are easily obtained by replacing $O^{s_j}_{a_i}$ and $O^*_{a_i}$ with $O^{s_j}_{\forall X}$, $O^{s_j}_{\exists X}$, etc.

Other two core concepts are those of *historic responsibility* and *retrospective responsibility*. In order to define these we will employ the notion of prospective responsibility and the notion of deliberate causal contribution; furthermore, we will employ a notion of *historic avoidability of causal contribution*, which requires some preliminary remark. Our attention is here focused on responsibility ascription for a state-of-affairs that obtained at some point in the past due to an agent's (or a group of agents') causal contribution, while it could have never obtained (neither in the past nor in the future). For instance, Mark and Emma stole a car two days ago, but three days ago it was still possible for both Mark and Emma to conduct their entire life without stealing any car. More generally,

Definition 7. *The causal contribution on ϕ of a group of agents $X \subseteq Agt$ is historically avoidable at a state w of a model $\mathfrak{M}$ iff:*

(I) there is a state $w' \prec w$ s.t., for all $a_i \in X$, we have $\mathfrak{M}, w' \vDash \neg C_{a_i}\phi$;
(II) for all $w'' \prec w'$ and for all $a_i \in X$, we have $\mathfrak{M}, w'' \vDash \neg C_{a_i}\phi$;

(III) there is a branch b stemming from w' s.t. for all $v \in b$ and for all $a_i \in X$, we have $\mathfrak{M}, v \vDash \neg C_{a_i}\phi$.

This notion of *historic avoidability* can be formally represented in $\mathcal{L}$ by the following expression, whose truth at a state w of a model in C_m guarantees properties (I)–(III) of Definition 7:

Historic Avoidability (every agent in a group)
$$\mathbb{HA}_{\forall X}\phi =_{def} PF \bigwedge_{a_i \in X}(\neg C_{a_i}\phi \wedge H\neg C_{a_i}\phi \wedge G\neg C_{a_i}\phi)$$

In the case of a single agent, the definition at issue boils down to:

Historic Avoidability (single agent)
$$\mathbb{HA}_{a_i}\phi =_{def} PF(\neg C_{a_i}\phi \wedge H\neg C_{a_i}\phi \wedge G\neg C_{a_i}\phi)$$

Normative sources affect responsibility attribution across time. A group of agents X can be held responsible for a certain state-of-affairs ϕ that is prohibited either with reference to a normative source that was in effect at the time in which some (or every) agent $a_i \in X$ deliberately contributed to ϕ or with reference to a normative source presently in effect, but intended to have also a retrospective validity. In representing the two cases, we restrict our attention to maximal normative sources (i.e., all-things-considered norms). In the first case, one has the following formal definitions of *historic responsibility*:

Historic Responsibility (some agent in a group)
$$\mathbb{HR}_{\exists X}\phi =_{def} P(\bigvee_{a_i \in X} C_{a_i}\phi \wedge \mathbb{HA}_{\forall X}\phi \wedge \mathbb{PR}_{\forall X}\neg\phi)$$

Historic Responsibility (every agent in a group)
$$\mathbb{HR}_{\forall X}\phi =_{def} P(\bigwedge_{a_i \in X} C_{a_i}\phi \wedge \mathbb{HA}_{\forall X}\phi \wedge \mathbb{PR}_{\forall X}\neg\phi)$$

In the second case, instead, one has the following definitions of *retrospective responsibility*:

Retrospective Responsibility (some agent in a group)
$$\mathbb{RR}_{\exists X}\phi =_{def} P(\bigvee_{a_i \in X} C_{a_i}\phi \wedge \mathbb{HA}_{\forall X}\phi) \wedge \mathbb{PR}_{\forall X}\neg\phi$$

Retrospective Responsibility (every agent in a group)
$$\mathbb{RR}_{\forall X}\phi =_{def} P(\bigwedge_{a_i \in X} C_{a_i}\phi \wedge \mathbb{HA}_{\forall X}\phi) \wedge \mathbb{PR}_{\forall X}\neg\phi$$

Historic and retrospective responsibility do not exclude each other: indeed, it can be the case that the relevant normative sources remain unmodified across time and thus both definitions can be applied to describe a certain scenario.

We provide also the simplified definition of historic responsibility in the case of a single agent; retrospective responsibility for a single agent can be obtained in an analogous way:

Historic Responsibility (single agent)
$$\mathbb{HR}_{a_i}\phi =_{def} P(C_{a_i}\phi \wedge \mathbb{HA}_{a_i}\phi \wedge \mathbb{PR}_{a_i}\neg\phi)$$

Furthermore, we can introduce corresponding notions of responsibility with reference to a specific normative source, such as:

Source-specific Historic Responsibility (single agent)

$\mathbb{HR}^{s_j}_{a_i}\phi =_{def} P(C_{a_i}\phi \wedge \mathbb{HA}_{a_i}\phi \wedge \mathbb{PR}^{s_j}_{a_i}\neg\phi)$

Simultaneous and *posterior alleviation* with respect to what is prescribed by a normative source that is derogated (s_j) can be defined as follows:

Simultaneous Alleviation (single agent)

$\mathbb{SA}^{s_j}_{a_i}\phi =_{def} P(C_{a_i}\phi \wedge \mathbb{HA}_{a_i}\phi \wedge \mathbb{PR}^{s_j}_{a_i}\neg\phi \wedge \neg\mathbb{PR}_{a_i}\neg\phi)$

Posterior Alleviation (single agent)

$\mathbb{PA}^{s_j}_{a_i}\phi =_{def} \mathbb{HR}^{s_j}_{a_i}\phi \wedge \neg\mathbb{PR}_{a_i}\neg\phi$

Notice that in the system RNS, we have the following *Second Fundamental Theorem*, due to A14 and A15:

$FT2\ (\phi \sim \psi) \rightarrow (N\phi \equiv N\psi)$, where N is any notion of responsibility/alleviation defined in the present section.

Therefore, responsibility/alleviation attribution is invariant under propositional synonymy. Let us now show how the framework works in terms of some examples.

Example 1: the special militia. Alan and Bill, the only two members of a special militia, simultaneously shot at a single victim, Colin, since they suspected that he was a spy. However, the military code of the special militia has always prohibited to kill spies. Neither of the two bullets which were fired by Alan and Bill was sufficient for killing, but the two bullets together led Colin to lose enough blood to die. Let k be the proposition that Colin is killed and $M = \{a, b\}$ be the special militia, where a is Alan and b is Bill; let w be the state of evaluation, in which Colin is already dead, and u be the state in which Alan and Bill shot Colin (hence $u \prec w$). We want to formally express the fact that the special militia is responsible for the death of Colin. At u it is true that $C_a k$ and $C_b k$ and that their causal contribution is historically avoidable, since we can imagine that nothing forced Alan and Bill to act in such a way and that Colin's murder could have never taken place. Hence, we have that $\bigwedge_{x \in M}(C_x k \wedge \mathbb{HA}_x k \wedge \mathbb{PR}_x \neg k)$ holds at u and that $P\bigwedge_{x \in M}(C_x k \wedge \mathbb{HA}_x k \wedge \mathbb{PR}_x \neg k)$ holds at w. Therefore, at w the special militia is historically responsible for the death of Colin. In this case, both Alan and Bill are individually responsible as well, even if none of the two causally determined Colin's death.

Example 2: the toxic compound. A toy company T consists of two factories, f and g (so $T = \{f, g\}$), and g used to produce toys with a compound that was recognized as toxic only few years ago, such as lead paint. Companies who have produced toys with lead paint are required to withdraw their products from the market, since they are responsible for the distribution. We want to claim that T is retrospectively responsible for the distribution of dangerous toys by virtue of the new legislation and so that T has to take action. Let w be the state at which we are evaluating things and l the proposition that lead paint is used in toys. We know that there is some state $u \prec w$ s.t. $C_g l$ holds at u; furthermore, in an indeterministic world the causal contribution of g on l is historically avoidable at

u, so $\mathbb{HA}_g l$ holds there as well. Finally, at u the legislation on toxic compounds (s) is such that the use of lead paint is not prohibited, though it is prohibited at w, due to successive scientific discoveries. Therefore, $\neg\mathbb{PR}_g^s\neg l$ holds at u and $\mathbb{PR}_g^s\neg l$ holds at w. In this scenario, at w, we can conclude that not only the factory g, but the company T itself is retrospectively responsible for the use of lead paint, and so has to take action. Indeed, the formula $\mathbb{RR}_{\exists T} l$ holds at w.

Example 3: the food thief. In 2011, a homeless (a) attempted to steal a small amount of food (t) in Italy, which counts as an offence according to the legal source regulating offences of this kind (s_1), such as small thefts, whether completed or attempted. However, in the Italian legal system, there is a norm (s_2) of so-called *state of necessity* which allows for exceptions to generally valid norms. As a matter of fact, a was judged innocent by the Supreme Court of Cassation in virtue of s_2: stealing a small amount of food when in extreme need does not constitute a crime.[5] Let w be the state at which the action of a is evaluated by the Supreme Court of Cassation. We can say that there is some previous state u s.t. $C_a t$ holds at u. The causal contribution of a on t is historically avoidable at u under the assumption of an indeterministic world and t is prohibited by s_1 at w, so $\mathbb{PR}_a\neg t$ holds at w. Therefore, even if at w one can attribute to a retrospective (as well as historic, since the relevant regulations have not changed from u to w) responsibility on the theft on the basis of s_1, the Supreme Court of Cassation sentences that a's responsibility is alleviated by the higher-normative source s_2 (i.e., $s_1 \ll s_2$). Hence, from the perspective of the Supreme Court, we have a case of simultaneous alleviation due to the interaction between two normative sources. This fact is represented by the truth of $\mathbb{SA}_a t$ at w.

Example 4: the two ships. This example is also known as "Raffles v. Wichelhaus" and is taken from [18]. In 1864 a buyer purchased bales of cotton that were to be sent from Bombay to Liverpool on a ship named the "Peerless". When the contract regulating the transaction was made there were two ships called the Peerless (though, the two parties were not aware of this fact): one of them was supposed to leave India in October, the other in December. While the buyer expected the goods to be on the October ship, the seller placed them on the December ship. The two parties interpreted the contract in two different ways. Technically speaking, while the buyer took the statements "the bales of cotton are placed on the Peerless" (p) and "the bales of cotton are placed on the ship which leaves India in October" (q) as bearing a relation of propositional synonymy, the seller did not acknowledge such a relation. In order to model the controversy here, we need to take *two* states of evaluation, w_{seller} and w_{buyer}, which represent the alternative interpretations of the contract (s) followed by the two parties. In the sketched model the states w_{seller} and w_{buyer} are *not* related by any temporal path (i.e., we do not have $w_{seller} \bowtie w_{buyer}$); they rather belong to two disjoint trees of the model, $\mathfrak{T}_{seller}$ and $\mathfrak{T}_{buyer}$, which are associated with the two different interpretations of the contract. If we represent the legal

---

[5] This case is discussed here: https://www.bbc.com/news/world-europe-36190557.

divergence in terms of historic responsibility, then we have that $p \sim q$ holds at w_{buyer} and that, in the light of the principle FT2, $\mathbb{RR}^s_{seller}\neg q$ entails $\mathbb{RR}^s_{seller}\neg p$ at such state. However, since $p \sim q$ does *not* hold at w_{seller}, then $\mathbb{RR}^s_{seller}\neg q$ does *not* entail $\mathbb{RR}^s_{seller}\neg p$ at such state.

5   Concluding Remarks

We developed a theoretical framework for the analysis of responsibility based on three main ingredients: causal contribution, context of evaluation (provided by several normative sources which may vary with time) and norm interpretation. We represented this framework within a simple system of temporal and multi-agent deontic logic, called RNS, where it is possible to define many fine-grained notions of responsibility attribution and alleviation. We supported RNS with a mechanism for conflict resolution based on a hierarchy of normative sources and showed that RNS can be characterized by a certain class of models. Finally, we illustrated how the formal definitions provided can be used to analyse heterogeneous examples of legal reasoning.

As far as future directions of research are concerned, we have not discussed a mechanism to handle defeasible norms that is provided, *in nuce*, by the present framework and that requires further investigation. Consider the following norms: (I) "a ought to bring about ϕ given ψ" and (II) "a ought not to bring about ϕ given ψ and χ." Since normative sources are just sets of norms, we can take a normative source s_1 which includes exactly (I) and a normative source s_2 which includes exactly (II). We can then formalize the two norms as $\psi \to O^{s_1}_a \phi$ and $(\psi \wedge \chi) \to O^{s_2}_a \neg\phi$. Then, if s_1 and s_2 are the only relevant normative sources, by taking $s_1 \ll s_2$, we get $(\psi \wedge \chi) \to (O^*_a \neg\phi \wedge \neg O^*_a \phi)$.

Another direction is to examine a richer framework of temporal logic, such as a STIT-based or a CTL-based one, which would allow us to provide more refined definitions of responsibility. From a philosophical perspective it would be relevant to examine what kind of indeterminism is needed for the very possibility of responsibility, taking the notion of avoidability as the starting point. Other directions would include examining various specifically legal concepts, which are the stock-in-trade of lawyers, and considering applications of our framework for responsibility attribution in the areas of multi-agent systems and autonomous vehicles (see, e.g., [9] and [14]).

Acknowledgements and Contribution. We are grateful to Olivier Roy, his group, and Timo Lang. Daniela Glavaničová was supported by the Slovak Research and Development Agency under the contract no. APVV-17-0057 and by the grant no. UK/414/2018. Matteo Pascucci was funded by the WWTF project MA16-028. The two authors equally contributed to the contents.

References

1. Alchourrón, C.E., Makinson, D.: Hierarchies of regulations and their logic. In: Hilpinen, R. (ed.) New Studies in Deontic Logic, vol. 152, pp. 125–148. Springer, Dordrecht (1981). https://doi.org/10.1007/978-94-009-8484-4_5

2. Baldoni, M., Baroglio, C., Boissier, O., May, K.M., Micalizio, R., Tedeschi, S.: Accountability and responsibility in agent organizations. In: Miller, T., Oren, N., Sakurai, Y., Noda, I., Savarimuthu, B.T.R., Cao Son, T. (eds.) PRIMA 2018. LNCS (LNAI), vol. 11224, pp. 261–278. Springer, Cham (2018). https://doi.org/10.1007/978-3-030-03098-8_16

3. Braham, M., Van Hees, M.: Responsibility voids. Philos. Q. **61**, 6–15 (2011)

4. Braham, M., Van Hees, M.: An anatomy of moral responsibility. Mind **121**, 601–634 (2012)

5. Cane, P.: Responsibility in Law and Morality. Hart Publishing, Oxford (2002)

6. Chromá, M.: Synonymy and polysemy in legal terminology and their applications to bilingual and bijural translation. Res. Lang. **9**, 31–50 (2011)

7. Cooper, D.E.: Collective responsibility. Philosophy **43**, 258–268 (1968)

8. de Lima, T., Royakkers, L., Dignum, F.: A logic for reasoning about responsibility. Logic J. IGPL **18**, 99–117 (2010)

9. Derakhshan, F., Bench-Capon, T., McBurney, P.: Dynamic assignment of roles, rights and responsibilities in normative multi-agent systems. J. Logic Comput. **23**(2), 355–372 (2011)

10. Faroldi, F.L.G.: Deontic modals and hyperintensionality. Logic J. IGPL **27**(4), 387–410 (2019)

11. Frege, G.: Über Sinn und Bedeutung. Zeitschrift für Philosophie und philosophische Kritik. **100**, 25–50 (1892)

12. Giordani, A.: Ability and responsibility in general action logic. In: Broersen, J., Condoravdi, C., Shyam, N., Pigozzi, G. (eds.) DEON 2018, pp. 121–138. College Publications, London (2018)

13. Goble, L.: Prima facie norms, normative conflicts, and dilemmas. In: Gabbay, D., Horty, J., Parent, X. (eds.) Handbook of Deontic Logic and Normative Systems, pp. 241–351. College Publications, London (2013)

14. Hevelke, A., Nida-Rümelin, J.: Responsibility for crashes of autonomous vehicles: an ethical analysis. Sci. Eng. Ethics **21**(3), 619–630 (2015)

15. Lorini, E., Longin, D., Mayor, E.: A logical analysis of responsibility attribution: emotions, individuals and collectives. J. Logic Comput. **24**, 1313–1339 (2014)

16. Lorini, E., Sartor, G.: Influence and responsibility: a logical analysis. In: JURIX 2015, pp. 51–60 (2015)

17. Oddie, G., Tichý, P.: The logic of ability, freedom and responsibility. Stud. Logica. **41**, 227–248 (1982)

18. Schane, S.: Ambiguity and misunderstanding in the law. Thomas Jefferson Law Rev. **25**, 167–193 (2002)

19. Sedlár, I.: Hyperintensional logics for everyone. Synthese, 1–24 (2019)

20. van Benthem, J.: The Logic of Time. Kluwer, Dordrecht (1983)

Decidable Verification of Agent-Based Data-Aware Systems

Francesco Belardinelli[1,2] and Vadim Malvone[2(✉)]

[1] Imperial College London, London, UK
[2] Laboratoire IBISC, Universite d'Evry, Évry, France
vadim.malvone@univ-evry.fr

Abstract. In recent years the area of knowledge representation and reasoning (KR&R) has witnessed a growing interest in the modelling and analysis of data-driven/data-centric systems. These are systems in which the two tenets of data and processes are given equal importance, differently from traditional approaches whereby the data content is typically abstracted away in order to make the reasoning task easier. However, if data-aware systems (DaS) are to be deployed in concrete KR&R scenarios, it is key to develop tailored verification techniques, suitable to account for both data and processes. In this contribution we consider for the first time to our knowledge the parameterised verification of DaS. In particular, we prove that – under specific assumptions – this problem is decidable by computing a suitable cut-off value. We illustrate the proposed approach with a use case from the literature on business process modelling.

1 Introduction

The ever increasing reliance of AI technologies on data acquisition, managements, and processing is having a profound impact on the nature and mission of artificial intelligence itself [28]. In recent years the area of knowledge representation and reasoning (KR&R) has witnessed a growing interest in the modelling and analysis of data-driven/data-centric/data-intensive systems [3,15,16]. This paradigm shift towards data-aware systems (DaS) has initiated in the area of business process modelling (BPM), in response to traditional approaches to service-oriented computing that typically abstract the data content away to reduce the complexity of the system description [30]. However, this data content is often essential to drive a business process. Hence, according to the data-aware perspective on BPM, the *data content* and the *processes* operating on it are seen as two equally relevant tenets in modelling systems [11,20]. This data-aware approach has proved fruitful also in applications to areas in KR&R, including commitments in negotiation [27], planning [9], and service-oriented computing [14], where processes are often thought of as *agents*, endowed with their own goals, plans to achieve them, as well as information about the external environment [29].

© Springer Nature Switzerland AG 2019
M. Baldoni et al. (Eds.): PRIMA 2019, LNAI 11873, pp. 52–68, 2019.
https://doi.org/10.1007/978-3-030-33792-6_4

Yet, if agent-based DaS are to be deployed in concrete KR&R scenarios, it is key to develop verification techniques, suitable to account for the two tenets of data and processes. Then, a critical issue in tackling this task lies in the infinite state space generated by the possibly infinite data content of DaS. Recently, several contributions have addressed this problem [3,7,10,26], also leading to the development of open-source toolkits for DaS verification [19,25]. Nonetheless, we identify a conceptual difficulty with most of the current approaches in the literature: data-aware systems are typically assumed to contain an actual infinity of data and to be able to reason about such an actual infinity. For instance, in [7,10] an infinite quantification domain is part of the system's description. But real-life scenarios actually deal only with a finite, possibly *unbounded*, quantity of data. Hence, the soundness and applicability of those theoretical results to concrete DaS scenarios cannot be taken for granted.

To provide an answer to the difficulties pertaining to reasoning about an actual infinite data domain, in Sect. 2 we introduce parameterised agent-based DaS (or P-AbDaS) as abstract systems, which are to be coupled with a (finite) data domain, in order to generate a concrete agent-based DaS (or C-AbDaS). Hence, differently from [7,10], the same P-AbDaS can be instantiated in possibly infinitely-many C-AbDaS, but all of them are finite. Further, to specify the behaviour of P-AbDaS we need both temporal operators to describe the system's evolution, and first-order features, including quantifiers and relation symbols, to account for data. Hence, in Sect. 3 we consider a first-order extension of the computation-tree logic CTL as the specification language for P-AbDaS, and then define the *parameterised* model checking problem for this setting, which we show to be undecidable in general. Then, in Sect. 4 we introduce techniques based on isomorphisms and finite interpretation that allow – under specific assumptions – for the existence of a *cut-off*, that is, a bound on the size of the quantification domain above which the truth value of formulas in first-order CTL does not change. The existence and value of the cut-off allow for a complete model checking procedure that checks the specification on increasingly larger domains, up to the cut-off value. We illustrate the formal machinery with a procurement scenario from the literature on BPM [21]. Finally, we conclude in Sect. 5 by discussing related work and pointing to future directions of research.

2   Agent-Based Data-Aware Systems

In this section we introduce parameterised agent-based data-aware systems (P-AbDaS) and define the corresponding model checking problem w.r.t. a first-order version of the temporal logic CTL. We first present the basic terminology on databases that is used throughout the paper [1].

Definition 1 (Database schema and instance). *A* database schema *is a finite set $\mathcal{D} = \{P_1/q_1, \ldots, P_n/q_n\}$ of relation symbols P with arity $q \in \mathbb{N}$.*

Given a countable interpretation domain Y, a $\mathcal{D}$-instance over Y is a mapping D associating each relation symbol P to a finite q-ary relation on Y, i.e., $D(P) \underset{fin}{\subseteq} Y^q$.

By Definition 1 a database instance can be thought of as a finite relational structure, in line with relational models of databases [1]. We denote the set of all $\mathcal{D}$-instances on domain Y as $\mathcal{D}(Y)$. The *active domain* $adom(D)$ of a $\mathcal{D}$-instance D is the *finite* set of all elements $u \in Y$ occurring in some predicate interpretation $D(P)$, that is, $adom(D) = \bigcup_{P \in \mathcal{D}} \{u \in Y \mid \langle u_1, \ldots, u, \ldots, u_q \rangle \in D(P)\}$. Hereafter, we assume w.l.o.g. that the active domain also includes a finite set $C \subseteq Y$ of constants, i.e., $C \subseteq adom(D)$. To describe the temporal evolution of agent-based data-aware systems, we introduce the *primed version* of a database schema $\mathcal{D}$ as the schema $\mathcal{D}' = \{P_1'/q_1, \ldots, P_n'/q_n\}$. Then, the *disjoint union* $D \oplus D'$ of $\mathcal{D}$-instances D and D' is the $(\mathcal{D} \cup \mathcal{D}')$-instance such that *(i)* $(D \oplus D')(P_i) = D(P_i)$, and *(ii)* $(D \oplus D')(P_i') = D'(P_i)$, where $\mathcal{D}'$ is the primed version of $\mathcal{D}$. Intuitively, D and D' represent the current and next state of the system respectively, represented as database instances.

To specify properties of databases, we now recall the syntax of first-order logic with equality and no function symbols. Let V be a countable set of individual variables and let a *term* be any element $t \in T = V \cup C$.

Definition 2 (FO-formulas). *Given a database schema $\mathcal{D}$, the formulas φ of the first-order language $\mathcal{L}_\mathcal{D}$ are defined by the following BNF:*

$$\varphi ::= P(t_1, \ldots, t_q) \mid t = t' \mid \neg\varphi \mid \varphi \rightarrow \varphi \mid \forall x \varphi$$

where $P \in \mathcal{D}$, $t_1, \ldots, t_q$ is a q-tuple of terms, and t, t' are terms.

We define the free and bound variables in a formula φ as standard, and write $\varphi(\boldsymbol{x})$ to denote that the free variables of φ are among $x_1, \ldots, x_n$.

To interpret first-order formulas on database instances, we introduce *assignments* as functions $\sigma : T \rightarrow Y$ from terms to elements in Y. We denote by σ_u^x the assignment such that *(i)* $\sigma_u^x(x) = u$; and *(ii)* $\sigma_u^x(x') = \sigma(x')$ for every $x' \neq x$. Also, we assume a Herbrandian interpretation of constants, that is, $\sigma(c) = c$ for all $c \in C$.

Definition 3 (Satisfaction of FO-formulas). *Given a $\mathcal{D}$-instance D, an assignment σ, and an FO-formula $\varphi \in \mathcal{L}_\mathcal{D}$, we inductively define whether D satisfies φ under σ, or $(D, \sigma) \models \varphi$, as follows:*

$(D, \sigma) \models P(t_1, \ldots, t_q)$	*iff*	$\langle \sigma(t_1), \ldots, \sigma(t_q) \rangle \in D(P)$
$(D, \sigma) \models t = t'$	*iff*	$\sigma(t) = \sigma(t')$
$(D, \sigma) \models \neg\varphi$	*iff*	$(D, \sigma) \not\models \varphi$
$(D, \sigma) \models \varphi \rightarrow \varphi'$	*iff*	$(D, \sigma) \not\models \varphi$ or $(D, \sigma) \models \varphi'$
$(D, \sigma) \models \forall x \varphi$	*iff*	for all $u \in adom(D)$, $(D, \sigma_u^x) \models \varphi$

A formula φ is true *in D, or $D \models \varphi$, iff $(D, \sigma) \models \varphi$ for all assignments σ.*

Notice that we adopt an *active domain* semantics, where quantifiers range over the active domain $adom(D)$ of D. This is a standard assumption in database theory [1]. Hereafter, we often write $(D, \boldsymbol{u}) \models \varphi$ whenever $\boldsymbol{x}$ are all the free variables in φ and $\sigma(\boldsymbol{x}) = \boldsymbol{u}$. In particular, the satisfaction of a formula only depends on its free variables.

We now introduce a notion of agent whose local information state is represented as a relational database. In particular, inspired by the literature in KR&R and BPM on the specification of agent actions in terms of pre- and post-conditions [2,3,21], we introduce the notion of *action type*.

Definition 4 (Action Type). *An action type is an expression* $\alpha(\boldsymbol{x}) ::= g(\boldsymbol{x}) \rightsquigarrow ef(\boldsymbol{x})$, *where:*

- *guard g is an FO-formula with free variables $\boldsymbol{x}$;*
- *effect ef is an expression built according to the BNF:*

$$ef ::= add(P, \boldsymbol{x}) \mid del(P, \boldsymbol{x}) \mid ef; ef \mid ef \cup ef$$

where, intuitively, $add(P, \boldsymbol{x})$ is the insertion of tuple $\boldsymbol{x}$ in relation P, $del(P, \boldsymbol{x})$ is the deletion of $\boldsymbol{x}$ from P, $ef; ef$ is the sequential composition, and $ef \cup ef$ is the non-deterministic choice.

We now introduce a set Ag of agents, operating on databases, each of them defined as follows:

Definition 5 (Agent). *An agent is a tuple $i = \langle \mathcal{D}_i, Act_i \rangle$, where*

- $\mathcal{D}_i$ *is the* local database schema;
- Act_i *is the finite set of* action types $\alpha(\boldsymbol{x})$, *whose guards and effects are built over $\mathcal{D}_i$.*

Intuitively, by Definition 5 we assume that at each moment agent i is in some local state $D \in \mathcal{D}_i(Y)$ that represents all the information she has about the global state of the system. In this respect we follow the typical approach to agent-based systems [17,31], but here we require that this information is structured as a database. Further, each agent has her own database schema $\mathcal{D}_i$, but the same relation symbol might appear in several schemas.

As we are interested in the interactions of agents among themselves and with the external environment, we introduce their synchronous composition.

Definition 6 (Parameterised AbDaS). *A parameterised agent-based data-aware system (or P-AbDaS) is a finite set Ag of agents defined as in Definition 5.*

To endow a P-AbDaS with a data content, thus obtaining a concrete Ab-DaS, we consider an infinite, countable interpretation domain $\mathcal{Y}$, which intuitively represents these data.

Definition 7 (Concrete AbDaS). *A concrete agent-based data-aware system (or C-AbDaS) is a tuple $\mathcal{P} = (Ag, Y)$, where (i) Ag is a P-AbDaS; and (ii) $Y \supseteq C$ is a finite subset of $\mathcal{Y}$.*

Notice that, differently from [7,10], we do not assume an actual infinity of elements in our models: each C-AbDaS only contains a finite set Y of elements.

However, in general we can obtain infinitely many C-AbDaS based on the same P-AbDaS, build on different domains $Y \subseteq_{fin} \mathcal{Y}$.

We now introduce some technical notions that will be used in the rest of the paper. Given a C-AbDaS $\mathcal{P} = (Ag, Y)$, the (global) *states* of $\mathcal{P}$ are tuples $s \in S = \prod_{i \in Ag} \mathcal{D}_i(Y)$, whereas *joint actions* $\alpha(\boldsymbol{u}) \in ACT(Y) = \prod_{i \in Ag} Act_i(Y)$ take values $\boldsymbol{u}$ from domain Y. Observe that every global state $s = \langle D_0, \ldots, D_n \rangle \in S$ can be thought of as a database instance on the *global* database schema $\mathcal{D} = \bigcup_{i \in Ag} \mathcal{D}_i$ such that $s(P) = \bigcup_{i \in Ag} \mathcal{D}_i(P)$, for every $P \in \mathcal{D}$. Then, we set s_i as the restriction of s to the relation symbols in $\mathcal{D}_i$. That is, we assume that each agent has a truthful, yet partial, view of the global database $\mathcal{D}$, since in general $\mathcal{D}_i$ is a subset of $\mathcal{D}$.

Further, the *transition relation* $\tau : S \times ACT(Y) \mapsto 2^S$ is defined such that $t = \langle D'_0, \ldots, D'_n \rangle \in \tau(s, \alpha(\boldsymbol{u}))$ iff for every $i \in Ag$, $(s_i, \boldsymbol{u}) \models g_i$, i.e., all guards are satisfied and the corresponding joint action is enabled, and applying the effects $ef_i(\boldsymbol{u})$. Specifically, if $ef_i = add(P, \boldsymbol{x})$ (resp. $del(P, \boldsymbol{x})$), then D'_i is obtained from D_i by performing the corresponding insertion (resp. deletion) in P with values $\boldsymbol{u}$. If $ef_i = ef'_i; ef''_i$, then t_i is obtained from s_i by applying first the effects in ef'_i, and then ef''_i. Similarly for $ef_i = ef'_i \cup ef''_i$.

Finally, we introduce the *successor relation* $\rightarrow$ on global states such that $s \rightarrow t$ if there exists $\alpha(\boldsymbol{u}) \in ACT(Y)$ such that $s \xrightarrow{\alpha(\boldsymbol{u})} t$, i.e., $t \in \tau(s, \alpha(\boldsymbol{u}))$. A *run* r from state s is an infinite sequence $s^0 \rightarrow s^1 \rightarrow \ldots$, with $s^0 = s$. For $n \in \mathbb{N}$, we define $r(n) = s^n$. Hereafter we assume that the relation $\rightarrow$ is serial. This can be ensured by using skip actions. Notice that, in what follows we restrict the set of global states as the set of reachable states only. The disjoint union $\oplus$ is extended to global states in a pointwise manner: for $s = \langle D_0, \ldots, D_n \rangle$ and $s' = \langle D'_0, \ldots, D'_n \rangle$, we define $s \oplus s'$ as $\langle D_0 \oplus D'_0, \ldots, D_n \oplus D'_n \rangle$.

Example 1. To illustrate the formal machinery introduced thus far, we present a business process inspired by a concrete IBM customer use case [21]. The order-to-cash business process specifies the interactions of three agents in an e-commerce situation relating to the purchase and delivery of a product: a manufacturer m, a customer c, and a supplier s. The process begins when c prepares and submits to m a *purchase order* (PO), i.e., a list of products c requires (action *createPO()*). Upon receiving a PO, m prepares a *material order* (MO), i.e., a list of components needed to assemble the requested products (action *createMO()*). Then, m forwards to s the relevant material order. Upon receiving an MO, s can either accept or reject it (actions *acceptMO()* and *rejectMO()*). In the former case she proceeds to deliver the requested components to m (action *shipMO()*). In the latter, she notifies m of her rejection. If an MO is rejected, m deletes it and then prepares and submits a new MO (action *deleteMO()*). Upon delivery of the components (action *receiveMO()*), m assembles the product and, provided the order has been paid for (action *payPO()*), delivers it to c (action *shipPO()*).

We can encode the order-to-cash business process as a P-AbDaS, where the data model is represented by means of database schemas, whose evolution is determined by an appropriate set of actions types. Formally the three agents can be defined as follows:

- $A_c = \langle \mathcal{D}_c, Act_c \rangle$, where
    - $\mathcal{D}_c\{Products(prod\_code, budget), PO(id, prod\_code, offer, status)\}$;
    - $Act_c = \{createPO(id, code), payPO(id), deletePO(id)\}$;
- $A_m = \langle \mathcal{D}_m, Act_m \rangle$, where
    - $\mathcal{D}_m = \{PO(id, prod\_code, offer, status), MO(id, prod\_code, price, status)\}$;
    - $Act_m = \{createMO(id, price), receiveMO(id), deleteMO(id), shipPO(id)\}$;
- $A_s = \langle \mathcal{D}_s, Act_s \rangle$, where
    - $\mathcal{D}_s = \{Materials(mat\_code, cost), MO(id, prod\_code, price, status)\}$;
    - $Act_s = \{acceptMO(id), rejectMO(id), shipMO(id)\}$.

In Table 1 we provide the detailed action types for all agents in the use case. As an example, according to action type $createPO()$ (item (1.a)), the customer can create a purchase order with a designed id only if there exists a product with the same id. Further, by using $createMO()$ the manufacturer can create a material order with a designed id if MO does not contain a tuple with same id in preparation status (item (2.a)).

Table 1. The list of actions in the order-to-cash scenario.

The actions of customer c:
1. $createPO(id, code) ::= Products(code, x) \wedge \neg \exists z PO(id, code, z, \text{submitted}) \rightsquigarrow$ $add(PO(id, code, x, \text{submitted}))$
2. $payPO(id) ::= (PO(id, x, y, \text{prepared}) \wedge PO(id, x, y', \text{submitted}) \wedge y = y') \rightsquigarrow$ $del(PO(id, x, y, \text{submitted})); add(PO(id, x, y, \text{paid}))$
3. $deletePO(id) ::= PO(id, x, y, \text{shipped}) \rightsquigarrow del(PO(id, x, y, \text{paid}))$

The actions of manufacturer m:
1. $createMO(id, price) ::= (PO(id, x, \text{offer}, \text{submitted}) \wedge \neg \exists z MO(id, z, price, \text{preparation})) \rightsquigarrow$ $add(MO(id, x, price, \text{preparation}))$
2. $receiveMO(id) ::= MO(id, x, y, \text{shipped}) \rightsquigarrow$ $del(MO(id, x, y, \text{preparation})); add(MO(id, x, y, \text{received})); add(PO(id, x, y, \text{prepared}))$
3. $deleteMO(id) ::= MO(id, x, y, \text{rejected}) \rightsquigarrow del(MO(id, x, y, \text{preparation}))$
4. $shipPO(id) ::= PO(id, x, y, \text{paid}) \rightsquigarrow del(PO(id, x, y, \text{prepared})); add(PO(id, x, y, \text{shipped}))$

The actions of supplier s:
1. $acceptMO(id) ::= MO(id, code, y, \text{preparation}) \wedge \neg \exists z MO(id, code, z, \text{accepted}) \wedge$ $Materials(code, y) \rightsquigarrow add(MO(id, code, y, \text{accepted}))$
2. $rejectMO(id) ::= MO(id, code, y, \text{preparation}) \wedge \neg \exists z MO(id, code, z, \text{rejected}) \wedge$ $\neg Materials(code, y) \rightsquigarrow add(MO(id, code, y, \text{rejected}))$
3. $shipMO(id) ::= MO(id, x, y, \text{accepted}) \rightsquigarrow del(MO(id, x, y, \text{accepted})); add(MO(id, x, y, \text{shipped}))$

3 The Verification of AbDaS

In this section we introduce the specification language for AbDaS and the corresponding model checking problem. We recall that we consider a set V of *individual variables* and a set C of *individual constants*. The terms $t_1, t_2, \ldots$ in T are either variables in V or constants in C.

Definition 8 (FO-CTL). *The FO-CTL formulas φ over a database schema $\mathcal{D}$ are defined as follows, where $P \in \mathcal{D}$:*

$$\varphi ::= P(t_1, \ldots, t_q) \mid \neg\varphi \mid \varphi \to \varphi \mid \forall x\varphi \mid AX\varphi \mid A\varphi U\varphi \mid E\varphi U\varphi$$

The language FO-CTL is a first-order extension of the propositional temporal logic CTL. The temporal formulas $AX\varphi$ and $A\varphi U\varphi'$ (resp. $E\varphi U\varphi'$) are read as "for all runs, at the next step φ" and "for all runs (resp. some run), φ until φ'". Given a formula φ, we denote the set of free and all variables as $fr(\varphi)$ and $var(\varphi)$ respectively, and introduce formulas $EX\varphi$, $AF\varphi$, $AG\varphi$, $EF\varphi$, and $EG\varphi$ as standard.

We now interpreted FO-CTL on concrete agent-based data-aware systems.

Definition 9 (Semantics of FO-CTL). *We define whether a C-AbDaS $\mathcal{P}$ satisfies a formula φ in a state s according to assignment σ, or $(\mathcal{P}, s, \sigma) \models \varphi$, as follows:*

$(\mathcal{P}, s, \sigma) \models P(t)$ *iff* $\langle \sigma(t_1), \ldots, \sigma(t_q) \rangle \in s(P)$

$(\mathcal{P}, s, \sigma) \models t = t'$ *iff* $\sigma(t) = \sigma(t')$

$(\mathcal{P}, s, \sigma) \models \neg\varphi$ *iff* $(\mathcal{P}, s, \sigma) \not\models \varphi$

$(\mathcal{P}, s, \sigma) \models \varphi \to \varphi'$ *iff* $(\mathcal{P}, s, \sigma) \not\models \varphi$ *or* $(\mathcal{P}, s, \sigma) \models \varphi'$

$(\mathcal{P}, s, \sigma) \models \forall x\varphi$ *iff*   *for all* $u \in adom(s)$, $(\mathcal{P}, s, \sigma_u^x) \models \varphi$

$(\mathcal{P}, s, \sigma) \models AX\varphi$ *iff*   *for all* r, *if* $r(0) = s$ *then* $(\mathcal{P}, r(1), \sigma) \models \varphi$

$(\mathcal{P}, s, \sigma) \models A\varphi U\varphi'$ *iff*   *for all* r, *if* $r(0) = s$ *then there is* $k \geq 0$ *s.t.* $(\mathcal{P}, r(k), \sigma) \models \varphi'$, *and for all* j, $0 \leq j < k$ *implies* $(\mathcal{P}, r(j), \sigma) \models \varphi$

$(\mathcal{P}, s, \sigma) \models E\varphi U\varphi'$ *iff*   *for some* r, $r(0) = s$ *and there is* $k \geq 0$ *s.t.* $(\mathcal{P}, r(k), \sigma) \models \varphi'$, *and for all* j, $0 \leq j < k$ *implies* $(\mathcal{P}, r(j), \sigma) \models \varphi$

A formula φ is true at state s, or $(\mathcal{P}, s) \models \varphi$, if $(\mathcal{P}, s, \sigma) \models \varphi$ for all assignments σ; φ is true in C-AbDaS $\mathcal{P}$, or $\mathcal{P} \models \varphi$, if $(\mathcal{P}, s) \models \varphi$ for every $s \in S$. Finally, $Ag \models \varphi$ iff $(Ag, Y) \models \varphi$ for all $Y \subseteq_{fin} \mathcal{Y}$.

Again, in Definition 9 we adopt an active domain semantics, whereby quantifiers range over the active domain $adom(s)$ of s.

Finally, we present the model checking problem for P-AbDaS with respect to the specification language FO-CTL.

Definition 10 (Parameterised Model Checking). *Given a P-AbDaS Ag, an infinite domain $\mathcal{Y}$, and an FO-CTL formula φ, determine whether $Ag \models \varphi$.*

Notice that the parameterised model checking problem requires in principle to check an infinite number of C-AbDaS built on the same P-AbDaS. Indeed, model checking P-AbDaS is undecidable in general: we remark without proof that P-AbDaS are expressive enough to encode Turing machines, and reachability of a halting state can then be expressed in FO-CTL similarly to [7,15]. Hence, it is of interest to investigate semantic restrictions on P-AbDaS that allow for a decidable model checking problem.

To this end, a key notion to decide parameterised model checking in general is the *cut-off*:

Definition 11 (Cut-off). *A natural number* $n \in \mathbb{N}$ *is a* cut-off *for P-AbDaS Ag and formula* ϕ *iff for all finite subsets* $Y \supseteq C, Y' \supseteq C$ *of* $\mathcal{Y}$, *if* $|Y| = n$ *and* $|Y'| \geq |Y|$, *then* $(Ag, Y) \models \phi$ *iff* $(Ag, Y') \models \phi$.

Note that, in Definition 11 we suppose $|Y'| \geq |Y|$ without considering that $|Y|$ is a subset of $|Y'|$. This is because we define the set of constants C to be in both $|Y|$ and $|Y'|$, and for this reason the intersection between $|Y'|$ and $|Y|$ cannot be empty.

The existence of the cut-off allows us to decide verification by checking all C-AbDaS up to size $|n|$, of which there exist finitely many instances. We devote the rest of the paper to finding sufficient condition for the existence of cut-offs.

We conclude this section by elaborating on Example 1.

Example 2. We can investigate properties of the order-to-cash business process by using specifications in FO-CTL. For instance, the following formula intuitively specifies that each material order MO has to match a corresponding purchase order PO:

$$AG \; \forall id, pc \; (\exists pr, s \; MO(id, pc, pr, s) \rightarrow \exists o, s' PO(id, pc, o, s'))$$

The next specification states that given a material order MO, it can be the case that eventually the corresponding PO will be shipped.

$$AG \; \forall id, pc \; (\exists pr, s \; MO(id, pc, pr, s) \rightarrow EF \; \exists o \; PO(id, pc, o, \mathsf{shipped}))$$

Hereafter we develop techniques to model check specifications in FO-CTL like the ones above.

4 Finding Cut-Offs

In this section we introduce model-theoretic notions that will be used to tackle the parameterised model checking problem for P-AbDaS. In particular, we recall some notions in [7].

Definition 12 (Isomorphism). *Two database instances* $D \in \mathcal{D}(Y')$, $D' \in \mathcal{D}(Y)$ *are* isomorphic, *or* $D \simeq D'$, *iff there exists a bijection* $\iota : adom(D) \mapsto adom(D')$ *s.t.:*

(i) ι *is the identity on the constants in* C;
(ii) for all $P \in \mathcal{D}$, $\boldsymbol{u} \in Y^q$, $\boldsymbol{u} \in D(P)$ *iff* $\iota(\boldsymbol{u}) \in D'(P)$.

When the above is the case, we say that ι *is a* witness *for* $D \simeq D'$. *Moreover, two global states* $s = \langle D_0, \ldots, D_n \rangle \in S$ *and* $s' = \langle D'_0, \ldots, D'_n \rangle \in S'$ *are* isomorphic, *or* $s \simeq s'$, *iff there exists a bijection* $\iota : adom(s) \mapsto adom(s')$ *such that for every* $j \in Ag$, ι *is a witness for* $D_j \simeq D'_j$.

By Definition 12 isomorphisms preserve the interpretation of constants as well as of predicates up to renaming of terms. Obviously, isomorphisms are equivalence relations. Given a function $f : Y \mapsto Y'$ defined on $adom(s)$, $f(s)$ denotes the instance in $\mathcal{D}(Y')$ obtained from s by renaming each $u \in adom(s)$ as $f(u)$. If f is also injective (thus invertible) and the identity on C, then $f(s) \simeq s$.

While isomorphic states share the same relational structure, two isomorphic states do not necessarily satisfy the same FO-formulas as satisfaction depends also on the values assigned to free variables. To account for this, we introduce the following notion.

Definition 13 (Equivalent assignments). *Given states $s \in S$ and $s' \in S'$, and a set $V' \subseteq V$ of variables, assignments $\sigma : T \mapsto Y$ and $\sigma' : T \mapsto Y'$ are equivalent for V' w.r.t. s and s' iff there exists a bijection $\gamma : adom(s) \cup \sigma(V') \mapsto adom(s') \cup \sigma'(V')$ such that:*

(i) $\gamma|_{adom(s)}$ is a witness for $s \simeq s'$;
(ii) $\sigma'|_{V'} = \gamma; \sigma|_{V'}$, where ; is function composition.

By Definition 13 equivalent assignments preserve both the (in)equalities of the terms in s, s' up to renaming. Clearly, the existence of equivalent assignments implies that s, s' are isomorphic. We say that two assignments are *equivalent for an FO-CTL formula* φ, omitting states s and s' when clear from the context, if these are equivalent for the free variables $fr(\varphi)$ in φ.

We now state the following standard result in first-order (non-modal) logic, i.e., isomorphic states satisfy exactly the same FO-formulas, when interpreted with equivalent assignments [1].

Proposition 1. *Given isomorphic states $s \in S$ and $s' \in S'$, an FO-formula φ, and assignments σ and σ' equivalent for φ, we have that*

$$(s, \sigma) \models \varphi \text{ iff } (s', \sigma') \models \varphi$$

An immediate consequence of Proposition 1 is that isomorphic states cannot be distinguished by FO-sentences. In the rest of the section we show how isomorphisms can actually be used to prove the preservation of the whole FO-CTL. Notice that this is in marked contrast with similar results in the literature [3,7], which need to assume some notion of (bi)simulation on the underlying transitions systems. Nothing similar is required here, we show that isomorphisms suffice. More specifically, in [7] the requirement of *uniformity* was put forward as a sufficient condition for bisimilar systems to satisfy the same formulas in FO-CTL. We now show that C-AbDaS satisfy uniformity unrestrictedly.

Lemma 1 (Uniformity). *All C-AbDaS $\mathcal{P}, \mathcal{P}'$ are uniform, that is, for every $s, t \in S$, $s' \in S'$, $t' \in \mathcal{D}(Y)$, if $t \in \tau(s, \alpha(\boldsymbol{u}))$ and $s \oplus t \simeq s' \oplus t'$ for some witness ι, then for every constant-preserving bijection ι' that extends ι to $\boldsymbol{u}$, we have that $t' \in \tau(s', \alpha(\iota'(\boldsymbol{u})))$.*

Proof. For illustration, we consider the case in which there is only one agent, i.e., $\alpha(\boldsymbol{u}) = g(\boldsymbol{u}) \rightsquigarrow ef(\boldsymbol{u})$. First of all, notice that if $s \oplus t \simeq s' \oplus t'$ then for every bijection ι' extending ι to $\boldsymbol{u}$, we have that $(s, \boldsymbol{u}) \models g(\boldsymbol{x})$ iff $(s, \iota'(\boldsymbol{u})) \models g(\boldsymbol{x})$ by Proposition 1. Hence, action $\alpha(\boldsymbol{u})$ is enabled in s iff $\alpha(\iota'(\boldsymbol{u}))$ is enabled in s'.

Now we prove by induction on the structure of $ef(\boldsymbol{u})$ that t' can be obtained by applying effects $ef(\iota'(\boldsymbol{u}))$ to s', and therefore $t' \in \tau(s', \alpha(\iota'(\boldsymbol{u})))$. For the base of induction, consider $ef(\boldsymbol{u}) = add(P, \boldsymbol{u})$. Then, t differs from s only for tuple $\boldsymbol{u}$ possibly added to the interpretation of P. Since $s \oplus t \simeq s' \oplus t'$, also t' differs from s' only for tuple $\iota'(\boldsymbol{u})$ added to the interpretation of P, and therefore $t' \in \tau(s', \alpha(\iota'(\boldsymbol{u})))$. As regards the base case for $ef(\boldsymbol{u}) = del(P, \boldsymbol{u})$, t differs from s only for tuple $\boldsymbol{u}$ possibly deleted from the interpretation of P. Since $s \oplus t \simeq s' \oplus t'$, again t' differs from s' only for tuple $\iota'(\boldsymbol{u})$ deleted from the interpretation of P, and therefore $t' \in \tau(s', \alpha(\iota'(\boldsymbol{u})))$.

As for the inductive case for $ef(\boldsymbol{u}) = ef_1(\boldsymbol{u}_1) \cup ef_2(\boldsymbol{u}_2)$, then t is obtained from s by applying either the effects in $ef_1(\boldsymbol{u}_1)$ or in $ef_2(\boldsymbol{u}_2)$. Then, by induction hypothesis, t' can be obtained from s' by applying either the effects in $ef_1(\iota'(\boldsymbol{u}_1))$ or in $ef_2(\iota'(\boldsymbol{u}_2))$, which is tantamount to $ef(\iota'(\boldsymbol{u}))$. Finally, for $ef(\boldsymbol{u}) = ef_1(\boldsymbol{u}_1); ef_2(\boldsymbol{u}_2)$, t is obtained from s by applying first the effects in $ef_1(\boldsymbol{u}_1)$ and then $ef_2(\boldsymbol{u}_2)$. Then, by induction hypothesis, t' can be obtained from s' by applying first the effects in $ef_1(\iota'(\boldsymbol{u}_1))$ and then $ef_2(\iota'(\boldsymbol{u}_2))$, which is tantamount to $ef(\iota'(\boldsymbol{u}))$.

Intuitively, the notion of uniformity in Lemma 1 captures the idea that actions take into account and operate only on the relational structure of states, irrespective of the actual data they contain. Because of this, uniformity has been compared to the notion of *genericity* in database theory, whereby in specific cases the answer to a query depends only on the structure of the database [1]. Actually, the result in Lemma 1 is stronger that the notion of uniformity in [7], which is restricted to states belonging to the same system. We are able to prove a stronger result, as we consider C-AbDaS built on the same P-AbDaS and therefore sharing the same actions, which is not the case in [7].

We now demonstrate some auxiliary lemmas that will be used in proving the main preservation result (Theorem 2). The first two guarantee that under appropriate conditions on the cardinality of the interpretation domains, equivalent assignments are preserved by the isomorphism relation. Hereafter we set $N_{Ag} = \sum_{i \in Ag} \max_{\alpha(\boldsymbol{x}) \in Act_i} \{|\boldsymbol{x}|\}$, i.e., N_{Ag} is the sum of the maximum number of parameters contained in the action types of each agent in Ag; whereas $\mathcal{P} = (Ag, Y)$ and $\mathcal{P}' = (Ag, Y')$ are C-AbDaS defined on the same P-AbDaS Ag.

Lemma 2. *Consider C-AbDaS $\mathcal{P}$ and $\mathcal{P}'$ defined on the same P-AbDaS Ag, isomorphic states $s \in S$ and $s' \in S'$, an FO-CTL formula φ, and assignments σ and σ' equivalent for φ w.r.t. s and s'. For every $t \in S$ such that $s \rightarrow t$, if $|Y'| \geq |adom(s) \cup \sigma(fr(\varphi))| + N_{Ag}$, then there exists $t' \in S'$ such that $s' \rightarrow t'$, $t \simeq t'$, and σ and σ' are equivalent for φ w.r.t. t and t'.*

Proof. First of all, let γ be a bijection witnessing that σ and σ' are equivalent for φ w.r.t. s and s', and suppose that $t \in \tau(s, \boldsymbol{\alpha}(\boldsymbol{u}))$ for some joint action $\boldsymbol{\alpha}(\boldsymbol{u})$. Now define $Dom(j) \doteq adom(s) \cup \sigma(fr(\varphi)) \cup \boldsymbol{u}$, and partition it into:

- $Dom(\gamma) \doteq adom(s) \cup \sigma(fr(\varphi))$;
- $Dom(\iota') \doteq \boldsymbol{u} \setminus Dom(\gamma)$.

Let $\iota' : Dom(\iota') \mapsto Y' \setminus Im(\gamma)$ be an invertible total function. Observe that $|Im(\gamma)| = |adom(s') \cup \sigma'(fr(\varphi))| = |adom(s) \cup \sigma(fr(\varphi))|$, thus from the fact that $|Y'| \geq |adom(s) \cup \sigma(fr(\varphi))| + N_{Ag}$, we have that $|Y' \setminus Im(\gamma)| \geq |Dom(\iota')|$, which guarantees the existence of ι'.

Next, define $j : Dom(j) \mapsto Y'$ as follows:

$$j(u) = \begin{cases} \gamma(u), \text{ if } u \in Dom(\gamma) \\ \iota'(u), \text{ if } u \in Dom(\iota') \end{cases}$$

Clearly, j is invertible. In particular, j is a witness for $s \oplus t \simeq s' \oplus t'$, for $t' = j(t)$. In particular, since $t \in \tau(s, \boldsymbol{\alpha}(\boldsymbol{u}))$, by uniformity we obtain that $t' \in \tau(s', \boldsymbol{\alpha}(j(\boldsymbol{u})))$. Thus, $s' \to t'$. Finally, by construction of t', σ and σ' are equivalent for φ w.r.t. t and t'. $\square$

The proof of Lemma 2 relies crucially on $\mathcal{P}$ and $\mathcal{P}'$ being uniform. Moreover, since $\mathcal{P}$ and $\mathcal{P}'$ are defined on the same P-AbDaS Ag, we do not need to assume that $\mathcal{P}$ and $\mathcal{P}'$ are bisimilar, as it is the case in [7, Lemma 3.9] for instance.

Then, Lemma 2 generalises to runs.

Lemma 3. *Consider C-AbDaS $\mathcal{P}$ and $\mathcal{P}'$ defined on the same P-AbDaS Ag, isomorphic states $s \in S$ and $s' \in S'$, an FO-CTL formula φ, and two assignments σ and σ' equivalent for φ w.r.t. s and s'. For every run r of $\mathcal{P}$, if $r(0) = s$ and for all $i \geq 0$, $|Y'| \geq |adom(r(i)) \cup \sigma(fr(\varphi))| + N_{Ag}$, then there exists a run r' of $\mathcal{P}'$ such that for all $i \geq 0$:*

(i) $r'(0) = s'$;
(ii) $r(i) \simeq r'(i)$;
(iii) σ and σ' are equivalent for φ w.r.t. $r(i)$ and $r'(i)$.

Proof. Let r be a run satisfying the lemma's hypothesis. We inductively build r' and show that the conditions (i)–(iii) are satisfied. For $i = 0$, let $r'(0) = s'$. By hypothesis, r is such that $|Y'| \geq |adom(r(0)) \cup \sigma(fr(\varphi))| + N_{Ag}$. Thus, since $r(0) \to r(1)$, by Lemma 2 there exists $t' \in S'$ such that $r'(0) \to t'$, $r(1) \simeq t'$, and σ and σ' are equivalent for φ w.r.t. $r(1)$ and t'. Let $r'(1) = t'$.

The case for $i > 0$ is similar. Assume that $r(i) \simeq r'(i)$ and σ and σ' are equivalent for φ w.r.t. $r(i)$ and $r'(i)$. Since $r(i) \to r(i+1)$ and $|Y'| \geq |adom(r(i)) \cup \sigma(fr(\varphi))| + N_{Ag}$, by Lemma 2 there exists $t' \in S'$ such that $r'(i) \to t'$, σ and σ' are equivalent for φ w.r.t. $r(i+1)$ and t', and $r(i+1) \simeq t'$. Let $r'(i+1) = t'$. It is clear that r' is a run in $\mathcal{P}'$.

Again, Lemma 3 differs from similar results in the literature (e.g., [7, Lemma 3.10]) as we do not need to assume that $\mathcal{P}$ and $\mathcal{P}'$ are bisimilar.

By Lemma 3 we can prove that, for sufficiently large domains, FO-CTL formulas cannot distinguish isomorphic C-AbDaS built on the same P-AbDaS.

Theorem 1. *Consider C-AbDaS $\mathcal{P}$ and $\mathcal{P}'$ defined on the same P-AbDaS Ag, isomorphic states $s \in S$ and $s' \in S'$, an FO-CTL formula φ, and two assignments σ and σ' equivalent for φ w.r.t. s and s'. If*

1. *for every run r such that $r(0) = s$, for all $k \geq 0$ we have $|Y'| \geq |adom(r(k)) \cup \sigma(fr(\varphi))| + |var(\varphi) \setminus fr(\varphi)| + N_{Ag}$;*
2. *for every run r' such that $r'(0) = s'$, for all $k \geq 0$ we have $|Y| \geq |adom(r'(k)) \cup \sigma'(fr(\varphi))| + |var(\varphi) \setminus fr(\varphi)| + N_{Ag}$;*

then $(\mathcal{P}, s, \sigma) \models \varphi$ iff $(\mathcal{P}', s', \sigma') \models \varphi$.

Proof. The proof is by induction on the structure of φ. We prove that if $(\mathcal{P}, s, \sigma) \models \varphi$ then $(\mathcal{P}', s', \sigma') \models \varphi$. The other direction can be proved analogously. The base case for atomic formulas follows by Proposition 1. The inductive cases for propositional connectives are immediate and thus omitted.

For $\varphi \equiv \forall x \psi$, assume that $x \in fr(\psi)$ (otherwise consider ψ, and the corresponding case), and no variable is quantified more than once (otherwise we can rename variables w.l.o.g.). Let γ be a bijection witnessing that σ and σ' are equivalent for φ w.r.t. s and s'. For $u \in adom(s)$, consider the assignment σ_u^x. By definition, $\gamma(u) \in adom(s')$, and $\sigma_{\gamma(u)}'^x$ is well-defined. Note that $fr(\psi) = fr(\varphi) \cup \{x\}$; so σ_u^x and $\sigma_{\gamma(u)}'^x$ are equivalent for ψ w.r.t. s and s'. Moreover, $|\sigma_u^x(fr(\psi))| = |\sigma(fr(\varphi))| + 1$. The same considerations apply to σ'. Further, $|var(\psi) \setminus fr(\psi)| = |var(\varphi) \setminus fr(\varphi)| - 1$, as $var(\psi) = var(\varphi)$, $fr(\psi) = fr(\varphi) \cup \{x\}$, and $x \notin fr(\varphi)$. Thus, both hypotheses (1) and (2) remain satisfied if we replace φ with ψ, σ with σ_u^x, and σ' with $\sigma_{\gamma(u)}'^x$. Therefore, by the induction hypothesis, if $(\mathcal{P}, s, \sigma_u^x) \models \psi$ then $(\mathcal{P}', s', \sigma_{\gamma(u)}'^x) \models \psi$. Since $u \in adom(s)$ is generic and γ is a bijection, the result follows.

For $\varphi \equiv AX\psi$, assume by contraposition that $(\mathcal{P}', s', \sigma') \not\models \varphi$. Then, there exists a run r' such that $r'(0) = s'$ and $(\mathcal{P}', r'(1), \sigma') \not\models \psi$. Since $|var(\varphi) \setminus fr(\varphi)| \geq 0$, by Lemma 3, there exists a run r such that $r(0) = s$, and for all $i \geq 0$, $r(i) \simeq r'(i)$ and σ and σ' are equivalent for ψ w.r.t. $r(i)$ and $r'(i)$. Since r is a run such that $r(0) = s$, it satisfies hypothesis (1). Moreover, the same hypothesis is necessarily satisfied by all the runs r'' such that for some $i \geq 0, r''(0) = r(i)$ (otherwise, the run $r(0) \to \cdots \to r(i) \to r''(1) \to r''(2) \to \cdots$ would not satisfy the hypothesis for r); the same considerations apply w.r.t hypothesis (2) and for all the runs r''' such that $r'''(0) = r'(i)$, for some $i \geq 0$. In particular, these hold for $i = 1$. Thus, we can inductively apply the hypothesis, by replacing s with $r(1)$, s' with $r'(1)$, and φ with ψ (observe that $var(\varphi) = var(\psi)$ and $fr(\varphi) = fr(\psi)$). But then we obtain $(\mathcal{P}, r(1), \sigma) \not\models \psi$, thus $(\mathcal{P}, r(0), \sigma) \not\models AX\psi$.

For $\varphi \equiv E\psi U\phi$, assume that the only variables common to ψ and ϕ occur free in both formulas (otherwise rename quantified variables w.l.o.g.). Let r be a run such that $r(0) = s$, and there exists $k \geq 0$ such that $(\mathcal{P}, r(k), \sigma) \models \phi$, and $(\mathcal{P}, r(j), \sigma) \models \psi$ for $0 \leq j < k$. By Lemma 3 there exists a run r' such that $r'(0) = s'$ and for all $i \geq 0$, $r'(i) \simeq r(i)$ and σ and σ' are equivalent for φ w.r.t. $r'(i)$ and $r(i)$. From each bijection γ_i witnessing that σ and σ' are equivalent for φ w.r.t. $r'(i)$ and $r(i)$, define the bijections $\gamma_{i,\psi} = \gamma_i|_{adom(r(i)) \cup \sigma(fr(\psi))}$

and $\gamma_{i,\phi} = \gamma_i|_{adom(r(i)) \cup \sigma(fr(\phi))}$. Since $fr(\psi) \subseteq fr(\varphi), fr(\phi) \subseteq fr(\varphi)$, it can be seen that $\gamma_{i,\psi}$ and $\gamma_{i,\phi}$ witness that σ and σ' are equivalent for respectively ψ and ϕ w.r.t. $r'(i)$ and $r(i)$. By the same argument used for the AX case above, hypothesis (1) holds for all the runs r'' such that $r''(0) = r(i)$, for some $i \geq 0$, and hypothesis (2) holds for all the runs r''' such that $r'''(0) = r'(i)$. Now observe that $|\sigma(fr(\phi))|, |\sigma(fr(\psi))| \leq |\sigma(fr(\varphi))|$. Moreover, by the assumption on the common variables of ψ and ϕ, $(var(\varphi) \setminus fr(\varphi)) = (var(\psi) \setminus fr(\psi)) \uplus (var(\phi) \setminus fr(\phi))$, thus $|var(\varphi) \setminus fr(\varphi)| = |(var(\psi) \setminus fr(\psi)| + |(var(\phi) \setminus fr(\phi)|$, hence $|(var(\psi) \setminus fr(\psi)|, |(var(\phi) \setminus fr(\phi)| \leq |var(\varphi) \setminus fr(\varphi)|$. Therefore hypotheses (1) and (2) hold also with φ uniformly replaced by either ψ or ϕ. Then, the induction hypothesis applies for each i, by replacing s with $r(i)$, s' with $r'(i)$, and φ with either ψ or ϕ. Thus, for each i, $(\mathcal{P}, r(i), \sigma) \models \psi$ iff $(\mathcal{P}', r'(i), \sigma') \models \psi$, and $(\mathcal{P}, r(i), \sigma) \models \phi$ iff $(\mathcal{P}', r'(i), \sigma') \models \phi$. Therefore, r' is a run such that $r'(0) = s'$, $(\mathcal{P}', r'(k), \sigma') \models \phi$, and for every j, $0 \leq j < k$ implies $(\mathcal{P}', r'(j), \sigma') \models \psi$, i.e., $(\mathcal{P}', s', \sigma') \models E\psi U\phi$.

For $\varphi \equiv A\psi U\phi$, assume by contraposition that $(\mathcal{P}', s', \sigma') \not\models \varphi$. Then, there exists a run r' such that $r'(0) = s'$ and for every $k \geq 0$, either $(\mathcal{P}', r'(k), \sigma') \not\models \phi$ or there exists j such that $0 \leq j < k$ and $(\mathcal{P}', r'(j), \sigma') \not\models \psi$. By Lemma 3 there exists a run r such that $r(0) = s$, and for all $i \geq 0$, $r(i) \simeq r'(i)$ and σ and σ' are equivalent for φ w.r.t. $r(i)$ and $r'(i)$. Similarly to the case of $E\psi U\phi$, it can be shown that σ and σ' are equivalent for ψ and ϕ w.r.t. $r(i)$ and $r'(i)$, for all $i \geq 0$. Further, assuming w.l.o.g. that all variables common to ψ and ϕ occur free in both formulas, it can be shown, as in the case of $E\psi U\phi$, that the induction hypothesis holds on every pair of runs obtained as suffixes of r and r', starting from their i-th state, for every $i \geq 0$. Thus, $(\mathcal{P}, r(i), \sigma) \models \psi$ iff $(\mathcal{P}', r'(i), \sigma') \models \psi$, and $(\mathcal{P}, r(i), \sigma) \models \phi$ iff $(\mathcal{P}', r'(i), \sigma') \models \phi$. But then r is such that $r(0) = s$ and for every $k \geq 0$, either $(\mathcal{P}, r(k), \sigma) \not\models \phi$ or there exists j such that $0 \leq j < k$ and $(\mathcal{P}, r(j), \sigma) \not\models \psi$, that is, $(\mathcal{P}, s, \sigma) \not\models A\psi U\phi$.

We can now immediately extend Theorem 1 to the model checking problem for C-AbDaS.

Theorem 2. *Consider C-AbDaS $\mathcal{P}$ and $\mathcal{P}'$ defined on the same P-AbDaS Ag, and an FO-CTL formula φ. If*

1. $|Y'| \geq \max_{s \in S} |adom(s)| + |var(\varphi)| + N_{Ag}$;
2. $|Y| \geq \max_{s' \in S'} |adom(s')| + |var(\varphi)| + N_{Ag}$;

then $\mathcal{P} \models \varphi$ iff $\mathcal{P}' \models \varphi$.

Proof. Equivalently, we prove that if $(\mathcal{P}, s_0, \sigma) \not\models \varphi$ for some σ, then there exists a σ' s.t. $(\mathcal{P}', s_0', \sigma') \not\models \varphi$, and viceversa. To this end, observe that hypotheses (1) and (2) imply, respectively, hypotheses (1) and (2) of Theorem 1. Further, notice that, by cardinality considerations, given the assignment $\sigma : T \mapsto Y$, there exists an assignment $\sigma' : T \mapsto Y'$ such that σ and σ' are equivalent for φ w.r.t. s_0 and s_0'. Thus, by applying Theorem 1 we have that if there exists an assignment σ such that $(\mathcal{P}, s_0, \sigma) \not\models \varphi$, then there exists an assignment σ' such that $(\mathcal{P}', s_0', \sigma') \not\models \varphi$. The converse can be proved analogously, as the hypotheses are symmetric.

Theorem 2 shows that P-AbDaS Ag can in principle be verified by assuming an interpretation domain of suitable size. Notice again that, since $\mathcal{P}$ and $\mathcal{P}'$ are defined on the same P-AbDaS Ag, differently from [7] we do not require any notion of bisimulation. Moreover, if we are able to bound the quantity $\max_{s \in S} |adom(s)|$ across Ag, then we obtain a cut-off value. These considerations motivate the following definition.

Definition 14 (Bounded P-AbDaS). *A P-AbDaS Ag is b-bounded, for $b \in \mathbb{N}$, if for all C-AbDaS $\mathcal{P}$ based on Ag, for all reachable states $s \in S$, $|adom(s)| \leq b$.*

Boundedness can be justified in terms of the underlying implementation of a P-AbDaS. Indeed, in the order-to-cash scenarios it is likely that there is a maximum number of purchase orders that the manufacturer can deal with at any single time. By assuming boundedness, next result follows from Theorem 2.

Theorem 3. *Consider a b-bounded P-AbDaS Ag over an infinite interpretation domain $\mathcal{Y}$. Then, $n = b + k + N_{Ag}$ is a cut-off for all formulas with at most k variables.*

By Theorem 3 to decide whether a specification φ is true in a bounded P-AbDaS Ag, we can check the corresponding C-AbDaS $\mathcal{P}$ based on increasingly bigger domains $Y \underset{inf}{\subset} \mathcal{Y}$, until we hit $|Y| = b + var(\varphi) + N_{Ag}$. If formula φ is true in all iteration, we can then conclude that φ is true in Ag.

Discussion. The assumption of boundedness to obtain decidability may appear restrictive. However, notice that in most implementation of data-aware systems, the bound is set by the system's specification in terms of memory. That is, we can safely assume that our system will never contain more than a certain amount of data, however large it can be, and use this bound to verify properties of interest. Unfortunately, the problem of deciding whether a system is b-bounded, for some $b \in \mathbb{N}$, is undecidable in general. Some restrictions on the specification of actions to obtain bounded systems have been explored in [3].

We conclude this section by elaborating on our running example.

Example 3. Consider again the order-to-cash scenario and suppose that the customer can request at most 5 products for each purchase order and the manufacturer can request at most 10 materials to the supplier. Note that, in principle the number of products could be infinite. Further, the total number of products and the total number of materials are both 20. So, we can fix a bound $b = 5 \cdot 4 + 10 \cdot 4 + 20 \cdot 2 + 20 \cdot 2 = 140$, and notice that the FO-CTL specifications in Example 2 contain at most 6 variables. Then, the value for the cut-off is $n = 146 + N_{Ag}$. Since the maximum number of parameters for the customer and the manufacturer is 2 and for the supplier is 1, then $n = 146 + 5 = 151$ is the total cut-off. As a result, to verify the FO-CTL specifications in Example 2 it is sufficient to model check them on C-AbDaS of domain size $|Y| = 151$.

5   Related Work and Conclusions

Amongst the first contributions to consider the verification of data-aware systems we mention [8,18]. This direction was then developed in [12,15], which apply syntactic restrictions on the system description and the specification language in order to obtain decidability. Closely related to the present contribution are [3,7,10], where sufficient conditions for decidable model checking of data-centric dynamic systems are given. Results on the verification of DaS have also appeared in [5,6,13], and then applied to the monitoring of commitments [27] and plan synthesis [9]. While we acknowledge the contribution of these works, there are two important differences in our approach w.r.t. the state of the art. Firstly, we here considered the parameterised model checking problem, where each system is parametric w.r.t. a *finite*, possibly different, interpretation domain; whereas in the references above each system carries its own infinite interpretation domain. Secondly, because of this technical shift, instead of introducing notions of bisimilarity to obtain finite abstractions [7], we rather explore the existence of cut-offs defined on the same agents as the parameterised AbDaS, but with a finite interpretation domain. We believe that this last problem is more interesting for practical applications because, rather than dealing with an actual infinity of data, data-aware systems usually encompass an unbounded number of elements, which is more naturally modelled as a parameterised model checking problem.

On the subject of parameterised model checking of agent-based systems, recently several methodologies and tools have been proposed [22,23]. These contributions are orthogonal, as while they do not model data-aware systems, they are capable of dealing with an arbitrary number of agents. As regards DaS, a method for the verification of parameterised agent-based systems, each encoded via infinite-state models, was presented in [24]. However, this approach only supports a non-quantified specification language and does not deal with (semi-)structured data as we do here. Finally, [4] reports on some preliminaries results on the verification of data-aware multi-agent systems. But decidability results are available only for a rather limited fragment of the specification language considered therein. The present contribution differs from the works above as, to the best of our knowledge, we introduce for the first time the problem of parameterised model checking for data-aware systems. As we motivated, this is a relevant question for verification, as we aim at guaranteeing the correct behaviour of data-aware systems no matter what the underlying data content is. To this end, we proved theoretical results on the preservation of specifications written in FO-CTL under cardinality constraints. Finally, we showed that such results guarantee the existence of a cut-off for the class of bounded P-AbDaS. We illustrate the relevance of the formal machinery through an application to an IBM use-case, the order-to-cash scenario.

We plan to extend the present work in several directions, including more expressive specification languages, possibly with some form of arithmetic, which is essential for real-life applications. Also of interest are the results in [22,23] that allow for the verification of systems with an arbitrary number of agents. We plan to explore such an extension of our present setting.

Acknowledgements. F. Belardinelli acknowledges the support of ANR JCJC Project SVeDaS (ANR-16-CE40-0021).

References

1. Abiteboul, S., Hull, R., Vianu, V.: Foundations of Databases. Addison-Wesley, Boston (1995)
2. Alur, R., Henzinger, T.: Reactive modules. Formal Methods Syst. Des. **15**(1), 7–48 (1999)
3. Bagheri, B., Calvanese, D., Montali, M., Giacomo, G., Deutsch, A.: Verification of relational data-centric dynamic systems with external services. In: PODS 2013, pp. 163–174. ACM (2013)
4. Belardinelli, F., Kouvaros, P., Lomuscio, A.: Parameterised verification of data-aware multi-agent systems. In: Proceedings of IJCAI (2017)
5. Belardinelli, F., Lomuscio, A., Patrizi, F.: An abstraction technique for the verification of artifact-centric systems. In: KR 2012, pp. 319–328 (2012)
6. Belardinelli, F., Lomuscio, A., Patrizi, F.: Verification of GSM-based artifact-centric systems through finite abstraction. In: Liu, C., Ludwig, H., Toumani, F., Yu, Q. (eds.) ICSOC 2012. LNCS, vol. 7636, pp. 17–31. Springer, Heidelberg (2012). https://doi.org/10.1007/978-3-642-34321-6_2
7. Belardinelli, F., Lomuscio, A., Patrizi, F.: Verification of agent-based artifact systems. J. Artif. Intell. Res. **51**, 333–376 (2014)
8. Bhattacharya, K., Gerede, C., Hull, R., Liu, R., Su, J.: Towards formal analysis of artifact-centric business process models. In: Alonso, G., Dadam, P., Rosemann, M. (eds.) BPM 2007. LNCS, vol. 4714, pp. 288–304. Springer, Heidelberg (2007). https://doi.org/10.1007/978-3-540-75183-0_21
9. Calvanese, D., Montali, M., Patrizi, F., Stawowy, M.: Plan synthesis for knowledge and action bases. In: IJCAI 2016, pp. 1022–1029 (2016)
10. Calvanese, D., De Giacomo, G., Montali, M., Patrizi, F.: First-order mu-calculus over generic transition systems and applications to the situation calculus. Inf. Comput. **259**(3), 328–347 (2018)
11. Cohn, D., Hull, R.: Business artifacts: a data-centric approach to modeling business operations and processes. IEEE Data Eng. Bull. **32**(3), 3–9 (2009)
12. Damaggio, E., Deutsch, A., Vianu, V.: Artifact systems with data dependencies and arithmetic. ACM TDS **37**(3), 22:1–22:36 (2012)
13. De Giacomo, G., Lespérance, Y., Patrizi, F.: Bounded situation calculus action theories and decidable verification. In: KR 2012, pp. 467–477 (2012)
14. De Masellis, R., Lembo, D., Montali, M., Solomakhin, D.: Semantic enrichment of GSM-based artifact-centric models. J. Data Semant. **4**(1), 3–27 (2015)
15. Deutsch, A., Hull, R., Patrizi, F., Vianu, V.: Automatic verification of data-centric business processes. In: ICDT 2009, pp. 252–267. ACM (2009)
16. Deutsch, A., Sui, L., Vianu, V.: Specification and verification of data-driven web applications. J. Comput. Syst. Sci. **73**(3), 442–474 (2007)
17. Fagin, R., Halpern, J., Moses, Y., Vardi, M.: Reasoning About Knowledge. The MIT Press, Cambridge (1995)
18. Gerede, C.E., Su, J.: Specification and verification of artifact behaviors in business process models. In: Krämer, B.J., Lin, K.-J., Narasimhan, P. (eds.) ICSOC 2007. LNCS, vol. 4749, pp. 181–192. Springer, Heidelberg (2007). https://doi.org/10.1007/978-3-540-74974-5_15

19. Gonzalez, P., Griesmayer, A., Lomuscio, A.: Verification of GSM-based artifact-centric systems by predicate abstraction. In: Barros, A., Grigori, D., Narendra, N.C., Dam, H.K. (eds.) ICSOC 2015. LNCS, vol. 9435, pp. 253–268. Springer, Heidelberg (2015). https://doi.org/10.1007/978-3-662-48616-0_16

20. Hull, R.: Artifact-centric business process models: brief survey of research results and challenges. In: Meersman, R., Tari, Z. (eds.) OTM 2008. LNCS, vol. 5332, pp. 1152–1163. Springer, Heidelberg (2008). https://doi.org/10.1007/978-3-540-88873-4_17

21. Hull, R., et al.: Business artifacts with guard-stage-milestone lifecycles: managing artifact interactions with conditions and events. In: Proceedings of DEBS, pp. 51–62. ACM (2011)

22. Kouvaros, P., Lomuscio, A.: Verifying emergent properties of swarms. In: Proceedings of IJCAI 2015, pp. 1083–1089. AAAI Press (2015)

23. Kouvaros, P., Lomuscio, A.: Parameterised verification for multi-agent systems. Artif. Intell. **234**, 152–189 (2016)

24. Kouvaros, P., Lomuscio, A.: Parameterised verification of infinite state multi-agent systems via predicate abstraction. In: Proceedings of AAAI 2017, pp. 3013–3020. AAAI Press (2017)

25. Lomuscio, A., Michaliszyn, J.: Model checking unbounded artifact-centric systems. In: KR 2014, pp. 488–497 (2014)

26. Montali, M., Calvanese, D.: Soundness of data-aware, case-centric processes. STTT **18**(5), 535–558 (2016)

27. Montali, M., Calvanese, D., De Giacomo, G.: Verification of data-aware commitment-based multiagent system. In: AAMAS 2014, pp. 157–164. IFAAMAS (2014)

28. O'Leary, D.E.: Artificial intelligence and big data. IEEE Intell. Syst. **28**, 96–99 (2013)

29. Shoham, Y., Leyton-Brown, K.: Multiagent Systems: Algorithmic, Game-Theoretic, and Logical Foundations. Cambridge University Press, Cambridge (2008)

30. Singh, M.P., Huhns, M.N.: Service-Oriented Computing: Semantics, Processes, Agents. Wiley, Hoboken (2005)

31. Wooldridge, M.: Computationally grounded theories of agency. In: Proceedings of ICMAS, pp. 13–22. IEEE Press (2000)

New Distributed Constraint Reasoning Algorithms for Load Balancing in Edge Computing

Khoi D. Hoang[1]([⊠]), Christabel Wayllace[1], William Yeoh[1], Jacob Beal[2],
Soura Dasgupta[3], Yuanqiu Mo[3], and Aaron Paulos[2], and Jon Schewe[2]

[1] Department of Computer Science and Engineering,
Washington University in St. Louis, St. Louis, USA
{khoi.hoang,cwayllace,wyeoh}@wustl.edu
[2] Raytheon BBN Technologies, Cambridge, USA
{jake.beal,aaron.paulos,jon.schewe}@raytheon.com
[3] Department of Electrical and Computer Engineering, University of Iowa,
Iowa City, USA
{soura-dasgupta,yuanqiu-mo}@uiowa.edu

Abstract. Edge computing is a paradigm for improving the performance of cloud computing systems by performing data processing at the edge of the network, closer to the users and sources of data. As data processing is traditionally done in large data centers, typically located far from their users, the edge computing paradigm will reduce the communication bottleneck between the user and the location of data processing, thereby improving overall performance. This becomes more important as the number of Internet-of-Things (IoT) devices and other mobile or embedded devices continues to increase. In this paper, we investigate the use of distributed constraint reasoning (DCR) techniques to model and solve the distributed load balancing problem in edge computing problems. Specifically, we *(i)* provide a mapping of the distributed load balancing problem in edge computing to a distributed constraint satisfaction and optimization problem; *(ii)* propose two DCR algorithms to solve such problems; and *(iii)* empirically evaluate our algorithms against a state-of-the-art DCR algorithm on random and scale-free networks.

Keywords: DisCSPs · DCOPs · Edge computing · Multi-agent systems

1 Introduction

Cloud computing is unequivocally the backbone of a large fraction of AI systems, where it provides computational functionality and data storage to the ever-growing number of Internet-of-Things (IoT), mobile, and embedded devices. In today's traditional cloud computing architecture, the compute and storage resources are typically housed in data centers that may be managed by different

M. Baldoni et al. (Eds.): PRIMA 2019, LNAI 11873, pp. 69–86, 2019.
https://doi.org/10.1007/978-3-030-33792-6_5

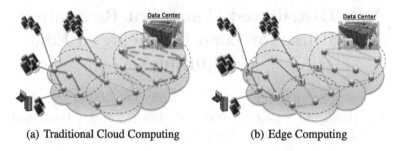

(a) Traditional Cloud Computing   (b) Edge Computing

Fig. 1. Illustration of cloud & edge computing paradigms. Figure adapted from [15] (Color figure online)

public and private organizations. For example, Amazon's AWS and Microsoft's Azure systems are two examples of popular cloud computing services that are provided by Amazon and Microsoft to the public for a fee.

As the number of IoT and similar devices continue to grow [6], so will the demand for cloud services. This increase in demand will eventually strain the bandwidth limitations to the data centers, thereby resulting in a drop in the quality of service of such services. To alleviate this limitation, researchers have proposed a new paradigm called *edge computing*, whereby the compute and storage resources are migrated from the data centers distant from users to compute resources that are closer to the user devices at the edges of the network. Figure 1(a) shows the traditional cloud computing paradigm, where the colors of the arrows denote the congestion in the network – green arrows represent uncongested links, yellow arrows represent marginally congested links, and red arrows represent very congested links. Figure 1(b) shows an edge computing paradigm, where services are hosted at resources at nodes labeled with 'S' and requests are routed to those nodes, resulting in decreased network congestion, and thus in increased performance of services. How to manage decisions about dispersal and placement of services in such a paradigm, however, is still an open problem.

In this paper, we model the distributed load balancing problem for edge computing as distributed constraint satisfaction and optimization problems, where agents that control nodes in the network need to coordinate to identify which node should host which services, subject to constraints on the capacity of the nodes and the requirement to satisfy all expected incoming requests. We also propose the *Distributed Constraint-based Diffusion Algorithm* (CDIFF) and *Distributed Routing-based Diffusion Algorithm* (RDIFF) to solve this problem and show results on random and scale-free graphs.

2   Background: DisCSP and DCOP

A *Distributed Constraint Satisfaction Problem* (DisCSP) [22] is a tuple $\langle \mathcal{X}, \mathcal{D}, \mathcal{C}, \mathcal{A}, \alpha \rangle$, where $\mathcal{X} = \{x_1, \ldots, x_n\}$ is a set of *variables*; $\mathcal{D} = \{D_1, \ldots, D_n\}$ is a set of finite *domains* (i.e., $x_i \in D_i$); $\mathcal{C} = \{c_1, \ldots, c_e\}$ is a set of *constraints* –

each constraint c_i is defined over its *scope* $\mathbf{x}^{c_i} \subseteq \mathcal{X}$ and specifies the *satisfying* combination of value assignments in its scope; $\mathcal{A} = \{a_1, \ldots, a_p\}$ is a set of *agents*; and $\alpha : \mathcal{X} \to \mathcal{A}$ is a function that maps each variable to one agent.

A *Distributed Constraint Optimization Problem* (DCOP) [7,13,16] generalizes DisCSPs by encoding the constraints as functions $c_i : \prod_{x \in \mathbf{x}^{c_i}} D_x \to \mathbb{R}_0^+ \cup \{-\infty\}$ that return a finite non-negative utility $\mathbb{R}_0^+$ for satisfying combination of value assignments and a negative infinity utility $-\infty$ for infeasible combination of value assignments. To ease readability, we assume that each agent controls exactly one variable. Thus, we will use the terms "variable" and "agent" interchangeably and assume that $\alpha(x_i) = a_i$.

A *solution* is a value assignment σ for all the variables $\mathbf{x}_\sigma \subseteq \mathcal{X}$ that is consistent with their respective domains. The utility $\mathcal{C}(\mathbf{x}_\sigma) = \sum_{c \in \mathcal{C}, \mathbf{x}^c \subseteq \mathbf{x}_\sigma} c(\mathbf{x}_\sigma)$ is the sum of the utilities across all the applicable constraints in $\mathbf{x}_\sigma$. A solution σ is a *complete solution* if $\mathbf{x}_\sigma = \mathcal{X}$. The goal of a DisCSP is to find a complete solution that satisfies all constraints while the goal of a DCOP is to maximize the sum of utilities across all constraints. Or, more formally, to find a complete solution $\mathbf{x}^* = \operatorname{argmax}_{\mathbf{x}} \mathcal{C}(\mathbf{x})$.

3 Load Balancing in Edge Computing

We now provide a simplistic description of the load balancing problem in edge computing architectures. For more detailed discussions, we refer readers to the following resources [17,18,21].

Assume that the network can be represented as a graph $G = \langle V, E \rangle$, where each vertex $v \in V$ corresponds to a compute node in the network that is able to host services and each edge $e \in E$ indicates that the two nodes connected by that edge can communicate directly with each other. Each node v has a capacity $cap(v)$ indicating the amount of available resources to host services. Some of the nodes in the graph are data centers, which are default nodes of these services. Some of the nodes $c \in C \subset V$ at the edge of the cloud are connected to pools of IoT devices, referred to as *client pools*. Further, we assume that an estimate of the load $load(v, s, c)$ of each service $s \in S$ induced by each client pool c at each node v is available.

The primary objective of the problem is to distribute the hosting of services across the compute network in such a way that all loads can be successfully served. The problem also has a secondary objective of minimizing the latency of the service requests where possible (i.e., services should be hosted as close to the client pools as possible).

4 Mapping to DisCSPs and DCOPs

We now show how one can model this problem as a DisCSP, which takes into account the primary objective only, as well as a DCOP, which additionally takes into account the secondary objective. To model this problem as a DisCSP:

- Each agent $a_v \in \mathcal{A}$ maps to a vertex $v \in V$ in the graph.
- Each variable $x_{v,s,c} \in \mathcal{X}$ maps to a pair $\langle v, s, c \rangle$ of vertex $v \in V$, service $s \in S$, and client pool $c \in C$.
- Each variable $x_{v,s,c}$ is controlled by agent a_v.
- The domain $D_{v,s,c}$ of each variable $x_{v,s,c}$ maps to the range of capacity $[0, cap(v)]$ of the vertex v.
- A constraint $\sum_{s \in S, c \in C} v_{v,s,c} \le cap(v)$ for each vertex $v \in V$ is imposed to ensure that agent a_v does not over-allocate resources to host services, where $v_{v,s,c}$ is the value assignment for variable $x_{v,s,c}$ in the solution.
- Finally, a constraint $\sum_{v \in V, s \in S, c \in C} v_{v,s,c} \ge \sum_{v \in V, s \in S, c \in C} load(v, s, c)$ is imposed to ensure that the total load can be satisfied by the network.

To model this problem as a DCOP, one needs to include an additional global soft constraint that takes as inputs the value assignments of all variables and outputs the utility:

$$\sum_{v \in V, s \in S, c \in C} \frac{v_{v,s,c}}{dist(v, c)} \tag{1}$$

where $dist(v, c)$ is the number of hops between nodes v and c in the graph G. While it may be better to use the latency between two nodes as the distance metric, latency is dependent on network traffic, which depends on the allocation of services based on the DCOP solution as well as the background traffic. These dependencies also rely on the network protocols employed. Since accurate models of these dependencies are unavailable, we use the number of hops as a proxy in this paper.

As the DCOP model subsumes the DisCSP model and, consequently, the DCOP algorithms will likely find solutions that are better than those found by DisCSP algorithms, it may seem that there is little value in discussing DisCSPs in this paper. However, we would like to highlight that the number of hops between all pairs of nodes, which is required in the DCOP formulation, require every agent to have complete knowledge about the entire network topology. Such an assumption violates a common requirement of distributed constraint reasoning approaches as well as our distributed load balancing problem – that an agent should have access to local information only. Therefore, our DCOP

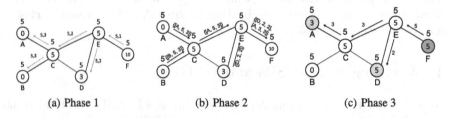

(a) Phase 1   (b) Phase 2   (c) Phase 3

Fig. 2. Illustration of CDIFF operations. Figure adapted from [15] (Color figure online)

model is actually not suitable for this application. Nonetheless, we propose the DCOP model so that we can evaluate our two DisCSP algorithms against an off-the-shelf optimal DCOP algorithm in terms of the quality of their solutions found with respect to the secondary objective of minimizing latency of service requests in the load balancing problem.

5   Proposed Algorithms

We now discuss our two DisCSP algorithms – *Distributed Constraint-based Diffusion Algorithm* (CDIFF) and *Distributed Routing-based Diffusion Algorithm* (RDIFF).

5.1   Distributed Constraint-Based Diffusion Algorithm (CDIFF)

This algorithm is inspired by other diffusion-based algorithms in the literature [3, 11,14]. At a high level, each overloaded agent (i.e., those agents that control nodes where $load(v) > cap(v)$) identifies to which subset of other agents that it should shed its excess load. Figure 2 illustrates its three phases, where numbers in circles are the current loads of the nodes and red numbers are the capacities. Node F is the overloaded agent, and nodes A, B, and D are possible nodes that can absorb the excess load from A.[1] We now describe the three phases at a high level:

Algorithm 1. CDIFF (D)

---

1 CDIFF-InitVars()
2 $newMap \leftarrow hostMap \leftarrow excessMap \leftarrow \emptyset$
3 **foreach** (s, l) *in* **D do**
4 $\quad\lfloor\ newMap \leftarrow newMap \cup \{(s, l, hop)\}$

5 $(excessMap, hostMap) \leftarrow$ KeepPossible($newMap$)
6 **if** $excessMap \neq \emptyset$ **then**
7 $\quad\lfloor\ phase \leftarrow 1$

8 send $(phase, excessMap)$ message to each neighbor $n \in$ **N**
9 **while** *true* **do**
10 $\quad$ **while** not received message from all neighbors **do**
11 $\quad\quad\lvert\quad msgs \leftarrow \emptyset$
12 $\quad\quad\lvert$ **if** received message m from neighbor n **then**
13 $\quad\quad\lvert\quad\lfloor\ msgs \leftarrow msgs \cup \{(m, n)\}$

14 $\quad$ **if** $phase = 0$ **then** CDIFF-ProcessPhase0($msgs$);
15 $\quad$ **else if** $phase = 1$ **then** CDIFF-ProcessPhase1($msgs$);
16 $\quad$ **else if** $phase = 2$ **then** CDIFF-ProcessPhase2($msgs$);
17 $\quad$ send $(0, null)$ message to each neighbor that the agent did not send a
$\quad\quad\lfloor$ message to in this cycle

---

[1] While the figure illustrates an example with only one overloaded region, our description below generalizes to the case where there are multiple overloaded regions.

Procedure. CDIFF-InitVars()

---

18 $Reject \leftarrow \emptyset$
19 $parent \leftarrow msg \leftarrow null$
20 $hop \leftarrow phase \leftarrow 0$
21 $Children \leftarrow \mathbf{N}$

- **Phase 1:** Each overloaded agent sends a message to all neighboring agents with the amount of excess load it needs to shed as well as a hop count indicator that is initialized to 1.[2] When an agent receives such a message for the first time, it will propagate the received information to its neighbors after incrementing the hop counter by 1. The agent will then ignore subsequent Phase 1 messages by other neighbors and respond to them after Phase 3. This propagation of information continues until it reaches either nodes with sufficient capacity to accept the excess load or nodes that have received information from a closer overloaded agent. At the end of this phase, the agents have built a directed spanning forest, with roots at every overloaded agent.[3] In the example in Fig. 2, node F is the sole root as it is the only overloaded agent and nodes A, B, and D are the leaves.

Procedure. CDIFF-ProcessPhase0($msgs$)

---

22 $(m, n) \leftarrow$ choose any $((type, map), sender)$ from $msgs$ where $type = 1$
23 $parent \leftarrow n$
24 $(excessMap, hostMap) \leftarrow$ KEEPPOSSIBLE($m.map$)
25 **foreach** $((type, map), n) \in msgs$ where $n \neq parent \wedge type = 1$ **do**
26 $\quad$ $Reject \leftarrow Reject \cup \{n\}$
27 $\quad$ send $(REJECT, null)$ message to n
28 $Children \leftarrow Children \setminus (Reject \cup \{parent\})$
29 **if** $parent \neq null$ **then**
30 $\quad$ **if** $excessMap \neq \emptyset \wedge Children \neq \emptyset$ **then**
31 $\quad\quad$ $phase \leftarrow 1$
32 $\quad\quad$ send $(phase, excessMap)$ message to each child $n \in Children$
33 $\quad$ **else**
34 $\quad\quad$ $phase \leftarrow 2$
35 $\quad\quad$ $newMap \leftarrow \emptyset$
36 $\quad\quad$ **foreach** $(s, load, h)$ in $hostMap$ **do**
37 $\quad\quad\quad$ $newMap \leftarrow newMap \cup \{(s, load, h + 1)\}$
38 $\quad\quad$ send $(phase, newMap)$ message to $parent$

---

[2] This indicator counts the number of hops a node is from the overloaded agent.
[3] If an agent receives this information from more than one neighbor at the same time, it breaks ties by identifiers.

- **Phase 2:** Each leaf agent v of the spanning forest sends a message to its parent with its node ID, its available capacity $cap(v) - load(v)$, and the number of hops it is away from its root. When an agent receives this information from all its children, it aggregates the information received so that the sum of available capacities is at most the amount of excess load needed to be shed, preferring nodes with smaller hop counts, and sends the aggregated information to its parent. This process continues until each root (i.e., the overloaded agent) receives the messages from all its children.
- **Phase 3:** Each root agent then sends a message to each of its children indicating the amount of excess load it intends to shed to them and their descendants in the spanning tree. This information gets propagated down to the leaves, which then terminates the algorithm. For example, in Fig. 2, node F sheds 5 units of load – 2 units to node D and 3 units to node A.

These three phases continue until all overloaded regions successfully shed their loads.

Algorithm 1 shows the pseudocode of CDIFF that is executed by each agent $a_v \in \mathcal{A}$. It takes as inputs its estimated load $\mathbf{D}_v$, which is a mapping of (s, l) indicating a load of $l \in \mathbb{R}_0^+$ for service $s \in S$. Additionally, we assume that the agent always knows about the set of neighboring agents $\mathbf{N}_v$. In the pseudocode, we drop the subscripts v since they always refer to the "self" agent. Each agent maintains the following key data structures:

- *parent* and *Children* refer to the agent's parent and set of children, respectively, in the spanning forest built in Phase 1 of the algorithm.
- *hop* refers to the number of hops the agent is away from the root of its tree.
- *phase* refers to the phase of the algorithm that the agent is currently in.
- *hostMap* and *excessMap* are sets of service s, load l, and hop h tuples (s, l, h); *hostMap* contains the information on how much load from each service will it host and *excessMap* contains the information on how much excess load for each service that it needs to shed.

Each agent first initializes its variables (lines 1–2). Then, it tries to host as much load as possible via the function KEEPPOSSIBLE (lines 3–5). The function takes as input the demand that it received aggregated with the hop value and updates how much of the demand it will host in *hostMap* as well as how much excess it must shed in *excessMap*. If it can host all demand, then it remains in Phase 0. Otherwise, it is overloaded and goes into Phase 1 (line 7). It then sends a message to each neighbor and goes into an infinite loop (or until timeout) where it runs the following processes in each cycle: It waits for messages from all neighbors; processes those messages based on its phase; and sends a message to each neighbor at the end of that process (lines 8–17).

If an agent is in Phase 0, it runs the CDIFF-PROCESSPHASE0 procedure. Upon receiving a message from a neighbor that is in Phase 1 (i.e., it is overloaded and is asking for help), the agent sets the neighbor as parent and checks how much excess load it can host from the parent. If the agent is able to host all the load, it then replies to its parent with its capacity availabilities (lines 34–38).

Procedure. CDIFF-ProcessPhase1($msgs$)

---

39 **foreach** $((type, map), n) \in msgs$ **do**
40   **if** $type = REJECT$ **then**
41 | $Children \leftarrow Children \setminus \{n\}$
42   **else if** $type = 1 \wedge n \neq parent$ **then**
43 | $Children \leftarrow Children \setminus \{n\}$
44 | send $(REJECT, null)$ message to n
45   **else if** $type = 2$ **then**
46 | store capacity availabilities from children

47 **if** $parent = null$ **then**
48   **if** $Children = \emptyset$ **then**
49 | send $(phase, excessMap)$ message to each neighbor $n \in \mathbf{N}$
50   **else**
51 | $phase \leftarrow 3$
52 | $plan \leftarrow$ shed load in $excessMap$ to $Children$ prioritizing smaller hop counts
53 | send $(phase, plan)$ message to each child $n \in Children$
54 **else if** $Children = \emptyset$ **then**
55 | $phase \leftarrow 2$
56 | $newMap \leftarrow \emptyset$
57 | **foreach** $(s, load, h)$ in $hostMap$ **do**
58 | $newMap \leftarrow newMap \cup \{(s, load, h + 1)\}$
59 | send $(phase, newMap)$ message to $parent$
60 **else**
61 | $phase \leftarrow 2$
62 | $aggPlan \leftarrow$ aggregated capacity availabilities from children
63 | send $(phase, aggPlan)$ message to $parent$

Otherwise, it propagates the request from the parent to other neighbors to ask for help (lines 30–32). If it receives such a message from more than one neighbor, then it breaks ties randomly, chooses to help only one of them and rejects the other requests (lines 22–27). Therefore, the request from the overloaded region (i.e., root of a tree) will be propagated throughout the network until it reaches agents with neighbors that are all not in Phase 0 (i.e., they are already part of the spanning forest). In such a case, the leaf agents will go into Phase 2 and respond to its parent with its available capacity (lines 34–38).

Procedure. CDIFF-ProcessPhase2($msgs$)

---

64 **foreach** $((type, map), n) \in msgs$ **do**
65   **if** $type = 1$ **then**
66   send $(REJECT, null)$ message to n
67   **else if** $type = 3$ **then**
68        $phase \leftarrow 3$
69        $(excessMap, hostMap) \leftarrow$ FollowPlan(map)
70        $plan \leftarrow$ shed load in $excessMap$ to $Children$ prioritizing smaller hop counts
71 send $(phase, plan)$ message to each child $n \in Children$
72 CDIFF-InitVars()

If an agent is in Phase 1, it runs the CDIFF-ProcessPhase1 procedure, where it goes into Phase 2 and send the aggregate available capacity received from all children to the parent (lines 54–63). This process continues until the information reaches the root, which will go into Phase 3, plans for how to shed its excess load, and sends the final plans back to its children (lines 51–53).

If an agent is in Phase 2, it runs the CDIFF-ProcessPhase2 procedure, where it goes into Phase 3, hosts as much load as possible based on the plan received from the parent, plans for how to shed its excess load based on the available capacities received from its children before, and sends those plans to its children (lines 68–71). The agent then reinitializes its variables, goes back into Phase 0 and is ready to help with new overloaded agents (line 72).

5.2 Distributed Routing-Based Diffusion Algorithm (RDIFF)

One limitation of CDIFF is that it does not take into account information of where the client pools are located when deciding where the overloaded agents should shed its load. As such, it is not able to optimize the secondary objective of our problem. RDIFF addresses this limitation by shedding not only the excess load of overloaded agents, but as much load as possible to the agents that are of close proximity to the client pools. To do so, the agents operate in the following manner:

- **Phase 1:** Each data center propagates its entire load received from each client pool back towards that client pool by back-tracing the paths the requests took from the client pool to the data center. At the end of this phase, the agents have built a directed graph, where each branch of the graph corresponds to the path requests from a client pool took to get to a data center.[4]
- **Phase 2:** Each client pool will host as much of the load it received as possible, up to its capacity, and sheds its excess load to its parent (the next node along the branch from client pool towards the data center). This process repeats until all of the excess load is hosted. In the worst case where none of the

---

[4] If there are multiple paths per client pool, we randomly choose one of them.

Algorithm 2. RDIFF (D)

---

73   $Parents \leftarrow Children \leftarrow \emptyset$
74   $hostMap \leftarrow pushMap \leftarrow excessMap \leftarrow 2DCMap \leftarrow \emptyset$
75   **foreach** (s, l, c) *in* **D do**
76   **if** c *is the "self" agent* **then**
77         $2DCMap \leftarrow 2DCMap \cup \{(s, l, c, c)\}$
78   **else**
79         $pushMap \leftarrow pushMap \cup \{(s, l, c, r)\}$

80   $(2DCMap, hostMap) \leftarrow \textsc{KeepPossible}(2DCMap)$
81   **while** *true* **do**
82   **foreach** $(s, l, c, r) \in pushMap$ **do**
83   **if** $\nexists n : (s, n, c, r) \in Children$ **then**
84             $Children \leftarrow Children \cup \{(s, n, c, r)\}$ where n is the neighbor that sent the request for service s from client pool c to server r
85   send $(1, (s, l, c, r))$ message to child n where $(s, n, c, r) \in Children$
86   **foreach** $(s, l, c, r) \in excessMap$ **do**
87   send $(2, (s, l, c, r))$ message to parent n where $(s, n, c, r) \in Parents$
88   **foreach** $(s, l, c, r) \in 2DCMap$ **do**
89   send $(DC, (s, l, c, r))$ message to $DC(s)$
90   send $(null, null)$ message to each neighbor that the agent did not send a message to in this cycle
91   **while** not received message from all neighbors **do**
92         $msgs \leftarrow \emptyset$
93   **if** received message m from neighbor n **then**
94             $msgs \leftarrow msgs \cup \{(m, n)\}$
95   RDIFF-PROCESSMESSAGES($msgs$);

---

agents along the branch has excess capacity, the data center will host the entire load.

Algorithm 2 shows the pseudocode of RDIFF that is executed by each agent $a_v \in \mathcal{A}$. It takes as inputs its estimated load $\mathbf{D}_v$, which is a set of mappings (s, l, c) indicating a load of $l \in \mathbb{R}_0^+$ for service $s \in S$ from client pool $c \in \mathcal{A}$. Note that this estimated load is different than that in CDIFF, where it now includes the information per client pool. Like for CDIFF, we assume that the agent knows about its set of neighboring agents $\mathbf{N}_v$. Also, the agent knows the data center $DC(s)$ for each service $s \in S$. In the pseudocode, we drop the subscripts v since they always refer to the "self" agent.

Each agent maintains the following key data structures:

- *Parents* refers to the sets of service s, agent a, client pool c, and server r tuples (s, a, c, r), where the agent a is the agent's parent for service s, client pool c, and server r in the directed graph built in Phase 1 of the algorithm.

Procedure. RDIFF-ProcessMessages($msgs$)

```
96   foreach ((type, map), n) ∈ msgs do
97       if type = 1 then
98           foreach (s, l, c, r) in map do
99               if c is the "self" agent then
100                  │ (excessMap, hostMap) ← KEEPPOSSIBLE({(s, l, c, r)})
101              else
102                  │ pushMap ← pushMap ∪ {(s, l, c, r)}
103              if ∄p : (s, p, c, r) ∈ Parents then
104                  │ Parents ← Parents ∪ {(s, n, c, r)}

105      else if type = 2 or type = DC then
106          foreach (s, l, c, r) in map do
107              if r is the "self" agent then
108                  │ (2DCMap, hostMap) ← KEEPPOSSIBLE({(s, l, c, r)})
109              else
110                  │ (excessMap, hostMap) ← KEEPPOSSIBLE({(s, l, c, r)})
```

- *Children* refers to a similar set as *Parents*, except that the agent a in the tuple is the agent's child for service s, client pool c, and server r in the directed graph built in Phase 1 of the algorithm.
- *hostMap*, *pushMap*, *excessMap*, and *2DCMap* are sets of service s, load l, client pool c, and server r tuples (s, l, c, r); *hostMap* contains the information on how much load l from each service s whose request originated from client pool c towards server r will be hosted; *pushMap* contains the information for how much load will be pushed from the server towards the client pool; *excessMap* contains the information for how much load will be pushed from the client pool towards the server; and *2DCMap* contains the information for how much load will be pushed from the server directly to the data center.

Each agent first initializes these variables (lines 73–74). Then, it tries to host as much of its own load as possible if it is the client pool. Excess load is aggregated into *2DCMap* in preparation to be pushed towards the data center (line 76–77). Loads from other client pools are aggregated into *pushMap* in preparation to be pushed out towards those client pools (line 79). It then goes into an infinite loop (or until timeout) where it runs the following processes in each cycle: It sends a message to each neighbor; waits for messages from all neighbors; and processes those messages (lines 81–95).

At the start, the agent will iterate through *pushMap* and send a Phase 1 message containing the amount of load to be pushed for each service, client pool, and server combination to the appropriate child (lines 82–85). Upon receiving this information, the child will aggregate that information into its own *pushMap* in preparation to be sent to its child in the next cycle (line 102). This process continues until it reaches the client pool, at which point, it hosts as much load as possible and stores the excess load in *excessMap* (line 100).

In the next cycle, the client pool will iterate through *excessMap* and send a Phase 2 message containing the load to be pushed towards the server to the appropriate parent (lines 86–87). Upon receiving this information, the parent will host as much load as well and pushes the excess to its parent in the next cycle (line 110). This process continues until all the load is hosted or it reaches the server. If the server does not have enough capacity to host all the load, then it stores the excess load in *2DCMap* (line 108).

In the next cycle, the server will iterate through *2DCMap* and send a DC message containing the amount to be pushed to the appropriate data center (line 89). As we assume that the data centers have infinite capacity, all the load will then be hosted.

6   Theoretical Results

We now discuss some of the theoretical properties of the algorithms, where we make the standard assumptions that: (1) messages sent are never lost and are received in the order that they were sent; and (2) there exists a path from each node of the network to every other node of the network.

Lemma 1. *In CDIFF, an agent with available capacity will eventually be part of the tree of an overloaded agent as long as one such overloaded agent exists.*

Proof (Sketch): Since overloaded agents send Phase 1 messages that are propagated throughout the network, the agent with available capacity will eventually receive one such message and insert itself into the spanning tree of the overloaded agent that initiated the series of messages that it received.

Lemma 2. *In CDIFF, an overloaded agent will shed some of its excess load if its tree includes agents with available capacity.*

Proof (Sketch): Since Phase 1 messages are repeatedly propagated throughout the network until they either reach agents with enough capacity to host all the overloaded services of the root agent or reach agents without any free neighbors (i.e., neighbors in Phase 0), the phase is guaranteed to end after a finite number of cycles since the network is of finite size. Then, Phase 2 messages are propagated from the leafs to the root of the tree, upon which the root sheds some of its load based on the available capacities of the agents in its tree in Phase 3.

Theorem 1. *CDIFF is guaranteed to find a satisfying solution if one exists.*

Proof (Sketch): Based on Lemmas 1 and 2, it is easy to see that all overloaded agents will eventually succeed at shedding their load assuming that there exists agents with available capacity.

Theorem 2. *RDIFF is guaranteed to find a satisfying solution if data centers have infinite capacity.*

Proof (Sketch): It is trivial to see that each server will successfully push its load to the client pools in Phase 1, and the agents along the path will host as much as possible in Phase 2. Should the combined capacities of the agents along the path be insufficient to host all the load, then the agent will send the excess load to the data center, which will be able to host it since it has infinite capacity.

Theorem 3. *If CDIFF and RDIFF finds a satisfying solution, it will take at most $O(|\mathcal{A}| \cdot d)$ cycles to do so, where d is the diameter of the network graph.*

Proof (Sketch): In the worst case, the network is a chain of length d and every agent $a_1, \ldots, a_{d-1}$ along the chain is overloaded except for one agent a_d at the end of the chain that has sufficient capacity. In this scenario, agent a_{d-1} will first succeed in shedding its load to a_d. Then, agent a_{d-2} will shed its load and so on until agent a_1 sheds its load. Each time an agent sheds its load, it will take $O(d)$ number of cycles to do so since each phase of the algorithms take $O(d)$ cycles and there is only a constant number of phases. Since there are $O(|\mathcal{A}|)$ overloaded agents, the total runtime is $O(|\mathcal{A}| \cdot d)$ cycles.

7 Related Work

Since our work is on the use of DCOPs for cloud computing applications, we will first discuss work at this intersection before broadening the discussion to other DCOP-based approaches on similar load balancing applications and other multi-agent approaches for cloud computing applications. Within this intersection, the work by Rust *et al.* [19] is most relevant, where they used DCOPs to model the problem of resiliently distributing computation nodes in edge computing scenarios. Specifically, given a dynamic network, where nodes in the network may fail and disappear over time, the goal is to identify k nodes to host replicated services (aside from the one currently hosting the service) such that the service is resilient to the node failures. There are several key differences between their work and ours: (1) Their approach allows for node failures while our approach assumes that the network remains unchanged over time. (2) Their approach seeks to only identify k replicas to host services and migrates services to one of the replicated nodes when the node hosting the service fails. In contrast, our approach seeks to distribute the load across all the nodes that are hosting services to ensure that all load can be served while optimizing for quality-of-service metrics like response times.

Within the broader application of DCOPs, aside from the many applications listed in the introduction, the most relevant one to our problem is the one on dynamic load balancing problems in wireless LANs [2]. In this problem, a set of access points need to coordinate and identify who should serve each mobile station in a set of such mobile stations. DCOPs are used to model this optimization problem, where the objective optimizes the received signal strength of each mobile station as well as distribute the load among all access points as evenly as possible. The key difference between their work and ours is that the sources of load in their problem are the mobile stations that physically move within an environment. In contrast, the sources of load in our problem are service requests made by clients within a fixed topology.

Finally, other multi-agent based approaches such as negotiation and auctions have also been used for resource allocation and load balancing problems in cloud computing [4,20] and grid computing [8,12]. The key difference is that these negotiation and auction-based approaches often assume that the agents are self-interested and seek to optimize their individual objective functions. In contrast, agents in our DCOP-based approach are completely cooperative, where the goal is to optimize a global objective function.

8   Experimental Results

In this paper, we empirically evaluate CDIFF and RDIFF algorithms against DPOP [16], a state-of-the-art complete DCOP algorithm. However, it is important to note that it will be impractical to use DPOP (or any other DCOP algorithm) as the information that they need to optimize their utility function, which is the number of hops between all pairs of nodes in the network, is often unavailable in practice. We therefore include the results of DPOP mostly as a way to quantify the quality of solutions found by CDIFF and RDIFF with respect to the optimal DCOP solution.[5]

We evaluate the algorithms on random networks [5] with a density p_1 of 0.5 and scale-free networks [1], where we randomly choose a node as the data center in random networks and choose the node with the most number of neighbors as the data center in scale-free networks. The data center initially hosts three

Table 1. Quality of solutions on random networks

$|\mathcal{A}|$	CDIFF				RDIFF				DPOP
	A	B	C	Total	A	B	C	Total	Total
5	0.32	0.25	0.34	0.91	0.33	0.29	0.38	1.00	1.59
10	0.29	0.29	0.32	0.90	0.23	0.30	0.35	0.88	–
15	0.28	0.33	0.27	0.88	0.39	0.38	0.34	1.11	–
20	0.23	0.33	0.34	0.90	0.35	0.34	0.34	1.03	–

Table 2. Quality of solutions on scale-free networks

$|\mathcal{A}|$	CDIFF				RDIFF				DPOP
	A	B	C	Total	A	B	C	Total	Total
5	0.28	0.28	0.31	0.87	0.29	0.27	0.36	0.92	1.56
10	0.27	0.23	0.30	0.80	0.26	0.25	0.33	0.84	–
15	0.14	0.15	0.18	0.47	0.19	0.18	0.23	0.60	–
20	0.21	0.21	0.23	0.65	0.20	0.19	0.24	0.63	–

---

[5] https://github.com/map-dcomp/map-code.

services A, B, and C, and will then redirect the service request to other nodes by following the solutions of the algorithms. We randomly place three client pools in both random and scale-free networks. Each client pool makes 10 batches of service requests, and each batch starts a minute after each other. Each batch has 20 requests per service, and each request induces a load of 0.1 units of resource. Each node has a capacity of 20 units of resource, and the data center has a capacity of 8 units. For all three algorithms, we set the thresholded capacity of nodes to be 55% of their actual capacity. A node is a considered overloaded if its predicted load is greater than its thresholded capacity.

We vary the number of agents $|\mathcal{A}|$, which are nodes in the graph, from 5 to 20, and we report the quality of solution measured using the utility function defined by Eq. (1) as well as the number of successful requests as a function of the number of hops between the client pool and the server that served the requests. All experiments were performed on an Intel Core i5, 2.0 GHz machine with 8 GB of RAM. Data points are averaged of over 20 instances.

Tables 1 and 2 tabulate the quality of solutions found by CDIFF, RDIFF, and DPOP on random and scale-free networks, respectively. As expected, DPOP finds the best solutions since it explicitly optimizes for the global utility function while CDIFF and RDIFF do not. Nonetheless, DPOP fails to solve the larger problems as it ran out of memory. In both networks, RDIFF is often able to find better solutions with larger utilities than CDIFF. The reason is that RDIFF sheds the excess load towards the edge, closer to the client pools. On the other hand, CDIFF sheds the excess load to nodes around the data center, which tends to be further away from the client pools. The difference in solution qualities between RDIFF and CDIFF is more pronounced in scale-free networks than in random networks. The reason is that the distance between client pools and data centers is often times larger in scale-free networks than in random graphs.

Table 3. Number of successful requests on random networks

$|\mathcal{A}|$	CDIFF					RDIFF					DPOP				
	0	1	2	3	Total	0	1	2	3	Total	0	1	2	3	Total
5	1805	683	845	127	3460	10407	230	354	50	11041	1290	1084	307	0	2681
10	1307	1241	728	59	3335	11652	503	296	49	12500	–	–	–	–	–
15	522	1391	799	49	2761	10607	976	523	33	12139	–	–	–	–	–
20	107	1286	977	0	2370	1362	1032	851	0	3245	–	–	–	–	–

Table 4. Number of successful requests on scale-free networks

$|\mathcal{A}|$	CDIFF				RDIFF				DPOP			
	0–3	4–6	7–10	Total	0–3	4–6	7–10	Total	0–3	4–6	7–10	Total
5	3681	0	0	3681	11687	0	0	11687	4576	0	0	4576
10	2929	187	0	3116	11171	92	0	11263	–	–	–	–
15	1834	452	30	2316	12065	181	0	12246	–	–	–	–
20	2315	383	74	2772	11359	172	24	11555	–	–	–	–

Tables 3 and 4 tabulate the number of successful requests as a function of the number of hops between the client pool and the server that served the requests. We make the following observations:

- RDIFF has a larger fraction of successful requests served closer to the client pool compared to CDIFF. In fact, in most cases, more than 80% of the requests were served in the node that is also the client pool (when the number of hops is zero). This observation is to be expected since RDIFF pushes the load towards the client pools while CDIFF diffuses the load around the data center.
- All three algorithms did not succeed in successfully serving all requests. A request is considered to be a failed request if it is not served within a pre-scribed time window, which occurs when the request is directed to a node that is busy serving other requests and have a large number of pending requests in its queue. This occurs during the execution of the algorithms before they found a load-balanced solution. During the execution time of the algorithms, the agents execute the default strategy of serving all requests at the data center, which is overloaded. As a result, the longer the execution time of an algorithm, the larger the number of failed requests due to the default strategy. Another reason for failed request is a mismatch between the *actual load*, which is based on the actual number of requests, and the *estimated load*, which is based on the number of requests in the past. Since the load-balanced solutions are based on estimated loads, some requests may fail if the actual load is underestimated.
- DPOP has the smallest number of successful requests compared to CDIFF and RDIFF. The reason is because it has the longest runtime. As a result, it has the most number of requests being directed to an overloaded data center.
- RDIFF has a larger number of successful requests than CDIFF. The reason is because there are more nodes with loads that are closer to the thresholded capacity in CDIFF than in RDIFF. In CDIFF, loads from all three services are congregated around the data center. In contrast, in RDIFF, load from each service is dissipated towards the client pool for that service.

In summary, these empirical results show that RDIFF is better than CDIFF in terms of both the DCOP utility function of, despite both algorithms not optimizing that function explicitly, as well as the number of successful requests served.

9 Conclusions and Future Work

In this paper, we proposed a distributed constraint reasoning approach to model and solve a distributed load balancing problem in edge computing. Our two algorithms, Distributed Constraint-based Diffusion Algorithm (CDIFF) and Distributed Routing-based Diffusion Algorithm (RDIFF), are guaranteed to find satisfying solutions (i.e., all the estimated load will be served by nodes in the network) under certain conditions. Further, despite not optimizing for the global objective function explicitly, because it is impractical to do so as the information needed to do so (= number of hops between all pairs or nodes in the network) is often unavailable in practice, RDIFF still found solutions that are within 60% of optimal. Experimental results also show that both CDIFF and RDIFF can scale better than DPOP, a state-of-the-art DCOP algorithm, and that RDIFF is better than CDIFF in terms of the number of successful requests served.

Future work includes integrating CDIFF and RDIFF into a single algorithm, where, like RDIFF, data centers propagate their entire loads received to their respective client pools. However, unlike RDIFF, which allocates the loads to the agents along the paths from the client pools to the data centers only, the integrated algorithm allocates the loads *around* the client pools like in CDIFF. This

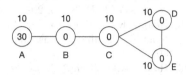

Fig. 3. Motivating scenario for integrating CDIFF and RDIFF

will likely result in more load being hosted closer to the client pools. Figure 3 illustrates such a motivating example, where, like the example in Fig. 2, numbers in circles are the current loads of the nodes and red numbers are the capacities. In this example, node A is the data center serving 30 units of load from a client pool at node D. RDIFF would have allocated 10 units of load to nodes B, C, and D, and cannot consider allocations to E since it is not on the path from A to D. In contrast, a better solution would be to allocate 10 units of load to C, D, and E, and such a solution would be found by the integrated algorithm. Finally, we also plan to improve all of these algorithms so that they are more resilient to dynamic changes [19] as well as proactively take into account anticipated future changes [9,10].

Acknowledgment. This research is supported by Defense Advanced Research Projects Agency (DARPA) contract HR001117C0049. The views, opinions, and/or findings expressed are those of the author(s) and should not be interpreted as representing the official views or policies of the Department of Defense or the U.S. Government. This document does not contain technology or technical data controlled under either U.S. International Traffic in Arms Regulation or U.S. Export Administration Regulations. Approved for public release, distribution unlimited (DARPA DISTAR 31530, 6/6/19).

References

1. Barabási, A.L.: Scale-free networks: a decade and beyond. Science **325**(5939), 412–413 (2009)
2. Cheng, S., Raja, A., Xie, J., Howitt, I.: DLB-SDPOP: a multiagent pseudo-tree repair algorithm for load balancing in WLANs. In: Proceedings of WIIAT, pp. 311–318 (2010)
3. Cybenko, G.: Dynamic load balancing for distributed memory multiprocessors. J. Parallel Distrib. Comput. **7**(2), 279–301 (1989)
4. Du, L., Bigham, J., Cuthbert, L., Nahi, P., Parini, C.: Intelligent cellular network load balancing using a cooperative negotiation approach. In: Proceedings of WCNC, pp. 1675–1679 (2003)

5. Erdös, P., Rényi, A.: On random graphs, i. Publicationes Mathematicae (Debrecen) **6**, 290–297 (1959)
6. Evans, D.: The internet of things: How the next evolution of the internet is changing everything. CISCO White Paper **1**(2011), 1–11 (2011)
7. Fioretto, F., Pontelli, E., Yeoh, W.: Distributed constraint optimization problems and applications: a survey. J. Artif. Intell. Res. **61**, 623–698 (2018)
8. Grosu, D., Das, A.: Auction-based resource allocation protocols in grids. In: Proceedings of ICDCS, pp. 20–27 (2004)
9. Hoang, K.D., Fioretto, F., Hou, P., Yokoo, M., Yeoh, W., Zivan, R.: Proactive dynamic distributed constraint optimization. In: Proceedings of AAMAS, pp. 597–605 (2016)
10. Hoang, K.D., Hou, P., Fioretto, F., Yeoh, W., Zivan, R., Yokoo, M.: Infinite-horizon proactive dynamic DCOPs. In: Proceedings of AAMAS, pp. 212–220 (2017)
11. Hu, Y., Blake, R.: An optimal dynamic load balancing algorithm. Technical report, SCAN-9509056 (1995)
12. Izakian, H., Abraham, A., Ladani, B.T.: An auction method for resource allocation in computational grids. Future Gener. Comput. Syst. **26**(2), 228–235 (2010)
13. Modi, P., Shen, W.M., Tambe, M., Yokoo, M.: ADOPT: asynchronous distributed constraint optimization with quality guarantees. Artif. Intell. **161**(1–2), 149–180 (2005)
14. Muthukrishnan, S., Ghosh, B., Schultz, M.H.: First-and second-order diffusive methods for rapid, coarse, distributed load balancing. Theory Comput. Syst. **31**(4), 331–354 (1998)
15. Paulos, A., et al.: A framework for self-adaptive dispersal of computing services. In: IEEE Self-Adaptive and Self-Organizing Systems Workshops (2019)
16. Petcu, A., Faltings, B.: A scalable method for multiagent constraint optimization. In: Proceedings of IJCAI, pp. 1413–1420 (2005)
17. Puthal, D., Obaidat, M.S., Nanda, P., Prasad, M., Mohanty, S.P., Zomaya, A.Y.: Secure and sustainable load balancing of edge data centers in fog computing. IEEE Commun. Mag. **56**(5), 60–65 (2018)
18. Rabinovich, M., Xiao, Z., Aggarwal, A.: Computing on the edge: a platform for replicating internet applications. In: Douglis, F., Davison, B.D. (eds.) Web Content Caching and Distribution, pp. 57–77. Springer, Dordrecht (2004). https://doi.org/10.1007/1-4020-2258-1_4
19. Rust, P., Picard, G., Ramparany, F.: Self-organized and resilient distribution of decisions over dynamic multi-agent systems. In: International Workshop on Optimization in Multiagent Systems (2018)
20. Shen, W., Li, Y., Ghenniwa, H., Wang, C., et al.: Adaptive negotiation for agent-based grid computing. J. Am. Stat. Assoc. **97**(457), 210–214 (2002)
21. Shi, W., Dustdar, S.: The promise of edge computing. Computer **49**(5), 78–81 (2016)
22. Yokoo, M., Durfee, E., Ishida, T., Kuwabara, K.: Distributed constraint satisfaction for formalizing distributed problem solving. In: Proceedings of ICDCS, pp. 614–621 (1992)

A Distributed and Clustering-Based Algorithm for the Enumeration Problem in Abstract Argumentation

Sylvie Doutre, Mickaël Lafages, and Marie-Christine Lagasquie-Schiex[✉]

IRIT, UT1-UT3, Toulouse, France
{doutre,mickael.lafages,lagasq}@irit.fr

Abstract. Computing acceptability semantics of abstract argumentation frameworks is receiving increasing attention. Large-scale instances, with a clustered structure, have shown particularly difficult to compute. This paper presents a distributed algorithm, *AFDivider*, that enumerates the acceptable sets under several labelling-based semantics. This algorithm starts with cutting the argumentation framework into clusters thanks to a spectral clustering method, before computing simultaneously in each cluster parts of the labellings. This algorithm is proven to be sound and complete for the stable, complete and preferred semantics, and empirical results are presented.

Keywords: Abstract argumentation · Algorithms · Clustering · Enumeration

1 Introduction

Argumentation is a reasoning model which has been of application in multi-agent systems for years (see [16] for an overview). The development of argumentation techniques and of their computation drives such applications.

Among the various argumentation models, the one that is considered in this paper has been defined by Dung [23]: an abstract argumentation framework (AF) considers arguments as abstract entities, and focuses on their attack relationships, hence representing arguments and their underlying conflicts by a directed graph. Which arguments can be accepted is defined by [23] as a collective notion, by a semantics: a set of arguments is collectively acceptable under the semantics. Four semantics (*grounded, stable, complete* and *preferred*) were defined by Dung, and a variety of other semantics have followed (see [6] for an overview). Several enrichments of the argumentation framework have also been proposed (*e.g.* [7,17]).

Supported by the ANR-11-LABEX-0040-CIMI project of the CIMI International Centre for Mathematics and Computer Science in Toulouse.

M. Baldoni et al. (Eds.): PRIMA 2019, LNAI 11873, pp. 87–105, 2019.
https://doi.org/10.1007/978-3-030-33792-6_6

The enumeration of all the acceptable sets of an AF under a given semantics is a problem that has received a lot of attention (see [21] for an overview). This problem has been shown to be computationally intractable for some of the above-mentioned semantics [25]. A competition, ICCMA, that compares argumentation solvers on their ability to solve this problem (and other decision problems) was created a few years ago.[1] The last editions of this competition have been analyzed: [12,34] highlight that some AF instances have been particularly hard to solve, and that others were not solved at all, considering the *preferred* semantics notably. Many of these instances are of Barabási–Albert (BA) type [1], which is a structure found in several large-scale natural and human-made systems, such as the World Wide Web and some social networks [4]. More generally, these hard graphs are non-dense, but contain parts which are dense:[2] such graphs have a *clustered structure*.

Recent algorithms, proposed for an efficient enumeration of the acceptable sets, are based on a cutting of the AF [18,24,27], along with, for some of them, the use of distributed, parallel computation in each part, to construct the acceptable sets [19]. In this research line, our paper presents a new "cutting and distributed computing" algorithm, called *AFDivider*, for the enumeration of the acceptable sets of an AF, under the *stable*, *preferred* and *complete* labelling semantics. The cutting of the AF is done in a new way, using spectral clustering methods. Compared to the existing approaches, the added value of *AFDivider* is its way to split the AF and thus to distribute the solving hardness of the whole AF into smaller parts, the reunifying process requiring less checks than the construction of the labellings over the whole AF. *AFDivider* is shown to be sound and complete. The algorithm has been empirically tested, and the results have been compared to those of two solvers of the ICCMA 2017 edition, *Pyglaf* [3] and *ArgSemSAT* [20].

The paper starts with presenting the background of this work (Sect. 2), before describing the algorithm (Sect. 3). Soundness and completeness of the algorithm are proven in Sect. 4. A preliminary empirical analysis is conducted (Sect. 5). Related works are presented in Sect. 6. Perspectives for future work are then opened.

2   Background

2.1   Abstract Argumentation

According to [23], an abstract argumentation framework consists of a set of arguments and of a binary attack relation between them.

---

[1] International Competition on Computational Models of Argumentation (ICCMA) http://argumentationcompetition.org/.

[2] The density in an argumentation graph is the ratio "number of existing attacks" over "number of potential attacks" (this last number is equal to n^2 with n being the number of arguments).

Definition 1 (AF). *An argumentation framework (AF) is a pair $\Gamma = \langle A, R \rangle$ where A is a finite[3] set of abstract arguments and $R \subseteq A \times A$ is a binary relation on A, called the attack relation: $(a, b) \in R$ means that a attacks b.*

Hence, an argumentation framework can be represented by a directed graph with arguments as vertices and attacks as edges. Figure 1 shows an example of an AF.

Acceptability semantics can be defined in terms of labellings [6,15].

Definition 2 (Labelling). *Let $\Gamma = \langle A, R \rangle$ be an AF, and $S \subseteq A$. A labelling of S is a total function $\ell : S \rightarrow \{in, out, und\}$. The set of all labellings of S is denoted as $\mathscr{L}(S)$. A labelling of Γ is a labelling of A. The set of all labellings of Γ is denoted as $\mathscr{L}(\Gamma)$.*

We write $in(\ell)$ for $\{a|\ell(a) = in\}$, $out(\ell)$ for $\{a|\ell(a) = out\}$ and $und(\ell)$ for $\{a|\ell(a) = und\}$.

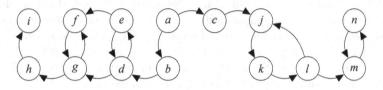

Fig. 1. Example of an argumentation framework *AF*.

Definition 3 (Legally labelled arguments, valid labelling). *An in-labelled argument is said to be legally in iff all its attackers are labelled out. An out-labelled argument is said to be legally out iff at least one of its attackers is labelled in. An und-labelled argument is said to be legally und iff it does not have any attacker that is labelled in and one of its attackers is not labelled out. A valid labelling is a labelling in which all arguments are legally labelled.*

Let $\Gamma = \langle A, R \rangle$ be an AF, and $\ell \in \mathscr{L}(\Gamma)$ be a labelling. Different kinds of labelling can be defined:

Definition 4 (Admissible, complete, grounded, preferred and stable labellings). *ℓ is an admissible labelling of Γ iff for any argument $a \in A$ such that $\ell(a) = in$ or $\ell(a) = out$, a is legally labelled. ℓ is a complete labelling of Γ iff for any argument $a \in A$, a is legally labelled. ℓ is the grounded labelling of Γ iff it is the complete labelling of Γ that minimizes (w.r.t $\subseteq$) the set of in-labelled arguments. ℓ is a preferred labelling of Γ iff it is a complete labelling of Γ that maximizes (w.r.t $\subseteq$) the set of in-labelled arguments. ℓ is a stable labelling of Γ iff it is a complete labelling of Γ which has no und-labelled argument.*

---

[3] According to [23], the set of arguments is not necessarily finite. Nevertheless, in this paper, it is reasonable to assume that it is finite.

Note that each complete labelling includes the grounded labelling. This property will be used by the algorithm presented in Sect. 3 in order to compute the AF labellings in a distributed way. Let $\Gamma = \langle A, R \rangle$ be an AF, and $\mathscr{L}(\Gamma)$ be its set of labellings, semantics can be defined.

Definition 5 (Semantics). *A semantics σ is a total function σ that associates to Γ a subset of $\mathscr{L}(\Gamma)$. The set of labellings under semantics σ, with σ being either the complete (co), the grounded (gr), the stable (st) or the preferred (pr) semantics, is denoted by $\mathscr{L}_\sigma(\Gamma)$. A labelling ℓ is a σ-labelling iff $\ell \in \mathscr{L}_\sigma(\Gamma)$.*

Example 1. Let us consider the AF given in Fig. 1. Table 1 shows the labellings corresponding to the different semantics (the other possible labellings are not given). Note that this AF has no stable labelling.

2.2 Clustering Methods

A *cluster* in a graph can be defined as a connected subgraph. Finding clusters is a subject that has been widely studied (see [31, 35]). The clustering approach implemented in our algorithm is based on a spectral analysis of a defined similarity matrix of the graph. We chose this clustering method as it is well suited for a non-dense graph (see Sects. 3.1 and 3.2 for more explanation). We give here a succinct description of this approach (for details, see [36]):

Table 1. Labellings of the *AF* of Fig. 1 under the grounded, complete, preferred and stable semantics.

	arguments														σ			
	a	*b*	*c*	*d*	*e*	*f*	*g*	*h*	*i*	*j*	*k*	*l*	*m*	*n*	*gr*	*co*	*pr*	*st*
ℓ_1	*in*	*out*	*out*	*out*	*in*	*out*	*in*	*out*	*in*	*und*	*und*	*und*	*out*	*in*		×	×	
ℓ_2	*in*	*out*	*out*	*in*	*out*	*in*	*out*	*in*	*out*	*und*	*und*	*und*	*out*	*in*		×	×	
ℓ_3	*in*	*out*	*out*	*out*	*in*	*out*	*in*	*out*	*in*	*und*	*und*	*und*	*und*	*und*		×		
ℓ_4	*in*	*out*	*out*	*in*	*out*	*in*	*out*	*in*	*out*	*und*	*und*	*und*	*und*	*und*		×		
ℓ_5	*in*	*out*	*out*	*und*	*und*	*und*	*und*	*und*	*und*	*und*	*und*	*und*	*und*	*und*	×	×		
ℓ_6	*in*	*out*	*out*	*und*	*und*	*und*	*und*	*und*	*und*	*und*	*und*	*und*	*out*	*in*		×		

- Computation of a similarity matrix of the graph. In this squared matrix, the values represent how much two nodes are similar according to a given similarity criterion, and the rows may be seen as the coordinates of the graph nodes in a similarity space.
- Computation of the Laplacian matrix of this similarity matrix. The rows of this Laplacian matrix represent how much a node is similar to the others and how much each of its neighbours contributes to its global similarity with its neighbourhood.
- Computation of the eigenvectors (see [33]) of the Laplacian matrix with their associated eigenvalues.

- These eigenvalues are sorted by increasing order. A number n of them is kept with their associated eigenvectors.[4]
- A matrix whose columns are the remaining eigenvectors is built. Its rows represent the new node coordinates in a space that maximizes the proximity between similar nodes. In that space, the euclidean distance between two nodes shows how much a node is similar to another.
- Then a simple algorithm of clustering such as *KMeans* is applied to that new data set, seeking for a partition into n parts, based on the coordinates of the nodes (see [30] for more information about *KMeans* algorithm).

An illustration of this method on the running example is given in Sect. 3.2 while the similarity criterion used is explicited in Sect. 3.1.

3 The Algorithm

This section presents the *AFDivider* algorithm designed for the *complete, stable* and *preferred* semantics (denoted by σ). It computes the semantics labellings of an AF by first removing trivial parts of the AF (the *grounded* labelling, as done in [18]), then cutting the AF into clusters and computing simultaneously in each cluster labelling parts, before finally reunifying compatible parts to get the σ-labellings of the whole AF. Each of these steps will be presented and then illustrated on the running example.

Algorithm 1: *AFDivider* algorithm.

Data: Let $\Gamma = \langle A, R \rangle$ be an AF and σ be a semantics
Result: $\mathscr{L}_\sigma \in 2^{\mathscr{L}(\Gamma)}$: the set of the σ-labellings of Γ

1   $\ell_{gr} \leftarrow ComputeGroundedLabelling(\Gamma)$
2   $CCSet \leftarrow SplitConnectedComponents(\Gamma, \ell_{gr})$
3 **for all** $\gamma_i \in CCSet$ **do in parallel**
4     $ClustSet \leftarrow ComputeClusters(\gamma_i)$
5     $\mathscr{L}_\sigma^{\gamma_i} \leftarrow ComputeCompLabs(\sigma, ClustSet)$
6   $\mathscr{L}_\sigma \leftarrow \varnothing$
7 **if** $\nexists \gamma_i \in CCSet$ s.t. $\mathscr{L}_\sigma^{\gamma_i} = \varnothing$ **then** $\mathscr{L}_\sigma \leftarrow \{\ell_{gr}\} \times \prod_{\gamma_i \in CCSet} \mathscr{L}_\sigma^{\gamma_i}$
8 **return** $\mathscr{L}_\sigma$

---

[4] Sorted in ascending order, the eigenvalue sequence represents how the similarity within clusters increases as the number of clusters grows. Obviously, the more clusters, the more homogeneous they will get, but also, the more cases to compute. A compromise between the number of clusters and homogeneity is needed. A heuristic (called "elbow heuristic") to find the appropriate number of dimensions to keep, consists in detecting the jump in the eigenvalues sequence.

3.1 Description

Given an argumentation framework $\Gamma = \langle A, R \rangle$, the *AFDivider* algorithm (Algorithm 1) starts with computing the grounded labelling of Γ (line 1). Indeed in each of the semantics σ we are interested in, the arguments labelled *in* or *out* in the grounded labelling are labelled in the same way in all the σ-labellings. It is a fixed part. Note that the function $ComputeGroundedLabelling(\Gamma)$ returns a partial labelling of Γ in which the arguments are labelled *in* or *out*. The *und*-labelled arguments according to the grounded semantics do not belong to ℓ_{gr}.

Γ is then split into disjoint sub-AFs obtained after removing the arguments labelled *in* or *out* in the grounded labelling (line 2). The *CCSet* variable is the set of connected components computed.

Given that there is no relation between them, the labelling computation of those connected components can be made in a simultaneous way (line 3) according to the chosen semantics.

For each of these connected components, a clustering is made (line 4) using the spectral clustering method presented in Sect. 2.2. The similarity matrix on which the spectral analysis relies is a kind of adjacency matrix where the directionality of edges is omitted and where the matrix values are the number of edges between two arguments. Basically, the more an argument will be related to another, the more similar the two arguments will be considered.

This similarity criterion is particularly relevant for non-dense graphs with a clustered structure. Indeed, it produces sparse matrices and as a consequence the eigenvector equation system to solve will be simplified as there will be many zero values. This is what motivated our choice for the spectral clustering method.

After this clustering process, $ComputeCompLabs$ (Algorithm 2) is called to compute in a distributed way all the labellings of the connected component according to σ (line 5).

Finally, given that ℓ_{gr} is a fixed part of all σ-labellings of Γ and that all the connected components are completely independent, to construct the σ-labellings of the whole AF, a simple Cartesian product is made (line 7) between the labellings of all the components and the grounded one.

If one of the components has no labelling then the whole AF has no labelling (so $\mathscr{L}_\sigma = \varnothing$).

Consider now Algorithm 2 that computes the component labellings in a distributed way, relying on the clustering made. The σ-labellings of each cluster are computed simultaneously (line 1). Unlike the case of connected components used in Algorithm 1, there exist attacks between clusters. In order to compute all the possible σ-labellings of a given cluster, every case concerning its inward attacks (attacks whose target is in the current cluster but the source is from another cluster) have to be considered. Given that the sources of an inward attack could be labelled *in*, *out* or *und* in their own cluster, the σ-labellings of the current cluster have to be computed for all the labelling combinations of inward attack sources.

Algorithm 2: *ComputeCompLabs* algorithm.

Data: Let *ClustSet* be a set of cluster structures for a component γ, σ be a semantics

Result: $\mathscr{L}_\sigma \in 2^{\mathscr{L}(\gamma)}$: the set of the σ-labellings of γ

1 **for all** $\kappa_j \in ClustSet$ **do in parallel** $\mathscr{L}_\sigma^{\kappa_j} \leftarrow ComputeClustLabs(\sigma, \kappa_j)$

2 $\mathscr{L}_\sigma \leftarrow ReunifyCompLabs(\bigcup_{\kappa_j \in ClustSet} \mathscr{L}_\sigma^{\kappa_j}, ClustSet)$

3 **if** $\sigma = pr$ **then** $\mathscr{L}_\sigma \leftarrow \{\ell | \ell \in \mathscr{L}_\sigma \text{ s.t. } \nexists \ell' \in \mathscr{L}_\sigma \text{ s.t. } in(\ell) \subset in(\ell')\}$

4 **return** $\mathscr{L}_\sigma$

Note that having "well shaped" clusters (*i.e.* clusters with few inter cluster attacks) reduces considerably the number of cases to compute, as there are few edges cut. Thus this algorithm is well suited for clustered non-dense graphs.

Once that, for all clusters, the *ComputeClustLabs* function has computed the σ-labellings for all the possible cases (this is done by calling any sound and complete procedure computing the semantics labellings), the *ReunifyCompLabs* function is called in order to reunify compatible labelling parts. Labelling parts are said to be compatible together when all the targets of the inter cluster attacks are legally labelled in the resulting reunified labelling.

A special step has to be done for the *preferred* semantics as this reunifying process does not ensure the maximality (w.r.t $\subseteq$) of the set of *in*-labelled arguments (so not all of the labellings produced in line 2 are *preferred* ones). A maximality check is done (line 3) in order to keep only the wanted labellings.

Note that, when computing the *stable* semantics, the set of labellings $\mathscr{L}_\sigma$ returned by the function *ReunifyCompLabs* may be empty. It happens when one of the component clusters has no *stable* labelling.

3.2 An Illustrating Example

In this section, the behaviour of our algorithms is illustrated on the AF given in Fig. 1 for the *preferred* semantics, as it is the most complex semantics of the three targeted ones.

The first step consists in computing the grounded labelling in order to eventually split the AF into sub-AFs. The grounded labelling of the AF restricted only to the *in*-labelled and *out*-labelled arguments is: $\ell_{gr} = \{(a, in), (b, out), (c, out)\}$.

Removing arguments a, b and c from the AF produces two connected components, as illustrated in Fig. 2.

Then simultaneously γ_1 and γ_2 are clustered using the spectral clustering method This is done by several steps. First, we consider the similarity matrices of γ_1 and γ_2 according to our criterion, *i.e.* the number of attacks between arguments. They may also be seen as the adjacency matrices of the weighted non-directed graphs obtained from γ_1 and γ_2 (see Fig. 3). Given that the AF relation density is low, the matrices are rather sparse.

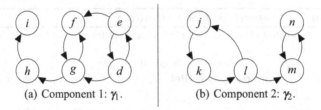

(a) Component 1: γ_1.   (b) Component 2: γ_2.

Fig. 2. Connected components resulting from the grounded removal pre-processing.

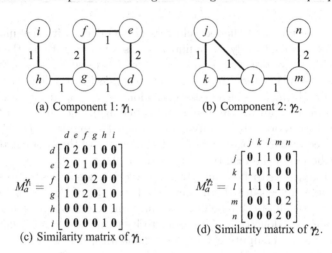

(a) Component 1: γ_1.   (b) Component 2: γ_2.

$$M_a^{\gamma_1} = \begin{array}{c} \\ d \\ e \\ f \\ g \\ h \\ i \end{array} \begin{array}{c} d\ e\ f\ g\ h\ i \\ \begin{bmatrix} 0\ 2\ 0\ 1\ 0\ 0 \\ 2\ 0\ 1\ 0\ 0\ 0 \\ 0\ 1\ 0\ 2\ 0\ 0 \\ 1\ 0\ 2\ 0\ 1\ 0 \\ 0\ 0\ 0\ 1\ 0\ 1 \\ 0\ 0\ 0\ 0\ 1\ 0 \end{bmatrix} \end{array}$$

(c) Similarity matrix of γ_1.

$$M_a^{\gamma_2} = \begin{array}{c} \\ j \\ k \\ l \\ m \\ n \end{array} \begin{array}{c} j\ k\ l\ m\ n \\ \begin{bmatrix} 0\ 1\ 1\ 0\ 0 \\ 1\ 0\ 1\ 0\ 0 \\ 1\ 1\ 0\ 1\ 0 \\ 0\ 0\ 1\ 0\ 2 \\ 0\ 0\ 0\ 2\ 0 \end{bmatrix} \end{array}$$

(d) Similarity matrix of γ_2.

Fig. 3. Step 1 of the spectral clustering.

Once the AF similarity matrix is constructed, data are projected in a new space in which similarity is maximised. If a certain structure exists in the data set, we will see in that space some agglomerates appear, corresponding to the node clusters. To do this projection, we compute the n smallest eigenvalues[5] of the Laplacian matrix obtained from the similarity matrix and the vectors associated with them (this n is an arbitrary parameter; in this example we have chosen to keep all the vectors, *i.e.* $n = 5$). Indeed, the eigenvectors found will correspond to the basis of that similarity space and the eigenvalues to the variance on the corresponding axes. Given that we are looking for homogeneous groups, we will consider only the axis on which the variance is low, and so the eigenvectors that have small eigenvalues. The space whose basis is the n selected eigenvectors (corresponding to the n smallest eigenvalues) is then a compression of similarity space (*i.e.* we keep only the dimension useful for a clustering).

---

[5] There exist algorithms, such as *Krylov-Schur* method, able to compute eigenvectors from smallest to greatest eigenvalue and to stop at any wanted step (*e.g.* the number of vectors found). With such an algorithm it is not necessary to find all the solutions as we are interested only in the small eigenvalues.

Let us take as an example the case of γ_2. Its degree matrix $M_d^{\gamma_2}$ and its Laplacian matrix $M_l^{\gamma_2}$ are given in Fig. 4.

$$
M_d^{\gamma_2} = \begin{array}{c} \\ j \\ k \\ l \\ m \\ n \end{array}
\begin{array}{c} j\ k\ l\ m\ n \\ \left[\begin{array}{ccccc} 2 & 0 & 0 & 0 & 0 \\ 0 & 2 & 0 & 0 & 0 \\ 0 & 0 & 3 & 0 & 0 \\ 0 & 0 & 0 & 3 & 0 \\ 0 & 0 & 0 & 0 & 2 \end{array}\right] \end{array}
$$

(a) Degree matrix of γ_2.

$$
M_d^{\gamma_2} - M_a^{\gamma_2} = M_l^{\gamma_2} = \begin{array}{c} \\ j \\ k \\ l \\ m \\ n \end{array}
\begin{array}{c} j\quad k\quad l\quad m\quad n \\ \left[\begin{array}{ccccc} 2 & -1 & -1 & 0 & 0 \\ -1 & 2 & -1 & 0 & 0 \\ -1 & -1 & 3 & -1 & 0 \\ 0 & 0 & -1 & 3 & -2 \\ 0 & 0 & 0 & -2 & 2 \end{array}\right] \end{array}
$$

(b) Laplacian matrix of γ_2.

Fig. 4. Step 2 of the spectral clustering for γ_2.

The eigenvalues of $M_l^{\gamma_2}$ sorted in ascending order are:

$$
\begin{array}{ccccc} \lambda_1 & \lambda_2 & \lambda_3 & \lambda_4 & \lambda_5 \end{array}
$$
$$
\left[2.476651 \times 10^{-16} \quad 5.857864 \times 10^{-1} \quad 3.000000 \quad 3.414214 \quad 5.000000 \right]
$$

and their associated eigenvectors are:

$$
\begin{array}{ccccc} v_1 & v_2 & v_3 & v_4 & v_5 \end{array}
$$
$$
\left[\begin{array}{ccccc}
-0.4472136 & 0.4397326 & 7.071068 \times 10^{-1} & 0.3038906 & 0.1195229 \\
-0.4472136 & 0.4397326 & -7.071068 \times 10^{-1} & 0.3038906 & 0.1195229 \\
-0.4472136 & 0.1821432 & -5.551115 \times 10^{-17} & -0.7336569 & -0.4780914 \\
-0.4472136 & -0.4397326 & -2.775558 \times 10^{-16} & -0.3038906 & 0.7171372 \\
-0.4472136 & -0.6218758 & -1.665335 \times 10^{-16} & 0.4297663 & -0.4780914
\end{array}\right]
$$

Now that the similarity space is found, the following step is to find how many groups we have in that space. This number can be founded using the eigenvalue sequence sorted in ascending order and identifying in this sequence the "best elbow" (*i.e.* the point that corresponds to a quick growth of the variance, see Fig. 5). In our example, the number of clusters determined by that heuristic is 2.

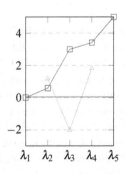

Fig. 5. Step 3 of the spectral clustering. (Color figure online)

To compute that "best elbow" we consider the second derivative (green line with triangles) of the ascending order sequence. As the second derivative represents the concavity of the eigenvalue sequence, we can take the first value of the second derivative above a certain threshold (red line without symbol) determined experimentally (*i.e.* the first position where the eigenvalue sequence is enough convex).

The first point of the second derivative, corresponding to the concavity formed by the first three eigenvalues, is the first value above the threshold; so we determine that the "best elbow" is in position 2.

Once the number of clusters is chosen, we must to find the partition of the set of arguments. This is done using a *KMeans* type algorithm [30][6] applied on the kept eigenvectors following the chosen number of clusters (see Fig. 6).

The matrix composed by the kept eigenvectors (the *two* first eigenvectors, 2 being the number of clusters):

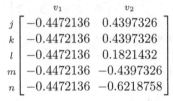

$$\begin{array}{c@{\quad}cc}
 & v_1 & v_2 \\
j & \begin{bmatrix} -0.4472136 & 0.4397326 \\ -0.4472136 & 0.4397326 \\ -0.4472136 & 0.1821432 \\ -0.4472136 & -0.4397326 \\ -0.4472136 & -0.6218758 \end{bmatrix} \\
k & \\
l & \\
m & \\
n &
\end{array}$$

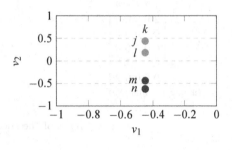

Fig. 6. Step 4 of the spectral clustering.

The lines of this matrix correspond to the coordinates of the nodes in the compressed similarity space. With a *KMeans* algorithm we can find groups of datapoint in that space and so have the partition of arguments we wanted (here $\{j, k, l\}$ and $\{m, n\}$).

The complete result given by the spectral clustering is shown in Fig. 7. κ_1 and κ_2 are the clusters determined from γ_1, and κ_3 and κ_4 are the ones from γ_2.

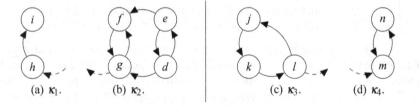

(a) κ_1.   (b) κ_2.   (c) κ_3.   (d) κ_4.

Fig. 7. Identified clusters.

After the clustering, the next step of our algorithm is the computation of *preferred* labellings. This computation is made simultaneously in the different clusters using an external solver (one of the best solvers identified in the ICCMA competition, see [34]). Recall that, for each cluster, every case concerning its inward attacks (attacks whose target is in the current cluster but the source is from another cluster) have to be considered. Given that the sources of an inward attack could be labelled *in*, *out* or *und* in their own cluster, the σ-labellings of the current cluster have to be computed for all the labelling combinations of inward attack sources. For instance, for κ_1 (resp. κ_4), three cases for h and so for i (resp. for m and so for n) must be considered. Whereas for κ_2 and κ_3, there is no inward attack, the computed labellings only depend on the content of the cluster. The tables in Fig. 8(a) show the computed labelling parts for each cluster.

---

[6] Given n observations, a *KMeans* algorithm aims to partition the n observations into k subsets such that the distance between the elements inside each subset is minimized. Here we have $n = 5$ and $k = 2$.

Notice that although three cases are computed for κ_4, only two labellings are obtained. This is due to the maximality of the *preferred* semantics. Indeed, even though m is attacked by an **und**-labelled argument, n may be labelled **in** as it defends itself against m. As a consequence, m would be labelled **out**.

The last step of our algorithm is the reunifying phase (line 2, Algorithm 2). In this step, the constructed labellings are those in which all the target arguments are legally labelled. As an example, $\ell_1^{\kappa_1}$ cannot be reunified with $\ell_2^{\kappa_2}$ as h would be illegally **out**-labelled. Figure 8(b) shows the valid reunified labellings for each component.

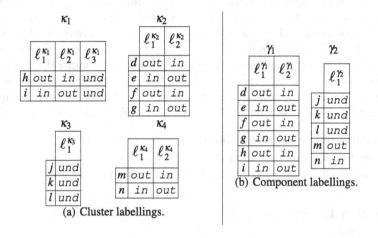

(a) Cluster labellings.   (b) Component labellings.

Fig. 8. Labellings computed using our algorithm.

In that particular example all the reunified labellings are maximal w.r.t $\subseteq$ of the set of *in*-labelled arguments, so the maximality check (line 3, Algorithm 2) does not change the set of labellings.[7]

Finally, the *preferred* labellings of the whole AF are constructed by performing a Cartesian product of the component labellings and of the grounded one. See the final computed *preferred* labellings in Table 1, Sect. 2.1 (labellings ℓ_1 and ℓ_2).

4   Soundness and Completeness

This section presents formal properties of *AFDivider*: soundness and completeness for the *complete*, the *stable* and the *preferred* semantics. Let σ be one of

---

[7] To highlight the necessity of the maximality check, let us take as minimal example the AF defined by $\langle\{a,b\},\{(a,b),(b,a)\}\rangle$ and a partition of it in which each argument is in a different cluster. For each cluster, we will have three possible labellings as the inward attack source may be labelled *in*, *out* or *und* in the other cluster. The reunifying phase will thus admit the labelling $\{(a,\mathbf{und}),(b,\mathbf{und})\}$ which is not a *preferred* labelling.

these three semantics. To be *sound* for σ means that the algorithm produces only σ-labellings. To be *complete* for σ means that the algorithm produces all the σ-labellings. In other words, given σ, *AFDivider* produces only and all the σ-labellings.

In order to prove these properties, we rely on the notions of *top-down* and *bottom-up* semantics decomposability introduced in [5] and then developed in [9]. In a few words, a semantics σ is said to be *top-down* decomposable if, for all AF Γ and for all its partitions into sub-AFs, the set of σ-labellings of Γ is included in the set of valid labellings obtained by reunifying the σ-labellings of its sub-AFs. A semantics σ is said to be *bottom-up* decomposable if, for all AF Γ and for all its partitions into sub-AFs, the set of valid labellings obtained by reunifying the σ-labellings of its sub-AFs is included in the set of σ-labellings of Γ. A semantics is said to be *fully* decomposable if it is *top-down* and *bottom-up* decomposable. These notions of *top-down* and *bottom-up* semantics decomposability can also be defined w.r.t. a specific type of partition. For instance, the partition selector denoted by $\mathscr{S}_{USCC}$ only produces partitions in which SCCs (Strongly Connected Components) are not split into different parts. In [9] it has been proven that:

- The *stable* and *complete* semantics are *fully* decomposable.
- The *preferred* semantics is *top-down* decomposable.
- The *preferred* semantics is *fully* decomposable w.r.t to $\mathscr{S}_{USCC}$.

Proposition 1. *AFDivider is sound and complete for the complete and the stable semantics.*

SKETCH OF PROOF. *Let σ be a fully decomposable semantics. Let $\Gamma = \langle A, R \rangle$ be an AF. Let ℓ_{gr} be the grounded labelling of Γ restricted to the in-labelled and out-labelled arguments. Let $\Omega = \{\omega_{gr}, \omega_1^1, \ldots, \omega_{n_1}^1, \ldots, \omega_1^k, \ldots, \omega_{n_k}^k\}$ be a partition of A such that ω_{gr} is the set of arguments labelled in ℓ_{gr} and such that for all i and j, ω_i^j is the set of arguments corresponding to the cluster j of the component i determined by the component clustering performed by AFDivider.*

Given that for all clusters, the labellings are computed for all possible labellings of the cluster inward attack sources, and given that σ is fully decomposable, the set of valid reunified labellings produced by AFDivider is equal to $\mathscr{L}_\sigma(\Gamma)$.

And so AFDivider is sound and complete for the complete and the stable semantics. ∎

Proposition 2. *AFDivider is sound and complete for the preferred semantics.*

SKETCH OF PROOF. *Let σ be the preferred semantics. Let $\Gamma = \langle A, R \rangle$ be an AF. Let ℓ_{gr} be the grounded labelling of Γ restricted to the in-labelled and out-labelled arguments. Let $\{\gamma_1, \ldots, \gamma_k\}$ be the set of all connected components obtained by AFDivider after removing ℓ_{gr}. Let $\Omega = \{\omega_{gr}, \omega_1^1, \ldots, \omega_{n_1}^1, \ldots, \omega_1^k, \ldots, \omega_{n_k}^k\}$ be a partition of A such that ω_{gr} is the set of arguments labelled in*

ℓ_{gr} and such that for all i and j, ω_i^j is the set of arguments corresponding to the cluster j of the component γ_i determined by the component clustering performed by AFDivider.

Given that the preferred semantics is top-down decomposable, and given that for all clusters, the labellings are computed for all possible labellings of the cluster inward attack sources, then for each component γ_i, $\mathscr{L}_{pr}(\gamma_i)$ is included in the set of valid reunified labellings produced by the function $ReunifyCompLabs$ (Algorithm 2, line 2). The maximality check (line 3) makes Algorithm 2 sound and complete for the preferred semantics.

Let $\Omega' = \{\omega_{gr}, \omega^1, \ldots, \omega^k\}$ be a partition of A such that ω_{gr} is the set of arguments labelled in ℓ_{gr} and such that for all i: $\omega^i = \bigcup_{j=1}^{n_i}(\omega_j^i)$. Let $S = \{(a,b)|\exists i \text{ s.t. } (a,b) \in (\omega_{gr} \times \omega^i) \cap R\}$ be the set of all attacks going from an argument labelled in ℓ_{gr} to an argument non present in ℓ_{gr}. Note that all the sources of these attacks are **out**-labelled in ℓ_{gr}. Let $\Gamma' = \langle A, R' \rangle$ with $R' = R \setminus S$, be the AF obtained from Γ when removing the attacks in S. Given that the sources of attacks removed to obtained Γ' from Γ are all **out**-labelled arguments, we have $\mathscr{L}_\sigma(\Gamma') = \mathscr{L}_\sigma(\Gamma)$. Note that $\Omega' \in \mathscr{S}_{USCC}(\Gamma')$. Indeed, for all i, $(\omega_{gr} \times \omega^i) \cap R' = \varnothing$ and for all $j \neq i$, $(\omega^j \times \omega^i) \cap R' = \varnothing$.

Given that the preferred semantics is fully decomposable w.r.t. $\mathscr{S}_{USCC}$ then the set of valid labellings obtained by reunifying the σ-labellings of the sub-AFs corresponding to Ω' equal to $\mathscr{L}_\sigma(\Gamma')$. Given that Algorithm 2 is sound and complete for the preferred semantics, the Cartesian product made in Algorithm 1 (line 7) computes exactly $\mathscr{L}_\sigma(\Gamma')$. As a consequence, Algorithm 1 computes exactly $\mathscr{L}_\sigma(\Gamma)$. AFDivider is thus sound and complete for the preferred semantics. ∎

5 Experimental Results

In this section we present some experimental results conducted with the *AFDivider* algorithm. The experiments have been made on some hard instances of the ICCMA competition, which are mostly of Barabási–Albert (BA) type. They all are non-dense and have a clustered structure.

To compute the labellings of a cluster given a particular labelling of its inward attack sources, we have used an already existing solver called *"Pyglaf"*, one of the best solvers at the ICCMA 2017 session, which transforms the AF labelling problem into a SAT problem [3]. In this paper, we compare our algorithm (using *Pyglaf*) with *Pyglaf* itself, and with *ArgSemSAT* [20], for the preferred, the complete and the stable semantics.

For each experiment, we used 6 cores of a Intel Xeon Gold 6136 processor, each core having a frequency of 3 GHz. The RAM size was 45GB. As at least two of the three used solvers are multithreaded (*Pyglaf* and *AFDivider*), we have chosen to compare them using both CPU and real time (the CPU time includes the user and the system times). Note that, for our algorithm, the durations cover both the clustering time and the computation of labellings time. The timeout has been set to 1 h for the real time.

Table 2. Experimental results (PR: preferred, CO: complete, ST: stable, MO : "Memory Overflow", TO: "stop with TimeOut", "—": "missing data"). The time result format is "minutes: seconds. centiseconds".

			i_1	i_2	i_3	i_4	i_5	i_6	i_7	i_8
PR	Nb lab. ($\approx$)		0.28×10^6	1.07×10^6	1.28×10^6	1.37×10^6	1.96×10^6	4.47×10^6	11.75×10^6	10.74×10^9
	AFDivider	end state	✓	✓	✓	✓	✓	✓	✓	MO
		CPU time	0:07.35	0:14.05	0:19.89	0:31.39	0:28.01	0:46.27	12:15.16	
		real time	0:05.84	0:27.98	0:20.42	0:35.05	0:31.31	1:09.10	12:39.21	
	Pyglaf	end state	✓	✓	✓	✓	✓	TO	TO	TO
		CPU time	0:45.33	6:18.60	11:06.51	15:21.07	54:49.31			
		real time	0:39.00	6:04.37	10:12.22	14:51.09	54:20.72			
	ArgSemSAT	end state	TO	TO	TO	TO	TO	TO	TO	TO
ST	Nb lab. ($\approx$)		Idem preferred case							
	AFDivider	end state	✓	✓	✓	✓	✓	✓	✓	MO
		CPU time	0:06.52	0:13.29	0:18.01	0:28.50	0:26.66	0:45.56	1:39.14	
		real time	0:06.26	0:13.20	0:18.78	0:31.02	0:29.46	0:50.79	1:48.30	
	Pyglaf	end state	✓	✓	✓	✓	✓	✓	✓	TO
		CPU time	0:05.43	0:17.31	0:24.78	0:31,50	0:41.69	1:13.10	3:35.76	
		real time	0:03.02	0:09.22	0:14.76	0:18.43	0:21.15	0:42.57	1:53.95	
	ArgSemSAT	end state	TO	TO	TO	TO	TO	TO	TO	TO
CO	Nb lab. ($\approx$)		0.80×10^9	5.22×10^9	9.31×10^9	11.93×10^9	16.18×10^9	49.58×10^9	-	22×10^{15}
	AFDivider	end state	MO	MO	MO	MO	MO	MO	MO	MO
	Pyglaf	end state	TO	TO	TO	TO	TO	TO	TO	TO
	ArgSemSAT	end state	TO	TO	TO	TO	TO	TO	TO	TO

Table 2 gives the obtained results on 8 significant instances:[8] i_1 to i_8 for respectively BA_120_70_1.apx, BA_100_60_2.apx, BA_120_80_2.apx, BA_180_60_4.apx, basin-or-us.gml.20.apx, BA_100_80_3.apx, amador-transit_20151216_1706.gml.80.apx and BA_-200_70_4.apx. Note that these instances have a number of labellings under the *preferred* and *stable* semantics that is particularly large (more than a hundred thousand), and even larger for the complete semantics.

In Table 2, it is worth noting that, first, none of the chosen instances is solved by *ArgSemSAT*; second, that none of the three solvers can provide results for the complete semantics; third, that our algorithm is far better than *Pyglaf* on those instances for the preferred semantics.[9] Actually, we can observe a real order of magnitude change which increases with the hardness of the instances: from 39 s to 5 s for i_1 and from almost one hour to 31 s for i_5 (i_6 to i_8 being unsolved by *Pyglaf* in less than one hour). The last chosen instance (i_8), with its more than ten billion *preferred* labellings, presents a memory representation challenge; a compressed representation of the labellings is to be found to tackle such instances. This is also the case for the complete semantics. Finally, concerning the stable semantics, *Pyglaf* and *AFDivider* give similar results: in term of real time, *Pyglaf* is slightly better except on i_7. Nevertheless, it is worth noting that, in term of CPU time, *AFDivider* is generally better than *Pyglaf*; this last point needs further studies.

Overall, these preliminary experimental results show that the AF clustering approach brings a real added value in terms of resolution time in the case of the preferred semantics, and that an additional analysis will be necessary for identifying how to improve the results for the other semantics.

6   Related Work

There exist many approaches for enumerating semantics labellings, but most of them are non-direct, in the sense that they reduce the semantics computation to other problems (most of the time to the SAT problem). Such non-direct approaches may use some kind of cutting process and even distributed computation (it is the case of *Pyglaf* [3]). Direct approaches, such as *AFDivider*, are less common. It is with the existing direct approaches that we compare in this section the *AFDivider* algorithm.

Here are some direct approach algorithms which use some kind of cutting techniques:[10] [24], that presents an algorithm based on a dynamic analysis of an argumentation framework; [27], where the algorithm computes the labellings of an AF following its SCC decomposition; [18], where the *R-PREF*

---

[8] *amador-transit_20151216_1706.gml.80.apx*   and   *basin-or-us.gml.20.apx*   are instances which come from real data of the traffic domain.

[9] Note that *Pyglaf* is also multi-core. Moreover, when we compare *Pyglaf* and *AFDivider*, we use a computer with the same number of cores. So the fact that there is a more important parallelization in *AFDivider* (so more threads) is not what explains the difference in runtime for the preferred semantics.

[10] For an overview on the different AF splitting possibilities see [8].

algorithm is based on [27]'s approach, with the addition of applying the decomposition process recursively when the labellings under construction break the SCCs; [19], where the *P-SCC-REC* algorithm, inspired by notions introduced in [5,10,28,29], is the parallelized version of *R-PREF*; [11], where the algorithm splits the AF in two parts (without breaking SCCs), and computes their labelling before reunifying them. Let us compare *AFDivider* with these approaches in two respects.

- First, on their ability to break SCCs: [27] and [11] do not do so; [18] and [19] can do so, given a current SCC and an ancestor labelling, but only when the ancestor labelling has some particular effects on the current SCC; [24] always breaks SCCs as at each step at most one argument is added or removed from the considered sub-AF. Nevertheless, this way of updating argument after argument in [24] generates a lot of computations and uses a lot of memory. *AFDivider*, and this is one of its advantages, breaks SCCs whenever it is well suited to have well shaped clusters.
- Second, on their ability to compute the labellings in a distributed way: [11,18, 24,27] are fully sequential. *AFDivider* and [19] use distributed computation, but in [19], the computation of one labelling is mainly sequential (it is very unlikely that the greedy phase suffices to generate a labelling). Furthermore parallelizing following labellings could overload the CPUs as the number of solutions in hard AF problems may be huge.

To conclude, what distinguishes best *AFDivider* from the other ones is that cutting the AF into clusters limits the combinatorial effect due to the number of labellings, to the cluster. The other approaches propagate this effect to the whole AF. This property makes *AFDivider* well suited for non-dense AF with a clustered structure. Indeed, in such a structure, the reunifying phase will be less expensive than exploring the whole AF to construct each of the labellings.

An incremental algorithm that computes labellings has been proposed in [2] but it does not concern the enumeration problem. Other works such as [14,22,37] might be related to our approach as they analyze some kind of AF matrices; however, it is not done in order to cluster the AF.

7   Conclusion

AFDivider is the first algorithm that uses spectral clustering methods to compute semantics labellings. After removing the trivial part of the AF (grounded labelling), the algorithm cuts the AF into small pieces (the identified clusters), then it computes simultaneously (in each cluster) labelling parts of the AF, before reunifying compatible parts to get the whole AF labellings. Soundness and completeness of this algorithm are proven for the *stable*, the *complete* and the *preferred* semantics.

We compared the behaviour of our algorithm with other ones that also use some kind of clustering. Among the various advantages of our method (its ability to break SCCs and to compute the labellings in a distributed way), we highlighted the fact that cutting the AF into clusters has the great advantage of limiting the solving hardness to the clusters. This algorithm is particularly well suited for non-dense AFs with a clustered structure, such as the ones which are among the hardest instances of the ICCMA competition.

An empirical analysis of *AFDivider* on the benchmarks of the competition is underway and some preliminary results are presented in this paper. Nevertheless, more exhaustive experiments are planned, in particular:

- an analysis of the impact of the partition on the solving time, from a random one to a clustered one; different clustering methods may also be compared;
- a complete comparison with the other existing solvers used in ICCMA competition including the 2019 edition (for instance, CoquiAAS [26], or μ-toksia [32], which is the winner of the 2019 edition);
- and finally the use of *AFDivider* for the other tasks, on the other semantics, of the competition (see [13]).

Another interesting question to answer is how to know in a reasonable time if an AF is well suited for the *AFDivider* algorithm. In fact, this is a double question: "what is a theoretical characterization of such an AF?" and "given an AF, what is the computational cost for checking whether it respects this characterization?".

Moreover, among future works, this approach may be extended to enriched argumentation frameworks (*e.g.* with a support relation or with higher-order interactions), and to other acceptability semantics.

References

1. Albert, R., Barabási, A.L.: Statistical mechanics of complex networks. Rev. Mod. Phys. **74**(1), 47 (2002)
2. Alfano, G., Greco, S., Parisi, F.: Efficient computation of extensions for dynamic abstract argumentation frameworks: an incremental approach. In: IJCAI, pp. 49–55 (2017)
3. Alviano, M.: The pyglaf argumentation reasoner. In: OASIcs-OpenAccess Series in Informatics, vol. 58 (2018)
4. Barabási, A.L., et al.: Network Science. Cambridge University Press, Cambridge (2016)
5. Baroni, P., Boella, G., Cerutti, F., Giacomin, M., van der Torre, L.W.N., Villata, S.: On input/output argumentation frameworks. In: COMMA, pp. 358–365 (2012)
6. Baroni, P., Caminada, M., Giacomin, M.: An introduction to argumentation semantics. Knowl. Eng. Rev. **26**(4), 365–410 (2011)
7. Baroni, P., Cerutti, F., Giacomin, M., Guida, G.: AFRA: argumentation framework with recursive attacks. Int. J. Approximate Reasoning **52**(1), 19–37 (2011)
8. Baroni, P., Giacomin, M., Liao, B.: Locality and modularity in abstract argumentation. In: Handbook of Formal Argumentation, pp. 937–979. College Publication (2018)
9. Baroni, P., Boella, G., Cerutti, F., Giacomin, M., Van Der Torre, L., Villata, S.: On the input/output behavior of argumentation frameworks. Artif. Intell. **217**, 144–197 (2014)

10. Baroni, P., Giacomin, M., Liao, B.: On topology-related properties of abstract argumentation semantics. a correction and extension to dynamics of argumentation systems: a division-based method. Artif. Intell. **212**, 104–115 (2014)
11. Baumann, R., Brewka, G., Wong, R.: Splitting argumentation frameworks: an empirical evaluation. In: Modgil, S., Oren, N., Toni, F. (eds.) TAFA 2011. LNCS (LNAI), vol. 7132, pp. 17–31. Springer, Heidelberg (2012). https://doi.org/10.1007/978-3-642-29184-5_2
12. Bistarelli, S., Rossi, F., Santini, F.: Not only size, but also shape counts: abstract argumentation solvers are benchmark-sensitive. J. Log. Comput. **28**(1), 85–117 (2018)
13. Bistarelli, S., Santini, F., Kotthoff, L., Mantadelis, T., Taticchi, C.: Int. Competition on Computational Models of Argumentation (2019). https://www.iccma2019.dmi.unipg.it/
14. Butterworth, J., Dunne, P.: Spectral techniques in argumentation framework analysis. COMMA **287**, 167 (2016)
15. Caminada, M.: On the issue of reinstatement in argumentation. In: JELIA, pp. 111–123 (2006)
16. Carrera, Á., Iglesias, C.A.: A systematic review of argumentation techniques for multi-agent systems research. Artif. Intell. Rev. **44**(4), 509–535 (2015)
17. Cayrol, C., Lagasquie-Schiex, M.C.: On the acceptability of arguments in bipolar argumentation frameworks. In: Godo, L. (ed.) ECSQARU, pp. 378–389 (2005)
18. Cerutti, F., Giacomin, M., Vallati, M., Zanella, M.: An SCC recursive meta-algorithm for computing preferred labellings in abstract argumentation. In: KR (2014)
19. Cerutti, F., Tachmazidis, I., Vallati, M., Batsakis, S., Giacomin, M., Antoniou, G.: Exploiting parallelism for hard problems in abstract argumentation. In: AAAI, pp. 1475–1481 (2015)
20. Cerutti, F., Vallati, M., Giacomin, M., Zanetti, T.: ArgSemSAT-2017 (2017)
21. Charwat, G., Dvořák, W., Gaggl, S.A., Wallner, J.P., Woltran, S.: Methods for solving reasoning problems in abstract argumentation-a survey. Artif. Intell. **220**, 28–63 (2015)
22. Corea, C., Thimm, M.: Using matrix exponentials for abstract argumentation. In: SAFA Workshop, pp. 10–21 (2016)
23. Dung, P.: On the acceptability of arguments and its fundamental role in nonmonotonic reasoning, logic programming and n-person games. Artif. Intell. **77**, 321–357 (1995)
24. Dvořák, W., Pichler, R., Woltran, S.: Towards fixed-parameter tractable algorithms for abstract argumentation. Artif. Intell. **186**, 1–37 (2012)
25. Kröll, M., Pichler, R., Woltran, S.: On the complexity of enumerating the extensions of abstract argumentation frameworks. In: IJCAI, pp. 1145–1152 (2017)
26. Lagniez, J.M., Lonca, E., Mailly, J.G.: CoQuiAAS v3.0. ICCMA 2019 Solver Description (2019)
27. Liao, B.: Toward incremental computation of argumentation semantics: a decomposition-based approach. Ann. Math. Artif. Intell. **67**(3–4), 319–358 (2013)
28. Liao, B., Huang, H.: Partial semantics of argumentation: basic properties and empirical. J. Logic Comput. **23**(3), 541–562 (2013)
29. Liao, B., Jin, L., Koons, R.C.: Dynamics of argumentation systems: a division-based method. Artif. Intell. **175**(11), 1790–1814 (2011)
30. Lloyd, S.: Least squares quantization in PCM. IEEE Trans. Inf. Theory **28**(2), 129–137 (1982)

31. Malliaros, F.D., Vazirgiannis, M.: Clustering and community detection in directed networks: a survey. Phys. Rep. **533**(4), 95–142 (2013)
32. Niskanen, A., Järvisal, M.: μ-toksia. Participating in ICCMA 2019 (2019)
33. Robert, M.K.: Elementary linear algebra. University of Queenland (2013)
34. Rodrigues, O., Black, E., Luck, M., Murphy, J.: On structural properties of argumentation frameworks: lessons from ICCMA. In: SAFA Workshop, pp. 22–35 (2018)
35. Schaeffer, S.E.: Graph clustering. Comput. Sci. Rev. **1**(1), 27–64 (2007)
36. Von Luxburg, U.: A tutorial on spectral clustering. Stat. Comput. **17**(4), 395–416 (2007)
37. Xu, Y., Cayrol, C.: Initial sets in abstract argumentation frameworks. J. Appl. Non-Classical Logics **28**(2–3), 260–279 (2018)

Dynamic Multi-Agent Systems: Conceptual Framework, Automata-Based Modelling and Verification

Rodica Condurache[1], Riccardo De Masellis[2(✉)], and Valentin Goranko[2,3]

[1] A. I. Cuza University of Iasi, Iaşi, Romania
rodica.b.condurache@gmail.com
[2] Stockholm University, Stockholm, Sweden
{riccardo.demasellis,valentin.goranko}@philosophy.su.se,
demasellis@gmail.com
[3] University of Johannesburg (visiting professorship),
Johannesburg, South Africa

Abstract. We study dynamic multi-agent systems (DMASs). These are multi-agent systems with explicitly dynamic features, where agents can join and leave the system during the evolution. We propose a general conceptual framework for modelling such DMASs and argue that it can adequately capture a variety of important and representative cases. We then present a concrete modelling framework for a large class of DMASs, composed in a modular way from agents specified by means of automata-based representations. We develop generic algorithms implementing the dynamic behaviour, namely addition and removal of agents in such systems. Lastly, we state and discuss several formal verification tasks that are specific for DMASs and propose general algorithmic solutions for the class of automata representable DMASs.

1 Introduction

A multi-agent system (MAS) comprises a set of agents acting and interacting in a common arena. Each agent is equipped with a set of available actions and all agents contribute with simultaneously performed actions, thus generating collectively action profiles causing state transitions in the system.

An overall objective in the area of formal methods for multi-agent systems (MASs), is to design frameworks for modelling of the structure and evolutions of such systems and to develop methods for algorithmic verification of properties of such abstract models specified in suitable formal (usually, logic-based) languages.

Traditionally, the set of agents in such frameworks – including the well-known concurrent game structures [2] and interpreted systems [6] – is assumed fixed during the system evolution. In many settings this is an essential limitation, as witnessed by the increasing interest in *parametric* MASs [1,5,10,12] where the set of agents is taken as a parameter and every instantiation of that parameter gives rise to a MAS. Parametric model-checking amounts to verifying a property

© Springer Nature Switzerland AG 2019
M. Baldoni et al. (Eds.): PRIMA 2019, LNAI 11873, pp. 106–122, 2019.
https://doi.org/10.1007/978-3-030-33792-6_7

irrespectively of the specific value of the parameter. However, even in this case, once the parameter is bound to a specific value, it does not change during the system evolution.

1.1 Our Contributions

In this work we take a step forward and consider truly *dynamic* MAS (DMASs), where agents can join and leave the system *during the evolution*. From a practical perspective, the dynamic feature naturally arises in many practical scenarios, such as: markets, where brokers joining and leaving the system dynamically impacts the price of goods and shares; sensor/computer networks where global properties of the network depends dynamically on the connections between components and the network topology; manufacturing [3], where adding/removing machines can enable or disable the capability of producing specific products; and others that we discuss further in the paper.

To the best of our knowledge, this is one of the first efforts to study and analyse such systems using formal methods. Thus, as a first main contribution, we present in detail a conceptual formalisation of DMASs. We believe that our framework is general enough to cover many scenarios and we provide several examples to support this claim. We note that, on the one hand, such a general framework provides a broad conceptual characterisation of DMASs, but on the other hand, such a generality makes it quite difficult to develop algorithmic procedures for them.

As a second main contribution, we ground the abstract modelling framework by proposing an automata-based approach for modelling DMASs and show how it provides automated procedures for adding and removing agents. We then providing concrete algorithms for implementing these dynamic features.

As a third main contribution, we formulate the main dynamic reasoning tasks that are specific for DMASs and propose general algorithmic solutions for the class of automata-representable DMASs.

1.2 Related Work

Our interest in parametric systems is mostly in the way they describe interactions among a bounded, but unknown, number of agents. Here we mention a few related works and lines of research.

Among the first works to consider verification of parametric systems is [1], where a counting abstraction is used and decidability of formal properties is achieved by using vector addition systems with states (VASS). In [12] strategic reasoning is considered but only for a restricted set of properties such as reachability, coverability and deadlock avoidance. In order to achieve decidability, assumptions on the system evolutions are made and, in particular, monotonicity with respect to a well-quasi-ordering. In [10] temporal epistemic properties on parameterized interpreted systems are checked irrespective on the number of agents by using cutoff techniques.

The idea of decoupling the interaction between agents from their internal evolution by means of signals/observations is inspired by modular interpreted systems [9], where however, no truly dynamic behaviour is considered, as the set of agents is fixed.

It is also worth mentioning the work in [3] where a sort of dynamic synthesis problem is solved: given a transducer representing a target behaviour to realize, and a set of transducer types, the output is the minimal number of actual transducers which, suitably (asynchronously) orchestrated, can realize the target behaviour. Another related work, though with different motivation and agenda, is [8] where *term-modal logics* are introduced for reasoning about systems with unspecified number of agents.

Other, more closely related works are discussed in Sect. 3.

2   Framework

This section is devoted to the formalization of a conceptual framework for dynamic MAS (DMAS). For the sake of readability, we first introduce the main components of a DMAS and defer its formal definition to the end of the section. Also, in order to illustrate the introduced concepts for the reader, we make use of a running example.

Example 1. Let us consider manufacturing plants [3] as dynamic multi-agent systems, where pieces of raw materials are processed by machines – the agents – and assembled in final products.

From a high-level perspective, we aim at providing a modular representation of agents in a DMAS, and we adapt concepts and terminology borrowed from object-oriented programming to our setting. To help the reader, we use different fonts to distinguish the introduced concepts.

- **Agent types** represent the abstract behavior of agents as autonomous and stand-alone entities, e.g., `robotManipulator` or `person`.
- *Agent roles* describe the part that an agent type could play within a DMAS, e.g., in the manufacturing plant agent type `robotManipulator` can play the role of a *roboticArm* with a laser as hand effector, or a the type `person` can play the role of *assemblyLineWorker*.
- **Agent instances** are actual concrete agents in a DMAS, characterized by a type, a role, and a unique identification, e.g., a `robotManipulator` in the role of a *roboticArm*, installed in a specific location of the plant.

We emphasize that an agent type is not a concrete agent, as it only describe the high-level features that agent instances of that type have. The same reasoning holds for agent roles. The conceptual difference between a type and a roles is that the former is not related to any specific DMAS, while the latter is DMAS-specific. Also, the same agent type (e.g., `person`) can play several roles depending on the DMAS it is employed in (e.g., *assemblyLineWorker* in the manufacturing plant or *trader* in a financial market) and vice-versa, the same role (*assemblyLineWorker*) can be performed by possibly different agent types (`robotManipulator` or `person`). Also, there may be several concrete instances of the same type and role, for example, several *roboticArms* in the plant. In the rest of the section we formalize such concepts.

2.1 Agent Types

Informally, an agent type describes the abstract behavior of an agent by itself, independently from the system it could be deployed in. Mathematically, it is akin to a Mealy machine, i.e. a finite state automaton, the transition function and outputs of which depends not only on its own actions, but also on the inputs, or *observations*, that come from the system in which it could be deployed to operate.

Definition 1 (Agent type).

$$T = \langle S_T, Act_T, avt_T, \mathcal{O}, \delta_T \rangle \ where:$$

- S_T *is a finite set of* internal *states;*
- Act_T *is a finite set of* action types;
- $avt_T : S_T \to 2^{Act_T} \setminus \emptyset$ *maps to each state a set of available action types;*
- $\mathcal{O}$ *is a set of* observations;
- $\delta_T : S_T \times Act_T \times \mathcal{O} \dashrightarrow S_T$ *is the partial transition function such that for each $s \in S_T$, $act \in avt_T(s)$ and $o \in \mathcal{O}$ we have that $\delta_T(s, act, o)$ is defined.*

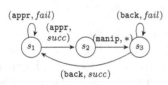

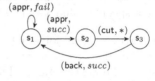

(a) Graphical representation of agent type robotManipulator.

(b) Graphical representation of the automaton instance of type robotManipulator with role *roboticArm* and parameter *handEffector* assigned to value *laser*.

Fig. 1. Graphical representation of an agent type and instance.

Example 2. Figure 1a shows a graphical representation of agent type robotManipulator. The circles are states and the transition function is rendered by arrows labeled with pairs (action, *observation*), where $*$ represent any value. The set of actions is $Act_T = \{appr, manip, back, noop\}$. Also, we assume a self-looping transition (noop, $*$) in any state, not represented in the picture for the sake of readability. The set of observations is $\mathcal{O} = \{fail, succ\}$. Intuitively, the abstract behavior of robotManipulator is as follows. In state s_1 it tries to reach for the object to manipulate by performing action appr. Its success in doing so depends on the system it is currently acting: if, e.g., the object is not available or there are obstacles in its path, then it observes *fail*, thus looping in s_1. If it observes *success*, then it successfully moves to s_2, where it can perform its (still abstract) action of manipulating the object. Finally, in state s_3 it goes back in its original position or not by performing action back depending on the observation, analogously to what happens in s_1.

We remark that observations are the interface with the external world and they allow to decouple the internal behavior of the agent from the possible events coming from the outside. To be more precise, we distinguish between *signals* that a DMAS produces, which will be formally defined later, and *observations* that agents have of signals coming from the other agents and the system. In other words, signals are global events that a DMAS generates while observations are the interpretation that agents have of signals. From now on, we denote by Σ the set of signals of a DMAS.

2.2   Agent Role, Agent Instances and Instance Creation Function

Unlike agent types, *roles* are conceptually related to a specific DMAS. Formally, a role is a set of parameter names $R = \{p_1, \ldots, p_m\}$, where each parameter can be thought as a characteristic element, or a feature, assigned to an agent in role R. As it will be shown later on, parameter names are assigned values when creating agent instances.

Example 3. In the manufacturing plant example, the role *roboticArm* is characterized by one parameter name only, *handEffector*. Any instance of *roboticArm* will have a specific value assigned to it, such as *laser* or *rotaryTool*.

When a new agent joins a DMAS, first an agent instance is created for it and then that instance is incorporated into the system. The latter operation is described in the next section, while here we focus on the former. The creation of the instance is an operation specific to each DMAS, called *instance creation function*: it takes as inputs a **type** T, a *role* R and an assignment β of values to parameters in R and returns an agent instance. An agent instance can be thought of as an automaton that *specializes* T. Indeed, there is a mapping between states of the automaton instance to states of the automaton type, and analogously for actions.

Definition 2. *An agent instance of type* $T = \langle S_T, Act_T, avt_T, \mathcal{O}, \delta_T \rangle$ *with role R and assignment β is an automaton:*

$$\mathsf{ag} = \langle \mathsf{S}, \mathsf{Act}, \alpha, \mathsf{avt}, \mathcal{O}, \mathsf{obs}, \delta \rangle \ \text{where:}$$

- S *is the set of local states;*
- Act *is the set of actions;*
- $\alpha : \mathsf{S} \cup \mathsf{Act} \to S_T \cup Act_T$ *is the abstraction function such that for each* $\mathsf{s} \in \mathsf{S}$ *we have* $\alpha(\mathsf{s}) \in S_T$ *and for each* $\mathsf{act} \in \mathsf{Act}$ *we have* $\alpha(\mathsf{act}) \in Act_T$;
- $\mathsf{avt} : \mathsf{S} \to 2^{\mathsf{Act}}$ *is consistent with* avt_T, *namely, for each* $\mathsf{act} \in \mathsf{Act}$ *and* $\mathsf{s} \in \mathsf{S}$, *if* $\mathsf{act} \in \mathsf{avt}(\mathsf{s})$, *then* $\alpha(\mathsf{act}) \in avt_T(\alpha(\mathsf{s}))$;
- $\mathsf{obs} : \mathsf{S} \times \Sigma \to \mathcal{O}$ *is the observation function, mapping local states and signals coming from the system to observations;*
- $\delta : \mathsf{S} \times \mathsf{Act} \times \mathcal{O} \dashrightarrow \mathsf{S}$ *it is such that:*
    - *it is defined for each available action in each state, namely for each* $\mathsf{s} \in \mathsf{S}$ *and* $\mathsf{act} \in \mathsf{avt}(\mathsf{s})$ *there exists* $o \in \mathcal{O}$ *such that* $\delta(\mathsf{s}, \mathsf{act}, o)$ *is defined;*

- *it is consistent with transition function δ_T through mapping α, viz. if $\delta(s, \mathsf{act}, o)$ is defined and equal to s', then $\delta_T(\alpha(s), \alpha(\mathsf{act}), o)$ is defined and equal to $\alpha(s')$.*

We remark that all components of an agent instance depend not only on the type, but also on the role and assignment. This is hidden in the definition because such a dependency is domain-specific and cannot, in general, be formally generalized.

Example 4. Figure 1b shows a graphical representation of the automaton instance of type `robotManipulator` with role *roboticArm* and parameter *handEffector* assigned to value *laser* in the DMAS manufacturing plant. The abstraction function is such that $\alpha(\mathsf{appr}) = \mathsf{appr}$, $\alpha(\mathsf{cut}) = \mathsf{manip}$ and $\alpha(\mathsf{back}) = \mathsf{back}$. We do not present here the whole observation function but we point out that, for each signal $\sigma \in \Sigma$, it is such that $\mathsf{obs}(\sigma, s_3) = success$. This is because robotic arms in the plant are placed in an obstacle-free area which makes the action of going back in the initial position always successful (as opposed to action `appr` that can fail if the object to manipulate is not present). For this reason, there is no $(\mathsf{loop}, fail)$ transition in state s_3. The diligent reader can easily verify that transition function δ satisfies the constraints of Definition 2.

We now have all the concepts needed to define a DMAS.

2.3   Dynamical Multi-Agent Systems

In a DMAS, agents can join and leave during the evolution. From a high-level perspective, at each time instant the system (global) state is characterized by the tuple of local states of the agent instances that are currently part of the system. At each step, either the instances concurrently perform an action that results in the system evolving in a new global state, or a single agent is added/removed to the system. In the first case, the step can be conceptually understood as a sequence of micro-steps:

1. each agent chooses and performs an action, thus generating an *action profile* π (formally defined later);
2. given π and the current global state, the system generates a signal σ;
3. the local state of each agent instance `ag` is updated according to the observation of σ and `ag`'s own action, which results in the new global state being computed.

When an agent is added, first its instance is generated by calling the system's *instance creation function* described before (by providing a type, a role, and an assignment of values to the role parameters) and then the instance is incorporated into the system by adding its initial state to the current global state. When an agent is removed from the system, its local state is simply removed from the system's global state.

There is a special agent instance in every DMAS that we call the *arena*: it is of type T_0 and role R_0 and it is *unique*, namely: there is only one instance of type T_0 with role R_0 in every DMAS; no other agent instances are of type T_0 or role R_0 and it cannot be removed, thus it is always present. In order to explain its purpose, let us consider the actual usage we intend to make of dynamic MAS, which is verifying formal properties. In a traditional MAS (global) system states are labeled with atomic propositions, but in our dynamic setting the states themselves are subject to change (as it will be clear later in this section) given that they depend on which, or how many, agents are currently present. Thus, the issue of how to express properties naturally arises, and we solve it by labelling the arena states with atomic propositions. The arena is like any other agent type and role but conceptually represents the ground where the agents play (or equivalently, the behavior of the fixed components that cannot be removed from the system). We note that such arena can be designed so as to incorporate properties that we are interested to check in a DMAS: it is sufficient to design specific arena states that are reached when the (un)desired conditions are met. E.g., in the factory example, we can model arena states that are reached whenever an agent instance fails an action, i.e., when it performs a transition with observation *fail*. Such a choice makes our framework suitable to model the effects that dynamic agents cause on the environment/arena they live in.

A DMAS $\mathfrak{D}$ has the following components:

- a set $\{T_0, T_1, \ldots, T_n\}$ of agent types;
- a set $\{R_0, R_1, \ldots, R_m\}$ of *roles*, where each R_i is a set of parameter names for $i \in \{0, \ldots, m\}$;
- a set of *domain* values for each parameter name;
- a finite set Σ of *signals*;
- a function sig mapping system (global) states and action profiles π to signals;
- an *instance creation function*;
- an *add protocol* add;
- a *remove protocol* rem.

We have already introduced the instance creation function: it takes a type T_j a role R_i and an assignment β for the parameters in R_i and produces an agent instance. More precisely, β assigns to each parameter in R_i a value from its domain. It remains to formalize the function sig and the add and remove protocols.

Signal Function. It intuitively defines the core behavior of the system as it tells which signals are produced for every possible joint action of the agent instances currently present in the system, regardless of how many they are and of which type and role. Given that the number of agent instances is unbounded, such a function is usually defined implicitly.

Let ST be the union of local states for every agent instance that may be present in the system. We note that such a set is finite and bounded by the number of roles, parameters and assignments. We denote $ST^n := ST \times \ldots \times ST$ (n times) and likewise ACT^n. The function sig^n outputs a signal for n agent instances in any state performing any action, as follows: $\text{sig}^n : ST^n \times ACT^n \dashrightarrow \Sigma$.

Lastly, we define $\mathsf{sig} := \bigcup_1^\infty \mathsf{sig}^n$ and with this definition at hand, we can now describe the behavior of a DMAS $\mathfrak{D}$ for a specific set of agent instances, which we call a *modular multi-agent structure* (MMAS).

Definition 3 (MMAS). *Let $\mathfrak{D}$ be a DMAS and let $\mathsf{Ag} = \langle \mathsf{ag}_0, \mathsf{ag}_1, \ldots, \mathsf{ag}_x \rangle$ be a tuple of agent instances where ag_0 is the arena and each $\mathsf{ag}_i \in \mathsf{Ag}$ is $\langle \mathsf{S}_i, \mathsf{Act}_i, \alpha_i, \mathsf{avt}_i, \mathcal{O}_i, \mathsf{obs}_i, \delta_i \rangle$. A modular multi-agent structure for $\mathfrak{D}$ with agents Ag is the tuple:*

$$\mathcal{G}_{\mathfrak{D}}(\mathsf{Ag}) = \langle Q, \Pi, \Delta \rangle \text{ where:}$$

- $Q \subseteq \mathsf{S}_0 \times \ldots \times \mathsf{S}_x$ *is the set of global states. Given a state $q \in Q$ we denote by $q(i)$ the state of agent ag_i.*
- $\Pi \subseteq \mathsf{Act}_0 \times \ldots \times \mathsf{Act}_x$. *An action profile for $q \in Q$ is any $\pi \in \Pi$ such that $\pi(i) \in \mathsf{avt}_i(q(i))$ for each $i \in \{0, \ldots, x\}$.*
- *Partial transition function $\Delta : Q \times \Pi \dashrightarrow Q$ is such that $\Delta(q, \pi)$ is defined and equal to q' iff:*
  - π *is an action profile for q and*
  - *for each $i \in \{1, \ldots, x\}$ the next state of agent ag_i is given by transition function δ_i from: ag_i current state $q(i)$; ag_i performed action $\pi(i)$ and from ag_i observation of the signal computed by sig function (which in turns depends on the whole current system state q and action profile π). Formally we have that $q'(i) = \delta_i(q(i), \pi(i), \mathsf{obs}_i(q(i), \mathsf{sig}(q, \pi)))$ for each $i \in \{1, \ldots, x\}$.*

Note how the evolution of the system is described by means of transition function Δ: the local state of each agent instance is updated according to its current local state, its action and the observation of the signal that is generated by the system, which in turn depends on the whole action profile.

We also remark that a modular multi-agent structure is parameterized by a tuple of agents Ag and thus it suffices to specify how to update such a tuple to handle the joining and leaving of agents. This is precisely the purpose of add and rem protocols.

Add and Remove Protocols. Let $\mathcal{G}_{\mathfrak{D}}(\mathsf{Ag})$ be a MMAS, the protocols define a new MMAS that is the result of adding/removing an agent to/from $\mathcal{G}_{\mathfrak{D}}(\mathsf{Ag})$. We remark that such protocols do not provide yet actual procedures for incorporating or removing an agent to an existing MMAS, as such procedures are domain-specific and may not be even computable, in general. In Sect. 4 we will be more concrete and will provide an actual algorithm for the add and rem protocols for a specific class of DMAS, namely those composed by using automata-based agent representation and techniques.

Definition 4 (Add protocol). *Let $\mathcal{G}_{\mathfrak{D}}(\mathsf{Ag})$ be a MMAS for a DMAS $\mathfrak{D}$ with $\mathsf{Ag} = \langle \mathsf{ag}_0, \ldots, \mathsf{ag}_x \rangle$ and let $q \in Q$ be the current state of $\mathcal{G}_{\mathfrak{D}}(\mathsf{Ag})$. The addition of agent instance $\mathsf{ag} \notin \mathsf{Ag}$ is defined by function:*

$$\mathsf{add}(\mathcal{G}_{\mathfrak{D}}(\mathsf{Ag}), q, \mathsf{ag}) \text{ which returns } (\mathcal{G}_{\mathfrak{D}}(\mathsf{Ag}) \oplus \mathsf{ag}, q') \text{ where:}$$

- $\mathcal{G}_{\mathfrak{D}}(\mathsf{Ag}) \oplus \mathsf{ag} = \mathcal{G}_{\mathfrak{D}}(\langle \mathsf{ag}_0, \ldots, \mathsf{ag}_x, \mathsf{ag} \rangle)$ *and*
- q' *is the new current state after the addition of* ag *and it is such that* $q'(i) = q(i)$ *for every* $i \in \{0, \ldots, x\}$.

Note that, in general, no constraint is put on the current state of the new agent after the addition. This is because such a state depends on the specific application, but intuitively, it functionally depends on q and ag.

Definition 5 (Remove protocol). *Let* $\mathcal{G}_{\mathfrak{D}}(\mathsf{Ag})$ *be a* MMAS *with* $\mathsf{Ag} = \langle \mathsf{ag}_0, \ldots, \mathsf{ag}_x \rangle$ *and let* $q \in Q$ *the current state of* $\mathcal{G}_{\mathfrak{D}}(\mathsf{Ag})$. *The removal of agent* $\mathsf{ag}_i \neq \mathsf{ag}_0$ *is defined by function*

$$\mathsf{rem}(\mathcal{G}_{\mathfrak{D}}(\mathsf{Ag}), q, \mathsf{ag}_i) \text{ which returns } (\mathcal{G}_{\mathfrak{D}}(\mathsf{Ag}) \ominus \mathsf{ag}_i, q') \text{ where:}$$

- $\mathcal{G}_{\mathfrak{D}}(\mathsf{Ag}) \ominus \mathsf{ag}_i = \mathcal{G}_{\mathfrak{D}}(\langle \mathsf{ag}_0, \ldots, \mathsf{ag}_{i-1}, \mathsf{ag}_{i+1}, \ldots, \mathsf{ag}_x \rangle)$ *and*
- q' *is the new current state after the removal of* ag_i *and it is obtained from* q *by dropping the element in position* i.

We note that if Ag and Ag' differ only on the order of agents, they still give rise to different $\mathcal{G}_{\mathfrak{D}}(\mathsf{Ag})$ and $\mathcal{G}_{\mathfrak{D}}(\mathsf{Ag}')$. However, since the behavior of a MMAS does not depend on the order of the agents, we say that $\mathcal{G}_{\mathfrak{D}}(\mathsf{Ag})$ and $\mathcal{G}_{\mathfrak{D}}(\mathsf{Ag}')$ are order-isomorphic iff Ag is a rearrangement of Ag' (we omit the details for lack of space). With such a notion at hand, we notice that the add and rem protocols enjoy the following property: for every set of agent instances Ag, every agent instance ag_1, ag_2 and every state $q \in Q$, adding an agent and then removing it results in the same MMAS: $\mathsf{rem}(\mathsf{add}(\mathcal{G}_{\mathfrak{D}}(\mathsf{Ag}), q, \mathsf{ag}_1), \mathsf{ag}_1) = (\mathcal{G}_{\mathfrak{D}}(\mathsf{Ag}), q)$.

3 Some Concrete Examples

In what follows we informally show how to model some existing frameworks as MMASs. The multi-agent systems that we model, although not all necessarily *dynamic*, are characterized by being parametric, namely systems whose evolution can be described symbolically regardless how many concrete agents are part of it. The purpose is solely to show the expressiveness of MMASs, therefore the translations are by no means efficient, nor unique.

*Homogeneous Dynamic Multi-Agent Systems (*HDMAS*).* We refer to the framework in [4], where homogeneity means that all agents have the same available actions at any given state and the actions have the same effects regardless of which agents perform them. The global state transitions are therefore determined only by the vector of numbers of agents performing each action and are specified symbolically, by means of conditions on these numbers, called *guards*. The internal states of the arena are the global states of the HDMAS. Conceptually, here the arena is passive, meaning that it does not perform actions. Technically, we allow for the same spurious action in every state. All agents are thus represented by the same agent type and the same agent role (with no parameters), i.e. the set of agents is homogeneous. The internal states of the agent type are again the global states of the HDMAS, whose action availability function follows from the HDMAS and so does the transition function. Signals and observations coincides. We have one for each guard and they are used to tell which guard is satisfied at each step. The global state of the MMAS is a tuple of agents states, but, being agent-homogeneous, such tuples are of the kind $\langle s, s, \ldots, s \rangle$, i.e., composed by the same state. The protocol for adding one agent appends one more element (the current state) to the tuple of the global states and updates the transitions to account for the new agent, according to the HDMAS transition function. The protocol for removing an agent takes no inputs and removes one state from the global MMAS state tuple and updates the transitions according to the HDMAS transition function, analogously to the addition.

*Open Multi-Agent Systems (*OMAS*)* [11]. These are dynamic MAS where agents can be added or removed during the system evolution by means of special transitions and their behaviour is described by means of automata similar to our agent types. At each time instant, the system is described by the tuple of local states of agents. However, we point out two main differences between OMAS and DMAS. The first concern the way the interaction between a possibly unbounded number of agents is achieved: in OMAS, agents evolutions depends on the projection of the joint action of all agents into a set rather than the joint action itself. Secondly, the (global) transition function of the whole system in OMAS is asynchronous, but synchronization between agents can be achieved by means of special actions. Each OMAS agent type can be modeled as a MMAS agent type. As the OMAS global transition function take into account only if every action has been performed by at least one agent, the corresponding MMAS transition function can be described with a finite number of signals and observations. The add, resp., rem protocols simply add, resp., remove, the agent local state from the tuple of global states.

Population Protocols [5]. These are homogeneous asynchronous systems where at each step only a pair of agents change state. The global transition relation thus comprises nondeterministically all possible interactions that can happen at each step among pairs of agents. As agents in a population are homogeneous, we need one agent type and one role only. We also equip the system with actions and signals to "resolve" the intrinsic nondeterminism of the protocol: at each step is the system that decides which pair of agents interact (and thus change state). In order to do so, however, each agent instance in a MMAS should be formally distinguishable, or otherwise the environment cannot specify *which* pair of agents change state (notice indeed that agent instances of the same type and role react to signals in the very same way). We can make agent instances distinguishable from each other by assigning for each of them different values to a special role parameter, although this requires an unbounded domain for that parameter whenever we want to model an unbounded number of agents to join/leave the system.

4   Automata-Based Representation

Here we use infinite word automata in order to model dynamic MMAS, following the general framework outlined in Sect. 2.

Definition 6. *A deterministic infinite word automaton is a tuple* $WA = \langle \Gamma, S, \gamma, Acc \rangle$ *where* Γ *is the input alphabet,* S *is the set of states,* $\gamma : S \times \Gamma \to S$ *is the transition function, and* Acc *is the accepting condition.*

For the chosen accepting condition, we denote by $\mathcal{L}(WA, s)$ the set of words accepted by the automaton WA starting from the state s. Here we consider Büchi accepting condition for the automata. We represent an agent as being a deterministic infinite word automaton as follows.

Let $\mathsf{ag} = \langle \mathsf{S}, \mathsf{Act}, \alpha, \mathsf{avt}, \mathcal{O}, \mathsf{obs}, \delta \rangle$ be an agent instance of type T, role R and assignment β. The interaction between the agent and the other agents in the system, as well as the arena, materialises in an infinite sequence of actions of the agent and observations over the signals sent by the system. Then, the automaton WA_{ag} corresponding to the agent ag is such that it accepts all words over actions and observations that describe possible interactions. That is, the alphabet of the automaton is $\Gamma = \mathsf{Act} \times \mathcal{O}$, $S = \mathsf{S} \cup \{\bot\}$ and γ is defined as

$$\gamma(\mathsf{s}, \mathsf{act} \cdot o) = \begin{cases} \delta(\mathsf{s}, \mathsf{act}, o) & \text{if } \mathsf{act} \in \mathsf{avt}(\mathsf{s}) \\ \bot & \text{otherwise} \end{cases}$$

and $\gamma(\bot, \mathsf{act} \cdot o) = \bot$ for any action act and observation o, where $\cdot$ denotes, from now on, the concatenation of two elements or tuples. The set of accepting states is $Acc = S \setminus \{\bot\} = \mathsf{S}$. Note that the state $\bot$ in the automaton mimics the fact that the agent ag played an unauthorized action.

Lemma 1. *The automaton* WA_{ag} *accepts exactly the paths in* ag.

Proof. Note that the transitions of WA_{ag} are equivalent to the ones in ag when the transition function in ag is defined, otherwise the sink state $\bot$ is reached. Therefore, since the accepting condition in WA_{ag} asks to not visit $\bot$ infinitely often, WA_{ag} accepts only executions corresponding to executions in ag.

4.1   Modular Multi-Agent Structures as Composition of Automata

Let $\mathfrak{D}$ be a dynamic MAS, $\mathsf{Ag} = \langle \mathsf{ag}_0, \mathsf{ag}_1, \ldots, \mathsf{ag}_x \rangle$ be a set of agent instances where ag_0 is the arena and each $\mathsf{ag}_i \in \mathsf{Ag}$ is $\langle S_i, \mathsf{Act}_i, \alpha_i, \mathsf{avt}_i, \mathcal{O}_i, \mathsf{obs}_i, \delta_i \rangle$. Let moreover $\mathcal{G}_{\mathfrak{D}}(\mathsf{Ag})$ the MMAS for Ag and $WA_i = \langle \Gamma_i, S_i, \gamma_i, Acc_i \rangle$ the word automaton for ag_i for $i \in \{1, \ldots, x\}$.

We model the MMAS $\mathcal{G}_{\mathfrak{D}}(\mathsf{Ag})$ by the synchronous composition of the automata WA_{ag_i} and we call the resulting automaton $WA_{\mathsf{Ag}} = \langle \Gamma, W, \gamma, Acc \rangle$. Note that $\mathcal{G}_{\mathfrak{D}}(\mathsf{Ag})$ is already by definition the synchronous (commutative) product of the agent instances ag from the set Ag of agents. Transitions are labelled with tuples of actions of the agent instances together with signals. Such signals are not only those generated by tuples of actions of agents in Ag, but they might be generated by other (longer) tuples of actions. This technical solution is used to solve the dynamic verification Problem 5 in Sect. 5. We therefore say that a signal σ is *compatible* with a state $w \in S_0 \times \ldots \times S_x$ and a tuple of actions $\pi \in \text{Act}_0 \times \ldots \times \text{Act}_x$ if there is some tuple $\pi' \in \text{ACT}^*$ such that $\sigma = \text{sig}(w, \pi \cdot \pi')$. Technically a state of WA_{Ag} is composed of local states of the agent instances together with symbol $\star$ when the state is reached by a signal generated by the currently present agents in Ag, or with symbol $+$ when the state is reached by a (compatible) signal generated when other agents are added. Also, if agent instances do not play available actions or the signal is not compatible with the current state and the actions played, then the next state in the automaton is the sink state $\bot$. In what follows, we use the usual notation $\pi(i)$ for the i-th component of the action profile. More precisely, $WA_{\text{Ag}} = \langle \Gamma, W, \gamma, Acc \rangle$ is defined as follows:

- alphabet $\Gamma = \text{Act}_0 \times \ldots \times \text{Act}_x \times \Sigma$ consisting of action profiles paired with signals;
- the set of states is $W = S_0 \times \ldots \times S_x \times \{\star, +\} \cup \{\bot\}$.
  States in W are denoted by $w \cdot c$, where $w \in S_0 \times \ldots \times S_x$, $w(i)$ is the i-th component of w and $c \in \{\star, +\}$.
- the transition function $\gamma : W \times \Gamma \rightarrow W$ is defined as follows:
  - $\gamma(\bot, \pi \cdot \sigma) = \bot$;
  - $\gamma(w \cdot c, \pi \cdot \sigma) = \bot$ if there exists $i \in \{0, \ldots, x\}$ such that $\gamma_i(w(i), \pi(i) \cdot \text{obs}_i(w(i), \sigma))) = \bot$ (instance ag_i is performing a non-available action) or σ is not compatible with w and π;
  - otherwise $\gamma(w \cdot c, \pi \cdot \sigma) = w' \cdot c'$ where $w'(i) = \gamma_i(w(i), \pi(i) \cdot \text{obs}_i(w(i), \sigma))$ for $i \in \{0, \ldots, x\}$ and $c' = \star$ if $c = \star$ and $\sigma = \text{sig}(w, \pi)$ and $c' = +$ otherwise;
- accepting set $Acc = W \setminus \{\bot\}$ consisting of all states but $\bot$.

A *run* in the automaton WA_{Ag} is a (infinite) sequence $\rho = (w_0 \cdot c_0)(\pi_0 \cdot \sigma_0)(w_1 \cdot c_1)(\pi_1 \cdot \sigma_1)(w_2 \cdot c_2)(\pi_2 \cdot \sigma_2) \ldots$ of states and actions and signals such that $c_0 = \star$ and $(w_{i+1} \cdot c_{i+1}) = \gamma(w_i \cdot c_i, \pi_i \cdot \sigma_i)$ for any $i \in \mathbb{N}$. It is then accepted if it visits infinitely often the states in Acc. That is, since the transitions in WA_{Ag} are such that, once in $\bot$ the automaton stays there, the run is accepted if it never visits the state $\bot$.

Adding Protocol. Let $WA_{\text{Ag}} = \langle \Gamma, W, \gamma, Acc \rangle$ be the automaton modelling the MMAS $\mathcal{G}_{\mathfrak{D}}(\text{Ag})$ for a given set of agents Ag, let $\overline{w} \cdot \star$ be a state in W, and let $WA_{\text{ag}} = \langle \Gamma, S, \gamma, Acc \rangle$ be the automaton for agent ag to be added to WA_{Ag}. The protocol for adding ag is then defined as: $\text{add}(WA_{\text{Ag}}, WA_{\text{ag}}, \overline{w} \cdot \star) = (WA'_{\text{Ag}+}, \overline{w}' \cdot \star)$ where $WA'_{\text{Ag}+} = \langle \Gamma', W', \gamma', Acc' \rangle$ is the new word automaton obtained after the addition of WA_{ag}, which intuitively is composed from the (old) word automaton WA_{Ag} by "attaching" to state $\overline{w} \cdot \star$ the word automaton $WA_{\text{Ag} \cup \{\text{ag}\}} = \langle \Gamma_{\text{Ag} \cup \{\text{ag}\}}, W_{\text{Ag} \cup \{\text{ag}\}}, \gamma_{\text{Ag} \cup \{\text{ag}\}}, Acc_{\text{Ag} \cup \{\text{ag}\}} \rangle$, that is, the automaton for agents $\text{Ag} \cup \{\text{ag}\}$. In other words, from state $\overline{w} \cdot \star$ the new automaton $WA'_{\text{Ag}+}$ "jumps" to $WA_{\text{Ag} \cup \{\text{ag}\}}$ in state $\overline{w}' \cdot \star$ and start behaving like it. The new current state $\overline{w}' = \overline{w} \cdot s$ is obtained by adding a state $s \in S$ of WA_{ag} to the old global state. Notice that the choice of the specific state s is up to the protocol itself, and depends on its inputs. More precisely, $WA'_{\mathsf{Ag}+} = \langle \Gamma', W', \gamma', Acc' \rangle$ where:

- $\Gamma' = \Gamma \cup \Gamma_{\mathsf{Ag} \cup \{\mathsf{ag}\}}$;
- $W' = W \cup W_{\mathsf{Ag} \cup \{\mathsf{ag}\}}$;
- $\gamma' : (W \cup W_{\mathsf{Ag} \cup \{\mathsf{ag}\}}) \times (\Gamma \cup \Gamma_{\mathsf{Ag} \cup \{\mathsf{ag}\}}) \rightarrow (W \cup W_{\mathsf{Ag} \cup \{\mathsf{ag}\}})$ is such that:
  - $\gamma'(w \cdot c, \pi \cdot \sigma) = \gamma(w \cdot c, \pi \cdot \sigma)$ for each w in W and every $\pi \cdot \sigma \in \Gamma$ such that $\gamma(w \cdot c, \pi \cdot \sigma) \neq \overline{w} \cdot \star$;
  - $\gamma'(w \cdot c, \pi \cdot \sigma) = \overline{w}' \cdot \star$ for each w in W and every $\pi \cdot \sigma \in \Gamma$ such that $\gamma(w \cdot c, \pi \cdot \sigma) = \overline{w} \cdot \star$;
  - $\gamma'(w \cdot c, \pi \cdot \sigma) = \gamma(w \cdot c, \pi \cdot \sigma)$ for each w in $W_{\mathsf{Ag} \cup \{\mathsf{ag}\}}$ and every $\pi \cdot \sigma \in \Gamma$.
- $Acc' = WA'_{\mathsf{Ag}+} \setminus \{\bot\}$.

Intuitively, the jump into the automaton $WA_{\mathsf{Ag} \cup \{\mathsf{ag}\}}$ is modelled by identifying states $\overline{w} \cdot \star$ and $\overline{w}' \cdot \star$ and defining the transitions at that merged state so that the incoming ones are those for state $\overline{w} \cdot \star$ in the automaton WA_{Ag} and the outgoing transitions are those from the state $\overline{w}' \cdot \star$ in $WA_{\mathsf{Ag} \cup \{\mathsf{ag}\}}$.

Removing Protocol. The removing protocol is modelled here by projecting away the state of the removed agent ag. Formally, we define the function $\mathsf{rem}(WA_{\mathsf{Ag}}, \mathsf{ag}, \overline{w} \cdot \star) = (WA'_{\mathsf{Ag}-}, \overline{w}' \cdot \star)$ where, analogously as before, $WA'_{\mathsf{Ag}-}$ is composed from the old automaton WA_{Ag} where we attach to state $\overline{w} \cdot \star$ the word automaton $WA_{\mathsf{Ag} \setminus \{\mathsf{ag}\}}$. Intuitively, $WA'_{\mathsf{Ag}-}$ behaves like WA_{Ag} until state $\overline{w} \cdot \star$ is reached, and then it "jumps" to $WA_{\mathsf{Ag} \setminus \{\mathsf{ag}\}}$ in state $\overline{w}' \cdot \star$ and start behaving like it. More precisely, $WA'_{\mathsf{Ag}-} = \langle \Gamma', W', \gamma', Acc' \rangle$ where:

- $\Gamma' = \Gamma \cup \Gamma_{\mathsf{Ag} \setminus \{\mathsf{ag}\}}$;
- $W' = W \cup W_{\mathsf{Ag} \setminus \{\mathsf{ag}\}}$;
- $\gamma' : (W \cup W_{\mathsf{Ag} \setminus \{\mathsf{ag}\}}) \times (\Gamma \cup \Gamma_{\mathsf{Ag} \setminus \{\mathsf{ag}\}}) \rightarrow (W \cup W_{\mathsf{Ag} \setminus \{\mathsf{ag}\}})$ is such that:
  - $\gamma'(w \cdot c, \pi \cdot \sigma) = \gamma(w \cdot c, \pi \cdot \sigma)$ for each w in W and every $\pi \cdot \sigma \in \Gamma$ such that $\gamma(w \cdot c, \pi \cdot \sigma) \neq \overline{w} \cdot \star$;
  - $\gamma'(w \cdot c, \pi \cdot \sigma) = \overline{w}' \cdot \star$ for each w in W and every $\pi \cdot \sigma \in \Gamma$ such that $\gamma(w \cdot c, \pi \cdot \sigma) = \overline{w} \cdot \star$;
  - $\gamma'(w \cdot c, \pi \cdot \sigma) = \gamma_{\mathsf{Ag} \setminus \{\mathsf{ag}\}}(w \cdot c, \pi \cdot \sigma)$ for each $w \in W_{\mathsf{Ag} \setminus \{\mathsf{ag}\}}$ and every $\pi \cdot \sigma \in \Gamma_{\mathsf{Ag} \setminus \{\mathsf{ag}\}}$;
- $Acc' = WA'_{\mathsf{Ag}-} \setminus \{\bot\}$.

5   Dynamic Verification of MMASs

Modelling dynamic multi-agent systems using automata enables us to solve some relevant and important decision problems that arise in the context of MMASs in a uniform way. Here we state and sketch solutions for the most important ones. All these problems can be solved using automata and game theory approaches. In what follows, we assume properties to be expressed in Linear-time Temporal Logic (LTL) where the atomic propositions are labels on the arena states, given that it is the only agent instance that is always present and never removed.

A classical verification problem is the one asking whether any interaction of the agents present in the model satisfies some required property:

Problem 1 (Verification). Let $\mathcal{G}_{\mathfrak{D}}(\mathsf{Ag})$ be a MMAS. Does the MMAS $\mathcal{G}_{\mathfrak{D}}(\mathsf{Ag})$ satisfy the property φ at a state q?

Problem 1 was already studied and proved to be solvable in PSPACE [13], thus the same technique can be used here by considering only states of $\mathcal{G}_{\mathfrak{D}}(\mathsf{Ag})$ marked with $\star$. In the following, we introduce some problems that are related to the changes that may appear in a MMAS when agents leave or new agents join.

5.1   Addition of Agents

Problem 2 (Verification of additions of agents). Let $\mathcal{G}_{\mathfrak{D}}(\mathsf{Ag})$ be a MMAS with its current state q and $\mathsf{ag} \notin \mathsf{Ag}$ be an agent instance. Does the addition of the agent ag in $\mathcal{G}_{\mathfrak{D}}(\mathsf{Ag})$ at the current state satisfy the property φ?

Theorem 1. *There is an algorithm that solves Problem 2 for all LTL properties in* ExpTime.

Proof. The problem is solved using the automata approach outlined here as follows. First, we build the automata WA_{Ag} and WA_{ag} for $\mathcal{G}_{\mathfrak{D}}(\mathsf{Ag})$ and ag and then apply the function add to compute the automaton $WA'_{\mathsf{Ag}+}$ and its current state $\overline{w}' \bullet \star$. Also, we set the accepting states for $WA'_{\mathsf{Ag}+}$ as being all states $w \bullet \star$ with $w \in W'$. That is, we only accept executions that correspond to the interaction of agents in the set Ag and call those "good" executions. Then, the problem is reduced to verifying whether $\mathcal{L}(WA'_{\mathsf{Ag}+}, \overline{w}' \bullet \star) \subseteq \mathcal{L}(\varphi)$ holds. The automaton $WA'_{\mathsf{Ag}+}$ has a size polynomial in the size of the input. However, the verification of the LTL formula φ on all "good" executions takes ExpTime.   □

Problem 3 (Existence of an agent satisfying a requirement). Let $\mathcal{G}_{\mathfrak{D}}(\mathsf{Ag})$ be the MMAS for $\mathfrak{D}$ and agents Ag. Is there an agent $\mathsf{a} \notin \mathsf{Ag}$ such that its addition in the current state $w \bullet \star$ of the MMAS $\mathcal{G}_{\mathfrak{D}}(\mathsf{Ag})$ guarantees the property φ?

Theorem 2. *There is an algorithm that solves Problem 3 for all LTL properties in* NExpTime.

Proof. There is a nondeterministic algorithm that guesses an agent type T, a role R, and an assignment β, such that for the resulting agent ag we can answer positively Problem 2. Note that, since the set of allowed types, roles, and domains are fixed in the DMAS $\mathfrak{D}$, when the domains are finite there is a finite number of agent instances that may be added to $\mathcal{G}_{\mathfrak{D}}(\mathsf{Ag})$. The complexity bound is a consequence of the nondeterministic choice and the verification in exponential time.   □

Problem 4 (Satisfiability of a property after addition of an agent). Let $\mathcal{G}_{\mathfrak{D}}(\mathsf{Ag})$ be the MMAS for $\mathfrak{D}$ and agents Ag. Is there a state in the MMAS WA_{Ag} and an agent $\mathsf{a} \notin \mathsf{Ag}$ such that the agents in $\mathsf{Ag} \cup \{\mathsf{a}\}$ can cooperate and ensure φ in the resulting MMAS?

Theorem 3. *There is an algorithm that solves Problem 4 for all LTL properties in* NExpTime.

Proof. The nondeterministic algorithm first guesses an agent instance (an agent type, a role, and an assignment) and a state s in WA_{Ag}, then it builds the automaton corresponding to the addition of the chosen agent, then guess a path in the resulting automaton and, finally, verifies in ExpTime that it satisfy the LTL condition.

Problem 5 (Stability). Let $\mathcal{G}_{\mathfrak{D}}(Ag)$ be the MMAS for $\mathfrak{D}$ and agents Ag. Can the agents in Ag ensure φ whenever an arbitrary number of agents of any type and role are added to the MMAS?

Theorem 4. *There is an algorithm that solves Problem 5 for all LTL properties in* 2ExpTime.

Proof. Solving Problem 5 can be reduced to solving a two-players game between a constructor and a spoiler on WA_{Ag}. The constructor proposes actions of the agents and spoiler plays signals. We remark that the spoiler in any state $w \cdot c$ can play signals that leads to a state marked with $+$, say $w' \cdot +$. This intuitively means that there exist agents which, added in $w \cdot c$, can perform actions leading to $w' \cdot +$. The objective of the constructor is therefore to play a strategy profile for the players in Ag such that for any actions of the spoiler, the state $\perp$ is never reached and the LTL formula is satisfied. Note, that this problem is equivalent to LTL synthesis for the agents in Ag against an environment where the objective is $\varphi \wedge \Box\neg$ff, where φ is the LTL formula given as input, $\Box$ is the "always" modality, and the property ff is true only in the state $\perp$. This problem is solved in 2ExpTime.

5.2   Removal of Agents

Problem 6 (Verification of removals of agents). Let $\mathcal{G}_{\mathfrak{D}}(Ag)$ be the MMAS for $\mathfrak{D}$ and agents Ag. Does the removal of agent $a \in Ag$ from the MMAS WA_{Ag} at its current state ensure the truth of formula φ at that state?

Theorem 5. *There is an algorithm that solves Problem 6 for LTL properties in* ExpTime.

Proof. The algorithm runs as follows: first it builds the automaton for the system and then verifies in ExpTime that all its executions satisfy the LTL formula.

Problem 7 (Satisfiability of a property after removal of an agent). Let $\mathcal{G}_{\mathfrak{D}}(Ag)$ be the MMAS for $\mathfrak{D}$ and agents Ag. Is there a state in WA_{Ag} and an agent $a \in Ag$ such that its removal from that state guarantees the property φ?

Theorem 6. *There is an algorithm that solves Problem 7 for LTL properties in* NExpTime.

Proof. The algorithm guesses the state in WA_{Ag} and the agent to be removed. Then, after building the automaton corresponding to the removal of the chosen agent, it verifies if all paths in it verify the LTL property φ.

6   Concluding Remarks

In this work we propose DMAS, a conceptual framework for modeling dynamic MAS the main features of which are being modular and automata-based. The latter enables using techniques and results from automata-based verification. We argue that DMASs are expressive enough to capture a wide range of scenarios and other frameworks in literature. However, we note that not all types of multi-agent systems can be modeled as DMASs. For instance, concurrent game structures (CGS), not being modular, make the removal of agents not generally implementable. Also, in dynamic reactive modules [7] the available actions of a module m depend not only on the state of variables of m, but also on the state of the variables of any other module m' to which m has access. Therefore, the behavior of m modeled as an agent instance may become undefined when module m' is removed, as DMASs do not feature a dynamic "availability function" of actions. Extending our framework to cover such cases is left for future work.

Acknowledgements. The work of Valentin Goranko and Riccardo De Masellis was supported by a research grant 2015-04388 of the Swedish Research Council.

We thank the reviewers for some helpful comments and suggestions.

References

1. Bloem, R., et al.: Decidability in parameterized verification. SIGACT News **47**(2), 53–64 (2016)
2. Bulling, N., Goranko, V., Jamroga, W.: Logics for reasoning about strategic abilities in multi-player games. In: Models of Strategic Reasoning: Logics, Games, and Communities, pp. 93–136 (2015)
3. De Giacomo, G., Vardi, M., Felli, P., Alechina, N., Logan, B.: Synthesis of orchestrations of transducers for manufacturing. In: Proceedings of the AAAI 2018, pp. 6161–6168 (2018)
4. De Masellis, R., Goranko, V.: Logic-based specification and verification of homogeneous dynamic multi-agent systems. arXiv:1905.00810 [cs.LO] (2019)
5. Esparza, J., Ganty, P., Leroux, J., Majumdar, R.: Model checking population protocols. In: 36th IARCS Annual Conference on FSTTCS, pp. 27:1–27:14 (2016)
6. Fagin, R., Halpern, J., Moses, Y., Vardi, M.: Reasoning about Knowledge. MIT Press, Cambridge (1995)
7. Fisher, J., Henzinger, T.A., Nickovic, D., Piterman, N., Singh, A.V., Vardi, M.Y.: Dynamic reactive modules. In: Katoen, J.-P., König, B. (eds.) CONCUR 2011. LNCS, vol. 6901, pp. 404–418. Springer, Heidelberg (2011). https://doi.org/10.1007/978-3-642-23217-6_27
8. Fitting, M., Thalmann, L., Voronkov, A.: Term-modal logics. Stud. Logica. **69**(1), 133–169 (2001)
9. Jamroga, W., Ågotnes, T.: Modular interpreted systems. In: Proceedings of AAMAS, pp. 131:1–131:8. ACM (2007)
10. Kouvaros, P., Lomuscio, A.: Parameterised verification for multi-agent systems. Artif. Intell. **234**, 152–189 (2016)
11. Kouvaros, P., Lomuscio, A., Pirovano, E., Punchihewa, H.: Formal verification of open multi-agent systems. In: Proceedings of AAMAS 2019, pp. 179–187 (2019)

12. Raskin, J., Samuelides, M., Van Begin, L.: Games for counting abstractions. Electr. Notes Theor. Comput. Sci. **128**(6), 69–85 (2005)
13. Sistla, A.P., Clarke, E.M.: The complexity of propositional linear temporal logics. J. ACM **32**(3), 733–749 (1985)

Usefulness of Information for Goal Achievement

Laurence Cholvy[1] and Célia da Costa Pereira[2(✉)]

[1] ONERA, Toulouse, France
Laurence.Cholvy@onera.fr
[2] Université Côte d'Azur, CNRS, I3S Lab., Sophia Antipolis, France
Celia.DA-COSTA-PEREIRA@univ-cotedazur.fr

Abstract. This paper focuses on modelling information usefulness. More precisely, it aims at characterizing how useful a piece of information is for a cognitive agent which has some beliefs and goals. The paper presents three different approaches. We take Information Retrieval as a particular application domain and we compare some existing measures with the usefulness measure introduced in the paper.

1 Introduction

Usefulness is a ubiquitous notion. For instance, in Data Mining, evaluating the interest of the extracted knowledge is necessary [9]; in Natural Language Processing, identifying useful terminology [19] is a prerequisite to any analysis. In Social Science, studying how people achieve effective conversational communication in common social situations is needed. Grice [10], introduced the maxim of quantity which emphasizes the fact that a speaker contribution must be as informative as required for the current purposes of the exchange, but not more informative. In the database domain, taking the goals and the preferences of the user who asks a query is necessary for generating cooperative answers [12]. In Information Retrieval (IR), the aim is to take into account a query expressed by a user and provide documents which best suit the user need i.e., which are the most useful ones. Initially, the *topical relevance* approach considered that relevant documents are those whose topics best match the topics of the user query [11]. This led to the *aboutness* measure. Then, other dimensions have been considered: *coverage*, which measures how strongly the user interests are included in a document [13]; *appropriateness*, which measures how suitable a document is with respect to the user interests [8]; and *novelty*, which measures how novel is the document with respect to what the system has already proposed to the user [4]. However, the user who asks a query is a cognitive agent [7,14]: he/she has some goals to achieve and he/she has some beliefs about the world.

C. da Costa Pereira—Acknowledges support of the PEPS AIRINFO project funded by the CNRS. This work has been carried out during her visit at the ONERA center of Toulouse.

M. Baldoni et al. (Eds.): PRIMA 2019, LNAI 11873, pp. 123–137, 2019.
https://doi.org/10.1007/978-3-030-33792-6_8

Moreover, these beliefs are generally incomplete and the user asks queries to the system in order to get new information which will help him/her achieve his/her goals.

In the present work, we consider a general framework in which there are two cognitive agents: one is the user who has some beliefs and some goals modelled as propositional formulas; the second is the system. The latter has some beliefs about the user's beliefs and goals. Its goal is to provide the user with information which is the most useful for him/her to achieve his/her own goals. This framework is general enough to model the paradigm of cooperative exchanges with a system (a speaker, a database, the search engine) who answers the query expressed by the user (the listener, the database user, the web user...) in which the system has to provide the most useful information to the user. Defining the concept of information usefulness in such a context is the main aim of this paper. More precisely, we take the system point of view and try to characterize how useful a piece of information can be for the user.

The paper is organised as follows. In Sect. 2 we give some preliminaries and state our working hypotheses. In Sects. 3, 4 and 5 we propose three different definitions of information usefulness, respectively called binary, ordinal and numerical. In Sect. 6, we consider the particular case of Information Retrieval and compares some measures defined there with ours. Some concluding remarks are given in Sect. 7.

2   Preliminaries

We consider a propositional language L of which a subset, L_G, is the language used to represent the goals. We consider an agent a with a goal set G_a, which is a finite set of positive literals from L_G. For example, *finish the state of the art of my article, prepare for Monday's class*. Moreover, agent a has a belief base B_a composed of two subsets B_a^m and B_a^g. B_a^m is the set of formulas from $L \setminus L_G$ which represents a's beliefs. For example, *I know modal logic* and *I know the Python language*. B_a^g contains as many formulas $l_g^1 \wedge \ldots \wedge l_g^{m_g} \to g$, where each l_g^i is a positive literal of $L \setminus L_G$, as there are $g \in G_a$. Such formulas represent the beliefs of a about what is needed to achieve its goals. For example, *to finish the state of the art (g) I need knowledge about modal logic (p) and BDI agents (q)* (i.e., $p \wedge q \to g$). The conjunction $l_g^1 \wedge \ldots \wedge l_g^{m_g}$ is called *premise* of g and it is noted $premise(g)$. Notice that, according to the previous assumptions, we consider that the agent knows how to achieve its goals (in G_a)—the agent knows which are the pieces of information it needs to achieve its goals. This means that the goals for which the agent does not know the information necessary to achieve them are not considered.

Definition 1. *Let C and C' be two conjunctions of literals. C is included in C', noted $C \subseteq C'$, iff all the literals of C are literals of C'. C is equal to C', noted $C = C'$, iff the literals of C are exactly the same as the literals of C'. The result of the intersection between C and C', noted $C \cap C'$, contains literals which are* *both in C and in C'. The result of the difference between C and C', noted $C \backslash C'$, contains literals which are in C but not in C'. The cardinality of a conjunction of literals C, noted $|C|$, corresponds to the number of literals in C.*

Definition 2. *Let S and S' be two sets of conjunctions of positive literals. $S \preceq^1 S'$ iff (i) $|S| \le |S'|$ and (ii) if $|S| = |S'|$ then there is a bijection $f : S \to S'$ such that: $\forall \psi \in S$ $\psi \subseteq f(\psi)$. $S \prec^1 S'$ iff $S \preceq^1 S'$ and $S' \not\preceq^1 S$.*

Definition 3. *Let S and S' be two sets of conjunctions of positive literals. $S \preceq^2 S'$ iff (i) $|S| \le |S'|$ and (ii) if $|S| = |S'|$ then there is a bijection $f : S \to S'$ such that: $\forall \psi \in S$ $|\psi| \le |f(\psi)|$. $S \prec^2 S'$ iff $S \preceq^2 S'$ and $S' \not\preceq^2 S$.*

Thus $S \preceq^1 S'$ (resp., $S \preceq^2 S'$) iff S does not have more elements than S'; if S and S' have the same number of elements, then the conjunctions in S are included in the conjunctions of S' (resp., are shorter than those of S'). Notice that $\preceq^1$ is a preorder but it is not total. Some sets of conjunctions are incomparable, such as $\{p, q \wedge r\} \not\preceq^1 \{r, s\}$ and $\{r, s\} \not\preceq^1 \{p, q \wedge r\}$. $\preceq^2$ is a total preorder.

Lemma 1. [1] *Let S and S' be two sets of conjunctions of positive literals.*

- *If $S \preceq^1 S'$ then $S \preceq^2 S'$*
- *If $S \preceq^1 S'$ and $S' \preceq^1 S$ then $S = S'$*
- *If $S \preceq^2 S'$ and $S' \preceq^2 S$ then $S = S'$*
- *$S \prec^1 S'$ iff (i) $|S| < |S'|$ or (ii) $|S| = |S'|$ and there is a bijection $f : S \to S'$ such that $\forall \psi \in S$ $\psi \subseteq f(\psi)$ and $\exists \psi_0 \in S$ $\psi_0 \subset f(\psi_0)$.*
- *$S \prec^2 S'$ iff (i) $|S| < |S'|$ or (ii) $|S| = |S'|$ and there is a bijection $f : S \to S'$ such that $\forall \psi \in S$ $|\psi| \le |f(\psi)|$ and $\exists \psi_0 \in S$ $|\psi_0| < |f(\psi_0)|$.*

Definition 4 (Missing Information). *Let a be an agent with its belief base B_a and its goal set G_a. Let $g \in G_a$ be such that $B_a \not\models g$. $Missing(B_a, g)$, is defined as follows:*

$$Missing(B_a, g) = \bigwedge_{l : l \in premise(g) \text{ and } B_a \not\models l} l$$

$Missing(B_a, g)$ is the conjunction of all the literals in the premise of g which cannot be deduced from B_a (i.e., which are not yet believed by the agent). Therefore, in the particular case in which $B_a^m = \emptyset$, $Missing(B_a, g) = premise(g)$, i.e., the missing piece of information to achieve g is $premise(g)$.

Notice that the notion of missing information is defined only for the goals that are not already achieved (i.e, goals such that $B_a \not\models g$). A missing information associated to a goal is then the conjunction of all the literals representing the information need to achieve that goal (not yet achieved), and only these ones. Moreover, we would like to stress out that, according to Definition 4, the formula whose conclusion is g can be written as: $Missing(B_a, g) \wedge \psi_{B_a,g} \to g$ with $\psi_{B_a,g} \in L \setminus L_G$, $B_a \models \psi_{B_a,g}$ and $B_a \not\models Missing(B_a, g)$.

---

[1] Proofs are omitted due to length limitation.

Proposition 1.

- *Let $\varphi \in L \setminus L_G$ be a formula and $g \in G_a$ be a goal of agent a. We have that $Missing(B_a \cup \varphi, g) \subseteq Missing(B_a, g)$.*
- *If $\psi \models \varphi$ then $Missing(B_a \cup \psi, g) \subseteq Missing(B_a \cup \varphi, g)$.*
- *Let $\varphi_1 \in L \setminus L_G$, $\varphi_2 \in L \setminus L_G$ be two formulas and $g \in G_a$ be a goal of agent a. We have that $Missing(B_a \cup (\varphi_1 \wedge \varphi_2), g) = Missing((B_a \cup \varphi_1) \cup \varphi_2), g)$.*

Definition 5 (Multiset of missing information). *Let a be an agent whose belief base is B_a and whose goal set is G_a. The multiset[2] of missing information to achieve the goals in G_a is: $Missing(B_a, G_a) = \{Missing(B_a, g_1), \ldots, Missing(B_a, g_k)\}$ with $\{g_1, \ldots, g_k\} = \{g_i \in G_a \text{ and } B_a \not\models g_i\}$.*

There is therefore as much missing information as there are unachieved goals, i.e., the cardinality of $Missing(B_a, G_a)$ corresponds to the number of goals that are not yet achieved. Actually, we would like to take into account the weight of the missing information and not only the number of missing information.

Example 1. Let us consider a propositional language whose letters are: p, q, r, g_1 and g_2 respectively meaning "I know the main papers about modal logic", "I know the main papers about BDI agents", "I know the Python language", "I can start writing the state of the art" and "My Monday's class is prepared". Let us consider $G_a = \{g_1, g_2\}$ and $B_a = \{p\} \cup \{p \wedge q \rightarrow g_1, r \rightarrow g_2\}$. We have that, $Missing(B_a, g_1) = q$, $Missing(B_a, g_2) = r$ and therefore, $Missing(B_a, G_a) = \{q, r\}$. This means that, in order to achieve its goals, the agent lacks knowledge about BDI agents and about the Python language.

The following proposition shows that adding a belief to the belief base B_a does not increase the number of missing conjunctions. Moreover, if this does not reduce it either, then it does not increase their size. Finally, if adding a belief to the belief base B_a reduces the number of missing conjunctions, then this means that such new belief allows to achieve one or more goals.

Proposition 2. *For all formula (piece of information) $\varphi \in L \setminus L_G$, we have:*

- *$|Missing(B_a \cup \varphi, G_a)| \leq |Missing(B_a, G_a)|$.*
- *$\forall \varphi$ if $|Missing(B_a \cup \varphi, G_a)| = |Missing(B_a, G_a)|$ then there is a bijection $f : Missing(B_a \cup \varphi, G_a) \rightarrow Missing(B_a, G_a)$ such that $\forall \psi \in Missing(B_a \cup \varphi, G_a)$ $\psi \subseteq f(\psi)$.*
- *If $|Missing(B_a \cup \varphi, G_a)| < |Missing(B_a, G_a)|$ then $\exists G_i \in G_a$ such that $Missing(B_a, g_i) \in Missing(B_a, G_a)$ and $B_a \cup \varphi \models g_i$.*

3   A Binary Approach

In this section, we characterize useful information for an agent in view of achieving its goals in two different ways. According to this binary approach, a piece of information is useful or not.

---

[2] Reminder: a multiset is a set whose elements can have several occurrences, such as $\{p, q, p\}$.

Definition 6. *Let a be an agent with its belief base B_a and its set of goals G_a. Formula $\varphi \in L \setminus L_G$ is U^1-useful for agent a iff $Missing(B_a \cup \varphi, G_a) \prec^1 Missing(B_a, G_a)$. We use the notation $U^1_{G_a, B_a}\varphi$ or, more simply, $U^1\varphi$, when there is no ambiguity.*

According to this definition, a formula φ in $L \setminus L_G$ is useful for a in view of achieving its goals G_a iff being aware of φ allows a to reduce its information need either by reducing the number of missing conjunctions or by simplifying them. Restricting useful information to formulas of $L \setminus L_G$ only amounts (i) to restrict to information the agent must acquire in order to achieve its goals and (ii) to rule out the fact that a goal can be achieved by a other than through the acquisition of information recommended in the formulas whose aims are the conclusions.

Definition 7. *Let a be an agent with its belief base B_a and its goals G_a. The formula $\varphi \in L \setminus L_G$ is U^2-useful for a iff $Missing(B_a \cup \varphi, G_a) \prec^2 Missing(B_a, G_a)$. We use the notation $U^2_{G_a, B_a}\varphi$ or $U^2\varphi$ when there is no ambiguity.*

According to this second definition, a formula φ of $L \setminus L_G$ is U^2-useful for a if knowing φ allows a to reduce its information need either by reducing the number of missing conjunctions or by reducing their size. However, the two previous definitions, based on different pre-orders, are equivalent as shown by the following proposition.

Proposition 3.
$$U^1\varphi \iff U^2\varphi.$$

Since $U^1\varphi$ and $U^2\varphi$ are equivalent, we will use just $U\varphi$ to denote both.

Example 2. **Example 1 (continued).** $Missing(B_a, G_a) = \{q, r\}$. $Missing(B_a \cup \{r\}, G_a) = \{q\}$. $Missing(B_a \cup \{q\}, G_a) = \{r\}$. $Missing(B_a \cup \{q \wedge r\}, G_a) = \emptyset$. Therefore, Ur, Uq and $U(q \wedge r)$. In addition, if x is a propositional letter of the language, we have $U(r \wedge x)$ which means that $r \wedge x$ is useful. Indeed, *knowing Python and Java* is useful for the agent because it allows the agent to achieve G_2.

The last remark in this example shows a limitation of this binary model. Indeed, r is useful and so is $r \wedge x$ because, like r, it reduces the agent's need for information. However, this could be questionable because $r \wedge x$ contains x, which does not result in reducing the agent's need for information. In other words, reading a document on Python and Java, certainly allows the agent to acquire useful information about Python to prepare the class, but leads the agent to read content about Java, not useful for achieving its goals. This limitation is emphasized by the following proposition.

Proposition 4. *Let φ_1 and φ_2 be two formulas of $L \setminus L_G$. If $U\varphi_1$ then $U(\varphi_1 \wedge \varphi_2)$.*

Some more results are given below.

Proposition 5.

- If φ is not useful then $Missing(B_a \cup \varphi, G_a) = Missing(B_a, G_a)$.
- If $\exists \psi \in Missing(B_a, G_a)$ such that $\varphi \models \psi$ then $U\varphi$.
- $\exists \varphi \; U\varphi \not\Rightarrow Missing(B_a, G_a) \models \varphi$.
- $\exists \varphi \; Missing(B_a, G_a) \models \varphi \not\Rightarrow U\varphi$.

The first point of this proposition shows that adding unnecessary information to the agent's belief base does not change missing information. The second point shows that any information that implies missing information is useful. In particular, any missing information is useful. The reverse is obviously not true. See Example 2: $r \wedge x$ is useful but does not belong to $Missing(B_a, G_a)$. Therefore, all missing information is useful, but some useful information is not missing. The third point illustrates the fact that useful information is not necessarily a logical consequence of the $Missing(B_a, G_a)$ set. Finally, the fourth point illustrates the fact that there are logical consequences of $Missing(B_a, G_a)$ set that are not useful.

4   An Ordinal Approach

In this section we are interested in a notion of *relative usefulness* by defining, in two different ways, a pre-order between the formulas. To compare two formulas φ_1 and φ_2, we compare the two sets of information that is missing once the piece of information is added to the belief base, i.e., we compare $Missing(B_a \cup \varphi_1, G_a)$ and $Missing(B_a \cup \varphi_2, G_a)$, by using either of the pre-orders $\preceq^1$ and $\preceq^2$. Here, the obtained definitions will not be equivalent (see Example 3).

Definition 8. *Let a be an agent, B_a be its belief base and G_a be its set of goals. Let φ_1 and φ_2 be two formulas of $L \setminus L_G$. φ_1 is at least as useful for a as φ_2, denoted by $\varphi_2 \preceq_u^1 \varphi_1$, iff $Missing(B_a \cup \varphi_1, G_a) \preceq^1 Missing(B_a \cup \varphi_2, G_a)$. φ_1 is strictly more useful for a than φ_2, denoted by $\varphi_2 \prec_u^1 \varphi_1$, iff $\varphi_2 \preceq^1 \varphi_1$ and $\varphi_1 \not\preceq^1 \varphi_2$. Finally, φ_1 is as useful for a as φ_2, denoted by $\sim_u^1$, iff $\varphi_2 \preceq_u^1 \varphi_1$ and $\varphi_1 \preceq_u^1 \varphi_2$.*

According to this definition, if one piece of information allows to achieve more goals than another, then it is more useful. If it makes it possible to achieve the same number of goals but if, for at least one goal, it makes it possible to reduce missing information, then it is more useful.

Obviously, $\varphi_2 \prec_u^1 \varphi_1$ iff $Missing(B_a \cup \varphi_1, G_a) \prec^1 Missing(B_a \cup \varphi_2, G_a)$ and $\varphi_2 \sim_u^1 \varphi_1$ iff $Missing(B_a \cup \varphi_1, G_a) = Missing(B_a \cup \varphi_2, G_a)$. $\preceq_u^1$ is a pre-order on all the propositional formulas but not a total pre-order. For example, in Example 3 below, $p \wedge q$ and $p \wedge r$ are incomparable. Indeed $Missing(B_a \cup (p \wedge q), G_a) = \{r\}$ and $Missing(B_a \cup (p \wedge r), G_a) = \{q\}$ and $\{r\} \not\preceq^1 \{q\}$ and $\{q\} \not\preceq^1 \{r\}$.

Definition 9. *Let a be an agent, B_a be its belief base and G_a be its set of goals. Let φ_1 and φ_2 be two formulas of $L \setminus L_G$. φ_1 is at least as useful for a as φ_2, denoted by $\varphi_2 \preceq_u^2 \varphi_1$, iff $Missing(B_a \cup \varphi_1, G_a) \preceq^2 Missing(B_a \cup \varphi_2, G_a)$. φ_1*

is strictly more useful for a than φ_2, denoted by $\varphi_2 \prec_u^2 \varphi_1$, iff $\varphi_2 \preceq_U^2 \varphi_1$ and $\varphi_1 \npreceq_U^2 \varphi_2$. Finally, φ_1 is as useful for a as φ_2, denoted by $\sim_u^2$, iff $\varphi_2 \preceq_u^2 \varphi_1$ and $\varphi_1 \preceq_u^2 \varphi_2$.

According to this definition, if one piece of information allows to achieve more goals than another, then it is more useful. If it achieves the same number of goals and if the missing information is generally shorter, then it is more useful. These two definitions are not equivalent as shown below.

Example 3. Let us suppose that: $B_a = \{p \wedge q \rightarrow g_1, p \wedge r \rightarrow g_2\}$ and $G_a = \{g_1, g_2\}$. We have for instance, $Missing(B_a \cup (p \wedge x), G_a) = \{q, r\}$ and $Missing(B_a \cup r, G_a) = \{p \wedge q, p\}$. Thus $r \prec_u^2 (p \wedge x)$ but $r \nprec_u^1 (p \wedge x)$.

Proposition 6. *If $\psi \models \varphi$ then $\varphi \preceq_U^1 \psi$ and $\varphi \preceq_U^2 \psi$.*

In particular $\varphi_1 \preceq_U^1 \varphi_1 \wedge \varphi_2$ and $\varphi_1 \preceq_U^2 \varphi_1 \wedge \varphi_2$. That is to say $\varphi_1 \wedge \varphi_2$ is at least as useful, in the sense of $\preceq_U^1$ (and of $\preceq_U^2$) than φ_1. However, we do not have $\varphi_1 \prec_U^1 \varphi_1 \wedge \varphi_2$ neither $\varphi_1 \prec_U^2 \varphi_1 \wedge \varphi_2$ as shown in the previous examples where $p \sim^1 p \wedge x$ and $p \sim^2 p \wedge x$.

5 A Numerical Approach

In this section, we follow a numerical approach by associating each piece of information with a usefulness degree. To begin with, we state some rationality postulates such a measure must satisfy. The general case will not be treated, and we will limit ourselves to calculating the degree of usefulness *of conjunctions of positive literals*. Let φ be a conjunction of positive literals. We define:

- $Cons(B_a, \varphi) = \{l \text{ positive literal of } L \setminus L_G : B_a \cup \varphi \models l\}$
- $N_1(\varphi) = \Sigma_{g \in G_a} |Cons(B_a, \varphi) \cap Missing(B_a, g)|$
- $N_2(\varphi) = \Sigma_{g \in G_a} |Missing(B_a, g) \setminus Cons(B_a, \varphi)|$
- $N_3(\varphi) = |\varphi \setminus \cup_{G \in G_a} Missing(B_a, g)|$

$Cons(B_a, \varphi)$ is the set of all the positive literals that are deducible after adding φ to B_a. $N_1(\varphi)$ counts the positive literals common to $Cons(B_a, \varphi)$ and to the missing information. The larger the $N_1(\varphi)$, the more φ reduces the missing information to achieve the goals. $N_2(\varphi)$ counts the positive literals of missing information that are not in $Cons(B_a, \varphi)$.
Notice that $N_2(\varphi) = \Sigma_{g \in G_a} |Missing(B_a, g)| - N_1(\varphi)$. Therefore, if $N_1(\varphi)$ increases, $N_2(\varphi)$ decreases. $N_3(\varphi)$ counts the positive literals of φ that are not literals of missing information. Adding them is therefore not useful to achieve the goals.

Let us consider again agent a whose belief base is B_a and goal set is G_a.

Definition 10. *The set of goals that a formula φ allows the agent to achieve is:*

$$E_{B_a, G_a}(\varphi) = \{g \in G_a, B_a \nvDash g \text{ and } B_a \cup \varphi \models g\}$$

We use $E(\varphi)$ when there is no ambiguity.

Let $U(\varphi)$ be a real number representing how much φ is useful for a. We have based our definition on the following postulates.

Monotonicity on the Number of Goals

(P1) $|E(\varphi_1)| < |E(\varphi_2)| \implies U(\varphi_1) < U(\varphi_2)$.

The number of goals that a piece of information allows an agent to achieve should influence the degree of usefulness of such a piece of information for the agent. Intuitively, a piece of information which allows to achieve a higher number of goals (with respect to another piece of information) should be more useful.

Monotonicity on the Quantity of Information Needed

(P2) $|E(\varphi_1)| = |E(\varphi_2)|$ and $N_1(\varphi_1) > N_1(\varphi_2) \implies U(\varphi_1) > U(\varphi_2)$.

The amount of missing information (needed information) provided by a formula should influence its degree of usefulness. Intuitively, when two formulas allow to achieve the same number of goals, one of them is more useful than the other if it reduces the amount of missing information more than the other.

Monotonicity on the Quantity of Useless Information

(P3) $|E(\varphi_1)| = |E(\varphi_2)|$ and $N_1(\varphi_1) = N_1(\varphi_2)$ and $N_3(\varphi_1) < N_3(\varphi_2) \implies U(\varphi_1) > U(\varphi_2)$.

The amount of useless information conveyed by a piece of information should also influence its degree of usefulness. Intuitively, when two formulas allow to achieve the same number of goals, a formula is more useful than another if it provides less useless information than the other. This idea agrees with the maxmin principle of Grice's. Useless information while not being harmful in view of reaching a goal may produce an overhead on whom has to process it which may be qualified as a cost.

Equality

P4 $|E(\varphi_1)| = |E(\varphi_2)|$ and $N_1(\varphi_1) = N_1(\varphi_2)$ and $N_3(\varphi_1) = N_3(\varphi_2) \implies U(\varphi_1) = U(\varphi_2)$.

Two pieces of information which allow to achieve the same number of goals, and which have exactly the same amount of useful and useless information should have the same degree of usefulness.

To sum up, according to **(P1)**, the higher the number of goals that a formula makes it possible to achieve, the higher its usefulness degree. According to **(P2)**, **(P3)** and **(P4)**, when two formulas allow to achieve the same number of goals (whether the goals are the same, different or even no goals at all), then the more a formula reduces missing information the more useful it is. Moreover, in case of equality, the most useful information is the one which brings the least useless information; finally, if they have the same number of useless pieces of information, then they have the same usefulness degree. These postulates are consistent because their premises are incompatible.

Notice that, according to these postulates, if $N_1(\varphi_1) = N_1(\varphi_2)$ and $N_3(\varphi_1) = N_3(\varphi_2)$ then $U(\varphi_1) = U(\varphi_2)$.

In the following, we provide the definition of a usefulness measure U which satisfies these postulates.

Definition 11. *Let a be an agent whose goals are in G_a and let φ be a conjunction of positive literals. We define the usefulness degree[3] by:*

$$U(\varphi) = \frac{1}{|G_a|+1}\left[|E(\varphi)| + \frac{N_1(\varphi)}{N_1(\varphi)+N_2(\varphi)+\frac{N_3(\varphi)}{N_3(\varphi)+1}}\right]$$

$N_1(\varphi)$ quantifies the useful part of φ for the agent, while $N_2(\varphi)$ quantifies the agent's disappointment (lack of needed information) towards φ and, finally, $N_3(\varphi)$ quantifies the disturbance caused to the agent by the unexpected and unnecessary content of φ. Our definition of usefulness takes these three aspects into consideration.

The intuitive idea behind this definition of usefulness is as follows. The usefulness of information can be seen as a calculation of the similarity between the information the agent needs to achieve its goals and the piece of information that arrives. The more direct or indirect elements (that can be deduced) there are in common between the two, the more useful the information will be. We would like to stress that this fact allows to account for the serendipity factor [17] in the definition of usefulness. Indeed, an agent gets (asks for) a piece of information to achieve a given goal, but if the received piece of information also helps achieve other goals then this fact is considered in the computation of the usefulness. However, the number of common elements is not always enough to distinguish the degrees of usefulness between two pieces of information. Indeed, in some cases it would also be necessary to take into account their differences. We have been inspired by Tversky's idea [18], according to which, in order to calculate the similarity between two objects A and B, we should consider, in addition to what they have in common, what distinguishes them, i.e., the features of A which are not features of B and vice-versa. This is the reason why we have considered these three values, $N_1(\varphi)$, $N_2(\varphi)$ and $N_3(\varphi)$, in our definition.

Remark 1. *We can notice that for any conjunction of positive literals φ we have:*

$$0 \le \frac{N_1(\varphi)}{N_1(\varphi)+N_2(\varphi)+\frac{N_3(\varphi)}{N_3(\varphi)+1}} \le 1.$$

$$\frac{N_1(\varphi)}{N_1(\varphi)+N_2(\varphi)+\frac{N_3(\varphi)}{N_3(\varphi)+1}} = 1 \implies E(\varphi) = G_a.$$

---

[3] Such a degree should be noted $U_{B_a,G_a}(\varphi)$ but we will note it $U(\varphi)$ when there is no ambiguity.

Proposition 7. *The measure $U(\varphi)$ proposed in Definition 11 satisfies postulates* **(P1)–(P4)**.

Example 4. Let us consider: $B_a = \{q\} \cup \{p \wedge q \rightarrow g_1, p \wedge r \rightarrow g_2\}$ and $G_a = \{g_1, g_2\}$. We have then $Missing(B_a, G_a) = \{p, p \wedge r\}$. We obtain $U(p \wedge r) = 1$, $U(p) = 5/6$, $U(p \wedge q) = U(p \wedge x) = 11/14$, $U(r) = 1/6$, $U(q \wedge r) = 1/7$, $U(q \wedge x) = U(q) = 0$. In other words, $p \wedge r$ is the piece of information that has the maximal degree of usefulness, which is explained by the fact that adding $p \wedge r$ allows to achieve both goals g_1 and g_2. The usefulness of p is lower than the usefulness of $p \wedge r$ but it is higher than those of the other formulas, because adding p allows to achieve a goal (g_1). On the other hand, $p \wedge q$, is less useful than p because of q: the agent already knows q therefore q is not useful anymore for the agent because not novel. The same reasoning holds for $p \wedge x$. Formula r instead is less useful because it only reduces missing information regarding one single goal. It is easy to understand that $q \wedge r$ is less useful than r once more because of the unnecessary information q. Obviously, q and $q \wedge x$ are not useful at all because they do not help progressing towards a goal.

Proposition 8. *If $U(\varphi_1) = U(\varphi_2)$ then $|E(\varphi_1)| = |E(\varphi_2)|$ and $N_1(\varphi_1) = N_1(\varphi_1)$, $N_2(\varphi_1) = N_2(\varphi_1)$, $N_3(\varphi_1) = N_3(\varphi_1)$.*

By this proposition, the only way two formulas can have the same usefulness is by having the same values for these three parameters. This shows that Definition 11 does not permit any compensation: a variation of one of these three values cannot be compensated by the variation of the others.

Particular Cases

- **When $B_a^m = \emptyset$:** In the case where $B_a^m = \emptyset$, i.e., when the only beliefs of the agent concern the agent's needs in terms of information about the way to achieve its goals, we have: $Missing(B_a, g) = premise(g)$ and $Cons(B_a, \varphi) = \varphi$. $U(\varphi)$ can then be written as:

$$U(\varphi) = \frac{1}{|G_a+1|} \cdot \left[|E(\varphi)| + \frac{N_1(\varphi)}{K + \frac{N_3(\varphi)}{N_3(\varphi)+1}} \right]$$

with $E(\varphi) = \{g \in G_a, premise(g) \subseteq \varphi\}$, $N_1(\varphi) = \Sigma_{G \in G_a} |\varphi \cap Premise(g)|$, $K = \Sigma_{g \in G_a} |premise(g)|$, $N_3(\varphi) = |\varphi \setminus \cup_{g \in G_a} Premise(g)|$

- **When $B_a^m = \emptyset$ and G_a is a singleton:** In this case, the agent has a single goal, g_0, and its only beliefs is the formula which expresses the information need for achieving that single goal. $U(\varphi)$ can then be written as follows:

$$U(\varphi) = \frac{1}{2} \cdot \left(n(\varphi) + \frac{|\varphi \cap premise(g_0)|}{|premise(g_0)| + \frac{|\varphi \setminus premise(g_0)|}{|\varphi \setminus premise(g_0)|+1}} \right)$$

with $n(\varphi) = 1$ if $premise(g_0) \subseteq \varphi$ and $n(\phi) = 0$ otherwise.

Example 5. Take $premise(g_0) = a \wedge b$. Then we have $U(c) = 0$, $U(a \wedge c) = 1/5$, $U(a) = 1/4$, $U(a \wedge b \wedge c) = 9/10$, $U(a \wedge b) = 1$. In other words, c is not useful at all because knowing c does not allow the agent to reach or get closer to its goal. $a \wedge c$ is a little more useful, because even if knowing c is not useful to the agent, knowing a allows it to get a little closer to its goal. a is more useful than $a \wedge c$ because it does not add unnecessary information. $a \wedge b \wedge c$ is even more useful because even if it adds unnecessary information, it allows the agent to achieve its goal. Finally, $a \wedge b$ is the most useful because it allows the agent to reach its goal and does not add any unnecessary information.

6   An Example of Application to Information Retrieval

In this section, we will first recall some relevance dimensions in information retrieval which have been used in the literature [8] to propose documents to a user (who now takes the place of what we called "agent" in the above general framework). We will then compare those dimensions with the usefulness measure we are proposing here. However, to have a fair comparison, we need to reformulate those dimensions in a logical setting [1].

6.1   A Refresher on Relevance Dimensions

The *aboutness* [5] dimension is a core notion in Information Retrieval. It is used to compute the topical matching between a document and a user query. However, its modeling gave raise to several distinct interpretations, which characterize a variety of Information Retrieval models, of which the *vector space model* is an example. Formally, in the vector space model, a piece of information or, more generally, a document d, can be represented as a vector of T elements, $d = [w_{1d}, \ldots, w_{|T|d}]$. The user interests are represented by a vector $q = [w_{1q}, \ldots, w_{|T|q}]$, $|T|$ being the size of the term vocabulary used. Different choices have been made in the literature regarding the values of w_{id}, for example: simply based on the presence or absence of a word in the document, in this case the vector contains values in $\{0, 1\}$, or based on the frequency of the word in the document and in the whole repository (TF-IDF) [2]. Here, we will use the vector space model interpretation, and, like in [8], in addition to the aboutness measure, we will consider the *appropriateness* dimension (proposed in [8]) and the *coverage* dimension (proposed in [13]). We have considered those three relevance dimensions because they explicitly account for the user query/goals. This is not the case for the *popularity* relevance dimension for example.

Aboutness. The term *aboutness* (*topical relevance*) is formally defined as follows. Let $d = [w_{1d} \ldots w_{|T|d}]$ and $q = [w_{1q} \ldots w_{|T|q}]$ representing document d and query q, respectively, with $|T|$ representing the size of the term vocabulary used. The measure of *aboutness* (*topical relevance*) is calculated by the standard cosine-similarity [15]:

$$\text{Aboutness}_{IR}(d, q) = \frac{\sum_{i=1}^{|T|}(w_{iq}.w_{id})}{\sqrt{\sum_{i=1}^{|T|} w_{iq}^2 \cdot \sum_{i=1}^{|T|} w_{id}^2}}. \tag{1}$$

Coverage. The *coverage* criterion is assessed on the document representation and on the user profile representation. It measures how strongly the user interests are included in a document.

$$\text{Coverage}_{IR}(d, q) = \frac{\sum_{i=1}^{|T|} \min(w_{iq}, w_{id})}{\sum_{i=1}^{|T|} w_{iq}}. \tag{2}$$

This function produces the maximum value 1 when the non null elements in q's vector also belong to d's vector. It produces the value zero when the two vectors have no common element. Moreover, the value of the function increases with the increase of the number of common elements.

Appropriateness. This dimension allows to measure how appropriate or how seemly a document is with respect to the user interests.

$$\text{Appropriateness}_{IR}(d, q) = 1 - \frac{\sum_{i=1}^{|T|} |w_{iq} - w_{id}|}{|T|}. \tag{3}$$

According to this definition, a piece of information is considered *fully appropriate* if it covers all the user interests. However, if in addition it covers other subjects, it is considered *less appropriate*.

6.2   Reformulation in Logic

We can consider a user query in information retrieval as the information needed to achieve a goal. This way, the premise of the goal can be represented by a formula that corresponds to the agent's information needed. Let φ and ψ be two conjunctions of positive literals of a propositional language. We have:

$$\text{Aboutness}_{Logic}(\varphi, \psi)) = \frac{|\varphi \cap \psi|}{\sqrt{|\varphi| \cdot |\psi|}},$$

$$\text{Coverage}_{Logic}(\varphi, \psi) = \frac{|\varphi \cap \psi|}{|\psi|},$$

$$\text{Appropriateness}_{Logic}(\varphi, \psi) = 1 - \frac{|\varphi \backslash \psi| + |\psi \backslash \varphi|}{|L|}.$$

After replacing the premises of the agent's goal by the formula ψ, the measure defined in Definition 11 is then re-written as follows:

$$U(\varphi, \psi) = \tfrac{1}{2} \cdot \left(n(\varphi) + \frac{|\varphi \cap \psi|}{|\psi| + \frac{|\varphi \backslash \psi|}{|\varphi \backslash \psi| + 1}} \right)$$

with $n(\varphi) = 1$ if $\psi \subseteq \varphi$ and $n(\phi) = 0$ otherwise.

More precisely, we consider a propositional language L that has $|T|$ propositional letters $p_1 \ldots p_{|T|}$ and a letter g_0 representing the goal of the user. A document d can then be represented by a formula noted φ_d defined as: $\varphi_d = \bigwedge_{i=1,\ldots,|T| \text{ and } w_{i,d}=1} p_i$. A query q can also be represented by a formula noted $premise(g_0)$ defined by $\psi_q = \bigwedge_{i=1,\ldots,|T| \text{ and } w_{i,q}=1} p_i$.

The following proposition allows us to reformulate in logic the three IR relevance dimensions we have considered from the literature.

Proposition 9.

$$\text{Aboutness}_{IR}(d, q) = \text{Aboutness}_{Logic}(\varphi_d, \psi_q)$$
$$\text{Coverage}_{IR}(d, q) = \text{Coverage}_{Logic}(\varphi_d, \psi_q)$$
$$\text{Appropriateness}_{IR}(d, q) = \text{Appropriateness}_{Logic}(\varphi_d, \psi_q)$$

Example 6. Let us consider again Example 5, with the propositional language whose letters are a, b, c and g_0. $\psi = a \wedge b$ and let us consider the five formulas: $\varphi_1 = c$, $\varphi_2 = a \wedge c$, $\varphi_3 = a$, $\varphi_4 = a \wedge b \wedge c$, and $\varphi_5 = a \wedge b$. The following table summarizes the values of the four measurements.

φ	About	Cov	Approp	U
$\varphi_1 = c$	0	0	0	0
$\varphi_2 = a \wedge c$	1/2	1/2	1/3	1/5
$\varphi_3 = a$	$\frac{1}{\sqrt{2}}$	1/2	2/3	1/4
$\varphi_4 = a \wedge b \wedge c$	$\frac{2}{\sqrt{6}}$	1	2/3	9/10
$\varphi_5 = a \wedge b$	1	1	1	1

A number of observations emerge from these results. First of all, we notice that two formulas can have identical degrees of coverage without their degrees of usefulness being identical. Thus, $Coverage(\varphi_2, \psi) = Coverage(\varphi_3, \psi)$ but $U(\varphi_2, \psi) \neq U(\varphi_3, \psi)$. Similarly, two formulas may have identical degrees of appropriateness without their degrees of usefulness being identical. Thus, $Appropriatemess(\varphi_3, \psi) = Appropriateness(\varphi_4, \psi)$ but $U(\varphi_3, \psi) \neq U(\varphi_4, \psi)$. We also notice that a and $a \wedge b \wedge c$ have identical appropriateness values although for different reasons: $appriopriateness(a, a \wedge b) = 2/3$ because a says nothing about b, whereas this is part of the user's information need, and $appriopriateness(a \wedge b \wedge c, a \wedge b) = 2/3$ because $a \wedge b \wedge c$, although providing all the information the user need to achieve his/her goal, it provides unnecessary information, c. On the other hand, these different reasons lead to different degrees of usefulness and, in particular, $U(a, a \wedge b)$ is much lower than $U(a \wedge b \wedge c, a \wedge b)$. Indeed, by definition, U favors information that allows the user need to be satisfied (this is fully the case with $a \wedge b \wedge c$ whereas it is partially the case with a). Even if $a \wedge b \wedge c$ provides unnecessary information, namely c, the user will be able to achieve his/her goal with it, unlike with a.

The following proposition provides some comparisons between the U measure and the IR ones.

Proposition 10. *Let φ and ψ be two conjunctions of literals.*

- $U(\varphi, \psi) = \text{Aboutness}(\varphi, \psi) = \text{Appropriateness}(\varphi, \psi) = 1 \Longleftrightarrow \varphi = \psi$.
- $\text{Coverage}(\varphi, \psi) = 1 \Longleftrightarrow \psi \subseteq \varphi$.
- $U(\varphi, \psi) = \text{Aboutness}(\varphi, \psi) = \text{Appropriateness}(\varphi, \psi) = \text{Coverage}(\varphi, \psi) = 0 \Longleftrightarrow \varphi \cap \psi = \emptyset$.
- $\text{Coverage}(\varphi_1, \psi) < \text{Coverage}(\varphi_2, \psi) \Longrightarrow U(\varphi_1, \psi) < U(\varphi_2, \psi)$.
- $\text{Appropriateness}(\varphi_1, \psi) \leq \text{Appropriateness}(\varphi_2, \psi)$ *and* $\text{Coverage}(\varphi_1, \psi) = \text{Coverage}(\varphi_2, \psi). \Longrightarrow U(\varphi_1, \psi) \leq U(\varphi_2, \psi)$.

7   Conclusion and Future Work

We have proposed three approches to define the notion of usefulness for a cognitive agent. A *binary approach*, which allows to classify a piece of information as being *useful or not*. An *ordinal approach*, which allows to compare two pieces of information in order to establish which one is more useful. Two different operators have been proposed in this case: a pre-order operator and a total order operator. However, and like for the binary approach, the proposed ordinal approach does not allow to consider unnecessary information. This is accounted for by the third approach by means of a numerical definition of usefulness. We have compared, through an easy to understand example, three IR measures from the literature with our numerical measure. The results of the comparison show that our numerical definition of usefulness, based on the cognitive aspects of the user, allows to capture in a single value different dimensions, without the need for eliciting an explicit priority order on the dimensions from the user. In addition, it allows to somehow account for the *serendipity* factor (see Example 4). Moreover, it also allows to account for *novelty* with respect to the user's beliefs, not only with respect to the past user interactions as usual in the literature (see again Example 4, in which the fact that a piece of information contains information already known by the user diminishes its usefulness).

An application of our framework that would be interesting to investigate is its use to reduce the needs to coordinate multiple *assistive agents* advising the same user [16]. Other possible applications would be in the case of the Information Flow Problem in multi-agent systems, in which there is a need to ensure an adequate exchange of information within a system [3], and in the case of BDI personal medical assistant agents, where one critical requirement is to (automatically) produce an accurate documentation [6].

We also plan to extend our framework in a more general case where premise of a goal is not restricted to a conjunction but may be a more complex formula. We also plan to consider weighted goals in order to take into account the importance of goals in the definition of information usefulness.

References

1. Abdulahhad, K., Berrut, C., Chevallet, J.-P., Pasi, G.: Modeling information retrieval by formal logic: a survey. ACM Comput. Surv. **52**(1), 15:1–15:37 (2019)
2. Baeza-Yates, R.A., Ribeiro-Neto, B.A.: Modern Information Retrieval - The Concepts and Technology Behind Search, 2nd edn. Pearson Education Ltd., Harlow (2011)
3. Búrdalo, L., Terrasa, A., Julián, V., Fornes, A.G.: The information flow problem in multi-agent systems. Eng. Appl. Artif. Intell. **70**, 130–141 (2018)
4. Clarke, C.L.A., et al.: Novelty and diversity in information retrieval evaluation. In: SIGIR, pp. 659–666. ACM (2008)
5. Cooper, W.S.: A definition of relevance for information retrieval. Inf. Storage Retrieval **7**(1), 19–37 (1971)
6. Croatti, A., Montagna, S., Ricci, A., Gamberini, E., Albarello, V., Agnoletti, V.: BDI personal medical assistant agents: the case of trauma tracking and alerting. Artif. Intell. Med. **96**, 187–197 (2018)
7. da Costa Móra, M., Lopes, J.G.P., Vicari, R.M., Coelho, H.: BDI models and systems: bridging the gap. In: Proceedings of ATAL 1998, pp. 11–27 (1998)
8. da Costa Pereira, C., Dragoni, M., Pasi, G.: Multidimensional relevance: a new aggregation criterion. In: Boughanem, M., Berrut, C., Mothe, J., Soule-Dupuy, C. (eds.) ECIR 2009. LNCS, vol. 5478, pp. 264–275. Springer, Heidelberg (2009). https://doi.org/10.1007/978-3-642-00958-7_25
9. Flouvat, F., Sanhes, J., Pasquier, C., Selmaoui-Folcher, N., Boulicaut, J.-F.: Improving pattern discovery relevancy by deriving constraints from expert models. In: ECAI. Frontiers in Artificial Intelligence and Applications, vol. 263, pp. 327–332. IOS Press (2014)
10. Grice, H.P.: Logic and conversation. In: Cole, P., Morgan, J.L. (eds.) Syntax and Semantics: Vol. 3: Speech Acts, pp. 41–58. Academic Press, New York (1975)
11. Huang, X., Soergel, D.: Relevance: an improved framework for explicating the notion. JASIST **64**(1), 18–35 (2013)
12. Minker, J.: An overview of cooperative answering in databases. In: Andreasen, T., Christiansen, H., Larsen, H.L. (eds.) FQAS 1998. LNCS, vol. 1495, pp. 282–285. Springer, Heidelberg (1998). https://doi.org/10.1007/BFb0056009
13. Pasi, G., Bordogna, G., Villa, R.: A multi-criteria content-based filtering system. In: SIGIR 2007: Proceedings of the 30th Annual International ACM SIGIR Conference on Research and Development in Information Retrieval, pp. 775–776 (2007)
14. Rao, A.S., Georgeff, M.P.: Modeling rational agents within a BDI-architecture. In: KR 1991, pp. 473–484 (1991)
15. Salton, G., McGill, M.: Introduction to Modern Information Retrieval. McGraw-Hill Book Company, New York (1984)
16. Subagdja, B., Tan, A.-H., Kang, Y.: A coordination framework for multi-agent persuasion and adviser systems. Expert Syst. Appl. **116**, 31–51 (2019)
17. Toms, E.G.: Serendipitous information retrieval. In: DELOS (2000)
18. Tversky, A.: Features of similarity. Psychol. Rev. **84**(4), 327–352 (1977)
19. Zhang, Z., Petrak, J., Maynard., D.: Adapted textrank for term extraction: a generic method of improving automatic term extraction algorithms. Procedia Comput. Sci. **137**, 102–108 (2018). Proceedings of the 14th International Conference on Semantic Systems 10th–13th of September 2018 Vienna, Austria

A Scheduler for Smart Homes with Probabilistic User Preferences

Van Nguyen[1], William Yeoh[2], Tran Cao Son[1], Vladik Kreinovich[3(✉)],
and Tiep Le[1,4]

[1] New Mexico State University, Las Cruces, NM, USA
{vnguyen,tson,tile}@cs.nmsu.edu
[2] Washington University in St. Louis, St. Louis, MO, USA
wyeoh@wustl.edu
[3] University of Texas at El Paso, El Paso, TX, USA
vladik@utep.edu
[4] Viome, Inc., Santa Clara, CA, USA
lebatiep@gmail.com

Abstract. Scheduling appliances is a challenging and interesting problem aimed at reducing energy consumption at a residential level. Previous work on appliance scheduling for smart homes assumes that user preferences have no uncertainty. In this paper, we study two approaches to address this problem when user preferences are uncertain. More specifically, we assume that user preferences in turning on or off a device are represented by Normal distributions. The first approach uses sample average approximation, a mathematical model, in computing a schedule. The second one relies on the fact that a scheduling problem could be viewed as a constraint satisfaction problem and uses depth-first search to identify a solution. We also conduct an experimental evaluation of the two approaches to investigate the scalability of each approach in different problem variants. We conclude by discussing computational challenges of our approaches and some possible directions for future work.

Keywords: Smart Home Scheduling · Probabilistic user preference

1 Introduction

Demand Side Management (DSM) is a portfolio of measures to improve the energy system at the consumption side. The initial goal of DSM is to cut the cost or energy consumption from the power grid, and that goal is a well-studied subject in smart grids (Department of Energy and Climate Change 2009a; 2009b). In recent years, with the rapid growth of technology and engineering such as Internet of Things, smart devices and ubiquitous computing, appliances in a household can communicate with each others. This creates a new environment in which each appliance can be considered as an agent, and the team of agents is able to collaborate to achieve a specific goal; for example, to execute a precomputed schedule of the appliances. It is not difficult to envision that in the near

© Springer Nature Switzerland AG 2019
M. Baldoni et al. (Eds.): PRIMA 2019, LNAI 11873, pp. 138–152, 2019.
https://doi.org/10.1007/978-3-030-33792-6_9

future, these agents can be controlled by a central server (or multiple servers) that can generate schedules of the appliances on the fly to improve the users' comfort while keeping energy consumption minimal.

In this paper, we aim at developing a scalable and efficient scheduling system for smart homes. The main difference between the proposed system and contemporary ones (see Sect. 6 for a discussion of current approaches) lies in that the former system will take user preferences into consideration under the assumption that the preferences are uncertain. This assumption is realistic since, as shown in the literature, user preferences could be approximately but not completely learned (see, e.g., [6,13,14,16]).

The present work could be considered as bridging the preference elicitation research and the development of smart home schedulers. This also provides a core component for the development of a comprehensive energy management system for smart grids in which individuals (e.g., homes, companies, etc.) can control their own energy consumption and, at the same time, coordinate with each other to lower the overall energy consumption, contributing to improved sustainability.

The main contributions of this paper are the following: (*i*) We provide a definition of a multi-objective *Smart Home Scheduling Problem* (SHSP) with probabilistic user preferences; (*ii*) We propose two approaches to solve SHSP, one based on *Sample Average Approximation* (SAA) and the other based on depth-first search; (*iii*) We present an empirical evaluation of the two approaches. Our empirical evaluation shows that the depth-first search based approach performs better than the sampling-based approach and thus provides a viable system for SHSP.

2   Smart Home Scheduling Problem

In this section, we define the *Smart Home Scheduling Problem* (SHSP) with probabilistic user preferences and its solutions.

Definition 1. *A scheduling problem P is a tuple $\langle A, E, T, C, L, D \rangle$, where*

- *A is a set of **appliances** (or **devices**), usually written as the set of integers $\{1, \ldots, |A|\}$.*
- *$E = (e_1, e_2, ..., e_{|A|})$ is a vector of positive real numbers, where each e_i represents the **energy consumption** of device i.*
- *T is a set of **time slots**, usually written as the set of integers $\{1, \ldots, |T|\}$.*
- *$C = (c_1, c_2, ..., c_{|T|})$ and $L = (l_1, l_2, ..., l_{|T|})$ are vectors of non-negative real numbers, where c_i and l_i represent the **cost** of 1 kWh and the maximum **permissible load** of all the devices at time i, respectively.*
- *D is an $|A| \times |A|$ matrix, called **dependency matrix**, each cell $D(i, j)$ represents a hard constraint between devices i and j. The relations/constraints can be one of the following types:*
  - *$\textbf{before}$ (resp. $\textbf{after}$) means that the device i must be turned on before (resp. after) device j.*

- **parallel** *(resp. **not-parallel**) means that the device i must run in parallel (resp. must not run in parallel) with the device j.*
- **nil** *if the usage of the device i is independent from that of the device j.*

Intuitively, a scheduling problem P represents the problem of when to turn on devices. P is said to have no dependency if every element in D is **nil**. In this paper, without the loss of generality, we will assume that each device in P is turned on exactly once within $|T|$ time slots. For simplicity of the presentation, we will also assume that each device is active for only one time slot. The definitions and propositions in this paper can easily adapted for systems with appliances that work in multiple time slots (e.g., the washing machine runs for two hours) or need to be turn off (e.g., the light bulbs). Furthermore, we assume that the matrix D is symmetric in the following sense: (*i*) If $D(i,j) = $ **before** (resp. $D(i,j) = $ **after**), then $D(j,i) = $ **after** (resp. $D(j,i) = $ **before**); (*ii*) If $D(i,j) = $ **parallel** (resp. $D(i,j) = $ **not-parallel**), then $D(j,i) = $ **parallel** (resp. $D(j,i) = $ **not-parallel**); and (*iii*) If $D(i,j) = $ **nil**, then $D(j,i) = $ **nil**. A user preference for a scheduling problem is defined as follows.

Definition 2. *A probabilistic user preference over a scheduling problem $P = \langle A, E, T, C, L, D \rangle$ is a tuple $\mathcal{C} = \langle N, \alpha, \beta, \lambda \rangle$, where*

- *N is an $|A| \times |T|$ matrix, called **preference matrix**, where each cell $N(i,j)$ is a Normal distribution $\mathcal{N}(\mu_{ij}, \sigma_{ij})$ representing the probability distribution of the user's preference in turning the device i on at time slot j.*
- *α, called the **cumulative satisfaction threshold**, is a number representing the minimum acquired cumulative preference required by a user from a schedule.*
- *β is a number in the interval $[0, 1]$ representing the **probability threshold**, which indicates the threshold of the probability that α will be achieved given a schedule in order for a user to accept that schedule.*
- *λ is a number indicating the **cost threshold** that a user could accept.*

Table 1 presents an example of preference matrix for $|A| = 4$ and $|T| = 3$.
Scheduling problems with probabilistic preferences are defined next.

Definition 3. *A Smart Home Scheduling Problem (SHSP) with probabilistic user preferences (or p-scheduling problem, for short) is a pair $(P, \mathcal{C})$, where P is a scheduling problem and $\mathcal{C}$ is a probabilistic preference over P.*

In this paper, for brevity, when we refer to SHSPs, we mean SHSPs with probabilistic user preferences.

We next define the notions of a schedule for P and when a schedule for P satisfies constraints in **dependency matrix** in D.

Definition 4. *Given a scheduling problem $P = \langle A, E, T, C, L, D \rangle$, a **schedule** for P is an $|A| \times |T|$ matrix H, where each cell $H(i,j)$ is either 0 (off) or 1 (on), representing the status of the device i at time slot j, and*

Table 1. An example of preference matrix N for $|A| = 4$ and $|T| = 3$. The two numbers in each cell of the table represent the Normal distribution for user preference to turn on an appliance at a time slot. For example, the preference to turn on device 1 at time 1 is $\mathcal{N}(10, 0.2)$.

		Time slots		
		1	2	3
Appliances	1	10, 0.2	9, 0.1	6, 0.15
	2	6, 0.01	8, 0.05	2, 0.78
	3	6, 0.51	7, 0.2	7, 0.99
	4	2, 0.41	6, 0.67	6, 0.09

- if $D(i,j) = \boldsymbol{before}$, then $H(i,t) = 1$ implies that $H(j,k) = 0$ for every $k \leq t$;
- if $D(i,j) = \boldsymbol{after}$, then $H(i,t) = 1$ implies that $H(j,k) = 0$ for every $k \geq t$;
- if $D(i,j) = \boldsymbol{parallel}$, then $H(i,t) = 1$ implies that $H(j,t) = 1$; and
- if $D(i,j) = \boldsymbol{not\text{-}parallel}$, then $H(i,t) = 1$ implies that $H(j,t) = 0$.

It is easy to see that the following observation holds under the assumption that each appliance is turned on exactly once among $|T|$ time slots.

Observation 1. *For each schedule H of a problem $P = \langle A, E, T, C, L, D \rangle$*

$$\forall i \in [1, |A|], \exists j \in [1, |T|] \text{ such that } H(i,j) = 1$$

$$\text{and } \forall j_1, j_2 \in [1, |T|], H(i, j_1) = H(i, j_2) = 1 \implies j_1 = j_2.$$

Definition 5. *The **Normal distribution of a schedule** H for a p-schedule problem $(P, \mathcal{C})$, with $P = \langle A, E, T, C, L, D \rangle$ and $\mathcal{C} = \langle N, \alpha, \beta, \lambda \rangle$, is defined by $\mathcal{N}_H(\mu_H, \sigma_H)$, where*

$$- \mu_H = \sum_{i=1}^{|A|} \sum_{j=1}^{|T|} \mu_{ij} \cdot H(i,j) \text{ and}$$

$$- \sigma_H = \sum_{i=1}^{|A|} \sum_{j=1}^{|T|} \sigma_{ij} \cdot H(i,j).$$

Intuitively, the distribution $\mathcal{N}_H(\mu_H, \sigma_H)$ represents the satisfactory of a user given the schedule H. Given a schedule H of a problem P, we define:

- the total energy consumption of all appliances at a given time slot j as:

$$e^H(j) = \sum_{i=1}^{|A|} e_i \cdot H(i,j). \tag{1}$$

- the cost at a given time slot j is

$$c^H(j) = c_j \cdot e^H(j). \tag{2}$$

Recall that the *complementary cumulative distribution function* (ccdf) of a real-valued random variable X is defined as $F_X(x) = Prob(X \geq x)$. We thus use $F_{\mathcal{N}_H(\mu_H, \sigma_H)}(\alpha)$ to represent the probability that the cumulative preference acquired by schedule H is greater than or equal to a cumulative satisfaction threshold α.

We are now ready to define the notion of satisfaction of a user preference by a schedule.

Definition 6. *Given a p-schedule problem* $\mathcal{P} = (P, \mathcal{C})$, *with* $P = \langle A, E, T, C, L, D \rangle$ *and* $\mathcal{C} = \langle N, \alpha, \beta, \lambda \rangle$ *over* P, *a schedule* H *satisfies* $\mathcal{C}$ *if it meets the following conditions:*

- **Power Safety:**
$$\forall j \in [1, |T|], e^H(j) \leq l_j. \tag{3}$$

- **User Preference:**
$$F_{\mathcal{N}_H(\mu_H, \sigma_H)}(\alpha) \geq \beta. \tag{4}$$

- **Cost Efficiency:**
$$f_c^H = \sum_{j=1}^{|T|} c^H(j) \leq \lambda \tag{5}$$

We say that a schedule H^* *is* optimal *if*

$$H^* = \operatorname*{argmin}_{H \in \mathcal{H}} \sum_{j=1}^{|T|} c^H(j) \tag{6}$$

where $\mathcal{H}$ *is the set of schedules satisfying Conditions* (3), (4), *and* (5).

Intuitively, Condition (3) requires that at any given time slot j, the total energy consumption of all appliances (i.e., $e^H(j)$) is at most equal to the given maximum load (i.e., l_j). Condition (4) states that the probability in which the cumulative preference acquired by H meets the cumulative satisfaction threshold (i.e., that accumulate preference is at least α) is at least β. Finally, Condition (5) indicates that the cost of the schedule must be at most λ.

In the next sections, we propose two methods to solve the SHSP. The first method is based on *Sample Average Assumption* (SAA) and the second method is based on depth-first search.

3   Solving SHSPs Using Sample Average Approximation

Sample Average Approximation (SAA) [5] is a method to solve an optimization problem of the form

$$\min_{x \in \Theta} \tilde{f}(x), \tag{7}$$

where $\Theta \subseteq \mathbb{R}^d$ $(d < \infty)$ and the real-valued function $\tilde{f}(\cdot)$ cannot be computed exactly, but can be estimated through a (stochastic) simulation.

Throughout this section, $(P,\mathcal{C})$ denotes a p-scheduling problem, where $P = \langle A, E, T, C, L, D \rangle$ is a scheduling problem and $\mathcal{C} = \langle N, \alpha, \beta, \lambda \rangle$ is a constraint over P.

Observe that in SHSPs, if the user preferences are deterministic (i.e., each cell of the matrix N is a real number), then a schedule that maximally satisfies the user preferences can be easily computed (e.g., as proposed in [18]). So, one way to use SAA in computing a solution of a SHSP $\mathcal{P} = (P,\mathcal{C})$ is to randomly generate deterministic samples from the given $\mathcal{P}$, compute their solutions, and take the average of these solutions as the solution of $\mathcal{P}$. From this realization, in order to solve a SHSP using SAA approach, we aim at formalizing the SHSP as a *Mixed Integer Linear Programming* (MILP). We start with some extra notations.

Definition 7. *Let N be a preference matrix of the size $|A| \times |T|$. A **sample** of N is an $|A| \times |T|$ matrix where the cell (i,j) is a value generated from the Normal distribution $\mathcal{N}(\mu_{ij}, \sigma_{ij})$.*

Given a sample and a schedule, the projection of the schedule on the sample is defined as follows.

Definition 8. *Let s be a sample matrix of N. The **projection** of a schedule H on s, denoted by $\mathfrak{H}$, is an $|A| \times |T|$ matrix, where, for each cell (i,j)*

$$\mathfrak{H}(i,j) = \begin{cases} s(i,j) \ if \ H(i,j) = 1 \\ 0 \ otherwise \end{cases} \tag{8}$$

Definition 9. *Let s be a sample matrix of N. The **cumulative preference** of a schedule H in s, denoted by C_s, is defined by*

$$C_s = \sum_{i=1}^{|A|} \sum_{j=1}^{|T|} \mathfrak{H}(i,j). \tag{9}$$

We define the indicator function for a sample s as follows.

$$f(s) = \begin{cases} 1 \ if \ C_s \geq \alpha \\ 0 \ otherwise \end{cases} \tag{10}$$

Let n be an integer and $\mathcal{S} = \{s_k\}_{k=1}^n$ be a sequence of samples of N. A schedule H is said to satisfy the user preference condition in $\mathcal{S}$ if

$$\sum_{k=1}^{n} f(s_k) \geq \frac{\beta \times n}{100} \tag{11}$$

The above allows us to transform a p-scheduling problem $\mathcal{P} = (P, \mathcal{C})$ to a MILP,[1] denoted as program Π:

$$\mathcal{S} = \{s_k\}_{k=1}^n \text{ is a sequence of } n \text{ samples of } N$$

$$\text{maximize} \sum_{k=1}^n f(s_k) \text{ subject to}$$

$$\sum_{j=1}^{|T|} H(i,j) = 1 \qquad \forall i = 1, ..., |A| \qquad \text{(from Definition 4)}$$

$$e(j) \leq l_j \qquad \forall j = 1, ..., |T| \qquad \text{(from Eq. 3)}$$

$$\sum_{j=1}^{|T|} c(j) \leq \lambda \qquad \text{(from Eq. 5)}$$

$$\sum_{i=1}^{|A|} \sum_{j=1}^{|T|} H(i,j) \cdot s_k(i,j) \geq \alpha \qquad \forall k = 1, ..., n$$

$$\sum_{k=1}^n f(s_k) \geq \frac{\beta \times n}{100} \qquad \text{(from Eq. 11)}$$

4   Solving SHSP Using Depth-First Search

In this section, we propose an approach to solving p-scheduling problems using *depth-first search* (DFS).[2] As in the previous section, $\mathcal{P} = (P, \mathcal{C})$ denotes a p-scheduling problem, where $P = \langle A, E, T, C, L, D \rangle$ is a scheduling problem and $\mathcal{C} = \langle N, \alpha, \beta, \lambda \rangle$ is a preference over P. Due to Observation 1, we can view $\mathcal{P}$ as a *Constraint Satisfaction Problem* (CSP), denoted by $csp(\mathcal{P})$, whose set of variables $\widetilde{H}_1, \ldots, \widetilde{H}_{|A|}$ and the domain of each variable is $\{1, \ldots, |T|\}$. Intuitively, each variable $\widetilde{H}_i$ encodes a schedule of the appliance i. It is easy to see that there is a one-to-one correspondence between a complete variable assignment $\widetilde{H} = \{\widetilde{H}_i = v_i \mid i = 1, \ldots, |A|\}$ of $csp(\mathcal{P})$ and a schedule H of $\mathcal{P}$ defined by

$$H(i,j) = 1 \quad \text{iff} \quad \widetilde{H}_i = j. \tag{12}$$

For this reason, we often use H and $\widetilde{H}$ interchangeably. We will begin with a theorem that helps in choosing the value of a variable in the expansion phase as well as pruning the search tree.

---

[1] Our proposed transformation from a p-scheduling problem $\mathcal{P} = (P, \mathcal{C})$ to a MILP does satisfy Conditions (3), (4), and (5), but ignores the dependency matrix D in P. We leave a proposal for a complete transformation for future work.

[2] One could also use other search algorithms as well because our core contribution here is to formulate the problem into a search problem and propose a number of pruning conditions that can be used with any search strategy.

Theorem 1. *Let* $\mathcal{N}(\mu_1, \sigma_1), \mathcal{N}(\mu_2, \sigma_2), ..., \mathcal{N}(\mu_n, \sigma_n)$ *be the Normal distributions of the random variables* $x_1, x_2, ..., x_n$, *respectively,* α *be a number, and* $K \in [1, n]$. *Then, the probability* $x_K \geq \alpha$ *is maximal when* $\dfrac{\mu_K - \alpha}{\sigma_K}$ *is maximal among* $\dfrac{\mu_1 - \alpha}{\sigma_1}, ..., \dfrac{\mu_n - \alpha}{\sigma_n}$.

Proof. Denote $\phi(\xi) = Prob(x < \xi)$ for a standard Normal distribution. It holds that

$$Prob(\mathcal{N}(\mu_K, \sigma_K) \geq \alpha) = Prob(\sigma_K \mathcal{N}(0, 1) + \mu_K \geq \alpha)$$

$$= Prob\left(\mathcal{N}(0, 1) \geq \frac{\alpha - \mu_K}{\sigma_K}\right) = 1 - \phi\left(\frac{\alpha - \mu_K}{\sigma_K}\right) \quad (13)$$

This implies that:

$$\max_K(Prob(\mathcal{N}(\mu_K, \sigma_K) \geq \alpha)) \Leftrightarrow \max_K \left(1 - \phi\left(\frac{\alpha - \mu_K}{\sigma_K}\right)\right)$$

$$\Leftrightarrow \min_K \left(\phi\left(\frac{\alpha - \mu_K}{\sigma_K}\right)\right)$$

$$\Leftrightarrow \min_K \left(\frac{\alpha - \mu_K}{\sigma_K}\right) \quad (14)$$

$$\Leftrightarrow \max_K \left(\frac{\mu_K - \alpha}{\sigma_K}\right)$$

How can Theorem 1 help us in searching for a schedule? Observed that if we were to use DFS to solve the CSP of $\mathcal{P}$, then each possible solution H corresponds to a complete assignment of the variables $\tilde{H}_i$ $(1 \leq i \leq |A|)$. So, Theorem 1 indicates that the schedule H with $\mathcal{N}(\mu_H, \sigma_H)$ that has large μ_H and small σ_H has the best chance to satisfy the user preferences than other schedules. More precisely, from Eqs. 4 and 13, we have the following:

$$F_{\mathcal{N}(\mu_H, \sigma_H)}(\alpha) \geq \beta \Leftrightarrow Prob(\mathcal{N}(\mu_H, \sigma_H) \geq \alpha) \geq \beta$$

$$\Leftrightarrow 1 - \phi(\frac{\alpha - \mu_H}{\sigma_H}) \geq \beta \Leftrightarrow \phi(\frac{\alpha - \mu_H}{\sigma_H}) \leq 1 - \beta \quad (15)$$

Consider a partial assignment $\tilde{H}'$ and assume that $\tilde{H}$ is a completion of $\tilde{H}'$, i.e., $\tilde{H}' \subseteq \tilde{H}$. Let

$$\mu_{\tilde{H}'}^{max} = \sum_{\tilde{H}_i = v_i \in \tilde{H}'} \mu(i, v_i) + \sum_{\tilde{H}_i = v_i \in \tilde{H} \setminus \tilde{H}', i \neq k} \max_{j=1,...,|T|} \mu(i, j) \quad (16)$$

$$\sigma_{\tilde{H}'}^{max} = \sum_{\tilde{H}_i = v_i \in \tilde{H}'} \sigma(i, v_i) + \sum_{\tilde{H}_i = v_i \in \tilde{H} \setminus \tilde{H}'} \max_{j=1,...,|T|} \sigma(i, j) \quad (17)$$

Assume that H is the schedule equivalent to $\tilde{H}$ as defined in (12). Clearly,

$$\mu_{\tilde{H}'}^{max} \geq \mu_H \text{ and } \sigma_{\tilde{H}'}^{max} \geq \sigma_H \quad (18)$$

Therefore,

$$\frac{\alpha - \mu_{\tilde{H}'}^{max}}{\sigma_{\tilde{H}'}^{max}} \leq \frac{\alpha - \mu_H}{\sigma_H} \tag{19}$$

which implies

$$1 - \phi\left(\frac{\alpha - \mu_{\tilde{H}'}^{max}}{\sigma_{\tilde{H}'}^{max}}\right) \geq 1 - \phi\left(\frac{\alpha - \mu_H}{\sigma_H}\right) \tag{20}$$

That leads to the following theorem, which is also the pruning condition based on user preference.

Theorem 2. *Assuming that $\tilde{H}'$ is a partial assignment of the variables in the CSP of a p-scheduling problem $\mathcal{P}$. If*

$$1 - \phi\left(\frac{\alpha - \mu_{\tilde{H}'}^{max}}{\sigma_{\tilde{H}'}^{max}}\right) < \beta$$

and $\tilde{H}$ is a completion assignment such that $\tilde{H}' \subseteq \tilde{H}$, then the schedule H corresponding to $\tilde{H}$ does not satisfy Condition (4).

Theorem 2 can then be used to eliminate a partial assignment $\tilde{H}'$ from consideration in the search for a solution. This is used in the algorithm that we present next.

Given a problem $P = \langle A, E, T, C, L, D \rangle$, we say that the number of dependencies of an appliance i, denoted by $d(i)$, is the number of elements in row i of D whose value differs from **nil**. Without loss of generality, we will assume that the appliances in A are listed in decreasing order of dependencies, i.e., if $1 \leq i < j \leq |A|$, then $d(i) \geq d(j)$. For a partial assignment $\tilde{H}'$, let

$$cost(\tilde{H}') = \sum_{\tilde{H}_i = v_i \in \tilde{H}'} c_{v_i} \cdot \left(\sum_{i=1}^{|A|} e_i \times |\{i \mid \tilde{H}_t = v_i \in \tilde{H}'\}|\right)$$

Notice that $cost(\tilde{H}')$ is the energy consumption of all appliances specified by $\tilde{H}'$. Due to the space limitation, we will only present the algorithm for computing an optimal solution for a p-scheduling problem $\mathcal{P} = (P, \mathcal{C})$.

In Algorithm 1, the function $ok(\tilde{H})$ returns **false** if one of the following conditions is satisfied: (i) $cost(\tilde{H}) > \lambda$ (cost efficiency requirement violated); (ii) the dependencies among current scheduled appliances do not satisfy the conditions in Definition 4 (dependency violated); and (iii) $1 - \phi\left(\frac{\alpha - \mu_{\tilde{H}}^{max}}{\sigma_{\tilde{H}}^{max}}\right) < \beta$ (user preference violated).

Intuitively, Algorithm 1 implements DFS by selecting a time slot for an appliance in each iteration of the overall **while-loop** (Lines 6–36), in the order $1, \ldots, |A|$. If all the time slots of the first appliance have been considered, then the search is complete (Line 8–10). For each device, the algorithm starts with the time slot whose preference distribution has maximal mean over other time slots that have not been considered (Line 18–19). When a time slot is assigned to an appliance, the algorithm uses Theorem 2 and other checks ($ok(.)$) to rule out whether the search should be continued or backtracked (the **loop** command, Lines 21–23) for a different time slot of the appliance or the previous appliance (Lines 21–23). When a backtrack to the previously considered appliance (Lines 11–17), the assignment of the current appliance is removed from the schedule and its set of time slots is reseted to **false** (Lines 12–15). If all appliances have been assigned some time slots, then we need to check whether the generated schedule satisfies the user preference and optimal (Lines 26–30).

Observe that if we add "**return** $\widetilde{H}$" to Line 29 of Algorithm 1, then it returns the first satisfiable schedule. Furthermore, additional bookkeeping on the dependencies (e.g., removing all time slots that violate the dependencies in the schedule from the set $c(i)$) could help prune certain selections. We did implement this measure in our implementation. Due to the verifications in Lines 21 and 26, it is easy to see that the following theorem holds.

Theorem 3. *Algorithm 1 is sound and complete.*

5   Experiments

We performed an empirical evaluation of the two proposed methods (labeled DFS and SAA) on randomly-generated problems (i.e., problems with randomly-generated energy consumption vectors E and preference matrices N).

We implemented DFS method using Python, and we used MATLAB Release 2017a, for SAA method, to solve the mixed integer linear programming proposed in program Π. The number of samples in SAA is 100. In our experiments, we investigate the runtime and success rates of the two approaches in the following four SHSP variants:

- *Variant 1*: There are 10 dependencies between the appliances and the goal is to find a satisfiable solution.
- *Variant 2*: All appliances are independent from each other and the goal is to find a satisfiable solution.
- *Variant 3*: There are 10 dependencies between the appliances and the goal is to find an optimal solution.
- *Variant 4*: All appliances are independent from each other and the goal is to find an optimal solution.

For each variant, we generated problems varying the number of appliances $|A| = 20, 25, 30, \ldots, 65$, set the horizon $|T| = 24$, and set $\alpha = 6.5 \cdot |A|$ and $\beta = 0.8$. Finally, we use costs from the literature [12].

We set a time limit of 10 min and 1 hour for problems whose goal is to find satisfiable and optimal solutions, respectively, and we report average runtimes and success rates (=number of instances successfully solved) of the two approaches.

Input : A p-scheduling problem $\mathcal{P} = (P, \mathcal{C})$
Output: An optimal schedule of $\mathcal{P}$

1 optimalValue $= +\infty$
2 optimalCandidate $=$ **nil**
3 Let $\widetilde{H} = \emptyset$
4 Let *checked* be a Boolean $|A| \times |T|$ matrix, initialized with **false**
5 $i = 1$
6 **while true do**
7 | Let $c(i) = \{k \mid checked(i, k) = \textbf{false}\}$
8 | **if** $c(i) = \emptyset \wedge i = 1$ **then**
9 | | **break**
10 | **end**
11 | **if** $c(i) = \emptyset \wedge i > 1$ **then**
12 | | Set $checked(i, k) = \textbf{false}$ for $k = 1, \ldots, |T|$
13 | | Identify x such that $\widetilde{H}_i = x$ belongs to $\widetilde{H}$
14 | | $\widetilde{H} = \widetilde{H} \setminus \{\widetilde{H}_i = x\}$
15 | | $i = i - 1$
16 | | **loop**
17 | **end**
18 | Let $j \in c(i)$ such that $\mu(i, j) = \max_{k \in c(i)} \mu(i, k)$
19 | $checked(i, j) = \textbf{true}$
20 | $\widetilde{H} = \widetilde{H} \cup \{\widetilde{H}_i = j\}$
21 | **if** $\neg ok(\widetilde{H})$ **then**
22 | | **loop**
23 | **end**
24 | **if** $i = |A|$ **then**
25 | | Let H be the schedule correspond to $\widetilde{H}$
26 | | **if** $F_{\mathcal{N}_H(\mu_H, \sigma_H)}(\alpha) \geq \beta \wedge f_c^H <$ optimalValue **then**
27 | | | optimalCandidate $= \widetilde{H}$
28 | | | optimalValue $= f_c^H$
29 | | | % **return** $\widetilde{H}$ if only satisfiable schedule is needed
30 | | **end**
31 | | Identify x such that $\widetilde{H}_i = x$ belongs to $\widetilde{H}$
32 | | $\widetilde{H} = \widetilde{H} \setminus \{\widetilde{H}_i = x\}$
33 | **else**
34 | | $i = i + 1$
35 | **end**
36 **end**
37 **if** optimalCandidate $=$ **nil then**
38 | **return** no optimal schedule found
39 **end**
40 **return** optimalCandidate;

Algorithm 1: Computing an Optimal Schedule for $\mathcal{P} = (P, \mathcal{C})$

Figure 1 shows the runtimes (in seconds) and Table 2 tabulates the success rates (in percentages) of the two approaches on the four variants. We only ran

SAA for Variant 2 because our formulation does not take into account dependencies between appliances (and is thus inapplicable for Variants 1 and 3) and it is not guaranteed to find optimal solutions since it is an approximation approach (and is thus inapplicable for Variants 3 and 4). Results for the number of appliances $|A| > 35$ for Variants 3 and 4 are not shown because none of the approaches successfully solved a single instance for those large problems within the time limit.

The results show that DFS is faster than SAA in Variant 2 and, thus, it is more scalable than SAA. In Variants 1 and 2, DFS maintains acceptable runtimes of within 40 seconds and success rates of approximately 80%. Not surprisingly, DFS is slower when solving the optimization problems of Variants 3 and 4 compared to the satisfaction problems of Variants 1 and 2. Similarly, DFS also has smaller success rates on the optimization problems.

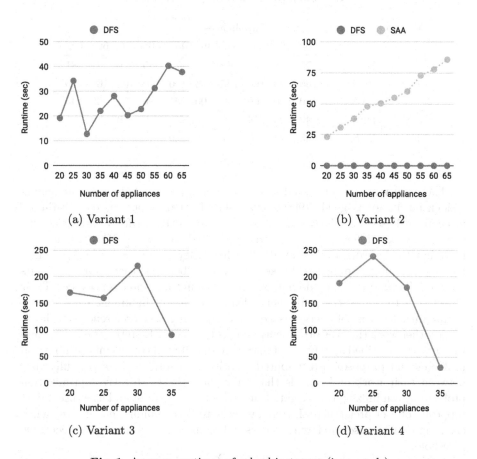

Fig. 1. Average runtimes of solved instances (in seconds)

6 Related Work

In the literature, existing works to solve SHSPs can be divided into three categories: *mathematical optimization, meta-heuristic search* and *heuristic search* [2]. Between these three categories, most of the work is in mathematical optimization, especially ones using MILP-based approaches. Some recent works [1,3,10,12] used MILP, while others have formulated the problem in convex programming [17] and quadratic programming [15] in which the cost or the energy consumption function is optimized. To a certain extent, our proposed SAA model can be considered as the first work that applies SAA mathematical model into solving SHSPs.

Table 2. Success rates (in percentages)

Variant	Approach	Number of appliances $|A|$									
		20	25	30	35	40	45	50	55	60	65
1	DFS	75	79	84	80	83	72	85	79	81	81
2	DFS	100	100	100	100	100	100	100	100	100	100
	SAA	100	100	100	100	100	95	86	81	69	46
3	DFS	42	25	14	5	0	0	0	0	0	0
4	DFS	35	23	15	7	0	0	0	0	0	0

There exist also several studies in applying search techniques in managing residential energy usage [4,7,9]. For example, Misra *et al.* presented a scheduling mechanism based on *Markov Decision Processes* (MDPs) for reducing energy expenses, which differs from our approach as we do not use MDPs [9]. Our work is similar to the work by Lee *et al.* [7], where they introduced a backtracking-based scheduling approach. The key differences between their work and ours are the following: (*i*) They do not take into account user preferences; (*ii*) Their objective is to reduce the peak energy load of homes or buildings, while ours is to minimize the cost of energy usage while satisfying user preference threshold.

Another work that is worth mentioning is the one by Fioretto *et al.* [4], where the authors described a mapping of SHSPs to distributed constraint optimization problems and proposed a distributed algorithm to solve it. The key difference between their work and ours is that they solve the bi-objective optimization problem by minimizing the weighted sum of both energy cost and user discomfort (opposite of user preference). Instead, we seek to only minimize energy cost while ensuring that the user preference (or user discomfort) is within some acceptable threshold.

With respect to the last general area of meta-heuristic search, researchers have proposed a scheduling method using genetic algorithm [8] and studied the application of particle swarm optimization [11] in determining a near-optimal solution for a multi-objective optimization problem like SHSPs.

7   Conclusions and Future Work

In this paper, we introduced two approaches to solve the *smart home scheduling problem* with *probabilistic user preferences*. More precisely, we consider the scheduling problem when user preferences for using (turning on/off) a device are Normal distributions. The first approach relies on *sample average approximation* (SAA) and the second approach uses *depth-first search* (DFS). We also propose pruning strategies, which we applied to our DFS algorithm. As these strategies are general for search-based approaches, they can also be applied to other heuristic search approaches aside from DFS. Our experimental results show that DFS is faster and scales better than SAA.

Future work includes more comprehensive evaluations, where we vary the α and β parameters of DFS and SAA as well as the degree of dependencies of the devices. We also plan to investigate improved optimization techniques for SAA. Finally, we also plan to consider an online extension of the problem, where some subset of preferences are elicited and schedules are provided in a repeated and interactive manner with users.

Acknowledgment. This research is partially supported by NSF grants 1242122, 1345232, 1619273, 1623190, 1757207, 1812618, and 1812619. The views and conclusions contained in this document are those of the authors and should not be interpreted as representing the official policies, either expressed or implied, of the sponsoring organizations, agencies, or the U.S. government. We would also like to thank Long Tran-Thanh for initial discussions that influenced the direction of this research.

References

1. Agnetis, A., De Pascale, G., Detti, P., Vicino, A.: Load scheduling for household energy consumption optimization. IEEE Trans. Smart Grid **4**(4), 2364–2373 (2013)
2. Beaudin, M., Zareipour, H.: Home energy management systems: a review of modelling and complexity. Renew. Sustain. Energy Rev. **45**, 318–335 (2015)
3. Costanzo, G.T., Zhu, G., Anjos, M.F., Savard, G.: A system architecture for autonomous demand side load management in smart buildings. IEEE Trans. Smart Grid **3**(4), 2157–2165 (2012)
4. Fioretto, F., Yeoh, W., Pontelli, E.: A multiagent system approach to scheduling devices in smart homes. In: Proceedings of the International Conference on Autonomous Agents and Multi-Agent Systems, pp. 981–989 (2017)
5. Kleywegt, A.J., Shapiro, A., Homem-de Mello, T.: The sample average approximation method for stochastic discrete optimization. SIAM J. Optim. **12**(2), 479–502 (2002)
6. Le, T., Tabakhi, A.M., Tran-Thanh, L., Yeoh, W., Son, T.C.: Preference elicitation with interdependency and user bother cost. In: Proceedings of the International Conference on Autonomous Agents and Multi-Agent Systems, pp. 1459–1875 (2018)
7. Lee, J., Kim, H.J., Park, G.L., Kang, M.: Energy consumption scheduler for demand response systems in the smart grid. J. Inf. Sci. Eng. **28**(5), 955–969 (2012)

8. Lujano-Rojas, J.M., Monteiro, C., Dufo-López, R., Bernal-Agustín, J.L.: Optimum residential load management strategy for real time pricing (RTP) demand response programs. Energy Policy **45**, 671–679 (2012)
9. Misra, S., Mondal, A., Banik, S., Khatua, M., Bera, S., Obaidat, M.S.: Residential energy management in smart grid: a Markov decision process-based approach. In: Proceedings of the IEEE International Conference on Green Computing and Communications; IEEE Internet of Things; and IEEE Cyber, Physical and Social Computing, pp. 1152–1157 (2013)
10. Molderink, A., Bakker, V., Bosman, M.G., Hurink, J.L., Smit, G.J.: Domestic energy management methodology for optimizing efficiency in smart grids. In: Proceedings of the IEEE Bucharest PowerTech, pp. 1–7 (2009)
11. Pedrasa, M.A.A., Spooner, T.D., MacGill, I.F.: Scheduling of demand side resources using binary particle swarm optimization. IEEE Trans. Power Syst. **24**(3), 1173–1181 (2009)
12. Sou, K.C., Weimer, J., Sandberg, H., Karl Henrik, J.: Scheduling smart home appliances using mixed integer linear programming. In: Proceedings of the IEEE Conference on Decision and Control and European Control Conference, pp. 5144–5149 (2011)
13. Tabakhi, A.M., Le, T., Fioretto, F., Yeoh, W.: Preference elicitation for DCOPs. In: Proceedings of the International Conference on Principles and Practice of Constraint Programming, pp. 278–296 (2017)
14. Tabakhi, A.M., Yeoh, W., Yokoo, M.: Parameterized heuristics for incomplete weighted CSPs with elicitation costs. In: Proceedings of the International Conference on Autonomous Agents and Multi-Agent Systems, pp. 476–484 (2019)
15. Tarasak, P.: Optimal real-time pricing under load uncertainty based on utility maximization for smart grid. In: Proceedings of the IEEE International Conference on Smart Grid Communications, pp. 321–326 (2011)
16. Truong, N.C., Baarslag, T., Ramchurn, G., Tran-Thanh, L.: Interactive scheduling of appliance usage in the home. In: Proceedings of the International Joint Conference on Artificial Intelligence, pp. 869–1467 (2016)
17. Tsui, K.M., Chan, S.C.: Demand response optimization for smart home scheduling under real-time pricing. IEEE Trans. Smart Grid **3**(4), 1812–1821 (2012)
18. Zhu, Z., Tang, J., Lambotharan, S., Chin, W.H., Fan, Z.: An integer linear programming based optimization for home demand-side management in smart grid. In: Proceedings of the IEEE PES Innovative Smart Grid Technologies, pp. 1–5 (2012)

Supply Chain Management World

A Benchmark Environment for Situated Negotiations

Yasser Mohammad[1,4(✉)], Enrique Areyan Viqueira[3], Nahum Alvarez Ayerza[1], Amy Greenwald[3], Shinji Nakadai[1,2], and Satoshi Morinaga[1,2]

[1] AIST, Tokyo, Japan
y.mohammad@aist.go.jp
[2] NEC Inc., Tokyo, Japan
[3] Brown University, Providence, USA
[4] Assiut University, Asyut, Egypt

Abstract. In the very near future, we anticipate that more and more artificially intelligent agents will be deployed to represent individuals and institutions. Automated negotiation environments are a mechanism by which to coordinate the behavior of such agents. Most existing work on automated negotiation assumes a context that is predefined, and hence, static. This paper focuses on the dynamic case, which we call *situated negotiation*, where agents need to decide not only how to negotiate, but with whom, and about what. We describe a common benchmark simulation environment for evaluating situated negotiation strategies, and evaluate several baseline strategies in the proposed environment.

1 Introduction

Negotiation is a process by which **self-interested** parties aim to reach an agreement. Self-interestedness implies a partial ordering over different possible outcomes, which in turn implies the existence of a continuous **utility function** that assigns a real value to all outcomes [6].

In **automated negotiation**, one or more of the negotiating parties is an artificially intelligent (AI) agent. Interest in automated negotiation is increasing, because of the growing use of AI to automate business operations [17], and the understanding that these agents must be capable of reaching agreements, if the businesses they represent are to be successful.

We refer to an instance of automated negotiation as a **negotiation thread**. A negotiation thread involves at least two agents (often called negotiators), each with its own utility function and **strategy**, negotiating about some **agenda**. A negotiation strategy is a mapping from the state of the negotiation, as understood by an agent, to the actions allowed by the negotiation **protocol** (sometimes called a **mechanism**). A negotiation agenda is the space of issues under consideration: e.g., in the context of supply chain management, the possible prices, quantities, and delivery dates.

Traditionally, automated negotiation research has focused on **context-free** negotiations. Such a negotiation is characterized by a single thread, in which

© Springer Nature Switzerland AG 2019
M. Baldoni et al. (Eds.): PRIMA 2019, LNAI 11873, pp. 153–169, 2019.
https://doi.org/10.1007/978-3-030-33792-6_10

agents endowed with static utility functions negotiate about a fixed agenda [3]. Here, the key research questions usually pertain to the design of an effective negotiation strategy [7].

To apply automated negotiation technology in realistic business settings, however, agents will need to decide not only *how* to negotiate, but with *whom* and about *what*. Furthermore, when an agent is simultaneously negotiating with multiple other agents, their utility in one negotiation is necessarily dynamic, as it depends on the success or failure of other negotiations [2]. We call such scenarios **situated negotiations** to emphasize the role of the context, or the *situation*, in the negotiation process.

In many settings, it may not be optimal, or even possible, to decompose a situated negotiation neatly. For example, consider an agent A that is negotiating with another agent B. If A receives an offer from a third agent C, it should be reluctant to accept any worse offer from B. In general, the availability of a third agent C as a potential or actual negotiation partner will affect the offers that A places and is willing to accept from B. Dividing a situated negotiation into a set of independent negotiations may lead to suboptimal behavior in all of them.

Different aspects of situated negotiations have been studied in the literature under different names, including *negotiation with outside options* [9], *one-to-many negotiation* [11], *negotiation in distributed environments* [10], *concurrent negotiations* [20], and was applied to complex multiagent resource allocation [2], distributed task allocation [8], cloud computing [2], and smart grids [1].

The first contribution of this paper is to present a common benchmark simulation environment called the Supply Chain Management (SCM) world that is rich enough to help illuminate the challenges faced by situated negotiators, while at the same time simple enough to focus the research effort on core problems. Availability of similar benchmark problems in other domains has proved useful in stimulating research and generating new ideas. Examples include the Face Recognition Grand Challenge (FRGC) [16], the Trading Agent Competition [18], The Robot World Cup Initiative (RoboCup), and the Automated Negotiation Agents Competition (ANAC) [7]. The second contribution of this paper is three baseline strategies and their evaluation in the proposed environment.

This paper is organized as follows. Section 2 defines situated negotiations in more detail. Section 3 outlines the objectives we believe a simulation should attain in order to serve as a useful benchmark for current and future research on situated negotiations. Section 4 describes the proposed benchmark problem that was designed to achieve these objectives. Section 5 describes the annual automated agent negotiation competition (ANAC) 2019 supply chain management league (SCML), an instantiation of these ideas. Section 6 introduces three strategies for this problem, and Sect. 7 evaluates the proposed strategies.

2 Situated Negotiations

Problems in automatic negotiation are usually studied without regard to the environment in which the negotiation takes place. From an engineering perspective, this abstraction is justifiable; it can make an otherwise intractable problem tractable. For example, external pressures to reach agreement quickly can be modeled by a negotiation *deadline*, an exponential discount factor on a *utility function*, as part of the *opponent model*, or in a *reservation value* (i.e., the value for failure to reach agreement). But in many negotiation scenarios, it is not so simple to encode the effect of the environment on the negotiation. Informally, the environment creates what we call **situated** negotiations. An agent is engaged in a situated negotiation if the utility function it uses to guide its negotiation is dynamic, and varies with the context in which the negotiation is situated.

A primary example of a situated negotiation is a negotiation under uncertainty. For example, when an agent is not endowed with perfect knowledge of the utility function of the entity it represents, and consequently engages in *preference elicitation* during the negotiation [14] to refine its estimate of its utility function, its current estimate is, in general, situation-dependent.

An agent's utility function is also situation-dependent when it is negotiating in the presence of an *outside option*, i.e., a **substitute**, whose value is either unknown or subject to change. For example, if an agent is negotiating about the price of a plane ticket from Tokyo to California, and in the midst of the negotiation there is an earthquake in Tokyo, the agent's utility function—specifically, its reservation value—may suddenly need to be updated.

An important type of situated negotiation is an **embedded** negotiation. In such a negotiation, an agent's utility function heavily depends on contextual information in that it depends on the collective outcome of multiple negotiations. We call such a utility function **global**. A key task of the agent, then, is to figure out a way to decompose this global utility function into **local** utility functions to be farmed out to the separate negotiation threads. This task is known to be notoriously difficult for autonomous bidders in simultaneous and sequential auctions [5], a special case of many-to-one automated negotiation in which the "one's" (i.e., the auctioneer's) strategy is public, but can be done effectively when integrated with an appropriate bidding strategy [19].

For example, imagine an agent that engages in two *concurrent* negotiations on behalf of someone planning to attend the Tokyo Olympics—one about plane tickets and the other about hotel reservations. The agent's global utility function may ascribe non-zero value only to both travel goods together, implying that the goods are **complements**. Regardless of how this global utility function is decomposed into local utility functions and then farmed out to the two separate negotiation threads, the negotiations are embedded because the conclusion of either would impact the agent's utility function in the other.

The matching market in the U.S. Navy detailing system, which allocates sailors to job vacancies, is an example of an embedded negotiation that marries concurrent negotiations with outside options [9]. In this system, vacancies are published and sailors apply to fill them. Commanders then choose among the applicants via concurrent bilateral negotiations. (Likewise, one can imagine a sequential version in which negotiations are conducted consecutively instead of concurrently, and where the utility function of each subsequent negotiation is affected by past outcomes and predictions about future outcomes.) Li *et al.* [9]

argue that relying on fixed reservation values in each negotiation thread for the duration of the concurrent negotiations is sub-optimal. On the contrary, the reservation value (and hence utility function) in one thread must be updated based on how negotiations unfold in the others.

What these scenarios have in common is that factors external to a negotiation thread itself affect aspects of that negotiation, which entail changes to the utility function. These scenarios are called **situated negotiations** in this paper, and are characterized by *dynamic utility functions that emerge endogenously during possibly concurrent and/or possibly consecutive negotiations.*

3   Design Objectives

The goal of this work is to advance the state-of-the-art in situated negotiation. To achieve this goal, we propose that researchers *benchmark* their progress using a *common* simulation environment. The primary advantage of a common environment is that it facilitates the comparison of agent negotiation strategies. The alternative would involve the arduous task of reimplementing strategies across domains. Moreover, when multiple research teams develop competing approaches, running them all on a common benchmark environment more closely resembles real-world negotiations among disparate parties.

We believe that any common benchmark environment that is intended to further research in autonomous agents and multi-agent systems (AAMAS) should satisfy three design objectives. First, it should model a real-world scenario, thereby increasing its relevance, and enabling researchers to jump start the (strategic) design process using existing intuitions. Second, it should be easy for researchers to run experiments to compare different mechanisms, different agent strategies/designs within a given mechanism, etc. Finally, it should support a canonical design and implementation, to facilitate collaboration among researchers and reproducibility of results.

For the special case of situated negotiation, the environment should model a negotiation scenario that involves one or more of the sub-problems depicted in Sect. 2; and if the scenario involves more than of these sub-problems, it should be relatively straightforward to isolate and study specific ones.

4   The SCM World: A Common Benchmark Environment

A **supply chain** is a sequence of processes by which raw materials are converted into finished goods. A supply chain is usually managed by multiple independent entities, whose coordination is called **supply chain management** (SCM). SCM exemplifies situated negotiation. The SCM world was built on top of an open-source automated negotiation platform called NegMAS [13] to serve as a common benchmark environment for the study of situated negotiation.

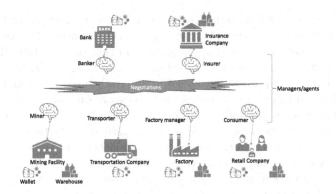

Fig. 1. The main entities and their managers (agents) in the SCM world simulation.

Entities. SCM consists of six types of entities and their corresponding **managers** (See Fig. 1): factories, mining facilities, retail companies, transportation companies, banks, and insurance companies. The relationship between these entities and their managers is one-to-one. All entities have accompanying **wallets** that store their cash. Moreover, factories, mining facilities, retail companies, and insurance companies have accompanying storage **warehouses**. In more detail:

Factories convert raw materials and intermediate products into intermediate and final products by running their manufacturing processes for some time, assuming all inputs, enough funds, and enough time are available to run the processes. They are managed by **factory managers**.

Mining facilities are capable of mining raw materials, which they do to satisfy their negotiated contracts. They are managed by **miners** that act only as sellers in the SCM world.

Retail companies are interested in consuming a subset of the final products to satisfy some predefined consumption schedule. They are managed by **consumers** that act only as buyers.

Transportation companies transport materials between warehouses. They are managed by **transporters** that represent service providers.

Banks provide loans to potential buyers.

Insurance companies insure managers against **breaches of contract** committed by other managers (e.g., failure of a seller to deliver promised products on time, insufficient funds in the buyer's wallet at the time of delivery, transportation delay by a transporter, etc).

Agents. In the SCM world, agents represent managers. The goal of each agent is to accrue as much profit as possible.

All trade in the SCM world is conducted through negotiations. Negotiations can be bilateral or multilateral, and can use any negotiation protocol—synchronous or asynchronous—to reach an agreement. As a special case, some (or all) agreements may be arrived at using auction protocols, allowing for direct comparison between the auction mechanisms and other negotiation protocols.

When an agreement is signed, it is converted into a contract. When a contract comes due, the simulator attempts to execute it. For a contract between a buyer and a seller, it moves the agreed upon quantity of that product from the seller's inventory to the buyer's, and the agreed upon price from the buyer's wallet to the seller's. For a transportation contract, it moves the products from the source to the destination (after any agreed upon transportation delay), and moves the transportation cost to the wallet of the transporter. If any of these executions fail, a breach of contract can occur. Breaches can also occur if either party decides not to honor the contract. In cases of potential breaches, the simulator may offer the agents involved an opportunity to renegotiate.

To find negotiation partners, agents may **request-a-negotiation** with potential trading partners directly, or publish their interest in negotiating on a public **bulletin board** that lists **call-for-proposals** (CFPs). Each such CFP specifies the publisher and the proposed negotiation issues. Interested agents then respond to the publisher with a request to negotiate. Requesting such a negotiation implies acceptance of the negotiation agenda.

Simulation. Before the start of the simulation, an initial balance is deposited in each agent's wallet, and catalog prices are posted for all products. In addition, each agent is assigned a private profile, which characterizes its production capabilities and/or its consumption preferences. Each SCM world simulation runs for multiple (say, 100) steps. During each step:

1. Agents make any outstanding loan payments, all contracts that come due are executed, and any breaches that arise are handled.
2. Agents then engage in negotiations for multiple steps (say, 10). During this time, they are also free to read the bulletin board, post CFPs, and respond to CFPs.
3. Finally, all production lines in all factories advance one time step, meaning required inputs are removed from inventory, generated outputs are stored in inventory, and production costs are subtracted from the factories' wallets. Moreover, transportation advancement is simulated.

Utility Functions. The SCM world does not endow agents with utility functions. On the contrary, all utility functions are endogenous, meaning they are engendered by the simulator's dynamics and agents' interactions. Endogenous utility functions that arise as the market evolves are a distinguishing feature of situated negotiations. In the SCM world, a major determiner of an agent's profits is its ability to position itself well in the market via successful negotiations, which in turn depends on the utility functions it uses to guide its negotiations.

Desiderata. The SCM world satisfies the generic AAMAS design objectives outlined in Sect. 3, as well as the ones that are specific to situated negotiations. First, it is possible to instantiate all the example situated negotiation scenarios described in Sect. 2. For example, by disabling banks, insurance companies, transportation companies, and factory managers, so that only miners and consumers negotiate about the price of a ready-made product to be delivered at a fixed time, it is possible to model *negotiation with outside options* [9], where the outside options are other agents trading the same product. Second, the environment is a simulation of a real-world marketplace in which business intuitions can be applied to generate and test automated negotiation strategies. Finally, a canonical implementation of the SCM world simulation is available as an open source library [13], to enhance reproducibility and provide a common platform to advance the state-of-the-art in situated negotiations.

5   ANAC 2019 SCM League

One way to expedite the widespread use of a common benchmark environment throughout a research community is to sponsor a competition in the environment. To this end, in 2019, the SCM league (SCML), based on the SCM world design was organized as part of the Automated Negotiation Agents Competition (ANAC) [7], held at the International Joint Conference on AI.

SCML '19 is one relatively simple instantiation of the SCM world. The simplifications were design choices aimed at reducing any complexity in the SCM world that did not immediately pertain to situated negotiations, so as to provide a relatively straightforward setting in which to develop innovative negotiation strategies, while at the same time ensuring a sufficient level of activity. Specifically, in SCML '19, activity was measured via **business size**, defined as the total monetary value of all successfully executed contracts. The design was then optimized in attempt to avoid **market blockage**, namely a business size of zero.

SCML '19 ignored logistics (i.e. no transportation companies were simulated). Instead, all products were transported between all entities free of charge, after a predefined constant delay (which was set to zero). In addition, warehouse capacity was infinite. The bank was disabled and all agents were initialized with large balances to avoid the need for loans. These simplifications, which sidestepped cash flow, storage limitations, and logistic complications, were intended to lower the barrier to entry in the initial year of the competition.

The insurance company was not removed from the simulation. Agents interacted with the insurance company via the ultimatum mechanism: i.e., the latter made a single final offer of an insurance policy, which the agent could accept or reject, without any possibility of haggling. All other agreements were reached via bilateral negotiations, using the **alternating offers protocol** [3], in which agents exchange offers and counteroffers.

The production graph used in SCML '19 was organized as a single chain, with a single raw material, a single finished good, and a set of intermediate products. To manufacture each product, there was but a single process that consumed one item of the product just before it in the chain.

The SCML development team designed the miners, the consumers, and the insurance company. The job of the participants was to develop a **factory manager**. The development team also provided a baseline factory manager, whose strategy is described in Sect. 6. This agent was an eager business partner, and thus participated in the competition to ensure sufficiently many trading opportunities, thereby increasing the business size metric.

The behavior of the built-in agents make SCML '19 a **pull economy**, meaning it is demand driven. Proactive consumers drive demand by posting buy CFPs. Baseline factory manager agents react by responding to the consumers' buy CFPs (offering to sell), and then post their own buy CFPs further down the chain. Miners at the far end of the chain are similarly reactive.

Consumers. Consumers in SCML '19 are proactive. They post buy CFPs, which drive the supply chain. The negotiation agendas that characterize these CFPs reflect the consumers' utility functions, which in turn are characterized by consumption schedules that usually cannot be fulfilled via a single factory during a single time step, but instead require multiple of one or the other or both, and hence create a situated negotiation scenario.

A consumer c's utility of consuming a finished good is determined by its profile π_c. This profile includes a predefined consumption schedule S_c that defines, for each step, a preferred quantity to consume, as well as overconsumption and underconsumption penalties, $\hat{O}_c$ and $\hat{U}_c$, respectively. Thus, the utility functions reward consumers who follow their schedules closely, and penalize deviations from them. These assumptions lead to the form of consumers' utility functions shown in Eq. 1.

Given an outcome (u, q, t), denoting unit price, quantity, and execution time, respectively, consumer c's utility is given by

$$
U_c(u, q, t) = \begin{cases} 0, & u < 0 \text{ or } q < 0 \text{ or } t < 0 \\ \alpha_u h_u^{\tau_u, \beta_u}(u) + \alpha_q h_q^{\tau_q, U, O}(q, S(t)), & \text{otherwise} \end{cases}
$$

$$(1)$$

The parameters α_*, where $*$ is the issue name (i.e., $* \in \{u, q\}$), are values in $(0, 1)$ drawn from a Dirichlet distribution that varies with the consumer. The parameters $\beta_u, \tau_u, \tau_q, U$, and O, are drawn from a normal distribution that likewise varies with the consumer.

The function $h_u^{\tau_u, \beta_u}$ is monotonic in the unit price, $x \in \mathbf{R}_0^+$: $h_u^{\tau_u, \beta_u}(x) = -(x/\beta_u)^{\tau_u}$. The function $h_q^{\tau_q, U, O}$ takes as input two quantities; the first is specified by the outcome, and the second, by the consumer's schedule at time t. This function has the following form:

$$
h_q^{\tau_q, U, O}(x, y) = \begin{cases} e^{-U\left(\frac{y-x}{y}\right)^{\tau_q}} & x \le y \wedge y \ne 0 \\ e^{-O\left(\frac{x-y}{y}\right)^{\tau_q}} & x \ge y \wedge y \ne 0 \end{cases}
$$

$$(2)$$

With every negotiation opportunity a fresh utility function is created based on the consumer's profile. Consequently, even if a consumer already engaged in a failed negotiated with another agent about an existing CFP, it will behave differently the next time, so their negotiation may as yet succeed.

Miners. Miners in SCML '19 are purely reactive. They wait for buy CFPs for the raw material to be posted, and respond, based on their utility functions, to all whose negotiation agendas are consistent with their mining abilities. Note that miners' utilities are not coupled across negotiations in the same way that consumers' are, because a miner's total profit across negotiations is simply the sum of its profits in its individual negotiations.

A miner m's utility of mining (i.e., generating) any quantity of a raw material is determined by its profile π_m. At a high-level, miners should prefer to mine fewer raw materials, as late as possible, which it should then aim to sell the highest possible prices. However, in an attempt to increase business size, miners preferred to mine more, rather than fewer, raw materials. These assumptions lead to the form of the miners' utility functions, described in Eq. 3, and generated in an analogous way to consumers'.

Given an outcome (u, q, t), denoting unit price, quantity, and execution time, respectively, miner m's utility is given by

$$
U_m(u, q, t) = \begin{cases} 0, & u < 0 \text{ or } q < 0 \text{ or } t < 0 \\ \alpha_u g_u(u) + \alpha_q g_q(q) + \alpha_t g_t(t), & \text{otherwise} \end{cases}
\tag{3}
$$

The parameters α_*, where $*$ is the issue name (i.e., $* \in \{u, q, t\}$), are values in $(0, 1)$ drawn from a Dirichlet distribution that varies with the miner. The parameters τ_* and β_*, where $*$ is again the issue name, are drawn from a normal distribution that likewise varies with the miner. The functions g_* are monotonic in the issue value, $x \in \mathbf{R}_0^+$: $g_*(x) = (x/\beta_*)^{\tau_*}$.

With the goal in mind of optimizing business size, the following design choices were made for SCML '19: Baseline factory managers *always* bought insurance. The insurance premium was relatively cheap (10% of the outcome's total value), and did not increase all that much with breaches, and breach penalties were minimal (2%). These choices effectively prevented market blockage, and favored larger business sizes, as shown in Sect. 7.

6   Strategies

There are inherent difficulties in building a realistic simulation environment. Figuring out how to best trade off time and/or space complexity for realism, for example, can be challenging.

SCM factory managers face multiple challenges, including: (1) strategic placement of CFPs (i.e., proactively initiating negotiation opportunities), (2) reacting to negotiation requests from others, (3) creating utility functions for negotiation threads, (4) negotiation strategies for each thread, (5) inventory control, and (6) production scheduling. An SCM agent strategy encompasses all the heuristics a factory manager uses to address these six challenges.

In this section, we describe three agents strategies we developed for the SCM world, as instantiated in SCML '19. The first was designed as a baseline strategy, upon which participating teams could base their design. This strategy tackled the embedded negotiation aspect of SCML (see Sect. 2), albeit heuristically. The second strategy focuses on procurement, and draws inspiration from the newsvendor model [15], by formulating a discrete optimization problem whose decision variables are the quantity of inputs to buy. The solution to this problem is useful in deciding what buy CFPs to post, and what sell CFPs to respond to. The third strategy tries to find a negotiation agenda—specifically, a price—that is both profitable from its point of view and, at the same time, acceptable to other agents. By working to artificially inflate prices, this strategy aims at altering the trading environment in which the agent is situated to promote itself.

Greedy Factory Manager: A Baseline. The **Greedy Factory Manager** (GFM) was designed to showcase all the components needed to design a factory manager for the SCM world. GFM was also intended to be run in all simulations so that it could ensure sufficient business size, even at the expense of being profitable. GFM's strategy overcontracts, which avoids starving factory managers at earlier levels in the supply chain, but results in many breaches of contract.

The GFM agent employs a reactive-seller, proactive-buyer strategy, much like consumers. It is *reactive* in that it requests negotiations with the publishers of all buy CFPs about the product it produces, as long as it can schedule the desired quantity of the product of interest to be manufactured within the proposed delivery time. When such a negotiation request is accepted, GFM calculates the utility of the potential sell contract as the marginal utility of its outcome, given all existing (buy and sell) contracts, pessimistically assuming that any ongoing negotiations will fail.In this way, the controller decomposes the agent's global utility function, which values the potential outcomes of multiple negotiations, into local utility functions, which values only one outcome. GFM then spawns a negotiator, endowed with the corresponding marginal utility as its utility function. These negotiators embody embedded negotiations, in the sense of Sect. 2.

After a sell contract is signed, the consumption schedules of the necessary inputs are increased accordingly, and GFM then *proactively* places buy CFPs, using the same placement strategy as consumers (Sect. 5). The utility of each potential buy contract is calculated using Eq. 1, taking as the target consumption schedule the production demands of all existing sell contracts. When it accepts another agent's request to negotiate, GFM spawns an internal consumer agent, which in turn spawns a negotiator with this utility function. Similar to consumers, the GFM controller couples these negotiators through utility functions that depend on a shared consumption schedule. Whenever a contract is signed or executes successfully, the utility functions of all ongoing negotiations are updated to reflect a change in production demands and production line occupancy. Likewise, GFM recalculates the marginal utilities of all potential sell contracts whenever a contract is signed or executes successfully.

GFM uses a simple time-based negotiation strategy [4]. At time step t, it offers an outcome with the minimum utility above the so-called **aspiration** level a, which deceases over time as follows: $a(t) = 1 - (t/T)^4$. Here T is the maximum number of negotiation steps, a value specified by the protocol. GFM accepts an offers if its utility is at least the utility of its own ensuing offer at the current aspiration level.

The GFM agent is so called because it uses a greedy heuristic to scheduling production. This heuristic aims to produce outputs as late as possible, in attempt to increase the negotiation power of the agent when buying inputs.

Newsvendor Model Agent. The **Newsvendor Model Agent** (NVM) takes inspiration from the newsvendor model [15], a classic model in operations research used to model the choice of an optimal inventory level for a perishable product (e.g., a newspaper). The NVM agent plans for some finite horizon, assuming that unsold inputs and outputs at the end of that horizon will have no value. Analogous to newsvendor models, an agent implementing this strategy tries not to over- or under-produce during its planning horizon. They do not want to stock too many products, as any excess (whatever does not sell) will go to waste; but they also do not want to stock too few, as any shortage will result in lost sales.

At each time step t, an SCML agent faces (at least) four decisions: the quantity of inputs to buy, y_{IN}^t; the price at which to buy those inputs, x_{IN}^t; the quantity of outputs to sell, y_{OUT}^t; and the price at which to sell those outputs, x_{OUT}^t. The goal of the NVM agent is to maximize its total expected profits over a finite time horizon, in the face of uncertain and non-stationary elastic demand.

The NVM agent models the uncertainty it faces at time step t by a joint distribution $G^t \doteq G_{P_{\text{IN}}, Q_{\text{IN}}, P_{\text{OUT}}, Q_{\text{OUT}}}^t$, where $G_{P_{\text{IN}}, Q_{\text{IN}}, P_{\text{OUT}}, Q_{\text{OUT}}}(P_{\text{IN}}^t \leq p_{\text{IN}}^t, Q_{\text{IN}}^t \leq q_{\text{IN}}^t, P_{\text{OUT}}^t \leq p_{\text{OUT}}^t, Q_{\text{OUT}}^t \leq q_{\text{OUT}}^t)$ is the cumulative probability that, at time t, q_{IN}^t units of the input IN will be sold at price p_{IN}^t per-unit, and q_{OUT}^t units of the output OUT will be sold at price p_{OUT}^t. We denote by $G_{P_{\text{OUT}}^t}$ (respectively, $G_{Q_{\text{OUT}}^t}, G_{P_{\text{IN}}^t}$, and $G_{Q_{\text{IN}}^t}$) the marginal distribution over output prices (respectively, output quantities, input prices, and input quantities). $G_{P_{\text{IN}}, Q_{\text{IN}}, P_{\text{OUT}}, Q_{\text{OUT}}}$ was estimated by a histogram, which was constructed from data obtained offline, via repeated simulations between one NVM agent and one GFM at each of the other levels in the production chain. For SCML '19, a histogram was a sufficient representation because of the small number of trading quantities entertainined by GFM agents.

Given a fixed time horizon T, a **plan of action** is defined as a collection of tuples $P = \{(x_t, y_t, z_t)\}_{t=1}^T$. This plan completely specifies for each time period $t = 1, \ldots, T$, the number x_t of inputs to buy, y_t of outputs to sell, and z_t of inputs to turn into outputs. A plan is **feasible** if it can be executed, i.e., if at every time step there are enough inputs to be bought, enough outputs to be sold, and enough inputs to be converted into outputs.

More formally, the goal of the NVM agent is to find a feasible plan that maximizes its total expected profits over the time horizon T:

$$\max_{\mathbf{x},\mathbf{y},\mathbf{z}} \mathbb{E}_{Q_{\text{IN}}^t, Q_{\text{OUT}}^t} \left[\sum_{t=1}^T p_{\text{OUT}}^t \min(y_t, Q_{\text{OUT}}^t) - p_{\text{IN}}^t \min(x_t, Q_{\text{IN}}^t) - \text{COST} \cdot z_t \right]$$

$$\text{s.t.} \quad z_t \leq \text{CAPACITY}$$

$$y_t \leq O_t = \sum_{k=1}^{t-1} z_k - y_k \tag{4}$$

$$z_t \leq I_t = \sum_{k=1}^{t-1} x_k - z_k$$

$$x_t, y_t, z_t \geq 0$$

All these constraints must hold for all time steps $t \in \{1, \ldots, T\}$, with initial conditions $O_1 = I_1 = y_1 = z_1 = 0$. Variables O_t and I_t are auxiliary variables representing the output, respectively the input, inventory levels at time t. The initial conditions specify that, at the beginning of the planning horizon, the agent has no inputs nor outputs in storage, and hence, cannot produce or sell outputs. Note that these initial conditions can easily be changed; thus, the agent can plan differently given non-zero storage. COST is the agent's private, per-unit production cost, while CAPACITY is the maximum number of inputs that can be converted into outputs during a single time step. The current version of NVM sets $p_{\text{IN}}^t = \mathbb{E}[P_{\text{IN}}^t]$ and $p_{\text{OUT}}^t = \mathbb{E}[P_{\text{OUT}}^t]$.

At each time t, NVM solves for an optimal plan of action.[1] Given this plan, the agent posts a single buy CFP with quantity range $(\max(1, y_1 - \delta_q), y_1 + \delta_q)$, price range between 0 and the expected catalog price $p_{\text{IN}}^t = \mathbb{E}[P_{\text{IN}}^t]$, and time range $(t + \underline{\delta}_t, t + \overline{\delta}_t)$.[2] Additionally, NVM requests negotiations with publishers of sell CFPs. With sufficient (e.g., unlimited) negotiation resources, it can conduct negotiations that are consistent with its optimal plan of action with any agent who is interested in negotiating about anything.

To estimate the utility of a potential buy contract, NVM uses an ad hoc function defined solely in terms of price, namely $u(p) = 1 - p$, which means the agent prefers lower prices, at all possible values of quantity and time. The utility of a potential sell contract is calculated in terms of both price and quantity, as $u(p, q) = e^{(p-1.5)}q$, if $p > 0$ and $-\infty$ otherwise. In other words, NVM prefers to sell many outputs at higher prices, provided the price is not zero. An independent copy of the relevant (buy or sell) utility function is used in all concurrent negotiations.

Like GFM, NVM operates as a reactive seller (requesting negotiations with all publishers of buy CFPs) and uses the built-in aspiration-level negotiator. Unlike GFM, upon receiving a delivery of inputs, it immediately sends the inputs to one of its production lines, where they are scheduled in a FIFO fashion.

Self-Adjustable Heuristic Agent (SAHA). Rather than redesign the various components of an agent (negotiators, utility functions, scheduler, etc.), the **self-adjustable heuristic agent** (SAHA) implements a high-level behavior on top of GFM. Specifically, SAHA imports the aspiration-level negotiator, the utility functions, and the baseline scheduler from GFM. The main focus of SAHA is then on strategic placement of CFPs with the intent of achieving a high profit margin. Moreover, the interaction of multiple SAHA agents, all aiming for higher profit margins, artificially inflates (deflates) the prices of its sell (buy) contracts.

When selling (buying) products, SAHA posts CFPs with progressively higher (lower) prices until the other agents start rejecting their proposals outright. SAHA then decreases (increases) prices until it enters into negotiations again, always seeking to post CFPs with prices near the highest (lowest) observed

---

[1] Details of the dynamic program we used to efficiently solve (4) for optimal plans are left for a longer version of this paper.

[2] These parameters were manually tuned to $\underline{\delta}_t = 5, \overline{\delta}_t = 15$, and $\delta_q = 5$.

acceptable price. We observed in our experiments that over time, the agent's buying and selling price ranges seem to stabilize. In more detail:

1. SAHA requests a negotiation with the publisher of a buy CFP for its outputs, or it counters with a modified negotiation agenda in its desired price range.
2. SAHA requests a negotiation with the publisher of a sell CFP for its inputs, up to a stock limit, again within its desired price range.
3. SAHA posts sell (buy) CFPs for all the outputs in inventory (inputs needed).
4. If SAHA enters into a negotiation and it fails, it reverts the desired price range for that product to its previous value.

The SAHA agent maintains a set of records based on past and current CFPs containing each product's minimum and maximum prices. Whenever a new CFP is posted, or the agent reaches an agreement, the records are updated with the new information, and the product price ranges for that product are recalculated, adding or subtracting an increment as follows: Buying Range $= [0, CP + \Delta_1 CP]$, where CP is the catalog price for the product and Δ_1 is the buy increment; ans Selling Range $= [M - \Delta_1 M, M + \Delta_2 M]$, where M is the maximum price observed for that product, Δ_1 is the buy increment and Δ_2 is the sell increment. The agent will create a set of 20 prices for the negotiation between those ranges in order to avoid a negotiation fail due to a timeout.

We tuned the agent's behavior by optimizing three hyperparameters: the minimum elapsed time until entering a negotiation; the maximum inventory level at any time; and the buy and sell increments used to create price ranges.

7   Experiments

This section describes a series of experiments that we ran to evaluate the three aforementioned agent strategies for managing a factory in the SCM world. The following round-robin design was employed. A set of N random world configurations were generated. For each configuration, two sets of factories, each of cardinality F, were selected. For each of the three possible combinations of agents (i.e., GFM vs. NVM, GFM vs. SAHA, and SAHA vs. NVM), two simulations were conducted, one with each of the two sets of factories managed by each of the two competing agents. In total, each of the N world configurations was simulated $3 \times 2 = 6$ times. An agent's score in a single simulation is the profit it

Table 1. Results of a Comparative Study using the SCML '19 settings.

Strategy	Median	Mean (±Std.)	Kolmogorov-Smirnov Test Statistic (p-value)		
			NVM	SAHA	GFM
NVM	**0.315**	0.221 (±0.636)	–	0.213 (0.046)	0.625 (1.359×10^{-14})
SAHA	0.168	**0.401** (±0.628)		–	0.588 (6.059×10^{-13})
GFM	−0.055	−0.107 (±0.154)			–

achieves as a fraction of its initial wallet balance (which was set to 1000 for these experiments, for all agents). All agents' scores in all simulations were collected and analyzed, as described in the following subsections.

In the first experiment, the settings used in the ANAC SCML '19 standard track league (Sect. 5) were used [12]. Twenty different world configurations were employed, with one factory per strategy per simulation ($F = 1$), leading to 120 world simulations and 240 scores per agent. A summary of the results of this experiment is presented in Table 1. SAHA achieved the highest average score while NVM achieved the highest median score. The difference in score distributions between SAHA and NVM was not statistically significant, according to a factorial two-sided Kolmogorov–Smirnov test with a Bonferroni multiple-comparisons correction ($t = 0.213, p = 0.046 > 0.05/3$). Both agents achieved higher scores than the baseline GFM agent ($p < 1.4 \times 10^{-14}$ for NVM, and $p < 6.1 \times 10^{-13}$ for SAHA).

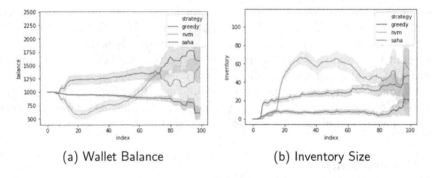

(a) Wallet Balance   (b) Inventory Size

Fig. 2. Evolution of wallet balance and inventory size over time.

Figure 2a shows the evolution of the three agents' wallet balances and inventory sizes over time. NVM's evolving wallet balances and inventory sizes accurately reflects its strategy: its wallet balance initially decreases while its inventory size increases, as it accrues inputs to manufacture into outputs; its wallet balance then begins to recover (around time step 20), when it starts to do more selling than buying. SAHA, in contrast, tries to create favorable market conditions from the beginning, and achieves a nearly monotonic increase in both its wallet balance and its inventory size. By the end of the simulations, NVM and SAHA tend to achieve similar wallet balances, and similar inventory sizes, thought

Table 2. Effect of the insurance company on the market.

Condition	Negotiations	Agreements	Contracts	Executed	Business size
Without Insurer	5867.5	3559	**1068.5**	397.5	2379.25
With Insurer	5299	**3781**	983	**472.5**	**3927.58**

NVM, because of its lookahead, does a better job of unloading excess inventory at the very end than SAHA. GFM's balance, on the other hand, *decreases* almost monotonically, due to its tendency to overcontract.

The insurance company was introduced into the SCM world to increase business size. To assess whether it was successful in achieving this goal, we reran the experimental design used in the comparative study, but without the insurance company. The results of this experiment are presented in Tables 2 and 3.

In Table 2, we see that although there were more agreements reached in the presence of the insurance company, there was also an 8% reduction in the number of contracts signed, likely because of the cost of insurance. (GFM and SAHA always buy insurance; NVM never does.) Nevertheless, there was also a 16% reduction in the number of breached contracts, because breaches at lower levels of the production chain did not automatically cause breaches at higher levels. This in turn led to a 65% increase in business size, which demonstrates that the insurance company did provide the benefits for which it was designed.

Table 3. Results of the Comparative Study without the insurance company.

Strategy	Median	Mean (±Std.)	Kolmogorov-Smirov Test Statistic (p-value)		
			NVM	SAHA	GFM
NVM	0.077	−0.044 (±0.524)	–	−0.37 (1.22×10^{-24})	0.448 (7.612×10^{-36})
SAHA	**0.257**	**0.421** (±0.477)		–	0.603 (1.247×10^{-64})
GFM	−0.050	−0.071 (±0.112)			–

We now briefly investigate how heavily each of the three agents relied on the insurance company (Table 3). SAHA appears to be least dependent, with its median profit increasing by 16.8%, and with almost no change in its mean profit. This robustness allowed SAHA to outperform both NVM and GFM, and the difference is statistically significant after a Bonferroni multiple-comparisons correction ($p < 1.3 \times 10^{-64}$ for NVM) and ($p < 7.7 \times 10^{-36}$ for GFM).

Our experimental results suggest that NVM and SAHA are more successful factory managers in the SCM world than the baseline GFM. NVM's performance has lower variance in the presence of the insurance company, while SAHA has better average performance and is especially robust to the omission of the insurance company. It remains to be seen, however, whether GFM might be more competitive if it were not parameterized to maximize business size.

Conclusion

This paper described a common benchmark simulation environment, which is available as an open-source library, and can thus serve as a sandbox to advance research on situated negotiations. We presented a set of desiderata we believe this kind of simulator should satisfy in order to be a useful model of real-world negotiation scenarios, and argued that the proposed benchmark satisfies them. We then described the SCM world, as well as SCML, an automated negotiation competition, that was run in 2019 using this benchmark. A baseline strategy for this competition, along with two other competitive entrants, were also described and evaluated. In future renditions of SCML, we expect to alter the SCM world simulation in light of the lessons learned in 2019. Ultimately, our goal is to design and build environments that isolate various aspects of situated negotiations to promote the development of automated negotiation strategies.

References

1. Adabi, S., Movaghar, A., Rahmani, A.M., Beigy, H., Dastmalchy-Tabrizi, H.: A new fuzzy negotiation protocol for grid resource allocation. J. Network Comput. Appl. **37**, 89–126 (2014)
2. An, B., Lesser, V., Irwin, D., Zink, M.: Automated negotiation with decommitment for dynamic resource allocation in cloud computing. In: Proceedings of the 9th AAMAS, pp. 981–988 (2010)
3. Aydoğan, R., Festen, D., Hindriks, K.V., Jonker, C.M.: Alternating offers protocols for multilateral negotiation. In: Fujita, K., et al. (eds.) Modern Approaches to Agent-based Complex Automated Negotiation. SCI, vol. 674, pp. 153–167. Springer, Cham (2017). https://doi.org/10.1007/978-3-319-51563-2_10
4. Faratin, P., Sierra, C., Jennings, N.R.: Negotiation decision functions for autonomous agents. Robot. Auton. Syst. **24**(3–4), 159–182 (1998)
5. Greenwald, A., Boyan, J.: Bidding algorithms for simultaneous auctions. In: Proceedings of the 3rd ACM Conference on Electronic Commerce, pp. 115–124 (2001)
6. Jaffray, J.Y.: Existence of a continuous utility function: an elementary proof. Econometrica **43**(5/6), 981–983 (1975)
7. Jonker, C.M., Aydogan, R., Baarslag, T., Fujita, K., Ito, T., Hindriks, K.V.: Automated negotiating agents competition (ANAC). In: AAAI, pp. 5070–5072 (2017)
8. Krainin, M., An, B., Lesser, V.: An application of automated negotiation to distributed task allocation. In: Proceedings of the 2007 IEEE/WIC/ACM International Conference on Intelligent Agent Technology, pp. 138–145 (2007)
9. Li, C., Giampapa, J., Sycara, K.: Bilateral negotiation decisions with uncertain dynamic outside options. IEEE Trans. Syst. Man. Cybern. Part C (Appl. Rev.) **36**(1), 31–44 (2006)
10. Li, M., Vo, Q.B., Kowalczyk, R., Ossowski, S., Kersten, G.: Automated negotiation in open and distributed environments. Expert Syst. Appl. **40**(15), 6195–6212 (2013)
11. Mansour, K., Kowalczyk, R.: A meta-strategy for coordinating of one-to-many negotiation over multiple issues. In: Wang, Y., Li, T. (eds.) Foundations of Intelligent Systems, pp. 343–353. Springer, Heidelberg (2011). https://doi.org/10.1007/978-3-642-25664-6_40
12. Mohammad, Y., Fujita, K., Greenwald, A., Klein, M., Morinaga, S., Nakadai, S.: ANAC 2019 SCML (2019). http://tiny.cc/f8sv9y
13. Mohammad, Y., Greenwald, A., Nakadai, S.: Negmas: a platform for situated negotiations. In: Twelfth International Workshop on Agent-Based Complex Automated Negotiations (ACAN2019) in Conjunction with IJCAI (2019)
14. Mohammad, Y., Nakadai, S.: Optimal value of information based elicitation during negotiation. In: Proceedings of the 18th International Conference on Autonomous Agents and MultiAgent Systems, AAMAS 2019, pp. 242–250. International Foundation for Autonomous Agents and Multiagent Systems (2019)

15. Petruzzi, N.C., Dada, M.: Pricing and the newsvendor problem: a review with extensions. Oper. Res. **47**(2), 183–194 (1999)
16. Phillips, P.J., Flynn, P.J., Scruggs, T., Bowyer, K.W., Worek, W.: Preliminary face recognition grand challenge results. In: 7th International Conference on Automatic Face and Gesture Recognition (FGR06), pp. 15–24. IEEE (2006)
17. PRNewswire: digital process automation market by component, business function, deployment type, organization size, industry vertical and region - global forecast to 2023 (2019). http://tiny.cc/573o9y
18. Wellman, M.P., Greenwald, A., Stone, P., Wurman, P.R.: The 2001 trading agent competition. Electron. Markets **13**(1), 4–12 (2003)
19. Wellman, M.P., Sodomka, E., Greenwald, A.: Self-confirming price-prediction strategies for simultaneous one-shot auctions. Games Econ. Behav. **102**, 339–372 (2017)
20. Williams, C., Robu, V., Gerding, E., Jennings, N.R.: Negotiating concurrently with unknown opponents in complex, real-time domains. Front. Artif. Intell. Appl. **242**, 834–839 (2012)

Coordination of Mobile Agents
for Simultaneous Coverage

Petra Mazdin[1]([⊠]) and Bernhard Rinner[2]([⊠])

[1] Karl Popper Kolleg on Networked Autonomous Aerial Vehicles,
University of Klagenfurt, Klagenfurt, Austria
`petra.mazdin@aau.at`
[2] Institute of Networked and Embedded Systems, University of Klagenfurt,
Klagenfurt, Austria
`bernhard.rinner@aau.at`

Abstract. Simultaneous environment coverage represents a challenging multi-agent application, in which mobile agents (drones) must cover surfaces by simultaneously capturing images from different viewpoints. It constitutes a complex optimization problem with potentially conflicting criteria, such as mission time and coverage quality, and requires dynamic coordination of agent tasks. In this paper, we introduce a decentralized coordination method, adaptive to a dynamic and a priori unknown 3D environment. Our approach selects the role an agent should take on and coordinates the assignment of agents to their computed viewpoints. Our main goal is to cover all detected objects in the environment at a certain quality as soon as possible. We evaluate the methods in AirSim in different setups and assess how the proposed methods respond to dynamic changes in the environment.

Keywords: Multi-agent system · Simultaneous coverage · Drones · Viewpoint constellations · Market-based task assignment · AirSim simulator

1 Introduction

Mobile robots represent a prototypical example of a multi-agent system, and we have witnessed their tremendous progress in research and applications over the last decades. Collaborative aerial robots or multi-drone systems (e.g. [21,25]) are a particularly challenging research field due to their flexibility, scalability and resource limitations.

This paper deals with *simultaneous coverage* of unknown environments which represents an important problem for multi-drone systems. In various applications, such as monitoring, inspection, 3D reconstruction, and depth measurements, drones with onboard cameras autonomously move in the environment to capture imagery of objects of interest with sufficient quality [15]. In case of dynamic environments, the capturing time of images is highly relevant, and estimation of the state of the environment or the objects of interest may become

© Springer Nature Switzerland AG 2019
M. Baldoni et al. (Eds.): PRIMA 2019, LNAI 11873, pp. 170–185, 2019.
https://doi.org/10.1007/978-3-030-33792-6_11

uncertain if the time lag of the individual image capturing is too large. Simultaneous coverage mitigates this problem by requiring concurrent image capturing from k different viewpoints and thus simplifies multi-view image analysis.

In our approach, objects of interest must be first detected and then covered by simultaneously captured images from k different viewpoints. Figure 1 depicts different stages of such coverage mission where drones explore the initially unknown environment (gray area) to detect objects (pink cuboids). Once an object has been detected, it needs to be observed in order to abstract its shape and to compute the required viewpoints (constellations) for the coverage. Finally, dynamic teams are formed and move along the paths to the assigned viewpoints. When the required viewpoint locations are reached, the drones simultaneously capture images with overlapping field of view (yellow area) and continue the mission. Dynamic coordination of tasks and paths is crucial, since simultaneous coverage constitutes a complex optimization problem with changing knowledge about the state of the environment.

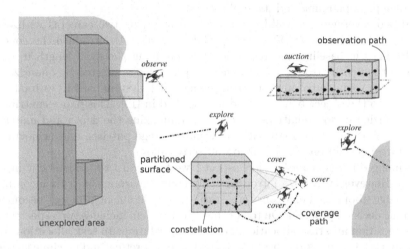

Fig. 1. Sketch of a simultaneous coverage mission where drones explore the environment, observe detected objects, compute constellations, and navigate along the constellations in dynamically assigned teams (here for $k = 3$ drones). (Color figure online)

Weyrer and Rinner [24] introduced a path planning algorithm and a model-predictive controller for a fixed team of two drones, and Mazdin and Rinner [16] proposed a market-based drone assignment for coverage in simple, a priori known 2D environments. The contribution of this paper can be summarized as follows: First, we expand the simultaneous coverage algorithm to 3D unknown environments where drones autonomously take on different roles. Second, the computation of the required viewpoints explores the tradeoff between achieved coverage quality and coverage area. Third, we introduce an adaptive market-based coordination approach for dynamic task assignment. Finally, we perform a simulation study of our approach using the multi-drone framework AirSim [22].

The paper is organized as follows: Sect. 2 briefly compares our contribution with the state of the art. Section 3 provides the formal problem definition, and Sect. 4 describes our approach. Section 5 discusses the achieved results, and Sect. 6 summarizes the contribution and discusses potential future work.

2   Related Work

Even with small-scale drones, leveraging onboard cameras is widely used for various inspection tasks of an object's surface, and the approaches differ whether a priori knowledge of the environment or the object's shape is considered. Heng et al. [13] propose an algorithm for simultaneous exploration and coverage in an unknown environment, whereas Bircher et al. [3] address the exploration of an unknown environment and extend their work to include the inspection of surfaces in [4]. An alternative approach to a similar exploration path planning problem can be found in [26]. Galceran and Carreras [10] survey the problem of coverage path planning and its applications.

Stereo coverage is a well-known topic of arranging two cameras with overlapping fields of view (FoV) [4,9,13]. Gallup et al. [11] introduce the concept of altering the baseline and resolution by modifying the focal length in order to keep the depth error constant, where depth error is affected by quantization noise [6,9]. Variable baseline stereo tracking vision system used to estimate the distance to the object being tracked is described in [19]. This paper contributes to optimizing of constellations in terms of minimizing the depth and matching error, increasing the overlap with adjacent coverage patches, and achieving as high target resolution as the mission objective allows.

Among different coordination aspects, we focus on task assignment in this paper. However, when we introduce a dynamic environment with incomplete knowledge about its behaviour, our static task assignment problem becomes a dynamic decision problem. On top of that, the problem includes two aspects: task decomposition and task allocation. Some of the solutions to task allocation comprise market-based approaches [12,17,20], game theoretical and machine learning approaches [14,23,27], optimization-based approaches [2,5,8], etc. We adopt the market-based approach from [16], due to its simplicity, dynamic response and decentralization. Moreover, we improve the approach by elaborating on the task decomposition aspect in terms of adaptation to the partial available environment knowledge of drones.

3   Problem Definition

The simultaneous coverage problem can be formalized as follows: A set of m drones $D = \{d_1, \ldots, d_m\}$ covers a 3D environment which includes a set of ground objects of interest $O = \{o_1, \ldots, o_p\}$, whose position and shape are initially unknown. We consider static objects that neither change their position nor shape, and semi-dynamic objects that don't change their position but may experience some dynamics of their shape, e.g. due to wind. After detection and sufficient observation, an object o_i is abstracted by a set of surfaces $S_i = \{s_{i1}, \ldots, s_{in}\}$. A constellation c_i represents the k viewpoints, i.e. the positions and orientations of the drones required to cover a surface or parts of it. A (part of a) surface is simultaneously covered if k drones visit the viewpoints of the corresponding constellation and capture overlapping images concurrently.

The mission is achieved when the specified area is fully explored and every surface of the detected objects has been simultaneously covered. The overall objective is to complete the mission as fast as possible and at a certain quality.

Solving the simultaneous coverage problem can be decomposed into several interdependent sub-problems: (1) exploring the environment, (2) detecting objects, abstracting surfaces and computing the required constellations, (3) assigning drones to constellations, and (4) covering all surfaces by following collision-free paths between the constellations. In our approach, drones autonomously take on different roles when contributing to the different sub-problems.

4 Approach

4.1 Mission Objective

Our overall objective is to cover every surface satisfying a certain quality as soon as possible. We have thus two sub-objectives: the mission duration and the coverage quality. We represent the mission duration objective by the number of constellation points J_{nc}, since the time it takes a drone to cover each point comprises the time to reach it, to decelerate and stabilize as well as to wait for the other $k-1$ drones in order to simultaneously capture images. The number of constellation points is dependent on the coverage quality: For achieving higher quality, more constellation points are necessary. We label the coverage quality, represented by the resolution δ, with J_{cq}, and formulate the mission objective as minimizing

$$J_{mo} = \lambda \cdot J_{nc} + (1 - \lambda) \cdot J_{cq}, \tag{1}$$

where $\lambda \in \mathbb{R} | 0 \leq \lambda \leq 1$ controls the effect of the two optimization goals. We define $J_{cq} = \frac{\delta_{max}}{\delta}$ to be within the limits imposed by simple camera model with image width w, minimum safe distance to the surface D_{max}, and the lens horizontal aperture angle α_H, i.e. $\delta_{max} = \frac{w}{2 \cdot D_{max} \cdot tan(\frac{\alpha_H}{2})}$ [24]. As we aim to minimize this objective, we need to increase δ to increase the coverage quality.

We estimate the number of constellation points J_{nc} by

$$J_{nc} = \frac{2 \cdot k \cdot \sum_{i=1}^{n} L_i \cdot \lambda_{as} \cdot H_i \cdot \delta^2}{w \cdot h}, \tag{2}$$

which depends on k, the resolution δ, image width w and height h, a sum $\sum_{i=1}^{n} L_i$ of lengths of all surfaces of an object o_i (double the value due to the requirement of at least 50% horizontal overlap), the object's height H_i, and a weight parameter $\lambda_{as} \geq 1$. As opposed to J_{cq}, a low value of δ reduces the mission duration. We use λ_{as} throughout the mission to tune the importance of maximizing additional covered area for the purpose of increasing the overlap with adjacent image patches. When λ_{as} is set to 1, we obtain no vertical additional area that leads to no overlap between images taken from two neighboring surfaces (in a vertical direction).

4.2   Selection of Drone Roles

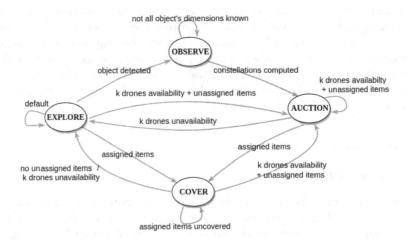

Fig. 2. Four drone roles and transition conditions.

In order to find a solution to the simultaneous coverage problem, we decompose it into smaller sub-problems and adopt a bottom-up approach by solving them individually. These sub-problems comprise exploration, object detection and observation, and coverage, and introduce different roles that drones can take on during the mission. Figure 2 depicts the drone roles and the predefined transition conditions by means of a state diagram. The default role of a drone d_i is *explore*, represented as d_i^e, where it moves in the environment following a given exploration strategy for detecting objects. Once an object has been detected, the drone changes its role to *observe* d_i^o, investigates the shape of the object in order to abstract surfaces, and computes constellation points. These points represent the positions and orientations of k cameras satisfying the quality constraints (cp. Sect. 4.3). Afterwards, the computed constellation points to cover the detected object(s) have to be assigned to appropriate drones. Therefore, the drone changes its role to *auction* d_i^a to perform this task assignment by means of different auction strategies (cp. Sect. 4.4). The assigned drones change to the *cover* role d_i^c and execute the necessary steps for covering the assigned surface(s).

Drone assignment is not successful if less than k drones are available for covering an object or surface, respectively. In this case, the drone can either change to *explore* or participate in the bidding of another auction drone. This drone periodically checks if a sufficient number of drones has become available and continues then with the auctioning of unassigned items as long as this condition is satisfied.

Only drones with role d_i^e and role d_i^a but an insufficient number of bidders can participate in the bidding. We further assume that drones with roles d_i^o and d_i^c cannot be interrupted by a bidding request.

4.3   Constellation Computation

Figure 3 sketches a constellation of three drones placed at positions $[x_i, y_i, z_i]$, separated by baselines b_{ij}, and at distance $\hat{y}$ to the surface. For simplicity, the covered partition of length L_p is perpendicular to the y axis, and the cameras' views are perpendicular to the surface. The covered partition $P_{sij} \subseteq S_{ij}$ is defined by the points $p_{xyz} = [x, y, z]$ which are visible to all k cameras. If we apply a simple camera model with focal length f, sensor dimensions $w \times h$ and aperture angles α_H and α_V, the following constraints between any camera pair i and j must hold:

$$|x - x_i - \frac{b_{ij}}{2}| \leq \frac{w\hat{y} - b_{ij}f}{2f},$$

$$y - y_i \geq \frac{b_{ij}f}{w}, \tag{3}$$

$$|z - z_i| \leq \frac{\hat{y}h}{2f}.$$

Note that these constraints impose an overlap in the cameras' FoV of at least 50%. The partition can be specified by the four corner points of P_{sij} as

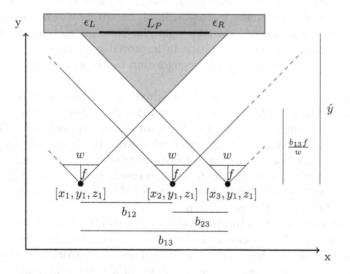

Fig. 3. Drone constellation with covered FoV represented in the xy plane. $k = 3$ drones, positioned at $[x_i, y_1, z_1]$, simultaneously cover the partition of length L_p.

$[x_P, y_P, z_P], [x_P + L_P, y_P, z_P], [x_P + L_P, y_P, z_P + H_P], [x_P, y_P, z_P + H_P]$, where L_P and H_P represent the width and the height of P_{sij}, respectively.

In our approach, we formulate the constellation computation problem as a multi-objective optimization problem, having three fitness functions to be minimized:

$$J_{co} = \lambda_{de} \cdot J_{de} + \lambda_{me} \cdot J_{me} - \lambda_{as} \cdot J_{as}, \tag{4}$$

where J_{de} represents the depth error, J_{me} represents the matching error, and J_{as} corresponds to the covered area.

We use a first order Taylor series approximation to estimate the depth error $J_{de} = \frac{\hat{y}^2}{b_{ij}f} \cdot \epsilon_d$ given the distance $\hat{y}$, the disparity error ϵ_d caused by the corresponding pixels' difference in x coordinates, baseline b_{ij}, and the focal length f. The matching error J_{me} depends on the parameters a and b describing matching performance and the relative viewing angle γ, and is approximated as $\frac{1}{a} \cdot (e^{-b|\gamma|} - 1)$ [18,24].

The third cost function component J_{as} rewards the additional area covered beyond the border of the partition P_{sij}. This additional overlap with adjacent image patches helps to improve the overall stitching of the images from the individual partitions. Basically, we want to increase both ϵ_R and ϵ_L in Fig. 3 and therefore subtract it in Eq. 4, as opposed to the other objectives.

With the equal height of the k constellation points, the y and z coordinates of the drones are given as $y_i = y_P - \frac{L_P}{\tan(\frac{\alpha_H}{2})}$ and $z_i = z_P + \frac{H_P}{2}$. Note that if $k = 1$ only J_{as} is taken into account aiming for an overlap with neighboring partitions of at least 50%.

Since constellation computation is an NP-hard multi-objective optimization problem, we address it with an efficient evolutionary algorithm NSGA-II (non-dominated sorting genetic algorithm-II), leading to Pareto optimal solutions [7]. This fast, elitist and parameterless algorithm is known for its low computational complexity with a simple but efficient constraint-handling method and fast non-dominated sorting procedure resulting in improved convergence. We limit the number of function evaluations of the algorithm based on the mission's update rate.

As previously stated, k controls the required simultaneously captured images for a surface. Thus, a larger k may provide more data about dynamic textures, occlusions, etc., which might be beneficial for certain applications. Therefore, we extend our constellation computation algorithm to be suitable for a larger k. Figure 4 depicts two relaxations for the constellation computation for $k = 3$ drones. We allow (a) asymmetric drone placements resulting in different baseline settings and (b) different distances between drones and the covered surface resulting in different target resolutions.

Since we consider 3D objects in the environment, we have to assure the coverage of all visible surfaces, including the top ones. We do so by projecting the top surface of the object as an additional vertical partition to the vertical surface being covered. However, we are aware of a lower achievable resolution due to the fact that the far most part of the top surface is further away than

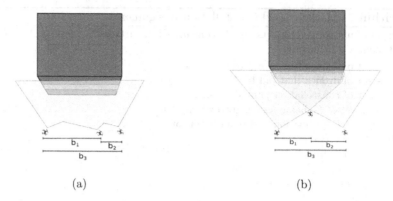

(a)   (b)

Fig. 4. Different constellation relaxations for $k = 3$: (a) different baselines, and (b) different distances to the surface.

the vertical surface. To assure corner detection in the images, we add another horizontal partition to the right of each surface.

4.4 Adaptive Task Assignment

After constellation computation has been completed, drone d_i changes its role to d_i^a and starts the assignment of available drones to constellations. We adopt a decentralized market-based assignment due to its scalability, efficiency, and suitability for dynamic settings [1]. Optimal assignment algorithms that reach the global optimum are mostly centralized. Many decentralized multi-agent task assignment methods employ auctioning mechanisms which have been applied to NP-hard problems (routing, scheduling, planning, etc.), or address problems where only partial knowledge about the environment is available, and therefore local information is exploited. Since our mission is defined in such a way, agents make decisions based on their current (local) knowledge. Due to the lack of knowledge, most often the global optimum solution is not found. When, on top of that, we consider a dynamic environment and only agents' local knowledge about it, the resulting assignment quality gets difficult to measure.

We adopt our previous approach [16], where we deployed a basic auction mechanism enabling drones to bid for constellations and introduced an object-based (OB) and surface-based (SB) variant. OB allocation assigns all constellation points of an object to the same team of k drones, whereas SB allocation assigns constellations individually to k drones.

Algorithm 1 describes our new adaptive allocation algorithm which is running on each drone d_i with unassigned constellations. As long as drone d_i has unassigned allocation items, it is free to explore around and periodically (line 7) broadcast the request for roles in order to find out the number of drones available for bidding (lines 8 to 11). If there are at least k drones available, d_i selects an object from O_i^a, computes the constellations of object o and initiates an auction

---

Algorithm 1. Market-based Constellation Assignment

Input: set of unassigned objects O_i^a of drone d_i, set of surfaces S_i for $o_i \in O_i^a$, auction T_a and request T_r timeout

1: $F_i^a \leftarrow$ set of drones free to bid to d_i
2: $B_i^a \leftarrow$ set of drones that bid to d_i
3: $C_i^a \leftarrow$ set of constellation points to assign
4: $S_i^a \leftarrow$ subset of S_i being assigned to winners in B_i^a
5: $t_a = 0, t_r = T_r \leftarrow$ auction and request timeout counter
6: **while** $O_i^a \neq \emptyset$ **do**
7:     **if** $t_r \geq T_r$ **then**
8:         $d_i \leftarrow d_i^e$
9:         $broadcast\_role\_request()$
10:        $t_r \leftarrow 0$
11:    $F_i^a \leftarrow update\_free\_drones()$
12:    **if** $|F_i^a| \geq k$ **then**
13:        $d_i \leftarrow d_i^a$
14:        $o \leftarrow select\_object(O_i^a)$
15:        $C_i^a \leftarrow compute\_constellations(o)$
16:        $broadcast\_constellations(C_i^a)$
17:        **if** $t_a < T_a$ **then**
18:            $t_a \leftarrow t_a + 1$
19:            $B_i^a \leftarrow update\_bids()$
20:            **if** $|B_i^a| \geq k$ **then**
21:                $S_i^a \leftarrow allocate\_surfaces()$
22:                $broadcast\_decision(S_i^a)$
23:                $wait\_for\_acknowledgment()$
24:                $O_i^a \leftarrow O_i^a \setminus o; t_r \leftarrow T_r$
25:                **break**
26:        **else**
27:            $d_i \leftarrow d_i^e$
28:            $t_r \leftarrow T_r; t_a \leftarrow 0$
29:    **else**
30:        $t_r \leftarrow t_r + 1$
31: $d_i \leftarrow d_i^e$

---

by broadcasting the constellations of o (lines 14 to 16). It does so as long as it has not received enough bids (lines 19 and 20) and the timeout t_a has not expired. If a sufficient number of bids has been received, d_i selects the k drones from B_i^a with the highest bid values and broadcasts a decision (lines 21 and 22).

We consider this part to be of importance when adapting to the dynamic change of roles and the current knowledge drones possess. This knowledge comprises a number of drones, their roles and locations, and the shape of the object and its constellations. Basically, we improve the task decomposition aspect of the task assignment problem by assigning a number of neighboring surfaces proportionally to the number of bids and their distances to the drones that bid. This way we parallelize the coverage when multiples of k drones bid. This is important because with such a dynamic environment and quick changes, especially in drones' movements, proceeding with an assumption made at the moment an object was ready to be assigned could prolong the mission.

Once the drone d_i receives an acknowledgment from all allocated drones (line 23), it removes the object from O_i^a and resets timer t_r to be ready to broadcast role requests again (line 24). If the timeout has exceeded, d_i keeps exploring and resets both timers to broadcast role requests again (lines 27 and 28). If all objects have been assigned, d_i changes its role to explore (line 31).

To consider the auction successful, drone d_i waits for the acknowledgments from all assigned drones. This acknowledgment mechanism also holds for the bidding drones. If they did not receive an acknowledgment from the drone d_i within a predefined timeout T_c, they cancel the bid and start exploring or submit a bid to another auction.

As stated above, due to the partial environment knowledge, we cannot aim for the global optimum solution, rather for the optimal solution given the knowledge a drone auctioneer possesses at the moment it starts the auction. One reason for a non-optimal outcome could be an unknown obstacle between assigned drones(s) and constellation points, which results in a prolonged flight time as compared to the estimated time of the drone bidder.

4.5   Exploration and Object Detection

We apply a simple heuristic for exploring the environment to detect objects of interest. The drones start exploring from the ground station in a random direction and move straight until they detect an object, encounter an obstacle, or reach the border of the environment. In the latter case, they rotate at a random angle to stay within the environment and continue exploration. For object and obstacle detection we exploit the drone's frontal camera. In particular, we leverage the API of AirSim to retrieve an uncompressed depth image from the left frontal camera, convert it to a gray-scale image, and remove the ground to show only the relevant part. We estimate the distance to a potential object by evaluating the corresponding pixel values and perform further analysis based on the size of the pixel cluster in the depth image. To investigate the shape of an object, the drone performs wall following by keeping the distance to the object fixed while moving around the object. Once wall following has reached the starting position, i.e. the path around the object has been closed, the drone ascends to estimate the height of the object.

We adapt the path planning approach [16] by considering online obstacle detection and avoidance. Whenever an object or obstacle is detected on the computed path towards a constellation point, we perform a similar wall following approach for bypassing the obstacle at a safe distance. If the path towards the constellation point is clear, the drone continues in a straight line.

5   Experiments

5.1   Experimental Setup

We use the open-source simulator Microsoft AirSim[1] (Aerial Informatics and Robotics Simulation) which is built on the Epic Games' Unreal Engine 4 (UE4)[2] for our simulation study. We created a virtual environment on a 64-bit Windows-10 platform (cp. Fig. 5), imported it to a Linux platform running Ubuntu 16.04 LTS, and added the AirSim plugin as a replacement for AirSim drone with the *SimpleFlight* built-in flight controller. As we aim for a fully decentralized system and want to deploy our algorithms on real drones, we incorporated the recent ROS2 version (distribution Bouncy Bolson)[3]. With this setup the drone agents are able to exchange messages at an update rate of 1 s which is very important for real-world missions. ROS2 is supposed to run under Windows. However, in our 64-bit Windows-10 setup, ROS2 showed unreliable performance, in particular, more than 50% of the messages were lost when running simulations with more than 4 drones. Therefore, we used the Windows platform only for creating the environment and the Linux platform for running the experiments and exchanging messages among the drone agents via ROS2.

Fig. 5. The virtual environment for our simulation study rendered by the Epic Games Unreal Engine 4.

For our simulation we use an environment of 240 m × 240 m and place building blocks of different sizes as objects of interest. The ground station is at the center from where all drones start their mission. The drones are equipped with cameras, GPS, an Inertial Measurement Unit (IMU), and a barometer. We perform experiments with varying $k \in \{1, 2, 3\}$ and for the object-based (OB), surface-based (SB), and adaptive (AD) auction variants. As baseline for

---

[1] https://github.com/Microsoft/AirSim.
[2] https://www.unrealengine.com.
[3] https://github.com/ros2/ros2.

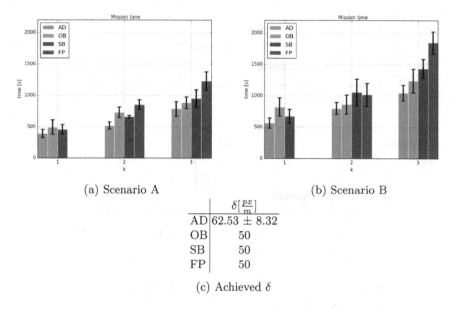

(a) Scenario A   (b) Scenario B

	$\delta[\frac{px}{m}]$
AD	62.53 ± 8.32
OB	50
SB	50
FP	50

(c) Achieved δ

Fig. 6. Average mission time with standard deviations for adaptive auction (AD), object-based (OB), surface-based (SB), and fixed pair (FP) assignment for scenario A (6a) and scenario B (6b). Achieved pixel resolution δ (6c).

the comparison we also run experiments with fixed teams of k drones (FP), i.e. offline assigned teams jointly explore the environment and simultaneously cover the detected surfaces and no dynamic assignment is necessary.

We measure the total mission time and the achieved pixel resolution δ as key performance metrics. We further measure the object coverage time, which is defined as the time period when an object has been detected until it is fully covered, as well as the times the drones operate in the four different roles. We compare our approach with two different settings: Scenario A is composed of 4, and Scenario B is composed of 6 unevenly distributed building blocks. We run the experiments with varying number of drones $m \in \{2, 4, 6, 8\}$. Important simulation parameters are fixed as follows: The timeout thresholds T_r, T_a and T_c are set to 3 s, 5 s and 10 s, respectively. We use the following camera parameters: $f = 1662.8$ px, $\alpha_H = 60°$, $w \times h = 1920 \times 1080$ px (full HD sensor). In order to give more priority to the mission's duration over coverage quality, we set λ to 0.7, whereas we set λ_{as} to be equal to 1.5 to ensure 50% of the vertical overlap. Both minimum distance between drones and a distance to objects are set to 3 m. We run 10 simulations for each experiment in order to lower the effect of randomness in exploration. Since we consider the mission to be successfully completed when the whole area is known and all objects have been covered, we terminate the experiments when all objects have been completely covered, assuming we know a priori the number of objects.

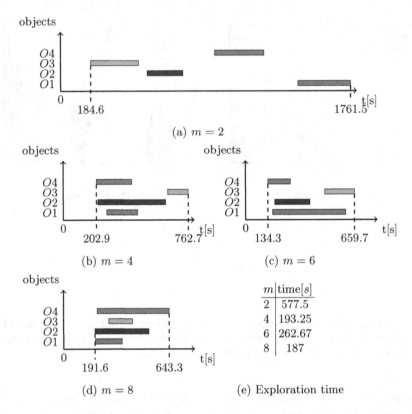

Fig. 7. Impact of number of drones m on time each object required to be fully covered from the moment it was ready to be assigned, and the average exploration time per drone (7e), for the environment setup from Scenario A.

5.2 Experimental Results

Figure 6 depicts the impact of k and the assignment variant (AD, OB, SB, and FP) on the overall mission time for both scenarios. It is rather intuitive that the coverage time increases with k as more drones have to be jointly assigned and potentially wait for each other at the assigned points. In the AD auction variant, we aim to take advantage of both the OB and the SB variant, and on top of that, adapt the coverage quality to mission requirements. As shown in Fig. 6a for $k = 1$ and $k = 2$ and in Fig. 6b for $k = 1$, the SB variant outperforms the OB variant due to a sufficiently large number of drones m. If the number of objects and hence unassigned tasks is relatively small as compared to the available drones, the OB variant outperforms the SB variant, since the auctioneering drones do not lose time on waiting for bids for each surface. In this case, assignment of drones for the whole object is more efficient.

Our AD variant outperforms the other variants since it adapts to the mission and its dynamics of discovering new objects. Furthermore, it achieves a higher pixel resolution δ as the fixed one of the other three variants (cp. Fig. 6c). Regarding a comparison between fixed and dynamic assignment, we analyze how the FP variant performs with varying k in our scenarios. For $k = 1$, the FP variant performs as the OB variant, since the same drone which has detected the object can also cover it. For $k = 2$, FP performs only slightly worse than OB or SB. For $k = 3$, the performance of FP deteriorates. The main reason for this degraded performance is that the FP variant explores the environment in fixed teams of k co-located drones and is therefore less effective in detecting objects as compared to the exploration with independent drones. Even though the FP variant's advantages in terms of shorter coverage time are not evident in the total mission time, drones did cover some objects faster for certain scenarios because of the proximity of the other $k - 1$ drone(s). Moreover, we have introduced two relaxations for $k = 3$: different baselines and different distances to the surface. From the coverage time perspective, the effect of these relaxations is negligible because the distance variation of a k constellation point for two relaxations is much smaller than the distances between the constellation points. However, the coverage quality can benefit from these relaxations, and we therefore applied both relaxations for our simulations with $k = 3$, i.e. variable distances at corners to increase the overlap and variable baselines for regular surfaces.

We further evaluated the scalability of our AD variant by varying $m \in \{2, 4, 6, 8\}$ for scenario A with $k = 2$. The horizontal bars in Fig. 7 show the object coverage time for all objects in order to visualize the overall mission execution and the effect of exploration for different m. The left value on the x axis represents the time when the first object has been detected, whereas the right value represents the overall mission time. For $m = k = 2$, we can clearly observe the sequential coverage of the four objects (Fig. 7a); the gaps in between correspond to the time required for detection and abstraction of surfaces. Figures 7b to d plot results for $m > k$, where objects can be covered in parallel. Note that coverage of a particular object can be interrupted due to too few drones available. Figure 7e summarizes the time drones explored the environment searching for objects. This exploration time does not decrease with increasing number of drones. It strongly depends on the uncertainty of the environment (i.e. random object placement) and chosen exploration method.

6 Conclusions

We have presented a decentralized coordination method to simultaneously cover a priori unknown environments aiming for minimizing the mission duration and maximizing the coverage quality. The allocation of drones to constellation points is a critical step for this problem. Our adaptive market-based assignment (AD) achieved a shorter mission duration as compared to surface-based (SB), object-based (OB) or fixed assignments (FP) in our simulation study, as well as a higher coverage quality. Since we apply our approach in initially unknown environments, the time required for exploration has a significant influence on the overall mission time. Thus, there is a tradeoff between exploration and coverage and the effort put into (concurrently) solving these sub-problems.

Simultaneous coverage represents a challenging multi-agent problem, and efficient solutions will leverage various applications including monitoring, inspection and reconstruction. As future work we intend to investigate in (i) coordinated exploration methods to decrease the object detection time, (ii) considering the object's semantics to adapt k and δ for each object individually, and (iii) in deploying our dynamic coordination in real multi-drone applications.

Acknowledgments. This work is supported by the Karl Popper Kolleg on Networked Autonomous Aerial Vehicles (uav.aau.at) at the University of Klagenfurt.

References

1. Badreldin, M., Hussein, A., Khamis, A.: A comparative study between optimization and market-based approaches to multi-robot task allocation. Adv. Artif. Intell. **2013**, 12 (2013). https://doi.org/10.1155/2013/256524
2. Berman, S., Halász, Á., Hsieh, M.A., Kumar, V.: Optimized stochastic policies for task allocation in swarms of robots. IEEE Trans. Robot. **25**(4), 927–937 (2009). https://doi.org/10.1109/TRO.2009.2024997
3. Bircher, A., Kamel, M., Alexis, K., Oleynikova, H., Siegwart, R.: Receding horizon "next-best-view" planner for 3D exploration. In: Proceedings of IEEE International Conference on Robotics and Automation, pp. 1462–1468. IEEE (2016). https://doi.org/10.1109/ICRA.2016.7487281
4. Bircher, A., Kamel, M., Alexis, K., Oleynikova, H., Siegwart, R.: Receding horizon path planning for 3D exploration and surface inspection. Auton. Robot. **42**(2), 291–306 (2018). https://doi.org/10.1007/s10514-016-9610-0
5. Capitan, J., Spaan, M.T., Merino, L., Ollero, A.: Decentralized multi-robot cooperation with auctioned POMDPs. Int. J. Robot. Res. **32**(6), 650–671 (2013). https://doi.org/10.1109/ICRA.2012.6224917
6. Chang, C., Chatterjee, S.: Quantization error analysis in stereo vision. In: Proceedings of Asilomar Conference on Signals, Systems & Computers, pp. 1037–1041. IEEE (1992). https://doi.org/10.1109/ACSSC.1992.269140
7. Deb, K., Pratap, A., Agarwal, S., Meyarivan, T.: A fast and elitist multiobjective genetic algorithm: NSGA-II. IEEE Trans. Evol. Comput. **6**(2), 182–197 (2002). https://doi.org/10.1109/4235.996017
8. Fonooni, B., Jevtić, A., Hellström, T., Janlert, L.E.: Applying ant colony optimization algorithms for high-level behavior learning and reproduction from demonstrations. Robot. Auton. Syst. **65**, 24–39 (2015). https://doi.org/10.1016/j.robot.2014.12.001
9. Freundlich, C., Zhang, Y., Zhu, A.Z., Mordohai, P., Zavlanos, M.M.: Controlling a robotic stereo camera under image quantization noise. Int. J. Robot. Res. **36**(12), 1268–1285 (2017). https://doi.org/10.1177/0278364917735163
10. Galceran, E., Carreras, M.: A survey on coverage path planning for robotics. Robot. Auton. Syst. **61**(12), 1258–1276 (2013). https://doi.org/10.1016/j.robot.2013.09.004
11. Gallup, D., Frahm, J.M., Mordohai, P., Pollefeys, M.: Variable baseline/resolution stereo. In: Proceedings of IEEE Conference on Computer Vision and Pattern Recognition, pp. 1–8. IEEE (2008). https://doi.org/10.1109/CVPR.2008.4587671
12. Gerkey, B.P., Mataric, M.J.: Sold!: auction methods for multirobot coordination. IEEE Trans. Robot. Autom. **18**(5), 758–768 (2002)

13. Heng, L., Gotovos, A., Krause, A., Pollefeys, M.: Efficient visual exploration and coverage with a micro aerial vehicle in unknown environments. In: Proceedings of IEEE International Conference on Robotics and Automation, pp. 1071–1078. IEEE (2015). https://doi.org/10.1109/ICRA.2015.7139309

14. Jiang, A.X., Procaccia, A.D., Qian, Y., Shah, N., Tambe, M.: Defender (mis)coordination in security games. In: Twenty-Third International Joint Conference on Artificial Intelligence (2013)

15. Khan, A., Rinner, B., Cavallaro, A.: Cooperative robots to observe moving targets: a review. IEEE Trans. Cybern. **48**(1), 187–198 (2018). https://doi.org/10.1109/TCYB.2016.2628161

16. Mazdin, P., Rinner, B.: Efficient and QoS-aware drone coordination for simultaneous environment coverage. In: Proc. IEEE Conference on Multimedia Information Processing and Retrieval, pp. 333–338. IEEE (2019). https://doi.org/10.1109/MIPR.2019.00066

17. McIntire, M., Nunes, E., Gini, M.: Iterated multi-robot auctions for precedence-constrained task scheduling. In: Proceedings of International Conference on Autonomous Agents & Multiagent Systems, pp. 1078–1086. International Foundation for Autonomous Agents and Multiagent Systems (2016)

18. Morel, J.M., Yu, G.: ASIFT: a new framework for fully affine invariant image comparison. SIAM J. Imaging Sci. **2**(2), 438–469 (2009). https://doi.org/10.1137/080732730

19. Nakabo, Y., Mukai, T., Hattori, Y., Takeuchi, Y., Ohnishi, N.: Variable baseline stereo tracking vision system using high-speed linear slider. In: Proceedings of IEEE International Conference on Robotics and Automation, pp. 1567–1572. IEEE (2005). https://doi.org/10.1109/ROBOT.2005.1570337

20. Nunes, E., Gini, M.: Multi-robot auctions for allocation of tasks with temporal constraints. In: Proceedings of AAAI Conference on Artificial Intelligence (2015)

21. Perez-Carabaza, S., Scherer, J., Rinner, B., Lopez-Orozco, J.A., Besada-Portas, E.: UAV trajectory optimization for minimum time search with communication constraints and collision avoidance. Eng. Appl. Artif. Intell. **85**, 357–371 (2019)

22. Shah, S., Dey, D., Lovett, C., Kapoor, A.: AirSim: high-fidelity visual and physical simulation for autonomous vehicles. In: Proceedings of Field and Service Robotics (2017)

23. Tambe, M.: Security and Game Theory: Algorithms, Deployed Systems, Lessons Learned. Cambridge University Press (2011). https://doi.org/10.1017/CBO9780511973031

24. Weyrer, M., Rinner, B.: UAV motion planning and control for multi-coverage of 3D environments. In: Proceedings of International Conference on Unmanned Aircraft Systems, pp. 939–946 (2018). https://doi.org/10.1109/ICUAS.2018.8453427

25. Yanmaz, E., Yahyanejad, S., Rinner, B., Hellwagner, H., Bettstetter, C.: Drone networks: communications, coordination, and sensing. Ad Hoc Networks **68**(1), 1–15 (2018). https://doi.org/10.1016/j.adhoc.2017.09.001

26. Yoder, L., Scherer, S.: Autonomous exploration for infrastructure modeling with a micro aerial vehicle. In: Wettergreen, D.S., Barfoot, T.D. (eds.) Field and Service Robotics. STAR, vol. 113, pp. 427–440. Springer, Cham (2016). https://doi.org/10.1007/978-3-319-27702-8_28

27. Zhang, C., Lesser, V.: Coordinated multi-agent reinforcement learning in networked distributed POMDPs. In: Proceedings of AAAI Conference on Artificial Intelligence (2011)

MCTS-Based Automated Negotiation Agent

Cédric L. R. Buron[1][(✉)], Zahia Guessoum[2,3], and Sylvain Ductor[4]

[1] Thales Research and Technology, 1 av. Augustin Fresnel, Palaiseau, France
`cedric.buron@thalesgroup.com`
[2] Lip6, Sorbonne Université, Paris, France
[3] CReSTIC, Université de Reims Champagne Ardennes, Reims, France
`zahia.guessoum@univ-reims.fr`
[4] Universidade Estadual do Ceará, Fortaleza, Brazil
`sylvain.ductor@uece.com.br`

Abstract. This paper introduces a new negotiating agent model for automated negotiation. We focus on applications without time pressure with multidimensional negotiation on both continuous and discrete domains. The agent bidding strategy relies on Monte Carlo Tree Search, which is a trendy method since it has been used with success on games with high branching factor such as Go. It also exploits opponent modeling techniques thanks to Gaussian process regression and Bayesian learning. Evaluation is done by confronting the existing agents that are able to negotiate in such context: Random Walker, Tit-for-tat and Nice Tit-for-Tat. None of those agents succeeds in beating our agent. Also, the modular and adaptive nature of our approach is a huge advantage when it comes to optimize it in specific applicative contexts.

Keywords: Automated negotiation · MCTS · Supply chain

1 Introduction

Negotiation is a form of interaction in which a group of agents with conflicting interests and a desire to cooperate try to reach a mutually acceptable agreement on an object of negotiation [2]. The agents explore solutions according to a predetermined protocol in order to find an acceptable agreement. Being widely used in economic domains and with the rise of e-commerce applications, the question of automating negotiation has gained a lot of interest in the field of artificial intelligence and multi-agent systems.

Many negotiation frameworks have been proposed [13]. They may be characterized along different aspects, whether concerning the set of participants (*e.g.* bilateral or multilateral), agent preferences (*e.g.* linear or not), issues of negotiated objects (*e.g.* discrete or continuous), or even the characteristics of the interaction protocol (*e.g.* globally bounded in time or number of rounds). They run negotiating agents that use strategies to evaluate the received information and

© Springer Nature Switzerland AG 2019
M. Baldoni et al. (Eds.): PRIMA 2019, LNAI 11873, pp. 186–201, 2019.
https://doi.org/10.1007/978-3-030-33792-6_12

make proposals. Several strategies have been proposed. Either fixed or adaptive, most of them rely on a known deadline (either in time or in rounds). However in several applications, the deadline of an agent may change over the negotiation. The negotiation horizon may vary depending on external elements such as other opportunities. To the best of our knowledge, these elements have not been taken into account so far.

In this paper, we propose to handle this issue by designing a loosely constrained adaptive strategy for automated negotiation. This strategy considers that: (1) the agent preferences are nonlinear, (2) the issues of negotiated objects can be both continuous and discrete and (3) the time pressure is undefined, and therefore the deadline of the negotiation. To cope with this objective, our agent is based on General Game Playing [11] and Machine Learning [2]. Its strategy relies on both Monte Carlo Tree Search (MCTS), a heuristic technique that has been used with success for many kinds of games (see for instance [5,23]), and opponent modeling techniques in order to be more efficient.

The paper is organized as follows. Section 2 describes our targeted industrial application. Section 3 provides some background on automated negotiation and AI strategies for games. Section 4 gives the theoretical and formal setting for bargaining in order to motivate the use of AI for games. Section 5 introduces our strategy. Section 6 gives some details on the agent implementation and shows its performance against a Random Walker agent, Tit-for-Tat agent and Nice Tit-for-Tat agent. The last section gives concluding remarks and perspectives.

2   Target Application

This work is part of an industrial project that addresses an economic application, the *factoring*. This application requires a solution that complies with the specific scope we consider here and which is neglected by the literature.

When a company sells goods or services to another company, it produces an invoice. The selling company is called *supplier* and the customer is called *debtor*. Each country may define a legal payment term of generally several weeks. Moreover, the principal may not pay within this payment term. In the supply chain, the debtor is often much larger than the supplier. It can therefore impose its own conditions at the expense of the supplier. The consequences are quite harmful for the latter: during those payment delays, its *working capital* is reduced and hence its capacity to produce, fulfill future orders or pay its own suppliers.

Factoring is an interesting answer to this issue. A funding company (called a *factor*) accepts to fund the invoices of the supplier, by paying them immediately less than their nominal amount and assuming the delay of payment of the principal. From the factor perspective – generally a bank or an investment fund – the principal can be seen as a short-term investment, where the risk of defaulting on payment depends on the reputation of the principal. Since we consider the case where the principal is much larger than the supplier, this risk is lower and the rate is more affordable for the supplier.

As this kind of funding may be recurrent, there is a strong interest in automating the negotiation between the supplier and the factor. Moreover, some recent works have shown an increase in the number of factoring marketplaces all around the world [8]. However, there are several specificities to this setting. The first specificity is the negotiation domain. Several elements are negotiated at the same time: the nominal amount to be funded and the discount rate are the primary elements of the negotiation. Also, for identical nominal amounts, a factor may ask the supplier to sell invoices of certain principals it trusts. Finally, when several invoices are available, the expected number of financing days may also be negotiated. Therefore, we consider complex issues that combine at the same time elements of various kinds: continuous (the discount rate), numeric (the numerical amount and the financing days), and categorical (the principal).

The second specificity is related to uncertainty and resource availability. Automated negotiation often considers a deadline, which defines the time allocated to the negotiation. Most of the negotiation strategies rely on this time pressure to compute a concession rate. In our application, time pressure is not constant over the negotiation. For the factor, the time pressure depends both on the money it has to invest and on the investment opportunities. If the factor has a lot of money and few opportunities, the time pressure increases: the factor sees not invested money as a loss. On the contrary, when resources are limited and opportunities are common, the factor tries to get a better discount rate and the time pressure decreases. For the supplier, the situation is even more unpredictable. Time pressure depends on its opportunities to get new credit lines (including bank loans) and even on the time the principal takes to pay it: the negotiation may be brutally interrupted at some point if the payment of an invoice makes it useless for the supplier.

Automated negotiation components relying either on a deadline commonly known by the agents, or on a deadline private to each of them is therefore not applicable to our target applications. In our target application the negotiation domain consists of numerical, continuous and categorical issues, the agent preferences are nonlinear, and the time pressure is dynamic.

3   Related Work

Our agent is at the meeting point of automated negotiation and Monte Carlo methods applied to games. In this section, we introduce both domains.

3.1   Automated Negotiation

Various authors have explored the negotiation strategies with different perspectives. Most of those works have identified three components that make up the "BOA" architecture [1]: a **Bidding strategy** defines the offers the agent sends to its opponent, an **Acceptance strategy** defines whether the agent accepts the offer it just received or if it makes a counterproposal, and an **Opponent modeling** models some features of the opponents, as its bidding strategy, its preference domain and its acceptance strategy. The latter aims to improve the efficiency of the bidding strategy and/or the acceptance strategy of the agent. The following subsections present the related work for each component.

Bidding Strategy. Bidding strategies may depend on several elements: the history, including the concessions made by the opponent and/or a negotiation deadline, the utility function of the agent, and the opponent model. Faratin *et al.* proposed the so-called tactics that mainly rely on the criticality of the resources, the remaining time before the deadline is reached or the concessions made by the opponent. All of them except the last rely on a known deadline. The latter has been extended to create more complex strategies, as the Nice tit-For-Tat agent [4], which uses learning techniques in order to improve it. Genetic algorithms [15] use generated proposals as individuals. They rely on the time pressure for the variation of their proposals and make some that are acceptable for their opponent.

This paper advances the state of the art in the bidding strategies by introducing and evaluating a strategy that considers the negotiation as a game and uses the very efficient Monte Carlo Methods.

Acceptance Strategy. Acceptance strategies can be divided into two main categories [3]. The first category is called "myopic strategies" as they only consider the last bid of the opponent. An agent may accept an offer when (1) it is better than the new one produced by its own bidding strategy, (2) it is better than the last one made by the agent, (3) it is above a predetermined threshold, or (4) it embodies any combination of the previous ones. The second category consists of "optimal strategies" [3] that rely on an opponent bidding strategy in order to optimize the expected utility. They are based on the concessions made by the opponent and a prediction that the expected utility of the agent should increase while the deadline is getting closer. So, the first category is not suitable for our context. We therefore propose to use the second category in our agent model.

Opponent Modeling. [2] presents an exhaustive review of the opponent modeling techniques related to automated negotiation. They are generally used to model (1) opponent bidding strategy, (2) its utility and (3) its acceptance strategy as well as private deadline and a reserve price, depending on which of these elements are relevant in each context.

There are two main methods to model adaptive **bidding strategy** which does not rely on the deadline: neural networks and time series-based techniques. Neural networks use a fixed number of previous offers as input, and the expected value for the next proposal as output. Time series methods can be generalized very easily. Among them, the Gaussian process regression is a stochastic technique which has been used with success by [24]. Due to its nature, it can generate various proposals at each negotiation turn. Those proposals are proportional to a likelihood provided by the regression. We select this technique to model the opponent bidding strategy since it is particularly adapted to the Monte Carlo Tree Search.

The opponent **utility** is generally considered as the weighted average of partial utility functions for each issue. Two families of methods are used to model them. The first one is based on the frequency of each value among the previous opponent bids. The methods of this family make the hypothesis that the most frequent values are the ones the opponent prefers, and that the most stable issues are the most important for it. They are relevant in the cases where the negotiation domain only consists of discrete issues; their extension to the continuous case is not suitable to complex domains, as it requires the definition of a distance function which depends on the negotiation domain. The second family of methods is based on Bayesian Learning [14]. It is well suited for the continuous case and can be easily extended to categorical domains. We use it as is for the numerical issues and make an extension for the categorical ones. The latter is presented in Sect. 5.1.

Their is two ways to learn the opponent **acceptance strategy**: either by assuming that the opponent has a myopic strategy or by using neural networks [9]. The latter is quite expensive in terms of computation time. The weights of the network must be updated each time the opponent makes a new proposal.

3.2   Monte Carlo Tree Search

Monte Carlo methods are regularly used as heuristics for games. Rémi Coulom [6] proposes a method to combine the construction of a game tree – a traditional method for games that has proved to be very to be effective – with Monte Carlo techniques. This method is called Monte Carlo Tree Search (MCTS) and it has been improved using various extensions [5], including pruning the less promising branches of the tree. It has met great success in games, particularly games with high branching factor [23].

MCTS consists of 4 steps. A **selection** is dedicated to the exploration of the already built part of the tree, based on a predefined strategy. While exploring a node, the algorithm chooses whether to explore a lower-level branch or expand a new branch. In the latter case, there is an **expansion** of a new node; it is created just below the last explored one. Once a new node has been expanded, a **simulation** of the game is performed until a final state is reached. Finally, outcomes of the final state are computed and a **backpropagation** of them is made over all the nodes that have been explored.

[16] presents a recent attempt to exploit MCTS for General Game Playing, with Automated Negotiation as a potential application. The negotiation domain considered is limited to a single-issue, discrete domain with complete information (each agent knows what is the optimal deal for its opponent). Our work is specifically made for recent evolution of Automated Negotiation, focusing thus on multi-issues, combining continuous, numerical and categorical domains with incomplete information (the agent has no information on the opponent utility profile). These differences have consequences on the technical aspects of these works. The referenced works use Upper Confidence Trees, inapplicable in our case since it imposes the number of possible moves at each step to be finite. Also, [16] does not require opponent modeling, since the opponent utility profile is known.

4 Negotiation as a Game

Monte Carlo Tree Search has been applied with success to extensive games. In this section, we show how it is possible to represent negotiation using this model. We first associate each aspect of negotiation to a game element. We then describe specificities of negotiation that prevent us from using most common MCTS selection, expansion and simulation strategies.

An extensive game [20] consists of a set of players, the set of all possible game histories, a function mapping each non-terminal history to the player who must play then and a preference profile. By using this definition, it is possible to define a bargaining $\mathcal{B}$ as an extensive game:

Definition 1 (Bargaining). *A bargaining can be represented as triple $\mathcal{B} = \left(H, A, (u_i)_{i \in [\![1,2]\!]} \right)$ where:*

1. *A is the set of two **players**: the buyer (player 1) and the seller (player 2),*
2. *H is the set of **possible histories** of the negotiation. Each history consists of the sequence of messages the agents sent to each other: proposals, acceptance and rejection messages. Terminal histories are the histories ending by acceptance or rejection, and infinite histories. Each message is a pair (α, c) where α is the speech act (performative) of the message and c is the content of the message, i.e. a list of couples (k, v) where k is the key of an issue of the negotiation domain and v is the corresponding value. The history can be divided in two parts, each part corresponding to the messages sent by one of the agents: $h_i = (\alpha, c)_i$,*
3. *the **player** function is based on the parity of the size of the history (we suppose that the buyer (player 1) always plays first). Therefore $\forall h \in H, player(h) = 2 - (|h| \mod 2)$ where $|h|$ is the size of h,*
4. *the **preference profile**, $u_i, i \in \{1, 2\}$, is an evaluation of terminal histories with regards to each player. If the history ends with an acceptance of the agent, u_i returns the utility associated by the agent, if not it returns a specific value that may depend on the engaged resources.*

The representation of bargaining as a game has already been investigated in [19, 22] for single issue bargaining. More complex domains has been initially dealt by making the assumption that the agents proposals are independent of the opponent's ones [10]. However in recent advances in automated negotiation, the agent bidding strategies are generally adaptive *i.e.* the proposals made by an agent depend on its opponent's ones.

However, negotiation is not a classical combinatorial game as Chess or Go. Its resolution is a challenge to the MCTS approach for three reasons. First, it is a non-zero sum game: agents try to find a mutually beneficial agreement which is often much better for both agents than their reserve utility *i.e.* the situation where the agents do not find an agreement. Second, it is an incomplete information game: the agent preference profiles are unknown to their opponents and generally modeled by them. These two specificities make it impossible to use the most common implementation of MCTS, the Upper Confidence Tree [17]. Last, we consider a large and complex domain that encompasses numeric, continuous and categorical issues, with nonlinear utility functions and possibly infinite game trees. This has several consequences on the way the tree is explored, in particular on the criterion followed to expand a new node.

5   MCTS-Based Agent

As we explained in the previous section, negotiation is a particular game. It is therefore required to adapt the heuristics traditionally used for games to its specificities. In this section, we present our automated negotiation agent relying on MCTS. The agent architecture is composed of three modules presented in Fig. 1. The bidding strategy module implements MCTS and uses the opponent modeling module. The latter consists of two submodules: one models the opponent utility, the other models its bidding strategy. The last module is the acceptance strategy, which makes a comparison between the last proposal from the opponent and the bid generated by the bidding strategy. Each of the agent submodules and their interactions are described in this section.

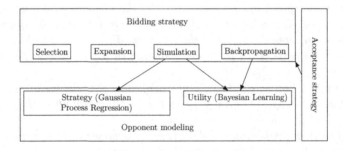

Fig. 1. Interaction between the modules of our agent

5.1   Opponent Modeling

In order to improve the efficiency of MCTS, we model both the bidding strategy and the utility of the opponent.

Bidding Strategy Modeling. The goal of this model is to predict what proposal the opponent will make at turn x_*. To do so, we use Gaussian Process Regression [21]. This method produces a Gaussian with the mean corresponding to the value predicted by the algorithm and a standard deviation corresponding to the uncertainty induced by the model.

The first step is to compute the covariance matrix K which represents the proximity between the turns $(x_i)_{i \in [\![1,n]\!]}$ of the sequence, based on a covariance function, also called kernel k. Let

$$K = \begin{pmatrix} k(x_1, x_1) & \ldots & k(x_1, x_n) \\ \vdots & & \vdots \\ k(x_n, x_1) & \ldots & k(x_n, x_n) \end{pmatrix} \tag{1}$$

we then compute the distance between the turn of the predicted proposal x_* and the previous turns in the vector K_*:

$$K_* = (k(x_*, x_1), \ldots, k(x_*, x_n)) \tag{2}$$

The Gaussian process regression relies on the supposition that all these values are the dimensions of a multivariate Gaussian. Using results on multivariate Gaussian, we can compute

$$\overline{y_*} = K_* K^{-1} \mathbf{y} \tag{3}$$

$$\sigma_*^2 = \mathrm{Var}(y_*) = K_{**} - K_* K^{-1} K_*^\top \tag{4}$$

where $K_{**} = k(x_*, x_*)$. The result corresponds to a Gaussian random variable with mean $\overline{y_*}$ and standard deviation σ_*.

One of the capital aspects of Gaussian process regression is the choice of the kernel. The most common ones are radial basis functions (RBF), rational quadratic functions (RQF), Matérn kernel and exponential sine squared (ESS). These kernels are used to define distance between the turns of the bargaining. We tested these four kernels on various negotiations among finalists of ANAC 2014 (bilateral general-purpose negotiation with nonlinear utilities). The Table 1 shows the results of GPR for each of the aforementioned kernels. We generated randomly 25 negotiation sessions and modeled two agents using each kernel. We got a total of 50 models by kernel. Each bid of each sequence is predicted using previous proposals and is used to predict following ones. The table shows average Euclidean distance between the actual proposals and the predicted sequences. The lower the value, the closer is the prediction to the actual proposal. The kernel that got the best result is the Rational Quadratic Function. Our agent therefore uses this one.

Table 1. Average Euclidean distance between actual proposals of a bargaining and values predicted by GPR, depending on the used kernel.

Kernel	RBF	RQF	Matérn	ESS
Avg. distance	43.288	**17.766**	43.228	22.292

This method also allows to make predictions on the categorical issues. The method presented in chapter 3 of [21] is also possible and relies on Monte Carlo method for some integration estimation.

Preference Profile Modeling. Bayesian learning described in [14] makes the only supposition that an agent makes concessions at roughly constant rate. Though this constraint may seem tough, it is relatively low in comparison with other methods.

The opponent utility is approximated by a weighted sum of triangular functions. A function t of $[a, b] \subset \mathbb{R}$ in $[0, 1]$ is called triangular if and only if:

- t is linear and either $t(a) = 0$ and $t(b) = 1$ or $t(a) = 1$ et $t(b) = 0$, or:
- there is some c in $[a, b]$ such that t is linear on $[a, c]$ and $[c, b]$, $t(a) = 0$, $t(b) = 0$ and $t(c) = 1$.

The method can be divided into two steps. First, the agent generates a predetermined number of hypotheses on the utility function. These hypotheses are composed of weighted sums of triangular functions (one per issue). Each issue is therefore associated with a weight and a triangular function.

The estimated utility of the opponent is the weighted sum of these hypotheses where each weight is the probability computed using Bayesian learning. This method does not make any supposition on the opponent strategy, which makes it more general than the frequency based techniques.

This method can be naturally extended to the categorical issues. Given a categorical issue $C = \{C_1, \ldots, C_n\}$, the partial utility function is chosen among the set of functions of $[0, 1]^C$.

Acceptance Strategy Model. Acceptance strategy is modeled in a very simple way: a simulated agent accepts the proposal from its opponent if and only if its utility is better than the utility generated by the bidding strategy model. This method presented by Baarslag et al. in [2] is not computationally expensive.

5.2   MCTS-Based Bidding Strategy

Monte Carlo methods are very adaptive, and achieve promising results in various games, including games with high branching factor. In this section, we describe the way we have adapted these methods to the negotiation context.

Raw MCTS. As we explained before, MCTS is a general algorithm and relies on several strategies. Each time an agent needs to take a decision, it generates a new tree and explores it using MCTS. The most common implementation of MCTS is Upper Confidence Tree (UCT). This method has proved to be very efficient, particularly for Go. Nevertheless, it expands a new node whenever it explores a node whose children have not all been explored, which is not applicable when issues are continuous. Beyond that, in the case where the branching factor is not small in comparison with the number of simulation, UCT keeps expanding a new node without exploring deeper nodes, which loses the interest of MCTS compared to flat Monte Carlo. In our context, it is therefore necessary to define a different implementation of MCTS:

Selection. For this step, we use progressive widening, as described by [7]. The expansion criterion of the progressive widening states that a new node is expanded if and only if:

$$n_p^\alpha \geq n_c \tag{5}$$

where n_p is the number of times the parent has been simulated, n_c is its number of children and α is a parameter of the model. If the result is that a new node is not expanded, the selected node is the node i maximizing:

$$W_i = \frac{s_i}{n_i + 1} + C \times n^\alpha \sqrt{\frac{\ln(n)}{n_i + 1}} \tag{6}$$

where n is the total number of simulations of the tree, s_i is the score of the node i and C is also a parameter of the model.

Expansion. The content of the expanded node is chosen randomly among all the possible bids of the domain with an even distribution.

Simulation. During the simulation, the model of the opponent bidding strategy is used in order to make the simulation more representative. The model of the opponent utility and its acceptance strategy are used to decide when it accepts a proposal.

Backpropagation. The backpropagation also uses the opponent utility model. The utility of both agents is computed and the scores of both agents is updated for each visited node. The utility of the agent itself is computed using its real preference profile.

Pruning. In order to explore only the interesting nodes for the agent, it is possible to use the knowledge of the agent on the game to prune the less promising branches of the tree. Though we do not have much information in our context, we decide that the opponent should find any offer it made acceptable. We therefore decide to prune all the branches of the tree where our agent makes a proposal less interesting than the best proposal received from the opponent: the goal is to use the best proposal of the opponent as a lower bound and to try to improve on this basic value.

6 Experiments

In order to evaluate our agent, we use the GENIUS [18] framework. We confront our agent with the only agents that do not require a deadline for their strategy to the best of our knowledge: two variants of the Tit-for-Tat agent and a RandomWalker agent. In this section, we describe the implementations of our agent and those three. We then describe in detail the experimental protocol and finally we present the achieved results.

6.1   Implementation

Our agent is developed in Java and consists of a set of independent modules connected to GENIUS platform thanks to interfaces. Figure 2 presents this architecture (the ✉ represents the messages sent and received by the agent). It consists of the components of Sect. 5: a module for the MCTS-based bidding strategy (with classes for the Monte Carlo Tree, its nodes, etc.), a module for opponent utility modeling and another one for the opponent bidding strategy modeling. We use the same acceptance strategy for both our agent and the model it uses for its opponent. As they are very simple, there is no module dedicated to them.

As MCTS are computationally expensive and take quite a long time, we parallelized them. The stochastic aspect of the opponent bidding strategy model ensures that two simulations going from the same branch of the tree are not similar, while still prioritizing the most probable values. The Gaussian process regression, which relies on matrix computation, has been developed using the Jama library[1]. The parameters of the kernel are optimized using the Apache Commons Math library utilities[2].

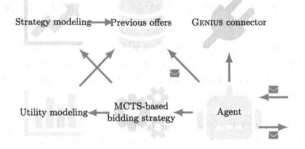

Fig. 2. Software architecture of the modules of our agent

The time taken by our agent for each round has been set empirically. When our agent makes a choice among 200 bids, there is generally one that results into a high utility both for it and its opponent. In order to explore the tree in depth, we let it enough time to generate about 50'000 simulations. Then, to make a proposal, our agent takes about 3 min. This duration meets the expectation of the real-world applications of our industrial partners. From these values, we get $\alpha = 0.489$.

6.2   Opponent's Description

In this section, we provide a description of the confronted agents. It is impossible to compare our agents with state-of-the-art ones, as they all rely on the

---

[1] http://math.nist.gov/javanumerics/.

[2] http://commons.apache.org/proper/commons-math/.

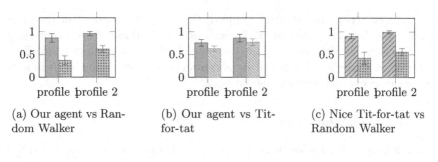

Fig. 3. Average utility of negotiating agents

supposition that there is a publicly known deadline. The only three agents able to negotiate without a given deadline are the RandomWalker, the Tit-for-Tat agent and its more evolved variant, the Nice Tit-for-Tat.

RandomWalker. The RandomWalker is described by Baarslag in [3] and makes random proposals.

Tit-for-Tat. Tit-for-tat agent was first described by Faratin *et al.* in [10]. This agent makes a concession whenever its opponent makes concessions itself. Several possible implementations are given. Here, when it has received fewer than 2 proposals the agent makes the most interesting proposal from its own perspective (it generates 10'000 random proposals and chooses the best one for its utility function). For the other proposals, the agent looks at the last two proposals of its opponent and computes the made concession. This concession may be positive or negative. It adds this concession to the utility of its own last proposal. It then searches for a proposal with the closest utility to this target value. In our implementation, 10'000 proposals are generated to this end.

Nice Tit-for-Tat. Nice Tit-for-Tat is somehow, a more evolved version of the Tit-for-Tat. It has been described by Baarslag *et al.* in [4]. The goal of this work is to comply with domains where mutual agreement is possible. The agent then uses the same opponent utility modeling as our agent and uses it to estimate the Nash point of the setting, *i.e.* the agreement maximizing the product of the utilities of the agents. The concession rate is computed between the first and the last bids of the opponent as the percentile of the distance between its first bid and the Nash point. The corresponding concession is made from the agent point of view. Among the equivalent offers, the utility model is also used in order to choose the best bid for the opponent among equivalent ones for the agent. The only difference with the version used in our experiments and the agent proposed in [4] is the acceptance strategy. Indeed, the strategy proposed in the original version which is presented in [3] depends on the deadline of the negotiation in order to take the time pressure into account. Here, we provide the Nice Tit-for-Tat with a simplified version of its acceptance strategy, which corresponds to the same acceptance strategy as our agent.

6.3 Experimental Protocol

GENIUS makes it possible to negotiate on numerical or categorical issues, but not yet on continuous ones. In order to evaluate our agent, we want to target a negotiation domain that is at the same time neutral enough to show the generic aspects of our work, but complex enough to motivate its use. ANAC is an international competition used to determine the effective negotiation strategies. The negotiation domain used in ANAC 2014 [12] fits well to this objective. Subsequent competitions focused on multilateral negotiation and specific application domains. In ANAC 2014 domain, issues are numerical, varying from 1 to 10. Several domains have been proposed, varying from 10 to 50 issues. In order to reduce computational complexity which is not the concern of this work, we use the 10-issue version. The utility functions are non-linear, and the reserve utility is set to 0, which is the minimal outcome value for the agents. As the time pressure is supposed to vary over time, we do not use a discount rate. While it does not exactly correspond to the targeted application, its complexity (10^10 possible proposals) makes a suitable test bench for our negotiation strategy. In order to simulate the fact that the time pressure is unknown to the agent, we put a very large deadline, so that it is never reached.

6.4 Results

Figure 3 displays the utility of the agents when negotiating with each other using a histogram. The results are averaged over 20 negotiation sessions with each profile, with error bars representing the standard deviation from the average.

Note that the two preference profiles are very different from each other, and not symmetrical at all. This specificity explains the fact that for all the agents in all configurations, utility is always higher with Profile 2 than it is with Profile 1.

As shown on Fig. 3a, our agent is able to beat the Random Walker in every situation, even when its preference profile is Profile 1 and Random Walker's is Profile 2. It is interesting to note that the negotiations with Random Walker are very short with only 3.1 proposals in average: 2.5 when it gets Profile 1 and 3.7 proposals when our agent gets Profile 2. This difference can be explained by the fact that it is easy to find agreements with very high results for Profile 1 (0.9 or more) and high results for Profile 2 (0.6). In most of the negotiations, the first proposal of our agent is of this kind. In that case, Random Walker is more likely to generate a proposal with utility lower than the one proposed by our agent and accepts it, generating a utility of 0.6 for Random Walker and a negotiation session consisting of a single proposal.

Negotiating with Tit-for-Tat is harder, as we can see on Fig. 3b. Our agent gets a lower utility than the Random Walker but is able to beat Tit-for-Tat. The expectation level of Tit-for-Tat also generates much longer negotiations: 34.2 proposals on average with 31.55 proposals when it gets Profile 1 and 36.85 proposals when our agent gets Profile 2. This result can be explained the same way as the results of the negotiation with Random Walker.

The negotiations with Nice Tit-for-Tat never ends: the agents keep negotiating forever. Our MCTS-based method refuses to make a concession significant enough to have a chance to be accepted by Nice Tit-for-Tat, considering the high expectation it has by using the Nash point. Reciprocally, Nice Tit-for-Tat, without time pressure, and dynamic adaptation of its acceptance strategy, does not accept the proposals of our agent. By looking at the internal state of the Nice Tit-for-Tat, we also see that its estimation of the Nash point is incorrect: it expects a utility above the real one.

We propose instead an indirect evaluation by confronting Nice Tit-for-Tat with Random Walker, in the same setting. The results are represented on Fig. 3c. The performances of both agents are comparable, considering the standard deviation of the series.

7 Conclusion

In this paper, we presented an automated negotiation agent able to negotiate in a context where agents do not have predetermined deadline, neither in time nor in rounds, and where the negotiation domain can be composed of numerical, continuous and categorical issues. We described this setting as an extensive game and described a negotiation strategy based on a specific implementation of MCTS relying on two opponent models and a pruning strategy. One of them is the Gaussian process regression, which relies on a covariance function. We tested several covariance functions and chose the one that provides better results in context similar to ours.

Experiments were run in the context of a large negotiation domain, with nonlinear utility functions using different preference profiles. The experimental results are promising: against all the agents that can negotiate in its negotiation domain, our agent outperformed Random Walker and Tit-for-Tat and draws with Nice Tit-for-Tat. This work therefore indicates that techniques from games such as MCTS can be used with success in automated negotiation. However, the modularity of the architecture and the variety of strategies proposed on General Game Playing and Machine Learning areas are a huge advantage when it comes to optimizing the agent for a specific application domain.

Among the perspectives of this work, we would like to create a customized version of our agent and adapt it to the context where the deadline is known, in order to make it available for these applications. Our agent can already be used in this context, but the fact that it does not exploit this information may make it less efficient than its opponents. Another possible direction would be to adapt it to the multilateral context. In fact, there would be little modification to make it available for a context of stacked alternate protocol or a many-to-many bargaining scenario, since MCTS has already been used in n-player games. The use of our agent in its industrial context, in particular with corresponding negotiation domains would yield very interesting results. Last, we would like to improve our agent by using MCTS variations. It would be interesting for instance to test other kinds of pruning. The use of traditional MCTS techniques such as Rapid Action Value Estimation or All Moves As First to reduce the number of simulations while keeping their intrinsic qualities would be interesting.

References

1. Baarslag, T.: Exploring the Strategy Space of Negotiating Agents: A Framework for Bidding, Learning and Accepting in Automated Negotiation. Ph.D. thesis, Delft University of Technology (2016)
2. Baarslag, T., Hendrikx, M.J.C., Hindriks, K.V., Jonker, C.M.: Learning about the opponent in automated bilateral negotiation: a comprehensive survey of opponent modeling techniques. Auton. Agents Multi-Agent Syst. 20(1), 1–50 (2015). https://doi.org/10.1007/s10458-015-9309-1
3. Baarslag, T., Hindriks, K.V.: Accepting optimally in automated negotiation with incomplete information. In: AAMAS 2013, pp. 715–722. International Foundation for Autonomous Agents and Multiagent Systems, Richland (2013). http://dl.acm.org/citation.cfm?id=2484920.2485033
4. Baarslag, T., Hindriks, K.V., Jonker, C.: A tit for tat negotiation strategy for real-time bilateral negotiation. In: Ito, T., Zhang, M., Robu, V., Matsuo, T. (eds.) Complex Automated Negotiations: Theories, Models, and Software Competitions, vol. 435, pp. 229–233. Springer, Heidelberg (2013). https://doi.org/10.1007/978-3-642-30737-9_18
5. Browne, C.C., et al.: A survey of Monte Carlo tree search methods. IEEE Trans. Comput. Intell. AI Games 4(1), 1–43 (2012). https://doi.org/10.1109/TCIAIG.2012.2186810
6. Coulom, R.: Efficient selectivity and backup operators in Monte-Carlo tree search. In: van den Herik, H.J., Ciancarini, P., Donkers, H.H.L.M.J. (eds.) CG 2006. LNCS, vol. 4630, pp. 72–83. Springer, Heidelberg (2007). https://doi.org/10.1007/978-3-540-75538-8_7
7. Couëtoux, A.: Monte Carlo Tree Search for Continuous and Stochastic Sequential Decision Making Problems. Ph.D. thesis, Université Paris XI (2013)
8. Dziuba, D.T.: Crowdfunding platforms in invoice trading as alternative financial markets. Roczniki Kolegium Analiz Ekonomicznych/Szkoła Główna Handlowa 49, 455–464 (2018)
9. Fang, F., Xin, Y., Xia, Y., Haitao, X.: An opponent's negotiation behavior model to facilitate buyer-seller negotiations in supply chain management. In: 2008 International Symposium on Electronic Commerce and Security (2008). https://doi.org/10.1109/ISECS.2008.93
10. Faratin, P., Jennings, N.R., Sierra, C.: Negotiation decision functions for autonomous agents. Robot. Auton. Syst. 24(3–4), 159–182 (1998). https://doi.org/10.1016/S0921-8890(98)00029-3
11. Finnsson, H.: Generalized Monte Carlo tree search extensions for general game playing. In: Proceedings of the Twenty-Sixth AAAI Conference on Artificial Intelligence, AAAI 2012, pp. 1550–1556. AAAI Press (2012). http://dl.acm.org/citation.cfm?id=2900929.2900948

12. Fukuta, N., Ito, T., Zhang, M., Fujita, K., Robu, V. (eds.): Recent Advances in Agent-based Complex Automated Negotiation. SCI, vol. 638. Springer, Cham (2016). https://doi.org/10.1007/978-3-319-30307-9
13. Guttman, R.H., Moukas, A.G., Maes, P.: Agent-mediated electronic commerce: a survey. Knowl. Eng. Rev. **13**(02), 147–159 (1998). https://doi.org/10.1007/3-540-58266-5_1. http://journals.cambridge.org/action/displayAbstract? fromPage=online&aid=71015&fileId=S0269888998002082
14. Hindriks, K., Tykhonov, D.: Opponent modelling in automated multi-issue negotiation using bayesian learning. In: Proceedings of the 7th International Joint Conference on Autonomous Agents and Multiagent Systems, vol. 1, pp. 331–338 (2008). http://dl.acm.org/citation.cfm?id=1402383.1402433
15. de Jonge, D., Sierra, C.: GANGSTER: an automated negotiator applying genetic algorithms. In: Fukuta, N., Ito, T., Zhang, M., Fujita, K., Robu, V. (eds.) Recent Advances in Agent-based Complex Automated Negotiation. SCI, vol. 638, pp. 225–234. Springer, Cham (2016). https://doi.org/10.1007/978-3-319-30307-9_14
16. de Jonge, D., Zhang, D.: Automated negotiations for general game playing. In: AAMAS 2017, Richland, SC, pp. 371–379 (2017). http://dl.acm.org/citation.cfm?id=3091125.3091183
17. Kocsis, L., Szepesvári, C.: Bandit based Monte-Carlo planning. In: Fürnkranz, J., Scheffer, T., Spiliopoulou, M. (eds.) ECML 2006. LNCS (LNAI), vol. 4212, pp. 282–293. Springer, Heidelberg (2006). https://doi.org/10.1007/11871842_29
18. Lin, R., Kraus, S., Baarslag, T., Tykhonov, D., Hindriks, K., Jonker, C.M.: Genius: an integrated environment for supporting the design of generic automated negotiators. Comput. Intell. **30**(1), 48–70 (2014). https://doi.org/10.1111/j.1467-8640.2012.00463.x
19. Nash Jr., J.F.: The bargaining problem. Econometrica J. Econ. Soc. **18**, 155–162 (1950)
20. Osborne, M.J., Rubinstein, A.: A Course in Game Theory, 12th edn. MIT Press, Cambridge (1994)
21. Rasmussen, C.E., Williams, C.K.I.: Gaussian Processes for Machine Learning. MIT Press, Cambridge (2006)
22. Rubinstein, A.: Perfect equilibrium in a bargaining model. Econometrica J. Econ. Soc. **50**, 97–109 (1982)
23. Silver, D., et al.: Mastering the game of go with deep neural networks and tree search. Nature **529**(7587), 484–489 (2016)
24. Williams, C.R., Robu, V., Gerding, E.H., Jennings, N.R.: Using Gaussian processes to optimise concession in complex negotiations against unknown opponents. In: IJCAI 2011, pp. 432–438 (2011). https://doi.org/10.5591/978-1-57735-516-8/IJCAI11-080

Automating Agential Reasoning: Proof-Calculi and Syntactic Decidability for STIT Logics

Tim Lyon$^{(\boxtimes)}$ and Kees van Berkel

Institut für Logic and Computation, Technische Universität Wien, 1040 Wien, Austria
{lyon,kees}@logic.at

Abstract. This work provides proof-search algorithms and automated counter-model extraction for a class of STIT logics. With this, we answer an open problem concerning syntactic decision procedures and cut-free calculi for STIT logics. A new class of cut-free complete labelled sequent calculi G3Ldm$_n^m$, for multi-agent STIT with at most n-many choices, is introduced. We refine the calculi G3Ldm$_n^m$ through the use of propagation rules and demonstrate the admissibility of their structural rules, resulting in the auxiliary calculi Ldm$_n^m$L. In the single-agent case, we show that the refined calculi Ldm$_n^m$L derive theorems within a restricted class of (forest-like) sequents, allowing us to provide proof-search algorithms that decide single-agent STIT logics. We prove that the proof-search algorithms are correct and terminate.

Keywords: Decidability · Labelled calculus · Logics of agency · Proof search · Proof theory · Propagation rules · Sequent · STIT logic

1 Introduction

Modal logics of STIT, an acronym for 'seeing to it that', have a long tradition in the formal investigation of agency, starting with a series of papers by Belnap and Perloff in the 1980s and culminating in [3]. For the past decades, STIT logic has continued to receive considerable attention, proving itself invaluable in a multitude of fields concerned with formal reasoning about agentive choice making. For example, the framework has been applied to epistemic logic [5], deontic logic [11,13], and the formal analysis of legal reasoning [5,12]. Surprisingly, investigations of the mathematical properties of STIT logics are limited [2,15] and its proof-theory has only been addressed recently [4,19]. What is more, despite AI-oriented STIT papers motivating the need of tools for automated reasoning about agentive choice-making [1,2,4], the envisaged automation results are still lacking. The present work will be the first to provide terminating, automated proof-search for a class of STIT logics, including counter-model extraction directly based on failed proof-search.

Work funded by the projects WWTF MA16-028, FWF I2982 and FWF W1255-N23.

M. Baldoni et al. (Eds.): PRIMA 2019, LNAI 11873, pp. 202–218, 2019.
https://doi.org/10.1007/978-3-030-33792-6_13

The *sequent calculus* [7] is an effective framework for proof-search, suitable for automated deduction procedures. Given the metalogical property of *analyticity*, a sequent calculus allows for the construction of proofs by merely decomposing the formula in question. In the present work, we employ the *labelled* sequent calculus—a useful formalism for a large class of modal logics [14,18]—and introduce labelled sequent calculi $\mathsf{G3Ldm}_n^m$ (with $n, m \in \mathbb{N}$) for multi-agent STIT logics containing limited choice axioms, discussed in [20].

In order to appropriate the calculi $\mathsf{G3Ldm}_n^m$ for automated proof-search, we take up a *refinement* method presented in [17]—developed for the more restricted setting of display logic—and adapt it to the more general setting of labelled calculi. In the refinement process the *external* character of labelled systems—namely, the explicit presence of the semantic structure—is made *internal* through the use of alternative, yet equivalent, *propagation rules* [17]. The tailored propagation rules restrict and simplify the sequential structures needed in derivations, producing, for example, shorter proofs. Moreover, one can show that through the use of propagation rules, the structural rules, capturing the behavior of the logic's modal operators, are admissible. In our case, the resulting refined calculi $\mathsf{Ldm}_n^m\mathsf{L}$ derive theorems using only forestlike sequents, allowing us to adapt methods from [17] and provide correct and terminating proof-search algorithms for this class of STIT logics.

In short, the contribution of this paper will be threefold: First, we provide new sound and cut-free complete labelled sequent calculi $\mathsf{G3Ldm}_n^m$ for all multi-agent STIT logics Ldm_n^m (with $n, m \in \mathbb{N}$) discussed in [20]—thus extending the class of logics addressed in [4]. Second, we show how to refine these calculi to obtain new calculi $\mathsf{Ldm}_n^m\mathsf{L}$, which are suitable for proof-search. Last, for each $n \in \mathbb{N}$, we provide a terminating proof-search algorithm deciding the single-agent STIT logic Ldm_n^1. Although [9] provides a polynomial reduction of Ldm_n^m into the modal logic $\mathsf{S5}$ (providing decidability via $\mathsf{S5\text{-}SAT}$), the present work has the advantage that it offers a syntactic decision procedure within the unreduced Ldm_n^m language and is modular, that is, it will allow us to extend our work to a variety of STIT logics. We conclude by discussing the prospects of generalizing the latter results to the multi-agent setting.

The paper is structured as follows: We start by introducing the class of logics Ldm_n^m in Sect. 2. In Sect. 3, corresponding labelled calculi $\mathsf{G3Ldm}_n^m$ are provided, which will subsequently be refined, resulting in the calculi $\mathsf{Ldm}_n^m\mathsf{L}$. We devote Sect. 4 to proof-search algorithms and counter-model extraction.

2   Logical Preliminaries

STIT logic refers to a group of modal logics using operators that capture agential choice-making. The STIT logics Ldm_n^m, which will be considered throughout this paper, employ two types of modal operators: First, they contain a *settledness* operator $\Box$ expressing which formulae are 'settled true' at a current moment. Second, they contain, for each agent i in the language, an atemporal—i.e., instantaneous—*choice* operator $[i]$ expressing that 'agent i sees to it that'.

This basic choice operator is referred to as the *Chellas* STIT [3]. Using both operators, one can define the more refined notion of *deliberative* STIT: i.e., $[i]_d\phi$ iff $[i]\phi \wedge \neg\Box\phi$. Intuitively, $[i]_d\phi$ holds when 'agent i sees to it that ϕ and it is possible for ϕ not to hold'. The multi-agent language for Ldm_n^m is defined accordingly:

Definition 1 (The Language $\mathcal{L}^m$ [10]). *Let $Ag = \{1, 2, ..., m\}$ be a finite set of agent labels and let $Var = \{p, q, r...\}$ be a countable set of propositional variables. $\mathcal{L}^m$ is defined via the following BNF grammar:*

$$\phi ::= p \mid \overline{p} \mid \phi \wedge \phi \mid \phi \vee \phi \mid \Box\phi \mid \Diamond\phi \mid [i]\phi \mid \langle i\rangle\phi$$

where $i \in Ag$ and $p \in Var$.

Notice, the language $\mathcal{L}^m$ consists of formulae in negation normal form. This notation allows us to reduce the number of rules in our calculi, enhancing the readability and simplicity of our proof theory. The negation of ϕ, written as $\overline{\phi}$, is obtained by replacing each operator with its dual, each positive atom p with its negation $\overline{p}$, and each $\overline{p}$ with its positive variant p [4]. Consequently, we obtain the following abbreviations: $\phi \to \psi$ *iff* $\overline{\phi} \vee \psi$, $\phi \leftrightarrow \psi$ *iff* $(\phi \to \psi) \wedge (\psi \to \phi)$, $\top$ *iff* $p \vee \overline{p}$, and $\bot$ *iff* $p \wedge \overline{p}$. We will freely use these abbreviations throughout this paper. Since we are working in negation normal form, diamond-modalities are introduced as separate primitive operators. We take $\langle i\rangle$ and $\Diamond$ as the duals of $[i]$ and $\Box$, respectively.

Following [10], since we work with instantaneous, atemporal STIT it suffices to regard only single choice-moments in our relational frames. This means that we can forgo the traditional branching time structures of basic, atemporal STIT logic [3]. In what follows, we define Ldm_n^m frames as those STIT frames in which $n > 0$ limits the amount of choices available to each agent to at most n-many choices (imposing no limitation when $n = 0$).[1]

Definition 2 (Relational Ldm_n^m Frames and Models). *Let $|Ag| = m$ and let $\mathcal{R}_i(w) := \{v \in W \mid (w, v) \in \mathcal{R}_i\}$ for $i \in Ag$. An Ldm_n^m-frame is defined as a tuple $F = (W, \{\mathcal{R}_i \mid i \in Ag\})$ where $W \neq \emptyset$ is a set of worlds $w, v, u...$ and:*

(**C1**) *For each $i \in Ag$, $\mathcal{R}_i \subseteq W \times W$ is an equivalence relation;*
(**C2**) *For all $u_1, ..., u_m \in W$, $\bigcap_i \mathcal{R}_i(u_i) \neq \emptyset$;*
(**C3**) *Let $n > 0$ and $i \in Ag$, then*

$$\text{For all } w_0, w_1, \cdots, w_n \in W, \bigvee_{0 \leq k \leq n-1, \ k+1 \leq j \leq n} \mathcal{R}_i w_k w_j$$

*An Ldm_n^m-model is a tuple $M = (F, V)$ where F is an Ldm_n^m-frame and V is a valuation assigning propositional variables to subsets of W, i.e. $V: Var \mapsto \mathcal{P}(W)$. Additionally, we stipulate that condition (**C3**) is omitted when $n = 0$.*

---

[1] For a discussion of the philosophical utility of reasoning with limited choice see [20].

$$\phi \to (\psi \to \phi) \quad (\overline{\psi} \to \overline{\phi}) \to (\phi \to \psi) \quad (\phi \to (\psi \to \chi)) \to ((\phi \to \psi) \to (\phi \to \chi))$$

$$(\text{S5}\Box) \ \Box(\phi \to \psi) \to (\Box\phi \to \Box\psi) \quad \Box\phi \to \phi \quad \Diamond\phi \to \Box\Diamond\phi \quad \Box\phi \lor \Diamond\overline{\phi}$$

$$(\text{S5}[i]) \ [i](\phi \to \psi) \to ([i]\phi \to [i]\psi) \quad [i]\phi \to \phi \quad \langle i\rangle\phi \to [i]\langle i\rangle\phi \quad [i]\phi \lor \langle i\rangle\overline{\phi}$$

$$(\text{IOA}) \ \bigwedge_{i \in Ag} \Diamond[i]\phi_i \to \Diamond(\bigwedge_{i \in Ag}[i]\phi_i) \quad (\text{Bridge}) \ \Box\phi \to [i]\phi \quad \frac{\phi}{\Box\phi} \quad \frac{\phi \quad \phi \to \psi}{\psi}$$

$$(\text{APC}_n^i) \ \Diamond[i]\phi_1 \land \Diamond(\overline{\phi}_1 \land [i]\phi_2) \land \cdots \land \Diamond(\overline{\phi}_1 \land \cdots \land \overline{\phi}_{n-1} \land [i]\phi_n) \to \phi_1 \lor \cdots \lor \phi_n$$

Fig. 1. The Hilbert calculus for Ldm_n^m [3,20]. A *derivation of* ϕ in Ldm_n^m from a set of premises Γ, is written as $\Gamma \vdash_{\text{Ldm}_n^m} \phi$, and is defined inductively in the usual way. When Γ is the empty set, we refer to ϕ as a *theorem* and write $\vdash_{\text{Ldm}_n^m} \phi$.

As in [10], the set of worlds W is taken to represent a single moment in which agents from Ag are making their decision. Following **(C1)**, for every agent i, the relation $\mathcal{R}_i$ is an equivalence relation; that is, $\mathcal{R}_i$ functions as a partitioning of W into what will be called *choice-cells* for agent i. Each choice-cell represents a set of possible worlds that may be realized by a choice of the agent. The condition **(C2)** expresses the STIT principle *independence of agents*, ensuring that any combination of choices, available to different agents, is consistent. The last condition **(C3)**, represents the STIT principle which limits the amount of choices available to an agent to a maximum of n. For a philosophical discussion of these principles we refer to [3, Chap. 7C].

Definition 3 (Semantic Clauses for $\mathcal{L}^m$ [4,10]). *Let M be an Ldm_n^m-model $(W, \{\mathcal{R}_i \mid i \in Ag\}, V)$ and let w be a world in its domain W. The satisfaction of a formula $\phi \in \mathcal{L}^m$ on M at w is inductively defined as follows:*

1. *$M, w \Vdash p$ iff $w \in V(p)$*
2. *$M, w \Vdash \overline{p}$ iff $w \notin V(p)$*
3. *$M, w \Vdash \phi \land \psi$ iff $M, w \Vdash \phi$ and $M, w \Vdash \psi$*
4. *$M, w \Vdash \phi \lor \psi$ iff $M, w \Vdash \phi$ or $M, w \Vdash \psi$*
5. *$M, w \Vdash \Box\phi$ iff $\forall u \in W, M, u \Vdash \phi$*
6. *$M, w \Vdash \Diamond\phi$ iff $\exists u \in W, M, u \Vdash \phi$*
7. *$M, w \Vdash [i]\phi$ iff $\forall u \in \mathcal{R}_i(w), M, u \Vdash \phi$*
8. *$M, w \Vdash \langle i\rangle\phi$ iff $\exists u \in \mathcal{R}_i(w), M, u \Vdash \phi$*

A formula ϕ is globally true on M (i.e. $M \Vdash \phi$) iff it is satisfied at every world w in the domain W of M. A formula ϕ is valid (i.e. $\Vdash \phi$) iff it is globally true on every Ldm_n^m-model. Last, Γ semantically implies ϕ, written $\Gamma \Vdash \phi$, iff for all models M and worlds w in W of M, if $M, w \Vdash \psi$ for all $\psi \in \Gamma$, then $M, w \Vdash \phi$.

It is worth emphasizing that the semantic interpretation of $\Box$ refers to the domain of the model in its entirety; i.e., ϕ is settled true iff ϕ is globally true. This is an immediate consequence of considering instantaneous STIT in a single-moment setting (cf. semantics where a relation $\mathcal{R}_\Box$ is introduced for $\Box$, e.g., [4]).

The Hilbert calculus for Ldm_n^m in Fig. 1 is taken from [20]. Apart from the propositional axioms, it consists of S5 axiomatizations for $\Box$ and $[i]$, for each $i \in Ag$. It contains the standard bridge axiom (**Bridge**), linking $[i]$ to $\Box$. Furthermore, it contains an independence of agents axiom (**IOA**), as well as an n-choice axiom (APC_n^i) for each $i \in Ag$. The rules are modus ponens and $\Box$-necessitation.

Theorem 1 (Soundness and Completeness [10,20]). *For any formula* $\phi \in \mathcal{L}^m$, $\Gamma \vdash_{\mathsf{Ldm}_n^m} \phi$ *if and only if* $\Gamma \Vdash \phi$.

3 Refinement of the Calculi $\mathsf{G3Ldm}_n^m$

In this section, we introduce the labelled calculi $\mathsf{G3Ldm}_n^m$ for multi-agent STIT logics (with limited choice). Our calculi are modified, extended versions of the labelled calculi for the logics Ldm_0^m (with $m \in \mathbb{N}$) proposed in [4] and cover a larger class of logics. The calculi $\mathsf{G3Ldm}_n^m$ possess fundamental proof-theoretic properties such as contraction- and cut-admissibility which follow from the general results on labelled calculi established in [14]. The main goal of this section is to refine the $\mathsf{G3Ldm}_n^m$ calculi through the elimination of structural rules, resulting in new calculi $\mathsf{Ldm}_n^m\mathsf{L}$ that derive theorems within a restricted class of sequents. As a result of adopting the approach in [10], the omission of the relational structure corresponding to the $\Box$ modality offers a simpler approach to proving the admissibility of structural rules in the presence of propagation rules (Sect. 3.2). Let us start by introducing the class of $\mathsf{G3Ldm}_n^m$ calculi.

3.1 The $\mathsf{G3Ldm}_n^m$ Calculi

We define labelled sequents Λ via the following BNF grammar:

$$\Lambda ::= x : \phi \mid \Lambda, \Lambda \mid \mathcal{R}_i xy, \Lambda$$

where $i \in Ag$, $\phi \in \mathcal{L}^m$ and x, y are from a denumerable set of labels $Lab = \{x, y, z, ...\}$. Labelled sequents consist exclusively of labelled formulae of the form $x : \phi$ and relational atoms of the form $\mathcal{R}_i xy$. For this reason, sequents can be partitioned into two parts: we sometimes use the notation $\mathcal{R}, \Gamma$ to denote labelled sequents, where $\mathcal{R}$ is the part consisting of relational atoms and Γ is the part consisting of labelled formulae. Last, we interpret the commas between relational atoms in $\mathcal{R}$ conjunctively, the comma between $\mathcal{R}$ and Γ in $\mathcal{R}, \Gamma$ implicationally, and the commas between labelled formulae in Γ disjunctively (cf. Definition 7).

The labelled STIT calculi $\mathsf{G3Ldm}_n^m$ (where $n, m \in \mathbb{N}$) are shown in Fig. 2. Note that for each agent $i \in Ag$, we obtain a copy for each of the rules ($\langle\langle i \rangle\rangle$), ($[i]$), ($\mathsf{refl}_i$), ($\mathsf{eucl}_i$), and ($\mathsf{APC}_n^i$). We refer to ($\mathsf{refl}_i$), ($\mathsf{eucl}_i$), (IOA), and ($\mathsf{APC}_n^i$) as the *structural rules* of $\mathsf{G3Ldm}_n^m$. The rule (IOA) captures the *independence of agents* principle. Furthermore, the rule schema (APC_n^i), limiting the amount of choices available to agent i, provides different rules depending on the value of n in $\mathsf{G3Ldm}_n^m$ (we reserve $n = 0$ to assert that the rule does not appear). When $n > 0$, the (APC_n^i) rule contains $n(n+1)/2$ premises, where each sequent $\mathcal{R}, \mathcal{R}_i x_k x_j, \Gamma$ (for $0 \leq k \leq n-1$ and $k+1 \leq j \leq n$) represents a different premise of the rule. As an example, for $n = 1$ and $n = 2$ the rules for agent i are:

$$\frac{}{\mathcal{R}, w : p, w : \overline{p}, \Gamma}\ (\mathsf{id}) \qquad \frac{\mathcal{R}, w : \phi \wedge \psi, w : \phi, \Gamma \qquad \mathcal{R}, w : \phi \wedge \psi, w : \psi, \Gamma}{\mathcal{R}, w : \phi \wedge \psi, \Gamma}\ (\wedge)$$

$$\frac{\mathcal{R}, w : \phi \vee \psi, w : \phi, w : \psi, \Gamma}{\mathcal{R}, w : \phi \vee \psi, \Gamma}\ (\vee) \qquad \frac{\mathcal{R}, \mathcal{R}_i wv, v : \phi, \Gamma}{\mathcal{R}, w : [i]\phi, \Gamma}\ ([i])^{\dagger}$$

$$\frac{\mathcal{R}, w : \Box\phi, v : \phi, \Gamma}{\mathcal{R}, w : \Box\phi, \Gamma}\ (\Box)^{\dagger} \qquad \frac{\mathcal{R}, w : \Diamond\phi, u : \phi, \Gamma}{\mathcal{R}, w : \Diamond\phi, \Gamma}\ (\Diamond) \qquad \frac{\mathcal{R}, \mathcal{R}_1 u_1 v, ..., \mathcal{R}_m u_m v, \Gamma}{\mathcal{R}, \Gamma}\ (\mathsf{IOA})^{\dagger}$$

$$\frac{\mathcal{R}, \mathcal{R}_i wu, w : \langle i \rangle \phi, u : \phi, \Gamma}{\mathcal{R}, \mathcal{R}_i wu, w : \langle i \rangle \phi, \Gamma}\ (\langle i \rangle) \qquad \frac{\mathcal{R}, \mathcal{R}_i ww, \Gamma}{\mathcal{R}, \Gamma}\ (\mathsf{refl}_i) \qquad \frac{\mathcal{R}, \mathcal{R}_i wu, \mathcal{R}_i wv, \mathcal{R}_i uv, \Gamma}{\mathcal{R}, \mathcal{R}_i wu, \mathcal{R}_i wv, \Gamma}\ (\mathsf{eucl}_i)$$

$$\frac{\left\{ \mathcal{R}, \mathcal{R}_i w_k w_j, \Gamma \ \middle| \ 0 \le k \le n-1, \ k+1 \le j \le n \right\}}{\mathcal{R}, \Gamma}\ (\mathsf{APC}_n^i)$$

Fig. 2. The $\mathsf{G3Ldm}_n^m$ labelled calculi. The superscript $\dagger$ on the $(\Box)$, $([i])$, and (IOA) rule names indicates an eigenvariable condition: the variable v occurring in the premise of the rule cannot occur in the context of the premise (or, equivalently, in the conclusion).

$$\frac{\mathcal{R}, \mathcal{R}_i w_0 w_1, \Gamma}{\mathcal{R}, \Gamma}\ (\mathsf{APC}_1^i) \qquad \frac{\mathcal{R}, \mathcal{R}_i w_0 w_1, \Gamma \qquad \mathcal{R}, \mathcal{R}_i w_0 w_2, \Gamma \qquad \mathcal{R}, \mathcal{R}_i w_1 w_2, \Gamma}{\mathcal{R}, \Gamma}\ (\mathsf{APC}_2^i)$$

Theorem 2. *The $\mathsf{G3Ldm}_n^m$ calculi have the following properties:*

1. *All sequents of the form $\mathcal{R}, w : \phi, w : \overline{\phi}, \Gamma$ are derivable;*
2. *Variable-substitution is height-preserving admissible;*
3. *All inference rules are height-preserving invertible;*
4. *Weakening and contractions are height-preserving admissible:*

$$\frac{\mathcal{R}, \Gamma}{\mathcal{R}, \mathcal{R}', \Gamma', \Gamma}\ (\mathsf{wk}) \qquad \frac{\mathcal{R}, \mathcal{R}', \mathcal{R}', \Gamma}{\mathcal{R}, \mathcal{R}', \Gamma}\ (\mathsf{ctr})_\mathsf{R} \qquad \frac{\mathcal{R}, \Gamma', \Gamma', \Gamma}{\mathcal{R}, \Gamma', \Gamma}\ (\mathsf{ctr})_\mathsf{F}$$

5. *The cut rule is admissible:*

$$\frac{\mathcal{R}, x : \phi, \Gamma \qquad \mathcal{R}, x : \overline{\phi}, \Gamma}{\mathcal{R}, \Gamma}\ (\mathsf{cut})$$

6. *For every formula $\phi \in \mathcal{L}^m$, $w : \phi$ is derivable in $\mathsf{G3Ldm}_n^m$ if and only if $\vdash_{\mathsf{Ldm}_n^m} \phi$, i.e., $\mathsf{G3Ldm}_n^m$ is sound and complete relative to Ldm_n^m.*

Proof. The proof is a basic adaption of [14] and can be found in the online appended version (available at https://arxiv.org/abs/1908.11360). $\qquad\square$

Proof-theoretic properties like those expressed in (4) and (5) of Theorem 2 are essential when designing decidability procedures via proof-search. In constructing a proof of a sequent, proof-search algorithms proceed by applying inference rules of a calculus bottom-up. A bottom-up application of the (cut) rule in a proof-search procedure, however, requires one to guess the *cut formula* ϕ, and thus risks non-termination in the algorithm. (One can think of similar arguments why (ctr)$_R$ and (ctr)$_F$ risk non-termination.) It is thus crucial that such rules are *admissible*; *i.e.* everything derivable with these rules, is derivable without them.

Remark 1. To obtain contraction admissibility (Theorem 2-(4)) labelled calculi must satisfy the *closure condition* [14]: if a substitution of variables in a structural rule brings about a duplication of relational atoms in the conclusion, then the calculus must contain another instance of the rule with this duplication contracted.

We observe that if we substitute the variable u for v in the structural rule (eucl$_i$) (below left), we obtain the rule (eucl$_i$)* (below right), when the atom $\mathcal{R}_i wu$ is contracted:

$$\frac{\mathcal{R}, \mathcal{R}_i wu, \mathcal{R}_i wu, \mathcal{R}_i uu, \Gamma}{\mathcal{R}, \mathcal{R}_i wu, \mathcal{R}_i wu, \Gamma} \text{ (eucl}_i) \qquad \frac{\mathcal{R}, \mathcal{R}_i wu, \mathcal{R}_i uu, \Gamma}{\mathcal{R}, \mathcal{R}_i wu, \Gamma} \text{ (eucl}_i)^*$$

Thus, following the closure condition, we must also add (eucl$_i$)* to our calculus. However, (eucl$_i$)* is a special instance of the (refl$_i$) rule, and hence it is admissible; therefore, we can omit its inclusion in our calculi. None of the other structural rules possess duplicate relational atoms in their conclusions under a substitution of variables, and so, each G3Ldm$_n^m$ calculus satisfies the closure condition.

3.2   Extracting the Ldm$_n^m$L Calculi

We now refine the G3Ldm$_n^m$ calculi, extracting new Ldm$_n^m$L calculi to which proof-search techniques from [17] may be adapted. In short, we introduce new rules to our calculi, called *propagation rules*, which are well-suited for proof-search and imply the admissibility of the less suitable structural rules (refl$_i$) and (eucl$_i$).

Propagation rules are special sequent rules that possess a nonstandard side condition, consisting of two components. For the first component (1), we transform the sequent occurring in the premise of the rule into an *automaton*. The labels appearing in the sequent determine the states of the automaton, whereas the relational atoms of the sequent determine the transitions between these states. The following definition, based on [17, Definition 4.1], makes this notion precise:

Definition 4 (Propagation Automaton). *Let Λ be a labelled sequent, $Lab(\Lambda)$ be the set of labels occurring in Λ, and $w, u \in Lab(\Lambda)$. We define a propagation automaton $\mathcal{P}_\Lambda(w, u)$ to be the tuple $(\Sigma, S, I, F, \delta)$ s.t. (i) $\Sigma := \{\langle i \rangle \mid i \in Ag\}$ is the automaton's alphabet, (ii) $S := Lab(\Lambda)$ is the set of states, (iii) $I := \{w\}$ is the initial state, (iv) $F := \{u\}$ is the accepting state, and (v) $\delta : S \times \Sigma \to S$ is the transition function where $\delta(v, \langle i \rangle) = v'$ and $\delta(v', \langle i \rangle) = v$ iff $\mathcal{R}_i vv' \in \Lambda$.*

We will often write $v \xrightarrow{\langle i \rangle} v'$ instead of $\delta(v, \langle i \rangle) = v'$ to denote a transition between states. A string is a, possibly empty, concatenation of symbols from Σ (where ε indicates the empty string). We say that an automaton accepts a string $\omega = \langle i_1 \rangle \langle i_2 \rangle \cdots \langle i_k \rangle$ iff there exists a transition sequence $w \xrightarrow{\langle i_1 \rangle} v \xrightarrow{\langle i_2 \rangle} \cdots \xrightarrow{\langle i_k \rangle} u$

from the initial state w to the accepting state u. Last, we will abuse notation and use $\mathcal{P}_\Lambda(w, u)$ equivocally to represent both the automaton and the set of strings ω accepted by the automaton, i.e. $\{\omega \mid \mathcal{P}_\Lambda(w, u) \text{ accepts string } \omega\}$. The use of notation can be determined from the context.

The second component (2) of the rule's side condition restricts the application of the rule to a particular language that specifies and determines which types of strings occurring in the automaton allow for a correct application of the propagation rule. We define this language accordingly:

Definition 5 (Agent i Application Language). *For each $i \in Ag$, we define the application language L_i to be the language generated from the regular expression $\langle i \rangle^*$, that is, $L_i = \{\varepsilon, \langle i \rangle, \langle i \rangle\langle i \rangle, \langle i \rangle\langle i \rangle\langle i \rangle, \cdots \}$ with ε the empty string.[2]*

Bringing components (1) and (2) together, a propagation rule is applicable only if the associated propagation automaton accepts a certain string—corresponding to a path of relational atoms in the premise of the rule—and the string is in the application language.

Definition 6 (Propagation Rule). *Let $i \in Ag$, $\Lambda_1 = \mathcal{R}, w : \langle i \rangle\phi, u : \phi, \Gamma$, and $\Lambda_2 = \mathcal{R}, w : \langle i \rangle\phi, \Gamma$. The propagation rule (Pr_i) is defined as follows:*

$$\frac{\mathcal{R}, w : \langle i \rangle\phi, u : \phi, \Gamma}{\mathcal{R}, w : \langle i \rangle\phi, \Gamma} \ (\mathsf{Pr}_i)^{\dagger\dagger}$$

The superscript $\dagger\dagger$ indicates that $\mathcal{P}_{\Lambda_k}(w, u) \cap L_i \neq \emptyset$ for $k \in \{1, 2\}$.[3]
We use $\mathsf{PR} := \{(\mathsf{Pr}_i) \mid i \in Ag\}$ to represent the set of all propagation rules.

The underlying intuition of the rule (applied bottom-up) is that, given some labelled sequent Λ, a formula ϕ is propagated from $w : \langle i \rangle\phi$ to another label u, if w and u are connected by a sequence of $\mathcal{R}_i$ relational atoms in Λ (with i fixed). In the corresponding propagation automaton $\mathcal{P}_\Lambda(w, u)$, this amounts to the existence of a string $\omega \in \mathcal{P}_\Lambda(w, u) \cap L_i$ which represents a sequence of transitions from w to u, such that all transitions are solely labelled with $\langle i \rangle$. To see how the language L_i secures the soundness of the rule, we refer to Theorem 4. For an introduction to propagation rules and propagation automata, see [17].

Let us make the introduced notions more concrete by providing an example:

Example 1. Let $\Lambda = \mathcal{R}_1 wu, \mathcal{R}_2 uv, \mathcal{R}_1 vz, w : \langle 1 \rangle\phi$. The propagation automaton $\mathcal{P}_\Lambda(w, z)$ is depicted graphically as (where the single-boxed node w designates the initial state and a double-boxed node z represents the accepting state):

---

[2] For further information on regular languages and expressions, consult [16].

[3] Observe that $\mathcal{P}_{\Lambda_1}(w, u) = \mathcal{P}_{\Lambda_2}(w, u)$. Hence, deciding which automaton to employ in determining the side condition is inconsequential: when applying the rule top-down we may consult Λ_1, whereas during bottom-up proof-search we may regard Λ_2.

$$\frac{}{\mathcal{R}, w : p, w : \overline{p}, \Gamma} \text{ (id)} \qquad \frac{\mathcal{R}, w : \phi \wedge \psi, w : \phi, \Gamma \qquad \mathcal{R}, w : \phi \wedge \psi, w : \psi, \Gamma}{\mathcal{R}, w : \phi \wedge \psi, \Gamma} \text{ (}\wedge\text{)}$$

$$\frac{\mathcal{R}, w : \phi \vee \psi, w : \phi, w : \psi, \Gamma}{\mathcal{R}, w : \phi \vee \psi, \Gamma} \text{ (}\vee\text{)} \qquad \frac{\mathcal{R}, w : \Box\phi, v : \phi, \Gamma}{\mathcal{R}, w : \Box\phi, \Gamma} \text{ (}\Box\text{)}^{\dagger} \qquad \frac{\mathcal{R}, w : \Diamond\phi, u : \phi, \Gamma}{\mathcal{R}, w : \Diamond\phi, \Gamma} \text{ (}\Diamond\text{)}$$

$$\frac{\mathcal{R}, \mathcal{R}_1 u_1 v, ..., \mathcal{R}_m u_m v, \Gamma}{\mathcal{R}, \Gamma} \text{ (IOA)}^{\dagger} \qquad \frac{\mathcal{R}, \mathcal{R}_i wv, w : [i]\phi, v : \phi, \Gamma}{\mathcal{R}, w : [i]\phi, \Gamma} \text{ (}[i]\text{)}^{\dagger}$$

$$\frac{\mathcal{R}, w : \langle i \rangle \phi, u : \phi, \Gamma}{\mathcal{R}, w : \langle i \rangle \phi, \Gamma} \text{ (Pr}_i\text{)}^{\dagger\dagger} \qquad \frac{\left\{ \mathcal{R}, \mathcal{R}_i w_k w_j, \Gamma \mid 0 \leq k \leq n-1, \, k+1 \leq j \leq n \right\}}{\mathcal{R}, \Gamma} \text{ (APC}_n^i\text{)}$$

Fig. 3. The labelled calculus $\mathsf{Ldm}_n^m\mathsf{L}$. The superscript $\dagger$ on the ($\Box$), ($[i]$), and (IOA) rules indicate that v is an eigenvariable. The $\dagger\dagger$ side condition is the same as in Definition 6. Last, we have ($[i]$), (Pr$_i$), and (APC$_n^i$) rules for each $i \in Ag$.

Observe that every string the automaton accepts must contain at least one $\langle 2 \rangle$ symbol. Since no string of this form exists in L_1, it is not valid to propagate the formula ϕ to z. That is, the sequent $\mathcal{R}_1 wu, \mathcal{R}_2 uv, \mathcal{R}_1 vz, w : \langle 1 \rangle \phi, z : \phi$ does not follow from applying the propagation rule (Pr$_1$) (bottom-up) to Λ.

On the other hand, consider the propagation automaton $\mathcal{P}_\Lambda(w, u)$:

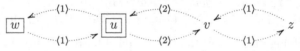

The automaton accepts the simple string $\langle 1 \rangle$, which is included in the language L_1. Therefore, it is permissible to apply the propagation rule (Pr$_1$) (bottom-up) and derive $\mathcal{R}_1 wu, \mathcal{R}_2 uv, \mathcal{R}_1 vz, w : \langle 1 \rangle \phi, u : \phi$ from Λ.

Remark 2. We observe that both of the languages $\mathcal{P}_\Lambda(w, u)$ and L_i are regular, and thus, the problem of determining whether $\mathcal{P}_\Lambda(w, u) \cap L_i \neq \emptyset$, is decidable [17]. Consequently, the propagation rules in PR may be integrated into our proof-search algorithm without risking non-termination.

The proof theoretic properties of $\mathsf{G3Ldm}_n^m$ are preserved when extended with the set of propagation rules PR (Lemma 1). Moreover, the nature of our propagation rules allows us to prove the admissibility of the structural rules (refl$_i$) and (eucl$_i$), for each $i \in Ag$ (resp. Lemmas 2 and 3), which results in the refined calculi $\mathsf{Ldm}_n^m\mathsf{L}$ (shown in Fig. 3). The proofs of Lemmas 1 and 2 are present in the online appended version (the latter is similar to the proof of Lemma 3 presented here).

Lemma 1. *The* $\mathsf{G3Ldm}_n^m$+PR *calculi have the following properties: (i) all sequents Λ of the form $\Lambda = \mathcal{R}, w{:}\ \phi, w{:}\ \overline{\phi}, \Gamma$ are derivable; (ii) variable-substitution is height-preserving admissible; (iii) all inference rules are* *height-preserving invertible; (iv) the* (wk), (ctr)$_R$ *and* (ctr)$_F$ *rules are height-preserving admissible.*

Lemma 2 ((refl$_i$)-**Elimination**). *Every sequent Λ derivable in* G3Ldm$_n^m$ + PR *is derivable without the use of* (refl$_i$).

Lemma 3 ((eucl$_i$)-**Elimination**). *Every sequent Λ derivable in* G3Ldm$_n^m$ + PR *is derivable without the use of* (eucl$_i$).

Proof. The result is proven by induction on the height of the given derivation. We show that the topmost instance of a (eucl$_i$) rule can be permuted upward in a derivation until it is eliminated entirely; by successively eliminating each (eucl$_i$) inference from the derivation, we obtain a derivation free of such inferences. Also, we evoke Lemma 2 and assume that all instances of (refl$_i$) have been eliminated from the given derivation.

Base Case. An application of (eucl$_i$) on an initial sequent (below left) can be re-written as an instance of the (id) rule (below right).

$$\frac{\mathcal{R}, \mathcal{R}_i wu, \mathcal{R}_i wv, \mathcal{R}_i uv, z : p, z : \overline{p}, \Gamma}{\mathcal{R}, \mathcal{R}_i wu, \mathcal{R}_i wv, z : p, z : \overline{p}, \Gamma} \text{ (eucl}_i) \qquad \frac{}{\mathcal{R}, \mathcal{R}_i wu, \mathcal{R}_i wv, z : p, z : \overline{p}, \Gamma} \text{ (id)}$$

Inductive Step. We show the inductive step for the non-trivial cases: ($\langle i \rangle$) and (Pr$_i$) (case (i) and (ii), respectively). All other cases are resolved by applying IH to the premise followed by an application of the corresponding rule.

(i) Let $\mathcal{R}_i uv$ be active in the ($\langle i \rangle$) inference of the initial derivation (below (1)). Observe that when we apply the (eucl$_i$) rule first (below (2)), the atom $\mathcal{R}_i uv$ is no longer present in $\Lambda = \mathcal{R}, \mathcal{R}_i wu, \mathcal{R}_i wv, u : \langle i \rangle \phi, v : \phi, \Gamma$, and so, the ($\langle i \rangle$) rule is not necessarily applicable. Nevertheless, we may apply the (Pr$_i$) rule to derive the desired conclusion since $\langle i \rangle \langle i \rangle \in \mathcal{P}_\Lambda(u,v) \cap L_i$. Namely, the fact that $\langle i \rangle \langle i \rangle \in \mathcal{P}_\Lambda(u,v)$ only relies on the presence of $\mathcal{R}_i wu, \mathcal{R}_i wv$ in Λ.

$$\frac{\dfrac{\mathcal{R}, \mathcal{R}_i wu, \mathcal{R}_i wv, \mathcal{R}_i uv, u : \langle i \rangle \phi, v : \phi, \Gamma}{\mathcal{R}, \mathcal{R}_i wu, \mathcal{R}_i wv, \mathcal{R}_i uv, u : \langle i \rangle \phi, \Gamma} (\langle i \rangle)}{\mathcal{R}, \mathcal{R}_i wu, \mathcal{R}_i wv, u : \langle i \rangle \phi, \Gamma} \text{ (eucl}_i)} \qquad (1)$$

$$\frac{\dfrac{\mathcal{R}, \mathcal{R}_i wu, \mathcal{R}_i wv, \mathcal{R}_i uv, u : \langle i \rangle \phi, v : \phi, \Gamma}{\mathcal{R}, \mathcal{R}_i wu, \mathcal{R}_i wv, u : \langle i \rangle \phi, v : \phi, \Gamma} \text{ (eucl}_i)}{\mathcal{R}, \mathcal{R}_i wu, \mathcal{R}_i wv, u : \langle i \rangle \phi, \Gamma} \text{ (Pr}_i)} \qquad (2)$$

(ii) Let Λ_1 be the first premise $\mathcal{R}, \mathcal{R}_i wu, \mathcal{R}_i wv, \mathcal{R}_i uv, x : \langle i \rangle \phi, y : \phi, \Gamma$ of the initial derivation (below (3)). In the (Pr$_i$) inference of the top derivation, we assume that $\mathcal{R}_i uv$ is active, that is, the side condition of (Pr$_i$) is satisfied because some string $\langle i \rangle^n \in \mathcal{P}_{\Lambda_1}(x,y) \cap L_i$ with $n \in \mathbb{N}$. (NB. For the non-trivial case, we assume that $\langle i \rangle^n \in \mathcal{P}_{\Lambda_1}(x,y)$ relies on the presence of $\mathcal{R}_i uv \in \Lambda_1$, that is, the automaton $\mathcal{P}_{\Lambda_1}(x,y)$ makes use of transitions $u \xrightarrow{\langle i \rangle} v$ or $v \xrightarrow{\langle i \rangle} u$ defined relative to $\mathcal{R}_i uv$.) When we apply the (eucl$_i$) rule first in our derivation (below (4)), we can no longer rely on the relational atom $\mathcal{R}_i uv$ to apply the (Pr$_i$) rule. However,

due to the presence of $\mathcal{R}_i wu, \mathcal{R}_i wv$ in $\Lambda_2 = \mathcal{R}, \mathcal{R}_i wu, \mathcal{R}_i wv, x : \langle i \rangle \phi, y : \phi, \Gamma$ we may still apply the (Pr_i) rule. Namely, since $\langle i \rangle^n \in \mathcal{P}_{\Lambda_1}(x, y)$, we know there is a sequence of n transitions $x \xrightarrow{\langle i \rangle} z_1 \xrightarrow{\langle i \rangle} \cdots z_{n-1} \xrightarrow{\langle i \rangle} y$ from x to y. We replace each occurrence of $u \xrightarrow{\langle i \rangle} v$ with $u \xrightarrow{\langle i \rangle} w \xrightarrow{\langle i \rangle} v$ and each occurrence of $v \xrightarrow{\langle i \rangle} u$ with $v \xrightarrow{\langle i \rangle} w \xrightarrow{\langle i \rangle} u$. There will thus be a string in $\mathcal{P}_{\Lambda_2}(x, y) \cap L_i$, and so, the (Pr_i) rule may be applied.

$$\frac{\dfrac{\mathcal{R}, \mathcal{R}_i wu, \mathcal{R}_i wv, \mathcal{R}_i uv, x : \langle i \rangle \phi, y : \phi, \Gamma}{\mathcal{R}, \mathcal{R}_i wu, \mathcal{R}_i wv, \mathcal{R}_i uv, x : \langle i \rangle \phi, \Gamma} (\mathsf{Pr}_i)}{\mathcal{R}, \mathcal{R}_i wu, \mathcal{R}_i wv, x : \langle i \rangle \phi, \Gamma} (\mathsf{eucl}_i) \tag{3}$$

$$\frac{\dfrac{\mathcal{R}, \mathcal{R}_i wu, \mathcal{R}_i wv, \mathcal{R}_i uv, x : \langle i \rangle \phi, y : \phi, \Gamma}{\mathcal{R}, \mathcal{R}_i wu, \mathcal{R}_i wv, x : \langle i \rangle \phi, y : \phi, \Gamma} (\mathsf{eucl}_i)}{\mathcal{R}, \mathcal{R}_i wu, \mathcal{R}_i wv, x : \langle i \rangle \phi, \Gamma} (\mathsf{Pr}_i) \tag{4}$$

$\square$

Theorem 3 (Cut-free Completeness of $\mathsf{Ldm}_n^m \mathsf{L}$). *For any formula $\phi \in \mathcal{L}^m$, if $\Vdash \phi$, then $x : \phi$ is cut-free derivable in $\mathsf{Ldm}_n^m \mathsf{L}$.*

Proof. Follows from Theorem 2, Lemma's 1–3, and the fact that, for each $i \in Ag$, the $(\langle i \rangle)$ rule is admissible, that is, the $(\langle i \rangle)$ rule is an instance of the rule (Pr_i). $\square$

Last, we must ensure that $\mathsf{Ldm}_n^m \mathsf{L}$ is sound. To prove this, we need to stipulate how to interpret sequents on Ldm_n^m-models. Our definition is based on [4]:

Definition 7 (Interpretation, Satisfaction, Validity). *Let M be an Ldm_n^m-model with domain W, $\Lambda = \mathcal{R}, \Gamma$ a labelled sequent, and Lab the set of labels. Let I be an interpretation function mapping labels to worlds: i.e. $I: Lab \mapsto W$.*

Λ is satisfied in M with I iff for all relational atoms $\mathcal{R}_i xy \in \mathcal{R}$, if $\mathcal{R}_i x^I y^I$ holds in M, then there must exist some $z : \phi$ in Γ such that $M, z^I \Vdash \phi$.

Λ is valid iff it is satisfiable in every M with any interpretation function I.

Theorem 4 ($\mathsf{Ldm}_n^m \mathsf{L}$ Soundness). *Every sequent derivable in $\mathsf{Ldm}_n^m \mathsf{L}$ is valid.*

Proof. We know by Theorem 2 that all rules of $\mathsf{Ldm}_n^m \mathsf{L}$, with the exception of (Pr_i), preserve validity. Details of the (Pr_i) case are given in the online appended version (available at https://arxiv.org/abs/1908.11360). $\square$

4   Proof-Search and Decidability

In this section, we provide a class of proof-search algorithms, each deciding a logic Ldm_n^1 (with $n \in \mathbb{N}$). (We use 1 to denote the agent in the single-agent setting.) In the single-agent case, the independence of agents condition is trivially satisfied, meaning we can omit the (IOA) rule from each calculus and from consideration during proof-search. We end the section by commenting on the more complicated multi-agent setting.

In what follows, we prove that derivations in $\mathsf{Ldm}_n^1\mathsf{L}$ need only use *forestlike* *sequents*. The forestlike structure of a sequent Λ refers to a graph corresponding to the sequent. This control in sequential structure is what allows us to adapt methods from [17] to $\mathsf{Ldm}_n^1\mathsf{L}$, and produce a proof-search algorithm that decides Ldm_n^1, for each $n \in \mathbb{N}$. Let us start by making the aforementioned notions precise.

Definition 8 (Sequent Graph). *We define a graph G to be a tuple (V, E, L), where V is the non-empty set of vertices, the set of edges $E \subseteq V \times V$, and L is the labelling function that maps edges from E into some non-empty set S and vertices from V into some non-empty set S'.*

Let $\Lambda = \mathcal{R}, \Gamma$ be a labelled sequent and let $Lab(\Lambda)$ be the set of labels in Λ. The graph of Λ, denoted $G(\Lambda)$, is the tuple (V, E, L), where (i) $V = Lab(\Lambda)$, (ii) $(w, u) \in E$ and $L(w, u) = i$ iff $\mathcal{R}_i wu \in \mathcal{R}$, and (iii) $L(w) = \phi$ iff $w : \phi \in \Gamma$.

Example 2. The sequent *graph* $G(\Lambda)$ corresponding to the labelled sequent $\Lambda = \mathcal{R}_1 xy, \mathcal{R}_1 zx, x : p, y : \overline{p} \vee q, z : r, z : \Diamond q$ is shown below:

Definition 9 (Tree, Forest, Forestlike Sequent, Choice-tree). *We say that a graph $G = (V, E, L)$ is a tree iff there exists a node w, called the root, such that there is exactly one directed path from w to any other node u in the graph. We say that a graph is a forest iff it consists of a disjoint union of trees.*

A sequent Λ is forestlike iff its graph $G(\Lambda)$ is a forest. We refer to each disjoint tree in the graph of a forestlike sequent as a choice-tree and for any label w in Λ, we let $CT(w)$ represent the choice-tree that w belongs to.

The above notions will be significant for our proof-search algorithms, for example:

Remark 3. When interpreting a sequent, each choice-tree that occurs in the graph of the sequent is a syntactic representation of an equivalence class of $\mathcal{R}_1$ (i.e., a choice-cell for agent 1). Using this insight, we know that if agent 1 is restricted to n-many choices, then if there are $m > n$ choice-trees in the sequent, at least two choice-trees must correspond to the same equivalence class in $\mathcal{R}_1$. We use this observation to specify how APC_n^1 is applied in the algorithm.

The following definitions introduce the necessary tools for the algorithms:

Definition 10 (Saturation, $\Box$-, [1]-realization, $\Diamond$-, $\langle 1 \rangle$-propagated). *Let Λ be a forestlike sequent and let w be a label in Λ.*

The label w is saturated iff the following hold: (i) If $w : \phi \in \Lambda$, then $w : \overline{\phi} \notin \Lambda$, (ii) if $w : \phi \vee \psi \in \Lambda$, then $w : \phi \in \Lambda$ and $w : \psi \in \Lambda$, (iii) if $w : \phi \wedge \psi \in \Lambda$, then $w : \phi \in \Lambda$ or $w : \psi \in \Lambda$.

A label w in Λ is $\Box$-realized iff for every $w : \Box\phi \in \Lambda$, there exists a label u such that $u : \phi \in \Lambda$. A label w in Λ is [1]-realized iff for every $w : [1]\phi \in \Lambda$, there exists a label u in $CT(w)$ such that $u : \phi \in \Lambda$.

A label w in Λ is $\Diamond$-propagated iff for every $w : \Diamond\phi \in \Lambda$, we have $u : \phi \in \Lambda$ for all labels u in Λ. A label w in Λ is $\langle 1 \rangle$-propagated iff for every $w : \langle 1 \rangle\phi \in \Lambda$, we have $u : \phi \in \Lambda$ for all labels u in $CT(w)$.

Definition 11 (n-choice Consistency). *Let Λ be a forestlike sequent and let our logic be Ldm_n^1 with $n > 0$. We say that Λ is n-choice consistent iff $G(\Lambda)$ contains at most n-many choice-trees.*

Definition 12 (Stability). *A forestlike labelled sequent Λ is stable iff (i) all labels w in Λ are saturated, (ii) all labels are $\Box$- and $[1]$-realized, (iii) all labels are $\Diamond$- and $\langle 1 \rangle$-propagated, and (iv) Λ is n-choice consistent.*

We are now able to define our proof-search algorithms for the logics Ldm_n^1. The algorithms are provided in Fig. 4 and are inspired by [17]. We emphasize that the execution of instruction 4 in Fig. 4 corresponds to an instance of the (Pr_1) rule. The algorithms are correct (Theorem 5) and terminate (Theorem 6). Last, Lemma 4 ensures that the concepts of realization, propagation, n-choice

---

Function Prove$_n$(Sequent $\mathcal{R}, \Gamma$) : Boolean

1. If $\mathcal{R}, \Gamma = \mathcal{R}, w : p, w : \bar{p}, \Gamma'$, return true.
2. If $\mathcal{R}, \Gamma$ is stable, return false.
3. If some label w in $\mathcal{R}, \Gamma$ is not saturated, then:
   (i) If $w : \phi \vee \psi \in \mathcal{R}, \Gamma$, but either $w : \phi \notin \mathcal{R}, \Gamma$ or $w : \psi \notin \mathcal{R}, \Gamma$, then let $\mathcal{R}, \Gamma' = \mathcal{R}, w : \phi, w : \psi, \Gamma$ and return Prove$_n(\mathcal{R}, \Gamma')$.
   (ii) If $w : \phi \wedge \psi \in \mathcal{R}, \Gamma$, but neither $w : \phi \notin \mathcal{R}, \Gamma$ nor $w : \psi \notin \mathcal{R}, \Gamma$, then let $\mathcal{R}, \Gamma_1 = \mathcal{R}, w : \phi, \Gamma$, let $\mathcal{R}, \Gamma_2 = \mathcal{R}, w : \psi, \Gamma$, and return false if Prove$_n(\mathcal{R}, \Gamma_i)$ = false for some $i \in \{1, 2\}$, and return true otherwise.
4. If some label w in $\mathcal{R}, \Gamma$ is not $\langle 1 \rangle$-propagated, then there is a label u in $CT(w)$ such that $u : \phi \notin \Gamma$. Let $\mathcal{R}, \Gamma' = \mathcal{R}, u : \phi, \Gamma$ and return Prove$_n(\mathcal{R}, \Gamma')$.
5. If some label w in $\mathcal{R}, \Gamma$ is not $\Diamond$-propagated, then there is a label u such that $u : \phi \notin \Gamma$. Let $\mathcal{R}, \Gamma' = \mathcal{R}, u : \phi, \Gamma$ and return Prove$_n(\mathcal{R}, \Gamma')$.
6. If there is a label w that is not $[1]$-realized, then there is a $w : [1]\phi \in \Gamma$ such that $u : \phi \notin \Gamma$ for every label $u \in CT(w)$. Let $\mathcal{R}', \Gamma' = \mathcal{R}, \mathcal{R}_1 wv, v : \phi, \Gamma$ with v fresh and return Prove$_n(\mathcal{R}', \Gamma')$.
7. If there is a label w that is not $\Box$-realized, then there is a $w : \Box\phi \in \Gamma$ such that $u : \phi \notin \Gamma$ for every label u in $\mathcal{R}, \Gamma$. Let $\mathcal{R}, \Gamma' = \mathcal{R}, v : \phi, \Gamma$ with v fresh and return Prove$_n(\mathcal{R}, \Gamma')$.
8. If $\mathcal{R}, \Gamma$ is not n-choice consistent, then let $\mathcal{R}_{k,j}, \Gamma = \mathcal{R}, \mathcal{R}_1 w_k w_j, \Gamma$ (with $0 \leq k \leq n - 1$ and $k + 1 \leq j \leq n$) and where each w_k and w_j are distinct roots of choice-trees in $\mathcal{R}, \Gamma$. Return false if Prove$_n(\mathcal{R}_{k,j}, \Gamma)$ = false for some k and j, and return true otherwise.

Fig. 4. The proof-search algorithms for Ldm_n^1 with $n > 0$. The algorithm for Ldm_0^1 is obtained by deleting line 8.

consistency, and stability are defined at each stage of the computation (Definitions 10–12). The proofs of Lemma 4 and Theorem 6 can be found in the online appended version.

Lemma 4. *Every labelled sequent generated throughout the course of computing* $\texttt{Prove}_n(w : \phi)$ *is forestlike.*

Theorem 5 (Correctness). (i) *If* $\texttt{Prove}_n(\texttt{w} : \phi)$ *returns* true, *then* $w : \phi$ *is* $\mathsf{Ldm}_n^1\mathsf{L}$*-provable.* (ii) *If* $\texttt{Prove}_n(\texttt{w} : \phi)$ *returns* false, *then* $w : \phi$ *is not* $\mathsf{Ldm}_n^1\mathsf{L}$*-provable.*

Proof. (i) It suffices to observe that each step of $\texttt{Prove}_n(\cdot)$ is a backwards application of a rule in $\mathsf{Ldm}_n^1\mathsf{L}$, and so, if the proof-search algorithm returns true, the formula $w : \phi$ is derivable in $\mathsf{Ldm}_n^1\mathsf{L}$ with arbitrary label w.

(ii) To prove this statement, we assume that $\texttt{Prove}_n(\texttt{w} : \phi)$ returned false and show that we can construct a counter-model for ϕ. By the assumption, we know that a stable sequent Λ was generated with $w : \phi \in \Lambda$. We define our counter-model $M = (W, \mathcal{R}_1, V)$ as follows: $W = Lab(\Lambda)$; $\mathcal{R}_1 uv$ iff $\mathcal{P}_\Lambda(u, v) \cap L_1 \neq \emptyset$; and $w \in V(p)$ iff $w : \overline{p} \in \Lambda$.

We argue that $F = (W, \mathcal{R}_1)$ is an Ldm_n^m-frame. It is easy to see that $W \neq \emptyset$ (at the very least, the label w must occur in Λ). Moreover, condition (C2) is trivially satisfied in the single-agent setting. We prove (C1) and (C3):

(C1) We need to prove that $\mathcal{R}_1$ is (i) reflexive and (ii) euclidean. To prove (i), it suffices to show that for each $u \in Lab(\Lambda)$ there exists a string ω in both $\mathcal{P}_\Lambda(u, u)$ and L_1. By Definition 4, we know that $\varepsilon \in \mathcal{P}_\Lambda(u, u)$ since u is both the initial and accepting state. Also, by Definition 5 we know that $\varepsilon \in L_1$. To prove (ii), we assume that $\mathcal{R}_1 wu$ and $\mathcal{R}_1 wv$ hold, and show that $\mathcal{R}_1 uv$ holds as well. By our assumption, there exist strings $\langle 1 \rangle^k \in \mathcal{P}_\Lambda(w, u) \cap L_1$ and $\langle 1 \rangle^m \in \mathcal{P}_\Lambda(w, v) \cap L_1$ (with $k, m \in \mathbb{N}$). It is not difficult to prove that if $\langle 1 \rangle^k \in \mathcal{P}_\Lambda(w, u)$, then $\langle 1 \rangle^k \in \mathcal{P}_\Lambda(u, w)$, and also that if $\langle 1 \rangle^k \in \mathcal{P}_\Lambda(u, w)$ and $\langle 1 \rangle^m \in \mathcal{P}_\Lambda(w, v)$, then $\langle 1 \rangle^{k+m} \in \mathcal{P}_\Lambda(u, v)$. Hence, we know $\langle 1 \rangle^{k+m} \in \mathcal{P}_\Lambda(u, v)$, which, together with $\langle 1 \rangle^{k+m} \in L_1$ (Definition 5), gives us the desired $\mathcal{R}_1 uv$.

(C3) By assumption we know Λ is stable. Consequently, when $n > 0$ for $\mathsf{Ldm}_n^1\mathsf{L}$, the sequent Λ must be n-choice consistent. Hence, the graph of Λ must contain $k \leq n$ choice-trees. Condition (C3) follows straightforwardly.

Since F is an Ldm_n^m-frame, M is an Ldm_n^m-model. We show by induction on the complexity of ψ that for any $u : \psi \in \Lambda$, $M, u \not\Vdash \psi$. Consequently, M is a counter-model for ϕ, and so, by Theorem 4, we know $w : \phi$ is not provable in $\mathsf{Ldm}_n^1\mathsf{L}$.

Base Case. Assume $u : p \in \Lambda$. Since Λ is stable, we know that $u : \overline{p} \notin \Lambda$. Hence, by the definition of V, we know that $u \notin V(p)$, implying that $M, u \not\Vdash p$.

Inductive Step. We consider each connective in turn. (i) Assume that $u : \theta \vee \chi \in \Lambda$. Since Λ is stable, it is saturated, meaning that $u : \theta, u : \chi \in \Lambda$. Hence, by IH $M, u \not\Vdash \theta$ and $M, u \not\Vdash \chi$, which implies that $M, u \not\Vdash \theta \vee \chi$. (ii) The case $u : \theta \wedge \chi \in \Lambda$ is similar to the previous case. (iii) Assume $u : \langle 1 \rangle \theta \in \Lambda$. Since

Λ is stable, we know that every label is $\langle 1 \rangle$-propagated. Therefore, for all labels $v \in CT(u)$ we have $v : \theta \in \Lambda$. By IH, $M, v \not\Vdash \theta$ for all $v \in CT(u)$. In general, the definition of $\mathcal{R}_1$ implies that $\mathcal{R}_1 xy$ iff $y \in CT(x)$. The former two statements imply that $M, v \not\Vdash \theta$ for all v such that $\mathcal{R}_1 uv$, and so, $M, u \not\Vdash \langle 1 \rangle \theta$. (iv) Assume that $u : \Diamond \theta \in \Lambda$. Since Λ is stable, every label is $\Diamond$-propagated, which implies that for all labels v in Λ, $v : \theta \in \Lambda$. By IH, this implies that for all $v \in W$, $M, v \not\Vdash \theta$. Thus, $M, u \not\Vdash \Diamond \theta$. (v) Assume $u : [1]\theta \in \Lambda$. Since Λ is stable, we know every label in Λ is $[1]$-realized. Therefore, there exists a label v in $CT(u)$ such that $v : \theta \in \Lambda$. By IH, we conclude that $M, v \not\Vdash \theta$. Moreover, since $\mathcal{R}_1 xy$ iff $y \in CT(x)$, we also know that $\mathcal{R}_1 uv$, which implies $M, u \not\Vdash [1]\psi$. (vi) Assume $u : \Box \theta \in \Lambda$. Since Λ is stable, we know that every label is $\Box$-realized. Consequently, there exists a label v such that $v : \theta \in \Lambda$. By IH, we conclude $M, v \not\Vdash \theta$; hence, $M, u \not\Vdash \Box \theta$. $\Box$

Theorem 6 (Termination). *For each formula* $w : \phi$, $\mathtt{Prove_n}(\mathtt{w}: \phi)$ *terminates.*

Corollary 1 (Decidability and FMP). *For each* $n \in \mathbb{N}$, *the logic* Ldm_n^1 *is decidable and has the finite model property.*

Proof. Follows from Theorems 5 and 6 above. The finite model property follows from the fact that the counter-models constructed in Theorem 5 are all finite. $\Box$

Additionally, from a computational viewpoint, it is interesting to know if completeness is preserved under a restricted class of sequents (cf. [6]). Indeed, Lemma 4, Theorems 5 and 6, imply that completeness is preserved when we restrict $\mathsf{Ldm}_n^1 \mathsf{L}$ derivations to forestlike sequents; that is, when inputting a formula into our algorithms, the sequent produced at each step of the computation will be forestlike. Interestingly, this result was obtained via our proof-search algorithms.

Corollary 2 (Forestlike Derivations). *For each* $n \in \mathbb{N}$, *if a labelled formula* $w : \phi$ *is derivable in* $\mathsf{Ldm}_n^1 \mathsf{L}$, *then it is derivable using only forestlike sequents.*

A Note on the Multi-agent Setting of $\mathsf{Ldm}_n^m \mathsf{L}$. As a concluding remark, we briefly touch upon extending the current results to the multi-agent calculi $\mathsf{Ldm}_n^m \mathsf{L}$. In the multi-agent setting (when $n = 0$), our sequents have the structure of *directed acyclic graphs* (i.e., directed graphs free of cycles), due to the independence of agents rule (IOA). In such graphs, one can easily recognize loop-nodes—i.e., a path from an ancestor node to the alleged loop-node such that both nodes are labelled with the same multiset of formulae—and use this information to bound the depth of the sequent during proof-search (cf. [17]).

The main challenge concerns the (IOA) rule, which when applied bottom-up during proof-search, introduces a fresh label v to the sequent. As a consequence, one must ensure that if proof-search terminates in a counter-model construction, this label v satisfies the independence of agents condition in that model. At first glance, one might conjecture that for every application of the (IOA) rule an additional application of the rule is needed to saturate the independence of agents condition. Of course, in such a case the algorithm will not terminate with a sequent that is readily convertible to a counter-model. Fortunately, it turns out that only finitely many applications of (IOA) are needed to construct a counter-model satisfying independence of agents. The authors have planned to devote their future work to answer this open problem for the multi-agent setting.

5 Conclusion

This paper introduced the first cut-free complete calculi for the class of multi-agent Ldm_n^m logics, introduced in [20]. We adapted propagation rules, discussed in [17], in order to refine the multi-agent $\mathsf{G3Ldm}_n^m$ labelled calculi and generate the proof-search friendly $\mathsf{Ldm}_n^m\mathsf{L}$ calculi. For the single agent case, we provided a class of terminating proof-search algorithms, each deciding a logic Ldm_n^1 (with $n \in \mathbb{N}$), including counter-model extraction from failed proof-search.

As discussed in Sect. 4, we plan to devote future research to leveraging the current results for the multi-agent setting and to provide terminating proof-search procedures for the entire Ldm_n^m class. As a natural extension, we aim to implement the proof-search algorithms from Sect. 4 in PROLOG (e.g., as in [8]). Additionally, we plan to expand the current framework to include deontic STIT operators (e.g., from [11,13]) with the goal of automating normative, agent-based reasoning. Last, it is shown in [2] that Ldm_0^1 has an NP-complete satisfiability problem and each logic Ldm_0^m, with $m > 0$, is NEXPTIME-complete. Along with expanding our proof-search algorithms to the class of all Ldm_n^m logics, we aim to investigate the complexity and optimality of our associated algorithms.

References

1. Arkoudas, K., Bringsjord S., Bello, P.: Toward ethical robots via mechanized deontic logic. In: AAAI Fall Symposium on Machine Ethics, pp. 17–23 (2005)
2. Balbiani, P., Herzig, A., Troquard, N.: Alternative axiomatics and complexity of deliberative STIT theories. J. Philos. Logic 37(4), 387–406 (2008)
3. Belnap, N., Perloff, M., Xu, M.: Facing the Future: Agents and Choices in Our Indeterminist World. Oxford University Press on Demand, Oxford (2001)
4. van Berkel, K., Lyon, T.: Cut-free calculi and relational semantics for temporal STIT logics. In: Calimeri, F., Leone, N., Manna, M. (eds.) JELIA 2019. LNCS (LNAI), vol. 11468, pp. 803–819. Springer, Cham (2019). https://doi.org/10.1007/978-3-030-19570-0_52
5. Broersen, J.: Deontic epistemic stit logic distinguishing modes of mens rea. J. Appl. Logic 9(2), 137–152 (2011)
6. Ciabattoni, A., Lyon, T., Ramanayake, R.: From display to labelled proofs for tense logics. In: Artemov, S., Nerode, A. (eds.) LFCS 2018. LNCS, vol. 10703, pp. 120–139. Springer, Cham (2018). https://doi.org/10.1007/978-3-319-72056-2_8
7. Gentzen, G.: Untersuchungen über das logische Schließen. Math. Z. 39(3), 405–431 (1935)
8. Girlando, M., Lellmann, B., Olivetti, N., Pozzato, G.L., Vitalis, Q.: VINTE: an implementation of internal calculi for lewis' logics of counterfactual reasoning. In: Schmidt, R.A., Nalon, C. (eds.) TABLEAUX 2017. LNCS (LNAI), vol. 10501, pp. 149–159. Springer, Cham (2017). https://doi.org/10.1007/978-3-319-66902-1_9

9. Grossi, D., Lorini, E., Schwarzentruber, F.: The ceteris paribus structure of logics of game forms. J. Artif. Intell. Res. **53**, 91–126 (2015)
10. Herzig, A., Schwarzentruber, F.: Properties of logics of individual and group agency. Adv. Modal Logic **7**, 133–149 (2008)
11. Horty, J.: Agency and Deontic Logic. Oxford University Press, Oxford (2001)
12. Lorini, E., Sartor, G.: Influence and responsibility: a logical analysis. In: Legal Knowledge and Information Systems, pp. 51–60. IOS Press (2015)
13. Murakami, Y.: Utilitarian deontic logic. Adv. Modal Logic **5**, 211–230 (2005)
14. Negri, S.: Proof analysis in modal logic. J. Philos. Logic **34**(5–6), 507–544 (2005)
15. Schwarzentruber, F.: Complexity results of stit fragments. Stud. Logica **100**(5), 1001–1045 (2012)
16. Sipser, M.: Introduction to the Theory of Computation. Course Technology (2006)
17. Tiu, A., Ianovski, E., Goré, R.: Grammar Logics in Nested Sequent Calculus: Proof Theory and Decision Procedures. CoRR (2012)
18. Viganò, L.: Labelled Non-classical Logics. Kluwer Academic Publishers, Dordrecht (2000)
19. Wansing, H.: Tableaux for multi-agent deliberative-stit logic. Adv. Modal Logic **6**, 503–520 (2006)
20. Xu, M.: Decidability of deliberative *stit* theories with multiple agents. In: Gabbay, D.M., Ohlbach, H.J. (eds.) ICTL 1994. LNCS, vol. 827, pp. 332–348. Springer, Heidelberg (1994). https://doi.org/10.1007/BFb0013997

Selfish Mining in Proof-of-Work Blockchain with Multiple Miners: An Empirical Evaluation

Tin Leelavimolsilp[1](✉), Viet Nguyen[2], Sebastian Stein[1], and Long Tran-Thanh[1]

[1] University of Southampton, Southampton SO17 1BJ, UK
{tin.leelavimolsilp,s.stein,l.tran-thanh}@soton.ac.uk
[2] Imperial College London, London SW7 2AZ, UK
viet.nguyen17@imperial.ac.uk

Abstract. Proof-of-Work blockchain, despite its numerous benefits, is still not an entirely secure technology due to the existence of Selfish Mining (SM) strategies that can disrupt the system and its mining economy. While the effect of SM has been studied mostly in a two-miners scenario, it has not been investigated in a more practical context where there are multiple malicious miners individually performing SM. To fill this gap, we carry out an empirical study that separately accounts for different numbers of SM miners (who always perform SM) and strategic miners (who choose either SM or Nakamoto's mining protocol depending on which maximises their individual mining reward). Our result shows that SM is generally more effective as the number of SM miners increases, however its effectiveness does not vary in the presence of a large number of strategic miners. Under specific mining power distributions, we also demonstrate that multiple miners can perform SM and simultaneously gain higher mining rewards than they should. Surprisingly, we also show that the more strategic miners there are, the more robust the systems become. Since blockchain miners should naturally be seen as self-interested strategic miners, our findings encourage blockchain system developers and engineers to attract as many miners as possible to prevent SM and similar behaviour.

Keywords: Selfish mining · Proof-of-Work blockchain · Agent-based model · Empirical multiplayer game

1 Introduction

With the aim to decrease reliance on financial institutions, blockchain was designed and used to securely approve and record transactions among Internet users [11]. A number of blockchain characteristics such as its security, transparency, and decentralised authority have drawn many researchers and developers to apply blockchain to a wide range of application areas, such as personal

M. Baldoni et al. (Eds.): PRIMA 2019, LNAI 11873, pp. 219–234, 2019.
https://doi.org/10.1007/978-3-030-33792-6_14

data management [1,16], Internet of Things [5], and decentralised platform as a service [14].

The success of blockchain is based on two elements: an application of a cryptographic puzzle, namely Proof-of-Work (PoW), and an economic incentive for miners, who are the underlying workforce of the system. The mining process is briefly described as follows. First, a miner composes a block which mainly consists of locally verified transactions. The block also refers to the latest block of the miner's locally stored blockchain as its parent block. The miner then performs a brute force search for a number that results in a hash value of the block lower than the globally set target. When such a number (which is a "Proof of Work" that the miner did) is found, the block together with the number is broadcasted. Subsequently, a recipient of the block verifies the block's transactions and the block's hash value. Once approved, the block is then appended to the recipient's locally stored blockchain. Later, the miner claims their mining reward (which is the aforementioned incentive) by referring to the block in their spending transaction. As such, every miner is fairly rewarded in proportion to a number of blocks that they managed to create or an amount of hash rate that they expended.[1]

One of the most fundamental and significant attacks against blockchain systems is *forking*, which is difficult in practice and widely known as the 51% attack. Since the mining protocol instructs everyone to trust the longest chain[2], a malicious miner simply needs to produce a blockchain longer than the current one. Once succeeded, part of the current blockchain will be replaced by the malicious miner's blocks. Consequently, all transactions and the mining reward of the replaced blocks have been nullified, and the malicious miner earns all mining reward from their blocks; thus resulting in a disproportionate reward distribution. However, forking is not easy since it requires at least a half of the total hash rate in the system [11]. As such, it resulted in a public belief that blockchain systems are strongly secure as long as no miner possesses more than 50% of the total hash rate.

Eyal and Sirer later demonstrated that forking is still possible with lower hash rates using their *Selfish Mining* (SM) strategy [6]. Essentially, SM hides and privately mines their own blocks in contrast to publicly forking the blockchain. Such hiding allows the malicious miner to gain an advantage by removing the chance of the successive blocks being mined by the others. In addition, SM gradually discloses their private blocks to keep the advantage as much as possible to themselves. Most importantly, it requires only 1/3 of the total hash rate to fork the blockchain and earn a higher mining reward than they should. Such a hash rate is significantly lower than 1/2 of the total hash rate for publicly forking,

---

[1] To be precise, there are two types of mining reward: namely, block reward and transaction fee [2]. While there will be no block reward per block in the future, miners will still be incentivized by the transaction fee to do their mining.

[2] In practice, a chain that is the most computationally expensive or has the highest difficulty sum is chosen [4]. If every block has the same computational difficulty, the actual verification reduces to selecting the longest blockchain.

and therefore greatly threatens the security of PoW blockchain systems. With a larger hash rate, SM is even more effective and can fork the blockchain more frequently. In the worst scenario, the mining economy and the system could collapse due to the disrupted distribution of the economic incentive.

Moreover, SM can be difficult to detect in practice. While the rate of orphaned blocks (i.e. blocks that were not part of the longest chain) is a main indicator of SM activity [8], it can point out a network instability or a high network delay that causes broadcasted blocks to arrive late or be lost. As such, the practicality of the detection method based on the orphaned block rate is not certain.

Despite the threats posed by SM, there are not sufficient investigations in a more practical context: that is, a case where SM being used individually and simultaneously by multiple miners. In particular, most research so far focused on a system with one malicious miner who performs SM and has another who follows Nakamoto's mining protocol [6,7,9,12,13,15]. In practice, multiple miners can perform SM at the same time. Whether SM is even more effective in such situation is not clearly known.

For this reason, we carry out an investigation on SM in the context of multiple miners. Particularly, we seek to know (a) the effectiveness of SM in such a context, (b) the minimum hash rate that SM requires to earn mining reward more than it should, and (c) the minimum hash rate that non-malicious miners require to prevent SM. We also consider strategic miners who choose either SM or Nakamoto's mining protocol depending on which gives a higher mining reward. We believe that such miners better represent the actual miners since earning mining reward is the main purpose of the mining and a higher reward would be more preferable.

The rest of this paper is structured as follows. First, a literature review of existing studies on SM is presented in Sect. 2. We then describe two models of PoW blockchain systems (where one considers strategic miners and the another does not) in Sect. 3 and some concepts that are necessary for our work in Sect. 4. Subsequently, our empirical results for each model are described and discussed in Sect. 5. We finally conclude this paper with our findings and interesting questions that remain to be solved in Sect. 6.

2   Related Work

After Eyal and Sirer's work, there has been further research on improving SM. To exemplify this, the optimised (two-miners) SM strategy was proposed and its effectiveness was slightly improved [7,13]. A combination of SM with other attacks was also designed to increase the effectiveness of the attack [12]. In general, such improvements further reduce the amount of required hash rate to successfully employ SM.

A number of studies also shed more light on SM under different contexts. For example, Göbel et al., who further explored the effect of network delay on the SM strategy, demonstrated that SM will be more successful if every miner in the

SM pool[3] helps propagate the hidden block [8]. Kiayias et al. also showed that, under the game-theoretical setting, every miner will follow Nakamoto's mining protocol if no one has greater than 30.8% of the total hash rate [9].

On the contrary, a number of improvements of Nakamoto's mining protocol have been suggested, but they are difficult to implement in practice [6,15]. In particular, the improvements raise the hash rate required for SM to be effective, but they needs a precise coordination among miners to adopt them at the same time.

Despite the significant body of work on SM, the idea of multiple miners individually and simultaneously employing SM has not been fully explored in the existing literature. In particular, most works so far studied SM or similar strategies in a setting with one malicious miner and one non-malicious miner [6,7,9,12,13,15]. To our knowledge, there is a small-scale study which was recently conducted in parallel [10]. Compared to their work, our findings are more robust due to a large number of malicious miners in the system and a fair treatment of the underlying network in our experiment. Our work also offers a game-theoretical analysis which is a natural extension when malicious miners are considered self-interested agents that act strategically to maximise their mining rewards.

3   Models of the PoW Blockchain Mining

In this section, we formally define two models of PoW blockchain mining where the difference between them lies in the miner's capability of choosing a mining strategy. To clearly observe SM under the effect of different numbers of miners, assumptions are made as follows:

1. A fully connected network of miners without any communication delay;
2. An equal amount of mining reward per block to the creator of every block in the blockchain; and
3. The same computational difficulty (the target hash value) for every block in the blockchain.

While we adopt Assumptions 2 and 3 for the sake of comparing results with the previous works, Assumption 1 is made to scope our study on the effect of varying the number of miners in the system. In particular, unlike previous works on two miners where the network can be easily addressed [6], modelling miner's network capabilities in a system of a large number of miners is not straightforward. Therefore, we assume such a perfect network and focus on the effect of different numbers of miners in the system.

---

[3] A pool is a group of miners whose mining processes are coordinated such that they receive their mining rewards more frequently but in a smaller chunk comparing to solo mining [3].

We consider two mining strategies: *Honest Mining (HM)* and *Selfish Mining (SM)*[4]. The first is Nakamoto's mining protocol where a miner always mines and publishes a new block from the last block of the longest blockchain. On the other hand, the latter (Algorithm 1) is a strategy that hides its recently created block to privately mine from it and then strategically publishes its hidden blocks to overwrite the currently longest chain [6]. That is, whenever SM receives a new block created by the others, SM also publishes its block with the expectation that it reaches and get accepted by the rest of the network quicker than the received block. In addition, SM publishes all hidden blocks to completely overwrite the other chain whenever possible.

Algorithm 1. Selfish Mining [6]

Initialise:

    public chain, *private chain* $\leftarrow$ all publicly known blocks

    privateBranchLength $\leftarrow 0$

    Mine from the tail block of the *private chain*

Upon any new block b:

    $\Delta \leftarrow$ length(*private chain*) - length(*public chain*)

    if b was created by the SM miner **then**

        Append b to *private chain*

        privateBranchLength $\leftarrow$ *privateBranchLen* $+ 1$

        if $\Delta = 0$ **and** *privateBranchLen* $= 2$ **then**

            publish all of the *private chain*

            privateBranchLength $\leftarrow 0$

    else

        Append b to *public chain*

        if $\Delta = 0$ **then**

            private chain $\leftarrow$ *public chain*

            privateBranchLength $\leftarrow 0$

        else if $\Delta = 1$ **then**

            publish the last block of *private chain*

        else if $\Delta = 2$ **then**

            publish all of the *private chain*

            privateBranchLength $\leftarrow 0$

        else

            Publish the 1st unpublished block in the *private chain*

    Mine from the tail of the *private chain*

Subsequently there are three types of miners: Honest miner, Selfish miner, and Strategic miner. By definition, Honest miner and Selfish miner perform HM and SM respectively; henceforth HM and SM will also be used to denote them. In contrast, *Strategic miner (StrM)* is a miner that performs either HM or SM

---

[4] We do not use the optimised (two-miners) SM [7,13] since it might not be optimal in our context of multiple miners. The method of obtaining an optimal strategy in this context is also not yet known and lies outside the scope of this work.

depending on which maximises its mining reward. Note that StrM will be referred only in the second model where we consider miners are capable of choosing their strategies.

3.1 Fixed Strategy Mining Model

Here, we describe the first model of the PoW blockchain mining process where every miner employs a fixed mining strategy. Formally, a Markov model of the fixed strategy mining $\mathcal{M} = (I, C, P, S, \mathbb{P}(\cdot), \mathbb{U}(\cdot))$ is as follows:

- $I = \{1, 2, ..., N\}$ denotes a set of all miners individually represented by a positive integer.
- $C = (c_i | c_i \in \{\mathrm{HM}, \mathrm{SM}\}, i \in I)$ is a list of miner's mining strategies where the i-th element is a mining strategy used by the i-th miner in I.
- $P = (p_i | p_i \in [0, 1], \sum_{i \in I} p_i = 1, i \in I)$ is a tuple of miner's *mining powers* where the i-th element is the i-th miner's proportion of the total hash rate. That is, P is a power allocation of miners in the system.
- S is a set of all states in this Markov model where each element $s \in S$ is a state of the blockchain. The initial state $s_0 \in S$ is the blockchain with only one block that is not owned by any miner in I.
- $\mathbb{P}(\cdot)$ is a state transition function where its probability mass is $\mathbb{P}(s_{t+1} | s_t) = p_i$, and the next state s_{t+1} is the current state s_t that includes the new block created by miner i. In other words, a state transition from s_t to s_{t+1} represents a discovery of a new block with respect to miner's mining powers.
- $\mathbb{U}(\cdot)$ is a utility function that computes a proportion of a miner's blocks in the longest blockchain:

$$\mathbb{U}(s_t, i) = \frac{b_i}{\sum_{i \in I} b_i} \tag{1}$$

where b_i is the total number of i-th miner's blocks in the longest chain. Since this is a stationary Markov model, the i-th miner's *mining reward* $\mathbb{U}(s_t, i)$ will converge given a sufficiently long time t and a state $s_t \in S$ that has only one longest chain of blocks. That is, there always exists the convergence time t where $\forall t_1, t_2 \in [t, \infty) : |\mathbb{U}(s_{t_1}, i) - \mathbb{U}(s_{t_2}, i)| \le \alpha$ and α is a negligible positive real. Note that the converged value will be used throughout our work.

3.2 Dynamic Strategy Mining Model

In contrast to the previous model, the model here considers the malicious miner's capability of choosing a mining strategy that maximises their mining reward. With a game-theoretical analysis, we account for a change of the SM miner's strategy in the previous model when they deem it is better off to use HM under some power allocations.

In particular, we extend the previous model such that every SM miner becomes a StrM miner who chooses their mining strategy given an information of other miners' strategies and all possible mining rewards that the StrM miner will receive in each outcome. In particular, an empirical normal-form game of the PoW mining is denoted by $\mathcal{G} = (I, C', P, \mathbb{A}(\cdot), \mathbb{U}'(\cdot))$ where I and P are the same as before and the rest are described as follows:

- $C' = (c_i'|c_i' \in \{\text{HM}, \text{StrM}\}, i \in I)$ is a list of miner's types where the i-th element indicates whether an i-th miner is a HM miner or a StrM miner.
- $\mathbb{A}(\cdot)$ is a function that maps a type of miner to a set of permissible strategies. Given an i-th miner's type $c_i' \in C'$, $\mathbb{A}(\cdot)$ performs a mapping as follows:

$$\mathbb{A}(c_i') = \begin{cases} \{\text{HM}, \text{SM}\} & \text{if } c_i' = \text{StrM}; \\ \{\text{HM}\} & \text{otherwise.} \end{cases}$$

A strategy profile is then denoted as $A = (a_i|a_i \in \mathbb{A}(c_i'), c_i' \in C', i \in I)$ or $A = (a_i, a_{-i})$ where a_i is the i-th miner's strategy and a_{-i} collectively denotes the rest.

- $\mathbb{U}' : I \times \mathcal{A} \mapsto [0, 1]$ is a payoff function that computes a miner's mining reward given $\mathcal{A}$ is a set of all possible strategy profiles with respect to I. Given a strategy profile $A \in \mathcal{A}$, the computation of $\mathbb{U}'(i, A)$ is simply done via the utility function $\mathbb{U}$ of the previously described model $\mathcal{M}$ where its strategy list C corresponds to A and other elements of the model are the same.

4   Power Threshold, Safety Level and Equilibrium

As mentioned in Sect. 1, we are interested in (a) the minimum mining power that enables SM/StrM miners to earn an unfairly large mining reward and (b) the minimum sum of HM miners' mining power that can prevent such an unfair outcome.

In more detail, an unfairly large mining reward in our models is one that exceeds the miner's mining power. Originally, a system of all HM miners will allocate a mining reward equal to their individual mining power (since everyone mines from the latest block and therefore the expected proportion of any miner's blocks is their mining power.) However, a miner with sufficiently high mining power can use SM and gain a mining reward that is higher than their mining power. Such an unfairly large reward will be demonstrated in the Sect. 5.

In our discussion, we then look for a *power threshold* which is the least mining power that lets a SM/StrM earn its unfairly large reward regardless of how much mining power the others possess. Consequently, a SM/StrM miner whose mining power reaches the power threshold will earn a mining reward more than they should.

Definition 1. *Given that $\hat{P}(p)$ is the set of all possible power allocations where a SM/StrM miner has mining power p, and $\mathbb{U}_{p,P}$ is the mining reward of the SM/StrM miner with mining power p in a power allocation P, a **power threshold** β is one that satisfies the following condition:*

$$\beta = \min \{ p \mid \forall P \in \hat{P}(p) : \mathbb{U}_{p,P} > p ; \quad \forall q \in [p, 1], \forall P' \in \hat{P}(q) : \mathbb{U}_{q,P'} > q \}$$

In other words, for every SM/StrM's mining power that yields mining reward larger than their power regardless of the other miner's power allocation, a power threshold is the least SM/StrM's power that also yields such a reward for every SM/StrM's power beyond the threshold.

Similarly, we also look for a *safety level* which is the least mining power of the HM-miner collective that prevents all SM/StrM from earning their unfairly large mining rewards. Once the safety level is reached, no SM/StrM miner will gain a mining reward higher than their mining power.

Definition 2. *Given that $\hat{P}(p_{HM})$ is the set of all possible power allocations where the sum of all HM miners' mining powers is p_{HM}, $p_{i,P}$ is an i-th miner's mining power in a power allocation P, and $I'(P)$ is the set of all SM/StrM miners in a power allocation P, a **safety level** γ is one that satisfies the condition below:*

$$\gamma = \min\{\, p_{HM} \mid \forall P \in \hat{P}(p_{HM}), \forall i \in I'(P) : \mathbb{U}_{i,P} \le p_{i,P}\,;$$
$$\forall q_{HM} \in [p_{HM}, 1], \forall P' \in \hat{P}(q_{HM}), \forall i' \in I'(P') : \mathbb{U}_{i',P'} \le p_{i',P'}\,\}$$

where $\mathbb{U}_{i,P}$ is a mining reward of the i-th miner with mining power p.

That is, for every mining power of the HM-miner collective that results in all SM/StrM's mining rewards no greater than their powers regardless of how much power an SM/StrM individually can have, a safety level is the collective's least power that also yields such SM/StrM's rewards for every HM-miner collective's power beyond the safety level.

In the dynamic strategy mining model (Sect. 3.2), we will retrieve an outcome of the game prior to an analysis of the safety level and the power threshold. In particular, we use the concept of pure-strategy ϵ-equilibrium (ϵ-PE) to derive the choice of miners' strategies that maximises their mining reward. The concept is also useful to disregard small fluctuations in the payoff value; such a fluctuation is caused by a stochastic nature of the PoW blockchain mining process and consequently could lead us to misinterpret the result.

Definition 3. *A pure-strategy ϵ-equilibrium (ϵ-PE) where $\epsilon > 0$ is a strategy profile $A^* = (a_i^*, a_{-i})$ that satisfies the following condition:*

$$\forall i \in I, \forall a_i \in \mathbb{A}(c_i') : \quad \mathbb{U}'(i, A^*) \ge \mathbb{U}'(i, (a_i, a_{-i})) - \epsilon$$

In other words, for each and every miner, there is no other mining strategy that allows them to gain a higher utility than the strategy in the pure-strategy ϵ-equilibrium by ϵ, given that the others' strategies are fixed.

Finally, an extra assumption where HM is more preferable to SM will be incorporated in the ϵ-PE analysis of the result. In Sect. 5, we will show the existence of multiple equilibria due to a negligible difference in StrM's mining reward between HM and SM under the same power allocation. Since there is neither an incentive nor a proper reason for the StrM to use SM instead of HM in such cases, we disregard such equilibria with SM by the *HM-preference assumption*, which is defined as follows:

Definition 4. *Given a pair of ϵ-equilibria $A^* = (a_i^*, a_{-i})$ and $A^{**} = (a_i^{**}, a_{-i})$ where $a_i^* \neq a_i^{**}$ (one i-th miner's choice is HM and the another is SM) in a model $\mathcal{G}$, an HM-preferable ϵ-equilibrium is the equilibrium where the i-th miner's choice is HM.*

5 Empirical Results and Discussion

To address our research question, we carry out discrete event simulations of the models such that different numbers of SM/StrM miners and different power allocations are accounted (Table 1).[5] In particular, each element in the Markov model that was described in Sect. 3 is varied, and a simulation where a state transition occurs at each timestep is performed. Each simulation setting is also repeatedly simulated 100 times to compute an average of the converged utility value. In a rare case of non-convergence, we use the value at the 200,000th timestep, which is analogous to 3–4 years in the Bitcoin system and well approximates the system behaviour compared to the results of others [6,13].

Table 1. Simulation parameters

	Parameter	Value
	α (Eq. 1)	0.0001
	ϵ (Definition 3)	0.0001
Power step	for 1, 2, 3 SM/StrM cases	0.01
	for 4 SM/StrM case	0.02
	for 5, 6, 7 SM/StrM cases	0.04
	for 8, 9 SM/StrM cases	0.05

Due to an extremely large number of simulations to cover all settings, we carry out simulations only for the base parameters and perform a permutation to cover all necessary results. To exemplify this, we swap the miner's utility of the model $\mathcal{M}_1$ with $C_1 = (\text{HM}, \text{SM})$ and $P_1 = (0.4, 0.6)$ and use it as a result of the model $\mathcal{M}_2$ where $C_2 = (\text{SM}, \text{HM})$ and $P_2 = (0.6, 0.4)$. We also treat a collective of HM miners as a single HM miner since their individual earnings are unnecessary in this work and an overall outcome of their individual minings is the same as a solo HM mining with their combined mining powers.

5.1 Fixed Strategy Mining

In general, the mining powers of SM and HM that yield an unfairly large mining reward decreases with the number of SM miners in the system. As shown in

---

[5] Note that modelling the underlying network is not in the scope of this work. Consequently, multiple broadcasted messages that occur in a single timestep will be processed in a uniformly random manner.

Fig. 1(a), the mean of SM's mining reward among different power allocations exponentially grows in an increase of SM's mining power until its convergence at one. However, the range of SM's mining power during the exponential growth gradually decreases with the number of SM miners. A similar trend in the HM's mining reward with respect to the HM's mining power is also observed and shown in Fig. 1(b).

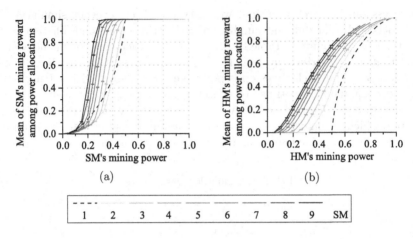

Fig. 1. Average of the SM's mining reward among different power allocations with specific SM's mining power (a) and an average of the HM's mining reward among different power allocations with specific HM's mining power (b) in a system with different numbers of SM. Standard error of the mean is shown as an error bar.

As shown by Liu et al. [10], our observation has also revealed a similar underlying cause of the trend of HM/SM's mining reward. Generally, the higher the number of miners, the less mining power each of them has. With a low mining power, SM is less likely to create a private chain longer than the other chains and therefore most of their computational resources are wasted. In turn, a mining power that HM/SM requires to earn an unfairly large reward becomes less in a system with a large number of miners.

Surprisingly, a number of SM miners can simultaneously get their unfairly large rewards under some power allocations. In particular, their mining powers in such a power allocation are equal and larger than a certain value. However, the range of such mining powers decreases and shortens as the number of SM increases, as shown in Fig. 2. We therefore hypothesise that this behaviour does not exist in a system with an extremely large number of miners.

5.2 Dynamic Strategy Mining

Previously, we have shown that a SM miner with low mining power earns less than their power. However, they might be able to earn more if they switch back

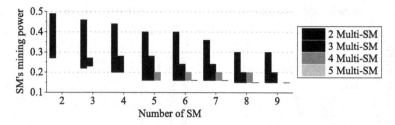

Fig. 2. Ranges of a mining power of multiple and profitable SM (Multi-SM) with respect to an increasing number of SM in the system. In such ranges, a number of SM miners (indicated by the number of Multi-SM) individually have equal mining power and simultaneously gain an unfairly large mining reward.

to HM instead. Such a switch can induce further strategy switches due to a change in mining reward. In this section, we use a game-theoretical concept of equilibria (Sect. 4) to tackle such strategy changes and discuss the outcome.

We first notice multiple equilibria in some specific power allocations and at least one equilibrium in every power allocation. As shown in Fig. 3(a), the average number of ϵ-PE per power allocation is always at least one. However, it becomes extremely large in power allocations where there is a StrM with a relatively high mining power.

In a following observation, we see that the large number of ϵ-PE is caused by a StrM miner expressing an indifference between HM and SM strategy where there is another StrM with a considerably large mining power. In such a situation, there is no significant difference in mining reward between HM and SM used by a StrM with a low mining power; which results in a moderate amount of StrM's SM over all ϵ-PE as depicted in Fig. 3(c). Consequently, the number of ϵ-PE is a combinatorial number of the StrM's HM/SM with low mining power and therefore grows in an increase of the number of StrM in the system, as shown in Fig. 3(a).

With the HM-preference assumption, a reasonable choice of StrM's strategy in ϵ-PE is obtained. In particular, StrM will no longer choose SM if there is no significant difference between HM's and SM's mining reward. The change of strategy in ϵ-PE is clearly demonstrated by a comparatively low number of ϵ-PE per power allocation in Fig. 3(b) and no SM strategy chosen by a StrM with mining power under 0.3 in Fig. 3(d).

Clearly, StrM prefers SM to HM and starts earning an unfairly large mining reward as their mining power increases. These are confirmed in Figs. 3(d) and 4(a). That is, StrM starts to choose SM once their mining power exceeds one-fourth. Once StrM possesses at least half of the total mining power, they always choose SM to reap the whole mining reward from the system.

Interestingly, the more StrM in the system, the more their mining strategy and their mining reward become similar to the case of one StrM. As demonstrated in Fig. 3(d), when the number of StrM miners increases, the transition of the StrM's strategy from HM to SM gradually becomes sharper similarly to

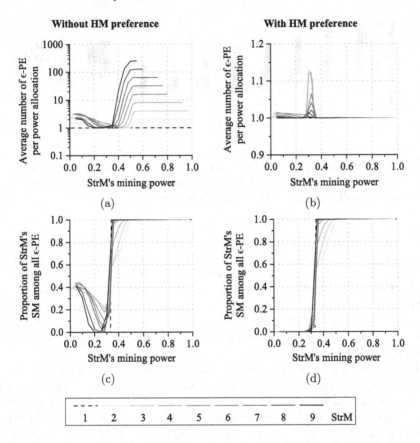

Fig. 3. Average number of ϵ-PE per power allocation (a, b) and an overall StrM's strategy in ϵ-PE (c, d) with different number of StrM in the system. Left figures (a, c) are results not under the HM-preference assumption, while right figures (b, d) are results under the HM-preference assumption.

the case of single StrM. Likewise, Fig. 4(a) shows a convergence of the mining reward of StrM with a mining power lower than $1/2$ to one of the case of one StrM.

In contrast, HM's mining reward does not converge to one in the case of single StrM. Instead, it converges to their mining power as the number of StrM increases. This is shown in Fig. 4(b), where the HM's mining reward with a mining power under 0.67 asymptotically approaches their power as the number of StrM increases.

Even with the HM-preference assumption, there still are multiple ϵ-PE for some power allocations. Such multiple equilibria are shown in Fig. 3(b) where an average number of ϵ-PE per power allocation is more than one for any StrM's mining power below 0.36. We find that multiple StrM with the same mining power larger than 0.3 together choose either HM or SM in such ϵ-PE. Since an

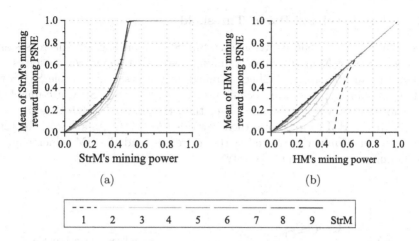

Fig. 4. Average of the StrM's mining reward among different ϵ-PE with specific StrM's mining power (a) and average of the HM's mining reward among different ϵ-PE with specific HM's mining power (b) in a system with different numbers of StrM. Standard error of the mean is shown as an error bar.

individual deviation from HM to SM or vice versa yields a comparatively low mining reward, multiple ϵ-PE with such StrM together choosing either HM or SM are formed.

On further inspection, an ϵ-PE where multiple StrM choose SM becomes less likely to occur as the number of StrM increases. Compared to the fixed strategy model's, a range of such StrM's mining power in this model is even less. As shown in Fig. 5, the mining-power range of multiple StrM that possess nearly equal power and together choose SM in ϵ-PE shortens in an increase of the number of StrM. Therefore, it is clear that this behaviour is highly unlikely to occur in the presence of a large number of StrM.

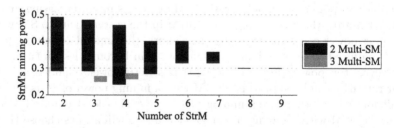

Fig. 5. Ranges of a mining power of multiple and profitable SM (Multi-SM) with respect to an increasing number of StrM in the system. In such ranges, a number of StrM miners (indicated by the number of Multi-SM) individually have equal mining power and simultaneously gain an unfairly large mining reward.

5.3   Safety Level and Power Threshold

As shown in Fig. 6, a safety level against SM/StrM monotonically decreases as a number of SM/StrM grows. Since a mining power that one miner possesses will decrease in an increasing number of miners in the system, multiple SM/StrM with a low mining power will become prominent. Such SM/StrM are unable to frequently create a private chain longer than the others (Sect. 5.1) and consequently choose HM to maximise their rewards (Sect. 5.2). As a result, the total mining power of miners performing HM increases, and the HM miner requires less mining power to prevent SM/StrM.

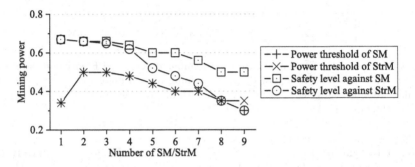

Fig. 6. Power thresholds and safety levels with respect to different numbers of SM/StrM in the system. No difference of a safety level between one with the HM-preference assumption and one without the assumption is found.

Moreover, the safety level is upper bounded by the case of one SM/StrM; that is, it is no greater than 2/3. Intuitively, the case of one SM/StrM is the most difficult to prevent since it is a coalition of all SM/StrM miners combining their mining power and working together against HM miners. The safety level in this case is therefore the greatest one.

Similarly, a power threshold of SM/StrM decreases in an increasing number of SM/StrM after the case of single SM/StrM in the system. Due to SM with a low mining power constantly wasting their effort, the amount of mining power which is required to secretly build the longest chain becomes less in turn.

However, the power threshold of StrM is strictly lower bounded at 1/3. A similar rationale can be applied here: HM with a mining power of 2/3 is the most difficult for SM and therefore a mining power of 1/3 is at least required. On the contrary, a StrM with a mining power lower than 1/3 will always choose HM, as shown in Fig. 3(d).

Clearly an upper bound of the power threshold of SM/StrM is 1/2, which corresponds to Nakamoto's analysis [11]. Any mining power beyond the threshold always allows SM/StrM to successfully create the longest chain.

6   Conclusions and Future Work

In this work, an empirical investigation of the Selfish Mining (SM) strategy employed by multiple malicious miners has been carried out. We separately considered two types of malicious miners where one (SM miner) always follow SM and the another (StrM miner) chooses to follow either Nakamoto's mining protocol or the SM strategy depending on which maximises its mining reward. Since our work accounted for a large number of malicious miners in the system, our findings (such as the case of multiple miners simultaneously and individually performing SM) are more practical than the other's so far.

The effectiveness of SM strategy varies when different types and different numbers of malicious miners are considered. In general, SM is more effective in the presence of a large number of SM miners than one in StrM miners since it can reap a larger amount of mining reward with the same hash-rate proportion. However, SM in a system with a low number of StrM miners is less effective than one in SM miners since it yields a smaller mining reward with the same hash-rate proportion.

Regardless of the type and the number of miners in the system, the least hash-rate proportion to perform and to prevent SM are no greater than $1/2$ and $2/3$ respectively. Additionally, both proportions monotonically decrease in an increasing number of malicious miners in the system. If only StrM miners are considered, then the least hash-rate proportion required for SM is strictly $1/3$. However, such a proportion reduces further than $1/3$ (as originally reported by Eyal and Sirer [6]) if SM miners are considered.

Despite the aforementioned, our result suggests that PoW blockchain systems are required to have a large number of miners to be more secure against SM. Since blockchain miners work for their mining reward, they are utility-maximising agents or StrM miners in our model. As shown in Sect. 5.2, SM is comparably less chosen in a presence of a large number of StrM miners. Together with the decreasing hash-rate proportion required for preventing SM, it can be concluded that a large number of miners can prevent SM and similar malicious mining strategies.

A number of interesting questions still remain to be investigated. As pointed out by Eyal and Sirer [6], a network capability of SM miners is also an important factor that affects the effectiveness of SM. This aspect will be taken into account in our future work. Moreover, an optimal SM strategy in the context of multiple miners, similar to that in the work of Sapirshtein et al. [13], is not yet known. With the optimal strategy, it remains to be seen whether our findings are still valid.

Acknowledgement. The authors gratefully acknowledge financial support from the EPSRC Doctoral Training Partnership, and the use of IRIDIS High Performance Computing Facility at the University of Southampton. We also would like to express our gratitude to all anonymous reviewers for their insightful comments.

References

1. Azaria, A., Ekblaw, A., Vieira, T., Lippman, A.: MedRec: using blockchain for medical data access and permission management. In: 2016 2nd International Conference on Open and Big Data, pp. 25–30 (2016)
2. Bitcoin Wiki: Mining (2018). https://en.bitcoin.it/wiki/Mining. Accessed 1 July 2019
3. Bitcoin Wiki: Pooled mining (2018). https://en.bitcoin.it/wiki/Pooled_mining. Accessed 14 June 2019
4. Bitcoin Wiki: Block (2019). https://en.bitcoin.it/wiki/Block. Accessed 13 June 2019
5. Christidis, K., Devetsikiotis, M.: Blockchains and smart contracts for the internet of things. IEEE Access **4**, 2292–2303 (2016)
6. Eyal, I., Sirer, E.G.: Majority is not enough: bitcoin mining is vulnerable. In: Christin, N., Safavi-Naini, R. (eds.) FC 2014. LNCS, vol. 8437, pp. 436–454. Springer, Heidelberg (2014). https://doi.org/10.1007/978-3-662-45472-5_28
7. Gervais, A., Karame, G.O., Wüst, K., Glykantzis, V., Ritzdorf, H., Capkun, S.: On the security and performance of proof of work blockchains. In: Proceedings of the 2016 ACM SIGSAC Conference on Computer and Communications Security, CCS 2016, pp. 3–16. ACM, New York (2016)
8. Göbel, J., Keeler, H.P., Krzesinski, A.E., Taylor, P.G.: Bitcoin blockchain dynamics: the selfish-mine strategy in the presence of propagation delay. Perform. Eval. **104**, 23–41 (2016)
9. Kiayias, A., Koutsoupias, E., Kyropoulou, M., Tselekounis, Y.: Blockchain mining games. In: Conitzer, V., Bergemann, D., Chen, Y. (eds.) Proceedings of the 2016 ACM Conference on Economics and Computation, EC 2016, pp. 365–382. ACM Press, New York (2016)
10. Liu, H., Ruan, N., Du, R., Jia, W.: On the strategy and behavior of bitcoin mining with n-attackers. In: Proceedings of the 2018 on Asia Conference on Computer and Communications Security, ASIACCS 2018, pp. 357–368. ACM, New York (2018)
11. Nakamoto, S.: Bitcoin: a peer-to-peer electronic cash system (2008). https://bitcoin.org/en/bitcoin-paper. Accessed 28 Nov 2015
12. Nayak, K., Kumar, S., Miller, A., Shi, E.: Stubborn mining: generalizing selfish mining and combining with an eclipse attack. In: 2016 IEEE European Symposium on Security and Privacy, pp. 305–320. IEEE Press, Los Alamitos (2016)
13. Sapirshtein, A., Sompolinsky, Y., Zohar, A.: Optimal selfish mining strategies in bitcoin. In: Grossklags, J., Preneel, B. (eds.) FC 2016. LNCS, vol. 9603, pp. 515–532. Springer, Heidelberg (2017). https://doi.org/10.1007/978-3-662-54970-4_30
14. Wood, G.: Ethereum: a secure decentralised generalised transaction ledger. Ethereum Project Yellow Paper **151**, 1–32 (2014)
15. Zhang, R., Preneel, B.: Publish or perish: a backward-compatible defense against selfish mining in bitcoin. In: Handschuh, H. (ed.) CT-RSA 2017. LNCS, vol. 10159, pp. 277–292. Springer, Cham (2017). https://doi.org/10.1007/978-3-319-52153-4_16
16. Zyskind, G., Nathan, O., Pentland, A.: Decentralizing privacy: using blockchain to protect personal data. In: 2015 IEEE Security and Privacy Workshops, pp. 180–184 (2015)

A Co-evolutionary Approach
to Analyzing the Impact of Rationality
on the Italian Electricity Market

Célia da Costa Pereira[1]([✉]), Sara Bevilacqua[2], Eric Guerci[3], Frédéric Precioso[1],
and Claudio Sartori[2]

[1] Université Côte d'Azur, CNRS, I3S Lab., Sophia Antipolis, France
{Celia.DA-COSTA-PEREIRA,frederic.precioso}@univ-cotedazur.fr
[2] Università di Bologna, Bologna, Italy
{sara.bevilacqua,claudio.sartori}@unibo.it
[3] Université Côote d'Azur, CNRS - GREDEG, Nice, France
eric.guerci@univ-cotedazur.fr

Abstract. We analyze the behavior of the Italian electricity market with an agent-based model. In particular, we are interested in testing the assumption that the market participants are fully rational in the economical sense. To this end, we suppose that while constructing its strategy the agent takes into account all the possible strategies the other (competitors) agents might adopt in the future, not only their last strategies, as it is done in the literature. This motivates us to propose a co-evolutionary approach to strategy optimization, which better reflects the way actual decision makers behave in reality. The experiments carried out corroborate our hypothesis and show an improvement in the results compared to the literature.

1 Introduction

The need for understanding the evolution of the prices in the electrical power markets has increased with the new trends of the electrical market in many countries [14,15]. Artificial Intelligence techniques have already proven to be effective in modeling the electricity market. Faia and colleagues proposed in [4] a Genetic Algorithm (GA) based approach to solve the portfolio optimization problem for simulating the Iberian electricity market. The results show that their GA based method is able to reach better results than previous implementations of Particle Swarm Optimization (PS) and Simulated Annealing (SA) methods. They also compared their results with the ones obtained with a deterministic approach. Santos and colleagues proposed in [13] a new version of the Multi-Agent System for Competitive Electricity Markets (MASCEM, [12]) with the aim of optimizing it with respect to the results as well as to the execution time, in order to face the highly demanding requirements from the decision support.

C. da Costa Pereira—Acknowledges support of the PEPS AIRINFO project funded by the CNRS.

M. Baldoni et al. (Eds.): PRIMA 2019, LNAI 11873, pp. 235–250, 2019.
https://doi.org/10.1007/978-3-030-33792-6_15

Other models have been proposed, like the one presented by Urielli and colleagues [18], in which the authors study the impact of the Time-Of-Use (TOU) tariffs in a competitive electricity marketplace. A very interesting and recent survey of potential design changes in the electricity market and their consequences, has been proposed by Ela and colleagues in [3].

In this paper, we propose a framework which helps analysing the behavior of the participants in the Italian electrical power market [16]. We would like to stress that our interest is in understanding how the market behaves as a consequence of the actions of its participants to make profit, and also in analysing the behavior of the market in order to maximize the social welfare from an economical rational point of view [17,19], i.e., with respect to the electricity producers as well as with respect to the electricity consumers. To this aim, we build upon our previous contribution [2], which reproduced and then extended an existing economical-based model of the Italian electricity market [8]. Instead of treating the strategies of the market competitors as already known (from the previous auctions) and fixed, here we adopt a more sophisticated setting, more in line with reality, whereby each market participant optimizes its strategy while trying to anticipate the strategies its competitors could adopt. This led us to devise a co-evolutionary approach to strategy optimization.

The paper is organized as follows. Section 2 briefly presents the three optimization methods used in the paper. Section 3 presents the mechanism of exchanges in the Italian market proposed in the literature. Section 4 presents the problem statement and Sect. 5 describes the co-evolutionary approach as well as the obtained results. Section 6 concludes the paper.

2   Some Background: A Brief Description of the Used Methods

In this section, we will briefly present the three methods used in our work to model the rationality of the market participants.

A *Genetic Algorithm (GA)* [7,9] is a computational technique inspired by biology. The basic idea of a GA is to mimic the Darwinian principle of survival of the fittest, according to which species with a high capacity of adaptation have a higher probability to survive and then to reproduce. The algorithm considers a population of individuals represented by their genes. Three operators can be used to mimic the evolution of these individuals: *mutation*, which randomly changes some bits of a gene, *crossover*, which mimics the sexual reproduction of the living beings, and *selection*, which consists of deciding which among the individuals in the population will survive in the next generation. This choice is made thanks to a *fitness function*, which is an objective function allowing to compute the extent to which an individual of the population is adapted to solve the considered problem.

In *Monte Carlo Optimization* [1], an approximation to the optimum of an objective function is obtained by drawing random points from a probability distribution, evaluating them, and keeping the one for which the value of the objective function is the greatest (if a maximum is sought for) or the least (if a minimum is sought for). As the number of points increases, the approximation converges to the global optimum.

Particle Swarm Optimization (PS) [10,11] is a meta-heuristic method inspired by the behavior or rules that guide groups of animals, for example bird flocks. According to these rules, the members of the swarm need to balance two opposite behaviors in order to reach the goal: individualistic behavior, in which each element searches for an optimal solution, and social behavior, which allows the swarm to be compact. Therefore, individuals take advantage from other searches moving toward a promising region. In this algorithm, the evolution of the population is re-created by the changing of the velocity of the particles. The idea is to tweak the values of a group of variables in order to make them become closer to the member of the group whose value is closest to the considered target. PS is similar to genetic algorithms (GAs). It is also a population-based method with the particularity that the elements of the population are iteratively modified until a termination criterion is satisfied.

3   The Italian Electricity Market

3.1   The Market Configuration

The reality of the Italian Electricity Market which takes place in the Italian Power Exchange (IPEX), considers a two-settlement market configuration with a generic forward market and the Day-Ahead Market (DAM). The DAM price value is commonly adopted as underlying for forward contracts; therefore, as in Guerci *et al.* [8], we will refer to DAM as the spot (i.e., immediate, instantaneous) market session for simplicity. The forward market session is modeled by assuming a common, zone-independent, and unique forward market price P^f for all market participants and by determining the exact historical quantity commitments for each generating unit.

Definition 1 (Generating Company).
A generating company (GenCo) is an agent g, (with $g = 1, 2, ..., G$, and G is the number of GenCos) which owns N_g generators[1]. The ith generator (where $i = 1, 2, \ldots, N_g$) has lower $\underline{Q}_{i,g}$ and upper $\overline{Q}_{i,g}$ production limits, which define the feasible production interval for its hourly real-power production level in MW (Mega Watt) $\hat{Q}_{i,g,h} = \hat{Q}^f_{i,g,h} + \hat{Q}^s_{i,g,h}$, with $\underline{Q}_{i,g} \leq \hat{Q}_{i,g,h} \leq \overline{Q}_{i,g}$ where $\hat{Q}^f_{i,g,h}$ and $\hat{Q}^s_{i,g,h}$ are respectively the quantity sold in the forward market and the quantity accepted in the DAM in each hour h.

It is assumed that the company g takes a long position in the forward market (it means that the company makes agreement with the market operator with large advance) for each owned generator i, corresponding to a fraction $f_{i,g,h}$ (where h indicates the hour of the day) of its hourly production capacity, that

---

[1] In the following we will use the terms *generator* and *power plant* interchangeably.

is $\hat{Q}^f_{i,g,h} = f_{i,g,h} \cdot \overline{Q}_{i,g}$. The value of such fraction varies throughout the day, indeed forward contracts are commonly sold according to standard daily profiles. The value of $f_{i,g,h}$ has been estimated by looking at historical data and thus corresponds to a realistic daily profile for each generator.

Definition 2 (Revenues for the forward and spot markets).
The revenue in Euro per hour ([€h]), $R^f_{g,h}$, from forward contracts for company g and given the unique forward market price P^f is:

$$R^f_{g,h} = \sum_{i=1}^{N_g} \hat{Q}^f_{i,g,h} \cdot P^f \tag{1}$$

The spot revenue, $R^s_{g,h}$, per hour for GenCo g is obtained as follows:

$$R^s_{g,h} = \sum_{z=1}^{Z} \hat{Q}^s_{z,g,h} \cdot P^s_{z,h} \tag{2}$$

where $P^s_{z,h}$ is the price in the spot market in zone z at hour h, and Z is the total number of zones.

Let $C_{i,g,h}$ $([€/h])^2$ be the total cost (of production) function of the ith generator of GenCo g. The total profit per hour, $\pi_{g,h}$, $[€/h]$ for GenCo g is computed as follows:

$$\pi_{g,h} = R^s_{g,h} + R^f_{g,h} - \sum_{i=1}^{N_g} C_{i,g,h}(\hat{Q}_{i,g,h}) \tag{3}$$

The considered set of thermal power plants, independently owned by GenCos, consists of up to 224 generating units, using 5 different technologies. The number of generation companies and generating units offering in the DAM varies throughout the day. Based on historical data, it has been determined for each period (day and hour) the thermal power plants that offered in DAM.[3] For each power plant in the dataset, information on the maximum and minimum capacity limits is available, as well as on the parameters needed to compute the cost.

3.2 Market Exchanges

A GenCo g submits to the DAM a bid consisting of a pair of values corresponding to the limit price P^s_i $([€/MW])$ and the maximum quantity of power $Q^s_i \leq \overline{Q}_{i,g} - \hat{Q}^f_{i,g}$ $([MW])$ that it is willing to be paid and to produce, respectively. After receiving all generators' bids, the market operator clears the DAM by performing a social welfare maximization, subject to the following constraints:

---

[2] The details about the function can be found in [8].
[3] Notice that bid data are publicly available on the power exchange website with a one-week delay, therefore, information about what plants were actually present and the like is supposed to be common knowledge.

– the zonal energy balance (Kirchhoff's laws),
– the maximum and minimum capacity of each power plant,
– the inter-zonal transmission limits.

It is worth noting that the Italian demand curve in the DAM is price-inelastic, i.e., it is unaffected when the price changes. Therefore, the social welfare maximization can be transformed into a minimization of the total reported production costs, i.e., of the bid prices (see Eq. 4). This mechanism determines both the unit commitments for each generator and the Locational Marginal Price (LMP) for each connection bus. However, the Italian market introduces two slight modifications. Firstly, sellers are paid the zonal prices (LMP), therefore, this fact has to be explicitly considered in the model, whereas buyers pay a unique national price (PUN, for *Prezzo Unico Nazionale*) common for the whole market and computed as a weighted average of the zonal prices with respect to the zonal loads. Secondly, transmission power-flow constraints differ according to the flow direction.

The factor to minimize by solving the linear program is the following:

$$\min \sum_{g=1}^{G} \sum_{i=1}^{N_g} P_{i,g,h}^s \hat{Q}_{i,g,h}^s, \tag{4}$$

which is subject to the following constraints:

– Active power generation limits: $\underline{Q}_{i,g} \leq \hat{Q}_{i,g,h} = \hat{Q}_{i,g,h}^s + \hat{Q}_{i,g,h}^f \leq \overline{Q}_{i,g}$ [MW]
– Active power balance equations for each zone z:
  $\sum_{g=1}^{G} \sum_{j \in z} \hat{Q}_{j,g,h}^s - Q_{z,load,h} = Q_{z,inject,h}$ [MW]
  being $\sum_{g=1}^{G} \sum_{j \in z} \hat{Q}_{j,g,h}^s$ the sum of all the productions over all generators located in zone z, $Q_{z,load,h}$, the load demand at zone z in hour h and $Q_{z,inject,h}$, the net oriented power injection in the network at zone z in hour h.
– Real power flow limits of line, l: $Q_{l,st} \leq \overline{Q}_{l,st}$ [MW] and $Q_{l,ts} \leq \overline{Q}_{l,ts}$ [MW] being $Q_{l,st}$ the power flowing from zone s to zone t of line l and $\overline{Q}_{l,st}$ the maximum transmission capacity of line l in the same direction. $Q_{l,st}$ are calculated with the standard DC power flow model [5].

The solution consists of the set of the active powers $\hat{Q}_{i,g,h}^s$ generated by each plant i and the set of zonal prices P_z^s (LMPs) for each zone $z \in [1, 2, \ldots, Z]$, where Z is the number of zones.

4   Problem Statement

In this section we will present a general statement of the problem of choosing the most competitive strategy for a GenCo.

4.1 Model Description

Each GenCo g must submit to the DAM a bid, i.e., a set of prices for each of its own power plants. Therefore, each GenCo has an action space for each power plant, which is a set of possible prices that the GenCo can choose. This set is represented by vector $AS_{i,g}$, which is obtained with the following product:

$$AS_{i,g} = MC_{i,g} \cdot MKset, \qquad (5)$$

where $AS_{i,g}$ represents the action space of power plant i of GenCo g, $MC_{i,g}$ is the marginal cost of the same power plant, and $MKset = [1.00, 1.04, \ldots, 5.00]$ is the vector with the mark-up levels. In this way, GenCos are sure not to propose a price lower than the costs.

The Multi-agent System. The multi-agent system is depicted in Fig. 1. The G GenCos are reported on the top of the figure. These GenCos repeatedly interact with each other at the end of each period $r \in \{1,\ldots,R\}$, that is they all submit bids to the DAM according to their current beliefs on opponents' strategies. At the beginning of each period r, GenCos need to study the current market situation in order to predict which strategies their competitors will adopt and identify the best reply to their opponents, to be played at period $r + 1$.

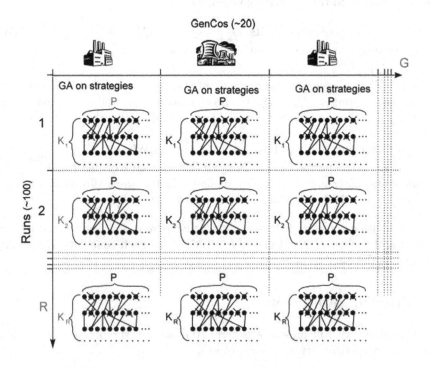

Fig. 1. A schematic representation of a simulation.

In order to choose the most competitive strategy, GenCos need to repeatedly solve the market for different private strategies and predicted strategies of their opponents, much in the same way as a chess player has to anticipate all possible moves of her/his opponent before deciding which move to play. This corresponds to an optimization problem.

4.2   The Optimization Process

The general purpose of the optimisation algorithm is to keep a large population of candidate strategies and to improve at the same time their fitness/performance in the market. Thus, a population of size P, (see Fig. 1), of strategies is defined, which evolves throughout the K_r generations.

Strategy. A strategy is a vector of prices in the action space, *one for each of the N_g power plants of GenCo g* (depicted as a black dot in Fig. 1).

Profit. The profit generated by GenCo g using strategy x, while its competitors are using the strategies collectively represented by y (a vector whose length is $\sum_{g' \neq g} N_{g'}$) can be computed based on Eq. 3. In the following, it will be convenient to denote such profit as $profit(x, y)$.

Selecting a Strategy. At the end of each period r, each GenCo bids to the market by selecting one strategy among its current population of candidates.

In [8] the selection is done according to a probabilistic choice model in order to favor the most represented strategy in the population (i.e., based on the *frequency probability*). In addition to the *frequency based* strategy of selection, in [2] a second strategy is used, *based on the value of the fitness of the individuals*, named *fitness-based* strategy. Here, like in [2], we also consider these two strategies.

5   Intelligent GenCos: A Co-evolutionary Approach

In this section, we will present an extension of the framework proposed in [2]. We will start with a brief explanation of our motivations and then we will present the methodology we have adopted.

5.1   Motivations

In previous work, like [2,8], it is supposed that the GenCos share their strategies: a GenCo constructed its strategy while making the hypothesis that the other GenCos maintain their last strategies. More precisely, the populations of strategies evolve separately and the profit of a GenCo depends on the strategies of the other GenCos. In particular, each GenCo considers, at time t, the strategies adopted by its competitors at time $t - 1$, not the ones it would expect its competitors to adopt at time t. In other words, the expectation of a GenCo is that *all the competitors will repeat the strategy they used at the previous auction.*

The framework we are proposing here allows instead to consider more realistic situations. The hypothesis we make is that each GenCo should consider, during the period in which it constructs its strategy, all the possible strategies the other GenCos might adopt. This way, the strategy under construction can be optimized against the most unfavorable competitors' current strategies.

This approach may be seen as a kind of adversarial reasoning. The difference is that in the game reasoning framework, the goal is to win against the opponent, but here there are no winners and losers: the goal for a GenCo is to obtain high profits as much as possible for its own characteristics and possibilities, while respecting all the constraints imposed by the market. Therefore, under this assumption, it is possible that the best strategy for a GenCo allows a competitor to obtain a higher profit. In what follows, we will notice that the results of the experiments made using this new framework for one particular configuration outperform the previous results, but we will first explain the fundamental ideas underlying our proposals.

5.2 Methodology

Here, instead of having G (where G is the number of GenCos) updating algorithms evolving with one different population for each GenCo, our proposal is to evolve G updating algorithms with two populations for each GenCo: the first population concerns the GenCo's own strategy, while the second population concerns the possible strategies of all the other GenCos. Therefore, the individuals of the second population represent the strategies of the remaining $G-1$ GenCos.

Benefits. Two benefits emerge from considering two populations. The first one is due to the introduction of the competitive aspect in the process. The second one is due to the fact that we can now account for the independence between GenCos unlike in [2], where GenCos were supposed to share their strategy with their competitors in order to allow for the evolution of the population. Our proposal is more in line with the reality of the Italian market, in which the companies do not share their strategies with competitors. Therefore, by adding a second population, GenCos can avoid sharing these precious information and they can reason by themselves.

Figure 2 illustrates the two populations: the GenCo's own population on the left-hand side and the population of its competitors on the right-hand side. Let x_i be one individual of Population 1 (red rectangle) and let y_j be one individual of Population 2 (blue rectangle). The fitness of an individual x_i of Population 1, $f^+(x_i)$, is to be maximized while the fitness of an individual of Population 2, $f^-(y_j)$, is to be minimized. $f^+(x_i)$ may correspond to the average of the profit that the GenCo would obtain if it adopts this strategy (x_i) by considering all the possible strategies y_j of its competitors:

Genco g

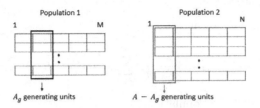

where A is the total number of generating units

Fig. 2. Schematic representation of the two populations of a GenCo (Color figure online)

$$f^+(x_i) = \frac{1}{N} \cdot \sum_{j=1}^{N} profit(x_i, y_j), \qquad (6)$$

where N in the size of Population 2 and $profit$ is the function that estimates the profit of GenCo g, given all generating units bids. The objective is to maximize the fitness $f^+(x_i)$ for each x_i in Population 1. Many other approaches can be adopted, for example by considering the different possible variations when computing the fitness. One particular example is to use the minimum instead of the average as follows:

$$f^+(x_i) = min_{j=1..N}(profit(x_i, y_j)) \qquad (7)$$

In this case, the best strategy in Population 1 corresponds to the most *robust strategy*, i.e., the one which guarantees the highest profit against the strongest competitor.

However, this new proposal increases considerably the execution time. Indeed, instead of solving a linear programming problem M times, we have now NM linear programming problems to solve.

Proposed Solution. In order to reduce the execution time, we have considered only the *best strategy among the competitors' strategies*. The best strategy for the agent will then be the one which allows the GenCo to achieve better results against the best of the competing strategies:

$$f^+(x_i) = profit(x_i, y_{best}) \qquad (8)$$

where y_{best} is the element of Population 2 with the lowest fitness or the element with the highest frequency. In this case, the linear programming problem is solved M times.

It should be recalled that our aim is to find the most robust strategy for the GenCo, i.e., the strategy which best replies to the competitors even if they all do their best to minimize the GenCo's profit. As for the fitness of individuals of Population 1, several possibilities can be considered to compute the fitness of individuals of Population 2:

– Compute the fitness as an average:

$$f(y_j) = \frac{1}{M} \cdot \sum_{i=1}^{M} profit(x_i, y_j) \tag{9}$$

where M is the size of Population 1.

– Choose the strategy with the maximum profit among all the possibilities:

$$f(y_j) = max_{i=1..M}(profit(x_i, y_j)) \tag{10}$$

– Estimate the fitness considering only the best strategy of Population 1, in order to reduce the computational effort of the two previous cases (from NM to N):

$$f(y_j) = profit(x_{best}, y_j), \tag{11}$$

where x_{best} is the element of Population 1 with the highest fitness value or with the highest frequency.

Many scenarios can be explored by mixing different approaches of computing the fitness from the two populations. Accordingly, the computational effort varies: in the best case (using Eqs. 8 and 11) the LP problem is solved NM times and in the worst case it is solved $(NM)^2$ times per iteration. Taking into account the generations of the genetic algorithm n_{gen}, the computational efforts become, respectively, $n_{gen} \cdot NM$ and $(n_{gen} \cdot NM)^2$ per iteration.

5.3   Evaluation of the Proposed Approach

To validate the proposed approach, we tested several combinations of fitness functions (f^+ and f^-), criteria for selecting one strategy from a population, and optimisation algorithms. The Hist line (red line) reports real values of the PUN. Two versions have been considered:

1. with f^+ defined as in Eq. 8, f^- as in Eq. 11:
    (a) *GAfreq1* : frequency-based strategy and genetic algorithm;
    (b) *GAfitness1* : f^+ fitness-based strategy and genetic algorithm;
    (c) *PSfreq1* : f^+ frequency-based strategy and swarm optimization;
    (d) *PSfirness1* : f^+ fitness-based strategy and swarm optimization;
    (e) *Monte Carlo.*
2. with f^+ defined as in Eq. 7, f^- as in Eq. 9:
    (a) *GAfreq2* : frequency-based strategy and genetic algorithm;
    (b) *GAfitness2* : fitness-based strategy and genetic algorithm;
    (c) *PSfreq2* : f^+ frequency-based strategy and swarm optimization;
    (d) *PSfirness2* : f^+ fitness-based strategy and swarm optimization;
    (e) *Monte Carlo.*

The remaining configurations have been left for future work.

Data. The demand of energy for each zone is provided in a *load* matrix with the following information: a first column which contains the zones, the second which contains the maximum limit prices and the third column which contains the demand quantities of electricity.

All the characteristics of the power plants are collected in a structure with the following features:

- the names of the GenCos (for example ATEL, EDISON, ...),
- the names of the used technologies (coal, combined cycle gas turbine, ...),
- the prices of the fuels,
- information related to the Italian power plants: the columns indicates respectively the zone, maximum production quantity, minimum production quantity, coefficient a, coefficient b, coefficient c (see 3), GenCo's id, technology index, and fuel index and power plant's id.
- the production quantity data from other power plants (i.e., not produced by the GenCo).

The PUN historical values used in the experiments are public data which can be found in [6].

Implementation and Results. The implementations have been done in MATLAB R2017a with Optimization and Global Optimization toolboxes. Experiments were performed on a computer running Windows 7 and based on an Intel©CoreTMi7-3610QM @2.30 GHz microprocessor with 8 GB main memory.

In all the simulations, the number of GenCos participating in the market varies between 15 and 19, while the number of power plants for each GenCo varies between 1 and 90. The three optimization methods use the Matlab default parameters and are allocated the same number of objective function evaluations.

The execution time varies a lot between different versions, since the execution effort varies. With two populations of 10 individuals, the combinations Version 1: (a)–(e) take about 16 s for the GA per iteration, 20 s for the PS and 6 s for Monte Carlo. The combinations Version 2: (a)–(e) require about 180 s per iteration for the GA, 240 s for the PS, and 55 s for Monte Carlo. In all the figures below, the real situation is plotted in red with the label *Hist*.

Figure 3 shows the results of genetic algorithm, particle swarm optimization and Monte Carlo optimization of IntelligentGenCo in Version 1. GAfitness1 (lilac line) is still low, GAfreq2 (dark-blue line) and GAfitness2 (dark-green line) still overestimate the PUN (historical red line). PSfreq1 (light-blue line), PSfreq2 (yellow line) and PSfitness2 (brown line) are quite good (see also Figs. 4 and 5), except for the overestimation in the off-peak hours. GAfreq1 (light-green line) is equivalent to the previous ones, but it overestimates the PUN also in peak hours. PSfitness1 (orange line) is again the best algorithm, since it is able to reproduce the PUN in off-peak hours. The main difference is in Monte Carlo (dark dashed line with crosses), which has basically the same trend of GAfitness1 in this version.

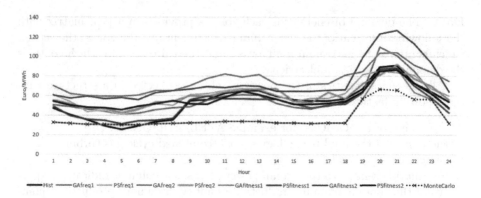

Fig. 3. Simulated PUNs for 2010-10-03, provided by IntelligentGenCo in Version 1 (Color figure online)

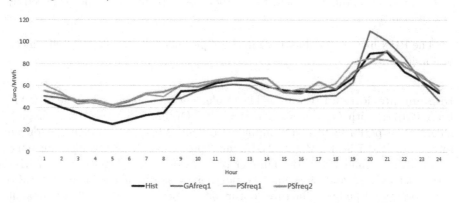

Fig. 4. Focus on the best frequency–based algorithms seen in Fig. 3. (Color figure online)

Figure 6 shows the results for the IntelligentGenCo's Version 2. In this version results are very different with respect to the previous cases: now no line clearly overestimates the historical values (red line), except in off-peak hours. This result could be a consequence of the adversarial behavior of GenCos. In Fig. 6, the lines relevant to the various algorithms lie very close to each other, especially in the central hours. Thus, the following detailed figures will focus on similar lines.

GAfitness1 (lilac line) is still low. Both PSfitness1 (orange line) and PSfitness2 (brown line) are low in off-peak hours, almost reaching the historical line (see Fig. 7).

The remaining genetic algorithms GAfreq1 (light-green line), GAfreq2 (dark-blue line) and GAfitness2 (dark-green line) are very close to each other, but only the last one is able to reach the peaks at 8pm and 9pm (as it could be seen in Fig. 8). The last three algorithms are very close to the historical line in the central hours, but they overestimate the off-peak hours (see Fig. 9). Both PSfreq1

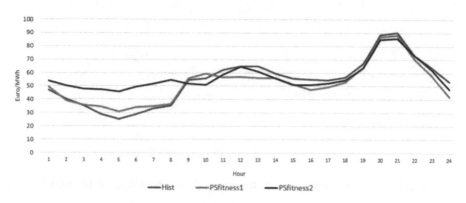

Fig. 5. Focus on the best fitness–based algorithms seen in Fig. 3. (Color figure online)

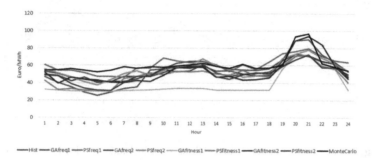

Fig. 6. Simulated PUNs for 2010-10-03, provided by IntelligentGenCo in Version 2 (Color figure online)

(light-blue line) and PSfreq2 (yellow line) underestimate the peak hours; on the contrary, Monte Carlo (black line) is good at these hours.

Evaluation of the RMSD. These considerations at the macro-level are supported by the evaluation of the root-mean-square deviation (RMSD) which is a frequently used measure of the difference between values predicted by a model and the actually observed values. The RMSD represents the sample standard deviation of the differences between predicted values and observed values. The formula we have used is the following:

$$RMSD = \sqrt{\frac{\sum_{h=1}^{24}(\hat{y}_h - y_h)^2}{24}} \tag{12}$$

where $\hat{y}_h$ and y_h are respectively the predicted value and the observed value of the PUN at hour h.

Table 1 shows the RMSD of all the 9 scenarios for the two versions of the co-evolutionary approach and compares them to the corresponding scenarios of two simple evolutionary approaches proposed in [2]. The *Approx* approach makes the

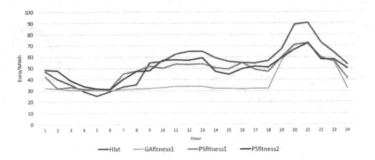

Fig. 7. Focus on the lowest algorithms seen in Fig. 6. (Color figure online)

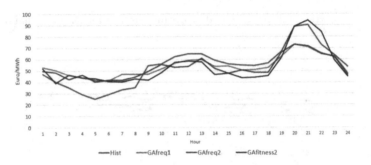

Fig. 8. Focus on the genetic algorithms seen in Fig. 6. (Color figure online)

same simplification as in [8], namely, that the vector of prices in the action space contains *only one* price for each collection of power plants situated in the same zone and using the same technology. The *Real* approach relaxes such constraint, as our co-evolutionary approach does.

We can noticed that for some optimization methods, the co-evolutionary approach gives less accurate predictions than the simple approach. This can be explained by the increased size of the optimization problem (the search space goes from just one vector of parameters to G vectors of parameters, i.e. the strategy of the GenCo itself and the strategies of all its competitors). It is important to notice that the comparison to previous work has been done by allowing the same number of objective function evaluations to each approach and configuration in order for the comparison to be fair. Nevertheless, it is interesting to

Table 1. RMSD of IntelligentGenCo methods for Versions 1 and 2.

Version	GAfreq1	PSfreq1	GAfreq2	PSfreq2	GAfitness1	PSfitness1	GAfitness2	PSfitness2	Montecarlo
1	9.58	9.87	21.89	9.83	18.11	**4.95**	22.62	9.97	19.51
2	9.61	11.60	9.51	9.32	18.91	9.51	9.41	9.11	13.04
[2] Approx	8.30	7.74	18.49	12.12	18.60	5.14	35.87	9.29	14.93
[2] Real	7.41	8.41	17.84	12.08	18.12	5.85	34.94	9.42	15.55

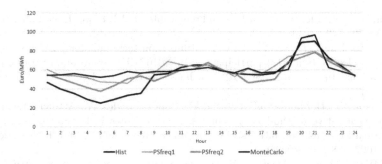

Fig. 9. Focus on selected algorithms seen in Fig. 6. (Color figure online)

notice that some optimization methods achieve improved results despite this increase in problem size. Indeed, PSfitness1 achieve the best accuracy among all tested combinations, improving over the simpler approaches of previous work. This confirms the potential of the co-evolutionary approach but also highlights the need to increase the number of objective function evaluations, if accurate predictions are sought for.

6 Conclusion

We have extended an existing agent-based model of the Italian electricity market and we have investigated the rationality of the market participants by comparing three optimization methods.

We can conclude that the planning for managing GenCos follows a *rational strategy*. It can be modeled as an optimization method using a co-evolutionary approach which better reflects the real behavior of the decision makers. We can also conclude that the particle swarm optimization method with a fitness-based strategy selection is the method which is capable to best simulate the behavior of the agents in the Italian electricity market—its results better fit the historical PUN values than all the others.

In addition to confirming the rationality of the market, our model could be used to predict the behavior of the Italian electricity market, for example by performing contingency analyses.

References

1. Betrò, B., Cugiani, M., Schoen, F.: Monte Carlo Methods in Numerical Integration and Optimization. Applied Mathematics Monographs, CNR. Giardini, Pisa (1990)
2. Bevilacqua, S., da Costa Pereira, C., Guerci, E., Precioso, F., Sartori, C.: Analysing the impact of rationality on the italian electricity market. In: Torra, V., Narukawa, Y., Pasi, G., Viviani, M. (eds.) MDAI 2019. LNCS (LNAI), vol. 11676, pp. 236–247. Springer, Cham (2019). https://doi.org/10.1007/978-3-030-26773-5_21

3. Ela, E., et al.: Electricity markets and renewables. IEEE Power Energ. Mag. 15(27), 1540–7977 (2015)

4. Faia, R., Pinto, T., Vale, Z.A.: GA optimization technique for portfolio optimization of electricity market participation. In: 2016 IEEE Symposium Series on Computational Intelligence, SSCI 2016, Athens, Greece, 6–9 December 2016, pp. 1–7 (2016)

5. Giulioni, G., Hernández, C., Posada, M., López-Paredes, A.: Artificial Economics: The Generative Method in Economics. Lecture Notes in Economics and Mathematical Systems, vol. 631, 1st edn. Springer, Heidelberg (2009). https://doi.org/10.1007/978-3-642-02956-1

6. GME - Gestore Mercati Energetici. Data access through. http://www.mercatoelettrico.org/it/download/DatiStorici.aspx

7. Goldberg, D.E.: Genetic Algorithms in Search Optimization and Machine Learning. Addison-Wesley, Boston (1989)

8. Guerci, E., Rastegar, M.A., Cincotti, S.: Agent-based modeling and simulation of competitive wholesale electricity markets. In: Rebennack, S., Pardalos, P.M., Pereira, M.V.F., Iliadis, N.A. (eds.) Handbook of Power Systems II, pp. 241–286. Springer, Heidelberg (2010). https://doi.org/10.1007/978-3-642-12686-4_9

9. Holland, J.H.: Adaptation in Natural and Artificial Systems. The University of Michigan Press, Ann Arbor (1975)

10. Kennedy, J.: Particle swarm optimization. In: Sammut, C., Webb, G.I. (eds.) Encyclopedia of Machine Learning and Data Mining, pp. 967–972. Springer, Boston (2017). https://doi.org/10.1007/978-0-387-30164-8

11. Kennedy, J., Eberhart, R.: Particle swarm optimization. In: Proceedings of IEEE International Conference on Neural Networks, Part IV, pp. 1942–1948 (1995

12. Santos, G., Pinto, T., Praça, I., Vale, Z.: A new approach for multi-agent coalition formation and management in the scope of electricity markets. Energy 36(8), 5004–5015 (2011)

13. Santos, G., Pinto, T., Praça, I., Vale, Z.: MASCEM: optimizing the performance of a multi-agent system. Energy 111(Supplement C), 513–524 (2016)

14. Silva, F., Teixeira, B., Pinto, T., Santos, G., Praça, I., Vale, Z.: Demonstration of realistic multi-agent scenario generator for electricity markets simulation. In: Demazeau, Y., Decker, K.S., Bajo Pérez, J., de la Prieta, F. (eds.) PAAMS 2015. LNCS (LNAI), vol. 9086, pp. 316–319. Springer, Cham (2015). https://doi.org/10.1007/978-3-319-18944-4_36

15. Sioshansi, F.P.: Evolution of Global Electricity Markets. Academic Press, Boston (2013)

16. Tribbia, C.: Solving the Italian electricity power exchange (2015)

17. Urieli, D.: Autonomous trading in modern electricity markets. AI Matters 2(4), 18–19 (2016)

18. Urieli, D., Stone, P.: Autonomous electricity trading using time-of-use tariffs in a competitive market. In: Proceedings of the Thirtieth AAAI Conference on Artificial Intelligence, Phoenix, Arizona, USA, 12–17 February 2016, pp. 345–352 (2016)

19. Vytelingum, P., Ramchurn, S.D., Voice, T., Rogers, A., Jennings, N.R.: Trading agents for the smart electricity grid. In: 9th International Conference on Autonomous Agents and Multiagent Systems (AAMAS 2010), Toronto, Canada, 10–14 May 2010, vol. 1–3, pp. 897–904 (2010)

Modelling Shared Decision Making in Medical Negotiations: Interactive Training with Cognitive Agents

Volha Petukhova[1]([✉]), Firuza Sharifullaeva[2], and Dietrich Klakow[1]

[1] Spoken Language Systems Group, Saarland University, Saarbrücken, Germany
{v.petukhova,dietrich.klakow}@lsv.uni-saarland.de
[2] Saarland Informatics Campus, Saarbrücken, Germany
s8fishar@stud.uni-saarland.de

Abstract. In the past decade, increasingly sophisticated models have been developed to determine which strategy explains human decision behaviour the best. In this paper, we model shared decision making in medical negotiations. Cognitive agents, who simulate various types of patients and are equipped with basic negotiation and decision making strategies, are tested in social learning setting. Human trainees were prompted to learn to make decisions analysing consequences of their own and partner's actions. Human-human and human-agent negotiations were evaluated in terms of the number of agreements reached and their Pareto efficiency, the number of the accepted negative deals and the cooperativeness of the negotiators' actions. The results show that agents can act as credible opponents to train efficient decision making strategies while improving negotiation performance. Agents with compensatory strategies integrate all available information and explore action-outcome connections the best. Agents that match and coordinate their decisions with their partners show convincing abilities for social mirroring and cooperative actions, skills that are important for human medical professionals to master. Simple non-compensatory heuristics are shown to be at least as accurate, and in complex scenarios even more effective, than the cognitive-intensive strategies. The designed baseline agents are proven to be useful in activation, training and assessment of doctor's abilities regarding social and cognitive adaptation for effective shared decision making. Implications for future research and extensions are discussed.

Keywords: Cognitive agents · Interactive social learning · Decision making

1 Introduction

Recently, the use of cognitive agents in interactive applications has gained lots of attentions. It has been proven that even very simple agents can exhibit complex emergent behavioural patterns [13,34]. Advanced cognitive agents are able

© Springer Nature Switzerland AG 2019
M. Baldoni et al. (Eds.): PRIMA 2019, LNAI 11873, pp. 251–270, 2019.
https://doi.org/10.1007/978-3-030-33792-6_16

to produce detailed simulation of human learning, prediction, adaptation and decision making [17,22,32]. They are also perfectly capable to play the role of a believable character in various human-agent settings. Cognitive agents have been beneficially used for training various human skills, e.g. negotiation and coordination skills in job interviews and trading [18,38], metacognitive skills in various learning settings and domains [31,37]. Cognitive agents allow creating and manipulating specific situations in which human social learning and human interactive behaviour can be studied. It has been also demonstrated that the integration of cognitive agents into a dialogue system has important advantages for effective implementation of complex (multi-agent) dialogue models [21].

In this paper, we address the use of cognitive agents to train efficient decision making strategies in asymmetric medical negotiations. Here, learning occurs through the partner's interpretation of own and others successes and failures, and through reflection on the action consequences for the interactive outcomes [1,4]. We designed baseline agents to investigate the effectiveness of various decision making strategies for the patient's therapy adherence behaviour. The agents are based on the recent developments in cognitive modelling. Cognitive models are developed producing detailed simulations of human decision making performance. We extend them to facilitate realistic social learning and interactive scenarios.

We first set a scene for our investigations discussing the important characteristics of medical interactions to be considered when designing social intelligent agents for the training of efficient decision making (Sect. 2). We review models of individual decision making and social learning aspects which are modelled to explain and predict changes in human behaviour in general. Subsequently, we present the concept of Shared Decision Making (SDM) in medical context. Section 3 discusses the design aspects related to the human-agent interaction giving a global outline of a set of negotiation tasks with increasing scenario complexity and performed interactive actions. Section 4 presents our baseline agents with details for decision making strategies selection and the agent's feedback. In Sect. 5, we present the results of the experiments evaluating baseline agents simulating various decision making strategies. Finally, we summarize our findings and outlines directions for the future research and development.

2   Decision Making and Social Learning

International research has produced great deal of models describing how individuals make decisions. The problem is approached at many levels, e.g. concentrating on psychological processes, and on biological and environmental factors. According to the most widely applied theories which attempt to explain and predict human behaviour and behavioural changes, Theory of Planned Behaviour [1] and Social Cognitive Theory [3], there are three key sets of decision-making determinants defined: (1) individual attitudes towards behaviour and its outcomes (A_p), (2) perceived social norms (PN) and (3) perceived behavioural control (PBC), see Fig. 1. A_p beliefs are concerned with the individually perceived *importance* of the behaviour given the known benefits, risks and threats and the perceived level of *readiness* to perform (execute) certain behaviour. Individual decision making is influenced by the individual beliefs (confidence) about abilities to perform and control behaviour and its outcome, i.e. *self-efficacy*. If an individual has developed positive attitudes towards a particular behavioural change, e.g. ceasing smoking, however believes he is not capable to maintain this behaviour, this will not lead to intention to perform this action. Outcome expectations and self-efficacy are very important determinants of health behaviour and depend on features such as perceived difficulty of the behaviour and/or the perceived certainty of its benefits [36].

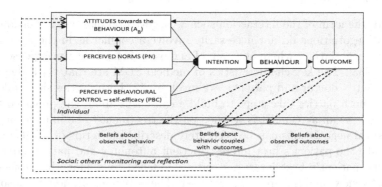

Fig. 1. Decision making and social learning model. Adapted from [30].

Perceptions about attitudes of others can influence the individual decision making. Learning that is facilitated by observation of, or in interaction with another individual or their products, is defined as social learning [14]. Individual experiences obtained through observation of successful or unsuccessful performance of others, *vicarious experiences*, may account for a major part of learning throughout life [1] and influence (self-)efficacy expectations. Social learning, however, depends on the ability of an individual to take another individual's perspectives and use other people's behaviour as a guide to their own. Thus, learning occurs through reflecting on experiences. The cognitive capacity to attribute mental states to self and others is considered as a key factor of social and cognitive adaptation and is known as Theory of Mind (ToM, [28]) skills. ToM abilities significantly influence decision-making processes, can enhance motivation and self-efficacy, and can be successfully trained in human-agent setting.

2.1   Asymmetries in Doctor-Patient Communication

In medical encounters, certain asymmetries and an imbalance in the knowledge and relationship between interlocutors are observed. Doctors empowered with institutional authority may expand the distance to their non-expert patients.

Differences in knowledge, inequity in social status and power may lead to miscommunication, have trust damaging effects and, after all, decrease patients' therapy adherence [29].

Recently, Shared Decision-Making (SDM) models have been evaluated showing that patient's active participation in the decision-making process is fundamental for the therapy's success [23]. The shift from therapy 'compliance' to 'adherence' implies that patients have more autonomy in defining and following their medical treatments.

2.2 Shared Decision Making: Monitoring Attitudes and Enhancing Self-efficacy

In SDM, the form of the interaction such as negotiation plays an important role. Medical negotiations do not necessarily involve a conflict as in the case of distributive negotiations where any gain of one party is made at the expense of the other(s) [33]. The key characteristics of medical SDM are that (1) at least two participants - doctor and patient - are involved; (2) both parties share information; (3) both parties take steps to build a consensus about the preferred treatment; and (4) an agreement is reached on the treatment to be implemented [9].

Medical negotiations can be accurately described in terms of a balancing of values like the patient's best interest, patient autonomy and patient adherence [39]. The patient's best interest is often modelled by taking the professional (doctor's) view on a patient's best interest. The patient's autonomy is respected based on an assessment of whether the patient will adhere to the treatment in question. To make it a shared decision, the patient will have to agree on and accept a compromise. The medical SDM can be best modelled as interest-based bargaining where parties reason about the interests of each other and, building a consensus, negotiate the best possible mutual agreement [20]. Interests include the needs, desires, concerns, and fears important to each side. Parties' preferences regarding the possible agreements may be not completely in conflict and they may be adapted depending on the perception of the preferences and behaviour of others. Thus, our model accounts for (1) participant's beliefs about perceived importance and desires concerning the certain behaviour and its outcomes (attitudes); (2) participant's beliefs about his abilities to perform this behaviour (self-efficacy); (3) and the beliefs of the same kind about his partner.

3 Design

3.1 Use Case and Scenarios

Patient's therapy non-adherence have different forms, e.g. skipping the intake of the prescribed medicines, the failure to keep appointments, to follow recommended dietary, lifestyle changes, recommended preventive health practices [12, 26].

The best practice for health behaviour change remains face-to-face interaction with an expert counsellor [5]. A medical professional dealing with a non-adherent patient should master negotiation skills in order to reach an efficient agreement by proposing regimen that are feasible to follow, showing an appropriate understanding of patient's condition and treatments, and exercising the right influence on patient's beliefs and attitudes taking patient's social, cognitive and economic constraints into account [8].

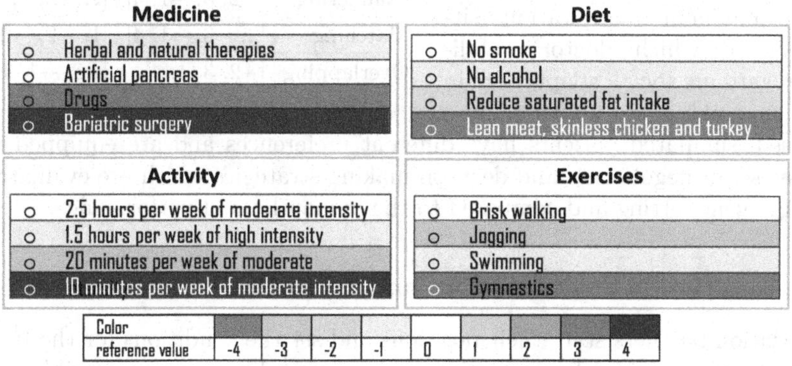

Fig. 2. Example of a participant's preference profile. (Color figure online)

The domain selected for our use case concerns the treatment of diabetes of Type 2. The patient-doctor negotiation scenario was designed based on the recommendations for patients according to the International Diabetes Federation (IDF, 2017) addressing four issues: (1) medication, (2) diet, (3) activity and (4) exercise recommendations. Each of these issues involves four important negotiation *options* with preferences assigned representing parties negotiation positions, i.e. preference profiles. Preferences are weighted in order of importance and defined as the participant's beliefs about *attitudes* towards certain behaviour and *abilities* to perform this behaviour. The goal of each partner is to find out the preference of each other and to search for the best possible mutual agreement.

Five scenarios of various complexity based different preference profiles were designed. The preferences strength was communicated to the negotiators through colours, see Fig. 2. The preferences values range from −4 for highly dispreferred (dark orange) options to 4 for highly preferred (dark blue) options. The preferences can be set by human participant and/or generated automatically by the system dependent what type of partner the human participant wants to negotiate with. A graphical user interface was designed where human trainees, including domain experts, can specify their preferences and select partner's preference profile, either conflicting, matching or overlapping. Three types of profiles are specified, see also Table 1:

- *Conflicting*: negotiators' preferences are completely the opposite to each other.
- *Matching*: preferences are of the same polarity, but different in strength.
- *Overlapping*: some preferences are of the same polarity and strength.

The human participant - doctor - negotiates with various agents who simulates various types of patients, selecting one option per issue. To create and manipulate various situations in which doctor's abilities regarding social adaptation in decision making are activated and

Table 1. Preferences profiles examples.

Type	Human	Agent
Conflicting	[−2, 3, −1, 4]	[2, −3, 1, −4]
Matching	[2, −3, −1, 4]	[1, −2, −2, 3]
Overlapping	[−2, 3, 1, 4]	[−2, −1, 1, 4]

assessed, simulated patients have different preferences and are equipped with a basic set of negotiation and decision-making strategies which are evaluated in human-agent setting and compared to the human-human performance.

3.2   Negotiation Space, Actions and Strategies

Negotiation partners state their positions and set the conditions for the further exchange. The obtained information serves to establish jointly possible values constituting the *negotiation space*. In medical negotiation, this happens when a doctor explores patient's attitudes and abilities: elicits description of preferable actions, encourages patient to share his experiences, and matches those with his professional expertise. The better all possible actions and parties experiences are explored and discussed, the better future agreements are reached. In our design, human trainees (doctors) negotiates therapeutic interventions which they believe are medically mandated and what they understand are desired by the patient. The success of the interactive 'claiming' and 'giving up' space depends not only on the medical competence of the doctor, but also on his social competences and ToM skills. Participants' tasks are to determine their own actions, to interpret partner's actions, and to adjust their behaviour accordingly. The agent achieves this by taking the perspective of its partner and using its own knowledge to evaluate the partner's strategy, i.e. apply ToM skills. The agent holds three sets of preference values: the agent's own preferences (zero ToM), the agent's beliefs about the partner's preferences (first-order ToM), and the agent's beliefs about the partner's beliefs about the agent's preferences (second-order ToM).

The successful medical negotiation involves adequate disclosure by both parties indicating their values as well as other relevant matters. We specified the set of actions based on the ISO 24617-2 dialogue act taxonomy [7] tailored to the medical counselling domain using the Roter Interaction Analysis System (RIAS, [30]). Table 2 provides an overview of actions modelled to be performed by the baseline agent and the categories proposed for future extensions (marked *). Semantic content of dialogue acts specifies (modalized) negotiation moves and their arguments expressing the importance, desires and abilities concerning the certain behaviour and its outcomes, i.e. patient's attitudes and self-efficacy assessments.

Table 2. Taxonomy of the agent's actions. Adapted from the ISO 24617-2 dialogue act taxonomy enriched with the RIAS categories proposed for future extensions (*).

Socio-emotional exchange (*)	Task-focused exchange	Semantic content			Global affect (*)
		Modality	Negotiation Move	Issue(options)	
Show approval	(open-ended) set question	Preference	(final) offer	Figure 2 related to:	Uncertainty
Give compliment	(forced) choice question	Ability	Exchange	Therapeutic regimen	Anxiety
Show empathy	Propositional questions	Necessity	Concession	lifestyle	Dominance
Show concern/worry	Check questions	Acquiescence	Deal		Attentiveness
Reassure/Encourage	Inform/Answer		Withdraw		Engagement
Ask for reassurance	(dis-)agreement				Friendliness
Show understanding	Advise				Anger
Show compassion	Suggest				
	Request/Instruct				
	Offer				
	Promise				

Negotiation moves types, sequences and the expressed modality are used to compute negotiation strategies. We consider negotiators as *cooperative* if they share information about their preferences with their opponents. A cooperative negotiator prefers the options that have the highest collective value. If not enough information is available to make this determination, he will elicit this information from his opponent. A cooperative negotiator will not engage in positional bargaining holding on to a fixed set of preferences regardless of the interests of others, instead, he will attempt to find issues where a compromise is possible. *Competitive* negotiators prefer to assert their own preferred positions rather than exploring the space of possible agreements. A competitive negotiator will ignore partner's interests and requests for information. Instead, he will find his own ideal position and insist upon it in the hope of making the opponent concede. He will threaten to end the negotiation. The competitive negotiator will accept an offer only if he can gain a significant number of points from it.

4   Baseline Agents

4.1   Agent's Knowledge and Memory

The baseline agents are designed using ACT-R cognitive architecture implemented in Java[1]. Agent's knowledge is encoded in instances. An instance consists of a representation of the current state of the world (what do I know, what do I know about others, what am I asked, what can I do, what has happened before), and an action to be taken in that situation (give information, run tests, examine something, reason about others, change attitude, etc.). An instance has a form of slot-value pairs representing context and actions. Table 3 depicts the structure of an instance.

Instances are stored in an ACT-R declarative memory which is represented as traces of instances used. At the beginning of the interaction, the agent may have no or weak assumptions about the partner's preferences, thus instances may be empty or partially filled in. As the interaction proceeds the agent builds up more knowledge, i.e. learns by observing actions of others, storing those as instances, or by trying out actions itself and adjusting its instances based on feedback.

4.2   Agent's Feedback

The agent's feedback actions are designed to assist the trainee (medical professional) to form a mental model of an agent (patient). By providing real-time feedback about the agent's cognitive state, the trainee should become aware of how his own actions influence patient's beliefs. This feedback comes in three forms: evaluation of agent's beliefs about trainee's preferences, evaluation of

---

[1] A Java Simulation and Development Environment for the ACT-R Cognitive Architecture - homepage http://cog.cs.drexel.edu/act-r/about.php.

Table 3. Instance definition.

Slot	Value [range]	Explanation
Strategy	[*cooperative*|*competitive*|*neutral*]	The strategy associated with the instance
Agent-move-value-agent	[−4, 4]	The number of points the agent's gets from his own move
Partner-move-value-agent	[−4, 4]	The number of points the partner's move brings to the agent
Partner-move-greater	[*true*|*false*]	True if the partner's move brings at least as much as the agent's one, otherwise - false
Next-move-value-agent	[−4, 4]	The number of points that the next best move can bring to the agent
Utility	[0, 17]	How valuable are the partner's suggestions made by now, see Eq. 4
Shared utility	[0, 1]	How valuable are both partner's suggestions for them, see Eq. 6
Agent-move	$(M_1, ..., M_n)$	The move that the agent should make in this context (2)
Partner-move	$(M_1, ..., M_n)$	The move that the agent believes the partner should make in this context (Table 2)
Compensation	[1, 4]	If the agent's move is of the concession or exchange type, what is the minimum utility that the agent should look for choosing an alternative option

patient's self-efficacy beliefs (possible actions) and evaluation of trainee's negotiation strategy.

Every time the trainee makes a move expressing his preferences, the agent matches it to its preferences and available strategies and computes the most plausible action(-s), it also provides alternatives and plans possible outcomes. Since the agent knows why certain actions are performed, it can explain why its and partner's choices lead to the specific outcome. Evaluation of trainee strategy provides the trainee with feedback about how the agent views their overall performance. Both participants operate under constrain that negotiation outcome should be acceptable for both partners. Thus, the interactions were evaluated in terms of the percentage of reached agreements[2], percentage of negative outcomes[3] and Pareto efficient outcomes[4].

The summative feedback is generated when a negotiation round is over and includes the assessment of the overall cooperativeness level, percentage of reached agreements and negative outcomes, and the Pareto efficiency scores. All scores accumulate with each negotiation round indicating the learning progress. In the feedback on the best possible outcome is included.

4.3 Action Selection Decisions

The decision-making process can be simple when randomly picking options out of the available ones, or complex when systematically rating different aspects of the available choices. Human decision-making strategies may depend on various factors, including how much time they have to make the decision, the overall complexity of the decision, and the amount of ambiguity that is involved. According to [25], decision makers choose strategies adaptively in response to different task demands, and often apply simplified shortcuts—heuristics—that allow fast decisions with acceptable losses in accuracy. Moreover, simple heuristics are often more or at least equally accurate in predicting new data compared to more complex strategies [10]. Simple heuristics are more robust, extracting only the most important and reliable information from the data, while complex strategies that weight all pieces of evidence extract much noise, resulting in large accuracy losses when making predictions for new data [27].

We implemented and assessed three decision-making strategies to simulate situations where different alternatives will be selected by the agent in a certain context in order to achieve acceptable outcomes: *recognition* or *activation*-based retrieval, *compensatory* models and *non-compensatory* heuristics.

When the agent has to make a decision, it activates his declarative knowledge and retrieves direct and vicarious experiences that are the most *active*, i.e. most recent and frequent. For every instance i in the set, the activation is computed as

$$A_i = B_i - MP \sum_{v,d}(1 - Sim(v,d)) \tag{1}$$

where MP, a mismatch penalty, reflects the amount of weighting given to the matching, i.e. the higher MP, the stronger the activation is affected by the similarity[5]. B_i, base level activation, is computed as

---

[2] We consider the agreement reached if parties agreed on all four issues.

[3] Negative deals are considered as flawed negotiation action, i.e. the sum of all reached agreements resulted in an overall negative value meaning that the partner made too many concessions and selected mostly dispreferred bright 'orange' options (see Fig. 2).

[4] The negotiation is Pareto efficient if none of the negotiators could have achieved a higher score for themselves without a reduction in score of the other negotiator.

[5] We set MP constant high at 5, consistent with the value used in Lebiere et al. (2000). To disable MP, it can be set at 0.

$$B_i = ln \sum_{j=1}^{n} t_{ij}^{-d} \tag{2}$$

where t_{ij} is the time elapsed since the j_{th} presentation or creation of the instance i, and d is the memory decay rate[6]. The similarity $Sim(v, d)$ between the goal value v and the actual value d held in the retrieved instance is computed as

$$Sim(v, d) = \frac{1.0}{((v - d)^2/2.0 + 1.0)} \tag{3}$$

The agent makes its next move based on the value of 'agent-move' slot, see Table 3. The ACT-R mechanisms effectively account for both the effects of recency - more recent memory traces are more likely to be retrieved, and frequency - if a memory trace has been created or retrieved more often in the past it has a higher likelihood of being retrieved. By disabling MP, the agent will be able to retrieve past instances for reasoning even when a particular situation has not been encountered before. An instance does not have to be a perfect match to a retrieval request to be activated. ACT-R can reduce its activation to compute partial matching [16]. If the value is missing in an instance, 'blending' is proposed as a generalization of the retrieval mechanism, allowing to retrieve values from multiple instances [19].

To assess alternative decision making strategies, procedural knowledge was incorporated and condition-action rules were defined. For example, the weighted-additive rule (WADD) is computed by, first, weighting the dimensions (i.e. issues or criteria) on their relative importance by summing preference values of all attributes specified within this dimension divided by their number and then multiplying the preference values with their respective importance weights. To form an overall evaluation, the products are summed and the option with the highest value is chosen, *weighted sum model* (WSM). The total importance of an alternative A_i^{WSM} is computed as

$$A_i^{WSM} = \sum_{j=1}^{n} w_j u_{ij} \tag{4}$$

where w_j denotes the relative importance of the dimension D_j and u_{ij} is the utility value of alternative A_i when it is evaluated with relation to the dimension D_j. In case all dimensions are considered of equal importance as in our case, equal-weight rule (EQW) is applied. In compensatory decisions, a negative value of one attribute can be compensated by an equal or higher value of another attribute. Thus, compensatory strategy involves a systematic evaluation of multiple attributes and works well if all information is available modelling rational decision choices the best.

---

[6] In the ACT-R community, 0.5 has emerged as the default value for the parameter d over a large range of applications, [2].

In contrast, non-compensatory strategies assume that decisions are often made based on the rejection of undesirable alternatives on the basis of one, or at most a few criteria. When faced with a more complex (multi-alternative) decision task, the subjects employed decision strategies designed to eliminate some of the available alternatives as quickly as possible and on the basis of a limited amount of information search and evaluation [6]. Here, values on the most salient dimension are processed first and alternatives that score lower are eliminated as unsatisfactory, also known as take-the-best (TTB) strategy. Values in other dimensions are not used for a compensation, thus a negotiator makes no trade-offs between attributes.

4.4   Negotiation Strategy Selection

In our first approach, the agent adjusts its negotiation strategy according to the perceived level of the opponent's cooperativeness. The agent starts neutrally, requesting the partner's preferences. If the agent believes the partner is behaving cooperatively, the agent will react with an cooperative negotiation move. If the agent experiences the partner as competitive, it will switch to a competitive mode. Such strategy is observed in human negotiation and coordination games [15,35] and we call it *matching coordination* (MC). In interactions, interlocutors often mirror decision making behaviour of their opponents, in particular, where a clear division of roles and an asymmetric distribution of interactional power is observed. To simulate the mirroring decision making, activation of declarative knowledge within ACT-R's declarative memory is used and the instance with the highest matching score M_{ip} is retrieved computed as

$$M_{ip} = A_i - MP \sum_{v,d} (1 - Sim(v,d)) \tag{5}$$

According to the compensatory decision-making model, in choice situations with multiple alternatives in multiple dimensions, if for a certain alternative in one dimensions scores are low and a higher score on another dimension can compensate for it, this alternative will be adopted. In other words, a high score on one dimension (e.g. medicine) can compensate a lower score on another dimension (e.g. diet). These are then combined to maximize a utility. For each dimensions, the overall scores are considered and alternatives with the highest scores are chosen [11]. Since, the goal of our decision-makers not to maximize their own utility but to achieve an acceptable, ideally Pareto efficient outcome, the negotiator will try to maximize the shared utility in one or multiple negotiation rounds across dimensions computed based on utility earned by both partners as a proportion of maximum utility possible

$$U_{shared} = \frac{u_{agent} + u_{trainee}}{maxU_{agent} + maxU_{trainee}} \tag{6}$$

Unlike the MC agent, the utility-based (UB) agent does not attempt to find the appropriate instance in the memory based on the similarity of the slots to the current context and the instance activation value. Decision will be made based on the accumulated agent's *utility* (u_{agent}) and the estimated *shared utility* (U_{shared}) values.

The agent starts by selecting options with the highest utility values, procedure which is regularly observed in human-human negotiations since it is always easier to bargain down than to bargain in. If the agent will continue to win points insisting on his preferences while ignoring the preferences of his partner's, after it collects enough points, e.g. it has already reached the amount of the half maximum score possible in the current scenario, it will switch to cooperative mode. Playing cooperatively, if the agent starts loosing too much, so that its utility score becomes lower than the half maximum score possible in the current scenario, it will switch to the competitive mode to compensate for its previous losses. We express the decisions to change a negotiation strategy as:

$$\text{SetStrategy}(u_{agent}, U_{shared}, \text{round}) = \begin{cases} \text{cooperative,} & \text{if } u_{agent} < \frac{1}{2} * \text{round} * (\max U_{agent}) \\ \text{competitive,} & \text{if } u_{agent} \geq \frac{1}{2} * \text{round} * (\max U_{agent}) \\ & \text{and } U_{shared} \geq \text{threshold} \\ \text{neutral,} & \text{otherwise} \end{cases}$$

Threshold for the shared utility value can be set via GUI; by default it set on 0.5, meaning that at least the half of the mutually acceptable agreements have to be reached.

To simulate repetitive negotiations, e.g. to analyse trainee's learning behaviour over time[7], we model cross-rounds decision making strategies based on the negotiation history. Thus, our strategy changing policies account for successes and failures of previous rounds taking the current round number into consideration.

To simulate non-compensatory decision-making, the agent insists on the options beneficial for it, until an agreement on exactly one option in each dimension is reached. Here, the 'exchange' actions are impossible. The options with negative scores are eliminated by the agent. This strategy may result in agent's position bargaining when it sticks to the preferred options with the hope that partner concedes, and if not it breaks the negotiation proposing the final offer playing 'take-or-leave-it' strategy. The agent's behaviour can be described as follows:

$$\text{SetStrategy}(u_{agent}, U_{shared}, u_{min}) = \begin{cases} \text{cooperative,} & \text{if } U_{shared} < \text{threshold and} \\ & u_{min} < u_{agent} \\ \text{competitive,} & \text{if } U_{shared} \geq \text{threshold} \\ \text{take-or-leave-it,} & \text{if } u_{agent} = 0 \end{cases}$$

The time (number of moves) until the agent breaks the negotiation is configurable via GUI, as well as its $utility_{min}$.

---

[7] In real life, doctors and patient often do not meet only once, but share certain interaction history with each other.

5 Evaluation

We conducted a set of small-scaled evaluation experiments with ten participants involved in human-human negotiations and different five participants in human-agent negotiations. None of the participants was familiar with the topic. The age of the participants varied from 23 to 32 years old.

In human-human setting, one participant was randomly assigned the role of a doctor, the other participant the role of a patient. Each participant received his cover story and instructions, as well as the preference profile for each scenario, as shown in Fig. 2. Participants were not allowed to share their preference information with each other. They were asked to negotiate an agreement with the highest possible value according to their preference information. Participants were allowed to break the negotiation if they feel that it is impossible to reach an agreement on the provided terms. No further rules on the negotiation process or time constraints were imposed. The interactions were recorded, transcribed and analysed. In total, we collected 25 human-human negotiations comprising about 575 speaking turns.

In human-agent negotiations, each human trainee in the doctor's role negotiated with the simulated patient (agent) getting instructions similar to ones in the human-human setting. A trainee negotiated with an agent who uses (1) a Matched Coordination decision making Strategy (MCS); (2) a Compensatory decision making Strategy (CS); and (3) a Non-Compensatory decision making Strategy (NCS). A human trainee played five rounds with each agent within five randomly selected scenarios of different complexity. Totally, 75 human-agent negotiations were collected comprising 2049 turns.

5.1 Results

We compared the agents and human performance on the *number of agreements* reached, the ability to achieve *Pareto efficient* outcomes, maintain a reasonable *level of cooperativeness* while avoiding *negative deals*.

The obtained results are summarized in Table 4. We observed that trainees spent on average more time negotiating with a human than with a simulated patient (23 vs 21.1 turns). In human-human setting, actions other than related to the negotiation task were observed. Along with task-related offers, human participants performed frequent feedback, turn and time management, discourse structuring acts concerned with topic switches moving from one issue to another and decisions to continue, delay, reschedule or terminate the ongoing discussion and/or whole interaction. Agents, by contrast, were designed to produce actions concerned with the negotiation task. Humans reached on average a lower number of agreements when negotiating with agents than negotiating with each other, 78% vs 86.3%. Negotiations with humans as well as with the NCS-agents were often terminated or threaded to be terminated when partners were not willing to concede. Participants negotiating with the MCS- and CS-agents reached a similar number of Pareto efficient agreements (close to 100%). In negotiations

Table 4. Comparison of human-human and human-agent negotiation performance.

Evaluation criteria	Human vs human	Human vs MCS-agent	CS-agent	NCS-agent
Number of dialogues	25	25	25	25
Mean dialogue duration (in #turns)	23.0	22.4	17.2	23.8
Number of offers/per round	16.0	15.7	10.7	16.4
Agreements (in %)	78.0	95.6	87.0	76.2
Pareto efficient agreement (in %)	82.4	99.9	95.0	76.0
Negative deals (in %)	21.0	47.8	21.7	33.3
Cooperativeness rate (in %)	39.0	65.5	66.0	54.2

with the NCS-agents, about 25% of outcomes were not Pareto efficient. Human participants showed a higher level of cooperativity when interacting with an agent, i.e. more than 50% of all actions are annotated as cooperative. We concluded that agents were useful for trainees to understand partner's attitudes and abilities, to explore the negotiation space more optimally and to adapt their behaviour accordingly. A higher number of negative deals was observed for human-agent pairs, 21% vs 33%, mostly when interacting with the MCS-agents. Agents with compensatory strategies performed the best showing that they allow to efficiently explore action-outcome connections - the behaviour which leads to a limited number of negative deals.

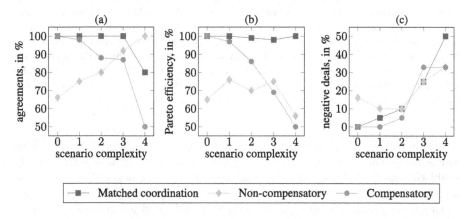

Fig. 3. The impact of scenario complexity on (a) the number of agreements reached; (b) Pareto efficiency of these outcomes; and (c) the number of negative deals accepted.

We assessed different decision making strategies applied in scenarios of various complexity. The scenario complexity has been computed taking the difference between agent's and trainee's preference profiles, i.e. the higher the difference the more complex the scenario, see also Table 1. The results depicted in Fig. 3 show that negotiations with all agents ended successfully, with a reasonable number of Pareto efficient agreements. When scenario was getting too complex, the NCS-agent was performing at least as accurate as the other two. Since non-compensatory decision-making does not require extensive cognitive efforts to evaluate attributes and reflect on the partner's behaviour, it may be applied rather effectively under 'unfavourable' conditions like time pressure, distractions or physical and psychological exhaustion.

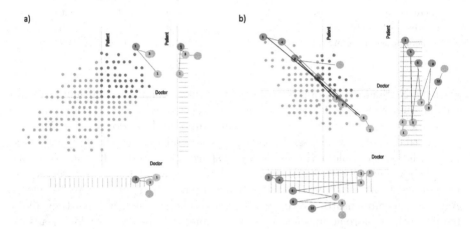

Fig. 4. Negotiation space for (a) a cooperative and (b) a competitive scenario. The top left panels show the possible negotiation outcomes in terms of the score for the patient (vertical) and the doctor (horizontal). Blue dots indicate outcomes that are acceptable to both negotiators, while red dots indicate unacceptable outcomes. Large dots show the possible outcomes for the patient (purple) and the doctor (yellow), as well as the final agreement (green). The sequence of offers made during the negotiation is indicated by connected dots. The panels on the right and the bottom show the same information from the perspective of the patient and the doctor, respectively. (Color figure online)

Asymmetries in preferences may not always yield the desired outcomes. This forces participants' to explore the negotiation space more thoroughly, apply sophisticated ToM skills. Figure 4 illustrates examples of negotiation scenarios, a cooperative and a competitive ones. Our results showed that in cooperative settings, negotiations tend to resolve more quickly and are more likely to be Pareto efficient. In competitive settings, on the other hand, negotiations tend to take more turns, and are more likely to result in an outcome that is not Pareto efficient. Our general observations showed that with a more cooperative CS- or MCS-agent, the trainee learns to adapt his behaviour acting more cooperatively and gains scores close to his maximum utility. A competitive CS-agent often challenges the human to compensate for his previous losses, but it is punished by loosing points. When a competitive human wants to take advantage of the cooperative MCS-agent, he starts to loose points and is enable to reach mutual agreements. In an NCS setting, the agent selects the competitive negotiation strategy more frequently and forces the human to act more competitively as well.

Our in-depth analysis of the logged interactions revealed that trainees used different negotiation tactics which resulted in different outcomes. Negotiators often delayed making complete agreements on the first discussed issue until the agreement on the next one is secured. They frequently revised their past offers. The order in which the issues are negotiated, i.e. negotiation agenda, might influence on the overall outcome. The most common strategy observed was issue-by-issue bargaining. Various negotiation tactics were concerned with the partners' alacrity to reveal or hide their preferences. When all preferences are brought on the negotiation table from the very beginning, agreements that are Pareto efficient were reached faster.

It has been noticed that not only asymmetries in preferences and participant's status may influence the decision making process, but participants of different gender and personality, and in different emotional state may adopt divergent strategies under identical conditions. To investigate relationships between participant's intrinsic characteristics and various dependent variables, a larger study needs to be conducted where personality traits will be assessed and specific emotions induced prior to the experiments.

Concerning the learning progress supported by the interaction with the agents, a follow up test-restest study with medical professionals and students will be performed. Our preliminary feedback indicates that most respondents think that the system presents an interesting form of skills training. The vast majority of users learned how to complete their tasks successfully in consecutive rounds.

6   Conclusions and Future Work

In this study, we investigated whether simple cognitive models can produce plausible simulations of human decision making performance acting as believable agents in human-agent interactive learning setting. Cognitive modelling of human intelligent behaviour not only enables better understanding of complex mental tasks, but also allow designing and controlling learning and interactive situations, scenarios and actors to assess human abilities for joint attention, social mirroring and cooperative actions - important in shared decision making process.

To facilitate realistic scenarios to study human social interactive behaviour, the agents who simulates different types of patients are equipped with different sets of preferences encoding desires and self-efficacy attitudes, and apply various negotiation and decision-making strategies. Human-human and human-agent negotiations were evaluated in terms of the number of agreements reached and their Pareto efficiency, the number of the accepted negative deals and the cooperativeness of the negotiators' actions. The results show that agents can act as credible opponents to train decision making for improved negotiation performance.

Agents with compensatory strategies, due to their ability to explore action-outcome connections systematically using all available information, approximate rational decisions the best. Agents that match and coordinate their decisions with their partners show powerful abilities for social mirroring and cooperative actions, skills that are important for human medical professionals to master. Simple non-compensatory heuristics are shown to be at least as accurate, and in complex scenarios even more effective, than more cognitive-intensive strategies. The designed baseline agents are proven to be useful in activation, training and assessment of doctor's abilities regarding social and cognitive adaptation for effective shared decision making.

Past research has indicated that people select strategies adaptively depending on the situation they face [25]. Our baseline agents, while already showing convincing human-like decision making behaviour, are rather constrained in their abilities for adaptation. The strategies were programmed rather than learned. In the future, we plan to assess the impact of various (pragma-)linguistic and interactive strategies on the adaptive decision-making behaviour while accounting for the interwoven relationship between multimodal language-specific schemes and emotional, social and cultural determinants. The design of sophisticated models of human decision-making behaviour have the potential to form the foundation for a new generation of interactive social systems.

References

1. Ajzen, I.: The theory of planned behavior. Organ. Behav. Hum. Decis. Process. **50**(2), 179–211 (1991)
2. Anderson, J., Bothell, D., Byrne, M., Douglass, S., Lebiere, C., Qin, Y.: An integrated theory of the mind. Psychol. Rev. **111**(4), 1036 (2004)
3. Bandura, A.: Social cognitive theory: an agentic perspective. Annu. Rev. Psychol. **52**(1), 1–26 (2001)
4. Bandura, A., Walters, R.: Social Learning Theory. Prentice-Hall Inc., Upper Saddle River (1977)
5. Bickmore, T., Giorgino, T.: Health dialog systems for patients and consumers. J. Biomed. Inform. **39**(5), 556–571 (2006)
6. Billings, R.S., Scherer, L.L.: The effects of response mode and importance on decision-making strategies: judgment versus choice. Organ. Behav. Hum. Decis. Process. **41**(1), 1–19 (1988)
7. Bunt, H., et al.: ISO 24617-2: a semantically-based standard for dialogue annotation. In: LREC, pp. 430–437. Citeseer (2012)
8. Burgoon, J.K., Pfau, M., Parrott, R., Birk, T., Coker, R., Burgoon, M.: Relational communication, satisfaction, compliance-gaining strategies, and compliance in communication between physicians and patients. Commun. Monogr. **54**(3), 307–324 (1987)
9. Charles, C., Gafni, A., Whelan, T.: Shared decision-making in the medical encounter: what does it mean? (or it takes at least two to tango). Soc. Sci. Med. **44**(5), 681–692 (1997)
10. Czerlinski, J., Gigerenzer, G., Goldstein, D.G.: How good are simple heuristics? In: Simple Heuristics That Make US Smart, pp. 97–118. Oxford University Press (1999)

11. Einhorn, H.J., Hogarth, R.M.: Behavioral decision theory: processes of judgement and choice. Annu. Rev. Psychol. **32**(1), 53–88 (1981)
12. Fawcett, J.: Compliance: definitions and key issues. J. Clin. Psychiatry (1995)
13. Hegselmann, R., Krause, U., et al.: Opinion dynamics and bounded confidence models, analysis, and simulation. J. Artif. Soc. Soc. Simul. **5**(3) (2002)
14. Hoppitt, W., Laland, K.N.: Social Learning: An Introduction to Mechanisms, Methods, and Models. Princeton University Press, Princeton (2013)
15. Kelley, H., Stahelski, A.: Social interaction basis of cooperators' and competitors' beliefs about others. J. Pers. Soc. Psychol. **16**(1), 66 (1970)
16. Lebiere, C., Wallach, D., West, R.: A memory-based account of the prisoner's dilemma and other 2x2 games. In: Proceedings of International Conference on Cognitive Modeling, pp. 185–193 (2000)
17. Lee, H., Betts, S., Anderson, J.: Learning problem-solving rules as search through a hypothesis space. Cogn. Sci. **40**(5), 1036–1079 (2015)
18. Lin, R., Kraus, S., Mazliah, Y., et al.: Training with automated agents improves people's behavior in negotiation and coordination tasks. Decis. Support Syst. **60**, 1–9 (2014)
19. Lovet, M., Reder, L.M., Lebiere, C.: Modeling working memory in a unified architecture. In: Models of Working Memory: Mechanisms of Active Maintenance and Executive Control, p. 135 (1999)
20. Makoul, G., Clayman, M.L.: An integrative model of shared decision making in medical encounters. Patient Educ. Couns. **60**(3), 301–312 (2006)
21. Malchanau, A.: Cognitive architecture of multimodal multidimensional dialogue management. Ph.D. thesis, University of Saarland, Saarbrücken (2018)
22. Marewski, J., Link, D.: Strategy selection: an introduction to the modeling challenge. Wiley Interdisc. Rev. Cogn. Sci. **5**(1), 39–59 (2014)
23. Mazur, D.J.: Shared Decision Making in the Patient-Physician Relationship: Challenges Facing Patients, Physicians, and Medical Institutions. American College of Physician Executives, Tampa, FL (2001)
24. Nowak, S.A., Matthews, L.J., Parker, A.M.: A general agent-based model of social learning. Rand Health Q. **7**(1) (2017)
25. Payne, J.W., Bettman, J.R., Johnson, E.J.: The Adaptive Decision Maker. Cambridge University Press, Cambridge (1993)
26. Peterson, A.M., Nau, D.P., Cramer, J.A., Benner, J., Gwadry-Sridhar, F., Nichol, M.: A checklist for medication compliance and persistence studies using retrospective databases. Value Health **10**(1), 3–12 (2007)
27. Pitt, M.A., Myung, I.J.: When a good fit can be bad. Trends Cogn. Sci. **6**(10), 421–425 (2002)
28. Premack, D., Woodruff, G.: Does the chimpanzee have a theory of mind? Behav. Brain Sci. **1**(04), 515–526 (1978)
29. Rodriguez-Osorio, C.A., Dominguez-Cherit, G.: Medical decision making: paternalism versus patient-centered (autonomous) care. Current Opin. Crit. Care **14**(6), 708–713 (2008)
30. Roter, D., Larson, S.: The roter interaction analysis system (rias): utility and flexibility for analysis of medical interactions. Patient Educ. Couns. **46**(4), 243–251 (2002)
31. Rus, V., Lintean, M., Azevedo, R.: Automatic detection of student mental models during prior knowledge activation in MetaTutor. In: International Working Group on Educational Data Mining (2009)
32. Salvucci, D., Taatgen, N.: Threaded cognition: an integrated theory of concurrent multitasking. Psychol. Rev. **115**(1), 101 (2008)

33. Sandman, L.: The concept of negotiation in shared decision making. Health Care Anal. **17**(3), 236–243 (2009)
34. Schelling, T.C.: The strategy of conflict. Prospectus for a reorientation of game theory. J. Conflict Resolut. **2**(3), 203–264 (1958)
35. Smith, L., Pruitt, D., Carnevale, P.: Matching and mismatching: the effect of own limit, other's toughness, and time pressure on concession rate in negotiation. J. Pers. Soc. Psychol. **42**(5), 876 (1982)
36. Strecher, V.J., McEvoy DeVellis, B., Becker, M.H., Rosenstock, I.M.: The role of self-efficacy in achieving health behavior change. Health Educ. Q. **13**(1), 73–92 (1986)
37. Van Helvert, J., et al.: Observing, coaching and reflecting: metalogue - a multi-modal tutoring system with metacognitive abilities. EAI Endorsed Trans. Future Intell. Educ. Environ. **16**(6) (2016)
38. de Weerd, H., Broers, E., Verbrugge, R.: Savvy software agents can encourage the use of second-order theory of mind by negotiators. In: CogSci (2015)
39. Wirtz, V., Cribb, A., Barber, N.: Patient-doctor decision-making about treatment within the consultation–a critical analysis of models. Soc. Sci. Med. **62**(1), 116–124 (2006)

Doxastic Group Reasoning via Multiple Belief Shadowing

Barbara Dunin-Kęplicz[1], Inga Rüb[1], and Andrzej Szałas[1,2(✉)]

[1] Institute of Informatics, University of Warsaw, Banacha 2, Warsaw, Poland
{keplicz,inga.rub,andrzej.szalas}@mimuw.edu.pl
[2] Department of Computer and Information Science, Linköping University,
Linköping, Sweden

Abstract. In real world situations an agent may need to switch between distinct roles and/or groups. This calls for a well-controlled and computationally-friendly adjustment of relevant beliefs, especially when groups' structures and organization evolve dynamically. A need for adaptability may also emerge from the impossibility of fixing agents' roles or teams at design time. In such changing circumstances reasoning about beliefs is a challenging issue.

A concept of belief shadowing, introduced in [8], address these phenomena with a use of $A \mathbin{as} B$ operator expressing that A acts as B. That is, beliefs of $A \mathbin{as} B$ are those of B, unless B does not know the doxastic status of a given belief, in which case the belief of A is binding. This simple construct turns out to be efficient for shallow and transient forms of belief change. Yet, while being convenient in situations when an agent plays a specific role or joins a given group, single shadowing hardly fits cases of multiple roles and/or multiple groups entered simultaneously without prioritizing them. As a remedy we introduce multiple shadowing together with a query language, δQL, where roles and groups are dealt with uniformly.

The multiple shadowing operator appears simple yet flexible for reasoning about the associated beliefs, which otherwise are rather complex and onerous to reason about.Importantly, the presented language is tractable. Possible applications of δQL as a lightweight tool for doxastic reasoning are pointed out.

Keywords: Doxastic reasoning · Belief change · Group reasoning · Rule-based languages · Tractable languages · Paraconsistent reasoning

1 A Modern View on Group Reasoning

The role of group reasoning is invaluable in situated systems where the outcomes depend on the decisions and behaviour of other autonomous agents and groups. No matter how the merit of group beliefs is understood, this notion gained a lot of attention in multi-modal epistemic logics, see [12,13,17,22,31,38] and references there.

© Springer Nature Switzerland AG 2019
M. Baldoni et al. (Eds.): PRIMA 2019, LNAI 11873, pp. 271–288, 2019.
https://doi.org/10.1007/978-3-030-33792-6_17

Among various notions of group reasoning, the strongest one - a common belief - captures the essence of mutuality between group members: consensus between them. As common belief permits to draw common conclusions from commonly believed premises, it enormously helps in building models of others. But this comes at an unacceptable price of super-polynomial complexity. Recently, the need of reducing complexity forced the evolution of group beliefs, as expressed in [11] with respect to group knowledge but applicable to doxastic reasoning as well:

"As the role of group knowledge has recently evolved, it may instead be useful for participants to preserve their individual beliefs, while at the same time being a member of a larger group structure with group beliefs that govern the group's behavior. Instead of "what every fool knows", group knowledge would then tend to express synthetic information extracted from the information delivered by individuals. Thus, more so than in classical epistemic and doxastic logical approaches, there should be a clear distinction between agents' individual informational stances and the groups' ones. Consensus is not a requirement anymore, as group members do not necessarily adopt group conclusions. It suffices that during the group's lifetime they obey them."

Table 1. Traditional vs new approach to group reasoning.

Traditional approach	The new approach
What every fool knows	What a wise person would believe in
Holistic knowledge	Synthetic information from individuals or groups, selected aspects
Consensus	Group members not forced to adopt group conclusions: only required to obey them during the group's lifetime
Omniscience	Incomplete and inconsistent beliefs allowed: information grabbed from others or resolved non-monotonically
Homogeneity	Reasoning adjusted to application domain and individualized
Reasoning intractable	Tractability guaranteed

The new approach to more distributed and focused forms of group beliefs is summarized in Table 1. To answer the question "what a wise person would believe in", agents' individual beliefs are pulled together to draw classical conclusions from the combined information like in distributed beliefs. Moreover, by adding non-deductive and possibly non-monotonic heuristic rules or methods of jumping to conclusion, e.g. originating from computational social choice, we can meaningfully extend the group reasoning capabilities. However, tractability remains an essential requirement here.

Now, all the intends and purposes lead to a new approach to group reasoning associated with the very nature of its dynamics, manifesting itself mostly in teamwork [12]. In order to maintain autonomy, agents must be equipped with: (1) mobility between groups/roles; (2) inheritance of the beliefs of others; (3) easiness of role changing.

Roughly speaking, agents typically move from one group to another while realizing their everyday activities, reflected in a sequence of goals to be performed by the dedicated groups. During this activity, agents may preserve a fair part of their individual beliefs, while adopting (inheriting) the appropriate group beliefs. This combination of beliefs will drive task accomplishing and problem solving in consecutive groups. As an agent may play a diversity of roles in these groups, it should be able to easily switch between them. This ability includes a critical analysis of consequences of these choices.

The above aspects call for a smooth belief change mechanism, ensuring computational efficiency. Classical, rather complicated, belief revision methods do not always meet this requirement what is an issue when the changes are transient. Therefore, to address related problems, we have created δQL rooted in the field of paraconsistent reasoning [5,6]. It is an extension to the existing query language 4QL$^{\text{Bel}+}$ [8], using the logic derived from [9]. 4QL$^{\text{Bel}+}$ is a doxastic extension of 4QL [28] allowing for a *single shadowing* operator 'as' and for relevant forms of constraints. In the paper we follow a research line on doxastic reasoning initiated in [9,10] and continued in [7,8,11].

One typically distinguishes groups and roles though both are semantically modeled as collections: a group is a collection of members, while a role is a collection of responsibilities/behaviors (see, e.g., [34]). Despite these differences, in δQL groups and roles are modeled uniformly with the use of belief bases and belief structures [9,10]. It is assumed that the initial belief bases associated with each agent/group involved in a new group structure may be transformed into a fused belief base via a dedicated *epistemic profile* (see Fig. 1). Epistemic profile is a conceptual, abstract entity that transforms a finite set of belief bases into a resulting one. For example, an epistemic profile may:

- transform initial "raw" beliefs into mature ones, e.g., as done in non-monotonic formalisms completing unknown beliefs and/or disambiguating inconsistencies [9,10];
- fuse beliefs of group members to obtain the resultant group beliefs;
- provide beliefs governing the group behavior, abstracting from individual beliefs.

Both a method of fusing group beliefs as well as of disambiguating inconsistencies has to be specifically defined in the epistemic profile.

When a group is formed and its belief base is established, the assignment of authority, positions, roles, responsibilities, etc., can be done via suitable relations and rules in the group's epistemic profile.

Figure 1 illustrates a natural group structure and a hierarchy of the agents/groups involved. The group G is superior to its members A_i/G_i. If a group member is a group itself then, recursively, it contributes to the hierarchy with its own structure. That way complex group topologies can be specified in

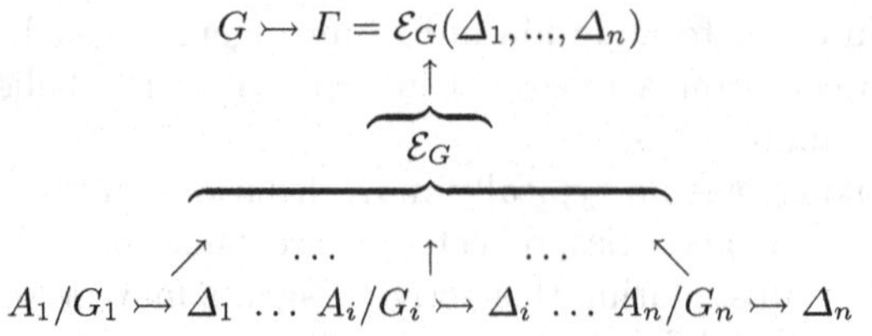

$$G \rightarrowtail \Gamma = \mathcal{E}_G(\Delta_1, ..., \Delta_n)$$

$$\underbrace{\mathcal{E}_G}$$

$$A_1/G_1 \rightarrowtail \Delta_1 \ ... \ A_i/G_i \rightarrowtail \Delta_i \ ... \ A_n/G_n \rightarrowtail \Delta_n$$

Fig. 1. Belief bases and epistemic profiles in group formation: A_i/G_i – agents/groups involved, Δ_i – their belief bases, $G, \mathcal{E}_G, \Gamma$ – the formed group, its epistemic profile and its belief base.

δQL. However, during reasoning it may occur that some beliefs of the G's members have to be shadowed by G's beliefs [8]. For this purpose, a belief operator, $\mathrm{Bel}[\Delta](\alpha)$, has been introduced in [8], where α is a formula, Δ is a belief base or a *shadowing expression* of the form:

$$\Delta_u \text{ as } \Delta_v \text{ as } ... \text{ as } \Delta_w. \tag{1}$$

The intuitive meaning of 'as' is:

the beliefs represented by Δ_u are shadowed by those represented by Δ_v, shadowed by ..., and finally shadowed by Δ_w.

In the sequel the single shadowing (1) will be extended to its multiple version, where a collection of belief bases may be shadowed by another collection of belief bases.

The 'as' operator is intended to help agents to easily switch between roles and teams. Namely, if Δ is a belief base of an agent A, and Γ is a belief base of a group/role G, then 'Δ as Γ' expresses the belief base of A acting as a member of the group or playing the role G. That is, beliefs specified by 'Δ as Γ' are those of Γ, unless a particular belief in Γ is unknown, in which case its doxastic status is taken from Δ. In other words, beliefs in Δ are shadowed by Γ.

The 'as' operator is computationally friendly: query evaluation in 4QL$^{\mathrm{Bel}+}$ is tractable [8]. However, it does not capture situations when an agent is a member of more than one group or plays a couple of roles simultaneously, without prioritizing beliefs. To fill this gap we define and analyze *multiple shadowing* allowing to express such phenomena while retaining tractability of query evaluation. For the sake of clarity, the operator 'as' of [8] will further be called *single shadowing*.

In summary, the original contribution presented here includes an analysis of the shadowing mechanism and an extension of shadowing towards multiple shadowing. The paper is structured as follows. Section 2 outlines the applied understanding of belief bases and provides a formal background. Then, in Sect. 3 we discuss single belief shadowing and extend it to multiple shadowing. We also recall the 4QL$^{\mathrm{Bel}+}$ rule language implementing, among others, doxastic reasoning with single shadowing, define its extension to δQL with multiple shadowing and show the tractability of the extended language. In Sect. 4 we outline some possible uses of multiple shadowing. Finally, in Sect. 5 we discuss related work and provide concluding remarks.

2 Belief Bases

2.1 Intuitions and Syntax

In contemporary situated systems one deals with realistic modeling of informationally-complex environments where data is obtained from sensors, cameras, measurement devices and other equipment. The issues pertaining the quality and accessibility of information originated from the sources of different characteristics and credibility often result in inconsistency or gaps in knowledge. Such an imperfect information will be abbreviated by $3i$, standing for incomplete and/or inconsistent information.

In the literature, belief bases are typically understood as finite sets of formulas in some formal language. Without restrictions such an approach is intractable. In order to maintain tractability, we follow [9,10], where belief bases are finite sets of worlds consisting of variable-free (ground) literals. That way disjunction and negation, typically leading to intractability, are used in a controlled manner.

We will use the classical first-order language, always assuming that domains are finite and consist of constants.[1] Let *Const* be a fixed finite set of constants denoting all domain elements, *Var* be a fixed set of variables and *Rel* be a fixed finite set of relation symbols. As standard in rule-base languages, an identifier starting with a capital letter denotes a variable. Formal definitions of basic syntax are presented below.

Definition 1 (Literals, $3i$-worlds). *By a positive literal we understand an expression of the form $r(\bar{e})$, where $r \in Rel$ and $\bar{e}$ is a tuple consisting of variables and/or constants. A* negative literal *is an expression of the form $\neg\ell$, where ℓ is a positive literal. Literals without variables are called* ground. *A $3i$-world is a finite set of ground literals.*   ◁

Importantly, since a $3i$-world allows to represent defective information, it can be applied to everyday situations abound with data gaps and inconsistencies.

Example 1 (Court Example). Prior to pronouncing judgement, the court examines case files of a particular lawsuit. It is not unusual that such a documentation involves discrepancies, notably between the witnesses' statements, and lacks answers to crucial questions. To illustrate how these imperfections can be expressed with a $3i$-world, w, we consider the following testimonies of witnesses:[2]

$$w = \left\{ \begin{array}{l} \text{capable(tom, murder)}, \neg\text{capable(tom, murder)}, \\ \neg\text{gun(tom)}, \text{capable(ben, murder)}. \end{array} \right\}.$$

---

[1] Note, however, that the semantics of the language will be non-classical.

[2] Of course, the multiplicity of testimonies could be useful in disambiguating potential inconsistencies. Here, for simplicity, we use sets, but multisets could be represented by adding integer parameter specifying the number of persons testifying a given fact.

Here the witnesses disagree whether Tom would be capable of committing the murder ('capable(tom, murder)' is *inconsistent* in w) and there is no disagreement that Ben would be. Furthermore, while it is known that Tom is not in possession of a gun, no one knows whether the same holds for Ben ('gun(ben)' is *unknown* in w).   ◁

Definition 2 (First-order Formulas). First-order formulas *are defined as the smallest set $\mathcal{F}$ of expressions containing literals and such that whenever $\alpha, \beta \in \mathcal{F}$, then also: $\neg\alpha, \alpha \wedge \beta, \alpha \vee \beta, \alpha \to \beta, \forall X(\alpha(X)), \exists X(\alpha(X)) \in \mathcal{F}$.*   ◁

Similarly to databases, our belief bases are equipped with constraints, i.e., formulas required to be true in all instances of belief bases. They ensure the integrity of belief bases at arbitrary abstraction levels: from worlds, through agents' belief bases up to complex groups' structures. Constraints are divided into *rigid* and *flexible* ones. Even though both have to be respected by a belief base, the difference occurs in the context of shadowing: flexible constraints are suspended by shadowing whereas rigid constrains cannot be violated.

Definition 3 (Belief Bases). *By a* belief base over a set of constants *Const we understand any pair $\Delta = \langle \mathcal{W}, \mathcal{C} \rangle$ consisting of:*

- $\mathcal{W} = \{w_1, \ldots, w_k\}$, *where $k \geq 1$ and for $i = 1, \ldots, k$, w_i is a 3i-world;*
- $\mathcal{C} = \mathcal{C}_R \cup \mathcal{C}_F$ *is a finite set of* rigid *and* flexible *constraints (i.e., formulas of the underlying logic).*

If $k = 1$ then Δ is deterministic *otherwise it is* indeterministic.   ◁

Example 2 (Example 1 Continued). Consider two additional 3i-worlds representing testimonies of two witnesses. The first one, Eve, is convinced that Ben is guilty (giving maximal 3 points in the scale of certainty to this charge), and believes that Tom cannot be the murderer, being at the same birthday party when the crime was committed:

$$\{\text{guilty(ben, murder, 3), guilty(tom, murder, 0)}, \atop \text{alibi(tom, birthday\_party)}\}. \tag{2}$$

The other person, who witnessed a destructive Tom's jealousy of the victim, is more inclined to accuse Tom rather than Ben, who has no known motives:

$$\{\text{guilty(ben, murder, 1), guilty(tom, murder, 2)}, \atop \text{motive(tom, jealousy)}\}. \tag{3}$$

These two worlds together constitute a belief base Δ representing the two alternative scenarios resulting from hearings. Note that the set of Δ's constraints is empty. Δ can be augmented with additional information possessed by the court, for example, of Ben's DNA being found in the crime scene:

$$\{(2), (3), \{\text{evidence(ben, dna)}\}\}.$$

◁

For reasoning about beliefs the following definition introduces doxastic formulas with the Bel[]() operator in its basic form.

Definition 4 (Basic Doxastic Formulas). *The set $\mathcal{D}_B$ of basic doxastic formulas is the smallest set containing literals, satisfying the condition that whenever $\alpha \in \mathcal{D}_B$ and Δ is a belief base then $\mathrm{Bel}[\Delta](\alpha) \in \mathcal{D}_B$, and closed under propositional connectives and quantifiers (like in Definition 2).*   ◁

2.2   Semantics of Belief Bases

In Sect. 2.1 we referred to inconsistency and the lack of knowledge. To cover these cases we will extend the language of classical logic with $\mathbf{t}$ ("true") and $\mathbf{f}$ ("false"), by two additional truth values: $\mathbf{i}$ ("inconsistent") and $\mathbf{u}$ ("unknown"). For simplicity, logical constants $\mathbf{f}, \mathbf{u}, \mathbf{i}, \mathbf{t}$ are identified with the corresponding truth values. The semantics of the logic, introduced in [29], is classical on $\mathbf{t}$ and $\mathbf{f}$. To define the semantics of formulas, let $v : Var \longrightarrow Const$ be an assignment of constants to variables and w be a $3i$-world. Then the *truth value* of a literal ℓ wrt w, v denoted by $\ell(w, v)$, is defined by:

$$\ell(w,v) \stackrel{\text{def}}{=} \begin{cases} \mathbf{t} \text{ when } v(\ell) \in w \text{ and } \neg v(\ell) \notin w; \\ \mathbf{i} \text{ when } v(\ell) \in w \text{ and } \neg v(\ell) \in w; \\ \mathbf{u} \text{ when } v(\ell) \notin w \text{ and } \neg v(\ell) \notin w; \\ \mathbf{f} \text{ when } v(\ell) \notin w \text{ and } \neg v(\ell) \in w, \end{cases}$$

where $v(\ell)$ stands for the literal obtained by substituting each variable X occurring in ℓ by the constant $v(X)$.

The semantics of negation is given by:[3]

$$\begin{aligned} \neg\alpha(w,v) = \mathbf{t} \text{ iff } \alpha(w,v) = \mathbf{f}; \\ \text{for } \tau \in \{\mathbf{u}, \mathbf{i}\} : \neg\alpha(w,v) = \tau \text{ iff } \alpha(w,v) = \tau. \end{aligned} \tag{4}$$

To define the semantics of other connectives and quantifiers, the *truth ordering*, reflecting the "amount of truth contained in a value", is needed. Technically, it is the transitive and reflexive closure of:

$$\mathbf{f} < \mathbf{u} < \mathbf{i} < \mathbf{t}. \tag{5}$$

Then, denoting by max, min the maximum and the minimum wrt ordering (5):

$$(\alpha \wedge \beta)(w,v) \stackrel{\text{def}}{=} \min\{\alpha(w,v), \beta(w,v)\}; \tag{6}$$

$$(\alpha \vee \beta)(w,v) \stackrel{\text{def}}{=} \max\{\alpha(w,v), \beta(w,v)\}; \tag{7}$$

$$(\alpha \rightarrow \beta)(w,v) \stackrel{\text{def}}{=} \neg\alpha(w,v) \vee \beta(w,v). \tag{8}$$

---

[3] For the sake of simplicity $\neg\neg\ell$ is identified with ℓ.

Since domains of belief bases are finite, the universal (existential) quantifier can be seen as an abbreviation of a conjunction (disjunction). If $\{a_1, \ldots, a_n\}$ is the domain and X/a_i denotes the substitution of the variable X by a_i then:

$$\forall X(\alpha(X))(w,v) \stackrel{\text{def}}{=} \min \{\alpha(X/a_i)(w,v) \mid i = 1, \ldots, n\};$$
$$\exists x(\alpha(X))(w,v) \stackrel{\text{def}}{=} \max \{\alpha(X/a_i)(w,v) \mid i = 1, \ldots, n\}. \tag{9}$$

The $\text{Bel}[\Delta]()$ operator fuses information from all its $3i$-worlds. *Information ordering*, being the reflexive and transitive closure of ordering shown in Fig. 2, reflects the process of gathering evidences from information sources.[4]

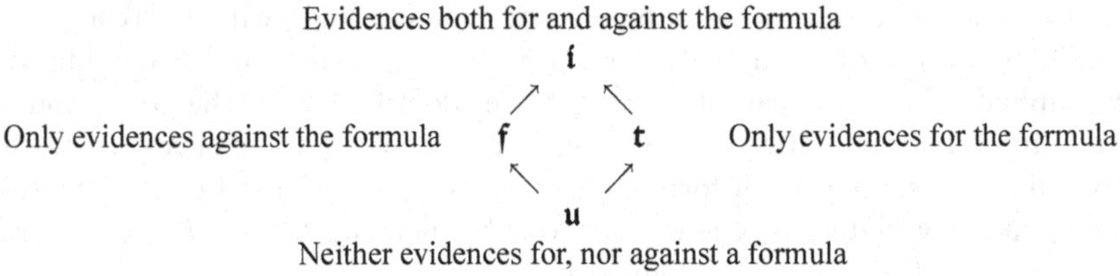

Evidences both for and against the formula

i

Only evidences against the formula   f   t   Only evidences for the formula

u

Neither evidences for, nor against a formula

Fig. 2. Information ordering.

Let $\Delta = \langle \mathcal{W}, \mathcal{C} \rangle$. The semantics of $\text{Bel}[\Delta]()$ is given by:[5]

$$(\text{Bel}[\Delta](\alpha))(v) \stackrel{\text{def}}{=} \begin{cases} \text{LUB}\{\alpha(w_i, v) \mid w_i \in \mathcal{W}\} & \text{assuming} \\ \quad \text{that all formulas of } \mathcal{C} \text{ are true in } \mathcal{W}; \\ u & \text{otherwise}, \end{cases} \tag{10}$$

where LUB denotes the least upper bound wrt information ordering.

Example 3 (Example 2 Continued). Assume that the $3i$-world (2) is extended by:

$$\neg\, \text{guilty(ben, murder, 1)}, \neg\, \text{guilty(ben, murder, 2)}. \tag{11}$$

Denote by Δ' the belief base with two $3i$-worlds: (i) the world (2) extended by (11), and (ii) the world (3). Then, e.g.,

$\text{Bel}[\Delta'](\text{guilty(ben, murder, 3)}) = \mathsf{t};$ $\text{Bel}[\Delta'](\text{guilty(ben, murder, 1)}) = i;$
$\text{Bel}[\Delta'](\text{guilty(ben, murder, 0)}) = u;$ $\text{Bel}[\Delta'](\text{guilty(ben, murder, 2)}) = \mathsf{f}.$ ◁

To finalize the definition of the semantics, let us recall the meaning of arbitrary formulas in a belief base.

Definition 5 (Meaning of Formulas in a Belief Base). *Let $v : Var \longrightarrow Const$ be an assignment of constants to variables and Δ be a belief base. Then the truth value of a formula α wrt Δ and v is defined by $\alpha(\Delta, v) \stackrel{\text{def}}{=} \text{Bel}[\Delta](\alpha)(v).$* ◁

---

[4] Evidence gathering proceeds bottom up: from the lack of information to false or true, and perhaps finally to inconsistency.

[5] The argument w is irrelevant here: $\text{Bel}[]()$ applies to belief bases rather than to worlds.

3   Belief Shadowing

3.1   Extending the Belief Operator

Single shadowing of beliefs is achieved by the use of the operator 'as', treated as a formal expression on belief bases [8]. These expressions are allowed to appear as the first argument of the Bel[]() operator. The idea is that in 'Δ_1 as Δ_2',

- the truth value of Bel[Δ_1 as Δ_2](α) is Bel[Δ_2](α) if the value of α can be determined in Δ_2, otherwise (when Δ_2 doesn't know the value of α), it is the value of Bel[Δ_1](α);
- the constraints of Δ_1 as Δ_2 consist of rigid constraints of Δ_1 and both rigid and flexible constraints of Δ_2.[6]

The following example informally illustrates some uses of single shadowing.

Example 4 (Examples 1, 2 Continued). Let us show how the as operator is able to express dilemmas preceding the verdict announcement, Assuming that there is a definite evidence to convict Ben of committing the murder, the judge, Jim, needs to impose a sentence. Being moved by unprecedented cruelty of the crime, Jim may be personally convinced that Ben deserves life imprisonment:

$$\text{Bel[jim]}(\text{deserves(ben, 'life\_ imprisonment')}) = \mathsf{t}. \tag{12}$$

However, as a judge, he has to follow the penal code, which stipulates that a murderer cannot be punished with more than 25 years of imprisonment:

$$\text{Bel[jim as judge]}(\text{deserves(ben, '25-years')}) = \mathsf{t}. \tag{13}$$

We can also imagine that Jim had been bribed by Ben or his companions. In this case, Jim may be prompted to impose a relatively milder penalty, so his beliefs change:

$$\text{Bel[jim as bribed]}(\text{deserves(ben, '25-years')}) = \mathsf{f}. \tag{14}$$

With shadowing one can prioritize roles/groups Jim belongs to wrt the discussed circumstances of the lawsuit. If Jim gives a priority to his role as a judge, his belief bases as a judge overshadow his other beliefs:

$$\text{Bel[jim as bribed as judge]}(\text{deserves(ben,'25-years')}) = \mathsf{t}. \tag{15}$$

With the same ordering on groups, Jim may believe he should deal with the bribe, e.g.:

$$\begin{aligned}\text{Bel[jim as bribed as judge]}(\text{find\_excuse}) &= \mathsf{t}, \\ \text{Bel[jim as bribed as judge]}(\text{return\_ bribe}) &= \mathsf{u}.\end{aligned} \tag{16}$$

When Jim gives a priority to his 'bribed' role, he intends to reduce Ben's punishment against the law. Therefore, beliefs of Jim as a bribed judge may include:

$$\text{Bel[jim as judge as bribed]}(\text{deserves(ben,'25-years')}) = \mathsf{f}. \tag{17}$$

---

[6] That way flexible constraints of Δ_1 are relaxed.

Note that the variant in which Jim's personal inclination to imprison Ben for life dominates other beliefs can be expressed as well. However, in practice it should not be possible for Jim to increase the punishment against the penal code: this limitation needs to be expressed as a rigid constraint, intrinsic for a judge profession.[7]

Formulas (12)–(17) apply the shadowing operator to express how Jim's beliefs vary with his role. However, without multiple shadowing it is not yet possible to express his beliefs when he is both bribed and a judge simultaneously, with no priority given to any of these roles.   ◁

Note that in Example 4, we used the 'as' operator to indicate various roles rather than groups entered by the judge.

In order to extend single to multiple shadowing, we first have to extend the Bel[]() operator to multiple belief bases.

Definition 6 (Extended Belief Operator). *Let $\mathbb{B}$ be a finite set of belief bases and α be a formula. By an* extended belief operator *we mean an expression* $\mathrm{Bel}[\mathbb{B}](\alpha)$ *with its meaning defined by:*

$$\left(\mathrm{Bel}[\mathbb{B}](\alpha)\right)(v) \stackrel{\text{def}}{=} \mathrm{LUB}\{(\mathrm{Bel}[\varDelta](\alpha))(v) \mid \varDelta \in \mathbb{B}\}, \tag{18}$$

where LUB *denotes the least upper bound wrt information ordering.*   ◁

Intuitively, when belief bases of an agent/group are shadowed, the rigid constraints must be obeyed wrt the shadowed belief bases. To explain the complex interplay among shadowing, constraints and beliefs, let us consider the next example.

Example 5 (Example 2 Continued). Assume that rigid constraints of the witness, say Eve, contain:

$$\forall X\big(\mathrm{guilty}(X, \text{ murder}, 3) \rightarrow \mathrm{deserves}(X, \text{'25-years'})\big). \tag{19}$$

Let Eve's personal beliefs concerning the case be limited to:

$$\{\mathrm{guilty}(\text{ben}, \text{ murder}, 3), \mathrm{deserves}(\text{ben}, \text{'25-years'})\}. \tag{20}$$

Then, of course, her rigid constraint (19) is obeyed. Assume further that a group consisting of Ben's circle of friends came to the sole conclusion that, no matter what, he does not deserve the sentence of 25-years long imprisonment. In such a case, the group's belief base, 'bcf', contains only the fact ¬deserves(ben,'25-years'). Then it should intuitively hold that (Eve as bcf)'s rigid constraint (19) should be violated. Namely, when she acts as a Ben's friend, her beliefs contain:

– guilty(ben, murder, 3) (being **u** in 'bcf' and **t** in (20)), and

---

[7] Questions on how to prioritize the groups as well as how to handle inconsistent rigid constraints are out of the scope of this work.

– ¬deserves(ben,'25-years') (being **t** in 'bcf').

Therefore, using (10), we have that for an arbitrary formula α:

$$\text{Bel[eve } \textbf{as } \text{bcf]}(\alpha) = \mathfrak{u}, \tag{21}$$

what looks like a feasible testimonial strategy for Eve as a Ben's friend.   ◁

We are now ready to define multiple shadowing.

Definition 7 (Multiple Shadowing). *Let* $\mathbb{B}_1, \ldots, \mathbb{B}_n$ *be nonempty sets of belief bases. Multiple shadowing is an expression of the form:*

$$\mathbb{B}_1 \textbf{ as} \ldots \textbf{ as } \mathbb{B}_n. \tag{22}$$

We assume that **as** *is left associative and its semantics is recursively defined by:*

$$\text{Bel[}\mathbb{B} \textbf{ as } \mathbb{B}'\text{]}(\alpha) \overset{\text{def}}{=} \begin{cases} \big(\text{Bel[}\mathbb{B}'\text{]}(\alpha)\big)(v) & \text{when this value is in } \{\mathfrak{t}, \mathfrak{i}, \mathfrak{f}\}; \\ \big(\text{Bel[}\mathbb{B}''\text{]}(\alpha)\big)(v) & \text{otherwise,} \end{cases}$$

where $v : Var \to Const$ *is an assignment of constants to variables, and* $\mathbb{B}''$ *is obtained from* $\mathbb{B}$ *by accepting as constraints the rigid constraints of* $\mathbb{B}$ *and all constraints of* $\mathbb{B}'$*, assuming that all these constraints are evaluated in uncon-strained (*$\mathbb{B}$ **as** $\mathbb{B}'$*).*   ◁

Definition 8 (Doxastic Formulas). *The set* $\mathcal{D}$ *of doxastic formulas is the smallest set containing literals, satisfying the condition that whenever* $\alpha \in \mathcal{D}$ *and* E *is a multiple shadowing expression then* $\text{Bel}[E](\alpha) \in \mathcal{D}$*, and closed under propositional connectives and quantifiers (like in Definition 2).*   ◁

Example 6 (Example 4 Continued). In Example 4 it has not been possible to avoid prioritizing roles. If we do not give priority to roles 'judge' and 'bribed', we can express Jim's role as a bribed judge using multiple shadowing:

$$\text{Bel[jim } \textbf{as } \text{judge, bribed]}\big(\text{deserves(ben, '25-years')}\big) = \mathfrak{i}. \tag{23}$$

The belief (23) combines (13)–(14) using information ordering.   ◁

3.2   The 4QL$^{\text{Bel}+}$ Rule Language

The 4QL$^{\text{Bel}+}$ language [8], implementing single shadowing, belongs to the 4QL family of rule languages whose unique features are, among others, the following:

– the presence of truth values **t**, **f**, **i**, **u**;
– an unrestricted use of negation in conclusions and premises of rules while retaining intuitive results and tractable query evaluation;
– simple and uniform tools (modules and external literals) allowing for lightweight versions of non-monotonic reasoning techniques both for heuristic completing missing information and disambiguation of inconsistencies.

Though full definitions of the languages are available (4QL in [28], $4QL^{Bel}$ in [7], and $4QL^{Bel+}$ in [8]), for clarity we recall most important constructs of these languages.

The building blocks of $4QL^{Bel+}$ programs are modules, which contain following sections: **constraints**, **domains**, **relations** (it specifies names and signatures of relations used in rules), **rules** and **facts**. Though facts can be expressed by rules, their separation from rules and simplified syntax makes the specifications more readable. It is also useful in formulating complexity results in Sect. 3.3.

An important feature of belief bases in $4QL^{Bel+}$ is that domains of their worlds become their own domains, accessible in their constraints. If a domain 'dom' appears in more than one world then corresponding belief base's domain is the union of all domains 'dom' from belief base's worlds (assuming the same types of domain elements).

$4QL^{Bel+}$ rules, specified in modules, have the following form, where ⟨*Formula*⟩ is an arbitrary formula of the logic presented in Sect. 2:

$$\langle Literal \rangle :- \langle Formula \rangle . \tag{24}$$

A rule of the form (24) is "fired" for its ground instances when the value of ⟨*Formula*⟩ contains some truth. As the effect, only ⟨*Literal*⟩ (if the value is **t**) or both ⟨*Literal*⟩ and ¬⟨*Literal*⟩ (if the value is **i**) are added to the set of conclusions. In the ⟨*Formula*⟩ part of rules the operator $Bel[E](\alpha)$ is allowed, where E is a belief base or a single shadowing expression of the form (1), and α is a formula.

As in the case of 4QL, the semantics of $4QL^{Bel+}$ modules is given by *well-supported models* in the sense of [28]. A $3i$-world is well-supported by a $4QL^{Bel+}$ program when it consists of ground literals (if any) assuming that all literals it contains are conclusions of a reasoning starting from facts. For each $4QL^{Bel+}$ program, its well-supported model exists, is uniquely determined, and can be computed in deterministic polynomial time wrt the size of all domains and number of modules [8]. Each $4QL^{Bel+}$ module uniquely specifies its well-supported model, so it can be identified with a $3i$-world. That way:

$4QL^{Bel+}$ modules can be used as a tool for concise and

uniform specification of $3i$-worlds. (25)

Taking the principle (25) into account, in the sequel modules can appear wherever $3i$-worlds are allowed, in particular as elements of Δ in a belief base $\Delta = \langle \mathcal{W}, \mathcal{C} \rangle$.

3.3   Extending $4QL^{Bel+}$ to δQL

Extending $4QL^{Bel+}$ by multiple shadowing is syntactically simple: wherever single shadowing can be used, multiple shadowing expressed as in (22) can be used as well. The extension of the semantics is also relatively straightforward: for multiple shadowing we use Definition 7. The resulting language is denoted by δQL.

Definition 9 (δQL Programs). *By a δQL program we understand any $4QL^{Bel+}$ program, additionally allowing multiple shadowing expressions in belief operators, as defined in Definition 7.*   ◁

We will also make a simplifying assumption that a module is treated as a belief base, consisting of a single 3i-world obtained as the well-supported model of the module and constraints listed in the **constraints** section of the module.

Let Π be a δQL program and n be the number of objects in all domains in Π. In the following complexity results we refer to data complexity. That is, we assume that Π is given and only the **facts** sections of Π modules may vary. This way n may vary, too, while, e.g, the number of 3i-worlds in Π is constant.

Lemma 1 (Tractability of Queries). *Given a δQL program Π, the values of expressions of the form $\mathrm{Bel}[E](\alpha)$ in the well-supported model of Π can be computed in deterministic polynomial time in n.*   ◁

The proof of the lemma is rather straightforward when α in $\mathrm{Bel}[E](\alpha)$ is a first-order formula. Then α is evaluated in each 3i-world occurring in E and then fused using information ordering. Since the number of worlds is constant, the complexity comes from evaluating α in 3i-worlds. Let w be such a 3i-world. Of course (see, e.g., [2]), the complexity of such an evaluation is deterministic polynomial in the size of w.[8] Since the query is fixed, the case when the $\mathrm{Bel}[](\ )$ operator is nested reduces to a constant number of recursive evaluations (the constant reflects the nesting depth).

Remark 1. Note that first-order queries can be encoded in standard non-recursive SQL, so query evaluation can indeed be efficiently implemented.   ◁

In order to query a δQL program, one has to compute its well-supported model. An extension of the method provided for 4QL [28] provides a tractable machinery for such computations. Therefore, the following theorem addressing data complexity of δQL is a consequence of Lemma 1.

Theorem 1 (Tractability of δQL). *Computing queries to any δQL program Π is deterministic polynomial in the number of objects in all domains of Π.*   ◁

4   Some Other Use-Cases

There is a broad spectrum of possible applications of multiple belief shadowing dealing with various aspects of doxastic reasoning. To briefly outline some of them we will assume that Δ and Γ, possibly with indices, are belief bases of agents A and roles/groups G, respectively.

---

[8] The time is logarithmic on a polynomially bounded number of processors running in parallel.

Conflict Recognition and Resolution. An immediate application of multiple shadowing is conflict recognition. For example,

- a difference on the truth values of beliefs $\text{Bel}[\Delta \text{ as } \Gamma_1](\alpha)$ and $\text{Bel}[\Delta \text{ as } \Gamma_2](\alpha)$ demonstrates a conflict among A's roles or groups G_1 and G_2 on a belief α;
- a difference on the truth values of beliefs $\text{Bel}[\Delta](\alpha)$ and $\text{Bel}[\Delta \text{ as } \Gamma](\alpha)$ demonstrates a conflict among A's belief α before and after joining the group G;
- when $\text{Bel}[\Delta \text{ as } \Gamma](\mathsf{t})$ results in u then an A's internal conflict manifesting itself in rigid constraints violation, is caused by entering the group G.

This indicates that a systematic approach to conflict recognition can be provided using multiple shadowing. Even though conflicts cannot be avoided in general, they may be sometimes resolved by changing hierarchy/priorities of groups/roles.

Hypothetical Reasoning. With the 'as' operator, it is possible to ask "what-if" questions, like the following ones:

- $\text{Bel}[\Delta \text{ as } \Gamma_1, \ldots, \Gamma_r](\alpha)$: what would be the belief of A expressed by α, when A becomes a member of given groups/takes given roles $G_1, \ldots, G_r$?
- $\text{Bel}[\Delta \text{ as } \Gamma'](\alpha)$: what would be the belief of A acting as G, expressed by α, when agents $A_1, \ldots, A_s$ joined/left the group? Here Γ' is obtained from Γ by adding/removing agents $A_1, \ldots, A_s$ to/from G.[9]

These questions are essential in different configurations. For instance, when asking whether the change of group structure is meaningful in a given situation and whether this potential difference is substantial.

Preference/Priorities Mining. Assume that an agent can freely join groups/take roles to maximize its utility, but it is not willing to reveal its priorities. With representative data sample concerning agent's behavior one can:

1. compute $\text{Bel}[E](\alpha)$ for typical (in a given context) shadowing expressions E and suitably selected formulas α;
2. compare the results with the actual agent's behavior and approximate relative frequencies of choices the agent made.

This way some indications pertaining agents' actual priorities to join a group or to accept a specific role may be provided.

---

[9] This calls for computing Γ' using the epistemic profile of G with the new set of agents, using their belief bases $\Delta_1, \ldots, \Delta_s$.

Access Control Under Defective Information. In some aspects our app-roach is close in spirit to that of [1] where access control in distributed systems has been investigated using classical truth values only. On the other hand, an explicit presence of inconsistency and ignorance allows one also to address phe-nomena related to the non-classical truth values. Even though both frameworks deal with roles, there are meaningful differences in their understanding and for-malization. Using δQL one can also:

- properly react on inconsistent or unknown results returned by disagreeing or defective servers; here non-monotonic rules formalizing access policies may be needed;
- ask queries about the access rights of ad hoc formed groups embedded in arbitrary shadowing contexts.

Moreover, our framework guarantees tractability what in [1] is achieved by rather serious restrictions imposed on the general formalisms.

5   Related Work and Conclusions

Beliefs and their modifications have been intensively investigated in many con-texts. Starting with definitions of different kinds of beliefs [12,13,17,22,31,38], sophisticated structures like belief sets and belief bases have been defined as a semantical reasoning foundations [18,19,35]. Our approach builds on paracon-sistent and paracomplete belief bases understood as in [7–10]. We extended them with multiple shadowing, creating a convenient reasoning engine with constraints serving as built-in safety tools.

Belief dynamics, reflecting changes in the environment, has been studied in a variety of contexts, including belief update and revision [16,20,21,25–27,30, 32]. Among others, the well known AGM [3] model was developed as a theoretical framework for adequate belief revision. A significant amount of AGM variants have been proposed [4,14,15], including paraconsistent ones [33,36,37].

An alternative framework, belief merging, is addressed in many sources (for an overview see [24]). The authors study merging several belief bases in the presence of integrity constraints while preventing potential inconsistencies. δQL is more flexible: both input belief bases and the resulting ones can be inconsistent. Also, the complexity of belief merging is typically high (see [23]) while δQL guarantees tractability.

Belief shadowing, combined with epistemic profiles [9,10] creates a unique, computationally friendly formal framework for modeling belief dynamics and evolution. In particular, rather than considering updates/revisions potentially affecting belief bases' as a whole, one can provide more focused solutions. On the one hand, a group belief base may be small, containing beliefs relevant to the group goal solely. On the other hand, it may represent a large body of beliefs, e.g., pertaining to a given role. Then, agents may inherit only relevant beliefs while shadowing the others.

Importantly, the presented multiple shadowing remains a lightweight mechanism:

- the 'as' operator itself does not invoke any computations: notably, it doesn't rely on any preprocessing nor modifications of agents', groups' or roles' belief bases;
- the computational cost appears only with query evaluation, which is tractable.

An algebra and logical calculus of principals and roles in the context of access control are presented in [1]. Among others, the authors consider expressions of the form A as R where A is a principal and R is a role. Principals may be atomic or defined by means of expressions. Besides our focus on beliefs, there are, however, many substantial differences between [1] and our approach, including the following ones:

- the framework of [1] is focused on access control and trust while we focus on more general beliefs which may concern security but are more dedicated to groups and the dynamics of their beliefs;
- the approach of [1] is two-valued while our framework allows us to address paraconsistent and paracomplete reasoning including non-monotonic ones;
- while [1] approach is computationally hard and making it tractable requires restrictions (e.g., by differentiating roles from other principals and restricting their use), our framework is tractable.

This paper pertains methodology and design choices related to the underlying paraconsistent four-valued logic, the understanding of belief bases and belief operators and the shadowing machinery. We have shown complexity results as an evidence of computational feasibility of the approach. Other properties, logical and metalogical, are left for further research. We also plan to extend the existing implementation of single shadowing to cover its multiple version, too.

From among may possible applications of multiple shadowing, especially those dealing with group dynamics are essential in MAS. Importantly, modeling group structures evolving over time is rather complex. We substantially reduce this complexity by creating a lightweight mechanism that allows one to operate on both individual and group beliefs, for example shadowing some of them while simultaneously keeping and access to the original beliefs. We have verified this process on a vast case study which will be a subject of an extended version of this paper.

Acknowledgments. The research reported in this paper has been supported by the Polish National Science Centre grant 2015/19/B/ST6/02589, the ELLIIT network organization for Information and Communication Technology, and the Swedish Foundation for Strategic Research FSR (SymbiKBot Project).

References

1. Abadi, M., Burrows, M., Lampson, B., Plotkin, G.: A calculus for access control in distributed systems. ACM Trans. Program. Lang. Syst. **15**(4), 706–734 (1993)
2. Abiteboul, S., Hull, R., Vianu, V.: Foundations of Databases: The Logical Level. Addison-Wesley, Boston (1995)
3. Alchourrón, C.E., Gärdenfors, P., Makinson, D.: On the logic of theory change: partial meet contraction and revision functions. J. Symb. Logic **50**(2), 510–530 (1985)
4. Aucher, G.: Generalizing AGM to a multi-agent setting. Logic J. IGPL **18**(4), 530–558 (2010)
5. Bertossi, L.E., Hunter, A., Schaub, T. (eds.): Inconsistency Tolerance. LNCS, vol. 3300. Springer, Heidelberg (2005). https://doi.org/10.1007/b104925
6. Béziau, J.Y., Carnielli, W., Gabbay, D. (eds.): Handbook of Paraconsistency. College Publications, London (2007)
7. Białek, Ł., Dunin-Kęplicz, B., Szałas, A.: Rule-based reasoning with belief structures. In: Kryszkiewicz, M., Appice, A., Ślęzak, D., Rybinski, H., Skowron, A., Raś, Z.W. (eds.) ISMIS 2017. LNCS (LNAI), vol. 10352, pp. 229–239. Springer, Cham (2017). https://doi.org/10.1007/978-3-319-60438-1_23
8. Białek, Ł., Dunin-Kęplicz, B., Szałas, A.: Belief shadowing. In: Weyns, D., Mascardi, V., Ricci, A. (eds.) EMAS 2018. LNCS (LNAI), vol. 11375, pp. 158–180. Springer, Cham (2019). https://doi.org/10.1007/978-3-030-25693-7_9
9. Dunin-Kęplicz, B., Szałas, A.: Taming complex beliefs. In: Nguyen, N.T. (ed.) Transactions on Computational Collective Intelligence XI. LNCS, vol. 8065, pp. 1–21. Springer, Heidelberg (2013). https://doi.org/10.1007/978-3-642-41776-4_1
10. Dunin-Kęplicz, B., Szałas, A.: Indeterministic belief structures. In: Jezic, G., Kusek, M., Lovrek, I., J. Howlett, R., Jain, L.C. (eds.) Agent and Multi-Agent Systems: Technologies and Applications. AISC, vol. 296, pp. 57–66. Springer, Cham (2014). https://doi.org/10.1007/978-3-319-07650-8_7
11. Dunin-Kęplicz, B., Szałas, A., Verbrugge, R.: Tractable reasoning about group beliefs. In: Dalpiaz, F., Dix, J., van Riemsdijk, M.B. (eds.) EMAS 2014. LNCS (LNAI), vol. 8758, pp. 328–350. Springer, Cham (2014). https://doi.org/10.1007/978-3-319-14484-9_17
12. Dunin-Kęplicz, B., Verbrugge, R.: Teamwork in Multi-Agent Systems. A Formal Approach. Wiley, Hoboken (2010)
13. Fagin, R., Halpern, J., Moses, Y., Vardi, M.: Reasoning About Knowledge. MIT Press, Cambridge (2003)
14. Fermé, E., Hansson, S.O.: AGM 25 years: twenty-five years of research in belief change. J. Philos. Logic **40**(2), 295–331 (2011)
15. Flouris, G., Plexousakis, D., Antoniou, G.: On generalizing the AGM postulates. In: Proceedings of the 2006 Conference on STAIRS 2006, pp. 132–143. IOS Press (2006)
16. Gärdenfors, P.: Conditionals and changes of belief. Acta Phil. Fennica **30**, 381–404 (1978)
17. Hadley, R.F.: The many uses of 'belief' in AI. Mind. Mach. **1**(1), 55–73 (1991)
18. Hansson, S.O.: Taking belief bases seriously. In: Prawitz, D., Westerståhl, D. (eds.) Logic and Philosophy of Science in Uppsala, pp. 13–28. Springer, Dordrecht (1994). https://doi.org/10.1007/978-94-015-8311-4_2
19. Hansson, S.O.: Revision of belief sets and belief bases. In: Dubois, D., Prade, H. (eds.) Belief Change, pp. 17–75. Springer, Dordrecht (1998). https://doi.org/10.1007/978-94-011-5054-5_2

20. Hansson, S.O.: A Textbook of Belief Dynamics. Theory Change and Database Updating. Kluwer Academic Publishers, Dordrecht (1999)
21. Herzig, A., Rifi, O.: Propositional belief base update and minimal change. Artif. Intell. **115**(1), 107–138 (1999)
22. Huber, F.: Formal representations of belief. In: Zalta, E.N. (ed.) The Stanford Encyclopedia of Philosophy. Stanford University, Spring 2016 Edition (2016)
23. Konieczny, S., Lang, J., Marquis, P.: Da^2 merging operators. Artif. Intell. **157**(1–2), 49–79 (2004)
24. Konieczny, S., Pino Pérez, R.: Merging information under constraints: a logical framework. J. Log. Comput. **12**(5), 773–808 (2002)
25. Lang, J.: Belief update revisited. In: Proceedings of the 20th IJCAI, pp. 2517–2522 (2007)
26. Liberatore, P.: The complexity of belief update. Artif. Intell. **119**(1), 141–190 (2000)
27. Liberatore, P.: A framework for belief update. In: Ojeda-Aciego, M., de Guzmán, I.P., Brewka, G., Moniz Pereira, L. (eds.) JELIA 2000. LNCS (LNAI), vol. 1919, pp. 361–375. Springer, Heidelberg (2000). https://doi.org/10.1007/3-540-40006-0_25
28. Małuszyński, J., Szałas, A.: Partiality and inconsistency in agents' belief bases. In: Barbucha, D., et al. (eds.) Proceedings of the 7th KES AMSTA Conference, pp. 3–17. IOS Press (2013)
29. Małuszyński, J., Szałas, A., Vitória, A.: A four-valued logic for rough set-like approximate reasoning. In: Peters, J.F., Skowron, A., Düntsch, I., Grzymała-Busse, J., Orłowska, E., Polkowski, L. (eds.) Transactions on Rough Sets VI. LNCS, vol. 4374, pp. 176–190. Springer, Heidelberg (2007). https://doi.org/10.1007/978-3-540-71200-8_11
30. Marchi, J., Bittencourt, G., Perrussel, L.: A syntactical approach to belief update. In: Gelbukh, A., de Albornoz, Á., Terashima-Marín, H. (eds.) MICAI 2005. LNCS (LNAI), vol. 3789, pp. 142–151. Springer, Heidelberg (2005). https://doi.org/10.1007/11579427_15
31. Meyer, J.J.C., van der Hoek, W.: Epistemic Logic for AI and Theoretical Computer Science. Cambridge University Press, Cambridge (1995)
32. Peppas, P.: Belief revision. In: van Harmelen, F., Lifschitz, V., Porter, B. (eds.) Handbook of KR, pp. 317–359. Elsevier, Amsterdam (2008)
33. Priest, G.: Paraconsistent belief revision. Theoria **67**(3), 214–228 (2001)
34. Sandhu, R.: Roles versus groups. In: Youman, C., Sandhu, R., Coyne, E. (eds.) Proceedings of the 1st ACM Workshop on Role-Based Access Control RBAC. ACM (1995)
35. Santos, Y.D., Ribeiro, M.M., Wassermann, R.: Between belief bases and belief sets: partial meet contraction. In: Proceedings of the International Conference on Defeasible and Ampliative Reasoning, vol. 1423, pp. 50–56. CEUR-WS.org (2015)
36. Testa, R.R., Coniglio, M.E., Ribeiro, M.M.: Paraconsistent belief revision based on a formal consistency operator. CLE E-Prints **15**(8), 01–11 (2015)
37. Testa, R.R., Coniglio, M.E., Ribeiro, M.M.: AGM-like paraconsistent belief change. Logic J. of the IGPL **25**(4), 632–672 (2017)
38. Wooldridge, M.: Reasoning About Rational Agents. MIT Press, Cambridge (2000)

Subset Spaces for Conditional Norms

Huimin Dong[1], R. Ramanujam[2], and Yì N. Wáng[1(✉)]

[1] Department of Philosophy, Zhejiang University, Hangzhou, China
huimin.dong@xixilogic.org, ynw@xixilogic.org
[2] Institute of Mathematical Sciences, Chennai, India
jam@imsc.res.in

Abstract. We introduce two notions of conditionals, forward conditional for deductive implication and backward conditional for abductive implication. The former is in regard to Lewis [16]'s conditional, while the latter is treated as a binary window modality. We introduce logics of forward and backward conditionals, interpreted over a point-set semantics (with explicit likelihood) from the logic of subset spaces. These conditionals and their logics have applications in the studies of conditional norms.

Keywords: Forward conditional · Backward conditional · Modal logic · Subset space · Logic of norms

1 Introduction

Multi-agent systems essentially involve situations where an agent observes the state of the system and decides to act, bringing about change in the system state [26]. Design of agents involves careful decisions on how agents *may* act in any given situation, as well as describing situations in which agents *must* act in specific ways. An example of the latter is a security leak: when an agent A receives from another agent B an item that was supposed to have been secret to B, this must be reported; in some cases, A must abort the program. Actions of the former kind are broader: A may be given the task of selling an item within a price range, without being told which of the several possibly contradictory ways of doing so.

Mundane as such considerations may seem, the underlying reasoning involves conundrums arising from deeper philosophical reflection on *norms, obligations and permissions*. The extensive literature on deontic logics [9] studies many such situations. A central issue in such studies is the logical relationship between the *must* and the *may*, when both are conditional [19]. This paper contributes to such logical studies of conditional norms by offering a topological semantics using subset spaces, which gives us a pleasing duality [1,6]: conditional obligations flow in the forward direction, and conditional permissions flow in the backward direction, and these can be treated in a uniform semantic framework.

There are many unconditional social norms: Thou shalt not kill, but even these need to be often qualified; for instance, soldiers are exempted in some situations. On the other hand, personal norms are typically conditional. When you see someone

© Springer Nature Switzerland AG 2019
M. Baldoni et al. (Eds.): PRIMA 2019, LNAI 11873, pp. 289–304, 2019.
https://doi.org/10.1007/978-3-030-33792-6_18

writhing in pain, it is perhaps obligatory for you to offer help. But if that person is accompanied, you are permitted to assume that the accompanying person would do whatever is necessary. If you are a doctor, you should perhaps rush to offer help anyway. In general, given that φ holds, it is obligatory to ensure ψ. This is a conditional, and often studied in deontic logic as a modality [8, 19].

Personal norms involve permissions as well, and again these are typically conditional: you are permitted to do many things in "good faith". That is, your action is *rationalizable* by showing it to be based on certain assumptions about the ideal state of the world. For instance, in the example above, the presence of an accompanying person A permits you to walk away, justified by your assumption that A would provide the required care. Note that this is only an assumption that may not actually hold; A might be someone who happened to be near, incapable of providing assistance, but yet, the assumption is justified in an ideal situation as perceived by you.

Such considerations lead us to a logic admitting two kinds of conditionals: a *forward* conditional that models what can be concluded given an assumption, and a *backward* conditional that models what conclusion can be traced back to an assumption. The former is related to the Lewis-Stalnaker conditional [2], and the latter is related to the 'window operator' used in modelling abductive reasoning [7] as logical inference.

In this paper, we model these two kinds of conditionals by using subset spaces [5, 18]. The actual state of the world is not known to the agent in its entirety, but comes with observations available to the agent, which are modelled as *neighbourhoods*. These neighbourhoods represent the uncertainty of the agent about the actual world. Subset spaces represent the intuition that these observations may be "extended" by the agent to imagine an "ideal counterpart" and infer accordingly. In general, at any neighbourhood, an open subset corresponds to a situation which the agent knows better, or considers subject to more stringent norms. Conversely, an open superset corresponds to a situation with greater uncertainty, admitting more possibilities. This is analogous to subset spaces in *topologic* wherein open subsets correspond to greater knowledge obtained by greater effort [5, 24]. The resulting logic gives us a uniform treatment of conditional norms while avoiding some of the classical conundrums arising from treating obligations and permissions as modal converse to each other.

In what follows, we present a propositional logic with the forward and backward conditionals. It shares many features of [16] that distinguish the forward conditional from classical implication, but is also distinct: a key axiom of Lewis's logic is invalid here. We show interesting properties that connect the two conditionals, and show how obligations and permissions are modelled in this logical framework.

Thus, the contribution of this paper is mainly conceptual: it attempts to isolate the *minimal* logical core of such forward and abductive backward reasoning by way of topological semantics. It is minimal in the sense of avoiding explicit reference to preferences, priorities etc, and the model has no elements other than simple subset structures. The logic is also minimal in the sense of avoiding modal quantification over neighbourhoods or across neighbourhoods.

The structure of the paper is as follows: we present the logic, and a set of examples illustrating the semantics. We present logical properties of the conditionals (like failure of monotonicity) that demonstrate their suitability for deontic reasoning, and place this proposal in relation to other work. We present some preliminary applications to reasoning about norms, permissions and obligations. The paper ends with a discussion on technical questions arising from the logic.

2 Logic of Forward and Backward Conditionals

In this section we study the logic of forward and backward conditionals, which is suitable for reasoning about deductive and/or abductive implications. We intend to study a minimal logic in this direction, and a unique agent is assumed in this paper. The logic can be extended to a setting with multiple agents, but that will distract us from the main issues involving conditionals, so we focus on the one agent setting here.

We assume a set P of atomic propositions.

Definition 1 (Language). *The language $\mathcal{L}$ has the following grammar rule:*

$$\varphi ::= p \mid \top \mid \bot \mid \neg\varphi \mid (\varphi \to \varphi) \mid (\varphi \multimap \varphi) \mid (\varphi \multimapinv \varphi)$$

where $p \in P$ is an atomic proposition, and $\top$ and $\bot$ are the constants for truth *and* falsity, *respectively. Boolean operators such as conjunction (denoted $\wedge$), disjunction (denoted $\vee$) and equivalence (denoted $\leftrightarrow$) are defined as usual.*

Binary modalities $\multimap$ and $\multimapinv$ are used to characterize forward and backward conditionals respectively. We read $(\varphi \multimap \psi)$ as "every *ideal* φ-assumption gives a certain ψ-conclusion," and $(\varphi \multimapinv \psi)$ as "every certain ψ-conclusion can be traced back to an *ideal* φ." Moreover, the forward conditional can be understood as a causal implication, in the sense that it addresses from the cause to the effect. In contrast, the backward conditional works as a justification for the implication, that is, tracing back to the cause from the effect.

Definition 2 (Subset Models). *A subset model (or model for short) is a tuple $M = (W, \mathcal{O}, V)$ such that:*

- *W is a non-empty set of* worlds;
- *$\mathcal{O} \subseteq \wp(W)$ is a set of subsets of W, called* open sets *or simply* opens;
- *$V : P \to 2^W$ is a valuation that maps every atomic proposition to a set of worlds.*

The pair $(W, \mathcal{O})$ in a subset model is called a subset space.[1]

For a given world $w \in W$, we define $\mathcal{O}_w$ to be the set of *(open) neighborhoods* of w, i.e., $\mathcal{O}_w = \{O \in \mathcal{O} \mid w \in O\}$. An *open subset* of a given set X of worlds is an open which is also a subset of X. The set of all open subsets of X is denoted sub(X).

---

[1] *Subset space* is a more general concept than *topological space*, in the sense that $\mathcal{O}$ can be any set of subsets of W in a subset space (W, O), while as a topological space, $\mathcal{O}$ must in addition satisfy several closure conditions. Therefore, all topological spaces are subset spaces, but not vice versa. Further note that the *opens* in a subset space may also lack the closure conditions.

Definition 3 (Satisfaction). *The satisfaction relation $\models$ is recursively defined as follows. For any model $M = (W, \mathscr{O}, V)$, any world $w \in W$ and any of its open neighborhoods $O \in \mathscr{O}_w$:*

$$
\begin{aligned}
&M, w, O \models p && \Longleftrightarrow w \in V(p) \\
&M, w, O \models \top && always \\
&M, w, O \models \bot && never \\
&M, w, O \models \neg\varphi && \Longleftrightarrow M, w, O \not\models \varphi \\
&M, w, O \models \varphi \rightarrow \psi && \Longleftrightarrow if\ M, w, O \models \varphi\ then\ M, w, O \models \psi \\
&M, w, O \models \varphi \multimap \psi && \Longleftrightarrow for\ all\ O' \in \mathscr{O}_w, if\ [\![\varphi]\!]_{O'} \in sub(O)\ then\ M, w, O' \models \psi \\
&M, w, O \models \varphi \bullet\!\!- \psi && \Longleftrightarrow for\ all\ O' \in \mathscr{O}_w, if\ M, w, O' \models \psi\ then\ [\![\varphi]\!]_{O'} \in sub(O)
\end{aligned}
$$

where $[\![\varphi]\!]_{O'} = \{w' \in O' \mid M, w', O' \models \varphi\}$. We say that a formula is valid*, if it is satisfied at a certain point set in a model, or otherwise* invalid*.*

It is not hard to see that the backward conditional has the flavor of the window operator, which can be traced back to [3, 12, 15].

We first test some trivial conditionals, with its antecedent or consequent a truth or falsity. This gives us the following observations.

Proposition 1. *For any model $M = (W, \mathscr{O}, V)$, any $w \in W$ and $O \in \mathscr{O}_w$, for any formulas φ, ψ and χ, the following hold:*

1. $M, w, O \models \top \multimap \varphi \Longleftrightarrow$ *for all $O' \in \mathscr{O}_w$, if $O' \subseteq O$ then $M, w, O' \models \varphi$*
2. $M, w, O \models \bot \multimap \varphi \Longleftrightarrow$ *for all $O' \in \mathscr{O}_w$, if $\emptyset \in \mathscr{O}$ then $M, w, O' \models \varphi$*
3. $\varphi \multimap \top$ *is valid*
4. $M, w, O \models \varphi \multimap \bot \Longleftrightarrow$ *for all $O' \in \mathscr{O}_w$, $[\![\varphi]\!]_{O'} \notin sub(O)$*
5. $M, w, O \models \varphi \bullet\!\!- \top \Longleftrightarrow$ *for all $O' \in \mathscr{O}_w$, $[\![\varphi]\!]_{O'} \in sub(O)$*
6. $\varphi \bullet\!\!- \bot$ *is valid*
7. $M, w, O \models \top \bullet\!\!- \varphi \Longleftrightarrow$ *for all $O' \in \mathscr{O}_w$, if $M, w, O' \models \varphi$ then $O' \subseteq O$*
8. $M, w, O \models \bot \bullet\!\!- \varphi \Longleftrightarrow$ *for all $O' \in \mathscr{O}_w$, if $M, w, O' \models \varphi$ then $\emptyset \in \mathscr{O}$*

Some of the above give natural sentences which can be of use in different contexts. For convenience we introduce some modal abbreviations:

$$
\begin{aligned}
\Box\varphi &:= \top \multimap \varphi \\
\boxplus\varphi &:= \varphi \bullet\!\!- \top \\
\boxminus\varphi &:= \varphi \multimap \bot
\end{aligned}
$$

We repeat the truth conditions of modalities $\Box$, $\boxplus$ and $\boxminus$, which are presented as follows:

$$
\begin{aligned}
&M, w, O \models \Box\varphi && \Longleftrightarrow for\ all\ O' \in \mathscr{O}_w, if\ O' \subseteq O\ then\ M, w, O' \models \varphi \\
&M, w, O \models \boxplus\varphi && \Longleftrightarrow for\ all\ O' \in \mathscr{O}_w, [\![\varphi]\!]_{O'} \in sub(O) \\
&M, w, O \models \boxminus\varphi && \Longleftrightarrow for\ all\ O' \in \mathscr{O}_w, [\![\varphi]\!]_{O'} \notin sub(O).
\end{aligned}
$$

The operator $\Box$ is the standard box operator used in the logic of subset spaces [5, 18], which is interpreted as a refinement to the current neighborhood. In our logic, a formula

$\square\varphi$ reads as "φ is true in all ideal counterparts." The formula $\boxplus\varphi$ states that the current situation is ideal regarding to φ, and the $\boxminus\varphi$ says the opposite.

Conditionals interact with boolean operators to a certain extent. We list some of these properties in the following proposition, together with some standard validity-preserving rules. Their proofs are routine applications of definitions and first-order reasoning, and are therefore omitted.

Proposition 2. *For all formulas φ, ψ and χ, the following hold:*

1. $(\varphi \multimap (\psi \to \chi)) \to ((\varphi \multimap \psi) \to (\varphi \multimap \chi))$ *is valid;*
2. $(\varphi \multimapdotinv (\psi \to \chi)) \to ((\varphi \multimapdotinv \chi) \to (\varphi \multimapdotinv \psi))$ *is valid;*
3. $(\varphi \multimap (\psi \land \chi)) \leftrightarrow ((\varphi \multimap \psi) \land (\varphi \multimap \chi))$ *is valid;*
4. $(\varphi \multimapdotinv (\psi \land \chi)) \leftrightarrow ((\varphi \multimapdotinv \psi) \lor (\varphi \multimapdotinv \chi))$ *is valid;*
5. $(\varphi \multimap (\psi \lor \chi)) \leftrightarrow ((\varphi \multimap \psi) \lor (\varphi \multimap \chi))$ *is valid;*
6. $(\varphi \multimapdotinv (\psi \lor \chi)) \leftrightarrow ((\varphi \multimapdotinv \psi) \land (\varphi \multimapdotinv \chi))$ *is valid;*
7. *if φ is valid, then $\psi \multimap \varphi$ is valid;*
8. *if $\neg\varphi$ is valid, then $\psi \multimapdotinv \varphi$ is valid;*
9. *if $\varphi \leftrightarrow \varphi'$ is valid, then $(\varphi \multimap \psi) \leftrightarrow (\varphi' \multimap \psi)$ is valid;*
10. *if $\varphi \leftrightarrow \varphi'$ is valid, then $(\varphi \multimapdotinv \psi) \leftrightarrow (\varphi' \multimapdotinv \psi)$ is valid.*

More interesting might be the properties of the forward conditional by itself, backward conditional by itself, and interactions between them. Some of these properties have already been presented in the previous proposition. We focus on several more in the following.

In our logic we interpret an open set as the ideal worlds observed by an agent. This gives a good reason for not allowing the empty set to be an open. We call a subset space $(W, \mathcal{O})$ with $\emptyset \notin \mathcal{O}$ a *satisfactory space*. A subset model based on a satisfactory space, i.e., a model $(W, \mathcal{O}, V)$ such that $(W, \mathcal{O})$ is a satisfactory space, is called a *satisfactory model*. We get a different logic if we interpret the formulas over the class of satisfactory models. It is easy to verify that $\bot \multimap \varphi$ becomes valid in the new logic (cf. Proposition 1(2)), and $\bot \multimapdotinv \varphi$ will mean that φ is false at the factual world in all of its neighborhoods (cf. Proposition 1(8)).

Proposition 3. *For any formulas φ, ψ, for any propositional formula α, the following hold:*

1. $(\varphi \multimapdotinv \psi) \to (\psi \multimap \varphi)$ *is not valid;*
2. $\varphi \multimap \varphi$ *is not valid, nor is $\alpha \multimap \alpha$ valid;*
3. $\alpha \to (\varphi \multimap \alpha)$ *is valid;*
4. $\neg\alpha \to (\varphi \multimapdotinv \alpha)$ *is valid;*
5. $\varphi \multimapdotinv \varphi$ *is not valid, nor is $\alpha \multimapdotinv \alpha$ valid.*

Proof. We leave some of the proofs to a technical appendix.

Some of these properties suggest that there are interesting subclasses of subset space models where formulas such as $\varphi \multimap \varphi$ are valid.

3 Examples of Truth Verification

In this section we illustrate how we can check the truth of formulas in some given subset models. We focus on the non-monotonicity and non-transitivity of the conditionals. This section is a technical exposition, we leave discussions of the intuition to the next section.

Let us start with a model $M = (W, \mathcal{O}, V)$ such that:

- $W = \{a, b, c, d, e\}$
- $\mathcal{O} = \{O_1, O_2, O_3, O_4, O_5, O_6\}$ with
  - $O_1 = \{a, b, c, d\}$
  - $O_2 = \{c, d, e\}$
  - $O_3 = \{a, b, d\}$
  - $O_4 = \{b\}$
  - $O_5 = \{c, e\}$
  - $O_6 = W = \{a, b, c, d, e\}$
- V is such that $V(p) = \{a, b, c, e\}$, $V(q) = \{c, d\}$ and $V(r) = \{b\}$.

Failure of Forward Monotonicity. We first verify that $M, a, O_1 \models p \multimap q$. By definition the set of neighborhoods of a is $\mathcal{O}_a = \{O_1, O_3, O_6\}$. The truth sets of p over each of the open neighborhoods are respectively:

$$
\begin{aligned}
\llbracket p \rrbracket_{O_1} &= \{w \in O_1 \mid M, w, O_1 \models p\} &= V(p) \cap O_1 &= \{a, b, c\} \\
\llbracket p \rrbracket_{O_3} &= \{w \in O_3 \mid M, w, O_3 \models p\} &= V(p) \cap O_3 &= \{a, b\} \\
\llbracket p \rrbracket_{O_6} &= \{w \in O_6 \mid M, w, O_6 \models p\} &= V(p) \cap O_6 &= \{a, b, c, e\}
\end{aligned}
$$

None of the truth sets of p over the neighborhood of a are open subsets of O_1 (for none of them is an open set). Therefore $M, a, O_1 \models p \multimap q$ holds for the precondition cannot be met.

Now consider the truth sets of $p \wedge r$ over the neighborhoods of a:

$$
\begin{aligned}
\llbracket p \wedge r \rrbracket_{O_1} &= \{w \in O_1 \mid M, w, O_1 \models p \wedge r\} &= V(p) \cap V(r) \cap O_1 &= \{b\} \\
\llbracket p \wedge r \rrbracket_{O_3} &= \{w \in O_3 \mid M, w, O_3 \models p \wedge r\} &= V(p) \cap V(r) \cap O_3 &= \{b\} \\
\llbracket p \wedge r \rrbracket_{O_6} &= \{w \in O_6 \mid M, w, O_6 \models p \wedge r\} &= V(p) \cap V(r) \cap O_6 &= \{b\}
\end{aligned}
$$

These truth sets of $p \wedge r$, being the same, is indeed an open subset of O, namely O_4. If we evaluate the truth of the formula $(p \wedge r) \multimap q$, we find that for all $O' \in \mathrm{sub}(O_1)$ such that $\llbracket p \wedge r \rrbracket_{O'} \in \mathrm{sub}(O)$ – namely O_1, O_3 and O_6 – we have $M, a, O' \not\models q$. To observe that $M, a, O' \not\models q$, it might be good to see that the truth of q is given by the valuation V which relies only on the factual world a. Since $a \notin V(q)$, $M, a, O' \not\models q$. That is to say, $M, a, O_1 \not\models (p \wedge r) \multimap q$.

This gives us a wanted result: there is a countermodel for the formula $(p \multimap q) \rightarrow ((p \wedge r) \multimap q)$, by making the antecedent true and the consequent false. This formula is a special case of $(\varphi \multimap \psi) \rightarrow ((\varphi \wedge \chi) \multimap \psi)$, which says that "whenever ψ is true in all ideal φ worlds, ψ is also true in all ideal $\varphi \wedge \chi$ worlds", which characterizes a *principle of monotonicity* for the forward conditional. Invalidity of this formula, as in our logic, shows an example of non-monotonicity of the forward conditional.

Failure of Forward Transitivity. This time we show that $(p \multimap q) \wedge (q \multimap r) \to (p \multimap r)$ is also not valid. We consider M, c, O_1 instead. The set of neighborhoods of c is $\mathscr{O}_c = \{O_1, O_2, O_5, O_6\}$. The truth sets of p over these are:

$$
\begin{aligned}
\llbracket p \rrbracket_{O_1} &= \{w \in O_1 \mid M, w, O_1 \models p\} &=& V(p) \cap O_1 &=& \{a, b, c\} \\
\llbracket p \rrbracket_{O_2} &= \{w \in O_2 \mid M, w, O_2 \models p\} &=& V(p) \cap O_2 &=& \{c, e\} \\
\llbracket p \rrbracket_{O_5} &= \{w \in O_5 \mid M, w, O_5 \models p\} &=& V(p) \cap O_5 &=& \{c, e\} \\
\llbracket p \rrbracket_{O_6} &= \{w \in O_6 \mid M, w, O_6 \models p\} &=& V(p) \cap O_6 &=& \{a, b, c, e\}
\end{aligned}
$$

Since $\llbracket p \rrbracket_{O_2}$ and $\llbracket p \rrbracket_{O_5}$ are both open subsets of O_1, to see whether $p \multimap q$ is true, we need to very whether $M, c, O_2 \models q$ and $M, c, O_5 \models q$ both hold. They are, for $c \in V(q)$. Thus, $M, c, O_1 \models p \multimap q$.

How about $M, a, O_1 \models q \multimap r$? Again, since the neighborhoods of c are O_1, O_2, O_5 and O_6, we consider the truth sets of q over them:

$$
\begin{aligned}
\llbracket q \rrbracket_{O_1} &= \{w \in O_1 \mid M, w, O_1 \models q\} &=& V(q) \cap O_1 &=& \{c, d\} \\
\llbracket q \rrbracket_{O_2} &= \{w \in O_2 \mid M, w, O_2 \models q\} &=& V(q) \cap O_2 &=& \{c, d\} \\
\llbracket q \rrbracket_{O_5} &= \{w \in O_5 \mid M, w, O_5 \models q\} &=& V(q) \cap O_5 &=& \{c\} \\
\llbracket q \rrbracket_{O_6} &= \{w \in O_6 \mid M, w, O_6 \models q\} &=& V(q) \cap O_6 &=& \{c, d\}
\end{aligned}
$$

None of these truth sets of q are open sets, and so $M, c, O_1 \models q \multimap r$ holds for very much the same reason as we showed $M, a, O_1 \models p \multimap q$.

Finally, we check whether $p \multimap r$ is satisfied in M, a, O_1. By similar argument, only $\llbracket p \rrbracket_{O_2}$ and $\llbracket p \rrbracket_{O_2}$ are open subsets of O_1, and all we need to do is to verify whether $M, c, O_2 \models r$ and $M, c, O_5 \models r$ both hold. This is not the case, for $c \notin V(r)$. Thus, $M, c, O_1 \not\models p \multimap r$.

We conclude that the transitivity of forward conditional is invalid, for $M, c, O_1 \not\models (p \multimap q) \wedge (q \multimap r) \to (p \multimap r)$. As we will explain in Sect. 4.2, transitivity is not a property we want for talking about norms.

Failure of Backward Monotonicity. We want to verify that $(r \multimapinv p) \to ((r \wedge q) \multimapinv p)$ is not valid. We consider M, c, O_1.

First we show that $M, a, O_1 \models r \multimapinv p$. Again, the neighborhoods of a are O_1, O_3, and O_6, and p is true at a in all these neighborhoods. The truth set of r over these neighborhoods are listed below:

$$
\begin{aligned}
\llbracket r \rrbracket_{O_1} &= \{w \in O_1 \mid M, w, O_1 \models r\} &=& V(r) \cap O_1 &=& \{b\} \\
\llbracket r \rrbracket_{O_3} &= \{w \in O_3 \mid M, w, O_3 \models r\} &=& V(r) \cap O_3 &=& \{b\} \\
\llbracket r \rrbracket_{O_6} &= \{w \in O_6 \mid M, w, O_6 \models r\} &=& V(r) \cap O_6 &=& \{b\}
\end{aligned}
$$

All these are an open subset of O_1, i.e., O_4, which gives us the wanted result.

How about $(r \wedge q) \multimapinv p$? It is not hard to see that $r \wedge q$ is true in no world, so the truth set of $r \wedge q$ is the emptyset which is not an open subset of O_1. It follows that $M, a, O_1 \not\models (r \wedge q) \multimapinv p$.

Therefore, $(r \multimapinv p) \to ((r \wedge q) \multimapinv p)$, and a more general version of it, $(\varphi \multimapinv \psi) \to ((\varphi \wedge \chi) \multimapinv \psi)$, is not valid. This reveals the non-monotonicity of the backward conditional.

Failure of Backward Transitivity. We show that $(q \bullet\!\!- r) \wedge (r \bullet\!\!- p) \to (q \bullet\!\!- p)$ is not valid. We consider M, a, O_1. Note that the set of neighborhoods of a is $\{O_1, O_3, O_6\}$ which has been discussed a few times above.

We first argue that $M, a, O_1 \models q \bullet\!\!- r$. This is because $b \notin V(r)$ and the premise of the interpretation is not met.

Now $M, a, O_1 \models r \bullet\!\!- p$ as well, for the truth sets of r over O_1, O_3 are O_6 are all open subsets of O_1, as we verified above.

Finally we show that $M, a, O_1 \not\models q \bullet\!\!- p$. Clearly p is true which meets the premise. But now the truth sets of q over the neighborhoods are:

$$
\begin{aligned}
[\![q]\!]_{O_1} &= \{w \in O_1 \mid M, w, O_1 \models q\} &= V(q) \cap O_1 &= \{c, d\} \\
[\![q]\!]_{O_3} &= \{w \in O_3 \mid M, w, O_3 \models q\} &= V(q) \cap O_3 &= \{d\} \\
[\![q]\!]_{O_6} &= \{w \in O_6 \mid M, w, O_6 \models q\} &= V(q) \cap O_6 &= \{c, d\}
\end{aligned}
$$

None of them are open subsets of O_1, which gives us the results.

That is to say, $(\varphi \bullet\!\!- \psi) \wedge (\psi \bullet\!\!- \chi) \to (\varphi \bullet\!\!- \chi)$, which characterizes the transitivity of the backward conditional, is not a valid formula. We shall discuss these in the next section.

4   Discussion on the Semantics

We have introduced a logic based on a subset space semantics, which has its root in the logic of subset spaces [5, 18]. While this semantics is also related to neighborhood semantics [4] (just as hinted by the names of the concepts of open set, neighbourhood, etc.) they have their technical pros and cons. In particular, subset space semantics has its advantage in jumping over open sets – especially useful when the open sets are used for fundamental notions in applications. Here we explain some of the properties of the logic and its relationship to the literature, from a semantical perspective, starting from the work on conditionals using a solution based on neighborhood semantics.

4.1   Interpreting the Conditionals

Conditionals have been studied extensively, at least originating from Ramsey in 1929 [20]. Consider the Ramsey example: "I will not eat cake, as it will upset my stomach." We cannot model this as the implication "If I eat cake, I will fall sick," as we cannot contradict it by making me eat and then showing I am not sick. Such assertions are modelled explicitly as conditionals. When we reason about what an agent ought to do, these considerations lead us to *ontic* conditionals, and *counterfactuals*: "Had I eaten cake, I might have fallen sick." This involves consideration of likely causes and likely effects.

Lewis provided a neighbourhood semantics to model the notion of *likelihood*. Likelihood is interpreted by spheres in Lewis' work [16, p. 14]:

> "Any particular sphere around a world i is to contain just those worlds that resemble i to at least a certain degree. This degree is different for different spheres around i. The smaller the sphere, the more similar to i must a world be to fall within it."

In Lewis' proposal, each most likely sphere is *explicitly* given as a neighbourhood in the model. We follow this idea, but subset spaces achieve the same purpose implicitly.

The *forward* conditional $\varphi \multimap \psi$ is to be interpreted as: "in the *ideal* situation φ conceived of by the agent, we can conclude ψ." We use forward conditionals to express sentences like "On sunny days during winter, my landlord does not stay at home" and "Before my landlord goes out, he turns off the heater in the house." A forward conditional indicates what is concluded from a certain amount of evidence.

The backward conditional $\varphi \multimapinv \psi$ is used to capture *abductive* reasoning as a justification arising from an implication. $\varphi \multimapinv \psi$ is intended to mean that ψ as a conclusion can be traced back to the *ideality* assumption φ. This backward conditional can be used to express, for instance: "Two friends who got into a row and have just been seen jogging together have made up," or a normative sentence like: "A student driver may drive on the highway when accompanied by a driving instructor." Notice that these sentences do not provide a description of *deductive* reasoning. From the observations that two friends got into a row and that they have been seen jogging together, it is *not necessary to infer* the conclusion that they have made up. Rather, the conclusion is *sufficient* as one of the best available explanations for the given observations. In other words, these *ideal* hypotheses can be safely assumed.

Although the key core of abduction is still controversial, such sufficiency of best explanation is a widely accepted principle [7] even in legal reasoning [23]. It is essential to note that under this principle, the forward conditionals are distinct from the backward conditionals. My landlord's going out during winter is by no means sufficient as a best explanation for good weather. Nor does turning off the heater in any way explain his going out. In contrast, that the two friends made up offers a best explanation for why they had been seen jogging together, despite their having had a row. In the normative context, according to the traffic regulation, a case that a student driver operates a motor vehicle on the highway is sufficient to infer her being accompanied by a driving instructor, because it is an *ideal* instantiation of such accompanying. Such a principle of *sufficiency* does help the tracing back of assumptions from what is concluded. This is the principle embodied in our semantics of conditionals using subset spaces.

4.2 Properties

Forward Conditional. We follow Lewis [16] in distinguishing material implication and the (forward) conditional, by listing certain classical properties of implication that fail for the conditional.

Failure of Monotonicity. $(\varphi \multimap \psi) \to ((\varphi \wedge \chi) \multimap \psi)$ is not valid. This is because the conjunction $\varphi \wedge \chi$ might correspond to an idealization (open subset) whereas φ might not. In this case the former conditional might hold trivially, whereas the stronger assumption might invalidate ψ. A detailed countermodel has been given in Sect. 3. This is a natural property we would like to have. Consider the sentences:

1. If you see food on the table in the common room then you eat it.
2. If you see food on the table in the common room meant for conference in the next room then you eat it.

The truth of the first does not necessarily imply that of the second.

Failure of Transitivity. $((\varphi \multimap \psi) \wedge (\psi \multimap \chi)) \to (\varphi \multimap \chi)$ is not valid. The invalidity of this property is also shown in Sect. 3. Consider the following sentences for the intuition behind it:

1. If you attend a conference, you look for free food in the common room.
2. If you see food on the table in the common room then you eat it.
3. If you attend a conference, you get to eat free food.

Failure of Contraposition. $(\varphi \multimap \psi) \to (\neg\psi \multimap \neg\varphi)$ is not valid, for there are models making $\varphi \multimap \psi$ true, but $\neg\psi \multimap \neg\varphi$ false. One of the main technical details here is that $\neg\varphi$ being false does not necessarily disallow the truth set of φ being an open subset (even the truth set for $\bot$, which is the empty set, can be an open). An intuitive case can be the following.

1. If you see food on the table in the common room then you eat it.
2. If you do not eat the food on the table in the common room, it is because you have not seen it.

Failure of Inconsistency. $(\varphi \multimap \psi) \wedge (\varphi \multimap \neg\psi)$ is not valid, for there could simply be no ideal φ worlds conceived by the agent. An intuitive example can be:

1. If you see food on the table in the common room then you can eat it.
2. If you see food on the table in the common room then you should not eat it.

Failure of Excluded Middle. $(\varphi \multimap \psi) \vee (\varphi \multimap \neg\psi)$ is not valid, for a similar reason for the failure of inconsistency. An example for the appropriateness of this property is as follows.

1. If you see food on the table in the common room then you can eat it.
2. If you see food on the table in the common room then you should not eat it.

One key axiom in Lewis' logic [16] is invalid in our logic: $(\varphi \multimap \psi) \to (\varphi \to \psi)$. This is perhaps not surprising since subset space models are weaker than Lewis' semantics. Our logic of forward conditionals closely resemble Lewis's logic of counterfactuals while remaining distinct.

Backward Conditional. The work on backward conditionals go back to the unary modality called *window operator* developed in [3,10,12,15]. This is essentially a universal modality, whose interest lies in the fact that its truth condition is the converse of the truth condition for "necessity" and in this sense offers a condition of "sufficiency." This has been used to capture notions like program negation or action negation, permission, etc. It is this sufficiency principle that underlies the semantics of the backward conditional proposed in this paper.

Logics of conditionals have generally not addressed sufficiency barring a few such as [11,13], which used conditionals for the notion of "counts-as". Our logic is distinguished from these, as their validity $(\psi \bullet\!\!- \varphi) \wedge (\chi \bullet\!\!- \varphi) \to ((\psi \wedge \chi) \bullet\!\!- \varphi)$ is invalid in our logic.

We can find a similar list of failures of properties with respect to the backward conditional; the explanations are similar, so we do not present them.

Paradoxes of Material Implication. Neither the forward nor the backward conditional escapes the problems of material implication, as revealed by the validities in Proposition 1 (3, 6), though ($\bot \multimap \varphi$) and ($\top \bullet\!\!- \varphi$) are indeed not valid. In this sense, both conditionals are types of material implication.

5   Applications

5.1   Modeling Interdependent Decisions

Here we apply our semantics to model the so-called "interdependent decision" discussed by Schelling [21], which illustrates the interaction of a number of self-interested players in a game. The following is a standard example of this.

Example 1 (Chicken Games). This game involves two players x and y. If x and y both drive straight, it results in disaster. So, if x keeps driving straight, then y better make a turn. If x makes a turn, then y is better off keeping straight, although y's making a turn would not cause any accident. What should y do given an action chosen by x? What can y do given that x is driving straight?

To describe this normative states in this example, we define two conditional norms by the forward and backward modalities as follows:

$$O(\psi/\varphi) := (\varphi \multimap \boxplus\psi)$$
$$P(\psi/\varphi) := (\varphi \bullet\!\!- \boxminus\neg\psi)$$

Here $O(\psi/\varphi)$ reads as: "It is obligatory to ψ given that φ" and $P(\psi/\varphi)$ as: "It is permitted to ψ given that φ." Notice that the modality $\boxplus$ goes through all ideal possibilities regarding to the given proposition. In contrast, $\boxminus\neg\psi$ captures that $\neg\psi$ is non-deal in an exclusive sense. Or, $\boxminus\neg\psi$ indicates a weaker sense of ideality by saying that ψ is not forbidden. So, it ought to be ψ, conditional on φ, when all ideal φ-cases force ψ being ideal among them. It is permitted to be ψ, conditional on φ, when the non-forbidden ψ cases can be traced back to the ideal φ cases. The proposal here follows the tradition of deontic duality suggested by [1,3], in form of conditional norms. As argued in [1], this idea of duality can well capture *rational* strategies in game theory. Here we show an application of modelling the chicken games. For instance, all ideal actions of one player's driving straight cause the other to swerve, in order to avoid crashing. As a *rational choice*, one oughts to swerve if the other is driving straight. While, as being *rationally recommended* [6], it is permitted for one to make a turn when the other does so, because one's non-forbidden swerving can be traced back to an ideal case of swerving made by the other. In the following we illustrate the conditional obligation and permission in this situation by using our semantics.[2]

The set T of all action tokens of swerving is $\{t_1, \ldots, t_n\}$, and the set S of all tokens of driving straight is defined as $\{s_1, \ldots, s_m\}$. A possible world (x, y) is a pair of strategies

---

[2] In literature, STIT-logic [22] offers a standard way to illustrate obligation and permission in games. But the connection between STIT and the approach we take has been aware [1,6]. We compare our account with STIT-logic in the future.

by the two players, in which the action token x is chosen by the first player and y by the second. In other words, each possible world is a strategy profile.

Let us consider the model $M = (W, \mathcal{O}, V)$ of this example as follows:

- $W = \{(x, y) \mid x, y \in T \cup S\}$ is the set of all strategy profiles.
- $O = \{(x, y) \in W \mid x \in T \text{ iff } y \in S\} \cup \{(x, y) \in W \mid x, y \in T\}$ is the set of all ideal strategy profiles, in which no disaster happens. Let $\mathcal{O} = \wp(O)$.
- $V(a : T) = \{(x, y) \in W \mid x \in T\}$, $V(b : T) = \{(x, y) \in W \mid y \in T\}$, and $V(b : S) = \{(x, y) \in W \mid y \in S\}$.

The sentence $a : T$ is read as "Agent a swerves" and $b : S$ as "Agent b drives straight." Similarly, the sentence $b : T$ says "Agent b swerves." At state (t, s) within ideality O, the sentence $(a : T) \multimap \boxplus(b : S)$ asserts a *rational* strategy, representing an obligation of $b : S$, agent b to drive straight, enforced by the given condition $a : T$, agent a to swerve. The permissions $(a : T) \bullet\!\!- \boxminus\neg(b : T)$ and $(a : T) \bullet\!\!- \boxminus\neg(b : S)$ both hold at (s, t) within O, which *rationally* recommend agent b to make a turn, or keep driving straight, conditional on agent a's swerve. The conditional obligation and permission we proposed obey a principle similar to "obligation as the weakest permission" [1]: If φ is obligatory and ψ is permitted, then, ideally speaking, the non-forbiddance for ψ is included in the ideality for φ. We left the comparison in the future work.[3]

5.2 Free Choice Permission Paradox Revisited

The conditional permission proposed in the previous section takes a weak sense of ideality in its assumption, such that what is permitted is decided by whether non-forbiddance implies ideality. This permission is weak, not only it defines ideality in a negative way (comparing with the affirmative way to define obligation), but also it only has half of the free choice properties [14]:

$$P(\psi/\varphi) \wedge P(\chi/\varphi) \to P(\psi \vee \chi/\varphi) \tag{FC}$$

The proof of this can be done by replacing $P(\psi/\varphi)$ back into the backward conditional $\varphi \bullet\!\!- \boxminus\neg\psi$. The crucial step here is that, given $[\![\neg\psi]\!]_{O'} \notin \text{sub}(O)$ and $[\![\neg\chi]\!]_{O'} \notin \text{sub}(O)$ for every $O' \in \mathcal{O}_w$, in addition to a world w and an open O, it is not possible to have an open $O'' \in \mathcal{O}_w$ such that $[\![\neg\psi]\!]_{O''} \cap [\![\neg\chi]\!]_{O''} \in \text{sub}(O)$. If this were possible, it would contradict the given assumption. This *"free choice"* property indicates that, given that ψ and χ are permitted conditional on φ, it implies that the disjunction of ψ and χ is still permitted, conditional on the same φ.

One merit of this is that this conditional permission does not confront the infamous *"free choice permission paradox"* [14]. It is permitted for someone to enter another's property (represented by letter E), conditional on the owner giving her consent (represented by letter C). However, in the paradox, this permission implies further permission to do anything more on entering (e.g. stealing, represented by S), since the permission

---

[3] Like the discussion in [1], we also model the chicken game by express agents implicitly. The reason is that our two deontic concepts can be discussed without the explicit modalities regarding to multi-agents, because it is *symmetric* for agents to choose strategies in chicken game.

of entering the house and doing anything she wants is based on this consent. In fact, this free choice property does not hold in our proposal. The converse of (FC) is not valid in our framework. See the following model $M = (W, \mathcal{O}, V)$ for this invalidity:

- $W = \{a, b, c, d, e\}$;
- $\mathcal{O} = \{\{a\}, \{a, b\}, \{a, b, e\}\}$ for the ideality in the entrance example;
- $V(C) = \{a, b, e\}$, $V(E) = \{a, b, c\}$ and $V(S) = \{c, d\}$.

Observe that model M is a satisfactory model such that $\emptyset \notin \mathcal{O}$. In this case, we have $M, a, \{a, b\} \models C \bullet\!\!- \boxminus\neg E$. This is so because $\{a, b, e\}$ should not be considered. While, on the other hand, the fine-grained permission $C \bullet\!\!- \boxminus\neg(E \wedge S)$ does not hold at a within ideality $\{a, b\}$. At this time we have to consider the ideality $\{a, b, e\}$. But then it gives $[\![C]\!]_{\{a,b,e\}} = \{a, b, e\} \notin sub(\{a, b\})$, even if $\forall O \in \mathcal{O}_a$ that $[\![\neg(E \wedge S)]\!]_O \notin sub(\{a, b, e\})$. We thus can conclude with a permission to enter the other's place with her consent; but to have the further permission, as we argued, we need to check carefully whether the non-forbiddance of this permission is still governed under the given ideal condition.

6   Conclusion

We have presented a logic of forward and backward conditionals with a subset space semantics. The logic is close to Lewis's and yet distinct, and the backward conditional offers novel perspectives. We have shown strong connections to deontic reasoning. Our claim to interest is that of minimality: a logic with few modalities or quantifiers and models with literally nothing apart from a system of subsets.

We have not presented technical results for the logic, such as a complete axiomatization of the valid formulas or a decision procedure for the satisfiability problem. For topological semantics, even checking truth of a formula in a given model presents interesting algorithmic challenges. In fact, succinct representations of models is an important issue for applications in systems. These are important issues, and we do intend to elaborate on them elsewhere. Here we have maintained a focus on conceptual discussion and relation to deontic reasoning that might be of relevance to multi-agent systems. There are also ways of extending our logic to reason about multiple agents. Work in [25] gives us a hint.

While we have sketched applications to reasoning about norms, obligations and permissions, further investigation will be needed to determine the effectiveness of such reasoning in multi-agent systems. In this sense, our proposal is preliminary rather than definitive, but we hope that this line of investigation may open up wider applications for logics of action [17].

Acknowledgement. Huimin Dong is supported by the China Postdoctoral Science Foundation (Grant No. 2018M632494), the National Social Science Fund of China (Grant No. 18ZDA290), the National Science Centre of Poland (Grant No. UMO-2017/26/M/HS1/01092), and the Fundamental Research Funds for the Central Universities of China. Yì N. Wáng acknowledges funding support by the National Social Science Foundation of China (Grant No. 16CZX048, 18ZDA290).

A   Some Proofs of Proposition 3

Clause 1. We show this by giving a counter model. Consider $M = (\{w\}, \mathscr{O}, V)$ such that $\mathscr{O} = \{\emptyset, \{w\}\}$, $V(p) = \emptyset$ and $V(q) = \{w\}$. We show $M, w, \{w\} \not\models (p \bullet\!\!- q) \to (q \multimap p)$. It suffices to show that if

$$\text{for all } O' \in \mathscr{O}_w, \text{ if } M, w, O' \models q \text{ then } \llbracket p \rrbracket_{O'} \in \mathrm{sub}(\{w\}), \tag{1}$$

then

$$\text{for all } O' \in \mathscr{O}_w, \text{ if } \llbracket q \rrbracket_{O'} \in \mathrm{sub}(\{w\}) \text{ then } M, w, O' \models p. \tag{2}$$

Since there is only one open neighborhood of w. Clause (1) is equivalent to:

$$\text{if } M, w, \{w\} \models q, \text{then } \llbracket p \rrbracket_{\{w\}} \in \mathrm{sub}(\{w\}) \tag{3}$$

By definition, $M, w, \{w\} \models q \iff w \in V(q)$ which is true, and $\llbracket p \rrbracket_{\{w\}} = \emptyset \in \mathrm{sub}(\{w\})$ is also true. So clause (3) holds.

Similarly, clause (2) is equivalent to the following:

$$\text{if } \llbracket q \rrbracket_{\{w\}} \in \mathrm{sub}(\{w\}), \text{ then } M, w, \{w\} \models p. \tag{4}$$

While $\llbracket q \rrbracket_{\{w\}} = \{w\} \in \mathrm{sub}(\{w\})$ holds, $M, w, \{w\} \models p$ does not. So clause (4) does not hold. Which shows that the given model M is such that $M, w, \{w\} \not\models (p \bullet\!\!- q) \to (q \multimap p)$.

Clause 2. Consider the formula $\bot \multimap \bot$. Given a model $M = (W, \mathscr{O}, V)$, $w \in W$ and $O \in \mathscr{O}_w$, by definition,

$$
\begin{aligned}
M, w, O \models \bot \multimap \bot &\iff \text{for all } O' \in \mathscr{O}_w, \text{ if } \llbracket \bot \rrbracket_{O'} \in \mathrm{sub}(O) \text{ then } M, w, O' \models \bot \\
&\iff \text{for all } O' \in \mathscr{O}_w, \text{if } \emptyset \in \mathscr{O} \text{ then } M, w, O' \models \bot \\
&\iff \text{for all } O' \in \mathscr{O}_w, \emptyset \notin \mathscr{O}
\end{aligned}
$$

To find a counter model, all we need is to make the empty set an open in a model and make sure that there is an open neighborhood of a world w. A candidate of such a model is $(\{w\}, \{\emptyset, \{w\}\}, V)$, where the valuation V is arbitrary.

This shows that $\varphi \multimap \varphi$ is not valid in general, and further that $\alpha \multimap \alpha$ is not valid even when α is propositional.

Clause 5. Consider the fomrula $\top \bullet\!\!- \top$. Given a model $M = (W, \mathscr{O}, V)$, $w \in W$ and $O \in \mathscr{O}_w$, by definition,

$$
\begin{aligned}
M, w, O \models \top \bullet\!\!- \top &\iff \text{for all } O' \in \mathscr{O}_w, \text{ if } M, w, O' \models \top \text{ then } \llbracket \top \rrbracket_{O'} \in \mathrm{sub}(O) \\
&\iff \text{for all } O' \in \mathscr{O}_w, W \in \mathrm{sub}(O)
\end{aligned}
$$

This is clearly not valid. We can easily find a counterexample, as long as $W \notin \mathscr{O}$.

References

1. Anglberger, A.J., Gratzl, N., Roy, O.: Obligation, free choice, and the logic of weakest permissions. Rev. Symb. Logic **8**, 807–827 (2015)
2. Arlo-Costa, H., Egré, P., Rott, H.: The logic of conditionals. In: Zalta, E.N. (ed.) The Stanford Encyclopedia of Philosophy. Metaphysics Research Lab, Stanford University, Summer 2019 Edition (2019)
3. van Benthem, J.F.A.K.: Minimal deontic logics. Bull. Sect. Logic **8**(1), 36–41 (1979)
4. Chellas, B.F.: Modal Logic: An Introduction. Cambridge University Press, Cambridge (1980)
5. Dabrowski, A., Moss, L.S., Parikh, R.: Topological reasoning and the logic of knowledge. Ann. Pure Appl. Logic **78**(1–3), 73–110 (1996)
6. Dong, H., Roy, O.: Three deontic logics for rational agency in games. Stud. Logic **8**(4), 7–31 (2015)
7. Douven, I.: Abduction. In: Zalta, E.N. (ed.) The Stanford Encyclopedia of Philosophy. Metaphysics Research Lab, Stanford University, Summer 2017 Edition (2017)
8. Fraassen, B.C.: The logic of conditional obligation. J. Philos. Logic **1**(3), 417–438 (1972)
9. Gabbay, D., Horty, J., Parent, X., van der Meyden, R., van der Torre, L.: Handbook of Deontic Logic and Normative Systems. College Publication, London (2013)
10. Gargov, G., Passy, S., Tinchev, T.: Modal environment for boolean speculations. In: Skordev, D.G. (ed.) Mathematical Logic and Its Applications, pp. 253–263. Springer, Boston (1987). https://doi.org/10.1007/978-1-4613-0897-3_17
11. Gelati, J., Rotolo, A., Sartor, G., Governatori, G.: Normative autonomy and normative coordination: declarative power, representation, and mandate. Artif. Intell. Law **12**(1–2), 53–81 (2004)
12. Goldblatt, R.I.: Semantic analysis of orthologic. J. Philos. Logic **3**(1), 19–35 (1974). https://doi.org/10.1007/BF00652069
13. Governatori, G., Gelati, J., Rotolo, A., Sartor, G.: Actions, institutions, powers: preliminary notes. In: International Workshop on Regulated Agent-Based Social Systems: Theories and Applications, RASTA 2002, pp. 131–147. Springer, Heidelberg (2002)
14. Hansson, S.O.: The varieties of permissions. In: Gabbay, D., Horty, J., Parent, X., van der Meyden, R., van der Torre, L. (eds.) Handbook of Deontic Logic and Normative Systems, vol. 1. College Publication, London (2013)
15. Humberstone, I.L.: Inaccessible worlds. Notre Dame J. Formal Logic **24**(3), 346–352 (1983). https://doi.org/10.1305/ndjfl/1093870378
16. Lewis, D.: Counterfactuals. Blackwell Publishers, Oxford (1973)
17. Makinson, D.: On a fundamental problem of deontic logic. In: Norms, Logics and Information Systems. New Studies on Deontic Logic and Computer Science, pp. 29–54 (1999)
18. Moss, L.S., Parikh, R.: Topological reasoning and the logic of knowledge. In: Moses, Y. (ed.) Proceedings of the 4th Conference on Theoretical Aspects of Reasoning about Knowledge (TARK), Monterey, CA, pp. 95–105. Morgan Kaufmann, San Francisco, March 1992. Preliminary report
19. Pigozzi, G., Van Der Torre, L.: Multiagent deontic logic and its challenges from a normative systems perspective. Ifcolog J. Logics Appl. **4**, 2929–2993 (2017)
20. Ramsey, F.P.: General propositions and causality. In: Mellor, D.H. (ed.) F. P. Ramsey: Philosophical Papers. Cambridge University Press, Cambridge (1990)
21. Schelling, T.C.: The Strategy of Conflict. Harvard University Press, Cambridge (1980)
22. Tamminga, A.: Deontic logic for strategic games. Erkenntnis **78**(1), 183–200 (2013)
23. Tuzet, G.: Legal abductions. In: Legal Knowledge and Information Systems, pp. 41–49. IOS Press, Amsterdam (2003)

24. Vickers, S.: Topology via Logic. Cambridge University Press, New York (1989)
25. Wáng, Y.N., Ågotnes, T.: Multi-agent subset space logic. In: Proceedings of IJCAI, pp. 1155–1161 (2013)
26. Wooldridge, M.: An Introduction to MultiAgent Systems, 2nd edn. Wiley, Hoboken (2009)

Integrating CP-Nets in Reactive BDI Agents

Mostafa Mohajeri Parizi[1](✉), Giovanni Sileno[1](✉), and Tom van Engers[1,2](✉)

[1] Informatics Institute, University of Amsterdam, Amsterdam, The Netherlands
{m.mohajeriparizi,g.sileno,vanengers}@uva.nl
[2] Leibniz Institute, University of Amsterdam/TNO, Amsterdam, The Netherlands

Abstract. Computational agents based upon the belief-desire-intention (BDI) architecture generally use reactive rules to trigger the execution of plans. For various reasons, certain plans might be preferred over others at design time. Most BDI agents platforms use hard-coding these preferences in some form of the static ordering of the reactive rules, but keeping the preferential structure implicit limits script reuse and generalization. This paper proposes an approach to add qualitative preferences over adoption/avoidance of procedural goals into an agent script, building upon the well-known notation of conditional *ceteris paribus* preference networks (CP-nets). For effective execution, the procedural knowledge and the preferential structure of the agent are mapped in an off-line fashion into a new reactive agent script. This solution contrasts with recent proposals integrating preferences as a *rationale* in the decision making cycle, and so overriding the reactive nature of BDI agents.

Keywords: BDI agents · Conditional preferences · Procedural goals · Goal adoption/avoidance · CP-Nets · Reactive agents

1 Introduction

In decision-making and intelligent systems design, when there are multiple ways to achieve a certain goal, the best course of action is usually identified as the one that adheres at best to the user's (or users') preferences. Unexpectedly, current computational models of intentional agents, based upon *belief-desire-intention* (BDI) architectures (e.g. AgentSpeak(L)/Jason [4,21], 2APL/3APL [9,16], GOAL [15]) exhibit a treatment of preferences still relatively underdeveloped with respect to solutions explored in other AI fields like planning or decision systems. All these platforms encode preferences in some form of hard-coded ordering, e.g. of plans, to be used for plan selection. By doing so, the structure of preferences *underlying* such ordering remains implicit, thus limiting transparency and traceability of the choices taken by the modeler, as well as reusability and generalization of the agent scripts (e.g. modifying the preferential structure without modifying the procedural knowledge). Additionally, leaving preferences implicit is particularly problematic if one is targeting institutional design tasks: BDI agents provide a natural model to reproduce behaviours

© Springer Nature Switzerland AG 2019
M. Baldoni et al. (Eds.): PRIMA 2019, LNAI 11873, pp. 305–320, 2019.
https://doi.org/10.1007/978-3-030-33792-6_19

reported in an actual social system, but, without mapping the explicit preferences of their social referents, one cannot make considerations about to what extent a certain policy is affecting individuals.

For these reasons, this paper aims to start reducing the *preference specification gap* for BDI agents, by proposing an extension to the BDI architecture that makes preferences first-class citizens, both w.r.t. representational and computational dimensions. For a similar purpose, Visser et al. [26] have recently proposed a method to integrate preferences as a *rationale* in the decision-making cycle to guide the selection of an intention amongst possible options. However, because the agent looks at its script at execution time, their solution builds upon *reflection*, and so disrupts the reactive nature of BDI agents. In contrast, we propose here a method to *pre-process* (offline) some input procedural knowledge together with an input preferential structure in order to construct a prioritized script. For simplicity, in this paper we will focus only on *procedural goals* and propositional descriptions. In future work, we will consider extensions to first order logic descriptions and declarative goals (achievement and maintenance).

The paper is structured as follows. Section 2 provides an introduction to the BDI architecture and the execution model for reactive agents, an overview of relevant preference representation methods, and presents an extension/modification to the syntax of AgentSpeak(L) to integrate preferences based on CP-nets. Section 3 presents a method to pre-process given procedural knowledge and preferential structure into an agent script. Section 4 presents an example of application. Notes about further developments conclude the paper.

2 Preliminaries

2.1 BDI Architecture and Execution Model

BDI frameworks are usually described in terms of an *agent theory* and an *agent computational architecture* [12]. The agent theory usually refer to Bratman's theory of practical reasoning [7], describing the agent's cognitive state and reasoning process in terms of its *beliefs*, *desires* and *intentions*. Beliefs are the facts that the agent believes to be true in the environment. Desires capture the motivational dimension of the agent, typically in the more concrete form of *goals*, representing procedures/states that the agent wants to perform/achieve. Intentions are selected conducts (or *plans*) that the agent commits to (in order to advance its desires). The agent architecture varies depending on the platform. In Jason [4], for instance, it consists of: perception and actuation modules, a *belief base*, *intention stacks* and an *event queue*. The associated BDI execution model, reproducing the agent's reasoning cycle, can be summarized as follows:

1. observe the external world and update the internal state (perception);
2. update the event queue with perceptions and exogenous events;
3. select events from the event queue to commit to;
4. select plans from the plan library that are relevant to the selected event;
5. select an intended means amongst the applicable plans for instantiation;

6. push the intended means to an existing or a new intention stack;
7. select an intention stack and pull an intention, execute the next step of it;
8. if the step is about a primitive action, perform it, if about a sub-goal post it to the event queue.

As this description exemplifies, an essential feature of BDI architectures is the ability to instantiate plans that can: (a) react to specific situations, and (b) be invoked based on their purpose [22]. Consequently, the BDI execution model naturally relies on a *reactive* model of computation (cf. *event-based programming*), usually in the form of some type of *event-condition-action* (ECA) rules.

2.2 Goal-Plan Rules

A general definition of reactive rules for BDI execution models can be derived from the notion of *goal-plan rules*, i.e. *uninstantiated specifications of the means for achieving a goal* [22], capturing the procedural knowledge (*how-to*) of the agent. A goal-plan rule *pr* is a tuple $\langle e, c, p \rangle$, where:

- e is the *invocation condition*, i.e. the event that makes the rule *relevant*;
- c, the *context condition*, is a first-order formula over the agent's belief base, which makes the rule *applicable*;
- p, the *plan body*, consisting of a finite and possibly empty sequence of steps $[a_1, a_2, ..., a_n]$ where each a_i is either a *goal* (an invocation attempting to trigger a goal-plan rule), or a *primitive action*.

A goal-plan rule pr_i is an *option* or a *possibility* for achieving a goal-event e, if the invocation condition of pr_i matches with e, and the preconditions pr_i matches the current state of the world, as perceived or encoded in the agent's beliefs. In BDI implementations, the preference between these optional conducts is specified through static rankings assigned by the designer, typically via the ordering of the rules in the code.

Syntax. This paper will refer to a syntax close to that of AgentSpeak(L) [21], introducing a few extensions. If g is the name of a *higher-level action*[1], !g is a procedural goal (also action-goal or *want-to-do*, usually distinguished from declarative goals/state-goals, or *want-to-be*), that can be referenced to in a plan of action, and +!g denotes the goal-event, that acts as triggering event (invocation condition) initiating the commitment towards a plan aiming to perform it. As an example of code, consider:

```
+!g : c <= !a.
+!g <= !b.
```

---

[1] Higher-level actions are those that can be decomposed in lower-level actions, e.g. the higher-level action "booking a travel arrangement" may have "booking a flight" and "reserving a hotel" as lower-level actions.

The script means that if the triggering event +!g occurs, if c holds, the agent commits to a, otherwise (that is, c does not hold) the agent commits to b.[2]

For the method proposed here, we will need to refer to conditions concerning adoption and avoidance of certain goals, therefore we extend the previous syntax with new elements for the conditional part of rules: !g denotes that g is currently adopted and is *active* (i.e. present in the intention stack), and not !g states that g is *not active* (i.e. absent from the intention stack). Thus, the rule:

```
+!a : !g, not !h, c <= !b.
```

means that when the goal a is invoked, if g is in the intention stack, h is not in it, and condition c holds, then the agent adopts the goal b.

In the standard syntax, there is no unique identifier to distinguish goal-plan rules (although Jason offers some *labeling* construct). There is also no standard way to have direct access to the plan component of a rule. A possible solution to identify a specific plan without explicit labeling is to refer to the invocation condition of the associated rule alongside its position, e.g. with respect to other rules with the same invocation condition. Consider for instance:

```
+!pay <= !cash.
+!pay <= !credit.
```

Assuming that there is no other rule with the same invocation condition before, the two plans of cash and credit for the pay goal will be respectively denoted as !pay[0] and !pay[1]. For more clarity, to better separate goal-adoption from the treatment of primitive actions, we will not consider primitive actions as part of preferences (a primitive action a will be denoted as #a).

2.3 Goal-Plan Graph (Procedural Knowledge)

In the BDI literature, the goal-plan structure expressing the procedural knowledge of an agent is often represented as *and-or* decision trees (see e.g. [8,26]): sequences of sub-goals in each goal-plan rule form the "and" edges (in order to complete that plan, all of the steps should be completed), different goal-plan rules relevant for a goal are the "or" edges (possible plan choices for a given goal). However, presenting the goal-plan dependencies as a tree is a too strong simplification on the possible relations between goals and plans. Procedural knowledge of a BDI agent is often structured by the designer in a manner that plans can be re-used. For example, a pay goal can be a sub-goal of any plan concerning buying or reserving something. Further, a tree structure assumes one root goal, when in reality the procedural knowledge structure does not always start from one single goal. Besides, exogenous events may initiate a goal at any level in the goal-plan

---

[2] Note the backward sense of the arrow "<="; although counter-intuitive with respect to the semantics of production rules, it highlights the underlying backward chaining of instrumental reasoning (the agent commits to a because it aims to perform g), and consequently, it suggests a priority of evaluation between the rules (the first plan, if applicable, is preferred to the second).

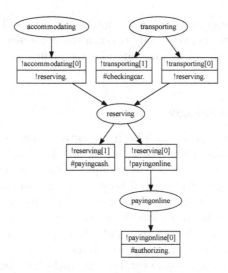

Fig. 1. Example of procedural knowledge illustrated in a goal-plan graph.

graph. This being said, we do assume different levels of granularity of goals and plans, i.e. that there exist higher-level goals/plans and lower-level goals/plans, in the spirit of *hierarchical task networks* (HTNs) [11]. For example, it is not sound having a plan about paying to contain the sub-goal of buying or a plan about preparing for a trip the sub-goal of going for a trip. This assumption is reflected in our representation disallowing loops and recursions in the goal-plan graph. With these constraints, the procedural knowledge of the agent can be modelled as a *directed acyclic graph* (DAG).

Example. Consider the simple script of an agent assisting the user to plan a holiday, e.g. to prepare travel and accommodating. Suppose that two plans are available for the travelling goal: flying and driving; for accommodating, only one: reserving a hotel; the driving plan only contains a primitive action (reminding of checking the car), but the flying plan has the sub-goal of reserving, which is shared with the accommodating plan, etc. The script would be written as:

```
+!travelling => !reserving.
+!travelling => #checking_car.
+!accommodating => !reserving.
+!reserving => !paying_online.
+!reserving => #checking_wallet.
+!paying_online => #authorizing.
```

The associated goal-plan graph is illustrated in Fig. 1 (goals are drawn with ellipses and plans with rectangles). Note how here we slightly modified the AgentSpeak(L) syntax ("=>" instead of "<="), to make clear that there is no priority of evaluation between these rules (see note 2). For simplicity, plans of this running example do not have any context conditions. This is not a limitation: because context conditions only concern the *applicability* of plans, but not their *preferability*, they can be integrated independently to the method that we will present.

2.4   Preference Languages

Several models of preferences have been presented in the computational literature, with various levels of granularity and expressiveness.[3]

The most straightforward *quantitative* approaches are based upon *utility theory* and *decision theory*, under which both planning and action selection problems have shown to be effectively expressed. Typically, by assigning a utility function to each action in each state, the agent/the planner system tries to *maximise* its utility by choosing actions that would result in higher total utility (including avoiding actions with negative utility, e.g. due to cost). The selected plan is called *policy* or *strategy*. Several recent works have investigated the integration of these types of preferences in a BDI architecture. In [10], the authors introduce a utility-based plan selection method triggered at run-time; a similar approach is followed in [8], but here plan selection depends on a given value system, including the case of possibly conflicting values. A hybrid quantitative method is provided by PDDL3 [13], an extension of the *planning domain definition language* (PDDL) [19]. PDDL3 preferences rely on *linear temporal logic* (LTL) over states of the environment. Although based on qualitative descriptions, these preferences are considered quantitative [2] because the valuation of each preference is expressed with a numerical value that corresponds to the number of violations of that preference. This valuation contributes to *preference aggregation strategies* in measuring the quality of a plan, alongside other plan attributes, e.g. resource usage.

While quantitative approaches bring clear advantages in non-deterministic environments or environments with a large state space, they also suffer from the non-trivial issue of translating user's preferences into utility functions. They do not directly support partial ordering and conditional preferences, which are the most natural constructs for humans to express preferences. This explains the existence of a family of *qualitative* proposals. An example of qualitative preference language is LPP [3], relying on first-order, linear temporal logic expressions and *situation calculus* to compute the event dynamics; aggregation is done through different strategy functions, including lexicographic orderings, but also numeric methods. In [25,26], LPP is used to specify preferences about properties of goals and resource usage, and this specification is used during the deliberation phase of a BDI agent.

Other preference models, as CP-nets (qualitative) [5] and GAI networks (quantitative) [14], are introduced specifically for taking into account dependencies and conditioning between preferences in terms of *compact representations* [20]. This is to address the problem of storing preferences in domains with a

---

[3] For a comprehensive overview (specifically in AI planning), see e.g. [6,17].

large number of features, separately from the problem of choosing from a set of alternative options. Whereas CP-nets have weak constraints, GAI networks build upon the assumption of *generalized additive independence*, and in doing so they enable computing the utility contribution of every single attribute/subset of attributes (they can be seen as the preferential counterpart of Bayesian networks). An additional interesting feature of both CP-nets and GAI-networks is the possibility to be illustrated as intuitive graphical models. To our knowledge, no work has yet attempted to embed these representational models in a BDI architecture. Because they rely on weakest assumptions, and they exhibit primarily a qualitative nature, this work will focus on CP-Nets.

CP-Nets. Conditional *ceteris paribus* preferences networks (CP-nets) are a compact representation of preferences in domains with finite *attributes of interest* [5]. An attribute of interest is an attribute in the world that the agent has some sort of preference over its possible values; in our example, *travelling* can be seen an attribute of interest, with possible values *driving* and *taking a flight*. CP-nets build upon the idea that most of the preferences people make explicit are expressed jointly with an implicit *ceteris paribus* ("all things being equal") assumption. For example, when people say "I prefer to fly rather than to drive", they do not mean at all costs and situations, but that they prefer to fly, all other things being equal to their current situation. CP-nets account also for *conditional preferences* between attributes and their values. An attribute A is said to be the parent of attribute B if preferences over B are conditional over values of A. An example of a preferential system could be "I prefer to go to a close location for holidays, and if I am going to a close location, I prefer to drive, but if I am going to a faraway location, I prefer to fly". Here preference over *location* is unconditional but the preference over *travelling* is conditional, so *location* is the parent of the *travelling* attribute; in practice, *location* is more important than *travelling*. In the graphical presentation of CP-nets, attributes A, B are seen as vertices, and, if A is a parent of B, there is an edge between two attributes A and B.

Syntax. Constraining our attention on procedural goals (*want-to-do*), the preferences we target are about *performance* or *omission* of *higher-order actions*. The attributes of interests for the CP-net are then the possible procedural goals of the agent. Each attribute has two possible values: (1) adoption of the goal, here denoted with the goal name "!g", (2) avoiding the goal, denoted as "not !g". A preference over performing an action g over omitting it in condition c can be written as a preference of adopting a (procedural) goal g over avoiding it in condition c:

!g > not !g : c.

In general, c might be an higher priority preferential attribute or a logical **true** in the case of an unconditional preference.

3   Prioritizing Procedural Knowledge with Preferences

Consider the unconditional preference "I prefer not to do any sort of travel (all the rest being equal)" and the conditional preference "If I am planning a travel, I prefer not to reserve anything". In the previous syntax, this becomes:

```
not !travelling > !travelling : true.
not !reserving > !reserving : !travelling.
```

In this case, the procedural dependency and preferential dependency map well together: in the procedural knowledge graph of the agent, travelling can only precede (i.e. is higher-order with respect to) reserving. At the time the agent is going to plan for reserving, it already knows whether it is reserving a travel by simply checking the presence of this goal in the intention stack. This is not true in the general case: the dependency between preferences may be inverse.

For instance, "I prefer not to pay online, but if I'm paying online, I prefer this to be for paying for a travel (i.e. instrumentally to a travelling goal). I also prefer not to be paying for a travel if it is not by paying online." This preferential structure is written as:

```
not !paying_online > !paying_online : true.
!travelling > not !travelling : !paying_online.
not !travelling > !travelling : not !paying_online.
```

As a procedural dependency, travelling precedes paying online, but as a preferential dependency, online payment is higher than travel. So at the time the agent is choosing to plan a travel, it has not started paying beforehand (either online or cash), that is, the goal of online payment is not yet adopted.

3.1   Plan Meta-data

To deal with this issue, we have considered four sets of *meta-data* for each goal-plan rule pr (and so for each plan p): (1) certain sub-goals as $CG(p)$, (2) possible sub-goals as $PG(p)$, (3) possible intents $PI(p)$ and (4) certain intents $CI(p)$. A certain sub-goal is a goal that will certainly be adopted in all refinements of a plan. A possible sub-goal is one that will possibly be adopted in some refinements of a plan. Possible intents of a plan are all the goals that at some point in their refinement (depending on context) may request the execution of the plan. Finally, we neglect the set of certain intents for a plan because a goal can be adopted for some exogenous event (e.g. an external request), hence, for any goal-plan rule, the only certain intent is the goal appearing in its invocation condition.

3.2   Calculating the Plan Meta-data

In order to calculate these sets, we draw on simple definitions from graph theory. The procedural knowledge is assumed to be an directed acyclic graph $G = \langle V, E \rangle$, where V is the set of vertices (goals and plans), and E the set of edges which either connect goals to plans (*relevant plans*) or plans to goals (*sub-goal*). The set

$r \subseteq V$ consists of root vertices (all goals that are never the sub-goal of any plan), and the set $l \subseteq V$ consists of the leaf vertices (plans that have no sub-goals). Being $v, v' \in V$ two vertices, we introduce three definitions:

- there is a *path* between v and v' is if there is a finite sequence of distinct edges that connect v to v'.
- v is said to *dominate* v' if all the paths from all members of r to v' in the graph pass through v; v is also said to be *dominator* of v'.
- v' is said to *post-dominate* v if all the paths from v to any member of l in the graph pass through v'; v' is also said to be *post-dominator* of v.

Let us assume two goals g and g' with $g \neq g'$ (e.g. !g1 and !g2) and denote with g_i and g'_j plans respectively for g and g' (e.g. !g1[i] and !g2[j]). The goal g is a *certain sub-goal* of a plan g'_i if g is the post-dominator of g'_i in the goal-plan graph (i.e. all paths from g'_i to a leaf node will visit g). A goal g is a *possible sub-goal* of g'_i if there is a path from g'_i to g and g is not a certain sub-goal of g'_i. A goal g is a *possible intent* of plan g'_i, if there is a path from g to g'_i in the goal-plan tree. By definition, because all g_i plans for a goal g have g as their single shared parent in the graph, then possible intents of these plans are always the same. Finally the only *certain intent* for each plan g_i is g itself.

For instance, w.r.t. our example, the possible intents of !reserving[0] are !accommodating and !travelling, that is, !reserving[0] can be executed while attempting to achieve either of these goals; !paying_online is a possible sub-goal for the plan !travelling[0], that is, based on the run-time environmental state and contextual conditions, adoption of !paying_online may or may not happen in the execution of !travelling[0], etc.

These four sets are mutually exclusive from each other. The set $CI(g_i)$ is mutually exclusive from other sets because $CI(g_i) = \{g\}$ and as a condition for a g' to be in $CG(g_i)$, $PG(g_i)$ or $PI(g_i)$, we have $g \neq g'$. The two sets $CG(g_i)$ and $PG(g_i)$ are mutually exclusive by definition, and $g' \in PG(g_i)$ if $g' \notin CG(g_i)$. Because the procedural graph is assumed to be a DAG, if there is a path from g to g'_i, there cannot be a path from g'_i to g, so we infer that $PI(g_i)$ is mutually exclusive from $CG(g_i)$ and $PG(g_i)$. We have then:

$$CG(g_i) \cap PG(g_i) \cap PI(g_i) \cap CI(g_i) = \emptyset$$

3.3 Rewriting the Agent Script

This section proposes a method to *embed* a given preferential structure into the procedural knowledge of the agent. Informally, the script is rewritten in a manner that the sequential priority between plans follows the explicit CP-net based specification provided by the modeler/programmer. Under the assumption that the preferential structure implied by the CP-net enables an effective *total ordering* of plans and the execution model of the agent dictates that plans are considered in a sequential manner (as in Jason/AgentSpeak(L)), more preferred goal-plan rules will be placed higher in the code. The resulting script is deterministic and keeps the reactivity of the agent intact as it only contains simple conditions on the intentional stack (in addition to contextual conditions).

In essence, the *preferability* of goal-plans is determined by the outcome associated with them. To find the best possible outcome of a goal-plan, the algorithm takes into account what will certainly follow that goal-plan (certain sub-goals), what may follow that goal-plan (possible sub-goals) and creates an outcome for each different run-time motivational contexts in which this goal-plan may be executed (possible intents).

Motivational Contexts. Prior to run-time, there is no certainty about the motivational context of the agent at the time of adopting a goal. To rectify this, we define the set $C(g)$ as the set of all *valid* combinations of the adoption/avoidance of goals present in $PI(g_i)$. The index i is omitted in $C(g)$ because all plans of a given goal share the same intents. Each member of $C(g)$ is representative of a possible motivational context that g may be adopted in. The "valid" qualification means that this combination can occur and this is deduced by the following simple rules. Given two goals $g', g'' \in PI(g_i)$:

- the adoption of g'' can occur together with that of g' if there is a path between them in the goal-plan graph;
- the adoption of g'' can occur together with the avoidance of g', iff g' is not a post-dominator of g'' and g' is not a dominator of g''.

Plan Outcomes. An *outcome o* is an assignment of values (adoption/avoidance) of the variables of W. If we define $Z \subseteq W$, either adoption or avoidance of all $z \in Z$ is present in o. An outcome is a partial outcome if $Z \subset W$ and a complete outcome if $Z = W$. For example, if $W = \{a, b, c\}$ then a possible complete outcome would be $\{!a, \text{not } !b, !c\}$. In order to find the preferential priorities between goal-plan rules, the motivational outcomes of each plan should be calculated. As $C(g)$ is the set of possible motivational contexts that a plan g_i may be executed in, we infer the outcome associated to each g_i in each $c \in C(g)$, from here on denoted as $o(g_i, c)$. To calculate the outcome $o(g_i, c)$, we follow the following steps:

1. add all elements of c;
2. add the adoption of all the values of $CG(g_i)$;
3. add the adoption of all the values of $CI(g_i)$;
4. add the avoidance of all variables that are not in other sets, i.e. all p such that $(p \in W) \wedge (p \notin (PG(g_i) \cup CG(g_i) \cup PI(g_i) \cup CI(g_i)))$.

The step 4 captures that all the goals that are not added in the other steps, are impossible to be adopted in the outcome of the plan and so they are considered avoided. Based on the definition of these steps and the mutual exclusion between these sets, after these steps, for each $w \in W$ (all goals) either adoption or avoidance of the w is present in $o(g_i, c)$, except the members of $PG(g_i)$. So o is a partial outcome if $PG(g_i) \neq \emptyset$. This reflects the fact that we can not be sure about the avoidance or adoption of a possible goal in a plan outcome.

Traditionally, an outcome is called *reachable* if an applicable goal-plan rule p exists such that all refinements of p will result in that outcome [27]. However, as observed in [18], this approach starts from a very pessimistic view, ignoring the fact that the agent itself (not an adversary) chooses which refinement to make, so instead of thinking what it might bring about in all refinements, we are interested in what is the best thing that can happen under some refinement. The best outcome here indicates the optimal outcome according to the preferences specified in the CP-net.

Optimal Outcome. To find the optimal complete outcome $o(g_i, c)$, we use the *forward sweep procedure* presented in [5]. Given the current partial outcome generated from the previous four steps, the method *sweeps* through the CP-net from top to bottom (i.e., from ancestors to descendants), setting each variable that is not present in partial outcome (i.e the members of $PG(g_i)$) to its most preferred valid value (adoption/avoidance) given the values of its parents. This procedure has been proven to return an optimal outcome given the partial outcome as constraint [5]. We only added the condition of validity, to ensure that an outcome can happen. By doing this, for each plan g_i of each goal g, we have a the set $C(g_i)$ representing the possible motivational contexts of g_i and for each $c \in C(g_i)$ we have exactly one optimal complete outcome, as $o(g_i, c)$.

Plan Priorities. At this point, we need to find a best-to-worst ordering between the outcomes of plans of each goal g for each condition $c \in C(g)$. As these are already complete outcomes with respect to the variables of W, we can easily use the *preferential comparison algorithm* presented in [5]. Under a certain condition $c \in C(g)$, given two outcomes $o(g_i, c)$ and $o(g_j, c)$ of two plans g_i and g_j so that $i \neq j$, we say g_i is preferred to g_j if $o(g_i, c)$ is preferred to $o(g_j, c)$, i.e. $g_i \succeq_c^g g_j$ iff $o(g_i, c) \succeq o(g_j, c)$.

Script Rewriting. After computing the $\succeq_c^g$ relation between all plans of each goal g, the script can be rewritten with respect to preferential structure. For all goals for which there is only one plan, no reordering is needed. For each goal g with more than one plan, if $C(g) = \emptyset$, only one ordering is needed and all plans of g are rewritten in the best-to-worst sequence according to $\succeq^g$, alongside their context condition. Otherwise if $C(g) \neq \emptyset$, for each $c \in C(g)$, first the condition over motivational context is written as a logical expression associated to c, encoded as the conjunction of all members of c. Then, same as before, all the plans of g are written in the best-to-worst sequence based on $\succeq_c^g$, possibly with their context condition.

4   Running Example

We illustrate the proposed method on a travel assistant agent, specified with the following preferences:

```
not !travelling > !travelling : true.
not !reserving > !reserving : !travelling.
!reserving > not !reserving : not !travelling.
```

```
!accommodating > not !accommodating : !reserving.
not !accommodating > !accommodating : not !reserving.
!paying_online > not !paying_online : !travelling.
not !paying_online > !paying_online : not !travelling.
```

Table 1. Example of plan meta-data

Plan	CG	PG	PI	CI
!travelling[0]	!reserving	!paying_online		!travelling
!travelling[1]				!travelling
!reserving[0]			!accommodating, !travelling	!reserving
!reserving[1]	!paying_online		!accommodating, !travelling	!reserving

The four sets of plan meta-data of the two goals *travelling* and *reserving* from the goal-plan graph of the agent are presented in Table 1. Other plans are omitted because the other goals have only one relevant plan, and then there is not need to rewrite their plans.

For both `travelling` plans, we have $PI(\cdot) = \emptyset$, and so $C(\cdot) = \emptyset$. We calculate the partial outcome based on the rules specified in Sect. 3.3:

$o(!travelling[0], true) =$
   $\{!travelling, !reserving, \; not \; !accommodating)$
$o(!travelling[1], true) =$
   $\{!travelling, \; not \; !reserving, not \; !accommodating, \; not \; !paying\_online)$

The outcome for $!travelling[1]$ is already complete. For $!travelling[0]$, based on the CP-net and the partial outcome, the most optimistic substitution for goal *paying_online* is the adoption of this goal, then the complete outcome will be

$o(!travelling[0], true) =$
   $\{!travelling, !reserving, \; not \; !accommodating, !paying\_online)$

Comparing these two outcomes with the *improving search* method shows that:

$$o(!travelling[1], true) \succeq o(!travelling[0], true)$$

which in turn gives that

$$!travelling[1] \succeq_{true} !travelling[0]$$

This means that, if the agent has to travel, the driving plan is always preferred and then should always be evaluated before for applicability. The *travelling* plans will be then rewritten as follows:

```
+!travelling <= #checkingcar.
+!travelling <= !reserving.
```

Next, for plans of the goal *reserving*, we have:

$$C(reserving) = \{\{!travelling, \; not \; !accommodating\},$$
$$\{not \; !travelling, \; not \; !accommodating\},$$
$$\{not \; !travelling, \; !accommodating\}\}$$

Considering the first element of $C(reserving)$, denoted as c_1, we have:

$$o(!reserving[0], c_1) =$$
$$\{!travelling, !reserving, \; not \; !accommodating, !paying\_online\}$$
$$o(!reserving[1], c_1) =$$
$$\{!travelling, !reserving, \; not \; !accommodating, \; not \; !paying\_online\}$$

Note that both outcomes are already complete: this is because the set PG is empty for both plans. Comparing these two outcomes we can see that:

$$o(!reserving[0], c_1) \succeq o(!reserving[1], c_1)$$

and then we have:

$$!reserving[0] \succeq_{c_1} !reserving[1])$$

This means that, at the point of reserving, if the agent has the intent of travelling but not the intent of accommodating, the plan with online payment is preferred to paying with cash and should be considered first. Finding the ordering for other motivational contexts c_2 and c_3, we will have:

$$!reserving[1] \succeq_{c_2} !reserving[0] \text{ and } !reserving[1] \succeq_{c_3} !reserving[0]$$

and because they result in an equivalent ordering, can be written as

$$!reserving[1] \succeq_{c_2 \vee c_3} !reserving[0]$$

To conclude, the *reserving* plans will be rewritten as follows:

```
+!reserving :
!travelling & not !accommodating
<= !paying_online.
<= #checkingwallet.

+!reserving :
(not !travelling & !accommodating) |
(not !travelling & not !accommodating)
<= #checkingwallet.
<= !paying_online.
```

To simplify the code, we omitted the repetition of the head of the rule for alternative plans associated with the same event/condition coupling, similarly to LightJason [1]. Additional simplifications of the contextual conditions may be obtained by boolean simplification and by considering the sequential evaluation of rules (see e.g. [24] for converting between *constraint-based* and *priority-based* rule-bases).

5   Conclusion and Further Developments

The paper presents an initial contribution towards the integration of the specification of qualitative conditional preferences, expressed as CP-nets, into a BDI agent script. This work focused merely on propositional logic and procedural goals (higher-order actions) and assumed an effective total-ordering on plans. Therefore, as a necessary step towards actual use, the proposal has to be extended in the near future to declarative goals (*achievement goals* and *maintenance goals*) and to *first-order logic* descriptions, and joint with an investigation on how to deal with conflicting partial ordering situations (e.g. forcing total ordering of plans at need calling for user's intervention). Additional investigation is also required for an analysis of the overall algorithmic complexity.

More in detail, for the extension to declarative goals, besides existing proposals in the MAS literature, we are investigating characterizations of *ought-to-do* and *ought-to-be* norms explored in deontic logic, and studies on the interactions between HTN (intuitively related to procedural goals) and STRIPS-like (intuitively related to achievement goals) representations. The core issue we are exploring at the moment concerns how to take into account side-effects, from first principles (primitive actions) to higher-order behavioural constructs, acknowledging that the aggregation of side-effects is non-trivial.

Further, in order to enable an extension to first-order logic, the preferential attitude towards propositional content (which, under a *ceteris paribus* assumption, captures a fully contextualized situation, albeit implicitly) has to be interpreted w.r.t. the internal objects of the proposition and this interpretation seems to bring different results depending on the specific decision-making context (that is, contextual conditions) in which the preference is evaluated; typically it modifies the selection of objects (i.e. in logic programming, it adds additional controls on the unification process), but in certain cases it might entail preparatory actions or sustain maintenance activities. For instance, "when you want to drink during winter, prefer to drink warm drinks rather than cold drinks"; then, if the agent doesn't have yet a drink, it is rational for him to choose a warm drink; but, if he knows already what he'll drink (respectively he is currently drinking), it is rational to attempt to make it warm (resp. keep it warm).

Said that, although the present contribution is a only a first step towards a generally applicable solution, the principle of aiming to a transformation compatible with the reactive nature of BDI agents is a novel technical contribution and sets an important precedent (a higher-level discussion on the separation of reflective from reactive components can be found in [23, Chap. 7]). Replacing reasoning functions usually implemented with reflective methods with reactive solutions is crucial for many application where computational efficiency is at stake, as for instance model execution for large-scale simulations. In principle, a similar approach could also be extended to other components of the BDI model for which certain authors resorted to reflective methods, like intent selection and event selection [28].

Acknowledgments. This paper results from work done within the NWO-funded project *Data Logistics for Logistics Data* (DL4LD, www.dl4ld.net), supported by the Dutch Top consortia for Knowledge and Innovation Institute for Advanced Logistics (TKI Dinalog, www.dinalog.nl) of the Ministry of Economy and Environment in The Netherlands and the *Commit-to-Data* initiative (commit2data.nl), and partly within the NWO-funded program VWDATA.

References

1. Aschermann, M., Dennisen, S., Kraus, P., Müller, J.P.: LightJason, a highly scalable and concurrent agent framework: overview and application. In: Proceedings of the 17th International Conference on Autonomous Agents and Multi-Agent Systems (AAMAS 2018), pp. 1794–1796 (2018)
2. Baier, J.A., McIlraith, S.A.: On domain-independent heuristics for planning with qualitative preferences. In: AAAI Spring Symposium: Logical Formalizations of Commonsense Reasoning, pp. 7–12 (2007)
3. Bienvenu, M., Fritz, C., McIlraith, S.A.: Planning with qualitative temporal preferences. In: Proceedings of the 10th International Conference on the Principles of Knowledge Representation and Reasoning (KR 2006), pp. 134–144 (2006)
4. Bordini, R.H., Hübner, J.F., Vieira, R.: *Jason* and the golden fleece of agent-oriented programming. In: Bordini, R.H., Dastani, M., Dix, J., El Fallah Seghrouchni, A. (eds.) Multi-Agent Programming. MSASSO, vol. 15, pp. 3–37. Springer, Boston, MA (2005). https://doi.org/10.1007/0-387-26350-0_1
5. Boutilier, C., Brafman, R.I., Domshlak, C., Hoos, H.H., Poole, D.: CP-nets: a tool for representing and reasoning with conditional ceteris paribus preference statements. J. Artif. Intell. Res. **21**, 135–191 (2004)
6. Brafman, R., Domshlak, C.: Preference handling - an introductory tutorial. AI Mag. **30**(1), 58 (2009)
7. Bratman, M.E.: Intention, Plans, and Practical Reason, vol. 10. Harvard University Press, Cambridge (1987)
8. Cranefield, S., Winikoff, M., Dignum, V., Dignum, F.: No pizza for you: value-based plan selection in BDI agents. In: Proceedings of the 26th International Joint Conference on Artificial Intelligence (IJCAI 2017), pp. 178–184 (2017)
9. Dastani, M.: 2APL: a practical agent programming language. Auton. Agent. Multi-Agent Syst. **16**(3), 214–248 (2008)
10. Deljoo, A., van Engers, T., Gommans, L., et al.: What is going on: utility-based plan selection in BDI agents. In: Proceedings of Workshops at the 31st AAAI Conference on Artificial Intelligence, pp. 711–718 (2017)
11. Erol, K., Hendler, J., Nau, D.S.: HTN planning: complexity and expressivity. In Proceedings of the 12th AAAI Conference on Artificial Intelligence, pp. 1123–1129 (1994)

12. Fisher, M., Bordini, R.H., Hirsch, B., Torroni, P.: Computational logics and agents: a road map of current technologies and future trends. Comput. Intell. **23**(1), 61–91 (2007)
13. Gerevini, A., Long, D.: Plan constraints and preferences in PDDL3. Technical report (2005)
14. Gonzales, C., Perny, P.: GAI networks for utility elicitation. In: Proceedings of the 9th International Conference on the Principles of Knowledge Representation and Reasoning (KR 2004), pp. 224–233 (2004)
15. Hindriks, K.V.: Programming rational agents in GOAL. In: El Fallah Seghrouchni, A., Dix, J., Dastani, M., Bordini, R.H. (eds.) Multi-Agent Programming, pp. 119–157. Springer, Boston, MA (2009). https://doi.org/10.1007/978-0-387-89299-3_4
16. Hoeve, E.T., Dastani, M.: 3APL platform. Master's thesis, University of Utrecht, The Netherlands (2003)
17. Jorge, A., McIlraith, S.A.: Planning with preferences. AI Mag. **29**(4), 25–36 (2008)
18. Marthi, B., Russell, S.J., Wolfe, J.: Angelic semantics for high-level actions. In: Proceedings of the 17th International Conference on Automated Planning and Scheduling, pp. 232–239 (2007)
19. McDermott, D., et al.: PDDL - the planning domain definition language. Technical report (1998)
20. Pigozzi, G., Tsoukiàs, A., Viappiani, P.: Preferences in artificial intelligence. Ann. Math. Artif. Intell. **77**(3–4), 361–401 (2016)
21. Rao, A.S.: AgentSpeak(L): BDI agents speak out in a logical computable language. In: Van de Velde, W., Perram, J.W. (eds.) MAAMAW 1996. LNCS, vol. 1038, pp. 42–55. Springer, Heidelberg (1996). https://doi.org/10.1007/BFb0031845
22. Rao, A.S., Georgeff, M.P.: BDI agents: from theory to practice. In: Proceedings of the First International Conference on Multi-Agent Systems (ICMAS 1995), pp. 312–319 (1995)
23. Sileno, G.: Aligning law and action. Ph.D. thesis, University of Amsterdam (2016)
24. Sileno, G., Boer, A., van Engers, T.: A constructivist approach to rule bases. In: Proceedings of the 7th International Conference on Agents and Artificial Intelligence (ICAART 2015) (2015)
25. Visser, S., Thangarajah, J., Harland, J.: Reasoning about preferences in intelligent agent systems. In: Proceedings of the International Joint Conference on Artificial Intelligence (IJCAI 2011), pp. 426–431 (2011)
26. Visser, S., Thangarajah, J., Harland, J., Dignum, F.: Preference-based reasoning in BDI agent systems. Auton. Agent. Multi-Agent Syst. **30**(2), 291–330 (2016)
27. Yang, Q.: Formalizing planning knowledge for hierarchical planning. Comput. Intell. **6**(1), 12–24 (1990)
28. Yao, Y., Logan, B.: Action-level intention selection for BDI agents. In: Proceedings of the 15th International Conference on Autonomous Agents and Multiagent Systems (AAMAS 2016), pp. 1227–1236 (2016)

SAT-Based Automated Mechanism Design for False-Name-Proof Facility Location

Nodoka Okada[1](✉), Taiki Todo[1,2], and Makoto Yokoo[1,2]

[1] Kyushu University, Fukuoka 819-0395, Japan
n-okada@agent.inf.kyushu-u.ac.jp, {todo,yokoo}@inf.kyushu-u.ac.jp
[2] RIKEN AIP, Tokyo, Japan

Abstract. In the literature of mechanism design, market mechanisms have been developed by professionals based on their experience. The concept of automated mechanism design (AMD), initiated by Sandholm (2002), is a ground-breaking computer-aided framework to develop market mechanisms. In this paper, we apply a very recent AMD approach based on Boolean Satisfiability (SAT) to the mechanism design of false-name-proof facility location. We first provide a general theoretical characteristic of false-name-proof mechanisms, which enables a quite compact representation of target mechanisms. Our approach successfully reproduces several known results in the literature on false-name-proof facility locations over discrete structures. Furthermore, some unknown mechanisms are discovered for locating a public good on a 2-by-2 grid, and an impossibility result is revealed for locating a public bad, with an additional mild assumption, on a 2-by-3 grid. Finally, we demonstrate the extendability of our approach, by providing a new false-name-proof mechanism for a slightly modified problem of locating a public good.

Keywords: Automated mechanism design · Boolean Satisfiability · SAT solver · Facility location · False-name-proofness

1 Introduction

Mechanism design, which is a well-known research direction in the literature of microeconomics, has been widely studied in recent years at the intersection of AI, theoretical computer science, and economics. The main goal of mechanism design is to develop (market) *mechanisms*, defined as mapping from agents' reports to a social outcome, so that some incentive property (and possibly with some objective function) is fulfilled such as strategy-proofness and/or false-name-proofness. Strategy-proofness requires that for each agent, reporting her true preference truthfully is a dominant strategy, i.e., a best response to every possible profile of the actions of the other agents. False-name-proofness refines strategy-proofness, which requires that using only a single (true) identity and reporting her true preference is a dominant strategy, even though adding arbitrarily many fake

© Springer Nature Switzerland AG 2019
M. Baldoni et al. (Eds.): PRIMA 2019, LNAI 11873, pp. 321–337, 2019.
https://doi.org/10.1007/978-3-030-33792-6_20

identities is possible. The application domain of mechanism design covers various problems in economics, from combinatorial auction to matching, exchange, and *facility location*.

Facility location is a mechanism design problem as well as a special case of voting. In the facility location problem studied in this paper, given a discrete graph, a mechanism builds a public good (or a public bad) on a vertex, based on the profile of agents' preferences. We also assume that agents' preferences are *distance-based, single-peaked* (or single-dipped); each agent's preference is characterized by her ideal vertex on the graph, where having a public good that is closer to (or a public bad further from) the ideal vertex is better for her. We focus on locating a facility in the *Pareto efficient* manner, which is a well-motivated requirement in the literature of economics. Given a profile of agents' preferences and a location returned by a Pareto efficient mechanism, there is no other vertex that is weakly better for all the agents and strictly better for at least one agent. See Sect. 3 for the formal definition of these preferences and Pareto efficiency.

Automated mechanism design (AMD), initiated by Sandholm (2002), is a ground-breaking computer-aided framework for developing market mechanisms. The task of developing/analyzing mechanisms usually requires deep knowledge of mathematics and game theory, which inhibits third parties who want to run new systems for their own problem that are generally far more complicated than those in textbooks from taking into account the incentives of potential participants. In AMD, on the other hand, the third parties simply list all the incentive conditions and the objective function, and input them to an AMD framework (solver). AMD then returns a complete description of a mechanism (if any) that maximizes the objective with respect to the given conditions.

The main objective of this paper is to develop, for facility location, an AMD framework that automatically provides deterministic, false-name-proof, and Pareto efficient facility location mechanisms. One of our main interests is focused on the existence of such mechanisms for a given underlying structure and a given domain of agents' preferences, not on the maximization of a given objective function. We therefore develop an AMD framework using a *Boolean Satisfiability* (SAT) solver, which is identical to the work Brandt et al. [11] did on voting. SAT is one of the most well-known NP-complete problems in the literature of computer science. A SAT instance, which is defined by a Boolean formula, is called 'satisfiable' if there is an assignment (also known as a *model*) for the Boolean variables that makes the formula true, and 'unsatisfiable' otherwise. Our SAT-based AMD framework takes the required conditions represented in a formula as input and returns 'satisfiable' if and only if there exists a mechanism that meets all the conditions.

The first contribution of this paper is on the theory side of the false-name-proof facility location. A naïve SAT encoding of the facility location problem needs to have a variable for each possible profile of the agents' preferences and each Pareto efficient vertex for the profile, resulting in exponentially many variables in terms of the number of agents. Since the property of false-name-proofness deals with an arbitrary number of fake identities, the size of the formula for designing false-name-proof mechanisms is unbounded. In this paper, however, we first provide critical theoretical guarantee on false-name-proof and Pareto efficient mechanisms. As long as we are interested only in the utility of each agent and not in the exact outcome returned by a mechanism, we can focus without loss of generality on a specific form of false-name-proof mechanisms, which makes the set of variables independent from the number of agents (Theorem 1). More specifically, such a mechanism can be defined as a mapping from a set of vertices that is ideal for at least one agent to the location of a facility. Based on this compact representation, the size of our SAT encoding is bounded.

We then show the validity, novelty, and applicability of our SAT-based AMD framework. For validity, we reproduce some known results in the literature of false-name-proof facility location, especially the existence for a public good on cycle graphs of length at most five, and the non-existence for a public good on cycle graphs of length at least six. For novelty, we show that our framework automatically finds unknown mechanisms for a public good (and a public bad) on a 2-by-2 grid, or equally, on a cycle graph of length four. For applicability, we find a new impossibility result by introducing an additional fairness property called *ontoness* as a clause, which requires that a facility be located at each vertex for at least one profile. Our new finding is that, for a 2-by-3 grid, no mechanism simultaneously satisfies false-name-proofness, Pareto efficiency, and ontoness for locating a public bad.

We also demonstrate the extendability of our framework by solving a slightly modified facility location. We focus on a cycle graph of length six, and assume that a specific vertex is *trusted*, meaning that any agent who considers it her ideal vertex does not act strategically and only reports her true preference using one identity. For example, such a situation may occur when a steering committee is deciding a time-slot for a faculty meeting on a day, where the committee has its own ideal slot, a.k.a., a status-quo solution. If a committee member also attends the faculty meeting, her ideal slot must be the status-quo, while it remains possible that she does not join the meeting. The status-quo corresponds to the trusted vertex in the modified facility location. Our framework identifies that there is an appropriate mechanism for this problem, which is in contrast to the impossibility explained in the previous paragraph.

The following is the organization of this paper. Section 2 describes previous work. Section 3 defines necessary notations and technical terms. In Sect. 4, the theoretical guarantee for a compact representation of false-name-proof and Pareto efficient mechanisms is presented. Section 5 explains the actual compact encoding for facility location. Section 6 reveals the validity, novelty, and applicability of our approach by presenting the known results in the literature that are automatically reproduced, some false-name-proof and Pareto efficient mechanisms that are newly found, and an impossibility result with an additional requirement. Section 7 reveals the extendability of our framework, by presenting a slightly modified facility location problem, for which our framework also returns a new mechanism. Section 8 overviews possible future directions.

2   Related Works

In recent years, the idea of AMD has been extended to various domains, with different AI tools. Sandholm's pioneering AMD paper [28] used the technique of mixed integer linear programming to represent combinatorial auction problems and solved them by an optimization package called CPLEX. Sandholm and Likhodedov [29] extended AMD to handle continuous bids. Albert et al. [1] is another recent extension of AMD, which relaxed an assumption of Cremer-McLean [13]. Albert et al. [2] further extended AMD for auctions by allowing some uncertainty on the distributions of bidders' types. Narasimhan et al. [23] used machine learning techniques to automatically design social choice and matching mechanisms. Shen et al. [30] used deep neural networks to automatically design auction mechanisms.

Computer-aided proof and verification are also promising directions, where some papers considered economics-related problems; for detail, please see Kerber et al. [18] and Geist and Peters [17]. In particular, SAT solvers have been widely applied to voting problems. Brandt et al. [11] obtained some impossibility theorems for voting where agents' preferences contain ties. Brandt et al. [10] reproduced Arrow's no-show paradox and showed a tight bound of the number of agents so that it could occur. Based on a SAT solver, Brandt and Geist [9] showed that no Pareto efficient and majoritarian mechanism satisfies a slightly modified version of strategy-proofness for multi-winner voting. Brandl et al. [8] further analyzed multi-winner voting with strategic abstention, where their proofs for impossibilities were automatically generated based on a minimal unsatisfiable set (MUS) of conditions in a SAT formula. Barthe et al. [7] used a programming language called HOARe2 to automatically provide a proof of some property for a given mechanism.

In traditional economic literature, the facility location problem has been studied on a continuous line, rather than discrete structures. Moulin [22] proposed generalized median voter schemes, which are the only deterministic, strategy-proof, Pareto efficient and anonymous mechanisms. Procaccia and Tennenholtz [26] proposed a general framework of approximate mechanism design, which evaluates the worst case performance of strategy-proof mechanisms from the perspective of competitive ratio. Some other researches also considered the location on grids [15,32] and cycles [4,5,14], while all these papers only focused on strategy-proof facility location.

Over the last decade, false-name-proofness has also been scrutinized in various mechanism design problems [6,33,36,37] as an incentive property for such open and anonymous environments as the internet. Bu [12] clarified a connection between false-name-proofness and population monotonicity in general social choice. Todo et al. [34] provided a complete characterization of false-name-proof and Pareto efficient mechanisms for the facility location problem with single-peaked preferences on a continuous line. Lesca et al. [20] also addressed false-name-proof mechanisms that are associated with monetary compensation. Sonoda et al. [31] considered the case of locating two homogeneous facilities. Ono et al. [25] studied discrete structures, while they focused on randomized mechanisms. Nehama et al. [24] clarified the network structures under which false-name-proof and Pareto efficient mechanisms exist for single-peaked preferences.

Locating a public bad has also been widely studied in both economics and computer science fields. Manjunath [21] characterized strategy-proof mechanisms on an interval. Lahiri et al. [19] studied a model for locating two public bads. Both Feigenbaum and Sethuraman [16] and Alcalde-Unzu and Vorsatz [3] considered cases where single-peaked and single-dipped preferences coexist. Roy and Storken [27] investigated the preference domain of voting for which strategy-proof, unanimous, and non-dictatorial mechanisms exist. Nevertheless, all of these works just focused on truthful mechanisms. To the best of our knowledge, this paper is the very first work on false-name-proof facility location with single-dipped preferences.

3 Preliminaries

In this section, we describe our model of the facility location problem. Let $\Gamma :=$ (V, E) be an undirected, connected graph, defined by the set V of vertices and the set E of edges. In particular, a cycle graph of length k is denoted as C_k. Agents' preferences are determined based on a distance function $d : V^2 \to \mathbb{N}_{\geq 0}$, such that for any $v, w \in V$, $d(v, w) := \#\{e \in E | e \in s(v, w)\}$, where $s(v, w)$ is the shortest path between v and w.

Since we consider false-name manipulations, we need to define both *potential* agents/identities and *participating* agents. Let $\mathcal{N}$ be the set of potential agents, and let $N \subseteq \mathcal{N}$ be a set of participating agents. Each agent $i \in N$ has a *type* $\theta_i \in V$. When agent i has type θ_i, agent i is said to be *located on* vertex θ_i. Let $\theta := (\theta_i)_{i \in N} \in V^{|N|}$ denote a profile of the agents' types, and let $\theta_{-i} := (\theta_{i'})_{i' \neq i}$ denote the profile without i's. Given θ, let $I(\theta) \subseteq V$ be a set of the vertices on which at least one agent is located, i.e., $I(\theta) := \bigcup_{i \in N} \theta_i$. Given θ and $v \in I(\theta)$, let θ_{-v} be a profile obtained by removing all the agents at the vertex v from θ. By definition, $I(\theta_{-v}) = I(\theta) \setminus \{v\}$.

Given Γ and $v \in V$, let $\succsim_v$ be the preference of the agent located on vertex v over the set V of outcomes, where $\succ_v$ and $\sim_v$ indicate the strict and indifferent parts of $\succsim_v$, respectively. A preference $\succsim_v$ is *single-peaked* (resp. *single-dipped*) under Γ if, for any $w, x \in V$, $w \succ_v x$ if and only if $d(v, w) < d(v, x)$ (resp. $d(v, w) > d(v, x)$), and $w \sim_v x$ if and only if $d(v, w) = d(v, x)$. That is, an agent located on v strictly prefers outcome w, which is strictly closer to (resp. farther from) v than other outcome x, and is indifferent between these outcomes when they are the same distance from v. By definition, for each possible type θ_i, the single-peaked (resp. single-dipped) preference is unique.

A (deterministic) mechanism is a mapping from the set of possible profiles to the set of vertices. Since each agent might pretend to be multiple agents in our model, a mechanism must be defined for different-sized profiles. To describe this feature, we define a mechanisms $f = (f_N)_{N \subseteq \mathcal{N}}$ as a family of functions, where each f_N is a mapping from $V^{|N|}$ to V. When a set N of agents participates,

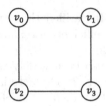

Fig. 1. 2-by-2 grid

the mechanisms f uses function f_N to determine the outcome. The function f_N takes profile θ of types jointly reported by N as an input, and returns $f_N(\theta)$ as an outcome. We denote f_N as f if it is clear from the context. We further assume that a mechanism f is anonymous, i.e., for any input θ and its permutation θ', $f(\theta') = f(\theta)$ holds.

We are now ready to define the two desirable properties of mechanisms: *false-name-proofness* and *Pareto efficiency*.

Definition 1. *A mechanism f is* false-name-proof *if for any N, θ, $i \in N$, $\theta_i \in V$, $\theta_i' \in V$, $\Phi_i \subseteq \mathcal{N}\backslash N$, and $\theta_{\Phi_i} \in V^{|\Phi_i|}$, it holds that $f(\theta) \succsim_{\theta_i} f(\theta_i', \theta_{\Phi_i}, \theta_{-i})$.*

The set Φ_i indicates the set of identities added by i for the manipulation. The property coincides with the canonical *strategy-proofness* when $\Phi_i = \emptyset$, i.e., agent i only uses one identity.

Definition 2. *An outcome $v \in V$ Pareto dominates $w \in V$ under θ if $v \succsim_{\theta_i} w$ for all $i \in N$ and $v \succ_{\theta_j} w$ for some $j \in N$. A mechanism f is* Pareto efficient *(PE) if for any N and θ, no outcome $v \in V$ Pareto dominates $f(\theta)$.*

Given θ, let $\mathrm{PE}(\theta) \subseteq V$ indicate the set of all the outcomes that are not Pareto dominated by any outcome.

4   Problem Reduction

In this section, we first provide a useful theorem that enables us to focus on a specific class of false-name-proof and Pareto efficient mechanisms. In words, we can focus on mechanisms that do not count the number of agents located on each vertex; they only care about whether at least one agent is located on each vertex. Due to this characteristic, the size of our SAT encoding can be drastically reduced. The description of a mechanism is simplified from a family of mappings $f = (f_N)_{N \subseteq \mathcal{N}}$, where each mapping $f_N : V^{|N|} \to V$, to a single mapping $f : 2^V \to V$.

We first formally define the characteristic of false-name-proof mechanisms.

Definition 3 (Ignoring Duplicate Ballots (IDB)). *A mechanism is said to be* ignoring duplicate ballots *(or satisfies IDB) if for any pair θ, θ', $I(\theta) = I(\theta')$ implies $f(\theta) = f(\theta')$.*

Example 1. Consider locating a public good (or a public bad) on a 2-by-2 grid (Fig. 1). Let $V = \{v_0, v_1, v_2, v_3\}$. Consider the following two mechanisms. For a given profile, the first mechanism checks the Pareto efficiency of each vertex in the order $v_0 \to v_3 \to v_1 \to v_2$ and locates the facility at the first Pareto efficient vertex. The second mechanism is a slight modification. For any profile θ such that $I(\theta) = \{v_1, v_2\}$, if $\#\{i \in N \mid \theta_i = v_1\} > \#\{i \in N \mid \theta_i = v_2\}$, it locates the facility at v_0; otherwise it locates the facility at v_3. For all the other profiles, it works as same as the first mechanism.

The former obviously satisfies IDB, since it does not count the number of agents at all. On the other hand, the latter does not satisfy IDB. For example, it returns v_0 for profile $\theta = (v_1, v_1, v_2)$, and v_3 for profile $\theta' = (v_1, v_2, v_2)$, where $I(\theta) = I(\theta') = \{v_1, v_2\}$.

The following theorem shows that, regardless whether the preference domain is single-peaked or single-dipped, focusing on mechanisms that satisfy IDB is without loss of generality, if we only consider agents' utilities under false-name-proof and Pareto efficient mechanisms.

Theorem 1. *Assume there exists a mechanism f that satisfies both false-name-proofness and Pareto efficiency but not satisfy IDB. Then, there also exists a mechanism f' that satisfies false-name-proofness, Pareto efficiency, and IDB simultaneously, and*

$$\forall \theta, \forall i \in N, f(\theta) \sim_{\theta_i} f'(\theta)$$

holds, regardless whether agents' preferences are single-peaked or single-dipped,

Proof. Since f violates IDB, there is a pair of profiles, θ and θ', such that

$$[I(\theta) = I(\theta')] \wedge [f(\theta) \nsim_{\theta_i} f(\theta')].$$

For any such pair θ and θ', the lemma below implies that

$$\forall v \in I(\theta), f(\theta) \sim_{\theta_i} f(\theta').$$

Therefore, we can easily construct a mechanism f' by switching the outcome for θ' as $f(\theta') := f(\theta)$, in which the utility does not change for every agent at any vertex.   □

Lemma 1. *Let Γ be an arbitrary graph. Assume that there is a false-name-proof and Pareto efficient mechanism f for Γ. Then, for any θ and any θ' such that $I(\theta') = I(\theta)$, it must be the case that*

$$\forall v \in I(\theta), f(\theta) \sim_v f(\theta'),$$

regardless whether agents' preferences are single-peaked or single-dipped.

Proof. Assume for the sake of contradiction that for some pair θ and θ' such that $I(\theta') = I(\theta)$ and some $v \in I(\theta)$, it holds that

$$f(\theta) \nsim_v f(\theta').$$

This implies that $f(\theta) \neq f(\theta')$.

Consider the profile $\theta'' := I(\theta)$, i.e., there is no duplication on any vertex in the set $I(\theta)$ of the vertices. By definition, θ'' is a subset of the profile of both θ and θ'. In other words, when the true profile is given as θ'', both θ and θ' are reachable by a manipulation of any agent.

Since $f(\theta) \neq f(\theta')$ holds, $f(\theta) \neq f(\theta'')$ or $f(\theta') \neq f(\theta'')$ holds. Without loss of generality, assume that $f(\theta) \neq f(\theta'')$. Since f is Pareto efficient and $\mathrm{PE}(\theta) = \mathrm{PE}(\theta'')$, there exists at least one vertex $u \in I(\theta)$, which may or may not be equal to v, such that $f(\theta) \succ_u f(\theta'')$. Since the agent at vertex u can manipulate and make the situation identical to profile θ, the mechanism violates false-name-proofness.   □

Applying Theorem 1 to Example 1, we can obtain the first mechanism from the second one by the procedure presented in the proof. Both the theorem and the lemma do not assume any specific structure of the underlying graph. Therefore, although we will focus on paths, hypergrids, and cycles in this paper, the conclusion of the theorem remains valid for any type of graphs like those considered by Nehama et al. [24].

Furthermore, most analysis of facility location mechanisms from the perspective of algorithmic mechanism design only consider agents' utilities, such as the social cost and the maximum cost [26]. Thus, focusing on mechanisms that satisfy IDM does not prevent such analysis.

Note that the theorem ignores any other information available to mechanism designers. In practice, however, possible situations can be found where the vertices in a given graph are not symmetric. For example, a mechanism designer may have her own preference among vertices, or there are opening costs of facility that are non-uniform among vertices. Even for such cases, we can slightly modify our SAT encoding so that the preferred vertex has a higher priority.

5   Compact SAT Encoding

Due to Theorem 1, we focus on finding deterministic mechanisms that satisfy IDB, which maps a subset of vertices into a vertex; formally $f : 2^V \to V$. We create an input file for a SAT solver by following the definition of the DIMACS CNF format. We first define the set of Boolean variables in the formula, and implement each condition as a clause. Our SAT-based AMD framework then returns 'satisfiable' if and only if there exists such an appropriate mechanism, and the assignment (model) of the Boolean values to the variables fully explains the behavior of the obtained mechanism.

Here we show how each property is implemented as a clause. At the end of this section, we also demonstrate the SAT encoding for false-name-proof facility location for a 2-by-2 grid.

5.1   Variables

In our SAT encoding, a Boolean variable $c_{S,v}$ is defined for a given set $S \in 2^V \setminus \emptyset$ of the vertices and a specific vertex $v \in \mathrm{PE}(S)$, where $\mathrm{PE}(S)$ indicates the set of Pareto efficient vertices when reported profile θ satisfies $I(\theta) = S$. A TRUE assignment to a variable $c_{S,v}$ means that the vertex v is chosen for the input S, and a FALSE assignment means that v is not chosen for S.

5.2 Constraints for Feasibility

Now we are ready to define the clauses of the formula. We first define those that guarantee the feasibility of a mechanism; i.e., a mechanism is a well-defined and single-valued. Specifically, for each input S, exactly one outcome v is returned.

Formally, we add the following two kinds of clauses. The first ones are for guaranteeing that the mechanism is well-defined, so that it returns at least one outcome for any given input S:

$$\forall S \in 2^V \setminus \emptyset, \quad \bigvee_{v \in \mathrm{PE}(S)} c_{S,v}, \tag{1}$$

and the second ones are for guaranteeing that the mechanism is single-valued, so that for each input S it returns at most one outcome:

$$\forall S \in 2^V \setminus \emptyset, \forall u, v \in \mathrm{PE}(S), \neg c_{S,u} \vee \neg c_{S,v}. \tag{2}$$

5.3 Constraints for False-Name-Proofness

Finally and most importantly, we define the clauses for false-name-proofness. Each clause that we add here indicates that, for any set S of vertices, for any vertex $u \in \mathrm{PE}(S)$ that is chosen as the outcome, for any manipulator at vertex $m \in S$, and for any set T of vertices after m arbitrarily chose her manipulation, it holds that any outcome v that is strictly better than u for the manipulator must not be realized.

To implement this property, it is useful to first define the set of *strictly better* outcomes for each vertex u and each vertex m at which a manipulator is located. Let $B(u, m) \subseteq V$ be the set of such strictly better outcomes:

$$B(u, m) := \{v \in V \mid v \succ_m u\}.$$

Let $R(S, m) \subseteq 2^V \setminus \emptyset$ be the set of *reachable profiles*, i.e., the sets of vertices to which the manipulator can make the situation identical from the current profile S. The possible manipulations include both preference misreporting using a single (true) identity and false-name-manipulations using multiple fake identities. Basically a reachable profile from S is a superset of S. If there is no agent (except the manipulator) located at m, a preference misreport can make the situation identical to $S \setminus \{m\}$. Furthermore, the identical profile S can be ignored, since the conditions are added by assuming that an outcome for input S is fixed to u. Therefore, the set of reachable profiles is formalized as follows:

$$R(S, m) := \{S' \in 2^V \mid [S' \neq S] \wedge [S' \supseteq (S \setminus \{m\})]\}$$

We are now ready to define the conditions for false-name-proofness using the above notations as a set of clauses.

$$\forall S \in 2^V, \forall u \in \mathrm{PE}(S), \forall m \in S, \forall T \in R(S, m), \forall v \in \mathrm{PE}(T) \cap B(u, m), \neg c_{S,u} \vee \neg c_{T,v}.$$

5.4 Example of SAT Encoding for 2-by-2 Grid

Let us demonstrate how a CNF file can be created, for a 2-by-2 grid (see Example 1), whose vertices are given as v_0, v_1, v_2, and v_3. For notation simplicity, we only write the indices of vertices, instead of their names, as $c_{123,1}$ to denote $c_{\{v_1,v_2,v_3\},v_1}$. First, we compute the set PE(S) of the Pareto efficient outcomes for each input S, and define the set of variables:

$$c_{0,0}, c_{1,1}, c_{2,2}, c_{3,3},$$

$$c_{01,0}, c_{01,1}, c_{02,0}, c_{02,2}, c_{03,0}, c_{03,1}, c_{03,2}, c_{03,3},$$

$$c_{12,0}, c_{12,1}, c_{12,2}, c_{12,3}, c_{13,1}, c_{13,3}, c_{23,2}, c_{23,3},$$

$$c_{012,0}, c_{012,1}, c_{012,2}, c_{013,0}, c_{013,1}, c_{013,3},$$

$$c_{023,0}, c_{023,2}, c_{023,3}, c_{123,1}, c_{123,2}, c_{123,3},$$

$$c_{0123,0}, c_{0123,1}, c_{0123,2}, c_{0123,3}.$$

We then define the feasibility constraints. For example, for the input $S = \{v_0, v_3\}$, the clause for well-definedness is

$$c_{03,0} \vee c_{03,1} \vee c_{03,2} \vee c_{03,3},$$

and the clauses for single-valuedness are

$$\neg c_{03,0} \vee \neg c_{03,1},$$
$$\neg c_{03,0} \vee \neg c_{03,2},$$
$$\neg c_{03,0} \vee \neg c_{03,3},$$
$$\neg c_{03,1} \vee \neg c_{03,2},$$
$$\vdots$$

We finally add the constraints as clauses. For example, let $S = \{v_1, v_2, v_3\}$ be the original profile, and let $m = v_1$ be the vertex where the manipulator is located. Then, for each vertex $u \in$ PE(S) $= \{v_1, v_2, v_3\}$, the set $B(u, v)$ of strictly better outcomes are:

$$B(v_1, v_1) = \emptyset$$
$$B(v_2, v_1) = \{v_0, v_1, v_3\}, B(v_3, v_1) = \{v_1\}.$$

Also, the set of reachable profiles from the above S by a manipulation of the manipulator at m is:

$$R(\{v_1, v_2, v_3\}, v_1) = \{\{v_2, v_3\}, \{v_0, v_2, v_3\}, \{v_0, v_1, v_2, v_3\}\}.$$

Thus, for $S = \{v_1, v_2, v_3\}$ and $m = v_1$, the clauses to be added for false-name-proofness are:

$$\neg c_{123,2} \vee \neg c_{23,3},$$
$$\neg c_{123,2} \vee \neg c_{023,0},$$
$$\neg c_{123,2} \vee \neg c_{023,3},$$
$$\neg c_{123,2} \vee \neg c_{0123,0},$$
$$\neg c_{123,2} \vee \neg c_{0123,1},$$
$$\neg c_{123,2} \vee \neg c_{0123,3},$$
$$\neg c_{123,3} \vee \neg c_{0123,1}.$$

Note that $\neg c_{123,1}$ is ignored as a first literal for the manipulator at v_1, since it corresponds to her ideal outcome. Finally we obtain 36 variables and 229 clauses for this problem on a 2-by-2 grid.

6   Obtained Results

We applied our SAT-based AMD framework to various problems of false-name-proof facility location. In this section three kinds of results are present. First, we successfully regenerate the existence/inexistence theorem on cycle graphs, demonstrating the validity of our approach. Second, we found new mechanisms on a 2-by-2 grid graph, demonstrating its novelty. Third, we devised a new impossibility result for a public bad on a 2-by-3 grid by additionally introducing a fairness property called *ontoness*, which demonstrates the applicability of our approach.

6.1   Validity: Regenerating Known Results

Todo et al. [35] showed that, regardless whether agents' preferences are single-peaked or single-dipped, there is no mechanism that satisfies false-name-proofness and Pareto efficient on cycle graph C_k for any integer $k \geq 6$. However, for any $k \leq 5$, there is such a mechanism. Our SAT-based framework successfully regenerates these results for any $k \leq 7$, i.e., it finds some mechanisms for $3 \leq k \leq 5$, and does not find any mechanism for $5 < k \leq 7$. For larger $k \geq 8$, it does not stop for more than a week. Indeed, the size of our compact SAT encoding is already quite large, where the number of variables is $O(2^n \times n)$ and the number of constraints is $O(2^n \times n^4)$.

6.2   Novelty: Finding New Mechanisms

Table 1 shows an actual assignment returned by the SAT solver for a public good on a 2-by-2 grid[1]. The behavior is slightly different from the first mechanism

---

[1] The domain of single-peaked preferences coincides with that of single-dipped ones on a 2-by-2 grid. Thus, the same mechanism also works for locating a public bad.

332 N. Okada et al.

Table 1. Showing behavior of a newly obtained mechanism for a public good on 2-by-2 grid, by listing all variables and assigned Boolean values. 'T' and 'F' indicates TRUE and FALSE, respectively.

$c_{0,0}$	T	$c_{1,1}$	T	$c_{2,2}$	T	$c_{3,3}$	T	$c_{01,0}$	T	$c_{01,1}$	F
$c_{02,0}$	T	$c_{02,2}$	F	$c_{03,0}$	T	$c_{03,1}$	F	$c_{03,2}$	F	$c_{03,3}$	F
$c_{12,0}$	F	$c_{12,1}$	F	$c_{12,2}$	F	$c_{12,3}$	T	$c_{13,1}$	F	$c_{13,3}$	T
$c_{23,2}$	F	$c_{23,3}$	T	$c_{012,0}$	T	$c_{012,1}$	F	$c_{012,2}$	F	$c_{013,0}$	T
$c_{013,1}$	F	$c_{013,3}$	F	$c_{023,0}$	T	$c_{023,2}$	F	$c_{023,3}$	F	$c_{123,1}$	F
$c_{123,2}$	F	$c_{123,3}$	T	$c_{0123,0}$	T	$c_{0123,1}$	F	$c_{0123,2}$	F	$c_{0123,3}$	F

described in Example 1. The only difference is for input $S = \{v_1, v_2\}$, where the first mechanism in Example 1 returns v_0 and the one shown in the above table returns v_3.

It has been unclarified whether such a slight modification also works, although the first mechanism in Example 1 was already proposed in Todo et al. [35].

Actually, based on the model enumeration function of a SAT solver, we found that there are *only* eight mechanisms; two of which are explained above, and the other six are obtained from the rotational symmetry. Future work will develop a new framework to automatically derive a human-readable description of a mechanism, rather than just showing the behavior in a table.

6.3 Applicability: An Impossibility with Additional Property

No work has formally analyzed false-name-proof location of a public bad on grid graphs, except for a 2-by-2 grid that is identical to cycle C_4. We therefore apply our framework to a 2-by-3 grid (Fig. 2) and obtained mechanisms satisfying both false-name-proofness and Pareto efficiency. However, in this subsection, we show a negative result, by introducing a well-known property on fairness between outcomes, so-called *ontoness*.

Ontoness requires that each outcome must be realized under some input. Formally, a mechanism f is said to be *onto* if for any outcome $v \in V$, there is at least one input $S \in 2^V$ such that $f(S) = v$. If ontoness is not satisfied, there exists at least one outcome that is never selected under any input. Such a mechanism is unfair for outcomes, e.g., voting for candidates and/or on sites for public bad locations. All the outcomes should be treated as fairly as possible, and if such an outcome that is never selected exists, the mechanism should run for all but that outcome.

Implementing the ontoness property in an CNF formula is quite easy. The only clause that is added to the SAT encoding in Sect. 5 is:

$$\forall v \in V, \bigvee_{S \in 2^V} c_{S,v}.$$

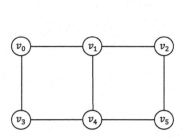

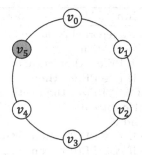

Fig. 2. 2-by-3 grid

Fig. 3. 6-cycle, where gray vertex v_5 is trusted.

Our framework then returns 'unsatisfiable,' that is, for a public bad location on a 2-by-3 grid, no deterministic mechanism simultaneously satisfies false-name-proofness, Pareto efficiency, and ontoness. Actually, any of the obtained mechanisms without introducing ontoness is not locating the facility at v_1 (or at v_4). This is reasonable and consistent with a result by Manjunath [21] for a continuous line; since agents' preferences are single-dipped, the public bad must be located at one of the extremes.

As we observed in this subsection, our SAT-based framework is quite applicable to various mechanism design problems. Indeed, obtaining such a new result is easy; by just adding a new condition, we obtain some new insights from our framework. To verify the consistency of any property, simply represent it as a set of clauses.

7   Extension to a New Variant of Facility Location

As we confirmed in the previous section, and was originally shown in Todo et al. [35], there is no mechanism that is false-name-proof and Pareto efficient on the cycle graph with six vertices. However, it might be possible in practice to restrict the set of manipulators. One such situation is to decide a meeting slot, where some core members might have preferred slot, as explained in Sect. 1. Another possibility is that a city is running its own collection of personal information; the citizens are therefore only allowed to report their true preference.

Here we demonstrate that our AMD approach is easily extendable to such a modified problem, which originally requires a complicated analysis from scratch in the traditional mechanism design. Our framework indeed returns many models for the modified problem, meaning that there are false-name-proof and Pareto efficient mechanisms.

The following are the details of the modified problem. One vertex in C_6 is trusted, e.g., the vertex v_5 in the cycle graph C_6 shown in Fig. 3, and the mechanism designer is going to locate a public good, i.e., agents' preferences are single-peaked. Each agent can still do false-name manipulations as in the

---

Algorithm 1. Mechanism found on cycle C_6 with trusted vertex v_5

Require: a reported profile θ'
Ensure: a location x
 1: **if** $v_3 \in \mathrm{PE}(\theta')$ **then return** v_3
 2: **else if** $v_4 \in \mathrm{PE}(\theta')$ **then**
 3:　　**if** $v_0 \in \mathrm{PE}(\theta')$ **then return** v_5
 4:　　**else return** v_4
 5:　　**end if**
 6: **else if** $v_1 \in \mathrm{PE}(\theta')$ **then return** v_1
 7: **else if** $v_0 \in \mathrm{PE}(\theta')$ **then return** v_0
 8: **else if** $v_5 \in \mathrm{PE}(\theta')$ **then return** v_5
 9: **else return** v_2
10: **end if**

---

previous problem, while those located at v_5 just report their true type v_5. Formally, the property to be satisfied is slightly modified as follows:

Definition 4. *A mechanism f is false-name-proof for the modified problem if for any N, θ, $i \in N$, $\theta_i \in V \setminus \{v_5\}$, $\theta_i' \in V$, $\Phi_i \subseteq \mathcal{N} \setminus N$, and $\theta_{\Phi_i} \in V^{|\Phi_i|}$, it holds that $f(\theta) \succsim_{\theta_i} f(\theta_i', \theta_{\Phi_i}, \theta_{-i})$.*

Almost identical encoding with Sect. 5 works, except for removing all the conditions on false-name-proofness with respect to the vertex v_5 where a manipulator is located, as Definition 4 did. Thus, the conditions to be added for the *modified* false-name-proofness is:

$$\forall S \in 2^V, \forall u \in \mathrm{PE}(S), \forall m \in S \setminus \{v_5\}, \forall T \in R(S, m), \forall v \in \mathrm{PE}(T) \cap B(u, m),$$

$$\neg c_{S,u} \vee \neg c_{T,v}.$$

After applying our framework, we obtained 160 models (i.e., mechanisms) for the problem. One of them appears in Algorithm 1, which can be represented as a simple form based on an if-then rule, except for the nested part in lines 2–5.

We briefly introduce how the mechanism prevents false-name manipulations, particularly by focusing on why the nested part need. The mechanism f first tries to locate the facility on the bottom of the diagonal line between v_5 and v_2, i.e., vertices v_3 and v_4. If v_3 is not Pareto efficient but v_4 is, then f also checks whether v_0 is also Pareto efficient. If so, it locates the facility at v_5; otherwise at v_4. Consider the profile $S = \{v_1, v_4, v_5\}$. Here, v_3 is not Pareto efficient and v_4 is. What if f locates the facility at v_4? Then, the agent at v_1 adds a fake identity at vertex v_3 (or v_2). This manipulation makes v_3 Pareto efficient, and moves the facility to v_3, which is beneficial for her. To remove this incentive, f also needs to check the Pareto efficiency of v_5. Indeed, $f(S) = v_5$, which is identical with v_3 for the manipulator at v_1.

Actually, we did a brute-force check for each model and confirmed that any obtained model must have such a nested form, i.e., it cannot be represented as a mechanism that sequentially checks the Pareto efficiency of each vertex, like that proposed in Nehama et al. [24].

8 Concluding Remarks

We proposed a SAT-based AMD framework for the false-name-proof facility location. We regenerated existing results, revealed many new findings, and further demonstrated that our framework can be easily extended to a modified problem. Our future work will include the automated proving of impossibility results, based on extracting a minimal unsatisfiable set. Establishing a general technique to provide a complete characterization of mechanisms, based on a model enumeration function of a SAT solver, would also be interesting.

Acknowledgments. This work is partially supported by JSPS KAKENHI Grants JP17H00761 and JP17H04695, and JST SICORP JPMJSC1607. The authors thank Ilan Nehama and Yuho Wada for their helpful comments and discussions. All errors are our own.

References

1. Albert, M., Conitzer, V., Lopomo, G.: Assessing the robustness of cremer-mclean with automated mechanism design. In: Proceedings of the AAAI 2015, pp. 763–769 (2015)
2. Albert, M., Conitzer, V., Stone, P.: Automated design of robust mechanisms. In: Proceedings of the AAAI 2017, pp. 298–304 (2017)
3. Alcalde-Unzu, J., Vorsatz, M.: Strategy-proof location of public facilities. Games Econ. Behav. **112**, 21–48 (2018)
4. Alon, N., Feldman, M., Procaccia, A.D., Tennenholtz, M.: Strategyproof approximation of the minimax on networks. Math. Oper. Res. **35**(3), 513–526 (2010)
5. Alon, N., Feldman, M., Procaccia, A.D., Tennenholtz, M.: Walking in circles. Discrete Math. **310**(23), 3432–3435 (2010)
6. Aziz, H., Paterson, M.: False name manipulations in weighted voting games: splitting, merging and annexation. In: Proceedings of the AAMAS 2009, pp. 409–416 (2009)
7. Barthe, G., Gaboardi, M., Arias, E.J.G., Hsu, J., Roth, A., Strub, P.-Y.: Computer-aided verification for mechanism design. In: Cai, Y., Vetta, A. (eds.) WINE 2016. LNCS, vol. 10123, pp. 279–293. Springer, Heidelberg (2016). https://doi.org/10.1007/978-3-662-54110-4_20
8. Brandl, F., Brandt, F., Geist, C., Hofbauer, J.: Strategic abstention based on preference extensions: positive results and computer-generated impossibilities. In: Proceedings of the IJCAI 2015, pp. 18–24 (2015)
9. Brandt, F., Geist, C.: Finding strategyproof social choice functions via SAT solving. In: Proceedings of the AAMAS 2014, pp. 1193–1200 (2014)
10. Brandt, F., Geist, C., Peters, D.: Optimal bounds for the no-show paradox via SAT solving. In: Proceedings of the AAMAS 2016, pp. 314–322 (2016)
11. Brandt, F., Saile, C., Stricker, C.: Voting with ties: strong impossibilities via SAT solving. In: Proceedings of the AAMAS 2018, pp. 1285–1293 (2018)
12. Bu, N.: Unfolding the mystery of false-name-proofness. Econ. Lett. **120**(3), 559–561 (2013)
13. Crémer, J., McLean, R.P.: Optimal selling strategies under uncertainty for a discriminating monopolist when demands are interdependent. Econometrica **53**(2), 345–361 (1985)

14. Dokow, E., Feldman, M., Meir, R., Nehama, I.: Mechanism design on discrete lines and cycles. In: Proceedings of the EC 2012, pp. 423–440 (2012)

15. Escoffier, B., Gourvès, L., Kim Thang, N., Pascual, F., Spanjaard, O.: Strategy-proof mechanisms for facility location games with many facilities. In: Brafman, R.I., Roberts, F.S., Tsoukiàs, A. (eds.) ADT 2011. LNCS (LNAI), vol. 6992, pp. 67–81. Springer, Heidelberg (2011). https://doi.org/10.1007/978-3-642-24873-3_6

16. Feigenbaum, I., Sethuraman, J.: Strategyproof mechanisms for one-dimensional hybrid and obnoxious facility location models. In: Proceedings of the AAAI 2015 Workshop on Incentive and Trust in E-Communities, pp. 8–13 (2015)

17. Geist, C., Peters, D.: Computer-aided methods for social choice theory. In: Trends in Computational Social Choice, chap. 13, pp. 249–267 (2017)

18. Kerber, M., Lange, C., Rowat, C.: An introduction to mechanized reasoning. J. Math. Econ. **66**, 26–39 (2016)

19. Lahiri, A., Peters, H., Storcken, T.: Strategy-proof location of public bads in a two-country model. Math. Soc. Sci. **90**, 150–159 (2017)

20. Lesca, J., Todo, T., Yokoo, M.: Coexistence of utilitarian efficiency and false-name-proofness in social choice. In: Proceedings of the AAMAS 2014, pp. 1201–1208 (2014)

21. Manjunath, V.: Efficient and strategy-proof social choice when preferences are single-dipped. Int. J. Game Theory **43**(3), 579–597 (2014)

22. Moulin, H.: On strategy-proofness and single peakedness. Public Choice **35**(4), 437–455 (1980)

23. Narasimhan, H., Agarwal, S., Parkes, D.C.: Automated mechanism design without money via machine learning. In: Proceedings of the IJCAI 2016, pp. 433–439 (2016)

24. Nehama, I., Todo, T., Yokoo, M.: Manipulations-resistant facility location mechanisms for ZV-line graphs. In: Proceedings of the AAMAS 2019, pp. 1452–1460 (2019)

25. Ono, T., Todo, T., Yokoo, M.: Rename and false-name manipulations in discrete facility location with optional preferences. In: An, B., Bazzan, A., Leite, J., Villata, S., van der Torre, L. (eds.) PRIMA 2017. LNCS (LNAI), vol. 10621, pp. 163–179. Springer, Cham (2017). https://doi.org/10.1007/978-3-319-69131-2_10

26. Procaccia, A.D., Tennenholtz, M.: Approximate mechanism design without money. ACM Trans. Econ. Comput. **1**(4), 18 (2013)

27. Roy, S., Storcken, T.: A characterization of possibility domains in strategic voting. J. Math. Econ. **84**, 46–55 (2019)

28. Sandholm, T.: Automated mechanism design: a new application area for search algorithms. In: Rossi, F. (ed.) CP 2003. LNCS, vol. 2833, pp. 19–36. Springer, Heidelberg (2003). https://doi.org/10.1007/978-3-540-45193-8_2

29. Sandholm, T., Likhodedov, A.: Automated design of revenue-maximizing combinatorial auctions. Oper. Res. **63**(5), 1000–1025 (2015)

30. Shen, W., Tang, P., Zuo, S.: Automated mechanism design via neural networks. In: Proceedings of the AAMAS 2019, pp. 215–223 (2019)

31. Sonoda, A., Todo, T., Yokoo, M.: False-name-proof locations of two facilities: economic and algorithmic approachess. In: Proceedings of the AAAI 2016, pp. 615–621 (2016)

32. Sui, X., Boutilier, C., Sandholm, T.: Analysis and optimization of multi-dimensional percentile mechanisms. In: Proceedings of the IJCAI 2013, pp. 367–374 (2013)

33. Todo, T., Conitzer, V.: False-name-proof matching. In: Proceedings of the AAMAS 2013, pp. 311–318 (2013)

34. Todo, T., Iwasaki, A., Yokoo, M.: False-name-proof mechanism design without money. In: Proceedings of the AAMAS 2011, pp. 651–658 (2011)
35. Todo, T., Okada, N., Yokoo, M.: False-name-proof facility location on discrete structures (2019). http://arxiv.org/abs/1907.08914
36. Tsuruta, S., Oka, M., Todo, T., Sakurai, Y., Yokoo, M.: Fairness and false-name manipulations in randomized cake cutting. In: Proceedings of the AAMAS 2015, pp. 909–917 (2015)
37. Yokoo, M., Sakurai, Y., Matsubara, S.: The effect of false-name bids in combinatorial auctions: new fraud in internet auctions. Games Econ. Behav. 46(1), 174–188 (2004)

Solving Coalition Structure Generation Problems over Weighted Graph

Emi Watanabe[1]([⊠]), Miyuki Koshimura[1], Yuko Sakurai[2], and Makoto Yokoo[1,3]

[1] Kyushu University, Fukuoka, Japan
watanabe@agent.inf.kyushu-u.ac.jp, {koshi,yokoo}@inf.kyushu-u.ac.jp
[2] National Institute of Advanced Industrial Science and Technology, Tsukuba, Japan
yuko.sakurai@aist.go.jp
[3] RIKEN Center for Advanced Intelligence Project (AIP), Tokyo, Japan

Abstract. Coalition Structure Generation (CSG), which is a leading research issue in the domain of coalitional games, divides agents into exhaustive and disjoint coalitions to optimize social welfare. This paper studies CSG problems over weighted undirected graphs in which the weight on an edge between any two connecting agents represents how well they work together in a coalition. The weight can have either a positive or a negative value. We examine two types of problems. One is a CSG without any restrictions on the number of coalitions, and another is a CSG with k coalitions where k is determined in advance. We present two methods to solve these problems: ILP formulation and MaxSAT encoding.

Keywords: Coalitional games · Coalition structure generation problem · Integer linear programming · MaxSAT

1 Introduction

The study of interactions among multiple self-interested agents who can form coalitions to achieve common goals is an important research topic in multi-agent systems. Coalitional game theory provides a mathematical framework for modeling and analyzing such interactions. Coalitional games have two major research issues. The first involves partitioning the agents into coalitions to maximize the sum of the values of all the coalitions. This is called the Coalition Structure Generation problem [22]. The second topic involves how to divide the value of the coalition among agents. Coalitional game theory provides various solution concepts, such as the core, the Shapley value, and the nucleolus.

Although coalitional games can apply many real-world services including supply chains and rescue-team formation, existing works have identified that many problems in coalitional games tend to be computationally intractable. A coalitional game is represented as a black-box function called a *characteristic function* that takes a coalition as an input and returns its value as an output. When we explicitly represent an arbitrary characteristic function for a game of n

© Springer Nature Switzerland AG 2019
M. Baldoni et al. (Eds.): PRIMA 2019, LNAI 11873, pp. 338–353, 2019.
https://doi.org/10.1007/978-3-030-33792-6_21

agents, $\Theta(2^n)$ values are required. Thus, a concise representation for the game, i.e., polynomial size with respect to the number of agents, is one key property from a representation scheme for coalitional games.

Several concise representation schemes for a characteristic function have been proposed: graphical representation [1,7,18], marginal contribution nets (MC-nets) [11], synergy coalition group (SCG) [4], an agent-type representation [25], and a representation based on Zero-suppressed Binary Decision Diagram (ZDD) [21]. Among these concise representations, a coalitional game over a graph, (often called a graph-restricted game) introduced by Myerson [18], is the most popular concise representation scheme. Here nodes indicate agents and edges indicate communication channels; that is, whether the two connecting agents actually communicate. Thus, a coalition is feasible if and only if it induces a connected subgraph of the underlying graph. Myerson also investigated the existence of a disconnected coalition as a set of disjoint, connected components and defined the value of a disconnected coalition as the sum of the values of connected components. Deng and Papadimitriou [7] proposed a coalitional game over a weighted undirected graph with an integer weight on each edge. The coalition's value is given by the sum of the weight of the edges contained in it. They analyzed the computational complexity of the problems associated with each solution concept.

In this paper, we study coalition structure generation over weighted undirected graphs in which the weight on an edge between any two connecting agents represents how well they work together in a coalition. The relations between pairs of agents are symmetric. The weight can be either positive or negative. A positive weight represents how much profit the two connecting agents make for the coalition to which they belong when they work together. A negative weight represents how much they subtract from the coalition. We allow the existence of a disconnected coalition as a set of disjoint, connected components and define the value of a disconnected coalition in the same manner as Myerson [18].

We study two types of problems to find the optimal coalition structure that maximizes the sum of the utilities obtained by the coalitions. The first problem is a well-known general *coalition structure generation (CSG)* problem. For the second, we fix the number of coalitions in a coalition structure to k which an organizer determines in advance. We call the latter the *k-coalition structure generation (k-CSG) problem*, which is a variant of the CSG problem introduced by Sless *et al.* [23]. Although Sless *et al.* proposed an algorithm for the k-CSG problem over a graph when the number of negative edges is limited, we address a k-CSG problem over a graph without such a limitation. When we assume that all the weights in the graph are positive and k is fixed, the k-CSG (minimum-weight k-cut) problem is polynomial time solvable [9]. Even if k is fixed, the k-CSG problem over a graph having positive and negative edges is NP-hard.

In this paper, we propose a 0–1 integer liner programming (ILP) formulation and MaxSAT encodings to solve the CSG and k-CSG problems. In our formulations, we introduce a symmetry breaking constraint to reduce the duplicated solutions. If n agents exist, there exist at most $n!$ duplicated solutions since the names of coalitions are indistinguishable. A symmetry breaking constraint reduces such duplicated solutions. For k-CSG problems, we also reformulate the existing ILP formulation for a graph clustering problem, proposed by Miyauchi et al. [17] and experimentally show that our formulation works well on k-CSG.

The rest of this paper is organized as follows. Related works are introduced in Sect. 2. The definitions and notations used in it are given in Sect. 3. In Sect. 4, we introduce the existing ILP formulation for clustering problems over graphs proposed by Miyauchi et al. [17]. In Sects. 5 and 6, we introduce 0–1 ILP formulation and MaxSAT encoding for general CSG and k-CSG problems, followed by an empirical evaluation in Sect. 7. Some final conclusions are presented in Sect. 8.

2   Related Works

Myerson [18] first established a coalitional game over a graph, as we described in Sect. 1. After his work, many researchers in computer science addressed such computationally intractable problems to find an optimal coalition structure or calculate solution concepts and proposed efficient algorithms for them [20]. Among various existing works, we introduce the works on CSG problems that are close to our study.

Voice et al. [26] proposed algorithms to enumerate and evaluate all of the feasible coalitions and find an optimal coalition structure over a sparse graph when a feasible coalition consists of a connected subgraph. Our experiments showed that the proposed algorithm evaluated all of the coalition values for up to 50 agents in a reasonable time and found an optimal coalition structure for 30 agents within 5.3 min on random trees. Bachrach et al. [2] considered the CSG problem over a weighted graph and showed that the optimization problem in a weighted graph game is NP-hard. Then they proposed approximate algorithms with constant factor approximations for such restricted graphs as planner, minor free, and bounded degree graphs. Sless et al. [23] considered a CSG problem with a fixed constant k of coalitions (k-CSG problem) for a weighted undirected graph. They proposed a polynomial time algorithm to find an optimal coalition structure for a nearly positive graph where the number of negative edges is limited. They also identified tractable instances and proposed a polynomial time algorithm to find the core stable solutions for them. We provide ILP formulation of k-CSG problems without any constraints on the negative edge in this paper.

If the agents in a coalition have to form a connected component, CSG problems over graphs are identical as the clique partitioning problem introduced by Grötschel and Wakabayashi [10]. Recently, Miyauchi et al. [17] proposed an ILP formulation and an ILP-based algorithm for the clique partitioning problem. We reformulate an ILP formulation for the k-CSG problem in Sect. 5.

Liao et al. presented two MaxSAT encodings for CSGs represented by MC-nets or embedded MC-nets: agent-based and rule-based [15]. The former encodes agent relations into propositional logic while the latter encodes rule relations between rules of MC-nets [16,19,24]. The rule-based encoding is applicable to only CSGs represented by MC-nets. In other words, we can not use it for CSGs by weighted graphs. Thus, we present an agent-based MaxSAT encoding in this work.

3   Model

Let $N = \{1, 2, \ldots, n\}$ be a set of agents. The game is represented as undirected weighted graph $G = (N, E, w)$. Each edge $(i, i') \in E$ is associated with weight $w_{i,i'} = w_{i',i} \in \mathbb{Q}$ where $\mathbb{Q}$ is the set of rational numbers. Weight $w_{i,i'}$ indicates the degree of the relationship strength between agents i and i'. Let coalition $S \subseteq N$ denote a subset of agents. We do not require the agents in coalition S to form a connected component. The value of S is the sum of the weights among the agents who belong to coalition S.

Definition 1 (Value of Coalition). *For any coalition of agents $S \subseteq N$, the value of S is given by*

$$v(S) = \sum_{(i,i') \in E[S]} w_{i,i'}.$$

where $E[S] = \{(i, i') \in E \mid i, i' \in S\}$.

We can extend graph G to a complete graph by adding zero-weighted edges to it without changing $v(S)$. Therefore, for simplicity, we assume every weighted graph G in this paper is complete.

We consider two types of coalition structure generation problems: a general coalition structure generation problem and a k-coalition structure generation problem where we restrict the number of coalitions in a coalition structure to k.

First we define a general coalition structure generation problem. Coalition structure CS is defined as a partition of N into disjoint and exhaustive coalitions.

Definition 2 (Coalition Structure). *Coalition structure $CS = \{S_1, S_2, \ldots\}$ satisfies the following conditions:*

$$\forall i, j \ (i \neq j), \ S_i \cap S_j = \emptyset, \ \bigcup_{S_i \in CS} S_i = N.$$

Denote the set of all coalition structures as $\Pi(N)$.

The value of coalition structure CS, $V(CS)$, is given by $V(CS) = \sum_{S_j \in CS} v(S_j)$.

Therefore, we define a general coalition structure generation problem (CSG) as follows.

Definition 3 (Coalition Structure Generation Problem (CSG)). *The coalition structure generation problem is the problem to find CS^* satisfies*

$$\forall CS, V(CS^*) \geq V(CS).$$

Next we define k-Coalition Structure Generation Problem (k-CSG). In it, the number of non-empty coalitions in a coalition structure is predefined as k. In other words, a coalition structure has to consist of exactly k coalitions. Let CS_k be a coalition structure with exactly k coalitions.

Definition 4. (k-Coalition Structure Generation Problem (k-CSG)). *The k-coalition structure generation problem is to find CS_k^* satisfying*

$$\forall CS, V(CS_k^*) \geq V(CS_k).$$

4   Existing ILP Formulations

We introduce the existing state-of-the-art ILP formulation and an ILP-based algorithm for the graph clustering problem, which have been proposed by Miyauchi *et al.* (2018).

A graph clustering problem finds an optimal partition that maximizes the sum of the weights on edges within the clusters in the partition for a given complete weighted undirected graph $G = (N, E, w)$ with the weight on edge $w : E \to \mathbb{Q}$. Such a problem is often called the clique partitioning problem. For it, Grötshel and Wakabayashi (1989) first proposed an ILP formulation, in which decision variable $z_{i,i'}$ for each edge (i, i') is introduced where $z_{i,i'} = 1$ if i and i' are in the same cluster and 0 otherwise. As constraints, we introduce the triangle inequality constraints for any $i, i', i'' \in N$. If i and i' are in the same cluster and i' and i'' are also in the same cluster, then i and i'' have to be in the same cluster. This constraint is represented by inequality $z_{i,i'} + z_{i',i''} - z_{i,i''} \leq 1$. Thus, the ILP formulation has $\binom{n}{2} = \Theta(n^2)$ variables and $3\binom{n}{3} = \Theta(n^3)$ triangle inequality constraints.

Miyauchi *et al.* proposed an ILP formulation and an ILP-based algorithm to reduce a set of triangle inequality constraints. The ILP formulation called $\mathrm{RP}(\tilde{G})$ has far fewer constraints than a previously proposed standard ILP formulation [10]. The ILP-based algorithm called $\mathrm{RP}^*(\mathrm{G})$+pp consists of two procedures. $\mathrm{RP}^*(\mathrm{G})$ first solves a ILP problem defined by modifying $\mathrm{RP}(\tilde{G})$ to further reduce a set of triangle inequality constraints and then decompose the partitions obtained by solving the ILP problem into weakly connected components to obtain an optimal solution as a post-processing. Miyauchi *et al.* also proved that both $\mathrm{RP}(\tilde{G})$ and $\mathrm{RP}^*(\mathrm{G})$+pp always find an optimal solution.

$\mathrm{RP}(\tilde{G})$: In the ILP formulation $\mathrm{RP}(\tilde{G})$, we assume that the weight on edge $w_{i,i'}$ is an integer value, i.e., $w_{i,i'} \in \mathbb{Z}$. A new graph, $\tilde{G} = (N, E, \tilde{w})$, is given where weight function $\tilde{w}_{i,i'}$ is defined so that for $(i, i') \in E$,

$$\tilde{w}_{i,i'} = \begin{cases} -\epsilon & \text{if } (w_{i,i'} = 0) \\ w_{i,i'} & \text{otherwise,} \end{cases}$$

where $\epsilon \in (0, 1/\binom{n}{2})$.

Zero-weighted edges in G become negative-weighted ones in $\tilde{G}$. This decreases the number of triangle inequality constraints for $\tilde{G}$ dramatically when there are a lot of zero-weighted edges in G.

$$\text{RP}(\tilde{G}): \ \max \sum_{i=1}^{n-1} \sum_{i'=i+1}^{n} \tilde{w}_{i,i'} z_{i,i'}$$

$$\text{s.t.} \quad z_{i,i'} + z_{i',i''} - z_{i,i''} \leq 1 \quad \forall (i,i',i'') \in T_{\geq 0}^1,$$
$$z_{i,i'} - z_{i',i''} + z_{i,i''} \leq 1 \quad \forall (i,i',i'') \in T_{\geq 0}^2,$$
$$-z_{i,i'} + z_{i',i''} + z_{i,i''} \leq 1 \quad \forall (i,i',i'') \in T_{\geq 0}^3,$$
$$z_{i,i'} \in \{0,1\} \qquad 1 \leq i < i' \leq n$$

where $T_{\geq 0}^1 = \{(i,i',i'') : 1 \leq i < i' < i'' \leq n, \ \tilde{w}_{i,i'} \geq 0 \text{ or } \tilde{w}_{i',i''} \geq 0\}$,

$\quad T_{\geq 0}^2 = \{(i,i',i'') : 1 \leq i < i' < i'' \leq n, \ \tilde{w}_{i,i'} \geq 0 \text{ or } \tilde{w}_{i,i''} \geq 0\}$, and

$\quad T_{\geq 0}^3 = \{(i,i',i'') : 1 \leq i < i' < i'' \leq n, \ \tilde{w}_{i',i''} \geq 0 \text{ or } \tilde{w}_{i,i''} \geq 0\}$.

Miyauchi *et al.* showed that $\text{RP}(\tilde{G})$ removed about 90% of the constraints, compared with a standard ILP formulation for correlation clustering instances where the weight of an edge is 1, 0, or -1 in their computational experiments.

RP*(G)+pp: In ILP-based algorithm RP*(G)+pp, we first solve the following ILP problem called RP*(G) in which the set of constraints is identical to $\text{RP}(\tilde{G})$.

$$\text{RP}^*(G): \ \max \sum_{i=1}^{n-1} \sum_{i'=i+1}^{n} w_{i,i'} z_{i,i'}$$

$$\text{s.t.} \quad z_{i,i'} + z_{i',i''} - z_{i,i''} \leq 1 \quad \forall (i,i',i'') \in T_{>0}^1,$$
$$z_{i,i'} - z_{i',i''} + z_{i,i''} \leq 1 \quad \forall (i,i',i'') \in T_{>0}^2,$$
$$-z_{i,i'} + z_{i',i''} + z_{i,i''} \leq 1 \quad \forall (i,i',i'') \in T_{>0}^3,$$
$$z_{i,i'} \in \{0,1\} \qquad 1 \leq i < i' \leq n$$

where $T_{>0}^1 = \{(i,i',i'') : 1 \leq i < i' < i'' \leq n, \ w_{i,i'} > 0 \text{ or } w_{i',i''} > 0\}$,

$\quad T_{>0}^2 = \{(i,i',i'') : 1 \leq i < i' < i'' \leq n, \ w_{i,i'} > 0 \text{ or } w_{i,i''} > 0\}$, and

$\quad T_{>0}^3 = \{(i,i',i'') : 1 \leq i < i' < i'' \leq n, \ w_{i',i''} > 0 \text{ or } w_{i,i''} > 0\}$.

As in $\text{RP}(\tilde{G})$, the number of triangle inequality constraints in RP*(G) decreases as the number of edges having positive edges decreases. However, RP*(G) may fail to obtain the optimal solution. Thus, we apply a post-processing, which we refer to as pp, to decompose the partition obtained by solving RP*(G) into a set of weakly connected components by a depth-first search[1] **pp** runs in time linear in the size of graph G. Miyauchi *et al.* showed that RP*(G)+pp was the fastest among the existing formulations and algorithms including RP$(\tilde{G})$ for the instances of bipartite graphs in the computational experiments.

5 ILP Formulation

In this section, we present our ILP formulations through which we introduce two types of decision variables, $x_{i,j}$ and $y_{i,i',j}$ for $1 \leq i < i' \leq n$ and $1 \leq j \leq n$.

$$x_{i,j} = \begin{cases} 1 & \text{if agent } i \text{ is in a coalition } S_j, \\ 0 & \text{otherwise.} \end{cases}$$

$$y_{i,i',j} = \begin{cases} 1 & \text{if agents } i \text{ and } i' \text{ are in coalition } S_j, \\ 0 & \text{otherwise.} \end{cases}$$

5.1 General CSG Problems

We introduce the following ILP problems for general CSG problems:

$$\max \sum_{i=1}^{n-1} \sum_{i'=i+1}^{n} \sum_{j=1}^{n} w_{i,i'} y_{i,i',j}$$

$$\text{s.t.} \ \sum_{j=1}^{n} x_{i,j} = 1 \ (1 \leq i \leq n) \tag{1}$$

$$y_{i,i',j} \leq x_{i,j} \quad (1 \leq i < i' \leq n, 1 \leq j \leq n) \tag{2}$$

$$y_{i,i',j} \leq x_{i',j} \quad \text{(as above)} \tag{3}$$

$$x_{i,j} + x_{i',j} \leq y_{i,i',j} + 1 \ \text{(as above)} \tag{4}$$

$$x_{1,1} = 1 \tag{5}$$

$$x_{i,j} = 0 \quad (2 \leq i < j \leq n) \tag{6}$$

$$x_{i,j} \leq \sum_{i'=1}^{i-1} x_{i',j-1} \ (2 \leq i,j \leq n) \tag{7}$$

Constraint (1) means that any agent must be in a coalition and that the number of coalitions it joins is exactly 1. Constraints (2), (3), and (4) mean that $y_{i,i',j}$ is 1 if and only if agents i and i' work together in coalition S_j and also 0 otherwise. The remaining constraints from (5) to (7) are for symmetry breaking constraints [8]. If n agents exist, at most n coalitions exist in a coalition structure. Thus, there exist at most $n!$ duplicated solutions, since the names of the coalitions are indistinguishable. We can reduce such duplicated solutions by adding symmetry breaking constraints which implies that the minimum agent

---

[1] In the search, we only examine components connected by edges with positive weights.

in S_j must be smaller than that in S_{j+1}. Thus, agent 1 must be in coalition S_1 and then agent 2 joins in either S_1 or S_2. If agent 2 cannot join in S_1, it is in S_2. If agents 1 and 2 are in S_1, agent 3 joins in either S_1 or S_2, and so on.

5.2 k-CSG Problems

We reformulate the above ILP formulation to work it for k-CSG problems. To obtain the optimal coalition structure with precise k coalitions, we change the maximum number of coalitions in a coalition structure from n to k in an objective function and add a new constraint (8). k coalitions must exist in a coalition structure, i.e., at least one agent must join any coalition:

$$\max \sum_{i=1}^{n-1} \sum_{i'=i+1}^{n} \sum_{j=1}^{k} w_{i,i'} y_{i,i',j}$$

$$\text{s.t. } \sum_{i=1}^{n} x_{i,j} \geq 1 \quad (1 \leq j \leq k) \tag{8}$$

$$\sum_{j=1}^{k} x_{i,j} = 1 \quad (1 \leq i \leq n) \tag{9}$$

$$y_{i,i',j} \leq x_{i,j} \qquad\qquad (1 \leq i < i' \leq n, 1 \leq j \leq k) \tag{10}$$

$$y_{i,i',j} \leq x_{i',j} \qquad\qquad \text{(as above)} \tag{11}$$

$$x_{i,j} + x_{i',j} \leq y_{i,i',j} + 1 \quad \text{(as above)} \tag{12}$$

$$x_{1,1} = 1 \tag{13}$$

$$x_{i,j} = 0 \qquad\qquad (2 \leq i < j \leq k) \tag{14}$$

$$x_{i,j} \leq \sum_{i'=1}^{i-1} x_{i',j-1} \quad (2 \leq i \leq n, 2 \leq j \leq k) \tag{15}$$

We also consider the reformulation of $\text{RP}(\tilde{G})$ for k-CSG problems and call it $\text{RP}_k(\tilde{G})$. We add k dummy nodes $D = \{n+1, \ldots, n+k\}$ where $n+j$ indicates coalition S_j, and introduce decision variable $z_{i,n+j}$ where $z_{i,n+j} = 1$ if i is in S_j and 0 otherwise $(1 \leq i \leq n, 1 \leq j \leq k)$. We also add dummy edges E_d between node i and dummy node $n+j$. Thus, $k \cdot n$ dummy edges are added to graph G. Although we assume the weight of a dummy edge is 0, we explicitly present dummy edges in a graph. Furthermore, we add a constraint where each dummy node must connect to at least one node to $\text{RP}(\tilde{G})$, i.e., $\sum_{i=1}^{n} z_{i,n+j} \geq 1$ must be satisfied for any $n+j$:

$$\mathrm{RP}_k(\tilde{G}) : \max \sum_{i=1}^{n-1} \sum_{i'=i+1}^{n} \tilde{w}_{i,i'} z_{i,i'}$$

$$\text{s.t. } \sum_{i=1}^{n} z_{i,n+j} \geq 1 \qquad (1 \leq j \leq k)$$

$$\sum_{j=1}^{k} z_{i,n+j} = 1 \qquad (1 \leq i \leq n)$$

$$z_{1,n+1} = 1$$

$$z_{i,n+j} = 0 \qquad (2 \leq i \leq n,\ i \leq j \leq k)$$

$$z_{i,n+j} \leq \sum_{i'=1}^{i-1} z_{i',n+j-1} \qquad (2 \leq i \leq n,\ 2 \leq j \leq k)$$

$$z_{i,i'} + z_{i',i''} - z_{i,i''} \leq 1 \quad \forall(i,i',i'') \in T^1_{\geq 0} \cup T^4_{\geq 0},$$

$$z_{i,i'} - z_{i',i''} + z_{i,i''} \leq 1 \quad \forall(i,i',i'') \in T^2_{\geq 0} \cup T^4_{\geq 0},$$

$$-z_{i,i'} + z_{i',i''} + z_{i,i''} \leq 1 \quad \forall(i,i',i'') \in T^3_{\geq 0} \cup T^4_{\geq 0},$$

$$z_{i,i'} \in \{0,1\} \qquad (1 \leq i < i' \leq n),$$

$$z_{i,n+j} \in \{0,1\} \qquad (1 \leq i \leq n,\ 1 \leq j \leq k),$$

$$\text{where } T^1_{\geq 0} = \{(i,i',i'') : 1 \leq i < i' < i'' \leq n,\ w_{i,i'} \geq 0 \text{ or } w_{i',i''} \geq 0\},$$

$$T^2_{\geq 0} = \{(i,i',i'') : 1 \leq i < i' < i'' \leq n,\ w_{i,i'} \geq 0 \text{ or } w_{i,i''} \geq 0\},$$

$$T^3_{\geq 0} = \{(i,i',i'') : 1 \leq i < i' < i'' \leq n,\ w_{i',i''} \geq 0 \text{ or } w_{i,i''} \geq 0\},$$

$$T^4_{\geq 0} = \{(i,i',n+j) : 1 \leq i < i' \leq n, 1 \leq j \leq k\}$$

6   MaxSAT Encoding

The Boolean Satisfiability Problem (SAT) was the first shown to be NP-complete [5]. SAT is represented by a Boolean formula, which is expressed in a *Conjunctive Normal Form (CNF)*, which consists of a conjunction (logic *and*) of one or more clauses. A *clause* is a disjunction (logic *or*) of one or more literals, and a *literal* is an occurrence of a Boolean variable or its negation. In this paper, a set of clauses is regarded as a conjunction of all the clauses in the set.

SAT determines whether any variable assignment that satisfies all clauses. Maximum Satisfiability (MaxSAT) is an optimal version of SAT [14]. Also, in practice, the problem instance is typically expressed as a set of hard and soft clauses where each soft clause has a bounded positive numerical *weight*. The problem is to find an assignment that satisfies all the hard clauses and maximizes the sum of the weights of the satisfied soft clauses.

Formally, we denote a MaxSAT formula by $\phi = \{(C_1, w_1), \ldots, (C_m, w_m), C_{m+1}, \ldots, C_{m+m'}\}$ where the first m clauses are soft and the rest are hard. With each soft clause C_i, Boolean variable b_i is associated such that $b_i = 1$ if clause C_i

is satisfied and otherwise $b_i = 0$. Solving MaxSAT instance ϕ amounts to finding an assignment that satisfies all $C_{m+1}, \ldots, C_{m+m'}$ and maximizes $\sum_{i=1}^{m} w_i b_i$.

We introduce Boolean variable $x_{i,j}$ for a pair of agent i and coalition S_j. If i is in S_j, $x_{i,j} = 1$, and otherwise, $x_{i,j} = 0$. We also introduce Boolean variable $y_{i,i',j}$ for a pair of agents i and i' where $i < i'$, and coalition S_j. If i and i' are in coalition j, $y_{i,i',j} = 1$, and otherwise, $y_{i,i',j} = 0$. To address negative weights in MaxSAT, which deals with only positive weights, we introduce Boolean variable $z_{i,i'}$ for a pair of agents i and i' whose edge's weight is negative. If i and i' are in the same coalition, $z_{i,i'} = 1$, and otherwise, $z_{i,i'} = 0$.

6.1 General CSG Problems

We introduce the following MaxSAT clauses for general CSG problems. This is essentially identical to the unary encoding in [3]:

- Soft clauses:
$$(y_{i,i',1} \vee \cdots \vee y_{i,i',n}, \; w_{i,i'}) \quad \text{if } w_{i,i'} > 0 \quad (1)$$
$$(\neg z_{i,i'}, \; -w_{i,i'}) \quad \text{if } w_{i,i'} < 0 \quad (2a)$$
- Hard clauses:

$$\neg y_{i,i',j} \vee z_{i,i'} \qquad\qquad (1 \leq j \leq n) \text{ if } w_{i,i'} < 0 \quad (2b)$$
$$x_{i,1} \vee \cdots \vee x_{i,n} \qquad\qquad (1 \leq i \leq n) \quad (3a)$$
$$\neg x_{i,j} \vee \neg x_{i,j'} \qquad\qquad (1 \leq i \leq n, 1 \leq j < j' \leq n) \quad (3b)$$
$$\neg x_{i,j} \vee \neg x_{i',j} \vee y_{i,i',j} \qquad (1 \leq i < i' \leq n, 1 \leq j \leq n) \quad (4a)$$
$$\neg y_{i,i',j} \vee x_{i,j} \qquad\qquad (\text{as above}) \quad (4b)$$
$$\neg y_{i,i',j} \vee x_{i',j} \qquad\qquad (\text{as above}) \quad (4c)$$
$$x_{1,1} \qquad\qquad\qquad\qquad (5a)$$
$$\neg x_{i,j} \qquad\qquad\qquad\qquad (1 < i < j \leq n) \quad (5b)$$
$$\neg x_{i,j} \vee x_{1,j-1} \vee \cdots \vee x_{i-1,j-1} \quad (2 \leq i, j \leq n) \quad (5c).$$

Soft clause (2a) denotes that value $-w_{i,i'} (> 0)$ is obtained when agents i and i' are in different coalitions. This coincides with the original meaning of the negative weights where the value is lost when i and i' are in the same coalition. Hard clause (2b) argues that if i and i' are in different coalition then there is no coalition S_j such that both i and i' are in S_j.

Hard clauses (3a) and (3b) mean that each agent must be in exactly one coalition. Hard clauses (4a), (4b), and (4c) argue that $x_{i,j} = x_{i',j} = 1$ if and only if $y_{i,i',j} = 1$. The remaining hard clauses (5a), (5b), and (5c) consider symmetry breaking. (5c) argues that if agent i is in coalition S_j then an agent smaller than i is in coalition S_{j-1}. This implies that the minimum agent in coalition S_{j-1} must be strictly smaller than that in coalition S_j.

6.2 k-CSG Problems

We obtained the MaxSAT clauses for k-CSG problems by replacing range $1 \leq j \leq n$ with $1 \leq j \leq k$ and adding hard clause (6) saying that no empty coalition exists as follows:

- Soft clauses:

$$(y_{i,i',1} \vee \cdots \vee y_{i,i',k}, \; w_{i,i'}) \quad \text{if } w_{i,i'} > 0 \quad (1)$$
$$(\neg z_{i,i'}, \; -w_{i,i'}) \quad\quad\quad\quad \text{if } w_{i,i'} < 0 \quad (2a)$$

- Hard clauses:

$$\neg y_{i,i',j} \vee z_{i,i'} \quad\quad\quad\quad (1 \le j \le k) \text{ if } w_{i,i'} < 0 \quad (2b)$$
$$x_{i,1} \vee \cdots \vee x_{i,k} \quad\quad\quad (1 \le i \le n) \quad\quad\quad\quad\quad\quad (3a)$$
$$\neg x_{i,j} \vee \neg x_{i,j'} \quad\quad\quad\quad (1 \le i \le n, 1 \le j < j' \le k) \quad (3b)$$
$$\neg x_{i,j} \vee \neg x_{i',j} \vee y_{i,i',j} \quad (1 \le i < i' \le n, 1 \le j \le k) \quad (4a)$$
$$\neg y_{i,i',j} \vee x_{i,j} \quad\quad\quad\quad (\text{as above}) \quad\quad\quad\quad\quad\quad\quad (4b)$$
$$\neg y_{i,i',j} \vee x_{i',j} \quad\quad\quad\quad (\text{as above}) \quad\quad\quad\quad\quad\quad\quad (4c)$$
$$x_{1,1} \quad\quad\quad\quad\quad\quad\quad\quad\quad\quad\quad\quad\quad\quad\quad\quad\quad\quad\quad\quad (5a)$$
$$\neg x_{i,j} \quad\quad\quad\quad\quad\quad\quad (1 < i < j \le k) \quad\quad\quad\quad\quad (5b)$$
$$\neg x_{i,j} \vee x_{1,j-1} \vee \cdots \vee x_{i-1,j-1} \quad (2 \le i \le n, 2 \le j \le k) \quad (5c)$$
$$x_{1,j} \vee \cdots \vee x_{n,j} \quad\quad\quad (1 \le j \le k) \quad\quad\quad\quad\quad\quad (6)$$

Note that $x_{i,j}$ and $y_{i,i',j}$ are introduced for $1 \le i < i' \le n$ and $1 \le j \le k$.

7 Experimental Evaluation

In this section, we experimentally evaluate the performance of our ILP formulations and MaxSAT encoding using two types of graph structures. For MaxSAT encoding, we apply two solvers, MaxHS [6] and RC2 on PySAT [12]. MaxHS is a MaxSAT solver that utilized a MIP solver, CPLEX along with a SAT solver, MiniSat. RC2 is a core-guided MaxSAT solver and won both the unweighted and weighted categories of the main track of MaxSAT Evaluation 2018.

We evaluated our ILP, RP*(G)+pp, MaxHS and RC2 for CSG problems, and our ILP, reformulated RP($\tilde{G}$), MaxHS and RC2 for k-CSG problems. All the tests were run on a machine: an Intel Xeon Gold 6130 CPU @ 2.10 GHz processor with 192 GB RAM, Ubuntu 18.04.2 LTS with a 60-s timeout. We used a mixed integer programming Gurobi package version 7.5.0.

We executed the first set of experiments for a real-world network called Wikipedia Requests for Adminship (WikiRfA) network [27]. This is a network among Wikipedia users where each link (i,j) has a weight corresponding to the vote of user i towards user j to become an administrator. A link's weight is given based on the intensity of the sentiment expressed in the vote [13]. The original graph is directed. For a pair of nodes i and j, we created an undirected link with weight $w_{i,j} + w_{j,i}$. Also, an original weight value is in the range $[-1, 1]$, which we modify into an integer in $[-100, 100]$.

Based on the original graph with about 10,000 nodes and 100,000 links, we selected a subgraph with n nodes by randomly choosing a root node and by adding neighboring nodes in a (bounded) breadth-first manner. For a root node (as well as for each of its descendants), we continue to add neighbors up to a given limit d (we set d to $0.2n$) until the number of chosen nodes became n. Let p denote the probability that an edge exists between a pair of nodes. In an obtained graph, p is about 15%. Thus, about 85% of the edges have positive weights

Table 1. Number of instances solved within 60 s (CSG)

		# nodes			
		20	30	40	50
OurILP	WikiRfA	100	100	100	100
	Random	100	100	100	28
RP*(G)+pp	WikiRfA	100	100	100	100
	Random	100	100	100	100
MaxHS	WikiRfA	100	100	100	100
	Random	100	100	100	100
RC2	WikiRfA	100	100	100	100
	Random	100	100	30	1

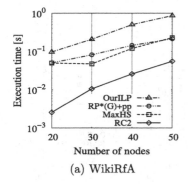
(a) WikiRfA

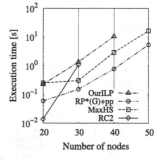
(b) Random graphs

Fig. 1. Average computational time (CSG)

We executed the second set of experiments for synthetic graphs where we randomly generate a graph with n nodes. For each pair of nodes, an edge exists with probability $p = 0.2$. The probability of edges having positive weight is 70% and the remaining 30% have negative weight. A positive/negative weight is chosen randomly from a range $[1, 100]/[-100, -1]$.

Thus, we have two types of graphs, WikiRfA and random. We set the amount of node n to 20, 30, 40, and 50. For each setting, we generated 100 instances. We finally experimented on 800 instances ($= 2 \times 4 \times 100$).

Table 1 shows the number of instances solved within 60 s and when we solved them as general CSG problems. Figure 1 plots the average computational time for 100 instances in each setting. The figures do not plot the time when at least one instance among the 100 instances was not solved within 60 s. Obviously, RC2 outperformed the others for WikiRfA and underperformed them for random. RP*(G)+pp and MaxHS work well for these general CSG problems.

Table 2 shows the number of instances solved within 60 s when we solved them as k-CSG problems where $k = 2, 5$. Figures 2 and 3 plot the average computational times for 100 instances in each setting. When solving WikiRfA instances

Table 2. Number of instances solved within 60 s (k-CSG)

		$n = 20$		$n = 30$		$n = 40$		$n = 50$	
		$k = 2$	$k = 5$	$k = 2$	$k = 5$	$k = 2$	$k = 5$	$k = 2$	$k = 5$
OurILP	WikiRfA	100	100	100	100	100	100	100	100
	Random	100	100	100	100	100	100	100	93
$RP_k(\tilde{G})$	WikiRfA	100	100	100	100	100	93	99	80
	Random	100	100	100	100	100	48	57	9
MaxHS	WikiRfA	100	100	100	100	100	99	100	94
	Random	100	100	100	100	100	75	100	51
RC2	WikiRfA	100	100	100	100	100	100	100	100
	Random	100	100	100	100	62	36	2	1

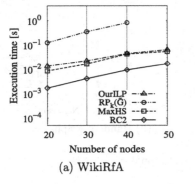

(a) WikiRfA

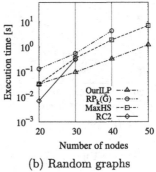

(b) Random graphs

Fig. 2. Average computational time (2-CSG)

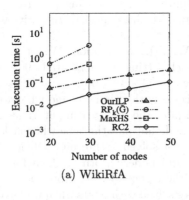

(a) WikiRfA

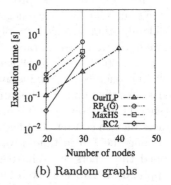

(b) Random graphs

Fig. 3. Average computational time (5-CSG)

as general CSG problems, RC2 outperformed the others. But it does not work on random graph instances. On the other hand, our ILP also performs well on both WikiRfA and random graph instances. Note that $RP_k(\tilde{G})$ does not work well on both the WikiRfA and random graph instances.

8 Conclusion

We considered two types of CSG, general CSG and k-CSG. A general CSG identifies a coalition structure so as to maximize its value. k-CSG examines only the coalition structures that consist of k coalitions. We introduced ILP and MaxSAT formulations for both CSGs, and evaluated them with a MIP solver Gurobi and two MaxSAT solvers, MaxHS and RC2. We used WikiRfA and random graphs as benchmark instances and compared our formulations with a state-of-the-art ILP formulation $RP^*(G)$ for general CSGs and its k-CSG version $RP_k(\tilde{G})$. Our experimental results show the following: (1) MaxHS and $RP^*(G)$ work well on instances in general CSG settings, (2) RC2 works well on WikiRfA instances in both general CSG and k-CSG settings; (3) our ILP formulation works well on instances in the k-CSG setting.

Future works will investigate the followings: (1) develop heuristics to enhance the performance, such as ordering agents, (2) decrease the number of constraints of both the ILP and MaxSAT formulations, (3) find out why each formulation or each solver changes its behaviour according to the type of benchmark.

Acknowledgment. This work was supported by JSPS KAKENHI Grant Numbers JP17H00761, JP17KK0008, JP19H04175, by JST SICORP JPMJSC1607, and by Kayamori Foundation of Informational Science Advancement.

References

1. Amer, R., Giménez, J.M.: A connectivity game for graphs. Math. Oper. Res. (MOR) **60**(3), 453–470 (2004). https://doi.org/10.1007/s001860400356
2. Bachrach, Y., Kohli, P., Kolmogorov, V., Zadimoghaddam, M.: Optimal coalition structure generation in cooperative graph games. In: Proceedings of the 27th AAAI Conference on Artificial Intelligence (AAAI-2013), pp. 81–87 (2013)
3. Berg, J., Järvisalo, M.: Cost-optimal constrained correlation clustering via weighted partial Maximum Satisfiability. Artif. Intell. **244**, 110–142 (2017)
4. Conitzer, V., Sandholm, T.: Complexity of constructing solutions in the core based on synergies among coalitions. Artif. Intell. **170**(6), 607–619 (2006)
5. Cook, S.A.: The complexity of theorem-proving procedures. In: Proceedings of the 3rd Annual ACM Symposium on Theory of Computing, pp. 151–158 (1971)
6. Davies, J., Bacchus, F.: Exploiting the Power of MIP Solvers in MAXSAT. In: Järvisalo, M., Van Gelder, A. (eds.) SAT 2013. LNCS, vol. 7962, pp. 166–181. Springer, Heidelberg (2013). https://doi.org/10.1007/978-3-642-39071-5_13
7. Deng, X., Papadimitriou, C.H.: On the complexity of cooperative solution concepts. MOR **19**(2), 257–266 (1994)

8. Gent, I.P.: A symmetry breaking constraint for indistinguishable values. In: In Proceedings of the 1st International Workshop on Symmetry in Constraint Satisfaction Problems, pp. 469–473 (2001)
9. Goldschmidt, O., Hochbaum, D.S.: A polynomial algorithm for the k-cut problem for fixed k. MOR **19**(1), 24–37 (1994)
10. Grötschel, M., Wakabayashi, Y.: A cutting plane algorithm for a clustering problem. Math. Program. **45**(1–3), 59–96 (1989). https://doi.org/10.1007/BF01589097
11. Ieong, S., Shoham, Y.: Marginal contribution nets: a compact representation scheme for coalitional games. In: Proceedings of the 6th ACM Conference on Electronic Commerce (EC-2005), pp. 193–202 (2005)
12. Ignatiev, A., Morgado, A., Marques-Silva, J.: PySAT: a Python toolkit for prototyping with SAT oracles. In: Beyersdorff, O., Wintersteiger, C.M. (eds.) SAT 2018. LNCS, vol. 10929, pp. 428–437. Springer, Cham (2018). https://doi.org/10.1007/978-3-319-94144-8_26
13. Kumar, S., Spezzano, F., Subrahmanian, V.S., Faloutsos, C.: Edge weight prediction in weighted signed networks. In: Proceedings of IEEE 16th International Conference on Data Mining (ICDM-2016), pp. 221–230 (2016)
14. Li, C.M., Manyà, F.: MaxSAT, hard and soft constraints. In: Biere, A., Heule, M., van Maaren, H., Walsh, T. (eds.) Handbook of Satisfiability, Frontiers in Artificial Intelligence and Applications, vol. 185, pp. 613–631. IOS Press, Amsterdam (2009)
15. Liao, X., Koshimura, M., Fujita, H., Hasegawa, R.: Solving the coalition structure generation problem with MaxSAT. In: IEEE 24th International Conference on Tools with Artificial Intelligence (ICTAI-2012), pp. 910–915 (2012)
16. Liao, X., Koshimura, M., Nomoto, K., Ueda, S., Sakurai, Y., Yokoo, M.: Improved WPM encoding for coalition structure generation under MC-nets. Constraints **24**, 25–55 (2019). https://doi.org/10.1007/s10601-018-9295-4
17. Miyauchi, A., Sonobe, T., Sukegawa, N.: Exact clustering via integer programming and maximum satisfiability. In: Proceedings of AAAI-18, pp. 1387–1394 (2018)
18. Myerson, R.B.: Graphs and cooperation in games. MOR **2**(3), 225–229 (1977)
19. Ohta, N., Conitzer, V., Ichimura, R., Sakurai, Y., Iwasaki, A., Yokoo, M.: Coalition structure generation utilizing compact characteristic function representations. In: Gent, I.P. (ed.) CP 2009. LNCS, vol. 5732, pp. 623–638. Springer, Heidelberg (2009). https://doi.org/10.1007/978-3-642-04244-7_49
20. Rahwan, T., Michalak, T.P., Wooldridge, M., Jennings, N.R.: Coalition structure generation: a survey. Artif. Intell. **229**, 139–174 (2015)
21. Sakurai, Y., Ueda, S., Iwasaki, A., Minato, S.-I., Yokoo, M.: A compact representation scheme of coalitional games based on multi-terminal zero-suppressed binary decision diagrams. In: Kinny, D., Hsu, J.Y., Governatori, G., Ghose, A.K. (eds.) PRIMA 2011. LNCS (LNAI), vol. 7047, pp. 4–18. Springer, Heidelberg (2011). https://doi.org/10.1007/978-3-642-25044-6_4
22. Sandholm, T., Larson, K., Andersson, M., Shehory, O., Tohmé, F.: Coalition structure generation with worst case guarantees. Artif. Intell. **111**(1–2), 209–238 (1999)
23. Sless, L., Hazon, N., Kraus, S., Wooldridge, M.: Forming k coalitions and facilitating relationships in social networks. Artif. Intell. **259**, 217–245 (2018)
24. Ueda, S., Hasegawa, T., Hashimoto, N., Ohta, N., Iwasaki, A., Yokoo, M.: Handling negative value rules in MC-net-based coalition structure generation. In: Proceedings of AAMAS-2012, pp. 795–804 (2012)
25. Ueda, S., Kitaki, M., Iwasaki, A., Yokoo, M.: Concise characteristic function representations in coalitional games based on agent types. In: Proceedings of the 22nd International Joint Conference on Artificial Intelligence (IJCAI-2011), pp. 393–399 (2011)

26. Voice, T., Ramchurn, S.D., Jennings, N.R.: On coalition formation with sparse synergies. In: Proceedings of AAMAS-2012, pp. 223–230 (2012)
27. West, R., Paskov, H.S., Leskovec, J., Potts, C.: Exploiting social network structure for person-to-person sentiment analysis. Trans. Assoc. Comput. Linguist. **2**, 297–310 (2014)

From Good Intentions to Behaviour Change
Probabilistic Feature Diagrams for Behaviour Support Agents

Malte S. Kließ[1], Marielle Stoelinga[2], and M. Birna van Riemsdijk[1,2(✉)]

[1] Delft University of Technology, Delft, The Netherlands
m.s.kliess@tudelft.nl
[2] University of Twente, Enschede, The Netherlands
{m.i.a.stoelinga,m.b.vanriemsdijk}@utwente.nl

Abstract. Behaviour support technology assists people in organising their daily activities and changing their behaviour. A fundamental notion underlying such supportive technology is that of *compliance* with behavioural norms: do people indeed perform the desired behaviour? Existing technology employs a rigid implementation of compliance: a norm is either satisfied or not. In practice however, behaviour change norms are less strict: E.g., is a new norm to do sports at least three times a week complied with if it is occasionally only done twice a week? To address this, in this paper we formally specify probabilistic norms through a variant of *feature diagrams*, enabling a hierarchical decomposition of the desired behaviour and its execution frequencies. Further, we define a new notion of *probabilistic norm compliance* using a formal *hypothesis testing* framework. We show that probabilistic norm compliance can be used in a real-world setting by implementing and evaluating our semantics with respect to an existing daily behaviour dataset.

1 Introduction

Behaviour support technology [7] is aimed at assisting people in organising their daily activities and changing their behaviour, for example to adopt a healthier lifestyle. While numerous behaviour support frameworks have been developed, they typically focus on a specific domain or type of behaviour, such as monitoring our diet, emergency monitoring, or forgetting to perform certain tasks [12]. In our work we aim to develop a *generic* framework for representing and reasoning about people's (desired) daily behaviour in order to allow an electronic partner (epartner for short) to provide personalised behaviour support [19]. A generic framework facilitates application across domains, and development of expressive representation and reasoning techniques in a principled way.

This work is partially financed by the Netherlands Organisation for Scientific Research (NWO) under the research programmes CoreSAEP (639.022.416), SEQUOIA (15474) and StepUp (628.010.006), as well as by the EU under the project 102112 SUCCESS.

M. Baldoni et al. (Eds.): PRIMA 2019, LNAI 11873, pp. 354–369, 2019.
https://doi.org/10.1007/978-3-030-33792-6_22

A central task an epartner needs to be able to do in order to provide person-alised behaviour support, is determine whether the user is *complying* with the desired target behaviour. The challenge we address in this paper is to formally define the fundamental components that are (at least) required for an epartner to perform this task, namely:

1. a description of the desired user behaviour, which can be self-reported, pre-scribed by a caregiver, or otherwise recorded;
2. a record of the actual daily routine or behaviour of the user;
3. a measure of compliance of what is actually being done to what is expected/desired to be done.

Inspired by research on normative multiagent systems [2], we refer to expres-sions of desired user behaviour as *(behaviour) norms* that may or may not be complied with by the user of the epartner.

Providing a comprehensive formal framework for representation of daily user behaviour for the purpose of behaviour support is a non-trivial task due to the potential complexity of this behaviour and the many facets that may be consid-ered, such as temporal aspects [6] and user values [17]. In this paper we focus on two key characteristics. First, representing the potentially complex *structure of daily behaviour* requires a way to decompose behaviour into its constituting parts [18]. Not all of these parts need to always be executed, some are optional while others are mandatory, and sometimes a choice needs to be made. Second, the nature of (desired) daily behaviour is often *habitual* [5,9], i.e., it concerns the frequency of a user's repeated behaviour over time. For example, a user may want to change his habit of having a late breakfast such that at least 80% of his breakfasts are early breakfasts, and needs to do work in the evening on four out of five workdays, i.e., 80% of the workdays.

Defining when a user's behaviour is compliant with such a specification of desired behaviour requires first of all a definition of compliance with respect to the basic specified behaviour structure. Second, in order to define compliance with respect to the frequency of performed behaviour, we propose a statistical approach (*probabilistic norm compliance*). This is because there will typically be some variation in user behaviour over time, which might lead to some deviations from the precise desired behaviour frequencies. The question we need to answer is when these deviations are still "ok", i.e., when we can consider the user to have adopted the specified habit. For example, if we consider the past 20 workdays out of which the user has worked 17 evenings. Is the user compliant with the behaviour norm, i.e, can we say the user has adopted the specified habit? What if we consider the past 6 days out of which the user has worked 5 evenings?

To address these challenges, this paper provides the following contributions:

1. We propose to use the well-studied formalism of *Feature Diagrams* [11] for daily behaviour representation. Feature Diagrams have been used widely in software engineering for modelling Software Product Lines [15]. In that con-text Feature Diagrams represent the different parts of a software product, and how they fit together to compose the overarching concept or final product.

We observe that this formalism also provides a natural way of representing the hierarchical structure of daily behaviour. (Sections 2 and 3)

2. We introduce a novel extension of Feature Diagrams called probabilistic Feature Diagrams in order to represent behaviour frequencies. We provide a formal semantics by means of hypothesis testing [10]. Hypothesis testing is a type of statistical model checking, normally used to verify performance characteristics of software. (Section 4)

3. We perform an experimental evaluation of our framework by implementing the Feature Diagram semantics with respect to an existing daily behaviour dataset [14], and show that our notion of probabilistic norm compliance can be used in this real-world setting. (Section 5)

2   Behaviour Hierarchies

Psychological research [18] has shown that people think about their behaviour in a hierarchical fashion, from abstract to more concrete. We have proposed to formalise hierarchical behaviour structures with the aim of allowing a behaviour support agent to represent the (actual and desired) daily behaviour of its user in a way that matches how the user thinks about their behaviour [6,8,9,17].

Behaviour hierarchies can be represented as trees, with an abstract behaviour as the root, and its nodes and leaves decomposing this behaviour into its more concrete parts and sub-behaviours. The leaves will consist of behaviours that do not need to be decomposed further. This type of decomposition is comparable to Goal Plan Trees (GPTs) [16]. The main difference is in the semantics: our structures are used to *describe* desired behaviour, yielding a logic-based semantics to assess whether a structure is satisfied with respect to a user's actual behaviour. In contrast, GPTs are used to *generate* (software) agent behaviour. Furthermore, our hierarchies should include relative frequencies to indicate how often a sub-behaviour should be performed with respect to its parent behaviour.

Example 1. Suppose that a user, let us call him John, decides that they want to change their daily routine at home: John has realized that he very often has a late breakfast and thus starts his workday rather late as well. As part of improving his daily routine for a workday, he commits to having an early breakfast most of the time (at least 80%) – on the days that he has time for breakfast at home. To help him achieve this, John also commits to do some work at home in the evenings on most days (4 days per week, i.e., 80%), so he can have a breakfast at home as well as get the work done he committed to for his job. John also needs to take some prescribed medication several times per week (3–4 days, i.e., 60–80%). This desired behaviour can be represented as follows:

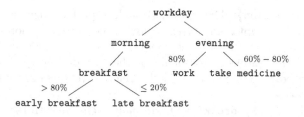

Fig. 1. Tree representation of Example 1

Note that this tree representation is lacking some information about the behaviour structure: namely, the sub-activities `early breakfast` and `late breakfast` form two *alternatives* of the activity `breakfast` (i.e., they cannot both occur on the same workday), while the sub-activities `work` and `take medicine` form two *options* of activities that may be done during the evening. Since for the evening activities, the rates of 80% and 60–80%, respectively, do not sum to (less than) 100%, it is easy to spot that there may be a different characterisation to these sub-activities as compared to the breakfast activities. However, should John plan to take medicine in the evening only once a week, changing the 60–80% to 20%, we need to express explicitly how these sub-behaviours should be interpreted. Similarly, we need to indicate whether an activity is supposed to be carried out as an *optional* or *mandatory* activity. For instance, John might occasionally skip eating breakfast at home in the morning, and take it to work, making this an *optional* activity.

In order to express such structural properties, one needs a more expressive syntactical framework, for which we propose to use Feature Diagrams.

3   Representing Daily Behaviour with Feature Diagrams

In previous work we have already proposed to formalise hierarchical behaviour structures for behaviour support agents [6,8,9,17]. Most of these works however do not provide formal semantics that expresses when such a structure is satisfied, or they do so for a structure with limited expressivity. Through our insight that the well-studied Feature Diagram formalism is suitable for representing behaviour hierarchies, in this paper we are able to propose both an expressive representation framework (Sect. 3.1) as well as an accompanying formal semantics (Sect. 3.2). In this section we provide a definition of Feature Diagrams that represents the behaviour structure. In the next section we add frequencies.

3.1   Syntax

The formal definition of a Feature Diagram we use here is based on Definition 3.2 of [11] and definitions for node types provided in [13]. In particular, the Feature Diagrams we present here are trees; nodes in our Feature Diagram represent (parts of) behaviours. Each node has a type associated with them from the set

$NT = \{\text{or}, \text{xor}, \text{option}\}$. The optional node type has edges that can either be of mandatory or optional type. That is, the decomposition of behaviour into parts is such that the sub-behaviours are either all independent parts of the behaviour (mandatory or optional), or they are options, possibly mutually exclusive ones (xor). The xor node is also referred to as an alternative node in the literature.

In Example 1, early breakfast is mutually exclusive with late breakfast, but taking them to be optional sub-nodes of the node breakfast would still allow both of them to be present. In this situation, we say that breakfast is of node type xor, meaning that precisely one of the sub-nodes are to be realised. Similarly, the node type or allows for at least one of the sub-nodes to be realised. For instance, taking evening in the example above to be of type or would mean that on any given evening of the workweek, John either takes medicine, or does some work, or both, but there is never (supposed to be) an evening on which he does not do either of these. Taking workday as an option node with mandatory links specifies that any workday requires something to be done in the morning and in the evening.

We formally define Feature Diagrams as follows, using a standard definition of the notion of a tree:

Definition 1 (Tree). *Let N be a set of behaviours and $E : N \times N$ a relation on N. We say that $\langle N, E \rangle$ is a tree, if E is antisymmetric, irreflexive and such that for any a, b, $c \in N$, if $(a,b) \in E$ and $(c,b) \in E$, then $a = c$. We use r to denote the root of a tree, i.e., the node $m \in N$ such that there is no $n \in N$ with $(n,m) \in E$. There can be precisely one such root node in any tree.*

Definition 2 (Feature Diagram, FD). *A Feature Diagram D is a structure $D = (N, E, \lambda, \mu)$ such that*

- *N is the set of nodes;*
- *$E \subseteq N \times N$ is the set of decomposition edges and $N^* \subseteq N$ is the set of nodes that are not leaves, i.e. $\forall n \in N^* \, \exists m \in N \, (n,m) \in E$;*
- *$\langle N, E \rangle$ is a tree;*
- *$\lambda : N^* \to NT$ is a labelling of the nodes, where $NT = \{\text{or}, \text{xor}, \text{option}\}$ is the set of node types;*
- *Let $N^{opt} \subseteq N$ be the set of nodes with label option, i.e., $\{n \mid n \in N, \lambda(n) = \text{option}\}$, and E^{opt} be the set of edges emerging from these nodes, i.e., $\{(n,m) \mid (n,m) \in E, n \in N^{opt}\}$. Then $\mu : E^{opt} \to \{\text{mandatory}, \text{optional}\}$ is a labelling of these edges.*

For a given node n, we will write $n \in D$ as shorthand for $n \in N$.

Usually, the formal Feature Diagrams are provided in graphical form; the relationships or, xor/alternative, optional, and mandatory are expressed using the following graphical representation:

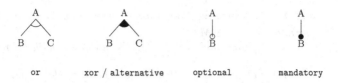

Fig. 2. Common representation of feature diagrams

Example 2. On th basis of the tree given in Example 1, we define the following Feature Diagram for the workday of John:

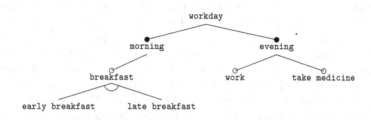

Fig. 3. Feature diagram representing the workday from Example 1

Note that the definition of Feature Diagrams as provided by Definition 2 does not allow for the representation of frequencies of Example 1, and thus we omit them here.

3.2 Semantics

The behavioural norms represented by Feature Diagrams are the ideal that the actual behaviour of the user will be compared to. We will therefore need to introduce what we mean by an *observation* or *model* of behavioural norms represented by a Feature Diagram. We can limit the observation to those behaviours that have a corresponding node in the Feature Diagram: behaviours that do not get mentioned in the diagram can be considered irrelevant for the question of whether a norm is complied with – any behaviour that is relevant for norm compliance should be recorded in the Feature Diagram right from the start.

Definition 3. *[Model/valid model] Let $D = (N, E, \lambda, \mu)$ be a Feature Diagram. A model of D is a subset $M \subseteq N$ of the nodes of D.*

A valid model is a subset $M \subseteq N$ such that

– *the root $r \in M$;*
– *if $n \in M$ and $\lambda(n) =$ or, then for at least one $m \in N$ with $(n, m) \in E$, $m \in M$;*
– *if $n \in M$ and $\lambda(n) =$ xor, then for precisely one $m \in N$ with $(n, m) \in E$, $m \in M$;*

- *if $n \in M$ and $\lambda(n) =$ option, then for all $m \in N$ with $(n,m) \in E$ and $\mu((n,m)) =$ mandatory, $m \in M$;*
- *if $m \in M$ with $m \neq r$, then also $n \in M$ for the unique n with $(n,m) \in E$.*

We will write $M \models D$ to indicate that M is a valid model of D.

We have omitted mentioning the optional edge type, since optional nodes need not be realized. Furthermore, the last point closes the model under predecessors in the tree: it guarantees that, e.g., if late breakfast as a subnode of breakfast, which in turn is a subnode of morning is present in a given model, then breakfast and morning are both guaranteed to be present.

A model of a Feature Diagram expresses the satisfaction of behaviour norms for a single instance of the behaviour represented by the tree. To formalise realisation of daily routines, i.e., satisfaction of Feature Diagrams over time, we introduce *traces* of models: each point in the trace will represent a single instance of user behaviour. E.g., if the behavioural norm the user wants assistance with is having early breakfasts on workdays, then a trace will consist of a sequence of valid models of the Feature Diagram representing this routine, one for each workday of the week. Note that the root of the Feature Diagram will be present in each sequent of the trace. Thus if the Feature Diagram represents a routine that is not done every day, we can either introduce a new root representing the day, which then occurs in every sequent of the trace – sometimes without any other element – or the sequents of the trace represent only those days on which the routine is – at least partially – executed in accordance with the specified Feature Diagram.

Definition 4 (Trace). *Let D be a Feature Diagram and let σ_i for $i \in \mathbb{N}$ be models of D. A trace on D is a sequence $\vec{\sigma} = \langle \sigma_0, \sigma_1, \ldots, \sigma_n, \ldots \rangle$. A trace $\vec{\sigma}$ on D satisfies D if for each $i \in \mathbb{N}$, $\sigma_i \models D$.*

There is an implied temporal ordering in this notion of trace: viewing the trace as a recording of observed behaviour, one can see the first sequent as the earliest observation, etc. Although we do not explicitly associate each index with a specific time, in most cases of monitoring daily behaviour it will be convenient to assume that each index stands for a specific day. Furthermore, we take traces in the formal definition to be countably infinite. In all practicality, we will then only be dealing with finite initial parts of traces. However, since we do not want to specify a maximal length, nor limit the number of times a specific behaviour can be recorded, we opt for $\mathbb{N}$ as the index set.

4   Probabilistic Feature Diagrams

The next step is to add frequencies into the Feature Diagrams. We do this by extending Definition 2 by a corresponding new component (Sect. 4.1). Then we define the semantics of these probabilistic Feature Diagrams through hypothesis testing (Sect. 4.2) by providing our new notion of probabilistic norm compliance (Sect. 4.3).

4.1 Syntax

Frequencies apply to edges of a Feature Diagram individually. An edge (n, m) with frequency p represents the norm to execute the behaviour represented by m with frequency p, relative to behaviour n. Frequencies may not only be seen as a point $p \in [0, 1]$, but could also refer to an interval in $[0, 1]$, e.g. $(1/2, 1]$ or $[1/3, 2/3]$, representing that the corresponding behaviour should be performed within this range. Edges are not required to have a frequency attached.

Definition 5 (probabilistic Feature Diagram, pFD). *Let $D = (N, E, \lambda, \mu)$ be a Feature Diagram. Let freq $: E \rightarrow I([0, 1])$ be a partial function assigning (relative) frequency intervals to edges in E.*

A probabilistic Feature Diagram $\mathcal{D} = \langle D, freq \rangle$ then is a Feature Diagram with the additional frequencies on the edges given by the function freq.

In case that q is either a singleton $[p, p]$, or of the form $[0, p)$, $(p, 1]$ (or their corresponding closed variants), we will simply denote these as p, $< p$, $> p$ (resp., $\leq p$, $\geq p$).

We impose a number of restrictions on frequencies, to avoid introducing contradictory information into the Feature Diagram. In particular, for xor nodes, we need to impose the restriction that the lower bounds of frequency intervals of its children add up to at most 1, and the upper bounds add up to 1. We can see frequencies as a normalised measure on the subnodes, relative to that node. The children of an xor node can be seen as a disjoint partition of the node, and thus frequencies summing up to some value larger than 1 would contradict this partition of the node. Since the frequency of the subnodes of some xor node are recording relative occurrence of the subnodes, having this restriction on the upper bounds guarantees that precisely one subnode will be done whenever the parent node is done. Furthermore, we do not allow a frequency $[0, 0]$ to be specified for an edge. This would indicate that the corresponding sub-behaviour should never be executed, which could contradict what are considered valid models according to Definition 3: a valid model might include the behaviour m of an edge (n, m), while adding a frequency $[0, 0]$ to this edge would express the contradictory information that this model is actually invalid. Third, we require that mandatory edges have frequency $[1, 1]$, as any other frequency would be contradicting the mandatory nature of the edge. We call probilistic Feature Diagrams that adhere to these restrictions *well-formed*.

Definition 6 (Well-formed probabilistic Feature Diagram, wpFD). *Let $\mathcal{D} = \langle D, freq \rangle$ with $D = (N, E, \lambda, \mu)$ be a probabilistic Feature Diagram. We say that $\mathcal{D}$ is a well-formed probabilistic Feature Diagram iff it satisfies the following constraints:*

- *if $\lambda(n) = $ xor for some $n \in D$, then $\sum_{(n,m) \in E} \inf freq((n, m)) \leq 1$ and $\sum_{(n,m) \in E} \sup freq((n, m)) = 1$;[1]*

---

[1] Note that we need to use the infimum here instead of the minimum, since the interval might be left-open.

- *There is no $e \in E$ such that freq$(e) = [0,0]$.*
- *If $e \in E$ and $\mu(e) = $ mandatory, then freq$(e) = [1,1]$.*

Example 3. Revisiting the Feature Diagram of Example 2, we are now able to work the frequencies back in, as given in Fig. 1, replacing the percentages given above by the corresponding frequency intervals:

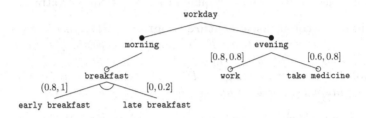

Fig. 4. Well-formed probabilistic feature diagram for the workday example

4.2   Hypothesis Testing for Probabilistic Feature Diagrams

Defining a semantics for the frequencies of a (well-formed) probabilistic Feature Diagram $\mathcal{D} = \langle D, freq \rangle$ requires a specification of the satisfaction of an edge (n, m) of D with frequency p with respect to a trace on D that represents the recorded behaviour of the user of the epartner over time. If these traces were infinite, we could calculate exactly whether the user behaviour indeed complies with the specified frequency by taking the ratio of the occurrence of m relative to n in the limit.

In practice however we need to evaluate compliance over varying finite time horizons, for example one week after the user has specified a new behaviour norm, but also after one month of trying to adopt a new habit, and possibly many other times. The observed frequencies will rarely be exactly equal to the desired frequency[2], since habitual user behaviour will often vary somewhat over time. In addition our sample size may prevent the possibility of exact compliance, e.g., if the desired frequency is 0.8 but we evaluate compliance over a trace of length 7. Nevertheless we want our epartner to be able to assess compliance in these cases.

To address these challenges, we employ a statistical technique called *hypothesis testing* [10]. Hypothesis testing is a type of statistical model checking to verify whether a system model satisfies a property of interest with a probability above or below a certain threshold value: the hypothesis. The core idea of statistical model checking is to use a computer program to repeatedly simulate

---

[2] At least when this frequency is a point. However also in case of an interval we need to ask whether it is justified to conclude (non-)compliance if the observed behaviour frequency is close to the edges of the interval.

the behaviour of the system model. For each of these simulations (samples), one can check whether or not the property of interest holds. One might see each such sample as a coin toss for which we can check whether it satisfies a certain property (let's say 'heads'). Using statistical techniques one can then determine whether it is justified to reject or accept the stated hypothesis, i.e., whether the true probability of the system exhibiting the property of interest can be assumed to be as stated by the hypothesis. For example, whether we can accept the hypothesis that the probability of the coin turning up heads is bigger than 0.7.

The idea of using hypothesis testing for defining the semantics of a probabilistic Feature Diagram now is to treat each state of a trace on the Feature Diagram as one possible sample: each state represents one instance of the user executing the behaviour specified by the Feature Diagram. Thus instead of repeatedly simulating a system model, we use repeated observations of the type of user behaviour expressed by the Feature Diagram. Recalling the user's intended behaviour of Example 1, the idea is that the epartner will construct a sequence $\langle \sigma_0, \sigma_1, \ldots, \sigma_t \rangle$ of length t after running for t days, monitoring only behaviour that is recorded in the Feature Diagram and thus relevant for monitoring norm compliance, and recording a separate model σ_j for each new day. The property of interest in our case is the occurrence of a behaviour m for a link (n, m) with some frequency, e.g., the user having `early breakfast`, in those states where n (`breakfast`) occurs (the sample size). This means we assume that these models are obtained via independent, identically distributed random processes as described above. Investigating to what extent we need to address possible dependencies between the creation of these models (e.g., once a user starts exhibiting non-compliant behaviour it is more likely that it will continue to do so) is left for future work.

Since hypothesis testing can only be used to verify whether the true probability is above or below a certain threshold value, for a frequency p that is a point we cannot conclude that the user behaviour is compliant. However, we *can* conclude that it is non-compliant, if it is (sufficiently) above or below p.

Hypothesis testing has previously been applied in the context of multi-agent systems to let agents hypothesise the likelihood that other agents will choose certain actions, based on their interaction history [1]. Instead, our work allows a behaviour support agent to assess whether observed user behaviour complies with given behaviour norms.

4.3 Semantics

In this section we formally define the semantics of probabilistic Feature Diagrams through hypothesis testing. Along the lines of [3,4], we first introduce the notion of a *j-sample* that takes the first j elements of the trace under consideration, allowing to select the sample we want to assess. Here, it is important that we do not 'mix and match' any specific parts of the trace, but pick j consecutive elements, without any discrimination. In a second step, the sample is processed through a statistic function T, which counts the number of times a node is included in the states of the selected part of the trace.

Definition 7. (j-Sample and Statistic). *Let $\mathcal{D} = \langle D, freq \rangle$ be a probabilistic Feature Diagram with $D = (N, E, \lambda, \mu)$, and let $\vec{\sigma}$ be a trace on D that satisfies D. The j-sample of $\vec{\sigma}$ is the initial sequence $\langle \sigma_0, \sigma_1, \ldots, \sigma_{j-1} \rangle$ of $\vec{\sigma}$ of length j. We denote the j-sample by $\vec{\sigma}(j)$.*

Let $\Sigma(D)$ be the set of traces on D and $\Sigma^{(j)}(D)$ be the set of j-samples of the traces. We define the statistic T on $\Sigma^{(j)}(D)$ and the nodes N of D by

$$T : \Sigma^{(j)}(D) \times N \to \mathbb{N}$$

$$T(\vec{\sigma}(j), m) = \sum_{s=0}^{j-1} \mathbb{1}_m(\sigma_s),$$

where

$$\mathbb{1}_m(\sigma) = \begin{cases} 1 & \text{if } m \in \sigma, \\ 0 & \text{otherwise.} \end{cases}$$

We can now use the statistic T to test for the hypothesis that the trace generated by the user's behaviour is compliant with the information in the probabilistic Feature Diagram $\mathcal{D}$ provided by the user. We opt here to use a test based on constructing confidence intervals for standard normally distributed random variables, which we will call Gauss-CI test, following the reasoning given by [10]. Given the properties of various tests described in [10], we opted for the Gauss-CI test since it works with a fixed sample size; in contrast to the model checking discussed there, the behavioural traces we deal with in this situation are indicating *past behaviour*, and we need our test to provide us with some answer towards (non-)compliance, so that a support system using the test can respond appropriately. This comes at the trade-off of drawing the wrong conclusion, or no conclusion at all, should the actual frequency of an activity be very close to the desired frequency. Since we would argue that a support system should not need a large sample of past behaviour before it can operate, we deem this acceptable.

Definition 8 (Gauss-CI test). *Let $\vec{\sigma}$, $\vec{\sigma}(j)$, $\mathcal{D}$ and T be as in Definition 7 above and let $\alpha \in [0, 1]$.*

Let $(n, m) \in E$ with $freq((n, m)) = p_m = [p_{0,m}, p_{1,m}]$. Let $T(\vec{\sigma}(j), n) = k$,

$$S_l(\vec{\sigma}(j), (n, m)) = (T(\vec{\sigma}(j), m) - k \cdot p_{0,m}),$$

$$S_u(\vec{\sigma}(j), (n, m)) = (T(\vec{\sigma}(j), m) - k \cdot p_{1,m}).$$

- *Let $l = l(\alpha, p_{0,m}) = \Phi^{-1}(\alpha) \cdot \sqrt{k \cdot p_{0,m} \cdot (1 - p_{0,m})}$ and $u = u(\alpha, p_{1,m}) = \Phi^{-1}(1 - \alpha) \cdot \sqrt{k \cdot p_{1,m} \cdot (1 - p_{1,m})}$, where Φ is the cumulative distribution function of the standard normal distribution.*
  We say that with confidence $(1 - \alpha)$, we reject the hypothesis that $p \geq p_{0,m}$ if $S_l(\vec{\sigma}(j), (n, m)) < l$, and we reject the hypothesis that $p \leq p_{0,m}$ if $S_l(\vec{\sigma}(j), (n, m)) > -l$.

We say that with confidence $(1 - \alpha)$, we reject the hypothesis that $p \geq p_{1,m}$ *if* $S_u(\vec{\sigma}(j), (n,m)) < -u$, *and we* reject the hypothesis that $p \leq p_{1,m}$ *if* $S_u(\vec{\sigma}(j), (n,m)) > u$.

- *We say that the test is* inconclusive *in all other cases.*

We will use the test defined above to give a formalization for our notion of *probabilistic norm compliance*. In essence, given some interval $[p_{0,m}, p_{1,m}]$, we want to be certain that the frequency p in our sample is not too low or too high, i.e. we want to rule out that $p < p_{0,m}$ or $p > p_{1,m}$. For this, we obtain 'confidence intervals' $[l, -l]$ and $[-u, u]^3$ for the values of $p_{0,m}$ and $p_{1,m}$, respectively. That is, if the statistic S_l is larger than $-l$, then we may assume – with error level α – that $p > p_{0,m}$, and similarly, we may assume $p < p_{1,m}$ if $S_u < -u$. If both inequalities hold, we can safely assume that the norm of doing the specified activity m with a frequency in the interval $[p_{0,m}, p_{1,m}]$ is complied with. Furthermore, if $S_l < l$, we may safely assume that the norm is not complied with, with a frequency that is too low, or similarly, we may assume that the frequency is too high in case $S_u > u$. In all other cases, the frequency p is too close to one of the endpoints $p_{0,m}$, $p_{1,m}$ to be certain that it is on the right side of the endpoint, and therefore the test will be inconclusive.

Definition 9 (Probabilistic Norm Compliance). *Let* $\mathcal{D} = \langle D, freq \rangle$ *be a probabilistic Feature Diagram with* $D = \langle N, E, \lambda, \mu \rangle$, $\vec{\sigma}$ *a trace on* D *satisfying* D *and* $\alpha \in [0,1]$ *an error level. Let* $(n,m) \in E$ *be an edge with* $freq((n,m)) = [p_0, p_1]$, *we say that*

- $\vec{\sigma}$ *is* compliant *with* $\mathcal{D}$ *for* (n,m), *if the test defined in Definition 8 rejects the hypotheses* $p \leq p_0$ *and* $p \geq p_1$;
- $\vec{\sigma}$ *is* non-compliant *with* $\mathcal{D}$ *for* (n,m), *if the test either does not reject* $p \leq p_0$ *or* $p \geq p_1$;
- $\vec{\sigma}$ *is* inconclusive *for* (n,m) *otherwise.*

With $S_l(\vec{\sigma}(j), (n,m))$ *and* $S_u(\vec{\sigma}(j), (n,m))$, $l(\alpha, p_0)$, $u(\alpha, p_1)$ *given as above, let the* compliance function *be the function* $R(\mathcal{D}, \vec{\sigma}, j, \alpha, (n,m))$ *defined by*

$$R(\mathcal{D}, \vec{\sigma}, j, \alpha, (n,m)) = \begin{cases} \text{compliant} & \text{if } S_l(\vec{\sigma}(j), (n,m)) > -l(\alpha, p_0) \\ & \text{and } S_u(\vec{\sigma}(j), (n,m)) < -u(\alpha, p_1), \\[2mm] \text{non-compliant-too-high} & \text{if } S_u(\vec{\sigma}(j), (n,m)) > u(\alpha, p_1), \\[2mm] \text{non-compliant-too-low} & \text{if } S_l(\vec{\sigma}(j), (n,m)) < l(\alpha, p_0), \\[2mm] \text{inconclusive} & \text{otherwise.} \end{cases}$$

Note that in the special case of $p_0 = p_1 = \bar{p}$, i.e. the interval is a singleton, the compliance function can never provide the value `compliant`, since we need to reject both $p \geq \bar{p}$ and $p \leq \bar{p}$, and thus in particular reject $p = \bar{p}$.

---

3 Note that we will have $l < 0 < u$, so the intervals are indeed sound.

5 Experimental Evaluation

5.1 Experimental Setup – Obtaining the Feature Diagram and Models

We will now proceed to put the formal definitions of the previous sections to the practice. Namely, we will evaluate an existing daily behaviour dataset [14] with our compliance function R given in Definition 9. The dataset consists of data about the execution of activities of daily living – e.g., eating and drinking, sleeping, working, watching tv, taking medicine, etc. – of several individuals (workday and weekend), over about 2 months. For this paper we have used the data in the file `data/edited_hh104_labour.xes.gz`, which has workday data of 43 days of user `hh104`. A typical entry for a single activity consists of a `start` event and a corresponding `complete` event (not shown here):

```
<event>
    <string key="concept:name" value="eatingdrinking"/>
    <string key="lifecycle:transition" value="start"/>
    <date key="time:timestamp"
          value="2011-06-15T07:11:45.000+02:00"/>
    <string key="work" value="eatingdrinking"/>
</event>
```

Since the dataset does not provide the Feature Diagrams corresponding to the desired behaviour of the user, we have reconstructed a possible Feature Diagram from the events given in the dataset. The sample entry above, for instance, indicates that the user had a meal on the morning of 15 June 2011, between 7:11 and 7:23. Thus we can take this entry as representing an instance of `breakfast`. We would separate the breakfasts into `early breakfast` in case the time of day is between 6 a.m. and 9 a.m., and classify a meal in the morning as `late breakfast` in case it takes place later than that but before noon. For this classification we only consider the start times of events.

Note that not all event entries of the dataset have been represented in the FD: for instance, we did not take any patterns for `sleep` into account here. We have picked values for the frequencies that might be considered desired behaviour for this user. For example, we noticed this user typically has breakfast rather late after doing some other activities, while it may be considered more healthy to start the day with breakfast. The resulting reconstructed probabilistic Feature Diagram is then that of Fig. 3.

To obtain the models, i.e., states of our trace and number of occurrences of the nodes in our Feature Diagram over this trace (the function T of Definition 7) we have made an implementation in the knowledge graph language Grakn (version 1.5.3 for Mac). The language allows to define an expressive schema in graph form over a given dataset. The tree structure of our Feature Diagrams lends itself well to implementation using knowledge graphs. We implement the Feature Diagram syntax and semantics as a Grakn schema. In order to obtain the models to make up our trace, we need to define when the nodes of our example Feature Diagram are satisfied with respect to the dataset, e.g., `early breakfast` holds on a certain date if the above event occurs in the dataset for that date. We specify this using Grakn rules. We obtain the number of occurrences of nodes in our trace using a query over our schema and the imported dataset.[4] With $j = 43$, i.e., taking all workdays present in our dataset, we obtain the following number of occurrences of nodes of our Feature Diagram: `workday`, `morning`, `evening`, `breakfast`: 43; `early breakfast`: 11; `late breakfast`: 32; `work`: 38; `take medicine`: 33.

5.2   Results in Probabilistic Norm Compliance

Given the numbers of occurrences, and the desired frequencies, we apply the testing framework given above. First we apply the statistic of Definition 7. Note that in this case, we have $j = k = 43$, since both the `breakfast` and `evening` nodes occur 43 times. Note that the nodes for `workday` and `morning` are left out here, since our Feature Diagram only specifies frequences for the leaf nodes with respect to their parents. We use Definition 8 to obtain confidence intervals for the values of the statistics. We calculate those values to two decimal places, using the `norm.ppf` function of Python's `scipy.stats` package to obtain values for Φ^{-1}. Finally, we use the Probabilistic Norm Compliance function R from Definition 9 in order to determine whether the sample data indicates compliance with the relative frequencies of the Feature Diagram. As an error level for our test, we pick a value of $\alpha = 0.05$, or 5%.

Node	k	T	α	p_0	p_1	l	S_l	u	S_u	R(esult)
early breakfast	43	11	0.05	0.8	1	-4.31	-23.4	0	-32	non-compliant-too-low
late breakfast	43	32	0.05	0	0.2	0	32	4.31	23.4	non-compliant-too-high
work	43	38	0.05	0.8	0.8	-4.31	3.6	4.31	3.6	inconclusive
take medicine	43	33	0.05	0.6	0.8	-5.28	7.2	4.31	-1.4	inconclusive
take medicine	43	33	0.3	0.6	0.8	-1.68	7.2	1.36	-1.4	compliant

We can see that for `breakfast`, the test result clearly indicates that the ratio of `early breakfast` is far too low, and symmetrically, `late breakfast` occurs too often in the data. However, for `work` and `take medicine` the test result indicates an inconclusive result. For `take medicine` the values indicate that this node is realized with a ration of at least 60%, but the actual rate is likely too close to the upper bound of 80% for the test to return meaningful results. In fact, as the last line in the table above shows, we can obtain a compliant result if the error level is substantially increased (to 30% in this case).

---

[4] The code is available from GitHub repository [20].

6   Conclusion

We have introduced Feature Diagrams as a way of expressing and assessing compliance with desired user behaviour. In order to represent relative frequencies we proposed a probabilistic extension of Feature Diagrams. Interpreting such a probabilistic Feature Diagram as a record of behavioural norms, we can use Hypothesis Testing methods to monitor compliance with these norms in daily behaviour. The methods demonstrated here allow not just to measure compliance itself, but also allow to give an estimate of whether non-compliant behaviour occurs with too low or too high a frequency, compared to the recorded values in the Feature Diagram.

Our experimental evaluation is based on a dataset that consists of such records of daily behaviour. While the Feature Diagram corresponding to this data was a reconstruction, the results presented in Sect. 5 nonetheless demonstrate that the concepts and methods used in this paper provide meaningful answers to the question of whether a pre-recorded behavioural norm is complied with by a user. The framework of probabilistic Feature Diagrams and Hypothesis testing methods can also provide us with meaningful results in the presence of a rather small set of data points.

Expanding from this proof of concept, we intend to investigate formal properties of this framework. We further plan a user study, investigating ease of use of the framework in the intended field of application, and assessing intuitiveness of the notion of probabilistic norm compliance for assessing satisfaction of behaviour norms.

References

1. Albrecht, S.V., Ramamoorthy, S.: Are you doing what i think you are doing? criticising uncertain agent models. In: Proceedings of the Thirty-First Conference on Uncertainty in Artificial Intelligence, Arlington, Virginia, United States, UAI 2015, pp. 52–61. AUAI Press (2015)
2. Andrighetto, G., Governatori, G., Noriega, P., van der Torre, L. (eds.) Normative Multi-Agent Systems, vol. 4 of Dagstuhl Follow-Ups. Schloss Dagstuhl-Leibniz-Zentrum fuer Informatik (2013)
3. Cheung, L., Stoelinga, M., Vaandrager, F.W.: A testing scenario for probabilistic processes. J. ACM 54(6), 29 (2007)
4. Gerhold, M., Stoelinga, M.: Model-based testing of probabilistic systems. Formal Asp. Comput. 30(1), 77–106 (2018)
5. Hull, C.L.: Principles of Behavior: An Introduction to Behavior Theory. Appleton-Century, New York (1943)
6. Kließ, M.S., Jonker, C.M., van Riemsdijk, M.B.A.: Temporal logic for modelling activities of daily living. In: Alechina, N., Nørvåg, K., Penczek, W. (eds.) 25th International Symposium on Temporal Representation and Reasoning, TIME 2018, vol. 120 of Leibniz International Proceedings in Informatics (LIPIcs), pp. 17:1–17:15. Schloss Dagstuhl-Leibniz-Zentrum fuer Informatik (2018)

7. Oinas-Kukkonen, Harri: Behavior change support systems: a research model and agenda. In: Ploug, Thomas, Hasle, Per, Oinas-Kukkonen, Harri (eds.) PERSUA-SIVE 2010. LNCS, vol. 6137, pp. 4–14. Springer, Heidelberg (2010). https://doi.org/10.1007/978-3-642-13226-1_3

8. Pasotti, P., Jonker, C.M., van Riemsdijk, M.B.: Action identification hierarchies for behaviour support agents. In: Third Workshop on Cognitive Knowledge Acquisition and Applications, Cognitum 2017 at IJCAI 2017 (2017)

9. Pasotti, P., van Riemsdijk, M.B., Jonker, C.M.: Representing human habits: towards a habit support agent. In: Proceedings of the 10th International Workshop on Normative Multiagent Systems, NorMAS 2016 (2016)

10. Reijsbergen, D., de Boer, P.-T., Scheinhardt, W., Haverkort, B.: On hypothesis testing for statistical model checking. Int. J. Softw. Tools Technol. Transfer $17(4)$, 377–395 (2015)

11. Schobbens, P., Heymans, P., Trigaux, J.: Feature diagrams: a survey and a formal semantics. In: 14th IEEE International Requirements Engineering Conference, RE 2006, pp. 139–148, September 2006

12. Shafti, Leila S., Haya, Pablo Alfonso, García-Herranz, Manuel, Alamán, Xavier: Personal ambient intelligent reminder for people with cognitive disabilities. In: Bravo, José, Hervás, Ramón, Rodríguez, Marcela (eds.) IWAAL 2012. LNCS, vol. 7657, pp. 383–390. Springer, Heidelberg (2012). https://doi.org/10.1007/978-3-642-35395-6_52

13. Sun, J., Zhang, H., Fang, Y., Wang, L.H.: Formal semantics and verification for feature modeling. In: 10th IEEE International Conference on Engineering of Complex Computer Systems, ICECCS 2005. IEEE, pp. 303–312 (2005)

14. Sztyler, T.T, Carmona, J.J.: Activities of daily living of several individuals (2015). https://data.4tu.nl/repository/uuid:01eaba9f-d3ed-4e04-9945-b8b302764176

15. ter Beek, M.H., Legay, A., Lafuente, A.L., Vandin, A.: Statistical analysis of probabilistic models of software product lines with quantitative constraints. In: Proceedings of the 19th International Conference on Software Product Line, SPLC 2015, New York, NY, USA, pp. 11–15. ACM (2015)

16. Thangarajah, J., Padgham, L., Winikoff, M.: Detecting & exploiting positive goal interaction in intelligent agents. In: Proceedings of the Second International Joint Conference on Autonomous Agents and Multiagent Systems, AAMAS 2003, pp. 401–408. ACM (2003)

17. Tielman, M.L., Jonker, C.M., van Riemsdijk, M.B.: What should i do? deriving norms from actions, values and context. In: Cassens, J., Wegener, R., Kofod-Petersen, A. (eds.) Proceedings of the Tenth International Workshop Modelling and Reasoning in Context, MRC 2018, no. 2134, pp. 35–40. CEUR Workshop Proceedings (2018)

18. Vallacher, R.R., Wegner, D.M.: What do people think they're doing? action identification and human behavior. Psychol. Rev. $94(1)$, 3–15 (1987)

19. van Riemsdijk, M.B., Jonker, C.M., Lesser, V.: Creating socially adaptive electronic partners: interaction, reasoning and ethical challenges. In: Proceedings of the Fourteenth International Joint Conference on Autonomous Agents and Multiagent Systems, AAMAS 2015, pp. 1201–1206. IFAAMAS (2015)

20. van Riemsdijk, M.B.: Feature diagrams for behaviour support agents in Grakn. https://github.com/mbirna/feature-diagrams-grakn (2019)

Identifying Belief Sequences in a Network of Communicating Agents

Gauvain Bourgne[1]($\boxtimes$), Yutaro Totsuka[2], Nicolas Schwind[3], and Katsumi Inoue[4]

[1] LIP6 UMR, CNRS & Sorbonne Université, 7606 Paris, France
gauvain.bourgne@lip6.fr
[2] Tokyo Institute of Technology, Tokyo, Japan
totsuka.y.aa@m.titech.ac.jp
[3] National Institute of Advanced Industrial Science and Technology, Tokyo, Japan
nicolas-schwind@aist.go.jp
[4] National Institute of Informatics/SOKENDAI, Tokyo Institute of Technology,
Tokyo, Japan
inoue@nii.ac.jp

Abstract. Belief Revision Games (BRGs) were recently introduced to simulate the dynamics of beliefs in a network of communicating agents. In a BRG, each agent expresses her beliefs as a propositional formula, which are iteratively revised according to the beliefs of her acquaintances. An appealing property of BRGs is that the belief sequence of each agent is always cyclic and thus can be finitely characterized. However, identifying such belief cycles is a hard task. This paper addresses the computational issues and focuses on the case where the revision policies of the agents are based on a well-known majority-based merging operator. In particular, we show how some evolution patterns in the belief sequences can be identified independently of the propositional language used by the agents to express their beliefs, allowing an exhaustive search of all possible belief cycle patterns. By further identifying beliefs that lead to similar belief cycles, we introduce algorithms to reduce the search space and perform an exhaustive analysis of the dynamics of beliefs in any given network.

1 Introduction

Belief Revision Games (BRGs) were introduced by Schwind et al. [5] in order to simulate dynamics of the beliefs of a group of communicating agents. In a BRG, agents synchronously revise their own belief states at each communication step by considering the beliefs of their acquaintances. Six classes of merging-based revision policies have been introduced, reflecting the importance an agent gives to her own beliefs in comparison with her acquaintances' beliefs. Simulating a BRG is done in a deterministic way, so that at some point the set of agents' beliefs falls into a so-called *global belief cycle*. The size of the global belief cycle can be viewed as a relevant indicator of the stability of the agents' beliefs.

In this paper, we are interested in studying how this size of such cycles is affected by the structural components of a BRG, independently of the propositional language used by the agent to express their beliefs, and making abstraction

M. Baldoni et al. (Eds.): PRIMA 2019, LNAI 11873, pp. 370–386, 2019.
https://doi.org/10.1007/978-3-030-33792-6_23

of the actual initial belief states of the agents. Thus given a *BRG structure* (i.e., a BRG without the agents' initial belief states), one could simply "simulate" all BRGs induced by it for all possible initial belief states, compute the size of the global belief cycle for each one of them, and return the maximal found number. But this raises two issues. First, computing the global belief cycle of a single BRG is a hard task. Second, given a BRG structure, there are infinitely many BRGs to simulate: indeed, the number of possible initial global belief states (modulo logical equivalence) that can instantiate a BRG structure is bounded only by the propositional language under consideration.

Our work addresses these computational issues. We focus on a broad family of BRGs where the revision policies used by the agents are based on a specific merging operator called the drastic majority operator [2]. Doing so, we show that the evolution of the global sequence of the agents' belief states does not strongly depend on the belief states themselves. More precisely, it is affected by the topological structure of the BRG, and whether subgroups of agents have consistent joint beliefs or not . This allows ones to greatly reduce the number of BRGs to explore given a BRG structure: $2^{2^n - 1}$, n being the number of agents. As this number is still huge, we introduce some ways to reduce the search space by grouping together global belief states leading to similar global belief cycles.

In the next section we provide some formal preliminaries on BRGs. In Sect. 3, we formalize the notion of BRG structure, and show that the evolution of all BRGs can be fully characterized by only considering a small number of representative BRGs from a given BRG structure. Section 4 focuses on the computation of the maximal size of global cycles of BRGs instantiating a BRG structure, and provides algorithms to compute and reduce the number of BRG sequences that need to be simulated to characterize all possible global belief cycles. These algorithms are tested in Sect. 5 with their implementation for a specific revision policy, showing that these reductions allows one to deal with BRGs with up to seven agents in less than ten minutes. We conclude in Sect. 6.

2 Preliminaries on Belief Revision Games

Given a propositional language $\mathcal{L}_\mathcal{P}$ built from a finite set $\mathcal{P}$ of variables and the usual connectives, formulae from $\mathcal{L}_\mathcal{P}$ are interpreted in the standard way, Ω denotes the set of all interpretations, $[\varphi]$ denotes the set of models of any $\varphi \in \mathcal{L}_\mathcal{P}$, $\models$ denotes logical entailment and $\equiv$ logical equivalence. A *belief base* (or *belief state*) is a formula from $\mathcal{L}_\mathcal{P}$ representing the beliefs of a given agent. A *profile* is a vector of belief bases representing the beliefs of different agents. A Belief Revision Game (BRG for short) is formalized as follows [5]:

Definition 1 (Belief Revision Game). *A Belief Revision Game (BRG) is a tuple $G = (V, A, \mathcal{L}_\mathcal{P}, B, \mathcal{R})$ where:*

- *$V = \{1, \dots, n\}$ is a finite set of* agents;
- *$A \subseteq V \times V$ is an irreflexive binary relation on V representing the* acquaintance relation *between the agents;*

- $\mathcal{L}_\mathcal{P}$ is a propositional language built from a finite set $\mathcal{P}$ of variables and the usual connectives;
- B is the (initial) global belief state, it is a mapping from V to $\mathcal{L}_\mathcal{P}$ where for each $i \in V$, $B(i)$ (also denoted by B_i) is the (initial) belief base of i;
- $\mathcal{R} = \langle R_1, \ldots, R_n \rangle$, where each R_i is the revision policy of agent i, i.e., a mapping from $\mathcal{L}_\mathcal{P} \times \mathcal{L}_\mathcal{P}^{in(i)}$ to $\mathcal{L}_\mathcal{P}$, with $in(i) = |\{j \mid (j,i) \in A\}|$ the in-degree of i, such that if $in(i) = 0$, then R_i is the identity function.

Let $G = (V, A, \mathcal{L}_\mathcal{P}, B, \mathcal{R})$ be a BRG. The *context of* $i \in V$, denoted by $\mathcal{C}_i$, is defined as the profile $\langle B_{i_1}, \ldots B_{i_{in(i)}} \rangle$ where $\{i_1, \ldots, i_{in(i)}\} = \{i_j | (i, i_j) \in A\}$ is the set of acquaintances of i. Then $R_i(B_i, \mathcal{C}_i)$ represents the belief base of i once "revised", after taking into account her own belief base B_i and her context $\mathcal{C}_i$. In a BRG, the agents' beliefs evolve stepwise, so that each agent i is associated with a *belief sequence* $(B_i^s)_{s \in \mathbb{N}}$, where B_i^s is the belief base of i at step s, $B_i^0 = B_i$, and $B_i^{s+1} = R_i(B_i^s, \mathcal{C}_i^s)$ for every $s \geq 0$, where $\mathcal{C}_i^s$ is the context of i at step s. Then $(B^s)_{s \in \mathbb{N}}$ denotes the *global belief sequence* of the BRG, where each B^s is the global belief state at step s. Schwind et al. [5] showed that in a BRG, the belief sequence of each agent is *cyclic*, which also means that the global belief sequence is also cyclic. Hence, any BRG G can be associated with a *global belief cycle*, denoted by $\mathrm{GCyc}(G)$, and defined as the first finite subsequence $(B^b, \ldots, B^e)$ found in the global belief sequence of G such that for every $j > e$ and every $i \in V$, we have $B_i^j \equiv B_i^{b+((j-b) \bmod (e-b+1))}$.

There are many ways an agent's revision policy R_i can be defined. Schwind et al. [5] introduced several classes of revision policies, each of which is characterized by a Belief Merging (BM) operator Δ. So let us first introduce some preliminary notions of BM operators. Formally, a BM operator Δ associates any formula μ (the *integrity constraint*) and any profile $\mathcal{C}$ with a new formula $\Delta_\mu(\mathcal{C})$ (the *merged base*). The purpose of a BM operator is to merge the (potentially conflicting) beliefs of a given group $\mathcal{C}$ while keeping a constraint μ satisfied. A set of standard properties (known as the IC postulates) are expected for BM operators, and such operators are called *IC merging operators* [3]. IC merging operators include a class of *distance-based* merging operators, which consist in selecting the models of the integrity constraint that are the "closest" to the input profile. These operators are characterized by a distance between interpretations and an aggregation function (see [2] for a number of instances of such operators).

Let us go back to BRGs and revision policies. Schwind et al. [5] have proposed six classes of revision policies R_Δ^k, each of which is based on a BM operator Δ:

$$R_\Delta^1(B_i^s, \mathcal{C}_i^s) = \Delta(\langle \mathcal{C}_i^s \rangle) \qquad R_\Delta^4(B_i^s, \mathcal{C}_i^s) = \Delta(\langle B_i^s, \Delta(\langle \mathcal{C}_i^s \rangle) \rangle)$$
$$R_\Delta^2(B_i^s, \mathcal{C}_i^s) = \Delta_{\Delta(\langle \mathcal{C}_i^s \rangle)}(\langle B_i \rangle) \qquad R_\Delta^5(B_i^s, \mathcal{C}_i^s) = \Delta_{B_i^s}(\Delta(\langle \mathcal{C}_i^s \rangle))$$
$$R_\Delta^3(B_i^s, \mathcal{C}_i^s) = \Delta(\langle B_i^s, \mathcal{C}_i^s \rangle) \qquad R_\Delta^6(B_i^s, \mathcal{C}_i^s) = \Delta_{B_i^s}(\langle \mathcal{C}_i^s \rangle)$$

These revision policies are ranked according to the relative importance given to an agent's own beliefs compared to the beliefs of her acquaintances.

In this paper, we focus on revision policies based on the *drastic majority operator* Δ^* [2]. This operator is defined for every profile $\mathcal{C}$ and every formula

Table 1. Computation of B_i^{s+1} when $R_i = R_{\Delta^*}^k$ for $k \in \{1, \ldots, 6\}$

R_i	case (a): $\varphi_{max}(\mathcal{C}_i^s) \wedge B_i^s \not\models \perp$ $(max = max_{B_i^s})$	case (b): $\varphi_{max}(\mathcal{C}_i^s) \wedge B_i^s \models \perp$ $(max > max_{B_i^s})$
$R_{\Delta^*}^1$	$\varphi_{max}(\mathcal{C}_i^s)$	$\varphi_{max}(\mathcal{C}_i^s)$
$R_{\Delta^*}^2$	$\varphi_{max}(\mathcal{C}_i^s) \wedge B_i^s$	$\varphi_{max}(\mathcal{C}_i^s)$
$R_{\Delta^*}^3$	$\varphi_{max}(\mathcal{C}_i^s) \wedge B_i^s$	$\varphi_{max}(\mathcal{C}_i^s) \vee (\varphi_{max(\mathcal{C}_i^s)-1}(\mathcal{C}_i^s) \wedge B_i^s)$
$R_{\Delta^*}^4$	$\varphi_{max}(\mathcal{C}_i^s) \wedge B_i^s$	$\varphi_{max}(\mathcal{C}_i^s) \vee B_i^s$
$R_{\Delta^*}^5$	$\varphi_{max}(\mathcal{C}_i^s) \wedge B_i^s$	B_i^s
$R_{\Delta^*}^6$	$\varphi_{max_{B_i^s}}(\mathcal{C}_i^s) \wedge B_i^s$	$\varphi_{max_{B_i^s}}(\mathcal{C}_i^s) \wedge B_i^s$

μ as a formula whole models are the models of μ satisfying the greatest number of bases from $\mathcal{C}$. Formally, given $k \geq 1$ and a profile $\mathcal{C}$, let $\varphi_k(\mathcal{C})$ be the formula defined as $\varphi_k(\mathcal{C}) = \bigvee_{J \subseteq \{1, \ldots, |\mathcal{C}|\}:|J|=k}(\bigwedge_{j \in J} B_j)$. By construction, the models of $\varphi_k(\mathcal{C})$ are precisely the set of all interpretations satisfying exactly k bases from $\mathcal{C}$. Then Δ^* is defined for every profile $\mathcal{C}$ and every formula μ as $\Delta_\mu^*(\mathcal{C}) = \mu \wedge \varphi_{max_\mu(\mathcal{C})}(\mathcal{C})$, where $max_\mu(\mathcal{C})$ is the maximal k such that $\mu \wedge \varphi_k(\mathcal{C})$ is consistent.

The drastic majority operator Δ^* is one of the most standard BM operators satisfying all IC postulates [3]. It corresponds to the distance-based merging operator $\Delta^{d_D, \Sigma}$ based on the drastic distance d_D between interpretations and using Σ as an aggregation function [2]. There is a number of works showing that Δ^* satisfies a number of additional properties. For instance, Δ^* satisfies some conditions of language independence [4], and some robustness properties from the viewpoint of strategy-proofness [1]. Moreover, when all agents in a BRG use a revision policy based on Δ^*, the BRG satisfies an appealing property of monotonicity [6]. This is why we focus on Δ^* in the rest of this paper and thus the specific revision policies $R_{\Delta^*}^k$, for $k \in \{1, \ldots, 6\}$. For the sake of reference, we provide in Table 1 the conditional outcome of a revised belief $R_{\Delta^*}^k(B_i^s, \mathcal{C}_i^s)$, for $k \in \{1, \ldots, 6\}$, $i \in V$ at any step $s \geq 0$. In this table, $\varphi_{max_\mu}(\mathcal{K})$ is used as a shorthand for $\varphi_{max_\mu(\mathcal{K})}(\mathcal{K})$ and $max_\top$ is shortened into max.

3   Characterizing Belief Sequences of BRG Structures

We are interested in this paper in identifying the structural components of a BRG that affect the *size* of its global belief cycle. We intend to show that the notion of *BRG structure* defined below is the key component for our purpose. Informally, a BRG structure can be viewed as more abstract notion of a BRG:

Definition 2 (BRG-structure). *A BRG-structure is a tuple* $S = (V, A, \alpha)$, *where V is a set of agents, A an acquaintance relation and α is an n-vector of numbers* $(\alpha_1, \ldots, \alpha_n)$ *where for each* $i \in V$, $\alpha_i \in \{1, \ldots, 6\}$.

Let us illustrate the notion of BRG structure through an example that will serve as a running example throughout the paper:

Example 1. We consider three agents Alice, Bob and Charles who communicate in a pairwise fashion as follows. Charles (agent 3) is an easily influenced agent, i.e., at each step he revises his beliefs according to Alice and Charles' without considering his own beliefs in the revision process. Bob (agent 2) is, on the contrary, reluctant to change: first, he only considers Bob's beliefs upon revision, and not Charles' ones; second, he is not ready to question his own beliefs, but may still expand his beliefs with Bob's ones, in case the resulting expanded beliefs remain consistent. Alice (agent 1) is ready to question her beliefs in a more parsimonious way than Charles: she values her beliefs and the beliefs of Bob and Charles equally. Formally, this corresponds to the BRG-structure $S = (V, A, \alpha)$ where $V = \{1, 2, 3\}$, $A = (V \times V) \setminus \{(3, 2)\}$, and $\alpha = (4, 6, 1)$. Hence, Alice (resp. Bob, Charles) is associated with the revision policy R^4 (resp. R^6, R^1).

Intuitively, a BRG structure characterizes the *behavior* of a BRG independently from an initial global belief state. Given our focus on Δ^*, the vector α fully characterizes the revision policy used for each agent in a BRG structure: for each agent i, $R_i = R^k_{\Delta^*}$. Therefore, a BRG structure $S = (V, A, \alpha)$ together with an initial global belief state B allows one to identify a BRG, denoted by $S(B)$, as $S(B) = (V, A, \mathcal{L_P}, B, \mathcal{R})$, where for each $i \in V$, $R_i = R^{\alpha_i}_{\Delta^*}$.

Given $\mathcal{L_P}$, we denote the set of all possible global belief states in $\mathcal{L_P}$ by $\mathbb{B}$. Then, given a BRG-structure S, For any $\mathcal{B} \subseteq \mathbb{B}$, we denote the maximum length of global belief cycle amongst all elements in $\mathcal{B}$ by $\mathrm{maxGCyc}(S, \mathcal{B}) = \max_{B \in \mathcal{B}} |GCyc(S(B))|$. Intuitively, the shorter length of global belief cycle, the more stable the agent's belief; a shorter global belief cycle reflects that all agents' beliefs oscillate amongst a smaller number of possible beliefs with the purely stable case corresponding to $\mathrm{maxGCyc}(S, \mathcal{B}) = 1$. Thus $\mathrm{maxGCyc}(S, \mathcal{B})$ represents the degree of unstability the beliefs could be in the BRG structure S amongst *all* possible initial beliefs $\mathcal{B}$. This enables us not only to simulate the diffusion of beliefs in a network of communicating agents, but also to analyze the impact of the networks and revision policies from the stability viewpoint. This paper mainly focuses on methods to calculate $\mathrm{maxGCyc}(S, \mathcal{B})$.

We will show that, as our revision policies are based on the drastic majority operator Δ^*, the global belief cycle in a BRG does not strongly depend on the initial global belief state itself, but depends on the underlying BRG structure, and whether subsets of agents have consistent beliefs or not. Given a BRG structure S, if two global belief states B and B' have a consistent intersection of beliefs for exactly the same subsets of agents, they should evolve in a similar fashion in the BRGs $S(B)$ and $S(B')$. We thus define the notion of *exclusive joint belief* of a given subset of agents $X \subseteq V$, which intuitively represents the common beliefs of all agents in X that are exclusive to this subset (i.e., no agent outside X shares any of these beliefs).

Definition 3 (Exclusive joint belief). *Given a set of agents V and a global belief state B over $\mathcal{L_P}$, the exclusive joint belief of $X \subseteq V$ w.r.t. B, denoted by $T_B(X)$, is defined as:* $T_B(X) = \bigwedge_{i \in X} B(i) \wedge \bigwedge_{i \in V \setminus X} \neg B(i).$

Property 1. Given V and a global belief state B over $\mathcal{L}_\mathcal{P}$, (a) for all X, Y in $2^V, X \neq Y \Rightarrow T_B(X) \wedge T_B(Y) \models \perp$ and (b) for all $i \in V$, $B(i) = \bigvee_{X \subseteq V : i \in X} T_B(X)$.

Example 2. Let $\mathcal{L}_\mathcal{P}$ be the propositional language generated from $\mathcal{P} = \{a, b, c\}$. Let B be the initial global belief state defined as $B = (bc, a, a\bar{b})$, [1] that is, $B_1 = bc$, $B_2 = a$, $B_3 = a\bar{b}$. We get that $T_B(\{1, 2, 3\}) = (bc) \wedge (a) \wedge (a\bar{b}) = ab\bar{b}c = \perp$ and $T_B(\{1, 2\} = (bc) \wedge (a) \wedge (\bar{a} \vee b) = abc$. Overall:

$$T_B(\{1, 2, 3\}) = \perp, \quad T_B(\{1, 2\}) = abc \quad T_B(\{1, 3\}) = \perp, \quad T_B(\{2, 3\}) = a\bar{b}$$
$$T_B(\{1\}) = \bar{a}bc, \quad T_B(\{2\}) = ab\bar{c}, \quad T_B(\{3\}) = \perp, \quad T_B(\emptyset) = \bar{a} \wedge (\bar{b} \vee \bar{c}).$$

For any revision policy $R_{\Delta*}^k$, the revised belief state of any agent is characterized solely by the consistency of the exclusive joint beliefs of non-empty subset of agents. To focus on this aspect in a succinct way, we introduce the language $\mathcal{L}_V$ as a propositional language over propositional variables a_i with $i \in V$. Each $X \subseteq V$ is associated with the formula $f_X \in \mathcal{L}_V$ defined a $f_X = \bigwedge_{i \in X} a_i \wedge \bigwedge_{i \in V \setminus X} \neg a_i$. It can be seen that for each $X \subseteq V$, f_X has a single model ω_X in which a_i is true iff $i \in X$. Then the set of all *non-empty* sets $X \subseteq V$ such that $T_B(X)$ is consistent can be represented as a disjunction of f_X (excluding $f_\emptyset$) and reciprocally.

Definition 4 (Consistency map). *Let V be a set of agents. A consistency map is a formula γ over $\mathcal{L}_V$ such that $\gamma \models \neg f_\emptyset$. An instance B of γ (denoted $B \in \|\gamma\|$) is any global belief state of V over some language $\mathcal{L}_\mathcal{P}$ such that $\forall X \in 2^{V*}, T_B(X) \not\models \perp \Leftrightarrow f_X \models \gamma$. Reciprocally, given a global belief state B of V over $\mathcal{L}_\mathcal{P}$, the consistency map of B, denoted γ_B is defined as $\gamma_B = \bigvee_{X \in 2^{V*} : T_B(X) \not\models \perp} f_X$.*

Definition 5 (Equiconsistency). *Let V be a set of agents, and let B and B' be two global belief states over $\mathcal{L}_\mathcal{P}$. B and B' are said to be equiconsistent, denoted by $B \approx B'$, iff B and B' share the same consistency map, that is, $\gamma_B \equiv \gamma_{B'}$.*

Hence, B and B' are equiconsistent iff $T_B(X)$ and $T_{B'}(X)$ are consistent for exactly the same subset of agents $X \subseteq V$, i.e., $T_B(X) \not\models \perp \Leftrightarrow T_{B'}(X) \not\models \perp$.

Example 3. Let us remark that the only consistent exclusive joint beliefs $T_B(X)$ with $X \neq \emptyset$ are such that $X \in \{\{1, 2\}, \{2, 3\}, \{1\}, \{2\}\}$. Thus $\gamma_B = f_{\{1,2\}} \vee f_{\{2,3\}} \vee f_{\{1\}} \vee f_{\{2\}} = a_1 a_2 \bar{a}_3 \vee \bar{a}_1 a_2 a_3 \vee a_1 \bar{a}_2 \bar{a}_3 \vee \bar{a}_1 a_2 \bar{a}_3 = a_1 \bar{a}_3 \vee \bar{a}_1 a_2$. Let $B' = (\bar{a}, a \vee b, a\bar{b})$. Its only consistent joint beliefs are $T_{B'}(\{1, 2\}) = \bar{a}b$, $T_{B'}(\{2, 3\}) = a\bar{b}$, $T_{B'}(\{1\}) = \bar{a}\bar{b}$ and $T_{B'}(\{2\}) = ab$. Thus $\gamma_{B'} = \gamma_B$ and $B \approx B'$.

Obviously enough, equiconsistency is an equivalence relation, so it partitions all possible global belief states into a set of equivalence classes, which can each be fully characterized as $\|\gamma\|$. A representative $B^\gamma \in \|\gamma\|$ of such a class should be succinct and easily derived from γ. Additionally, whenever two representatives B_1 and B_2 both have a consistent exclusive joint belief for some $X \in 2^{V*}$, theses

---

[1] For shorter notations in the examples, ab stands for $a \wedge b$, and $\bar{b}$ stands for $\neg b$.

beliefs should be the same (i.e. $T_{B_1}(X) = T_{B_2}(X)$). The idea is to build such canonical global belief states over the language $\mathcal{L}_V$. As each set of interpretation of $\mathcal{L}_V$ (excluding only $\omega_\emptyset$) gives rise to an equiconsistency class, this is the most succinct language we can use to ensure we can build representatives for all equiconsistency classes. Of particular interest is the equiconsistency class $\|\neg f_\emptyset\|$, where each subset of agents has a consistent exclusive joint belief. We define its representative B^{max} such that for all $i \in V$, $B^{max}(i) = a_i$. Then, representatives B^γ of other classes $\|\gamma\|$ should ensures for all X, $T_{B^\gamma}(X) = T_{B^{max}}(X) = f_X$ if $f_X \models \gamma$ and $\bot$ otherwise. Then $\forall X \in 2^{V*}$, $T_{B^\gamma}(X) = f_X \wedge \gamma$, which gives $\forall i \in V, B'(i) = a_i \wedge \gamma'$ (which is also true for B^{max} as $a_i \wedge \neg f_\emptyset = a_i \wedge \neg \bigwedge_{i \in V} \neg a_i = a_i$). As a result, we define the notion of canonical global belief base as follows:

Definition 6 (Canonical global belief base). *Let S be a BRG-structure and γ be a consistency map. The representative of the equiconsistency class $\|\gamma\|$, denoted B^γ is defined as the global belief state over $\mathcal{L}_V$ such that for all i, $B^\gamma(i) = a_i \wedge \gamma$. The global belief state $\mathbb{B}_V = \{B^\gamma | \gamma \in \mathcal{L}_V, \neg f_\emptyset \models \gamma\}$ is called the canonical global belief base of V.*

Example 4. Consider again $\gamma = \gamma_B = a_1\bar{a}_3 \vee \bar{a}_1 a_2$. We have $B^\gamma = (a_1 \wedge \gamma, a_2 \wedge \gamma, a_3 \wedge \gamma)$, or equivalently, $B^\gamma = (a_1\bar{a}_3, a_2\bar{a}_1 \vee a_2\bar{a}_3, \bar{a}_1 a_2 a_3)$.

The next result shows how equiconsistency of two global belief states B, B' reflects on BRGs $S(B), S(B)$ derived from a BRG structure S:

Theorem 1. *Let $S = (V, A, \mathcal{R}^\alpha_{\Delta*})$ be a BRG structure and let B and B' be two global belief states over $\mathcal{L}_P$. If $B \approx B'$, then $\forall s, \forall i, B_i^s \equiv \sigma(B_i'^s)$, where B^s (resp. B'^s) is the global belief state of the BRG $S(B)$ (resp. $S(B')$) at step s and σ is a mapping $\mathcal{L}_P \mapsto \mathcal{L}_P$ such that $\forall \varphi \in \mathcal{L}_V, \sigma(\varphi) = \bigvee_{X \in \mathcal{M}_{B'}(\varphi)} T_B(X)$ with $\mathcal{M}_{B'}(\varphi) = \{X \subseteq V | T_{B'}(X) \models \varphi\}$.*

Proof. (sketch) We first prove that $\forall X \subseteq V$, $\forall X \subseteq V, \sigma(T_{B'}(X)) \equiv T_B(X)$ using Property 1.a and $B \approx B'$ and from then $\forall \varphi, \psi, \sigma(\varphi \vee \psi) \equiv \sigma(\varphi) \vee \sigma(\psi)$. We prove $\sigma(B_i'^s) \equiv B_i^s$ by recurrence on s. If $s = 0$, Property 1.b gives $\sigma(B_i'^0) = \sigma(\bigvee_{X \subseteq V : i \in X} T_{B'}(X)) \equiv \bigvee_{X \subseteq V : i \in X} \sigma(T_{B'}(X)) \equiv \bigvee_{X \subseteq V : i \in X} T_B(X) = B_i^0$.

Assuming $\forall s \leq p, \forall i, \sigma(B_i'^s) \equiv B_i^s$ (which gives $\forall X, \sigma(T_{B'^s}(X)) \equiv T_{B^s}(X)$), we remark that for all k and s, by denoting N_i the acquaintances of i, we can express both $\varphi_k(\mathcal{C}_i^s)$ and $B_i^s \wedge \varphi_k(\mathcal{C}_i^s)$ as disjunction of exclusive joint beliefs $T_{B^s}(X)$ by using Property 1.b. So $\forall i, \forall k, \sigma(\varphi_k(\mathcal{C}_i'^p)) = \varphi_k(\mathcal{C}_i^k)$ and likewise for $B_i^p \wedge \varphi_k(\mathcal{C}_i^p)$. Together with $B' \approx B$, this also implies $max(\mathcal{C}_i'^p) = max(\mathcal{C}_i^p)$ and $max_{B_i'^p}(\mathcal{C}_i'^p) = max_{B_i^p}(\mathcal{C}_i^p)$. As, using Table 1, B_i^{p+1} and $B_i'^{p+1}$ can be expressed by the same expressions over $\varphi_k(\mathcal{C}_i^p)$ and B_i^p (resp. $\varphi_k(\mathcal{C}_i'^p)$ and $B_i'^p$), $\sigma(B_i'^{p+1}) \equiv B_i^{p+1}$ and the recurrence is proved.

Corollary 1. *For any BRG-structure S and set of global belief states $\mathcal{B}$, we have $maxGCyc(S, \mathcal{B}) = maxGCyc(S, \bigcup_{B \in \mathcal{B}} \|\gamma_B\| \cap \mathbb{B}_V)$.*

Instead of computing the global belief cycle of every $B \in \mathcal{B}$, we can then compute the ones of the representatives of their equiconsistency class. If $\mathcal{L}_\mathcal{P}$ has n_v propositional variables and V has n agents, the set $\mathbb{B}$ of all possible global belief states over $\mathcal{L}_\mathcal{P}$ is of size $(2^{2^{n_v}})^n$, (there are 2^{n_v} interpretations in $\mathcal{L}_\mathcal{P}$, thus $2^{2^{n_v}}$ possible formulas modulo equivalence for each one of the n agents), while $\mathbb{B}_V$ is of size 2^{2^n-1} (number of subsets of the $2^n - 1$ models of $\mathcal{L}_V$ different from $\omega_\emptyset$). When $n_v \geq n$, we get that $\mathrm{maxGCyc}(S, \mathbb{B}) = \mathrm{maxGCyc}(S, \mathbb{B}_V)$. Hence, we can always decrease the search space below $2^{(2^n)-1}$. This is important as it gives us a upper bound of search space solely depending on the number of agents.

4 Focusing on Belief Cycles

In order to compute all possible belief cycles of a BRG-structure independently from the language, one can thus iterate over the canonical global belief base $\mathbb{B}_V$ and use Theorem 1, decreasing the search space to less than $2^{(2^n)-1}$. Since this is still a prohibitive upper bound, we investigate in this section some methods to reduce furthermore the search space. The main idea is to focus on the belief cycle and regroup all equiconsistency classes that leads or belong to similar cycles.

4.1 Step Operator

Given the intuition that each step of the belief sequence will lead to the same cycle, we define the *step* operator.

Definition 7 (Step operator). *Given a BRG-structure $S = (V, A, \alpha)$, the step operator is defined as a mapping of any global belief state B to $step_S(B)$ defined as the representative of $\|\gamma_{B^1}\|$ where B^1 be is the global belief state at step 1, i.e., after the first revision of the initial beliefs, of BRG $S(B)$.*

If $\mathcal{B}$ is a set of global belief states, $step_S(\mathcal{B})$ will stand for $\{step_S(B)|B \in \mathcal{B}\}$. Since the belief sequence of $S(B^1)$ is included in the one of $S(B)$, they have the same belief cycle (possibly with an offset). Thus, $MaxGCyc(S, \mathcal{B}) = MaxGCyc(step_S(\mathcal{B}))$. Moreover, as different initial beliefs might be revised in equiconsistent first step, we have $|\mathcal{B}| \leq |step_S(\mathcal{B})|$. By applying $step_S$ iteratively as long as the size decrease, we can thus reduce the number of global belief state whose global cycle must be computed to determine $MaxGCyc(S, \mathcal{B})$. This is shown in Algorithm 1. We do not detail the actual computation of $\mathrm{maxGCyc}(S, \mathcal{B}')$ once $\mathcal{B}'$ has been reduced as we used a straightforward approach (a classic search for a maximum where for all B in $\mathcal{B}$ we compute $|\mathrm{GCyc}(S(B))|$ by simulating the BRG until reaching a previous state).

Please note that even if we get $step_S(B) = B$, this does not mean that $|\mathrm{GCyc}(S(B))| = 1$, as $B^1 \approx B$ does not imply $B^1 \equiv B$. For instance, consider $S = (V : \{1,2\}, A : \{(1,2),(2,1)\}, \alpha : (1,1))$ and $B = (a_1\bar{a}_2, \bar{a}_1 a_2)$. Then $B^1 = (\bar{a}_1 a_2, a_1\bar{a}_2)$. Although $B^1 \approx B$ (as $\gamma_{B^1} = \gamma_B = f_{\{1\}} \vee f_{\{2\}}$), clearly $B_1^1 \not\equiv B(1)$.

4.2 Computing $step_S(B)$

Consider a BRG-structure S and $B \in \mathbb{B}_V$. We define $\varphi_k^i = \varphi_k(\mathcal{C}_i)$ where $\mathcal{C}_i = \langle B_{i_0}, \ldots, B_{i_{in(i)}} \rangle$ is the context of agent i in BRG $S(B^{max})$. We have

$$\varphi_k^i = \bigvee_{J \subseteq \{1,\ldots,in(i)\}:|J|=k} \bigwedge_{j \in J} a_{i_j}$$

Algorithm 1. General structure of *step* reduction

Input: BRG-structure S, set of global belief states $\mathcal{B}$
Output: maxGCyc$(S, \mathcal{B})$
1: size $\leftarrow |\mathcal{B}| + 1$
2: $\mathcal{B}' \leftarrow \mathcal{B}$
3: **while** size $\geq |\mathcal{B}'|$ **do**
4:    size $\leftarrow |\mathcal{B}'|$
5:    $\mathcal{B}' \leftarrow step_S(\mathcal{B}')$
6: **return** maxGCyc$(S, \mathcal{B}')$

If $k > in(i)$, φ_k^i is an empty clause, *i.e.* $\forall k > in(i), \varphi_k^i = \perp$. Moreover, $\varphi_0^i = \bigwedge_{j \in \emptyset} a_{i_j}$ is an empty conjunction, *i.e.* $\varphi_0^i = \top$. Note that this stays true when $\mathcal{C}_i$ is empty. In such case, $\varphi_0^i = \top$ and $\forall k > 0, \varphi_k^i = \perp$. Now if we consider any $B \in \mathbb{B}_V$, we can derive $\varphi_k(\mathcal{C}_i)$ from φ_k^i as $\varphi_k(\mathcal{C}_i) = \varphi_k^i \wedge \gamma_B$. From Table 1, $R_{\Delta^*}^\alpha(B_i, \mathcal{C}_i)$ can be expressed by a formula involving some $\varphi_k(\mathcal{C}_i)$ and B_i, depending on the choice of k (either $max(\mathcal{C}_i)$ or $max_{B_i}(\mathcal{C}_i)$) and the consistency of $B_i \wedge \varphi_{max}(\mathcal{C}_i)$ (determining which column to use). We represent this formula with $next_S$:

Definition 8 (Operator $next_S$). *Let S be a BRG-structure, γ be a consistency map and $\kappa = ((k_1, \delta_1), \ldots, (k_n, \delta_n))$ a vector of pairs (k_i, δ_i) where k_i is a positive integer and $\delta_i \in \{\top, \perp\}$ is a boolean. We define $next_S$, taking γ and κ as arguments to output a global belief state, as: $\forall i \in V, (next_S(\gamma, \kappa))_i = n_{S,\kappa}^{\alpha_i}(i) \wedge \gamma$ where $n_{S,\kappa}^{\alpha_i}(i)$ is given depending on α_i as*

- $n_{S,\kappa}^1(i) = \varphi_{k_i}^i$
- $n_{S,\kappa}^2(i) = \varphi_{k_i}^i \wedge (a_i \vee (\neg \delta_i))$
- $n_{S,\kappa}^3(i) = (\varphi_{k_i}^i \wedge a_i) \vee (\neg \delta_i \wedge (\varphi_{k_i}^i \vee (a_i \wedge \varphi_{k_i-1}^i)))$
- $n_{S,\kappa}^4(i) = (\varphi_{k_i}^i \wedge a_i) \vee (\neg \delta_i \wedge (\varphi_{|k_i|}^i \vee a_i))$
- $n_{S,\kappa}^5(i) = a_i \wedge (\varphi_{|k_i|}^i \vee \neg \delta_i)$
- $n_{S,\kappa}^6(i) = \varphi_{k_i}^i \wedge a_i$

Definition 9. *Let S be a BRG-structure, γ be a formula over $\mathcal{L}_V$ and κ be a vector of n pairs $((k_1, \delta_1), \ldots, (k_n, \delta_n))$ of positive integers and booleans.*

Agent i is said to be k_i-group consistent for γ ($GCons_S^i(k_i, \gamma)$) iff (a) $\alpha_i < 6$ and $(\varphi_{k_i}^i \wedge \gamma \not\models \perp)$; or (b) $\alpha_i = 6$ and $(\varphi_{k_i}^i \wedge a_i \wedge \gamma \not\models \perp)$; or (c) $k_i = 0$.

Boolean δ_i is said to be adequate for i wrt to (k_i, γ) ($Adq_S^i(\delta_i, k_i, \gamma)$) iff $\delta_i \Leftrightarrow (\alpha_i = 1) \vee [\varphi_{k_i}^i \wedge a_i \wedge \gamma \not\models \perp]$. This property is decomposed in $PAdq_S^i(\delta_i, k_i, \gamma)$:

$\delta_i \Rightarrow (\alpha_i = 1) \vee [\varphi^i_{k_i} \wedge a_i \wedge \gamma \not\models \bot]$ and $NAdq^i_S(\delta_i, k_i, \gamma): \neg\delta_i \Rightarrow (\alpha_i \neq 1) \wedge [\varphi^i_{k_i} \wedge a_i \wedge \gamma \models \bot]$.

κ satisfies the consistency conditions for γ $(CCond_S(\kappa, \gamma))$ iff for all i, $GCons^i_S(k_i, \gamma)$ and $PAdq^i_S(\delta_i, k_i, \gamma)$; κ satisfies the inconsistency conditions for γ $(ICond_S(\kappa, \gamma))$ iff for all i, $\neg GCons^i_S(k_i + 1, \gamma)$ and $NAdq^i_S(\delta_i, k_i, \gamma)$.

The unique vector κ satisfying both consistency and inconsistency conditions $(CCond_S(\kappa, \gamma)$ and $ICond_S(\kappa, \gamma))$ is said to be maximal wrt γ and denoted $\kappa^{max}_{S,\gamma}$. It ensures: $\forall i$, $GCons^i_S(k_i, \gamma)$ and $\neg GCons^i_S(k_i, \gamma)$ and $Adq^i_S(\delta_i, k_i, \gamma)$.

Property 2. Let S be a BRG-structure, γ_1 and γ_2 be two formulas over $\mathcal{L}_V$, and κ a vector of n pairs of integers and booleans. If $\gamma_1 \models \gamma_2$ then $CCond_S(\kappa, \gamma_1) \Rightarrow CCond_S(\kappa, \gamma_2)$ and $ICond_S(\kappa, \gamma_2) \Rightarrow ICond_S(\kappa, \gamma_1)$.

Theorem 2. Let S be a BRG-structure such that $\alpha_i > 1$ for all agent i that receive no influence (C_i empty). Given a canonical global belief state $B \in \mathbb{B}_V$, if we denote by B^1 the global state of BRG $S(B)$ at step 1 and by $\kappa_{max} = \kappa^{max}_{S,\gamma_B}$ the maximal vector wrt consistency map γ_B: $B^1 = next_S(\gamma_B, \kappa_{max})$.

Proof. (sketch) We need to prove $B^1_i = (next_S(\gamma_B, \kappa_{max}))(i)$ for all i by showing that the definitions of κ_{max} ensures that $n_{S,\kappa_{max}} \wedge \gamma_B$ matches Table 1. We have 5 cases: $\alpha_i = 1$; $\alpha_i \in \{2, \ldots, 5\}$ and $\delta_i = \top$ or $\bot$; $\alpha_i = 6$ and $\delta_i = \top$ or $\bot$. We just illustrate here with the case $\alpha_i \in \{2, \ldots, 5\}$ and $\delta_i = \top$. First as $\alpha_i < 6$, $GCons^i_S(k_i, \gamma)$ and $\neg GCons^i_S(k_i, \gamma)$ means $\varphi^i_{k_i} \wedge \gamma_B \not\models \bot$ (which include case $k_i = 0$ as $\varphi^i_0 = \top$) and $\varphi^i_{k_i+1} \wedge \gamma_B \models \bot$. Thus $k_i = max(C_i)$. Then $\delta_i = \top$ means that $PAdq^i_S(\delta_i, k_i, \gamma)$ ensures $\varphi^i_{k_i} \wedge a_i \wedge \gamma_B = \varphi_{max}(C_i) \wedge B_i$ is consistent (case (a) of Table 1). Then $n_{S,\kappa_{max}}(i)$ can be simplified to $\varphi^i_{k_i} \wedge a_i$ for all possible values of $\alpha_i \in \{2, \ldots, 5\}$. Thus $B^1_i = \varphi_{max}(C_i) \wedge B^i_s = \varphi^i_{k_i} \wedge a_i \wedge \gamma_B = (next_S(\gamma_B, \kappa_{max}))(i)$.

Using this theorem, we can implement line 5 of Algorithm 1: for each $B \in \mathcal{B}$ we compute $step_S(B)$ by determining for all i the correct (k_i, δ_i) of κ to apply $B^1_i = next_S(\kappa, \gamma_B)$ and return representative $B^{\gamma_{B^1}}$. We call this method DStepRed.

Example 5. We take BRG-structure S from Example 1. Then $\varphi^1_2 = a_2 a_3$, $\varphi^1_1 = a_2 \vee a_3$, $\varphi^2_1 = a_1$, $\varphi^3_2 = a_1 a_2$ and $\varphi^3_1 = a_1 \vee a_2$. Consider $\gamma = a_1 \bar{a}_3 \vee \bar{a}_1 a_2$. We have $\varphi^1_2 \wedge \gamma \not\models \bot$ and $\varphi^1_2 \wedge a_1 \wedge \gamma = a_1 a_2 a_3 \wedge \gamma \models \bot$; $\varphi^2_1 \wedge a_2 \wedge \gamma = a_1 a_2 \wedge \gamma \not\models \bot$; $\varphi^3_2 \wedge \gamma = a_1 a_2 \not\models \bot$. Thus $\kappa_{max} = \kappa^{max}_{S,\gamma} = ((2, \bot), (1, \top), (2, \top))$. Then $(B^\gamma)^1 = next_S(\gamma, \kappa_{max})$:

$$(B^\gamma)^1 = (n^4_{S,\kappa_{max}}(1) \wedge \gamma, \qquad n^6_{S,\kappa_{max}}(2) \wedge \gamma, \quad n^1_{S,\kappa_{max}}(3) \wedge \gamma)$$
$$= (\bot \vee (\neg\bot \wedge ((a_2 a_3) \vee a_1)) \wedge \gamma, \quad (a_1) \wedge a_2 \wedge \gamma, \quad (a_1 a_2) \wedge \gamma)$$
$$= (\bar{a}_1 a_2 a_3 \vee a_1 \bar{a}_3, \qquad a_1 a_2 \bar{a}_3, \qquad a_1 a_2 \bar{a}_3)$$

$T_{(B^\gamma)^1}(\{1, 2, 3\}) = a_1 a_2 \bar{a}_3$ and $T_{(B^\gamma)^1}(\{1\}) = \bar{a}_1 a_2 a_3 \vee a_1 \bar{a}_2 \bar{a}_3$ are the only consistent $T_{(B^\gamma)^1}(X)$, so we get $\gamma_{step_S(B)} = f_{\{1,2,3\}} \vee f_{\{1\}} = a_1 a_2 a_3 \vee a_1 \bar{a}_2 \bar{a}_3$.

4.3   Exact Reduction Using Consistency Map Intervals

If we go further and try to compute $steps(\mathcal{B})$ without iterating elements in $\mathcal{B}$, we must group together elements sharing some similarity.

Definition 10 (Consistency map interval). *A consistency map interval* $\mathcal{I} = (\gamma^-, \gamma^+)$ *is defined as a pair of consistency maps* γ^- *and* γ^+ *such that* $\gamma^- \models \gamma^+$. γ^- *and* γ^+ *are called respectively the* lower *and* upper *bounds of* $\mathcal{I}$.

A global belief state B *is an* instance *of* $\mathcal{I} = (\gamma^-, \gamma^+)$ *(denoted by* $B \in \|(\gamma^-, \gamma^+)\|$*) iff* $\gamma^- \models \gamma_B \models \gamma^+$. B^{γ^-} *and* B^{γ^+} *are called respectively the* skeptical *and* credulous instances *of* $\mathcal{I}$.

Such an interval represents all consistency maps that are bounded (in term of entailment) by γ^- and γ^+. Intuitively, the models of γ^- (resp. $\neg\gamma^+$) represents the subgroups of agents that have consistent (resp. inconsistent) exclusive joint beliefs for all instances of the interval. Other subgroups (those X s.t. $f_X \models \gamma^+$ but $f_X \not\models \gamma^-$) are undetermined.

Example 6. Let $\gamma^- = f_{\{1,2\}} \vee f_{\{2,3\}} = a_1 a_2 \bar{a}_3 \vee \bar{a}_1 a_2 a_3$ and $\gamma^+ = \neg f_\emptyset \wedge \neg f_{\{1,2,3\}}$. We have $\gamma^- \models \gamma^+ \models \neg f_\emptyset$. Thus $\mathcal{I} = (\gamma^-, \gamma^+)$ is a consistency map interval representing global belief states where $\{1,2\}$ and $\{2,3\}$ have consistent exclusive joint beliefs but $\{1,2,3\}$ does not. Note that $B = (bc, a, a\bar{b})$ from previous examples is an instance of $\mathcal{I}$ since $\gamma^- \models \gamma_B \models \gamma^+$ (as $\gamma_B = f_{\{1,2\}} \vee f_{\{2,3\}} \vee f_{\{1\}} \vee f_{\{2\}}$).

This allow us to express and calculate multiple global belief states at the same time. The set of all instances of $\mathcal{I} = (\gamma^-, \gamma^+)$ will be denoted $\|\mathcal{I}\|$. The following theorem will be used to compute $step(\|\mathcal{I}\|)$, without iterating all $B \in \mathcal{B} = \|\mathcal{I}\|$.

Theorem 3. *Let S be a BRG-structure and $\mathcal{I} = (\gamma^-, \gamma^+)$ be a consistency map interval. If there exists a vector $\kappa = \{(k_1, \delta_1), \ldots, (k_n, \delta_n)\}$ that satisfies the consistency conditions for γ^- and the inconsistency conditions for γ^+ (i.e. if there exists κ such that $CCond_S(\kappa, \gamma^-)$ and $ICond_S(\kappa, \gamma^+)$), then*

$$step_S(\|\mathcal{I}\|) = \|(\gamma_{next_S(\gamma^-, \kappa)}, \gamma_{next_S(\gamma^-, \kappa)})\| \cap \mathbb{B}_V$$

Proof. (sketch). Let $\mathcal{I}'$ stand for $(\gamma_{next_S(\psi^-, \kappa)}, \gamma_{next_S(\psi^+, \kappa)})$. First, let us prove that $step(\|\mathcal{I}\|) \subseteq \|\mathcal{I}'\| \cap \mathbb{B}_V$. Let $B \in \|\mathcal{I}\| \cap \mathbb{B}_V$. By definition, we have $\gamma^- \models \gamma_B \models \gamma^+$. Then Property 2 gives $CCond_S(\kappa, \gamma^-) \Rightarrow CCond_S(\kappa, \gamma_B)$ and $ICond_S(\kappa, \gamma^+) \Rightarrow ICond_S(\kappa, \gamma_B)$. Thus κ is maximal for γ_B. Hence (given Theorem 2), $B^1 = next_S(\gamma_B, \kappa)$. Then, we prove the lemma: $\forall X \neq \emptyset, T_{next_S(\gamma, \kappa)}(X) = F_{S,\kappa}(X) \wedge \gamma$ where $F_{S,\kappa}(X) = \bigwedge_{i \in X} n_{S,\kappa}(i) \wedge \bigwedge_{i \in V \setminus X} \neg n_{S,\kappa}(i)$. This allows us to derive: $\forall X, T_{next_S(\gamma^-, \kappa)}(X) \models T_{next_S(\gamma_B, \kappa)}(X) \models T_{next_S(\gamma^+, \kappa)}(X)$. As $\forall B', \gamma_{B'} = \bigvee_{X \in 2^{V^*}: T_{B'}(X) \not\models \perp} f_X$, this implies $\gamma_{next_S(\gamma^-, \kappa)} \models \gamma_{B^1} \models \gamma_{next_S(\gamma^+, \kappa)}$. As $\gamma_{B^1} = \gamma_{step_S(B)}$ we conclude $step(B) \in \|\mathcal{I}'\|$. Now, to prove $step(\|\mathcal{I}\|) \supseteq \|\mathcal{I}'\| \cap \mathbb{B}_V$, we take $B' \in \|\mathcal{I}'\| \cap \mathbb{B}_V$ and define $\gamma = \bigvee_{Y \subseteq V: T_{B'}(Y) \not\models \perp} F_{S,\kappa}(Y) \wedge \gamma^+$. Let's note $\gamma'^- = \gamma_{next_S(\gamma^-, \kappa)}$ the lower bound of $\mathcal{I}'$ and $B'^- = B^{\gamma'^-}$ its skeptical instance. $B' \in \|\mathcal{I}'\|$

gives $\gamma'^- \models \gamma_{B'}$, so $\forall X \in 2^{V*}, (f_X \models \gamma'^-) \Rightarrow (f_X \models \gamma_{B'})$, which means $\forall X \in 2^{V*}, (T_{B'^-}(X) \not\models \bot) \Rightarrow (T_{B'}(X) \not\models \bot)$. This is also true for $X = \emptyset$, as for any canonical B'', $\neg T_{B''}(\emptyset) = \bigvee_{i \in V} B''(i) = \gamma_{B''}$ and as any consistency map verifies $\neg f_\emptyset \models \gamma_{B''}$ we know that $T_{B''}(\emptyset) \models f_\emptyset \not\models \bot$. As result, $\bigvee_{Y \subseteq V: T_{B'^-}(Y) \not\models \bot} F_{S,\kappa}(Y) \models \bigvee_{Y \subseteq V: T_{B'}(Y) \not\models \bot} F_{S,\kappa}(Y)$. Given $\gamma^- \models \gamma^+$, we thus get: $\mathcal{F} = \bigvee_{Y \subseteq V: T_{B'^-}(Y) \not\models \bot} F_{S,\kappa}(Y) \wedge \gamma^- \models \gamma$. Then rewriting $F_{S,\kappa}(Y)$ in terms of $T_{next_S(\gamma^-,\kappa)}$ we can prove $\mathcal{F} = \neg T_{next_S(\gamma^-,\kappa)}(\emptyset) \vee (F_{S,\kappa}(\emptyset) \wedge \gamma^-) = \gamma^-$ and thus $\gamma^- \models \gamma$. As $\gamma = (\bigvee_{Y \subseteq V: T_{B'}(Y) \not\models \bot} F_{S,\kappa}(Y)) \wedge \gamma^+$ we also have $\gamma \models \gamma^+$ and thus $B^\gamma \in \|\mathcal{I}\|$. As above, this entails that $(B^\gamma)^1 = next(\gamma,\kappa)$ and thus $\gamma_{steps(B^\gamma)} = \gamma_{next(\gamma,\kappa)}$. Then, using lemma $T_{next_S(\gamma,\kappa)}(X) = F_{S,\kappa}(X) \wedge \gamma$, we compute $T_{next_S(\gamma,\kappa)}(X) = \bigvee_{Y \subseteq V: T_{B'}(Y) \not\models \bot} (T_{next_S(\gamma^+,\kappa)}(X) \wedge T_{next_S(\gamma^+,\kappa)}(Y))$. Given Property 1, we can deduce that $T_{B'}(X) \models \bot$ entails $T_{next_S(\gamma,\kappa)}(X) \models \bot$. Besides, if $T_{B'}(X) \not\models \bot$ then $T_{next_S(\gamma,\kappa)}(X) = T_{next_S(\gamma^+,\kappa)}(X) \not\models \bot$ (because $T_{B'}(X) \not\models \bot$ gives $T_{B'^{\gamma^+}} \not\models \bot$ with $\gamma'^+ = \gamma_{next_S(\gamma^+,\kappa)}$). Following from this, we get $\gamma_{B'} = \gamma_{next(\gamma,\kappa)} = \gamma_{steps(B^\gamma)}$. Thus, as B' is canonical, $B' \in steps_S(\|\mathcal{I}\|)$.

Finding a unique κ such that $CCond_S(\kappa,\gamma^-)$ and $ICond_S(\kappa,\gamma^+)$ means that for any $B \in \|(\gamma^-,\gamma^+)\|$ this κ is maximal wrt γ_B and thus $steps_S(B) = B^\gamma_{next_S(\gamma_B,\kappa)}$. Since $next_S$ preserves the entailment relation on different γ, we can transfer the bounding of γ_B by the skeptical and credulous bounds to an equivalent bounding of the $\gamma_{step(B)}$. However, such a vector may not exist. Then, we have to change the bounds by forcing some undetermined subgroups of agents X to have either consistent or inconsistent $T_B(X)$ for all instances and try again for both cases. In the worst case, we may not find a correct κ until we reach $\gamma^- \equiv \gamma^+$. Algorithm 2 details function ESTEP returning $steps_S(\|\mathcal{I}\|)$ as a set of consistency maps intervals. Using it, we can again implement line 5 of Alg. 1 by representing $\mathcal{B}$ as a set of $\mathcal{I}$ (for instance $\mathbb{B} = \{\|(\bot, \neg f_\emptyset,)\|\}$) and using ESTEP on each of them. We call this version ESTEPRED.

Example 7. We use $\mathcal{I}$ from previous example. $\kappa = ((2, \bot, (1, \top), (2, \top))$ satisfies $CCond_S(\kappa,\gamma^-)$ and $ICond_S(\kappa,\gamma^+)$. For any γ of $\mathcal{I}$, $next_S(\kappa,\gamma) = (((a_2 a_3) \vee a_1)) \wedge \gamma, a_1 a_2 \wedge \gamma, (a_1 a_2) \wedge \gamma)$. Thus $next_S(\kappa,\gamma^-) = (\bar{a}_1 a_2 a_3 \vee a_1 a_2 \bar{a}_3, a_1 a_2 \bar{a}_3, a_1 a_2 \bar{a}_3)$, giving $\gamma_{next_S(\kappa,\gamma^-)} = f_{\{1,2,3\}} \vee f_{\{1\}}$ as in previous example. Likewise, $next_S(\kappa,\gamma^+) = (\bar{a}_1 a_2 a_3 \vee a_1 \bar{a}_3 \vee a_1 \bar{a}_2, a_1 a_2 \bar{a}_3, a_1 a_2 \bar{a}_3)$ will also give $\gamma_{next_S(\kappa,\gamma^+)} = f_{\{1,2,3\}} \vee f_{\{1\}}$ that we note γ'. Thus in this case: $steps_S(\|\mathcal{I}\|) = \|(\gamma',\gamma')\| \cap \mathbb{B}_V = \{B^{\gamma'}\}$.

4.4 Approximate Reduction

The problem of the previous procedure is that a common κ may not exist forcing us to branch over two cases of computations. To alleviate this, we consider the set of all vectors that are maximal for the consistency maps of some instances of our interval. But then applying the $next_S$ operator with the same κ on the bounds do not give us tight bounds anymore. Nonetheless, we can still get a tighter upper bound by using the notion of restriction of a consistency map.

382   G. Bourgne et al.

Algorithm 2. Computation of $step(\|\mathcal{I}\|)$ with exact reduction

---

Input: BRG-structure S, a consistency map intervals $\mathcal{I} = (\gamma^-, \gamma^+)$
Output: $step(\|\mathcal{I}\|)$ expressed as a set of consistency map intervals G'
1: **function** ESTEP(γ^-, γ^+)
2:    $(\kappa, Valid) \leftarrow ((0, \bot)^n, \top)$
3:    **for all** $i \in V$ **do**
4:        $(k_i, \delta_i) \leftarrow (in(i), \top)$
5:        **while** $\neg GCons_S^i(k_i, \gamma^-)$ **do** $k_i \leftarrow k_i - 1$
6:        **if** $\neg Adq_S^i(\delta_i, k_i, \gamma^-)$ **then** $\delta_i \leftarrow \neg \delta_i$
7:        $Valid \leftarrow IConds(\kappa, \gamma^+)$
8:        **if** $\neg Valid$ **then break**
9:        $\kappa[i] \leftarrow (k_i, \delta_i)$
10:        $(B^+[i], B^-[i]) \leftarrow (n_{S,\kappa}(i) \wedge \gamma^+, n_{S,\kappa}(i) \wedge \gamma^-)$
11:    **if** $Valid$ **then**
12:        **return** $\{(\text{ConsMap}(B^-), \text{ConsMap}(B^+))\}$
13:    **else**
14:        $X \leftarrow \text{getUnset}(\gamma^-, \gamma^+)$ ▷ get X s.t. $f_X \not\models \gamma^+$ and $f_X \models \gamma^-$
15:        **return** ESTEP$(\gamma^- \vee f_X, \gamma^+) \cup$ ESTEP$(\gamma^-, \gamma^+ \wedge \neg f_X)$

Definition 11 (Restriction to κ of a consistency map). *Given a BRG structure S and a vector $\kappa = ((k_1, \delta_1), \ldots, (k_n, \delta_n))$, we define*

$$\rho_{S,\kappa} = \bigwedge_{i \in V : \alpha_i < 6} \neg \varphi_{k_i+1}^i \wedge \bigwedge_{i \in V : \alpha_i = 6} \neg(a_i \wedge \varphi_{k_i+1}^i) \wedge \bigwedge_{i \in V} (\delta_i \vee \neg(a_i \wedge \varphi_{k_i}^i)).$$

Given a consistency map γ, the restriction of γ to κ is defined as $\gamma_{|\kappa} = \gamma \wedge \rho_{S,\kappa}$.

Taking the restriction of γ consists in removing some models from $[\gamma]$ to ensure the inconsistency of the formulas used in the inconsistency conditions $IConds$, while still keeping all other models of the original consistency map.

Property 3. Let S be a BRG-structure and κ a vector $\kappa = ((k_1, \delta_1), \ldots, (k_n, \delta_n))$ such that $\forall i, \alpha_i = 1 \rightarrow \delta_i = \top$. Given a consistency map γ we have:

$$IConds(\kappa, \gamma) \Leftrightarrow \gamma \models \rho_{S,\kappa}.$$

Theorem 4. *Let S be a BRG-structure and $\mathcal{I} = (\gamma^-, \gamma^+)$ be a consistency map interval. Let K be a set of vectors $\kappa = \{k_1, \ldots, k_n\}$ such that each κ satisfies consistency conditions for γ^+ and inconsistency ones for γ^- (i.e. $CConds(\kappa, \gamma^+)$ and $IConds(\kappa, \gamma^-)$), then:*

$$steps(\|\mathcal{I}\|) \subseteq \bigcup_{\kappa \in K} \|(\gamma_{next_S(\gamma^-,\kappa)}, \gamma_{next_S(\gamma^+_{|\kappa},\kappa)})\| \cap \mathbb{B}_V.$$

Proof. We denote by $\mathcal{I}'_\kappa$ the consistency map interval $(\gamma_{next_S(\gamma^-,\kappa)}, \gamma_{next_S(\gamma^+_{|\kappa},\kappa)})$. Consider an instance B of $\mathcal{I}$. Let $\kappa_B = \kappa_{S,\gamma_B}^{max}$ be its maximal vector wrt to γ_B. By definition, we get $CConds(\kappa_B, \gamma_B)$ and $IConds(\kappa_B, \gamma_B)$. From Property 3, we get $\gamma_B \models \rho_{S,\kappa_B}$, so $\gamma_B = \gamma_B \wedge \rho_{S,\kappa_B}$. As $B \in \|\mathcal{I}\|$, we have

$\gamma^- \models \gamma_B$ and $\gamma_B \models \gamma^+$, so $\gamma_B \wedge \rho_{S,\kappa_B} = \gamma_B \models \gamma^+ \wedge \rho_{S,\kappa_B} = \gamma^+_{|\kappa_B}$. Thus: $\gamma^- \models \gamma_B \models \gamma^+_{|\kappa_B}$. As in proof of Th. 3 we can express $T_{next_S(\gamma,\kappa_B)}$ as $F_{S,\kappa_B} \wedge \gamma$ to get $\gamma_{next_S(\gamma^-,\kappa_B)} \models \gamma_{next_S(\gamma_B,\kappa_B)} \models \gamma_{next_S(\gamma^+_{|\kappa_B},\kappa_B)}$. As $\kappa_B = \kappa^{max}_{S,\gamma_B}$, Theorem 2 ensures $\gamma_{next_S(\gamma_B,\kappa_B)} = \gamma_{B^1} = \gamma_{step(B)}$ and thus $step(B) \in \|\mathcal{I}'_{\kappa_B}\|$. Given $\gamma^- \models \gamma_B \models \gamma^+$ and Property 2, $ICond_S(\kappa_B,\gamma_B)$ yields $ICond_S(\kappa_B,\gamma^-)$ and $CCond_S(\kappa_B,\gamma_B)$ yields $CCond_S(\kappa_B,\gamma^+)$. This proves $\kappa_B \in K$ and thus (as $steps_S(B) \in \mathbb{B}_V$): $steps_S(B) \in \bigcup_{\kappa \in K} \|\mathcal{I}'_\kappa\| \cap \mathbb{B}_V$.

Using this theorem, we can directly compute a superset of $steps_S(\mathcal{B})$ in all cases. However, computing a superset might give us some additional incorrect global belief states. Still, when performing an exhaustive search (i.e. when our target $\mathcal{B}$ is $\mathbb{B}$), such additional belief states are at worse redundant. Algorithm 3 details the procedure. When doing an exhaustive search we can thus use ASTEP instead of ESTEP, a variant called ASTEPRED.

Algorithm 3. Computation of a superset of $step(\mathcal{B})$ with approximate reduction

---

Input: BRG-structure S, a consistency map intervals $\mathcal{I} = (\gamma^-,\gamma^+)$
Output: a superset G' of $step(\|\mathcal{I})\|)$ given as a set of consistency map intervals
1: **function** ASTEP(γ^-,γ^+)
2:     **for all** $i \in V$ **do**
3:         $K_i \leftarrow \emptyset$
4:         $k \leftarrow in(i)$
5:         **while** $\neg GCons^i_S(k,\gamma^+)$ **do** $k \leftarrow k - 1$
6:         $max \leftarrow k$
7:         **while** $\neg GCons^i_S(k,\gamma^-)$ **do** $k \leftarrow k - 1$
8:         $min \leftarrow k$
9:         **for all** $k \in \{min, max\}$ **do**
10:            **if** $PAdq^i_S(\top,k,\gamma^+)$ **then** $K_i \leftarrow K_i \cup \{(k,\top)\}$
11:            **if** $NAdq^i_S(\bot,k,\gamma^-)$ **then** $K_i \leftarrow K_i \cup \{(k,\bot)\}$
12:     $G' \leftarrow \emptyset$
13:     **for all** $\kappa \in K_1 \times \ldots \times K_n$ **do**
14:         **for all** $i \in V$ **do**
15:            $B^+[i] \leftarrow n_{S,\kappa}(i) \wedge \gamma^+ \wedge \rho_{S,\kappa}$; $B^-[i] \leftarrow n_{S,\kappa}(i) \wedge \gamma^-$
16:         $G' \leftarrow G' \cup \{(\text{ConsMap}(B^-),\text{ConsMap}(B^+))\}$
17:     **return** G'

Example 8. Using same S, we now take consistency map interval $\mathcal{I}_2 = (\gamma^-_2,\gamma^+)$ where $\gamma^-_2 = f_{\{1,2\}} = a_1 a_2 \bar{a}_3$ and $\gamma^+ = \neg f_\emptyset \wedge \neg f_{\{1,2,3\}}$ as before. We can check that the set of all κ satifying $CCond_S(\kappa,\gamma^+)$ and $ICond_S(\kappa,\gamma^-_2)$ is $K = \{\kappa_1,\kappa_2\}$ where $\kappa_1 = ((2,\bot),(1,\top),(2,\top))$ as before and $\kappa_2 = ((1,\top),(1,\top),(2,\top))$. For κ_1, we have $\rho_{S,\kappa_1} = \neg\varphi^1_3 \wedge \neg\varphi^3_3 \wedge \neg(a_2 \wedge \varphi^2_3 \wedge \neg(a_1 \wedge \varphi^1_2)) = \neg f_{\{1,2,3\}}$. Thus $\gamma^+_{|\kappa_1} = \gamma^+$ and $\gamma_{next_S(\gamma^+_{|\kappa_1},\kappa_1)} = \gamma' = f_{\{1,2,3\}} \vee f_{\{1\}}$. Then $next_S(\kappa_1,\gamma^-_2) = (a_1 a_2 \bar{a}_3, a_1 a_2 \bar{a}_3, a_1 a_2 \bar{a}_3)$ means $\gamma_{next_S(\gamma^-_2,\kappa_1)} = f_{\{1,2,3\}}$. With

κ_2, $n_{S,\kappa_2}^4(1)$ becomes $\varphi_1^1 \wedge a_1 = a_1 a_2 \vee a_1 a_3$. Thus $next_S(\kappa_2, \gamma_2^-)$ will be $(a_1 a_2 \bar{a}_3, a_1 a_2 \bar{a}_3, a_1 a_2 \bar{a}_3)$ and $\gamma_{next_S(\gamma_2^-, \kappa_1)} = f_{\{1,2,3\}}$. Besides, $\rho_{S,\kappa_2} = \neg \varphi_2^1 \wedge \neg \varphi_3^3 \wedge \neg (a_2 \wedge \varphi_2^2) = \neg(a_2 a_3) = \neg f_{\{2,3\}} \wedge \neg f_{\{1,2,3\}}$. So $\gamma_{|\kappa_2}^+ = \neg f_{\emptyset} \wedge \neg f_{\{2,3\}} \wedge \neg f_{\{1,2,3\}}$. Thus $next_S(\kappa_2, \gamma_2^-) = (a_1 a_2 \bar{a}_3 \vee a_1 \bar{a}_2 a_3, a_1 a_2 \bar{a}_3, a_1 a_2 \bar{a}_3)$ which gives $\gamma_{next_S(\gamma_{|\kappa_2}^+, \kappa_2)} = \gamma'$. In this case, we get the same consistency interval at next step for both κ_1 and κ_2. Thus $steps_S(\|\mathcal{I}_2\|) \subseteq (\|(f_{\{1,2,3\}}, \gamma')\| \cap \mathbb{B}_V = \{B^{f_{\{1,2,3\}}}, B^{\gamma'}\}$.

We propose MixStepRed as a compromise between Algorithms 2 and 3 using a parameter t. For each computation of $steps_S(\|\mathcal{I}\|)$, it chooses between EStep or AStep depending on the number u of non determined joint exclusive beliefs in $\mathcal{I}$ (i.e. $u = |\{X | f_X \not\models \gamma^+ \text{ and } f_X \models \gamma^-\}|$). If $u \leq t$, exact reduction will be used, otherwise, it will be approximate reduction. The underlying intuition is that EStep is costly because of its potential branching, whose depth is limited by u in the worst case, thus EStep is faster with smaller u.

5 Experiments

We have implemented the algorithms that are presented above for $R_{\Delta^*}^1$, setting $t = 16$ for MixStepRed. We also provided a naive implementation (Naive) where $maxGCyc(S, \mathbb{B})$ is computed in a simple loop for each $B \in \mathbb{B}$ without applying any reduction beforehand. We compared the performances of these algorithms for computing $maxGCyc(S, \mathbb{B})$ on different BRG-structures (with $\forall i, \alpha_i = 1$). For structures of 4 agents, we used all possible non-isometric simple directed networks satisfying $\forall i, in(i) > 0$ (126 networks). For 5 to 7 agents, we randomly produced 1000 simple directed networks (with $in(i) > 0$ for all nodes).

A comparison of these five algorithms is given in Table 2. The experiments were conducted on 1.4GHz Intel Core i5 processors with 4GB Memory. A timeout was set to ten minutes for each BRG-structure and one hour for each

Table 2. Comparison of computational performances

		Naive	DStepRed	EStepRed	AStepRed	MixStepRed $t = 16$
$n = 4$	Samples solved	126	126	126	126	n/a
	Average(ms)	1 445	177.4	10.06	**9.325**	n/a
	SD(ms)	394.2	67.89	54.06	**53.96**	n/a
$n = 5$	Samples solved	0	0	1000	1000	1000
	Average(ms)	n/a	n/a	3 431	35.2	**11.71**
	SD(ms)	n/a	n/a	11 700	62.05	**23.46**
$n = 6$	Samples solved	0	0	0	1000	1000
	Average(ms)	n/a	n/a	n/a	2 692	**309**
	SD(ms)	n/a	n/a	n/a	5 741	**524**
$n = 7$	Samples solved	0	0	0	13	**52**
	Average(ms)	n/a	n/a	n/a	79 960	**46 260**
	SD(ms)	n/a	n/a	n/a	98 170	**90 660**

algorithm. *"Sample solved"* shows how many samples were successfully solved within the time limits in each case. *"Average"* and *"SD"* give the average computation time for each sample and its standard deviation(SD). For $n = 4$, MIXSTEPRED with $t = 16$ is not used since the chosen threshold would be meaningless in this context.

From the result, we can see that although DSTEPRED gives better result than NAIVE, consistency map intervals are needed to go beyond $n = 4$. Indeed, for $n = 5$, the number of canonical global belief states is $2^{2^5-1} = 2^{31}$ (roughly 4×10^9) and this gets worse with higher n (around 10^{19} for $n = 6$ and 10^{38} for $n = 7$). By using consistency map intervals, other algorithms avoid the necessity to enumerate the elements of such a huge space, reducing the number of instances to be checked to less than 320 on almost all instances. As n gets bigger, the branching needed by ESTEPRED becomes too time and memory consuming, and ASTEPRED fares better. MIXSTEPRED with $t = 16$ appears a very good compromise and can analyze BRG-structure of size up to 7 (solving 52 structures of size 7 in less than an hour with 10 min time out for each structure). Note that standard deviation is quite high as computation time is highly dependent on the BRG-structure and thus varies a lot from one to the other.

The following table inspects the answers given by our algorithms for $\mathrm{maxGCyc}(S, \mathbb{B})$. It indicates the overall maximum and average for all tested structures and the percentage of BRG-structures whose maximal cycle size is less or equal to 1, 2, or n. For $n = 4$ we could test all possible networks, but we only got an empirical approximation for $n = 5$ or $n = 7$. Still, this shows that in most configurations, BRGs using only R^1 have a maximal cycle size close to 2 and that very long cycles only happens in very specific structures. Moreover, it proves that some BRG-structures are intrinsically stable: they can ensure that all BRG built upon them are stable, that is, have a belief cycle size of 1.

	Overall maximum	Average	Percent. at 1	Percent. ≤ 2	Percent. $\leq n$
$n = 4$	8	2.23	14.3	83.3	94.4
$n = 5$	12	2.38	13.5	77.5	94.0
$n = 6$	12	2.42	13.5	74.4	97.9

6   Conclusion

We proposed in this paper some analysis of the possible dynamics of beliefs in a network of communicating agents (with given behaviours), checking all possible initial beliefs. By introducing the notion of equiconsistency class, we can solve this problem independently from the language. Further reductions, using step operator to focus on the belief cycle itself and grouping together similar beliefs via consistency maps intervals, were implemented and compared, allowing consistently fast result for 6 agents, and solutions for up to 7 agents (for a search space of size 2^{2^n-1}). Future work could further improve this by using compact representations in the implementation and or refining the analysis. Indeed, while we focused here on maximum global cycle size, using Theorem 1 we could actually say more by memorizing the σ to get a function linking the belief cycles of $S(B)$ and $S(steps_S(B))$: all possible initial global belief sets can be partitioned in families converging to a similar global belief cycle, getting an exhaustive representing of all possible unfoldings of the BRG-structure S.

References

1. Everaere, P., Konieczny, S., Marquis, P.: The strategy-proofness landscape of merging. J. Artif. Intell. Res. **28**, 49–105 (2007)
2. Konieczny, S., Lang, J., Marquis, P.: DA2 merging operators. Artif. Intell. **157**, 49–79 (2004)
3. Konieczny, S., Pino Pérez, R.: Merging information under constraints: a logical framework. J. Logic Comput. **12**, 773–808 (2002)
4. Marquis, P., Schwind, N.: Lost in translation: language independence in propositional logic - application to belief change. Artif. Intell. **206**, 1–34 (2014)
5. Schwind, N., Inoue, K., Bourgne, G., Konieczny, S., Marquis, P.: Belief revision games. In: AAAI 2015, pp. 1590–1596 (2015)
6. Schwind, N., Inoue, K., Bourgne, G., Konieczny, S., Marquis, P.: Is promoting beliefs useful to make them accepted in networks of agents? In: IJCAI 2016, pp. 1237–1243 (2016)

Non-monotonic Collective Decisions

Matteo Cristani[1], Francesco Olivieri[2(✉)], and Guido Governatori[2]

[1] Department of Computer Science, University of Verona, Verona, Italy
[2] Data61-CSIRO, Brisbane, Australia
francesco.olivieri@data61.csiro.au

Abstract. The social choice theory has focused in the past on the problem of devising methods to determine how individual preferences are transformed into collective ones. In some investigations, scholars provided methods for expressing the social choice function, that, given a set of individual preferences, computes the resulting collective choice. Other studies focused on determining under which conditions the social choice function is efficiently computable.

In this paper, we concentrate on the specific case of collective decisions, when we assume that the agents are *rational*: they do not express random preferences, and they do not make random choices. In this context, we define four logical problems derived and study their computational complexity: (1) Determining the rationality of a given choice, (2) Establishing a possible rational maximal subset of a given choice, (3) Computing the votes on a rational proposal, and (4) Determining a priori the winning conditions of a given rational choice.

1 Introduction

When groups of individuals collaborate, it is required that the individual choices are combined into collective decisions. A *choice* and a *decision* are not the same process. A choice is the *"expression of a preference"*, whilst a decision is the *"deliberation of a choice"*. For instance, we can have the preference of caviar and champagne for lunch, but not the money to buy them. We thus decide to have a club sandwich with a glass of wine, that is a valid (though not the optimal) alternative. This is a common sense notion of choice and decision for individuals, but does this apply to collectivities in the same way?

In the above simple scenario, decisions can be graded, based on money availability. Rational are those alternatives that can be afforded. In many cases this is not possible because some of alternatives are unacceptable, for they violate general assumptions (rules) about the world. Suppose that we have to choose what clothing to wear while going out for dinner. It would be acceptable, for the restaurant's dress code, to wear a suit with a tie, or a tuxedo with a bowtie. We can make a choice between two groups of alternatives: {*suit, tuxedo*}, and {*tie, bowtie*}. Important here is to note that not all (four) combinations are acceptable: wearing a suit with a bowtie, or a tuxedo with a tie are *irrational* choices, as they do not match the dress code.

© Springer Nature Switzerland AG 2019
M. Baldoni et al. (Eds.): PRIMA 2019, LNAI 11873, pp. 387–404, 2019.
https://doi.org/10.1007/978-3-030-33792-6_24

Both decision making processes devised above, in which we have measures on the alternatives, or conditions to exclude some of them, have been dealt with in *Decision Theory*, the field of study that focuses on the problems of making decisions in presence of multiple, and possibly conflicting, criteria. The combination of acceptability based on criteria matching and weights is incorporated in the well-known notion of *Pareto Optimality*, where an alternative is said to be optimal when all the necessary criteria are matched and weighted with the maximal value among the admissible alternatives.

Although this field has been study in depth (including studies on computational aspects of the above sketched problems), the problem of rationality of choices in collective decision making still lacks literature in the fields of multi-agent systems, as well as computational logic. A conceptualisation of collective decision making is provided by the *Social Choice Theory* [3], where individual choices are combined into collective decisions. The individual choices are analysed in order to guarantee social welfare, by extension of the notion of Pareto optimality, called *Social Choice Function*. A Social Choice Function takes the individual choices of a collectivity, and deliberates a decision. A well known result of Social Choice Theory is the famous *Arrow's Impossibility theorem*, stating that there is no Social Choice Function able to guarantee the social welfare (the satisfaction of members of a collectivity) under certain general conditions.

Collective decisions are more complex to make than individual ones. In collective decision making, we need not only to evaluate the alternatives, but also to deliberate one choice that is *accepted* by the individuals who collaborate. In this paper, we deal with the problem of making collective decisions with some degree of *rationality*, namely in a way that not only provides choices accepted by the collectivity, but also compatible with common sense, in particular with a commonly accepted set of general rules considered reasonable by the collectivity.

In Social Choice Theory, scholars usually assume that the agents act in a rational way: their choices are rational to some extent. One way of relaxing this unrealistic assumption (agents have, many times, irrational choices) is by assuming that the choices need to satisfy some logical constraints: a rational choice should be consistent with some logical assumptions. We hence devote our attention to non-monotonic logic systems, as they can cope with exceptions and potentially conflicting information.

If we assume that a set of individuals collaborate, then it is natural to imagine that they have a commonly accepted background. For instance, they share methods as in scientific collaborations, or ethical principles as in social movements, or legal background as in political activities. We envision a system in which collaborating individuals share the common knowledge with an intelligent system able to perform reasoning on the choices of the individuals against the common background, therefore helping the decision process. Such a system can be viewed as a voting system, as we show in the rest of the paper.

We assume a form of rationality that is of *higher order*: when a choice is conflicting with the commonly accepted background, then it is not considered and can be reduced to an acceptable subset. We show that if a system of decision support is able to filter the choices of the individuals acting on a platform as sketched above, it would be a valid method to improve the welfare in the system itself, always within the theoretical limitations offered by the Arrow's Impossibility theorem.

We now introduce the running example of this work, to show how the logical framework we are going to develop takes these aspects into consideration, and specifically on the concept of choice.

Example 1. A group of friends (Alice, Bob, Jill, John, Julia, Mary, and Mark) will spend the evening together, and needs to decide: (1) the food for dinner, (2) the beverages to drink, and (3) the movies to watch. The possible choices are as follows. (1) Dinner: *Indian, Italian,* and *Chinese.* (2) Beverages: *beer, wine,* and *coke.* (3) Movies: *The Avengers (A), The Great Gatsby (B), The Hitchhikers' Guide to the Galaxy (C),* and *Red (D).* The individual choices are expressed in Table 1, while Fig. 1 depicts such a scenario.

Table 1. The agents' individual choices

Agent	Dinner	Drink	Film
Alice	Italian	Coke	(C)
Bob	Indian	Beer	(D)
John	Italian	Wine	(B)
Mary	Chinese	Beer	(A)
Jill	Italian	Coke	(C)
Mark	Indian	Wine	(A)
Julia	Italian	Wine	(C)

Fig. 1. The choices over the possible components for the a group of friends.

We assume that, despite the individual preferences, the group has to come up with collective decisions: they all must eat the same food, drink the same beverage, watch the same movie. These assumptions, whilst potentially unrealistic, are useful to highlight the results of this work.

When we deal with collective decisions, the Pareto optimal of one agent can be different from the Pareto optimal of another agent. Accordingly, we cannot try to use *object rank* as a means for solving the problem of optimal choice, as shown in [10].

We can combine the choices mentioned in Example 1 in $3 \times 3 \times 4 = 36$ different ways, but we have only 7 actual choices (precisely 1 for each individual). We may decide, for instance, to order Italian, drink wine and watch The Hitchhikers's Guide to the Galaxy. This corresponds to one specific combination of choices obtained by sequencing the choices on the columns from Dinner to Movie (as shown in [16]) and choose the most preferred of each column. Now, Julia is completely satisfied with this choice. To the contrary, Alice has preferred dinner and film but not beverage, Bob has only preferred drink, John has only preferred dinner, Jill has preferred food and film, Mary has only preferred beverage, and Mark has no preference satisfied.

A method that makes a decision while preserving the *social welfare* should be able to guarantee some degree of satisfaction to each of the individuals. Social choice theory is a widely recognised method to provide room for those processes in which a group of individuals makes a collective decision. The problem of Social Choice Function has been dealt with different perspectives and for different purposes. For many of these investigations, the base of the study is some sort of assumption on the existence of one kind of *collective rationality* that, to some extent, guarantees the applicability of a Social Choice Function. In other terms, it provides room to a decision process that, while assuming individual rationality, extends it by guaranteeing collective rationality. We can consider these computational approaches, and specifically those cases in which the computation of the collective decision has been valued for multi-agent systems, *Artificial Intelligence* for collective decision making. Conversely, the idea of rationality is considered for systems that make use of Social Choice Function to compute an acceptable collective decision, and therefore belong to the field of Decision Theory.

In this paper, we look at the rationality of choices made both individually, and collectively, in a *logical framework* where we delimit the perimeter of rationality to the notion of *plausibility*. We consider rational choices in a very general way, and then embed them onto a well-known logical framework, Defeasible Logic, that has been used for non-monotonic reasoning, as well as for modelling multi-agent systems in many research efforts so far [13,15]. Based on this framework, we consider a general problem to be addressed: Is an individual choice *rational*? This problem can be shown to correspond to the notion of *rational voting*, when an individual evaluates their choice against a proposal in a collaboration setting. In the rest of the paper, we also discuss consequences of this setting: What happens when a choice is irrational?

We devise a method for reducing it to a rational subset. We show how a decision process can be implemented in one specific case: the *majority principle* as Social Choice Function. We also study a method for deciding whether a proposal to be advanced for individual choices is a valid collective decision under the *majority principle*. These problems result hard from a computational viewpoint.

The rest of the paper is organised as follows: Sect. 2 discusses the employed formalism, and shows how to adapt it to the context. Section 3 defines four computational problems, provides the corresponding algorithms, and proves their complexities. Section 4 discusses related work, while Sect. 5 summarises, and sketches further work.

2   Basic Definitions

The basic setting of the theory presented in this paper is a multi-agent system: agents of the system employ a commonly accepted background in the form of a *defeasible theory*.

The background is formed by indisputable facts and commonly accepted rules that are considered plausible by every agent involved in the discussion. This theory is specified by a Defeasbile Logic. Defeasible Logic is a rule-based skeptical approach to non-monotonic reasoning. It is based on a logic programming-like language and is a simple, efficient, but flexible formalism capable of dealing with many intuitions of non-monotonic reasoning in a natural and meaningful way [2].

Set PROP defines propositional atoms, while Lab is a set of arbitrary labels. The set Lit = PROP $\cup\{\neg p | p \in$ PROP$\}$ denotes the set of literals. The *complement* of a literal q is denoted by $\sim q$; if q is a positive literal p, then $\sim q$ is $\neg p$, and if q is a negative literal $\neg p$ then $\sim q$ is p.

A defeasible theory D is a tuple $(F, R, >)$. $F \subseteq$ Lit are the facts which are always-true pieces of information. R contains three types of rules: strict rules, defeasible rules, and defeaters. A rule is an expression of the form '$r :$ $A(r) \hookrightarrow C(r)$', where r is the name of the rule, the *arrow* $\hookrightarrow \in \{\rightarrow, \Rightarrow, \rightsquigarrow\}$ is to denote, resp., strict rules, defeasible rules and defeaters, $A(r)$ is the (finite) set of antecedents of the rule, and $C(r)$ is its consequent (a single literal). A strict rule is a rule in the classical sense: whenever the antecedent holds, so is the conclusion. A defeasible rule is allowed to assert its conclusion unless there is contrary evidence to it. A defeater is a rule that cannot be used to draw any conclusion, but can provide contrary evidence to complementary conclusions. Lastly, $> \subseteq R \times R$ is the *superiority relation*, a binary and antisymmetric relation, which exact purpose is to solve conflicts among rules with opposite conclusions. We use the following abbreviations on R: R_s is to denote the set of strict rules in R, R_{sd} the set of strict and defeasible rules, and $R[q]$ is the set of rules in R s.t. $C(r) = q$.

A *derivation* (or *proof*) is a finite sequence $P = P(1), \ldots, P(n)$ of *tagged literals* of the type $+\Delta q$ (q is definitely provable), $-\Delta q$ (q is definitely not provable, or refuted), $+\partial q$ (q is defeasibly provable) and $-\partial q$ (q is defeasibly refuted). The proof conditions below define the logical meaning of such tagged literals.

Given a proof P, we use $P(n)$ to denote the n-th element of the sequence, and $P(1..n)$ to denote the first n elements of P. $\pm\Delta$ and $\pm\partial$ are called *proof tags*. Given $\# \in \{\Delta, \partial\}$ a proof tag, the notation $D \vdash \pm\#q$ means that there is a proof P in D such that $P(n) = \pm\#q$ for an index n.

In what follows, we only present the proof conditions for the positive tags: the negative ones are obtained via the principle of *strong negation*. This is closely related to the function that simplifies a formula by moving all negations to an inner most position in the resulting formula, and replaces the positive tags with the respective negative tags, and the other way around.

The proof conditions for $+\Delta$ describe just forward chaining of strict rules.

$+\Delta$: If $P(n+1) = +\Delta q$ then
    (1) $q \in F$, or
    (2) $\exists r \in R_s[q]$ s.t. $\forall a \in A(r)$. $+\Delta a \in P(1..n)$. P(1..n).

Literal q is definitely provable if either (1) is a fact, or (2) there is a strict rule for q, whose antecedents have all been definitely proved. Literal q is definitely refuted if (1) is not a fact, and (2) every strict rule for q has at least one definitely refuted antecedent.

The conditions to establish a defeasible proof $+\partial$ have a structure similar to arguments.

$+\partial$: If $P(n+1) = +\partial q$ then
    (1) $+\Delta q \in P(1..n)$, or
    (2) (2.1) $-\Delta\sim q \in P(1..n)$ and
        (2.2) $\exists r \in R_{sd}[q]$ s.t. $\forall a \in A(r) : +\partial a \in P(1..n)$, and
        (2.3) $\forall s \in R[\sim q]$. either
            (2.3.1) $\exists b \in A(s) : -\partial b \in P(1..n)$, or
            (2.3.2) $\exists t \in R$ s.t. $\forall c \in A(t) : +\partial c \in P(1..n)$ and $t > s$

A literal q is defeasibly proved if, naturally, it has already strictly proved. Otherwise, we need to use the defeasible part of the theory. Thus, first, the opposite literal cannot be strictly proved (2.1). Then, there must exist an *applicable* rule supporting such a conclusion (2.3)[1]. We now need to check that all counter-arguments (i.e., the rules supporting the opposite conclusion) are either *discarded* (condition (2.3.1), or defeated by a stronger, applicable rule for the conclusion we want to prove (2.3.2).

We introduce here a defeasible theory that is the background of Example 1.

Example 2. We assume that the group of friends described in Table 1 has already decided to get together for the evening, and we represent that with the fact '*evening_together*'. Further on, we introduce the rules that express the components of the evening:

---

[1] We say that a rule is *applicable* when all its antecedents have been proved within the current derivation step. Symmetrically, we say that a rule is *discarded* if at least one of its antecedents has been defeasibly refuted.

- R.1: *evening_together → have_dinner*
- R.2: *evening_together → drink_beverages*
- R.3: *evening_together → watch_film.*

Each of the admissible choices for each of the components is provided in the form of a single defeasible rule, derived from the literals *have_dinner*, *drink_beverages*, *watch_film.*

- r.1: *have_dinner ⇒ italian_cuisine*
- r.2: *have_dinner ⇒ indian_cuisine*
- r.3: *have_dinner ⇒ chinese_cuisine*
- r.4: *drink_beverages ⇒ coke*
- r.5: *drink_beverages ⇒ beer*
- r.6: *drink_beverages ⇒ wine*
- r.7: *watch_film ⇒ The_avengers*
- r.8: *watch_film ⇒ The_great_Gatsby*
- r.9: *watch_film ⇒ The_hitchhikers_guide_to_the_galaxy*
- r.10: *watch_film ⇒ Red.*

Moreover, we introduce exclusion rules, to describe the fact that each of the dining, drinking and film options cannot be shared.

- r.11: *italian_cuisine ⇒ ¬ indian_cuisine*
- r.12: *italian_cuisine ⇒ ¬ chinese_cuisine*
- r.13: *indian_cuisine ⇒ ¬ italian_cuisine*
- r.14: *indian_cuisine ⇒ ¬ chinese_cuisine*
- r.15: *chinese_cuisine ⇒ ¬ italian_cuisine*
- r.16: *chinese_cuisine ⇒ ¬ indian_cuisine*
- r.17: *coke ⇒ ¬ beer*
- r.18: *coke ⇒ ¬ wine*
- r.19: *beer ⇒ ¬ coke*
- r.20: *beer ⇒ ¬ wine*
- r.21: *wine ⇒ ¬ coke*
- r.22: *wine ⇒ ¬ beer*
- r.23: *The_avengers ⇒ ¬ The_great_Gatsby*
- r.24: *The_avengers ⇒ ¬ The_hitchhikers_guide_to_the_galaxy*
- r.25: *The_avengers ⇒ ¬ Red*
- r.26: *The_great_Gatsby ⇒ ¬ The_avengers*
- r.27: *The_great_Gatsby ⇒ ¬ The_hitchhikers_guide_to_the_galaxy*
- r.28: *The_great_Gatsby ⇒ ¬ Red*
- r.29: *The_hitchhikers_guide_to_the_galaxy ⇒ ¬ The_avengers*
- r.30: *The_hitchhikers_guide_to_the_galaxy ⇒ ¬ The_great_Gatsby*
- r.31: *The_hitchhikers_guide_to_the_galaxy ⇒ ¬ Red*
- r.32: *Red ⇒ ¬ The_avengers*
- r.33: *Red ⇒ ¬ The_great_Gatsby*
- r.34: *Red ⇒ ¬ The_hitchhikers_guide_to_the_galaxy.*

We have some rules for combining food, drink and film, shared by the friends having evening together.

- r.35: *italian_cuisine* $\Rightarrow$ *wine*
- r.36: *wine* $\Rightarrow \neg$ *indian_cuisine*
- r.37: *The_avengers* $\Rightarrow$ *chinese_cuisine*

Agents express their preferences on the shared theory by means of choices as in Definition 1. Choices may be, or not, rational, in the sense that we provide in Definition 2.

Definition 1 *(Choice)*. *Given a defeasible theory T, that constitutes the common background of a multi-agent system, a choice, is a finite set of literals that does not contain any contradiction (e.g., both l and $\neg l$).*

Definition 2 *(Rational choice)*. *We say that a choice C, expressed by an agent is* rational *with respect to a given background theory T, when it is possible to set the superiority relation on T, to define a theory T' in such a way that all the literals in P are defeasibly proved by T'.*

We adopt here the definition of *choice* expressed in the Social Choice Theory literature. Consider a setting in which an individual advances a proposal for the decision, that consists in expressing their choice, in order to make the individuals collaborating in the system *vote* for that choice. Voting consists in choosing a proposal advanced by another individual who expresses her choice to the individuals collaborating in the system. To devise rationality of the vote we consider the notion of *compatibility*.

Given two choices C_1 and C_2, we hereafter define the notion of *compatibility*.

- When $C_1 \subseteq C_2$, we say that C_1 is *strongly compatible* with C_2.
- When $C_2 \subseteq C_1$, we say that C_1 is *weakly compatible* with C_2.

hgConsider an agent that has choice C and votes for proposal P. If $P \subseteq C$ (the proposal is strongly compatible with the choice), the agent then obtains *only things they desire*, but possibly not everything (when $C \backslash P \neq \emptyset$). Conversely, if $C \subseteq P$ (P is weakly compatible with C), now the agent obtains *everything they desire*, but possibly also things that they did not include in their choice.

In fact, if an agent makes a choice that contains a literal l, they cannot vote for a rational proposal P that contains the opposite literal $\neg l$, their choice is strongly compatible with: this means that P contains both l and $\neg l$, therefore the proposal is irrational.

Guaranteeing satisfaction of the individuals under strong compatibility is more difficult than it is with weak one. When the compatibility is strong, and two individuals have no elements in common on their choices, then only the empty proposal is accepted by both. The setting we devise is as follows:

- Every agent has their own *choice*;

- Some agents advance their *proposals*, that consist in expressing their own choice;
- Every agent *votes* for one of the proposals, or none of them.

To illustrate how the model we propose in this paper works, we provide a formalisation of Example 1.

Example 3. Choices introduced by Table 1 can be expressed as follows:

- Alice {*italian_cuisine, coke, The_hitchhikers_guide_to_the_galaxy*}
- Bob {*indian_cuisine, beer, Red*}
- John {*italian_cuisine, wine, The_great_Gatsby*}
- Mary {*chinese_cuisine, beer, The_avengers*}
- Jill {*italian_cuisine, coke, The_hitchhikers_guide_to_the_galaxy*}
- Mark {*indian_cuisine, wine, The_avengers*}
- Julia {*italian_cuisine, wine, The_hitchhikers_guide_to_the_galaxy*}

Example 4. Rational choices are introduced by the exclusion and the combination rules given in Example 2. In particular, Alice and Jill's choices conflict with rule r.35, while Mark's choice conflicts with rules r.36 and r.37. Therefore, the only rational choices can be Bob's, John's, Mary's, and Julia's. To settle the choice of Bob, we need to guarantee that a rule deriving *indian_cuisine* prevails over the rules deriving ¬*indian_cuisine*, and the same for *beer* and *Red*. This is done by the following superiority relation, superimposed on the background.

In Sect. 3, we use the above defined setting to discuss computational problems related to them (Table 2).

Table 2. The choices listed in Example 1.

Agent/superiority	Agent/superiority	Agent/superiority	Agent/superiority
Bob: r.2 > r.11	John: r.1 > r.13	Mary: r.3 > r.12	Julia: r.1 > r.13
Bob: r.2 > r.16	John: r.1 > r.15	Mary: r.3 > r.14	Julia: r.1 > r.15
Bob: r.5 > r.17	John: r.6 > r.18	Mary: r.5 > r.17	Julia: r.5 > r.16
Bob: r.5 > r.22	John: r.6 > r.20	Mary: r.5 > r.22	Julia: r.5 > r.17
Bob: r.10 > r.25	John: r.8 > r.23	Mary: r.7 > r.26	Julia: r.9 > r.24
Bob: r.10 > r.28	John: r.8 > r.30	Mary: r.7 > r.29	Julia: r.9 > r.27
Bob: r.10 > r.31	John: r.8 > r.33	Mary: r.7 > r.32	Julia: r.9 > r.34

3   Collective Decision Making

We model the notion of *rational voting* by means of the setting devised in Sect. 2. In this section, we provide some relevant computational problems related to the introduced notion of rationality in vote and proposal expressions.

Definition 3. *Given a defeasible theory T that constitutes the commonly accepted background of a multi-agent system, and a choice C expressed by one of the agents, the problem of deciding whether C is rational w.r.t. T is named the* Rationality Detection Problem *(RDP)*.

RDP can be solved by superimposing a superiority relation on the theory T, so that T derives each literal in the choice of the agent. To do so, since T can already have a superiority relation, it may be necessary to *revise* such a superiority relation until we either: obtain a theory that actually derives all the literals, or conclude that such a revision does not exist, and therefore establish that the choice is not rational.

Comparing this problem to other ones analogously defined, as in [11, 12], we can prove the statement in Theorem 1. In the following, when referring to the problem of revising preference in a defeasible theory to derive one literal, we name this problem the *Preference Revision Problem*. That problem has been proven to be NP-complete in [11].

Theorem 1. *RDP is NP-complete.*

Proof. We prove this by showing that RDP can be polynomially reduced to the Preference Revision Problem of [11]. Given a set of literals, we aim at proving that these are derivable from the commonly accepted theory, once revised the superiority relation. We have a polynomial method on deterministic machine to establish whether a given superiority relation (superimposed on the commonly accepted theory) derives the whole set of literals, as this is the known problem of computing the extension of a defeasible theory, which is linear in the number of literals and rules in a theory. In [11], the authors provide an oracle for polynomially computing the superiority relation revision on a non-deterministic machine to derive a single literal, in the same configuration. Nevertheless, the number of literals does not influence the behaviour of the oracle. In fact, the oracle chooses the correct combination of superiority pairs for opposite literals. The number of these choices is, in the worst case, quadratic in the number of literals. This proves that the RDP problem is in NP. Moreover, the computation of the revision as shown above can be transformed into the revision of preferences in a linear number of steps, and this completes the proof that RDP is NP-complete.

We devise here a brute-force method to solve RDP on deterministic machines. Consider all the possible superiority relation pairs generated by combining every literal that appears at the head of at least one rule in the positive form, and in at least one rule in the negative form. In the worst case, these pairs are of the same order of the number of literals. Consequently, the number of rules obtained by the full combinatorics of the rules is $O(2^n)$ with n number of literals in the choice. For each combination computed as described above, we compute the extension of the theory, and we then check whether the choice is a subset of that extension. If we find such a combination, we have constructed the superiority relation and solved the RDP Problem.

Once a voter has analysed their choice, to evaluate the meaningfulness of their proposal they want to advance, and to realised whether that the choice is irrational, one possible reformulation of the problem may be: can I reduce the requests in the choice to a subset that results rational? If so, can I do this in a computationally effective manner? The problem defined informally above is formalised in Definition 4.

Definition 4. *Given a defeasible theory T, that constitutes the commonly accepted background of a multiple agent system, and an irrational preference C expressed by one of the agents, the problem of computing the maximal rational subsets of C is named the* Rationality Maximisation Problem (RMP).

We can solve the problem with a rather natural technique: we systematically remove one literal at a time from the original choice until we obtain a subset that results rational. Once we have such a subset, we continue to remove literals from the original choice until we have completed the process for one single literal. We further look at pairs of literals, but only for those that did not succeed as singletons. When concluded, we now proceed by considering triples, excluding those that contain one pair already included. This step ends when we reach a number k of elements to be removed, for which no set of elements can be removed that does not contain a subset already included in the step $k-1$. Once we have reached the step $k = n - 1$, we stop. At that step it would not be possible to find any further subset to delete.

Example 5. If we look at Alice's choice, the obvious selection is the literal *coke*, that, once removed, provides a rational choice, consisting in the expression: my preference is for Italian food, and I wish to watch the Hitchhikers Guide to the Galaxy, but I have no preference for beverages.

Theorem 2. *RMP is EXPTIME.*

Proof. RMP cannot be easily reduced to a NP-complete problem, and it has a non-polynomial space occupancy, due to the need to consider, in the worst case scenario, a number of subsets of the same size of the subsets of the choice, that is $O(2^n)$, with n number of literals in the choice. Also the size of the output of RMP can be exponential. We thus perform a total of steps that is bounded by the number of possible subsets of the choice. For each of these subsets, we can perform the algorithm sketched in the discussion above, to perform in an exponential time the correctness of the choice. Overall, we shall have a sequence of exponential size ($O(2^n)$) of exponential steps (each of $O(2^n)$), making therefore the result an exponential size of the original size of the choice ($O(2^{2n}) = O(2^n)$).

Data: An irrational choice, a background defeasible theory.
Result: The set of all maximal subsets of the input choice that are rational.
for *Every subset E of C of size i, incrementing i at each step* **do**
> Consider E only when no subset E' recorded at step (i-1) is contained in E;
> **if** *C−E is rational* **then**
>> | record C-E and E
>
> **end**
> **if** *At step i we did not add elements to the collection* **then**
>> | break
>
> **end**

end
Return All the recorded subsets;
Algorithm 1: RMPComp: an algorithm to compute maximal rational choices from an irrational one.

The implementation of the method devised in the proof of Theorem 2 is described in Algorithm 1.

Let us step forward onto the other level of the problems exposed here. When the choices are known to be rational, as in the case in which every individual has made their choice compared against the background theory by means of the method devised above, we can formulate the notion of Definition 5.

Definition 5. *Given a defeasible theory T that constitutes the commonly accepted background of a multiple agent system, and a finite set S of rational choices expressed as proposals, the problem of determining the result of the expression of rational choices by the agents, by applying a social choice function f, able to transform the individual votes for the proposals into a collective decision is called the* Collective Decision Problem (CDP).

For this case, the input to Algorithm 2 are choices that are assumed to be rational, and so do the proposals to be voted.

Data: A set of rational choices, a set of rational proposals, a background defeasible theory, a parameter for Strong/Weak comparability.
Result: The majority choices, if any.
for *every choice C* **do**
> **for** *every proposal P* **do**
>> **if** *C is Strongly/Weakly compatible with P* **then**
>>> | add a vote for P
>>
>> **end**
>
> **end**

end
Return All the proposals that received more than 50% of the votes;
Algorithm 2: RatVot: an algorithm to establish majority applied to MAS.

Theorem 3. *The CDP is polynomially solvable on rational proposals and rational votes, for the* majority *Social Choice Function.*

Proof. The proof that the algorithm RatVot correctly computes all, and only, the proposals that are rational and can pass the majority Social Choice Function filter is straightforward, and left therefore to the reader. The Algorithm clearly steps on a number of elements that are the choices, and a number of proposals. If we consider these as inputs, the computation is $O(p \cdot c)$ where p is the number of advances proposals, and c the number of rational choices involved in the vote. The claim is a direct consequence of the structure of the algorithm where two cycles are nested to each other of length respectively p and c.

To see how some proposals are rationally voted, we go back to Example 1.

Example 6. The friends of Example 1 vote in a rational way for three alternatives: [*italian_cuisine, wine, The_hitchhikers_guide_to_the_galaxy*] (A1, advanced by Julia, [*indian_cuisine, beer, Red*] (A2, advanced by Bob) and [*chinese_cuisine, beer, The_avengers*] (A3, advanced by Mary). The rational choices are obtained by reducing the expectations of Alice and Jill to dinner and film choices, and for Mark to film. Votes are in the third column. Note that the expectations of Alice and Jill are the only maximal subsets we can consider, whilst Mark may choose to reduce the expectations in two other ways: (1) only food choice to *Indian cuisine*(and thus voting for A2), or (2) only to *wine*(and thus voting for A1). If we value *strong* compatibility, and consider proposals for *Indian cuisine* and *beer* (B1, advanced by Bob), and for *Chinese cuisine* and *The Avengers* (B2, advanced by Mary), we have the votes on fourth column (Table 3).

Table 3. The rational votes in Example 1.

Agent	Choice	Vote (w)	Vote (s)
Alice	{*Italian cuisine, The hitchhikers guide to the galaxy*}	A1	–
Bob	{*Indian cuisine, beer, Red*}	A2	B1
John	{*Italian cuisine, wine, The great Gatsby*}	–	–
Mary	{*Chinese cuisine, beer, The avengers*}	A3	B2
Jill	{*Italian cuisine, The hitchhikers guide to the galaxy*}	A1	–
Mark	{*The avengers*}	–	B2
Julia	{*Italian cuisine, wine, The hitchhikers guide to the galaxy*}	A1	–

The winning alternatives are A1, and B2.

RMP problem is interesting from a methodological viewpoint. If a program to be voted is not rational, we can reduce it to a rational maximal subset. Once we have obtained a reduction of the choice, it becomes interesting to understand whether it is possible to aggregate a majority around the proposal. This problem is formalised in the definition below.

Definition 6. *Given a defeasible theory T, that constitutes the commonly accepted background of a multi-agent system, and the choices expressed by the agents in the system, the problem of computing a rational proposal that, under a given Social Choice Function f, satisfies f, is named the* Winning Proposal Definition Problem *(WPDP).*

The outcome of a voting system as devised here is not one single proposal that wins. We may observe also empty outcomes, without any winning proposals, or multiple outcome, where more than one proposal wins. Clearly, in both these cases we need some further selection process, but just the first step, under the control of rationality, is more complex than single winner systems (see [14] for the most general case).

Theorem 4. *WPDP is NP-hard for the* majority *Social Choice Function.*

Proof. To prove the claim, we need to devise a method that results exponential on deterministic machines. A simple approach consists in using the same method of rational choices, and subsequently computing votes for the single proposal by means of Algorithm 2. We consider a rational proposal, and try to see whether this has a majority consensus. If this is the case, then the algorithm has finished. Therefore, if we have an oracle that can compute a proposal (the number of possible proposals is evidently exponential in the number of literals), then, by means of the mentioned algorithm, we can compute the solution in polynomial time. This proves the claim.

It might appear interesting to analyse the rationality in presence of revision operators able to introduce, eliminate, and/or substitute rules. However, this configuration is not harder than the one we described here. Assume that we wish to derive a set of literals, and that we can manipulate the rules. We can simply introduce one rule for each of the desired literals derived from the set of facts. This setting can always be obtained by the revision of the rules. Formally, we introduce an extended notion of rationality of a choice.

Definition 7. *A choice is* r-rational *(rational including revision of rules) when there is a revision of the rules that derives all the literals in the choice.*

r-RDP is the problem of deciding whether a choice is r-rational on a given background. The above reasoning can be used to derive the following.

Proposition 1. *r-RDP is polynomially solvable.*

4   Related Work

In the recent past, many scholars have dealt with multi-agent systems from the viewpoint of preference aggregation and social choice theory. In [7], the authors deal with the basic issue that we addressed here: the collective decision problem in presence of varying preference expressions. The basic result of the investigation is that the application of multiple criteria methods, along with different methods to aggregate preferences, is generally very effective in defining a collective process of decision. What is missing in that study is that the authors do not address the specific problem of *logical analysis* of admissible choices, and the computational aspects of this logical analysis. This approach has been followed in this paper.

The field of social choice has been expanding rapidly as a research topic in the wider community of AI, and specifically in the multi-agent systems, especially with respect to socio-technical systems, where humans and bots can interact at the same level. Social choice theory is a very wide theme (for a rather complete analysis of the viewpoints developed in this field see [4]). Many investigations have focused upon the problems of how to define the social choice function, and on the difficulties determined by certain conditions that are superimposed on the social function itself, to the most famous negative result in this field, the Arrow's impossibility theorem [3], that has been investigated in terms of consequences in multi-agents systems widely as well [8,10].

There is also a wide literature in computational communities including multi-agent systems, that observes phenomena such the one we discussed, to an initial extent, in Sect. 3, when we introduced the Winning Proposal Definition Problem. In particular, the authors of [6] have dealt with the problem of *election manipulation*, a very complex topic that also deserves consideration in multi-agent systems. Similarly, the manipulation of coalition has been studied from many different viewpoints (see [19] for an example).

In particular, there are many important recent investigations regarding *preferences* and their underlying mathematics [1,7,9,16], and on their specific applications to AI, as generally discussed by Rossi *et al.* in [17], and then applied to the definition of social choice problems [5,16,18].

Overall, we may look at the current literature regarding revision of preferences in non-monotonic logic, as an immature research topic, especially when applied to multi-agent systems. Scholars have dealt with many different aspects of social choice, but the notion of rationality, as developed in this investigation, is rather novel in the community of agents.

5   Conclusions and Further Work

This work introduced a method that can be used for implementing a form of rationality in collective decisions, based upon the notion of *rational choice*, and the concept of *rational voting*. The approach we adopted is completely centred on the revision of preferences in the non-monotonic setting of Defeasible Logic.

We showed that some relevant problems defined on the above mentioned framework are computationally hard, and that one specific problem, under certain conditions, is polynomially solvable. We also showed that the intrinsic computational complexity of the approach defines the worst case scenario: the revision of rules reduces the complexity to polynomial.

Further work may include many different aspects, including, in particular, an ample analysis of the simplified sub-cases for which some of the problems introduced in this paper have better computational complexity. In the second step, the investigation should consider extensions to the language. There are several possible extensions, including: (1) the introduction of *degrees of acceptance* in the literals of choices, (2) the introduction of *priorities* among the elements of one choice, and (3) the optimisation of the superiority revision, namely the minimisation of revision steps.

There is, however, an aspect of further work that deserves some extensive discussion, for it is one of the crucial changes in the form of defeasible logics as studied in the recent past: the distinction between defeasible rules employed to represent plausible interpretation of the reality, and those that are used to introduce prescriptions to the behaviour of agents. Although this distinction has been dealt with in the current literature of logic and AI (see [2] for a large discussion), the applications of these aspects to the representation of voting issues and collective decisions is yet lacking.

In such a distinction, a given rule might state '*Usually women like beer less than men*' is a factual description, though, possibly, just plausible, and therefore significantly different from a rule that states '*Every action has an opposite and equal reaction*', which has more the flavour of a *strict* rule. This should be differentiated from a normative rule such as '*Citizens cannot wear war weapons*'. Law makers aim, where possible, at changing the second type of rules, and therefore a political proposal consists in the introduction of new normative rules. However, the ultimate purpose of political actions is to affect the reality. Consider that a law is introduced that increases the level of recognised competence for a certain class of workers (for instance, in Australia, yoga instructors must now have 500 h of certified training, whereas before was only 200). This will impact on the life of many people: some may undergo further training and education to continue within their current field, some may chose not to undertake further study and will consequently loose their job, since less people will have the required level to teach, the job will likely pay more.

It may also be the case that votes are expressed not only based on the rationality (but possibly within the rationality boundary) but also considering the *intention* included in the norm change proposals.

The purpose of such an investigation would be threefold:

- Determine what difference may be devised in terms of revision process, when such a distinction is introduced;
- Establish whether a revision process applies to normative part without interfering with the non-normative part;
- Establish whether the reality could be modified by the introduction of a normative set of rules, and by specifically introducing those rules by collective decisions.

Another important aspect that has not yet been investigated is the distinction between negative and positive choice elements. A negative literal expresses two different desires: the desire for the literal to become false, regardless of the nature of the positive literal corresponding to it, and the desire for the literal *not to become true*. For instance, consider the situation where, in a normative system, there is a law that forces women to wear certain types of clothing. Certain people may be disappointed that such an illiberal norm is not suppressed.

References

1. Andréka, H., Ryan, M., Schobbens, P.Y.: Operators and laws for combining preference relations. J. Logic Comput. **12**(1), 13–53 (2002)
2. Antoniou, G., Billington, D., Governatori, G., Maher, M.J.: Representation results for defeasible logic. ACM Trans. Comput. Logic **2**(2), 255–287 (2001)
3. Arrow, K.J.: A difficulty in the concept of social welfare. J. Polit. Econ. **58**(4), 328–346 (1950)
4. Chevaleyre, Y., Endriss, U., Lang, J., Maudet, N.: A short introduction to computational social choice. In: van Leeuwen, J., Italiano, G.F., van der Hoek, W., Meinel, C., Sack, H., Plášil, F. (eds.) SOFSEM 2007. LNCS, vol. 4362, pp. 51–69. Springer, Heidelberg (2007). https://doi.org/10.1007/978-3-540-69507-3_4
5. Chevaleyre, Y., Endriss, U., Lang, J., Maudet, N.: Preference handling in combinatorial domains: from AI to social choice. AI Mag. **29**(4), 37–46 (2008)
6. Conitzer, V., Sandholm, T., Lang, J.: When are elections with few candidates hard to manipulate?. J. ACM **54**(3) (2007). https://doi.org/10.1145/1236457.1236461. ISSN 0004-5411
7. Dong, Y., Zhang, H.: Multiperson decision making with different preference representation structures: a direct consensus framework and its properties. Knowl.-Based Syst. **58**, 45–57 (2014)
8. Endriss, U.: Judgment aggregation (2016)
9. Fono, L., Andjiga, N.: Fuzzy strict preference and social choice. Fuzzy Sets Syst. **155**(3), 372–389 (2005)
10. Geist, C., Endriss, U.: Automated search for impossibility theorems in social choice theory: ranking sets of objects. J. Artif. Intell. Res. **40**, 143–174 (2011)
11. Governatori, G., Olivieri, F., Cristani, M., Scannapieco, S.: Revision of defeasible preferences. Int. J. Approximate Reasoning **104**, 205–230 (2019)
12. Governatori, G., Olivieri, F., Scannapieco, S., Cristani, M.: The hardness of revising defeasible preferences. In: Bikakis, A., Fodor, P., Roman, D. (eds.) RuleML 2014. LNCS, vol. 8620, pp. 168–177. Springer, Cham (2014). https://doi.org/10.1007/978-3-319-09870-8_12
13. Governatori, G., Olivieri, F., Scannapieco, S., Rotolo, A., Cristani, M.: The rationale behind the concept of goal. TPLP **16**(3), 296–324 (2016)
14. Munda, G.: Social multi-criteria evaluation: methodological foundations and operational consequences. Eur. J. Oper. Res. **158**(3), 662–677 (2004)
15. Olivieri, F., Cristani, M., Governatori, G.: Compliant business processes with exclusive choices from agent specification. In: Chen, Q., Torroni, P., Villata, S., Hsu, J., Omicini, A. (eds.) PRIMA 2015. LNCS (LNAI), vol. 9387, pp. 603–612. Springer, Cham (2015). https://doi.org/10.1007/978-3-319-25524-8_43
16. Pini, M., Rossi, F., Venable, K., Walsh, T.: Aggregating partially ordered preferences. J. Logic Comput. **19**(3), 475–502 (2009)

17. Rossi, F., Venable, K., Walsh, T.: A Short Introduction to Preferences. Between Artificial Intelligence and Social Choice. Synthesis Lectures on Artificial Intelligence and Machine Learning, vol. 14, pp. 1–102. Morgan & Claypool Publishers, San Rafael (2011)
18. Wang, Y.M., Yang, J.B., Xu, D.L.: A preference aggregation method through the estimation of utility intervals. Comput. Oper. Res. **32**(8), 2027–2049 (2005)
19. Zuckerman, M., Procaccia, A., Rosenschein, J.: Algorithms for the coalitional manipulation problem. Artif. Intell. **173**(2), 392–412 (2009)

A Coalitional Algorithm for Recursive Delegation

Juan Afanador[1]([✉])[iD], Nir Oren[1][iD], and Murilo S. Baptista[2][iD]

[1] Department of Computing Science, University of Aberdeen,
AB24 3UE Aberdeen, Scotland
{r01jca16,n.oren}@abdn.ac.uk
[2] Department of Physics, University of Aberdeen, AB24 3UE Aberdeen, Scotland
m.baptista@abdn.ac.uk

Abstract. Within multi-agent systems, some agents may delegate tasks to other agents for execution. Recursive delegation designates situations where delegated tasks may, in turn, be delegated onwards. In unconstrained environments, recursive delegation policies based on quitting games are known to outperform policies based on multi-armed bandits. In this work, we incorporate allocation rules and rewarding schemes when considering recursive delegation, and reinterpret the quitting-game approach in terms of coalitions, employing the Shapley and Myerson values to guide delegation decisions. We empirically evaluate our extensions and demonstrate that they outperform the traditional multi-armed bandit based approach, while offering a resource efficient alternative to the quitting-game heuristic.

1 Introduction

Delegation within multi-agent systems involves a *delegator* handing over a task to a *delegatee*. While a single delegation event is often considered in works dealing with trust [2,4], we address situations where agents are allowed to pass the task onwards until it is eventually executed—a process termed *recursive delegation*. In [1], it has be shown that existing trust mechanisms can be improved within such recursive settings through a game theoretic treatment of the problem. Here, we extend the basic recursive delegation scenario to include an explicit reward rule associated with successful delegation, subject to an equally explicit resource constraint.

To exemplify the applications our approach may capture, consider a distributed network composed of heterogeneous sensors with distinct capabilities [6,8]. These sensors can repeatedly delegate a task across the network, but must do so mindful of their energy consumption (and timeliness of response), as well as the quality of the information returned (with the latter serving as a reward in this context). Upon receiving a task, a sensor must decide whether to delegate the task onwards or execute it (by sensing), attentive to the constraints and rewards attached to its decision.

© Springer Nature Switzerland AG 2019
M. Baldoni et al. (Eds.): PRIMA 2019, LNAI 11873, pp. 405–422, 2019.
https://doi.org/10.1007/978-3-030-33792-6_25

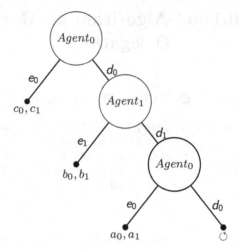

Fig. 1. Quitting game in extensive form

Non-cooperative games in the form of quitting games have already been applied to the study of recursive delegation [1]. Compared to nested multi-armed bandits, the former display greater efficiency, producing higher probabilities of successful delegation with lower levels of regret [1]. These techniques, however, do not take explicit resource constraints and rewards into account, whereas in our work, we not only introduce such additional aspects, but also formulate a coalitional alternative to non-cooperative decision making in recursive delegation domains.

The remainder of this paper is structured as follows. In the next section we describe the non-cooperative approach to recursive delegation. In Sect. 3, we present our implementation of the Shapley and Myerson values as coalitional algorithms for recursive delegation. Section 4 empirically compares the different approaches, Sect. 5 discusses our results alongside directions for future work, and Sect. 6 gathers our main conclusions.

2   Recursive Delegation as a Quitting Game

Adversarial techniques to reason about recursive delegation are built on an adaptation of quitting games; a class of stochastic games [17]. Players of a quitting game have two available actions, either choosing to continue the game (action d), or quitting the game altogether (action e). The former action allows the game to repeat, while the other brings the game to an end. After each game, all players receive whatever rewards they have earned.

A two-player game in extensive form is illustrated in Fig. 1. Here, either player selecting action e leads to the realisation of their respective rewards. Both players playing d leads to the continuation of the same game (denoted by ↻).

In an n-player game, the *strategy* of player i is a probability measure $x_{i(t)}$: $\mathbb{R}_0^+ \to [0,1]$ representing the likelihood of playing d at iteration t. A profile or vector of strategies $\mathbf{x}_t$ would then produce a stream of rewards r_{S_t}, contributed by the subset of players S who have chosen not to quit the game by iteration t. The expected reward of player i at iteration t thus becomes $w_{i(t)}(\mathbf{x}_t) := \mathbb{E}_{\mathbf{x}}[r_{S_t}]$. Let us note in passing that the subscript $i(t) := i \circ t : \{0, \dots, T-1\} \to \{0, \dots, n-1\}$ indicates the value of a variable associated with player i at iteration t, and that it is attached to said variable whenever the index's omission, or its simplification, seems ambiguous.

For $\epsilon \ll b_0/c_0$, $a_0 > 0$, $a_1 < c_1$, $c_0 < b_0$, $a_1 \geq b_1$ and $x_0 \ll 1$, the stationary profile $\mathbf{z} \equiv \langle x_0, d_1 \rangle$—where $Agent_0$ delegates the task with very low probability, while $Agent_1$ systematically chooses to delegate—is produced [18]. That is, the expected reward of $\mathbf{z}$ plus an overhead $\epsilon > 0$ is at least that of any other strategy $y_{i(t)}$ for every player i, or equivalently $w_{i(t)}(\mathbf{z}) \geq w_{i(t)}(\mathbf{x}_{-i(t)}, y_{i(t)}) - \epsilon$. Thereby, the profile $\mathbf{z}$ describes an ϵ-equilibrium [10].

Quitting games share many facets of recursive delegation, effectively capturing self-embedded instances of strategic interaction which resemble the replication of delegation requests along a *delegation chain*, i.e., the sequence of delegatees who receive delegation requests involving the same task. Unlike a standard quitting game, however, delegation requires distinct strategic scenarios, where players alternate between the delegator and delegatee roles, as opposed to the continuation of the game between the two original players. The adjustment to this scenario is conducive to the definition of a *Delegation Game* [1].

Definition 1 (Delegation Game). *The tuple $\Gamma_d = \langle N, A, (u_i, r_i)_{i \in N}, \boldsymbol{x} \rangle$ encodes a delegation game among $|N|$ players, where every player has the following attributes:*

Actions: $A := \{d, e\}$ *and* $A_i = A, \forall i \in N$. $\Delta(A)$ *is the collection of all probability distributions over the set of available actions.*

Rewards: $r_i : \times_{j \in D \subset N} \Delta(A_j) \to \mathbb{R}, \forall i \in N$ *is a Lebesgue measurable function representing the gains of player i when a group of agents $D \subset N$ have received a delegation request.*

Strategy: $x_i : A_i \to [0,1], \forall i \in N$ *is the probability of player i playing action d.*

Profile: $\boldsymbol{x}_t := \langle x_{i(t)} \rangle_{i \in N}$. *Profiles induce a probability distribution $\boldsymbol{P}_x \in \Delta(A)$ over the set of actions, which permits the computation of the expected rewards $w_{i(t)}(\boldsymbol{x}_t) := \mathbb{E}_x[r_{i(t)}]$.*

Updating Rule: $u_{i(t)} : \times_{j \in D_{t-1}} A_j \times \mathbb{R} \to \Delta(A)$ *is a measurable set-valued function that dictates the transition from one state of the system to a potentially different profile.*

When rewards are subject to a stochastic process, the selection of an action has to be expressed in terms of strategic profiles $(\mathbf{x}_t)$. The probability distribution these profiles induce is then used to calculate the expected rewards $(w_{i(t)})$. By comparing expected rewards in the manner of an ϵ-equilibrium, delegators and delegatees select their strategies, which once played provoke the respective information states to update $(u_{i(t)})$.

The entire delegation and learning process based on delegation games is captured by the DIG algorithm presented in [1]. As may be apparent, neither quitting games nor the algorithm take explicit account of the costs associated with exploration or the rewarding mechanism motivating the decision to delegate; we introduce these considerations in the next section.

3   Recursive Delegation as a Coalitional Game

Our approach posits that delegation is a recursive process whereby agents play delegate actions based on their collective implications, subject to restrictions and incentives conditioning the agents capacity to generate value by executing the delegated task. We proceed to describe how coalitions are formed, and state the allocation and distribution rules devised to reflect the delegation structure contained in Definition 1. To illustrate our ideas, let us revisit the opening example on sensor networks.

For the efficient design of one such network, the main aspects typically considered are (1) the features of the sensors as mobile nodes; (2) the limitations these nodes may face in terms of energy consumption, memory size to buffer data, or wireless transmission capacity [19]; and (3) the metrics used to assess the impact of their individual contributions on the overall data-gathering performance of the system [13]. We account for (1) by introducing explicit value allocation rules stating each node's potential to generate sensing data. The idea being that in, e.g., event-driven applications, nodes near active locations may have higher sensing rates, thereby inducing delegation.

Constraints in the form of fixed amounts of a productive resource enabling delegation—electrical energy, most notably—reflect (2). Although wireless charging allows nodes to transmit energy across the network, thereby internalising these budgetary restrictions into the functioning of the sensors themselves [9], we opt to deal with resource constraints as extrinsic to the system. The reason for this is that, in a single-task environment, indefinite delegation is undesirable, and self-sustainability in regard to the productive resource becomes subsidiary. In multi-objective applications, however, these considerations might be relevant, as multiple tasks may compete for the same productive resources involved in delegation.

The criteria used to model the selection of delegatees respond to (3). As presented in Sect. 2, mixed strategies serve as metrics to compute ϵ-equilibria for the quitting-game approach. Alternatively, as shown in [1], the largest Gittins Index can be used to select a suitable delegatee in multi-armed bandit (MAB) models. As will be introduced in Sect. 3.2, the Shapley and Myerson values serve the same purpose in our coalitional game. We now proceed to outline the design features associated with aspects (1) and (2).

3.1   Delegation and Allocation Rules

Given a set of allocation rules, resource constraints and the definition of a solution concept, we present a general framework for reasoning about delegation

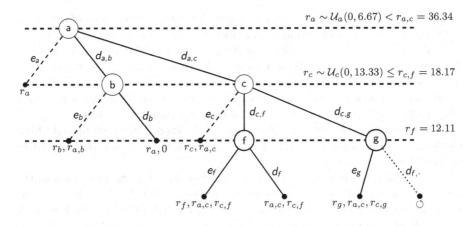

Fig. 2. Delegation game in extensive form

under these conditions. To do so, consider the tree in Fig. 2 which describes a delegation network of agents $N \equiv \{a, b, c, f, g, \ldots, m\}$ whose decisions consume a limiting resource C.

To capture task execution, we introduce *dummy agents* into our representation of the network. These dummy agents appear as solid unlabeled nodes in Fig. 2. A task reaching a dummy agent must be executed (as it cannot be further delegated), and is recorded as carried out by the agent who generates the delegation request.

Consider agent a, the originator of the delegation process, also termed the *root*. This agent can play e_a and perform the task itself, i.e., delegate to the dummy agent. It can also delegate the task to b, in which case b might accept the task by playing e_b, or reject it by playing d_b, thus returning the task to a and forcing a to perform the task itself (via action e_a). Alternatively, a could delegate to c, whence the task may reach f who could, in turn, proceed as b. The task may also be further delegated to g who, had decided not to play e_g, could pass on the task via d_f until a terminal node appears, some other node plays an execute action, or the constraints are no longer satisfied. In this context, *coalitions*, i.e., groups of players treated as strategic units, amount to delegation chains; we refer to the mechanism underlying this process of formation of delegation chains—and coalitions, by implication—as the *quitting structure* of the game.

Now let us turn to the nature of the rewards underpinning the assessment of a decision's profitability. The delegation game in [1] did not make direct reference to the way in which rewards were formed. Agents reached out to one another unconcerned with allocation and distribution rules, inasmuch as the only interactions affecting the calculation of their expected rewards were those with their immediate neighbours. Our proposal, on the contrary, is said to be coalitional because agents acknowledge the contributions of all delegatees in the same delegation chain. We therefore assign a (global) value V for playing the game, and introduce extrinsic rules for its allocation and the distribution of rewards emanating from it.

More precisely, let V be the largest value delegatees are capable of achieving as terminal nodes of a delegation chain. Since globally known from the beginning, the value of the game is initially apportioned among delegators and potential delegatees following a directly proportional distribution rule. The further away from the root, the larger the value an agent can generate, thereby incentivising delegation. In the sensors case, this accounts for flexible and diverse architectures of sparsely distributed nodes capable of generating value in the sense of [15] and [5], depending on their sensing rates—those with lower rates pick up data from the higher sensing agents roaming the network, while others act as data centres or base stations (c.f., [13, 20]).

By contrast, the distribution of the final outcome of delegation, that is, the actual set of rewards, obeys an inversely proportional rule. The closer to the root, the larger the share of the game's value, implying that the task is more profitable the sooner it is executed. In terms of the sensor network, this rule reflects problems of data latency and long delivery delay. If the time elapsed between data being buffered and uploaded to base stations is too long, it might be preferable to generate a greater number of delegation queries to proximate sensors [19].

To detail our argument, we now provide an example of the operation of these two rules which substantiates our approach $w.l.o.g.$ Let us, first, designate the initial allocations of V over all $n \equiv |N|$ agents by $\{v_i\}_{i \in N}$. These values are realised by the terminal node of any delegation chain as $outcomes$ $\{o_i\}_{i \in N}$. The rewards $\{r_i\}_{i \in N}$ accrued to the members of any chain are obtained from the outcome associated with the chain's terminal node. That is, each player's potential to produce the value of the game is conveyed through their respective outcomes, which propagate across the delegation chain in the form of rewards. The following steps illustrate the calculation of rewards in the subgraph spanned by $\{a, b, c, f, g\}$, up to a hypothetical third level of delegation for a game with value $V = 100$:

1. Distribute V proportionately among all agents, depending on their position along the tree:

$$\frac{v_a}{1} = \frac{v_b}{2} = \cdots = \frac{v_g}{5} = \frac{V}{1 + 2 + \cdots + 5},$$

   i.e., $v_a = 6.67, v_b = 13.33, v_c = 20, v_f = 26.67, v_g = 33.33$

2. Sample the outcomes from a uniform distribution between v_i (computed above) and V:

$$o_i \sim \mathcal{U}_i(v_i, V), \forall i \in \{a, b, c, f, g\},$$

   e.g., $o_a = 57.89, o_b = 75.31, o_c = 68.22, o_f = 66.63, o_g = 80.77$

3. Once a potential coalition/delegation chain forms, e.g., $\{a, c, f\}$, distribute the outcome yielded by the agent executing the task in an inversely proportional manner:

$$\frac{r_{a,c}}{1} = \frac{r_{c,f}}{1/2} = \frac{r_f}{1/3} = \frac{o_f}{1 + 1/2 + 1/3}, \text{i.e., } r_a = 36.34, r_c = 18.17, r_f = 12.11$$

More generally, our proportional rule implies that the value of the game is allocated according to the relation $\frac{v_i}{i+1} = \frac{V}{T_n}$, where $T_k := \sum_{j=1}^{k} j = \frac{k(k+1)}{2}$. The inversely proportional rule requires individual rewards to satisfy $\frac{r_{i,j}}{i} = \frac{o_k}{H_k}$, where $H_k := \sum_{i=1}^{k} \frac{1}{i}$ and $r_i \equiv r_{i,j}$ for every $i = j \in N$. Insofar as these two rules depict the structure of incentives behind delegation, they will frame the evaluation of our coalitional algorithm against the corresponding benchmarks; namely, the original quitting-game based approach in [1], and the MAB model also presented in [1] which extends the numerical approximation to the Gittins Index introduced in [3].

In consequence, aspect (1) is encapsulated in the interplay of equations $\frac{v_i}{i+1} = \frac{V}{T_k}$ and $\frac{r_{i,j}}{i} = \frac{o_k}{H_k}$, i.e., the value allocation and reward generation rules, respectively. Aspect (2), for its part, is incorporated into our framework via the explicit recognition of the value of the game V, and the straightforward imposition of a numerical parameter $K \in \mathbb{R}_0^+$ constraining the generation of delegation requests and the production of rewards out of V. Having established the relational characteristics of the agents in our delegation networks, and the rules or conditions that mediate their interactions—as per design aspects (1) and (2) outlined at the outset of this section—we go on to present the criterion and computational procedures delegators use to select a delegatee among its neighbours—thus reflecting aspect (3).

3.2 Recursive Delegation as a Coalitional Game

The initial allocation of values and the definition of rewards may circumscribe the delegator's decision, but the guiding principle behind delegation is given by the solution concept used to select one or another delegatee. We employ the Shapely and Myerson values to this effect. Computing these values allows us to map potential rewards to groups of agents, so the advantages of forming a particular delegation chain can be assessed.

In a coalitional setting, potential delegation chains are treated as coalitions, i.e., groups of agents who evaluate the collective aspect of task completion/delegation. In spite of the individual nature of the rewarding scheme, the completion of the task is considered a common objective, and the network-wide impact of the resources expended in achieving the task is acknowledged by delegators. Hence, in the form of neighbouring conditions, pre-existing valuations of available coalitions, and an internal mechanism for extracting individual contributions, these elements provide the basis of a delegation game of coalitions (DEC):

Definition 2 (Delegation Game of Coalitions). *A Delegation Game of Coalitions is a tuple* $\Gamma_c = \langle N, V; \mathcal{B}, \nu \rangle$, *characterised by the following elements:*

Value of the game: $V \in \mathbb{R}_0^+$, *gives the maximum value delegation can yield.*

Coalitional Structure: *A partition $\mathcal{B}$ of the set of agents $N = \{1,\ldots,n\}$ conforming to the quitting structure of delegation.*

Outcomes: $o_i : \Delta(\{w_i\}_{i \in N}) \rightarrow \mathbb{R}_0^+$ *for every $i \in N$, are obtained from the stochastic process dictating the allocation of the value of the game. $\Delta(\{w_i\}_{i \in N})$ is the collection of potential distributions over the set of admissible distributions of V.*

Characteristic Function: $\nu : 2^n \rightarrow \mathbb{R}^+$, *associates every coalition $D \subset \mathcal{B}$ with the expected value of its aggregated reward, i.e., $\nu(D) = \sum_{i \in D} \mathbb{E}[o_i]$.*

The coalitional structure of DEC encompasses those combinations of agents compatible with the quitting structure of delegation described in Sect. 3.1. The characteristic function links the expected rewards to the corresponding coalition(s) in the set of all permutations of agents, mapping invalid ones (e.g., those where a delegator comes last) to zero. The rewarding rule $\psi : \{o_i\}_{i \in D \subset \mathcal{B}} \rightarrow \mathbb{R}_0^+$, assigns rewards to the members of coalitions D belonging to the partition of the game $\mathcal{B}$. In the abstract, the solution concept is but a mapping $\phi : U \rightarrow \mathbb{R}^n$ with $U := \{\Gamma_c : n \subseteq \mathbb{R}^+\}$, while in our experiments it takes the form of the Shapley and the Myerson values.

Definition 3 (Shapley Value [14]). *The Shapley Value of a coalitional game $\Gamma = \langle N; \nu \rangle$ –such as DEC– is a solution concept that retrieves the individual contribution of any player, subject to the coalitional structure of the game given by all subsets $D \subseteq N$. It can be computed as follows for every player $i \in N$.*

$$Sh_i(N;\nu) := \sum_{D \subseteq N} g_D[\nu(D) - \nu(D \setminus \{i\})]; \quad g_D := \frac{(|D| - 1)!(n - |D|)!}{n!}. \quad (1)$$

That is, players foreign to a coalition D can be arranged in as many as $(n - |D|)!$ ways. In turn, within D all those players different from player i can be sorted in $(|D| - 1)!$ ways. The contribution of player i to the coalition is given by the difference between the aggregated value of D and that of the subsets (coalitions) excluding player i. The total number of such subsets amounts to $(|D| - 1)!(n - |D|)!$. To obtain the corresponding average contribution, the sum over all possible coalitions is divided by the number of all admissible combinations of players, i.e., $n!$.

The Myerson Value is a refinement of the Shapley Value. The Myerson Value exclusively targets graph-restricted games, i.e., coalitional games whose coalitions can only reflect specific subgraphs of the underlying general graph of interactions [11]. The idea being that coalitions are highly dependent on their context. This means that the characteristic function should only be defined over connected components $\mathcal{S}(N)$, as given by the topology of the network enabling delegation. Connectedness, in this sense, refers to the existence of a path connecting any pair of non-adjacent nodes, such as a and g in Fig. 2.

Definition 4 (The Myerson Value [11]). *Let* $\Gamma = \langle N, \nu \rangle$ *be a coalitional game. The Myerson Value (My_i) of Γ, corresponds to the Shapley Value for the characteristic function defined over connected coalitions i.e., $My_i(N; \nu) = Sh_i(N; \nu_M)$ such that*

$$\nu_M(D) = \begin{cases} \nu(D) & if D \in \mathcal{S}(N) \\ \sum_{K_i \in K(D)} \nu(K_i) & otherwise \end{cases}$$

The Shapely Value provides a means of differentiating individual contributions to a delegation chain within multi-agent systems, while incorporating the quitting structure of delegation outlined in Sect. 3.1. The Myerson Value implements the same procedure over a subset of players which not only conform to the quitting structure, but also respond to a particular configuration of the system laid out before the first delegation request had been issued.

Algorithm 1. Coalition Formation

Input: i: Index of the agent seeking coalitions, *path*: Length of the last delegation chain.

Output: *coalition*: Sequence of agents receiving a delegation request.

```
 1: function CFORM(i)
 2:     k ← i.delegatee
 3:     coalition ← {j, k}
 4:     max_length ← U(2, 3)
 5:     path_length ← len(coalition)
 6:     while path_length < max_length do
 7:         if k.out_neighbours ≠ ∅ then
 8:             m ← sample(k.out_neighbours)
 9:             coalition ← coalition ∪ {m}
10:             k ← m
11:             path_length ← len(coalition)
        return coalition
```

Our implementation of the Shapley and Myerson values requires a procedure to obtain the quitting structure of the game. Such procedure is given by Algorithm 1. It stipulates the formation of coalitions as a retrospective endeavour which looks into past delegation chains, permitting agents to recursively select new coalition members among their neighbours' neighbours (lines 6–11). Every agent foresees a coalition/delegation chain of length at most three (line 4); that is, itself, its immediate neighbour, and its neighbour's neighbour, intending to reflect myopic behaviour on the part of delegators.

Algorithm 2 implements DEC with the Myerson Value. Its Shapley version would only see the solution concept changed to Eq. (1) (in line 4 of the *DEL* function). The computation of both the Myerson and Shapley values follow the divide-and-conquer approach of [16], which performs a recursive backtrack in a depth-first search for the delegation chains rooted at delegator j.

Our algorithm strives to find the largest contributions among all the delegation chains allowed by the quitting structure, subject to a resource constraint (line 3) and the allocation rules introduced before. Its inputs correspond to said resource constraint (K), the value of the game (V), and the set of probabilities of successful execution describing each delegatee's ability to perform the delegated task $(\{s_i\}_{i \in [n]})$.

As our algorithm requires the initialisation of individual outcomes (o_i), rewards (r_i) and neighbourhoods $(P_i \equiv \{a_i, ad_i\}$, where ad_i represents the neighbours of agent $a_i)$, we have grouped those procedures under *Init_DEC*. After intialising counters of successful and failed execution (line 5), as well as the sets containing potential coalitions and actual delegatees (line 6), we apply the value allocation rule in line 7 to every agent in the system, followed by the sampling of outcomes as indicated in our opening example (line 8), so the distribution rule in line 9 enables the initialisation of the rewards on the basis of each agent's outcome.

We enter the main procedure *DEC* through a "while" statement at line 3. This statement guarantees that the game is played for as long as there is available productive resource K to effect a delegation request. Delegators employ the function *DEL* to allocate the delegation request. First, they seek a fitting coalition of three players at the most, by invoking the function *CForm* in line 2. Then, delegators compute the Myerson value of the resulting coalition (line 4), and proceed to select the delegatee who makes the largest contribution (line 5). If the selected delegatee is not its dummy agent, the delegation request is replicated (line 8) and the rewards obtained via our distribution rule in line 9.

We leave our core function at line 6, where the probability of successful execution of the selected delegatee (a_m) is contrasted against the state of nature as given by the probability $1 - \delta$. Not unlike the Delegation Game of [1], in our algorithm a favourable state of nature secures the execution of the task by the appointed delegatee, otherwise defaulting to the delegator itself, triggering the α and β counters as well as those keeping track of the fraction of the productive resource consumed throughout delegation; a rate of consumption equal to the ratio between the number of successful interactions and the total number of visits to the chosen delegatee (lines 8 and 11 resp.). Past this stage, the outcomes are once again sampled (line 12), and the characteristic function of the game is learned (line 14). This process repeats until the limiting resource is depleted.

Algorithm 2. Delegation Game of Coalitions Under Myerson

Input: V: Value of the game, K: A real number denoting the resource constraint, s_i: Probability of successful execution of agent i.

Output: S: Sequence of agents receiving a delegation request. ν: Set of values of the characteristic function.

1: **function** INIT_DEC(K, V)
2:    $\nu \leftarrow \emptyset$
3:    $Constraint \leftarrow K,\ Consumption \leftarrow 0$
4:    **for** $j = 1 \rightarrow n$ **do**
5:      $\alpha_j \leftarrow 0,\ \beta_j \leftarrow 0$
6:      $D_j \leftarrow \emptyset,\ S_j \leftarrow \emptyset$
7:      $v_j \leftarrow (j+1)V / \sum_{i \in [n]} i$
8:      $o_j \leftarrow \mathcal{U}(0, v_j)$
9:      $r_j \leftarrow j o_j / \sum_{i \in [n]} 1/i$
10:     $P_j \leftarrow \{a_j, ad_j\}$

1: **function** DEL(P_k)
2:    $coalition \leftarrow$ CFORM(k)
3:    $D_k \leftarrow D_k \cup \{coalition\}$
4:    $my_k \leftarrow My_k(|D_k|; \sum_{i \in D_k} r_i)$
5:    $m \leftarrow \operatorname{argmax}_{i \in ad_k}(my_i)$
6:    $S_k \leftarrow S_k \cup \{a_m\}$
7:    **if** $m \neq k$ **then**
8:      **return** DEL(P_{m}, s_m)
9:      $r_m \leftarrow k o_m / \sum_{i \in coalition} 1/i$
10:   **else**
11:     $r_m \leftarrow o_m$
12:   **return** (m, r_m, S_k)

1: **procedure** DEC$(K, V; \{s_k\}_{k \in [n]})$
2:    INIT_DEC(K, V)
3:    **while** $Constraint \geq Consumption$ **do**
4:      **for** $j = 1 \rightarrow n$ **do**
5:        $(m, r_m, S_j) \leftarrow$ DEL(P_j, s_j)
6:        **if** $s_m > 1 - \delta$ **then**
7:          $\alpha_j \leftarrow \alpha_j + 1$
8:          $Consumption \leftarrow Consumption + \frac{1}{\alpha_m + \beta_m}$
9:        **else**
10:         $\beta_j \leftarrow \beta_j + 1$
11:         $Consumption \leftarrow Consumption + \frac{1}{\alpha_j + \beta_j}$
12:        Update outcomes
13:        $S \leftarrow S_j \cup \{S_j\}$
14:        $\nu \leftarrow \nu \cup \{\sum_{k \in D_j} r_k\}$
15:      $Constraint \leftarrow Constraint - Consumption$
     return (S, ν)

---

4   Evaluation

4.1   Experimental Set-Up

Our objective remains establishing whether the coalitional approach of
Algorithm 2 can outperform DIG given the new constraints and rules. The evaluation of Algorithm 2 was carried out over Random Networks and Directed Trees
extending up to 4 levels of delegation, with a branching factor of 5 neighbours
per delegator among a population of 156 agents; as such is the number of nodes
in a tree-like layout including its root. The levels of the limiting resource were
allowed to range within 500 and 800 units, whereas the value of the game varied
from 800 to 1000 units. Our algorithm and contrasting benchmarks were tested
for the span of 100 runs elapsing 1000 trials, so as to stay consistent with the
experimental design of [1].

The systems under consideration are made up of agents arranged in either
4-level trees rooted at the first delegator in the network, or ad-hoc graphs whose
edges are generated as delegation progresses and whose respective dynamics are
dictated by the algorithms used to make delegation decisions. Directed Trees
offer a structured environment for accommodating agents who establish a relation of precedence upon delegating. Random Networks, instead, are discovered
as agents delegate—the probability of delegating arising form each algorithm
simultaneously dictates the probability of spanning an edge from a delegator to
a delegatee. The benchmarks used to compare our approach include the DIG
algorithm in [1] and the adaptation of the Gittins Index also proposed in [1], but
originally formulated in [3]. This selection circumscribes multi-armed bandits
and non-coalitional game-theoretic models whenever recursive delegation takes
place in constrained environments.

4.2   Results

Figure 3 depicts the behaviour of the probabilities of successful delegation (PSD),
alongside the ratio between the amount of productive resource expended in delegating and the value of the game generated through delegation (E/R). These
two variables define our criteria of performance. The curves they describe stop
at different trials due to the resource constraints faced by all agents and the
ways in which the algorithms make use of said resource—every delegate action
consumes a productive resource, when this budget is depleted, delegators cannot
delegate the task onwards. That is, the delegation process effectively comes to
an end; a situation which coalitional games had to face at a much later point in
time than their benchmarking algorithms.

In Random Networks and Directed Trees, DIG displays superior performance
compared to the MAB approach (DID) and the coalitional alternatives. It attains
larger rewards and higher probabilities of successful delegation. The great variability of this result, however, casts doubts on the efficiency of DIG. Directed
Trees provide a structured environment for all algorithms to explore. In situations like this, previous knowledge of their neighbours' connectivity allows agents

to expend less resources while exploring potential delegation chains. We find that the limiting resource not only lasts longer but leads to more stable delegation chains where tasks are more likely to be successfully executed (Fig. 3a).

Figure 3a and b indicate that Myerson does not perform remarkably well on tree-like structures, despite being designed to better cope with fixed delegation patterns. It appears that in the early stages of delegation ($T < 50$ for Fig. 3a) productive but costly coalitions were formed, which on account of the functioning of the algorithm would stifle exploration and trap delegators in chains with relatively poor capacity to adapt to delegation under tightening resource constraints.

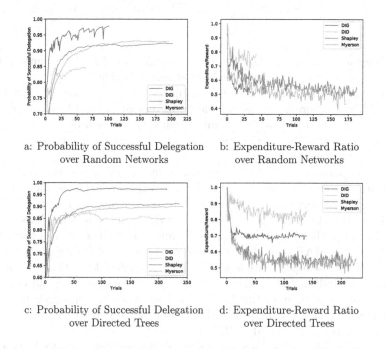

a: Probability of Successful Delegation   b: Expenditure-Reward Ratio
over Random Networks   over Random Networks

c: Probability of Successful Delegation   d: Expenditure-Reward Ratio
over Directed Trees   over Directed Trees

Fig. 3. Comparative performance between topologies

Myerson, Shapley and DIG make use of the limiting resource until roughly the same trial. The difference being that DIG succeeds in generating at least one extra quarter of the value attained by the best performing coalitional algorithm (Shapley). A difference further reflected in the levels of regret associated with these results (Table 1).

Random Networks, on the other hand, allow agents to select their own neighbours, and potential delegatees, based on an intrinsic property, i.e., the strategies and distribution of the Gittins Index for DIG and DID, respectively; or an external one as in the cases of Shapley and Myerson. Under these conditions agents rely more heavily on exploration, often incurring greater costs, particularly for

Table 1. Minimum credible intervals of the mean posterior PSD, reward and regret

Group	Network structure	PSD	Rewards	Regrets
Directed trees	DIG	0.92 ± 0.008	435 ± 0.19	$4.398 \pm 5e^{-5}$
	DID	0.827 ± 0.012	377 ± 0.62	$12.996 \pm 2e^{-5}$
	Shapley	0.889 ± 0.010	355 ± 0.33	$10.361 \pm 3e^{-5}$
	Myerson	0.858 ± 0.011	358 ± 0.04	$10.27 \pm 3e^{-5}$
Random networks	DIG	0.966 ± 0.006	387 ± 0.42	$2.971 \pm 2e^{-4}$
	DID	0.794 ± 0.014	219 ± 0.69	$8.810 \pm 1e^{-4}$
	Shapley	0.890 ± 0.010	330 ± 0.41	$8.975 \pm 3e^{-4}$
	Myerson	0.889 ± 0.010	329 ± 0.31	$9.702 \pm 2e^{-4}$

DIG. Delegators employing DIG guarantee a higher PSD at the expense of lesser rewards, which also implies a lower level of regret (Table 1).

Only the coalitional algorithms maintain the behaviour displayed over Directed Trees. There is a considerable improvement in their levels of (cumulative) regret which does not significantly reduce the reward obtained. Coalition formation as a criterion of delegation seems to traverse in an equally exhaustive manner both types of topologies.

As DID operates exclusively on a learning-by-observing mechanism, contrary to DIG agents who interact strategically, it struggles to traverse the delegation network when subject to resource constraints, often being confined to local maxima. We believe this is also the reason behind the high levels of the Expenditure-Reward ratio (E/R) encountered in Fig. 3b and c, as well as the insufficient performance of the MAB heuristic compared to the levels of PSD reported in [1].

Despite DIG's appropriateness for use in recursive delegation, the relative variability of PSD noted at the beginning of this section, and the decline in the levels of rewards, motivate further analysis when transitioning from trees to unstructured environments. For this reason, we opted to conduct a test of correlation between PSD and E/R.

Our test consists of a Bayesian reformulation of Pearson's for a Gaussian mixture of the prior of the correlation coefficient [12], centered in accordance with the corresponding distribution of the observations plotted in Fig. 3. PSD and E/R were fitted to a bivariate t-distribution with uninformative normal, uniform, and exponential priors for their respective means, variances and normality parameters, as per the BEST model put forward in [7]. All hyperparameters were obtained from the outputs of our original simulations (unreported). Figure 4 provides direct access to the posterior distribution of the correlation coefficient, in terms of the coefficient's 95% credible intervals. The results of the No-U-Turn sampler (unreported) guarantee the convergence of distributions, allowing for a direct interpretation of the mean posterior.

There exists a stronger correlation between efficient resource expenditure and increments in the likelihood of a successful delegation, when coalitional algorithms are used on Random Networks. Notwithstanding this behaviour, with a posterior probability of 86%, higher correlation values (0.24 > 0.15) are likely to be encountered in the same structures when agents use DIG (Fig. 4).

With respect to the same criterion, Shapley and Myerson can be considered more efficient in the use of the limiting resource. DIG, however, secures desirable levels of PSD while employing relatively concurrent levels of the resource at a rapid pace. Were the limiting resource apt for alternative uses, a coalitional approach to delegation would be more appropriate than a non-cooperative one, but in any case more pertinent than a MAB-based procedure. In this sense, the Shapley and Myerson algorithms are considered approximate solutions to the (recursive) delegation problem.

Finally, to elaborate on our last claim let us examine Fig. 5. It reports the difference between the mean rewards produced by DIG and those produced by DEC, using the same statistical model of the modified Pearson's test [12]. Our results indicate that the group means are not credibly different. Over both Directed Trees and Random Networks, approximately 50% of the posterior probability is greater than zero, suggesting that the gap between the root's mean reward under DIG and the coalitional alternatives is not significantly different from zero. Furthermore, the means of the group distributions range between 41 and 79 units of value, which is less than a third of the average reward earned by the root per trial. So, on grounds of efficiency and value generation capacity, both implementations of DEC are on a par with DIG.

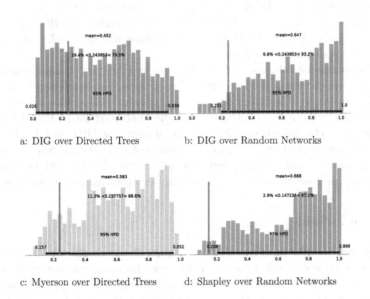

a: DIG over Directed Trees   b: DIG over Random Networks

c: Myerson over Directed Trees   d: Shapley over Random Networks

Fig. 4. Posterior distributions of the correlation statistic for PSD and R/E

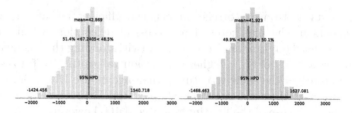

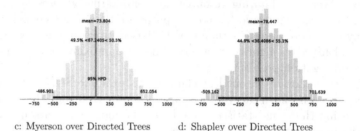

a: Myerson over Random Networks   b: Shapley over Random Networks

c: Myerson over Directed Trees   d: Shapley over Directed Trees

Fig. 5. Posterior distributions of the differences of means against DID

5   Discussion and Future Work

So far we have provided empirical evidence demonstrating that the quitting-game approach to recursive delegation retains all the desirable properties reported in [1], though mediated by the intensive use of the limiting resource. Our algorithm, on the other hand, guarantees the delegated task is carried out with a probability within reasonable limits ($PSD \approx 0.9$), while interactions can be sustained for longer periods of time ($T > 200$).

The resource-use efficiency of the Shapley and Myerson values is upheld by the mechanism dictating the formation of coalitions. The time complexity of this sampling process is quasilinear on restricted graphs and polynomial on random networks, due to the linear structure of the coalitions formed by DEC, thus conforming to the neighbour sampling complexity of DIG and DID [1]. The impact of more intricate coalitions on the levels of PSD, within complex systems where agents not only delegate but engage in multiple interactions dependent on the same productive resource, remain to be determined in future work.

6   Conclusions

In this paper, we introduce resource constraints alongside allocation and rewarding rules to recursive delegation. We further present a conceptual framework to cater for collective responses to these conditions. Quitting-game and multi-armed-bandit based approaches are used as benchmarks for evaluating the performance of adaptations of the Shapley and Myerson values to recursive delegation.

Our results indicate that over predefined networks of agents (Directed Trees) and unstructured environments (Random Networks), the quitting game approach attains greater rewards and higher probabilities of successful delegation. This is possible, however, only with the intensive use of the productive resource limiting delegation. In scenarios where constraints are decisive for the operation of multi-agent systems, coalitional games provide a second-best, yet more resource-efficient, alternative.

References

1. Afanador, J., Baptista, M., Oren, N.: An adversarial algorithm for delegation. In: Lujak, M. (ed.) AT 2018. LNCS (LNAI), vol. 11327, pp. 130–145. Springer, Cham (2019). https://doi.org/10.1007/978-3-030-17294-7_10
2. Alonso, R., Matouschek, N.: Optimal delegation. Rev. Econ. Stud. **75**(1), 259–293 (2008)
3. Brezzi, M., Lai, T.L.: Optimal learning and experimentation in bandit problems. J. Econ. Dyn. Control **27**(1), 87–108 (2002)
4. Castelfranchi, C., Falcone, R.: Towards a theory of delegation for agent-based systems. Robot. Autonomous Syst. **24**(3–4), 141–157 (1998). https://doi.org/10.1016/S0921-8890(98)00028-1
5. Chen, H., Ta, S., Sun, B.: Cooperative game approach to power allocation for target tracking in distributed mimo radar sensor networks. IEEE Sens. J. **15**(10), 5423–5432 (2015)
6. Etuk, A., Norman, T.J., Oren, N., Sensoy, M.: Strategies for truth discovery under resource constraints. In: Proceedings of the 2015 International Conference on Autonomous Agents and Multiagent Systems, pp. 1807–1808. International Foundation for Autonomous Agents and Multiagent Systems (2015)
7. Kruschke, J.K.: Bayesian estimation supersedes the t test. J. Exp. Psychol. Gen. **142**(2), 573 (2013)
8. Li, J., Mohapatra, P.: Analytical modeling and mitigation techniques for the energy hole problem in sensor networks. Pervasive Mob. Comput. **3**(3), 233–254 (2007)
9. Li, Z., Peng, Y., Zhang, W., Qiao, D.: Study of joint routing and wireless charging strategies in sensor networks. In: Pandurangan, G., Anil Kumar, V.S., Ming, G., Liu, Y., Li, Y. (eds.) WASA 2010. LNCS, vol. 6221, pp. 125–135. Springer, Heidelberg (2010). https://doi.org/10.1007/978-3-642-14654-1_17
10. Maschler, M., Solan, E., Zamir, S.: Game Theory. Cambridge University Press, Cambridge (2013). https://doi.org/10.1017/CBO9780511794216
11. Myerson, R.B.: Graphs and cooperation in games. Math. Oper. Res. **2**(3), 225–229 (1977)
12. Sedgwick, P.: Pearson's correlation coefficient. BMJ **345**, e4483 (2012)
13. Shah, R.C., Roy, S., Jain, S., Brunette, W.: Data mules: modeling and analysis of a three-tier architecture for sparse sensor networks. Ad Hoc Netw. **1**(2–3), 215–233 (2003)
14. Shapley, L.S.: A value for n-person games. Contrib. Theory Games **2**(28), 307–317 (1953)
15. Shi, H.Y., Wang, W.L., Kwok, N.M., Chen, S.Y.: Game theory for wireless sensor networks: a survey. Sensors **12**(7), 9055–9097 (2012)

16. Skibski, O., Michalak, T.P., Rahwan, T., Wooldridge, M.: Algorithms for the Shapley and Myerson values in graph-restricted games. In: Proceedings of the 2014 International Conference on Autonomous Agents and Multi-agent Systems, pp. 197–204. International Foundation for Autonomous Agents and Multiagent Systems (2014)
17. Solan, E., Vieille, N.: Quitting games. Math. Oper. Res. **26**(2), 265–285 (2001)
18. Solan, E., Vieille, N.: Quitting games-an example. Int. J. Game Theory **31**(3), 365–381 (2003)
19. Vecchio, M., Viana, A.C., Ziviani, A., Friedman, R.: DEEP: density-based proactive data dissemination protocol for wireless sensor networks with uncontrolled sink mobility. Comput. Commun. **33**(8), 929–939 (2010)
20. Ye, F., Luo, H., Cheng, J., Lu, S., Zhang, L.: A two-tier data dissemination model for large-scale wireless sensor networks. In: Proceedings of the 8th Annual International Conference on Mobile Computing and Networking, pp. 148–159. ACM (2002)

Short Papers

Compact Frequency Memory
for Reinforcement Learning
with Hidden States

Hüseyin Aydın[1]($\boxtimes$), Erkin Çilden[2], and Faruk Polat[1]

[1] Department of Computer Engineering, Middle East Technical University,
Üniversiteler Mah. Dumlupınar Blv. No:1, 06800 Ankara, Turkey
{huseyin,polat}@ceng.metu.edu.tr
[2] STM Defense Technologies Engineering and Trade Inc.,
Mustafa Kemal Mah. 2151. Cd. No:3/A, 06530 Ankara, Turkey
erkin.cilden@stm.com.tr

Abstract. Memory-based reinforcement learning approaches keep track of past experiences of the agent in environments with hidden states. This may require extensive use of memory that limits the practice of these methods in a real-life problem. The motivation behind this study is the observation that less frequent transitions provide more reliable information about the current state of the agent in ambiguous environments. In this work, a selective memory approach based on the frequencies of transitions is proposed to avoid keeping the transitions which are unrelated to the agent's current state. Experiments show that the usage of a compact and selective memory may improve and speed up the learning process.

Keywords: Reinforcement Learning · Memory-based learning · Compact Frequency Memory

1 Introduction

Reinforcement Learning (RL) [9] suffers from the limited information on the resulting granularity of the agent's state space for both continuous domains and the domains with hidden state space. When the ambiguity in the perception of the agent (also known as perceptual aliasing [1]) is inherent for the problem, finding a solution without using an internal memory becomes extremely difficult, or even impossible in some cases.

There are a number of memory-based method categories trying to cope with the perceptual aliasing problem. *Finite size history* is one of the simplest memory-based approaches [5]. Instead of keeping the current observation, the agent uses a chain of last n steps as the current observation. Recurrent-Q is another method that uses *Long Short-Term Memory (LSTM)* [2]. LSTM is a Recurrent Neural Network (RNN) variant used to filter out the irrelevant information about the state space. Yet another memory-based method category

© Springer Nature Switzerland AG 2019
M. Baldoni et al. (Eds.): PRIMA 2019, LNAI 11873, pp. 425–433, 2019.
https://doi.org/10.1007/978-3-030-33792-6_26

is the *variable-length history* family. In this approach, the size of the internal memory can be altered depending on dynamically changing memory requirement for the underlying learning procedure. Nearest Sequence Memory (NSM) and Utile Suffix Memory (USM) algorithms are examples of this category (also called *instance-based* methods) where all raw data of the agent's experience are kept in the form of action-reward-observation tuples [7].

All of the methods above tend to keep the recent or all the experiences of the agent collected throughout the learning process. Unfortunately, especially for problems with large state space, it becomes difficult to determine the size and content of the memory required to provide a distinctive clue about the current state of the agent. Although keeping all the history of the agent overcomes this problem, the estimated state, namely the information unit constructed by the agent to distinguish its current state, can be arbitrarily complex [6].

In this study, a selective memory approach based on transition frequencies is proposed via a more compact and reliable memory for the learning agent.

2   RL and Problems with Hidden State

RL refers to a family of algorithms mostly built on the assumption that the agent's current state depends solely on the previous one, called the *Markov property*, as in the Markov Decision Process (MDP) model. An MDP is defined as a tuple $\langle S, A, T, R \rangle$, where S is the finite set of states, A is the finite set of possible actions, $T : S \times A \times S \rightarrow [0,1]$ is the transition function that gives the probability of making transition from one state to another by taking some action, and $R : S \times A \rightarrow \Re$ is the reward function that gives the reward taken by the agent in some state doing some action. $\Re$ denotes the total expected reward which the agent tries to maximize.

Although MDP provides a well defined model to construct a solution for a given problem, it is not realistic since the assumption that the agent has the complete knowledge about its current state does not always hold. Partially Observable MDP (POMDP) is a generalization over MDP which enables to build up models for problems where there is an observation semantics over the state-action space, mimicking the limited sensor capabilities of a learning agent. A POMDP is defined as a tuple $\langle S, A, T, R, \Omega, O \rangle$, where S, A, T, R define an MDP and Ω is the finite set of observations, $O : S \times A \rightarrow \Pi(\Omega)$ is the observation function, which gives, for each action and resulting state, a probability distribution over possible observations [4]. A specific interpretation of POMDP model assumes that the underlying state space and transition function is entirely unknown, thus leaving only the observations and rewards for the agent to obtain feedback from the environment. Obviously, MDP is a special form of POMDP where every state is associated with a unique observation.

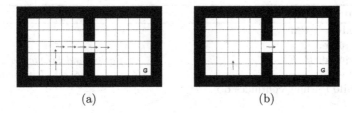

(a)   (b)

Fig. 1. (a) The transitions form the memory in NSM and USM (b) The transitions used in the CFM

3   Compact Frequency Memory

Being in an unknown city, a tourist needs some reference points to find a path to his/her destination. These reference points should be distinguishable among others. This case is similar to that of a learning agent in an unknown environment. If a solution exists for the given problem with hidden states, the agent may find its path to the goal more easily by using *relatively* reliable reference points. Usually, the most reliable information comes from the unique transitions which occur in only one state in the environment. However, by using not only unique transitions but also less frequent ones, the agent may still distinguish the aliased states which lead to the same observation.

Consider the domain given in Fig. 1 where the agent gets an observation for the current location based on the surrounding obstacles. The agent should know whether it passed through the door to the neighboring room where the goal state resides. In order to do so, methods like NSM and USM keep track of all of the transitions between the starting state and the current one. However, by the elimination of the frequent transitions in the environment and keeping significant transitions as in Fig. 1b, the agent can obtain more reliable and efficient information about its current path. Keeping the recent one or two transitions also fails to provide information about the agent's current path if the agent keeps moving to east in the same environment. The fixed size of memory can be increased for the domain, but this approach is not scalable for larger domains.

Algorithm 1 explains how CFM works during the learning process. The agent keeps track of the frequency of every transition in the domain, based on observations and actions. Then it compares the frequencies of all transitions with a given threshold to select the infrequent ones. This selection is repeated periodically, because the agent may experience a useful transition for the first time with the discovery of a new path in a very large domain. In this way, the information gathered from a new transition can be preserved. After generating a set of infrequent transitions, the agent uses this set to form a state estimation about its current state. The state estimation is composed of last n significant transitions and the recent observation. If the current transition is also significant and is not the same as the last one, then it is updated by removing the oldest transition. After the construction of the state estimation with current selections from infrequent transitions and the current observation, the regular Q update can be applied on this estimation.

Algorithm 1. CFM Algorithm

1: **procedure** CFM
2:     **require:** α, γ
3:     **require:** P, FT ▷ *Period and Frequency Threshold*
4:     $IP \leftarrow \emptyset$ ▷ *set of infrequent pairs*
5:     **while** learning continues **do**
6:         $t \leftarrow 0$
7:         $CS \leftarrow \emptyset$ ▷ *current selection from infrequent pairs*
8:         **while** episode continues **do**
9:             take action a_t, observe o_t and r_t
10:             apply regular Q update on the estimation (CS, o_t)
11:             increase the frequency count of the pair (o_t, a_t)
12:             **if** $(o_t, a_t) \in IP$ **then**
13:                 **if** $(o_t, a_t) \neq (o_{t-1}, a_{t-1})$ **then**
14:                     remove $argmin_t(o_t, a_t)$ from CS
15:                     add (o_t, a_t) to CS
16:                 **end if**
17:             **end if**
18:             $t \leftarrow t + 1$
19:         **end while**
20:         **if** episode number matches with P **then**
21:             **for** each pair p_i in transition pairs **do**
22:                 $nf_{p_i} = \frac{(f_{p_i} - min_j f_{p_j})}{(max_j f_{p_j} - min_j f_{p_j})}$ ▷ *normalized f*
23:                 **if** $nf_{p_i} < FT$ **then**
24:                     $IP = IP \cup \{p_i\}$
25:                 **end if**
26:             **end for**
27:         **end if**
28:     **end while**
29: **end procedure**

The idea of building up a memory using infrequent transitions is based on the assumption that for most of the problems with hidden states, there are less frequent unaliased states than aliased ones. If this assumption does not hold for a domain where the transitions are observed almost uniformly, CFM reduces to the fixed sized memory-based Q-learning.

4   Experiments

Experiments are carried out on two different settings. In the first one, although the problem domains are relatively small, the aliased states make the problems difficult or even impossible to solve without a memory. In these domains, CFM is compared with both memory-based (NSM and USM) and memoryless (Q-Learning [10] and Sarsa(λ) [6]) approaches. In the latter setting, larger domains are used in experimentation where NSM and USM approaches cannot be scaled to perform learning in a reasonable time and Q-Learning is not able to converge a memoryless policy. Therefore, in these domains only the results of CFM and Sarsa(λ) are provided. Experimentation shows that CFM finds near-optimal solutions for the given problems and it is more scalable than the memory-based approaches.

4.1 Relatively Small Domains

In the first setting of the experimentation, the two domains given in Fig. 2a and 2b are used. First one is McCallum's hallway navigation (mhn) domain which includes 23 states and 9 distinct observations [7]. In this domain, the methods with an internal memory usage have advantages due to the ambiguity. Only Sarsa(λ) algorithm achieves to get similar results with memory-based approaches by the help of its eligibility trace mechanism. The second domain is small 2 rooms which is downsized version of 2 rooms problem [8] and less complex than McCallum's domain. However, in this domain, there are 51 states and 11 distinct observations. Thus, perceptual aliasing is higher and the memory-based approaches suffer from redundantly growing state space during the learning. The environment yields different reward values for hitting a wall, passing to a neighboring state, and reaching the goal state, which are -0.1, -0.01, 5 for mhn domain and -1, -0.1, 1 for the small 2 rooms domain respectively.

For each problem domain, 50 experiments were executed for 1000 episodes. For every experiment, the agent was initially placed some random starting state

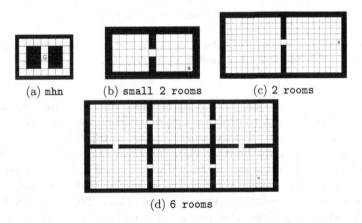

(a) mhn   (b) small 2 rooms   (c) 2 rooms

(d) 6 rooms

Fig. 2. The domains used in experimentation.

Table 1. Average elapsed time (msec) for an episode

	NSM	USM	CFM	Sarsa(λ)	Q
mhn	1.22	21.21	0.89	0.30	19.91
small 2 rooms	1237.00	4256.43	1.60	0.78	1.75

Table 2. Average memory usage (KB) for memory-based methods within an episode

	NSM	USM	CFM
mhn	413.55	64.97	**0.54**
small 2 rooms	1444.81	294.63	**0.70**

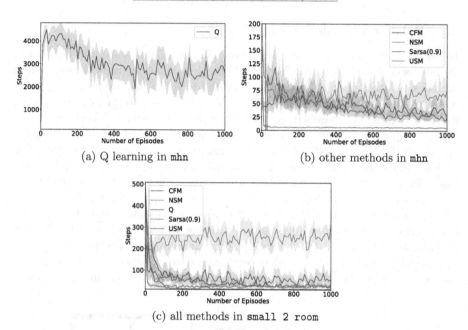

(a) Q learning in mhn

(b) other methods in mhn

(c) all methods in small 2 room

Fig. 3. Learning performances of Q-learning (a) and other methods (b) in mhn domain and all methods in small 2 room domain (c) in terms of number of steps

(in the left room for the small 2 rooms domain) other than the goal state and expected to find its path to goal state represented by the letter G. ϵ-greedy is used for action selection strategy, where ϵ is set as 0.1. The discount factor γ is chosen as 0.9 for all methods. In each domain λ value for Sarsa(λ) is set as 0.9. NSM uses the learning rate α of 0.9 while all other methods use 0.05. Since NSM uses a different semantic for the value update, this does not harm the fair comparison between this method and the others. The other NSM specific parameter which represents the number of neighbors, k, is chosen as 4. The maximum fringe depth for USM method is set as 4. The threshold and period parameters of the CFM are configured as 0.2 and 20 for the given domains. The memory length of CFM is set as 1, namely only one transition is used by CFM for the state estimation.

The time spent in the learning process is as important as finding an optimal and near-optimal solution for the given problem. Table 1 shows the average elapsed time (msec) for the methods in an episode. CFM clearly takes significantly less time than the other memory-based methods.

The last measurement examined for this experimentation setup is the memory usage of the NSM, USM and CFM methods. For the measurement of the NSM method, the number of nodes in the history chain is counted. The memory usage of USM consists of a similar history chain but also the official and fringe nodes in the tree. Each of the nodes in NSM and USM requires 12 Bytes (the total size of 2 int and a float in a standard C++ implementation). The memory required by CFM is the number of all transitions in the domain to keep track of the frequencies (12 Bytes for each transition) and the number of the selected infrequent transitions (8 Bytes for each transition). Obviously, this setup underestimates the memory usage of NSM and USM since it ignores the memory required for linking the nodes. However, even with this measurement, the memory usage of CFM is significantly less than NSM and USM. Table 2 shows that memory requirement of CFM is less than the other methods, which indicates that CFM is more scalable for the larger domains.

Figure 3a, b and c show the learning performances of the methods in terms of the number of steps to goal in mhn and small 2 rooms domains respectively. Shaded areas in these figures are bootstrapped confidence intervals for the results. For each domain, CFM finds a similar solution to the other methods which use a complex memory like USM and NSM or Sarsa(λ) which imitates a memory by trace mechanism. Since Q method does not have neither of these properties, it suffers from poor learning performance in mhn domain.

4.2 Larger Domains

In order to show the scalability of CFM method, two larger domains, namely 2 rooms and 6 rooms [8] given in Fig. 2c and d are used. For these problems, a different observation semantic is applied where the observation of each state is determined by the four different distance category to surrounding walls as in the study [3]. It is assumed that the doors yield unique observations in these domains. First one includes 201 states and 38 distinct observations where the second one has 606 states and 43 distinct observations.

In each domain, 50 experiments are executed for 10000 episodes. ϵ is set as 0.1. The agent is placed in a random state in left and left-upper room for the first and second domain respectively and expected to find its path to goal state represented by the letter G. Both methods use the learning rate α as 0.01. λ is chosen as 0.9 for the Sarsa(λ), like in the small domains. The threshold and period parameters of CFM is configured as 0.1 and 100 respectively. The memory length of CFM is set as 1.

Figure 4 shows the learning performances of both methods in terms of number of steps to goal. Despite being slower in 2 rooms domain, CFM reaches a similar near-optimal solution. On the other hand, CFM outperforms Sarsa(λ) in 6 rooms domain as can be seen in Fig. 4b. This indicates that even Sarsa(λ) which uses a powerful tracing mechanism may suffer from the aliased states in a very large domain, where CFM is effected less via its compact memory.

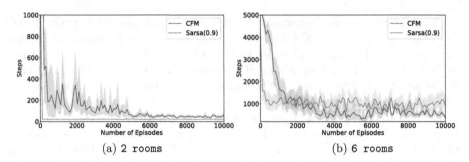

(a) 2 rooms   (b) 6 rooms

Fig. 4. Learning performances of CFM and Sarsa(λ) in larger domains in terms of number of steps

5 Conclusion

In this work, an efficient memory-based method, Compact Frequency Memory algorithm is proposed for POMDP based reinforcement learning with hidden state interpretation. Experiments show that the learning performance of the algorithm is promising. Furthermore, it does not only take much less time than the other memory-based methods for its computations and but also needs less memory. Therefore, CFM is empirically proven to be more scalable than the other well-known memory-based methods.

An immediate follow-up study is to analyze the statistical meaning of transition frequencies for a rich and diverse set of problem domains. As another future work, we aim to enhance the learning performance of the CFM with an additional trace mechanism for the infrequent transitions.

Acknowledgment. The authors would like to thank Alper Demir for helpful discussions.

References

1. Chrisman, L.: Reinforcement learning with perceptual aliasing: the perceptual distinctions approach. In: AAAI 1992 (1992)
2. Hochreiter, S., Schmidhuber, J.: Long short-term memory. Neural Comput. **9**(8), 1735–1780 (1997)
3. James, M.R., Singh, S.: SarsaLandmark: an algorithm for learning in POMDPs with landmarks. In: AAMAS 2009 (2009)
4. Kaelbling, L.P., Littman, M.L., Cassandra, A.R.: Planning and acting in partially observable stochastic domains. Artif. Intell. **101**(1), 99–134 (1998)
5. Lin, L.J., Mitchell, T.M.: Memory approaches to reinforcement learning in non-Markovian domains. Technical report, Carnegie Mellon University (1992)
6. Loch, J., Singh, S.P.: Using eligibility traces to find the best memoryless policy in partially observable Markov decision processes. In: ICML 1998 (1998)
7. McCallum, A.K.: Reinforcement learning with selective perception and hidden state. Ph.D. thesis, University of Rochester (1996)

8. Menache, I., Mannor, S., Shimkin, N.: Q-Cut—dynamic discovery of sub-goals in reinforcement learning. In: Elomaa, T., Mannila, H., Toivonen, H. (eds.) ECML 2002. LNCS (LNAI), vol. 2430, pp. 295–306. Springer, Heidelberg (2002). https://doi.org/10.1007/3-540-36755-1_25
9. Sutton, R.S., Barto, A.G.: Reinforcement Learning: An Introduction. MIT Press, Cambridge (1998)
10. Watkins, C.J.C.H.: Learning from delayed rewards. Ph.D. thesis, King's College, Cambridge, UK (1989)

Leveraging Symmetric Relations
for Approximation Coalition Structure
Generation

Changder Narayan[1(✉)], Aknine Samir[2(✉)], and Dutta Animesh[1(✉)]

[1] National Institute of Technology Durgapur, Durgapur, West Bengal, India
narayan.changder@gmail.com, animeshnit@gmail.com
[2] LIRIS Lab., Lyon 1 University, Villeurbanne, France
samir.aknine@univ-lyon1.fr

Abstract. Cooperative game theory studied the Coalition Structure Generation (CSG) problem in a characteristic function form, where each coalition is associated with a value. Given n agents, there are $2^n - 1$ coalitions. Hence, in the CSG problem, given a set of $2^n - 1$ coalitions, each associated with a value, we have to find a maximal valued disjoint set of coalitions with the same union as the whole set. The first best approximation ratio obtainable in $O(2^n)$ time is $\frac{2}{n}$ from the optimal [8]. Later, Adams et al. [1] presented an algorithm which is capable of generating a solution with a value of $\frac{2}{3}$ of the optimal in $O(\sqrt{n}2.83^n)$ time, a solution with a value $\frac{1}{2}$ of the optimal in $O(\sqrt{n}2.59^n)$ time and a $\frac{1}{8}$ approximation in $O(2^n)$ time. This paper sheds new light on the CSG problem by exploiting the combinatorics and symmetry and proposes an approximate *halfway dynamic programming* (HDP) algorithm with time complexity $O(2^{\frac{3n}{2}}) \approx O(2.83^n)$ with an approximation ratio of $1 - \frac{4}{n}$.

Keywords: Coalition formation · Coalition structure generation

1 Introduction

Coalition formation involves the coming together of collectives of agents to achieve both their individual and common goals. It is a key concept in multi-agent systems. Coalition formation can be applied to many real-world problems. Various algorithms have been proposed to solve the CSG problem. Michalak et al. [3] proposed a hybrid version of IDP [4] and IP [7] called ODP-IP and showed empirically that it is faster than other algorithms.

This paper advances the state of the art in the following ways: (1) we propose a new approximate algorithm HDP for the CSG problem with approximation ratio $(1 - \frac{4}{n})$, given n agents. (2) we prove that the time complexity of HDP algorithm is $O(2.83^n)$. (3) we develop a novel marriage function, which operates on all the coalitions of size[1] $\lceil \frac{n}{2} \rceil$, and returns most of the time the optimal

---

[1] If n is even, it picks coalitions of size $n/2$, n is odd, it chooses the coalitions of size $\lceil \frac{n}{2} \rceil$ and $\lceil \frac{n}{2} \rceil - 1$.

© Springer Nature Switzerland AG 2019
M. Baldoni et al. (Eds.): PRIMA 2019, LNAI 11873, pp. 434–442, 2019.
https://doi.org/10.1007/978-3-030-33792-6_27

coalition structure. (4) we show that HDP algorithm fails occasionally to give an exact result.

2   CSG Problem Formulation

Let $\mathcal{A}$ be the set of agents $\mathcal{A} = \{a_1, a_2, \ldots, a_n\}$, n the number of agents in $\mathcal{A}$. We denote any coalition $\mathcal{C} = \{a_1, a_2, \ldots, a_l\}$ as a coalition of agents, where $l \leq n$. Let v be a characteristic function, where v assigns a real value $v(\mathcal{C})$ to each coalition $\mathcal{C}$. Formally, $v \colon 2^{\mathcal{A}} \to \mathbb{R}$. A coalition structure $(\mathcal{CS})$ over $\mathcal{A}$ is a partitioning of $\mathcal{A}$ into a set of disjoint coalitions $\{\mathcal{C}_1, \mathcal{C}_2, \ldots, \mathcal{C}_k\}$, where $k = |\mathcal{CS}|$. In other words, $\{\mathcal{C}_1, \mathcal{C}_2, \ldots, \mathcal{C}_k\}$ satisfies the following constraints: (1) $\mathcal{C}_i, \mathcal{C}_j \neq \emptyset$, $i, j \in \{1, 2, \ldots, k\}$. (2) $\mathcal{C}_i \cap \mathcal{C}_j = \emptyset$, for all $i \neq j$. (3) $\bigcup_{i=1}^{k} \mathcal{C}_i = \mathcal{A}$. The value of any coalition structure $\mathcal{CS} = \{\mathcal{C}_1, \mathcal{C}_2, \ldots, \mathcal{C}_k\}$ is defined by $v(\mathcal{CS}) = \sum_{\mathcal{C}_i \in \mathcal{CS}}(v(\mathcal{C}_i))$. The optimal solution of CSG is a coalition structure $\mathcal{CS}^* \in \Pi^{\mathcal{A}}$, where $\Pi^{\mathcal{A}}$ denotes the set of all coalition structures over $\mathcal{A}$. Thus, $\mathcal{CS}^* = \arg\max_{\mathcal{CS} \in \Pi^{\mathcal{A}}} v(\mathcal{CS})$. The CSG problem is then the problem of finding such $\mathcal{CS}^*$. Finally, $\{a_1, a_2, \ldots, a_n\}$ and $\{1, 2, \ldots, n\}$ are used interchangeably throughout this paper.

3   Approximation Technique

The approximation algorithm we propose uses DP technique and produces two tables, the partition table P_t and the optimal value table V_t. $P_t(\mathcal{C})$ stores one optimal partition of each coalition $\mathcal{C}$. There can be more than one optimal partition of a coalition $\mathcal{C}$, $P_t(\mathcal{C})$ stores any one of them. $V_t(\mathcal{C})$ stores the optimal value of a coalition $\mathcal{C}$. Let $\mathcal{C}'' = \left\{ \mathcal{C}' | \mathcal{C}' \subset \mathcal{C} \text{ and } 0 \leq |\mathcal{C}'| \leq \frac{|\mathcal{C}|}{2} \right\}$, table V_t for each coalition $\mathcal{C}$ is constructed as follows:

$$V_t(\mathcal{C}) = \begin{cases} v(\mathcal{C}) & \text{if } |\mathcal{C}| = 1 \\ \arg\max_{\mathcal{C}' \in \mathcal{C}''}\{V_t(\mathcal{C}') + V_t(\mathcal{C} \setminus \mathcal{C}')\} & \text{otherwise} \end{cases}$$

Our approximation technique follows DP approaches up-to halfway and then we use a sophisticated *Marriage* function.

***Marriage* Function:** Any coalition can be stored in the partition table with any of its different possible partitions (into two halves or as the coalition itself). For example, in Fig. 1, the coalition $\{2, 3, 4\}$ is stored as $P_t(\{2, 3, 4\}) = \{2\}\{3, 4\}$. We call each half a component. For example in $\{\{2\}\{3, 4\}\}$, we denote $\{2\}$ and $\{3, 4\}$ as two different components of the coalition $\{2, 3, 4\}$. Algorithm 1 details the working procedure of this function. *Marriage* function is used between two disjoint coalitions of size $\lceil \frac{n}{2} \rceil$ and $n - \lceil \frac{n}{2} \rceil$.

Size	Coalition (C)	$v(C)$	Splitting	Optimal partition P_t	Optimal value V_t
1	{1}	24	$V_t[\{1\}] = 24$	{1}	24
	{2}	35	$V_t[\{2\}] = 35$	{2}	35
	{3}	20	$V_t[\{3\}] = 20$	{3}	20
	{4}	41	$V_t[\{4\}] = 41$	{4}	41
2	{1,2}	47	$v[\{1,2\}] = 47$, $\;V_t\{1\} + V_t\{2\} = 59$	{1}{2}	59
	{1,3}	43	$v[\{1,3\}] = 43$, $\;V_t\{1\} + V_t\{3\} = 44$	{1}{3}	44
	{1,4}	79	$v[\{1,4\}] = 79$, $\;V_t\{1\} + V_t\{4\} = 65$	{1,4}	79
	{2,3}	52	$v[\{2,3\}] = 52$ $\;V_t\{2\} + V_t\{3\} = 55$	{2}{3}	55
	{2,4}	65	$v[\{2,4\}] = 65$ $\;V_t\{2\} + V_t\{4\} = 76$	{2}{4}	76
	{3,4}	75	$v[\{3,4\}] = 75$, $\;V_t\{3\} + V_t\{4\} = 61$	{3,4}	75
3	{1,2,3}	85	$v[\{1,2,3\}] = 85$, $\;V_t\{1\} + V_t\{2,3\} = 79$ $V_t\{2\} + V_t\{1,3\} = 79, V_t\{3\} + V_t\{1,2\} = 79$	{1,2,3}	85
	{1,2,4}	110	$v[\{1,2,4\}] = 110$, $\;V_t\{1\} + V_t\{2,4\} = 100$ $V_t\{2\} + V_t\{1,4\} = 114$, $\;V_t\{4\} + V_t\{1,2\} = 100$	{2}{1,4}	114
	{1,3,4}	92	$v[\{1,3,4\}] = 92$, $\;V_t\{1\} + V_t\{3,4\} = 99$ $V_t\{3\} + V_t\{1,4\} = 99, V_t\{4\} + V_t\{1,3\} = 85$	{1}{3,4}	99
	{2,3,4}	108	$v[\{2,3,4\}] = 108$, $\;V_t\{2\} + V_t\{3,4\} = 110$ $V_t\{3\} + V_t\{2,4\} = 96, V_t\{4\} + V_t\{2,3\} = 96$	{2}{3,4}	110
4	{1,2,3,4}	131	$v[\{1,2,3,4\}] = 131, V_t\{1\} + V_t\{2,3,4\} = 134$ $V_t\{2\} + V_t\{1,3,4\} = 134, V_t\{3\} + V_t\{1,2,4\} = 134$ $V_t\{4\} + V_t\{1,2,3\} = 126, V_t\{1,2\} + V_t\{3,4\} = 134$ $V_t\{1,3\} + V_t\{2,4\} = 120, V_t\{1,4\} + V_t\{2,3\} = 134$	{1,2}{3,4}	134

Fig. 1. Working principle of DP and IDP algorithms computing P_t and V_t for four agents $A = \{1, 2, 3, 4\}$. Locally optimal results are shaded with green color. Red shade indicates splits that are considered by DP, but not IDP. (Color figure online)

3.1   HDP Algorithm

We now explain HDP algorithm in details. HDP algorithm runs for coalitions of size $1, 2, \ldots, \lceil \frac{n}{2} \rceil$ (as shown in lines 1–12 of Algorithm 2). Next, HDP picks all the coalitions of size $n, \ldots, \lceil \frac{n}{2} \rceil$ and each time HDP considers the rest of the unassigned agents, i.e. complement of the chosen coalition. Lines 14–23 describe how HDP evaluates and computes the maximum valued coalition structure found so far. Lines 24–30 elaborate on how to check all the feasible coalition structures from two disjoint coalitions $\mathcal{X}$ and $\mathcal{Y}$ of size $\lceil \frac{n}{2} \rceil$ and $n - \lceil \frac{n}{2} \rceil$ using the *Marriage* function. In the marriage process, HDP checks the size of the merged coalition. If this size is greater than or equal to $\lceil \frac{n}{2} \rceil$, then no need to use the *Marriage* operation because the same coalition structure has already been computed by HDP, as shown in lines 14–23 of Algorithm 2. Finally, lines 31–39 find the optimal coalition structure. Figure 2 pinpoints exactly how HDP searches the subspaces. One issue in HDP is that few search spaces are not explored by HDP as shown in Fig. 2 (spaces marked with gray color). Example 1 details how the *Marriage* function partially searches remaining subspaces.

Example 1. In our example shown in Fig. 1, all the compatible pairs of size 2 are checked using the *Marriage* function as follows. HDP picks the coalitions $\{1, 3\}$ and $\{2, 4\}$ and finds that they are stored as $\{1\}\{3\}$ and $\{2\}\{4\}$. First, the

Algorithm 1. Marriage function.

Input: Given two disjoint coalitions $\mathcal{X}$ and $\mathcal{Y}$ of size $\lceil \frac{n}{2} \rceil$ and $n - \lceil \frac{n}{2} \rceil$, where coalitions $\mathcal{X}$ and $\mathcal{Y}$ are stored in the partition table P_t as $\{\{x_1\}\{x_2\}\}$ and $\{\{y_1\}\{y_2\}\}$ or as they are.

Output: Maximum valued $\mathcal{CS}$ from the coalitions $\mathcal{X}$ and $\mathcal{Y}$ and its value.

Used variables: val and CS_o are used to keep track of values and coalition structures obtained so far from coalitions $\mathcal{X}$ and $\mathcal{Y}$.

```
1:  val ← V_t(X) + V_t(Y)
2:  CS_o ← {{X}{Y}}
3:  for Each component i in X = {{x_1}{x_2}} do
4:      for Each component j in Y = {{y_1}{y_2}} do
5:          if |i ∪ j| < ⌈n/2⌉ then
6:              if V_t(i ∪ j) + V_t(X \ i) + V_t(Y \ j) > val then
7:                  val ← V_t(i ∪ j) + V_t(X \ i) + V_t(Y \ j)        ▷ see footnote a.
8:                  CS_o ← {{i ∪ j}{X \ i}{Y \ j}}
9:              end if
10:         end if
11:     end for
12: end for
13: return CS_o, val
```

^{a} This line merges each component of $\mathcal{X}$ with another component of $\mathcal{Y}$ one at a time and leaves the other parts unchanged.

component $\{1\}$ of the coalition $\{1,3\}$ is merged with the components $\{2\}$ and $\{4\}$ of the coalition $\{2,4\}$. HDP creates these coalition structures $\{\{1,2\}\{3\}\{4\}\}$ and $\{\{1,4\}\{2\}\{3\}\}$. Next, the component $\{3\}$ of the coalition $\{1,3\}$ is merged with the components $\{2\}$ and $\{4\}$ of the coalition $\{2,4\}$. Then HDP creates these coalition structures $\{\{2,3\}\{1\}\{4\}\}$ and $\{\{3,4\}\{1\}\{2\}\}$. HDP calculates values for all these coalition structures as follows: $V_t\{1,3\} + V_t\{2,4\} = 44 + 76 = 120$, $V_t\{1,2\} + V_t\{3\} + V_t\{4\} = 59 + 20 + 41 = 120$, $V_t\{1,4\} + V_t\{2\} + V_t\{3\} = 79 + 35 + 20 = 134$, $V_t\{2,3\} + V_t\{1\} + V_t\{4\} = 55 + 24 + 41 = 120$, and $V_t\{3,4\} + V_t\{1\} + V_t\{2\} = 75 + 24 + 35 = 134$.

Computational Efficiency of HDP: HDP evaluates the coalitions of size $1, \ldots \lceil \frac{n}{2} \rceil$, where each coalition of size i needs $2^{i-1} - 1 = O(2^i)$ steps. So, the total operations performed is as follows: $\sum_{i=1}^{m} \binom{n}{i} 2^i$, where, $m = \lceil n/2 \rceil$. The bound for the above summation is calculated as follows: $\frac{\binom{n}{m} 2^m + \binom{n}{m-1} 2^{m-1} + \cdots + \binom{n}{0} 2^0}{\binom{n}{m} 2^m} ==$

$1 + \frac{m}{(n-m+1)2} + \frac{m(m-1)}{(n-m+1)(n-m+2)2^2} + \cdots + \frac{m!}{n^{\underline{m}}!2^m} = \leq 1 + \frac{m}{(n-m+1)2} + \left(\frac{m}{(n-m+1)2} \right)^2 +$

$\cdots + \left(\frac{m}{(n-m+1)2} \right)^m$. It is a partial sum of a geometric series. Therefore, $\sum_{i=0}^{m} \binom{n}{i} 2^i \leq \binom{n}{m} 2^m \frac{1 - r^{m+1}}{1-r}$, where $r = \frac{m}{(n-m+1)2}$. The central term in the series is the largest one and it is proved that $\binom{n}{n/2} \equiv O(2^n)$ because it follows

Algorithm 2. Halfway dynamic programming algorithm

Input: Set of all possible non-empty subsets of n agents $(2^n - 1)$. The value of any coalition $\mathcal{C}$ is $v(\mathcal{C})$. If no $v(\mathcal{C})$ is specified then $v(\mathcal{C}) = 0$. $\mathcal{A}$ denotes a set of n agents.
Output: Optimal coalition structure $\mathcal{CS}^*$ and the value of $\mathcal{CS}^*$.

1: **for** $i = 1$ to $\lceil \frac{n}{2} \rceil$ **do**
2:      **for each** $\mathcal{C}, \mathcal{C} \subseteq A$, where $|\mathcal{C}| = i$ **do**
3:          $V_t(\mathcal{C}) \leftarrow v(\mathcal{C})$
4:          $P_t(\mathcal{C}) \leftarrow \mathcal{C}$
5:          **for each** $\mathcal{C}', \mathcal{C}' \subset \mathcal{C}$ **do**
6:              **if** $V_t(\mathcal{C}') + V_t(\mathcal{C} \setminus \mathcal{C}') > V_t(\mathcal{C})$ **then**
7:                  $V_t(\mathcal{C}) \leftarrow V_t(\mathcal{C}') + V_t(\mathcal{C} \setminus \mathcal{C}')$
8:                  $P_t(\mathcal{C}) \leftarrow \{\mathcal{C}', \mathcal{C} \setminus \mathcal{C}'\}$
9:              **end if**
10:         **end for**
11:     **end for**
12: **end for**
13: $Maximum \leftarrow 0$
14: **for** $j = n$ downto $\lceil \frac{n}{2} \rceil$ **do**
15:     **for each** coalition $\mathcal{X}$, where $|\mathcal{X}| = j$ **do**
16:         $\mathcal{Y} \leftarrow \mathcal{A} \setminus \mathcal{X}$
17:         $\text{Temp}_{value} \leftarrow V_t(\mathcal{X}) + V_t(\mathcal{Y})$
18:         **if** $\text{Temp}_{value} > Maximum$ **then**
19:             $Maximum \leftarrow \text{Temp}_{value}$
20:             $\mathcal{CS}_{Temp} \leftarrow \{\mathcal{X}, \mathcal{Y}\}$
21:         **end if**
22:     **end for**
23: **end for**
24: **for each** coalition $\mathcal{Z}$, where $|\mathcal{Z}| = \lceil \frac{n}{2} \rceil$ **do**
25:     Apply $Marriage(\mathcal{Z}, \mathcal{A} \setminus \mathcal{Z})$
        // $v_{\mathcal{Z}, \mathcal{A} \setminus \mathcal{Z}}$, and $\mathcal{CS}_p$ are the $\mathcal{CS}$ value and the $\mathcal{CS}$ returned by $Marriage(\mathcal{Z}, \mathcal{A} \setminus \mathcal{Z})$
26:     **if** $v_{\mathcal{Z}, \mathcal{A} \setminus \mathcal{Z}} > Maximum$ **then**
27:         $Maximum \leftarrow v_{\mathcal{Z}, \mathcal{A} \setminus \mathcal{Z}}$
28:         $\mathcal{CS}_{Temp} \leftarrow \mathcal{CS}_p$
29:     **end if**
30: **end for**
31: $\mathcal{CS}^* \leftarrow \{\mathcal{CS}_{Temp}\}$
32: **for each** $\mathcal{C}, \mathcal{C} \in \mathcal{CS}^*$ **do**
33:     **if** $|\mathcal{C}| > \lceil \frac{n}{2} \rceil$ **then**
34:         $\mathcal{CS}^* \leftarrow (\mathcal{CS}^* \setminus \mathcal{C}, \mathcal{C})$
35:     **end if**
36:     **if** $P_t(\mathcal{C}) \neq \{\mathcal{C}\}$ **then**
37:         $\mathcal{CS}^* \leftarrow (\mathcal{CS}^* \setminus \mathcal{C}, P_t(\mathcal{C}))$
38:     **end if**
39: **end for**
40: Return $\mathcal{CS}^*, Maximum$.

from Wallis product $\binom{n}{n/2} \sim \frac{2^n}{\sqrt{\pi n/2}}$ as $n \to \infty$. Therefore, the total number of splitting operations is $\binom{n}{m}2^m$. Replacing the value of $m = n/2$, we get $\binom{n}{m}2^m = \binom{n}{n/2}2^{n/2} \Rightarrow 2^n \times 2^{n/2} = 2^{3n/2} \approx O(2.8284^n) \approx O(2.83^n)$. It then remains to check $\frac{2^n}{2}$ coalitions, so total $O(2^n)$ steps are necessary for this stage. Finally, HDP checks all the coalitions in the middle level. We know that in the middle level there are $O(2^n)$ possible coalitions, each requires four *Marriage* operations in the worst-case. Hence, we have total 4×2^n operations, which is an order of 2^n. So the total time complexity is $O(2^{3n/2}) + O(2^n) + O(2^n) = O(2^{3n/2}) \approx O(2.83^n)$.

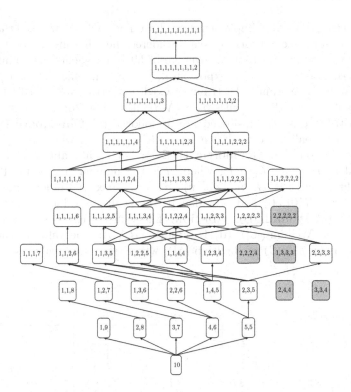

Fig. 2. Searched subspaces after evaluation of all the coalitions of size $\lceil \frac{n}{2} \rceil$. White colored subspaces are fully searched. Gray colored subspaces are not yet searched. *Marriage* function partially searches these gray colored subspaces in time $O(2^n)$.

Approximation Guarantees: Suppose HDP has found the coalition structure $\mathcal{CS}'$ and let $\mathcal{CS}^*$ be the optimal coalition structure. HDP ensures that if the optimal coalition structure contains a coalition of size greater than $\lceil \frac{n}{2} \rceil$, HDP will find it. Similarly, if the optimal coalition structure contains all singleton coalitions, HDP will also find it. Now, suppose the size of all the coalitions in the optimal coalition structure is less than $\lceil \frac{n}{2} \rceil$. Let's assume that $\mathcal{C}^*$ is the maximum valued coalition. If the optimal coalition structure contains all the coalitions of size two, then the maximum value of the optimal coalition structure is $\lceil \frac{n}{2} \rceil v(C^*)$. Now, in the middle level, HDP evaluates all the coalitions of size $\lceil \frac{n}{2} \rceil$ and then performs the *Marriage* operation. If all the coalitions of size $\lceil \frac{n}{2} \rceil$ are stored as they are, then the *Marriage* operation is not possible and the maximum value of $\lceil \frac{n}{2} \rceil$ sized coalitions is $(\frac{n}{4} - 1)v(C^*)$. So the maximum guaranteed value of the coalition structure found by HDP is $(n/2 - 2)v(C^*)$. Consequently, the approximation ratio is $\frac{(n/2-2)v(C^*)}{(n/2)v(C^*)} = \frac{n-4}{n} = 1 - \frac{4}{n}$.

4   Experimental Evaluation

Both the algorithms were implemented in Java. For ODP-IP, we used the code in Java provided by the authors [3]. We considered the following distributions and for each distribution we took an average of 50 tests: agent-based uniform [5], agent-based normal [3], beta, exponential, gamma, modified normal [5], modified uniform [1], Normally Distributed Coalition Structures (NDCS) [6], Single Valuable Agent (SVA) with β (SVA-β) [9] and uniform [2] distributions. Other distributions we considered are as follows: (a) **Chi-square** (χ^2): The value of each coalition C is drawn from $v(C) \sim \chi^2(\nu)$, where $\nu = |C|$ is the degree of freedom. (b) **Geometric (GEO):** For each coalition C, a value is generated as $rv = U(|C|/n, 1)$, where n is the number of agents. The value of a coalition $v(C) = Geometric(rv) * rv * |C|$, next a random number r is generated $r \sim U(0, 50)$ and is added to the coalition value $v(C)$ with probability 0.2. (c) **Weibull Distribution:** The value of coalition C is drawn as $v(C) \sim |C| \times$ Weibull $(|C|)$. (d) **Rayleigh (RAL):** The value of each coalition C is drawn as $v(C) \sim$ Rayleigh (M), where M = Mode value is defined as $10 * \sqrt{\frac{2}{\pi}} * |C|$.

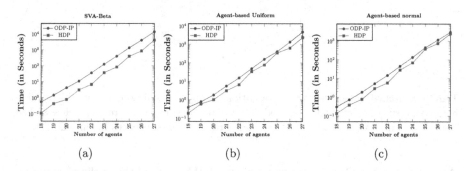

(a)   (b)   (c)

Fig. 3. Time performance of ODP-IP vs. HDP in the interval 18–27 agents. Here, time is measured in seconds and plotted *on a log scale*. To show the differences of runtimes we have only plotted three distributions.

The behavior of ODP-IP and HDP as follows: for instance, for Chi-square dataset, HDP's average runtime gain over ODP-IP is 58.23% for less than 21 agents, and for other sets ODP-IP outperforms HDP. In exponential distribution, the average runtime gain of HDP is 42.35% over ODP-IP for less than 17 agents. A similar pattern is found for geometric, Weibull, modified uniform, NDCS, Raleigh, double exponential and normal distributions. In these cases, HDP is better than ODP-IP for less than 19 agents with an average runtime gain of 49.17%. In other cases ODP-IP outperforms HDP. For Gamma distribution average runtime gain is 50.38% below 15 agents and for other sets ODP-IP is superior. In the modified normal distribution, HDP runtime gain is 55.46% for less than 16 agents. For the case of SVA-β distribution, HDP works well for all sets of agents, having an average performance gain of 230% over ODP-IP. On average for less than 14 agents HDP performance is better than ODP-IP with an average runtime gain of 54.626% for beta distribution, and below 17 agents the average runtime gain is 50.89% in the case of normal distribution. Moreover, experimental results show that HDP gains maximum 2380 s, and 9582 s in Agent-based uniform distribution, and SVA-β distribution for $n = 27$ agents (cf. Fig. 3). We have also compared the ratio between HDP generated coalition structure value and the optimal coalition structure value. We observed that in the fail cases this ratio is always greater than 0.99.

5 Conclusion

In this paper, we have presented a new algorithm for approximate coalition structure generation with worst case time ($O(2.83^n)$). Our approach is based on the new *Marriage* function with the help of dynamic programming. We proved that after the HDP algorithm has computed the optimal solution to all subproblems consisting of $\lceil \frac{n}{2} \rceil$ agents, then our algorithm generates an $1 - \frac{4}{n}$ approximation solution. We compared the performance of HDP algorithm to ODP-IP [3] and found that most of the time, HDP generates an exact result.

Acknowledgments. The research presented in this article is funded by "Visvesvaraya PhD Scheme for Electronics & IT", grant no: PhD-MLA/4(29)/2015-16. Samir Aknine was supported by Univ. Lyon 1.

References

1. Adams, J., et al.: Approximate coalition structure generation. In: Proceedings of the 24th AAAI Conference on Artificial Intelligence, pp. 854–859. AAAI (2010)
2. Larson, K.S., Sandholm, T.W.: Anytime coalition structure generation: an average case study. J. Exp. Theor. Artif. Intell. **12**(1), 23–42 (2000)
3. Michalak, T., Rahwan, T., Elkind, E., Wooldridge, M., Jennings, N.R.: A hybrid exact algorithm for complete set partitioning. Artif. Intell. **230**, 14–50 (2016)
4. Rahwan, T., Jennings, N.R.: An improved dynamic programming algorithm for coalition structure generation. In: AAMAS, vol. 3, pp. 1417–1420 (2008)

5. Rahwan, T., Michalak, T.P., Jennings, N.R.: A hybrid algorithm for coalition structure generation. In: AAAI, pp. 1443–1449 (2012)
6. Rahwan, T., Ramchurn, S.D., Dang, V.D., Giovannucci, A., Jennings, N.R.: Anytime optimal coalition structure generation. In: AAAI, vol. 7, pp. 1184–1190 (2007)
7. Rahwan, T., Ramchurn, S.D., Jennings, N.R., Giovannucci, A.: An anytime algorithm for optimal coalition structure generation. J. Artif. Intell. Res. **34**, 521–567 (2009)
8. Sandholm, T., Larson, K., Andersson, M., Shehory, O., Tohmé, F.: Coalition structure generation with worst case guarantees. Artif. Intell. **111**(1), 209–238 (1999)
9. Travis, S.: Coalition structure generation in characteristic function games. Ph.D. thesis, Graduate School of Vanderbilt University (2012)

Deception/Honesty Detection and (Mis)trust Building in Manipulable Multi-Agent Argumentation: An Insight

Ryuta Arisaka[✉], Makoto Hagiwara, and Takayuki Ito

Nagoya Institute of Technnology, Nagoya, Japan
ryutaarisaka@gmail.com, {hagiwara.makoto,ito.takayuki}@nitech.ac.jp

Abstract. In manipulable multi-agent argumentation, each agent may transmit deceptive information to others for tactical motives. We contemplate epistemic states and their roles in deception/honesty detection and (mis)trust-building. We propose the use of intra-agent preferences for handling deception/honesty detection and inter-agent preferences for determining which agent(s) to believe in more. We illustrate how deception/honesty in an argumentation of an agent, if detected, may alter the agent's perceived trustworthiness, and how that may affect agents' judgement as to which arguments they should accept. A detailed comparison to an earlier study on deception detection highlights wider applicability of our approach.

1 Introduction

From marketing to politics, exploitation of incomplete information through selective communication of arguments is ubiquitous. By withholding disadvantageous information [7,8], half-truths, and through various other tactical ruses, one can obtain greater strategic advantages. Such manipulation plays a significant role in real-life argumentation. However, very few attempts at modelling manipulable or deceptive argumentation [5,6,8] currently exist in the literature of formal argumentation. To further the research in this field, we contemplate epistemic states and their roles in deception/honesty detection and (mis)trust-building. We propose the use of multiple preferences to serve different purposes: intra-agent preferences for handling deception/honesty detection and inter-agent preferences for determining which agent(s) to believe in more. We illustrate how deception/honesty in an argumentation of an agent, if detected, could alter the agent's perceived trustworthiness, and how that may affect agents' judgement as to which arguments they should accept. A detailed comparison to an earlier formulation of deception detection [8] highlights wider applicability of our approach. In this paper we focus not on formalisation (which is found in [2]) but on the intuition behind it.

© Springer Nature Switzerland AG 2019
M. Baldoni et al. (Eds.): PRIMA 2019, LNAI 11873, pp. 443–451, 2019.
https://doi.org/10.1007/978-3-030-33792-6_28

2   Technical Preliminaries

Abstract Argumentation considers an argumentation as a graph where a node is an argument and an edge is an attack of the source argument on the target argument [4]. Let $\mathcal{A}$ denote the class of abstract entities that we understand as arguments, then a (finite) Dung argumentation is a pair (A, R) with $A \subseteq_{\text{fin}} \mathcal{A}$ and $R \subseteq A \times A$. We denote the class of all Dung argumentations by $\mathcal{F}^D$. From here on, we denote: a member of $\mathcal{A}$ by a; a finite subset of $\mathcal{A}$ by A; and a member of $\mathcal{F}^D$ by F^D, all with or without a subscript. This "with or without" convention shall be assumed for any other symbol without explicit mentioning. For any $(A, R) \equiv F^D$, we denote by 2^{F^D} the following set: $\{(A_1, R_1) \mid A_1 \subseteq A \text{ and } R_1 \subseteq R \cap (A_1 \times A_1)\}$, i.e. all sub-Dung-argumentations of F^D.[1]

Assume that the following notations are for any chosen $(A, R) \in \mathcal{F}^D$. $a_1 \in A$ is said to attack $a_2 \in A$ if and only if, or iff, $(a_1, a_2) \in R$. $A_1 \subseteq A$ is said to be conflict-free iff there is no $a_1, a_2 \in A$ such that $(a_1, a_2) \in R$. $A_1 \subseteq A$ is said to defend $a_x \in A$ iff every $a_y \in A$ attacking a_x is attacked by at least one member of A_1. $A_1 \subseteq A$ is said to be: admissible iff A_1 is conflict-free and defends all its members; complete iff A_1 is admissible and includes every argument it defends; preferred iff A_1 is a maximally complete set; and grounded iff A_1 is the set intersection of all complete sets. Let Sem be $\{\text{co}, \text{pr}, \text{gr}\}$, and let $D : \text{Sem} \times \mathcal{F}^D \to 2^{2^{\mathcal{A}}}$ be such that $D(\text{s}, (A, R))$ is the set of: all (A) complete, (B) preferred, or (C) grounded, sets of (A, R) if s is (A) co, (B) pr or (C) gr. $D(\text{co}, (A, R))$, $D(\text{pr}, (A, R))$ and $D(\text{gr}, (A, R))$ are called the complete semantics, the preferred semantics and the grounded semantics of (A, R). For a chosen $\text{s} \in \text{Sem}$, $a_1 \subseteq A$ is said to be: credulously acceptable iff there exists some $A_1 \in D(\text{s}, (A, R))$ such that $a \in A_1$; and skeptically acceptable iff $a \in A_1$ for every $A_1 \in D(\text{s}, (A, R))$. We may simply say $a\ (\in A)$ is acceptable in s when a is at least credulously acceptable in s.

Attack-Reverse Preference. Suppose $(\{a_1, a_2\}, \{(a_1, a_2)\})$ with two arguments and an attack. For any member s of Sem, we obtain that a_1 but not a_2 is acceptable. Suppose, however, that some agent observing this argumentation still prefers to accept a_2. The agent could conceive an extension of this argumentation, $(\{a_1, a_2, a_3\}, \{(a_1, a_2), (a_3, a_1)\})$ with some argument a_3: *I (= the agent) doubt it in the absence of any evidence.*, which attacks a_1. For $\text{s} \in \text{Sem}$, a_2 (and a_3) but not a_1 then become acceptable.

To achieve the same effect, we can apply attack-reverse preference [1]. Assume a partial order $\leq_p$ over A in some (A, R), then $R' \subseteq A \times A$ is said to be $\leq_p$-adjusted R iff it is the least set that satisfies the following conditions. We define that $a_1 <_p a_2$ iff $a_1 \leq_p a_2$ and not $a_2 \leq_p a_1$.

- $(a_1, a_2) \in R'$ if $(a_1, a_2) \in R$ and (not $a_1 <_p a_2$).   – $(a_2, a_1) \in R'$ if $(a_1, a_2) \in R$ and $a_1 <_p a_2$.

---

[1] "and" instead of "and" is used when the context in which the word appears strongly indicates classic-logic truth-value comparisons. Similarly for or (disjunction) and not (negation).

By setting $\leq_p$ to be such that $a_1 <_p a_2$ in $(\{a_1, a_2\}, \{(a_1, a_2)\})$, it is easy to see that $\leq_p$ expresses the agent's preference: under $\leq_p$-adjusted $\{(a_1, a_2)\}$, which is $\{(a_2, a_1)\}$, a semantics with some $\mathsf{s} \in \mathsf{Sem}$ makes a_2 but not a_1 acceptable.

Epistemic Agent Argumentation. Let $\mathcal{E}$ be a class of abstract entities that we understand as agents. Let e refer to a member of $\mathcal{E}$, and let E refer to a finite subset of $\mathcal{E}$. Meanwhile, let $\mathsf{getArg} : \mathcal{F}^\mathsf{D} \to 2^\mathcal{A}$ and $\mathsf{getR} : \mathcal{F}^\mathsf{D} \to 2^{\mathcal{A} \times \mathcal{A}}$ be such that $\mathsf{getArg}((A, R)) = A$, and that $\mathsf{getR}((A, R)) = R$ for any $(A, R) \in \mathcal{F}^\mathsf{D}$. Then an epistemic agent argumentation (e.g. [3]) with agents' semantics is $(F^\mathsf{D}, E, h_\mathbf{E}, f_\mathbf{A}, f_\mathsf{s})$ where: $h_\mathbf{E} : E \to (2^{F^\mathsf{D}} \setminus (\emptyset, \emptyset))$ is such that $\mathsf{getR}(h_\mathbf{E}(e)) = \mathsf{getR}(F^\mathsf{D}) \cap (\mathsf{getArg}(h_\mathbf{E}(e)) \times \mathsf{getArg}(h_\mathbf{E}(e)))$, and that $\mathsf{getArg}(h_\mathbf{E}(e_1)) \cap \mathsf{getArg}(h_\mathbf{E}(e_2)) = \emptyset$ if $e_1 \neq e_2$; and where $f_\mathbf{A} : E \to 2^{F^\mathsf{D}}$ is such that $h_\mathbf{E}(e) \in 2^{f_\mathbf{A}(e)}$, and that $\mathsf{getR}(f_\mathbf{A}(e)) \cap (\mathsf{getArg}(h_\mathbf{E}(e)) \times \mathsf{getArg}(h_\mathbf{E}(e))) = \mathsf{getR}(h_\mathbf{E}(e))$ for $e \in E$. Meanwhile, $f_\mathsf{s} : E \to \mathsf{Sem}$ indicates the type of semantics, $f_\mathsf{s}(e)$, which the agent e adopts when computing acceptability semantics. The purpose of $h_\mathbf{E}$ is to express agents' local scopes. $f_\mathbf{A}(e)$ is the argumentation e is aware of, which naturally subsumes $h_\mathbf{E}(e)$, and the attacks in $f_\mathbf{A}(e)$ match $\mathsf{getR}(h_\mathbf{E}(e))$ exactly as far as $\mathsf{getArg}(h_\mathbf{E}(e))$ are concerned. $f_\mathbf{A}(e)$ for $e \in E$ is called local agent argumentation of e in the global argumentation F^D.

3   Epistemic States and Agent Preferences for Deception/Honesty Detection and (Mis)trust Building

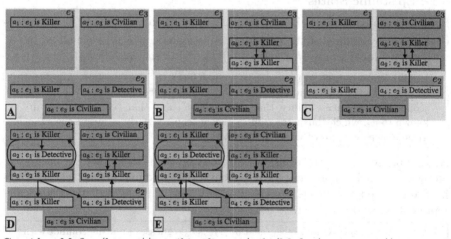

Consider Mafia (https://en.wikipedia.org/wiki/Mafia_(party_game)), its end game, as our example. We assume the following setting with 3 agents.

Common Knowledge Among Them. One agent is a killer, and the other two agents are civilians, of which at most one can be a detective - no player but detective itself, if in the game, knows for certain that there is a detective. Team Mafia comprises just the killer, and Team Innocent consists of the civilians.

Agents' Knowledge. All three of them know which role they have been assigned to. Killer knows that the other two are not a killer. Detective, if in Team Innocent, knows who the ordinary civilian (to be simply described civilian hereafter) and who the killer are by its ability. It also knows the killer knows it is the killer, and that the civilian knows it is a civilian. However, no civilians know the role of the other players.

Argumentations. Each agent may entertain argumentations generally consisting of a set of arguments, e.g. "Agent e_1 is Killer.", and attacks among them. They may also announce argumentations publicly. Arguments and attacks in a public announcement may not be actual, e.g. even if "e_2 is Killer" is just a guess or known to be untrue to e_3, e_3 may still put the argument forward, and similarly for an attack. Any argumentation announced publicly is known to every agent.

In the end, each agent chooses with its own semantics (that is, its own judgement criteria to decide which arguments to accept) who the killer to be hanged is. If there is an agent chosen by the other two, then the team the chosen agent belongs to loses, and the team the chosen agent does not belong to wins. It is everybody's interest to let its team win, to which end they thus conduct argumentation.

We illustrate epistemic states and intra-/inter-agent preferences, and how they are used for: deception/honesty detection; and updates on agent-to-agent trusts.

3.1 Epistemic States

Suppose e_1 is Killer, e_2 is Detective and e_3 is (ordinary) Civilian. Their knowledge at the beginning of the end game is as follows, which is visualised in $\boxed{A}$ with agents' local scopes ($h_{\mathbf{E}}(e_1) = \{a_1\}, h_{\mathbf{E}}(e_2) = \{a_4, a_5, a_6\}, h_{\mathbf{E}}(e_3) = \{a_7\}$).

> **Initial knowledge.** Argument a_1: "e_1 is Killer", is in e_1's scope. Argument a_4: "e_2 is Detective", is in e_2's scope. Argument a_7: "e_3 is Civilian", is in e_3's scope. By Detective's ability, that "e_1 is Killer", and that "e_3 is Civilian" are known to e_2, which thus appear in e_2's local scope. Clearly, e_2 also knows that a_1 is known to e_1 and that a_7 is known to e_3.

Now, suppose a sequence of argumentations by them as follows. At each step, an agent publicly announces an argumentation (argument(s), attack(s)). Publicly announced arguments are coloured brighter in all figures. We graphically represent $(a_1, a_2) \in R$ by $a_1 \rightarrow a_2$.

> 1. e_3 *says:* "e_2 is Killer" (argument a_9). It is e_3's guess, in mutual conflict with an alternative: "e_1 is Killer" (argument a_8). See $\boxed{B}$.
> 2. e_2 *says:* "e_2 is Detective" (a_4) as a counter-argument to a_9, and then that "e_1 is Killer" (a_5). See $\boxed{C}$.
> 3. e_1 *responds:* "e_1 is Detective" (argument a_2), and (i.e. due to ability of Detective) that "e_2 is Killer" (argument a_3), as a counter-argument to a_4 and a_5. See $\boxed{D}$. e_1 is aware that a_3 is actually in mutual conflict with a_1 as well as that a_2 is attacked by a_1.
> 4. e_2 *insists:* "e_1 is Killer" (a_5) as a counter-argument to a_3 and a_2. See $\boxed{E}$.

Local Agent Argumentations. Each agent sees all publicly announced argumentations together with its own, thus, for $\boxed{\text{E}}$, we have $\boxed{\text{E1}}$, $\boxed{\text{E2}}$ and $\boxed{\text{E3}}$ as the local argumentations of e_1, e_2 and respectively e_3.

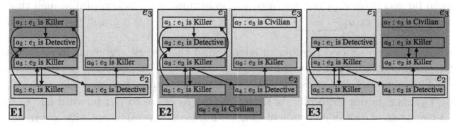

3.2 Intra-agent Preferences

To talk of the role of intra-agent preferences, suppose e_1 applies its own semantics s, say pr (preferred semantics; see Sect. 2), to the argumentation in $\boxed{\text{E1}}$ to tell which arguments are acceptable. By its definition (see Sect. 2), e_1 considers either $\{a_1, a_4, a_5\}$ (e_1 is Killer and e_2 is Detective) acceptable or else $\{a_2, a_3, a_9\}$ (e_1 is Detective and e_2 is Killer) acceptable. For a rational judgement and not for a strategic purpose, however, the second option is strange to say at the very least, since it contradicts e_1's factual knowledge a_1 (e_1 is Killer). If we are to prioritise factual arguments over the others, some attacks should turn out to be spurious. Detective e_2 who knows a_1 is factual to e_1 should also refute a_3.

For fact-prioritised reasoning by an agent of the argumentation it is aware of, we use an attack-reverse preference per agent, to prefer arguments that it knows factual (to some agent) over the other arguments found in its local agent argumentation. $\boxed{\text{E1}}$, $\boxed{\text{E2}}$ and $\boxed{\text{E3}}$ with preference-adjusted attack relations are as shown in $\boxed{\text{E1}'}$, $\boxed{\text{E2}'}$ and $\boxed{\text{E3}'}$.

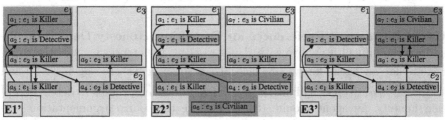

Since both e_1 and e_2 know that e_1 is Killer, i.e. e_1 knows a_1 to be factual to e_1, while e_2 knows a_1 to be factual to e_1 and a_5 to be factual to e_2,[2] the attack from a_3 to a_1 is not in $\boxed{\text{E1}'}$ or $\boxed{\text{E2}'}$. Additionally, in $\boxed{\text{E2}'}$, the attack from a_3 to a_5 is not present, and the attack from a_3 to a_4 is reversed, since e_2 knows a_4 and a_5 are factual to e_2. By contrast, attacks in $\boxed{\text{E3}'}$ remain unchanged from $\boxed{\text{E3}}$, since e_3 knows only that a_7 is factual to e_3.

---

[2] e_1 cannot be certain a_5 is factual to e_2, since, firstly, there may or may not be Detective in a game, and, secondly, it could be Civilian who is bluffing to be Detective.

On Deception, and Intra-agent Preferences. A method of deception detection in two-party argumentation is in Section 5 of [8], with which an argument a_x an agent e_1 puts forward as an acceptable argument is detected by an agent e_2 to be deceptive if e_1 has put forward an argument a_y as acceptable such that $\underbrace{a_x \to \cdots \to a_y}_{2k+1}$ or $\underbrace{a_y \to \cdots \to a_x}_{2k+1}$ for $k \in \mathbb{N}$ (when there is a graph path between a_x and a_y with an odd number of edges), and that every argument in the path has been originally put forward by e_x.

This approach can produce counter-intuitive results. For example, consider e_3, Civilian, in our example. As shown in $\boxed{\text{B}}$, e_3 chose to put forward a_9 (e_2 is Killer) as an acceptable argument. There, however, was an alternative argument a_8 (e_1 is Killer) that could have been put forward instead. These two arguments are in mutual conflict, and only one of them may be acceptable at one moment. But suppose, hearing the argumentation by e_2 and e_1, that e_3 develops an impression that e_1 is more likely the Killer, since a_4 attacks a_9. Suppose e_3 then changes its mind, and puts forward a_8 as an acceptable argument, then a_9 becomes non-acceptable. While, initially, a_8 was not considered acceptable and a_9 acceptable (call it Scenario 1), and later the acceptability statuses were swapped (call it Scenario 2), the change was due to context change, i.e. Scenario 1 seemed more likely to e_3 at the beginning of the game, and Scenario 2 seemed more likely once the additional information was gained. For example once at $\boxed{\text{C}}$, e_3 could have announced a_8 acceptable, but that should not lead to e_3's deceptive intention in former announcement of a_9. The method in [8] produces a false positive in this kind of a situation. A false negative can also result. In our example, when e_1 declares e_2 Killer (see $\boxed{\text{D}}$), deceptive intention of e_1 should be already evident to e_2, as it knows that "e_1 is Killer" is factual to e_1. However, e_1 does not announce a_1 to obviously contradict itself in public. But then the publicly known arguments a_2 and a_3 do not attack each other, and thus, according to the proposed approach, e_2 will not detect e_1's deception.

Use of Intra-agent Preferences for Deception/Honesty Detection. We address the difficulties above with the intra-agent preferences to prioritise arguments that an agent knows are factual (to some agent); see again $\boxed{\text{E1}'}$ and $\boxed{\text{E2}'}$, where a_1 attacks a_3 but not vice versa. For concrete steps to detect deception/honesty, an agent should: (**Step 1**) have the source argumentation (the one with respect to which detection is conducted) and the target argumentation (the one in which deception/honesty may be detected); (**Step 2**) calculate the semantics of the two argumentations; (**Step 3**) restrict them to those arguments for which detection is taking place. This restriction is necessary since the two argumentations may cover more arguments. It is also necessary to not restrict the two argumentations from a start since the agent's rational judgement as regards acceptability statuses of the concerned arguments is based on them as a whole; and (**Step 4**) finally calculate the presence of deception/honesty by applying an appropriate criterion to compare the restricted semantics.

Let us first inspect deception detection by considering the transition from $\boxed{C}$ to $\boxed{D}$ induced by e_1's public announcement.

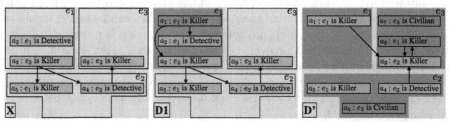

Suppose it is e_2 that wants to check e_1's deception. **Step 1.** Since e_2 needs to see any discrepancy between what e_1 has claimed in public and what e_2 perceives e_1 actually thinks, the source argumentation is the argumentation consisting only of all the previous public announcements including e_1's, as shown in $\boxed{X}$, while the target argumentation is e_2's (opponent) model of e_1's local agent argumentation. For the detection purpose, both must be already preference-adjusted by what e_2 considers is e_1's intra-agent preference, i.e. e_2's model of e_1's intra-agent preference. Thus, it is a requirement that the domain of f_s in Sect. 2 should be generalised from E to $E \times E$. Here, let us just assume that the source/target argumentation is $\boxed{X}/\boxed{D1}$.[3] **Step 2.** The semantics of the source argumentation is $\{\{a_2, a_3, a_9\}\}$, and that for the target argumentation is $\{\{a_1, a_4, a_5\}\}$ for a chosen $s \in$ Sem. **Step 3.** Note e_2 is checking the arguments in e_1's public announcement, which are a_2 and a_3. Hence, the restriction of the semantics to them yields $\{\{a_2, a_3\}\}$ (source) and $\{\emptyset\}$ (target). **Step 4.** Recall that a semantics $(= \{A_1, \ldots, A_n\})$ expresses non-deterministic possibilities, that each A_i in the semantics is judged possibly acceptable. Thus, deception by e_1 is detected by e_2 certainly only when the target semantics restricted to a_2 and a_3 (these are what e_2 considers e_1 considers possibly acceptable) contains no member of the source semantics restricted to a_2 and a_3 (these are what e_2 considers e_1 claims in public to be possibly acceptable), which holds good in this case because $\{\emptyset\} \cap \{\{a_2, a_3\}\} = \emptyset$.

The differentiation of arguments allows us to also express detection of honesty (as truthfulness to arguments known to be factual). Suppose an alternative transition from $\boxed{C}$ with e_1's (rather silly) announcement of $a_1 :$ "e_1 is Killer." into $\boxed{D'}$. The first three steps of honesty detection are the same as of deception detection. Suppose e_2 is the detector, and suppose e_2's preference-adjusted model of e_1 (the target argumentation) is $(\{a_1, a_4, a_5, a_6, a_7, a_9\}, \{(a_1, a_9), (a_4, a_9)\})$, where a_1 is considered factual to e_1. The semantics of the source argumentation is $\{\{a_1, a_4, a_5\}\}$, and that of the target argumentation is $\{\{a_1, a_4, a_5, a_6, a_7\}\}$. Since e_2 is checking the argument in e_1's public announcement, they are restricted by

---

[3] Recall e_2 knows e_1 knows a_1; as such, a_1 appears in e_2's model of e_1's preference-adjusted local agent argumentation. Recall also it is a common knowledge that Killer does not know whether there be Detective; as such, from e_2's perspective, neither a_4 nor a_5 is known by e_1 to be factual to e_2.

$\{a_1\}$, yielding $\{\{a_1\}\}$ (source) and $\{\{a_1\}\}$ (target). **Step 4.** For detection of honesty with respect to factual arguments, each member A_i of restricted source semantics $(\{A_1, \ldots, A_n\})$, which e_1 has publicly claimed acceptable, must consist only of the arguments factual to e_2, since, if not, they can be just e_1's guesses and bluffing to e_2. A_i containing any guesses is, insofar as it is potentially deceptive, not certain honesty. Moreover, the source and the target semantics must exactly match; in particular, the latter cannot contain strictly greater a number of members than the source argumentation[4] which would imply e_1's withholding of factual information, which again can be potentially a deceptive behaviour. In this example ($\boxed{D'}$), a_1 is known to be factual to e_2, and the two restricted semantics match exactly, so e_2 detects e_1's honesty. These two criteria ensure that e_3 does not detect e_1's honesty at $\boxed{D'}$, since a_1 is not known factual to e_3.

3.3   Inter-agent Preferences and Detected Deception/Honesty

For inter-agent preferences, say e_3 wants to decide which set(s) of arguments to publicly accept at $\boxed{E}$ (to decide which agent should be hanged). e_3 then obtains all the public argumentations announced up to $\boxed{E}$ (which is $\boxed{X}$ plus two attacks from a_5 to a_3 and from a_5 to a_2), as the basis of its reasoning. It then adjusts it by its intra-agent preference, to obtain its model of the public argumentation, which in this particular example is again $\boxed{X}$ plus two attacks from a_5 to a_3 and from a_5 to a_2, because e_3 cannot tell whether any arguments by e_1 or e_2 are factual. In the argumentation, e_3 sees a_3 and a_5 in mutual conflict. With $\mathsf{s} = \mathsf{pr}$, $\{a_2, a_3, a_9\}$ (e_2 is Killer) and $\{a_4, a_5\}$ (e_1 is Killer) are two possible judgement.

Now, when e_1, e_2 and e_3 are all strangers to each other, it is likely that e_3 with $\mathsf{s} = \mathsf{pr}$ will just have to choose one of the two. If, however, e_3 has gathered information from previous interactions with them to the point where e_3 considers e_2 a liar and e_1 an honest agent, then it is more likely that e_3 will trust e_1 more, to accept $\{a_2, a_3, a_9\}$ (e_2 is Killer).

The trustworthiness of e_1 perceived by e_3 can be expressed numerically. Let $\mathbb{Z}$ be the class of all integers, with a function $v_{\mathbf{E}} : E \times E \to \mathbb{Z}$, then the numerical trust e_3 gives e_1 can be expressed by $v_{\mathbf{E}}(e_3, e_1)$. Suppose also $v_{\mathbf{E}}(e_3, e_2)$ such that $v_{\mathbf{E}}(e_3, e_2) < v_{\mathbf{E}}(e_3, e_1)$. By enforcing that a greater numerical value implies a greater trust, we can express that e_3 trusts e_1 more, and can define an inter-agent preference per agent to break mutually conflicting arguments in favour of the agent(s) it trusts more.

There is an impact of deception/honesty detection on perceived trustworthiness: $v_{\mathbf{E}}(e_1, e_2)$ for any $e_1, e_2 \in E$ can increase, or decrease, by some $n \in \mathbb{N}$ due to e_1's detection of e_2's honesty, or deception. The change in the trustworthiness in turn influences agents' decision as to which arguments they should accept.

---

[4] Since every public argumentation is known to every agent, the converse is not possible.

4   Conclusion

A notion of deception detection within argumentation was defined in [8]. We have made detailed comparisons to it in Sect. 3, and proposed an alternative approach with intra-agent preferences. We also illustrated how deception/honesty of e_1 detected by e_2 affects e_2's perception of e_1's trustworthiness. Our study supports the need for multiple preferences for manipulable argumentation.

References

1. Amgoud, L., Vesic, S.: Rich preference-based argumentation frameworks. Int. J. Approximate Reasoning **2**, 586–606 (2014)
2. Arisaka, R., Hagiwara, M., Ito, T.: Formulating manipulable argumentation with intra-/inter-agent preferences. CoRR, abs/1909.03616 (2019)
3. Arisaka, R., Satoh, K., van der Torre, L.: Anything you say may be used against you in a court of law. In: Pagallo, U., Palmirani, M., Casanovas, P., Sartor, G., Villata, S. (eds.) AICOL 2015-2017. LNCS (LNAI), vol. 10791, pp. 427–442. Springer, Cham (2018). https://doi.org/10.1007/978-3-030-00178-0_29
4. Dung, P.M.: On the acceptability of arguments and its fundamental role in non-monotonic reasoning, logic programming, and n-person games. Artif. Intell. **77**(2), 321–357 (1995)
5. Kontarinis, D., Toni, F.: Identifying malicious behavior in multi-party bipolar argumentation debates. In: Rovatsos, M., Vouros, G., Julian, V. (eds.) EUMAS/AT -2015. LNCS (LNAI), vol. 9571, pp. 267–278. Springer, Cham (2016). https://doi.org/10.1007/978-3-319-33509-4_21
6. Kuipers, A., Denzinger, J.: Pitfalls in practical open multi agent argumentation systems: malicious argumentation. In: COMMA, pp. 323–334 (2010)
7. Rahwan, I., Larson, K.: Mechanism design for abstract argumentation. In: AAMAS, pp. 1031–1039 (2008)
8. Sakama, C.: Dishonest arguments in debate games. In: COMMA, pp. 177–184 (2012)

Self-vehicle Positioning Using Smart Infrastructures

Assia Belbachir[1] and Marcia Pasin[2(✉)]

[1] Institut Polytechnique des Sciences Avancées, Ivry-Sur-Seine, France
`assia.belbachir@ipsa.fr`
[2] Universidade Federal de Santa Maria, Santa Maria, Brazil
`marcia@inf.ufsm.br`

Abstract. Localization is crucial to many vehicular applications and is usually carried out using the Geographical Positioning System (GPS). However, when the GPS signal is unavailable, other solutions can be applied such as camera images and Inertial Navigation System (INS) to know about its movement in order to calculate the actual positions. However, such techniques can be costly in consumption in terms of processing time and energy. Moreover, INS is subject to cumulative errors. In order to improve positioning, information coming from other sensors can be a solution. Thus, this paper proposes a self-adaptive protocol for vehicle localization using smart infrastructure support in GPS free environments. In this context, an autonomous vehicle with unknown localization interacts with the infrastructure sensors to infers its position. Experiments with the adaptive protocol were conducted in a robotic platform. Our obtained results are promising and the maximum error percentage that our localization protocol gets from all our experiments is equal to 0.3%, which indicated an effective value for the precision metric.

Keywords: Localization · Vehicular networks · Adaptive approaches

1 Introduction

Localization is crucial to many vehicular applications and is usually carried out using the Geographical Positioning System (GPS). A critical situation occurs when a vehicle temporarily loses its GPS position information, which might lead it to crash. In such situations, it is required that the vehicle relies on fall-back systems and regains stable drive as soon as possible.

Most of the developed fall-back systems uses heavyweight mechanisms to compensate the GPS failure, such as infrared and visual cameras [7], a laser range scanner [5]. In general, available approaches use camera images or the last known position to locate a vehicle on a pre-loaded map and the embedded Inertial Navigation System (INS) to know about its movement in order to calculate the actual position. However, this technique is subject to cumulative error. Considering that vehicles in vehicular networks have memory, energy and

© Springer Nature Switzerland AG 2019
M. Baldoni et al. (Eds.): PRIMA 2019, LNAI 11873, pp. 452–459, 2019.
https://doi.org/10.1007/978-3-030-33792-6_29

time constraints, a desirable localization protocol should rather use lightweight mechanisms.

Having mentioned the drawbacks of these recent studies, we found that the existing distributed localization for collaborative vehicles is still unsatisfactory. A desirable protocol should neither demand fast propagation of up-to-date time information nor keeping track of the vehicle's neighboring, in order to avoid cumulative error. Moreover, such a protocol is strictly required to have low computational and communication overhead as well as small memory footprint. Thus, in this paper, we focus on range-based localization of vehicle without GPS coverage, that is in the communication range of $n \geq 3$ anchor infrastructures (e.g. traffic lights, antennas) whose positions are known. We conceptualize this single-hop procedure as comprising two step process, as suggested in [6]: at the first step, the vehicle communicates with the anchor and obtains its relative distance measurements by using any ranging method and the position information of the anchor. In the second step, the vehicle applies a localization algorithm and estimates its potential position.

To this end, we consider the problem of localization of a vehicle from a different perspective. We handle this problem as a *search process* in which each vehicle is trying to find the right coordinates *without knowing their correct values*. Due to the dynamics nature of the vehicular networks, e.g., where vehicles move continuously and thus the coordinate values are subject to changes quite frequently, an adaptive search technique is required for the search process. We employ the technique of Adaptive Value Tracking (AVT) [1,3,9], which finds and tracks a dynamic searched value in a given search space through successive feedback. The searched value for us is the position of a dynamic vehicle.

In summary, in this paper:

(*i*) we propose a self-localization protocol namely Adaptive Localization Protocol (ALP), which is not subject to cumulative error and

(*ii*) we evaluate the proposed algorithm in a controlled environment using a robotic platform.

By combining this simple mechanism, we observed an efficient localization of a vehicle without GPS coverage in our robotic platform.

The remainder of this paper is organized as follows. Section 2 introduces the localization problem and its usual solution. The ALP protocol is described in Sect. 3. Implementation and obtained results are described in Sect. 4. Conclusions are presented in Sect. 5.

2   Problem Statement and Solution

Usually, localization in vehicular networks relies in the GPS signal. However, when GPS signal is unavailable or inaccurate, location may fall on alternative methods applied with the support of sensors networks.

Using information from sensors, a trilateration technique can be implemented if at least the positions of three anchors are known, and a communication channel between each anchor and a vehicle v can be established. In this scenario, a vehicle v has an unknown position and needs to calculate it using three anchors of the infrastructure. The value d_i represents the Euclidian distance between the vehicle and each anchor a_i. These values are used to calculate the vehicle position.

If the anchors have communication facilities available, each distance d_i can be computed using two techniques: Time of Arrival (TOA) and Round Trip Time (RTT). A typical solution is to measure the TOA, which is the time a radio signal takes to travel from the transmitter antenna to the vehicle v. However, the vehicle v must calculate the TOA using its local and transmitter clock, which requires having both clocks synchronized. Since clock synchronization is challenging in distributed systems, alternatively the RTT can be used to compute the TOA. However, the displacement of an RTT message may introduce even more noise into the expected results.

To deal with this limitation, we proposed a lightweight cooperative positioning service based on trilateration and an intelligent noise learning technique AVT [3]. Basically, in this approach, the ALP approximates, until it reaches stabilization, the position dealing with a changing error.

The outcome of the self-localization service can be used by other vehicular network services, such as a vehicle tracking system. Tracking can be defined as a sequence of vehicle positions taking at time intervals from a starting point to an arrival point, given journey. These positions can be provided by GPS or, alternatively, by the application of trilateration approaches via communication devices. With these computed positions, it is possible to trace the vehicle path.

3 Self-positioning Using Adaptive Value Protocol

In this section, we describe the behavior of our proposed solution. This scheme is depicted in Fig. 1. Basically, when a vehicle v gets out of GPS coverage, it first broadcasts a "GPS failure" message (1) to all its neighbors (candidate anchors) (2) and starts its Adaptive Localization Protocol (ALP). A neighbor can be a traffic light, a vehicle, an antenna, etc. When a neighbor receives a message, it first checks/stabilizes itself (3) in its current position. Each neighbor that knows its position, it propagates a message with this information through the network (4). So, the vehicle v waits for the 3 first neighbors answers to be able to compute its localization (5). In this phase, the failing vehicle still goes on localizing itself using ALP (6). Upon having started receiving GPS signal, the failing vehicle stops executing ALP and goes on its mission using GPS.

In ALP, it uses a *search process* that finds the actual position of a mobile vehicle where the collected information and measurements are noisy. We propose a robust and efficient adaptive position tracking technique which the goal is to localize vehicles without GPS coverage by communicating with the infrastructure (stable position). The proposed approach handles single-hop localization as a two steps *search process* using Adaptive Value Tracking (AVT) [1,3,9].

Step 1: Ranging. In this step, the vehicle communicates with the infrastructure and estimates its relative distances by using a particular ranging method.

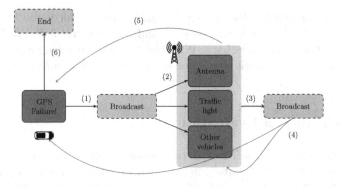

Fig. 1. Architecture of the proposed solution with exchanged messages.

However, due to network dynamics, the quality of its estimations are affected by the measurement noise. In order to get more robust estimates, we propose to handle the ranging as search process during which the relative distance d^* is searched inside the search space $[d_{min}, d_{max}]$ using the AVT, where d_{min} and d_{max} are the minimum and maximum distances that can be measured physically by the ranging method.

The ranging steps between a vehicle and a particular infrastructure are summarized as follows. If the distance value $\hat{d}$, which is estimated by using the available hardware e.g., ultrasonic transmitters and receivers, is higher than the range value proposed by the avt used for tracking the relative distance of the mobile node, an increase feedback $f \uparrow$ for increasing the distance, if it is smaller then a decrease feedback $f \downarrow$ for decreasing the distance, otherwise a good feedback $f \approx$ for indicating that the current range value is good is sent. Employing this algorithm, the value proposed by the avt of the mobile node converges to the actual distance value in finite amount of time.

Step 2: Adaptive Localization. The second step of the localization procedure is the localization algorithm that estimates the relative position of the vehicle. This estimation is based on trilateration, hence position and ranging data from three infrastructures are required. Thus, we assume that the vehicle is within the range of three infrastructures and applied the Ranging Algorithm to obtain its relative estimated distance. Therefore, the vehicle requires three AVTs in order to track these relative distances. Moreover, we also assume that the position information of all three infrastructures are obtained via communication.

The localization steps of the vehicle are summarized in the following. Having estimated its relative distances and obtained the positions of the infrastructure, a trilateration is sufficient to estimate the coordinate (x, y) of the vehicle. However, the estimation error of the ranging step affects the quality of this estimation. In order to have a robust and stable estimation, we propose to estimate these coordinates as a search process during which the actual coordinate (x^*, y^*) is searched for within the search spaces $[x_{min}, x_{max}]$ and $[y_{min}, y_{max}]$ respectively by using two AVTs. At any time, the avt_x and avt_y can propose the coordinate

(x, y). The error between the estimated $\hat{x}$ and $\hat{y}$ values calculated by the trilateration and the values proposed by avt_x and avt_y are calculated to inform the AVTs about the current feedback. With these steps, the value proposed by avt_x and avt_y of the mobile node converges to the actual position in finite amount of time.

4   Experimental Evaluation

Usually, the outcome of self-localization services can be evaluated in terms of accuracy and precision. Accuracy is the quantification of how close the samples are to the target, which is the value θ accept as correct. To determine whether an experimental value has accuracy, it must be compared with the correct value θ.

Given θ, and $\hat{\theta}$ as the measured value, we can compute the Root Mean Squared Error (RMSE) [2], which is given by:

$$RMSE = \sqrt{\frac{1}{n} \Sigma_{i=1}^n (\hat{\theta} - \theta)^2} \tag{1}$$

where $\hat{\theta} = (avt_x, avt_y)$ is the measured value for the positioning parameter θ, and n represents the number of repeated experiments. The final RMSE indicates the error of a reading. The higher the RMSE value, the worse the accuracy.

In the other hand, precision [8] quantifies how close replicate samples are to each other. Precision in localization services can be determined by the standard deviation, which indicates how much in average, the localization measurements differ from each other. High standard deviations indicate low precision, while low standard deviations indicate high precision.

In order to evaluate our approach, we implement the ALP in an indoor environment using an Arduino[1] and RaspberryPi 3[2] platforms, in an intersection scenario. Typically, in indoor environments, it does not make sense to use only the GPS for location because the GPS accuracy and precision can compromise the experiment. Thus, the ultrasonic sensor is commonly used for localization. However, available low cost ultrasonic sensors have limited range. Yet, their accuracy and precision are reduced.

Figure 2 depicts the material architecture of our vehicle. The infrastructure of our environment is represented in Fig. 3, with an intersection and a vehicle. An intersection contains four traffic lights which are controlled by an Field-Programmable Gate Array (FPGA) card. At each view, that represents a stretch of road related to one traffic light, there are embedded sensors in order to count the number of vehicles that are in the view (one sensor in the entrance of the view and another at the end of the view). These sensors are connected to the FPGA, thus the vehicle counting process is also done in the FPGA card. Our vehicle has an Arduino board connected to a RaspberryPi 3 board and two sensors (one ultrasonic model HC-RS04 and one camera). For each traffic light, we embedded

---

[1] https://www.arduino.cc.
[2] https://www.raspberrypi.org.

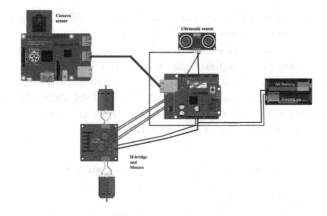

Fig. 2. Illustration of the material architecture of robot (vehicle).

Fig. 3. Illustration of the target platform.

an ultrasonic sensor. At each time the vehicle pass by the traffic light, the traffic light using its ultrasonic sensor estimates the distance of the vehicle from its position. Using the known position of at least three traffic lights, the vehicle is able to estimate its position.

The vehicle follows a predefined round trajectory. We repeated 20 times our experiments in order to check the position accuracy. Each traffic light has the ability to send its estimated range and also its estimated position to the vehicle. Thus, our vehicle is able to estimate its position during its trajectory while using ALP. The communication between the infrastructure and the vehicle is done using Wi-Fi, where the exchanged information is only the estimated distance from the vehicle to the infrastructure.

In this target scenario, we evaluate three types of methods: State estimation, trilateration and ALP. State estimation considers only the information from the odometer. Thus, in this case, trilateration is executed using the odometer support. However, near the traffic light the vehicle can communicate and estimate its position by trilateration. The vehicle is getting its distance from three traffic light, which allows to the vehicle to estimates its position (Each traffic light has a fixed position). The ALP communicates with the traffic light and can correct its position from its explained process (see Sect. 3).

The three methods, State estimation, trilateration and ALP, were evaluated based on the Root Mean Squared Error (RMSE) [2], which is a measure of accuracy, and standard deviation, which is a measure for precision. Thus, we conducted different experiments to evaluate the RMSE, increasing the number of tours that are required to our robot to execute its trajectory: 1 tour, 5 tours and then 10 tours. Results are depicted in Table 1.

Table 1. Statistical obtained results for vehicle localization with regard to accuracy.

Tours N.	RMSE (x, y)(cm)		
	State estimation (Odometry)	Trilateration	ALP
1	(1, 1.01)	(1.22, 1.24)	**(0.7, 0.71)**
5	(2, 2.01)	(1, 1.02)	**(0.89, 0.90)**
10	(2.23, 2.24)	(1.87, 1.87)	**(1.22, 1.23)**

We also measured the standard deviation for the same previously described scenarios. Our approach presented low error values due to the fast adaptation of the estimation algorithm in both x and y coordinates. Knowing that the platform size is 4 meters × 4 meters the maximum error percentage that ALP gets from all our experiments is equal to 0.3%, which indicated an effective value for the precision metric.

From our experiments, we can conclude that the localization approach ALP has less error in terms of vehicle positioning in a whole trip. Thus, ALP achieved better accuracy. Additionally, we proved that our ALP can be efficient even if the vehicle is moving.

As a second experiment we implemented a method to regulate the traffic light [4]. The method changes the duration of the traffic light according to the density of vehicles in the view. We implemented this method on our platform using the ALP information. The obtained results are adapting the traffic light according to the dense traffic.

5 Conclusions

In this paper, we describe an ALP for self-vehicle localization, which not require support of GPS coverage. Localization, without GPS support, is particularly useful in tunnels, underground parking and in situations where there is shading or interference in GPS signals. GPS-free location and GPS outcome improvement are also useful in miniaturized scenarios, where only the GPS outcome is not suitable.

The proposed ALP is based on trilateration and AVT. Trilateration is used to determine the position of the vehicle and AVT is used to minimize the errors occurred during the interdistance transmission between the infrastructure and vehicles. The particularity in our case of study is that all the vehicles are continuously moving that makes it hard to use not real time algorithms. The obtained results show that compared to state estimation (Odometry) and trilateration, our approach has better performance and it is showed with the computation of RMSE.

As future work, we would like to evaluate our solution in a scenario with several heterogeneous resources, with different sensors and communication capabilities. We believe that ALP will be able to extract adequate data and to fit scalability required demand.

References

1. Agliamzanov, R., Gürcan, O., Belbachir, A., Yildirim, K.S.: Robust and efficient self-adaptive position tracking in wireless embedded systems. In: Proceedings of the 2015 8th IFIP Wireless and Mobile Networking Conference (WMNC), pp. 152–159, October 2015
2. Baechler, G., et al.: Combining range and direction for improved localization. In: Proceedings of the 2018 IEEE International Conference on Acoustics, Speech and Signal Processing (ICASSP), pp. 3484–3488, April 2018
3. Belbachir, A., Pasin, M., Seghrouchni, A.E.F.: Lightweight cooperative self-localization as support to traffic regulation for autonomous car driving. In: Ivanović, M., Bădică, C., Dix, J., Jovanović, Z., Malgeri, M., Savić, M. (eds.) IDC 2017. SCI, vol. 737, pp. 73–79. Springer, Cham (2018). https://doi.org/10.1007/978-3-319-66379-1_7
4. Belbachir, A., El-Fallah-Seghrouchni, A., Casals, A., Pasin, M.: Smart mobility using multi-agent system. Procedia Comput. Sci. **151**, 447–454 (2019)
5. Bry, A., Bachrach, A., Roy, N.: State estimation for aggressive flight in GPS-denied environments using onboard sensing. In: Proceedings of the IEEE International Conference on Robotics and Automation, ICRA 2012 (2012)
6. Ledeczi, A., Maroti, M.: Wireless sensor node localization. Philosophical Transactions of the Royal Society A: Mathematical. Physical and Engineering Sciences, vol. 370, pp. 85–99. The Royal Society, London (2012)
7. Merino, L., Caballero, F., Martinez-de Dios, J.R., Ferruz, J., Ollero, A.: A cooperative perception system for multiple UAVs: application to automatic detection of forest fires. J. Field Rob. **23**, 165–184 (2006)
8. Taylor, J.R.: An introduction to error analysis: the study of uncertainties in physical measurements, 2nd edn. University Science Books, Sausalito (1997)
9. Yildirim, K.S., Gürcan, O.: Efficient time synchronization in a wireless sensor network by adaptive value tracking. IEEE Trans. Wireless Commun. **13**(7), 3650–3664 (2014)

A Combined Netflow-Driven and Agent-Based Social Modeling Approach for Building Evacuation

Julie Dugdale[2], Mahyar T. Moghaddam[1]([✉]), Henry Muccini[1], and Hrishikesh Narayanankutty[3]

[1] University of L'Aquila, 67100 L'Aquila, Italy
{mahtou,henry.muccini}@univaq.it
[2] University of Grenoble Alps, 38401 Grenoble, France
julie.dugdale@imag.fr
[3] Amrita Vishwa Vidyapeetham University, Kerala 690525, India
hrishikesh9409@gmail.com

Abstract. In an emergency, finding safe egress pathways in a short period of time is crucial. In this paper we use a network flow (netflow) algorithm that acts as the core of a real-time recommender system to be used by building occupants and decision-making bodies. However, a purely optimization approach can lack realism since building occupants may not evacuate immediately, stopping to look for their friends or trying to assess if the alert is for real or just a drill, etc. Furthermore, they may not always follow the recommended optimal paths. Thus, in order to assess the egress in a physical space and to test our evacuation algorithms, we use a simulation-optimization (S/O) approach. The model allows us to test more realistic evacuation scenarios and compare them with an optimal approach. The S/O uses both a netflow algorithm and an agent-based approach to model and simulate individual human behaviours. People are modeled as agents with specific characteristics, such as social attachment to others, variation in speed of movement, etc. Furthermore, a Belief-Desire-Intention (BDI) agent architecture is used to model the individual differences in people and to more accurately describe the heterogeneity of the building occupants in terms of their current beliefs about the situation and goals. The real geospatial data obtained from three experiments is set as the model input. The results confirm the usefulness of using such S/O approach to improve design-time and real-time evacuation systems.

Keywords: Agent-based modeling · Network optimization · Emergency evacuation

© Springer Nature Switzerland AG 2019
M. Baldoni et al. (Eds.): PRIMA 2019, LNAI 11873, pp. 460–468, 2019.
https://doi.org/10.1007/978-3-030-33792-6_30

1   Introduction

The safe evacuation of people and personnel from the premises takes precedence when dealing the mitigation and disaster risk management. The evacuation time of people from a scene of an emergency is crucial. In order to reduce evacuation time, better and more robust evacuation algorithms are developed. Such algorithms are used to model agents' exit patterns and strategies in order to evaluate their movement behaviour.

This paper extends the work in [1–3] that explores the collaboration between Internet of Things architectures [4,5] and safety critical systems. Specifically we look at incorporating our netflow algorithm that can be used in a computer simulation for designing buildings, and also in real-time building evacuation. The algorithm decomposes both the space (building plan) and the time dimension into finite elements: unit cells and time slots. The space element is monitored by sensors, whose data constantly feed into the algorithm to show the best evacuation routes to the occupants. However, such a system may lack accuracy since: *(i)* a purely optimization approach can lack realism as building occupants may not immediately evacuate; *(ii)* occupants may not always follow the recommended optimal paths due to various behavioural and organizational issues; *(iii)* the physical space may prevent an effective emergency evacuation.

To deal with the above-mentioned challenges, we introduce a simulation-optimization (S/O) approach. The S/O is an umbrella term for techniques used to optimize stochastic simulations [6]. Our S/O approach allows us to test more realistic evacuation scenarios and compare them with an optimal approach. We simulate the optimized netflow algorithm under different realistic behavioral agent-based modeling (ABM) constraints, such as social attachment [7] to others, variation in speed of movement, etc. The paper furthermore presents a correlation between evacuation time and the influence of human, social, physical and temporal factors.

This paper makes the following contributions:

- Following an empirical study, we suggest mitigating solutions to reduce the evacuation time.
- Taking into account the discovered real problems, we model various agents and their interactions during an emergency.
- We add the netflow algorithm to the ABM simulation engine and assess its efficiency under various scenarios, comparing it with other generally used algorithms such as shortest path.
- We evaluate our work by using the real case study of an exhibition venue in Italy.

The work is simulated using the PedSim microscopic pedestrian simulation tool and customized in order to incorporate the aforementioned constraints.

The structure of the paper is as follows. Section 2 presents the background and Sect. 3 specifies the conceptual model including agents and their constraints. The application of the model to a real exhibition venue is presented in Sect. 4 and conclusions are drawn in Sect. 5.

2   Background

Focusing on the agent-based modeling for emergency management domain, we consider the following key characteristics in our scenarios [8]: *(i)* pedestrian agents start to move faster than normal; *(ii)* agents may start to push against each other and things can quickly become physical in nature; *(iii)* dealing with a bottleneck becomes uncoordinated; *(iv)* jams become common in passageways, the front of the building and exit doors may become clogged sometimes preventing escape; *(v)* evacuation time is severely slowed, either wholly or partially, and often injured and slower agents become obstacles; *(vi)* herding of agents occur, i.e., agents tend to blindly follow the mass crowd [8]; *(vii)* alternate paths or exits are often ignored or not used due to such herding behavior and panic; *(viii)* physical pressure up to 4,450 N/m can build up due to clogging [8,9], which can even alter a topological structure, e.g. destroying steel barriers and brick walls [10].

The above-mentioned conditions are considered in this paper. The ABM S/O technique is used as it offers flexibility to model both micro and macro levels of a system [11]. In our current ABM S/O, social force models are considered for agent dynamics and interaction [12]. The advantage of using an ABM simulation model compared to a mathematical model is because nonlinear relationships and heterogeneous behaviors can be better modeled and understood through the multiple complex interactions. In this study, we compare the ABM S/O approach with our previously proposed optimization algorithm [1]. In emergency routing domain, pioneering work was conducted by Choi et al. [13], who modeled a building evacuation problem by dynamic flow maximization where arc capacities may depend on flows in incident arcs. Regarding Internet of Things based software architectures for evacuation handling, Lujak et al. [14] propose a distributed architecture for situation-aware evacuation guidance in smart buildings. They use WiFi, RFiD and Beacon for identification and sensing purposes.

3   Conceptual Model

This section describes the various agents and the behavior model used for pedestrian modeling during a critical scenario. The simulation concerns the Alan Turing building, which can house a maximum of 1008 agents. For ease of readability and clarity, two types of abstract agents are defined: *TopologyAgents* and *GameAgents*.

TopologyAgents are limited to the topology of the building and include obstacles, walls, doors, passageways, emergency exits, etc. These agents are associated with certain characteristic forces and traits. For instance, wall force acts on pedestrian agents so that they cannot pass through unless a huge amount of GameAgent force (see below) is applied. Other traits include passageway flow capacity, total door flow capacity, etc.

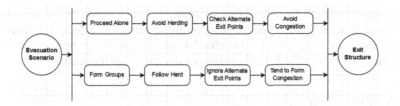

Fig. 1. Game agent behaviour pattern.

GameAgents are typically the active pedestrian agents that are modeled using the *BDI* architecture. They are associated with characteristic traits such as movement speed, perceptive radius, social force (personal and inter-personal radius), so that agents do not pass through each other. Since agents only use perceptive radius to navigate, they will continue towards the desired goal unless an event triggers them to act otherwise. Figure 1 shows the agents' behaviour pattern diagram. Game agents typically follow two types of behavior patterns: one to group and the other to follow an independent path. Game agents often interact with topological agents during an evacuation scenario. As shown in Fig. 2, there is a direct correlation between the various elements of a topology agent and how game agents proceed along the topography. This interaction between topological elements and game agents are described in simulated scenarios in the application section.

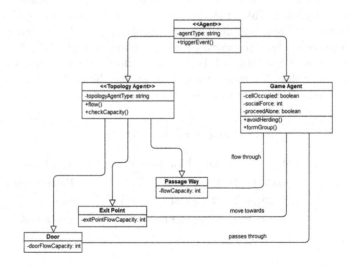

Fig. 2. Interaction between game agents and topological agents

To make simulations as realistic as possible, we incorporate social grouping into our scenarios. Game agents tend to make their decisions and movement as a result of *herding* [15]. Hence, this factor is explored in our scenarios and simulations to model S/O egress paths, as described in the next section.

4   Application

Our proposed model has been applied to the infrastructure design and evacuation management of Alan Turing building (University of L'Aquila, Italy), which is sometimes used for exhibitions. The building consists of 29 rooms, 4 main corridors, 4 emergency exits and 34 sets of Internet of Things sensors and actuators (See [16]). In order to investigate our approach we address 2 research questions.

The first question provides an experimental baseline for our simulation:

RQ1: What are the operational delays associated with the selected physical space?
The second research question is centered around the S/O approach:
RQ2: What is the evacuation time under various social ABM scenarios?

4.1   Answer to RQ1: Empirical Evaluation

This section describes the set of experiments to create a baseline for our proposed approach. To answer the above-mentioned points, we located security personnel all around the building. Table 1 shows the global evacuation time of three evacuation tests with different populations and disaster types. We observed that, the evacuation lasted 9 min in the worst case. The simulation type in Table 1, implies specific procedures to be followed. For instance, the earthquake evacuation takes a little bit longer than fire evacuation, since people should first find an internal shelter and further follow the evacuation recommendations.

Table 1. Empirical findings.

Test#	Date	Started	Finished	#Evacuees	Test type
1	22.03.2018	10:45	10:52	225	Earthquake
2	29.05.2018	11:37	11:43	200	Fire
3	07.03.2019	11:05	11:14	380	Earthquake

Taking into account the aforementioned results, the following sub-section describes modeling the physical space by S/O approach.

4.2   Answer to RQ2: ABM Scenario Simulation

This section describes the various social ABM simulation cases that form the *S/O* approach. We consider Alan Turing building with a real population (*GameAgents*) of: 200, 225 and 380 persons. All agents and scenarios use the following parameters:

- *Walking Velocity* - ranged between 0.7 m/s to 1.2 m/s, in accordance with the average walking speed in [17,18]. The walking speed of people, according to Tolea et al. [18], is based on a variety of factors that include not only a generic health disposition and disabilities, but also other social and psychological factors such as education and lifestyle.
- *Social Force* - an individual agent's radius is arbitrarily set to 0.2 m. This value is obtained using the *biacromial diameter* given in [19], so that agents do not pass through each other, whilst maintaining a minimum discernible distance from each other. This force further facilitates setting the maximum number of agents mapped per cell, room and passage-flow.
- *Wall Force* - wall force is set 0.1 m, i.e., agents cannot pass beyond 0.1 m from the wall, to prevent agents from sticking to walls and passing through obstacles.
- Door Flow Capacity - 1.2 p/m/s, [20].
- Cell capacity - 1.25 p/m², [21].

All agents use the ***Belief-Desire-Intention*** agent architecture as follows:

- *Belief* - Agents believe that a disaster is unfolding and must somehow escape the immediate surroundings. Agents have beliefs about where they are in a building based on their *perceptions* of the environment.
- *Desire* - Agents have the basic desire or *goal* to reach an exit point that would allow them to safely exit the building.
- *Intention* - Agents seek to find the shortest and/or optimal paths to reach the exit points (based on the algorithms presented in [1]).

The following simulations were carried out using ***PedSim Microscopic Simulator*** on a Core i7 2.7 GHz computer with 16Gb of RAM memory under Windows 10 pro 64-bits. In this set of simulations, we simulate both social attachment and grouping. A group of agents is a single immutable entity that consistently move together. We consider random groups consisting of 3 to 7 agents. The agents walking velocity is randomly varied between 0.7 m/s and 1.2 m/s. According to Wagnild et al. [17], walking velocity highly depends on the company and the speed of the slowest person in the group.

From Fig. 3a, evacuating 200 agents takes 2 min and 12.5 s and 1 min and 57.5 s for shortest paths and netflow respectively. Figure 3b corresponds to the evacuation simulation of 225 agents. In this case, the evacuation surprisingly takes less time than the case with 200 agents (1 min and 57.5 s with shortest paths and 1 min and 47.5 s with netflow). Although other simulations with the same settings led to expected results, i.e., higher evacuation time with a larger

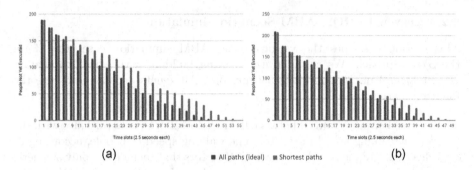

Fig. 3. Ideal vs. shortest paths evacuation considering grouping and attachment, case 1: N = 200 (a) and case 2: N = 225 (b).

number of agents, it was interesting to include this particular set of results to show that: randomized grouping and attachment constraints may increase or decrease congestion and evacuation time.

In a third set of simulations, we set the agent population as 380 (Fig. 4). In this case the evacuation time increased to 2 min and 52.5 s using shortest paths and 2 min and 7.5 s with netflow.

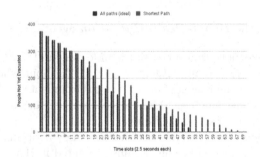

Fig. 4. Ideal vs. shortest paths evacuation considering grouping and attachment, case 3: N = 380.

Findings: *(a)* the results from the *S/O* approach confirm that network flow algorithm avoids congestion in building bottlenecks, whilst shortest path slows down the evacuation due to its inability to properly manage overcrowding. *(b)* grouping and attachment slowed down the evacuation in comparison with optimal case (see [16]).

5   Conclusion

From the scenario and cases, the netflow driven micro agent simulation optimized with the applied realistic constraints, presents a realistic approach to evacuation compared to the shortest path approach. Based on these results, we can design topologies and evacuation systems that are better suited to accommodate the required crowd of pedestrians. This work can be extended to non-standard buildings with additional constraints. The internet of things system helps counting the number of persons in each block and detecting their location (cell numbers). This can further be dynamically fed into the simulator for real-time optimization of exit paths. Obtaining such data, the simulations can be shifted from design-time to a real-time egress path evaluation.

References

1. Muccini, H., Arbib, C., Davidsson, P., Moghaddam, M.T.: An IoT software architecture for an evacuable building architecture. In: Proceedings of the 52nd Hawaii International Conference on System Sciences, HICSS (2019)
2. Arbib, C., Moghaddam, M.T., Muccini, H.: IoT flows: a network flow model application to building evacuation. In: Dell'Amico, M., Gaudioso, M., Stecca, G. (eds.) A View of Operations Research Applications in Italy, 2018. ASS, vol. 2, pp. 115–131. Springer, Cham (2019). https://doi.org/10.1007/978-3-030-25842-9_9
3. Arbib, C., Henry, M., Moghaddam, M.T.: Applying a network flow model to quick and safe evacuation of people from a building: a real case. In: RSFF, vol. 18, pp. 50–61 (2018)
4. Muccini, H., Moghaddam, M.T.: IoT architectural styles. In: Cuesta, C.E., Garlan, D., Pérez, J. (eds.) ECSA 2018. LNCS, vol. 11048, pp. 68–85. Springer, Cham (2018). https://doi.org/10.1007/978-3-030-00761-4_5
5. Muccini, H., Spalazzese, R., Moghaddam, M.T., Sharaf, M.: Self-adaptive IoT architectures: an emergency handling case study. In: Proceedings of the 12th European Conference on Software Architecture: Companion Proceedings, p. 19. ACM (2018)
6. Amaran, S., Sahinidis, N.V., Sharda, B., Bury, S.J.: Simulation optimization: a review of algorithms and applications. Ann. Oper. Res. **240**(1), 351–380 (2016)
7. Mawson, A.R.: Mass Panic and Social Attachment: The Dynamics of Human Behavior. Routledge, London (2017)
8. Helbing, D., Farkas, I., Vicsek, T.: Simulating dynamical features of escape panic. Nature **407**(6803), 487 (2000)
9. Elliott, D., Smith, D.: Football stadia disasters in the United Kingdom: learning from tragedy? Ind. Environ. Crisis Q. **7**(3), 205–229 (1993)
10. Cocking, C., Drury, J.: Talking about Hillsborough: 'panic'as discourse in survivors' accounts of the 1989 football stadium disaster. J. Community Appl. Soc. Psychol. **24**(2), 86–99 (2014)
11. Bonabeau, E.: Agent-based modeling: methods and techniques for simulating human systems. Proc. Nat. Acad. Sci. **99**(suppl 3), 7280–7287 (2002)
12. Helbing, D., Farkas, I.J., Molnar, P., Vicsek, T.: Simulation of pedestrian crowds in normal and evacuation situations. Pedestrian Evacuation Dyn. **21**(2), 21–58 (2002)

13. Choi, W., Hamacher, H.W., Tufekci, S.: Modeling of building evacuation problems by network flows with side constraints. Eur. J. Oper. Res. **35**(1), 98–110 (1988)
14. Lujak, M., Billhardt, H., Dunkel, J., Fernandez, A., Hermoso, R., Ossowski, S.: A distributed architecture for real-time evacuation guidance in large smart buildings. Comput. Sci. Inf. Syst. **14**(1), 257–282 (2017)
15. Helbing, D., Buzna, L., Johansson, A., Werner, T.: Self-organized pedestrian crowd dynamics: experiments, simulations, and design solutions. Transp. Sci. **39**(1), 1–24 (2005)
16. Arbib, C., Arcelli, D., Dugdale, J., Moghaddam, M., Muccini, H.: Real-time emergency response through performant IoT architectures. In: International Conference on Information Systems for Crisis Response and Management (ISCRAM) (2019)
17. Wagnild, J., Wall-Scheffler, C.M.: Energetic consequences of human sociality: walking speed choices among friendly dyads. PloS One **8**(10), e76576 (2013)
18. Tolea, M.I., et al.: Sex-specific correlates of walking speed in a wide age-ranged population. J. Gerontol. B Psychol. Sci. Soc. Sci. **65**(2), 174–184 (2010)
19. Patil, S.S., Jadhav, P.P., Dongare, S.S., Deokar, R.B.: Correlation of stature to arm span and biacromial shoulder width in young adults of Western Indian population. Int. J. Educ. Res. Health Sci. **3**(2), 64–70 (2017)
20. Ye, J., Chen, X., Yang, C., Wu, J.: Walking behavior and pedestrian flow characteristics for different types of walking facilities. Transp. Res. Rec. **2048**(1), 43–51 (2008)
21. Daamen, W., Hoogendoorn, S.: Emergency door capacity: influence of door width, population composition and stress level. Fire Technol. **48**(1), 55–71 (2012)

Imperfect Information in Alternating-Time Temporal Logic on Finite Traces

Francesco Belardinelli[1,2]([⊠]), Alessio Lomuscio[2], Aniello Murano[3], and Sasha Rubin[4]

[1] Laboratoire IBISC, UEVE, Courcouronnes, France
[2] Department of Computing, Imperial College London, London, UK
`francesco.belardinelli@imperial.ac.uk`
[3] DIETI, Università degli Studi di Napoli, Naples, Italy
[4] School of Computer Science, University of Sydney, Sydney, Australia

Abstract. We introduce a logic to reason about strategic abilities in finite games under imperfect information. We interpret Alternating-time Temporal Logic on interpreted systems with final states, where agents only have partial observability of the system's global state. We consider the model checking problem in this setting. We prove that the complexity results available for the case of infinite traces carry over to the finite traces case. We show that when only public actions are allowed, the verification problem under perfect recall becomes decidable.

1 Introduction

In this paper we further the line of work initiated in [5] and introduce a novel semantics for Alternating-time Temporal Logic (ATL) interpreted on finite traces, under both the *objective* and *subjective* interpretation of imperfect information [19]. Indeed, in negotiation, coordination, planning, business processes, as well as other AI-inspired applications, agents typically have imperfect information regarding the current state of the system. More precisely, we extend interpreted systems—a well-studied framework to reason about imperfect information [15]—with final states. Then, strategy operators in ATL only range on paths that end in a final state. We consider the model checking problem in this setting. In Sect. 3 we show that the complexity of model checking ATL on finite traces (under imperfect information, for both perfect and imperfect recall) is the same as for infinite traces, a result that echoes [5]. Yet, our decision procedures only use ordinary automata, operating on finite words, instead of infinite words or trees, thus sidestepping intrinsic difficulties of model checking ATL on infinite traces, due to automata operating over infinite words or trees, e.g., the determinisation of Büchi automata, which has proved to be resistant to efficient implementation [26], and emptiness of alternating parity tree automata [14]. Finally, in Sect. 4 we prove that, when agents can only perform public actions, then verification becomes decidable even under imperfect information and perfect recall. This result, which builds on [4,6], is relevant, e.g., to the theoretical foundations of planning with public actions [20].

© Springer Nature Switzerland AG 2019
M. Baldoni et al. (Eds.): PRIMA 2019, LNAI 11873, pp. 469–477, 2019.
https://doi.org/10.1007/978-3-030-33792-6_31

Related Work. Recently, a wealth of contributions in formal methods for AI have focused on LTL$_f$, a variant of the linear-time temporal logic LTL interpreted on finite traces (see, e.g., [10]). This logic has been applied to planning [2,3,7, 11,17], and in business process modelling [8,23–25]. For a thorough comparison of the finite- and infinite-trace semantics for LTL, see [9].

Differently from [11], where model checking LTL$_f$ is considered w.r.t. finite traces, here our models for ATL are interpreted systems. This modelling choice allows for the representation of complex strategic behaviours in multi-agent systems. Actually, interpretations on finite traces were originally considered in the context of the branching-time temporal logic CTL* [27]. These investigations were further pursued in [13], but—to the best of our knowledge—there is no work that tackles their model checking problems. Motivated by strategic reasoning over finite traces, [18] introduced iterated Boolean games with LDL goals over finite traces. Differently from us, the authors focus on the existence of Nash equilibria, rather than the verification of general ATL specifications. Further, [21] developed a verification approach for finite traces of multi-agent systems in the LDL$_f$K specifications language, which is more limited in that it does not have strategic operators, and more general in that it allows LDL operators (while we only allow LTL operators).

Closely related to the present contribution is [5], where a semantics for ATL on finite traces is presented for the case of concurrent game structures of *perfect information*. Here, we analyse the arguably more complex case of interpreted systems with imperfect information. Moreover, the restriction to public actions to retain decidability of ATL in contexts of imperfect information and perfect recall has been put forward in [4,6], even though only in relation with infinite traces. We here apply the same intuition to a semantics on finite traces. In general, automata-theoretic decision procedures working on finite traces present several advantages. More precisely, the procedures in Sects. 3 and 4 avoid determinisation and solving emptiness of alternating tree automata, such as Safraless decision procedures [16,22]. These procedures, while undeniably elegant, are still complex and tailored to reasoning about infinite traces. In contrast, just like [10], our algorithms are simpler: they only involve automata operating on *finite words*, and use the standard constructions on these, such as the classic subset construction for determinisation. We consider this a significant technical improvement.

2   ATL on Interpreted Systems with Final States

Given a set X of elements, let $u \in X^+$ denote a non-empty finite sequence on X. Then, we write u_i for its ith element, i.e., $u = u_1 u_2 \ldots$, and $|u| \in \mathbb{N}$ for its length. The first element of u is denoted by $first(u)$, and its last by $last(u)$. We write $u_{\geq i}$ for its suffix $u_i u_{i+1} \ldots$ starting in u_i, and $u_{\leq i}$ for its prefix $u_1 \ldots u_i$. The empty sequence is denoted by ϵ. For a vector $v \in \prod_i X_i$ we denote its ith element by $v(i)$. The powerset of X is denoted by $\mathbb{P}(X)$.

We extend the formalisms of interpreted systems [15] with final states, similarly to the definition of finite automata. In what follows we fix a set AP of atomic propositions (or *atoms*).

Definition 1 (IS$_f$). *An* interpreted system (IS) *with final states is a tuple* $M = \langle Ag, \{L_a, act_a, P_a, \tau_a\}_{a \in Ag}, S_0, F, \lambda \rangle$, *where* $Ag = \{1, \ldots, n\}$ *is a finite set of* agents *and for every* $a \in Ag$:

- L_a *is the finite set of* local states $l, l', \ldots$ *of agent* a.
- act_a *is the finite non-empty set of* actions *of agent* a. *Then, let Jact denote the set* $act_1 \times \ldots \times act_n$ *of* joint actions, *and Act the set* $\cup_{a \in Ag} act_a$ *of all* actions.
- $P_a : L_a \to \mathbb{P}(act_a) \backslash \{\emptyset\}$ *is the* local protocol *for agent* a, *specifying which actions* a *can execute from each local state.*
  If $j \in P_a(l)$ *we say that action* j *is* available *to agent* a *in local state* $l \in L_a$.
- $\tau_a : L_a \times Jact \to L_a$ *is the (partial)* local transition function *such that* $\tau_a(l, J)$ *is defined iff action* $J(a)$ *is available to* a *in local state* l. *That is,* τ_a *returns the next local state for agent* a *from local state* l *following a joint action* J *by all agents.*

Further, let $S = L_1 \times \ldots \times L_n$ *be the set of* global states, $S_0 \subseteq S$ *is the set of* initial (global) states *and* $F \subseteq S$ *is the set of* final (global) states. *Finally,* $\lambda : AP \to \mathbb{P}(S)$ *is the* valuation function.

We now recall some standard terminology about interpreted systems, that will be used hereafter. The induced *global transition function* is the partial function $\tau : S \times Jact \to S$ such that $\tau(s, J)$ is defined iff for every agent $a \in Ag$, action $J(a)$ is available to agent a in local state $s(a)$. If defined, $\tau(s, J)$ is the global state s' such that $s'(a) = \tau_a(s(a), J)$ for every agent $a \in Ag$. A *history* is a finite sequence $h \in S^+$ of global states starting in an initial state, and respecting the global transition function, i.e., $h(1) \in S_0$ and for every $n < |h|$ there exists a joint action $J \in Jact$ such that (i) all agent actions are allowed by the respective individual protocols (i.e., $J(a) \in P_a(h_a(n))$), and (ii) $h(n + 1) = \tau(h(n), J)$. For agent $a \in Ag$ and $n < |h|$, let $h_a(n)$ be the local state of agent a in the nth global state of h. We denote with $Hist$ the set of all histories. A *trace* is a history π that ends in a final state, i.e., $last(\pi) \in F$. Hereafter, we define strategic quantifiers to range over traces, i.e., finite sequences ending in final states. We denote the set of all traces by $Traces$.

Finally, we introduce an indistinguishability relation $\sim_a$ on S, for every agent $a \in Ag$, such that $s \sim_a s'$ iff $s(a) = s'(a)$, that is, two states are indistinguishable for agent a iff a's local state is the same in both states [15]. We extend $\sim_a$ to histories in a synchronous, point-wise manner: for $h, h' \in Hist$ define $h \sim_a h'$ if $|h| = |h'|$ and $h(i) \sim_a h'(i)$ for all $i \leq |h|$. Finally, for a history h, let $last([h]_{\sim_A}) \subseteq S$ denote the set of states $last(h')$ for which there exists $a \in A$ with $h' \sim_a h$.

We now introduce the language ATL* and its fragment ATL [1]. We then provide them with an interpretation on the finite traces generated by the interpreted systems with final states introduced in Sect. 2.

Definition 2 (ATL*). *The history (φ) and trace (ψ) formulas over AP and Ag are built using the following BNF, where $p \in AP$ and $A \subseteq Ag$:*

$$\varphi ::= p \mid \neg\varphi \mid \varphi \wedge \varphi \mid \langle\langle A \rangle\rangle \psi$$
$$\psi ::= \varphi \mid \neg\psi \mid \psi \wedge \psi \mid X\psi \mid \psi U \psi$$

The class of ATL* *formulas is the set of all and only history formulas.*

Traces formulas are built by using the *temporal operators* "next" X and "until" U. The *strategy quantifier* $\langle\langle A \rangle\rangle$ is read as "the agents in coalition A can enforce ...". We introduce the following abbreviations: $[A]\psi ::= \neg\langle\langle A \rangle\rangle\neg\psi$ (read "no matter what the agents in A do ..."), "weak next" $\widetilde{X}\psi ::= \neg X \neg\psi$, "releases" $\psi R \psi' ::= \neg(\neg\psi U \neg\psi')$, "eventually" $F\psi ::= \text{true} U \psi$, and "globally" $G\psi ::= \text{false} R \psi$.

Hereafter we consider also the ATL fragment of ATL*, where trace formulas ψ are restricted as follows: $\psi ::= X\varphi \mid \widetilde{X}\varphi \mid \varphi U \varphi \mid \varphi R \varphi$.

Notice that operators $\widetilde{X}$ and R have to be assumed as primitive in ATL. We discuss the reason why in Remark 2, but we need first to introduce the formal semantics of ATL.

Definition 3 (Strategies). *A (perfect recall or memoryfull) uniform strategy for agent a is a function $\sigma_a : Hist \rightarrow act_a$ such that for every history $h, h' \in Hist$, (i) action $\sigma_a(h)$ is available to agent a: $\sigma_a(h) \in P_a(last(h_a))$, and (ii) $h \sim_a h'$ implies $\sigma_a(h) = \sigma_a(h')$.*

A (uniform) strategy σ is *positional* or *memoryless* if for all $h, h' \in Hist$, $last(h) = last(h')$ implies $\sigma(h) = \sigma(h')$. The set of all memoryfull (resp. memoryless) strategies is denoted as Σ_R (resp. Σ_r). For $A \subseteq Ag$ and $y \in \{R, r\}$, let $\sigma_A : A \rightarrow \Sigma_y$ denote a *joint strategy* associating a (memoryfull or memoryless) strategy σ_a with each agent $a \in A$. For history $h \in Hist$ and joint strategy σ_A, let $\text{out}_{obj}(h, \sigma_A)$, called the *objective outcomes of σ_A from h*, include all traces π (recall that traces are histories that end in final states) consistent with σ_A and h, that is, $\pi_{\leq |h|} = h$, and for every $i \geq |h|$ there exists $J_i \in Jact$ such that $\pi_{i+1} \in \tau(\pi_i, J_i)$ and for every $a \in A$ we have $J_i(a) = \sigma_A(a)(\pi_{\leq i})$. Then, let the set $\text{out}_{subj}(h, \sigma_A)$ of *subjective outcomes of σ_A from h* be defined as $\bigcup_{i \in A, h' \sim_i h} \text{out}_{obj}(h', \sigma_A)$. That is, we consider all (objective) outcomes from any history that is indistinguishable from the current history for some agent a in coalition A. The distinction between objective and subjective outcomes has been introduced in [19], to which we refer for an in-depth discussion.

We can now define the interpretation of formulas on the finite trace semantics.

Definition 4. *Fix an IS_f M with final states. For $x \in \{obj, subj\}$ and $y \in \{R, r\}$, we define, by induction on the structure of formulas, the relation $(M, h, m) \models_{xy} \phi$, where $h \in Hist$, ϕ is a formula, and $m \leq |h|$,*

$(M, h, m) \models_{xy} p$	iff	$p \in \lambda(h(m))$
$(M, h, m) \models_{xy} \neg\varphi$	iff	$(M, h, m) \not\models_{xy} \varphi$
$(M, h, m) \models_{xy} \varphi \wedge \varphi'$	iff	$(M, h, m) \models_{xy} \varphi$ and $(M, h, m) \models_{xy} \varphi'$

$(M,h,m) \models_{xy} \langle\!\langle A \rangle\!\rangle \psi$ *iff*   for some joint strategy $\sigma_A \in \Sigma_y$,
                                        for all traces $\pi \in \mathrm{out}_x(h_{\leq m}, \sigma_A)$, $(M, \pi, m) \models_{xy} \psi$

$(M,h,m) \models_{xy} \neg\psi$ *iff* $(M,h,m) \not\models_{xy} \psi$

$(M,h,m) \models_{xy} \psi \wedge \psi'$ *iff* $(M,h,m) \models_{xy} \psi$ and $(M,h,m) \models_{xy} \psi'$

$(M,h,m) \models_{xy} \mathrm{X}\,\psi$ *iff* $h_{>m} \neq \epsilon$ and $(M,h,m+1) \models_{xy} \psi$

$(M,h,m) \models_{xy} \psi \,\mathrm{U}\, \psi'$ *iff*   for some j, $m \leq j \leq |h|$, $(M,h,j) \models_{xy} \psi'$, and
                                        for all k, $m \leq k < j$ implies $(M, \pi, k) \models_{xy} \psi$

For a formula ϕ, we write $M \models_{xy} \phi$ to mean that $(M, s, 1) \models_{xy} \phi$, for every $s \in S_0$; whereas ϕ is a validity, or $\models_{xy} \phi$, iff $M \models_{xy} \phi$ for every IS_f M with final states.

Remark 1. Notice that the clause for formulas $\langle\!\langle A \rangle\!\rangle \psi$ in Definition 4 is well-defined as traces are histories in particular.

Moreover, in the case of the memoryless semantics, we can show that a *history* formula φ is true in history h, at point m, iff φ is true at state $h(m)$, that is,

$$(M,h,m) \models_{xr} \varphi \text{ iff } (M, h(m), 1) \models_{xr} \varphi$$

So, for the memoryless semantics, we can forget about the past when evaluating history formulas (which are then really state formulas). However, this is not the case in general when we assume perfect recall.

Remark 2. As anticipated above, it is well-known that, differently from the case of infinite traces, on finite traces the next operator X is not self-dual. In particular, according to the semantics for $\models_f$ given in [10] in LTL$_f$ we have that

$$\models_f \mathrm{X}\,\psi \to \neg\mathrm{X}\,\neg\psi \text{ but } \not\models_f \neg\mathrm{X}\,\neg\psi \to \mathrm{X}\,\psi$$

This remark justifies the introduction of *weak next* $\widetilde{\mathrm{X}}\,\psi$ as $\neg\mathrm{X}\,\neg\psi$ (thus, e.g., differently from the case of infinite traces, $\langle\!\langle A \rangle\!\rangle \widetilde{\mathrm{X}}\,\varphi$ is no longer equivalent to $\langle\!\langle A \rangle\!\rangle \mathrm{X}\,\varphi$).

Remark 3. Finite traces have already been considered in the framework of interpreted systems in [21], even though without final states, or what is equivalent in our notation, assuming all states are final. Then, all finite executions are accounted for in the semantics. Unfortunately, in branching-time logics this modelling choice brings about the collapse of truth in the current state and truth in all possible future states, as remarked in [5] (for instance, if all states are final). Hence, here we restrict the range of strategy operators on executions terminating in a final state only.

That said, it is not hard to see that the semantics with final states can be simulated by the special case in which all states are final. This can be done by introducing a fresh atom $final$ that labels the final states, and replacing each formula of the form $\langle\!\langle A \rangle\!\rangle \psi$ by $\langle\!\langle A \rangle\!\rangle (\mathrm{F}\,\mathrm{G}\,final \to \psi')$, where ψ' is the result of applying the translation recursively to ψ. Indeed, this works because a finite trace ends in a final state iff it satisfies $\mathrm{F}\,\mathrm{G}\,final$. Note, however, that this translation does not preserve the fragment ATL since e.g., the translation of the ATL formula $\langle\!\langle A \rangle\!\rangle \mathrm{G}\,q$ is the ATL* formula $\langle\!\langle A \rangle\!\rangle (\mathrm{F}\,\mathrm{G}\,final \to \mathrm{G}\,q)$ which is not in ATL.

We observe that [21] does not suffer from the collapse of modalities as they focus on an epistemic extension of linear-time LDL$_f$.

3 The Model Checking Problem

We now state the decision problem that we will analyse in the rest of the paper.

Definition 5 (Model Checking). *Given an IS_f M and a formula φ, model checking M against φ on finite traces, w.r.t. the objective (resp. subjective) interpretation and perfect (resp. imperfect) recall amounts to determining whether $M \models_{xy} \varphi$ for $x = obj$ (resp. $x = subj$) and $y = R$ (resp., $y = r$).*

We investigate the model checking problem by considering imperfect recall first and then perfect recall. Since the resulting computational complexity is the same for the subjective and objective interpretation (notice that for checking strategy formulas $\langle\!\langle A \rangle\!\rangle \psi$ we need to consider all states indistinguishable from the current one, of which there are only linearly many), in the following we focus on the objective interpretation.

Theorem 1 (ATL$_r$). *Model checking ATL$_r$ is Δ_2^P-complete.*

We now consider the full language of ATL*.

Theorem 2 (ATL$_r^*$). *Model checking ATL$_r^*$ is PSPACE-complete.*

In the case of perfect recall, the model checking problem is undecidable for both languages, as it is the case for infinite traces [12].

Theorem 3 (ATL$_R$). *Model checking ATL$_R$ is undecidable.*

By Theorem 3 the following immediately holds.

Corollary 1 (ATL$_R^*$). *Model checking ATL$_R^*$ is undecidable.*

The following table summarizes the complexity results for the model checking problem of ATL and ATL* on finite traces.

	r	R
ATL	Δ_2^P-complete	undecidable
ATL*	PSPACE-complete	undecidable

Observe that the complexity results are the same as those for infinite traces. However, it should be noted that the algorithms tackling decidable cases sidestep intrinsic difficulties in model checking ATL/ATL* that are due to automata operating over infinite words or trees, e.g., determinisation of Büchi automata, which has been resistant to efficient implementation [26], or emptiness of alternating parity tree automata, [14]. This may in turn lead to more efficient implementations.

4   Decidability via Public Actions

We now identify a subclass of the class of interpreted systems with final states for which the model checking problem is decidable even under the assumptions of imperfect information and perfect recall. Specifically, this is the class of interpreted systems with public actions [4,6].

Definition 6 (IS with Public Actions). *An interpreted system with public actions (and final states) is a tuple $\langle Ag, \{L\_pr_a, act_a, pb\_act_a, P_a, \tau_a\}_{a \in Ag}, S_0, F, \lambda \rangle$ such that $\langle Ag, \{L_a, act_a, P_a, \tau_a\}_{a \in Ag}, S_0, F, \lambda \rangle$ is an IS with final states where, for every agent $a \in Ag$:*

1. *$pb\_act_a \subseteq act_a$ is the set of* public actions *of agent a;*
2. *$L_a = L\_pr_a \times \prod_{b \in Ag}(pb\_act_b \cup \{\epsilon\})$ is the set of local states;*
3. *the local transition function τ_a satisfies the property that $\tau_a(l,j) = (p', j')$ implies that for all $b \in Ag$, if $j_b \in pb\_act_b$ then $j'_b = j_b$ and otherwise $j'_b = \epsilon$.*

Intuitively, the set L_pr_a consists of the *private (local)* states of agent a. Then, the full local state of a comprises her private state and all public actions that have been played by any agent in the previous round.

Then, the following class of IS_f is the focus of this section.

Definition 7 (PAIS). *Let* public-action interpreted systems *be the class of interpreted systems with public actions (and final states) such that $act_a = pb\_act_a$ for all $a \in Ag$.*

We remark briefly that rounds in a number of community card games (bridge, poker, etc.) can as well be encoded as PAIS.

Here is the main result of this section:

Theorem 4. *The model-checking problem for* ATL^*_R *on PAIS is* 2EXPTIME-*complete.*

As for the lower bound, we use the fact that concurrent game structures (CGS) of perfect information can be embedded into PAIS by using a polynomial reduction. We here provide only a sketch of proof, and refer to [1] for a presentation of CGS. Intuitively, given a CGS G, the local state of each agent in the associated PAIS IS_f is defined as the current state of the CGS. Further, all actions in the CGS can be assumed to be public. Then, the transition relation in IS_f just mimics the one in G. We can check that the size of the state space of IS_f is polynomial (indeed linear) in the size of G. In particular, it can then be shown that the two structures satisfy the same formulas in ATL^*_R. Finally, model checking CGS against ATL^*_R, interpreted on finite traces, is 2EXPTIME-hard (c.f., [5]), since the latter can encode the synthesis problem for LTL_f, which is 2EXPTIME-hard [10].

5   Conclusions

In this contribution we introduced a novel interpretation of Alternating-time Temporal Logic under imperfect information, based on finite traces. To do so, we extended the framework of Interpreted Systems with final states, representing intuitively notable check-points in the system's execution. Then, we analysed the corresponding model checking problem for various flavours of ATL, depending on syntax and memory. We remarked that the complexity results obtained are analogous to those available for the case of infinite traces, with the notable difference that the related decision procedures make use of finite automata only, rather than infinite ones. Most importantly, for the specific case of IS_f with public actions only, we were able to obtain decidability also for the case of imperfect information and perfect recall, which is undecidable in general.

In future work we plan to test our intuition that manipulations on finite automata are more amenable to practical model checking through an implementation.

Acknowledgements. The authors acknowledge support of ANR JCJC Project SVeDaS (ANR-16-CE40-0021). Alessio Lomuscio is supported by a Royal Academy Chair in Emerging Technologies.

References

1. Alur, R., Henzinger, T., Kupferman, O.: Alternating-time temporal logic. J. ACM **49**(5), 672–713 (2002)
2. Bacchus, F., Kabanza, F.: Using temporal logics to express search control knowledge for planning. Art. Int. **116**(1–2), 123–191 (2000)
3. Baier, J.A., McIlraith, S.A.: Planning with first-order temporally extended goals using heuristic search. In: AAAI, pp. 788–795 (2006)
4. Belardinelli, F., Lomuscio, A., Murano, A., Rubin, S.: Verification of multi-agent systems with imperfect information and public actions. In: AAMAS, pp. 1268–1276 (2017)
5. Belardinelli, F., Lomuscio, A., Murano, A., Rubin, S.: Alternating-time temporal logic on finite traces. In: IJCAI, pp. 77–83 (2018). https://doi.org/10.24963/ijcai.2017/14
6. Belardinelli, F., Lomuscio, A., Murano, A., Rubin, S.: Decidable verification of multi-agent systems with bounded private actions. In: AAMAS, pp. 1865–1867 (2018)
7. Camacho, A., Triantafillou, E., Muise, C., Baier, J., McIlraith, S.: Non-deterministic planning with temporally extended goals: LTL over finite and infinite traces. In: AAAI, pp. 3716–3724 (2017)
8. De Giacomo, G., De Masellis, R., Grasso, M., Maggi, F.M., Montali, M.: Monitoring business metaconstraints based on LTL and LDL for finite traces. In: Sadiq, S., Soffer, P., Völzer, H. (eds.) BPM 2014. LNCS, vol. 8659, pp. 1–17. Springer, Cham (2014). https://doi.org/10.1007/978-3-319-10172-9_1
9. De Giacomo, G., De Masellis, R., Montali, M.: Reasoning on LTL on finite traces: insensitivity to infiniteness. In: AAAI, pp. 1027–1033 (2014)

10. De Giacomo, G., Vardi, M.Y.: Synthesis for LTL and LDL on finite traces. In: IJCAI, pp. 1558–1564 (2015)
11. De Giacomo, G., Vardi, M.: Linear temporal logic and linear dynamic logic on finite traces. In: IJCAI, pp. 854–860 (2013)
12. Dima, C., Tiplea, F.: Model-checking ATL under imperfect information and perfect recall semantics is undecidable. CoRR abs/1102.4225 (2011). http://arxiv.org/abs/1102.4225
13. Emerson, E.A., Halpern, J.Y.: "sometimes" and "not never" revisited: on branching versus linear time temporal logic. J. ACM **33**(1), 151–178 (1986)
14. Emerson, E., Jutla, C., Sistla, A.: On model checking for the μ-calculus and its fragments. Theor. Comp. Sci. **258**(1–2), 491–522 (2001)
15. Fagin, R., Halpern, J., Moses, Y., Vardi, M.: Reasoning About Knowledge. MIT, Cambridge (1995)
16. Filiot, E., Jin, N., Raskin, J.: Antichains and compositional algorithms for LTL synthesis. Formal Methods Syst. Des. **39**(3), 261–296 (2011)
17. Gerevini, A., Haslum, P., Long, D., Saetti, A., Dimopoulos, Y.: Deterministic planning in the fifth international planning competition: PDDL3 and experimental evaluation of the planners. Artif. Intell. **173**(5–6), 619–668 (2009). https://doi.org/10.1016/j.artint.2008.10.012
18. Gutierrez, J., Perelli, G., Wooldridge, M.: Iterated games with LDL goals over finite traces. In: AAMAS, pp. 696–704 (2017)
19. Jamroga, W., van der Hoek, W.: Agents that know how to play. Fund. Inf. **62**, 1–35 (2004)
20. Kominis, F., Geffner, H.: Multiagent online planning with nested beliefs and dialogue. In: ICAPS, pp. 186–194 (2017)
21. Kong, J., Lomuscio, A.: Model checking multi-agent systems against LDLK specifications on finite traces. In: AAMAS, pp. 166–174 (2018)
22. Kupferman, O., Piterman, N., Vardi, M.: Safraless compositional synthesis. In: CAV, pp. 31–44 (2006)
23. Montali, M., Pesic, M., van der Aalst, W., Chesani, F., Mello, P., Storari, S.: Declarative specification and verification of service choreographiess. ACM Trans. Web (TWEB) **4**(1), 3 (2010)
24. Pesic, M., Bosnacki, D., van der Aalst, W.: Enacting declarative languages using LTL: avoiding errors and improving performance. In: SPIN, pp. 146–161 (2010)
25. Pesic, M., van der Aalst, W.M.P.: A declarative approach for flexible business processes management. In: Eder, J., Dustdar, S. (eds.) BPM 2006. LNCS, vol. 4103, pp. 169–180. Springer, Heidelberg (2006). https://doi.org/10.1007/11837862_18
26. Tsai, M.H., Fogarty, S., Vardi, M., Tsay, Y.K.: State of Büchi complementation. LMCS **10**, 4 (2014). https://doi.org/10.2168/LMCS-10(4:13)2014
27. Vardi, M.Y., Stockmeyer, L.: Improved upper and lower bounds for modal logics of programs. In: STOC, pp. 240–251 (1985)

TAMER: Task Allocation in Multi-robot Systems Through an Entity-Relationship Model

Branko Miloradović, Mirgita Frasheri, Baran Cürüklü, Mikael Ekström,
and Alessandro Vittorio Papadopoulos$^{(\boxtimes)}$ (iD)

Mälardalen University, Västerås, Sweden
{branko.miloradovic,mirgita.frasheri,baran.curuklu,mikael.ekstrom,
alessandro.papadopoulos}@mdh.se

Abstract. Multi-robot task allocation (MRTA) problems have been studied extensively in the past decades. As a result, several classifications have been proposed in the literature targeting different aspects of MRTA, with often a few commonalities between them. The goal of this paper is twofold. First, a comprehensive overview of early work on existing MRTA taxonomies is provided, focusing on their differences and similarities. Second, the MRTA problem is modelled using an Entity-Relationship (ER) conceptual formalism to provide a structured representation of the most relevant aspects, including the ones proposed within previous taxonomies. Such representation has the advantage of (i) representing MRTA problems in a systematic way, (ii) providing a formalism that can be easily transformed into a software infrastructure, and (iii) setting the baseline for the definition of knowledge bases, that can be used for automated reasoning in MRTA problems.

1 Introduction

In the past decades, the interest in Multi-Agent Systems (MASs) has grown due to their suitability in representing applications where actors have different interests, and to their distributed nature that increases performance, scalability, and robustness [12]. Earlier papers from the 1980s and 1990s mostly focused on the properties and collaborative behaviour of MASs putting the emphasis on the specific aspects of the problem to be solved, e.g., communication, topology, robot group composition, and collaborative behaviour. Proposed solutions were usually verified in simulation environments.

As the complexity of the MAS missions started to increase, e.g., in terms of number of required agents, number of tasks to be completed, heterogeneity of capabilities required to complete some tasks, etc., more attention has been

This work was supported by the Aggregate Farming in the Cloud (**AFarCloud**) European project, with project number 783221 (Call: H2020-ECSEL-2017-2), DPAC research profile funded by KKS (20150022), the FIESTA project funded by KKS, and the UNICORN project. Projects are supported by ECSEL JU and the VINNOVA.

M. Baldoni et al. (Eds.): PRIMA 2019, LNAI 11873, pp. 478–486, 2019.
https://doi.org/10.1007/978-3-030-33792-6_32

devoted to the multi-robot task allocation (MRTA) problem, which has become an established research direction [2]. In order to tame such an emerging complexity, several taxonomies have been proposed in the literature. Gerkey and Matarić [5] introduced the first taxonomy for MRTA problems, proposing three main dimensions that specified the type of tasks, type of robots, and type of assignment. Other taxonomies have been proposed in the following years, further highlighting the complexity of the MRTA problem. However, most of them are do not build on previous ones, leading to a fragmented and possibly overlapping set of taxonomies.

This paper surveys the existing taxonomies, in order to capture the important dimensions of MRTA problem configurations and to understand differences and similarities. In addition, this paper presents the Task Allocation in Multi-Robot System Entity-Relationship (TAMER) model, an Entity-Relationship (ER) model that captures the most relevant aspects of the surveyed MRTA taxonomies. The goal of TAMER is to provide a unified view of the existing taxonomies, and a tool to classify and relate the different dimensions in a more structured and systematic way. Adding new dimensions on top of existing taxonomies requires a clear understanding of how they could fit in the big picture. In fact, newly proposed aspects may overlap with, may be coupled with, or may contain certain properties already captured by other dimensions. TAMER simplifies such process providing a more formal approach to tame the complexity of the MRTA taxonomy problem. TAMER offers a general model that includes the different dimensions proposed by the surveyed taxonomies (Sect. 2), and it can be thought of as a unifying approach to the MRTA taxonomy problem, allowing for extending the classification with new dimensions in a non-redundant way, in the attempt of providing a unique framework for the definition of the relevant dimensions in MRTA problems.

The contribution of this paper is twofold: (i) To provide an overview of MRTA taxonomies, analysing how the research axes evolved over the past few decades, and identifying differences and similarities among them (Sect. 2); (ii) To formalize the MRTA problem through TAMER, an ER conceptual model that includes the most relevant aspects of the identified MRTA research axes (Sect. 3).

2 Overview of the MRTA Taxonomies

The categorization of the MRTA problems across various dimensions has been extensively investigated by several researchers in the past three decades. Earlier taxonomies [1,3,12], from the 1990s and the beginning of 2000s, focus more on the communication, the cooperation, and the robot capabilities dimensions. Table 1 summarizes the main surveyed taxonomies, and the respective proposed dimensions. In these taxonomies, the task allocation dimension plays a minor role. The work presented by Gerkey and Matarić [5] is the first one to shift the focus from former dimensions, into the direction of task allocation. This trend has been followed in the past decade and a half, expanding the original MRTA dimensions [6,7,10].

Table 1. Summary of the proposed dimensions classification in MRTA taxonomies.

Dimension	Dudek et al. [3]	Cao et al. [1]	Stone et al. [12]	Lau & Zhang [8]	Gerkey & Mataric [5]	Landén et al. [7]	Korsah et al. [6]	Nunes et al. [10]
Group composition	✓	✓						
Robot capabilities	✓	✓	✓		✓			
Communication	✓	✓	✓					
Topology	✓	✓	✓					
Cooperation		✓	✓		✓		✓	
Resources	✓		✓	✓				
Environment		✓				✓		
Allocation				✓	✓	✓		✓
Task interrelatedness			✓			✓	✓	✓

The group composition represents a crucial aspect of a MAS, and has been addressed explicitly as the group architecture and size [1], collective composition [3], and degree of heterogeneity [12]. The robot group composition has been addressed in the original MRTA taxonomy with the introduction of Single-Robot (SR) and Multi-Robot (MR) tasks, and Single-Task (ST) and Multi-Task (MT) robots dimensions. In order to have heterogeneity in the robot group composition, individual robots must have different capabilities. The range of robot capabilities is very broad going from the ability to model other agents and learning [1], processing ability [3], to the ability to perform tasks concurrently [5].

The communication and topology dimensions were an important part of early taxonomies, however, with the shift of focus towards task allocation and task interrelatedness, the communication was usually assumed to be failure-free and it did not have an effect on the problem configuration or solution design. Nevertheless, these dimensions are of major importance in MASs and they have been divided into several sub-dimensions. They include the way of interaction [1], the communication range, bandwidth, and topology [3], and the communication language and protocols [12].

Another fundamental aspect in MASs is the interaction among agents, which can be intentional or emergent [1]. Furthermore, agents can have competitive or benevolent behaviour, negotiate and make commitments in order to reach their goals [12]. In later papers, the cooperation is usually assumed to be intentional and benevolent [5,6] or it is not been taken into account at all [7,10]. When resources are finite [8], resource conflict may arise [1], thus a resource manager is needed [12]. Conflicts can be related to sharing space, objects, equipment, or communication. If agents are physical units acting within an environment, geometric problems may occur [1]. The environment is classically classified as static or dynamic [7]. Sudden and unplanned changes in the environment may have different consequences on the problem configuration, ultimately leading to a task re-allocation.

Another major part of the MRTA taxonomy is the task allocation dimension. This dimension can be further divided into Instantaneous Assignment (IA) and

Time-Extended Assignment (TA) [5]. If the allocation is done by an agent, then the allocation is internal and is considered as a task in MAS, otherwise, it is assumed that the allocation process is external [7].

In order to cover the gaps that were left by the taxonomy proposed by Gerkey and Matarić [5], by not addressing interrelated utilities and task constraints, several different taxonomy additions were proposed [6,7,10]. Landén *et al.* [7] defined unrelated utilities and interrelated utilities as well as independent tasks and constrained tasks. On the other hand, Korsah *et al.* [6] covered both of these dimensions with a single dimension: the degree of interrelatedness. Although not identical, these concepts are related, so both utilities and constraints have an impact on the degree of interrelatedness between both agents and tasks. Instead of utility, Lau and Zhang [8] express the degree of objective fulfilment in profit. Although Gerkey and Matarić [5] state that their work does not include inter-relatedness between tasks explicitly, it can be noted that MR tasks do require some sort of synchronization between robots, while MT robots must have intra-related schedules in the case of TA. In addition, Nunes *et al.* [10] distinguish between temporal and ordering constraints, by adding Time Windows (TW) and Synchronization Precedence (SP) under TA. Furthermore, MRTA problem can be deterministic if the output of the model is completely determined by the initial conditions or stochastic if a model of the uncertainty is available. Despite the importance of uncertainty in robotics, most MRTA models are deterministic and deal with uncertainty only at execution time. Finally, all constraints can be divided into hard and soft constraints.

3   The TAMER Model

The TAMER model (shown in Fig. 1) aims at covering the relevant aspects of the MRTA problem, by adopting a systematic approach to unify the different dimensions presented in the former taxonomies. TAMER is an Entity-Relationship

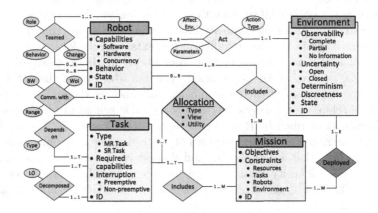

Fig. 1. The TAMER model.

(ER) model that defines the relevant entities of MRTA, and how they relate among them. TAMER unifies the previously proposed taxonomies, in a unique taxonomy that makes sure that the different dimensions are all necessary and sufficient to describe the fundamental problem configuration. TAMER also includes for all the entities and relationships a minimal set of attributes that captures the most relevant aspects presented in former taxonomies. Note that the proposed set of attributes does not aim for completeness, but it represents a core set that can be easily extended thanks to the TAMER approach.

3.1   Entities

TAMER consists of four entities: (i) *Robot*, (ii) *Environment*, (iii) *Task*, and (iv) *Mission*.

Robot. The *Robot* entity consists of the state, behaviour and capability attributes[1]. The state attribute covers those variables that are considered of interest in a particular context, e.g., velocity, position, orientation, and battery level. Different contexts might require different sets of variables, thus the state attribute is not specified in detail. The behaviour refers to the level of autonomy displayed by a robot. A robot might be able to display a particular level of autonomy that is fixed over time, or the level of its autonomy can be adaptive. Due to changing circumstances, the dependencies among robots can change, and, as a result, the autonomy levels change as well [4]. Both adaptive and fixed autonomy have an impact on the cooperation among the agents. Whereas the former allows for dynamic patterns and different levels of cooperation, the latter implies fixed patterns and a predefined level of cooperation.

The capability attribute covers the abilities of a robot, both at the hardware and software levels. These abilities can correspond to different levels of abstraction. For instance, at a low-level an ability might refer to processing power, concurrency, and/or computational resources, whereas at a high-level an ability might relate to being able of doing some action, e.g., grasping a mug.

Environment. The *Environment* entity is characterized by the following attributes: state, observability, uncertainty, determinism, discreteness, and additional constraints. As for the state attribute, different variables that describe the environment could be relevant in different contexts, e.g., the location of dynamic obstacles at a specific timestamp. The observability attribute takes values such as complete, partial, or no information. The uncertainty, on the other hand, refers to the dynamics in the environment, i.e., whether the environment does not change (closed) or changes overtime (open). Determinism, discreetness are characteristics described by Russell and Norvig [11, Chapter 2]. The additional constraints attribute serve the purposes of describing the environment in terms of rules and laws that are applicable and shape how the problem is formulated.

Task. The task entity consists of type required capabilities, and interruption attribute. The task type attribute is identical to the Gerkey and Matarić [5]

---

[1] All entities have an ID attribute, that uniquely distinguishes between instances of the same entity. The ID is not further discussed in this paper.

definition of SR and MR tasks. Required capabilities attribute describes the capability a robot needs to possess in order to execute a certain task. If a task can be temporarily interrupted without requiring its cooperation, in order to do some other task, then the task being interrupted is said to be preemptive. Preemptive tasks are of very common occurrence in real-time systems.

Mission. Mission entity encapsulates mission objectives, available resources, and constraints that are part of the problem domain. This is where the problem configuration as well as the objectives are defined. Mission constraints are constraints, which are imposed by some external actor, which is configuring the mission problem, e.g., human operator. These constraints can relate to resources, robots, tasks, and environment. For example, a constraint, which says that robot i can use at most 50% of its battery is considered to be resource constraint. Similarly, a set of n tasks to be completed is a task constraint. TW are another example of task constraints. A robot constraint may restrict, e.g., the number of robots that can be used in a specific mission. Specific constraints can be imposed regarding environment, e.g., in the form of forbidden areas, which must not be visited, or crossed.

3.2   Relationships

TAMER also includes nine relationships: (i) *Teamed*, (ii) *Communicate with*, (iii) *Act*, (iv) *Depends on*, (v) *Decomposed*, (vi) *Allocation*, (vii) *Includes Robot*, (viii) *Includes Task*, and (ix) *Deployed*.

Teamed. Robots can be part of teams within a MAS, and as such be in a *Teamed* relationship with one another. Attributes that characterize such relationship are state, behaviour, role, and dynamics. The state of a team could be specified by the size of the team, its composition in terms of robot capabilities, and the behaviour of the team. This attribute is similar to the behaviour attribute of the robot entity, however in this case it refers to the overall behaviour of the team that emerges from the local robot behaviours. The role attribute describes what hierarchical position a robot has in a particular team, e.g., leader or peer. The dynamics attribute refers to whether the team can change in time in terms of composition or hierarchy, among other variables.

Communicate with. *Communicate with* is also a relationship between robots, and has four attributes: type, range, bandwidth, and way of interaction. Communication type includes broadcast and one-to-one communication. Range and bandwidth describe physical properties of the communication channel. Way of interaction expresses whether a robot communicates directly with another robot, or indirectly, e.g., stigmergy where communication happens via the environment. The problem can depend on the upper bound of the bandwidth and range, which is a characteristic of a specific environment. Notice that the specification of this relationship defines the network topology, i.e., which robot communicates with whom.

Act. The *Act* relationship connects the robot and the environment entities to each other. A robot can act in an environment, and as a result have an impact on the state of the environment. Similarly, the environment can act on the robot and affect its state. This relationship is characterized by the type of action, parameters of the action, and affect on environment. A specific action can be described by a set of parameters, e.g., the action name could be one such parameter which defines what the action is. More parameters could be specified depending on the need. The *affect on the environment* attribute distinguishes between active and passive actions on the environment. The former covers actions that change the environment, whereas the latter covers actions that do not change the environment, e.g., a robot's movement.

Depends on. *Depends on* is a relationship between task entities describing their dependencies. This relationship has a *type* attribute. The type attribute, specifies what is the type of task dependency, i.e., *inter-dependent* (there are dependencies within robot's schedule), and *cross-schedule dependent* (there are dependencies within different robots' schedules). These dependencies can be utility related, synchronous, or time windows. Ordering constraints are treated as a special case of synchronization constraints.

Decomposed. Tasks can be atomic or divisible. The representation of the tasks is a design choice, and it may depend on the final purpose of the modeling. Tasks that are considered atomic from a high-level planning perspective, can be seen as divisible at the low level perspective, e.g., when agents need to coordinate to complete a more complex task. For example, Miloradović *et al.* [9] considered MR tasks as atomic in a high-level mission planning approach, while Zlot [13] deal with the task decomposition and allocation with Logical Operators (LO).

Allocation. The main relationship in the taxonomy that binds together mission, task, and robot entity is the allocation. The allocation can assign $0 \dots T$ tasks to $0 \dots R$ robots. If 0 tasks are assigned to 0 robots it means there is no allocation, hence no mission. However, it is still possible to have 0 tasks allocated to m robots, meaning that these m robots will not be used in a mission. The allocation consists of allocation type (IA or TA), allocation view (internal, external [7], or hybrid) and utility function.

Includes. The *includes* relationship connects the mission with the robot and task entities. This defines which tasks and robots are included in the mission. To have a mission, there must be at least 1 task allocated to at least 1 robot.

Deployed. After the allocation is done for a defined mission, through the *deployed* relationship the mission is deployed in the environment for execution. This means that missions are further constrained and shaped by the specific environment they should be executed in.

3.3 Discussion

The MRTA problem needs to consider all the presented aspects in order to represent a specific deployment. MRTA algorithms are in charge of populating the allocation relationship, based on the set of available robots, on the mission composed of the different tasks, and on the description of the environment.

The need for the TAMER model is motivated by the emerging complexity, both of the MRTA taxonomies and MAS missions. Most of the proposed taxonomies analyze the MRTA problem from different angles, and possibly introducing additional dimensions that are indirectly covered by other ones. TAMER model has several advantages. First, it allows for a systematic and structured representation of MRTA taxonomies. In fact, the taxonomies presented in Sect. 2 are included or can be reduced to specific instances of the TAMER model, avoiding redundancies and overlaps. For example, different topologies of communication are not directly represented in the TAMER model, but are a result of the relation *Communicate with*, that specifies the adjacency matrix of the communication topology, including additional attributes, such as the Range, the Bandwidth, and the Way of Interaction. Also, in TAMER all the attributes are assumed to be able to vary over time, while keeping a consistent knowledge base of the problem configuration.

The second important advantage of TAMER is that it adopts a classical approach for data/knowledge representation. As a result, TAMER defines a complex data structure that can be used for the definition of software infrastructures in MRTA problems, and for MRTA algorithms. Moreover, the TAMER model can be extended to include additional semantics to enable automated reasoning in MRTA problems.

Finally, TAMER adds two additional research axes: Multi-Mission problems and Multi-Environment problems. It allows multiple missions to be defined and deployed in the multiple or shared environment with the possibility of sharing robots and resources among the missions. The multi-mission and multi-environments aspects have not been extensively explored.

4   Conclusion

This work provides an overview of the main taxonomies for MRTA problems, analyzing and relating the different components (in this paper referred to as axes, or dimensions) proposed in the literature. Such dimensions may overlap or represent different aspects of the MRTA problem, but they seldom provide a general view on it. In order to tame the emerging complexity coming from the different taxonomies, we proposed TAMER, an ER model that provides a unified view on the MRTA problem, with the aim of remove potential redundancies in the classification, as well as a structured way to add or remove additional dimensions. As future work, TAMER can be extended to define a knowledge base for enabling automated reasoning in MRTA problems.

References

1. Cao, Y.U., Fukunaga, A.S., Kahng, A.B.: Cooperative mobile robotics: antecedents and directions. Auton. Robots **4**(1), 7–27 (1997). https://doi.org/10.1023/A:1008855018923
2. Dasgupta, P.: Multi-robot task allocation for performing cooperative foraging tasks in an initially unknown environment. In: Jain, L.C., Aidman, E.V., Abeynayake, C. (eds.) Innovations in Defence Support Systems -2. SCI, vol. 338, pp. 5–20. Springer, Heidelberg (2011). https://doi.org/10.1007/978-3-642-17764-4_2

3. Dudek, G., Jenkin, M., Milios, E.: A taxonomy of multirobot systems. In: Robot Teams: From diversity to Polymorphism, pp. 3–22 (2002)
4. Frasheri, M., Curuklu, B., Ekström, M., Papadopoulos, A.V.: Adaptive autonomy in a search and rescue scenario. In: 12th IEEE SASO (2018)
5. Gerkey, B.P., Matarić, M.J.: A formal analysis and taxonomy of task allocation in multi-robot systems. Int. J. Robot. Res. 23(9), 939–954 (2004)
6. Korsah, G.A., Stentz, A., Dias, M.B.: A comprehensive taxonomy for multi-robot task allocation. Int. J. Robot. Res. 32(12), 1495–1512 (2013)
7. Landén, D., Heintz, F., Doherty, P.: Complex task allocation in mixed-initiative delegation: a UAV case study. In: Desai, N., Liu, A., Winikoff, M. (eds.) PRIMA 2010. LNCS (LNAI), vol. 7057, pp. 288–303. Springer, Heidelberg (2012). https://doi.org/10.1007/978-3-642-25920-3_20
8. Lau, H.C., Zhang, L.: Task allocation via multi-agent coalition formation: taxonomy, algorithms and complexity. In: ICTAI, pp. 346–350 (2003)
9. Miloradović, B., Çürüklü, B., Ekström, M.: A genetic mission planner for solving temporal multi-agent problems with concurrent tasks. In: Tan, Y., Takagi, H., Shi, Y., Niu, B. (eds.) ICSI 2017. LNCS, vol. 10386, pp. 481–493. Springer, Cham (2017). https://doi.org/10.1007/978-3-319-61833-3_51
10. Nunes, E., Manner, M., Mitiche, H., Gini, M.: A taxonomy for task allocation problems with temporal and ordering constraints. Robot. Auton. Syst. 90, 55–70 (2017)
11. Russell, S.J., Norvig, P.: Artificial Intelligence: A Modern Approach. Pearson Education Limited, Malaysia (2016)
12. Stone, P., Veloso, M.: Multiagent systems: a survey from a machine learning perspective. Auton. Robots 8(3), 345–383 (2000). https://doi.org/10.1023/A:1008942012299
13. Zlot, R.M.: An auction-based approach to complex task allocation for multirobot teams. Ph.D. thesis, Carnegie Mellon University, Pittsburgh, PA (2006)

A Modeling Environment for Reified Temporal-Causal Networks: Modeling Plasticity and Metaplasticity in Cognitive Agent Models

Jan Treur[(✉)]

Social AI Group, Vrije Universiteit Amsterdam, Amsterdam, The Netherlands
j.treur@vu.nl
https://www.researchgate.net/profile/Jan_Treur

Abstract. Plasticity is a crucial adaptive characteristic of the brain. Relatively recently mechanisms have been found showing that plasticity itself is controlled by what is called metaplasticity. In this paper a modeling environment is introduced to develop and simulate reified temporal-causal network models that can be applied for cognitive agent models. It is shown how this environment is a useful tool to model plasticity combined with metaplasticity.

1 Introduction

Real-world cognitive agents are often adaptive, described by adaptation principles. For example, mental or neural networks equipped with a Hebbian learning mechanism [5] are able to adapt connection weights over time and learn in this way. This is usually called *plasticity* (modeled by the middle layer in the example in Fig. 1). In some circumstances it is better to learn fast, but in other circumstances it is better to stay stable and persist what has been learnt in the past. To control this, a type of (higher-order) adaptation called *metaplasticity* is used (highest layer in Fig. 1); e.g., [1, 6].

In [8, 11] any form of adaptation had to be added by specific procedural program code like usually is done for adaptive networks; there was no standard or principled way to explicitly specify adaptive causal relations. To offer a more principled way to specify adaptive networks, recently the notion of *network reification* was proposed as an addition to the temporal-causal network modeling approach, and illustrated by some case studies that were implemented in a more or less ad hoc - proof of concept – manner [9, 10]. These initial explorations suggest that this notion of network reification could be useful to model in a systematic and transparent manner from a network-oriented perspective, cognitive and social agent processes that are adaptive of any order, and in particular those involving plasticity and metaplasticity (e.g., see Fig. 1).

Following this, the current paper introduces a specification format based on declarative mathematical relations and a modeling environment for reified temporal-causal networks, implemented in Matlab in a principled and structure-preserving manner. Due to this dedicated overall Network-Oriented Modelling approach for adaptive networks, no procedural, algorithmic or programming skills are needed to

© Springer Nature Switzerland AG 2019
M. Baldoni et al. (Eds.): PRIMA 2019, LNAI 11873, pp. 487–495, 2019.
https://doi.org/10.1007/978-3-030-33792-6_33

design cognitive agents or social networks which show complex adaptive behaviour of any order.

In the paper, in Sect. 2 the reified temporal-causal network architecture is explained in some detail. After this, more details are described of the specification format (Sect. 3) and the implemented modeling environment and its computational reified network engine (Sect. 4) developed. Finally, Sect. 5 is a discussion.

2   Modeling Adaptive Processes by Reified Networks

A conceptual representation of the network structure of a temporal-causal network model involves three main characteristics of the network structure; see [8], Chapter 2, or [11]. First, for the *connectivity characteristics* of the network, connection weights $\omega_{X,Y}$ are used as a labels for connections from X to Y. Second, for the *aggregation characteristics* of a network, for each state Y a combination function $c_Y(..)$ is used to aggregate (and modulate) causal impacts on state Y; they can contain parameters **p**. Third, for the *timing characteristics* of a network, for each state Y a *speed factor* η_Y is used for timing of the causal effects. The difference equations used for simulation and mathematical analysis incorporate these three types of network characteristics $\omega_{X,Y}$, $c_Y(..)$, η_Y:

$$Y(t + \Delta t) = Y(t) + \eta_Y[c_Y(\omega_{X_1,Y}X_1(t), \ldots, \omega_{X_k,Y}X_k(t)) - Y(t)]\Delta t$$

Here $X_1, \ldots, X_k$ are the states from which state Y gets its incoming connections. For aggregation a library with a number (currently 35) of standard combination functions are available as options, but also own-defined functions can be added.

Modeling adaptive networks asks for a dedicated network architecture in which different levels of adaptivity or plasticity can be modeled. Such an architecture has been proposed based on the notion of network reification [9, 10]. Reification (e.g., [4]), in general means making an abstract notion concrete. For network models this is done by introducing additional states in the network that explicitly represent characteristics of the network such as *connectivity*, *aggregation*, and *timing*, and makes them adaptive:

- **Adaptation of a connection weight** $\omega_{X,Y}$: reified connection weight representations $\mathbf{W}_{X,Y}$
- **Adaptation of a speed factor** η_Y: reified speed factor representations $\mathbf{H}_Y$
- **Adaptation of a combination function** $c_Y(..)$: reified combination function weight representations $\mathbf{C}_{i,Y}$ (for the ith combination function used)
- **Adaptation of a combination function parameter** p_Y: reified combination function parameter representations $\mathbf{P}_{i,j,Y}$ (for the jth parameter of the ith combination function for Y)

In a graphical representation in a 3D format these new states are depicted in a second plane above the plane for the base network; see the blue plane in the example model depicted in Fig. 1, also indicated as the first reification level. This step can be repeated so that a third plane is added for second-order reification (see the purple third plane in Fig. 1). Three types of causal connections are distinguished: upward causal connections, downward causal connections and leveled (horizontal) causal connections. The downward causal connections have their own fixed role and meaning in the sense that they are causally effectuating one of the four types of adaptations listed above.

Combination functions are built as a weighted average from a number of basic combination functions $bcf_i(..)$ available in a library; these weights can be prespecified as constant values or can be adaptive based on reification states. Examples of basic combination functions often used are the *euclidean combination function* $\mathbf{eucl}_{n,\lambda}(\dots)$ with order $n > 0$ and scaling factor $\lambda > 0$ (generalising the linear scaled sum function for $n = 1$) and the *advanced logistic sum* combination function $\mathbf{alogistic}_{\sigma,\tau}(\dots)$ with steepness parameter $\sigma > 0$ and excitability threshold parameter τ:

$$\mathbf{eucl}_{n,\lambda}(V_1,\dots,V_k) = \sqrt[n]{\frac{V_1^n + \dots + V_k^n}{\lambda}}$$

$$\mathbf{alogistic}_{\sigma,\tau}(V_1,\dots,V_k) = \left[\frac{1}{1+e^{-\sigma(V_1+\dots+V_k-\tau)}} - \frac{1}{1+e^{\sigma\tau}}\right](1+e^{-\sigma\tau})$$

Here the V_i denote the single impacts $\omega_{X_i,Y}X_i(t)$ on state Y for each of the incoming connections from states $X_1, \dots, X_k$. Moreover, for Hebbian learning ('neurons that fire together, wire together'), among others the following combination function is available (used for the reification state $\mathbf{W}_{X,Y}$ in the middle layer in Fig. 1):

$$\mathbf{hebb}_\mu(V_1, V_2, W) = V_1 V_2 (1 - W) + \mu W$$

where V_1, V_2 indicate the single impacts from the connected states (base states at the bottom layer in Fig. 1) and W the connection weight (represented by reification state $\mathbf{W}_{X,Y}$ in the middle layer in Fig. 1), and μ is a persistence parameter. In Fig. 1:

- $\mathbf{W}_{X,Y}$ plays the role of connection weight for the connection from X to Y
- $\mathbf{H}_Y$ the role of speed factor for Y
- $\mathbf{C}_{i,Y}$ the role of combination function weight of $bcf_i(..)$ for Y
- $\mathbf{P}_{i,j,Y}$ the role of combination function parameter value; examples of such reified parameters used in Fig. 1 are the excitability parameters τ (reified by the two $\mathbf{T}$ states in the middle plane) and the persistence parameter μ (reified by the $\mathbf{M}$ state in the upper plane)

These values are used in the computations for base states Y depending on their role. For any base state Y the following *universal combination function* $\mathbf{c}^*_Y(..)$ is used:

$$\mathbf{c}^*_Y(H, C_1, \dots, C_m, P_{1,1}, P_{2,1}, \dots, P_{1,m}, P_{2,m}, W_1, \dots, W_k, V_1, \dots, V_k, V) =$$
$$H \frac{C_1 bcf_1\left(P_{1,1},P_{2,1},W_1V_1,..,W_kV_k\right) + \dots + C_m bcf_m\left(P_{1,m},P_{2,m},W_1V_1,..,W_kV_k\right)}{C_1 + \dots + C_m} + (1-H)\ V$$

where

- H is used for the speed factor reification $\mathbf{H}_Y(t)$
- C_j for the combination function weight reification $\mathbf{C}_{i,Y}(t)$

490   J. Treur

- $P_{i,j}$ for the combination function parameter reification $\mathbf{P}_{i,j,Y}(t)$
- W_i for the connection weight reification $\mathbf{W}_{X_i,Y}(t)$
- V_i for the state value $X_i(t)$ of base state X_i
- V for the state value $Y(t)$ of base state Y

This universal combination function is used in the following *universal computational (difference) equation* (leaving t out of most of the notation):

$Y(t + \Delta t) = Y(t) +$
$\quad [\mathbf{c} *_Y(\mathbf{H}_Y, \mathbf{C}_{1,Y}, \ldots, \mathbf{C}_{m,Y}, \mathbf{P}_{1,1,Y}, \mathbf{P}_{2,1,Y}, \ldots, \mathbf{P}_{1,m,Y}, \mathbf{P}_{2,m,Y}, \mathbf{W}_{X_1,Y}, \ldots, \mathbf{W}_{X_k,Y}, X_1, \ldots, X_k,$
$Y(t)) - Y(t)]\Delta t$
$\quad = Y(t) + \mathbf{H}_Y$

$[\dfrac{\mathbf{C}_{1,Y}\mathrm{bcf}_1(\mathbf{P}_{1,1,Y}, \mathbf{P}_{2,1,Y}, \mathbf{W}_{X_1,Y}X_1, .., \mathbf{W}_{X_k,Y}X_k) + \ldots.. + \mathbf{C}_{m,Y}\mathrm{bcf}_m(\mathbf{P}_{1,m,Y}, \mathbf{P}_{2,m,Y}, , \mathbf{W}_{X_1,Y}X_1, .., \mathbf{W}_{X_k,Y}X_k)}{\mathbf{C}_{1,Y} + \ldots.. + \mathbf{C}_{m,Y}} - Y(t)]\Delta t$

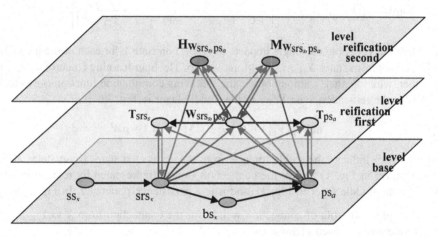

Fig. 1. Overview of an example reified network architecture addressing plasticity and metaplasticity for a cognitive agent model, with: (1) *base level* (lower plane, pink), (2) first reification level (middle plane, blue) for *plasticity* of the weight ω of the base connection from srs_s to ps_a and the excitability thresholds τ of these two base states (by the **W** state and the two **T** states), and (3) second reification level (upper plane, purple) for *metaplasticity* for the first-order adaptation speed η and the persistence μ (by the **H** state and **M** state). The upward causal connections (blue) and downward causal connections (red) define the interlevel relations. For more explanation of this example network, see [13]. (Color figure online)

In these formulas, by its place in the formula, each role indeed contributes a different type of effect according to its intended semantics. In Sect. 3 it is shown how in a network model design, the roles of these reification states are specified by *role matrices* **mb** (base connection role), **mcw** (connection weight role), **ms** (speed factor role), **mcfw** (combination function weight role), and **mcfp** (combination function parameter role).

Note that in a reified network the specific names of the reification states are computationally irrelevant: in this network modeling style the connections and their roles define meaning and processing, not the state names. This may be considered in contrast to reification in logic-based languages like (meta)Prolog [2, 7] where usually syntactical structures of names are processed.

3   Specification Format for a Reified Temporal-Causal Network

In role matrices it is specified which other states have impact on a given state (the incoming arrows in Fig. 1), but distinguished according to their role: *base* or *non-base* connections, from which for the latter a distinction is made for the roles *connection weight, speed factor, combination function weight* and *combination function parameter reification* (see also Fig. 1). Role matrices enable to apply structure-preserving implementation. The matrices all have rows according to the numbered states X_1, X_2, X_3, ...

For a given application a limited sequence of combination functions is specified by **mcf** = [....], for the example **mcf** = [1 2 3], where the numbers 1, 2, 3 refer to the numbering in the function library which currently contains 35 combination functions, the first three being $\mathbf{eucl}_{n,\lambda}(\ldots)$, $\mathbf{alogistic}_{\sigma,\tau}(\ldots)$, $\mathbf{hebb}_{\mu}(\ldots)$. In Box 1 the role matrices **mcfw** and **mcfp** (3D matrix) are shown. The first role matrix **mb** for *base connectivity* specifies on each row for a given state from which states at the same or a lower level it has incoming connections; see Box 1. For example, in the third row it is indicated that state X_3 (= bs_s) only has one incoming base connection, from state X_2 (= srs_s). As another example, the fifth row indicates that state X_5 (= W_{srs_s,ps_a}) has incoming base connections from X_2 (= srs_s), X_4 (= ps_a) and from X_5 itself, and in that order, which is important as the Hebbian combination function $\mathbf{hebb}_{\mu}(\ldots)$ used here is not symmetric.

In a similar way the four types of role matrices for *non-base connectivity* (i.e., connectivity from reification states at a higher level of reification: the downward arrows in Fig. 1), were defined: role matrices **mcw** for connection weights and **ms** for speed factors, and role matrices **mcfw** for combination function weights and **mcfp** for combination function parameters (see Box 1).

Within each role matrix a difference is made between cell entries indicating (in red) a reference to the name of another state that as a form of reification represents in a dynamic manner an adaptive characteristic, and entries indicating (in green) fixed values for nonadaptive characteristics. Indeed, in Box 1 it can be seen that the red cells of the non-base role matrices are filled with the (reification) states X_5 to X_9 of the first and second reification levels. For example, in Box 1 the name X_5 in the red cell row-column (4, 1) in role matrix **mcw** indicates that the value of the connection weight from srs_s to ps_a (as indicated in role matrix **mb**) can be found as value of the fifth state X_5. In contrast, the 1 in green cell (5, 1) of **mcw** indicates the static value of the connection weight from X_2 (= srs_s) to X_5 (= W_{srs_s,ps_a}). Similarly, role matrix **ms** indicates (in red) that X_8 represents the adaptive speed factor of X_5, and (in green) that the speed factors of all other states have fixed values. For more explanation about this role matrix specification format and the above example, see [12, 13] or the forthcoming book [14].

mb	base connectivity	1	2	3	4
X_1	ss_s	X_1			
X_2	srs_s	X_1			
X_3	bs_s	X_2			
X_4	ps_a	X_2	X_3		
X_5	$\mathbf{W}srs_s,ps_a$	X_2	X_4	X_5	
X_6	$\mathbf{T}srs_s$	X_2	X_4	X_6	
X_7	$\mathbf{T}ps_a$	X_2	X_4	X_7	
X_8	$\mathbf{HW}srs_s,ps_a$	X_2	X_4	X_5	X_8
X_9	$\mathbf{MW}srs_s,ps_a$	X_2	X_4	X_5	X_9

mcw	connection weights	1	2	3	4
X_1	ss_s	1			
X_2	srs_s	1			
X_3	bs_s	1			
X_4	ps_a	X_5	1		
X_5	$\mathbf{W}srs_s,ps_a$	1	1	1	
X_6	$\mathbf{T}srs_s$	-0.4	-0.4	1	
X_7	$\mathbf{T}ps_a$	-0.4	-0.4	1	
X_8	$\mathbf{HW}srs_s,ps_a$	1	1	-0.4	1
X_9	$\mathbf{MW}srs_s,ps_a$	1	1	1	1

mcfw	combination function weights	1 eucl	2 alogistic	3 hebb
X_1	ss_s	1		
X_2	srs_s		1	
X_3	bs_s		1	
X_4	ps_a		1	
X_5	$\mathbf{W}srs_s,ps_a$			1
X_6	$\mathbf{T}srs_s$		1	
X_7	$\mathbf{T}ps_a$		1	
X_8	$\mathbf{HW}srs_s,ps_a$		1	
X_9	$\mathbf{MW}srs_s,ps_a$		1	

ms	speed factors	1
X_1	ss_s	0.5
X_2	srs_s	0.5
X_3	bs_s	0.2
X_4	ps_a	0.5
X_5	$\mathbf{W}srs_s,ps_a$	X_8
X_6	$\mathbf{T}srs_s$	0.3
X_7	$\mathbf{T}ps_a$	0.3
X_8	$\mathbf{HW}srs_s,ps_a$	0.5
X_9	$\mathbf{MW}srs_s,ps_a$	0.1

mcfp	function	1 eucl		2 alogistic		3 hebb	
	parameter	1 n	2 λ	1 σ	2 τ	1 μ	2
X_1	ss_s	1	1				
X_2	srs_s			5	X_6		
X_3	bs_s			5	0.2		
X_4	ps_a			5	X_7		
X_5	$\mathbf{W}srs_s,ps_a$					X_9	
X_6	$\mathbf{T}srs_s$			5	0.7		
X_7	$\mathbf{T}ps_a$			5	0.7		
X_8	$\mathbf{HW}srs_s,ps_a$			5	1		
X_9	$\mathbf{MW}srs_s,ps_a$			5	1		

Box 1. Specification in role matrices format for the example reified network for plasticity and metaplasticity

4 The Computational Reified Network Engine

The computational reified network engine developed takes a specification in the format as described in Sect. 3 and runs it. First each role matrix (which can be specified easily as table in Word or in Excel) is copied to Matlab in two variants: a *values matrix* for the static values (adding the letter **v** to the name) in the green cells, and an *adaptivity matrix* for the adaptive values represented by reification states (adding the letter **a** to the name) in the red cells. For example, from **mcw** two matrices **mcwa** (adaptivity matrix) and **mcwv** (values matrix) are derived in this way. The numbers in **mcwa** indicate the state numbers of the reification states where the values can be found, and in **mcwv** the numbers indicate the static values directly. States X_j are represented in Matlab by their index number j. Empty cells are filled with NaN (Not a Number) indications. During a simulation, for each step from k to $k + 1$ (with step size Δt, in Matlab dt) based on the above role matrices first for each state X_j the right values (either the fixed value, or the adaptive value) are assigned to:

`s(j, k)`	speed of X_j
`b(j, p, k)`	value for the pth state connected to state X_j
`cw(j, p, k)`	connection weight for the pth state connected to state X_j
`cfw(j, m, k)`	weight for the mth combination function for X_j
`cfp(j, p, m, k)`	the pth parameter value of the mth combination function for X_j

Then, as a second part of the computational reified network engine, for the step from k to $k + 1$ the following is applied; here X(j,k) denotes $X_j(t)$ for t = t(k) = kdt:

```
for m=1:1:nocf
cfv(j,m,k) = bcf(mcf(m), squeeze(cfp(j, :, m, k)),
                 squeeze(cw(j, :, k)).*squeeze(b(j, :, k)));
end
    % This calculates the combination function values cfv(j,m,k) for
each combination function mcf(m) for state j at k
aggimpact(j, k) =
dot(cfw(j, :, k), cfv(j, :, k))/sum(cfw(j, :, k));
    % The aggregated impact for state j at k as inproduct of com-
bination function weights and combination function values, scaled
by the sum of these weights
X(j,k+1) =
X(j,k) + s(j,k)*(aggimpact(j,k) - X(j,k))*dt;
    % The iteration step from k to k+1 for state j
t(k+1) = t(k)+dt;
    % Keeping track of time
```

Note that functions with multiple groups of arguments here in Matlab get vector arguments where groups of arguments become vectors of variable length. For example, the basic combination function $bcf_i(P_{1,i}, P_{2,i}, W_1V_1, \ldots, W_kV_k)$ as expressed in Sect. 3 becomes bcf(i, p, v) in Matlab with vectors p = $[P_{1,i}, P_{2,i}]$ for function parameters and v = $[W_1V_1, \ldots, W_kV_k]$ for the values of the function arguments. This format bcf(i, p, v) is used as the basis of the combination function library developed (currently numbered by i = 1 to 35). As can be seen, the structure of the code of this computational reified network engine is quite compact, based on the universal difference equation discussed in Sect. 3: structure-preserving implementation. The combination function library used contains 35 functions at the time of writing. To obtain a general format easily usable within the simulations these functions were numbered and rewritten in the standard *basic combination function* form bcf(i, **p**, **v**) where i is the number of the function, **p** is its vector of parameters an **v** is a vector of values. A more detailed description of the software and a complete specification of the current combination function library can be found at [12].

5 Discussion

In this paper a modeling environment for reified temporal-causal networks was introduced, and applied to model a cognitive agent with plasticity and metaplasticity known from neuroscientific literature; e.g., [1, 6]. The environment includes a new specification format for reified networks and comes with a newly implemented dedicated computational reified network engine, which can simply run such specifications. Moreover, a library of currently 35 combination functions is offered, which can be used; this library can also be extended easily. Using this software environment, the development process of a model can focus in a declarative manner on the reified network specification and therefore is quite efficient, while still all kinds of complex (higher order) adaptive dynamics are covered without being bothered by implementation details. In a forthcoming book [14], more details and many more examples for this modeling approach will be presented.

Application may extend well beyond the neuro-inspired cognitive agents area, as also in Social Science cases are reported where network adaptation is itself adaptive; for example in [3] the second-order adaptation concept called 'inhibiting adaptation' for network organisations is described. For further work, it would be interesting to explore the applicability of the introduced modeling environment for such social agent domains as well.

References

1. Abraham, W.C., Bear, M.F.: Metaplasticity: the plasticity of synaptic plasticity. Trends Neurosci. **19**(4), 126–130 (1996)
2. Bowen, K.A., Kowalski, R.: Amalgamating language and meta-language in logic programming. In: Clark, K., Tarnlund, S. (eds.) Logic Programming, pp. 153–172. Academic Press, New York (1982)
3. Carley, K.M.: Inhibiting adaptation. In: Proceedings of the 2002 Command and Control Research and Technology Symposium, pp. 1–10. Naval Postgraduate School, Monterey, CA (2002)
4. Galton, A.: Operators vs. arguments: the ins and outs of reification. Synthese **150**, 415–441 (2006). https://doi.org/10.1007/s11229-005-5516-7
5. Hebb, D.O.: The organization of behavior: A neuropsychological theory. Wiley, New York (1949)
6. Magerl, W., Hansen, N., Treede, R.D., Klein, T.: The human pain system exhibits higher-order plasticity (metaplasticity). Neurobiol. Learn. Mem. **154**, 112–120 (2018)
7. Sterling, L., Beer, R.: Metainterpreters for expert system construction. J. Logic Program. **6**, 163–178 (1989)

8. Treur, J.: Network-Oriented Modeling: Addressing Complexity of Cognitive, Affective and Social Interactions. UCS. Springer, Cham (2016). https://doi.org/10.1007/978-3-319-45213-5

9. Treur, J.: Network reification as a unified approach to represent network adaptation principles within a network. In: Fagan, D., Martín-Vide, C., O'Neill, M., Vega-Rodríguez, M.A. (eds.) TPNC 2018. LNCS, vol. 11324, pp. 344–358. Springer, Cham (2018). https://doi.org/10.1007/978-3-030-04070-3_27

10. Treur, J.: Multilevel network reification: representing higher order adaptivity in a network. In: Aiello, L.M., Cherifi, C., Cherifi, H., Lambiotte, R., Lió, P., Rocha, Luis M. (eds.) COMPLEX NETWORKS 2018. SCI, vol. 812, pp. 635–651. Springer, Cham (2019). https://doi.org/10.1007/978-3-030-05411-3_51

11. Treur, J.: The ins and outs of network-oriented modeling: from biological networks and mental networks to social networks and beyond. In: Nguyen, N.T., Kowalczyk, R., Hernes, M. (eds.) Transactions on Computational Collective Intelligence XXXII. LNCS, vol. 11370, pp. 120–139. Springer, Heidelberg (2019). https://doi.org/10.1007/978-3-662-58611-2_2

12. Treur, J.: Design of a software architecture for multilevel reified temporal-causal networks (2019). https://www.researchgate.net/publication/333662169

13. Treur, J.: Network-oriented modeling of plasticity and metaplasticity (2019). https://www.researchgate.net/publication/335473145

14. Treur, J.: Network-Oriented Modeling for Adaptive Networks: Designing Higher-Order Adaptive Biological, Mental and Social Network Models. Studies in Systems, Decision and Control, vol. 251, pp. 314. Springer, Heidelberg (2020, to appear). https://doi.org/10.1007/978-3-030-31445-3, https://www.researchgate.net/publication/334576216

The Choice Between Bad and Worse: A Cognitive Agent Model for Desire Regulation Under Stress

Nimat Ullah[(⊠)][iD] and Jan Treur[iD]

Vrije Universiteit Amsterdam, Amsterdam, The Netherlands
nimatullah09@gmail.com, j.treur@vu.nl

Abstract. It is a proven fact in social sciences that desires for food intake can occur as a result of negative emotions. On the other hand, a negative emotion like anxiety also brings along psychological health issues. In such a situation it's quite a feasible option to get rid of the worse before the bad. In this paper, a cognitive agent model for food desire regulation is presented wherein Hebbian learning helps in breaking the bond between anxiety/stress and desire for food intake as a result. Simulation results of the model illustrate the food desire and its regulation.

Keywords: Desire regulation · Hebbian learning · Expressive suppression · Reappraisal · Cognitive agent model

1 Introduction

Emotional eating refers to the eating caused by some kind of emotions [1]. Emotions in general are considered the drivers for performing some action [2]. On the other hand, emotional eating, is referred to as interference between the optimal response to the environment and emotions [3]. It's not only overeating that is associated to emotions like anxiety and stress, less or no eating is also considered to be a possible consequence of such negative emotions [4]. Schachter and his colleagues termed decreased eating as a "natural response" to negative emotions. Contrary to a healthy individual, overeating has been associated to individuals with eating pathology, i.e. binge eating disorder [1], [5]. People turn to eating to escape from negative emotions [6] i.e. overeating is employed as a strategy to get rid of negative emotions. Overeating, as an emotion regulation (ER) strategy, has both pros and cons. Studies like [7] have found that binging improves mood. In contrast, there are various studies like [8] which are of the view that binging, despite improving mood, further deteriorates mood. Similarly, [9] is also of the view that increase in anxiety can lead to overeating which further worsens mood as a consequence.

This paper focuses on exploring how emotional eating takes place and how it can lead to an infinite loop between anxiety, eating and stress. A computational model for the difficult process of breaking the cycle of negative ER strategies is presented wherein Hebbian learning [10] plays a vital role in selection of a middle way. Section 2 of the paper presents a theoretical explanation and base for the model. Section 3

M. Baldoni et al. (Eds.): PRIMA 2019, LNAI 11873, pp. 496–504, 2019.
https://doi.org/10.1007/978-3-030-33792-6_34

presents the computational model, Sect. 4 presents a scenario and simulation experiments of the model for the scenario. Finally, Sect. 5 concludes the paper.

2 Background

Emotion leads us to different situations whereby the ER strategy employed for regulating those emotions has a profound effect on personality and health [11]. Its efficient regulation has positive [12] and dysregulation has wide range of negative [13] psychological health consequences.

Overeating is one such activity which can be used as a strategy to regulate negative emotions like anxiety and stress, for example, as the outcome of noneffective ER strategies [9]. In either case overeating is referred to as a maladaptive strategy [1], especially in the long run [14]. It is interesting to note that in case of normal individuals in terms of emotions, weight and restrained eating, the effect of negative emotions can be both increased and decreased eating [15]. Restrained eaters (i.e., dieters etc.) have more tendency to turn to eating in case of negative emotions [16] which further expose them to even more negative emotions like anxiety, stress and feelings of guilt after eating [8]. Similarly, other studies like [17] also support the notion that restrained eaters turn to overeating when they feel negative emotions but feeling of guilt, in case of restrained eaters, makes the eating rather less enjoyable and more like a guilt [18].

Digging the relation of eating and emotion deeper, studies like [3] conclude their experiment with the remarks that those asked to suppress their emotions ate more comfort food as compared to those who were asked to reappraise their emotions. Shedding more light on the problem, [3] state that the "emotions per se did not affect food intake, which indicates that applying the maladaptive ER strategy of suppression was responsible for higher (food) intake". Studies conducted on the eating behaviours of non-restrained healthy eaters [19] and eating behaviours of restrained eaters [20] also support the same relation of overeating and emotions as [3]. On the basis of the findings from studies conducted on the problem, it can be said that adaptive strategies like reappraisal not only decrease negative emotions, it can also prove helpful in preventing emotional eating [19], which usually leads to obesity and more stress, otherwise. Endorsing the findings of [3], [19] conclude that maladaptive strategies like suppression are responsible for overeating, while adaptive strategies like reappraisal can be used to prevent emotional eating.

3 The Cognitive Agent Model

The cognitive agent model presented below is based on literature and, with the help of Hebbian learning [21], leads to a (relatively) stable situation. It has been designed by Network-Oriented Modeling based on temporal-causal networks [22], see also [23].

In [22, 23] the interpretation of connections based on causality and dynamics forms a basis of the structure and semantics of the considered networks. Nodes in a network are interpreted here as states that vary over time, and connections are interpreted as causal relations that define how each state can affect other states over time. This type of network has been called a temporal-causal network; note that the word temporal here refers to the causality, not to the network, networks that themselves change over time are called adaptive networks. For a conceptual description of the model, see Fig. 1; for an explanation of the states, see Table 1.

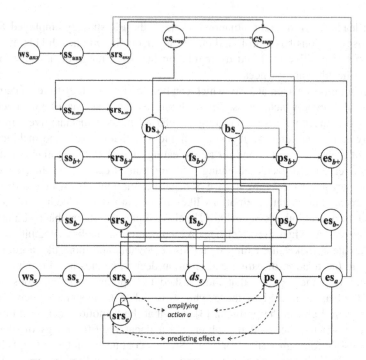

Fig. 1. Computational agent model as a temporal-causal network

The model in Fig. 1 can be best described by the scenario given in Sect. 4; the red lines represent negative connections. This model regulates food desires in both high and low intensity anxiety triggered by a scary event ws_{anx}. World state ws_s represents a constant stimulus, i.e., some food which is there. The belief state bs_+ represent a positive belief about food and bs_- represent a negative belief about food. If positive belief about food increases, a desire for food develops and the person goes for eating but if the negative belief about food increases, the person doesn't go for eating. Belief state bs_+ increases the desire for food intake with the help of a positive as-if-body loop and similarly bs_- for a negative body loop.

Furthermore, control states cs_{reapp} and cs_{supp} represent the control of reappraisal and suppression for regulation of food emotions, respectively. Reappraisal of food beliefs gets activated under conditions of relatively low intensity of anxiety and it makes the person avoid eating by cognitive change. The control state for suppression gets activated by a high intensity of anxiety and suppresses expression of food emotion. It does stop the person from eating for a while but finally, the person has to go for eating [24] as a rebound effect, which makes the person feel stressed. This cycle from feeling anxious to eating and to feeling stressed generally keeps repeating as shown in Fig. 3 if there's no learning involved in all this process. This cycle can be avoided where the person with some help of Hebbian learning [10], becomes an addictive eater to reduce anxiety at the cost of a moderate level of stress. The bad in the title refers to this moderate level of stress and worse refers to the high level of anxiety.

Table 1. Overview of the states and their explanation

Name	Description	Name	Description
ws_s	World state for stimulus s	srs_{b+}	Srs for positive body state b
ss_s	Sensing state for stimulus s	fs_{b+}	Feeling state for positive body state b
srs_s	Sensory representation state for the stimulus s	ps_{b+}	Preparation state for positive body state b
srs_e	srs for the predicted effect e (reward)	es_{b+}	Execution for positive body state b
ds_s	Desire state for stimulus s	bs_+	Positive belief about stimulus s
ps_a	Preparation state for physical action a in the real world	bs_-	Negative belief about stimulus s
es_a	Execution state for action a in the real world	$ss_{b.strs}$	Sensor state of body for stress $strs$
ss_{b-}	Sensor state for negative body state b	$srs_{b.strs}$	Srs of body for stress $strs$
srs_{b-}	srs for negative body state b	ws_{anx}	World state with trigger for anxiety anx
fs_{b-}	Feeling state for negative body state b	ss_{anx}	Sensor state for trigger for anxiety anx
ps_{b-}	Preparation state for negative body state b	srs_{anx}	Sensory representation state for anxiety anx
es_{b-}	Execution for negative body state b	cs_{reapp}	Control state for reappraisal
ss_{b+}	Sensor state for positive body state b	cs_{supp}	Control state for suppression

This kind of decision making and its predicted effect has been extensively summarized by [22], Chapter 6. The kind of valuation of the available courses of actions and the activation of the amygdala can be found in [25]. Similarly, a stimulus has an associated predicted effect to each of its associated responses [26] which either encourages or discourages a person to go or not go for a specific action. In the light of these findings, the connection from ps_a to srs_e to ps_a plays this role of valuing by predicting and then amplifying the preparation state ps_a.

4 Scenarios and Simulations Results

The cognitive agent model in Fig. 1 has been used to simulate the following scenario, which is based on the various findings from literature, and partly on [9].

> "Anna wants to lose her weight to look attractive, so she undergoes a dietary plan. Every time her coworker brings some pastries, her desire for food arises but she efficiently controls her food desires by reappraising her belief about food and putting her dietary goals in front of her. However, it becomes difficult for her when she has a particularly anxious week. She tries to suppress her desire for food but it proves maladaptive and she ends up in eating. After eating she feels stressed because she was on diet, she neither enjoyed the food nor complied with her dietary plans."

Figures 2, 3 and 4 show only the most representative states for the purpose of clarity.

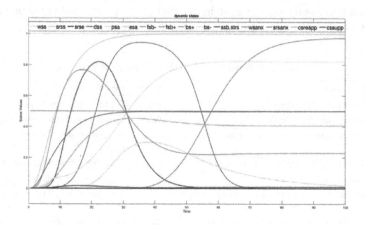

Fig. 2. Reappraisal to handle negative emotions

Figure 2 explains reappraisal being employed for down-regulating the positive belief about food while on diet. In this figure, it can be seen that the desire for food (ds_s) increases as the belief state bs_+ increases. Initially, the state bs- about food is quite low which means that the person may go for eating but when the control state cs_{reapp} for reappraisal gets activated, it changes the person's belief about food. First, the bs_+ decreases, as a result of which, ds_s also decreases. bs_+ and bs_ are inversely related to each other, and increase of bs_ means that negative belief about food has increased and the person will not go for eating. For low intensity of emotion, reappraisal is quite an adaptive strategy, which requires less physiological activation and decreases undesired belief about the stimulus.

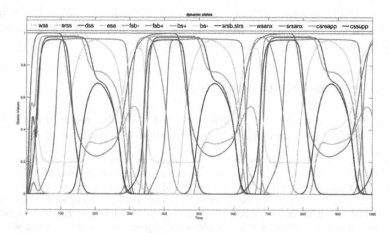

Fig. 3. Expressive suppression without Hebbian learning

Figure 3 gives insight of the second part of the scenario, where the person has particularly an anxious week. In this figure, it can be observed that initially when the intensity of food emotion is still low but increasing, reappraisal gets activated. It also, to some extent, increases bs. and decreases bs+ about food. Moving on, as the intensity of emotion increases, the control state cs_{supp} for suppression gets activated. This cs_{supp} just suppresses the expression of emotion which means the bs+ about food still remains high. Resultantly, the desire state ds_s also remains high. The increase of ds_s makes the person go for eating by activating es_a (execution of action). It decreases his anxiety, but, as per literature, restrained eaters feel more stressed and guiltier after eating. So, here as well, stress state $srs_{b.strs}$ gets activated. This cycle of suppression, eating and stress will go on if the person has no flexibility in ER strategies and employ an alternative but adaptive strategy.

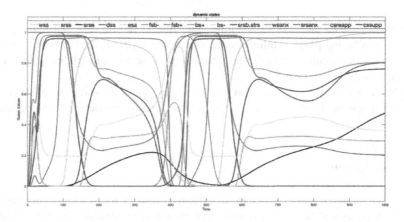

Fig. 4. Expressive suppression with Hebbian learning

Figure 4 shows how some people become habitual overeater because of negative emotions like anxiety and stress. It can be seen that as es_a (eating) takes place, srs_{anx} decreases and the $srs_{b.strs}$ increases but at the same time reward state srs_e also gets activated. Eating proves a kind of reward against anxiety. In the next moment, the person tries and somehow recovers from eating because of feeling stressed due to eating. But as the anxiety again increases so the person again goes for eating. This time the reward state srs_e, on the basis of his previous learned experience, goes much higher which makes the person fully get involved in eating. This makes the anxiety go down but stress remains high as shown in literature in case of constrained eaters. Although breaking the cycle of anxiety, suppression of food emotions and stress in this case the person becomes a habitual eater in case of external anxiety triggers, which is one of the main reasons of obesity.

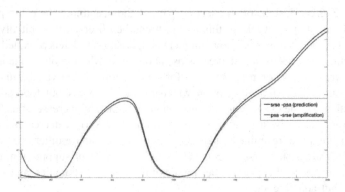

Fig. 5. Hebbian learning while using expressive suppression

Figure 5 shows the Hebbian learning over time. It can be seen that initially when the eating is taking place, a little amount of learning takes place. The next time when the person turns to eating he never turns back because he has learned that he feels better (comparatively) when he eats.

The various tables of connection weight values and other values to reproduce the above simulation results are available at https://www.researchgate.net/publication/335473229.

5 Conclusion

The cognitive agent model gives an in-depth overview of the working mechanism of two most compared and comparatively experimented regulation strategies. Using in any situation regulation strategies that are in the end not effective, in general has negative consequences which can make the situation worse. In the case of desire for food, especially in case of a restrained eater, it leads to an almost unbreakable cycle of emotion and overeating which ultimately leads to obesity that itself is an unacceptable psychological and physical state of health for many.

The simulations were performed using the dedicated software environment for temporal-causal network models described in [27]. Simulation results make it very clear that sometimes it's not the emotion but the strategy that is responsible for a certain state of mind. The results also demonstrate the role of reward as a result of Hebbian learning. The learning (over time) and the reward, helps the person in choosing (relatively) stable situation in comparison to continuous anxiety, eating and stressful episodes. At the same time the reported results also highlight the importance of a broader repertoire of strategies so that the learning can help in better decision making on the choice of emotion regulation strategies.

References

1. Wiser, S., Telch, C.F.: Dialectical behavior therapy for binge-eating disorder. J. Clin. Psychol. **55**(6), 755–768 (1999)
2. Ekman, P.: An argument for basic emotions. Cogn. Emot. **6**(3–4), 169–200 (1992)
3. De Ridder, D., Evers, C.: Stressed spelled backward is desserts: affective determinants of eating behavior. In: Williams, D.M., Rhodes, R.E., Conner, M.T. (eds.) Affective Determinants of Health Behavior. Oxford University Press, Oxford (2018)
4. Schachter, S., Goldman, R., Gordon, A.: Effects of fear, food deprivation, and obesity on eating. J. Pers. Soc. Psychol. **10**(2), 91–97 (1968)
5. Herman, C.P., Polivy, J.: Restraint and excess in dieters and bulimics. In: Pirke, K.M., Ploog, D., Vandereycken, W. (eds.) The Psychobiology of Bulimia Nervosa, pp. 33–41. Springer, Heidelberg (1988). https://doi.org/10.1007/978-3-642-73267-6_5
6. Heatherton, T.F., Baumeister, R.F.: Binge eating as escape from self-awareness. Psychol. Bull. **110**(1), 86–108 (1991)
7. Deaver, C.M., Miltenberger, R.G., Smyth, J., Meidinger, A., Crosby, R.: An evaluation of affect and binge eating. Behav. Modif. **27**(4), 578–599 (2003)
8. Macht, M., Dettmer, D.: Everyday mood and emotions after eating a chocolate bar or an apple. Appetite **46**(3), 332–336 (2006)
9. Aldao, A., Sheppes, G., Gross, J.J.: Emotion regulation flexibility. Cognit. Ther. Res. **39**(3), 263–278 (2015). https://doi.org/10.1007/s10608-014-9662-4
10. Hebb, D.O.: The organization of behavior: a neuropsychological theory. Wiley, Oxford (1949)
11. Suri, G., Sheppes, G., Young, G., Abraham, D., McRae, K., Gross, J.J.: Emotion regulation choice: the role of environmental affordances. Cogn. Emot. **32**(5), 963–971 (2018)
12. Koole, S.L.: The psychology of emotion regulation: an integrative review. Cogn. Emot. **23**(1), 4–41 (2009)
13. Gross, J.J.: Handbook of Emotion Regulation. Guilford Publications, New York (2013)
14. Evers, C., Marijn Stok, F., De Ridder, D.T.D.: Feeding your feelings: emotion regulation strategies and emotional eating. Pers. Soc. Psychol. Bull. **36**(6), 792–804 (2010)
15. Macht, M.: How emotions affect eating: a five-way model. Appetite **50**(1), 1–11 (2008)
16. Boon, B., Stroebe, W., Schut, H., Jansen, A.: Food for thought: Cognitive regulation of food intake. Br. J. Health Psychol. **3**, 27–40 (1998)
17. Yeomans, M.R., Coughlan, E.: Mood-induced eating. Interactive effects of restraint and tendency to overeat. Appetite **52**(2), 290–298 (2009)
18. Lindeman, M., Stark, K.: Loss of pleasure, ideological food choice reasons and eating pathology. Appetite **35**(3), 263–268 (2000)
19. Taut, D., Renner, B., Baban, A.: Reappraise the situation but express your emotions: impact of emotion regulation strategies on ad libitum food intake. Front. Psychol. **3**, 359 (2012)
20. Svaldi, J., Tuschen-Caffier, B., Lackner, H.K., Zimmermann, S., Naumann, E.: The effects of emotion regulation on the desire to overeat in restrained eaters. Appetite **59**(2), 256–263 (2012)
21. Abro, A.H., Treur, J.: A cognitive agent model for desire regulation applied to food desires. In: Criado Pacheco, N., Carrascosa, C., Osman, N., Julián Inglada, V. (eds.) EUMAS/AT-2016. LNCS (LNAI), vol. 10207, pp. 251–260. Springer, Cham (2017). https://doi.org/10.1007/978-3-319-59294-7_20
22. Treur, Jan: Network-Oriented Modeling: Addressing Complexity of Cognitive, Affective and Social Interactions. UCS. Springer, Cham (2016). https://doi.org/10.1007/978-3-319-45213-5

23. Treur, J.: The ins and outs of network-oriented modeling: from biological networks and mental networks to social networks and beyond. Trans. Comput. Collective Intell. **32**, 120–139 (2019). https://doi.org/10.1007/978-3-662-58611-2_2

24. Soetens, B., Braet, C.: 'The weight of a thought': food-related thought suppression in obese and normal-weight youngsters. Appetite **46**(3), 309–317 (2006)

25. Morrison, S.E., Salzman, C.D.: Re-valuing the amygdala. Curr. Opin. Neurobiol. **20**(2), 221–230 (2010)

26. Bechara, A., Damasio, H., Damasio, A.R.: Role of the amygdala in decision-making. Ann. N. Y. Acad. Sci. **985**, 356–369 (2003)

27. Mohammadi Ziabari, S.S., Treur, J.: A modeling environment for dynamic and adaptive network models implemented in Matlab. In: Proceedings of the Fourth International Congress on Information and Communication Technology, ICICT 2019. Advances in Intelligent Systems and Computing. Springer, London (2019)

Modeling Higher-Order Adaptive Evolutionary Processes by Multilevel Adaptive Agent Models

Jan Treur[(⊠)]

Social AI Group, Vrije Universiteit Amsterdam, Amsterdam, The Netherlands
j.treur@vu.nl
https://www.researchgate.net/profile/Jan_Treur

Abstract. In this paper a fourth-order adaptive agent model based on a multilevel reified network model is introduced to describe different orders of adaptivity of the agent's biological embodiment, as found in a case study on evolutionary processes. The adaptive agent model describes how the causal pathways for newly developed features affect the causal pathways of already existing features. This makes these new features one order of adaptivity higher than the existing ones. A network reification approach is shown to be an adequate means to model this.

1 Introduction

In the literature many examples can be found of first-order adaptive agent models, in different (e.g., cognitive, mental, social) domains. The current paper focuses on a case study of an adaptive agent model with biological embodiment to describe evolutionary processes, and the orders of adaptation that are recognized in them; e.g., [3, 4]. The case study addresses how the existence of pathogens has led to the adaptation of developing a defense system with an internal immune system and an external behavioural immune system [1]. Pregnancy led to the adaptation of temporary suppression of the internal defense system to give the (half-foreign) conceptus a chance to get embedded. Moreover, above that, as another adaptation, for the first trimester of pregnancy a strong feeling of disgust was developed to still strengthen the overall defense system by strengthening, in particular, the external component of it; see [1].

The case study is analysed in some depth and modeled by a fourth-order adaptive agent model making use of a multilevel reified network model. For this model different scenarios were simulated. In Sect. 2 the case study itself is briefly discussed. In Sect. 3 reified network models are briefly summarised. Section 4 introduces the fourth-order adaptive agent model, and Sect. 5 the simulations with it. An Appendix addresses mathematical analysis of the model's emerging behaviour and verification of the model based on that; see https://www.researchgate.net/publication/335473231.

© Springer Nature Switzerland AG 2019
M. Baldoni et al. (Eds.): PRIMA 2019, LNAI 11873, pp. 505–513, 2019.
https://doi.org/10.1007/978-3-030-33792-6_35

2 Higher-Order Adaptation in Evolutionary Processes

Viewed from a distance, an evolutionary process is an adaptation process that is changing the physical world by creating new causal pathways or blocking existing causal pathways. This can be described as changing the causal connections in such causal pathways from 0 or very low to high, or conversely. The adaptive aspect is exerted by the selection pressure, which makes that for given circumstances organisms with more favourable causal pathways for these circumstances become more dominant. Then they determine more the average causal pathways of the population: this leads to a shift in the average pathways by changes in the causal connections in these pathways. From [9] it is suggested that three levels of adaptation might be considered applicable for the first trimester of pregnancy. However, also the occurrence of pathogens can be considered a form of adaptation for the wider ecological context. Therefore, the following four adaptation orders can be distinguished:

First-Order Adaptation. Pathogens occur, with causal pathways negatively affecting the causal pathways for good health.

Second-Order Adaptation. An internal defense system occurs, with causal pathways which negatively affect the causal pathways used by pathogens.

Third-Order Adaptation. For pregnancy, causal pathways are added to make the defense system's causal pathways less strong as the half-foreign conceptus might easily be identified as a kind of parasite and attacked.

Fourth-Order Adaptation. Disgust during (first trimester) pregnancy adds causal pathways by which potential pathogens in the external world are avoided so that less risks are taken for entering of pathogens while the internal defense system is low functioning. This strengthens the overall defense system by strengthening the external defense system (the behavioural immune system) by which the pathogens are addressed outside the body. this makes the causal pathway from (first trimester) pregnancy to suppress the causal pathways of the overall defense system less strong as the external component of the defense system strengthened by disgust is not addressed by it.

So, can this be used as a basis for a fourth-order reified adaptive network model? This will be addressed in Sect. 4.

3 Reified Adaptive Temporal-Causal Network Models

The designed adaptive agent model to model these evolutionary processes makes use of a Network-Oriented Modeling approach. The Network-Oriented Modeling approach used is based on reified temporal-causal network models [7, 8]. A temporal-causal network model in the first place involves representing in a declarative manner states and connections between them that represent (causal) impacts of states on each other, as assumed to hold for the application domain addressed. The states are assumed to have (activation) levels, usually in the interval [0, 1], that vary over time. The following three main characteristics *connectivity*, *aggregation*, and *timing* of a network structure define a conceptual representation of a temporal-causal network model [6, 9]:

- **Connectivity** Each connection from a state X to a state Y has a connection weight value $\omega_{X,Y}$ representing the strength of the connection.
- **Aggregation** For each state a combination function $c_Y(..)$ is chosen to combine the causal impacts of other states on state Y.
- **Timing** For each state Y a speed factor η_Y is used to represent how fast state Y is changing upon causal impact.

The notion of *network reification* [7] is a means to model adaptive networks in a more transparent manner within a Network-Oriented Modelling perspective. This concept is used in different scientific areas in which it has been shown to provide substantial advantages in expressivity and transparency of models, and, in particular, within AI; e.g., [2, 5, 13]. Specific cases of reification from a linguistic or logical perspective are representing relations between objects by objects themselves, or representing more complex statements by objects or numbers.

For network models, reification can be applied by reifying network structure characteristics for connectivity, aggregation and timing (e.g., $\omega_{X,Y}$, $c_Y(..)$, η_Y indicated above) in the form of additional network states (called *reification states*, indicated by $W_{X,Y}$, C_Y, H_Y, respectively) within an extended network. According to the specific network structure characteristic represented, *roles* **W**, **C**, **H** are assigned to reification states: *connection weight reification, combination function reification, speed factor reification*, or values, respectively. Also a role **P** for *combination function parameters* is used. For more details, also see [10, 11], or the forthcoming book [12]. Multilevel reified networks can be used to model networks which are adaptive of different orders [8]. As discussed in Sect. 4 (see Box 1), a format based on *role matrices* **mb** (for base role), **mcw** (for connection weight role **W**), **mcfw** (for combination function weight role **C**), **mcfp** (for combination function parameter role **P**), and **ms** (for speed factor role **H**), is used to specify a reified network model according to these roles.

4 An Agent Model for Fourth-Order Adaptive Processes

Inspired by the information in Sect. 2 but abstracting from specific details, a fourth-order reified adaptive network for these evolutionary processes has been designed. As pointed out in Sect. 2, evolutionary adaptation usually concerns affecting existing causal pathways by adding new causal pathways that weaken or strengthen the existing causal pathways. This makes that levels of adaptation are created where the causal pathways at one adaptation level are adapted by the causal pathways at the next level. The adaptation of a causal pathway can be done by strengthening or weakening one or more causal connections within such a causal pathway. This fits well in a reified network architecture where for each level, for connection weights in causal pathways at that level, reification states are introduced at the next level. The general pattern then becomes in a simple form (for the main example, see Fig. 1):

Base level: causal pathway by a causal connection from a to b

First adaptation level: causal pathway by a causal connection from a_1 to $W_{a,b}$; this $W_{a,b}$ represents the causal connection from a to b from the base level

Second adaptation level: causal pathway by a causal connection from a_2 to $\mathbf{W}_{a_1}$, $\mathbf{W}_{a,b}$; this $\mathbf{W}_{a_1,\mathbf{W}_{a,b}}$ represents the causal connection from a_1 to $\mathbf{W}_{a,b}$ from the first adaptation level

Third adaptation level: causal pathway by a connection from a_3 to $\mathbf{W}_{a_2,\mathbf{W}_{a_1,\mathbf{W}_{a,b}}}$; this $\mathbf{W}_{a_2,\mathbf{W}_{a_1,\mathbf{W}_{a,b}}}$ represents the connection from a_2 to $\mathbf{W}_{a_1,\mathbf{W}_{a,b}}$ from the second adaptation level

Fourth adaptation level: causal pathway by a causal connection from a_4 to $\mathbf{W}_{a_3,\mathbf{W}_{a_2,\mathbf{W}_{a_1,\mathbf{W}_{a,b}}}}$; this $\mathbf{W}_{a_3,\mathbf{W}_{a_2,\mathbf{W}_{a_1,\mathbf{W}_{a,b}}}}$ represents the causal connection from a_3 to $\mathbf{W}_{a_2,\mathbf{W}_{a_1,\mathbf{W}_{a,b}}}$ from the third adaptation level

This general pattern for hierarchical adaptation processes for causal pathways will be used to obtain a more specific reified network model for the multilevel adaptation processes described in Sect. 2.

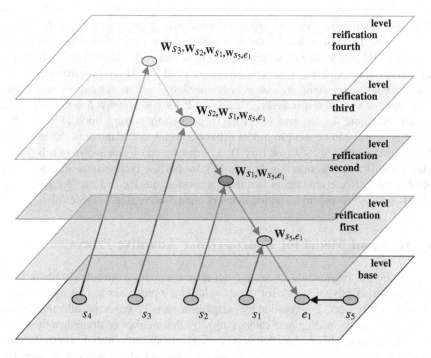

Fig. 1. Reified network model for fourth-order adaptation in an evolutionary context

In the considered reified network model four levels are considered, where for each level its causal pathway can be changed by causal pathways at one level higher. To limit the complexity of the overall model, the causal pathways at each level are kept simple, modeled by just one causal connection covering the whole pathway. Table 1 explains the states of the network model. Figure 1 shows a picture of the conceptual graphical representation of the reified network model. It includes four reification states at four levels which each reify the connection weight of the causal pathway one level lower:

- $\mathbf{W}_{s_5,e_1}$ first reification level state representing the causal connection from s_5 to e_1 from the base level
- $\mathbf{W}_{s_1,\mathbf{W}_{s_5,e_1}}$ second reification level state representing the causal connection from s_1 to $\mathbf{W}_{s_5,e_1}$ from the first reification level
- $\mathbf{W}_{s_2,\mathbf{W}_{s_1,\mathbf{W}_{s_5,e_1}}}$ third reification level state representing the causal connection from s_2 to $\mathbf{W}_{s_1,\mathbf{W}_{s_5,e_1}}$ from the second reification level
- $\mathbf{W}_{s_3,\mathbf{W}_{s_2,\mathbf{W}_{s_1,\mathbf{W}_{s_5,e_1}}}}$ fourth reification level state representing the causal connection from s_3 to $\mathbf{W}_{s_2,\mathbf{W}_{s_1,\mathbf{W}_{s_5,e_1}}}$ from the third reification level

Box 1 shows the role matrices **mb** (base connectivity), **mcw** (connection weights), **ms** (speed factors), **mcfw** (combination function weights), **mcfp** (combination function parameters). Each role matrix has a format in which in each row for the indicated state it is specified which other states (red cells) or values (green cells) affect it, and according to which role. In particular, in role matrix **mcw** the red cells indicate which states X_i play the role of the reification states for the weights of the connection indicated in that cell in **mb**.

Table 1. The states and their explanations

state		explanation	level
X_1	s_1	Occurrence of pathogens	
X_2	s_2	Occurrence of internal defense system	
X_3	s_3	Occurrence of pregnancy	Base
X_4	s_4	Occurrence of disgust	level
X_5	s_5	Contextual circumstances	
X_6	e_1	Health level, on a causal pathway with a connection from s_5 for context	
X_7	$\mathbf{W}_{s_5,e_1}$	Reification state for the weight of the base level connection from s_5 for context to $e1$ for health level, on a causal pathway with a connection from s_1 for pathogens	First reification level
X_8	$\mathbf{W}_{s_1,\mathbf{W}_{s_5,e_1}}$	Reification state for the weight of the first reification level connection from s_1 for pathogens to $\mathbf{W}_{s_5,e_1}$, on a causal pathway with a connection from s_2 for internal defense system	Second reification level
X_9	$\mathbf{W}_{s_2,\mathbf{W}_{s_1,\mathbf{W}_{s_5,e_1}}}$	Reification state for the weight of the second reification level connection from s_2 for internal defense system to $\mathbf{W}_{s_1,\mathbf{W}_{s_5,e_1}}$, on a causal pathway with a connection from s_3 for pregnancy	Third reification level
X_{10}	$\mathbf{W}_{s_3,\mathbf{W}_{s_2,\mathbf{W}_{s_1,\mathbf{W}_{s_5,e_1}}}}$	Reification state for the weight of the third reification level connection from s_3 for pregnancy to $\mathbf{W}_{s_2,\mathbf{W}_{s_1,\mathbf{W}_{s_5,e_1}}}$, on a causal pathway with a connection from s_4 for disgust	Fourth reification level

For the specific context described in Sect. 2, these elements are associated to the following:

- in environmental context s_5 a causal pathway from s_5 leads to a good health e_1
- pathogen state s_1 leads to disturbing the causal pathway to a good health effect (e_1)
- well functioning internal defense system (s_2) blocks the causal pathway for the effect of pathogens s_1 on the health pathway to e_1

- pregnancy in the first trimester s_3 needs less blocking of the effect of pathogens
- disgust s_4 is needed to compensate for the less blocking of foreign material

Box 1 Role matrices for the fourth-order adaptive network model

mb	base connectivity	1
X_1	s_1	X_1
X_2	s_2	X_2
X_3	s_3	X_3
X_4	s_4	X_4
X_5	s_5	X_5
X_6	e_1	X_5
X_7	$\mathbf{W}_{s_5,e_1}$	X_1
X_8	$\mathbf{W}_{s_1,W_{s_5,e_1}}$	X_2
X_9	$\mathbf{W}_{s_2,W_{s_1,W_{s_5,e_1}}}$	X_3
X_{10}	$\mathbf{W}_{s_3,W_{s_2,W_{s_1,W_{s_5,e_1}}}}$	X_4

mcw	connection weights	1
X_1	s_1	1
X_2	s_2	1
X_3	s_3	1
X_4	s_4	1
X_5	s_5	1
X_6	e_1	X_7
X_7	$\mathbf{W}_{s_5,e_1}$	X_8
X_8	$\mathbf{W}_{s_1,W_{s_5,e_1}}$	X_9
X_9	$\mathbf{W}_{s_2,W_{s_1,W_{s_5,e_1}}}$	X_{10}
X_{10}	$\mathbf{W}_{s_3,W_{s_2,W_{s_1,W_{s_5,e_1}}}}$	1

mcfw	combination function weights	1 alogistic	2 compid
X_1	s_1	1	
X_2	s_2	1	
X_3	s_3	1	
X_4	s_4	1	
X_5	s_5	1	
X_6	e_1	1	
X_7	$\mathbf{W}_{s_5,e_1}$		1
X_8	$\mathbf{W}_{s_1,W_{s_5,e_1}}$		1
X_9	$\mathbf{W}_{s_2,W_{s_1,W_{s_5,e_1}}}$		1
X_{10}	$\mathbf{W}_{s_3,W_{s_2,W_{s_1,W_{s_5,e_1}}}}$		1

mcfp combination function parameters		1 alogistic		2 compid	
	function	1	2	1	2
	parameter	σ	τ		
X_1	s_1	18	0.2		
X_2	s_2	18	0.2		
X_3	s_3	18	0.2		
X_4	s_4	18	0.2		
X_5	s_5	18	0.2		
X_6	e_1	8	0.5		
X_7	$\mathbf{W}_{s_5,e_1}$				
X_8	$\mathbf{W}_{s_1,W_{s_5,e_1}}$				
X_9	$\mathbf{W}_{s_2,W_{s_1,W_{s_5,e_1}}}$				
X_{10}	$\mathbf{W}_{s_3,W_{s_2,W_{s_1,W_{s_5,e_1}}}}$				

ms	speed factors	1
X_1	s_1	0.08
X_2	s_2	0.05
X_3	s_3	0.015
X_4	s_4	0.008
X_5	s_5	0.2
X_6	e_1	0.5
X_7	$\mathbf{W}_{s_5,e_1}$	0.05
X_8	$\mathbf{W}_{s_1,W_{s_5,e_1}}$	0.05
X_9	$\mathbf{W}_{s_2,W_{s_1,W_{s_5,e_1}}}$	0.004
X_{10}	$\mathbf{W}_{s_3,W_{s_2,W_{s_1,W_{s_5,e_1}}}}$	0.004

iv	initial values	1
X_1	s_1	0.2
X_2	s_2	0.1
X_3	s_3	0.11
X_4	s_4	0.1
X_5	s_5	0.5
X_6	e_1	0
X_7	$\mathbf{W}_{s_5,e_1}$	0.8
X_8	$\mathbf{W}_{s_1,W_{s_5,e_1}}$	0.8
X_9	$\mathbf{W}_{s_2,W_{s_1,W_{s_5,e_1}}}$	0.8
X_{10}	$\mathbf{W}_{s_3,W_{s_2,W_{s_1,W_{s_5,e_1}}}}$	0.8

5   Simulation Experiments

Simulations have been performed using the dedicated software environment for reified network models described in [10, 11] and in the forthcoming [12]. The scenario considered here focuses on a time period in which subsequently pathogens occur, a defense system against them is developed, pregnancy occurs, and disgust (in the first trimester of pregnancy) occurs. So, there are four orders of adaptation:

- Adaptation 1 Pathogens are introduced   first-order adaptation
- Adaptation 2 Defense system is developed   second-order adaptation
- Adaptation 3 Pregnancy   third-order adaptation
- Adaptation 4 Disgust   fourth-order adaptation

The red line in Fig. 2 indicates the health level. Before adaptation 1 health is good, after adaptation 1 health becomes bad, after adaptation 2 health becomes good again, after adaptation 3 health becomes worse again, and after adaptation 4 health becomes better again. The simulation results for this scenario are shown in Fig. 2.

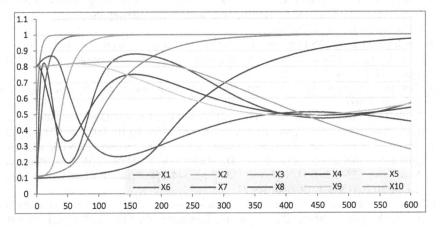

Fig. 2. Simulation with pathogens, internal defense system, pregnancy, and disgust occurring (Color figure online)

6   Discussion

In this paper a fourth-order adaptive agent model based on a multilevel reified network model was introduced to describe different orders of adaptivity found in a case study on evolutionary processes; e.g., [3, 4]. The adaptive agent model describes how the causal pathways for newly developed features in this case study affect the causal pathways of already existing features, which makes the pathways of these new features one order of adaptivity higher than the existing ones, as they adapt the previous adaptation. More details can be found at https://www.researchgate.net/publication/335473231. The network reification approach has shown to be an adequate means to model this in a transparent manner. In future research it can be explored how the adaptive agent model introduced here can be extended and whether this also works for other evolutionary case studies.

From a more general perspective, this paper illustrates how higher-order adaptive agent models can be designed making use of reified network models to specify their functionality and a dedicated Network-Oriented Modeling environment [10, 11]. In the current paper, the agent's embodiment was addressed from a biological perspective. Application for a similar approach to model higher-order adaptive mental and social processes for agents can be found in [8], and in the forthcoming book [12].

References

1. Aarøe, L., Petersen, M.B., Arceneaux, K.: The behavioral immune system shapes political intuitions: why and how individual differences in disgust sensitivity underlie opposition to immigration. Am. Polit. Sci. Rev. **111**(2), 277–294 (2017)
2. Galton, A.: Operators vs. arguments: the ins and outs of reification. Synthese **150**, 415–441 (2006). https://doi.org/10.1007/s11229-005-5516-7
3. Fessler, D.M.T., Clark, J.A., Clint, E.K.: Evolutionary psychology and evolutionary anthropology. In: Buss, D.M. (ed.) The Handbook of Evolutionary Psychology, pp. 1029–1046. Wiley, Hoboken (2015)
4. Fessler, D.M.T., Eng, S.J., Navarrete, C.D.: Elevated disgust sensitivity in the first trimester of pregnancy: evidence supporting the compensatory prophylaxis hypothesis. Evol. Hum. Behav. **26**(4), 344–351 (2005)
5. Sterling, L., Beer, R.: Metainterpreters for expert system construction. J. Logic Program. **6**, 163–178 (1989)
6. Treur, J.: Network-Oriented Modeling: Addressing Complexity of Cognitive, Affective and Social Interactions. UCS. Springer, Cham (2016). https://doi.org/10.1007/978-3-319-45213-5
7. Treur, J.: Network reification as a unified approach to represent network adaptation principles within a network. In: Fagan, D., Martín-Vide, C., O'Neill, M., Vega-Rodríguez, M.A. (eds.) TPNC 2018. LNCS, vol. 11324, pp. 344–358. Springer, Cham (2018). https://doi.org/10.1007/978-3-030-04070-3_27
8. Treur, J.: Multilevel network reification: representing higher order adaptivity in a network. In: Aiello, L.M., Cherifi, C., Cherifi, H., Lambiotte, R., Lió, P., Rocha, L.M. (eds.) COMPLEX NETWORKS 2018. SCI, vol. 812, pp. 635–651. Springer, Cham (2019). https://doi.org/10.1007/978-3-030-05411-3_51
9. Treur, J.: The ins and outs of network-oriented modeling: from biological networks and mental networks to social networks and beyond. In: Nguyen, N.T., Kowalczyk, R., Hernes, M. (eds.) Transactions on Computational Collective Intelligence XXXII. LNCS, vol. 11370, pp. 120–139. Springer, Heidelberg (2019). https://doi.org/10.1007/978-3-662-58611-2_2
10. Treur, J.: Design of a software architecture for multilevel reified temporal-causal networks (2019). https://www.researchgate.net/publication/333662169
11. Treur, J.: A modeling environment for reified temporal-causal networks modeling plasticity and metaplasticity in cognitive agent models. In: Proceedings of the 22nd International Conference on Principles and Practice of Multi-Agent Systems, PRIMA 2019. Lecture Notes in Artificial Intelligence. Springer, Heidelberg (2019)

12. Treur, J.: Network-Oriented Modeling for Adaptive Networks: Designing Higher-Order Adaptive Biological, Mental, and Social Network Models. Studies in Systems, Decision and Control, vol. 251, p. 314. Springer, Heidelberg (2020, to appear). https://doi.org/10.1007/978-3-030-31445-3, https://www.researchgate.net/publication/334576216
13. Weyhrauch, R.W.: Prolegomena to a theory of mechanized formal reasoning. Artif. Intell. **13**, 133–170 (1980)

Emergent Privacy Norms
for Collaborative Systems

Onuralp Ulusoy[(⊠)] and Pınar Yolum

Utrecht University, Utrecht, The Netherlands
{o.ulusoy,p.yolum}@uu.nl

Abstract. Managing privacy of users in online systems is a major aspect of cyber-security. Typical approaches to privacy are concerned with giving users options of informed consent, wherein users define their private data, how they want them to be used, and so on. However, in collaborative systems, such as online social networks, managing privacy exhibits problems beyond traditional consent, since a content being shared (such as a group picture or a multi-party business contract) might belong to more than a single entity, with different privacy policies. Recent approaches to preserve privacy in such settings rely on multiagent agreement technologies, which require a new decision to be formed for every content that will be shared, making them difficult to scale for real life applications. Accordingly, this paper proposes a normative approach for maintaining privacy in collaborative systems that do not require a decision to be formulated from scratch for each content. Instead, the system generates social norms based on previous decisions. The agents are free to follow the social norms as well as their own privacy policies. We show over multiagent simulations that our approach extracts social norms successfully and enables successful privacy decisions to be taken.

Keywords: Privacy · Multiagent systems · Norm emergence

1 Introduction

Collaborative systems, such as online social networks (OSNs), contain tremendous amount of content. These content, being shared by the OSN users, can be related to multiple people, as in the example of a group picture. However, these kind of content also might contain private information of people, either explicitly or implicitly. Hence, the decision of sharing or not sharing a content should be decided collaboratively by the users who are affected by it.

Collaborative privacy management mechanisms aim to resolve the conflicts in such cases. Finding a suitable resolution is usually a challenging task, since satisfying privacy protection constraints of some users might result in not sharing content that other users wanted to share, which is also undesirable by OSN providers since it would cause fewer content to be shared in the network. Multiagent agreement technologies, such as argumentation [6], negotiation [5,14] or

© Springer Nature Switzerland AG 2019
M. Baldoni et al. (Eds.): PRIMA 2019, LNAI 11873, pp. 514–522, 2019.
https://doi.org/10.1007/978-3-030-33792-6_36

auctions [13,17] have been successfully used for resolving privacy disputes. But, these approaches have two major drawbacks. First, they require each agent to actively participate in the decision making mechanism whenever a content is relevant to them. This is a large overhead for systems where a large set of content is shared regularly. For example, if nude pictures are never shared, it is redundant to deliberate on an incoming nude picture. Second, they ignore the relations and background knowledge available to the agents that are involved in the system as well as the values of the society that cannot be reflected with individual decisions of the agents. For example, a group of friends might share their Friday outing pictures regularly without a need to come to a mutual agreement on whether this is private or not every single time. To overcome the listed deficiencies, we propose to use normative multiagent systems where privacy decisions are taken based on the norms that are generated from the privacy decisions in the system. It is well known that human societies are guided and controlled by the norms [11]. Since privacy decisions over OSNs are correlated with the society behavior; extracting the norms from previous privacy actions could make them useful for future privacy decisions. If the norms are not applicable in a given situation (based on the content type or the individuals involved), the system still employs an existing collaborative privacy management mechanism to make a decision.

2   Privacy Norms

A typical collaborative system is online social networks, where users share content about themselves as well as others. A generic OSN consists of three main elements: users, a set of relations between the OSN users and content that is shared within the social networks of the users. Users can have privacy expectations that can vary based on the type of content as well as the other users to whom the content is exposed. For example, a user might not want her holiday pictures to be shown to colleagues, but might be fine with work pictures to be shown. In OSNs, it is common for a content to contain private information of users, either explicitly (e.g., geotagging or name tagging) or implicitly (e.g., finding about the location from the visible objects in the background, content's sharing time implying extra information about the co-owners and so on). When a single content contains private information of more than one user, conflicts might occur; some users wanting to share a content in the OSN while others want to share it with only a limited number of users, or even not share it at all. This requires a decision mechanism to be in place, so that for a new content the system can reach a *privacy decision* as to how it will be shared and with whom.

To reach privacy decision effectively and efficiently, we design a normative multiagent system, where privacy expectation of users for sharing content are being managed by software agents [6]. We represent a content with (i) a content type matrix which stores the contextual properties of the content, such as holiday, work, and so on and (ii) a set of co-owner agents whose privacy is possibly being affected by the content and thus should have a say about content's privacy decision. The system contains norms to capture the privacy preferences.

Informally, privacy norms capture the acceptable behaviour for sharing a particular type of content with a particular set of users. The acceptable behavior need not always be understood as the expected behavior of the majority. If a community is formed by privacy aware agents, an agent's request to not share a content might be complied by the others who initially wanted the content to be shared. If such an example occurs frequently, it can emerge as a norm and can be enforced to future decisions with the same context, where agents are not that privacy aware. In literature, privacy related access control mechanisms either enforces the strongest action (e.g., majority action) or rule based privacy decisions (e.g., deny overriding other actions). Minority protecting norms can aid a mechanism to differ from previous works in this sense, which could be beneficial for the goal of more satisfactory privacy decisions.

We adopt Tuomela's categorization of norms; where personal norms contain *m-norms* (i.e. moral norms) and *p-norms* (i.e. prudential norms), while social norms contain *r-norms* (i.e. rule norms) and *s-norms* (i.e. social norms) [16]. We formally represent them similar to existing formalisms [2,9], such that a set of preconditions determine the activation of a sharing action to be taken. Since our focus is more on the emergence of norms rather than their violation, we do not include norm sanctions explicitly. Thus, we employ *s-norms* as social norms, while *m-norms* contain all privacy requirements of individual agents.

s-norms are related to the common understanding of the society that apply to every individual. For example, in a given society, a norm of not sharing content that contains alcohol might emerge. *s-norms* are 3-tuple norms represented as $s<rType, cClass, act\{share,noShare\}>$, where $rType$ is the main relationship context between the co-owners for a content, $cClass$ is the specific class of the similar contents and act is the assigned action of the norm, which could be either sharing or not sharing the content. *s-norms* emerge depending on the previous collaborative decisions within the OSN. We employ $rType$ since *s-norms* are generated according to an overview of the societal decisions and $cClass$ because the norms pertain to the generic behavior of the society.

m-norms are based on individuals' own preferences (i.e., understanding of what is right to do). An agent might prefer not to share a content that it thinks is offensive to others. We represent *m-norms* as 3-tuple as well: $m<rType, cType, act\{share,noShare\}>$, where $rType$ is the main relationship type, $cType$ is the major content type, and act is the action to take when these conditions are satisfied.

3   Normative Privacy Decision

The agents' personal privacy expectations are represented as *m-norms* and stored in a personal *m-norm* base, which can only be changed or updated by the agent itself. *s-norm* base contains the social norms, which emerge based on the privacy decisions of the individual agents. There is a single *s-norm* base in the system. The normative decision mechanism process progresses with every incoming content. Initially, agents only have *m-norms*. *s-norms* emerge over time based on the actions of the agents. All types of norms have a lifecycle, where they are created, updated, or removed from the respective norm base. Our approach enables agents to make a privacy decision based on the norms in the system first and if that is not possible reverts to a collaborative decision mechanism.

When an agent wants to share a content, which is co-owned by other agents, the *uploader* agent checks if it is desirable for all the co-owners to share the content, considering the norms. This is done by considering the type of the content and the relationship with other co-owners. Since two types of norms are in effect, there can easily be conflicts among these norm-bases. For example, an agent's *m-norm* might permit sharing a content publicly, whereas the *s-norm* in the system might prescribe otherwise.

In this work, we assume *s-norms* dominate the *m-norms*, since we are interested in understanding the benefits of making privacy decisions using societal norms. Using this ordering, the uploader agent checks its *s-norm* base to see if a norm matching with the content type matrix exists. If so, it is applied without triggering the collaborative privacy decision mechanism within the system. It might be the case that none of the norms in the social norm base are applicable to make a decision. In that case, the decision mechanism is triggered and the final decision is made according to the collaborative privacy mechanism, which makes use of *m-norm* bases of all co-owner agents. In the latter case, the outcome of the mechanism also updates the *s-norm* base of the OSN, where new possible norms can be formed for future co-owned content.

It is crucial for norms to be identified and managed accurately. *m-norms* are private to each user and thus managed individually. The management of *s-norms* are more challenging because they emerge and die based on the users' interactions. *s-norms* reflect the privacy choices of the society as a whole and emerge based on the previous privacy decisions that are taken by the users on a given content type. For example, if in many occasions, the users that are colleagues do not share content about their holiday, this can emerge as an *s-norm* in the society. Since the OSN provider has access to all the privacy decisions in the system, the lifecycle of an *s-norm* can be managed by the OSN provider. Given the previous privacy decision, how can an OSN generate *s-norms*? To achieve this, we develop Algorithm 1. Algorithm 1 generates the norms from decisions using the intuition that we place all content over a multidimensional space according to their content type matrix dimensions and the relationship type of the co-owner agents. This space contains all the decisions considering its various properties as dimensions. Next, we cluster this space such that each cluster contains content that have similar attributes. Then, the clusters can be assigned as *s-norm* classes, and can be checked for normative behavior; i.e., qualified majority of the content in the same cluster result in the same type of sharing action. We call this type of clusters as *normative clusters*. To ensure that generated norms are still in effect, the algorithm is run periodically and the *s-norm* base is updated accordingly.

OSNs contain a tremendous amount of content; thus, continuously clustering the content space would require massive computing power. Since dimensions of *s-norms* are interrelated (e.g., content type matrix dimensions), neighbor clusters could have similar normative behavior and contextual properties. This enables us to relax the problem precision requirements, allowing us to not necessarily find the optimum solution for a few borderline decisions, but place them in one of the closest cluster. This approach also turns up beneficiary for our goal, since a borderline privacy decision between two clusters would mean that the decision is in a similar distance from both clusters and not strongly related with a single one. On the contrary with the privacy decisions in the center of the clusters, these kind of privacy decisions could belong to both of the clusters with weak ties. To achieve this, we employ *k-means* algorithm to cluster content and then check the clusters for normative behavior. k-means is a clustering method where n number of elements in a unidimensional or multidimensional space are partitioned into k clusters, where each element is assigned to the nearest mean of the elements in a cluster [15]. Note that the size of the clusters is important as they affect the number of clusters. Having few clusters with large amounts of content would result in not discovering normative behavior, while clustering with fewer number of content in each cluster would result in increased complexity. We address this by starting with a small number of clusters and increasing the number of clusters iteratively. The iteration for elements in a cluster ends when the threshold for minimum number of agents that a cluster can contain is reached, or a normative behavior is already found.

Algorithm 1: Generation of s-norms

    Input: mk, minimum number of clusters
    Input: t, threshold for min. number of agents in a cluster
    Input: $pDec$, previous privacy decisions within OSN
    Output: $cList$, a set of clusters generated from $pDec$

1 **while** *pDec **not** empty* **do**
2   tempcList = k-Means(mk,pDec)
3   **foreach** *cluster **in** tempcList* **do**
4   isNormative = checkNormative(cluster)
5   **if** *(isNormative = true **or** size(cluster) < t)* **then**
6   add(cluster,cList)
7   **foreach** *item **in** cluster* **do**
8   remove(item,pDec)

9   mk += 1
10 **return** $cList$

Algorithm 1 takes the minimum cluster count parameter (mk), the minimum size threshold parameter for a single cluster (t) and all the previous privacy mechanism based decisions $(pDec)$ as input. It then assigns all the items in $pDec$ to a cluster in the output cluster list $(cList)$. In each iteration, a temporary list of clusters are assigned with k-means algorithm, where all items in $pDec$ are clustered and the number of clusters are given as mk. In line 3, a for loop begins, which checks the temporary cluster assignments, and determines if the cluster shows a normative behavior, or the size of the cluster is below t value. If one of these conditions are satisfied for a temporary cluster, the cluster is added to *cList* in line 6 and all the items of the cluster are removed from *pDec*, ending an iteration. If there are still remaining items in *pDec*, another iteration starts to determine new clusters, until all items from the initial *pDec* are assigned to a cluster in *cList* output. When a new content comes, agents find the most similar cluster, according to its content type matrix and the relation between the co-owners. If this is a normative cluster, then agents can decide according to the related normative action.

4 Evaluation

Our main goal is to reduce the necessity of applying collaborative privacy management algorithms by identifying the emergent norms within OSNs. We study the emergence of norms through multiagent simulations in an environment we developed in Java. Each agent in the simulation represents a user. The users, and thus the agents are related to each other through one relationship. Each agent has a set of *m-norms* that are generated automatically. Each content in the OSN is related to a set of contexts with varying levels and is thus represented with a content type matrix. In real life, this information would come from the features or tags of the content. Here, we assume that the matrix, where major content type categories are predefined is given. For n number of content type categories, a content is placed in an n-dimensional space which enables the mechanism to both find out similar content types and match privacy requirements of agents with the content in consideration. Each content has a set of co-owners, which are the agents with private information represented in the content.

We include 100 agents and 10000 contents for each of our simulations, where each content is randomly assigned to 2 to 5 co-owners, and a 4 dimensional content type matrix, while each dimension has a value between 0 and 100, representing the significance of the content to the given type, 100 being the most. We represent each agent's privacy requirements with *m-norms*, while the simulation checks the evolution of *s-norms*. Each simulation follows the flow in Sect. 2. For simplicity, we employ majority voting as the collaborative privacy mechanism in our evaluations.

Societal normative behavior for privacy emerges when a set of agents have a similar idea of privacy; e.g., prefer to share similar content. If agents have totally different views about privacy, we do not expect norms to emerge. On the other hand, if all agents share the same idea of privacy, then there would be a few norms that could govern the entire population. We expect many populations to stand between these two cases. To account for this, we introduce a variable to capture the homogeneity of a given society. If the homogeneity of the society is 0%, then all the agents in the population can have different privacy choices. We ensure this by allowing them to randomly make a choice about sharing or not sharing

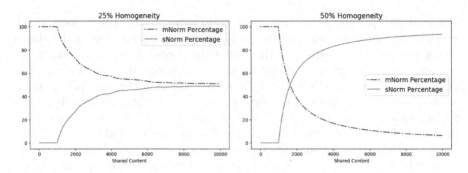

Fig. 1. Percentage of norm types over different levels of homogeneity.

a given content. We run the simulations with several levels of homogeneity. The simulation starts forming *s-norms* using Algorithm 1 after 1000th content shared in the OSN and reruns it after every 250 content for updating the *s-norm* base of the OSN. For each homogeneity level, we run 5 simulations and measure the percentage of our norm types over the number of content shared within the environment. This shows the necessary level of homogeneity for social norms to emerge.

Figure 1 plots the percentage of decisions that are taken by *m-norms* and *s-norms* as new content is introduced to the system for populations with two homogeneity levels. We omit other homogeneity levels for brevity as these two levels are sufficient enough to capture the trend. The plots show that if a quarter of the community shows homogeneous behavior, almost half of the decisions can be made according to social norms, reducing the need to use a decision mechanism to half. When half of the community behaves the same, only less than 10% of the decisions require a collaborative decision mechanism, and social norms can be decisive for more than 90% of privacy decisions.

5 Discussion

We have investigated how a normative approach can cope with privacy protection in a multiagent system that contains collaboration, cooperation and competition aspects for the agents at the same time. We apply our method thoroughly for the OSN domain, and evaluate it over multiagent simulations in terms of to what extent the privacy issues can be resolved with norms and their correctness in their resolutions.

Engineering privacy in ubiquitous information systems has become a research interest after millennium, mostly because internet becoming a part of a daily life with OSNs, smart devices etc. and causing massive amount of private information to be accessible by the others. Langheinrich [7] investigates the open issues for privacy-respecting approaches for ubiquitous computing. Spiekermann and Cranor [12] and Gurses [4] study the grounds of engineering privacy, explaining how information related domains can be designed and employ privacy-preserving methods. Paci *et al.* [10] provide an extensive survey for literature about access control over community centric collaborative systems; laying down the key issues and giving a roadmap for future challenges. Bahri *et al.* [3] show the challenges of preserving privacy over decentralized OSNs, and provides a review of previous work done for overcoming these challenges. These studies all show that privacy is an important aspect of information systems and should be tackled to prevent violations.

Sen and Airiau [11] pioneered the work of norm emergence, where they show that even when the population size and heterogeneity vary, social norms can emerge. Mashayekhi *et al.* [8] investigate norm emergence in traffic domain, where agents enter and leave and no known network structure among them exists. Ajmeri *et al.* [1] study norm emergence factoring in the context of the agents, taking in the sanctions into account. Our findings here show that for privacy norms to emerge, it is enough for the population to have a low level of homogeneity in how they perceive privacy.

An interesting direction is to study norm emergence when agents' privacy expectations can change over time as they learn new facts, face new norms or as their relationships change. Another direction is to enable agents to judge the social norms based on their own privacy values. We also aim to implement a mechanism of forgetting for norms, where social norms can fade over time. These would bring us closer to accommodating groups with different privacy norms to coexist in a society.

References

1. Ajmeri, N., Guo, H., Murukannaiah, P.K., Singh, M.P.: Robust norm emergence by revealing and reasoning about context: socially intelligent agents for enhancing privacy. In: Proceedings of the International Joint Conference on AI (IJCAI) (2018)
2. Alechina, N., Dastani, M., Logan, B.: Programming norm-aware agents. In: Proceedings of the 11th International Conference on Autonomous Agents and Multiagent Systems. AAMAS 2012, International Foundation for Autonomous Agents and Multiagent Systems, Richland, SC, vol. 2, pp. 1057–1064 (2012)
3. Bahri, L., Carminati, B., Ferrari, E.: Decentralized privacy preserving services for online social networks. Online Soc. Netw. Media **6**, 18–25 (2018)
4. Gurses, S., Troncoso, C., Diaz, C.: Engineering privacy by design. Comput. Priv. Data Prot. **14**(3), 25 (2011)
5. Kekulluoglu, D., Kokciyan, N., Yolum, P.: Preserving privacy as social responsibility in online social networks. ACM Trans. Internet Technol. **18**(4), 42:1–42:22 (2018)
6. Kökciyan, N., Yaglikci, N., Yolum, P.: An argumentation approach for resolving privacy disputes in online social networks. ACM Trans. Internet Technol. **17**(3), 27:1–27:22 (2017)
7. Langheinrich, M.: Privacy by design — principles of privacy-aware ubiquitous systems. In: Abowd, G.D., Brumitt, B., Shafer, S. (eds.) UbiComp 2001. LNCS, vol. 2201, pp. 273–291. Springer, Heidelberg (2001). https://doi.org/10.1007/3-540-45427-6_23

8. Mashayekhi, M., Du, H., List, G.F., Singh, M.P.: Silk: a simulation study of regulating open normative multiagent systems. In: Proceedings of the International Joint Conference on AI (IJCAI), pp. 373–379 (2016)
9. Morales, J., Lopez-Sanchez, M., Rodriguez-Aguilar, J.A., Wooldridge, M., Vasconcelos, W.: Automated synthesis of normative systems. In: Proceedings of the 2013 International Conference on Autonomous Agents and Multi-agent Systems. AAMAS 2013, International Foundation for Autonomous Agents and Multiagent Systems, Richland, SC, pp. 483–490 (2013)
10. Paci, F., Squicciarini, A., Zannone, N.: Survey on access control for community-centered collaborative systems. ACM Comput. Surv. **51**(1), 6:1–6:38 (2018)
11. Sen, S., Airiau, S.: Emergence of norms through social learning. In: Proceedings of the International Joint Conference on AI (IJCAI), vol. 1507, p. 1512 (2007)
12. Spiekermann, S., Cranor, L.F.: Engineering privacy. IEEE Trans. Softw. Eng. **35**(1), 67–82 (2009)
13. Squicciarini, A.C., Shehab, M., Paci, F.: Collective privacy management in social networks. In: Proceedings of the 18th International Conference on World Wide Web WWW 2009, pp. 521–530. ACM, New York (2009)
14. Such, J.M., Rovatsos, M.: Privacy policy negotiation in social media. ACM Trans. Auton. Adapt. Syst. **11**(1), 4:1–4:29 (2016)
15. Tan, P.N., Steinbach, M., Kumar, V.: Introduction to Data Mining, 1st edn. Addison-Wesley Longman Publishing Co., Inc., Boston (2005)
16. Tuomela, R.: The Importance of Us: A Philosophical Study of Basic Social Norms. Stanford University Press, Stanford (1995)
17. Ulusoy, O., Yolum, P.: Pano: privacy auctioning for online social networks. In: Proceedings of the 17th International Conference on Autonomous Agents and Multi-Agent Systems. AAMAS 2018, International Foundation for Autonomous Agents and Multiagent Systems, Richland, SC, pp. 2103–2105 (2018)

Estimating Missing Environmental Information by Contextual Data Cooperation

Davide Andrea Guastella[1,2]([✉]), Valérie Camps[1], and Marie-Pierre Gleizes[1]

[1] Institut de Recherche en Informatique de Toulouse, Université de
Toulouse III - Paul Sabatier, Toulouse, France
{davide.guastella,camps,gleizes}@irit.fr
[2] Università degli Studi di Palermo, Palermo, Italy

Abstract. The quality of life of users and energy consumption could be optimized by a complex network of sensors. Nevertheless, smart environments depend on their size, so it is expensive to provide enough sensors at low cost to monitor each part of the environment. We propose a cooperative multi-agent solution to estimate missing environmental information in smart environment when no *ad-hoc* sensors are available. We evaluated our proposal on a real dataset and compared the results to standard state-of-the-art solutions.

Keywords: Smart city · Cooperative multi-agent systems · Missing information estimation

1 Introduction

The concept of *Smart City* emerged in recent years as a way to exploit Information and Communication Technology (ICT) for improving services offered by a city and reducing its ecological footprint. Smart city initiatives are implemented by coupling *Ambient Intelligence* (AmI) and *Internet Of Things* (IoT). The idea behind AmI is to provide an environment with an interconnected network of coordinated IoT devices where the boundary between software and society blends and often disappears. As such, the environment is enriched with artificial intelligence to support humans in their everyday life [3,9]. The computational power of IoT devices coupled with widespread connectivity has increased significantly the development of initiatives to support smart cities. Such initiatives usually implement a monitoring activity of the environment in order to act on it in order to improve the energetic consumption, that is constantly increasing in the recent years [10], and ensure comfort to users. Nevertheless, the necessary devices can be intermittent, so they cannot guarantee continuous operability. In this case, it is necessary to provide accurate estimation of the values that ambient devices would provide if they were available. These estimations must be provided at real-time so that users can access to the information at any time [7]. In fact, a

M. Baldoni et al. (Eds.): PRIMA 2019, LNAI 11873, pp. 523–531, 2019.
https://doi.org/10.1007/978-3-030-33792-6_37

continuous monitoring of the environment can be useful when conceiving system to support smart city initiatives [6].

In this paper we propose a solution to estimate environmental information where ad hoc sensors are not available by using mobile and intermittent devices recurrent as well as historical data. Our proposal addresses the following challenges: (*i*) *intermittent data*: we exploit agents to provide accurate estimations when intermittent devices are used; (*ii*) *distributed processing*: each agent has its own local view of the environment, so that the estimation processes in different parts of the environment are independent and (*iii*) *online learning*: agents are capable of learning the dynamic of the environment at real-time without pre-processing data.

2   Proposition

To better understand the addressed problematic of estimating missing information in smart environments, let us consider a dataset of temperatures perceived by an *ad-hoc* device. If the device cannot provide information due to a malfunction at time i, the historical data perceived from the same device and other nearby devices can be correlated in order to provide an accurate estimation for the missing information. In this manner the system is able to evaluate an information that the device would provide if it worked.

Our proposal is based on a cooperative multi-agent system where each agent exploits data windows containing consecutive information in time, called *Ambient Context Windows* (ACW), in order to find recurrent dynamics in the historical data. ACWs are used to provide accurate estimations for missing information.

The rest of the section is organized as follow. In Sect. 2.1 we provide the definitions of the elements composing the proposed system, then in Sect. 2.2 we describe the general steps of our proposal.

2.1   Definitions

Definition 1 (Ambient Context Window). *An* Ambient Context Window *(ACW) C_i contains homogeneous environmental information perceived by an agent in a time window $T = [t_k, t_i]$, $k < i$. An ACW has $|C_i| = |T|$ homogeneous context entries, one for each time instant.*

Definition 2 (Context Entry). *A* Context Entry *$E_t^i \in \mathbb{R}$ is a punctual information perceived at time $t \in T$, where T is the time window of the ACW C_i. The value of a context entry can be any type of environmental information such as temperature, humidity, lightness etc.*

Definition 3 (ACW Distance). *The distance between two ACWs is defined as the absolute difference in time between the context entries divided by the number of entries γ of the two ACWs. The smaller the difference is, the more similar two ACWs are. The context distance between two ACWs C_i and C_k is defined by to the following formula:*

$$d\left(C_i, C_k\right) = \frac{\sum_{l \in [1,\gamma]} \left|E_l^i - E_l^k\right|}{\gamma}$$

where $\gamma = |C_i| = |C_k|$.

The distance d satisfies the following properties: (i) $d(C_i, C_k) \geq 0$, (ii) $d(C_i, C_k) = 0 \iff C_i = C_k$, (iii) $d(C_i, C_k) = d(C_k, C_i)$, (iv) $d(C_i, C_p) \leq d(C_i, C_k) + d(C_k, C_p)$ where C_i, C_k, C_p are ACWs for information times i, k, p respectively. Therefore d is a metric.

Definition 4 (Ambient Context Agent). *An Ambient Context Agent (ACA$_i$) identifies an ACW related to the information i in the dataset. Its goal is to provide environmental information. A cooperative behavior allows ACAs to provide environmental information even if a real device is unavailable.*

2.2   HybridIoT System Overview

In the proposed HybridIoT system, we suppose that data perceived by ambient devices are stored in a database and that the unavailability of a real device generates an exception as the ACAs is not able to provide an information. This exception is solved by exploiting the *Adaptive Multi-Agent System Approach* (AMAS) [5]. In this approach, an exception is considered as a *Non-Cooperative Situation* (NCS) that has to be solved in a local and cooperative way. In our problem, an incompetence NCS occurs when an ACA us unable to provide an environmental information (because no *ad hoc* sensor is available or it encountered a problem).

The main steps of the solution we propose are depicted in Fig. 1.

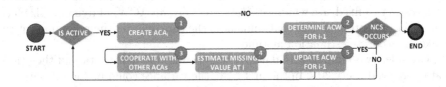

Fig. 1. The main steps of the proposed technique.

When data are available, ACAs are created on the fly and associated to the available information (step ①). Then the agent determines a context window that is representative of the information perceived (step ②). When data are not available due to the unavailability of the device or even a missing device, an exception we denote as *Non-Cooperative Situation* occurs; in this case the ACA cooperates with other agents (step ③) in order to provide an accurate estimation for the missing information (step ④). Once the information has been estimated, the ACW is being updated by the agent (step ⑤).

When the information at time i is not available, the ACA_i has to cooperate with other ACAs by comparing their ACWs in order to determine an accurate estimation. These ACAs are chosen according to the distance between their ACWs and the ACW related to the agent that encountered a NCS. In this way the estimation is evaluated using the ACWs that are the most similar to ACA_i. The set ξ contains the ACWs that minimize the distance from the ACW that contains an information to be estimated.

When the set ξ of ACAs has been evaluated, a weight w is computed by a cooperative process between the ACA_i (that encountered a NCS) and the other ACAs by using each related ACW $C_k \in \xi = \{C_n, ..., C_p\}$, $n < p < i$, for which the distance $d(C_i, C_k)$ is minimized. The weight w is computed as follow:

$$w = \frac{\sum_{C_j \in \xi} \left(E_k^j - E_{k-1}^j \right) \cdot d\left(C_i, C_j\right)}{\sum_{C_j \in \xi} d\left(C_i, C_k\right)}$$

where C_i is the ACW containing the information to be estimated at time i, $C_j \in \xi$, $|\xi| = 10$, is the j-th most similar context window to C_i for which the distance $d(C_i, C_j)$ is minimized and E_k^j and E_{k-1}^j are respectively the kth and $(k-1)^{th}$ context entries of the ACW $C_j \in \xi$ where $k = |C_j|$. Finally, let C_k be the ACW containing an information to be estimated; the estimated context entry E_i^k at time i is computed as follows:

$$E_i^k = E_{i-1}^k + w.$$

Once the information at time i has been estimated, the ACA_i evaluates a dynamic ACW, containing a number of information that is not specified *a priori* (step ⑤). The relevance of dynamic size context windows is motivated by the fact that their use allows to obtain accurate estimations for missing information with respect to fixed size windows. More precisely, an ACW_i of dynamic size has a number of context entries that influences the capability of the related agent to make an accurate estimation at time i.

Consider two temperature datasets, one containing daily data and the other data perceived every 30 s. In the first case, the variance could be high. Contrary, in the second case the difference between each sample is relatively low, so as the variance. In this case the ACW of an ACA_i contains many samples while still providing a good estimation of the value at time i.

For an information at time i our solution creates a set $\Lambda_i = \{C_{i,0}, C_{i,1}, ..., C_{i,\lambda-2}\}$ of ACWs, where $|C_{i,k}| = k + 2$. We have fixed $\lambda = 16$, thus Λ_i contains a maximum of 15 contextual windows. Each ACW in Λ_i has at least 2 entries, that is the minimum number of information that can be used in the estimation process. The process of evaluation of dynamic size ACWs gives as output a context window $C_{i,k} \in \Lambda_i$ that minimizes the variance between the information. We verified through experiments that using 15 context windows is sufficient in order to find an ACW that best represent the information to which it is related.

Estimating accurate values for missing information depends on the evaluation of appropriate ACWs of variable size that better describe the information with which they are associated. Moreover, the evaluation of dynamic size ACWs depends on the availability of data, whether they are estimated or real. For this reason, our proposal is divided into two interdependent and coupled subsystems.

3   Experimental Results

The proposed framework has been evaluated using a dataset of 196 real temperature samples from 80 weather stations located in the region of Emilia Romagna, Italy, provided by the ARPAE service [4]. Data from this dataset are acquired daily by weather stations.

To evaluate our method, we applied a k-fold cross validation, whose partitions the original sample in k subsamples. Among the k subsamples, a single subsample is retained as the validation data for testing the classifier, and the remaining $k-1$ subsamples are used as training data. During the training phase, agents assemble the contexts windows for each information. The test phase is then repeated k times, with each of the k subsamples used exactly once as the test data. The k results from the folds are then averaged to produce a single performance estimation [8]. In our experiments, we used a k value of 5, 10 and 15.

The proposed solution has been coded in Java and the experiments were carried out on a computer equipped with i7 − 7820HQ, 32 GB RAM and Windows 10. The estimation of a missing value is practically instantaneous and the evaluation of the solution using cross-validation requires about one second for each station.

The solution has been coded without considering any particular optimization technique. Since the proposed solution has been tested on a single machine, we did not consider any computational overhead of agents such as communication. Moreover, in our proposal the communication between agents is asynchronous and we consider the communication costs as unitary, thus irrelevant for the estimations of missing values. Also, we did not use any specific agent-based technology and our solution is based on a cooperative resolution process between agents, which is technology independent. This allows us to prove the effectiveness of the proposed estimation technique rather than focusing on a specific agent-based architecture to address the estimation problem.

Figure 2 shows the mean error and standard deviation for the regional dataset. The mean error among the considered stations is $-0.092°$, the mean standard deviation is $1.3043°$.

3.1   Comparison to Standard Solutions

We compared the obtained results to different state-of-the-art solutions by using the KNIME analytic platform, a modular environment which enables easy visual assembly and interactive execution of a data pipeline [1].

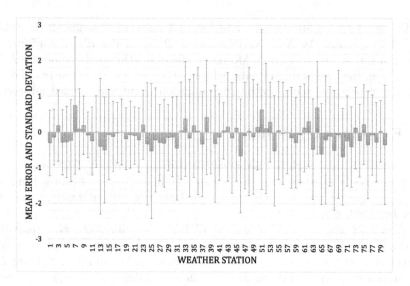

Fig. 2. Mean error bar and standard deviation of temperatures (degree Celsius) for the regional dataset.

A k-fold cross validation has been applied, as a specific node is available in KNIME, using 5, 10 and 15 validation iterations. We verified that when using such number of validation iterations the test set contains enough variation with respect to the training set.

For linear regression, the related node does not provide any configuration. For polynomial regression, we used a maximum polynomial degree of 2. For fuzzy rules, we used the *Best Guess* method to handle missing values [2], which computes the optimal replacement value by projecting the fuzzy rule (with missing value(s)) onto the missing dimension of all other rules. Also, we used *Product Norm* as rule to combine the membership values of each fuzzy interval for one rule and compute a final output across all rules and *Volumn Border Based* as shrink method to reduce rules in order to avoid conflicts between rules of different classes; this shrink method applies the volume loss in terms of the support or core region borders. These parameters gave us good results for the used dataset.

In order to compare to the state-of-art we used the four stations that gave the worst results using our method. The results of the comparison for the regional dataset are shown in Fig. 3. For the four stations considered, our proposal outperforms the results obtained by the state-of-the-art solutions.

In order to evaluate the effectiveness of dynamic ACWs, we used the same 4 stations shown in Fig. 3. We applied a k-fold cross validation using dynamic size ACWs, then we used fixed size ACWs containing a maximum of 3, 7, 10 entries respectively for each experiment. Figure 4 shows the results of the experiments using fixed size and dynamic size ACWs.

Even if using fixed size ACWs our proposal is able to make sufficiently good estimations; the system outperforms the results when using dynamic size ACWs.

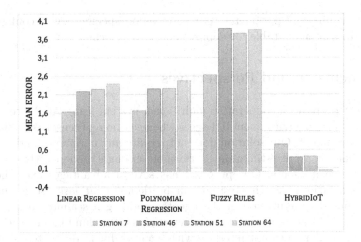

Fig. 3. Comparison of the mean error (degree Celsius) for our solution and standard techniques obtained from the regional dataset.

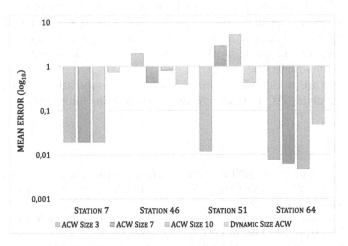

Fig. 4. Comparison of the mean error (degree Celsius) from 4 stations of the regional dataset using ACWs of fixed size (3, 7 and 10) and dynamic size ACWs. The mean error axis uses a logarithmic scale (base 10) as the error is significantly low.

Dynamic size ACWs have a twofold advantage. As we said in the previous section, they are able to better describe the dynamics of the information. Furthermore, when using dynamic size ACWs it is not necessary to specify the size of the context windows. In fact, the system must operate even when considering devices that have different frequency rate at which they perceive information. This is important in order to ensure that the system can operate in large-scale, open environments. In this manner our proposal is able to self-calibrate, thus it does not require any parameter that depends on specific device configuration, making the system suitable for deployment at large-scale.

4 Conclusion and Perspectives

This paper proposes a cooperative multi-agent system using ACWs to estimate missing data from environmental devices whenever no real sensor is available in a smart environment. Our solution does not require any parameter and is capable of providing accurate estimation at runtime through a cooperative resolution process between agents. Our proposal has several advantages over the state-of-the-art solutions: (i) the system can be deployed at large scale thanks to the distributed computation of the agents, enabling a seamless integration in smart cities; (ii) agents have a partial view of the surrounding environment, so their computation does not interfere with agents which are located in different and delocalized environments; (iii) the cooperation allows to estimate accurate information at real-time. Contrary to classical solutions in which data are a passive entity, in our proposal, data become an active part of the system as the agents identify them. As such, agents are able to cope with non-availability of real sensors; (iv) although we considered only a temperatures dataset, the system is generic enough to work with any kind of environmental information without any modification.

In our future works we aim at improving the cooperation process between ACAs by involving ACAs that perceive heterogeneous information.

References

1. Berthold, M.R., et al.: KNIME - the konstanz information miner: version 2.0 and beyond. ACM SIGKDD Explor. Newslett. **11**(1), 26–31 (2009). https://doi.org/10.1145/1656274.1656280
2. Berthold, M.R., Huber, K.P.: Missing values and learning of fuzzy rules **06**(2), 171–178. https://doi.org/10.1142/S021848859800015X
3. Bikakis, A., Antoniou, G.: Defeasible contextual reasoning with arguments in ambient intelligence. IEEE Trans. Knowl. Data Eng. **22**(11), 1492–1506 (2010). https://doi.org/10.1109/TKDE.2010.37
4. Bressan, L., Valentini, A., Paccagnella, T., Montani, A., Marsigli, C., Tesini, M.: Sensitivity of sea-level forecasting to the horizontal resolution and sea surface forcing for different configurations of an oceanographic model of the Adriatic Sea. Adv. Sci. Res. (Copernicus) **14**, 77–84 (2017). https://doi.org/10.5194/asr-14-77-2017
5. Georgé, J.P., Gleizes, M.P., Camps, V.: Cooperation. In: Di Marzo Serugendo, G., Gleizes, M.P., Karageorgos, A. (eds.) Self-Organising Software: From Natural to Artificial Adaptation, pp. 193–226. Springer, Heidelberg (2011). https://doi.org/10.1007/978-3-642-17348-6
6. Guastella, D., Camps, V., Gleizes, M.P.: Multi-agent systems for estimating missing information in smart cities. In: Proceedings of the 11th International Conference on Agents and Artificial Intelligence (ICAART), pp. 214–223. SciTePress (2019). https://doi.org/10.5220/0007381902140223

7. Guastella, D.A., Valenti, C.: Estimating missing information by cluster analysis and normalized convolution. In: 2018 IEEE 4th International Forum on Research and Technology for Society and Industry (RTSI), pp. 1–6. IEEE, September 2018. https://doi.org/10.1109/RTSI.2018.8548454

8. Moreno-Torres, J., Sáez, J.A., Herrera, F.: Study on the impact of partition-induced dataset shift on k-fold cross-validation. IEEE Trans. Neural Netw. Learn. Syst. **23**, 1304–1312 (2012). https://doi.org/10.1109/TNNLS.2012.2199516

9. Sabatucci, L., Seidita, V., Cossentino, M.: The four types of self-adaptive systems: a metamodel. In: De Pietro, G., Gallo, L., Howlett, R.J., Jain, L.C. (eds.) KES-IIMSS 2017. SIST, vol. 76, pp. 440–450. Springer, Cham (2018). https://doi.org/10.1007/978-3-319-59480-4_44

10. Tomazzoli, C., Cristani, M., Karafili, E., Olivieri, F.: Non-monotonic reasoning rules for energy efficiency. J. Ambient Intell. Smart Environ. **9**(3), 345–360.https://doi.org/10.3233/AIS-170434. (IOS Press)

Semantics of Extended Argumentation Frameworks Defined by Renovation Sets

Hengfei Li[1] and Jiachao Wu[2(✉)]

[1] School of Computer Science and Technology, Shandong Jianzhu University,
Jinan 250101, China
[2] Department of Mathematics, Shandong Normal University,
Jinan 250014, China
wujiachao1981@hotmail.com

Abstract. Dung's theory of abstract argumentation frameworks plays an increasingly important role in artificial intelligence. Extended argumentation frameworks extend Dung's AF by considering attacks on attacks. In this paper we introduce a new EAF semantics that deals with infinite deductive defence. This EAF semantics is underpinned by a new notion called renovation sets. Based on this, the concepts of conflict-freeness and acceptability are re-defined.

1   Introduction

Dung's abstract argumentation frameworks (AFs) [6] play a key role in a large variety of more specific formalisms ranging from non-monotonic reasoning to logic programming and game theory, and Dung's theory has been regarded as a powerful tool for theoretical analysis of argumentation. A number of variations of AFs have been proposed in recent years. There is a particular strand of work that extends AFs by allowing attacks on attacks. For example, Modgil's extended argumentation frameworks [9] consider (one level) attacks on attacks. Attacks on attacks and so on (higher levels) are allowed in argumentation frameworks of [1–5,7,8]. For convenience, we will refer to this type of argumentation frameworks as extended argumentation frameworks (EAFs).

In general, the semantics of EAFs is obtained in two different ways. One is to transform the framework into another framework whose semantics is already well established [2,5,7]. It is worth noting that the extensions obtained in this way contain both arguments and attacks, which is different from the AF semantics. In [8] and [9], the semantics of an EAF is built in another way in which a key notion is the acceptability of attacks. The extensions obtained in this way are subsets of all the arguments *Args*.

In this paper, we explore EAF semantics defined in the second way. More specifically, we examine the semantics of EAFs that contain "infinite inductive defence".

In [8], the inductive defence (i-defence) is only inductively defined for finite steps and there is no discussion on infinite cases. However, there are such cases that worth looking at.

© Springer Nature Switzerland AG 2019
M. Baldoni et al. (Eds.): PRIMA 2019, LNAI 11873, pp. 532–540, 2019.
https://doi.org/10.1007/978-3-030-33792-6_38

Example 1. Consider the EAF on the right-hand side of Fig. 1. X_i, Y_i, $i = 0, 1, 2, \ldots$ and Z are arguments and $Y_0 \to Z$ and α_i, β_i, $i = 0, 1, 2, \ldots$ denote attacks. Intuitively, the set $S = \{X_i \colon i = 0, 1, 2, ..\}$ defends Z, which is also valid in Modgil's system [9]. The defending process is for infinite steps. But in the system of [8], such defence is rejected.

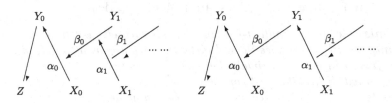

Fig. 1. Examples of infinite attacks on attacks.

In the EAF on the left-hand side of Fig. 1, the infinite inductive defence cannot be characterized by Modgil's system, i.e., there exist cases that Modgil's system cannot cover. Therefore, we aim to find a new semantics system to cover such cases.

In general, Modgil's method cannot be applied to any EAF because the reinstatement sets do not always exist. As we know, the elements of the reinstatement sets are the attacks "defeat^S". And the "defeat^S"s are the remaining attacks after omitting some attacks by $S \subseteq Args$. For example, in the EAF on the right-hand side of Fig. 1, β_i omits α_i for each $i \in \mathbb{N}$, and the remaining set $\{(Y_0, Z)\} \cup \{\beta_i \colon i = 0, 1, 2, ...\}$ contains all the defeat^S w.r.t. $S = Args$. But in some other EAFs, it will be much more complex. For instance, in the EAF on the left-hand side of Fig. 1, when β_0 is omitted by α_1 w.r.t. $S = Args$, should α_0 be kept as a defeat^S or not? If it is not kept, then all the α_is and β_is will be omitted, which is not our intention. If it is kept, what about β_0? Should it be kept by β_1? There seems no rational answer to this question.

In this paper, instead of finding rational ways to obtain the defeat^{S}s, we build "reinstatement sets" on all attacks. And such "reinstatement sets" are called *renovation sets* here. With the renovation sets, a new system of EAF semantics, which covers the "infinite i-defence", is introduced.

The contents are organized as follows. We recall basic notions of AFs and EAFs in the next section. In Sect. 3, we first introduce the notion of renovation sets. We then present our new semantics. We discuss how our work is compared with related works in Sect. 4 and we conclude in Sect. 5.

2   Basic Notions

In this section, we recall basic notions of Dung's AFs and EAFs of Hanh et al.

Definition 1. *An AF is a tuple $(Args, Atts)$ where $Args$ is a set of arguments and $Atts$ is a binary attack relations on $Args$, i.e., $Atts \subseteq Args \times Args$.*

Definition 2. *[Conflict-freeness] A set $S \subseteq Args$ is conflict-free iff there are no attacks between elements of S, i.e., $\forall A, B \in S$, $(A, B) \notin S$.*

Definition 3. *[Acceptability] A set $S \subseteq Args$ defends (or accepts) an argument $A \in Args$ iff for every argument $B \in Args$ attacking A, there exists $C \in S$ attacking B, i.e., $\forall B \in Args$ with $(B, A) \in Atts$, $\exists C \in S$, s.t. $(C, B) \in S$.*

Definition 4. *Given an AF $(Args, Atts)$. A set $E \subseteq Args$ is*

- *admissible iff it is conflict-free and defends each element in it;*
- *complete iff it is admissible and includes every argument it defends;*
- *preferred iff it is a maximal admissible extension;*
- *grounded iff it is the least complete extension;*
- *stable iff it is conflict-free and attacks each argument not in it.*

As discussed, there are different types of EAFs proposed by different researchers. In this paper, we will build our semantics based on the EAFs of Hanh et al. [8].

Definition 5. *An extended argumentation framework of Hanh et al. (H-EAF) is a pair $(Args, \mathcal{R})$ where $Args$ is a set of arguments and $\mathcal{R} = \cup_{i=0}^{\infty} \mathcal{R}_i$ is defined recursively as:*

$$\mathcal{R}_0 \subseteq Args \times Args,$$
$$\mathcal{R}_i \subseteq Args \times \mathcal{R}_{i-1}, \text{ for } i = 1, 2, \ldots$$

Before moving on, we introduce some symbols that will be used in the remainder of this paper. Let α be an attack relation, $trg(\alpha)$ and $src(\alpha)$ denote respectively the target and the source argument. Let $(Args, \mathcal{R})$ be an H-EAF, $\alpha, \beta \in \mathcal{R}$, $\chi \in Args \cup \mathcal{R}$. We say: α directly attacks χ iff $\chi = trg(\alpha)$; α indirectly attacks β iff $trg(\alpha) = src(\beta)$ and $\alpha \rightarrow_R \chi$ iff α directly or indirectly attacks χ.

3   New Semantics of EAFs

Key questions in defining a semantics for H-EAFs include how the notion of conflict-free should be generalized and what does it mean for an argument to be acceptable? In the following, we will restrict our attention to these two questions.

3.1   Renovation Sets

We first consider when an attack can be recognized to be valid. The following notion—renovation sets—plays a role similar to the "i-defence of an attack" in [8].

Definition 6. *[Renovation Sets] Let $(Args, \mathcal{R})$ be an H-EAF, $S \subseteq Args$ and $\alpha \in \mathcal{R}$. We say $\{\alpha_i, i = 1, 2, \ldots\} \subseteq \mathcal{R}$ is a renovation set of α w.r.t. S, denoted as R_S^α, if:*

1. $\alpha \in R_S^\alpha$;
2. $src(\alpha_i) \in S$, $\forall \alpha_i \in R_S^\alpha$;
3. $\forall \alpha_i \in R_S^\alpha$, $\forall \beta \in \mathcal{R}$, if $trg(\beta) = \alpha_i$, then $\exists \alpha_j \in R_S^\alpha$, s.t. $\alpha_j \rightarrow_R \beta$.

In the above, the set R_S^α can be finite, infinite.

Example 2. Consider the H-EAFs in Fig. 1. In each of them, $\{\alpha_i\}_{i \in \mathbb{N}}$ is a renovation set of every α_i w.r.t. $S = \{X_i, i = 0, 1, ...\}$. $\{\beta_i\}_{i \in \mathbb{N}}$ is a renovation set of each β_i w.r.t. $\{Y_i, i = 0, 1, ...\}$. And $\{\alpha_i, i = 0, 1, ...\} \cup \{\beta_j, j = 0, 1, ...\}$ is a renovation set of each α_i or β_j w.r.t. *Args*.

The following example shows that our renovation sets are distinct from the reinstatement sets in [9], even if in an EAF of [9].

Example 3. Consider the EAF of Fig. 2(a), which is a classical example in [9]. $R = \{\alpha_1, \alpha_2\}$ is a renovation set of both α_1 and α_2 w.r.t. $\{A, B, C, D\}$. But R is not a reinstatement set of α_1 w.r.t. $\{A, B, C, D\}$ in the semantics of [9].

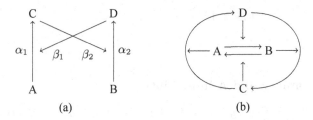

(a)   (b)

Fig. 2. Examples of renovation sets.

3.2 Conflict-Free Sets

Definition 7. *[Conflict-freeness] Let $(Args, \mathcal{R})$ be an H-EAF. $S \subseteq Args$ is weakly conflict-free, iff $\forall A, B \in S$, one of the following satisfies:*

1. $(A, B) \notin \mathcal{R}$;
2. $(A, B) \in \mathcal{R}$, but $\exists \alpha \in \mathcal{R}$ s.t. $trg(\alpha) = (A, B)$ and $\exists R_S^\alpha$.

A weakly conflict-free set S is called conflict-free if the second condition is strengthened to

2'. $(A, B) \in \mathcal{R}$, but $\exists \alpha \in \mathcal{R}$ s.t. $trg(\alpha) = (A, B)$, $\exists R_S^\alpha$ and $\neg \exists R_S^{(A,B)}$.

Example 4. In each H-EAF in Fig. 1, $S = \{X_i, Y_i: \ i = 0, 1, 2, ...\}$ is weakly conflict-free, but not conflict-free, because $\mathcal{R}$ is a renovation set of both α_0 and β_0.

Example 5. Consider the H-EAF in Fig. 2(a). The set $S = \{A, B, C, D\}$ is obviously weakly conflict-free; but S is not conflict-free, for $\{\alpha_1, \alpha_2\}$ is a renovation set of each element in it. On the other hand, $S' = \{A, C\}$ is not weakly conflict-free, thus not conflict-free here.

Example 6. Consider the conflict-freeness of the set $S = \{A, B, C\}$ in the H-EAF of Fig. 3. It is weakly conflict-free, for $\{\alpha, \beta, \gamma\}$ is a renovation set of β w.r.t. S. But it is not conflict-free, for $\{\alpha, \gamma\}$ is a renovation set of α w.r.t. S.

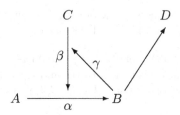

Fig. 3. Examples of conflict-free sets.

3.3 Acceptability and Admissibility

Generally, a set $S \subseteq Args$ defends A in two ways: For any $(B, A) \in \mathcal{R}$, S inductively attacks B, or S inductively attacks the attack (B, A).

Definition 8. *[Acceptability] In an H-EAF $(Args, \mathcal{R})$, $A \in Args$ is acceptable (or defended) w.r.t. $S \subseteq Args$, if it satisfies the following two conditions:*

- *For any $B \in Args$ attacking A, there exists an α s.t. $src(\alpha) \in S$, $\alpha \rightarrow_R (B, A)$ and there is a renovation set of α w.r.t. S.*

(⋆) If $trg(\alpha) = (B, A)$, then there are no renovation sets of (B, A) w.r.t. Args, i.e., $\nexists R_{Args}^{(B,A)}$.

Example 7. In every H-EAF in Fig. 1, the set $\{X_i : i = 0, 1, ...\}$ defends Z.
But $Args \setminus \{Z\}$ does not defend Y_0.

Example 8. In the graph in Fig. 2(a), the set $\{A, B, C, D\}$ does not defend C or D.

The condition (⋆) is important here as the Fundamental Lemma would be invalid without it.

Definition 9. *Given an H-EAF $(Args, \mathcal{R})$, a conflict-free set $E \subseteq Args$ is admissible, iff it defends every element in it.*

In the H-EAFs with infinite attack sequence, the condition "w.r.t. *Args*" in (⋆) cannot be weakened to "w.r.t. *S*".

Example 9. Consider the EAF in Fig. 4. The set $S = Args \setminus \{B\} = \{A, C\} \cup \{X_i, i = 0, 1, ...\} \cup \{Y_i, i = 0, 1, ...\}$ is obviously conflict-free and admissible.

According to Definition 9, S does not defend B, because $\{\gamma, \delta\} \cup \{\alpha_i, i = 0, 1, ...\}$ is a renovation set of γ w.r.t. *Args*. It also shows that *Args* is *not admissible*.

In the condition (⋆), if "w.r.t. *Args*" is replaced by "w.r.t. *S*", we will have S defends B, because $\{\alpha, \beta\} \cup \{\beta_i, i = 0, 1, ...\}$ is a renovation set of α w.r.t. S and there is no renovation set of γ w.r.t. S. The fact that the set $Args = S \cup \{B\}$ is not admissible shows the invalidity of the Fundamental Lemma.

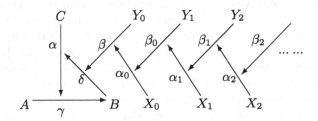

Fig. 4. Examples of admissible sets.

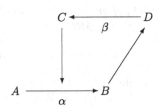

Fig. 5. Examples of c-stable extensions.

3.4   The Semantics

Definition 10. *Given an H-EAF* $(Args, \mathcal{R})$. *A conflict-free set* $E \subseteq Args$ *is called*

admissible *iff every argument in* E *is acceptable w.r.t.* E, *i.e.,* $E \subseteq F(E)$.
preferred *iff* E *is a set inclusion maximal admissible extension.*
complete *iff* E *is admissible and each argument defended by* E *belongs to* E, *i.e.,* $E = F(E)$.

grounded *iff* E *is the least complete extension.*
c-stable *iff* $\forall B \notin E$, $\exists A \in E$ *s.t.* $(A, B) \in \mathcal{R}$ *and* $\exists R_E^{(A,B)}$.
stable *iff it is admissible and c-stable.*

Example 10. In the H-EAF of Fig. 5, the set $S = \{A, B, C\}$ is c-stable, because S is conflict-free and $(B, D) \in \mathcal{R}$. On the other hand, $\{\alpha, \beta\}$ is a renovation set of α w.r.t. *Args*. According to Definitions 8 and 9, S is not admissible. Thus S is not stable.

4   Discussion

In this section, we briefly compare our semantics to the semantics systems of [8] and [9].

EAFs in [9] extends AFs by adding attacks from arguments to Dung's attacks. They are special EAFs with $\mathcal{R}_2 = \emptyset$ and some other constraints. First, our renovation sets are distinct from the reinstatement sets in [9]. Consider the EAF of Fig. 2(a). $R = \{\alpha_1, \alpha_2\}$ is a renovation set of both α_1 and α_2 w.r.t. $\{A, B, C, D\}$. But R is not a reinstatement set of α_1 w.r.t. $\{A, B, C, D\}$ in [9]. Second, in [9], a set is conflict-free if it is conflict-free in our semantics, but not vice versa. Consider Fig. 2(a). The set $\{A, B, C, D\}$ is not conflict-free in [9], but it is conflict-free in our semantics. Consequently the acceptability in the two semantics systems are distinct in general.

In general, our semantics improves the semantics in [8] by covering the infinite inductive defence. The relation between the "i-defence" in [8] and our renovation sets is in Propositions 1 and 2.

Proposition 1. *In an H-EAF, if an attack α is i-defended by $S \subseteq Args$, there is a renovation set of α w.r.t. S, i.e. $\exists R_S^\alpha$. But not vice versa.*

The following example shows the second part of this proposition.

Example 11. Consider the graphs in Fig. 2. In Fig. 2(a), $\{\alpha_1, \alpha_2\}$ is a renovation set of both α_1 and α_2 w.r.t. $\{A, B, C, D\}$. But $\forall k \in \mathbb{N}$, neither of them is i-defended by $\{A, B, C, D\}$ within k-steps, because none of them is i-defended within 0-steps. Thus neither α_1 nor α_2 is i-defended.

Similarly, in Fig. 2(b), the set $S = \{(A, B), (B, A), (C, D), (D, C)\}$ is a renovation set of each element in it, w.r.t. the set $\{A, B, C, D\}$. But neither of them is i-defended by $\{A, B, C, D\}$.

Our renovation sets can be classified as follows:

Definition 11. *Let R_S^α be a renovation set of an attack $\alpha \in \mathcal{R}$ w.r.t. $S \subseteq Args$. Then R_S^α is called*

finite *if there is a finite sequence $(S_0 = \{\alpha\}, S_1, ..., S_n)$, satisfying:*
    1. $\forall i = 0, 1, ..., n$, $S_i \subseteq R_S^\alpha$;

2. $\forall \beta \in S_i$ *with* $i < n$. *If* $\exists \gamma \in \mathcal{R}$ *with* $trg(\gamma) = \beta$, *then* $\exists \beta' \in S_{i+1}$ *with* $\beta' \to_R \gamma$; *and*

3. $\forall \beta \in S_n$, $\nexists \gamma \in \mathcal{R}$ *s.t.* $trg(\gamma) = \beta$.

We simply say R_S^α *renovates* α *within finite (or n) steps.*
infinite *if it is not finite.*

Note: A finite renovation set of α may contain infinite elements. But it has some finite subset, which is a renovation set of α. For example, given R_S^α and R_S^β, $R_S^\alpha \cup R_S^\beta$ is also a renovation set of α w.r.t. S, no matter R_S^β is finite or infinite.

Example 12. In the H-EAFs in Fig. 1, $\mathcal{R}$ is an infinite renovation set of each attack in it.

Example 13. In the H-EAF of Fig. 2(a), $\{\alpha_1, \alpha_2\}$ is an infinite renovation set of α_2. Because if $S_0 = \{\alpha_2\}$, then $S_1 = \{\alpha_1\}$. It follows that $S_2 = \{\alpha_2\}$, $S_3 = \{\alpha_1\}$,... The sequence $\{S_0, S_1, ...\}$ is endless.

For finite renovation sets, we have the following property, which strengthens Proposition 1.

Proposition 2. *In an H-EAF, an attack* α *is i-defended by a set* $S \subseteq Args$ *(within k-step), iff there is a finite renovation set of* α *w.r.t.* S, *which renovates* α *(within k-steps).*

Proposition 2 shows that the concept of i-defence in [8] can be described with finite renovation sets. This means that the semantics system introduced in [8] can also be expressed with finite renovation sets.

5   Conclusion

In this paper we focused on the semantics of extended argumentation frameworks with higher level attacks. We first introduced the notion of *renovation sets*. Based on it, we redefined the notions of conflict-free sets and acceptability. We then defined a new EAF semantics. We studied basic properties. We discussed how our work is related to Modgil's semantics system [9] and the semantics of Hanh et al. [8]. The main contribution lies in the novel notion of renovation sets and the new EAF semantics.

Acknowledgment. This work is supported by the NSFC (11601288) and the Natural Science Foundation of Shandong (ZR2016AQ21). The authors appreciate Professor P. Baroni, Professor C. Cayrol and Professor M. Giacomin for their constructive advice. They thank the anonymous reviewers for their helpful comments.

References

1. Baroni, P., Caminada, M., Giacomin, M.: An introduction to argumentation semantics. Knowl. Eng. Rev. **26**(4), 365–410 (2011)
2. Baroni, P., Cerutti, F., Giacomin, M., Guida, G.: AFRA: argumentation framework with recursive attacks. Int. J. Approximate Reasoning **52**(1), 19–37 (2011)
3. Cayrol, C., Cohen, A., Lagasquie-Schiex, M.C.: Towards a new framework for recursive interactions in abstract bipolar argumentation. In: Proceedings of COMMA 2016, pp. 191–198. IOS Press (2016)
4. Cohen, A., Gottiferedi, S., García, A.J., Simari, G.R.: On the acceptability semantics of argumentation frameworks with recursive attack and support. In: Proceedings of COMMA 2016, pp. 231–242. IOS Press (2016)
5. Cohen, A., Gottifredi, S., García, A.J., Simari, G.R.: An approach to abstract argumentation with recursive attack and support. J. Appl. Logic **13**(4), 509–533 (2015)
6. Dung, P.M.: On the acceptability of arguments and its fundamental role in nonmonotonic reasoning, logic programming and n-person games. Artif. Intell. **77**(2), 321–357 (1995)
7. Gabbay, D.M.: Semantics for higher level attacks in extended argumentation frames part 1: overview. Stud. Logica. **93**(2–3), 357 (2009)
8. Hanh, D., Dung, P.M., Hung, N.D., Thang, P.M.: Inductive defense for sceptical semantics of extended argumentation. J. Logic Comput. **21**(2), 307–349 (2010)
9. Modgil, S.: Reasoning about preferences in argumentation frameworks. Artif. Intell. **173**(9–10), 901–934 (2009)

Smart RogAgent: Where Agents and Humans Team Up

Chiara Capone[1], Rafael H. Bordini[1,2], Viviana Mascardi[1(✉)],
Giorgio Delzanno[1], Angelo Ferrando[3], Luca Gelati[4], and Giovanna Guerrini[1]

[1] Università degli Studi di Genova, Genoa, Italy
`caponechiara94@libero.it, rafael.bordini@edu.unige.it,`
`{viviana.mascardi,giorgio.delzanno,giovanna.guerrini}@unige.it`
[2] PUCRS, Porto Alegre, Brazil
`rafael.bordini@pucrs.br`
[3] University of Liverpool, Liverpool, UK
`angelo.ferrando@liverpool.ac.uk`
[4] Edutainment Formula s.r.l., Genoa, Italy
`luca.gelati.slp@gmail.com`

Abstract. The increasing diffusion of team building as a means to enhance social relations and define roles within teams, and the cost of setting up a real team building event, raises the pressing need of simulating team building activities in order to assess the effectiveness of different formats, run in different contexts and under different conditions, before one is selected for a particular scenario.

The selection of a software platform employing software abstractions which are close to the real entities involved in a team building event, including human beings and their roles, goals, and organisations, paves the way to substituting some simulated entity with its real counterpart, moving from simulation to a hybrid application where real entities and their software "alter egos" can co-exist.

We present the design of Smart RogAgent, a JaCaMo multi-agent system aimed at simulating rogaining, a special kind of team building activity. Once fully developed, Smart RogAgent will have the potential to allow artificial intelligent agents to enter human teams, and vice versa, providing the technological support for the creation of hybrid human-agent teams in a principled way.

Keywords: Team building · Hybrid human-agent teams · Simulation · Roles · Organisations · Artefacts

Rafael H. Bordini gratefully acknowledges the support of CAPES for his sabbatical period at the Universities of Genova and Oxford and the visiting researcher position at the University of Genova; Giorgio Delzanno, Giovanna Guerrini, and Viviana Mascardi gratefully acknowledge the "Boosting Computational Thinking with Pervasive and Collaborative Technologies 2017–2019" Project funded by the University of Genova.

© Springer Nature Switzerland AG 2019
M. Baldoni et al. (Eds.): PRIMA 2019, LNAI 11873, pp. 541–549, 2019.
https://doi.org/10.1007/978-3-030-33792-6_39

1   Introduction and Motivation

The term *team building* [6,15] identifies various types of activities used to enhance social relations and define roles within teams.

To make team building as effective as possible, evidence-based practices should be followed, which include [8]:

- *clarify needs of the teams to identify which components (i.e., problem-solving, interpersonal relationship management, goal setting, or role clarification) are most needed for team improvement;*
- *guide the team to develop tangible action plans/agreements;*
- *follow up on plans/agreements to maintain accountability.*

Rogaining [11] is one way to implement team building activities. In "standard" rogaining, individuals or teams are given printed maps showing up to 50 checkpoints spread over a large area. Teams navigate between checkpoints, getting as many points as possible before the clock stops. Teams travel entirely on foot, navigating by map and compass between checkpoints in terrains that vary from open farmland to hilly forest.

A variant of this standard outdoor format is "slow rogaining" that we invented in 2018 to meet security and insurance requirements when the activity is carried out inside a building and involves underage students. We experimented for the first time with slow rogaining in February 2019, during a School Work Experience Stage[1] organised by the Computer Science Course at DIBRIS – Dipartimento di Informatica, Bioingegneria, Robotica e Ingegneria dei Sistemi, University of Genova, and involving about 140 students. In slow rogaining, team members are forbidden both to run and to wander around the building in an uncontrolled way: to accumulate points, intellectual ability is more important than speed and orienteering skills. Each checkpoint is in fact associated with a challenge which depends on the educational/technical/physical goals that the slow rogaining event aims to achieve. Each challenge comes with a maximum time to be completed, which was 30 min in our setting.

The ever increasing diffusion of team building in general, and rogaining in particular, raises two major needs:

1. making rogaining smarter due to technological support that does not distort its nature, but rather makes it more inclusive, and more enjoyable for "digital natives";
2. having clues about the effectiveness of different rogaining formats, run in different contexts and under different conditions, *before* they are put in practice.

---

[1] Stage di Alternanza Scuola Lavoro del Corso di Studi in Informatica, Università di Genova, "Team Building 6.0: la Collaborazione tra Persone, la Collaborazione tra Macchine, e la Collaborazione tra Macchine e Persone", https://unige.it/comunicati-stampa/stage-informatica, https://www.youtube.com/watch?v=jdfLx7Jg1G8, https://www.youtube.com/watch?v=2F-8HPR1ySA, accessed on September 2019.

The first need is being addressed by SR-App, the Smart Rogaining App resulting from a collaboration of the academic authors and Luca Gelati's Edutainment Formula s.r.l. company. SR-App supports both the standard and the slow rogaining formats, and its functionalities have been tested following an orchestrated crowdsourced testing approach [10]. In 2019, it has been used in 8 rogaining events involving from 1 large team with 22 members, up to 13 teams with 6–9 members. SR-App is undergoing a continuous improvement process, with new features and functionalities designed and added as soon as they are identified as relevant.

The second need is addressed in this paper which presents the design of Smart RogAgent, a JaCaMo multi-agent system [2,3] where agents simulate human participants, groups of a JaCaMo organisation simulate teams, and the environment – which plays a fundamental role in rogaining – can be simulated as well, in a realistic way. In fact, an advantage of the approach is that we can move from a simulation to a useful system application to support human/agent teamwork by using the JaCaMo artefacts as a bridge to real sensors and effectors so the agents in the system can actually perceive and effect changes in a real-world environment.

Once fully developed, Smart RogAgent will have the potential for satisfying, besides simulation and 'what-if' analysis requirements, a much more ambitious goal: *allowing artificial intelligent agents to enter human teams (or vice versa!), leading to hybrid teams.*

By hybrid team we do not just mean a team where some agent supports or replaces some human in performing some task, according to some pre-defined fixed strategy. Rather, we mean a team where both agent and human functionalities relevant for the team success are in principle indistinguishable, and both agents and humans may play roles required to achieve the team goals, as in a "purely" human team. In fact, we expect that teams in the future, be them in leisure, sport, rescue, first aid, emergency management, and any other scenarios, will include both human and artificial participants with some intelligent capabilities, autonomy, duties, and rights. By integrating the functionalities of SR-App, which already provides an interface between the software backend and the humans into Smart RogAgent, we will be able to obtain a framework for "hybrid smart rogaining" involving humans and agents, taking a first step towards a platform for hybrid team building.

The paper is organised in the following way: Sect. 2 describes the application domain, namely smart and slow rogaining. Section 3 describes the architecture of Smart RogAgent. Section 4 discusses some possible developments of our work, and concludes.

2   The Context: Smart and Slow Rogaining

Both smart and slow rogaining events involve the organisers, the teams that will attend the event by using SR-App (one SR-App instance per team, given that team members cannot split and hence each team can be uniquely identified via the credentials used to access SR-App), and the domain experts who design and manage the challenges. A rogaining event consists of five main stages, described below.

Event Setup. Besides managing the logistics of the event and devising its educational goals, to be achieved through the challenges, the organisers collect the names and personal information of the candidates who would like to join the event, perform a selection process (in case there is a limited number of participants allowed), form the teams, and decide – together with the domain experts – where challenges will be located in the event area. Each team consists of a variable number of members (the same for a given event, but the group size can vary from one event to another), which, in the events we organised, was between 5 and 22.

Briefing. Once the event has been set up, the participants, the organisers and the domain experts meet in some pre-agreed "meeting point" for a briefing. The organisers explain the rules of the rogaining activity and its ultimate goals.

Team Preparation. Teams spend about 30 min for designing their strategy to accumulate points. Depending on the adopted format, one team member may act as the "team oracle". Team oracles do not engage in the activity on the field: we introduced them in our format to be inclusive of team members who have mobility impairment, allowing them to take an active and important role in their team. All team oracles know how many points each competing team is scoring, where each of the teams is located on the map, which team is currently working at which challenge (which can be faced only by one team at a time, after reserving the challenge and reaching it on time). This information is different from that available to "on the field" members, i.e., members that enter the game and face challenges, who only know where challenges are placed on the map. An oracle can help the other members of the team to refine or replan the team strategy by considering where the other teams are, and how well they are doing.

Game. After the team preparation stage, the organisers give the "three... two... one... must go!" directive, and on the field team members enter the actual game, following the team strategy. Points can be accumulated in three different ways:

1. By reaching a checkpoint and completing the associated challenge. Completion is certified via SR-App by one of the domain experts running the challenge.
2. By answering queries that are randomly picked from a repository, and displayed by SR-App with a configurable frequency (usually, one every 4 or 5 min).
3. By helping other teams, upon request, to answer one of those queries. This third approach to earn points has two more advantages: (i) it allows a team to come to know in advance queries that the team might be asked to answer later on, given that they are sent to teams in random order but picked from the same repository; and (ii) it conveys the positive message that, by helping others, we also help ourselves.

On the field members may play different roles at different times. Depending on the content of the challenge, whose details are unknown to the teams – including the oracle – until they reach the challenge location, one member might be more suitable to lead the team towards the solution of that challenge, or might be better employed to solve some subtask of the challenge, or to answer the random queries delivered via SR-App, or might even remain idle during one of the challenges. Besides "challenge leaders" and "query leaders", also one "team leader" usually emerges from the team interactions. These three roles are dynamic, and are only adopted during the game: one member may act as the team leader for some time, and might be substituted after some time (either after a cooperative or a "strong-armed" process) by another member.

Debriefing. When all the teams come back to the meeting point, a debriefing takes place, usually followed by a peer-evaluation stage and by the announcement of the winner team.

3 Smart RogAgent Architecture

The architectural components and the roles to be modelled in Smart RogAgent are in a one-to-one correspondence with the components and roles presented in Sect. 2. Despite the complexity of smart and slow rogaining, the Smart RogAgent design turns out to be clear and natural thanks to the adoption of agents, roles, workspaces, organisations, and artefacts as main design abstractions, and JaCaMo – which already supports all of them – as development platform. A JaCaMo multi-agent system results in fact from an agent organisation programmed in Moise [7], organising autonomous agents programmed in Jason [4], which share a distributed artefact-based environment programmed in CArtAgO [13]. Human beings (organisers and team members) are modelled as Jason agents, teams are modelled as Moise organisations, and the resources accessed by agents are modelled as CArtAgO artefacts. We note again that team members are not allowed to split and face various challenges concurrently: each team is uniquely identified via the team credentials used to access SR-App.

Figure 1 shows the architecture of Smart RogAgent: the workspace where on the field team members work is the same as the one where domain experts (not modelled in this Smart RogAgent version) organise their challenges. We name it *outdoor workspace*, although in some cases the experience might take place in an indoor environment as well. The other workspace is the *control room workspace* where the team oracles and the organisers are placed.

The team formation algorithm is encapsulated within a *team formation artefact* that the organisers can access when the rogaining event is set up. Each *challenge* takes place in a different location of the event area, and each such location is modelled as a different artefact that agents can observe and act upon. Team members can interact with the challenge only when they are close to it, in the simulated space. The *static map* is an artefact that can be read by anyone, and only shows where challenges are located. The *dynamic map* also gives information on where teams are located, the status of each challenge (free or currently

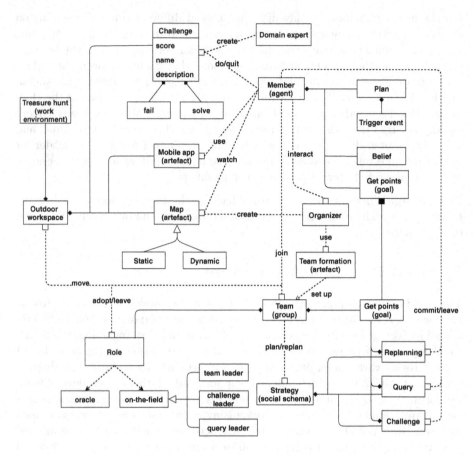

Fig. 1. Smart RogAgent architecture.

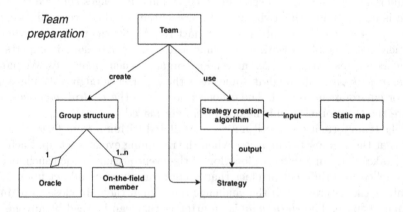

Fig. 2. Smart RogAgent team preparation.

occupied by some team), the expected time of completion of each challenge, and the points earned by each team. This dynamic map is also an artefact, but it can be accessed only by agents in the control room workspace, namely team oracles and organisers. Finally, one instance of the SR-App artefact is associated with each team, to implement receiving and answering to queries, as well as the "helping other teams in query answering" functionalities.

The roles that on the field team members can play are the *team leader*, the *challenge leader*, and the *query leader*. The team leader is not really a settled role, in fact it emerges during the game progress according to how the members behave and interact with others. The other two roles are also decided at runtime, in fact they are adopted, possibly by different agents, each time a team reaches a challenge. These roles can change, for example, depending on the subject and difficulty of the chosen challenge. The *on-the-field* team members other than the current challange/query leaders will support either the resolution of the challenge or query answering. *Team oracles* have a complete view of the situation on the field and thanks to this they can suggest the next move in case of replanning a strategy, for example.

The simulation process consists of the following stages: the organisers set up the rogaining event by exploiting the team formation artefact and by communicating to each participant the team they belong to. Then each team exploits some strategy creation algorithm in order to choose jointly the best strategy for the team to follow and to arrange an initial internal structure. Figure 2 shows such *team preparation* stage, while Fig. 3 shows the *game* phase of Smart RogAgent.

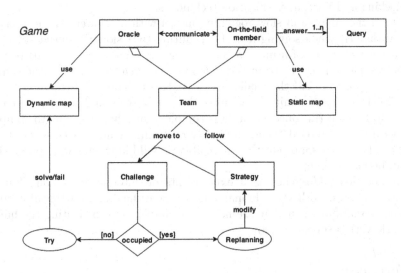

Fig. 3. Smart RogAgent game.

4   Conclusions and Future Developments

There is a vast literature on modelling/optimising teams in MASs, including seminal work on team-oriented programming, e.g., [12], approaches based on game theory [14], and recent proposals for addressing cooperative multi-agent reinforcement learning problems [9], also by exploiting neuro-evolutionary approaches [5]. A recent survey on the topic [1] discusses team composition, team formation, and their relationship with team performance, taking the points of view of both computer science and organisational psychology into account. Despite the large amount of work on the topic, we are not aware of systems which can both simulate "pure" human-centred team building activities, and provide – once properly consolidated – a software platform to support hybrid human-agent teams. Smart RogAgent addresses this need and, although its development is still ongoing, we see great potential in this research direction, confirmed by the collaboration with the Edutainment Formula s.r.l. company which is investing time and resources in making team building smarter. A multi-agent platform in general, and JaCaMo in particular, seem the most natural choice to achieve this goal.

Besides completing the development of Smart RogAgent and carrying out a systematic testing of its functionalities, many further activities populate our agenda:

– extending the model with probabilities for teams to be able to solve a given challenge: this would open up the possibility to exploit probabilistic model-checking and runtime-verification techniques;
– extend the smart and slow rogaining model with a "slower" stage in such a way that (i) when solving a problem during the "slower", initial stage, the team wins a piece of a map (a tile) of a smart rogaining game; (ii) to build the complete map, the team is divided into sub-teams (based on the skills of the components and the challenges) that try to acquire all the map tiles in parallel (a "team monitor" monitors the global state and sends instructions to sub-teams); (iii) once the map is complete, or when the time to complete it expires, a standard "smart and slow rogaining" game starts, where teams can only use the map that they were able to build in the "slower" part, which can be incomplete;
– run sociological/psychological experiments on interactions among humans and machines, both when humans are aware of having an artificial agent in their team, and when they are not (for example, by substituting the human oracle with a software one).

References

1. Andrejczuk, E., Berger, R., Rodriguez-Aguilar, J.A., Sierra, C., Marín-Puchades, V.: The composition and formation of effective teams: computer science meets organizational psychology. Knowl. Eng. Rev. **33**, e17 (2018)

2. Boissier, O., Bordini, R.H., Hübner, J.F., Ricci, A., Santi, A.: Multi-agent oriented programming with JaCaMo. Sci. Comput. Program. **78**(6), 747–761 (2013)
3. Boissier, O., Bordini, R.H., Hübner, J.F., Ricci, A.: Dimensions in programming multi-agent systems. Knowl. Eng. Rev. **34**, e2 (2019)
4. Bordini, R.H., Hübner, J.F., Wooldridge, M.: Programming Multi-agent Systems in AgentSpeak using Jason. Wiley Series in Agent Technology. Wiley, Hoboken (2007)
5. Bryant, B.D., Miikkulainen, R.: A neuroevolutionary approach to adaptive multi-agent teams. In: Abbass, H.A., Scholz, J., Reid, D.J. (eds.) Foundations of Trusted Autonomy. SSDC, vol. 117, pp. 87–115. Springer, Cham (2018). https://doi.org/10.1007/978-3-319-64816-3_5
6. Druskat, V.U., Wolff, S.B.: Building the emotional intelligence of groups. Harvard Bus. Rev. **79**(3), 80–91 (2001)
7. Hübner, J.F., Sichman, J.S., Boissier, O.: Developing organised multiagent systems using the MOISE$^+$ model: programming issues at the system and agent levels. IJAOSE **1**(3/4), 370–395 (2007)
8. Lacerenza, C.N., Marlow, S.L., Tannenbaum, S.I., Salas, E.: Team development interventions: evidence-based approaches for improving teamwork. Am. Psychol. **73**(4), 517 (2018)
9. Lee, H.R., Lee, T.: Improved cooperative multi-agent reinforcement learning algorithm augmented by mixing demonstrations from centralized policy. In: Proceedings of AAMAS 2019, pp. 1089–1098 (2019)
10. Leotta, M., Petito, V., Gelati, L., Delzanno, G., Guerrini, G., Mascardi, V.: Orchestrated crowdsourced testing of a mobile web application: a case study. In: Programming, pp. 17:1–17:6. ACM (2019)
11. Phillips, N., Phillips, R.: Rogaining Cross-Country Navigation. Outdoor Recreation in Australia (2000). ISBN 0-9593329-2-8
12. Pynadath, D.V., Tambe, M., Chauvat, N., Cavedon, L.: Toward team-oriented programming. In: Jennings, N.R., Lespérance, Y. (eds.) ATAL 1999. LNCS (LNAI), vol. 1757, pp. 233–247. Springer, Heidelberg (2000). https://doi.org/10.1007/10719619_17
13. Ricci, A., Piunti, M., Viroli, M.: Environment programming in multi-agent systems: an artifact-based perspective. Auton. Agent. Multi-Agent Syst. **23**(2), 158–192 (2011)
14. Semsar-Kazerooni, E., Khorasani, K.: Multi-agent team cooperation: a game theory approach. Automatica **45**(10), 2205–2213 (2009)
15. Tannenbaum, S.I., Beard, R.L., Salas, E.: Team building and its influence on team effectiveness: an examination of conceptual and empirical developments. In: Advances in Psychology, vol. 82, pp. 117–153. Elsevier (1992)

Coordination in Collaborative Work by Deep Reinforcement Learning with Various State Descriptions

Yuki Miyashita[1,2]([✉]) and Toshiharu Sugawara[1]([✉]) [iD]

[1] Computer Science and Engineering, Waseda University, Tokyo 1698555, Japan
{y.miyashita,sugawara}@isl.cs.waseda.ac.jp
[2] Shimizu Corporation, Tokyo 1040031, Japan

Abstract. Cooperation and coordination are sophisticated behaviors and are still major issues in studies on multi-agent systems because how to cooperate and coordinate depends on not only environmental characteristics but also the behaviors/strategies that closely affect each other. On the other hand, recently using the multi-agent deep reinforcement learning (MADRL) has received much attention because of the possibility of learning and facilitating their coordinated behaviors. However, the characteristics of socially learned coordination structures have been not sufficiently clarified. In this paper, by focusing on the MADRL in which each agent has its own deep Q-networks (DQNs), we show that the different types of input to the network lead to various coordination structures, using the *pickup and floor laying problem*, which is an abstract form related to our target problem. We also indicate that the generated coordination structures affect the entire performance of multi-agent systems.

Keywords: Multi-agent deep reinforcement learning · Coordination · Cooperation · Divisional cooperation · Deep Q networks

1 Introduction

It is desirable for the agents themselves to identify the appropriate cooperative actions through experience and form a regime for cooperation, because identifying appropriate coordination structures is difficult and complicated. On the other hand, advances in computer and networking technologies have led to the proposals of applications by collaborating with multiple agents [1,3,6]. We are also developing applications in which a number of cooperative robots work in a large construction site to help human builders/workers. This also aims to cope with the shortage of workers and robots are expected to compensate for labor shortages.

Recent ongoing techniques using deep reinforcement learning (DRL) have produced several successful results in many applications [4,5]. Even in multi-agent learning, some researches have extended these single-agent DRL

© Springer Nature Switzerland AG 2019
M. Baldoni et al. (Eds.): PRIMA 2019, LNAI 11873, pp. 550–558, 2019.
https://doi.org/10.1007/978-3-030-33792-6_40

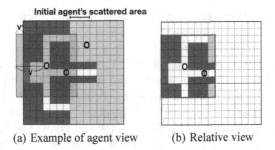

(a) Example of agent view   (b) Relative view

Fig. 1. Environmental state and relative views. (Color figure online)

approaches to multi-agent DRL (MADRL) approaches [2,7]. In the case of multi-agent learning, we always need to consider the fact that high dimensional state-action space has to be explored. Furthermore, the appropriate behaviors are highly dependent on the behaviors of the other agents, which may also vary with the learning progresses of individual agents; thereby, the current positive training data may become negative or noisy next time. However, it is still unclear how the observations of agents and data input to the deep Q-networks (DQNs) affect the generated coordination behaviors and structures in MADRL.

Therefore, we focus on a *multi-agent pickup and floor laying problem*, which is an abstract form of multi-robot working in a construction site. A challenge to tackle here is investigating how agents with concurrent learning using individual DQNs can establish spatial coordination regimes and generate the social norms and coordination behaviors to avoid the negative effects. We also attempt to see how the types of information as the inputs to the networks affect the resulting coordination and cooperative behaviors. For this purpose, we prepare some types of input structures and agents' observable views and then combine the locally observable environmental data with various own beliefs such as the (estimated) absolute location and the locations of tasks observed in the past.

Our experimental results show that cooperative structures emerged in the *pickup and floor laying problem* using distributed MADRL, and the emerging cooperative structures were affected by the input types of the state descriptions fed to their DQNs. For example, agents could establish divisional cooperation by segmentation when agents have absolute locations. In addition, if agents included the trajectory of their movements in the state descriptions, all the agents could establish a social norm with which each agent could incorporate the one-way rule into their behavior without direct communication; therefore, they could skip the redundant activities to avoid collisions.

2   Problem Formulation

We introduce an abstract laying floors problem by using multiple robot in construction sites, called the *pickup and floor laying problem*. In this problem, each agent moves to the given storage area, picks the flooring material up, delivers it to the location where the flooring material has not been installed yet, and then lays it. Then, agents repeat this sequence of tasks until the installation is completed. An example environment of our problem is shown in Fig. 1(a). The environment is a lattice consisting of $N \times N$ cells where the black (hollow) circles are agents, black cells are obstacles, green cells are the storage area where agents can pick flooring material up, and yellow cells are the installation area in which only one piece of material must be placed at each cell. To simplify the description, a piece of material is called a *task* and laying the material is called *executing a task* or *task execution*. We also introduce discrete time $t \geq 0$.

Let $I = \{1, \ldots, n\}$ be the set of n agents. Agent $i \in I$ can hold only one task. The set of its possible actions are denoted by $A = \{up, right, down, left\}$. In Fig. 1(a), the agent with a task is represented as a hollow circle whose inside is green. Agents can pick up a task at any green cell, and the materials will not run out. Right after i has picked up a task, it moves to the installation area and executes the task at a cell where no material has been laid on *empty cell*, represented as a yellow cell in Fig. 1(a). When i successfully executes the task, it receives a reward $r > 0$. Then, the empty cell is changed to the executed cell which is represented as a white cell in Fig. 1(a).

Formally, this problem is specified as a tuple $\langle I, m, N, E, \{S_i\}, \{A_i\} \rangle$, where m is the number of cells in the installation area, $E(\ni e)$ is the set of all possible states including all agents and the states of all cells. We assume that agent $\forall i \in I$ can itself observe the limited local area whose center is i; the state of i's local area at time t is denoted by $s_{i,t}$, which is the subset of the entire state e_t ($s_{i,t} \subset e_t$, where e_t is the entire environment at time t). Let S_i be the set of all local states of i. Finally, we define $\mathcal{A} = A_1 \times \cdots \times A_n \ni a_t = (a_{1,t}, \ldots, a_{n,t})$ as a product of actions, where A_i is the set of all possible actions by $i \in I$. We assume $A_i = A$ for $\forall i \in I$.

Every time agents take joint actions a_t in e_t, they may receive a *reward* $r_i(e_t, a_t)$, and then e_t changes to e_{t+1}. The value of the reward depends on only the current state $e_t \in E$ and joint action $a_t \in \mathcal{A}$. Then, i selects and takes an action on the basis of only the observed local state at t. Because we consider MADRL, the agents individually learn the Q-values to improve the coordinated/cooperative behaviors to obtain more rewards using their own DQNs. The policy π_i of i is usually expressed as the function whose domain is the set of the local state S_i, and range is the set of actions A.

The pickup and floor laying problem proceeds as follows. The storage area (3 cells) and the installation area (108 cells) are specified as shown in Fig. 1(a). Initially ($t = 0$), all agents in I are scattered randomly in a specific area, which is shown in Fig. 1(a) as the 3×15 cell region on the left in the installation area. Let e_t be the entire state of the environment at t. All agents take the following steps simultaneously.

(1) At time t, agent $\forall i \in I$ decides the action $a_{i,t}$ in e_t on the basis of its own policy, so $a_{i,t} = \pi_i(b_{i,t}) \in A$, where $b_{i,t}$ is the belief about the environment and is generated from the observed state $s_{i,t}$ (and is usually identical to $s_{i,t}$ unless otherwise stated).

(2) When i enters the storage area, i automatically picks up one task ψ_i and keeps holding it until arriving at one of the empty cells in the installation area. On the other hand, when i holding ψ_i arrives at an empty cell, i executes ψ_i (so the flooring material is laid) and changes to holding nothing. Then, i receives reward $r_{i,t} = r$, and the empty cell changes to the executed cell.

(3) After all agents move at t, e_t changes to the next state e_{t+1}.

(4) If $t \geq H$ or all cells in the installation area are laid with the flooring materials at t, an epoch ends; otherwise, $t = t + 1$ and go back to Step (1) for the next round, where positive integer H indicates the maximal rounds per epoch.

(5) After the epoch has ended, the environment is initialized, and another epoch will start from Step (1).

We iterate this problem for $F > 0$ epochs. The objective of agents is to maximize the rewards they receive.

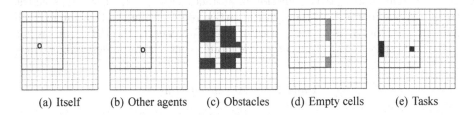

| (a) Itself | (b) Other agents | (c) Obstacles | (d) Empty cells | (e) Tasks |

Fig. 2. Input structure for relative view

3   View Representation

Agent i has a limited range of observation that is specified by the *observable range size* V_i, where V_i is a non-negative integer. Agents can locate all cells, other agents, tasks that other agents have, the storage area, and the installation area correctly within this range. This corresponds to i's observed data $s_{i,t}$. Figure 1(a) shows an example of i's observable range whose size is $V_i = V$. The blue square is the observable range, and i itself is at its center. In this example, the range covers the outside of the environment whose size is $(2V + 1) \times V'$, where $V' = 1$, but i cannot obtain any information on this subregion. We introduce two types of views, $v_{i,t}$, as inputs to DQNs.

Relative Views. Agent i with the *relative view* (RV) generates its view $v_{i,t}$ for input to the local DQN by composing its observed state $s_{i,t}$ and the entire map, as shown in Fig. 1(b). The unobservable regions are assumed to be blank (filled up with 0's). However, we assume that this RV includes the abstract map of the environment and that i's current location is part of its belief. The actual input to the local DQN consists of five channels of $N \times N$ lattices, as shown in Fig. 2, which contains only the location of itself (Fig. 2(a)), other agents (Fig. 2(b)), obstacles (Fig. 2(c)), the empty cells in the installation area (Fig. 2(d)). The fifth lattice represents the tasks that some agents hold and tasks in the storage area (Fig. 2(e)). Thus, the DQN in agent i can see whether i holds a task from the fifth lattice. In those lattice inputs, the characteristic cells are represented as 1, except for obstacle cells, which are represented as -1.

Historic Relative Views. We also introduce the arranged RV, which is the integration of the RV with part of the trajectory of itself. We call it the *historic relative view* (HRV). Agent i with the HRV adds such memorized trajectory data to two lattices of the RV input. First, in the lattice of the location of itself (Fig. 2(a)), i's current location is represented as 1. The i's location k ticks ago is represented as β^k if $\beta^k > \delta$, where $0 < \beta < 1$ is the decay rate, and δ is the threshold to decide whether to reflect the trajectory into the HRVs. If the agent visited a certain location more than twice in the last k ticks, the maximal value is used. Only when agent i holds a task, its trajectory is also added into the input of lattice that represents the location of obstacles (Fig. 2(c)); their values on the trajectory are identical to those in the lattice representing the location of itself and the past locations on the trajectory β^k. To generate the HRV, we assume that agents store the locations at a time more recent than a predetermined time.

Table 1. Network architecture.

Layer	Input	Filter size	Stride	Activation	Output
Convolutional	$N \times N \times 5$	2×2	1		$N \times N \times 32$
Convolutional	$N \times N \times 32$	2×2	1		$N \times N \times 32$
Max pooling	$N \times N \times 32$	2×2	2		$N/2 \times N/2 \times 32$
FCN	$N/2 \times N/2 \times 32$			ReLu	512
FCN	512			ReLu	256
FCN	256			Liner	4

Table 2. Learning parameters.

Parameter	Value
Discount factor for DQN γ_q	0.95
Initial value $\varepsilon_i = \varepsilon_{i,0}$	0.99999
Decay rate γ_ε	0.9999995
Lower limit ε_l	0.02
Update parameter at every η steps	4
Learning rate for RMSprop l_r	0.00001
Momentum for RMSprop α	0.90
ε for RMSprop ε_{rms}	1e-07

Table 3. Experimental parameters.

Parameter	Value
Size of environment N	15
No. of agents n	8
No. of executed cells m	108
Reward r	1
Memory capacity d	2000
Mini batch size u	32
Epoch length H	800
Sum of epochs F	25,000
Trajectory decay rate β	0.9
Lower threshold for trajectory δ	0.05

4   Experiments and Discussion

4.1   Experimental Setting

We experimentally compare the performances (i.e., the total number of tasks executed by all agents and the time required to complete the installation of floor materials) when different types of inputs are fed to the DQNs. The architecture of the DQN is specified in Table 1. The parameter values defined in these experiments are listed in Tables 2 and 3. We set the number of agents $n = 8$, and the environment used in these experiments is identical to that in Fig. 1(a).

We use the double DQN [8] with experience replay, i.e., target network parameters are periodically copied from the main Q-network parameters every H time steps, and update network parameter at every η steps by adapting RMSprop, and using the u number of random sampled experience data from its own memory. As the learning strategy, we use the ε-greedy strategy with decay, where $\varepsilon = \varepsilon_{i,t-1} = \gamma_\varepsilon^t$. When $\varepsilon_{i,t}$ falls below the lower limit ε_l, $\varepsilon_{i,t}$ is fixed to ε_l.

4.2   Performance Comparison

We first examined whether eight agents using RVs could improve the performance over epochs, what coordination structures have emerged, and how the observable range size V affected the performance and coordination structures. Figure 3 plots the moving average lines of total executed tasks using the values of 100 recent epochs from 1 to 25000 when $V = 4, 7, 10$, and 15. Note that since $N = 15$, agents with $V = 15$ can observe the entire environment. As shown in

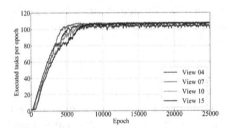

Fig. 3. Executed tasks per epoch (RVs).   Fig. 4. Required time to complete (RVs).

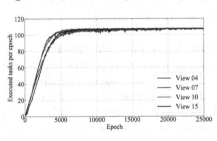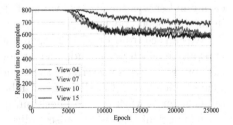

Fig. 5. Executed tasks per epoch (HRVs).   Fig. 6. Required time to complete (HRVs).

this figure, the agents with the RVs could improve the performance, and agents could execute tasks in the installation area regardless of the observation range size. A closer look shows that when $V = 7$, the performances converged slightly faster. This result suggests that there are appropriate values to speed up convergence. Furthermore, we plotted the required time to complete the installation in Fig. 4, where each plot is the moving average value of the time required every 100 epochs when $V = 4, 7, 10$, and 15. We can see that agents could gradually decrease the required time. The performance when $V = 15$ looks slightly shorter, but generally the performances were almost identical except for $V = 4$.

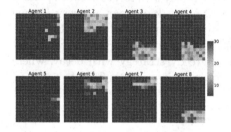
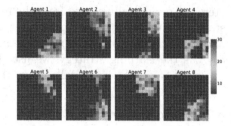

Fig. 7. Executed locations (RVs)   **Fig. 8.** Executed locations (HRVs)

In the second experiment, we verified the performance of collaborative work when agents used HRVs. We plotted the number of executed tasks and the time required for the eight agents with the HRVs in Figs. 5 and 6 to complete them. As shown in Fig. 5, agents with HRVs improved performance over epochs like those with the RVs, but their convergence was slightly faster than that of the agents with the RVs (Fig. 3). However, by comparing Figs. 6 and 4, we can confirm that there is no obvious difference in their times required.

4.3 Emerged Coordination Structures

From the results of the two experiments, the difference in the performance does not seem so large; however, we found that the coordination structures they learned were quite different. Figures 7 and 8 are the heatmaps indicating the numbers of executed tasks by each agent at individual cells when $V = 15$, where each number was the average value of the executed tasks during every 50 epochs in the last 5000 epochs.

We can see from Fig. 7 that agents with the RVs established divisional cooperation, i.e., each agent finds its own locations at which to execute tasks. In the case of agents with the HRVs, the structure of divisional cooperation appeared weakly. Generally, the division of labor may be efficient because it prevents duplication of work and competition, and work without division of labor tends to be inefficient because it causes collision and conflict. However, the results were rarely different in our experiments.

4.4   Discussion

We presented that two types of coordination structure emerged from the difference of input information despite decentralized concurrent MADRL. In the nature of the multi-agent pickup and floor laying problem, collisions and actions for collision avoidance on the narrow routes considerably negatively affect the entire performance; thus, agents generated coordination behaviors that do not cause collisions. The agents with the RVs could establish divisional cooperation on the basis of locational segmentation (or spatial divisional cooperation). Although we omit the graphs due to the page limitation, the agents with the RVs almost uniquely fixed the route for the round trip, and the agents with the HRVs also established the coordination structure in which agents circulate using one-way routes through environments to go back and forth between the storage and installation areas.

To understand the negative effect of collision avoidance, we counted the number of states immediately before collisions, i.e., the states in which two agents could not move onto neighboring cells due to the existence of another agent at the next cell. We call this number the *near collision count* (NSC). Then, we confirmed that the larger observable range size could decrease the NSC. Furthermore, we found that the agent with the HRVs whose range size is 15 ($V = 15$) resulted in the lowest NSC. This indicated that movement along circulation paths was effective in terms of collision avoidance. However, the performance of agents with HRVs was no obvious different form those with the RVs because their circulation paths forced the agents to take longer paths.

Agents with the RVs always took their own routes. This could lead to less collision, but since eight agents shared the three routes, there were a few chances to collide with another agent. We considered that agents with the RVs could establish the distributed work places to reduce the redundant movement in the installation area but could not solve the inefficiency by collision avoidance.

5   Conclusion

We presented that various strategic coordination/cooperation structures emerged in the pickup and floor laying problem with MA-DRL with various types of inputs which were constructed from the observed *views* with the local beliefs. In this framework, agents learn the action-value pairs concurrently by using their own DQNs without direct communication. We showed that various coordination structures were generated; for example, they generated the dividing work places to avoid redundant efforts, or they generated a social norm to regulate agents' behaviors so that no collision occurs. These structures were generated using the *view* including the entire map with their own locations and require these data to be established as social behaviors.

In future work, we would like to verify the robustness and scalability of the agent's learning in our problem when the environment changes because the construction site will change its structure day by day.

Acknowledgement. This work was partly supported by JSPS KAKENHI Grant Number 17KT0044.

References

1. Agmon, N., Kraus, S., Kaminka, G.A.: Multi-robot perimeter patrol in adversarial settings. In: 2008 IEEE International Conference on Robotics and Automation, pp. 2339–2345. IEEE (2008)
2. Foerster, J., Nardelli, N., Farquhar, G., Torr, P., Kohli, P., Whiteson, S., et al.: Stabilising experience replay for deep multi-agent reinforcement learning. arXiv preprint arXiv:1702.08887 (2017)
3. Giuggioli, L., Arye, I., Heiblum Robles, A., Kaminka, G.A.: From ants to birds: a novel bio-inspired approach to online area coverage. In: Groß, R., et al. (eds.) Distributed Autonomous Robotic Systems. SPAR, vol. 6, pp. 31–43. Springer, Cham (2018). https://doi.org/10.1007/978-3-319-73008-0_3
4. Gu, S., Holly, E., Lillicrap, T., Levine, S.: Deep reinforcement learning for robotic manipulation with asynchronous off-policy updates. In: 2017 IEEE International Conference on Robotics and Automation (ICRA), pp. 3389–3396. IEEE (2017)
5. Lample, G., Chaplot, D.S.: Playing FPS games with deep reinforcement learning. In: AAAI, pp. 2140–2146 (2017)
6. Liu, M., Ma, H., Li, J., Koenig, S.: Task and path planning for multi-agent pickup and delivery. In: Proceedings of the 18th International Conference on Autonomous Agents and MultiAgent Systems, pp. 1152–1160. IFAAMAS (2019)
7. Palmer, G., Tuyls, K., Bloembergen, D., Savani, R.: Lenient multi-agent deep reinforcement learning. In: Proceedings of the 17th International Conference on Autonomous Agents and MultiAgent Systems, pp. 443–451. IFAAMAS (2018)
8. Van Hasselt, H., Guez, A., Silver, D.: Deep reinforcement learning with double q-learning. In: AAAI, Phoenix, AZ, vol. 2, p. 5 (2016)

Learning to Explain Anger: An Adaptive Humanoid-Agent for Cyber-Aggression

Fakhra Jabeen[✉], Jan Treur, and Charlotte Gerritsen

Vrije Universiteit, 1081 HV Amsterdam, The Netherlands
fakhraikram@yahoo.com, {j.treur, cs.gerritsen}@vu.nl

Abstract. Social media is one of the widely used channels for interpersonal communication, and to give personal feedback. However, negative feedback can affect esteem and mental health of a person. This paper presents a computational network model of a humanoid agent for getting inappropriate feedback, who learns to react with a level of competence on aggression due to feedback. This model can serve as an input to detect and handle cyber-aggression.

Keywords: Cyber-aggression · Agent based modelling · Computational model

1 Introduction

Computer-mediated communication (CMC) is interpersonal communication, usually within the context of social media, and varies from peer-to-peer to peer-to-community. Individual expressiveness in a perceived anonymity, provides many opportunities to give positive or negative feedback, which may have a lifelong impact on the esteem of a person [1]. Agent-based modeling is able to provide support to humans and can be used to address aggression in educational to commercial sectors as well as in the cyber-world [2].

Aggression is general an unwanted behavior, which can be of any form like cyber-bullying [3] or responsive behavior upon negative critics [4]. Typically, anger arouses due to certain behavior of others, which threatens the ego of a person. Such behavior may hurt the selfesteem of a person, and may result in severe mental health issues including stress and anxiety [2]. To illustrate it further, consider online replies from customer care. Not all customers give positive feedback on a product. So, how customer care should react on negative feedback, is still a burning question [5]. Vulnerability of CMC towards misunderstanding the text or tone of a message, can cause stress and anger among individuals [6]. Network-oriented modeling [7] has addressed many biological and cognitive processes, and here we would like to address (a) mental organization of an agent to express or explain his anger and (b) how mental processes are learned to achieve a level of competence.

In the paper, Sect. 2 discusses related work, while Sect. 3 presents the proposed agent-based network model of cyber-aggression. Section 4 explains simulation results. Section 5 concludes the paper.

M. Baldoni et al. (Eds.): PRIMA 2019, LNAI 11873, pp. 559–567, 2019.
https://doi.org/10.1007/978-3-030-33792-6_41

2 Related Work

This section addresses aggression in a human due to negative feedback or critics from a psychological, social and neurological perspective.

By the psychological perspective, aggressive behavior is the outcome of a person with threatened egotism [8]. Cyber-aggression is usually less empathetic than face-to-face aggression, as aftermaths are not very obvious. Literature shows that feeling angry over a harmful behavior of another person, is a natural emotion [3, 9, 10]. It is good to suppress negative feelings. However, at times it is better to express your anger [9, 10], because anger suppression may cause mental illness [2]. A managed expression and a courteous negotiation might actually help others, while keeping selfesteem high [5, 9]. A prosocial response is always appreciated and can be learned over a period of time [11].

While looking into the cognitive-neuroscience perspective, the amygdala is observed to "play a critical role on emotional stimuli", deciding how to process the information, in a positive, negative or a neutral way [12]. Unlike in post-traumatic stress, the frontal cortex is implicated in regulation of response of a threat. The orientation of this anger is directed towards punishment, causing activations in the amygdala, prefrontal and posterior cingulate cortices. During threat, the amygdala-hypothalamus and the periaqueductal-gray become active [4] along with the hippocampus. Some neurotransmitters are also involved. As an example, 5-hydroxytryptamine (5-HT) predisposes an individual for impulsive aggression. Dopamine is responsible for modulating initiation, execution and consequences of such behavior, while noradrenaline is involved for fighting/attacking behavior [13].

Considering the social perspective of aggression, it is worthy to discuss that adolescents must learn to manage their physiological and cognitive arousal in a way that they can achieve some level of competence [11]. Mental processes depict feelings, emotions and actions of an individual. A person is able to feel and to decide his actions through prediction of these feelings [9]. This is learnt over time and experience, through 'hebbian learning' [14]; however this should be modulated at the level of maturity [15]. Based upon the literature mentioned above, we aim to design a temporal-causal network model (addressed in Sect. 3), that represents a real-time agent, who is able to get angry and her or his possible responses to a negative feedback.

3 Temporal-Causal Network Model

This section presents a temporal-causal network model, that show how an agent should behave when she or he encounters a negative feedback. At the end of the section, a mathematical representation of the model is also depicted.

A temporal-causal network model is based on a conceptual representation of states and connections. In a real-world scenario, these connections designate a causal relationship among the states. A value of a state is an aggregated impact of all influencing states, certain activation levels, over a period of time characterized by [7]:

Connection weight $\omega_{X,Y}$ indicates connection strength or magnitude by which a state X influences state Y. The magnitude usually varies between 0 and 1. A suppression effect on Y is categorized by a negative connection weight.

Speed factor η_Y indicates how fast a state Y changes its value by some causal impact; usual values range between 0 and 1.

Combination function $c_Y(..)$ is chosen to compute the causal (aggregated) impact of all incoming states (X_i: $i = 1\ldots n$) for state Y. Certain standard combination functions are already defined, and can be used to compute the aggregated impact of Y.

Figure 1 presents the conceptual representation of the model of an agent, who reacts with anger, to keep his or her ego high on certain negative feedback. A concise explanation of each state in the proposed model is shown along with reference in Table 1.

Aggression is not an instantaneous process or behavior. It starts with certain stimulus world states ws_s; ws_{fb}, and tries to influence the social repute ws_r of a person. Corresponding sensory states and sensory representation states are identified by ss_s, ss_{fb}, ss_r; and srs_s, srs_{fb}, srs_r respectively. State srs_r activates ps_r, the preparation state for the social repute of an agent. On the one hand srs_{fb} tries to lower the state of positive belief bs_{pos} of oneself, while on the other hand, it triggers negative beliefs about the received feedback via state bs_{neg}. State bs_{neg} activates the preparation states ps_{am}, ps_{com} and feeling state for anger fs_a. To maintain the self-worth of oneself, feeling state fs_a plays its role in expression of anger in two ways along with body expressions.

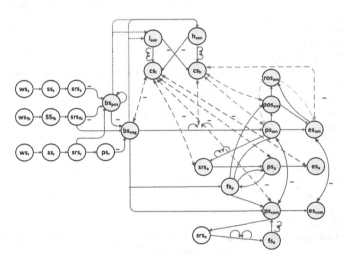

Fig. 1. Temporal-causal network model of the agent (Color figure online)

An expression can be an impulsive (ps_{com} and es_{com}; e.g. public reply) [10] or judicious (ps_{am}, es_{am}; e.g. personal message). In an impulsive reaction, state ps_{com} is activated by bs_{neg} and is amplified by representation and feeling states srs_e, fs_e of the predicted effect e. Secondly, bs_{neg} triggers anger management states ps_{am}, and es_{am} (for instance censoring a comment) [9]. State ps_{am} is completely intact with the self-control mechanisms through prior- and retrospective-ownership states pos_{am} and ros_{am}, making

es_{am} fully aware for the behavior. Moreover, state fs_a prepares (ps_a) to express anger (es_a) (like V shaped raised brows [16]).

The control states cs_l and cs_h provide regulation at two sensitivity levels for feedback: i.e. low (l_{sen}) and high (h_{sen}). Sensitivity is a measure that reflects in how far esteem is affected bs_{pos} due to negative belief bs_{neg}. Sensitivity of input directs the brain to choose between cs_l or cs_h, that may vary with the type of reaction; i.e., an impulsive, or a judicious, or both. As the model aims to explain and control the anger, emotion regulation [17] was used along with its expression. A low sensitive feedback activates cs_l, and uses a reappraisal strategy, to re-evaluate the negative belief bs_{neg}. It suppresses the respective body states $ps_a;$ and es_a and communication states $ps_{com};$ es_{com}. For a highly sensitive feedback, two different types of suppressions are used. Initially, cs_h tries to suppress anger-management states ps_{am}, pos_{am}, and es_{am}. Moreover, due to hebbian learning (experience of the agent), as a level of competence is attained, and cs_h suppresses the connection between bs_{neg} and ps_{am} by state connection modulation and anger (fs_a) is controlled (not suppressed). States cs_h and cs_l have bi-directional arrows indicating monitoring and suppression of a state or a connection. Monitoring and regulation is shown by blue and green arrows from and to control states cs_l and cs_h. While red arrows show suppression (negative connections).

Table 1. Categorical explanation of states.

Category and state	Literature
Stimulus	*"stimulus is sensed and leads to representation"* [7]
ws_i World state i = stimulus (s)/negative feedback (fb)/repute (r)	
ss_i Sensory state for i	
srs_i Representation state for i	
Valuation	*"response .. frontal cortex .. reactive aggression."* [4]
bs_{pos} Positive belief	
bs_{neg} Negative belief	
Control states	*dopamine (DA) may modulate... this behavior.* [13] p. 4
l_{sen} Low sensitive	
h_{sen} High sensitive	
cs_l; cs_h l = low; h = high	
Expression of anger (feeling a)	*DA and 5-HT neurotransmission may interact to mediate*
srs_a Representation state	*aggression"* [13] p. 4
ps_a Preparation state	
fs_a Feeling state	
es_a Expression execution state	
Anger communication (with predicted effect e)	*"hypofunction of 5HT ..individuals to impulsive*
srs_e Representation of effect e	*aggression."* [13] p. 3
fs_e Feeling state for effect e	
ps_{com} Preparation state for com	
es_{com} Execution state for com	
Anger management/Explanation (amicable expression am)	*"Initiation, execution, and consequences of aggression ... DA neurons"*
ps_{am} Preparation state	[13] p. 3
pos_{am} Prior-ownership state	
ros_{am} Retrospective-ownership state	
es_{am} Execution state	

For the computation of impacts of states, the magnitude of the connection weights and the speed factor values are between 0 to 1, and Δt is assumed to be 0.4. The state values of ws_s, ws_r, bs_{pos} are initialized by 1, and ws_{fb} is given values of 0 (no) or 1 (yes) feedback. We used two type of combination functions: (a) for states ss_s, ss_{fb}, ss_r, srs_s, srs_{fb}, srs_r, and ps_r we used the identity function $\mathbf{id}(V) = V$, while rest of the states use (b) **alogistic** function with activation threshold τ and steepness σ as:

$$\mathbf{alogistic}_{\sigma,\tau}(V_1,\ldots,V_k) = \left[\frac{1}{1+e-\sigma(V_1+\ldots+V_k-\tau)} - \frac{1}{1+e^{\sigma\tau}}\right](1+e^{-\sigma\tau})$$

where V_i, $(i =1 \ldots k)$, indicate variables for single impacts $\omega_{Xi,Y}X_i(t)$.

The numerical representation of the network cab be described as [7]:

1. At every time point t, activation value of state X is represented by $X(t)$, and its value ranges between [0-1].
2. To compute activation for $X \rightarrow Y$ at time t, we use the product of weight of connection $X \rightarrow Y$: $\omega_{X,Y}$ and value $X(t)$ of X at time t:

$$\mathbf{impact}_{X,Y}(t) = \omega_{X,Y}X(t)$$

3. The aggregated impact on Y is determined by the (multiple) incoming states X_1 to X_k, using the combination function $c_Y(..)$ of state Y by:

$$\mathbf{aggimpact}_Y(t) = c_Y(\mathbf{impact}_{X1,Y}(t), ., \mathbf{impact}_{Xk,Y}(t))$$
$$= c_Y(\omega_{X1,Y}X_1(t), ., \omega_{Xk,Y}X_k(t))$$

where $c_Y(...)$ is the combination function of Y.
4. The effect on Y is exerted gradually using speed factor η_Y to obtain the causal effect of Y after Δt:

$$Y(t+\Delta t) = Y(t) + \eta_Y[\mathbf{aggimpact}_Y(t) - Y(t)] \text{ and } \mathbf{d}Y(t)/\mathbf{d}t = \eta_Y[\mathbf{aggimpact}_Y(t) - Y(t)]$$
$$(1)$$

So, the difference and differential equations are:

$$Y(t+\Delta t) = Y(t) + \eta_Y[c_Y(\omega_{X1,Y}X_1(t),,\ldots,\omega_{Xk,Y}X_k(t)) - Y(t)]$$
$$\mathbf{d}Y(t)/\mathbf{d}t = \eta_Y[c_Y(\omega_{X1,Y}X_1(t),,\ldots,\omega_{Xk,Y}X_k(t)) - Y(t)]$$

Software environments developed in Matlab and Python are available (and are widely used) to automate the model and perform simulation experiments.

4   Simulation Experiments

This section describes the simulation of real world scenarios. Simulation experiments are used to verify the dynamic properties of a model by taking two real world processes into account: (a) impulsive aggression (b) or judicious aggression. It is worth to mention here, that aggression scenarios vary from case-to-case, which means that in some situations the following scenarios can be independent of each other, while in others they may go along before he learns to explain it. Moreover, aggression can recur with the passage of time, but for simplicity, each simulation scenario is independently represented with one occurrence, i.e. two episodes: (a) without and (b) with feedback. Following are two scenarios explained with respect to two episodes.

4.1   Scenario I: Impulsive Aggression

On an undesirable comment (may be a text message, or a feedback), an impulsive reaction is expected as it influences the esteem of a person [1]. This impulsive reaction can be a peer-to-peer communication. For example:

> "Erica's ... anger arousal ... intentions to pick on her, and ruminations about responding ... Erica seemed to filter out positive aspects of social situations ... two girls turned toward her, but Erica focused on a third girl who seemed to have "made a face and rolled her eyes." This led to Erica's mounting anger, and she felt justified as she made a sarcastic "diss" of her outfit..." [11]

In Fig. 2 the model is initially stable in episode 'a', when a person doesn't observe any negative feedback (states: ss_s, ss_r, srs_s, srs_r). However, the second episode 'b' starts when ws_{fb} is observed, which activates the related states ss_{fb} and srs_{fb}, and lowers bs_{pos} and activates bs_{neg} at $t = 240$. State bs_{neg} (violet curve) triggers ps_{com} and fs_a, which amplifies ps_{com} and ps_a. As a result, es_{com} and es_a are activated at $t = 250$. State cs_l becomes active; per literature fs_a is not suppressed. However, ps_{com} and es_{com} are suppressed by cs_l. It can be observed that initially ps_a, es_a are suppressed, but they continue to grow with fs_a. This indicates an angry impulsive reaction without lowering fs_a.

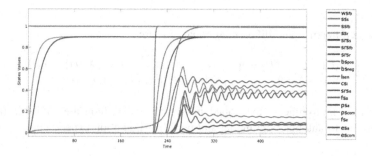

Fig. 2. Expressing anger: before and after feedback (Color figure online)

4.2 Scenario II: Judicious Aggression

For this scenario, we searched the literature, which focused on certain management skills to explain anger [5, 9]. For example a favorable reply to a poor feedback of snowshoes can be like:

> "Thank you so much for ...Unfortunately, depending on the type of snow you are encountering, it can clog even the best footwear. We would like to provide our customers with some customer friendly information to help you..." [18]

Like the first scenario, our model shows aggression when bs_{neg} is activated. Initially arousal is explained through ps_{com} and es_{com}. However, anger state fs_a continues to grow between peers at time point $t = 320$ to 480. So there is a judicious reaction (e.g. sending private message), by anger-management states ps_{am}, pos_{am}, ros_{am}, and es_{am}. The agent learns during the course to manage his or her aggression. As the anger is controlled, cs_h suppresses $bs_{neg} \rightarrow ps_{am}$, affecting rest of the states (at time point $t = 480$) (Fig. 3).

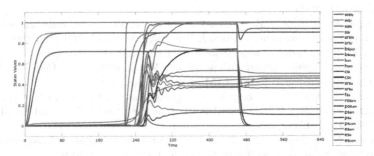

Fig. 3. A cautious expression: before and after feedback (Color figure online)

Here, a hebbian learning effect is also evident, concerning the states bs_{neg}, ps_{am} and fs_a. When cs_l suppresses bs_{neg}, state ps_{am} is initially affected (pink curve). However, this connection continues to learn (by experience), to reach its highest value 1. When cs_h identifies that further learning isn't possible, it plays its role to suppress the connection $bs_{neg} \rightarrow ps_{am}$ at time point $t = 480$. Here anger fs_a is controlled, however, ps_{com} and es_{com} are not much suppressed due to srs_e.

5 Conclusion

A temporal-causal network model [7] was presented explaining the influence of negative feedback, and a defensive reaction by a humanoid-agent. Threatened egotism is considered as one of the major causes of aggression. Feedback is perceived anonymous in social media, but it has limitless exposure. If it is negative, it can arouse angry feelings among peers. As a reaction, of angry feelings an impulsive or a cautious response is expected. An impulsive reaction is usually monitored by predicted effects, while learning plays an important role in a judicious reaction. Cautious or judicious reaction is justified and require a level of competence. This model can be a basis to detect and support anger.

As a future work, we aim to study the model with the perspective of real world data, that how a negative critic can play role in arousing aggression among peers. Moreover, we aim to address recurrence of anger and analyze it with respect to behaviors observed in social media. Lastly, we would also like to explore machine learning techniques that can be helpful in detecting anger, and devise a supporting mechanism for the victims and the aggressors.

References

1. Jabeen, F.: How happy you are: a computational study of social impact on self-esteem. In: Staab, S., Koltsova, O., Ignatov, D.I. (eds.) SocInfo 2018. LNCS, vol. 11186, pp. 108–117. Springer, Cham (2018). https://doi.org/10.1007/978-3-030-01159-8_10
2. Mishna, F., Regehr, C., Lacombe-Duncan, A., Daciuk, J., Fearing, G., Van Wert, M.: Social media, cyber-aggression and student mental health on a university campus. J. Mental Health **27**, 222–229 (2018)
3. Sinaceur, M., Tiedens, L.Z.: Get mad and get more than even: when and why anger expression is effective in negotiations. J. Exp. Soc. Psychol. **42**, 314–322 (2006)
4. Blair, R.J.R.: Considering anger from a cognitive neuroscience perspective: considering anger from a cognitive neuroscience perspective. Wiley Interdisc. Rev. Cogn. Sci. **3**, 65–74 (2012). https://doi.org/10.1002/wcs.154
5. Park, J., et al.: Managing bad news in social media: a case study on domino's pizza crisis. In: Proceedings of the 6th International AAAI Conference on Weblogs and Social Media, pp. 282–289 (2012)
6. Johnson, N.A., Cooper, R.B., Chin, W.W.: Anger and flaming in computer-mediated negotiation among strangers. Decis. Support Syst. **46**, 660–672 (2009)
7. Treur, J.: Network-Oriented Modeling. UCS. Springer, Cham (2016). https://doi.org/10.1007/978-3-319-45213-5
8. Baumeister, R.F., Smart, L., Boden, J.M.: Relation of threatened egotism to violence and aggression: the dark side of high self-esteem. Psychol. Rev. **103**(1), 5–33 (1996)
9. Dekay, S.H.: How large companies react to negative Facebook comments. Corp. Commun. Int. J. **17**(3), 289–299 (2012)
10. Völlink, T., Bolman, C.A.W., Dehue, F., Jacobs, N.C.L.: Coping with cyberbullying: differences between victims, bully-victims and children not involved in bullying. J. Commun. Appl. Soc. Psychol. **23**, 7–24 (2013)
11. Feindler, E.L., Engel, E.C.: Assessment and intervention for adolescents with anger and aggression difficulties in school settings. Psychol. Sch. **48**, 243–253 (2011)
12. Gainotti, G.: Emotions and the right hemisphere: can new data clarify old models? Neuroscientist **25**, 258–270 (2019)
13. Jones, L.J., Norton, W.H.J.: Using zebrafish to uncover the genetic and neural basis of aggression, a frequent comorbid symptom of psychiatric disorders. Behav. Brain Res. **276**, 171–180 (2015)
14. Hebb, D.: The Organization of Behavior. Wiley, New York (1949)
15. Treur, J., Mohammadi Ziabari, S.S.: An adaptive temporal-causal network model for decision making under acute stress. In: Nguyen, N.T., Pimenidis, E., Khan, Z., Trawiński, B. (eds.) ICCCI 2018. LNCS (LNAI), vol. 11056, pp. 13–25. Springer, Cham (2018). https://doi.org/10.1007/978-3-319-98446-9_2

16. LoBue, V., Larson, C.L.: What makes an angry face look so … angry? Examining visual attention to the shape of threat in children and adults. Vis. Cogn. **18**, 1165–1178 (2010). https://doi.org/10.1080/13506281003783675
17. Gross, J.J.: Emotion regulation: current status and future prospects. Psychol. Inq. **26**, 1–26 (2015)
18. Examples, Best Practices for Responding to Negative Reviews on Amazon & Beyond, Channel Signal. https://channelsignal.com/blog/examples-best-practices-of-responding-to-negative-reviews-on-amazon-beyond/

SPSC: A New Execution Policy for Exploring Discrete-Time Stochastic Simulations

Yu-Lin Huang$^{(\boxtimes)}$, Gildas Morvan, Frédéric Pichon, and David Mercier

Univ. Artois, EA 3926, Laboratoire de Génie Informatique et d'Automatique de l'Artois (LGI2A), Béthune, France
{ylin.huang,gildas.morvan,frederic.pichon,david.mercier}@univ-artois.fr

Abstract. In this paper, we introduce a new method called SPSC (Simulation, Partitioning, Selection, Cloning) to estimate efficiently the probability of possible solutions in stochastic simulations. This method can be applied to any type of simulation, however it is particularly suitable for multi-agent-based simulations (MABS). Therefore, its performance is evaluated on a well-known MABS and compared to the classical approach, *i.e.*, Monte Carlo.

Keywords: Stochastic simulation · Multi-agent-based simulation · Solution space exploration

1 Introduction

Multi-agent-based simulations (MABS) are widely used in various fields to study complex systems [6]. Most of them are combined with stochasticity to represent non fully controllable phenomena and use a discrete-time approach to facilitate model construction. Such model can generally be described as taking some initial conditions and some parameter set as inputs, in order to return outputs at each time step (*c.f.* Fig. 1).

Before running into exploration of the parameter set or the initial condition space, we must first analyze outcomes from a fixed parameter set and initial conditions. Let us denote a stochastic simulation outputs (called observables in the following) at a final time step T as a random vector $\boldsymbol{X}_T$. Then a key question to address is: what is the probability $\mathbb{P}(\boldsymbol{X}_T \in \mathcal{S}) = \theta_{\mathcal{S}}$ of a specific solution $\mathcal{S}$?

The classical method to handle this question is Monte Carlo simulation (MC) [7]. It consists in simulating a number n of replications and building an estimator $\hat{\theta}_{\mathcal{S}}$ of $\theta_{\mathcal{S}}$ defined as:

$$\hat{\theta}_{\mathcal{S}} = \frac{1}{n} \sum_{i=1}^{n} \mathbb{1}_{\mathcal{S}}(\boldsymbol{X}_T^i) \tag{1}$$

© Springer Nature Switzerland AG 2019
M. Baldoni et al. (Eds.): PRIMA 2019, LNAI 11873, pp. 568–575, 2019.
https://doi.org/10.1007/978-3-030-33792-6_42

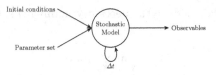

Fig. 1. Illustration of a discrete-time stochastic simulation

where $\mathbb{1}_S$ is the indicator function of the set S and $\boldsymbol{X}_T^i$ the value of observables in the ith replication. The issue with this approach is that for the estimator to be good, the number n has generally to be large, as illustrated in Sect. 2.

Some methods have been developed to speed-up the computation of such simulations, such as splitting [3] or polyagent [5]. However, they look for specific solutions (rare or mean), assume a particular modeling approach (Markov chains or agent-based) and require some low-level manipulations of the model.

In this paper, we propose a policy that simulates an authorized number N of replications and is as generic as the MC approach yet provides a better estimator when computational resources are limited (*i.e.* small N).

The paper is organized as follows: Sect. 2 recalls and illustrates a standard approach to determine the required number of replications in Monte Carlo simulation for a single observable. The design principles and the approach proposed to answer the above-mentioned issues are presented in Sect. 3 and then applied to a classical MABS in Sect. 4. Section 5 concludes the paper.

2   Monte Carlo Simulation, How Many Replications?

We recall in this section a standard approach to determine the number $n(X_{T,i})$ of replications to obtain a good estimator $\hat{\theta}_{S_i}$ of the probability $\mathbb{P}(X_{T,i} \in S_i) = \theta_{S_i}$ of some solution S_i where $X_{T,i}$ is one observable of the vector $\boldsymbol{X}_T$. Suppose a desired relative error ϵ for the estimator $\hat{\theta}_{S_i}$ at confidence level $1 - \alpha$:

$$\mathbb{P}(\frac{|\hat{\theta}_{S_i} - \theta_{S_i}|}{\theta_{S_i}} \leq \epsilon) \geq 1 - \alpha. \tag{2}$$

The minimal value for $n(X_{T,i})$ to verify (2) can be determined by applying the following algorithm [1, p. 449]:

1. Simulate n_0 replications. (n_0 observations $X_{T,i}^1, \ldots, X_{T,i}^{n_0}$)
2. Compute

$$n(X_{T,i}) = \lceil (\frac{Z_{1-(\frac{\alpha}{2})} \cdot s_i}{\epsilon \cdot \overline{X}_{T,i}})^2 \rceil \tag{3}$$

where $Z_{1-(\alpha/2)}$ is the $100(1 - \alpha/2)$ quantile of the normal distribution, s_i stands for the sample standard deviation over the n_0 observations and $\overline{X}_{T,i}$ is the sample mean value over the n_0 observations. The conventional values for n_0, ϵ and α are respectively 150, 0.05 and 0.05.

Afterward, we can then deduce the necessary number n satisfying every observable as:

$$n = \max_{X_{T,i} \in \boldsymbol{X}_T} n(X_{T,i}) \tag{4}$$

To illustrate this algorithm, let us take an academic example. We consider an environment containing vegetation and 2 types of agents: preys consuming the vegetation and predators hunting preys for food. Both preys and predators can move without restriction in the environment. This model has been implemented on the SIMILAR platform [4] and is based on the NetLogo wolf sheep predation model [8]. The set of observables here consists of the populations of different species at each time step. The necessary number n for some arbitrarily chosen parameter set and initial state of the simulation, using the conventional values for n_0, ϵ and α, is 3600 (c.f. Table 1). However, if we want a more precise estimation, the necessary number n of replications increases drastically: for example, considering a relative error $\epsilon = 0.005$ yields a necessary number of replications $n = 7249285$.

Table 1. Determination of the necessary number of replications for the prey predator model implemented on the SIMILAR platform. The parameters applied are $n_0 = 150$, $\epsilon = 0.05$ and $\alpha = 0.05$.

$X_{T,i}$	s_i	$\overline{X}_{T,i}$	$n(X_{T,i})$
Number of preys	697.83	783.77	1219
Number of predators	196.95	128.67	**3600**

3 A New Execution Policy for Stochastic Simulations

In this section, we introduce a new execution policy for stochastic simulations called SPSC (Simulation, Partitioning, Selection, Cloning). This approach relies on a decomposition of the probability of interest that we explain first.

3.1 Decomposition of the Probability of Interest

The probability $\mathbb{P}(\boldsymbol{X}_T \in \mathcal{S})$ concerns the observables with respect to a specific solution $\mathcal{S}$ at some final time step T. Thanks to the law of total probability, considering some intermediate time step j before T, we can write

$$\mathbb{P}(\boldsymbol{X}_T \in \mathcal{S}) = \sum_{\mathcal{S}_j \in \mathscr{P}_j} \mathbb{P}(\boldsymbol{X}_T \in \mathcal{S} | \boldsymbol{X}_j \in \mathcal{S}_j) \mathbb{P}(\boldsymbol{X}_j \in \mathcal{S}_j) \tag{5}$$

where $\mathscr{P}_j$ is a partition of the state space of the random vector $\boldsymbol{X}_j$.

More generally, considering all time steps before T, we can obtain the following decomposition by assuming a discrete-time system where $\boldsymbol{X}_i$ depends only on $\boldsymbol{X}_{i-1}$:

$$\mathbb{P}(\boldsymbol{X}_T \in \mathcal{S}) = \sum_{\substack{\mathcal{S}_{T-1} \in \mathscr{P}_{T-1} \\ \vdots \\ \mathcal{S}_1 \in \mathscr{P}_1}} \prod_{i=0}^{T-1} \mathbb{P}(\boldsymbol{X}_{i+1} \in \mathcal{S}_{i+1} | \boldsymbol{X}_i \in \mathcal{S}_i) \qquad (6)$$

where $\mathscr{P}_i$, $i = 1, ..., T - 1$, is a partition of the state space of $\boldsymbol{X}_i$, $\mathcal{S}_T = \mathcal{S}$ and $\mathcal{S}_0$ is the initial state of the simulation.

3.2 SPSC: Simulation, Partitioning, Selection, Cloning

Inspired by the decomposition (6), we split the time interval $[0, T]$ into m pieces: $[t_{(0)}, t_{(1)}], [t_{(1)}, t_{(2)}], ..., [t_{(m-1)}, t_{(m)}]$ where $t_{(0)} = 0 < t_{(1)} < ... < t_{(m-1)} < t_{(m)} = T$. Then, for each interval $[t_{(i)}, t_{(i+1)}]$ the following steps are applied (c.f. Figs. 2 and 3):

Simulation. Simulate N replications from $t_{(i)}$ to $t_{(i+1)}$, $i \in \{0, \ldots, m-1\}$, where N corresponds to the number of replications we authorize for the simulation.

Partitioning. At time $t_{(i+1)}$, form a partition of the space of observables of these N replications. This can be done by applying a clustering algorithm.

Selection. Choose one or multiple representative replications (which we call delegates) from each partition and discard the other replications.

Cloning. Clone the selected delegates to obtain N replications in total.

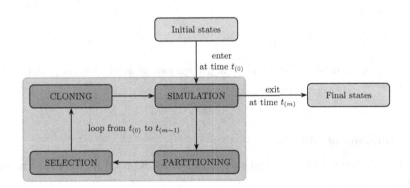

Fig. 2. SPSC process diagram

Once the iterations are finished, we have created for each $t_{(i)}$ a partition $\mathscr{P}_{(i)}$ for the state space of $\boldsymbol{X}_{t_{(i)}}$. For an element $\mathcal{S}_{(i)} \in \mathscr{P}_{(i)}$ of the partition at time step $t_{(i)}$, after the selection and cloning steps, it has n_i cloned replications.

Besides, among these n_i cloned replications, after evolving to the next time step $t_{(i+1)}$, some of them (n_{i+1} replications) belong to some element $\mathcal{S}_{(i+1)} \in \mathscr{P}_{(i+1)}$. We propose to use the numbers n_i and n_{i+1} to approximate the conditional probability $\mathbb{P}(\boldsymbol{X}_{t_{(i+1)}} \in \mathcal{S}_{(i+1)} | \boldsymbol{X}_{t_{(i)}} \in \mathcal{S}_{(i)})$ by:

$$\hat{P}(\boldsymbol{X}_{t_{(i+1)}} \in \mathcal{S}_{(i+1)} | \boldsymbol{X}_{t_{(i)}} \in \mathcal{S}_{(i)}) = \frac{n_{i+1}}{n_i} \tag{7}$$

Finally, we define an estimator $\hat{\theta}_{\mathcal{S}}$ for $\mathbb{P}(\boldsymbol{X}_T \in \mathcal{S})$ using a similar decomposition as that of Eq. (6), based on time steps $t_{(i)}$ and (7):

$$\hat{\theta}_{\mathcal{S}} = \sum_{\substack{\mathcal{S}_{(m-1)} \in \mathscr{P}_{(m-1)} \\ \vdots \\ \mathcal{S}_{(1)} \in \mathscr{P}_{(1)}}} \prod_{i=0}^{m-1} \hat{P}(\boldsymbol{X}_{t_{(i+1)}} \in \mathcal{S}_{(i+1)} | \boldsymbol{X}_{t_{(i)}} \in \mathcal{S}_{(i)}) \tag{8}$$

where $\mathcal{S}_{(m)} = \mathcal{S}$ and $\mathcal{S}_{(0)} = \mathcal{S}_0$.

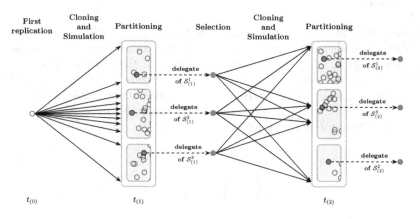

Fig. 3. Illustration of the first and second iterations of SPSC, starting from a single initial state.

3.3   Implementation

We describe here a simple implementation of SPSC used in the experiment in Sect. 4:

Simulation. No special action is taken in this step.

Partitioning. N replications provide N instances of observables. To form a partition in the space of observables, we can take advantage of existing unsupervised learning algorithm which can separate instances by multiple subgroups. The well-known clustering process *kmeans* has been chosen to fulfill the task. The number of cluster k is preset to 15.

Selection. From any element $\mathcal{S}_{(i)} \in \mathscr{P}_{(i)}$ of an intermediate partition, we select the replication which is the nearest to the center using euclidean distance on the space of observables.

Cloning. After partitioning and selection, k delegates are obtained to be cloned. To come back to N replications in total, we clone each delegate $\lfloor \frac{N}{k} \rfloor$ times. If k does not divide N, we select randomly the remainder number $N - k * \lfloor \frac{N}{k} \rfloor$ of delegates to produce one more clone per selected delegate.

The time interval $[0, T]$ is homogeneously split into $m = 5$ pieces (*i.e.* $\forall i \in \{0, 1, \ldots, 5\}$, $t_{(i)} = i \times \frac{T}{5}$).

4   Experiment

Let us take the prey predator model mentioned previously in Sect. 2 as an example. As this model is well-known and well-studied, we can give some possible solutions before launching simulations:

$\mathcal{S}_1$: Extinction of preys and predators, only vegetation remains.

$\mathcal{S}_2$: Predators go extinct, preys live without nature enemy's harass.

$\mathcal{S}_3$: All species survive and form a stable ecosystem.

Now the question is, for an arbitrary parameter set and initial condition, what is the probability of these solutions at a given time step (*e.g.* $T = 1000$)? To answer this question, the MC approach recalled in Sect. 2 is generally used.

In the following, we compare the performances of MC and SPSC. The validation is done by comparing the outputs of these methods with the same limited number of replications $N = 50$. By repeating the simulations 1000 times, we will be able to compare statistically the results obtained by MC and SPSC. Two performance measures are considered here: (1) The detection rate of a specific solution $\mathcal{S}$. (2) The precision of the probability estimator for a specific solution. Before evaluating these performance measures, we have done 30000 replications using MC in order to provide reference values for the comparisons:

$$P_{ref}(\mathcal{S}_1) \approx 0.0065, P_{ref}(\mathcal{S}_2) \approx 0.0126, P_{ref}(\mathcal{S}_3) \approx 0.981 \qquad (9)$$

The detection rates obtained with MC and SPSC policies, *i.e*, the capacity of identifying a specific solution, from $N = 50$ replications are summed up in Table 2. The first three columns indicate the detection rate of single solutions and the last column indicate the detection rate for the three solutions simultaneously. We can then deduce that SPSC explores more efficiently the solution space.

To evaluate the precision of the probability estimator, the absolute error between the probability estimator outcomes and the references is computed:

$$Err(\mathcal{S}_i) = |\hat{P}(\mathcal{S}_i) - P_{ref}(\mathcal{S}_i)|. \qquad (10)$$

Furthermore, to gain an entire vision on the three solutions simultaneously, we consider also the mean of three solutions relative errors:

$$\overline{Err} = \sum_{1 \leq i \leq 3} |\frac{\hat{P}(\mathcal{S}_i) - P_{ref}(\mathcal{S}_i)}{P_{ref}(\mathcal{S}_i)}|. \tag{11}$$

Table 2. Detection rates obtained with MC and SPSC when launching 50 replications.

	$\mathcal{S}_1$	$\mathcal{S}_2$	$\mathcal{S}_3$	$\mathcal{S}_1$, $\mathcal{S}_2$ and $\mathcal{S}_3$
MC	0.236	0.455	1	0.102
SPSC	0.332	0.617	1	0.203

Histograms of these errors for the policies SPSC and MC are shown in Fig. 4.

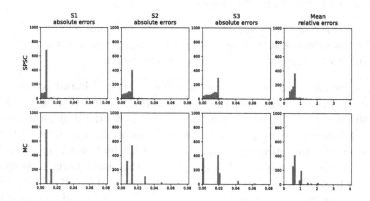

Fig. 4. Comparison of errors

We can notice that the distribution of errors are not normal nor symmetric. Thus, to compare the errors from MC and SPSC policies, the Wilcoxon-Mann-Whitney test is applied with the threshold $\alpha = 0.05$. The test results are presented in Table 3 with p-value and alternative hypotheses, we can then conclude that SPSC yields better probability estimates for each solution than MC.

Table 3. Hypothesis and p-value given by Wilcoxon-Mann-Whitney test.

Target solution	Alternative hypotheses	p-value	Conclusion
$\mathcal{S}_1$	$Err_{SPSC} < Err_{MC}$	2.2e−16	$Err_{SPSC} < Err_{MC}$
$\mathcal{S}_2$	$Err_{SPSC} < Err_{MC}$	3.163e−16	$Err_{SPSC} < Err_{MC}$
$\mathcal{S}_3$	$Err_{SPSC} < Err_{MC}$	9.849e−09	$Err_{SPSC} < Err_{MC}$
$\mathcal{S}_1$, $\mathcal{S}_2$ and $\mathcal{S}_3$	$\overline{Err}_{SPSC} < \overline{Err}_{MC}$	2.2e−16	$\overline{Err}_{SPSC} < \overline{Err}_{MC}$

5   Conclusions and Perspectives

We have introduced a generic policy called SPSC for executing stochastic simulations that deals with the weakness of MC when the number of replications is limited. It treats simulations as black boxes and therefore, does not rely upon *a priori* knowledge. We have also presented a simple implementation of SPSC and run it on a classic stochastic MABS model. By comparing the results obtained with SPSC and with MC, we can conclude that SPSC gives a better solution probability estimation and can reveal more different solutions than MC.

The first perspectives of this work are related to the impact of the parameters (N, k, etc.), the partitioning algorithm as well as the selection and cloning strategies on the performance. For instance, instead of having the same number of clones for each delegate, we could clone more the delegates from small partitions and less the delegates from large partitions. Theoretical properties of the proposed solution as well as its interest for multimodal transport simulation will also be investigated.

Moreover, since we deal with small sample size at each intermediate time step, we could take advantage of modern tools [2] for statistical inference to compute the estimator $\hat{\theta}_S$.

Acknowledgement. This work is partly funded by the ELSAT2020 project, which is co-financed by the European Union with the European Regional Development Fund, the French state and the Hauts de France Region Council.

References

1. Banks, J., Carson II, J., Nelson, B., Nicol, D.: Discrete-Event System Simulation, 5th edn. Pearson, Upper Saddle River (2010)
2. Kanjanatarakul, O., Denœux, T., Sriboonchitta, S.: Prediction of future observations using belief functions: a likelihood-based approach. Int. J. Approx. Reason. **72**, 71–94 (2016)
3. L'Ecuyer, P., Le Gland, F., Lezaud, P., Tuffin, B.: Rare Event Simulation using Monte Carlo Methods, chap. Wiley, Splitting Techniques (2009)
4. Morvan, G., Kubera, Y.: On time and consistency in multi-agent-based simulations. CoRR arXiv:1703.02399 (2017)
5. Dyke Parunak, H.: Pheromones, probabilities, and multiple futures. In: Bosse, T., Geller, A., Jonker, C.M. (eds.) MABS 2010. LNCS (LNAI), vol. 6532, pp. 44–60. Springer, Heidelberg (2011). https://doi.org/10.1007/978-3-642-18345-4_4
6. Railsback, S., Grimm, V.: Agent-Based and Individual-Based Modeling: A Practical Introduction. Princeton University Press, Princeton (2011)
7. Rubinstein, R.Y., Kroese, D.P.: Simulation and the Monte Carlo Method, 3rd edn. Wiley, New York (2016)
8. Wilensky, U.: NetLogo wolf sheep predation model. Center for Connected Learning and Computer-Based Modeling, Northwestern University, Evanston, IL (1997). http://ccl.northwestern.edu/netlogo/models/WolfSheepPredation

Computational Complexity of Hedonic Games on Sparse Graphs

Tesshu Hanaka[1]($\boxtimes$), Hironori Kiya[2], Yasuhide Maei[2]($\boxtimes$), and Hirotaka Ono[2]

[1] Department of Information and System Engineering, Chuo University,
1-13-27 Kasuga, Bunkyo-ku, Tokyo, Japan
hanaka.91t@g.chuo-u.ac.jp
[2] Graduate School of Informatics, Nagoya University,
Furo-cho, Chikusa-ku, Nagoya, Japan
kiya.hironori@f.mbox.nagoya-u.ac.jp, maei.yasuhide@a.mbox.nagoya-u.ac.jp,
ono@i.nagoya-u.ac.jp

Abstract. The additively separable hedonic game (ASHG) is a model of coalition formation games on graphs. In this paper, we intensively and extensively investigate the computational complexity of finding several desirable solutions, such as a Nash stable solution, a maximum utilitarian solution, and a maximum egalitarian solution in ASHGs on sparse graphs including bounded-degree graphs, bounded-treewidth graphs, and near-planar graphs. For example, we show that finding a maximum egalitarian solution is weakly NP-hard even on graphs of treewidth 2, whereas it can be solvable in polynomial time on trees. Moreover, we give a pseudo fixed parameter algorithm when parameterized by treewidth.

Keywords: Hedonic games · Coalition formation · Social network · PLS-completeness · Parameterized algorithm

1 Introduction

In this paper, we investigate the computational complexity of additively separable hedonic games on sparse graphs from the viewpoint of several solution concepts.

Given the set of agents, the coalition formation game is a model of finding a partition of the set of agents into subsets under a certain criterion, where each of the subsets is called a *coalition*. Such a partition is called a *coalition structure*. The *hedonic game* is a variant of coalition formation games, where each agent has the utility associated with his/her joining coalition. In the typical setting, if an agent belongs to a coalition where his/her favorite agents also belong to, his/her utility is high and he/she feels comfortable. Contrarily, if he/she does not like many members in the coalition, his/her utility must be low;

A full version of the paper is available in [13]. This work was partially supported by JSPS KAKENHI Grant Numbers JP17K19960, 17H01698, 19K21537.

M. Baldoni et al. (Eds.): PRIMA 2019, LNAI 11873, pp. 576–584, 2019.
https://doi.org/10.1007/978-3-030-33792-6_43

since he/she feels uncomfortable, he/she would like to move to another coalition. Although the model of hedonic games is very simple, it is useful to represent many practical situations, such as formation of research team [2], formation of coalition government [14], clustering in social networks [3,15,16], multi-agent distributed task assignment [18], and so on.

The *additively separable hedonic game* (ASHG) is a class of hedonic games, where the utility forms an additively separable function. In ASHG, an agent has a certain *valuation* for each of the agents, which represents his/her preference. The valuation could be positive, negative or 0. If the valuation of agent u for agent v is positive, agent u prefers agent v, and if it is negative, agent u does not prefer agent v. If it is 0, agent u has no interest for agent v. The utility of agent u for u's joining coalition C is defined by the sum of valuations of agent u for other agents in C. This setting is considered not very but reasonably general. Due to this definition, it can be also defined by an edge-weighted directed graph, where the weight of edge (u, v) represents the valuation of u to v. If a valuation is 0, we can remove the corresponding edge. Note that the undirected setting is possible, and in the case the valuations are symmetric; the valuation of agent u for agent v is always equal to the one of agent v for agent u.

In the study of hedonic games, several solution concepts are considered important and well investigated. One of the most natural solution concepts is *maximum utilitarian*, which is so-called a global optimal solution; it is a coalition structure that maximizes the total sum of the utilities of all the agents. The total sum of the utilities is also called *social welfare*. Another concept of a global optimal solution is *maximum egalitarian*. It maximizes the minimum utility of an agent among all the agents. That is, it makes the unhappiest agent as happy as possible. Nash-stability, envy-free and max envy-free are more personalized concepts of the solutions. A coalition structure is called *Nash-stable* if no agent has an incentive to move to another coalition from the current joining coalition. Such an incentive to move to another coalition is also called a *deviation*. Agent u feels envious of v if u can increase his/her utility by exchanging the coalitions of u and v. A coalition structure is *envy-free* if any agent does not envy any other agent. Furthermore, the best one among the envy-free coalition structures is also meaningful; it is an envy-free coalition structure with maximum social welfare.

Of course, it is not trivial to find a coalition structure satisfying above mentioned solution concepts. Ballester studies the computational complexity for finding coalition structures of several concepts including the above mentioned ones [5]. More precisely, he shows that determining whether there is a Nash stable, an individually stable, and a core stable coalition structure is NP-complete. In [19], Sung and Dimitrov show that the same results hold for ASHG. Aziz et al. investigate the computational complexity for many concepts including the above five solution concepts [4]. In summary, ASHG is unfortunately NP-hard for the above five solution concepts. These hardness results are however proven without any assumption about graph structures. For example, some of the proofs suppose that graphs are weighted complete graphs. This might be a problem, because graphs appearing in ASHGs for practical applications are so-called social networks; they are far from weighted complete graphs and known to be rather sparse or tree-like [1,10]. What if we restrict the input graphs of ASHG to sparse graphs? This is the motivation of this research.

In this paper, we investigate the computational complexity of ASHG on sparse graphs from the above five solution concepts. The sparsity that we consider in this paper is as follows: graphs with bounded degree, graphs with bounded treewidth and near-planar graphs. The degree is a very natural parameter that characterizes the sparsity of graphs. In social networks, the degree represents the number of friends, which is usually much smaller than the size of network. The *treewidth* is a parameter that represents how tree-like a graph is. As Adcock, Sullivan and Mahoney pointed out in [1], many large social and information networks have tree-like structures, which implies the significance to investigate the computational complexity of ASHG on graphs with bounded treewidth. Near-planar graphs here are p-apex graphs. A graph G is said to be p-apex if G becomes planar after deleting p vertices or fewer vertices. Near-planarity is less important than the former two in the context of social networks, though it also has many practical applications such as transportation networks. Note that all of these sparsity concepts are represented by parameters, i.e., treewidth, maximum degree and p-apex. In that sense, we consider the parameterized complexity of ASHG of several solution concepts in this paper.

This is not the first work that focuses on the parameterized complexity of ASHG. Peters presents that Nash-stable, Maximum Utilitarian, Maximum Egalitarian and Envy-free coalition structures can be computed in $2^{\text{tw}\Delta^2} n^{O(1)}$ time, where tw is the treewidth and Δ is the maximum degree of an input graph [17]. In other word, it is *fixed parameter tractable (FPT)* with respect to treewidth and maximum degree. This implies that if both of the treewidth and the maximum degree are small, we can efficiently find desirable coalition structures. This result raises the following natural question: is finding these desirable coalition structures still FPT when parameterized by either the treewidth or the maximum degree?

This paper answers the question from various viewpoints. Different from the case parameterized by treewidth and maximum degree, the time complexity varies depending on the solution concepts. For example, we can compute a maximum utilitarian coalition structure in $\text{tw}^{O(\text{tw})} n$ time, whereas computing a maximum egalitarian coalition structure is weakly NP-hard even for graphs with treewidth at most 2. Some other results of ours are summarized in Table 1. For more details, see Sect. 1.1. Also some related results are summarized in Sect. 1.2.

1.1   Our Contribution

We first study (symmetric) NASH STABLE on bounded degree graphs. We show that the problem is PLS-complete even on graphs with maximum degree 7. PLS is a complexity class of a pair of an optimization problem and a local search for it. It is originally introduced to capture the difficulty of finding a locally optimal solution of an optimization problem. In the context of hedonic games, a

Table 1. Complexity of ASHGs

Concept	Time complexity to compute	Reference
Nash stable	NP-hard	[19]
	PLS-complete (symm)	[11]
	PLS-complete (symm, $\Delta = 7$)	[Theorem 1]
	$\text{tw}^{O(\text{tw})}n$ **(symm, FPT by treewidth)**	[Corollary 1]
Max Utilitarian	strongly NP-hard (symm)	[4]
	strongly NP-hard (symm, 3-apex)	[Theorem 2]
	$\text{tw}^{O(\text{tw})}n$ **(FPT by treewidth)**	[Theorem 3]
Max Egalitarian	strongly NP-hard	[4]
	weakly NP-hard (symm, 2-apex, vc $= 4$)	[Theorem 6]
	weakly NP-hard (symm, planar, pw $= 4$, tw $= 2$)	[Theorem 5]
	strongly NP-hard (symm)	[Theorem 7]
	linear (symm, tree)	[Theorem 8]
	P (tree)	[Theorem 9]
	$(\text{tw}W)^{O(\text{tw})}n$ **(pseudo FPT by treewidth)**	[Theorem 10]
Envy-free	trivial	[4]
Max Envy-free	**weakly NP-hard (symm, planar, vc $= 2$, tw $= 2$)**	[Theorem 4]
	strongly NP-hard (symm)	[Theorem 7]
	linear (symm, tree)	[Theorem 8]

deviation corresponds to an improvement in local search, and thus PLS or PLS-completeness is also used to model the difficulty of finding a stable solution.

We next show that MAX UTILITARIAN is strongly NP-hard on 3-apex graphs, whereas it can be solved in time $\text{tw}^{O(\text{tw})}n$, and hence it is FPT when parameterized by treewidth tw. For MAX ENVY-FREE, we show that the problem is weakly NP-hard on series-parallel graphs with vertex cover number at most 2 whereas finding an envy-free partition is trivial [4].

Finally, we investigate the computational complexity of MAX EGALITARIAN. We show that MAX EGALITARIAN is weakly NP-hard on 2-apex graphs with vertex cover number at most 4 and planer graphs with pathwidth at most 4 and treewidth at most 2. Moreover, we show that MAX EGALITARIAN and MAX ENVY-FREE are strongly NP-hard even if the preferences are symmetric. In contrast, an egalitarian and envy-free partition with maximum social welfare can be found in linear time on trees if the preferences are symmetric. Moreover, MAX EGALITARIAN can be computed in polynomial time even if the preferences are asymmetric. In the end of this paper, we give a pseudo FPT algorithm when parameterized by treewidth.

1.2 Related Work

The *coalition formation game* is first introduced by Dreze and Greenber [9] in the field of Economics. Based on the concept of coalition formation games, Banerjee, Konishi and Sönmez [6] and Bogomolnaia and Jackson [7] study some stability and core concepts on hedonic games. For the computational complexity on hedonic games, Ballester shows that finding several coalition structures including Nash stable, core stable, and individually stable coalition structures is NP-complete [5]. For ASHGs, Aziz et al. investigate the computational complexity of finding several desirable coalition structures [4]. Gairing and Savani [11] show that computing a Nash stable coalition structure is PLS-complete in symmetric AGHGs whereas Bogomolnaia and Jackson [7] prove that a Nash stable coalition structure always exists. In [17], Peters designs parameterized algorithms for computing some coalition structures on hedonic games with respect to treewidth and maximum degree.

2 Preliminaries

2.1 Hedonic Game

An *additively separable hedonic game* (ASHG) is defined on a directed edge-weighted graph $G = (V, E, w)$. Each vertex $v \in V$ is called an *agent*. The weight of an edge $e = (u, v)$, denoted by w_e or w_{uv}, represents the valuation of u to v. An ASHG is said to be *symmetric* if $w_{uv} = w_{vu}$ holds for any pair of u and v. Any symmetric ASHG can be defined on an *undirected* edge-weighted graph. We denote an undirected edge by $\{u, v\}$. Note that any edge of weight 0 is removed from a graph.

Let $\mathcal{P}$ be a partition of V. Then $C \in \mathcal{P}$ is called a *coalition*. We denote by $C_u \in \mathcal{P}$ the coalition to which an agent $u \in V$ belongs under $\mathcal{P}$, and by $E(C_u)$ the set of edges $\{(u, v) \cup (v, u) \in E \mid v \in C_u\}$. In ASHGs, the utility of an agent u under $\mathcal{P}$ is defined as $u_{\mathcal{P}}(u) = \sum_{v \in N(u) \cap C_u} w_{uv}$, which is the sum of weights of edges from u to other agents in the same coalition. Also, the *social welfare* of $\mathcal{P}$ is defined as the sum of utilities of all agents under $\mathcal{P}$. Note that the social welfare equals to exactly twice the sum of weights of edges in coalitions.

Next, we define several concepts of desirable solution in ASHGs.

Definition 1 (Nash-stable). *A partition $\mathcal{P}$ is Nash-stable if there exists no agent u and coalition $C' \neq C_u$ containing u, possibly empty, such that $\sum_{v \in N(u) \cap C_u} w_{uv} < \sum_{v \in N(u) \cap C'} w_{uv}$.*

As an important fact, in any symmetric ASHG, a partition with maximum social welfare is Nash-stable by using the potential function argument [7].

Proposition 1. *In any symmetric ASHG, a partition with maximum social welfare is Nash-stable.*

Thus, if we can compute a partition with maximum social welfare in a symmetric ASHG, then we also obtain a Nash-stable partition.

Definition 2 (Envy-free). *We say an agent $u_1 \in C_{u_1}$ envies $u_2 \in C_{u_2}$ if the following inequality holds: $\sum_{v \in N(u_1) \cap C_{u_1}} w_{u_1 v} < \sum_{v \in N(u_1) \cap (C_{u_2} \setminus \{u_2\} \cup \{u_1\})} w_{u_1 v}$. That is, u_1 envies u_2 if the utility of u_1 increases by replacing u_2 by u_1. A partition $\mathcal{P}$ is* envy-free *if any agent does not envy an agent.*

NASH-STABLE, ENVY-FREE, MAX ENVY-FREE, MAX UTILITARIAN, and MAX EGALITARIAN are the following problems: Given a weighted graph $G = (V, E, w)$, find a Nash-stable partition, an envy-free partition, an envy-free partition with maximum social welfare, a maximum utilitarian partition, and a maximum egalitarian partition, respectively.

2.2   Graph Parameters and Parameterized Complexity

For the basic definitions of parameterized complexity such as the classes FPT and XP, and some definitions of graph parameters such as treewidth $\mathrm{tw}(G)$ and pathwidth $\mathrm{pw}(G)$, we refer the reader to the book [8].

A *vertex cover* S is the set of vertices such that every edge has at least one vertex in S. The size of minimum vertex cover in G is called *vertex cover number*, denoted by $\mathrm{vc}(G)$. The following proposition is a well-known relationship between treewidth, pathwidth, and vertex cover number.

Proposition 2. *For any graph G, it holds that $\mathrm{tw}(G) \leq \mathrm{pw}(G) \leq \mathrm{vc}(G)$.*

Proposition 3. *Let p be some constant. For any p-apex graph G, $\mathrm{tw}(G) \leq 3.183\sqrt{n} + p - 1$. Moreover, a tree decomposition of such width can be computed in polynomial time.*

Proposition 3 implies that there is a $2^{O(\sqrt{n} \log n)}$-time algorithm for any p-apex graph if there is a $\mathrm{tw}^{O(\mathrm{tw})}$-time or even an $n^{O(\mathrm{tw})}$-time algorithm. Therefore, MAX UTILITARIAN and MAX EGALITARIAN with restricted weights can be solved in time $2^{O(\sqrt{n} \log n)}$ on p-apex graphs from Theorems 3 and 10.

3   Nash-Stable

Any symmetric ASHG always has a Nash-stable partition by Proposition 1. However, finding a Nash-stable solution is PLS-complete [11]. In this section, we prove that NASH-STABLE is PLS-complete even on bounded degree graphs.

Theorem 1. *Symmetric* NASH-STABLE *is PLS-complete even on graphs with maximum degree $\Delta = 7$.*

4   Max Utilitarian

We first show that MAX UTILITARIAN is strongly NP-hard on 3-apex graphs.

Theorem 2. MAX UTILITARIAN *is strongly NP-hard on 3-apex graphs even if the preferences are symmetric.*

Then we give an FPT algorithm for MAX UTILITARIAN parameterized by treewidth. Our algorithm is based on dynamic programming on a tree decomposition for connectivity problems such as STEINER TREE [8]. In our dynamic programming, we keep track of all the partitions in each bag.

Theorem 3. *Given a tree decomposition of width* tw, MAX UTILITARIAN *can be solved in time* $\text{tw}^{O(\text{tw})}n$.

By Proposition 1, symmetric NASH-STABLE is also solvable in time $\text{tw}^{O(\text{tw})}n$.

Corollary 1. *Given a tree decomposition of width* tw, *symmetric* NASH-STABLE *can be solved in time* $\text{tw}^{O(\text{tw})}n$.

5   Max Envy-Free and Max Egalitarian

In [4], Aziz et al. show that finding an envy-free partition is trivial because a partition of singletons is envy-free. However, finding a *maximum* envy-free partition is much more difficult than finding an envy-free partition.

Theorem 4. MAX ENVY-FREE *is weakly NP-hard on series-parallel graphs of vertex cover number 2 even if the preferences are symmetric.*

Next, we show that MAX EGALITARIAN is weakly NP-hard on series-parallel graphs of pathwidth 4. Note that the class of series-parallel graph is equivalent to graphs with treewidth 2.

Theorem 5. *In the symmetric hedonic games,* MAX EGALITARIAN *is weakly NP-hard on series-parallel graphs of pathwidth 4 even if the preferences are symmetric.*

Note that the pathwidth and the treewidth of H' are bounded, but the vertex cover number is not bounded. We can similarly show We also show that MAX EGALITARIAN is also weakly NP-hard on bounded vertex cover number graphs.

Theorem 6. MAX EGALITARIAN *is weakly NP-hard on 2-apex graphs of vertex cover number 4 even if the preferences are symmetric.*

Aziz et al. show that *asymmetric* MAX EGALITARIAN is strongly NP-hard [4]. We show that *symmetric* MAX ENVY-FREE and *symmetric* MAX EGALITARIAN remain to be strongly NP-hard. To show this, we give a reduction from 3-PARTITION, which is strongly NP-complete [12].

Theorem 7. MAX ENVY-FREE *and* MAX EGALITARIAN *are strongly NP-hard even if the preferences are symmetric.*

Since $\mathrm{tw}(G) \leq \mathrm{vc}(G)$, MAX ENVY-FREE is weakly NP-hard on graphs of $\mathrm{tw}(G) = 2$ by Theorem 4. Also, MAX EGALITARIAN is weakly NP-hard on graphs of $\mathrm{tw}(G) = 2$ by Theorem 5. However, we show that symmetric MAX ENVY-FREE and symmetric MAX EGALITARIAN on trees, which are of treewidth 1, are solvable in linear time. Indeed, we can find an envy-free and maximum egalitarian partition with maximum social welfare. Such a partition consists of connected components of a forest obtained by removing all negative edges from an input tree.

Theorem 8. *Symmetric* MAX ENVY-FREE *and symmetric* MAX EGALITARIAN *are solvable in linear time on trees.*

Note that linear-time solvability does not hold for asymmetric cases, though asymmetric Max Egalitarian on trees can be solved in near-linear time.

Theorem 9. MAX EGALITARIAN *can be solved in time* $O(n \log W)$ *on trees.*

Theorems 5 and 6 mean that MAX EGALITARIAN is weakly NP-hard even on bounded treewidth graphs. On the other hand, we show that there is a pseudo FPT algorithm for MAX EGALITARIAN when parameterized by treewidth.

Theorem 10. *Given a tree decomposition of width* tw, MAX EGALITARIAN *can be solved in time* $(\mathrm{tw}W)^{O(\mathrm{tw})}n$ *where* $W = \max_{u \in V} \sum_{v \in N(u)} |w_{uv}|$.

Theorem 10 implies that if W is bounded by a polynomial in n, MAX EGALITARIAN can be computed in time $n^{O(\mathrm{tw})}$.

References

1. Adcock, A.B., Sullivan, B.D., Mahoney, M.W.: Tree-like structure in large social and information networks. In: ICDM 2013, pp. 1–10 (2013)
2. Alcalde, J., Revilla, P.: Researching with whom? Stability and manipulation. J. Math. Econ. **40**(8), 869–887 (2004)
3. Aziz, H., Brandt, F., Harrenstein, P.: Fractional hedonic games. In: AAMAS 2014, pp. 5–12 (2014)
4. Aziz, H., Brandt, F., Seedig, H.G.: Computing desirable partitions in additively separable hedonic games. Artif. Intell. **195**, 316–334 (2013)
5. Ballester, C.: NP-completeness in hedonic games. Games Econ. Behav. **49**(1), 1–30 (2004)
6. Banerjee, S., Konishi, H., Sönmez, T.: Core in a simple coalition formation game. Soc. Choice Welfare **18**(1), 135–153 (2001)
7. Bogomolnaia, A., Jackson, M.O.: The stability of hedonic coalition structures. Games Econ. Behav. **38**(2), 201–230 (2002)
8. Cygan, M.: Parameterized Algorithms. Springer, Switzerland (2015). https://doi.org/10.1007/978-3-319-21275-3
9. Dreze, J.H., Greenberg, J.: Hedonic coalitions: optimality and stability. Econometrica **48**(4), 987 (1980)

10. Dunbar, R.I.M.: Neocortex size as a constraint on group size in primates. J. Hum. Evol. **22**(6), 469–493 (1992)
11. Gairing, M., Savani, R.: Computing stable outcomes in hedonic games. In: Kontogiannis, S., Koutsoupias, E., Spirakis, P.G. (eds.) SAGT 2010. LNCS, vol. 6386, pp. 174–185. Springer, Heidelberg (2010). https://doi.org/10.1007/978-3-642-16170-4_16
12. Garey, M.R., Johnson, D.S.: Computers and Intractability: A Guide to the Theory of NP-Completeness. W. H. Freeman & Co., New York (1979)
13. Hanaka, T., Kiya, H., Maei, Y., Ono, H.: Computational complexity of hedonic games on sparse graphs (2019). arxiv.org/abs/1908.11554
14. Le Breton, M., Ortuño-Ortin, I., Weber, S.: Gamson's law and hedonic games. Soc. Choice Welfare **30**(1), 57–67 (2008)
15. McSweeney, P.J., Mehrotra, K., Oh, J.C.: A game theoretic framework for community detection. In: ASONAM 2012, pp. 227–234 (2012)
16. Olsen, M.: Nash stability in additively separable hedonic games and community structures. Theory Comput. Syst. **45**(4), 917–925 (2009)
17. Peters, D.: Graphical hedonic games of bounded treewidth. In: AAAI 2016, pp. 586–593 (2016)
18. Saad, W., Han, Z., Basar, T., Debbah, M., Hjorungnes, A.: Hedonic coalition formation for distributed task allocation among wireless agents. IEEE Trans. Mob. Comput. **10**(9), 1327–1344 (2010)
19. Sung, S.C., Dimitrov, D.: Computational complexity in additive hedonic games. Eur. J. Oper. Res. **203**(3), 635–639 (2010)

Strategies for Energy-Aware Multi-agent Continuous Cooperative Patrolling Problems Subject to Requirements

Lingying Wu[✉] and Toshiharu Sugawara[✉] [iD]

Computer Science and Engineering, Waseda University, Tokyo 169-8555, Japan
lingying.wu@isl.cs.waseda.ac.jp, sugawara@waseda.jp

Abstract. This paper proposes a method of autonomous strategy learning for multiple cooperative agents integrated with a series of behavioral strategies aiming at reduction of energy cost on the premise of satisfying quality requirements in continuous patrolling problems. We improved our algorithm of requirement estimation to avoid concentration of agents since they are given the knowledge of the work environment in advance. The experimental results show that our proposal enables the agents to learn to select appropriate behavioral planning strategies according to performance efficiency and energy cost, and to individually estimate whether the given requirement is reached and modify their action plans to save energy. Furthermore, agents with the new requirement estimation method could achieve fair patrolling by introducing local observations.

Keywords: Multi-agent systems · Continuous patrolling · Cooperation · Learning · Energy efficiency

1 Introduction

Cooperative robotics have recently attracted considerable attention. Coordination between multiple robots on their decision-making is crucial for them to achieve the optimal performance of the group as a whole in complex and large scale tasks [1]. In this study, we tackle the multi-agent *continuous cooperative patrolling problem* (CCPP) addressed by Sugiyama et al. [4], in which agents autonomously decide their action plans and continuously move around a given area for given purposes. This is an abstract problem for complex real-world applications that require appropriate coordination and cooperation between agents, such as cleaning, security, and surveillance patrolling tasks.

Realistic scenarios in the multi-agent patrolling problem field must be considered when deploying actual systems in real-world [2]. With regard to real-world applications which suffer from the trade-off between level of perfection and energy efficiency, comparing with accomplishing the tasks perfectly by ignoring energy usage, people usually place a higher value on reduction of energy cost.

Despite the fact that multi-agent patrolling has been investigated from various perspectives over the years, most of the studies lay emphasis on enhancing

© Springer Nature Switzerland AG 2019
M. Baldoni et al. (Eds.): PRIMA 2019, LNAI 11873, pp. 585–593, 2019.
https://doi.org/10.1007/978-3-030-33792-6_44

Table 1. List of notations used in this paper.

Symbol	Description
$d(v_i, v_j)$	Length of the shortest path between v_i and v_j
$v^i(t)$	Position of agent i at time t
v^i_{tar}	Target node of agent i
P_v	Probability of event occurrence (PEO)
$L_t(v)$	Number of unprocessed events
$EL_t(v)$	Expected value of $L_t(v)$
$D(s)$	Level of task completeness when using strategy s
$C(s)$	Total energy cost when using strategy s
$D^{|A|}_{req}$	Requirement of task completeness level

the performance in task completeness, and the issue of energy minimization has not been sufficiently studied. Mei et al. [9] presented an energy-efficient motion planning approach which selects the next target node based on orientation information and reduces repeated coverage. Cabreira et al. [3] proposed an energy-aware decentralized real-time search approach for cooperative patrolling problem using multiple unmanned aerial vehicles, which saves energy by minimizing the number of turns (Table 1).

Concerning the multi-agent CCPP, Yoneda et al. [8] proposed the autonomous reinforcement learning of target decision strategies called *adaptive meta-target decision strategy* (AMTDS). Sugiyama et al. extended the method by incorporating environmental learning [5], simple negotiation for task allocations [4], and learning of appropriate activity cycle [6]. However, energy usage was not taken into consideration in these studies, so agents always made an all-out effort and dedicated to performing the tasks perfectly by ignoring energy efficiency.

Previously, we [7] have presented a methodology for solving the multi-agent CCPP subject to the quality requirement from the viewpoint of energy cost reduction. However, we found that agents with this method could not maintain fairness in terms of patrolling quality when applying the method to a large and complicated environment. This paper proposes a new requirement estimation method to deal with the fairness problem. The experimental results demonstrate that the new algorithm could achieve fair task execution in a large and complex environment by introducing local observations.

2   Model

We use the multi-agent CCPP model [4], in which multiple autonomous agents move around the environment and visit locations with required and non-uniform frequencies. There are several important assumptions including that agents know the structure of the environment, their own position, and other's positions, that periodical return is required, and that sophisticated coordination should be avoided. Please refer to our previous paper [7] for detailed explanation of the assumptions.

2.1 Models of Environment and Agent

Agents move and work in an environment described by graph $G = (V, E)$, where $V = \{v_1, ...v_m\}$ is the set of nodes with coordinates $v = (x_v, y_v)$, and E is the set of edges which agents traverse. We introduce a discrete time unit called *tick*. In one tick, events occur on nodes, agents decide their action plan, and they can move to one of the neighboring nodes along the edges then work on the nodes they visit. Each node owns a value of *probability of event occurrence* (PEO) denoted as $\{P_v \mid v \in V, 0 \le P_v \le 1\}$, and the number of unprocessed events can be defined based on P_v. Environments with different characteristics can be expressed using these probabilities.

Let $A = \{1, ..., n\}$ be a set of agents. In this paper, agents are given the values of PEO in advance but do not know the actual value of $L_t(v)$. Instead, they estimate it by calculating the expected value, $EL_t(v)$, from P_v and $t_{visit}(v)$, the most recent time any agent (may not be i) visited and worked on the node v. $EL_t(v)$ at any future time t is defined by

$$EL_t(v) = P_v \cdot (t - t_{visit}(v)). \tag{1}$$

Note that even if agents are not given P_v, they can learn through experience during patrolling [5].

Agents have their own rechargeable batteries and have to periodically return to the charging bases to insure continuous patrolling. The detailed description of batteries is omitted since it is identical to that described in [7].

2.2 Path Planning Strategies

Agents create the plans for their paths in two stages: *target decision* and *path generation*. In the former stage, agent i decides the target node, v_{tar}^i, based on (1) on which node the largest number of events is expected to occur or (2) which node in unlikely to be visited by other agents in a short amount of time. Then, i generates the appropriate path from the current node to v_{tar}^i. We use simple strategies since proposing planning algorithms was not part of our main purpose.

Random Selection (R). Agent i randomly selects v_{tar}^i among all nodes V.

Probabilistic Greedy Selection (PGS). Agent i estimates the value of expected number of unprocessed events and select the one with the highest value.

Prioritizing Unvisited Interval (PI). Agent i selects the node that have not been visited recently.

Balanced Neighbor-Preferential Selection (BNPS). BNPS is an advanced version of PGS. The idea is that if agent i estimates that there exist nodes with higher values of expected unprocessed events in the neighborhood using the learned threshold, i selects v_{tar}^i from those nodes. Otherwise, i selects v_{tar}^i using PGS. A detail explanation is described in Yoneda et al.'s study [8].

Before agent i generates the path to v_{tar}^i, it checks the amount of remaining battery to makes sure that v_{tar}^i is reachable. Otherwise, i sets v_{tar}^i to its charging base, v_{base}^i, and returns to charge its battery. Since the path generation strategy is out of the scope of this paper, please refer to [7] for detailed explanation.

2.3 Performance Measures

Our purpose is to minimize the overall energy cost on the premise of satisfying the requirement for task completeness, which corresponds to the amount of unprocessed events in the work environment. Accordingly, we evaluate the proposed methods in two aspects: *level of task completeness* and *total energy consumption*. The definitions are omitted since they are identical to that in [7].

Even though smaller values of these measures are considered better, there is still a trade-off between level of perfection and energy cost. In our energy-aware CCPP model, agents are expected to cooperatively conduct the tasks to the requested extent with less energy. Given a value of *requirement level*, $D_{req}^{|A|} > 0$, instead of minimizing $D(s)$, agents work towards to minimize $C(s)$ and keep $D(s)$ small enough to satisfy the condition $D(s) \leq D_{req}^{|A|}$.

3 Proposed Methods

Our proposal includes a succession of decision-making algorithms which are called while agents execute their actions according to the generated plans. Figure 1 shows the flowchart of the action selection process with the proposed methods. First, agents estimate whether the given requirement of quality is reached and evaluate their' self-importance. Based on the preceding results, agents decide the following action by taking into account the status of the environment and themselves. Next, there are two

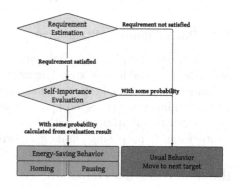

Fig. 1. Action selection in agents.

types of behavioral strategies which can be adopted by agents as a substitute for moving to the next target with the intention of reducing the energy cost. We only describe the new method of requirement estimation due to page limitation.

The main difference between the previous method [7] and the new one is that we incorporate local observations to the algorithm of *requirement estimation*, which is the process of estimating whether the requirement level is reached. We found that if the previous strategy is applied to a large and complicated environment, the agents cannot maintain fairness in the matter of patrolling but gather to specific regions. However, we prefer agents to perform uniform patrols by taking into account the importance of areas where events easily happen. Therefore, the new method is introduced aiming to avoid concentration of agents and achieve fair patrolling.

3.1   Requirement Estimation

As we expect the agents to reduce energy cost while satisfy the given requirement at the same time, it is necessary for agents to estimate the current status of the environment to decide the next action. Each agent independently estimated the total number of unprocessed events and then judges whether the requirement is satisfied on the basis of $D_{req}^{|A|}$. We introduce a novel algorithm of requirement estimation based on agents' local estimation to improve fairness. The previous algorithm is called *requirement estimation* (RE) [7], and the new algorithm is named, *requirement estimation with local observations* (RE/LO).

For agent i at time t, i generates a set $V_{est}(v^i(t)) \subset V$ comprising N_r nodes, where N_r is a positive integer which indicates the number of reference nodes. Referring to larger number of nodes gives a more accurate estimation result, but also requires more expensive computational resources. RE and RE/LO differ in the range of reference nodes when forming $V_{est}(v^i(t))$. An agent with RE/LO only selects the nearby nodes when it is far from the charging base. The farther the agent is from the charging base, the smaller range of area is used for estimation. With the minimal length of reference range given as d_{min}, the set of reference nodes is defined by

$$V_{est}(v^i(t)) = \{v \in V \mid d(v, v^i(t) \le d_{ref})\}, \tag{2}$$

where d_{ref} is the length of reference range calculated by

$$d_{ref} = max(max\{d(v, v_{base}^i) \mid v \in V\} - d(v^i(t), v_{base}^i), \ d_{min}). \tag{3}$$

The estimated value is obtained from the average of $EL_t(v)$ in $V_{est}(v^i(t))$:

$$EV_t^i = \frac{\sum_{v \in V_{est}(v^i(t))} EL_t(v)}{N_r}. \tag{4}$$

i judges that the requirement has been achieved only when the following condition is satisfied:

$$EV_t^i \le D_{req}^{|A|}. \tag{5}$$

If so, i then proceeds to *self-importance evaluation*. Otherwise, i selects the next target node with one of the target decision strategies and generates a path to the destination.

4   Experiments

The proposed methods are applied to an area cleaning application and evaluated in a simulation environment. It is experimentally demonstrated that the methods enable agents to cooperatively reduce energy cost and satisfy the given requirement at the same time. We also compare the two algorithms for requirement estimation, RE and RE/LO, and show that agents with RE/LO could perform fairer patrol.

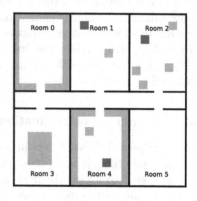

Fig. 2. Experimental environment.

4.1   Experimental Settings

Due to page limitation, we only describe the difference between this paper and our previous work [7], but omit the specifications of parameters, agents, and batteries. Differently from our previous work, we prepared a large and more complex environment consists of a corridor and six rooms labeled by *Room N* (where $N = 0,...5$) with different characteristics. The environment is represented by a two-dimensional grid space with several obstacles, where G is defined as a 101×101 grid. We set $p(v)$ for $v \in V$ as

$$p(v) = \begin{cases} 0 & \text{if } v \text{ was in a black region,} \\ 10^{-3} & \text{if } v \text{ was in a red region,} \\ 10^{-4} & \text{if } v \text{ was in a yellow region, and} \\ 10^{-6} & \text{otherwise.} \end{cases} \tag{6}$$

Figure 2 shows the distribution of colored regions. The experimental results given below are the averages of ten independent trials based on different random seeds.

4.2   Evaluation of Energy-Aware Strategies

The proposed methods are evaluated by comparing the performance of three agent behavioral regimes: usual behavior, energy-aware strategy with homing behavior, and energy-aware strategy with pausing behavior. We use the same values for parameters in energy-aware strategies as our previous paper [7].

Figure 3 plots the performance measures, which are the total dirt amount and overall energy consumption, for each target decision strategy and agent behavior. The dotted red line represents the given requirement of cleanliness which is set to 1200, and the dotted green line represents the theoretical maximal value of energy consumption. Note again that the smaller performance values are better. The results indicate that the proposal of energy-aware strategies successfully saves energy while agents could still satisfy the given requirement of remaining dirt. Since the main proposal of this paper is the RE/LO method, further discussion on the results is omitted due to page limitation.

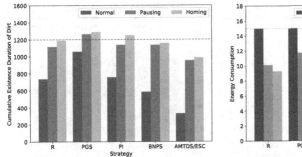
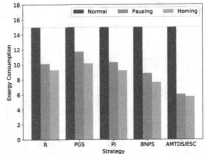

Fig. 3. Performance measures.

4.3 Requirement Estimation with Local Observations

We investigate the advantages and impact of introducing local observations by comparing the performances of the two algorithms for requirement estimation, RE and RE/LO. We only show the results for the case of using the homing behavior. Figure 4 plots the sum of P_v in each room, which corresponds to how easily the room becomes dirty due to page limitation. Figure 5 compares the amount of remaining dirt in each room by each algorithm in percentage.

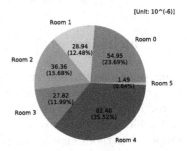

Fig. 4. Sum of P_v in each room.

As shown in Fig. 5(a), since agents are given the probability of dirt accumulation in advance and they have the knowledge about dirty regions, those with greedy strategies including PGS and BNPS tend to gather to the dirty rooms such as Room 0 and Room 4 and rarely clean the rooms with low probability of dirt accumulation such as Room 5. As a result, agents patrol in a biased manner and cause the cleanliness of the rooms where dirt hardly accumulates worse than those rooms which easily become dirty.

Although introduction of local observations does not significantly influence the overall performance, as shown in Fig. 5(b), agents using AMTDS/ESC with RE/LO could fairly clean all the rooms so that the resulting amount of remaining dirt in each room is comparatively closer to the sum of accumulation probability than that by agents using AMTDS/ESC with RE. Estimating the total dirt amount from local observations affects agents decision-making when they are far from the charging base. This somehow prompts agents to work more in the relatively clean rooms instead of going back to the charging base when they judge the requirement is satisfied from the viewpoint of the whole environment, and thus avoids concentration of agents at the dirty rooms and unfair patrols.

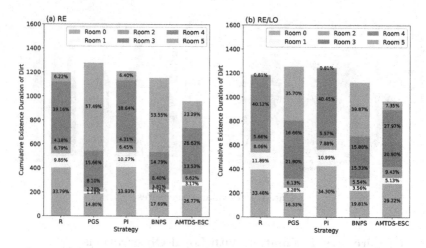

Fig. 5. Cumulative existence duration of dirt in each room.

5 Conclusion

This paper intent to solve the multi-agent CCPP subject to quality requirement from the aspect of energy cost reduction. We improved the previous method by introducing a new algorithm for requirement estimation to avoid biased patrol and achieve fair task execution. The experimental results confirmed that the proposed methods enabled agents to reduce the energy cost while cooperatively maintaining the given requirement of quality perfection and work fairly in a large and complex environment with local observations. Concentration of agents at rooms with high values of PEO can be avoided by incorporating local observations into requirement estimation.

More work needs to be done regarding the issue of environmental learning since our algorithms require the knowledge about the work environment, which restricts the range of application and flexibility of the proposed methods. Also, we plan to tackle the problem of importance evaluation conducted autonomously and individually by each agent. With this functionality, a continuous system will be able to autonomously eliminate old robots and introduce new ones without affecting the overall performance.

Acknowledgement. This work was partly supported by JSPS KAKENHI (17KT0044).

References

1. Almeida, A., et al.: Recent advances on multi-agent patrolling. In: Bazzan, A.L.C., Labidi, S. (eds.) SBIA 2004. LNCS (LNAI), vol. 3171, pp. 474–483. Springer, Heidelberg (2004). https://doi.org/10.1007/978-3-540-28645-5_48

2. Iocchi, L., Marchetti, L., Nardi, D.: Multi-robot patrolling with coordinated behaviours in realistic environments. In: 2011 IEEE/RSJ International Conference on Intelligent Robots and Systems, pp. 2796–2801, September 2011
3. Milech Cabreira, T., Stift Kappel, K., Ferreira, P.R., Brisolara de Brisolara, L.: An energy-aware real-time search approach for cooperative patrolling missions with multi-UAVs. In: 2018 Latin American Robotic Symposium, 2018 Brazilian Symposium on Robotics (SBR) and 2018 Workshop on Robotics in Education (WRE). pp. 254–259, November 2018
4. Sugiyama, A., Sea, V., Sugawara, T.: Effective task allocation by enhancing divisional cooperation in multi-agent continuous patrolling tasks. In: 2016 IEEE 28th International Conference on Tools with Artificial Intelligence (ICTAI), pp. 33–40, November 2016
5. Sugiyama, A., Sugawara, T.: Meta-strategy for cooperative tasks with learning of environments in multi-agent continuous tasks. In: Proceedings of the 30th Annual ACM Symposium on Applied Computing, SAC 2015, pp. 494–500. ACM, New York (2015)
6. Sugiyama., A., Wu., L., Sugawara., T.: Learning of activity cycle length based on battery limitation in multi-agent continuous cooperative patrol problems (2019)
7. Wu, L., Sugiyama, A., Sugawara, T.: Energy-efficient strategies for multi-agent continuous cooperative patrolling problems. In: Knowledge-Based and Intelligent Information & Engineering Systems: Proceedings of the 21st International Conference, KES-2019. Budapest, Hungary, September 2019
8. Yoneda, K., Sugiyama, A., Kato, C., Sugawara, T.: Learning and relearning of target decision strategies in continuous coordinated cleaning tasks with shallow coordination. Web Intell. **13**(4), 279–294 (2015)
9. Mei, Y., Lu, Y.-H., Lee, C.S.G., Hu, Y.C.: Energy-efficient mobile robot exploration. In: Proceedings of the 2006 IEEE International Conference on Robotics and Automation (ICRA 2006), pp. 505–511, May 2006

Deep False-Name-Proof Auction Mechanisms

Yuko Sakurai[1]($\boxtimes$), Satoshi Oyama[2], Mingyu Guo[3], and Makoto Yokoo[4]

[1] National Institute of Advanced Industrial Science and Technology, Tokyo, Japan
yuko.sakurai@aist.go.jp
[2] Hokkaido University/RIKEN, Sapporo, Japan
oyama@ist.hokudai.ac.jp
[3] University of Adelaide, Adelaide, Australia
mingyu.guo@adelaide.edu.au
[4] Kyushu University/RIKEN, Fukuoka, Japan
yokoo@inf.kyuhu-u.ac.jp

Abstract. We explore an approach to designing false-name-proof auction mechanisms using deep learning. While multi-agent systems researchers have recently proposed data-driven approaches to automatically designing auction mechanisms through deep learning, false-name-proofness, which generalizes strategy-proofness by assuming that a bidder can submit multiple bids under fictitious identifiers, has not been taken into account as a property that a mechanism has to satisfy. We extend the RegretNet neural network architecture to incorporate false-name-proof constraints and then conduct experiments demonstrating that the generated mechanisms satisfy false-name-proofness.

Keywords: Mechanism design · Deep learning · False-name-proofness

1 Introduction

Mechanism design, a subfield of microeconomic theory and game theory, focuses on designing mechanisms that result in desirable outcomes even if the agents act strategically. One desirable property that mechanisms have to satisfy is *strategy-proofness*: for a bidder, declaring her true valuation is a dominant strategy, i.e., an optimal strategy regardless of the other bidders' actions. The Vickrey-Clarke-Groves (VCG) mechanism is well-known to be a strategy-proof mechanism that can be applied to combinatorial auctions, in which multiple items are simultaneously offered, and a bidder can bid on any bundle of items. In the VCG mechanism, an allocation is determined that maximizes the social surplus, i.e., the sum of all participants' utilities including that of the auctioneer. A winner pays the smallest amount she would have had to bid to win her bundle of items.

The problem is, in anonymous settings such as the Internet, a bidder can pretend to be multiple bidders. We refer to such a manipulation as *false-name bidding*. False-name bids are bids submitted under fictitious identifiers, e.g., multiple e-mail addresses. It is difficult to detect false-name bids since identifying

© Springer Nature Switzerland AG 2019
M. Baldoni et al. (Eds.): PRIMA 2019, LNAI 11873, pp. 594–601, 2019.
https://doi.org/10.1007/978-3-030-33792-6_45

each participant on the Internet is virtually impossible. We say a mechanism is *false-name-proof* if, for each bidder, declaring her true valuations by using a single identifier is a dominant strategy. Unfortunately, Yokoo *et al.* [9] showed that the VCG mechanism is not false-name-proof and that no false-name-proof mechanism satisfies Pareto efficiency. Thus, several false-name-proof mechanisms have been proposed [6,8].

We consider the design of *false-name-proof* auctions through deep learning. Several multi-agent systems researchers recently used deep learning in the automated design of optimal auction mechanisms [3,4,7]. Conitzer and Sandholm [1,2] introduced the automated mechanism design (AMD) approach in which the problem of finding a mechanism to satisfy desirable properties is formulated as a linear program. However, Guo and Conitzer [5] showed that the AMD approach does not have sufficient scalability in terms of memory requirement and computational time. Thus, methods based on the AMD approach apply limited and specialized problem settings with a small number of agents and items. To overcome the scalability problem, Dütting *et al.* [3] recently proposed a data-driven approach to using deep neural networks called the *RegretNet framework* for the AMD problem of optimal auctions to maximize the expected revenue.

We have extended the RegretNet framework to incorporate false-name-proofness into designing combinatorial auctions that maximize the expected revenue. As far as the authors know, this is the first attempt to use machine learning for the design of false-name-proof auction mechanisms. Many of the existing manually designed mechanisms have been criticized for their relatively low revenue. It is thus important to examine how much revenue the machine-learning generated mechanisms can attain. In our experiments, we generated mechanisms for two problem settings. We found that when bidders' valuations are limited, the generated mechanism is closely similar to the Adaptive Reserve Price mechanism [6].

2 Preliminaries

2.1 Model

Let $N = \{1, 2, \ldots, n\}$ be the set of bidders and let $M = \{1, 2, \ldots, m\}$ be the set of items. A bidder $i \in N$ has a valuation function $v_i : 2^M \to \mathbb{R}_+$; i.e., $v_i(B)$ denotes bidder i's valuation for a bundle of items $B \subseteq M$. V_i denotes the space of a possible valuation function for bidder i. $v = (v_1, \ldots, v_n)$ denotes a profile of valuations, and $v_{-i} = (v_1, \ldots, v_{i-1}, v_{i+1}, \ldots, v_n)$ denotes the profile of valuations except for bidder i. We assume that a valuation function v_i normalized by $v_i(\emptyset) = 0$ satisfies *free disposal*, i.e., $v_i(B') \geq v_i(B)$ for all $B' \supseteq B$. We also assume that each bidder is single minded; i.e., she has at most one minimal bundle with a positive value. Here, minimal bundle B for bidder i with $v_i(B)$ satisfies $v_i(B') < v_i(B)$ for $\forall B' \subset B$. Bidder i's valuation function v_i is drawn independently from distribution F_i. We assume that an auctioneer knows the distributions $F = (F_1, \ldots, F_n)$.

Each bidder reports her bid $b_i(B)$ for any bundle of items $B \subseteq M$. $v_i(B) = b_i(B)$ is not guaranteed since a bidder might report her bid b_i untruthfully. Let $b = (b_1, \ldots, b_n)$ be the profile of bids and $b_{-i} = (b_1, \ldots, b_{i-1}, b_{i+1}, \ldots, b_n)$ be the profile of bids except for bidder i. We consider a randomized mechanism for a combinatorial auction. A combinatorial auction mechanism $\mathcal{M}(a, p)$ consists of a randomized allocation rule a and a payment rule p. When a set of n bidders participates, the randomized allocation rule is defined as $a : \mathbb{R}^{nm} \to [0, 1]^{nm}$, and the payment rule is defined as $p : \mathbb{R}^{nm} \to \mathbb{R}_+^n$. $a_i(B) \in [0, 1]$ denotes the probability that bidder i obtains bundle B and $p_i(B)$ is bidder i's payment for bundle B.

To satisfy the allocation feasibility requirement, the following conditions must be satisfied: (1) the probability that item $j \in M$ is allocated to a set of bidders N is at most 1 and (2) the total allocation to agent $i \in N$ is at most 1.

$$\sum_{i \in N} \sum_{B \subseteq M : j \in B} a_i(B) \leq 1, \ \forall j \in M \tag{1}$$

$$\sum_{B \subseteq M} a_i(B) \leq 1, \ \forall i \in N \tag{2}$$

The expected utility of bidder i with valuation function v_i is given by

$$u_i(v_i, b) = \sum_{B \subseteq M} v_i(B) \cdot a_i(B) - p_i(b). \tag{3}$$

Next, let us introduce three properties of mechanisms.

Strategy-Proofness (SP): A mechanism $\mathcal{M}(a, p)$ is strategy-proof if it maximizes a bidder's utility regardless of the other bidders' reports; i.e., $\forall i \in N$, $\forall b_i$, $\forall v_i$, $u_i(v_i, (v_i, b_{-i})) \geq u_i(v_i, (b_i, b_{-i}))$.

Individual Rationality (IR): A mechanism $\mathcal{M}(a, p)$ is *individually rational* if no bidder suffers any loss; i.e., $\forall N$, $\forall i \in N$, $\forall v_i$, $\forall b_{-i}$, $u_i(v_i, (v_i, b_{-i})) \geq 0$ holds.

False-Name-Proofness (FNP): A mechanism $\mathcal{M}(a, p)$ is false-name-proof if it maximizes a bidder's utility by reporting a true valuation function using a single identifier; i.e., if for all $k + 1$ valuation functions of $v_i, b_{id_1}, \ldots, b_{id_k}$ where b_{id_j} is a false-name bid and $k \leq n$, $u_i(v_i, (v_i, b_{-i})) \geq u_i(v_i, (b_{id_1}, \ldots, b_{id_k}, b_{-i}))$. We assume that the number of false-name bids k is at most the number of items n. This is a reasonable assumption because false-name bids are made for obtaining items.

Example 1. Consider a combinatorial auction with two items. We denote $b_i = ((b_i(\{1\}), b_i(\{2\}), b_i(\{1, 2\})))$ and $a_i = ((a_i(\{1\}), a_i(\{2\}), a_i(\{1, 2\})))$.
Case 1: Bidders 1 and 2 submit bids $b_1 = (0, 0, 10)$ and $b_2 = (0, 0, 8.4)$, respectively. A mechanism $\mathcal{M}(a, p)$ outputs $a_1 = (0, 0, 1)$ and $a_2 = (0, 0, 0)$ as an allocation rule and $p_1 = 8.4$ and $p_2 = 0$ as a payment rule. If we assume that the bidders reported their valuations truthfully, the expected utility of bidder 1 is $10 \times 1 - 8.4 = 1.6$ and the expected utility of bidder 2 is 0.

Case 2: Bidders 1 and 2 submit bids $b_1 = (0, 0, 9)$ and $b_2 = (0, 0, 8.4)$, respectively. A mechanism $\mathcal{M}(a, p)$ outputs $a_1 = (0, 0, 0.9)$, $a_2 = (0, 0, 0)$, $p_1 = 8.4$, and $p_2 = 0$. If we assume that bidder 1 misreported her valuation and that her true valuation is her bid in Case 1, her expected utility is $10 \times 0.9 - 8.4 = 0.6 < 1.6$.

Case 3: Bidders 1, 2, and 3 submit $(5, 0, 5)$, $(0, 0, 8.4)$, and $(0, 5, 5)$, respectively. A mechanism $\mathcal{M}(a, p)$ outputs $a_1 = (0.9, 0, 0)$, $a_2 = (0, 0, 0)$, $a_3 = (0, 0.9, 0)$, $p_1 = 4$, $p_2 = 0$, and $p_3 = 4$. If we assume that bidders 1 and 3 are false-name bids from bidder 1 in Case 1, the probability that bundle $\{1, 2\}$ is allocated to her is $a_1(\{1\}) \cdot a_2(\{2\}) + a_1(\{2\}) \cdot a_2(\{1\}) + a_1(\{1, 2\}) + a_2(\{1, 2\})$. Thus, her expected utility is $v_1(\{1, 2\}) \times 0.81 - (p_1 + p_2) = 10 \times 0.81 - 8 = 0.01 < 1.6$.

Although we show only three cases, we can say that mechanism $\mathcal{M}(a, p)$ satisfies SP and FNP if it is robust against all possible misreports and false-name manipulations.

2.2 Existing False-Name-Proof Mechanisms

The existing false-name-proof combinatorial auction mechanisms were manually developed [6,8,9]. We introduce two representative mechanisms.

Minimal Bundle (MB) [8]: First, $B \subseteq M$ is allocated to bidder i, where B is a minimal bundle of i. Then, $B^* \subseteq M \setminus B$ is allocated to another bidder i' who has the highest remaining valuation, where B^* is a minimal bundle of i', and so on. The payment for an allocated bundle B is equal to the highest valuation of another bidder for a bundle that is minimal and conflicting with B.

Adaptive Reserve Price (ARP) [6]: The basic idea of ARP is to base the reserve prices on the other bidders' bids. The reserve price on the set of all items is determined by doubling the second highest bid among ones for each single item. If a bidder makes the highest bid for the set of all items that exceeds this reserve price, she wins. Otherwise, the reserve price for singe items with the highest and the second highest bids is set as half of the highest bid for the set of all items. If the highest or/and second highest bids for any single item exceed the reserve price, she/they win. No other items are allocated.

3 RegretNet Framework

The *RegretNet* framework proposed by Dütting *et al.* [3] comprises two separate networks for the allocation and payment rules. Both networks are simultaneously trained using samples from the value distribution by maximizing expected revenue subject to SP.

Let $(a^w, p^w) \in \mathcal{M}$ be an auction with parameters $w \in \mathbb{R}^d$ and some $d \in \mathbb{N}$. The *loss function* is defined as the negated expected revenue $\mathcal{L}(a, p) = -\mathbf{E}_{v \sim F}[\sum_{i \in N} p_i^w(v)]$. With the other bids fixed, the *expected ex post regret* of SP rgt_sp$_i$ for bidder i is defined as the maximum excess in her utility, considering all possible misreports of her valuation functions: rgt_sp$_i(a^w, p^w) = $

$\mathbf{E}[\max_{b_i \in V_i} u_i^w(v_i, (b_i, v_{-i})) - u_i^w(v_i, (v_i, v_{-i}))]$. An auction satisfies SP if and only if $\mathrm{rgt\_sp}_i(a^w, p^w) \leq 0$ for any $i \in N$. For IR, Dütting *et al.* incorporated the IR constraint in the networks.

In practice, $\mathcal{L}(a, p)$ and $\mathrm{rgt\_sp}_i(a^w, p^w)$ can be estimated from a sample of valuation profiles $S = \{v^{(1)}, \ldots, v^{(L)}\}$ drawn independently from F. Thus, the learning problem is defined as

$$\min_{w \in \mathbb{R}^d} \widehat{\mathcal{L}}(a^w, p^w) \quad \text{s.t.} \quad \widehat{\mathrm{rgt\_sp}}_i(a^w, p^w) = 0, \quad \forall i \in N, \tag{4}$$

where

$$\widehat{\mathcal{L}}(a^w, p^w) = -\frac{1}{L} \sum_{l=1}^{L} \sum_{i=1}^{n} p_i^w(v^{(l)}), \tag{5}$$

$$\widehat{\mathrm{rgt\_sp}}_i(a^w, p^w) = \frac{1}{L} \sum_{l=1}^{L} \max_{b_i \in V_i} u_i^w(v_i^{(l)}, (b_i, v_{-i}^{(l)})) - u_i^w(v_i^{(l)}, v^{(l)}). \tag{6}$$

Dütting *et al.* used the *augmented Lagrangian method* to solve this learning problem. The Lagrangian function for the optimization problem with a strategy-proof constraint is defined as

$$\widehat{\mathcal{L}}(a^w, p^w) + \sum_{i \in N} \lambda_i \widehat{\mathrm{rgt\_sp}}_i(a^w, p^w) + \frac{\rho}{2} (\sum_{i \in N} \widehat{\mathrm{rgt\_sp}}_i(a^w, p^w))^2, \tag{7}$$

where $\lambda \in \mathbb{R}^n$ is a vector of Lagrangian multipliers and $\rho > 0$ is a fixed parameter used to control the weight of the quadratic penalty.

4   Introducing False-Name-Proof Constraints

In neural network training, the size of the input must be constant. This creates difficulties in introducing false-name-proof constraints since false-name bids change the number of bids an auction receives. If the maximum number of bids has already been received, a false-name constraint cannot be generated because more bids cannot be accepted.

To overcome this problem, we use subsets of the actual bids as *virtual bids* and then generate false-name bids for them. For example, if the number of actual bidders n is 3, we use subsets of size 2 and generate false-name bids for each of the two bidders. We randomly generate a certain number of false-name bids for each virtual bid and introduce the false-name-proof constraint for the virtual bids. Let us assume that bidder i submits k false-name bids by using $id_1, \ldots, id_k$. We restate $v = (v_1, \ldots, v_i, v_0, \ldots, v_0, \ldots, v_n)$ and $b = (b_1, \ldots, b_{id_1}, \ldots, b_{id_k}, \ldots, b_n)$, where v_0 is a *null bidder* whose valuation for any bundle is zero; i.e., $v_0(B) = 0$, for any $B \subseteq M$. We define the expected regret for FNP as

$$\mathrm{rgt\_fnp}_i(a^w, p^w) = \mathbf{E}[\max_{b_{id_i} \in V_i} u_i(v_i, (b_{id_1}, \ldots, b_{id_k}, b_{-i})) - u_i(v_i, (v_i, b_{-i}))]. \tag{8}$$

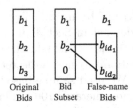

Fig. 1. Generating false-name-proof constraints

Table 1. Results with existing mechanisms, where A denotes results of allocation for bidders 1, 2, and 3 and P denotes results of payment for bidders 1, 2, and 3

Bids			ARP		MB		VCG	
Bidder 1	Bidder 2	Bidder 3	A	P	A	P	A	P
$(0,0,10)$	$(0,0,0)$	$(0,0,8.4)$	$(\{1,2\},\emptyset,\emptyset)$	$(8.4,0,0)$	$(\{1,2\},\emptyset,\emptyset)$	$(8.4,0,0)$	$(\{1,2\},\emptyset,\emptyset)$	$(8.4,0,0)$
$(5,0,5)$	$(0,5,5)$	$(0,0,8.4)$	$(\{1\},\{2\},\emptyset)$	$(4.2,4.2,0)$	$(\emptyset,\emptyset,\{1,2\})$	$(0,0,5)$	$(\{1\},\{2\},\emptyset)$	$(3.4,3.4,0)$
$(4,0,4)$	$(0,5,5)$	$(0,0,8.4)$	$(\emptyset,\emptyset,\{1,2\})$	$(0,0,5)$	$(\emptyset,\emptyset,\{1,2\})$	$(0,0,5)$	$(\{1\},\{2\},\emptyset)$	$(3.4,4.4,0)$

An auction satisfies FNP in expectation if and only if $\mathrm{rgt\_fnp}_i(a^w, p^w) \leq 0$ for any $i \in N$.

Figure 1 illustrates how false-name constraints are generated in an auction with two items and three bidders. We repeat the same process for six cases because there are three possible choices of two bidders and two possible choices of a bidder who makes false-name bids. The false-name bids (b_{id_1}, b_{id_2}) are randomly sampled from V_i. We sample a certain number of false-name bids for each case and assume that the expected regret for FNP is not positive; i.e., $\mathrm{rgt\_fnp}_i(a^w, p^w) \leq 0$.

We define the Lagrangian function for the optimization problem with strategy-proof and false-name-proof constraints as

$$\widehat{\mathcal{L}}(a^w, p^w) + \sum_{i \in N} \lambda_i \widehat{\mathrm{rgt\_sp}}_i(a^w, p^w) + \frac{\rho}{2} (\sum_{i \in N} \widehat{\mathrm{rgt\_sp}}_i(a^w, p^w))^2$$
$$+ \sum_{i \in N} \mu_i \widehat{\mathrm{rgt\_fnp}}_i(a^w, p^w) + \frac{\sigma}{2} (\sum_{i \in N} \widehat{\mathrm{rgt\_fnp}}_i(a^w, p^w))^2, \qquad (9)$$

where $\widehat{\mathrm{rgt\_fnp}}_i(a^w, p^w) = \frac{1}{L} \sum_{l=1}^{L} \max_{b_{id_i} \in V_i} u_i^w(v_i^{(l)}, (b_{id_1}, \ldots, b_{id_k}, v_{-i}^{(l)})) - u_i^w(v_i^{(l)}, v^{(l)})$, $\lambda, \mu \in \mathbb{R}^n$ is a vector of Lagrangian multipliers, and $\rho, \sigma > 0$ is a fixed parameter to control the weight of the quadratic penalty.

5   Experiments

We implemented a learning algorithm for our false-name-proof mechanisms that maximize the expected revenue in the RegretNet framework [3][1]. Specifically,

---

[1] https://github.com/saisrivatsan/deep-opt-auctions.

we extend the training algorithm by introducing false-name-proof constraints into the objective function defined in Sect. 4. In our experiments, we focused on combinatorial auctions with two items and three bidders for simplicity. We considered two different valuation settings: a discretized valuation setting and a uniform distribution setting. We used sample-based optimization for both misreports and false-name bids and generated 100 random misreports and 100 false-name bids for each valuation profile. The batch size and number of batches were set to 128 and 5000, respectively. The number of training iterations was 400, 000.

Table 2. Results for discretized setting

Bids			Bidder 1		Bidder 2		Bidder 3	
Bidder 1	Bidder 2	Bidder 3	a_1	p_1	a_2	p_2	a_3	p_3
$(0,0,10)$	$(0,0,0)$	$(0,0,8.4)$	$(0.000,0.000,1.000)$	8.630	$(0.000,0.000,0.000)$	0.000	$(0.000,0.000,0.000)$	0
$(5,0,5)$	$(0,5,5)$	$(0,0,8.4)$	$(0.858,0.000,0.000)$	3.919	$(0.000,0.796,0.000)$	3.559	$(0.000,0.000,0.142)$	1.189
$(4,0,4)$	$(0,5,5)$	$(0,0,8.4)$	$(0.320,0.000,0.000)$	1.281	$(0.000,0.361,0.000)$	1.603	$(0.000,0.000,0.639)$	5.370

Table 3. Results for uniform distribution setting

Bids			Bidder 1		Bidder 2		Bidder 3	
Bidder 1	Bidder 2	Bidder 3	a_1	p_1	a_2	p_2	a_3	p_3
$(0,0,1)$	$(0,0,0)$	$(0,0,0.84)$	$(0.035,0.000,0.770)$	0.580	$(0.000,0.000,0.000)$	0.000	$(0.000,0.000,0.000)$	0.000
$(0.5,0,0.5)$	$(0,0.5,0.5)$	$(0,0,0.84)$	$(0.253,0.000,0.030)$	0.135	$(0.000,0.454,0.000)$	0.220	$(0.000,0.000,0.000)$	0.001
$(0.4,0,0.4)$	$(0,0.5,0.5)$	$(0,0,0.84)$	$(0.000,0.000,0.000)$	0.001	$(0.000,0.472,0.000)$	0.230	$(0.000,0.000,0.000)$	0.003

5.1 Discretized Setting

The valuations of bidders were uniformly sampled from a finite valuation set:

$$V = \{(0,0,0), (4,0,4), (0,4,4), (5,0,5), (0,5,5), (0,0,8.4), (0,0,10),$$

where each tuple contains $(v_i(\{1\}), v_i(\{2\}), v_i(\{1,2\}))$.

The average expected social surplus was 7.425, and the average expected revenue was 7.030 for independently generated test data. To clarify the property of the generated mechanism, we present the results for three existing mechanisms (VCG, MB, and ARP). While the VCG mechanism is vulnerable to false-name manipulation, MB and ARP satisfy FNP, as shown in Table 1. We chose three bid cases, as shown in Tables 1 and 2. The second and third cases can be considered as the situation in which bidder 1 in the first case $(0,0,10)$ submitted false-name bids by using bidders 1 and 2. In Table 2, we show the results with three-decimal accuracy. We checked all cases of possible false-name manipulation and found that the generated mechanism satisfied FNP. For example, the utility of bidder 1 in the first case $(0,0,10)$ was 1.37, but her utility when she submitted $(5,0,5)$ and $(0,5,5)$ became negative $(10 \times 0.858 \times 0.796 - 3.919 - 3.669 = -0.648)$.

While we cannot exactly compare the generated mechanism with the existing mechanisms since the latter are deterministic, we can see that the results of the former are closely similar to those of the ARP mechanism.

5.2 Uniform Distribution Setting

The bidder valuations were real numbers sampled from finite intervals. We first uniformly sampled a class of agents from three bidder classes: single-minded bidder for item 1, item 2, and bundle $\{1, 2\}$, respectively. For the first class of agents, valuation was in the form $(v_i(\{1\}), 0, v_i(\{1\}))$, where $v_i(\{1\}) \sim U[0, 1]$. The second class of agents had valuations $(0, v_i(\{2\}), v_i(\{2\}))$, where $v_i(\{2\}) \sim U[0, 1]$. The third class of agents had valuations $(0, 0, v_i(\{1, 2\})))$, where $v_i(\{1, 2\})) \sim U[0, 2]$. The average expected social surplus was 1.021, and the average expected revenue was 0.755 for the test set. Table 3 shows the results for three cases of bids by the generated mechanism. It satisfied FNP. The allocation and the price for each agent were lower than the results in the discretized setting. This is because the space of possible valuations was wider than that in the discretized setting.

6 Conclusion

We explored an approach to designing false-name-proof combinatorial auction mechanisms using deep learning techniques. We extended the existing Regret-Net framework to handle false-name-proof constraints and then evaluated the generated mechanisms, demonstrating that they satisfy false-name-proofness. In future work we will extend our approach to more complicated settings.

Acknowledgments. This work was partially supported by JSPS KAKENHI Grant Numbers JP17H0 0761, JP17KK0008 and JP18H03337, by the Kayamori Foundation of Informational Science Advancement, and by the Telecommunications Advancement Foundation. We thank Paul Dütting and his coauthors for sharing the source code for the RegretNet framework.

References

1. Conitzer, V., Sandholm, T.: Complexity of mechanism design. In: UAI, pp. 103–110 (2002)
2. Conitzer, V., Sandholm, T.: Self-interested automated mechanism design and implications for optimal combinatorial auctions. In: ACM EC, pp. 132–141 (2004)
3. Düetting, P., Feng, Z., Narasimhan, H., Parkes, D., Ravindranath, S.S.: Optimal auctions through deep learning. In: ICML, pp. 1706–1715 (2019)
4. Feng, Z., Narasimhan, H., Parkes, D.C.: Deep learning for revenue-optimal auctions with budgets. In: AAMAS, pp. 354–362 (2018)
5. Guo, M., Conitzer, V.: Computationally feasible automated mechanism design: General approach and case studies. In: AAAI, pp. 1676–1679 (2010)
6. Iwasaki, A., et al.: Worst-case efficiency ratio in false-name-proof combinatorial auction mechanisms. In: AAMAS, pp. 633–640 (2010)
7. Manisha, P., Jawahar, C.V., Gujar, S.: Learning optimal redistribution mechanisms through neural networks. In: AAMAS, pp. 345–353 (2018)
8. Yokoo, M.: Characterization of strategy/false-name proof combinatorial auction protocols: price-oriented, rationing-free protocol. In: IJCAI, pp. 733–739 (2003)
9. Yokoo, M., Sakurai, Y., Matsubara, S.: Robust combinatorial auction protocol against false-name bids. Artif. Intell. J. **130**(2), 167–181 (2001)

Ubiquitous Computing and Multi-agent Systems: Clarification of the Lexicon

Nathan Aky[1]($\boxtimes$), Denis Payet[1], Sylvain Giroux[2], and Rémy Courdier[1]

[1] Laboratoire de Mathématiques et d'Informatiques, Université de la Réunion,
Saint-Denis, France
{nathan.aky,denis.payet,remy.courdier}@univ-reunion.fr
[2] DOMUS Laboratory, Department of Computer Science, University of Sherbrooke,
Sherbrooke, Canada
Sylvain.Giroux@usherbrooke.ca

Abstract. Ambient computing and Internet of Things have reached a level of maturity and a dynamic activity of research and engineering actors. Their goal is to create interactions between a set of distributed devices in an environment, in order to assist human activities. Multi-agent system is an interesting tool for coordinating devices and services for this purpose, because of its adaptation, autonomy and decentralized specifications. However, it is sometimes difficult to understand and share the same idea when it comes to terms such as "Ubiquitous Computing," "Ambient Computing" or the "Internet of Things." As a result, it can be really difficult to browse the literature through research engines and to make a bibliographical study without missing important papers.

That is why we want to address this first problem by means of a glossary proposal, synthesizing and unifying the extensively cited definitions of the lexicon belonging to these domains. Relaying on this terminology clarification, we present the relationship between the multi-agent approach and ubiquitous computing.

Keywords: Ambient agents · Ubiquitous computing · Multi-agent systems · Scientific lexicon · Internet of Things

1 Introduction

The democratization of devices with computational capabilities and their miniaturization have allowed the various actors of the research to imagine environments where such a set of devices, defined as "intelligent", would assist mankind in everyday life, in the most natural and intuitive way. We are talking about *ubiquitous computing.*

This strong dynamic has allowed the emergence of many applied solutions. MediaCups [1], the first connected cups, or more contemporary smartphones can be referred as examples among these. From such enthusiasm also results in the

Supported by Région Réunion.

appearance of a large number of articles dealing with fields related to ubiquitous computing, such as robotics, home assistance or the study of human-machine interactions.

This is why Sect. 2 of this article deals with the state of the art of the lexicon, sometimes inconstant, that we draw on this domain. It will expose a glossary of the main terms of the terminology. From that lexicon, we show the relationship between multi-agent system and ambient intelligence in Sect. 3. Finally, Sect. 4 consists of a conclusion of the work presented and proposals of raised prospects.

Moreover, the purpose of our contribution is to do a synthetic analysis and reformulation work. As objective as possible, our will is to consolidate the definitions outlined in the citations of the previous sections, to form a glossary of main terms related to ubiquitous computing, because we think that it is a necessary step to set out the link between ubiquitous computing and multi-agent systems.

The lexicon is created in order to avoid encroachment of types and definitions, from a non-exhaustive selection of articles. We have selected the best-referenced articles on the *Google Scholar* website, with a preference for articles with different definitions or typology.

2   State of the Art of Ubiquitous Computing

2.1   From Ubiquitous Computing

In [2], Mark Weiser describes ubiquitous computing as the idea of integrating computers into everyday physical objects. Later, Mark Weiser will point out that ubiquitous computing is a future world where users interact, in an invisible way, with a multitude of interconnected computers [6].

Later in 2010, Krumm [3] described ubiquitous computing as "the third era" of computing. This era, which represents the era in which we find ourselves, is characterized by the explosion of the use of embedded connected computers (such as smartphones) and thus by the use of several computers per person. The terms "Ubiquitous Computing" and "Pervasive Computing" are equivalent according to [3]. This idea of evolution of computing in time is echoed by Lyytinen and Yoo [4].

In [5], for the author "ubiquitous computing" described an information system to access information or to perform tasks anywhere. This system offers an intuitive use that seems invisible to the user. He defines several criteria for a system to be part of ubiquitous computing.

This is a conceptualization that we find interesting, but which we will return to in next Sect. 2.2, dealing with ambient intelligence. Indeed, we find that definitions, although they share a common idea, may slightly differ. The authors lasts cited speaks of an information system. But we propose to build on the definitions given by Krumm, Lyytien and Yoo defining *Ubiquitous Computing* as a period or an era. We made this choice because we aimed categorical differentiation between every term, that appear in this field.

That is why we propose to define ubiquitous computing as:

Ubiquitous Computing (*Period*) :
An era in which the democratization and miniaturization of
computers make it possible to offer users a distributed, intuitive and
possibly invisible use of computers.

The terms "ubiquitous computing", "pervasive computing" and "diffuse computing" are equivalent.

2.2   To Ambient Intelligence

Before studying ambient intelligence, we propose to define what intelligence is. Thus, according to [7], intelligence is the fact to perform rational actions, that is to say, which aims to maximize a performance measure, based on evidence acquired during a perception and a priori integrated knowledge.

According to Olson et al. [8], the concept of ambient intelligence was initiated at a conference organized by the research teams of Philips. Ambient intelligence has been described as the enrichment of an environment by technology (sensors, processors, actuators, etc.) in order to build a system for capturing and processing data, and for making decisions, to the benefit of users in this environment.

Since 2001, the European Commission's Information Society Technologies Advisory Group introduced the concept of ambient intelligence [11,12] and envisioned its impact on our societies in the future.

Finally, according to Aarts and Wichert [14]: "Ambient Intelligence (AmI) is about sensitive, adaptive electronic environments that respond to the actions of persons and objects and cater for their needs. This approach includes the entire environment and associates it with human interaction." This vision is shared by the author of [9]. Moreover, the book [10,13] and [14], pointed out the necessity of "various devices embedded in the environment collectively use the distributed information and the intelligence inherent in this interconnected network," in a context of ambient intelligence.

These authors also determined 3 criteria for the implementation of ambient intelligence [14]:

- Perception of the situation
- Ubiquitous access
- Natural interaction

Even if all these definitions are in imperfect agreement, the typology given by these authors are not evident. Thus, some speak of a "concept," or of what could be a research field and most define it by its goal. This is why we propose to distinguish between the domain, the set of services and the environment through the following definitions:

Ambient Intelligence (*Set of services*) :
A set of IT services which is interconnected, context-aware and
naturally interactive and intelligent [7], in order to assist human
activities. These services are based on a *smart environment*.

Ambient Computing (*Domain*) :
Emerging scientific domain of ubiquitous computing that aims to create ambient intelligence. This is an area touching many related fields such as: home assistance, robotics or artificial intelligence.

Smart Object (*Physical object*) :
Generally, an object whose original design has no direct link with computing, but which has been augmented with computational and communication capabilities. This is the basic block for building a *smart environment*.

Smart Environment (*Network*) :
A collection of interconnected smart objects, physically situated, that provide data capture, action and computing capabilities to a set of services.

Moreover, we can find the terms "smart environment," "responsive environment" and "intelligent environment" which are equivalent.

In the case where we want to communicate about the ambient intelligence and smart environment together, we propose to call it "ambient intelligence system". In this case, the definition is:

Ambient Intelligence System (*Services with network*) :
A smart environment exploited by ambient intelligence which aims to assist human activities.

2.3   Internet of Things

The authors of [15,17] and [16], give us explicit definitions which would allow us to assert that the Internet of Things is a network of objects that perceive and act in the physical world while offering services, becoming an integral part of the Internet. Given the definition of a smart environment mentioned above, we can intuitively assume that the Internet of Things is a smart environment.

Moreover, the authors, Atzori et al. [17], are in agreement with what we are advancing in this article and note an "apparent fuzziness," which comes from the different interests, finalities and backgrounds of the actors of the sector, whether they are from the research or business worlds.

In view of these definitions of the "Internet of Things," we propose the following reworking, which fits into all the terms we have defined above:

Internet of Things (*Network*) :
A world-wide *smart environment*, which aims to interconnect *smart objects* by means of the Internet standards of communication.

In the same way, Guinard and Trifa [18] highlight the "need for a common language that can be understood," by all the heterogeneous objects of the Internet of Things. Later they stated with Wilde [19] in 2010, that they : "propose to reuse and adapt patterns commonly used for the Web, and introduce an architecture for the Web of Things." This vision is confirmed by the survey [20].

Based on the definition we made of the Internet of Things, we propose to define the Web of Things as follows:

Web of Things (*Standards*) :
Integration of Web standards and technologies to design Web services based on interconnected smart objects belonging to the Internet of Things.

As we now defined an explicitly categorized vocabulary and definitions of main keywords of ubiquitous computing, we can use it to clarify the relationship between ubiquitous computing and multi-agent systems. It is the subject of the next section.

3   Multi-agent Systems

3.1   State of the Art

The authors of [21] have highlighted the fact that the term "agent" could have fluctuating definition. If we reread Russell and Norvig's book [7] about agents, it simply states that: "An agent is something that perceives and acts in an environment." According to this definition, we can presume that a multi-agent system is a system composed of several of these agents, and which possibly have social interactions between them. The definition is in line with the Ferber's point of view [22] of an agent: "an agent can be a physical or virtual entity that can act, perceive its environment (in a partial way) and communicate with others, is autonomous and has skills to achieve its goals and tendencies." The vision given by [21] and [23] is more restrictive because they define agents as autonomous software. The authors [21] outline the following criteria to characterize an agent:

- **autonomous**: it operates without the direct intervention of humans and has control over its actions and internal state.
- **social**: it cooperates with other agents.
- **reactive**: it perceives its environment and responds in a timely fashion to modify the environment.
- **proactive**: it is able to exhibit goal-directed behavior by taking initiative in addition to its perceives of its environment.

Unifying all these definitions, we propose to define multi-agent system as follows:

Multi-Agent System (*Set of software*) :
Computer system composed of multiple software, capable of autonomous, social and possibly reactive and proactive action. In most cases, the multi-agent system is based on an environment.

3.2   Relation Between Multi-agent Systems and Ambient Intelligence

Firstly, having regard to the state of the art we established on the fields of ubiquitous computing, ambient intelligence and multi-agent systems, we can suppose that an ambient intelligence system is a kind of multi-agent system. In this case, we can make the following comparisons about ambient intelligence services:

- Ambient intelligence services are autonomous, because they can operate without the direct intervention of humans.
- Ambient intelligence is social, because the services that compose it are interconnected.
- These services act and perceive their environment through actuators and sensors devices in real time, so they are reactive.
- They are proactive because these services aim to accomplish a goal.

Moreover, this ambient intelligence system is composed by agents (the services) that operate in an environment (composed by smart objects). So we come to the conclusions that an ambient intelligence system is a case of a multi-agent system. It is possible to take into account the users into the system. They are considered as agents, components of the system.

Secondly, many articles prove the interest of the multi-agent paradigm for ambient computing. Authors of the handbook [25] made a state of multi-agent systems in the service of ambient intelligence and describe multiple use cases.

Most of them use multi-agent paradigm in order to design ambient intelligence systems. For example, Piette et al. [24] proposed to use multi-agent approach for the deployment of services in a smart environment. On this topic they affirmed: "In real systems, privacy, autonomy, robustness and scalability are essential. That is why we identified MAS as a suitable solution."

In the same way, Satoh [26] submitted his framework which aims to construct distributed, large-scale, mobile application thanks to dynamic agents. These agents can migrate through computers of a network, so they are defined as "mobile agents."

The article from Calvaresi et al. [27] is an implementation of the multi-agent approach in a concrete framework of ambient intelligence. The context of this implementation is telereahibilitation of older adults, using these technologies to assist them.

Moreover, they are many articles, as evidence, that discuss about implementation of multi-agent approach to the Internet of Things. The authors of [28,29] and [30] and proposed to integrate agent-based approach to the Internet of Things, in order to deal with the heterogeneity and scalability problem.

Finally, another use of multi-agent system serving ambient intelligence is the simulation of this kind of system. Jamont and Occello proposed this kind of approach. In [31], they introduce a hardware/software hybrid multi-agent based simulation in order to design embedded agent societies exploit smart environments.

4   Conclusion and Prospect

After an overview of the different terms related to ubiquitous computing, we showed a scattering in terms of interpretations. This phenomenon of scattering makes it more difficult to build the state of the art, particularly because of the difficulty to bring out all the articles with different key words, despite the implementation of similar concepts.

This moved us towards the construction of a lexicon synthesizing and aggregating the definitions outlined in the citations of the previous sections.

From there, we showed the interest of this clarification by emphasizing the relationship between multi-agent system and ambient intelligence. This enabled us to determine that ambient intelligence is a particular case of multi-agent system.

Among the possible prospects, it seems interesting to strengthen the link between multi-agent systems and ambient intelligence, in particular by the proposal of meta-models and meta-languages describing smart environments to optimize the exploitation of these, which also goes through a more in-depth study of human/computer interactions, ethics and security issues.

References

1. Gellersen, H.-W., Beigl, M., Krull, H.: The MediaCup: awareness technology embedded in an everyday object. In: Gellersen, H.-W. (ed.) HUC 1999. LNCS, vol. 1707, pp. 308–310. Springer, Heidelberg (1999). https://doi.org/10.1007/3-540-48157-5_30
2. Weiser, M.: The computer for the 21st century. IEEE Pervasive Comput. **1**(1), 19–25 (2002)
3. Krumm, J.: Ubiquitous Computing Fundamentals. Chapman and Hall/CRC, Boca Raton (2016)
4. Lyytinen, K., Youngjin, Y.: Ubiquitous computing. Commun. ACM **45**(12), 63–96 (2002)
5. Poslad, S.: Ubiquitous Computing: Smart Devices, Environments and Interactions. Wiley, Hoboken (2011)
6. Weiser, M.: Some computer science issues in ubiquitous computing. Commun. ACM **36**(7), 75–84 (1993)
7. Russell, S.J., Peter, N.: Artificial Intelligence: A Modern Approach. Pearson Education Limited, Malaysia (2016)
8. Olson, N., et al.: Semantic web, ubiquitous computing, or internet of things? A macro-analysis of scholarly publications. J. Documentation **71**(5), 884–916 (2015)
9. Weber, W., Jan, R.: Ambient Intelligence. Springer, Heidelberg (2005). https://doi.org/10.1007/b138670
10. Waldner, J.-B.: Nanocomputers and Swarm Intelligence. Wiley, Hoboken (2013)
11. IST Advisory Group: Scenarios for Ambient Intelligence in 2010, European Commission (2001)
12. IST Advisory Group: Ambient Intelligence: From Vision to Reality, European Commission (2003)
13. Ramos, C., et al.: Ambient intelligence-the next step for artificial intelligence. IEEE Intell. Syst. **23**(2), 15–18 (2008)

14. Aarts, E., Reiner, W.: Ambient intelligence. Technology guide, pp. 244–249. Springer, Heidelberg (2009). https://doi.org/10.1007/978-3-642-05408-2
15. Gubbi, J., et al.: Internet of Things (IoT): a vision, architectural elements, and future directions. Future Gener. Comput. Syst. **29**(7), 1645–1660 (2013)
16. Zanella, A., et al.: Internet of things for smart cities. IEEE Internet Things J. **1**(1), 22–32 (2014)
17. Atzori, L., et al.: The internet of things: a survey. Comput. Networks **54**(15), 2787–2805 (2010)
18. Guinard, D., Vlad, T.: Towards the web of things: web mashups for embedded devices. In: Workshop on Mashups, Enterprise Mashups and Lightweight Composition on the Web (MEM 2009), in Proceedings of WWW (International World Wide Web Conferences), Madrid, Spain, vol. 15 (2009)
19. Guinard, D., et al.: A resource oriented architecture for the Web of Things. In: IoT (2010)
20. Zeng, D., et al.: The web of things: a survey. JCM **6**(6), 424–438 (2011)
21. Bellifemine, F.L., et al.: Developing Multi-Agent Systems with JADE, vol. 7. Wiley, Hoboken (2007)
22. Ferber, J., Gerhard, W.: Multi-Agent Systems: An Introduction to Distributed Artificial Intelligence, vol. 1. Addison-Wesley, Reading (1999)
23. Wooldridge, M.: An Introduction to Multiagent Systems. Wiley, Hoboken (2009)
24. Piette, F., et al.: A multi-agent approach for the deployment of distributed applications in smart environments. In: Badica, C., et al. (eds.) International Symposium on Intelligent and Distributed Computing, vol. 678. Springer, Cham (2016). https://doi.org/10.1007/978-3-319-48829-5_4
25. Nakashima, H., et al.: Handbook of Ambient Intelligence and Smart Environments. Springer, Boston (2009). https://doi.org/10.1007/978-0-387-93808-0
26. Satoh, I.: MobileSpaces: a framework for building adaptive distributed applications using a hierarchical mobile agent system. In: Proceedings 20th IEEE International Conference on Distributed Computing Systems, IEEE (2000
27. Calvaresi, D., et al.: Real-time multi-agent systems for telerehabilitation scenarios. Artif. Intell. Med. **96**, 217–231 (2019)
28. Fortino, G., et al.: Integration of agent-based and cloud computing for the smart objects-oriented IoT. In: Proceedings of the 2014 IEEE 18th International Conference on Computer Supported Cooperative Work in Design (CSCWD), IEEE (2014)
29. Kwan, J., et al.: An agentified use of the Internet of Things. In: IEEE International Conference on Internet of Things (iThings) and IEEE Green Computing and Communications (GreenCom) and IEEE Cyber, Physical and Social Computing (CPSCom) and IEEE Smart Data (SmartData), IEEE (2016)
30. Khalfi, E.M., et al.: Designing the web of things as a society of autonomous real/virtual hybrid entities. In: Proceedings of the 2014 International Workshop on Web Intelligence and Smart Sensing, ACM (2014)
31. Jamont, J.-P., Michel, O.: A multiagent tool to simulate hybrid real/virtual embedded agent societies. In: Proceedings of the 2009 IEEE/WIC/ACM International Joint Conference on Web Intelligence and Intelligent Agent Technology, vol. 2. IEEE Computer Society (2009)

Explainable ASP

Jérémie Dauphin[1]([✉]) and Ken Satoh[2]

[1] CSC, University of Luxembourg, Esch-sur-Alzette, Luxembourg
jeremie.dauphin@uni.lu
[2] National Institute of Informatics, Tokyo, Japan
ksatoh@nii.ac.jp

Abstract. Despite its proven relevance, ASP (answer set programming) suffers from a lack of transparency in its outputs. Much like other popular artificial intelligence systems such as deep learning, the results do not come with any explanation to support their derivation. In this paper, we use a given answer set as guidance for a simplified top-down procedure of answer set semantics developed by Satoh and Iwayama to provide not only an explanation for the derivation (or non-derivation) of the atoms, but also an explanation for the consistency of the whole answer set itself. Additionally, we show that a full use of the Satoh-Iwayama procedure gives an explanation of why an atom is not present in any answer set.

1 Introduction

The ASP reasoning system has proved useful in many situations (Erdem 2016). However, much like AI paradigms such as deep learning, it fails to provide explanations for any of its outputs. In critical domains such as self-driving vehicles and legal reasoning, providing such an explanation to justify the results of systems of increasing complexity is crucial for well-informed decision-making and future improvements of the systems.

In this paper, we treat a proof sequence of top-down proof of the Satoh-Iwayama procedure (Satoh 1993) as such an explanation. We additionally simplify the procedure by considering a given answer set as input to guide the procedure. This mechanism is based on the notion of "well-supportedness" (Fages 1991), which identifies a sequence of rules in derivation of an atom in the answer set.

Additionally, the procedure also produces an explanation not only for the presence of a certain literal in a given answer set, but also for the consistency of said answer set (we call this a "credulous explanation"). Indeed, while providing justifications for how a literal is being derived in a given answer is important, it is also crucial to show how the given answer set avoids deriving inconsistencies

The work of Jérémie Dauphin was supported by the H2020 Marie Skłodowska-Curie grant number 690974 for the project MIREL.

K. Satoh—This work was partially supported by JSPS KAKENHI Grant Number 17H06103.

M. Baldoni et al. (Eds.): PRIMA 2019, LNAI 11873, pp. 610–617, 2019.
https://doi.org/10.1007/978-3-030-33792-6_47

and thus satisfies integrity constraints. For debugging purposes, issues might sometimes arise in this part of the logic program, rather than in the derivation of a literal of interest.

Consider the following example logic program: $\bot \leftarrow q$

$$p \leftarrow \sim q$$
$$q \leftarrow \sim p$$

Suppose that $\bot \leftarrow q$ has been added by mistake instead of $\bot \leftarrow p$. Then, we have an extension $\{p\}$. We would like to know why p is derived but without considering the integrity constraint of $\bot \leftarrow p$, we cannot detect the mistake.

2   Preliminaries

In this section, we briefly present some definitions from the state of the art. The basic building blocks are *atoms*, elementary propositions which may be true or false. A *literal* is either an atom a or its weak negation $\sim a$. Weak negation means that $\sim a$ holds iff there is no derivation of a.

Definition 1. *Let l be a literal. We denote the* inverse *of the literal as $\tilde{l}$ where*

- *if l is a positive literal then $\tilde{l} = \sim l$ (negation of l);*
- *if l is a negative literal of the form $\sim l'$, then $\tilde{l} = l'$.*

Definition 2. *A rule R is an expression of the form:*

$$H \leftarrow B_1, B_2, ..., B_k, \sim A_1, ..., \sim A_m$$

Where B_i and A_j are all atoms, and H is either an atom or $\bot$ (meaning contradiction*). We call H the* head *of the rule denoted as $head(R)$ and a set of literals, $B_1, B_2, ..., B_k, \sim A_1, ..., \sim A_m$: the* body *of the rule denoted as $body(R)$. We also denote a set of positive literals in the rule, $B_1, B_2, ..., B_k$ as $pos(R)$ and a set of literals appearing negatively in the rule, $A_1, ..., A_m$ as $neg(R)$.*

If $H = \bot$, we call the rule an integrity constraint*:*

$$\bot \leftarrow B_1, B_2, ..., B_k, \sim A_1, ..., \sim A_m.$$

A *logic program T* is a set of such rules and integrity constraints.

Definition 3. *Let I be a set of atoms. We say that I satisfies the body of a rule R (denoted as $I \models body(R)$) iff $pos(R) \subseteq I$ and $neg(R) \cap I = \emptyset$.*

Definition 4. *Given a logic program T, a* model *of T is a set of atoms M s.t. $p \in M$ iff $\exists r \in T$ s.t. $head(R) = p$ and $M \models body(R)$.*
If a model of T is minimal in the set inclusion sense, we call it a minimal model*. If a minimal model is unique, we call it the* least model*.*

Definition 5. *Given a logic program T, an* answer set *M is a set of atoms s.t.* $\perp \notin M$ *and*

$$M = min(T^M)$$

where

- *$T^M = \{head(R) \leftarrow pos(R) | R \in T \text{ and } neg(R) \cap M = \emptyset\}$, which we also call the* reduct *of T w.r.t. M;*
- *$min(T)$: the least model of T.*

So the answer sets are the models which are exactly the least models of the program reduct in their respect. Note that since the reduct is a positive logic program, it is guaranteed to have a least model.

We now introduce the notion of *resolution*.

Definition 6. *Given a logic program T and a literal l, the* resolution *of T w.r.t. l is:*

- *If l is a positive literal:*
  $resolve(l, T) = \{H \leftarrow B_1, ..., B_{i-1}, B_{i+1}..., B_k, \sim A_1, ..., \sim A_m | H \leftarrow B_1, ..., B_k, \sim A_1, ..., \sim A_m \in T \text{ and } l = B_i\}$
- *If l is a negative literal of the form $\sim l'$:*
  $resolve(l, T) = \{H \leftarrow B_1, ..., B_k, \sim A_1, ..., \sim A_{i-1}, A_{i+1}, ..., \sim A_m | H \leftarrow B_1, ..., B_k, \sim A_1, ..., \sim A_m \in T \text{ and } l' = A_i\} \cup \{\perp \leftarrow B_1, ..., B_k, \sim A_1, ..., \sim A_m | H \leftarrow B_1, ..., B_k, \sim A_1, ..., \sim A_m \in T \text{ and } l' = H\}$

In the cases where l is a positive literal, the resolution is the set of rules containing l in the positive part of the body, but with l removed from the body. In the cases where l is a negative literal, the resolution is the set of rules containing l either in the negative part of the body of the head, but with it again removed. The aim is to identify the rules affected by the fixing of l's truth value and consider their simplified version, where l's truth value has been taken into account.

3   Overview of the Full Version of the Satoh-Iwayama Procedure

We reproduce the Satoh-Iwayama top-down procedure (Satoh 1993) as a basis for producing explanations. The procedure has the following characteristics:

- the procedure answers whether there is an answer set which satisfies a query.
- the procedure is correct for a consistent logic program.
- for a finite and consistent logic program, if there is an answer set which satisfies a query, the procedure always answers "yes".

It consists of the subprocedures *derive, literal_con, rule_con* and *delete_con*. Note that Δ in the procedure expresses the literals derived by the recursive subprocedure calls. So Δ is used in order to ensure that literals are only computed once, thus avoiding redundant computations.

For *derive*(p, Δ), given an atom p and a set of literals Δ, we do the following:

1. Check whether p has already been computed, in which case we can stop.
2. Otherwise, select a rule with p as its head:

$$p \leftarrow p_1, ..., p_m, \sim q_1, ..., \sim q_n$$

3. Check if every positive literal p_i in its body can be derived by calling *derive*.
4. Check if every negative literal $\sim q_j$ in its body can be consistently assumed to be false by calling *literal_con*.
5. Check that the head becoming true does not lead to contradiction by calling *literal_con*.

For *literal_con*(l, Δ), given a literal l and a set of literals Δ, we do the following:

1. Check if l has already been computed, in which case we can stop.
2. Otherwise, add l to Δ.
3. Check the consistency of rules which are obtained by the resolution of l and the program by calling *rule_con*. This is used to check that l being true does not lead to any contradiction.
4. Check the consistency of deleted rules in the program by l by calling *deleted_con*. This is used to check consistency of implicit deletion of a rule by assuming l which might lead to contradiction.

For *rule_con*(R, Δ), given a rule R and a set of literals Δ, we show one of the following:

Case 1. A positive literal in the body of R can be consistently assumed to be false by calling *literal_con*.
Case 2. A negative literal in the body of R is derived by calling *derive*.
Case 3. Every positive literal in the body of R is derived and every negative literal in the body of R can be consistently assumed to be false and the assumption that the head becomes true does not lead to contradiction by calling *derive* and *literal_con*.

Cases 1 and 2 are for when the rule is not applicable, while case 3 ensure that in the cases where the rule is applicable, it does not lead to any contradiction.

For *deleted_con*(R, Δ), given a rule R and a set of literals Δ, we show one of the following:

Case 1. The head of a deleted rule R is derived by another rule by calling *derive*.
Case 2. The head of a deleted rule R can be consistently assumed to be false by calling *literal_con*.

This subprocedure simply ensures that the rule R being no-longer applicable, due to the inverse of a literal in its body having been set to true, does not cause any issues.

For a detailed account of the procedure, we refer the reader to the original work (Satoh 1993).

4   Answer Set Guided Method of Producing Explanation Why an Atom is Derived in a Given Answer Set

In our work, we focus on causal explanations, and thus consider a causal trace to be an explanation. We base this on the following quote:

> To explain an event is to provide some information about its causal history. In an act of explaining, someone who is in possession of some information about the causal history of some event - *explanatory information*, I shall call it - tries to convey it to someone else. - Lewis (1986)

We first give a definition of well-supportedness from Fages (1991). Identifying supporting rules provides us with a first step towards explanation, and allows us to speed up the second part of the explanation process.

Definition 7. *Let T be a logic program. We say that a set of atoms I is* well-supported *if there exists a strict well-founded partial order $\prec$ on I such that for any atom $A \in I$ there exists a rule $R \in T$ called* a supporting rule *for A in T s.t. $head(R) = A$ and $I \models body(R)$ and for every $B \in pos(R)$, $B \prec A$.*

We call such a set of atoms I a *well-supported model*.

Theorem 1. *(Fages 1991) Let T be a logic program. A set of atoms I is an answer set iff I is a well-supported model.*

Since we consider only positive literals in the body of a supporting rule in the definition of a well-supported model M for a logic program T, we can instead look at the corresponding rules from T's reduct with respect to M, and then return their original equivalents. Given an answer set, we can compute the set of corresponding supporting rules in linear time by slightly adapting the algorithm 2 of Downling (1984). By first taking the reduct according to the given answer set, we are able to apply their algorithm for checking the satisfiability of positive logic programs. The algorithm works by marking edges as they are visited, and we can re-use this marking to identify the supporting rules.

Now, we give an answer set guided method of producing an explanation of why an atom is derived in a given answer set. We can use the knowledge of having the answer set known in advance in order to skip some selection operations in the original procedure. This allows us to speed up the process and save a considerable amount of computations.

It consists of simplified versions of the above four subprocedures, with the main difference being that we now have a global variable M representing the answer set of interest. This allows many branching choices to be reduced to single paths in the proof tree, saving many unnecessary computations. We briefly sketch the improvements from the original procedure.

For *simple_derive*(p, Δ), we can now select a supporting rule with respect to M instead of trying all rules with p as their heads. Since it is a supporting rule, we are guaranteed to be able to apply it, and hence won't need to backtrack and restart the process. This reduce a potential exponential branching to a single operation guaranteed to succeed.

The subprocedure *literal_con*(l, Δ) remains identical to the original one, as in this case the knowledge on the answer set does not provide any help.

For *simple_rule_con*(R, Δ), we can guide the procedure towards the relevant case from the three possibilities, since we know from the answer set which of the three cases is the applicable one.

The case of *simple_deleted_con*(R, Δ) is similar to the previous one, in the sense that the answer set tells us which of the two cases to pursue.

5   Examples of Explanations

We show examples of explanations. For a more user-friendly interface, we translate the subprocedure calls into natural language sentences.

Let T be: $\{p \leftarrow \sim q; q \leftarrow \sim p; r \leftarrow q; r \leftarrow \sim r\}$.

We show a credulous explanation for the derivation of q in the answer set $\{q, r\}$. To justify q, we first check which rule should be applied and since $q \leftarrow \sim p$ is a supporting rule for q given the answer set M, we choose the rule without making a selection of other rules[1]. Then, to derive q from the rule $q \leftarrow \sim p$, we first check the consistency of $\sim p$. To do this consistency check, we check the consistency of the resolvents of $\sim p$ w.r.t. T, which are $0 \leftarrow \sim q$[2] and $q \leftarrow$.

1. To show the consistency of $0 \leftarrow \sim q$, we show a derivation of q[3]. Then,
   (a) we can identify the supporting rule, $q \leftarrow \sim p$, for q given M and show the consistency of $\sim p$. This is done since $\sim p$ is already assumed
   (b) we check the consistency of assuming q as follows:
       i. we check the consistency of resolvent of q w.r.t. T, which is $r \leftarrow$. Then, we check the consistency of assuming r. This is done by consistency check of deleting $r \leftarrow \sim r$. This is successful since r is already assumed.
       ii. we check the consistency of deleted rule, $p \leftarrow \sim q$. In this case, thanks to M, we can determine that p should be false and it is proved since p is already assumed to be false.
2. the consistency of $q \leftarrow$ is proved since q is already assumed.

---

[1] In this example, $q \leftarrow \sim p$ is the only rule for deriving q but even if there were other rules, we can identify this rule given M.

[2] We display 0 instead of $\perp$ for notational consistency with the meta-interpreter output of the Satoh-Iwayama procedure.

[3] Since we know that $q \in M$, we can speed up the process by skipping the other checks.

And finally, we check the consistency of assuming q, which is immediate since q is already assumed.

We now show a cautious explanation for why there is no answer set including p for a logic program T. To show this, we need to show that every derivation of p leads to a contradiction. Since there is only one rule to derive p, that is $p \leftarrow \sim q$, we show consistency of assuming $\sim q$ as follows:

1. we need to check for consistency of the resolvents for $\sim q$ w.r.t. T, that is, $p \leftarrow$ and $0 \leftarrow \sim p$, as follows:
   (a) for $p \leftarrow$, deriving p does not lead to contradiction so p is assumed.
   (b) for $0 \leftarrow \sim p$, we already assume p so it is consistent.
2. we need to check consistency of a deleted rule by $\sim q$. w.r.t. T, that is, $r \leftarrow q$. To do so, we need to check whether r is either true or false. However, both checks fail in the following reasons:
   (a) in order to show r, we could use either $r \leftarrow q$ or $r \leftarrow \sim r$. But the first rule cannot be used since $\sim q$ is already assumed. For the second rule, we need to assume $\sim r$ to derive r. Then, we need to check resolvents of $\sim r$ w.r.t. T, that is $0 \leftarrow q$ and $0 \leftarrow \sim r$ and $r \leftarrow$:
      i. $0 \leftarrow q$ is consistent since $\sim q$ is already assumed.
      ii. $0 \leftarrow \sim r$ leads to contradiction since $\sim r$ is already assumed, therefore, showing r is failed.
   (b) in order to show $\sim r$, we should show that $\sim r$ is consistently assumed but then we iterate a part of the above checking to show r, the procedure is failed.
3. Therefore, r is neither true nor false and so derivations of $\sim$ and p are failed.

Thus, there is no answer set including p.

6   Related Work

In this section, we compare our approach with works mentioned in the excellent survey of explanations in ASP made by Fanndinno and Schulz (2019).

Pontelli (2009) gives a method of producing a graph-based explanation (called off-line justification) of the truth value of an atom w.r.t. a given answer set and extends the method to give a justification of atoms during the computation of an answer set (called on-line justification). In off-line justification, all the rule application steps used to derive an atom is included in the graph. On the other hand, Schulz (2016) decomposes each derivation of an atom into a part whether only assumptions to derive an atom are considered. Then, they define attack tree justification to give an overall explanation. Cabalar (2014) gives a method of giving an explanation by causal graphs. They give an algebraic characterization of combining causal graphs.

These approaches represent a graph (or a tree) for an explanation about derivation of a literal whereas our approach not only gives a derivation of a literal but also gives a derivation for the consistency of assuming the literal. Moreover, our approach is more procedural in which we give a credulous explanation by proof sequence of why a literal is derived in a given answer set and maintain consistency. We also give a cautious explanation why a literal is not included in any answer set. In the cautious explanation, we could use the previous methods above by giving an explanation why an atom is not included in each answer set after computing all the answer sets. However, this would cause a complex explanation whereas our proof procedure could share a common derivation to simplify the explanation.

7   Conclusion

We show methods of giving credulous and cautious explanations in ASP. We modify the Satoh-Iwayama's top-down procedure for answer set to produce a credulous explanation using a guidance of a given answer set. We also show a full use of the Satoh-Iwayama procedure to produce a cautious explanation.

We would like to apply these methods for applying ASP in a critical domain and show usefulness of our approach as a future work. Additionally, we would like to consider Miller's work on what constitutes an explanation in AI (Miller 2018) in order to produce multiple kinds of explanations.

References

Cabalar, P., Fandinno, J., Fink, M.: Causal graph justifications of logic programs. Theory Pract. Logic Program. **14**(4–5), 603–618 (2014)

Dowling, W.F., Gallier, J.: Linear-time algorithms for testing the satisfiability of propositional horn formulae. J. Logic Program. **1**(3), 267–284 (1984)

Erdem, E., Gelfond, M., Leone, N.: Applications of answer set programming. AI Mag. **37**(3), 53–68 (2016)

Fages, F.: A new fixpoint semantics for general logic programs compared with the well-founded and the stable model semantics. New Gener. Comput. **9**(3–4), 425–443 (1991)

Fandinno, J., Schulz, C.: Answering the "why" in answer set programming - a survey of explanation approaches. Theory Pract. Logic Program. **19**(2), 114–203 (2019)

Pontelli, E., Son, T.C., El-Khatib, O.: Justifications for logic programs under answer set semantics. Theory Pract. Logic Program. **9**(1), 1–56 (2009)

Satoh, K., Iwayama, N.: A correct goal-directed proof procedure for a general logic program with integrity constraints. In: Lamma, E., Mello, P. (eds.) ELP 1992. LNCS, vol. 660, pp. 24–44. Springer, Heidelberg (1993). https://doi.org/10.1007/3-540-56454-3_2

Schulz, C., Toni, F.: Justifying answer sets using argumentation. Theory Pract. Logic Program. **16**(1), 59–110 (2016)

Miller, T.: Explanation in artificial intelligence: insights from the social sciences. Artificial Intelligence (2018)

Lewis, D.: Causal explanation. Philos. Pap. **2**, 214–240 (1986)

Block Argumentation

Ryuta Arisaka[1]([✉]), Francesco Santini[2], and Stefano Bistarelli[2]

[1] Nagoya Institute of Technology, Nagoya, Japan
ryutaarisaka@gmail.com
[2] University of Perugia, Perugia, Italy
{francesco.santini,stefano.bistarelli}@unipg.it

Abstract. We advance the point of view: *an argument as an argumentation and vice versa*, to formulate Block (Bipolar) Argumentation (BBA), a bipolar argumentation theory that recursively instantiates an abstract argument with a bipolar argumentation. Multiple occurrence of the same argument(ation) can become issues in such a self-similar argumentation theory, for which we consider a graphical (syntactic) constraint, in relation to which we define its acceptability semantics. For some highlight, acceptability of unattacked arguments is not always warranted once this kind of a constraint must be taken into account.

1 Introduction

In this work, we advance the point of view: *an argument as an argumentation and vice versa*, which, despite the presence of substitution theories [7,8], has not been generally pursued. In abstract argumentation theory [6], an argumentation is represented by a graph with a node representing an argument with its nature left unspecified. Our point-of-view instantiates any argument with an argumentation recursively, which is theoretically the most general instantiation possible with the formal vocabulary of a given argumentation theory. We consider bipolar argumentation, with attack and support, so we name our theory *Block Bipolar Argumentation* (BBA). Formulation is in Sect. 3. There, we reflect on multiple occurrence of the same argument(ation)s in a given argumentation which can be, under some interpretation of it, seen raising internal consistency issues. We propose the use of a graphical (syntactic) constraint to address them, and define acceptability semantics in relation to it. Acceptability of unattacked arguments is not outright warranted once that kind of a constraint must be taken into account. More details including semantic constraints are in [1].

2 Technical Preliminaries

Let $\mathcal{A}$ be a class of abstract entities we understand as arguments. Its member is referred to by a, and its finite subset by A, each with or without a subscript and/or a superscript. This "with or without" convention shall be assumed for any other symbol. A bipolar argumentation (e.g. see [5]) is a tuple (A, R, R^s)

© Springer Nature Switzerland AG 2019
M. Baldoni et al. (Eds.): PRIMA 2019, LNAI 11873, pp. 618–626, 2019.
https://doi.org/10.1007/978-3-030-33792-6_48

with two binary relations R and R^s over A. For any (A, R, R^s), $A_1 \subseteq A$ is said to attack, or support, $A_2 \subseteq A$ if and only if, or iff, there exist $a_1 \in A_1$ and $a_2 \in A_2$ such that $(a_1, a_2) \in R$ (for attack), or $(a_1, a_2) \in R^s$ (for support).

An extension-based acceptability semantics of (A, R, R^s) is a member of 2^{2^A}. When R^s is not taken into account, a semantics of (A, R, R^s) is effectively that of (A, R), Dung's argumentation framework [6], where $A_1 \subseteq A$ is said to defend $a_x \in A$ iff each $a_y \in A$ attacking a_x is attacked by at least one member of A_1, and said to be conflict-free iff A_1 does not attack A_1. $A_1 \subseteq A$ is said to be: admissible iff it is conflict-free and defends every $a \in A_1$; complete iff it is admissible and includes all arguments it defends; preferred iff it is a maximal complete set; and grounded iff it is the set intersection of all complete sets. Complete/preferred/grounded semantics is the set of all complete/preferred/grounded sets.

A label-based acceptability semantics [4] for Dung's (A, R) makes use of the set $\mathcal{L}$ of three elements, say $\{+, -, ?\}$, and the class Λ of all functions from $\mathcal{A}$ to $\mathcal{L}$. While, normally, it is $\{\mathsf{in}, \mathsf{out}, \mathsf{undec}\}$, by $\{+, -, ?\}$ we avoid direct acceptability readings off them. $\lambda \in \Lambda$ is said to be a complete labelling of (A, R) iff both of the following hold: (A) $\lambda(a) = +$ iff $\lambda(a_p) = -$ for every $a_p \in A$ that attacks a; and (B) $\lambda(a) = -$ iff there is some $a_p \in A$ with $\lambda(a_p) = +$ that attacks a. $A_1 \subseteq A$ is the set of all arguments that map into $+$ under complete labelling iff A_1 is a complete set, thus a label-based semantics provides the same information as an extension-based semantics does, and more because of $-/?$ distinction.

In bipolar argumentation where R^s properly matters for an acceptability semantics, the notion of support is given a particular interpretation which influences the semantics; see [5] for a survey of some popular interpretations.

3   Block (Bipolar) Argumentation

Let $\mathbb{N}$ be the class of natural numbers including 0. Let $\mathcal{X}$ be a class of an uncountable number of abstract entities. It will be assumed that every member of $\mathcal{X}$ is distinguishable from any other members. Further, every member of $\mathcal{X}$ has no intersection with any others. Lack of these assumptions is not convenient if one wants to judge equality of two arguments.

Definition 1 (Arguments and argumentations). *We define a (block) argument $a \in \mathcal{A}$ to be either $(\{x\}, \emptyset, \emptyset)$ for some $x \in \mathcal{X}$, or $(\{a_1, \dots, a_n\}, R, R^s)$ for some $a_1, \dots, a_n \in \mathcal{A}$ and some binary relations R and R^s over $\{a_1, \dots, a_n\}$. We say $a \in \mathcal{A}$ is unitary iff a is some $(\{x\}, \emptyset, \emptyset)$.*

We define a Block (Bipolar) Argumentation (BBA) to be some argument $(A, R, R^s) \in \mathcal{A}$. We say that it is finite iff the number of occurrences of symbols is finite in A. We denote the class of all finite BBAs by $\mathcal{A}^{BBA}$, a subclass of $\mathcal{A}$, and may refer to its member particularly by a^{BBA}.

The viewpoint of this paper towards an argument and an argumentation has been, since the beginning, that either of them may be the other. There is no contradiction when we describe $\mathcal{A}$ as the class of arguments in Sect. 2, and here call them also argumentations.

3.1   Representation of Argument(ation)s

As the same member of $\mathcal{A}$ may occur more than once in $a^{BBA} \in \mathcal{A}$, a description of the kind: "a in a^{BBA}" is ambiguous. To refer to arguments in a specific position in a^{BBA} in a one-to-one manner, we assign a unique integer sequence to each $a \in \mathcal{A}$ that occurs in a^{BBA}.

Definition 2 (Flat representation). *Let $\langle \mathbb{N} \rangle$ denote the class of all sequences of natural numbers (an empty sequence is included), whose member may be referred to by $\langle m \rangle$. We use '.' for sequence concatenation. Let $\varpi : \mathcal{A} \to 2^{\mathcal{A} \times \langle \mathbb{N} \rangle}$ be such that $\varpi(a)$ is a minimal set that satisfies both: (1) $(a, 0) \in \varpi(a)$; and (2) For any $(a_p, \langle m \rangle) \in \varpi(a)$, if a_p is not unitary and is some $(\{a_1, \ldots, a_{n_p}\}, R_x, R_x^s)$, then $(a_i, \langle m \rangle.n_i) \in \varpi(a)$ for every $1 \le i \le n_p$ such that all $n_1, \ldots, n_{n_p}$ are distinct. For any a, we say that $\varpi(a)$ is its flat representation.*

We can now refer to any argument a in a^{BBA} uniquely, no matter how often it occurs in a^{BBA}, for, suppose $(a, \langle m_1 \rangle), (a, \langle m_2 \rangle) \in \varpi(a)$ with $\langle m_1 \rangle \neq \langle m_2 \rangle$, then a at the position specified by $\langle m_1 \rangle$ is different from a occurring at the position specified by $\langle m_2 \rangle$. We note that a flat representation will be used only for the purpose of uniquely identifying an argument that occurs in a given a^{BBA}.

3.2   Characterisation of Complete Sets (with No Constraints)

We characterise complete sets with no constraints initially.

Definition 3 (Arguments, attacks and supports in $\langle m \rangle$). *Let $Arg : \mathcal{A}^{BBA} \times \langle \mathbb{N} \rangle \to 2^{\mathcal{A}}$ be such that $Arg(a^{BBA}, \langle m \rangle) = A_p$ iff $((A_p, R, R^s), \langle m \rangle) \in \varpi(a^{BBA})$ for some R and R^s. Let $Attck, Spprt : \mathcal{A}^{BBA} \times \langle \mathbb{N} \rangle \to 2^{\mathcal{A} \times \mathcal{A}}$ be such that:*

$$Attck(a^{BBA}, \langle m \rangle) = \{(a_1, a_2) \in R \mid \exists((A, R, R^s), \langle m \rangle) \in \varpi(a^{BBA}). \; a_1, a_2 \in A\}$$
$$Spprt(a^{BBA}, \langle m \rangle) = \{(a_1, a_2) \in R^s \mid \exists((A, R, R^s), \langle m \rangle) \in \varpi(a^{BBA}). \; a_1, a_2 \in A\}$$

For any a^{BBA} and any $\langle m \rangle$, we say: a_1 attacks, or supports, a_2 in $\langle m \rangle$ iff $(a_1, a_2) \in Attck(a^{BBA}, \langle m \rangle)$ (attack), or $(a_1, a_2) \in Spprt(a^{BBA}, \langle m \rangle)$ (support).

While there are three typical interpretations (deductive, necessary, evidential) of support (see in [5]), they enforce a strong dependency between arguments and the arguments that support them concerning their acceptance. Our interpretation of support here is weaker, almost supplementary, as in the following definitions. Informally, it is not necessary that an argument be in a complete set when its supporter/supportee is in the set, unlike in deductive/necessary support. A supporter can, however, prevent an argument attacked by an attacker from being strongly rejected (with labels, it concerns the difference of whether the argument gets − (which leads to strong rejection) or ?). This interpretation is motivated by a real-life example, which will be looked at in Sect. 3.3. Extension-based complete set characterisation is:

Definition 4 (Extension-based complete set when no constraints). *For any a^{BBA} and any $\langle m \rangle$, we say: A_1 defends a in $\langle m \rangle$ iff $A_1 \subseteq Arg(a^{BBA}, \langle m \rangle)$ and $a \in Arg(a^{BBA}, \langle m \rangle)$ and every a_1 attacking a in $\langle m \rangle$ is: attacked by at least some $a_2 \in A_1$; and not supported by any $a_3 \in A_1$.*[1]

We say that A_1 is: conflict-free in $\langle m \rangle$ iff $A_1 \subseteq Arg(a^{BBA}, \langle m \rangle)$ and $(a_1, a_2) \notin Attck(a^{BBA}, \langle m \rangle)$ for any $a_1, a_2 \in A_1$. We say that A_1 is standard complete in $\langle m \rangle$ iff $A_1 \subseteq Arg(a^{BBA}, \langle m \rangle)$ and A_1 is conflict-free and includes all arguments it defends in $\langle m \rangle$.

We can also have a label-based characterisation with $\mathcal{L}$ $(= \{+, -, ?\})$. The idea is to have one-to-one correspondence with extension-based complete set characterisation above. Theorem 1 notes the correspondence of the two characterisations.

Definition 5 (Complete labelling when no constraints). *Let Λ be the class of all $\lambda : \mathcal{A} \times \langle \mathbb{N} \rangle \to \mathcal{L}$ such that, for any a and any $\langle m \rangle$, we have $\lambda((a, \langle m \rangle)) = l$ for some l. For any a^{BBA} and any $\lambda \in \Lambda$, we say that λ is a standard complete labelling of a^{BBA} iff every $(\{a_1, \ldots, a_n\}, \langle m \rangle) \in \varpi(a^{BBA})$ satisfies both of the following: (A) $\lambda((a_i, \langle m \rangle.n_i)) = +$, $1 \leq i \leq n$, iff every a_j, $1 \leq j \leq n$, attacking a_i in $\langle m \rangle$ satisfies $\lambda((a_j, \langle m \rangle.n_j)) = -$; and (B) $\lambda((a_i, \langle m \rangle.n_i)) = -$, $1 \leq i \leq n$, iff there exists some $1 \leq j \leq n$ such that $\lambda((a_j, \langle m \rangle.n_j)) = +$ and that a_j attacks a_i in $\langle m \rangle$ and there is no $1 \leq k \leq n$ such that $\lambda((a_k, \langle m \rangle.n_k)) = +$ and that a_k supports a_i in $\langle m \rangle$.*

Theorem 1 (Correspondence). *For any a^{BBA} and $\langle m \rangle$, $A_1 \subseteq Arg(a^{BBA}, \langle m \rangle)$ is standard complete in $\langle m \rangle$ only if there is some standard complete labelling λ of a^{BBA} such that $\lambda((a_p, \langle m \rangle.n)) = +$ is equivalent to $a_p \in A_1$ for any $(a_p, \langle m \rangle.n) \in \varpi(a^{BBA})$. Conversely, λ is a standard complete labelling of a^{BBA} only if, for every $(a, \langle m \rangle) \in \varpi(a^{BBA})$, $\{a_p \in Arg(a^{BBA}, \langle m \rangle) \mid \exists n \in \mathbb{N}.\lambda((a_p, \langle m \rangle.n)) = +\}$ is a standard complete set in $\langle m \rangle$.*

3.3 Graphical (Syntactic) Constraint

Multiple occurrence of an argument in a given a^{BBA} can be seen to cause internal consistency issues under some interpretation of argument(ation)s in a^{BBA}.

Example 1. During the trial over the death of Kim Jong-Nam[2], a certain argumentation was deployed by a suspect's defence lawyer as he cast a blame on Malaysian authorities for having released only portions of CCTV footage of the fatal attack. The argumentation was broadly:

Prosecutor: the CCTV footage released by Malaysian Police shows a suspect walking quickly to an airport restroom to wash hands after attacking the victim with VX (toxic chemical compound), which produces an impression

---

[1] "and" instead of "and" is used in this paper when the context in which it appears strongly indicates truth-value comparisons. It follows the semantics of classical logic conjunction. Similarly for "or" (disjunction).

[2] https://en.wikipedia.org/wiki/Assassination_of_Kim_Jong-nam.

that the suspect, contrary to her own statement that she thought she was acting for a prank video, knew what was on her hands.

Defence Lawyer: however, the CCTV footage in its entirety shows the suspect adjusting her glasses after the attack, with VX on her hands, which counter-evidences her knowledge of the substance. Since Malaysian authorities know of the omitted footage, they are clearly biased against the suspect, intentionally tampering with evidence.

Assume the following arguments:

a_1: After the victim was attacked with VX, the suspect walked quickly to a restroom for washing hands.

a_2: The suspect knew VX was on her hands.

a_3: The suspect was acting for a prank video.

a_4: The suspect adjusted her glasses with VX on her hands before walking to restroom.

a_5: Malaysian authorities are biased against the suspect, tampering with evidence by intentional omission of relevant CCTV footage.

a_6: a_1 supports a_2. a_7: a_4 attacks a_2. a_8: a_7 attacks a_6.

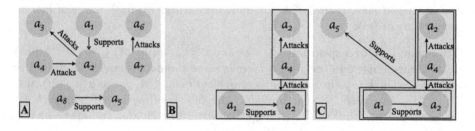

This example can be modelled as in $\boxed{A}$ with a_{1-5} considered unitary. Malaysian Police uses a_1 for a_2 (a_1 supports a_2) to dismiss a_3 (a_2 attacks a_3). All these three arguments are made available to the audience. The defence lawyer uses a_4 to counter a_2. a_4 is also available to the audience as attacking a_2. He then uses a_7 to attack Malaysian Police' a_6. This is also presented to the audience. Finally, he uses a_8 for a_5. Non-unitary arguments of the kinds of a_6, a_7 and a_8 are themselves argumentations making use of already appeared a_{1-4} and attack/support among them. "a_7 attacks a_6" could be detailed as in $\boxed{B}$, and "a_8 supports a_5" as in $\boxed{C}$.

For the internal consistency, if the defence lawyer argued instead: "The fact: [the suspect adjusted her glasses with VX on her hands before walking to restroom confirms her knowledge of the substance on her hands] attacks the argument: [she did not know VX was on her hands because, after attacking the victim with VX, she walked quickly to a restroom for washing hands].", i.e. the argument: "a_4 supports a_2" attacks the argument: "a_1 attacks a_2", we would see at once that the two inner arguments "a_4 supports a_2" and "a_1 attacks a_2" are factually inconsistent with the attack/support relations among a_{1-4}.

Consequently, one may like to impose certain constraints to enforce argument's dependency on the same argument that occurs in a given argumentation. For example, we may impose a constraint that an inner argument making use of already presented argumentation(s), i.e. outer argumentation(s), must correctly make use of the arguments and the attack/support relations in the argumentation, e.g. if "a_1 supports a_2" but not "a_1 attacks a_2" has been presented, a_1, a_2, and "a_1 supports a_2" may all be used in an inner argument as referring to a part of the outer argumentation, but not "a_1 attacks a_2", to prevent the factually inconsistent arguments from getting justified.

To characterise this graphical constraint, we need firstly to tell equality of two arguments.

Definition 6 (Equality). *Let* $Eq : \mathcal{A} \times \mathcal{A}$ *be such that* $Eq(a_1, a_2)$ *iff (1)* $a_1 = a_2 = (\{x\}, \emptyset, \emptyset)$ *for some* $x \in \mathcal{X}$ *or (2) If* a_1 *is some* $(\{a_1'', \ldots, a_n''\}, R_1, R_1^s)$, *then* a_2 *is some* $(\{a_1', \ldots, a_n'\}, R_2, R_2^s)$ *with: (A)* $Eq(a_i'', a_i')$; *(B)* $(a_i'', a_j'') \in R_1$ *iff* $(a_i', a_j') \in R_2$; *and (C)* $(a_i'', a_j'') \in R_1^s$ *iff* $(a_i', a_j') \in R_2^s$, *for* $1 \leq i, j \leq n$.

With this, we can identify whether $a_2 \in \mathcal{A}$ is a sub-graph, i.e. sub-argumentation, of $a_1 \in \mathcal{A}$ up to Eq. For our technical purpose, it suffices to simply learn whether, for a_i denoting $(A_i \equiv \{a_1^i, \ldots, a_{n_i}^i\}, R_i, R_i^s)$, $i \in \{1, 2\}$, the set members of A_2 form a subset of A_1 equivalent up to Eq, and whether the two binary relations over the set members of A_2 are equivalent up to Eq as those over A_1 for the set members shared between A_1 and A_2, which leads to the definition below.

Definition 7 (Partial-graph). *Let* $\searrow : \mathcal{A} \times \mathcal{A}$ *be such that* $((A_1, R_1, R_1^s), ((A_2, R_2, R_2^s)) \in \searrow$, *written synonymously as* $(A_1, R_1, R_1^s) \searrow (A_2, R_2, R_2^s)$, *iff* $A_2 = \{a_1', \ldots, a_{n_2}'\}$ *and* $A_1 = \{a_1, \ldots, a_{n_1}\}$ *satisfy: (A)* $|A_2| \leq |A_1|$; *(B) For each* a_i', $1 \leq i \leq n_2$, *there exists some* a_j, $1 \leq j \leq n_1$, *such that* $Eq(a_i', a_j)$; *(C) For each two* a_{i_1}', a_{i_2}', $1 \leq i_1, i_2 \leq n_2$, *if* $(a_{i_1}', a_{i_2}') \in R_2$, *then there exist some* a_{j_1}, a_{j_2}, $1 \leq j_1, j_2 \leq n_1$ *such that* $(a_{j_1}, a_{j_2}) \in R_1$, *that* $Eq(a_{i_1}', a_{j_1})$, *and that* $Eq(a_{i_2}', a_{j_2})$; *and (D) For each two* a_{i_1}', a_{i_2}', $1 \leq i_1, i_2 \leq n_2$, *if* $(a_{i_1}', a_{i_2}') \in R_2^s$, *then there exist some* a_{j_1}, a_{j_2}, $1 \leq j_1, j_2 \leq n_1$ *such that* $(a_{j_1}, a_{j_2}) \in R_1^s$, *that* $Eq(a_{i_1}', a_{j_1})$, *and that* $Eq(a_{i_2}', a_{j_2})$. *We say that* a_2 *is a partial-argumentation of* a_1 *iff* $a_1 \searrow a_2$.

Now, let $\sqsupseteq : (\mathcal{A} \times \langle \mathbb{N} \rangle) \times (\mathcal{A} \times \langle \mathbb{N} \rangle)$ be such that $((a_p, \langle m_p \rangle), (a_q, \langle m_q \rangle)) \in \sqsupseteq$, synonymously written as $(a_p, \langle m_p \rangle) \sqsupseteq (a_q, \langle m_q \rangle)$, iff $\langle m_p \rangle . \langle m_r \rangle = \langle m_q \rangle$ for some $\langle m_r \rangle$. Let us say: $(a_p, \langle m_p \rangle) \sqsupset (a_q, \langle m_q \rangle)$ iff $(a_p, \langle m_p \rangle) \sqsupseteq (a_q, \langle m_q \rangle)$ and $(a_q, \langle m_q \rangle) \not\sqsupseteq (a_p, \langle m_p \rangle)$. With these definitions, we obtain:

Definition 8 (Graphical constraints). *For any* a^{BBA}, *we say* $(a_2, \langle m_2 \rangle) \in \varpi(a^{BBA})$ *satisfies* **G** *iff both of the following hold: (A) if* $\langle m_2 \rangle \neq 0$ *and if* a_2 *is not unitary, then there exists some* $(a_1, \langle m_1 \rangle) \in \varpi(a^{BBA})$ *such that* $(a_1, \langle m_1 \rangle) \sqsupset (a_2, \langle m_2 \rangle)$ *and that* $a_1 \searrow a_2$; *and (B) every* $(a_p, \langle m_2 \rangle . n) \in \varpi(a^{BBA})$ *satisfies* **G**.

Example 2 (Graphical constraint). Let a^{BBA} be the argumentation in $\boxed{A}$. Its flat representation 'can' be the set of all the following: $(a^{BBA}, 0)$; $(a_i, 0.i)$ for $1 \leq i \leq 8$; $(a_1, 0.6.1)$ and $(a_2, 0.6.2)$; $(a_2, 0.7.1)$ and $(a_4, 0.7.2)$; $(a_6, 0.8.1)$ and $(a_7, 0.8.2)$; $(a_1, 0.8.1.1)$ and $(a_2, 0.8.1.2)$; and $(a_2, 0.8.2.1)$ and $(a_4, 0.8.2.2)$.

Then it holds that any $(a, \langle m \rangle) \in \varpi(a^{\mathsf{BBA}})$ satisfies **G**, since: (1) there is nothing to show for $(a^{\mathsf{BBA}}, 0)$ as the sequence is 0; (2) there is also nothing to show for $(a_i, 0.i)$, $1 \leq i \leq 5$, as $a_{1,\ldots,5}$ are unitary; (3) $a^{\mathsf{BBA}} \searrow (\{a_1, a_2\}, \emptyset, \{(a_1, a_2)\})$ for $(a_6, 0.6)$; (4) there is nothing to show for $(a_i, 0.6.i)$, $1 \leq i \leq 2$, as a_1 and a_2 are unitary; (5) $a^{\mathsf{BBA}} \searrow (\{a_2, a_4\}, \{(a_4, a_2)\}, \emptyset)$ for $(a_7, 0.7)$; (6) there is nothing to show for $(a_2, 0.7.1), (a_4, 0.7.2)$, as a_2 and a_4 are unitary; (7) $a^{\mathsf{BBA}} \searrow (\{a_6, a_7\}, \{(a_7, a_6)\}, \emptyset)$ for $(a_8, 0.8)$; (8) and similarly for all the rest.

For comparison, however, replace a_6 with a_x denoting $(\{a_1, a_2\}, \{(a_1, a_2)\}, \emptyset)$, a_7 with a_y denoting $(\{a_2, a_4\}, \emptyset, \{(a_4, a_2)\})$, as per our earlier discussion, and also replace a_8 with a_z denoting $(\{a_x, a_y\}, \{(a_y, a_x)\}, \emptyset)$. Denote the BBA which differs from a^{BBA} only by a_x, a_y and a_z by a_1^{BBA}. Assume $(a_x, 0.6), (a_y, 0.7), (a_z, 0.8) \in \varpi(a_1^{\mathsf{BBA}})$. Then none of them satisfy **G**, as a_1 supports a_2 and a_4 attacks a_2 in $\mathsf{Arg}(a_1^{\mathsf{BBA}}, 0)$, and there is no other shorter sequence of 0.6 and 0.7 occurring in the flat representation of a_1^{BBA}.

3.4   Generalisation of Standard Complete Labelling

Let us refine our earlier definition of standard complete labelling with the graphical constraint. We define C to be $\{\mathbf{G}\}$, and refer to its subset by C.

Definition 9 (Complete labelling). *For any a^{BBA}, any $\lambda \in \Lambda$ and any C, we say that λ is a complete labelling of a^{BBA} under C iff every $(\{a_1, \ldots, a_n\}, \langle m \rangle) \in \varpi(a^{\mathsf{BBA}})$ satisfies all the following conditions.*

- *$\lambda((a_i, \langle m \rangle.n_i)) = +$, $1 \leq i \leq n$, iff both of the following hold:*
  - *Every a_j, $1 \leq j \leq n$, attacking a_i in $\langle m \rangle$ satisfies $\lambda((a_j, \langle m \rangle.n_j)) = -$.*
  - *$\mathbf{G} \in C$ materially implies that $(a_i, \langle m \rangle.n_i)$ satisfies $\mathbf{G}$.*
- *$\lambda((a_i, \langle m \rangle.n_i)) = -$, $1 \leq i \leq n$, iff there exists some $1 \leq j \leq n$ such that $\lambda((a_j, \langle m \rangle.n_j)) = +$ and that a_j attacks a_i in $\langle m \rangle$ and there is no $1 \leq k \leq n$ such that $\lambda((a_k, \langle m \rangle.n_k)) = +$ and that a_k supports a_i in $\langle m \rangle$.*

Thus, any argument that violates the graphic constraint will not be assigned $+$ if $\mathbf{G} \in C$. For both $+$ and $-$, the first condition matches exactly the condition given for a standard complete labelling.

Clearly, a complete labelling is a generalisation of a standard complete labelling, as the two exactly match when $C = \emptyset$.

3.5   Acceptability Semantics

Definition 10 (Types of complete sets and acceptability semantics). *For any a^{BBA}, we say that $A_1 \subseteq \mathsf{Arg}(a^{\mathsf{BBA}}, 0)$ is: complete under C iff there exists a complete labelling $\lambda \in \Lambda$ of a^{BBA} under C such that $A_1 = \{a \in \mathcal{A} \mid \exists n \in \mathbb{N} \ \exists (a, 0.n) \in \varpi(a^{\mathsf{BBA}}). \ \lambda((a, 0.n)) = +\}$; grounded under C iff it is the set intersection of all complete sets under C; and preferred under C iff it is a maximal complete set under C. We call the set of all complete/grounded/preferred sets under C complete/grounded/preferred semantics under C.*

Note that ultimately we need to tell which subsets of $\mathsf{Arg}(a^{\mathsf{BBA}}, 0)$ are acceptable: this explains why we only look at $\langle m \rangle = 0$ for the semantics.

Theorem 2. *For any a^{BBA} and C, there exists at least one complete set under C, and if $\mathbf{G} \in C$, there may exist some unattacked $a \in \mathsf{Arg}(a^{\mathsf{BBA}}, 0)$ not in a complete set.*

The following example shows a concrete example where an unattacked argument is not justified under $C = \{\mathbf{G}\}$.

Example 3 (Acceptability semantics). (Continued) For the argumentation a^{BBA} in $\boxed{\mathbf{A}}$ with the same flat representation, there is some $\lambda_1 \in \Lambda$ with: $\lambda_1((a_i, 0.i)) = +$ for $i \in \{1, 4, 5, 7, 8\}$; $\lambda_1((a_6, 0.6)) = -$; and $\lambda_1((a_j, 0.j)) = ?$ for $j \in \{2, 3\}$, such that it is a complete labelling of a^{BBA}, and there is no $\lambda \in \Lambda$ which, if it is a complete labelling of a^{BBA}, differs from λ_1 for those members $(a_k, 0.k)$, $1 \le k \le 8$, of $\varpi(a^{\mathsf{BBA}})$. The complete semantics of a^{BBA} under any C is $\{\{a_1, a_4, a_5, a_7, a_8\}\}$.

Meanwhile, for a_1^{BBA}, there is some $\lambda_2 \in \Lambda$ with: $\lambda_2((a_i, 0.i)) = +$ for $i \in \{1, 4, 5\}$; and $\lambda_2((a_j, 0.j)) = ?$ for $j \in \{2, 3, x, y, z\}$, such that it is a complete labelling of a_1^{BBA} under $\{\mathbf{G}\}$. There is no $\lambda_x \in \Lambda$ which, if it is a complete labelling of a_1^{BBA} under $\{\mathbf{G}\}$, differs from λ_2 for those members of $\varpi(a_1^{\mathsf{BBA}})$. The complete semantics of a_1^{BBA} under $C = \{\mathbf{G}\}$ is then $\{\{a_1, a_4, a_5\}\}$.

4 Conclusion

Abstract argumentation does not specify the nature of an argument, which can be instantiated in some way. We presented block argumentation which recursively instantiates an argument generally by an argumentation, which is theoretically the most general instantiation possible with the vocabulary of a given abstract argumentation theory (namely, $\mathcal{A}$ and binary relations among the members of any subclass of it). Unitary arguments may be further instantiated by other languages. The key is to express the dual roles of an argument: as an argument and as an argumentation (similar emphasis is given for coalition formation [2]) and how they influence acceptability semantics.

Temporal/modal argumentation networks [3], as far as we are aware, is the first abstract argumentation study that hinted at the possibility that an unattacked argument may not be outright accepted. Unlike our graphical constraint, they enforce acceptance of some arguments. Such semantic dependency can be generalised with semantic constraints, the detail of which is found in [1].

For future work, we plan to cater for specific applications, and also consider introduction of probabilistic or dynamic approaches.

Acknowledgement. We thank anonymous reviewers for helpful comments. The last two authors have been supported by project *"Rappresentazione della Conoscenza e Apprendimento Automatico (RACRA)"* ("Ricerca di base" 2018–2020).

References

1. Arisaka, R., Bistarelli, S., Santini, F.: Block argumentation. CoRR abs/1901.06378 (2019). http://arxiv.org/abs/1901.06378
2. Arisaka, R., Satoh, K.: Coalition formability semantics with conflict-eliminable sets of arguments. In: AAMAS, pp. 1469–1471 (2017)
3. Barringer, H., Gabbay, D.M.: Modal and temporal argumentation networks. Argum. Comput. **3**(2–3), 203–227 (2012)
4. Caminada, M.: On the issue of reinstatement in argumentation. In: Fisher, M., van der Hoek, W., Konev, B., Lisitsa, A. (eds.) JELIA 2006. LNCS (LNAI), vol. 4160, pp. 111–123. Springer, Heidelberg (2006). https://doi.org/10.1007/11853886_11
5. Cayrol, C., Lagasquie-Schiex, M.C.: Bipolarity in argumentation graphs: towards a better understanding. In: SUM, pp. 137–148 (2011)
6. Dung, P.M.: On the acceptability of arguments and its fundamental role in non-monotonic reasoning, logic programming, and n-person games. Artif. Intell. **77**(2), 321–357 (1995)
7. Gabbay, D.M.: Fibring argumentation frames. Stud. Logica **93**(2–3), 231–295 (2009)
8. Gabbay, D.M.: Semantics for higher level attacks in extended argumentation frames part 1: overview. Stud. Logica **93**(2–3), 357–381 (2009)

DyNeMoC: Statistical Model Checking for Agent Based Systems on Graphs

Yenda Ramesh[ID], Nikhil Anand[ID], and M. V. Panduranga Rao[(✉)][ID]

Indian Institute of Technology, Hyderabad, India
{cs16resch11005,cs17mtech11021,mvp}@iith.ac.in

Abstract. We report a tool for analysing through statistical model checking, complex dynamical systems on graphs that can be modelled as multi-agent systems. We discuss techniques to leverage the fact that we restrict the tool to dynamics on graphs for performance improvements. The query language that the tool provides is a probabilistic version of bounded linear temporal logic.

We also introduce the notion of population sampling on agents for statistical model checking. To the best of our knowledge, this feature has not been reported previously in literature. Finally, we report experimental results on running examples that illustrate our ideas and the utility of the tool.

Keywords: Statistical model checking · Agent based systems · Graphs · Complex networks · Sampling

1 Introduction

Agent based modeling and simulations have gained traction in recent times for analyzing systems that defy closed form analytical approaches [9]. There are several elegant tools that facilitate such models and simulations [2,8].

Statistical model checking is essentially a sampling based technique of analyzing a system model against requirements (interchangeably, queries) specified in some logic. It has gained a lot of traction in the recent past since it avoids the state space explosion associated with numerical approaches for stochastic systems [7,11].

While analysis through modeling and simulation can be quite inaccurate, when used in conjunction with statistical model checking it increases our confidence in the model, and therefore the underlying system. A lot of agent based systems can be described as dynamic phenomena that happen on a graph. Examples include pursuit-evasion problems and the spread of epidemics across a network of cities. The motivation behind our work is to custom-build a tool to cater to such applications. While there are tools that combine generic (stochastic) agent based systems and (statistical) model checking [4,5,10], we report a tool called DyNeMoC (Model Checker for Dynamical phenomena on Networks) that is built specifically for analyzing agent based systems on graphs. This opens

© Springer Nature Switzerland AG 2019
M. Baldoni et al. (Eds.): PRIMA 2019, LNAI 11873, pp. 627–634, 2019.
https://doi.org/10.1007/978-3-030-33792-6_49

up the possibility of customized functionality for problems over graphs, and performance speed-ups. Firstly, in addition to queries at the granularity of agents, we can naturally ask queries pertaining to individual nodes. This makes for very intuitive use when dealing with such systems. Secondly, restricting focus to a variant of problems allows for increased efficiency in terms of time and space requirements for the simulations. The key advantage of focusing on graph based systems lies in the increased efficiency of the simulation engine through multi-threaded execution.

Our second contribution is methodological in nature. In a large agent based system, the biggest bottleneck in terms of speed is updating attributes for every agent. Speeding this up has been investigated in depth in the past. The model checking phase adds to the running time. While some formulas can be inexpensive to evaluate, formulas that involve huge agent populations may not be. Such agent based systems lend themselves to analysis through sampling–instead of polling every agent, samples of the agent population can be used to see if a formula is satisfied by the system. However, this comes at the cost of another source of inaccuracy in addition to the one inherent in statistical model checking. This approach is therefore useful when accuracy is not a stringent requirement, but speed is. We investigate the trade-off between accuracy and running time with this approach.

The rest of the paper is arranged as follows. Section 2 discusses the tool, its implementation and experimental results. Section 3 discusses the sampling approach and Sect. 4 concludes the paper with future directions.

2   DyNeMoC: The Tool

We begin with a brief and informal primer about a probabilistic version of bounded linear temporal logic (BLTL) [3]–we will encode the requirements that we expect of the system behavior as formulas in this logic. A BLTL formula has the following syntax:

$$\phi := \top \mid a \mid \neg\phi \mid \phi_1 \vee \phi_2 \mid \phi_1 U^{\leq k}\phi_2$$

Here, a is an atomic proposition that evaluates to *true* or *false* at any stage of execution of the system; and one can construct propositional formulas using Boolean operators $\vee$ and $\neg$. The bounded until formula $\phi_1 U^{\leq k}\phi_2$ evaluates to *true* for a run of the simulation, if the formula ϕ_2 becomes true at some point i in time before k and until that time (for all time $0 \leq t < i$), ϕ_1 is true. A probabilistic BLTL formula then is $Pr_{\geq\theta}(\phi)$ for $\theta \in [0, 1]$ and ϕ a BLTL logic formula. This formula evaluates to *true* if the system satisfies ϕ with probability at least θ. An estimation version is $Pr_{=?}(\phi)$–what is the probability that the systems satisfies the formula ϕ? In this paper, we focus on queries of this type. A simple technique for answering this estimation problem is to execute the system B times; if the system satisfies the query b of these times, the estimated probability would be b/B. For p the actual probability and p' the estimated probability and given $\epsilon > 0, \delta > 0$, a folklore application of the Chernoff-Hoeffding bound says that $Pr(|p - p'| > \epsilon) < \delta$ if B is at least $\frac{\ln 2/\delta}{\epsilon^2}$.

As mentioned previously we wish to build a simulation-cum-statistical-model-checking tool for dynamical phenomena on graphs. A weighted directed graph $G = (V, E)$ defines the *location graph* of the model. Vertices model geographic *locations* and edges between them model connectivity between the locations. Each location hosts a dynamically changing number of agents. The weight on an edge, drawn from the set of natural numbers, model the number of agents that can travel per unit time across the directed edge. As an example, the vertices can model cities, and the agents model the populations in each city.

The user gives the following inputs to the tool: $(G, I, A, R, \phi, \delta, \epsilon)$ where:

1. G is the location graph as described above. This is specified in a configuration file.
2. Each agent A is defined by k *attributes* $A = (A_1, A_2, \ldots, A_k)$. In our tool, the first attribute is always the location. The rest of the attributes are defined by the user. The other typical attribute would be neighborhood of the agent–the agents in that location that it can interact with.
3. R is a set of modification rules for each agent (type): $R = (R_1, R_2, \ldots, R_k)$.
4. I is a procedure for initializing the attributes of the agents.
5. Finally, the user defines the statistical model checking query ϕ and the confidence parameters ϵ and δ.

While inputs 1, 2 and 5 are specified in a configuration file, 3 and 4 are specified as code.

The tool provides two variants of an Atomic Proposition Evaluator, *Agent-Based* and *LocationBased*. Both these variants are essentially efficiently computable Boolean functions. The *AgentBased* version evaluator takes as input $(AgentId, AttName, AttVal, \bowtie)$. If an agent with id *AgentId*, has for attribute *AttName* a value that matches ($\bowtie$) with the required threshold *AttVal*, the tuple is evaluated to *true*, else it is evaluated to *false*. The *LocationBased* version is similar, but takes the location id's and location attributes and values. Figure 1 shows the architecture of the tool.

The tool can be accessed at "https://github.com/cs16resch11005/Dyne MOC". The running example that we use for illustrating an application of the tool is that of an epidemic spread over a geography of fifty cities. Naturally, the vertices of the location graph model the cities, the edges and their weights model the connectivity and capacity respectively. In our example, we use a completely connected location graph with infinite edge capacities. The model has one agent for each individual of the population. Apart from current location, the other attributes of an agent include list of neighbors and health status with respect to an ongoing epidemic: susceptible, infected or recovered. The movement of each agent is stochastic in nature. The modification rules therefore are concerned with movement of the agent between cities, how it connects in the agent network in destination city, and disease transmission rules. The total population is hundred thousand, with two thousand people in each city. Within a

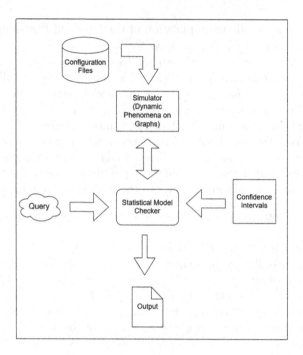

Fig. 1. Architecture of DyNeMoC

city, inter-agent connections are modelled as a Barabasi-Albert graph. An agent leaves a city with probability p, and goes to every other city with probability $p/49$ each and stays back in the same city with probability $1 - p$. The epidemic spread is modeled as follows. At every step, a susceptible agent is infected with probability $\frac{\text{number of infected neighbors}}{\text{total number of neighbors}}$ and an infected agent recovers on the dth time unit with probability $1 - (1 - (\frac{1}{t_r})^d)$ where t_r is the mean recovery period specific to the disease.

2.1   Implementation Details

The sequential algorithm for agent based modeling and the statistical model checking component is fairly straightforward. Each step of the simulation consists of two substeps, perceive and update. In the perceive step, every agent perceives the values of the attributes of other agents, including, if present, the environment. In the update substep, the agent updates its attributes based on the values of its influencing attributes. Both substeps are executed sequentially for each agent. At the end of each simulation step the probabilistic BLTL formula is evaluated and if it is satisfied, a counter is incremented. This is repeated B times, and the estimate of the probability that the system satisfies the formula is outputted as b/B.

Parallelization. In order to exploit the prevalent multicore architecture, we experimented with two different strategies for thread allocation. The first one is simply a random allocation. An array comprising all the agents is divided equally among all the threads. The threads then process the agents allotted to them, one by one. Despite its simplicity, there are some disadvantages to this approach. Neighbors of an agent can be scattered anywhere in the array, and updating needs a linear search to find them. The larger problem that can arise in case of asynchronous updates is that the attributes of an agent's neighbor can be locked by another thread. This can cause waiting delays. To overcome this, we experiment with a second, location based thread allocation strategy as detailed in Algorithm 1. The listing assumes an availability of one thread per location. When this is not true, then threads are allocated to locations by rotation. A thread i is allocated a linked list $L[i]$ of all agents in location i. Additionally, one linked list $Outgoing[i][j]$ is maintained for every other thread $j \neq i$. An agent migrating from i to j is added to $Outgoing[i][j]$ and deleted from $L[i]$. The entry corresponding to agent i is updated in a "master" array containing all agents. Maintaining this array is useful for evaluating queries involving individual agents.

At the end of one round of simulation, thread i consolidates its list by concatenating $Outgoing[j][i]$ (for all j) to $L[i]$. Since each thread has possession of the entire neighborhood, and an independent list for its migrating agents, this obviates the waits associated with locks. The only wait for all threads to terminate, to do the concatenation operation. When migration probability for agents is low, then location based allocation is beneficial. As migration probability increases, this advantage is lost.

Algorithm 1. One Run of the Location Based Allocation algorithm

---

1: **procedure** LocationBasedAllocation
2:    Create a thread pool with no. of threads = no. of cores
3:    $numLocations \leftarrow$ no. of locations in G
4:
5:    **ParFor** Each Thread i
6:        Initialize Linked List $L[i]$ of Agents in Location i.
7:        Initialize $Outgoing[i][j]$ array of incoming agents for $j \neq i$. //This is initially empty.
8:        **while** not end of Agent Linked List for i **do**
9:            **if** there is a change in location for agent A_r from i to j **then**
10:                Update other attributes
11:                Update Master Agent Array
12:                $Outgoing[i][j] \leftarrow A_r$
13:                Delete A_r from this linked list (in $O(1)$ time).
14:            Update other attributes
15:        **if** thread pool is terminated **then**
16:            Merge Linked List $L[i]$ with $Outgoing[j][i]$ for all j.
17:    **EndParFor**
18:    Shutdown thread pool

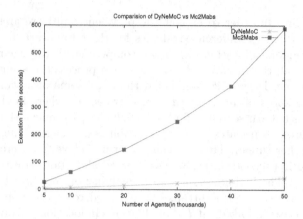

Fig. 2. DyNeMoC vs MC^2MABS

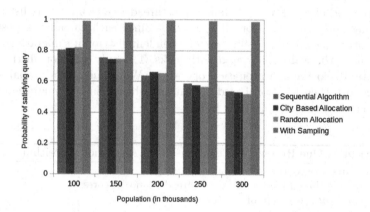

Fig. 3. Probability that the query ϕ is satisfied

Results and Comparison. The experiments were conducted on ubuntu 16.04 LTS (64-bit) with a memory of 8GiB and the Intel(R) Core(TM) i7-7700 CPU 3.60 GHz processor and a disk of 1TB. The geography contained 50 completely connected cities. Two percent of the population was infected at random to initiate the spread of the epidemic. The patients can recover by themselves with a mean recovery rate $t_r = 0.005$. With δ and ϵ set to 0.03, B turns out to be 2335 (runs). We ran the query $Pr_{=?}[\text{True}U^{\leq 300}\text{All agents are healthy}]$. We used a similar simulation set-up for MC^2MABS and the results are shown in Fig. 2. Results indicate that the time taken for the two thread allocation strategies are comparable, at least for smaller simulation scenarios. We expect location based allocation to be clearly beneficial when the updates are asynchronous.

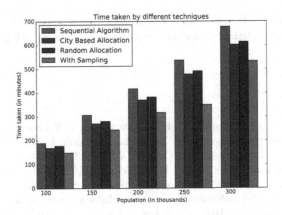

Fig. 4. Time taken for evaluating the query

3   Sampling

In queries that involve checking attributes of a sizeable fraction of the agent population, instead of polling all the agents for evaluation of a formula, what is the loss in accuracy that if we only sample the population? While the time taken to update all the agents cannot be avoided, there could be significant savings for evaluating the query. Such queries are natural in investigating dynamical phenomena of the kind we described previously. Indeed, such an approach would be analogous to sampling in surveys in real world populations.

While several sampling techniques exist, we have implemented and tested the simple random sampling and stratified sampling techniques. For arriving at the sample size for simple random sampling, we seek a confidence level of 99% (translating to a z-score of 2.58) and an error margin of 2%. This yields a sample size of about 4000 for a population of 100000.

As can be seen in Fig. 4, the gain in the total time taken for simulation plus query evaluation improves, but not by much. However, the time taken for only evaluating the query registers a drop. This comes at a cost of reduced accuracy. Figure 3 shows that the probability estimate is higher than the other techniques because of higher false positives. In some applications, for example in the case of qualitative queries, and when accuracy is not crucial, such estimates would suffice.

4   Conclusions and Future Work

Applications of an initial version of this tool were reported at other venues [1,6]. We intend to apply this to a more comprehensive study of problems in epidemic and epidemic-like phenomena in various domains like computer security, robot motion planning, pursuit evasion and other graph based problems. Extension of the framework to asynchronous updates would be useful in putting various thread allocation strategies to test. Finally, a rigorous analysis of the combined effect of sampling and statistical model checking on the accuracy-efficiency trade-off is also in order.

References

1. Arora, S., Jain, A., Ramesh, Y., Panduranga Rao, M.V.: Specialist cops catching robbers on complex networks. In: Aiello, L.M., Cherifi, C., Cherifi, H., Lambiotte, R., Lió, P., Rocha, L.M. (eds.) COMPLEX NETWORKS 2018. SCI, vol. 812, pp. 731–742. Springer, Cham (2019). https://doi.org/10.1007/978-3-030-05411-3_58
2. Borshchev, A.: Anylogic 7: new release presentation. In: Proceedings of the 2013 Winter Simulation Conference: Simulation: Making Decisions in a Complex World, WSC 2013, pp. 4106–4106. IEEE Press, Piscataway (2013). http://dl.acm.org/citation.cfm?id=2675807.2675980
3. Clarke Jr., E.M., Grumberg, O., Peled, D.A.: Model Checking. MIT Press, Cambridge (1999)
4. Herd, B., Miles, S., McBurney, P., Luck, M.: MC²MABS: a monte carlo model checker for multiagent-based simulations. In: Gaudou, B., Sichman, J.S. (eds.) MABS 2015. LNCS (LNAI), vol. 9568, pp. 37–54. Springer, Cham (2016). https://doi.org/10.1007/978-3-319-31447-1_3
5. Herd, B., Miles, S., McBurney, P., Luck, M.: Quantitative analysis of multiagent systems through statistical model checking. In: Baldoni, M., Baresi, L., Dastani, M. (eds.) EMAS 2015. LNCS (LNAI), vol. 9318, pp. 109–130. Springer, Cham (2015). https://doi.org/10.1007/978-3-319-26184-3_7
6. Ramesh, Y., Anand, N., Panduranga Rao, M.V.: Statistical model checking for dynamical processes on networks: a healthcare application. In: 11th International Conference on Communication Systems & Networks, COMSNETS 2019, Bengaluru, India, 7–11 January 2019, pp. 720–725 (2019)
7. Sen, K., Viswanathan, M., Agha, G.: On statistical model checking of stochastic systems. In: Etessami, K., Rajamani, S.K. (eds.) CAV 2005. LNCS, vol. 3576, pp. 266–280. Springer, Heidelberg (2005). https://doi.org/10.1007/11513988_26
8. Tisue, S., Wilensky, U.: Netlogo: design and implementation of a multi-agent modeling environment. In: Proceedings of Agent 2004 (2004)
9. Wooldridge, M.: An Introduction to MultiAgent Systems, 2nd edn. Wiley, Hoboken (2009)
10. Wooldridge, M., Fisher, M., Huget, M.P., Parsons, S.: Model checking multi-agent systems with MABLE. In: Proceedings of the First International Joint Conference on Autonomous Agents and Multiagent Systems: Part 2, AAMAS 2002, pp. 952–959 (2002). https://doi.org/10.1145/544862.544965
11. Younes, H.L.S., Kwiatkowska, M., Norman, G., Parker, D.: Numerical vs. statistical probabilistic model checking: an empirical study. In: Jensen, K., Podelski, A. (eds.) TACAS 2004. LNCS, vol. 2988, pp. 46–60. Springer, Heidelberg (2004). https://doi.org/10.1007/978-3-540-24730-2_4

An Adaptive Cognitive Agent Model for Development of a Hoarding Disorder and Recovery from it by Therapy

Alex Italiaander and Jan Treur[✉]

Social AI Group, Vrije Universiteit Amsterdam, Amsterdam, The Netherlands
aitaliaander@outlook.com, j.treur@vu.nl
https://www.researchgate.net/profile/Jan_Treur

Abstract. In this paper, an adaptive cognitive agent model is presented that describes both the process of development of a hoarding disorder and recovery from it by therapy. The adaptive agent model was evaluated by simulation experiments and comparison of them with expected patterns known from the literature. Moreover, mathematical analysis was performed of the equilibria of the agent model and used to verify the model. The model can be the basis for a virtual agent model that may support a therapist in their training or in their professional life.

1 Introduction

Hoarding Disorder (HD) can be described as excessive collection and acquisition of objects and a persistent inability to discard them because of a perceived need to save them, resulting in clutter. Attempts by caregivers or family to discard the clutter can cause distress, anxiety and conflict. It can lead to fire hazards and danger for one's physical and mental health. They perceive avoidance behavior as the solution to their problems, but this causes short-term relief and long-term pain.

Rodriguez et al. [4] found that treatments for Hoarding Disorder were underutilized, because the clients did not find the available treatments acceptable. This causes a delay in seeking treatment, which in turn causes progressive worsening of the hoarding behavior. In order to improve treatment and the mental health issues and safety conditions of hoarders, it may be valuable to gain more insight in what Hoarding Disorder fundamentally is and what happens during the process of decision making when needing to discard a possession. By gaining insight in self-help treatment for Hoarding Disorder it may be utilized more to maximize treatment outcomes.

Learning to cope with emotions the right way is essential in overcoming hoarding tendencies. In order to do this, Singh, Hooper and Jones [6] wrote a self-help guide using cognitive behavioral techniques. The Cognitive Behavioral Treatment (CBT) techniques in this book deal with hoarding by gradually eliminating unhelpful rituals that people with Hoarding Disorder use to cope with their emotions.

In this paper, an adaptive cognitive agent model is shown for the underlying mechanisms. It is adaptive both for developing the disorder, and for recovery from it by therapy. It analyzes Hoarding Disorder in a computational manner and simulates the processes assumed to play a role in the disorder, its development, and recovery from it.

© Springer Nature Switzerland AG 2019
M. Baldoni et al. (Eds.): PRIMA 2019, LNAI 11873, pp. 635–643, 2019.
https://doi.org/10.1007/978-3-030-33792-6_50

2 Background of Hoarding

Hoarding Disorder is defined as "the acquisition of, and failure to discard, a large number of possessions of limited apparent value, the presence of living spaces that are sufficiently cluttered as to preclude use of those areas for intended purposes, and significant distress or impairment in functioning caused by hoarding." [2]. Typically, a hoarder will save items that seem invaluable or useless to any other person (e.g. old newspapers, notes or trash). When confronted with the clutter, a hoarder may experience intense distress and/or anxiety [3]. Generally, there is limited space in active living areas, which can cause safety concerns like mobility limitations for first aid, fire and of course health risks (bad hygiene, pest or mold). However, even if the clutter interferes with the hoarder's day to day life, they may not be distressed about this at all. The lack of insight plays a role in this. "In Hoarding Disorder, insight refers to the level or degree the individual is aware of the consequences of the symptoms (e.g., safety for self and others or consequences of family members) in addition to hoarding-related beliefs (e.g., about the importance of possessions)." ([9], p. 26).

Singh found that most participants of his study stated that they have had help or support for their hoarding problems in the past, but that these had been ineffective [6]. Rodriguez supports this: "Only three treatments and services were deemed acceptable: individual CBT, professional organizing, and self-help book. However, these three just barely made the *a priori* cutoff of 6 on the Likert scale, suggesting there is an important gap between available resources and acceptability of these resources for clients with hoarding behaviors." ([4], p. 8) This gap, combined with the lack of insight, causes a delay in seeking treatment. When treatment is delayed, the hoarding behavior will get the chance to worsen progressively [11].

Primarily, the context of the situation is an important factor to consider when we speak about the development of hoarding. This includes early life experiences, personality traits (such as impulsiveness, perfectionism and dependency), familial history, comorbidity and individual vulnerabilities (such as genetic influences or traumatic life experiences). For this thesis, these factors are out of scope, since they are based on the context of the situation.

One of the most important factors of Hoarding Disorder is the 'belief' the hoarder has about their possessions. Individuals who hoard seem to deliberately consider each possession and assign a belief to each single one of them. This makes it more difficult for them to discard these possessions as specific conditions are set on when and why objects should be discarded. When talking about a belief, we refer to the meaning(s) a hoarder assigns to their possessions. In other words, the specific beliefs the hoarder attached to their possessions refer to the type of hoarding they are affected by. According to Frost, hoarders make decisions about their possessions based on the value of the object; it's instrumental, intrinsic or sentimental value [1]. This paper focuses on instrumental hoarding only. Instrumental hoarders judge the likelihood of future need of their possessions as higher than non-hoarders. They think they may need the item in the future. If the needed belonging will be discarded, their beliefs about the consequences and/or wastefulness can make them feel many negative emotions such as distress, sadness, grief, anger and fear.

Emotion plays an important role in Hoarding Disorder. In [5] it is found that "fear of decision-making interacted with general emotional reactivity to predict total hoarding symptoms and difficulty discarding. These findings support the idea that HD individuals experience a wide array of negative emotions more intensely." [5]. For people with Hoarding Disorder, most of the coping mechanisms the brain finds most optimal only bring short-term relief and long-term pain. Sometimes the ways of coping used by hoarders to help with uncomfortable emotions only perpetuate their hoarding problems, which results in a low level of tolerance of these feelings. For clarification, negative emotions (e.g., anxiety, distress, anger, sadness, helplessness and guilt) and positive emotions (e.g., happiness, emotional attraction to possessions and happy memories) are considered two different categories of emotions in this study. When an individual with HD has more trouble coping with negative emotions (e.g., during discarding possessions) it causes negative reinforcement of the hoarding behavior. A person with HD who has more difficulty coping with positive emotions (e.g., shopping online during a sale and wanting to buy many items) will lead to additional acquiring and will create a positive reinforcement pattern of the hoarding behavior.

Making any kind of decision is hard for individuals who have Hoarding Disorder. Tolin et al. [8] found that hoarding participants of his study exhibited abnormal activity in frontal and temporal regions when deciding whether to discard possessions. These brain regions are part of a network of structures that regulate decision-making and self-awareness, identify the emotional significance of a stimulus and generate an emotional response [8]. The deficits in decision-making, emotional response and emotional regulation are the core of the problem of being unable to discard possessions.

High levels of fear of decision-making combined with experiencing negative emotions more intensely can cause for an individual to have more difficulty discarding possessions and to start procrastinating. This negative reinforcement of the hoarding behavior will always lead to avoidance behavior. Behavioral avoidance is an important feature of hoarding behavior. Singh explains in his book that it "comes from a perceived fear of the intensity of the difficulty [a hoarder] may face or a prediction of how the situation will turn out, and a belief that [they] will not have the ability to deal with it or the discomfort [they] might experience." [6]. By saving possessions, the hoarder allows him- or herself to avoid making a decision.

The cognitive agent models introduced here are mainly inspired by the cognitive behavioral model created by Steketee and Frost [7]. "According to a cognitive behavioral model of compulsive hoarding, manifestations of hoarding (acquisition, saving, clutter) result from basic deficits or problems in (a) information processing, (b) beliefs about and attachments to possessions, and (c) emotional distress and avoidance behaviors that develop as a result." [7].

3 Modeling Hoarding, Its Development and Therapy

The functionality of the processes within the cognitive agent model was based on the Network-Oriented Modeling approach temporal-causal networks from [10]. Pictures can be found in Fig. 1. As the mental processes within the agent (1) contain essential cycles, and (2) are adaptive, the Network-Oriented Modeling based on temporal-causal networks fits well to this domain. The temporal-causal model shows the process of decision making as discussed. The model has ten states that are based on the background of hoarding and the model of Steketee and Frost, which suggests that "strong negative emotional reactions to possessions (e.g., anxiety, grief, guilt) lead to avoidance of discarding and organizing, while strong positive emotions (pleasure, joy) reinforce acquiring and saving possessions." [7]. The most prominent features of Hoarding Disorder covered here are: Problematic beliefs about possessions, Information processing deficits, Emotion processing deficits and emotional distress, Avoidance behaviors, Acquiring and saving behaviors, Decision making deficits. In addition to these states there are two adaptive connection weights for development of hoarding, and two for recovery of it by therapy. They are indicated in the pictures by the arrows pointing to an ω.

Figure 1 shows the basic conceptual model of the process of decision-making in humans, without specific weights of the connections. Some assumptions have been made, for sake of simplicity.

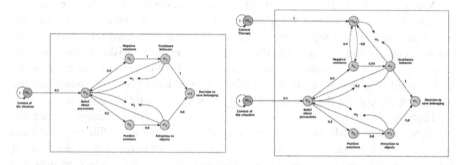

Fig. 1. Left: Graphical conceptual model of the process and development of decision making in a person with hoarding disorder. Over time the backward connections to the belief become stronger due to the learning. Right: The adaptive cognitive agent model with therapy. During therapy, the connection from Avoidance behaviour to the control state for the negative emotions becomes stronger due to the learning. When this connection becomes strong enough, therapy is not needed anymore, as the person can regulate these emotions by him or herself.

The simulation starts when the person grabs a possession. They need to try to make an instant decision about whether to discard it or not, as explained in the Main Scenario. This triggers belief state bs_p, which quickly triggers their particular emotions the person feels about the object; fs_n and/or fs_p. Negative feelings have an impact on preparation state behavioral avoidance, pr_1, and positive feelings have an impact on the amount of the attraction they feel towards the object, which is preparation state pr_2. The complex part of this model, represented by persistence (or extinction rate), is that the belief state is influenced back by the avoidance behavior and object attraction states, which represents a reinforcement cycle that can be negative (when enforced by avoidance behavior) or positive (when enforced by the object attraction). The two preparation states determine whether the threshold will be met and, thus, the decision will be made to save the belonging, which is execution state es_1. In this case, the higher the extinction rate, the greater the chance of not only developing, but also persisting Hoarding Behavior. Unlearning behavior with a high persistence value can be really difficult, however, can be learned to control using control states.

For therapy extra states and connections have been added to the model; see Fig. 1, right. The idea is that under guidance of the therapy the person strengthens his or her regulation skills, in particular the connection from Avoidance behavior to the control state (which suppresses the negative emotions for an object). If the therapy is successful, this connection will become strong enough to do regulation without the therapy. This is a second form of learning in the model, in addition to the learning for developing the disorder. The parameters used in the conceptual representations show some of the characteristics of the context they describe, however, they have been simplified to their essence for this study. These parameters can take the form of the connection weights, speed factors and threshold σ or steepness τ in logistic sum functions and have specific constant values for a given scenario. In order to simulate different scenarios to explore different situations, in this case decision-making in humans with hoarding disorder, these constant values should be varied, but they do not change over time.

The characteristics represented by the parameters can change over time as a result of developing the disorder or of treatment. Therefore, Hebbian learning is applied for these adaptation processes. It is used not only to show how hoarding is (or is not) developed in the brain, but also to see how a certain type of therapy may affect the disorder. Hebbian learning is based on the principle that 'neurons that fire together, wire together' and interprets the adapting connection weight characteristics as states that now can change over time, so the characteristics become variables [10], Ch. 2. A Hebbian connection between states X_1 and X_2 is indicated by ω_{X_1,X_2} or just by ω; it needs a *persistence rate* μ and *learning rate* (or speed) η. The formula used (in differential equation format) for calculating the Hebbian learning values is

$$\mathbf{d}\omega(t)/\mathbf{dt} = \eta[X_1(t)X_2(t)(1 - \omega(t)) - (1 - \mu)\omega(t)]$$

Note that if an equilibrium state is reached ($\mathbf{d}\omega(t)/\mathbf{dt} = 0$ and $\mathbf{d}Y(t)/\mathbf{dt} = 0$ for all ω and Y), from the above the following relation can be derived for the equilibrium values:

$$\omega = \frac{X_1 X_2}{1 - \mu + X_1 X_2} \quad \text{with a maximal value of} \quad \frac{1}{2 - \mu}$$

This relation was used for verification of the model by checking the different values from a simulation. For example, for $\mu = 0.99$, as often was set, the maximal value would be 0.9901. It can be seen in the simulations that indeed the values of the adaptive connection weights stayed below this value.

4 The Simulation Experiments

Four simulation experiments were done in order to test the model and run simulations of the treatment; two of them are discussed in Sect. 4. More can be found at https://www.researchgate.net/publication/335473135. The first shows how Hoarding Disorder gets developed by showing a reinforcement process underlying hoarding behavior. The second scenario shows a simulation of the treatment on the reinforcement cycle, by strengthening an emotion regulation cycle.

First, some background and context of the situations of the individuals involved in the simulations. Person Y is based on the patient who was covered in the case study by [11]. Person Y is a classic example of an individual who developed Hoarding Disorder, specifically instrumental disorder, but did not seek for help for a long period of time until it got out of hand. Person Y_{neg} is how we call person Y from now on, the individual from the case study by Vilaverde. Person Y_{neg} has problematic beliefs about his possessions, specifically about the possible use of these items in the future, which was the reason he could not discard them. This is a common belief among instrumental hoarders. Person Y_{neg} gets anxious whenever somebody else discards his possessions. This indicates deficits in information processing and emotion processing.

Scenario 2 (Figs. 2 and 3) concerns a simulation of the process of decision making in person Y_{neg}, which, if this behavioral pattern would be repeated for a long period of time, can make them develop instrumental hoarding. An instrumental hoarder has strong beliefs on not only the future usability, but also the wastefulness and consequences of discarding such an item. "Heightened general emotional reactivity and more intense emotional reactions to imagined discarding were associated with both difficulty discarding and acquisition." [5]. The beliefs combined with a fear of decision making and deficits in emotion processing can cause strong emotional reactions to the discarding of possessions, since an instrumental hoarder not only has trouble coping with negative emotions, but also experiences emotions more intensely than non-hoarders. The strong emotional reactions result in avoidance behavior regarding discarding and organizing, which can turn into a negative reinforcement cycle of acquiring items, but not discarding them when the persistence rate is high enough.

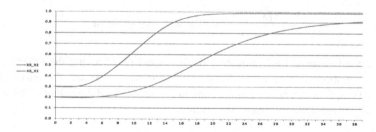

Fig. 2. The learnt connection weights of hoarding in person Y_{neg}: the connection from positive feeling state fs_p to belief bs_p (blue) and from negative feeling state fs_n to belief bs_p (green) (Color figure online)

For person Y_{neg}, the Hebbian persistence value is very high, that is 0.99, with speed factor 0.8. This entails that Y_{neg}'s brain has a strong tendency to learn from their negative reinforcement cycle as shown in Fig. 2. As can be seen it comes very close to 1 but not exact, as predicted by the analysis at the end of Sect. 3.

In order to cognitively restructure the beliefs hoarders have about their items, some of the techniques in [6] deal with emotion regulation. As we discussed in Sect. 2, people with Hoarding Disorder have deficits in the processing and regulating of their emotions. Using the Network-Oriented Modeling approach, emotion regulation can be simulated using control states. This can be done by modeling the processes involved in the detection of perceiving an undesired amount of emotional feeling and reacting to that with inhibition of the feeling state. Scenario 4 shows a simulation of the process of decision making in person Y_{neg}, as in Scenario 2, however, in this scenario the CBT treatment is incorporated (Fig. 4).

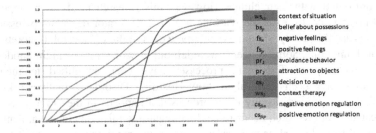

ws_a	context of situation
bs_p	belief about possessions
fs_n	negative feelings
fs_p	positive feelings
pr_1	avoidance behavior
pr_2	attraction to objects
cs_j	decision to save
ws_j	context therapy
cs_{fn}	negative emotion regulation
cs_{fp}	positive emotion regulation

Fig. 3. Simulation of Scenario 2: how instrumental hoarding develops in person Y_{neg}

For Y_{neg}, the Hebbian persistence value is very high, that is 0.99 with speed factor 0.8. This entails that Y_{neg}'s brain has a strong tendency to learn from their negative reinforcement cycle of acquiring items, but not discarding them. The decision is made a little late, due to the avoidance behavior.

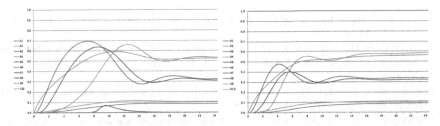

Fig. 4. Left Simulation of Scenario 4: treatment of instrumental hoarding in person Y_{neg} Right: Simulation of Scenario 4: test of treatment effect of instrumental hoarding in person Y_{neg} (Color figure online)

Person Y_{neg} picked up the treatment very well. The explanation for this may be that his lack of insight was not too bad, since they at least acknowledged that their collection of items was exaggerated. As seen in Fig. 4, the dark blue line (which represents the execution state of the decision) does not get activated, since it falls just below 0.1.

5 Discussion

There is not one single reason for why people hoard. The disorder can express itself in many ways. However, the reason that individuals with Hoarding Disorder experience a strong connection to possessions and a perceived need to save them is mainly due to decision-making deficits, information processing deficits, problematic beliefs about possessions and deficits in processing emotions. High levels of fear of decision making combined with experiencing negative emotions more intensely causes an inability or difficulty in discarding possessions. Avoidance behavior and/or a strong connection to the possessions causes for a hoarder's brain to develop coping mechanisms that bring temporary relief, but with that also comes reinforcement of the hoarding behavior.

Training the brain to eliminate unhelpful rituals using the cognitive behavioral therapy by Singh may work as self-treatment for people with Hoarding Disorder, when used to cope with their anxiety and other uncomfortable emotions that they encounter when confronted with their clutter. However, this research needs to be repeated to support this theory, for example with the use of a moderator or clean-up sessions.

Results of this study should be interpreted in light of several (theoretical and practical) limitations. Some concepts were left out of scope to prevent the models from getting too complex. The brain processes have been simplified to their core. Assumptions have been made about how Hoarding Disorder actually works in the brain, since this process, as any other process that happens in the brain, is extremely complicated. More research needs to be done regarding this domain. Treatment should be extended to additional help in order to lessen the emotional reactions. The patient will benefit from additions to the therapy, including psychoeducation, motivational interviewing, classic cognitive techniques focused on dysfunctional beliefs, and exposures targeting sorting and discarding, and they could also benefit from pharmacological interventions.

References

1. Frost, R.O., Hartl, T.L.: A cognitive-behavioral model of compulsive hoarding. Behav. Res. Ther. **34**, 341–350 (1996)
2. Mataix-Cols, D., Fernández de la Cruz, L.: Hoarding disorder has finally arrived, but many challenges lie ahead. World Psychiatry J. World Psychiatric Assoc. (WPA) **17**(2), 224–225 (2018)
3. Rachman, S., Elliott, C.M., Shafran, R., Radomsky, A.S.: Separating hoarding from OCD. Behav. Res. Ther. **47**(6), 520–522 (2009)
4. Rodriguez, C.I., et al.: Acceptability of treatments and services for individuals with hoarding behaviors. J. Obsessive Compuls. Relat. Disord. **11**, 1–8 (2016)
5. Shaw, A.M., Timpano, K.R., Steketee, G., Tolin, D.F., Frost, R.O.: Hoarding and emotional reactivity: the link between negative emotional reactions and hoarding symptomatology. J. Psychiatr. Res. **63**, 84–90 (2015)
6. Singh, S., Hooper, M., Jones, X.C.: Overcoming Hoarding: A Self-Help Guide Using Cognitive Behavioural Techniques. Robinson, London (2015)
7. Steketee, G., Frost, R.: Compulsive hoarding: current status of the research. Clin. Psychol. Rev. **23**(7), 905–927 (2003)

8. Tolin, D.F., Stevens, M.C., Villavicencio, A.L., Norberg, M.M., Calhoun, V.D., Frost, R.O., et al.: Neural mechanisms of decision making in hoarding disorder. Arch. Gen. Psychiatry **69**, 832–841 (2012)
9. Tompkins, M.A.: Clinician's Guide to Severe Hoarding. Springer, New York (2015). https://doi.org/10.1007/978-1-4939-1432-6
10. Treur, J.: Network-Oriented Modeling: Addressing Complexity of Cognitive, Affective and Social Interactions. Springer, Cham (2016). https://doi.org/10.1007/978-3-319-45213-5
11. Vilaverde, D., Gonçalves, J., Morgado, P.: Hoarding disorder: a case report. Front. Psychiatry **8**, 1–5 (2017). https://doi.org/10.3389/fpsyt.2017.00112

Author Index

Printed in the United States
By Bookmasters